HAGUE'S HISTORY OF THE LAW IN SOUTH AUSTRALIA 1837 – 1867

Ralph M. Hague

With a foreword
by the Honourable Justice John Perry

With a foreword to the 2019 Hardback edition
by the Honourable Justice Martin Hinton

And a biography of the author
by Helen Whitington

Illustrations compiled and captioned
by Bruce Greenhalgh

BARR SMITH
PRESS
UNIVERSITY
of ADELAIDE

Barr Smith Press
Barr Smith Library
University of Adelaide
South Australia
5005
www.library.adelaide.edu.au
press@adelaide.edu.au

First published 2005
Hardback Edition 2019

Designed by Bruce Greenhalgh
Printing and publication overseen by John Emerson

Barr Smith Library of The University of Adelaide
Cataloguing
Hague, R. M.
Hague's History of the Law in South Australia 1837-1867

Includes bibliographical references and index.

ISBN 978-1-925261-88-2

1. Law – South Australia – History. 2. Justice, Administration of – South Australia – History. 3. Lawyers – South Australia – Biography. 4. Lawyers – South Australia – History. 5. South Australia – Constitutional History. 6. South Australia – Politics and government – History. 7. South Australia – Judges – History. 8. South Australia- Judges - Biography
I. Hague, R. M. II. Title

342.9423
KL416.K2S

Publication of this book was assisted by:
The Law Foundation of South Australia
The Courts Administration Authority of South Australia
The John Bray Law Network of the University of Adelaide Alumni Association
The University of Adelaide

Contents

Chapter

Acknowledgments

Transforming Ralph Hague's typewritten manuscript into a finished publication was no small task and could not have been completed without the help of many people. We would like to express our gratitude to the following people:

Mrs Lois Schmidt, the Brown family (Katrina Brown, Joanne Quinn, Robert and Marilyn Brown), Valerie Esau, William Esau, John Stokes, Pamela McLaren, Gerald Fischer, the Late Professor Alex Castles, His Honour Judge Bishop, Tony Kimberlin, Janet Newman, Christine Grassi, Robert Fisher, Georgia Hale, the Honourable Justice John Perry, Michael Farrow, Joanne Cook, Master Peter Norman, Deanne Hanchant-Nichols, Ken Barlow, Sharon Bubner, Margaret Allen, Bronwyn Halliday, Jenny D'Arcy, Michael Talbot, Faye Lush, Saima Mahmud, Monty Smith, Rebecca Blight, Jane Stephenson, Greg Willson, John Gallehawk, Dr John Emerson, Kelvyn Prescott, the late Honourable Andrew Wells and Mrs E. Wells, Brian Magarey, Michael Treloar, the Honourable Elliot Johnson, Caroline Milne, Sandy Hancock, the Honourable Justice Thomas Gray, Robert Edwards, Iris Stevens, Stewart Munro, Jackie Curran, Bill Othams, Helen Bruce, Susan Woodburn, Hazel Hodges, His Honour Judge Brendan Burley, the Honourable Brian Cox, Cheryl Hoskin, Elsie Bennett, Judie Cox, Clive Brooks, Sharon Polkinghorne, Iris Stevens, Barbara Russell, Susan Sideris, Ross and Cecily Hicks, Rosemary and John Eyre, Erica Micklem, Pamela Reid, John Scales, Elizabeth Ormsby, Caroline Milne, Renée Amyot, John Marshall, Maggie Ragless, Prue McDonald, Rob Cameron, Maria Fedczyszyn, Leanne Baehnisch, John Edge, Chris Tonkin, Ray Choate and anyone who has contributed but unintentionally been left from this list.

Illustrations

We wish to acknowledge and thank the following contributors of illustrations to this publication:

Adelaide City Council Archives (ACCA)
Alexander Turnbull Library, National Library of New Zealand, Te Puna Matauranga o Aotearoa (ATLNZ)
Allport Library and Museum of Fine Arts, State Library of Tasmania (SLT)
Art Gallery of South Australia (AGSA)
City of Mitcham, Mitcham Historical Society
City of Norwood, Payneham and St Peters Civic Collection
Department of Administrative and Information Services (DAIS)
Department of the Premier and Cabinet (DPC)
Helen Whitington
Jane Stephenson
La Trobe Pictures Collection, State Library of Victoria (SLV)
Lois Schmidt
Mitcham Historical Society
Mouldens Solicitors
Mount Lofty House
National Library of Australia (NLA)
National Portrait Gallery, London (NPG)
News Corporation
Pamela Oborn
Roger Vaughan Picture Library (RVPL)
South Australian Police Historical Society (SAPHS)
State Library of South Australia (SLSA)
State Records (SR)
Supreme Court Library of South Australia (SCLSA)
Supreme Court of South Australia (SC)
The Brown Family
Tony Kimberlin
University of Adelaide (UA)
Valerie Esau

The abbreviations listed above are used to acknowledge the source of the illustrations in the main text. A full list of illustrations is included – see contents.

Preface

It is not unusual for a long time to elapse between an author finishing a work and that work being published. But the nearly seventy years it has taken for Ralph Meyrick Hague's *History of the Law in South Australia 1837 – 1867* to be published is notable and begs some explanation. That explanation is even more warranted when it is considered that this is a posthumous publication of a work that failed in its initial goal of gaining a doctorate for its author.

When Hague submitted his *History* to the University of Adelaide for the Bonython Prize (which was the Law Faculty's de facto doctorate) in 1936 he did so as somebody accustomed to academic success and with designs on a career in academia. The rejection of his work, which had less to do with its merit than with the narrow thinking of the time, thwarted that career and might have consigned the *History* to oblivion. But Hague understood the value of his work for he not only deposited a copy with what became the State Library but also continued to research the subject using the *History* as a basis for further monographs.

Over time others discovered the value of Hague's work and slowly it became recognized for what it was; a pioneering work born of meticulous and original research and delivered in an elegant and sometimes witty style. It became one of the foundations of a growing appreciation and study of Australian legal history.

Until this publication, however, the *History* remained in the form that Hague deposited it with the State Library; namely some 1500 pages of typewritten manuscript. In this form the *History* is a daunting work with a bare table of contents as its only navigational tool. The *History* was worthy of publication in a more attractive and accessible form. The decision, then, by the John Bray Law Chapter and, in particular Justice Gray, was more overdue than surprising. This publication aims to honour Hague, preserve his work and to take it to a wider audience.

The publication is distinguished from the usual mode of history presentation in a number of ways. Firstly, very little editing of Hague's manuscript has been done. Discrepancies between sections of the typescript, reflecting preparation over several years, have been rendered consistent throughout. Typographical errors have been corrected and the punctuation around Hague's interpolations into quoted texts has been simplified. Apart from these small changes the publication is faithful to Hague's typescript.

Performing a fuller edit was considered but rejected because of a desire to honour the author and preserve his unique style. The endnotes presented are essentially those listed in the typescript, which were incomplete and less than detailed. It was not practical to produce a full and detailed set of references although some amendments were made. Accordingly, the endnotes are not of a standard that would normally be expected. They are reproduced, however, for the possible benefit they may give to researchers. Illustrations and marginal notes were included to give the book a visual dimension, and to assist the reader. Images and reproductions of documents are used to convey an understanding of the times Hague described in words alone

Hague originally titled his work *The Early History of Law in South Australia.* It was retitled, possibly when deposited at the State Library, as *History of the Law in South Australia 1837 – 1867*. This second title is the one the work is commonly known by and is the title used in most (if not all) references to the *History* and because of this the decision was made to use the latter title.

Helen Whitington's biography of Hague was produced to satisfy the anticipated desire of readers to know something of the man who wrote the *History*. It also recognises that the story of the *History* and Hague's life are themselves part of South Australian legal history. It was not written as an authoritative biography but as a means of understanding the man not only through his work and career but also through his interests and relationships.

This publication is, in some ways, an imperfect work. The only real alternative to this, though, was not to publish the *History* at all and therefore to continue the neglect of this important work and to deny the benefits its publication creates. The publication should not be judged on its imperfections but on how well it educates, entertains and fosters a greater understanding and study of South Australian legal history.

Bruce Greenhalgh
Historical Collection Librarian
Supreme Court Library South Australia

Foreword

Ralph Hague's *History of the Law in South Australia 1837-1867* is a fascinating and perceptive narrative of the early legal history of South Australia

Completed in about 1936, the work remained unpublished at the time of his death in March 1997.

Hague begins with an account of the establishment of the province of South Australia. This was the culmination of the earnest endeavours of a group of idealists, who, as he reminds us, were dubbed disparagingly by James Stephen, as the Wakefield Theorists.

In the early chapters, he lays bare the intricate obscurities of the Foundation Act, no doubt a product in part of the unedifying wrangles between the promoters and the Colonial Office. His description of this is brought into sharp relief by a series of graphic pen portraits of the major protagonists such as Gilles, Wakefield, Gouger, Lord Howick and Lord Stanley.

He is equally graphic in his portrayal of the first Governors, beginning with Hindmarsh. He depicts Hindmarsh in a cruelly unflattering light, presiding over what he describes as "administrative pandemonium", marked by endless bickering between public officials.

But it is in his description of the judges and court officials, and their dealings with each other and with the Commissioners, wherein lies the strength of this work.

Hague's brush darts across the canvas, painting pictures of eccentric, larger than life characters. His description of their personalities and their lives causes me to reflect on the staid, carefully correct existence which most judges lead today.

It is hard to imagine such an adventurous and impetuous figure as Sir John Jeffcott, the province's first judge, who killed a man in a duel and stood in the dock on a charge of murder, taking up a position on today's Supreme Court bench.

Jeffcott's dramatic and untimely death by drowning while navigating the swirling breakers of the Murray mouth, left acting Justice Henry Jickling marooned on the Supreme Court bench. Hague quotes the description of Jickling which appeared in *The South Australian* as a man "inebriated with the exuberance of his own verbosity".

In his treatment of Jeffcott's successors in office, it is Hague's description of Mr Justice Boothby which is perhaps the most illuminating. The reader is left in no doubt about the extent of the havoc wrought by Boothby's eccentric ways and stubborn adherence to his bizarre views as to the application of English law to the Colonies.

Replete with quotations from contemporary journals, embellished by his own sharply perceptive writing, this book is a testimony to the dedicated scholarship of a man I knew as a quiet, unassuming lawyer whose talents are only now being recognised.

The book makes an invaluable contribution to our appreciation of the early legal history of the State.

Full credit is due to the John Bray Law Chapter of the Alumni Association of the University of Adelaide, more particularly to its former President, Justice Tom Gray, whose idea it was to publish the book; to Bruce Greenhalgh of the Supreme Court Library staff who prepared the manuscript for publication and selected the illustrations; and to Helen Whitington who wrote the biography of the author which is incorporated in the book.

The Honourable Justice John Perry
Supreme Court Chambers
Adelaide

Foreword to the 2019 Hardback Edition

I was very pleased to be asked to write a brief foreword to the second edition of *Hague's History of the Law in South Australia 1837-1867*.

I recall first diving into *Hague's History* when as Solicitor-General I was required to trace the origins and content of the executive power of the State in order to understand the power that a contemporary Governor may wield on the advice of his or her Ministers.

On another occasion I turned to Hague for his treatment of the establishment of the Supreme Court for the purpose of tracing the scope and content of the Court's jurisdiction.

More recently it was the work Hague had done on the first petit and grand juries that assisted in an analysis of the protection afforded by trial by jury.

In each case the origins of important legal institutions were critical to understanding the structure and purpose of contemporary equivalents. From its very beginning, the Province-cum-State has enjoyed a constitutional structure intended to allow for its people to grow and flourish. When change is proposed, as it is from time to time, we are fortunate to have *Hague's History* on hand so we can comfortably plot the course from where we have come and better pilot our way forward.

The Honourable Justice Martin Hinton
Supreme Court Chambers
Adelaide

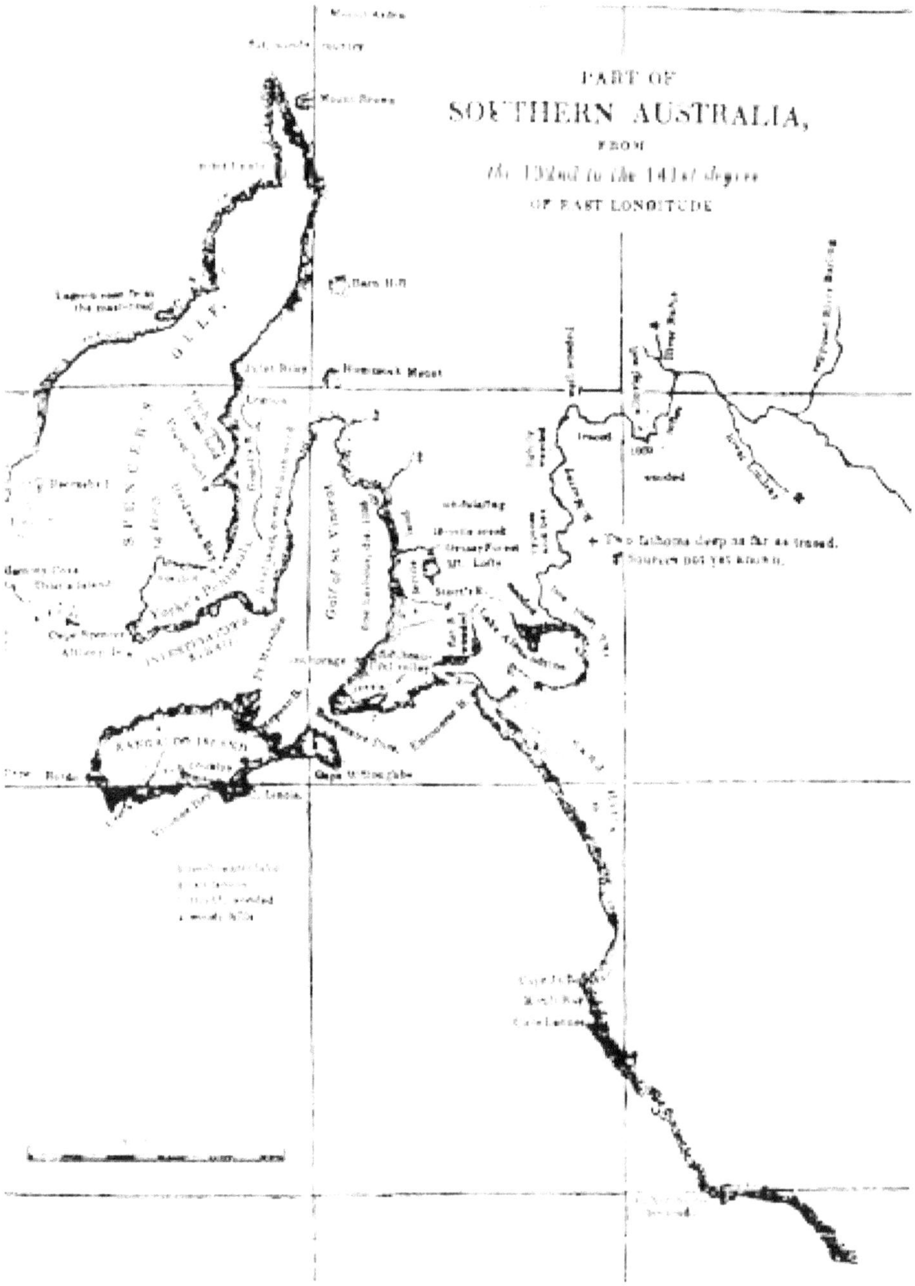

Part of Southern Australia, from the 132nd to the 141st degree of east longitude, (detail) from a pamphlet published by the Colonization Commissioners in 1835 addressed to “small farmers and others” promoting the merits of emigration to South Australia (SLSA)

Chapter 1.1

Historical Background

'It is unique'

The Province of South Australia was created pursuant to the provisions of an Act of the Imperial Parliament, passed in 1834.[1] By universal consent this Act has been condemned — by some as an obscure and misshapen blunder, by others as "a document of masterly ambiguity, if not of deep guile" — and to the pernicious influence of its dubious drafting have been traced many of the troubles which threatened to ruin the colony at its outset. "The chief and original error" — reported the Select Committee of the House of Commons which in 1841 inquired into the turbid affairs of South Australia — "was committed in the Act itself." [2]

George Fife Angas called it "a dead letter on the Statute Book, an order of the Imperial Government to make bricks without straw"— expressions which sufficiently show his opinion of it, although in truth the Act was far from being a mere inert and stillborn legislative corpse.[3] Sir Charles Cooper declared it to have been the cause of the virulent ill-feeling which racked the colony during the governorship of Captain John Hindmarsh. The Act, he said, in the tone of mild expostulation which was almost the severest form of disapprobation of which he was constitutionally capable: "... was constructed in England, whose legislators are famed for their wisdom, but when it was opened it created surprise".[4]

Nearly a century later, when it came under the critical scrutiny of the High Court, the Act was still creating surprise. "It seems very singular to me," said Sir Samuel Griffith as he puzzled over it. "It is unique," he was assured by Sir Josiah Symon.[5]

When an attempt was made to put the Foundation Act into operation, its construction was discovered to be to the last degree difficult and obscure. Its twenty-six sections formed a series of trous-de-loup upon the spikes of which those whose duty it was to expound the statutes became successively impaled. The well-known method of dealing with loose acts of Parliament is to drive a coach and six through them. Adopting this metaphor, it may be said that there was for some years a steady stream of traffic through the Foundation Act; nor was it one-way traffic only. The coaches frequently went in different directions. They all drove into the labyrinth at the same entrance; they did not all emerge at the same exit. Some did not emerge at all, but went round and round in a "circulus inextricabilis", seeking in vain a practicable way out. "An Act of Parliament can do no wrong," loyally said Lord Holt, but honesty compelled him to add that "it may do several things that look pretty odd", and the Foundation Act illustrated the second half of his dictum.

Why was the Act such a broad highway to doubts and difficulties? Why was Coke's admirable precept neglected, that Acts of Parliament should be plainly and clearly, and not cunningly and darkly, penned? Dr Grenfell Price half-heartedly hints at a sinister plot by Edward Gibbon Wakefield and his brother Daniel, who prepared the first draft of the Act, deliberately to produce ambiguity, presumably in order to give a wider scope for the unfettered development of their schemes.[6] This seems an opinion which is unsupported by fact, unjust to the Wakefields and quite unnecessary for the solution of the question. Successful ambiguity would be even harder to attain than honest precision. No doubt Edward Gibbon Wakefield was not a man to have scrupled to stoop to such a course had he thought it would further his purposes, but his heart was set on the success of his work, and he was too great a statesman not to foresee the disasters which would attend a colony whose constitutional foundations were laid in uncertainty.

The shortcomings of the Act can be fully and reasonably explained without resorting to any such theory.

In the first place, notwithstanding the copious resources of legal verbiage, it is almost impossible to prepare an act that will meet all exigencies and will be impervious to attack. Every day's experience teaches us that the most reasonable expectations may be baffled by events which could not be anticipated. That there would be sins of omission in the Act was inevitable. No-one in his right senses could contend that there should have been compressed into a two-page statute the whole of a complicated scheme for the establishment of a colony, upon a hitherto untried system, in an unexplored wilderness at the other side of the world. No complaint could be made that it was a mere skeleton: the charge is that it was a skeleton which had some bones missing altogether, and many others very poorly articulated. In part this was due to the maltreatment it received in the course of its passage through the Colonial Office and through Parliament. The Bill in its final form was vastly different from the original draft. "We struck out this provision"—wrote Wakefield—"because it displeased somebody, altered another to conciliate another person, and inserted a third because it embodied somebody's crotchets." [7]

The colonists were tired of waiting. "The ardour of individuals," James Mill soundly observed, "where anything is to be risked, is more easily excited than upheld." Daily the ranks of prospective emigrants were thinned by vexatious and expensive delays. The survivors were desperate for an act at almost any cost, provided only there was left sufficient of their original plan to enable them to hope for the successful foundation of a colony on the lines which they proposed, and they were as little inclined to pay attention to intricate questions of legal or constitutional verbiage as they were to the gloomy predictions of the Duke of Wellington, implicit in his laconic statement that if they wanted to go to South Australia, and make damned fools of themselves, let them.[8]

To cap all, the Act was the tainted offspring of a miserable and vicious compromise between two parties whose views upon the government of the proposed colony were as immiscible as oil and water. The Colonial Office maintained that South Australia, like other Crown colonies, should be ruled from England, through a governor and nominated Council. Contrariwise, an essential feature of the Wakefield theory of colonisation (the superiority of which, it was claimed, South Australia would demonstrate) was colonial self-government, and "We are being sold to the Colonial Office!" was the faction cry of those who were in the habit of congregating about the Adelphi to discuss the new principles. James Stephen ("Mr Mother-Country", "Mr Over-Secretary Stephen", "King Stephen", as he was variously called) has usually been taken as typifying the Colonial Office, and he was cautious, conservative, aristocratic; the majority of those who had actively taken up the scheme for the founding of South Australia were radicals, whose enthusiasm Stephen disliked, and whose political principles he distrusted.

(Sir) James Stephen (1789–1859)
An opponent of Wakefield's scheme, Stephen served in the Colonial Office as, variously, counsel, assistant undersecretary and undersecretary between 1825 and 1847.

The Adelphi was an important urban development designed by the Adam brothers in 1768 for a section of the Thames River bank. The South Australian Commissioners' office in the precinct was the site of much early discussion on the colony. Once a favoured area for writers and artists, the Adelphi has all but been demolished. (SLSA)

> 'The Wakefield theorists considered that, in attempting to wring a new colony from the Colonial Office, they were struggling with "the judgments of ignorance, the insults of pride, and the delays of idleness'" Stephen and his satellites believed that they were fighting a handful of revolutionary dreamers, who desired, from reasons by no means devoid of self-interest, to found a colony which would become a charge upon the mother-country, and would "erect within the British monarchy a government purely republican".' [9]

Years of higgling took place. The Colonial Office doggedly insisted that the government of the colony and the administration of the law must be left in the hands of the Crown, and that no part of the expense of the colony should fall upon England. Necessarily the plans and schemes which were presented by the Wakefield party for the approval of the Secretary of State became successively less and less democratic in their nature.[10]

Edward Gibbon Wakefield (1796–1862)
Wakefield is shown here displaying the style that may have tempted a young heiress. His more admirable pursuits included his theorizing on colonization that lead to the formation of the South Australian Association and the establishment of the Province. Drawing by A Wivell, London, 1823. (NLA)

Negotiations had been begun in 1831, not by Wakefield but by Anthony Bacon, an officer who had fought at Waterloo and was subsequently to distinguish himself in the struggle in Portugal between Don Miguel and Pedro IV. His plan for founding an Australian colony appears to have been modelled on the South Sea Bubble Company, "for carrying on an Undertaking of Great Advantage, but no one to know what it is", and Major Bacon himself (like Arnold Bennett, who used modestly to say that the best was good enough for him) asked only to be appointed the Governor of the colony, with the power to make its laws and appoint its officers. The Colonial Office frowned on this adventure, and coldly replied that no encouragement could be given:

> '... to schemes which have for their object the extension of the number of His Majesty's settlements abroad, and which, whether founded in the outset by individuals, or by the Government, are always liable to end in becoming in some way or other a source of expense to the revenue of this country.'[11]

Bacon then joined the party headed by Wakefield and Robert Gouger, and in June 1831 Gouger forwarded to Lord Howick a draft of a proposal to establish a colony by means of a chartered company, to carry out Wakefield's principles as to land and emigration. A local elective assembly was suggested, to be established when the male adult population reached 5,000 (later raised to 10,000). The first Governor was to be recommended by the company and appointed by the Crown, and, as a sop to make the request for an assembly more palatable, it was proposed that the Governor, until the meeting of the Assembly, should have supreme power "unencumbered by any Colonial Council to divide and weaken his responsibility". Until one year after the meeting of the local Assembly, all the expenses of government would be borne by the company; thenceforward the Governor would be appointed by the Crown, and the colonists would pay for their own government.

Robert Gouger (1802–1846)
Gouger was an important campaigner for the establishment of South Australia and publicist of Wakefield's theories. He arrived in South Australia in November 1836 as the first Colonial Secretary and Member of the Executive Council. Appointed a Justice of the Peace on 2 January 1837 he decided the first case in the colony.

This scheme was received with favour, but while the matter was still under official consideration the colonisers prematurely announced that the Government had approved of the scheme. When an explanation was requested, Bacon admitted that the assertion of the Government's sanction had been made to attract capital, and the Colonial Office would not go on with what looked suspiciously like a mere scheme for making money for its promoters.[12]

In July 1832 the provisional committee of the South Australian Land Company put forward a proposal for a chartered company, with a capital of £500,000. The company wanted power to constitute courts and to make laws for the government of the colony, until the population reached 50,000, when an assembly was to be established, under a governor nominated by the Crown. For revenue purposes a perpetual tax of 6d per acre would be reserved upon every original sale of land.[13]

James Stephen had strong objections. He disliked the system of chartered companies. Adam Smith had said that "the government of an exclusive company of merchants is, perhaps, the worst of all governments for any country whatever", and Stephen agreed with him. He thought the scheme "wild and impracticable", the proposals far too wide. There was no security for the proper use by the company of its powers of legislation, and the requests of the promoters showed "either a remarkable heedlessness or a singular degree of confidence". In his view the proper form of government of such a colony must be an official council, to be superseded later, perhaps, by an assembly, but not until the colony was firmly and successfully established. As for the power to erect courts, that could not possibly be granted; "the administration of justice ought to be studiously reserved to His Majesty".[14]

Lord Stanley (14th Earl of Derby) (1799–1869)
Edward George Geoffrey Smith Stanley's long political career as a Conservative saw him serve as Prime Minister three times. Before this he was Colonial Secretary from 1833 to 1834 and from 1841 to 1845. (NLA)

Upon these objections being communicated, the company immediately abandoned the obnoxious claims, "reserving only the principles of submitting all grants of land to a sale, the application of the proceeds of sale to the furtherance of emigration, and the eventual privilege of a legislative assembly". The reply was final:

> 'The very readiness with which the objectionable points have been abandoned, contrasted with their prominent appearance in the plan as fundamental principles, unavoidably induces in the mind of the Secretary of State a serious misgiving as to the maturity of their knowledge and counsels on the very important subject which they have submitted to his consideration ... It does not appear to His Lordship that any advantage will arise from continuing the correspondence on this subject.' [15]

It was not until Lord Stanley became Secretary of State in 1833 that the proposals for a joint stock company could be renewed, with modified provisions as to the government of the colony. All the public officers were to be appointed by the Crown, and it now appeared "highly desirable that the whole power and responsibility of the Government should devolve upon the Governor until the Colony shall be thought sufficiently advanced to receive the grant of a legislative assembly". Of the subscribed capital of £500,000, one half was to be employed in the purchase of lands and the other half used as a fund for the government of the colony and the construction of public works, the advances made to the colony to be considered a public debt. This plan the Colonial Office would not consider unless the company agreed to purchase the land, whether they settled it or not, by fixed instalments to be paid within a limited period—a demand with which the company could not comply.[16]

In November 1833 the South Australian Association was formed, and their proposals were laid before the Colonial Office in February 1834. The powers they asked were much less extensive than those of previous schemes. A corporation of trustees, the South Australian Commission, was to manage the economic side of the scheme and have power to make laws, constitute courts and appoint judges and officers, but their laws were to be placed before the Colonial Office for approval before being transmitted to the colony. The Crown would appoint the first Commissioners and vacancies would be filled by the remainder of the Commissioners, subject to the Crown's approval.[17]

Stanley replied that, unless the Government of the colony was left entirely in the hands of the Crown until it was able to govern itself, he would decline to proceed any further.[18] "He would only allow the economic side of Wakefield's system to be based on the centralised administration of a Crown Colony."[19] All hope of a chartered colony had therefore to be abandoned. "It was clear to us," said Wakefield, "that the part of our South Australian plan to which the Colonial Office most objected was a provision for bestowing on the colonists a considerable amount of local self-government. As we could not move an inch without the sanction of that Office, we now resolved to abandon the political part of our scheme, in the hope of being able to realise the economical part."[20]

Although the Wakefield party grudgingly consented to cede the power of government to the Colonial Office, it remained to be decided how the expenses of government were to be met. Provision for this had been made without difficulty in the schemes for a chartered company, but now the only means of obtaining money to establish and carry on the government of the colony was to borrow on the security of the land sales and the future revenue of the colony, for the Colonial Office flatly refused to give any financial assistance. Upon this point a deadlock was imminent:

> 'Stanley, on the one hand, would not move until sufficient money was subscribed and guaranteed to carry on the colonial government for ten years, so as to prevent all expense to the mother-country. The Association, on the other hand, could not promise to raise the money until they knew what kind of an Act of Parliament they were going to get.' [21]

But in June 1834 Stanley was succeeded at the Colonial Office by Thomas Spring Rice, with whom terms of compromise were arranged. A Bill purporting to embody these terms was introduced into the House of Commons and, after a hazardous passage through Parliament, it became law on 15th August 1834.

Thomas Spring-Rice (1790–1866)
A Whig politician, Spring-Rice was only Colonial Secretary for a few months but spent over four years as Chancellor of the Exchequer up to 1839.

So far the attitude of the Colonial Office had been clear and definite - the government of the colony must be left to the Crown. Upon this point it appeared to everyone that the Wakefield party, whilst retaining their principles as to land and emigration, had been forced to give way. The Foundation Act, however, proved to have quite unexpected qualities, and the Secretary of State gradually discovered that, owing to the language used in the Act, he had retained merely the shadow of authority while the substance had escaped him and had passed into the hands of the South Australian Commissioners.

Following 8 pages – The Foundation Act (4 & 5 Wm IV c.95)

ANNO QUARTO & QUINTO

GULIELMI IV. REGIS.

CAP. XCV.

An Act to empower His Majesty to erect *South Australia* into a *British* Province or Provinces, and to provide for the Colonization and Government thereof.

[15th *August* 1834.]

WHEREAS that Part of *Australia* which lies between the Meridians of the One hundred and thirty-second and One hundred and forty-first degrees of East Longitude, and between the Southern Ocean and Twenty-six Degrees of South Latitude, together with the Islands adjacent thereto, consists of waste and unoccupied Lands which are supposed to be fit for the Purposes of Colonization: And whereas divers of His Majesty's Subjects possessing amongst them considerable Property are desirous to embark for the said Part of *Australia*: And whereas it is highly expedient that His Majesty's said Subjects should be enabled to carry their said laudable Purpose into effect: And whereas the said Persons are desirous that in the said intended Colony an uniform System in the Mode of disposing of Waste Lands should be permanently established: Be it therefore enacted by the King's most Excellent Majesty, by and with the Advice and Consent of the Lords Spiritual and Temporal, and Commons, in this present Parliament assembled, and by the Authority of the same, That it shall and may be lawful for His Majesty, with the Advice of His Privy Council, to erect within that Part of *Australia* which lies between the Meridians of the One hundred and thirty-second and One hundred and forty-first Degrees of East Longitude, and between the Southern Ocean and the Twenty-six Degrees of South Latitude, together with all and every the Islands adjacent thereto, and the Bays and Gulfs thereof, with the Advice of His Privy Council, to establish One or more Provinces and to fix the respective Boundaries of such Provinces; and that all and every

His Majesty may establish One or more Provinces in that part of Australia herein described.

9 O Person

Person who shall at any Time hereafter inhabit or reside within His Majesty's said Province or Provinces shall be free, and shall not be subject to or bound by any Laws, Orders, Statutes, or Constitutions which have been heretofore made, or which hereafter shall be made, ordered, or enacted by, for, or as the Laws, Orders, Statutes, or Constitutions of any other Part of *Australia*, but shall be subject to and bound to obey such Laws, Orders, Statutes, and Constitutions as shall from Time to Time, in the Manner herein-after directed be made, ordered, and enacted for the Government of His Majesty's Province or Provinces of *South Australia*.

His Majesty may empower Persons resident in the Colony to make Laws.

II. And be it further enacted, That it shall and may be lawful for His Majesty, His Heirs and Successors, by any Order or Orders to be by Him or Them made with the Advice of His or Their Privy Council, to make, ordain, and, subject to such Conditions and Restrictions as to Him and Them shall seem meet, to authorize and empower any One or more Persons resident and being within any One of the said Provinces to make, ordain, and establish all such Laws, Institutions, or Ordinances, and to constitute such Courts, and appoint such Officers, and also such Chaplains and Clergymen of the Established Church of *England* or *Scotland*, and to impose and levy such Rates, Duties, and Taxes, as may be necessary for the Peace, Order, and good Government of His Majesty's Subjects and others within the said Province or Provinces; provided that all such Orders, and all Laws and Ordinances so to be made as aforesaid, shall be laid before the King in Council as soon as conveniently may be after the making and enacting thereof respectively, and that the same shall not in anywise be contrary or repugnant to any of the Provisions of this Act.

Such Laws to be laid before the King in Council.

Commissioners may be appointed to carry this Act into execution.

III. And be it further enacted, That it shall be lawful for His Majesty, His Heirs and Successors, by Warrant under the Sign Manual, to be countersigned by His Majesty's Principal Secretary of State for the Colonies, to appoint Three or more fit Persons to be Commissioners to carry certain Parts of this Act, and the Powers and authorities herein-after contained, into execution, and also from Time to Time at Pleasure to remove any of the Commissioners for the Time being, and upon every or any Vacancy in the said Number of Commissioners, either by Removal or by Death or otherwise, to appoint some other fit Persons to the said Office; and until such Appointment, it shall be lawful for the surviving or continuing Commissioners or Commissioner to act as if no such Vacancy had occurred.

Style of Board of Commissioners.

IV. And be it further enacted, That the said Commissioners shall be styled "The Colonization Commissioners for *South Australia*", and the said Commissioners or any Two of them may sit from Time to Time, as they deem expedient, as a Board of Commissioners for carrying certain Parts of this Act into execution.

All Proceedings to be sealed.

V. And be it further enacted, That the said Commissioners shall cause to be made a Seal of the said Board, and shall cause to be sealed or stamped therewith all Rules, Orders, and Regulations made by the said Commissioners in pursuance of this Act; and all such Rules, Orders, and Regulations, or Copies thereof, purporting to be sealed or stamped with the Seal of the said Board, shall be received as

10

Evidence

Evidence of the same respectively without any further proof thereof; and no such Rule, Order, or Regulation, or Copy thereof, shall be valid, or have any Force or Effect, unless the same shall be so sealed or stamped as aforesaid.

Commissioners to make Orders for the Sale of Land.

VI. And be it further enacted, That the said Commissioners shall and they are hereby empowered to declare all the Lands of the said Province or Provinces (excepting only Portions which may be reserved for Roads and Footpaths) to be Public Lands, open to Purchase by *British* Subjects, and to make such Orders and Regulations for the surveying and Sale of such Public Lands at such Price as the said Commissioners may from Time to Time deem expedient, and for the letting of the Common of Pasturage of unsold Portions thereof as to the said Commissioners may seem meet, for any period not exceeding Three Years; and from Time to Time to alter and revoke such Orders and Regulations, and to employ the Monies from Time to Time received as the Purchase Money of such Lands, or as Rent of the Common of Pasturage of unsold Portions thereof, in conducting the Emigration of poor Persons from *Great Britain* or *Ireland* to the said Province or Provinces: Provided always, that no Part of the said Public Lands shall be sold except in public for ready Money, and either by Auction or otherwise as may seem best to the said Commissioners, but in no Case, and at no Time for a lower Price than the Sum of Twelve Shillings Sterling *per English* Acre: Provided also, that the Sum *per* Acre which the said Commissioners may declare during any Period to be the upset or selling Price at which Public Lands shall be sold shall be an uniform Price; (that is to say,) the same Price *per* Acre whatever the Quantity or Situation of the Land put up for Sale: Provided also, that the whole of the Funds from Time to Time received as the Purchase Money of the said Lands, or as the Rent of the Common of Pasturage of unsold Portions thereof, shall constitute an "Emigration Fund," and shall, without any Deduction whatsoever, except in the Case herein-after provided for, be employed in conveying poor Emigrants from *Great Britain* or *Ireland* to the said Province or Provinces: Provided also, that the poor Persons who shall by means of the said "Emigration Fund" be conveyed to the said Province or Provinces shall, as far as possible, be adult Persons of the Two Sexes in equal Proportions, and not exceeding the Age of Thirty Years.

Funds received as Purchase Money to form a Fund for conveying poor Emigrants to the Province.

No poor Person to be allowed a Passage from Fund unless Family also conveyed.

VII. And be it further enacted, That no poor Person having a Husband or Wife (as the case may be), or a Child or Children, shall, by means of the said "Emigration Fund," obtain a Passage to the said Province or Provinces, unless the Husband or Wife (as the Case may be), or the Child or Children of such poor Person, shall also be conveyed to the said Province or Provinces.

A Resident Commissioner to be appointed.

VIII. And be it further enacted, That it shall be lawful for His Majesty, His Heirs and Successors, by Warrant under the Sign Manual, to be countersigned by His Majesty's Principal Secretary of State for the Colonies, to appoint a Commissioner of Public Lands to be resident in the said Colony, and to act under the Orders of the said Board of Commissioners as herein-after directed.

IX. And

Treasurer and other Officers may be appointed and removed.

IX. And be it further enacted, That the said Commissioners shall and they are hereby empowered to appoint such Person or Persons as they may think fit Treasurer, Assistant Surveyors, and other Officers, for carrying this Act into execution respecting the Disposal of the said Public Lands and the Purchase Money thereof, and to remove such Treasurer or Assistant Surveyors or other Officers at their Discretion, and on every or any Vacancy in the said Office of Treasurer, Assistant Surveyor, or other Officer, by Removal or by Death or otherwise, to appoint, if they see fit, some other Person to the said Office.

Powers may be delegated to Colonial Commissioner.

X. And be it further enacted, That it shall and may be lawful for the said Commissioners to delegate to the said Colonial Commissioner, Assistant Surveyor, or other Officer, or to any of them, such of the Powers and Authorities with respect to the Disposal of the Public Lands of the said Province or Provinces as the said Commissioners shall think fit; and the Powers and Authorities so delegated, and the Delegation thereof, shall be notified in such Manner, and such Powers and Authorities shall be exercised at such Places, for such Periods and under such Circumstances, and subject to such Regulations, as the said Commissioners shall direct; and the said Commissioners may at any Time revoke, recall, alter, or vary all or any of the Powers and Authorities which shall be so delegated as aforesaid.

Treasurers to receive and pay all Monies, and to give Security.

XI. And be it further enacted, That all Monies under the Controul of the said Board of Commissioners shall be received and paid by the Treasurers who may be appointed by the said Board, and who shall give Security for the faithful Discharge of their Duties to such Amount and in such Manner as to the said Commissioners may seem fit.

Accounts to be audited.

XII. And be it further enacted, That all Accounts of the said Treasurer shall be submitted to the Lords of His Majesty's Treasury, and be audited in the same Manner as other Public Accounts.

Appointment of Officers.

XIII. And be it further enacted, That the said Commissioners may and they are hereby empowered from Time to Time to appoint a Secretary, Treasurer, and all such Clerks, Messengers, and Officers as they shall think fit, and from Time to Time, at the Discretion of the said Commissioners, to remove such Secretary, Treasurer, Clerks, Messengers, and Officers, or any of them, and to appoint others in their Stead.

Commissioners to take Oath.

XIV. And be it further enacted, That every Commissioner and Colonial Commissioner to be appointed from Time to Time shall, before he shall enter upon the Execution of his Office, take the following Oath before one of the Judges of His Majesty's Court of Common Pleas, or one of the Barons of the Court of Exchequer, or (in the Case of such Colonial Commissioners) before the Judge of one of His Majesty's Courts in the said Province or Provinces; (that is to say,)

'I *A. B.* do swear, That I shall faithfully, impartially, and honestly, 'according to the best of my Skill and Judgment, execute and 'fulfil all the Powers and Duties of a Commissioner [*or* Colonial 'Commissioner, *as the Case may be*,] under an Act passed in the 'Fifth Year of the Reign of King *William* the Fourth, intituled '[*here set forth the Title of this Act*].'

XV. Pro-

4 & 5 GULIELMI IV. Cap. 95. 793

Salaries to be fixed by Lords of Treasury.

XV. Provided always, and be it further enacted, That the Salaries to be paid to all such Persons as may be appointed to any Office under this Act shall be fixed by the Lords of His Majesty's Treasury, and by them shall be revised from Time to Time as they may deem expedient.

Proceedings of Commissioners to be reported to Secretary of State, and laid before Parliament.

XVI. And be it further enacted, That the said Comissioners shall, at least once in every Year, and at such other Times and in such Form as His Majesty's Principal Secretary of State for the Colonies shall direct, submit to the said Secretary of State a full and particular Report of their Proceedings; and every such Report shall be laid before both Houses of Parliament within Six Weeks after the Receipt of the same by the said Secretary of State, if Parliament be then sitting, or if Parliament be not sitting, then within Six Weeks after the next Meeting thereof.

Until Sale of Lands, Money to be raised by Bond for conveying out poor Emigrants.

XVII. And be it further enacted, That it shall and may be lawful for the said Commissioners, previously and until the Sale of Public Lands in the said Province shall have produced a Fund sufficient to defray the Cost of conveying to the said Province or Provinces from Time to Time such a Number of poor Emigrants as may by the said Commissioners be thought desirable, from Time to Time to borrow and take up on Bond or otherwise, payable by Instalments or otherwise, at Interest not exceeding Ten Pounds *per Centum per Annum*, any Sum or Sums of Money not exceeding Fifty thousand Pounds, for the sole Purpose of defraying the Costs of the Passage of poor Emigrants from *Great Britain* or *Ireland* to the said Province or Provinces, by granting and issuing to any Person or Persons willing to advance such Monies Bonds or obligatory Writings under the Hands and Seals of the said Commissioners or of any Two of them, which Bonds or other obligatory Writings shall be termed "*South Australia* Public Lands Securities;" and all such Sum or Sums of Money not exceeding in the whole Fifty thousand Pounds so borrowed or taken up by means of the Bonds or Writings obligatory aforesaid, for the sole Purpose aforesaid, shall be borrowed on the Credit of and be deemed a Charge upon the whole of the Fund to be received as the Purchase Money of Public Lands, or as the Rent of the Common of Pasturage of unsold Portions thereof; and it shall and may be lawful for the said Commissioners from Time to Time to appropriate all or any Part of the Monies which may be obtained by the Sale of Public Lands in the said Province or Provinces to the Payment of Interest on any such Sum or Sums borrowed and taken up as aforesaid, or to the Repayment of such Principal Sum or Sums.

Power to borrow Money to pay Expenses of Colony.

XVIII. And be it further enacted, That for defraying the necessary Costs, Charges, and Expenses of founding the said intended Colony, and of providing for the Government thereof, and for the Expenses of the said Commissioners (excepting always the Purpose whereunto the said Emigration Fund is made solely applicable by this Act), and for defraying all Costs, Charges, and Expenses incurred in carrying this Act into execution, and applying for and obtaining this Act, it shall and may be lawful for the said Commissioners from Time to Time to borrow and take up on Bond or otherwise, payable by Instalments or otherwise, at Interest not exceeding Ten Pounds *per Centum per Annum*, any Sum or Sums of Money required for the

9 P Purposes

Purposes last aforesaid, not exceeding in the whole the Sum of Two hundred thousand Pounds, by granting or issuing to any Person or Persons willing to advance such Monies Bonds or obligatory Writings under the Hands and Seals of the said Commissioners or any Two of them, which Bonds or other obligatory Writings shall be termed "*South Australia* Colonial Revenue Securities;" and all such Sum or Sums of Money by the said Commissioners so borrowed and taken up as last aforesaid shall be and is and are hereby declared to be a Charge upon the ordinary Revenue or Produce of all Rates, Duties, and Taxes to be levied and collected as herein-before directed within the said Province or Provinces, and shall be deemed and taken to be a Public Debt owing by the said Province to the Holders of the Bond or Bonds or other Writings obligatory by the said Commissioners granted for the Purposes last aforesaid.

Commissioners may reduce Rate of Interest.

XIX. And be it further enacted, That it shall and may be lawful for the said Commissioners at any Time to borrow or take up any Sum or Sums of Money for any of the Purposes of this Act at a lower Rate of Interest than any Security or Securities previously given by them under and by virtue of this Act which may then be in force shall bear, and therewith to pay off and discharge any existing Security or Securities bearing a higher Rate of Interest as aforesaid.

Lands of Colony to be deemed a collateral Security.

XX. And be it further enacted, That in case it should so happen that the said Commissioners shall be unable to raise by the Issue of the said Colonial Revenue Securities the whole of the said Sum of Two hundred thousand Pounds, or that the ordinary Revenue of the said Province or Provinces shall be insufficient to discharge the Obligations of all or any of the said Securities, then and in that Case, but not otherwise, the Public Lands of the said Province or Provinces then remaining unsold, and the Monies to be obtained by the Sale thereof, shall be deemed a collateral Security for Payment of the Principal and Interest of the said Colonial Debt: Provided always, that no Monies obtained by the Sales of Public Lands in the said Province or Provinces shall be employed in defraying the Principal or Interest of the said Colonial Debt so long as any obligation created by the said *South Australian* Public Lands Securities shall remain undischarged: Provided also, that in case, after the Discharge of all Obligations created by the said *South Australian* Public Lands Securities, any Part of the Monies obtained by the Sale of Public Lands in the said Province or Provinces shall be employed to discharge any of the Obligations created by the said Colonial Revenue Securities, then and in that Case the Amount of such Deduction from the said Emigration Fund shall be deemed a Colonial Debt owing by the said Province to the Colonization Commissioners for *South Australia*, and be charged upon the ordinary Revenue of the said Province or Provinces.

Commissioners may sue and be sued in the Name of One Commissioner or of their Clerk or Secretary.

XXI. And be it further enacted, That the Commissioners nominated and appointed by His Majesty as aforesaid may sue and be sued in the Name or Names of any One of such Commissioners, or of their Secretary, Clerk or Clerks for the Time being; and that no Action or Suit to be brought or commenced by or against any of the said Commissioners in the Name or Names of any One of such Commissioners, or their Secretary or Clerk, shall abate or be discontinued by the Death or Removal of such Commissioner, Secretary, or Clerk, or any of them, or by the Act of such Commissioner, Secretary, or Clerk,

or

or any of them, without the Consent of the said Commissioners, but that any One of the said Commissioners, or the Secretary or Clerk for the Time being to the said Commissioners, shall always be deemed to be the Plaintiff or Defendant (as the Case may be) in every such Action or Suit: Provided always, that nothing herein contained shall be deemed, construed, or taken to extend to make the Commissioners who shall sign, execute, or give any of the Bonds or obligatory Writings so hereby authorized or directed to be given personally, or their respective Estates, Lands, or Tenements, Goods and Chattels, or such Secretary or Clerk, or their or either of their Lands and Tenements, Goods and Chattels, liable to the Payment of any of the Monies so borrowed and secured by reason of their giving any such Bonds or Securities as aforesaid, or of their being Plaintiff or Defendant in any such Action as aforesaid; but that the Costs, Charges and Expenses of every such Commissioner, Secretary, or Clerk, by reason of having been made Plaintiff or Defendant, or for any Contract, Act, Matter, or Thing whatsoever made or entered into in the *bonâ fide* Execution of this Act, from Time to Time be defrayed by the said Commissioners out of the Money so borrowed and taken up as aforesaid.

Convicts [not] to be transported to the Colony.

XXII. And be it further enacted, That no Person or Persons convicted in any Court of Justice in *Great Britain* or *Ireland*, or elsewhere, shall at any Time or under any Circumstances be transported as a Convict to any Place within the Limits herein-before described.

A Constitution to be established when there shall be Fifty thousand Inhabitants.

XXIII. And be it further enacted, That it shall and may be lawful for His Majesty, by and with the Advice of His Privy Council, to frame, constitute, and establish a Constitution or Constitutions of Local Government for any of the said Provinces possessing a Population of Fifty thousand Souls, in such Manner, and with such Provisoes, Limitations, and Restrictions, as shall to His Majesty, by and with the Advice of His Privy Council, be deemed meet and desirable: Provided always, that the Mode herein-before directed of disposing of the Public Lands of the said Province or Provinces by Sale only, and of the Fund obtained by the Sale thereof, shall not be liable to be in anywise altered or changed otherwise than by the Authority of His Majesty and the Consent of Parliament: Provided also, that in the said Constitution of Local Government for the said Province or Provinces, Provision shall be made for the Satisfaction of the Obligations of any of the said Colonial Revenue Securities which may be unsatisfied at the Time of framing such Constitution of the said Province or Provinces.

20,000l. to be invested in Exchequer Bills as a Security upon the Mother Country.

XXIV. And be it further enacted, That for the purpose of providing a Guarantee or Security that no Part of the Expense of founding and governing the said intended Colony shall fall on the Mother Country, the said Commissioners shall and are hereby empowered and required, out of the Monies borrowed and taken up as aforesaid on the Security of the said *South Australian* Colonial Revenue Securities, to invest the sum of Twenty thousand Pounds in the Purchase of Exchequer Bills or other Government Securities in *England*, in the Names of Trustees to be appointed by His Majesty; and the said Trustees shall hold the said Exchequer Bills, or other Government Securities so long as may seem fit to His Majesty's Principal Secretary of State for the Colonies; or shall, in Case

Case it shall seem fit to His Majesty's Principal Secretary of State for the Colonies, dispose of the same for any of the purposes to which the Monies raised by the Issue of the said *South Australian* Colonial Revenue Securitites are hereby made applicable: Provided always, that if the said Secretary of State should dispose of any Part of the said Twenty thousand Pounds, a Sum or Sums equal to the Sum or Sums so disposed of shall be invested in the Names of the said Trustees by the said Commissioners, so that the said Guarantee or Security Fund of Twenty thousand Pounds shall not at any Time be reduced below that Amount: Provided always, that the Interest and Dividends accruing from Time to Time upon the said Exchequer Bills, or other Government Securities, shall be paid to the said Commissioners, and by them be devoted to the Purposes to which, as herein-before directed, the Monies to be raised by the Issue of the aforesaid *South Australian* Colonial Revenue Bonds are made applicable.

If after Ten Years from the passing of this Act the Population shall be less than 20,000 natural born Subjects Lands to be liable to be disposed of by His Majesty.

XXV. And be it further enacted, That if after the Expiration of Ten Years from the passing of this Act the Population of the said Province or Provinces shall be less than Twenty thousand natural born Subjects, then and in that Case all the Public Lands of the said Province or Provinces which shall then be unsold shall be liable to be disposed of by His Majesty, His Heirs and Successors, in such Manner as to him or them shall seem meet: Provided always, that in case any of the Obligations created by the said *South Australian* Public Lands Securities should then be unsatisfied the Amount of such Obligations shall be deemed a Charge upon the said unsold Public Lands, and shall be paid to the Holders of such Securities out of any Monies that may be obtained by the Sale of the said Lands.

Powers of Commissioners not to commence until the Money is raised, except for that Purpose.

XXVI. And be it further enacted, That until the said Commissioners shall, by the granting and issuing of Bonds and Writings obligatory as aforesaid, that is to say, "*South Australian* Colonial Revenue Securities," have raised the Sum of Twenty thousand Pounds, and have invested the same in the Purchase of Exchequer Bills, or other Government Securities, as herein-before directed, and until the Persons intending to settle in the said Province or Provinces and others shall have invested, (either by Payment to the said Commissioners, or in the Names of Trustees to be appointed by them), for the Purchase of Public Lands in the said Province or Provinces, the Sum of Thirty-five thousand Pounds, none of the Powers and Authorities hereby given to His Majesty, or to the said Commissioners, or to any Person or Persons, except as respects the Exercise by the said Commissioners of such Powers as are required for raising Money by means of and on the Security of the Bonds or Securities last aforesaid, and for receiving and investing the aforesaid Sum of Thirty-five thousand Pounds for the Purchase of Public Lands, shall be of any Effect, or have any Operation whatsoever.

The Foundation Act can be conveniently analysed under the following heads:

A. The system of colonisation.
B. The method of government.
C. The self-supporting system.[1]

A. The System of Colonisation

(1) Three or more fit persons, to be styled the "Colonization Commissioners for South Australia", were to be appointed by the Crown to carry out the provisions of the Act.

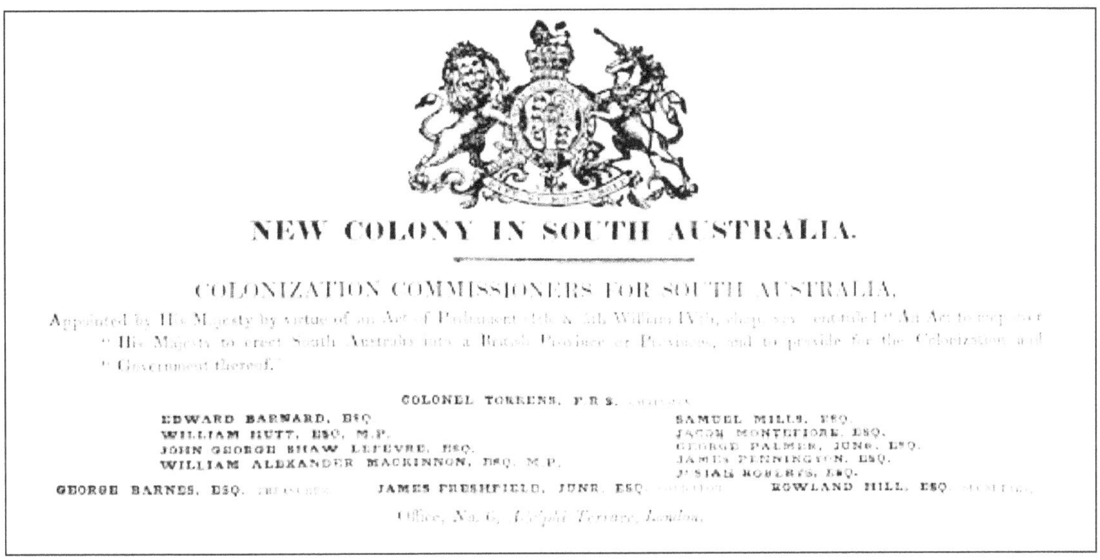
NEW COLONY IN SOUTH AUSTRALIA.

COLONIZATION COMMISSIONERS FOR SOUTH AUSTRALIA.

COLONEL TORRENS, F.R.S.

EDWARD BARNARD, ESQ.
WILLIAM HUTT, ESQ. M.P.
JOHN GEORGE SHAW LEFEVRE, ESQ.
WILLIAM ALEXANDER MACKINNON, ESQ. M.P.

SAMUEL MILLS, ESQ.
JACOB MONTEFIORE, ESQ.
GEORGE PALMER, JUNR. ESQ.
JAMES PENNINGTON, ESQ.
JOSIAH ROBERTS, ESQ.

GEORGE BARNES, ESQ. JAMES FRESHFIELD, JUNR. ESQ. ROWLAND HILL, ESQ.

Heading to information for prospective emigrants to South Australia published by the Commission in December 1835. (SLSA)

(2) The Commissioners were empowered:

(a) To declare all the lands of the province (except portions reserved for roads and footpaths) to be public lands open to purchase by British subjects.

(b) To make orders and regulations for the survey and sale of such lands at such price as they deemed sufficient; provided that no part of the public lands should be sold except in public for ready money, either by auction or otherwise as the Commissioners should determine, but in no case and at no time for a lower price than 12s per acre.

(c) To let the common of pasturage of unsold portions of land for any period not exceeding three years.

(d) To employ the whole of the purchase money or rent received as an "Emigration Fund" for conducting the emigration of poor persons from Great Britain and Ireland to the province.

(e) To appoint officers. They were authorised:

(i) By section IX "to appoint such person or persons as they may think fit Treasurer, Assistant Surveyors, and other officers, for carrying this Act into execution respecting the disposal of the said Public Lands and the Purchase Money thereof".

(ii) By section XIII to appoint "a Secretary, Treasurer, and all such clerks, messengers and officers as they shall think fit".

By section VIII the King was empowered to appoint a Commissioner of Public Lands, to be resident in the colony and to act under the orders of the Commissioners.

The salaries of the officers appointed under the Act were to be fixed by the Treasury.

(f) To delegate to the Colonial Commissioner or other officers such of the powers and authorities with respect to the disposal of the public lands of the province as they thought fit.

(3) At least once a year the Commissioners were to submit to the Secretary of State for the colonies a "full and detailed report" of their proceedings to be laid before Parliament.

B. The Method of Government

(1) By section I every person inhabiting or residing in the province "shall be free and shall not be subject to or bound by any laws orders statutes or constitutions which have been heretofore made or which hereafter shall be made ordered or enacted by for or as the laws orders statutes or constitutions of any other part of Australia, but shall be subject to and bound to obey such laws orders statutes and constitutions as shall from time to time, in the manner hereinafter directed, be made ordered and enacted for the government of His Majesty's Province of South Australia".

(2) Section II empowered the King, with the advice of the Privy Council, "to make ordain, and, subject to such conditions and restrictions as to him shall seem meet, to authorise and empower any one or more persons" resident in the province:

(a) to make, ordain and establish all such laws, institutions or ordinances; and

(b) to constitute such courts or appoint such officers; and

(c) to impose and levy such rates, duties and taxes "as may be necessary for the peace order and good government of the Province".

All such ordinances, laws and orders were to be laid before the King in Council and were not to be contrary or repugnant to any of the provisions of the Act.

(3) A constitution of local government was to be established when the population reached 50,000.

(4) No convicts were at any time or under any circumstances to be transported to the province.

Robert Dighton's *A Fleet of Transports under Convoy* depicts convicts at Newgate Gaol. No convicts were transported to South Australia but Newgate Gaol figures in the colony's history. This is where an imprisoned Edward Gibbon Wakefield formulated his system of colonisation and wrote *A Sketch of a Proposal for Colonizing Australasia* and *A Letter from Sydney*. (NLA)

C. The Self-Supporting Principle

(1) Until the sale of lands, the Commissioners were empowered to borrow at interest not exceeding ten per cent per annum up to £50,000 for the sole purpose of defraying the costs of the passage of poor emigrants by issuing bonds to be termed "South Australian Public Lands Securities".

All sums borrowed "shall be borrowed on the credit of and be deemed a charge upon the whole of the Fund" to be received as purchase moneys and rent; and the Commissioners might appropriate moneys from the sale of public lands to the payment of interest on, or repayment of, any sums borrowed.

(2) To defray the necessary costs, charges and expenses of founding the colony and providing for its government and the

expenses of administration, the Commissioners were empowered to borrow up to £200,000 at interest not exceeding ten per cent by issuing bonds to be termed "South Australian Colonial Revenue Securities". The sums so borrowed were to be charged upon the ordinary revenue or produce of all rates, duties and taxes to be levied and collected in the colony and were deemed to be a public debt owing by the province to the holders of the bonds.

(3) The lands of the colony and the moneys obtained by their sale were to be a collateral security for the payment of the colonial debt.

(4) Out of the moneys borrowed on the security of the "South Australian Colonial Revenue Securities", £20,000 was to be invested in the names of trustees to be appointed by the Crown; and this sum was to be at the disposal of the Secretary of State for the colonies as a guarantee against the government incurring any expense.

(5) The powers of the Commissioners were not to commence (except for the purpose of raising money) until the guarantee fund of £20,000 had been duly invested and £35,000 had been subscribed for the purchase of lands.

King William IV and Queen Adelaide (ACCA)

Chapter 1.3

Historical Background

Quarter deck government

Father Paul Sarpi read the Scriptures with such care that, it being his custom to draw a line under passages which he considered important, there was not a single word in his New Testament but was underlined. If any querulous person took a pen and set out to underline all the passages in the Foundation Act which caused trouble, his scoring might not be so meticulously thorough, but there would be few sections left unmarked. Its creators might well have chanted in unison, "We have done those things which we ought not to have done, and we have left undone those things which we ought to have done." Difficulties arose both in providing for subjects upon which the Act was silent and in endeavouring to ascertain what it meant when it spoke. Several writers have investigated the economic and financial deficiencies of the Act, and it is only proposed here to mention some of the legal and constitutional difficulties to which it gave rise.

Officialdom was puzzled from the outset. How was the province to be created? There was no precedent for the establishment of a colony in the manner indicated by the Act. Section I (in ungrammatical language) empowered the King, with the advice of the Privy Council, "to erect and establish within the boundaries prescribed one or more provinces" and to fix the respective boundaries of such provinces. Nothing was said about the instrument by which the provinces were to be created. Parliament had usurped the prerogative of the Crown by authorising the King to do that which he could have done, by a Commission under the Great Seal, without Parliamentary assistance.[1] Long consideration by the law officers was necessary before the decision was reached that the colony should be established by the issue of Letters Patent, defining its boundaries.[2]

Then how many provinces were there to be and how were the boundaries to be fixed? No-one had any adequate knowledge of the country, and the fixing of boundaries could be nothing more than guesswork. In the House of Commons one member had expressed the opinion that a "cabbage garden" or at the most sixty or one hundred square miles of territory would be quite enough "for these gentlemen to play their pranks in", and the Colonial Office were disposed to restrict the area to be granted for the experiment. The Commissioners hastened to obtain the opinion of Sir William Follett (Solicitor-General in 1835 and afterwards Attorney-General) that under the Act the provinces must be proclaimed once for all and that the government had no power to erect only a small portion of the territory into a province, leaving the remainder in abeyance to be added at a future time or made into another province, if the colony proved a success.[3]

Next, a legislature to be nominated by the Crown was to be established. Should it be official, unofficial or a mixture of both? And if official, what officers were to be members? The Commissioners wisely recommended that, as the Council was to conform to the instructions of the Colonial Office, no officers of the Commissioners should be members, so as to prevent any clashing, but it was eventually provided by an Order in Council on 23 February 1936 that the Council should consist of:

(1) The Governor or officer administering the government.
(2) The Judge.
(3) The Colonial Secretary.
(4) The Advocate-General.
(5) The Resident Commissioner.

Any three of them (of whom the Governor should be one) could make laws and ordinances, appoint officers and impose and levy rates, duties and taxes. All laws were to be introduced into the Council by the Governor and transmitted for the approval of the Crown at home.[4]

The following instructions were prescribed for the conduct of business by the Council:

(1) Each law was to be confined to a single subject matter.
(2) A law once disallowed was not to be re-enacted without leave.
(3) No law was to continue in force for less than two years, except in cases of necessity.
(4) No revenue law was to be lightened without leave.
(5) Acts of an extraordinary nature, prejudicial to the prerogative or the property of the subject, affecting trade or shipping, or of a private nature, were to be reserved for the consent of the Crown.

In the exercise of the prerogative of mercy the Judge was to report upon the trial of everyone sentenced to death. His report was to be considered at the next Council and the advice of the members taken but the Governor was finally to decide on his own deliberate judgment whether the sentence should be executed.[5]

Again, the method by which the officers of the colony were to be appointed worried the law officers for more than three months, before they finally advised that the Governor should be appointed, like the governors of other Crown colonies, by Letters Patent, and the other officers by an Order in Council. This latter mode of appointment they described as "very inconvenient and so far as we know without precedent" and they recommended that a bill should be introduced to amend the Act on this point.[6]

These questions were mainly matters of legal forms; there were difficulties far more serious to be faced. The powers given to the Commissioners by the Act were very large, but when the Act was examined there was a total absence of any provision to secure the due exercise of those powers.

> 'So large an administrative power in the discharge of so important a public trust ought not to have been confided to any other hands than those of the recognised authorities of the country. To devolve them upon a Board, the members of which were to be appointed and removed at the pleasure of the Crown, but over whose proceedings the responsible Ministers of the Crown could exercise no adequate control, was in effect to relieve the Government from its proper responsibility, and transfer it to persons of whose fitness for the office Parliament could take no assurance beyond the judgment of the Ministry for the time being, though the public faith was, to a great extent, implicated in their acts, and pledged to their engagements.'[7]

Robert Torrens (1780-1864) Economist, politician, soldier and newspaper proprietor, Torrens was an early promoter of schemes for the colonization of South Australia and emigration to colonies generally. He became Chairman of the Colonization Commissioners in 1835. (SLSA)

When Colonel Robert Torrens went to the Colonial Office to see Hay, "the ancient foe to South Australia", with a list of those whom it was proposed should be appointed Commissioners, Hay very naturally said that it would be necessary to ascertain in what way the Commissioners could be held responsible for the due execution of their duties. Supposing they suddenly resigned, for instance, the colony would be left stranded and the Government would have to come to the rescue. To the enthusiastic colonists Hay's sensible objections seemed merely obstructive. Further consideration by the Colonial Office opened up another question, and on 16 February 1835 Hay wrote to Colonel Torrens:

> 'Lord Aberdeen considers it to be an essential preliminary to the further discussion of the subject, that it should be distinctly understood whether the proposed Commissioners are or are not to be accountants to the Crown, and personally responsible for the receipt and application of the money to arise from the sale of lands in the proposed colony.'

Robert William Hay (1786-1861) Undersecretary at the Colonial Office from 1825 to 1836.

Although there was no express direction to be found in the Act, he presumed that:

> '... all the money which they shall receive as Commissioners must be considered as part of the King's revenue, and that the Commissioners, not being a body corporate, must be regarded only as His Majesty's agents (though appointed under the authority of Parliament) for the management, receipt and expenditure of that part of the revenue of the Crown.'

He thought the matter of "such essential importance, and involved in such obscurity, as to require a solution of the question on the highest accessible authority before the discussion advances further".[8]

Colonel Torrens submitted the matter to J.W. Freshfield (afterwards solicitor to the Commissioners), who advised:

> 'I have no hesitation in stating it as my opinion that the Commissioners are not to be accountants to the Crown, nor responsible for the receipt and application of the money made subject to their control by the Act of Parliament; of course, they would be liable for any personal corruption in the exercise of their powers, and for the application of the money to purposes not within the authority of the Act, but that liability is common to every person accepting a trust.' [9]

This opinion was forwarded to the Colonial Office and sent on to the Lords of the Treasury. There the matter slumbered until the colonists became impatient, and Robert Gouger went to see Sir Thomas Fremantle at the Treasury. An entry in John Brown's journal describes the interview and shows how little attention the Government officials had given to the South Australian scheme. Gouger complained of the delay and said that the question was a simple one — where was the responsibility to rest? Sir Thomas Fremantle said that:

John Brown (1801–1879)
A businessman and campaigner for the colonization of South Australia, Brown became the first Emigration Officer and one of those who opposed Hindmarsh. He was, variously, on Adelaide's first municipal council, a mine owner, the editor of the *Southern Australian* and the manager of an insurance company.

> '... he concluded that the Commissioners here would be as necessarily responsible for the loan and other monies they might raise as the Directors of any Land Company. And upon Gouger expressing astonishment at his confounding two offices so wholly dissimilar, it appeared that he had actually viewed the colony in the light of a land speculation for the benefit of individuals under the sanction of a Chater [sic]. Gouger then begged that as this view was wholly erroneous, he would allow him to wait while he sent for an Act of Parliament that the mistake might be at once rectified, and the impression removed. Fremantle accordingly sent, and confessed that he had not viewed it as a public and government Commission before.' [10]

Eventually the Treasury confirmed Freshfield's opinion and agreed that:

> '... so long as the powers in the South Australian Commissioners by the Act 4 & 5 Wm IV c.95 in regard to the moneys to be raised and applied under its provisions are duly exercised, and not exceeded by the Commissioners, they will not be personally responsible or accountable to the Crown for those moneys.'[11]

This decision was a surprise to the Colonial Office. Worse still was the gradual realisation that not only were the Commissioners free from any liability to account to the Crown for the expenditure of moneys coming to their hands but that they had complete and sole control over those moneys.

For some time neither the Commissioners nor the Colonial Office saw the full significance of the provisions of the Act. The Colonial Office believed that the Commissioners were limited to dealing with sales of land and emigration, while all questions of government remained under the direction of the Secretary of State. The only difference between the mode of government of South Australia and any other Crown colony, they thought, was that instead of the moneys required for the expenses of government being paid by the Treasury they would be drawn (until the colony was able to support itself) from the fund which the Commissioners were to raise, the Colonial Office having control of this revenue fund.

Most of the colonists who troubled themselves about constitutional matters probably came to South Australia holding this opinion. In the first number of *The Register*, for instance, which was published in June 1836 and contained information about the colony for the instruction of emigrants, it was said that:

> 'South Australia is to be governed precisely as the other colonies of the Crown, not possessing a legislative assembly, that is, by a Governor appointed by the King, assisted by a Legislative Council';

(Sir) Rowland Hill (1795–1879)
Hill served as Secretary for the South Australian Commission from 1834 to 1839 but is best known for his reform of the postal system and invention of stamps. (NPG)

and that the powers of the Governor would be the same as those of other governors with the exception of the disposal of public lands.[12]

At first the Commissioners, who were themselves divided in opinion about the construction of the Act, acquiesced in this view and were subservient to the Colonial Office. By the end of 1835 it had begun to dawn on them that they had, perhaps, larger powers than they had expected. Brown noted in his journal on 24 November 1835:

> 'A long discussion with the Governor, Mr Hill, Fisher, Stephens, Kingston and myself about writing to the Colonial Office to request their sanction to the Commissioners purchasing a vessel to accompany the first expedition as a small surveying vessel. The propriety of establishing a precedent for submitting all expenses to the permission of the Colonial Office was the question—in fact, whether the Commissioners are to have the direction of Government expenditure or the Office. The letter, tho' written by the Governor, was withheld until the Board considered it again.'

Lord Glenelg (1778–1866)
Charles Grant was Secretary of State from April 1835 to February 1839. Despite success with the abolition of slavery in the West Indies his performance as Colonial Secretary was often criticised, particularly regarding Canada, and he was forced to resign from office.

Here the point was directly raised, but the Commissioners did not take the matter up with the Colonial Office for some months.

In January 1836 Lord Glenelg said he would consent to the proclamation of the colony provided three things at least were embodied in an amending act:

(1) Regulations for the protection of the Aborigines, whose existence had been completely overlooked in the Foundation Act.
(2) Provision for the appointment of officers in a simpler and more convenient way.
(3) The reservation to the Treasury of power to apply towards the civil government and administration of justice so much of the proceeds of sale of land as might be made necessary by the deficiency of other public resources.[13]

At this stage the Colonial Office still had no doubt that the Commissioners were limited to controlling land and emigration. Lord Glenelg did not ask for an act giving the Crown control of the revenue fund because he assumed that the Crown had the power to dispose of it: he only wanted power to supplement it from the land fund if it proved insufficient.

Sir George Grey (1799-1882)
A Whig politician who, in 1836, was Colonial under-secretary to Spring Rice. He was to become Colonial Secretary from 1854 to 1855 and also served as the Home Secretary. In that post he carried the Bill that brought an end to transportation. (RVPL)

The last of his three points, however, caused consternation among the Wakefield party, to whom the land fund was sacrosanct. Torrens said that unless the Colonial Office abandoned this demand the colony was ended. He interviewed Sir George Grey and told him that any alteration in the appropriation of the land fund would bring about the immediate resignation of the Commissioners and the whole scheme would collapse.[14] Surprised at this strong opposition, the Colonial Office allowed the matter of an amending act to drop.

It was not until June 1836 that the Commissioners definitely asserted that the control of the funds raised pursuant to the Act (except so far as related to the salaries of the officers, which were fixed by the Treasury) was placed in their hands entirely. The claim was referred to the law officers (Sir John Campbell and Sir R.M. Rolfe), and Lord Glenelg was startled to find that their opinion was that the disposition of the fund to be raised under the 18th section of the Act to provide for the expenses of government rested with the Commissioners.

> 'The Commissioners will be liable for any wilful misapplication of the money; but so long as they bona fide apply it for the purposes indicated in the 18th section, they appear to us to have a discretion as to its application.' [15]

This unforeseen interpretation of the Act placed the Colonial Office in an extremely awkward position.[16] Lord Glenelg wrote that he could only anticipate "very great confusion and difficulty from the anomalous system which has been introduced into this branch of the public business".[17]

Two courses were open to him:

(1) To have an amending act passed to give the Colonial Office control of the fund for the expenses of government.
(2) To acquiesce in the complete control of the Commissioners and throw all the responsibility on them.

To have taken the first course would have involved a complete reconstruction of the Act. Out of the revenue fund had to be paid not only the governmental expenses but the preliminary costs of land sales and surveys, because by section 6 of the Act the whole of the money derived from the sale of lands had to be devoted to emigration. The Colonial Office did not want to take over the supervision of these expenses, for the division of authority would then simply be reversed and the Commissioners would have to embark upon enterprises, without control of the funds from which the expenses of them were to come. Further, thousands of pounds had been invested upon the basis of the scheme as set out in the original act. Seven vessels had sailed with over two hundred emigrants, and it was impossible to hold up emigration while the question was discussed in Parliament. Any step which might delay further progress or cast doubt upon the stability of the scheme would be ruinous. It is not surprising that Lord Glenelg shrank from such a course, and it is only fair to take it that he acted as much from a genuine belief that the best thing to be done in the emergency was to relinquish full control to the Commissioners, as from any Pontius-Pilate-like desire to shirk responsibility and wash his hands of the whole matter.

View on the Glenelg plains ca. 1837 by J.A. Thomas (NLA)

The Commissioners suggested it was desirable to have the point definitely decided by an amending act, but they received no reply.[18] The Colonial Office treated the whole matter as settled by the opinion of the law officers. The Commissioners became the real rulers of the colony and thus "an unbusinesslike Board gained the complete control of the complicated scheme of an almost unworkable Act of Parliament". All the dispatches and enactments which the Governor sent home to the Colonial Office were passed on to the Commissioners for their approval or condemnation. The only control which the Colonial Office retained was that the Commissioners were the nominees of the Secretary of State and might be removed by him.

(Sir) James Hurtle Fisher (1790-1875)
A lawyer who became the first Resident Commissioner, Fisher's tenure of the position ended with the arrival of Governor Gawler in 1838. He returned to the bar and in 1840 became the first mayor of Adelaide and subsequently held various political offices until his retirement in 1865. (SLSA)

Although the Colonial Office cannot be blamed, perhaps, for the course they took, there was no excuse for their failure to notify the Governor of the changed circumstances. James Hurtle Fisher, the Resident Commissioner, was advised of it by the Commissioners in August 1836, but the Governor sailed in the *Buffalo* firmly believing, as the Colonial Office had believed, that on the administrative side he was supreme and that he had, as representative of the Crown, complete control of this branch of affairs in the colony. It was not until March 1838 that Hindmarsh was informed of the volte-face which the Colonial Office had made; and then he only discovered it from Fisher.[19]

The worst error of the Foundation Act was the division of authority which it created. Edward Gibbon Wakefield said later that "according to the manner, I will not say system, in which South Australia has been governed, every body seems to have been fully relieved of responsibility to any body";[20] and the Select Committee of the House of Commons reported in 1841:

> 'In endeavouring to convey the necessary powers to the Commissioners without trespassing upon the Prerogative of the Crown, the Act created an inconvenient division of authority, and the powers of Administration were so parted between the two, that they could not be effectually exercised by either. The raising of a Revenue by means of Rates, Taxes and Duties, the appropriation of the Revenue so raised, and the general administration of the Government, were vested by the Act in a Local Board, appointed by the Crown, and subject to the authority of the Queen in Council; whilst the administration, not of the Land Fund only, but of the Fund out of which all the necessary expenses of Government for Surveys, Salaries, Police, Public Works &c were to be defrayed, was confided in England to the Commissioners, and in the Colony to a Commissioner, appointed indeed by the Crown, but acting only under their instructions, and subject only to their authority. Thus whilst one department was made responsible for the payment of the Colonial Debt, another had the management of the Fund out of which it was to be paid; and whilst one was responsible for conducting the Public Service, the money by means of which it was to be conducted was placed under the control of another. If the Revenues of

> the Colony were mismanaged by the Local Government, the Commissioners could not satisfy the Public Creditor; if the Funds raised on the security of those Revenues were mismanaged by the Commissioners, the Government could not conduct the Public Service. Nor is it to be forgotten, that the evils to be apprehended from the conflict of authorities so ill-adjusted, which must be great in any case, were greatly aggravated in this by the distance at which they were exercised, and the length of time before a difficulty arising in South Australia could be removed by a fresh instruction from England.' [21]

The Commissioners afterwards pleaded that the Foundation Act was not sufficiently explicit to enable them, in their instructions to the Resident Commissioner, to draw any precise line between the limits of the authority of the Governor on the one hand and of the Resident Commissioner on the other, but the fact that the Act was not sufficiently distinct was only an additional reason why they should have taken care to define those limits which the Act had left obscure.

In this state of affairs the only hope for success in the colony lay in the selection of able officers who would work together amicably. Dr Price has pointed out the difficulties with which the Commissioners were faced in making the appointments—their fields of choice limited to men prepared to emigrate, willing to accept moderate salaries and able to maintain themselves at their own expense for a considerable time; the services of those who had assisted in the colonisation movement to be rewarded; patronage to be dispensed to men with money who could buy land or bonds. "Qualifications, on the whole, were measured by bank balances rather than ability." The various official positions were filled only after months of jealous scheming which laid the foundation for quarrels in the colony. Captain John Hindmarsh was appointed Governor; and James Hurtle Fisher, a London solicitor, Resident Commissioner. Of the other officers it is necessary to mention only Charles Mann (Advocate-General, Crown Solicitor and Public Prosecutor, at a salary of £300 a year), Robert Gouger (Colonial Secretary), Osmond Gilles (Colonial Treasurer) and John Brown (Emigration Agent).

Charles Mann (1799–1860) A campaigner for colonization and the first South Australian Advocate General. After clashing with Hindmarsh he resigned on 13 November 1837. He continued to work in law, both in private practice and in a number of judicial offices. He was also co-editor of the *Southern Australian* with Brown.

Osmond Gilles (1788-1866) The first Colonial Treasurer (1836 to 1839) contrasted his failings as an official with his success as a businessman. Gilles was hot tempered but also a religious man known for his generosity.

The division of authority in the colony created by the Foundation Act was aggravated by the political prejudices of the officers. The Governor was an out-and-out Tory. Most of the officers were middle-class liberals and radicals of varying shades of opinion. Brown and Gilles were the most violent; they suspected Mann, who was at first the most moderate of the liberals, of being tainted with a tinge of Toryism. In between these extremes fell most of the others. Gilles, during his term as Colonial Treasurer, even went to the ridiculous length of attempting to have the Royal Arms removed from government proclamations.[22] Stevenson, the Governor's secretary, reported to the Colonial Office, with his usual asperity:

> 'Poor Gilles is a mere mischievous fool, whose propensity to intoxication and whose conduct when in that state makes it perfectly impossible for any gentleman to have the slightest connection with him. His common expression is, 'I have the support of Wakefield and Torrens, and care not a damn for any bugger of the Colonial Office.'" [23]

Though holding the most extreme views, the Colonial Treasurer was too erratic to be dangerous, and after Gilles had by his conduct antagonised the Resident Commissioner and his supporters, Hindmarsh turned him into a useful ally.

Long before the Governor sailed it was obvious that he was going to meet with decided opposition in the colony. Hindmarsh's energy, his splendid naval record, his frank and open appearance, had made a good impression at first and offset the disadvantage that he was not quite well enough known to the public to be an advertisement for the colony.[24] But within a few months he had managed to offend both the Commissioners and most of the prominent colonists. Angas had advanced him considerable sums of money and he thus became tied to the support of the South Australian Company against the Commissioners. He cared little about the economic details of the Wakefield plan and incurred the displeasure of a compact clique of its sponsors—Fisher, Brown, the Morphetts, George Strickland Kingston, Mann, Gilbert, Dr Wright. Hindmarsh thought them a set of unpleasant radicals who needed to be disciplined; they resented what they termed "quarter-deck government" and were suspicious that the Governor was trying to obtain complete power for the Colonial Office with himself as its representative. By November 1835 Brown, Morphett, Kingston and Rowland Hill were discussing plans for the formation of a society in the colony to oppose and check Hindmarsh if he acted "with greater promptitude decision and activity than may be compatible with sound and good judgment" or "from impulse or partiality, that may occasion differences of opinion, and possibly so that the colony may not be always benefitted", and by the end of the year Brown was expressing his conviction that Hindmarsh would not last long as Governor—"Indeed I should feel some anxiety about our future progress if I thought otherwise."[25]

Hindmarsh was not unaware of this opposition. "I began to perceive on the part of the Commissioners," he said, "a rising jealousy which manifested itself in a variety of ways."[26] He said, after his recall, that he would have resigned had not Torrens persuaded him that the Commissioners' duties were only as to land, emigration and the raising of money, and that the Commissioners would have nothing to do with the Government of the colony, which "once established would be on precisely the same footing as the

(Sir) John Morphett
(1809–1892)
From 1834 Morphett was an advocate for the province and he became an influential landowner and politician. One of four non-official members of the Legislative Council in 1841 his political career continued until 1873.

Sir) George Strickland Kingston
(1807–1880)
The Deputy-Surveyor-General to the new colony. Kingston also served as town surveyor and colonial architect. His political career began in the Legislative Council in 1851 and continued until 1880. "Paddy" Kingston is remembered as the "father" of South Australia's constitution and the father of Charles Cameron Kingston who was a major contributor to Australian federation and the federal constitution.

Dr Edward Wright
(c1788–1859)
A failed applicant for the position of the province's first medical officer, Wright, nevertheless, came to the colony in September 1836 to practice. His career was a chequered one due to his wayward character and bouts of drunkenness and at one time he was tried for murder.

Thomas Gilbert (c1787–1873)
Gilbert arrived in South Australia in 1836 to take the position of Colonial Storekeeper. He later became the first Postmaster. (SLSA)

government of any other colony".[27] The Governor consoled himself, therefore, with the belief that when he got to South Australia he would be able to rule with a free hand and be as completely master there as he had been of his ships of war. He took pains, however, to conciliate Gouger, in whom he saw a dangerous rival to his authority in the colony, and shortly before the *Buffalo* sailed Brown wrote disgustedly of Gouger:

> 'I find that he is all thick with Hindmarsh again, and that Hindmarsh abuses Torrens, Wakefield and Hill in no measured terms. What is perhaps more extraordinary, Gouger actually thinks that Hindmarsh is right, and the Commissioners wrong! So fatally prone is he to new friendships and new views. In 6 months he is quite as likely to head a party to get rid of the Governor. At present, however, the Governor and the Colonial Office are all in all. One melancholy reflection follows all this but too closely. How is this colony to succeed with these people as leaders?' [28]

John Hill was the boatswain of the *Buffalo* and hoisted the flag on Proclamation Day. The *Buffalo* was launched in 1813 as a merchant ship named the *Hindustan*. Acquired and renamed by the Royal Navy it served until it was wrecked at Mercury Bay in New Zealand in 1840. (SLSA)

Historical Background

'most romantic and beautiful'

The story of the voyage of the *Buffalo* has been told in detail by Stevenson (whose statements must be taken with suspicion), and sidelights on it, from another angle, are to be found in letters from Hindmarsh to Angas.[1] The Governor complained that Stevenson and his wife had made themselves thoroughly unpopular with everyone on board, and he bitterly regretted that he had asked them to dine at his table, for Mrs Stevenson was a perpetual annoyance to him.

George Stevenson (1799–1856) Appointed secretary to Governor Hindmarsh and Clerk of the Council Stevenson was, more notably, the original editor of the *South Australian Gazette and Colonial Register*, the Province's first newspaper. (SLSA)

'This unfortunate tempered woman always sits at my right hand and tho' she will hardly speak to me she speaks at me in the most insolent way you can imagine, so much so that poor as I am I would not have taken her for a thousand pounds.' [2]

He had two consolations. One was watching the embarrassment of Stevenson, "who sits on the opposite side of the table upon thorns", dreading his wife would provoke an outburst of vice-regal rage. The other was that Stevenson "has made himself a perfect scapegoat for me, as I am sure I could hardly do any unpopular act but it would be attributed to his advice".[3]

Stevenson, on the other hand, was contemptuous about Hindmarsh. "The poor man," he said, "does not know his own mind for two hours together. This is a sad failing for one in authority to be overpowered with."[4] He and Fisher came to the conclusion that the Governor was never less likely to do anything than when he announced it to be his "firm determination".[5] From Rio de Janeiro, Stevenson wrote to Angas that a fatal error had been made in the appointment of Governor: "The colony cannot hope to flourish to the extent it ought to, or to go on in peace and tranquillity under Captain Hindmarsh." [6]

There was a childishness in Hindmarsh's character, he said, which "while it renders him jealous to the utmost of the *appearance* of authority totally deprives him of the *reality*". With his tongue in his cheek, Stevenson added: "The sooner a successor is provided the better it will be for all parties. Would you but take the office, what a colony would it not be?" [7]

After leaving Rio, arguments began about Hindmarsh's powers. The Royal Instructions issued to him on 6 July 1836 had instructed him to preside at the council and contained a clause directing him, in case he saw sufficient cause to dissent from the major part or the whole of the council upon any question, to execute his powers in accordance with his own judgment. The Governor maintained that all appointments were in his hands and that he was not obliged to ask the council's advice or approval.

> 'I have told him plainly my opinion'—wrote Stevenson—'which is that subject to his right of proposing, and the power of pardoning or remitting the sentences of convicts, all executive as well as legislative acts must be done by him in Council. By the Royal Instructions he has power to carry his propositions into law even against the opinion and voice of the 'whole or major part' of his advisers—being obliged, however, in such a case to assign his reasons for so acting to the Secretary of State at home—a check, which if not quite sufficient against temporary acts of folly or despotism, is at least fully as regards their permanence.'

The Governor was not pleased with Stevenson's views.

> 'He says he is determined to act singly and uncontrolled—that he has Lord Glenelg's and Mr Stephen's authority for so doing, and will not, to use his own words, 'abate an inch of his Master's prerogative', forgetting perhaps that His Majesty has in this instance expressly delegated his authority, prerogative and all, to others. But it is in vain to argue with him on this point, or indeed on any other.' [8]

By December 1836 Stevenson was writing that "it seems more and more desirable that The Governor's powers should be defined strictly, or some strange antics we shall have".[9]

The relations between Hindmarsh and Fisher had not been improved by the voyage, which began inauspiciously with "a dust about a water-closet". Hindmarsh had contracted to cater for Fisher and his family for a lump sum and was annoyed at finding that he was losing money on it. He complained to Angas:

George Fife Angas (1789–1879)
A merchant, banker and landowner, Angas was an early supporter of the colony and the capital and immigrants he introduced to the settlement were crucial to its success. He did not arrive in South Australia until 1851, although by then he had substantial interests and two sons in the colony. He entered the Legislative Council in 1851 continuing to hold a seat there until 1866.

> 'I sat upwards of six months next but one to Mr Fisher, and I never heard him join in any general conversation whatever, rarely speaking, except upon the high attributes of the Commissioners, and the little or no power of the Crown in So. Australia, quibbling upon the meaning of words, and really expatiating upon the grand subject of feeding rabbits. Is this a man to carry out our great principle? I assure you that I think a worse selection could hardly have been made to represent the Commissioners. I wish Torrens was in his place, I wish Wakefield was, or any other man who understood what he was about.'

He charitably added that he believed "the poor man is unconscious of his error".[10]

Christmas Day 1836 was celebrated on the *Buffalo* with a display of "violence and ruffianism without parallel", the Governor's "profanity and abominable oaths " driving the passengers to seek refuge in their cabins;[11] but by 28 December, when the *Buffalo* anchored at Holdfast Bay, the storm had blown over. Those colonists who had already arrived, some two hundred in number, assembled on the beach in the scorching heat of a summer's day to receive their Governor. Shortly after two o'clock he landed; his commission was read; and the British flag hoisted to the accompaniment of a salute from the guns of the *Buffalo*, a straggling feu de joie from a party of marines, and the ringing cheers of the colonists. From the convenient shade of a gum tree, the establishment of the government was proclaimed. Everyone was delighted with the affability of the Governor, who shook hands all round, and in a hearty and genial manner congratulated the colonists on their good fortune in having such a fine country. At the open air luncheon which followed, toasts were proposed and drunk with rapidity and tremendous enthusiasm, and when the Governor himself gave—"May the present unanimity continue as long as South Australia exists," the plain rang with the acclamations.[12]

J.M Skipper's painting of Gouger's tent and hut at Holdfast Bay ca. 1837. The "Old Gum Tree" is shown on the left but the tree on the right is more likely to have been the true Proclamation Tree. (SLSA)

The colonists deluded themselves. If there was any unanimity induced by the excitement of the landing, it vanished with the setting of the sun. The evening was devoted by many to a drunken carousal, and those who went to bed at all that night rose to find that the Reign of Squabble had begun. For eighteen months Governor Hindmarsh presided over an administrative pandemonium. The emigrants were, in the words of Milton, "on the sudden transported under another climate to be tossed and turmoiled with their unballasted wits in the fathomless and unquiet deeps of controversy".

The public officials of the colony bickered amongst themselves with childish obstinacy, until South Australia was brought to the very verge of irretrievable ruin. "The administration of Hindmarsh," as Mr Rudall says, "was distinguished by little that was beneficial to the prosperity of the new settlement, by much that was injurious to its success, and principally by a continuous series of official quarrels which reduced the government to hopeless confusion."[13]

(Sir) John Hindmarsh (1785–1860)
Hindmarsh was a naval hero who became South Australia's first Governor, a position he held from July 1836 until his recall in June 1838. (SLSA)

The character of Hindmarsh was for a long time hidden under several layers of fuscous biographical varnish. Allen, for instance, in his *History of Australia* published in 1882 depicted him as a quarrelsome muddler, recalled in disgrace, and blamed him alone for: "... all the public and private quarrels, all the waste of time, all the stoppage of the surveys, all the delay in putting people in possession of their land" and said that they all arose: "out of his inordinate love of power, out of his objection to allow anybody to have a share with him in it, out of his unscrupulous opposition to all who did not defer to his wishes in everything; out of his constant intermeddling and intriguing".[14]

The modern view has been kinder. Admittedly the Governor had defects of character which militated against his success. By temperament he was obstinate and by training he was imperious and impatient of opposition. Like Dampier, his idea of a consultation with his officers was to swear at them if his opinions were questioned. Quick-tempered and changeable:

> 'Distracting thoughts by turns his bosom rules,
> Now Fired by wrath, and now by reason cooled.'

Colonel William Light (1786–1839)
Light was appointed Surveyor General after narrowly missing the position of Governor. Although his time as surveyor was productive it was far from happy – he resigned in 1838 in dispute with the Commissioners - and contributed to his failing health. (AGSA)

His acts were often hasty and ill-advised. He thought (and did not trouble to conceal it) that the colonial officials, with the exception of the Judge, Colonel Light, and one or two others, were a contemptible set—an opinion which was not entirely unfounded, for they were, in varying degrees, insolent, inexperienced and inefficient.[15]

But as James Stephen subsequently said, his case was hard. To a large extent he was the victim of circumstances over which he had little control—hostile officers, an unsurveyed country, an empty Treasury, lack of support from the Colonial Office. It was not to be expected that a colony could be founded without some mishaps and calamities. "The infirmity of human nature"—as Bentham has remarked—"renders all plans precarious in the execution, in proportion as they are extensive in design."

The honesty and good intentions of Governor Hindmarsh were never seriously questioned, and one may apply to him the words which John Dunmore Lang wrote of Bligh:

> 'That Governor Bligh was a passionate man, extremely irascible in his disposition, and disposed occasionally to give utterances to his angry feelings in language unbecoming an officer and a gentleman, I willingly admit; but that he had any other end in view than the administration of impartial justice, and the general welfare of the colony he was deputed to govern, I can find no ground whatever for believing.' [16]

It is perhaps not very useful to speculate upon Hindmarsh's probable success if he could have governed South Australia like an ordinary Crown colony:

> 'How easy 'tis when Destiny proves kind,
> With full spread sails to run before the wind'

But his efficiency later as Governor of Heligoland shows, as Hodder wrote, that "if he had been so situated as to have been able to act on his own responsibility and exercise an independent judgment he would have proved a much more successful administrator of the affairs of the infant colony".[17]

On the other hand, history has been kind to Fisher. The scandals of his administration of the Commissioners' business were forgotten, and he lived to become Sir James, and the Father of the Colony. Yet his conduct was more reprehensible than the Governor's. For Hindmarsh there was some excuse—he was a sailor, unused to the intricacies of civil administration; Fisher was a shrewd man of business, with a professional training. It is always difficult to estimate character. "To judge a man", as Montaigne said, "we must a long time follow, and very curiously mark his steps." The available evidence, however, tends to show that the opinion which Sir John Jeffcott, the Judge, formed of the Governor and Fisher was substantially an accurate and just one: "I told you, as you will recollect, from the beginning"—he wrote to Kermode in Van Diemen's Land—"that Fisher was a wily attorney, the very worst class of person that could have been selected for the office, who, by dint of writing and special pleading and splitting hairs upon every insignificant point, wishes to put the Governor, who is a bluff, straightforward, but not very prudent sailor, into a false position." [18]

Fisher appears to have made no effort to cooperate with the Governor; he devoted his activities to finding ways and means of asserting his claim to independent authority. On the voyage out while Hindmarsh showed and freely discussed his instructions, Fisher lay low and concealed his, and the true position, from the Governor, although it must have been patent to him that the Governor was under a misapprehension through ignorance of the most recent developments in the relations between the Colonial Office and the Commissioners. In the colony Fisher would not supply information to the Governor about the progress of emigration, the surveys, and other matters of which the Governor should have been informed.[19] He carried on private trading in addition to his official duties, and without giving much credit to the slanderous statements spread by Stevenson, who described the Resident Commissioner as:

> '... a needy weak man, grasping at every occasion to promote his own selfish interests, bound down to almost all the individual officers of the colony by pecuniary obligations and forced to act as they directed in fear of exposure'[20]

there seems little doubt that he was partial to his sons and friends, and that his conduct of the Commissioners' affairs called for a close scrutiny. The official inquiry into his administration dragged on for many years, and the result was "not proven" rather than an acquittal on the merits.[21] His failure to report to the Commissioners was inexcusable, and in their opinion was alone sufficient to justify his dismissal.[22] As soon as they learned of the troubles in the colony, the Commissioners hastened to write to Fisher impressing on him that "it is the wish of the Commissioners that you, and every other officer acting under their authority, should at all times treat Captain Hindmarsh with proper respect", but their admonition came too late to be of any effect.[23] Fisher's behaviour was quite unjustifiable and on him must fall a considerable part of the censure for the disgraceful scenes of the first two years of the colony.

It would be futile to narrate at length all the quarrels between the Governor and the Resident Commissioner and their respective partisans; most of them are of little other importance than to show the foolish and wrong-headed obstinacy of almost every person concerned in them. Apart from petty squabbles of a more or less private nature, they fall into two groups—geographical and political. The latter will be dealt with in the course of the two following chapters, the former can be here dismissed in a short space. They centred round the position of the capital and its distance from the port. Colonel Light had been entrusted by the Commissioners with the selection of the capital site. The Governor's attitude, as expressed to Stevenson, was that

> 'he did not care a ----- for any order of the Commissioners and he would fix the seat of Government where *he* pleased: it was only his private confidence in Colonel Light's discretion that would lead him to submit to his decision'.[24]

This erroneous view brought about quarrels with Light and Fisher. All parties agreed upon the fascinations of the site selected for the capital. In April 1837 Fisher wrote to the Commissioners:

> 'The situation of Adelaide is most romantic and beautiful, and what is of more consequence the soil all around it is most excellent; as indeed is nearly the whole of what I have seen, and far exceeding in rickness [sic] and quality anything that we had most sanguinely anticipated.' [25]

And two months later he reported:

> 'There are very few that come here that are not pleased with the place altogether, and it would be surprising to me if they were not for there is really everything which can be desired with the exception of comfortable habitations which I trust we shall not be many months longer without.' [26]

From the beginning, however, Hindmarsh was convinced that it was a mistake for the capital to be so far distant from the Port. In his first dispatch to Lord Glenelg he wrote:

> 'The spot selected is perhaps the most beautiful of the whole but it is upwards of six miles from the harbour ... It is true that from the harbour to the right bank of the river there is an easy communication over a perfect flat. The Resident Commissioner has expressed his opinion that this distance of six miles from the harbour is an advantage. I, however, entertain quite a different opinion.' [27]

Similarly to Angas the Governor wrote:

> 'Adelaide is to be on the bank of a beautiful stream with thousands of acres of the richest land I ever saw. Altogether a more beautiful spot can hardly be imagined.'

But its drawback was the distance to the Port.[28] It seems to have been assumed in England that the first city would be established on the coast or on a navigable river, and the instructions issued by the Commissioners to Light and Fisher did not contemplate the selection of a site miles from a harbour. Light's orders were to lay out the city first. The Governor wanted the harbour mapped and charted immediately. He had "the strongest objection to a Capital without a Port, which could not be obviated unless some land near the Harbour should also be surveyed in order to connect the two together in some way or other". Light was summoned before the council and ordered to survey the port; he declined to leave his work at Adelaide. Fisher was asked to permit the *Rapid*, the Commissioners' ship, to be used in charting the harbour; he ignored the request.[29] Thus, as the Commissioners said in their third annual report:

> 'The Governor had scarcely landed when a Governor's party and a Commissioner's party were formed. The partisans of the former imagined that they were upholding the royal prerogative and maintaining the power of the Crown, by forcing a departure from the regulations and instructions by which the Commissioners gave the selection of the site of the capital to the Surveyor General and left to private enterprise the laying out of all secondary towns. While, on the other hand, the partisans of the latter acted as if they thought that to limit and oppose the exercise of the executive authority was to vindicate the peculiar principles of colonization embodied in *the South Australian Act.*'[30]

The Governor said the trouble was all due to Fisher's "ridiculously exalted notions of the Commissioners' powers". Influenced by Stevenson, whose opinion was that the site was good for a farm but useless for a commercial city, Hindmarsh still had hopes that somewhere on the coast a better location for a capital might be found. In his more excited moments he threatened that unless his views were acceded to he would sail away to Port Lincoln with all the officers of the Government;[31] but he had sense enough to realise that something would have to be done without delay. He accordingly called a public meeting of land purchasers, following a requisition written by Stevenson but signed by Edward Stephens. The requisition urged that Colonel Light could not have thoroughly examined the whole coastline in three months and that Adelaide had been chosen only because it was the best site that had been so far discovered. The settlers, it was argued, should wait until it was certain that all available sites had been inspected.

> 'Adelaide is unquestionably a beautiful spot and for agricultural purposes altogether unexceptionable. But it can never be a great commercial city. It is six miles at least distant from a harbour which if safe at present, at least, entirely destitute of fresh water, and not capable of receiving ships of a heavy tonnage. A supply of water could, it is true, be brought to it from Adelaide—a canal might be dug or a railroad formed—the bar could be deepened. All this could be done and will be

done if no better place exists. But the point to be determined at the outset is, does a better place exist? Adelaide may be chosen—we may erect houses and commence canals to connect it by sea, and some fine morning may bring us the news that at Encounter Bay or Boston Bay, at Pt Drummond or on Spencer's Gulph, a splendid harbour with abundance of fine land has been discovered. What then becomes of Adelaide? Will its being the seat of government save it? Bring the ships to our doors if possible—that is the paramount consideration—the essential ingredient to commercial and colonial prosperity. Adelaide is an excellent place if there be no other—but that alternative is still open. When the coast is completely examined, then, but not before, fix the site of the principal city.'

George French Angas's sketch of Adelaide as seen from the Torrens ca. 1844. (SLSA)

The Governor declined to preside at the meeting, but sent a sensible letter in which he pointed out that although it would have been much better if the colony had been properly surveyed a year before the emigrants left England, "yet practically we must have nothing to do with such considerations, but grapple manfully with the case as we find it, and not conjure up difficulties that will lead to nothing but endless dissension". It would be disastrous to retard the survey. The comfort and health of the colonists, after living so long on salt provisions, depended upon raising a supply of vegetables as soon as possible. "Scarcely a seed is yet in the ground, nor will there be, I must fear, till you find yourselves upon your own land."[32]

The Governor's suggestion, to which Light eventually agreed, was that a certain number of acres should be surveyed at the Port, but Fisher refused his consent to this. Although he had been deprived of the power of selecting the site, the Governor thought he still had power to force the Resident Commissioner to fall into line with his views. He took care, he said, to let Light and Fisher know his opinion that although they might survey where they pleased "it required the royal prerogative to give franchises or to make a town".[33] He couched his ultimatum, as Dr Price says, in language worthy of James I:

> 'The thing is so self-evidently just that to refuse it would, of course, be the reverse. I consider that that portion of the prerogative left in my hands is like the whole prerogative itself, to be exercised for the protection and for the benefit of the people. Therefore, whether that portion left to me gives me power to say anything about the site of the town or not is a legal question. But I distinctly say that unless a portion of land be surveyed at the harbour I will not give my consent.'

The meeting, while passing a resolution in favour of the site chosen by Light, also requested that some of the city acres should be surveyed at the harbour, and Fisher was persuaded to agree to this. Hindmarsh considered it a personal triumph, and magnanimously wrote to Lord Glenelg begging him to overlook Fisher's errors.

The acres at the Port were duly surveyed, but the Governor's troubles were only beginning. At the meeting of preliminary purchasers held to determine the mode of selection of land, Samuel Stephens (the manager of the South Australian Company) and the Governor had a violent quarrel, and the Governor threatened to have him taken into custody. "It is a bad thing for us that the Governor is not a different character"—wrote John Barton Hack.

> 'He seems very well intentioned, but is hasty and headstrong to an excess and appears to have no command over himself. His power of doing mischief is fortunately very limited.'[34]

John Barton Hack (1805–1884)
A farmer and businessman who arrived in 1837 and became one of the pioneers of primary industry in South Australia.

On 27 March 1837, the Governor informed Fisher that the papers were all prepared for the proclamation of the Port, and copies were in the hands of the printer. This was a step of some importance to the community, for captains were unwilling to take their vessels into the Port until it was proclaimed.[35] Fisher, however, observed that in the draft proclamation names had been given to different parts of the land adjoining the harbour, and he replied: "I think it is right to state before the Proclamation is issued that I consider His Excellency has not the power to attach a name to any portion of the land within the Province, but that such power is vested in me."

Fisher's contention was that although the naming of unappropriated lands might in general be a prerogative of the Crown, yet that right had been delegated to the Commissioners and not to the Governor, by the vesting of the land in them; and further, that he could not convey country lands without describing them, and could not describe them without the power of naming them.[36]

Hindmarsh was touched on a sensitive spot. He had busied himself in drawing up lists of naval heroes and victories from which the chief geographical features were to be named; and, perhaps with a touch of humour, he proposed to give the names of the Commissioners to the uninviting mud flats and swamps which surrounded the harbour—for example, Torrens Island, Lefevre's Peninsula.[37] He told Fisher that he had "no sort of doubt but that the right alluded to (of naming) is retained by the Crown"; but as confusion would result if they both proceeded to give names, the proclamation of the Port must be delayed until this point was decided, even if it meant waiting for a decision by the authorities at home.[38]

> 'Your assumption of the power to name the places in the colony makes it impossible for the Governor to proceed in exercising what has been hitherto considered one of the most undoubted rights of the Crown; under this view His Excellency does not think it possible to comply with your request and send you the form of the Proclamation it was his intention to have issued; although His Excellency has resolved to suspend the exercise of the right he possesses, as His Majesty's representative, till he receives instructions on the point, still he cannot consent to be in any shape a party to the names fixed by yourself, whose right of interference on the subject he altogether denies.' [39]

At the same time as his claim to the right of naming, Fisher announced to the Council that the officers of the Government were dependent on him for payment of their salaries, and that he was authorised to pay them by bills at sixty days' sight on the Commissioners' treasurer in England. Hindmarsh protested bitterly against the indignity of the King's representative being paid by an inferior officer in the employment and under the control of the Commissioners, and the breach between him and the Resident Commissioner was further widened. "I have done everything in my power to maintain a good understanding with Mr Fisher," the Governor claimed;[40] but by now they were irreconcilable. "With Mr Fisher the Governor is quite at variance," Gouger reported to Angas, "and scarcely a day passes without some unpleasantness publicly arising between them."[41]

The Governor conceded that the Resident Commissioner had full control over the survey and disposal of land, but he contended that

Fisher ought to be entirely separate from, and possess no right of interfering with, the government of the colony, for all the rights which had not been expressly given by Parliament to the Commissioners remained with the Crown. He attributed Fisher's conduct to:

(1) A desire to accumulate importance as the representative of the Commissioners.[42]

'Mr Fisher'—the Governor wrote—'from the ridiculously exalted notions of the Commissioners' powers that he entertains, thought he could do anything, indeed he has often repeated that the Crown had not power to remove either any one of the Commissioners or myself or any one appointed by the Commissioners.' [43]

(2) 'A wish to obtain favour with a party holding violent democratical opinions and opposed to all governments but their own.'

(3) His legal training. 'Much of the difficulty around me,' he said, 'is to be ascribed to Mr Fisher's extreme narrow mindedness. He considers the Commissioners as his clients and as such he is ready to take advantage of any flaw in a word or other opportunity for their benefit. Was there ever a more absurd view of the case?'[44]

In a long letter to Angas in April 1837 he repeats this complaint: 'He has monopolised all power in his own hands. He has interfered in every and in the mostn [sic] trifling Act of Government, and I should say knows nothing about the principles of our Colony, which are that the Commissioners authority should sell the land, and apply the money to sending out labour, without being interfered with by the Government, but on the other hand the remainder of the King's prerogative remains intact and ought not to be meddled with by the Commissioner's representative. Mr F, however, acts as tho' the Proprietorship of the Land gives him a right to all other power, in fact, he can't get out of the Solicitor's Office, and considers the Commissioners as his clients, for whom he will grab all he can. He is indeed a weak man, incapable of comprehending any question beyond a deed or a mortgage. He has had the folly to place himself at the head of the violent party here, who would oppose an Angel were he only called Governor.' [45]

And in a later letter to Angas, he said ruefully: 'I am sorry to tell you that I have no bed of roses. Mr Fisher the Resident Commissioner is anything but what he ought to be. He heads a party opposed to all Government but their own.' [46]

The Commissioners had unfortunately thought it advisable, since their officers were the principal capitalists in the colony, to tolerate as a temporary measure the conjunction of private speculations and mercantile pursuits with official duties—a practice which was not stopped until 1840.[47] This inevitably placed Fisher in a position where his interest conflicted with his duty, and he was accused of favouritism and profiteering. "He should not be permitted"—wrote the Governor—"to hold land agencies, or to be the concealed or avowed partner of traders or employed in a private business of any sort whatever." [48]

On the other hand, Fisher's party could not find words strong enough for their denunciations of Hindmarsh, and they could only think that his appointment must have taken place when some malignant star was in the ascendant.

> 'As to the Governor himself'—Brown wrote to Wakefield—'I hold to what I have often said, that the time will come when we shall be glad to subscribe to get rid of him. He is wholly unfit for his office and has come out for himself only and not for the colony ... He meddles with the duties of every officer without understanding the business of any.' [49]

And in another letter to Wakefield he said:

> 'You know my opinion of him before I sailed. I never thought or expressed myself with half the strength that those who then supported him have since done. Fisher is a cautious man, Col Light has been for years on friendly terms with Hindmarsh, Gouger was ready to back his chief in anything, and Stephens, the Company's manager was prejudiced in his favour. Mann also was biassed in favour of the representative of His Majesty, both from the nature of his office and the slight shade he has of Toryism. Yet all these have declared that after making every allowance the conduct and character of our Governor, as Governor, is disgusting. He is mentally, morally, and educationally unfit for his post; and the colony is suffering and will suffer greatly by his continuance. To tell you all that he does that becomes not a Governor, would be to send you a diary of his proceedings.' [50]

Though his testifying to his own merits carries little weight, Fisher protested vehemently that he had been actuated only by motives of spotless purity:

> 'No object of ambition, no desire to annoy the Governor nor any sort of ill-feeling towards His Excellency, in short no other than the most pure and honest feeling has influenced me, and if in any one particular you shall think I have been mistaken

> you must ascribe it to an error of the head and not of the heart.' [51]

He was certainly placed in a position of embarrassment, for as representative of the Commissioners he thought himself bound to support their rights and powers, although this necessarily brought him, in his capacity as a member of the Council, into conflict with the Governor. To some extent, too, Fisher was forced into opposition to the Governor by his Instructions, which left him little discretionary power and compelled him to obtain the sanction of the Commissioners to almost every item of expenditure.[52] In his original Instructions he had been directed that he must "from the necessity of the case be in a great measure guided by circumstances of which it is impossible that they (the Commissioners) should have any accurate foreknowledge"; and in every case not specified he was to do what seemed to him to be most in accordance with the principles of the act and his regulations, "always remembering that any departure from these principles will be considered as an act of negligence or of misconduct".[53] But, complained Brown to Wakefield:

> 'The Resident Commissioner's original Instructions have been virtually superseded by a voluninous [sic] detail of such petty requirements that he cannot do his duty to the colony and adhere to them ... Why, his hands are so tied that he cannot order, however vitally important, the most trifling matter without first sending home an estimate for the approval of those who can have no guide whereby to form a judgment, either as to price or necessity of the work, be it what it may. Some great change is essential at home. If this colony fail now after what certainly has been an excellent beginning, it must be from an adherence on the part of the Commissioners to the miserable policy which has crippled every exertion we have had to make. It is felt in every department, and has irritated or disgusted every officer ... There are, and there must be, occasions constantly arising in such an undertaking, that require discretionary powers and resources that no minute restrictions can possibly provide ... By reducing their representative to a cypher the Commissioners are doing more to play into the hands of the Colonial Office and to destroy there our power in the Colony, than twenty heads like our Governor could effect; and the time will arrive when the folly of giving one inch will be apparent. At all events, one certain evil will be Mr Fisher's resignation.' [54]

This important letter is dated 10 April 1837. On the following day Fisher informed the Governor that he proposed to forward to Lord Glenelg his resignation of his office as a member of the Council on the plea that his numerous other duties required his undivided attention and time. Hindmarsh hastened to accept the resignation which he promised to lay "by the first opportunity" before Lord Glenelg.[55] A number of the colonists (including Light, Gouger, Mann, the Hacks, Finniss, Brown, Kingston, Gilles and Henry Jickling) at once addressed a letter to Fisher expressing their confidence in him and urging him to withdraw his resignation.

> 'In the present infant state of the colony they cannot learn that it is your intention to withdraw from so important a position in its government, without expressing their fears that their interests, and the general success of the great undertaking, in which they have engaged, will thereby be vitally effected ... The success of the colony mainly depends upon a preservation of every power vested in the Colonization Commissioners by the Act of Parliament; while the step you propose to take will deprive them of the only direct means of representing their opinions and intentions in the legislature of the Colony, which the Colonial Government as at present constituted admits or secures.'

Further, they considered:

> '... the appointment in question, being held directly under an Order of His Majesty in Council, you cannot be relieved from its duties until a communication be made to and answered by His Majesty's Government; and that by that time the more settled state of the colony or a change in its legislature may render your continuance in the Government perfectly compatible with your other duties.' [56]

Fisher accordingly wrote withdrawing his resignation. Hindmarsh was furious and declared that Fisher only resigned so that his party, headed by Brown, could get up a demonstration in his favour.[57] He had hopes that Fisher's resignation might have been legally irrevocable, and sarcastically informed the Advocate-General that the Resident Commissioner "had seen fit to signify his determination to persist in endeavouring to fulfil the arduous duties which devolve upon him at any sacrifice of time and personal comfort", and that the Governor, "being always desirous of acting in harmony with the colonists, has not the slightest objection to the Resident Commissioner's resuming his seat at the Council, provided that you, as the legal adviser of the Government, consider he can do so after the steps which have been taken". Mann replied that Fisher's letter was not a resignation but merely a notice of his intention to forward his resignation. The Governor curtly said that the question was not as to the reading of Fisher's letter but whether, taking his resignation for granted, the Governor must readmit him . Mann having then advised that Fisher should be allowed to resume his seat, the Governor reluctantly directed Gouger to notify the Resident Commissioner, and was angry when he found that Gouger had added an unauthorised sentence to the communication, that His Excellency hoped that Fisher would continue to give to the consultations of the Council the great benefit of his advice and assistance.[58]

In this posture, the affairs of the colony stood when the Judge, Sir John Jeffcott, arrived in the colony. Since Jeffcott and his successor, Henry Jickling, were ex officio members of the council, it was inevitable that they should become involved in the political dissensions which racked the community, and the part which they played in the Reign of Squabble falls to be described in the course of the next two chapters.

Oct. 28th 1950.

Dear Mr Hague,

Thank you very much for your letter, and also for the draft — & though I was not able to find Jickling an obituary, I am glad I managed to be able to help you — I am sure I enjoyed the search as much as you could have enjoyed receiving the results — I, too, got so interested, especially in the unfortunate Jeffcott — I don't wonder he got involved with what he would have called "the ladies" He had just enough romance about him to attract any woman — & a spice of Byronic misery that went frightfully well in his particular day — And quite a dashing fellow, too — Absolutely irresistible — I wonder he didn't do more damage than he did —!

I hope you enjoyed the cricket — Here we are settling down to the frost & fog of this most unpleasant season of the year — The leaves are falling fast — I am going once again to Blenheim Palace on Monday — & though I shall see the end of the year going through the Park to work each morning next week — I am expecting to be frozen most of the day — It is so cold

Hague continued to research and write on early South Australian legal history long after he had completed the *History*. Margaret Franklin of London was one who assisted with his research and in this letter to Hague she comments on the character and fascination of Jeffcott. (UA)

Sir John Jeffcott

A duel

When Sir John Jeffcott, after he had been knighted, went to the Heralds College to get his arms, an anecdote, ingenious rather than probable, was narrated to him. He was told that he was descended from a certain Geffe of Normandy. According to legend, Geffe was one day out hunting with the King when, outstripping the others, he killed a huge boar. Delighted with his prowess, the King exclaimed, "Well done, Geffe! Caught!" and: ".. henceforth that family was called Jeffcut or Jeffcot, and their crest was changed from a tiger to a boar".

Geffe or his descendants must have crossed to England sometime before the 16th century, for the family of Jeffcott is then found settled in Northamptonshire, whence a branch spread to Ireland. In England the Jeffcotts were principally distinguished in the Church; in Ireland they settled in County Kerry as plain country gentlemen and farmers. John William Jeffcott, the future Judge of South Australia, was of the Irish branch and was born at Kerry in 1796, the eldest of five children. The next in age was his brother William, who afterwards became Sir William and was a judge at Port Philip and Singapore.[1]

Jeffcott entered Trinity College, Dublin, on 2 January 1815 as a "pensioner"—one who paid a fixed sum annually—which indicated that he was probably the son of a person of moderate means. He obtained the degrees of BA (1819) and MA (1821). In February 1830 he was appointed Chief Justice of Sierra Leone and was "installed" at Freetown on 26 April.[2] Although styled Chief Justice, he was the only judge in the colony, and found his principal work in the Vice-Admiralty Court, which obtained a flow of business from the attempts to put down slaving on the African coast. As Recorder of Freetown he tried civil causes there and was Chairman of the Quarter Sessions, and from time to time he visited Gambier to hold a circuit court. Law was administered in Sierra Leone with blissful uncertainty; the enactments of the Council were not printed or published, and the only record of them was a single manuscript copy, to which few of the Magistrates of the colony had any opportunity of referring.[3]

Contemporary authorities are almost unanimous in describing the climate of Sierra Leone as destructive. "Much as we desire the improvement of the blacks," said one, "we protest against its being attempted by sending our countrymen to certain destruction in this most pestiferous of all pestiferous places." Sydney Smith's jest was that Sierra Leone always had two governors, one just arrived in the colony and the other just arrived in England. But Jeffcott appears to have liked it. The West African climate, he told John Barton Hack later, was not in the least unhealthy except in the rainy season, and he preferred it to that of Florence.

After three years in the colony, he returned to England on leave. Apparently his services were recognised as valuable, for on 1 May 1833 he was knighted, at the early age of 37.[4]

He was on his way to Plymouth to embark on the return voyage to Sierra Leone, when an event occurred which ruined his career and embittered the few years of life which remained for him. He had become engaged to be married, but the engagement was broken off by the girl or her family. Rumours spread concerning Jeffcott's conduct in the affair. Two days before he was to sail, he stopped at Exeter. A friend, Robert Holland, dined with him at his hotel, and over brandy and water and cigars Jeffcott asked him if he had heard any of the rumours. Holland admitted that he had, and upon being pressed repeated some words spoken by a Dr Hennis, that "it was merely a blind to a respectable family for Jeffcott to assert that he was going to Bristol, and that he had no more a vote for Dublin University than he (Dr Hennis) had". The first part of this has now much the same cabalistic meaning as Mr Pickwick's "Chops and tomato sauce", and it is impossible to say to what it refers; but Jeffcott resented it. Next morning he accosted Hennis and asked him whether he had used the words. Hennis admitted he had, but attempted to make an explanation. Jeffcott in rage called him a "calumniating scoundrel", and they parted in anger. Returning at once to his hotel, Jeffcott wrote a letter to Hennis which betrays evident signs of the haste and feeling with which it was composed, and is interesting as a specimen of the manner in which affairs of honour were conducted:

Dr Peter Hennis (c1803–1833)
Like Jeffcott, Hennis was of Irish origin and settled in Exeter as a young doctor. He became a local hero during the cholera outbreak in 1832.

> 'Street's Clarence Hotel,
> May 10
>
> Sir,
>
> In a conversation with a gentleman of character and respectability, and I believe hitherto of unquestionable veracity, I was last night, to my great astonishment, informed that you had, about three months ago stated to my informant, that the reason why a certain affair in which the name of a most respectable family is involved, to which I need not more particularly allude, was broken off, was that I had given that family a false statement of my pretensions; that I had, among other things, asserted I had a vote for the University of Dublin, which in your opinion I had no more than you, meaning, I presume, that I had no vote, and that I had stated what was not true, and that you considered that I was, in fact, a mere adventurer. I can scarcely imagine that a person holding the station in society that you do, or that any man who ought by

Jeffcott's Fiancé
The woman to whom Jeffcott was first engaged was Flora MacDonald, granddaughter of the Jacobite heroine of the same name.

> profession and education to be a gentleman, could have gone so gratuitously out of his way to traduce the character of any individual behind his back, to whom to his face you had made professions, if not of friendship, at least of cordiality and goodwill, and whose only previous intercourse with you was consulting you professionally in the first instance, and meeting you afterwards once or twice when you called professionally at the house of his friends. You will, therefore, I feel satisfied, see the propriety, from regard to your own character, of coming at once to an explicit understanding upon the subject of this letter, and stating to me whether you did or did not use the expressions attributed to you. If you did not, you cannot I am sure, as a gentleman, hesitate to disavow them promptly and unequivocally. If on the other hand, you are prepared to maintain them, you will see the propriety of letting me know so without delay, as I am at present alone in Exeter, and I am ordered to embark tomorrow morning on board His Majesty's ship Britomart at Plymouth.
>
> I have the honour to be,
> Your most obedient servant,
> J.W. Jeffcott'.

This letter was dispatched and Jeffcott, with two friends, Holland and Milford, went to walk in the cathedral precincts and wait for a reply. Meanwhile Hennis, before he received the letter, had sent one of his friends, named Irving, with an explanatory note to the effect that he had ascertained that Sir John Jeffcott's conduct had been throughout most honourable and that there was no ground whatever for any imputations against him. Irving found Jeffcott at the cathedral.

> 'I shook hands with him, and congratulated him upon his knighthood. I told him I had come to him from Dr Hennis, upon which he quickly turned round and asked if I came as Dr Hennis's friend.'

Irving and Milford went to one side, and Irving read Hennis's explanation, which he said he hoped would be sufficiently satisfactory to Jeffcott to induce him to retract the epithet which he had applied to Hennis that morning. Milford then showed Irving a copy of Jeffcott's letter and Irving decided that he must return to his principal for further instructions. He went away and came back with a Captain Halstead, and they both attempted to settle the matter amicably, urging Milford to persuade Jeffcott to accept the explanation. Milford said he feared it was no use, but went to discuss the matter with Jeffcott. He returned to report that Jeffcott would neither accept the explanation nor retract his words about Hennis and, according to the accepted standards of honour, only one course was left. They suspected Irving might inform against them, so no hint was given to him that the parties were going to fight, and he thought the incident was going to pass over without bloodshed. About four o'clock that day he saw Jeffcott with Holland and Milford getting into a post-chaise, and thinking he was leaving for Plymouth he wished him a happy voyage.

Pistols and Diaries
The pistols used in the duel are probably still in existence having been advertised for sale in the 1950's. In 2002 Jeffcott's journals were supposedly uncovered with revealing excerpts made public. But the diaries proved to be a hoax, compiled by a journalist with an interest in the duel and the trial.

The duel was fought with pistols at twenty paces, in the late afternoon of Friday, 10 May 1833 on a deserted racecourse at Haldon, near Exeter. Hennis fell wounded in the right side. Probably he went with the intention of merely standing his opponent's fire, for he did not shoot. Jeffcott was overcome as he realised the fatal consequences in which his hot temper had involved him, and he fell to the ground and implored Hennis to forgive him. Hennis struggled to his feet and shook hands, but the effort was too much for him and he collapsed. He was carried back to Exeter to die, and Jeffcott fled for his life. The seconds, Holland, Milford and Halstead, were arrested and tried for murder before Mr Justice Patteson at the Exeter Assizes in July 1833. A warrant was issued for Jeffcott's arrest, but he had gone into hiding, probably with a married sister in Cornwall.[5]

The Exeter trial was a remarkable and important one. At the end of the 18th century Baron Hotham had told a jury that the acquittal of an officer who had killed another in a duel would be "lovely in the sight both of God and man". Judges and juries alike were loath to hang a man when they felt that he could not have refrained from fighting without sacrificing his honour. During the 19th century, however, duelling gradually began to die out, and between 1830 and 1840 a series of clear pronouncements by eminent judges that, in the case of a deliberate duel where one of the parties was killed, both the party who actually killed him and the seconds were equally guilty of murder, helped to hasten the end of the wretched system.

The direction of Mr Justice Patteson to the jury was outspoken and to the point.

> 'It is impossible'—said a writer in the *Law Magazine*—'to speak too highly of the intrepid honesty and severe rectitude of Mr Justice Patteson on this occasion. Those who know that wise and amiable Judge best, can not suppose that it was from any indifference or want of sympathy for the situation of the prisoners, or without much pain and violence to his own feelings that he did his duty on this occasion; but he did it nevertheless.' [6]

The Judge plainly told the jury that their verdict must be murder or nothing.

> 'It is no answer to the charge of murder in a deliberate duel to say that it was done solely to vindicate reputation. If you are

> satisfied on the evidence that the three gentlemen went out to Haldon, knowing that Sir John Jeffcott and Dr Hennis were about to fight a duel there, without heat or irritation, but deliberately aiding or assisting the affair on a point of honour, after vainly endeavouring to effect an amicable arrangement, I cannot tell you in point of law it is anything short of murder.'

The position of the prisoners was desperate, for the completeness of the evidence against them seemed to place an acquittal out of the question, but after deliberating for a few minutes the jury announced that they found Milford and Holland not guilty. Halstead's name was then put to them. The foreman had given such careful attention to the proceedings that he turned to his fellows with a puzzled air, and said, "Halstead? Who's he? I never heard of he!" Another juryman prompted him, "Never mind, say they're all not guilty," and a verdict of acquittal was duly recorded. There was not the slightest doubt of the prisoners' guilt, and they escaped solely through the ignorance of the jury, who subsequently stated the ground of their verdict to be that "they (the accused) never titched him (Hennis)".

The trial and its results aroused widespread interest and a general feeling that it was high time that the farce of verdicts in direct opposition to the facts proved in evidence and the law laid down by the Judge should cease.

> 'A severer or a milder course'—said a contemporary—'an enforcement of the law so rigorous as to put an end to duels altogether, or a toleration of them within certain limits, and subject to certain moderate punishments, would be alike preferable to the present solemn mockery of justice, the scene of absurdity and want of conscience, which trials like this at Exeter exhibit.' [7]

Public feeling at the time was very hostile to Jeffcott and, although the facts proved at the trial somewhat restored his reputation, he was clearly the aggressor. Dr Hennis and his second made every effort consistent with honour to avoid a duel, but Jeffcott's impetuous temper was too strong. He was an Irishman, and duels were so frequent in that land of fire-eaters that the rhyme ran:

> 'After being fired at once or twice,
> The ear becomes more Irish, and less nice'.

His second, Milford, was equally hot-headed, and abruptly cut short Halstead's attempts to arrange a settlement by saying that the business should have been settled at nine that morning.

Jeffcott concealed himself for several months and a pitiable enough time he must have had as he lay in hiding.

> 'There is no subtle drug which can engender

Hennis's Death
Jeffcott had shot on the call of "prepare" not on the agreed "fire" which did not help his cause. Nor did the fact that Hennis's death was greatly lamented by a public which had benefited from his selfless medical work. As he lay dying up to two hundred people gathered at his residence awaiting news, a similar number attended his funeral and thousands lined the streets for the funeral procession.

Immunity from memory's lashing whips.'

After the acquittal of the seconds, the charge against him was allowed to drop. He had a powerful friend in Daniel O'Connell (a schoolfellow of Jeffcott's father at Kerry), who strongly defended him, saying that "a more humane, kind, and excellent man did not exist".[8] O'Connell was sympathetic not only because of his friendship with the Jeffcott family but because he himself had had the misfortune to kill a man in a duel. Jeffcott emerged a ruined and embittered man. He had lost his position as Judge. Socially he was shunned. He fell into difficulties with his creditors, and was driven from pillar to post in his efforts to avoid duns, and eventually to escape arrest for debt. Anxious to get away from England, where his name had become so notorious, he sought for another position in the colonies, but the odium of the duel was a stumbling block in the way of another responsible judicial position. He first applied for the position of Judge in the proposed colony of South Australia in April 1834, but during the long delay that followed the passing of the Foundation Act he disappears from view.[9] His application was abandoned, perhaps because his creditors had driven him to the Continent.

Daniel O'Connell (1775-1847)
The "Liberator" was an Irish politician of great influence – his support being crucial to the Whigs holding office from 1835 to 1841. The first Catholic in modern history to sit in the House of Commons, he campaigned successfully for the Catholic Emancipation Act of 1829 and unsuccessfully for the repeal of the Act of Union. (NLA)

Sir John Jeffcott (SCLSA)

Chapter 2.2

Sir John Jeffcott

'impossible to respect'

On 23 July 1835 Colonel Torrens, the Chairman of the Colonisation Commission for South Australia, informed Lord Glenelg (the Secretary of State for the Colonies) that there were three applicants for the office of Judge in the new colony and that the Commissioners had decided to leave the appointment to the Colonial Office, without selecting any one for particular recommendation. The three candidates were Daniel Wakefield of King's Bench Walk, Temple; Henry Jickling of Chancery Lane; and Henry Walter Parker of Old Square, Lincoln's Inn. Lord Glenelg dawdled over the docimasy and a month later the Commissioners urged the matter again. They "ventured to press the subject" on His Lordship's attention, "because in the progress of their undertaking they daily feel the want of such legal advice and co-operation as would be at once secured to them by now naming the future Judge".[1]

Daniel Wakefield (1798-1858)
Like his brother Edward, Daniel never came to South Australia but settled in New Zealand where he continued his legal career and eventually became a judge.

Daniel Wakefield, under the immediate superintendence of his brother, had drafted the Act for the creation of the colony. As a member of the colonisation movement and the brother of its originator, he had strong claims to recognition.

> 'I feel it my right to bear witness'—wrote Aubrey Beauclerk, one of the first committee of the South Australian Association—' to his indefatigable exertions in its favour, and if it be successful I think I may say, he and his brother have the chief merit of the Plan. My own knowledge of Mr Wakefield warrants me in saying that for those years that I have known him I know of no man more impartial or more strictly honest in his principles.'

Sir Henry Lytton Bulwer (1801-1872)
Well regarded and well travelled, Bulwer sat in Parliament from 1830 to 1837 and from 1868 to 1871 but is best remembered for his diplomatic work between those two terms, particularly in Turkey and the USA.

Sir Henry Lytton Bulwer also wrote in support of Wakefield that he had:

> '... laboured hard at advancing the project of this colony and showed in so doing very considerable talent. I really do not think from all that I know, that a better person could be sent.'

In Lord Glenelg's opinion, however, Daniel Wakefield's claims were no doubt to some extent offset by the impolicy of appointing as Judge the brother of a criminal whose sensational escapades and imprisonment were still fresh in the public memory. Bulwer tactfully mentioned the subject and tried to push it aside; "he (Daniel Wakefield) feels some delicacy in saying that he was abroad at the time of his brother's affair with Miss Turner and of course that has nothing to do with it".[2]

Daniel was confident of his success.

> 'I have to tell you' — wrote Nina Wakefield to her aunt in

August 1834—'that Dodo (Daniel) expects to obtain the appointment of Judge-in-chief in South Australia, in which case he turns colonist immediately.' [3]

It was unfortunate for him that Gouger had quarrelled with Edward Gibbon Wakefield, and nursed feelings of resentment.

'Torrens asked me'—wrote Gouger—'to meet the Wakefields at a reconciliation dinner, but this I refused. I told Torrens that I never again would meet them as friends; if I met them in public life for the furtherance of a public object, well and good; but I would not meet them in private life.'

This was written on 20 June 1835, and on 9 July Gouger noted in his journal with satisfaction that two of the Commissioners, Angas and Montefiore, would oppose Wakefield's application. The Wakefields, too, were not popular with many of the intending colonists who, while they recognised the abilities of the brothers, were jealous of their interference. John Brown sneeringly wrote of Daniel as "our Judge (!)". When the Commissioners met on 14 July to consider the question of the appointment, Gouger records that:

Jacob Montefiore (1801-1895) A Colonization Commissioner and businessman who, with brother Joseph, made a fortune in real estate and helped found the Bank of Australasia. Montefiore Hill is named after him and, consequently, the house that stands on the hill, which became the long-term residence of Sir Samuel Way.

'Wakefield was proposed by Torrens as candidate for Judge. This was universally disliked, and after a great deal of conversation, in which all present took part (excepting myself and Hill), it was agreed that he should be offered a compensation in money for the labour he had performed, and, it was added by Lefevre, that it was to be hoped the hint was taken.' [4]

The hint was not taken and Daniel persisted with his application.

Montefiore as it was in 1895. Way bought the house in 1872 and lived there until his death in 1916. It now forms part of the Adelaide University's residential Aquinas College. (SLSA)

The second candidate, Henry Jickling, was also a supporter of the colonisation movement. Although his intellectual qualifications were high, personal defects of manner and appearance placed him out of the race, and his candidature does not seem to have been taken very seriously by anyone but himself.

With Jickling eliminated and Daniel Wakefield's chances prejudiced by the indifference of the Commissioners, the opposition of Gouger and many of the colonists, and the blot of his brother's record, the appointment went to Parker. "Daniel did not come to judgment until twenty years afterwards, when he was appointed a judge in New Zealand." Parker had the strong support of Governor Hindmarsh. He was an able young man of twenty-six who had been called at Gray's Inn only three years before, but was already known as "a rising barrister of recognised talent". A judgeship, he said, was a position which "since entering the law it has ever been my ambition to attain".[5] He had been interested in emigration and the Australian colonies, and in 1833 he published a book on *Van Diemen's Land: its Rise, Progress and Present State*, which went to a second edition in the following year. He had also written the chapters in Clark's *Colonial Law* (1834) dealing with the Australian colonies. Apparently he was well-to-do and a part-owner of the *Morning Chronicle*, a paper which gave considerable space to colonial matters.[6]

In thanking Lord Glenelg for the appointment, Parker referred to the expense and inconvenience to which he would be put in going to South Australia, and asked that his salary should commence from the date of his embarkation for the colony.[7] This was refused, and he promptly resigned. In giving his reasons for this step, "to avoid the imputation of caprice", he uttered a prophetic warning:

> 'When I solicited the appointment I felt that I had nothing whatever to do with the principles on which the colony was to be founded, & that the duties of the Judge would be quite independent of the Commissioners appointed to found the Colony, & to regulate the sale of land. My sentiments in that respect are unaltered, but it is evident some members of the Commission do not coincide in their opinion, as they now act in direct opposition to those officers (though recommended to the Government by themselves) who will receive their appointments immediately from the Crown. It is this state of things that has produced in my mind a deep conviction that dissensions will be the result in the Colony. In embarking my fortune in a new Settlement, it could not be expected that the path would be smooth, but as the prospects of dissension are already lowering, I must beg your Lordship to permit me to withdraw from an undertaking which promises to be attended with much unhappiness to all concerned in it.'[8]

Hindmarsh was distressed and hastened to write to Lord Glenelg:

> 'Feeling satisfied that Mr Parker's resignation of the office of Judge was caused only by reasons that will disappear as soon as we leave England, and being thoroughly impressed with a deep sense of the injury his resignation will do the colony I take the liberty to implore Your Lordship to suspend the acceptance of it.' [9]

Parker, however, refused to withdraw his resignation; and event, the most undoubted interpreter of prophecy, fulfilled his gloomy predictions.

A curious rumour spread among the colonists and was noted by Brown:

> 'The report is that Parker has resigned, and the reason given is that Palmer or some other of the Commissioners shut a door in his face! This is nonsense, for as Fisher properly construed it, either it was or was not an intentional insult. If not, he is a weak man; if it was, he is no gentleman, or he has taken quietly an affront for which he ought to have pulled Palmer's nose or any other nose.' [10]

Upon hearing that the judgeship was again vacant, Jickling hastened to renew his application.[11] Daniel Wakefield had married in September 1835, and his wife and her parents had persuaded him to remain in England;[12] but there were fresh candidates in the field. One was a barrister named Harrison, who was sponsored by Lefevre, one of the Commissioners. Another was Richard Davies Hanson, who had been an early worker in the colonisation movement and was popular with the intending colonists, a number of whom joined in urging his claims.

> 'As proprietors of land in South Australia'—they wrote to the Commissioners—'we feel deeply interested in the success of the colony and we consider that much of that success both in the first settlement and in its future progress will depend upon a thorough knowledge of and attachment to the principles of the Colony in those who fill the more important offices ... In addition to ample legal requirements, Mr Hanson has been a strenuous and active friend of the colony for a considerable period.'

Hanson, however, was a solicitor only, and not a barrister, and this was a serious objection. Edward Gibbon Wakefield said that it was not insuperable, having been overcome in other cases.

> 'The great point now'—wrote Brown—'is to get precedents if possible of the appointment of attorneys to the office of Judge.

Wakefield says there are, but where we don't know.'[13]

Hanson's friends made great efforts on his behalf, and scurried to and fro, canvassing the Commissioners for their support.

> 'The lightning's locomotive powers
> Were slow to their agility'.

Lefevre was interviewed and said that he had put Harrison forward without knowing of Hanson's services in the formation of the new colony; he promised to recommend both. An attempt was made through Gouger to get Jickling to withdraw. Hutt obtained a written promise from Lord Glenelg to keep the appointment open. All the obliquities of Eastern negotiation were resorted to in the hope of securing Hanson the position.

(Sir) John George Shaw-Lefevre
(1797-1879)
A man of learning and long service with the Government, Lefevre was an undersecretary to Stanley at the Colonial Office and a Colonization Commissioner. (NPG)

> 'Everything promises well'—wrote Brown, after a meeting of the Commissioners had been held to consider the matter. 'Palmer remarked that not being a barrister was no objection, and Fisher said that it was a recommendation.'[14]

Hanson and his supporters were to receive some setbacks. Governor Hindmarsh was not favourable, and he had influence with Lord Glenelg, to whom he wrote:

> 'Mr S.B. Harrison is a barrister of some eminence and of high character. Mr Lefevre has had some conversation with him and approves highly of him. I think I can therefore recommend him to your Lordship's notice. Of the other Gentlemen, Mr Hanson is not a Barrister, nor do I consider him so eligible as Mr Harrison. The third gentleman, Mr Jickling, is certainly much inferior to both.'[15]

Still more serious was the reappearance of Sir John Jeffcott. On 25 April 1836 Brown reported:

> 'Today Sir John Jeffcote came to the office and informed Mr Hill that he had had the Judgeship offered him, wishing to know the salary, the probability of a house being built for him &c. E. Wakefield also came to say that O'Connell who dined with him yesterday said that his old friend Jeffcote had been appointed.'

(Sir) William Hutt
(1801-1882)
An M.P. from 1832 to 1874, Hutt was an important supporter of schemes for colonization. He was a Colonization Commissioner and, like his brother John, an unsuccessful applicant for the governorship in place of Hindmarsh. John, however, was to become Governor of Western Australia.

This was a totally unexpected turn.

> 'I think that Jeffcote having O'Connell's interest considers that it must be all powerful, and reckons too much on it. Glenelg never would act thus with a letter to Hutt existing stating that the thing should be kept open.'[16]

Jeffcott had not yet been appointed, but he was eager to obtain the post.

> 'I am aware'—he wrote to James Stephen—'that the salary is very inferior to that of my former office; but in my actual position, on which I need not dwell as you are so well acquainted with it, I need hardly say that I should most cheerfully and gratefully accept it.' [17]

Another event followed which completely ruined Hanson's chances. In some manner the Commissioners were informed that Hanson had been dismissed (apparently on account of his religious or political views) from a firm of solicitors, Bartlett and Beddome, with whom he had been employed several years before. Brown, who describes at length the scheming and intriguing that went on, records under the date of 28 April 1836:

> 'We went to Hutt's in the morning but found that Wakefield was before us & that Hutt was closeted with him impenetrably. W afterwards came to the rooms & saw Torrens & the result of it all is that something passed yesterday at the Board which nobody can tell or will tell, but it was sufficiently to the prejudice of Hanson to make his appointment uncertain. W says that all he can get at is that it would be well for H to get a recommendation from the parties with whom he was 3 years ago. Now this was Beddome and I suspect he has said something against H. It also appears that Mills has spoken to Gouger saying that there is something against H. All this mystery is too bad; for Wakefield was obliged to promise not to mention even what he has, or he would have learned nothing.'

On 4 May Hanson went to see Beddome:

> 'He received him cordially, expressed no objection to giving a certificate of his qualifications, and hinted at no reservation, but wished to consult his partner. H called, therefore, again at 1. Beddome's tone was altered & he would only write a letter which while it spoke highly of H's legal and mental qualifications, restricted their testimony to those points only. With this Hanson felt nothing more could be done.'

Brown and Wakefield urged that Angas's assistance should be obtained, and they interviewed him and asked for his aid. Bartlett and Beddome were Angas's solicitors, but he either could or would do nothing.

> 'Thus the matter is over; and the pique or ill feeling of one individual loses him a provision for life for which he was amply fitted.' [18]

O'Connell's powerful influence overcame the objections to Jeffcott on the score of duelling and debt. In other respects, Jeffcott was well qualified for the position—an able lawyer, young and energetic, of pleasing and attractive manners, experienced in colonial life. He was appointed on 27 May 1836 at a salary of £500 a year, to commence on his arrival in the colony. The Commissioners grumbled at the amount of the salary. It had originally been proposed by them to fix the Judge's salary at £400 a year, and they said that Lord Glenelg had named £500 on account of the "peculiar fitness" of Parker to fill the office, and that, Parker having resigned, the salary should revert to £400. To this Glenelg refused to agree.

> 'The arrangement in question was sanctioned by Her Majesty's Government without any reference to a question of a merely personal nature; and therefore his Lordship does not consider that a change in the person of the Judge would justify an alteration in the salary attached to the office.' [19]

John Rundle (1791-1864) Adelaide's premier shopping street is named after Rundle who at one time owned the landmark 'Beehive Corner' on its corner with King William Street. The South Australian Company, formed by George Fife Angas, was instrumental in the establishment of the colony through its land purchases and supply of settlers. A successful mixture of business and philanthropy it continued for over a hundred years and exerted considerable economic and political power.

Many of those interested in the colony objected to the appointment. John Rundle, MP for Tavistock and a director of the South Australian Company, was particularly outspoken.

> 'I am very much pained'—he wrote to Sir George Grey—'at hearing that Sir J. Jeffcott has been sent out as Chief Justice to South Australia. This appointment is very much regretted by every one feeling, as I do, a lively interest in the moral and religious welfare of that interesting colony. I feel that nothing can be more injurious than filling this Chief Seat of Justice with a Man whom it is impossible to respect & I do hope that the Colonial Office will at an early period repair the mischief by recalling him. I am told that besides the taint which justly attaches to his character on the score of duelling he was so deeply in Debt as not to be able to show publicly in London previous to his departure. [20]

In another letter to James Stephen, Rundle refers to Jeffcott's financial embarrassments, and says:

> 'Altho' they were assigned as the cause of his being the last to join Ship still I do not consider them as the most serious Ground of Objection to his Appointment, knowing the feeling entertained respecting Sir J. Jeffcott in Exeter in consequence of the duel in which he killed Dr Ennis. I know nothing since the formation of the Colony which has been so injurious to its rising popularity as the Appointment of Sir J. Jeffcott to the high and responsible situation which he fills. It has been frequently urged as a Ground of Distrust as to the Administration of the Laws of that Colony & has thereby been

> injurious to the operations of the South Australian Company ... Mr Angas, our Chairman, whose warm interest in the affairs of the Colony is well known, fully concurs in the view which I take in this unfortunate Appointment, & intends shortly being in London when he hopes for the Honor of an interview with you.' [21]

Jeffcott had been directed to accompany the Governor in the *Buffalo*;[22] but as soon as his appointment was announced and his creditors understood that he had a salaried situation and was about to leave England, they redoubled their efforts. The Colonial Office was pestered for his address. One man had been unsuccessfully chasing him for three years with a writ for the recovery of £50 lent to him.[23] Another wrote:

> 'Sir John Jeffcott, the Judge, going to Van Diemen's Land, is endeavouring to quit the country without effecting proper arrangements as to a pecuniary matter of some moment with a near relation';

and wanted to be informed where Jeffcott was to be found and by what ship he would sail.[24] Jeffcott's letters at this time are headed "Ostend": presumably he had retired to the Continent to escape the pressing attentions of his creditors. It was impossible for him to sail on the *Buffalo*, for his creditors and their bailiffs would have been waiting on the wharf. The Commissioners advanced him a quarter's salary, and he obtained permission from the Colonial Office to arrange his own passage at a later period, on the understanding that he must pay his own expenses and arrive in the colony about a month after the *Buffalo*.[25]

Just before the *Isabella* sailed from Spithead on 3 September 1836, the Judge of the Supreme Court was rowed out to the ship by a boatman after dark and stole quietly on board. His arrangements for a passage had been secretly made at the last moment in order to defeat his creditors. All the berths had been booked and he had to sleep on a sofa in the saloon.[26] John Barton Hack and his family were also passengers on the *Isabella*, and through his diary we obtain glimpses of Jeffcott during the voyage. Sir John, he recorded, "seemed disposed to make the best of inconveniences, and proved to be a pleasant and gentlemanly man ... very civil to us".[27] The ship put in at St Jago, one of the Cape de Verde islands, where Jeffcott toyed with the idea of leaving the ship to cross to the Gambier coast, and come on later to the Cape, and thence by the next ship to Australia. Bad wine at St Jago made him ill, but he nevertheless attempted to bathe among the rocks on the shore. This could be done only by lying down on the rocks and allowing the surf to break over him, a procedure which resulted in his being well bruised. Hack had gone with him, but after watching the Judge he prudently declined to follow his example. There was little to relieve the monotony of the long voyage, although there were certainly distractions in the evening:

'Are sorry to have discovered we have bugs in our cabin, which begin to be troublesome'—noted Hack, stoically adding—'but as we had expected this, ought not to complain.'

The *Isabella* reached Hobart Town on 1 January 1837 and Jeffcott spent several months in Van Diemen's Land, probably staying with his relatives the Kermodes at Mona Vale, for when he left for South Australia he was engaged to marry his cousin Anne Kermode.

Mona Vale, the Kermodes' home in Van Diemen's Land (Tasmania) (SLT)

The Exeter Guildhall where Jeffcott was to be tried for murder still stands today and is the seat of the local council. This drawing was done around 1840 by an anonymous artist. (projects.ex.co.uk)

Chapter 2.3

Sir John Jeffcott

'a gentleman by birth'

The Judge arrived in Adelaide on 21 April 1837.[1] Further misfortune had overtaken him, for all his personal belongings, books and furniture, valued at about £400, were lost when the *Isabella* was wrecked at Portland in March.[2] Hindmarsh granted him £150 to replace the law books, which were not to become Jeffcott's property but were to be retained at the Judge's chambers. The remainder of the loss Jeffcott had to bear himself, as he had not insured—an extremely heavy blow falling upon him, as it did, at a time when he had made over to his creditors half of his salary and had only £5 a week on which to live and maintain his position.[3]

It was particularly unfortunate for the colony that Jeffcott had delayed his arrival so long. Had he come out with the Governor on the *Buffalo* many of the quarrels which enlivened and disgraced the administration of Hindmarsh would never have occurred. As the two principal officers of the Crown, the Governor and the Judge were drawn together, and their official connection was strengthened by private friendship. The Governor took from Jeffcott, whom he could regard as his equal, advice which he would have resented had it come from anyone else in the colony, and Jeffcott soon obtained a considerable ascendancy over him. While Jeffcott was in South Australia, the Governor was restrained in his behaviour and acted prudently; as soon as Jeffcott left, Hindmarsh was in difficulties. It was while the Judge was on a visit to Van Diemen's Land that the Governor rashly suspended Brown and Gouger, a step which Jeffcott declared (and probably rightly) would never have been taken had he been in the colony to advise the Governor. If the Governor had been able to talk over his powers with Jeffcott on the *Buffalo* during the voyage to the colony, instead of being provoked by Fisher and Stevenson to maintain extreme views, he would have been spared some of his worst blunders.

It is worthy of note that of all the public officers of the colony Jeffcott is the only one who emerges unscathed from the mud-throwing and ink-slinging which characterises Hindmarsh's term as Governor. Gouger, Gilles, Mann, Fisher, Kingston, Stevenson, Brown, the Governor himself—all were freely and violently criticised and abused by their respective opponents. Even Light was attacked, although he disdained to descend to the miserable squabbling in which the others indulged. Yet not a line is to be found derogatory to Jeffcott, though it may well be supposed that if anything could have been said against him Fisher and his partisans would not have been slow to say it, for they knew that the Judge was the Governor's adviser and supporter. In Jeffcott's past, too, they had an easily available source for insulting remarks. Brown wrote to Edward Gibbon Wakefield that "we want a man like Hanson just now, when so much depends upon our first movements", but he admitted that Jeffcott was "a very agreeable and gentlemanly fellow".[4] The Judge's title and position gave him influence and dignity, and it is possible that his formidable reputation as a duellist may have helped to earn him the tribute of silence. But Hindmarsh was not protected from insult by his rank or his acknowledged bravery, and it is more likely that Jeffcott's success was due principally to personal attributes of character. He was of a different class from Fisher, Mann, Gilles, Brown and their friends. He was a gentleman by birth and education. Colonel Light and the Governor were the only men in the colony who could claim to rank with him in social standing. Accustomed to colonial life, he took pains to be courteous to everyone in the small community and to keep on good terms with all parties, and succeeded in giving strong support to the Governor without incurring the enmity of the Governor's opponents.

Before the Judge reached the colony, the Governor had made an unfortunate mistake in turning to Stevenson for advice and assistance. Although during the voyage out Hindmarsh and Stevenson had been contemptuous of each other, their opinions now underwent a sudden change. 'I find Stevenson a really clever man and of infinite use to me'—wrote the Governor.[5] Stevenson was undoubtedly a clever man but he was also an intriguer and was detested by Fisher and his friends, who were enraged when the Governor began to confer office after office upon his secretary. "Stephenson the Pluralist", he was dubbed by John Barton Hack. "Why such a cabal has been got up against Mr Stevenson, I really am at a loss to guess," ingenuously said the Governor.[6]

Stevenson fully reciprocated the hostility of the colonists.

> 'I have no wish to remain here'—he wrote in November 1837—'as however beautiful the climate and country, the people are the veriest set of—I need not describe them.'[7]

As he found benefits coming his way, Stevenson, who had clamoured so loudly for the Governor's recall, changed to the view that:

> '... he has been but scurvily treated, that is the truth of it ... He is not a strong-minded man nor a well-informed man certainly, but I think he is good-hearted at the bottom, and wishes to do if he can what is right.'[8]

The colonists saw with dismay this "long-faced beetle-browed Scotchman" becoming a power behind the throne, and their protests forced Stevenson to give up the position of Protector of Aborigines which Hindmarsh had conferred upon him—illegally, said Fisher.[9] In reply to a letter of objections from John Morphett, the Governor wrote, with more optimism than foresight, that he hoped:

> '... that those high anticipations formed in England of the

David McLaren (1785-1850) A devout Baptist, McLaren left South Australia in 1841 declaring it, "a dangerous place for Christians". His term as Manager of the SA Company was a successful one, however, highlighted by the building of the New Port (Port Adelaide) and a road to the port. (SLSA)

> Province having the great advantage of a pure and liberal government will be fully realised; moreover as it is clear that more than one person must be concerned in the reign of concord, His Excellency is quite sure it will never be found that its interruption will have been his fault'.[10]

There would have been dissensions in the colony even if Stevenson had never come there, but his baneful influence and bitter pen undoubtedly exacerbated the feeling against the Governor. David McLaren later wrote of Stevenson: "He is the cause of all the mischief, and the cause in particular of the Governor's ruin." [11]

At an early date Stevenson antagonised Mann, the Advocate-General, on whose advice the Governor should have been able to depend. Hindmarsh said that the trouble arose from Stevenson's brusque way of speaking, at which Mann was too quick to take offence.

> 'Stevenson has so much talent and knowledge that he finds it difficult to support Mann's Law Priggery ... I shall have more and more difficulty to keep them clear of each other.' [12]

Being quite inexperienced in civil administration, the Governor was an easy mark for a man as clever as Stevenson. Too often Stevenson's advice coincided with the secret wishes of the Governor and, supported and encouraged by it, Hindmarsh took steps which sober consideration should have convinced him could only lead to useless strife. There was imperative need for the arrival of the Judge to offset the influence which the secretary had obtained over his master.

Jeffcott was at once on good terms with the Governor.

> 'On my arrival here'—he wrote—'I found the Governor, His Excellency Capt Hindmarsh, RN, Knight of the Hanoverian Order, &c, in a mud hut—which consisted of only two rooms, in which were stowed besides himself, Mrs Hindmarsh, and her three daughters, young Hindmarsh, and a maid-servant. How they found room surpasses my comprehension. In the hut I dined with His Excellency in company with Capt Crozier, Commander of HMS Victor. We passed a very merry day, and had the pleasure of hearing the young ladies sing and accompany themselves on the guitar in the evening.' [13]

John Barton Hack took him out riding, and the Judge was delighted with the country.[14]

> 'The site of this incipient city (Adelaide) where I now write, in a tent be it said, is most beautiful, and looks quite like an English park. Nothing can be finer than the rich pastures spread over the land in all directions.' [15]

Jeffcott stayed in South Australia for only six weeks. Brown, in a letter to Wakefield, reporting the arrival of the Judge from Hobart, said: "He is engaged to a lady there, and intends returning with her in the spring, that is in September." Jeffcott's plans, however, were upset by the loss of his belongings, which caused him to obtain leave from Hindmarsh to return to Van Diemen's Land almost immediately to replenish his wardrobe.

Hack's property "Echunga Springs", from a sketch by Governor Gawler – this was a large and valuable property that attested to Hack's success as a pioneer. However, the depression of the early 1840s saw a reversal of his fortune and he finished his working life in government posts. (NLA)

During his stay in the colony he was not idle. He found the Governor was, in Gouger's words, "without a real friend in the Province", and he set himself to smoothing down the friction between Hindmarsh and his officers.[16] He encouraged the Governor to make overtures of friendship towards his enemies, and persuaded him to give a ball and invite all the officers to it. It was a sore point with the Resident Commissioner's party that the Governor never invited them to dine at his house. To a large extent it was innocently explained by the Governor's poverty and the size of his hut, but minds eager to find fault construed it as an insult. Their complaints upon this subject are not easy to understand, for Brown himself wrote to Wakefield of the miserable fare provided at the Governor's table. An Indian judge who visited the colony could only get at Government House a scanty meal of ship's pork and bad sherry, while Mr Fisher was able to provide a dinner of "Stewed Kangaroo, Roast Emu, Quails, Chicken, Claret and Champagne".[17]

The ludicrous controversy over the naming of the various streets and geographical features was compromised by submission to a committee of colonists. Jeffcott on behalf of the Governor proposed Hindmarsh's list of names—"a pocketful of royal and naval heroes" and "a journal of our Governor's life and adventures". King William Street and Victoria Square were loyally named without dissent, but when Jeffcott then proposed "Duncan Street" and "Howe Street" he was overruled by the majority, and "Grote Street" and "Wakefield Street" were substituted. Hindmarsh's heroes were completely outvoted.[18] Jeffcott himself was commemorated by Jeffcott Street in North Adelaide, Kermode Street honoured his fiancée, and in O'Connell Street he acknowledged his debt to his benefactor.

Port Adelaide in 1841 by Edward Opie. (NLA)

The naming question having been disposed of, the long overdue proclamation of the Port was issued by the Governor. A memorial had been presented to Fisher complaining of the delay in the proclamation, the signatories including Gilles, Kingston and Brown.[19] The Governor sent each a letter censuring them, as public officers, for putting their names to a document attacking him. Gilles apologised, but Brown and Kingston sent replies which indicate their attitude to this "attempt at old-fashioned Tory tyranny". Kingston denied that he owed any responsibility to the Governor and expressed regret that "His Excellency should attempt to restrain the free expression of opinion—a line of policy which is at all times unwise and oppressive". Brown was stronger:

> 'In accepting office, I conceive that I relinquished no right of expressing my opinions, publicly or privately, upon any subject. Any requisition tending to forward what I conceive to be the interests of the colony ought to have and will have my signature, be it addressed to whom it may, and the right of such expression of my opinion I will never relinquish.' [20]

At the end of May 1837 the Governor informed Lord Glenelg that he did not receive from the officers of the colony the support which they should render to him, and that:

> '... if I did not possess the cordial assistance of Sir John Jeffcott, whose upright and honorable behaviour I have every reason to admire, I should be alone in the Council and out of doors'. [21]

Besides assisting the Governor by his advice both as a friend and as a member of the Council, Jeffcott had his judicial duties to perform. Almost immediately he was called upon to hold a court to relieve the *Buffalo* of offenders who, for want of a gaol, had been imprisoned on board the vessel. On 6 May 1837 the Council ordered a special commission of gaol delivery to be issued under the seal of the province, and pursuant to this Jeffcott held the first Criminal Sessions, on 13 May, at the Resident Commissioner's office, which was used as a courtroom. "All together, it went off very well," was Brown's verdict.[22]

South Australia was the first of the Australian colonies into which trial by jury, as known to the law in England, was completely introduced. In New South Wales there had been military juries, and other juries of an anomalous nature, and grand juries had existed for a few years under a ruling of Chief Justice Forbes. His opinion was not approved by the authorities at home, and the Act 9 Geo IV c.83, while it gave the Supreme Court of New South Wales power to order trial by jury in civil cases if either of the parties asked for it, did away with grand juries, and it was not until 1839 that trial by jury was introduced in its entirety. There were obvious objections to jury trial in a convict settlement.

> 'You are aware'—said Jeffcott in his address to the Grand Jury at Adelaide—'that in the neighbouring colonies it has been considered inexpedient to concede the full right of trial by jury. The reasons which have been considered as justifying such a restriction elsewhere do not, however, happily prevail here; and I feel no slight degree of satisfaction in being able to congratulate the free inhabitants of South Australia, not on being admitted to, but in being able to claim as their birthright

> the full and unrestricted privileges of the British constitution amongst which not the least valuable is that which has justly been styled the palladium of English liberty, trial by jury, an institution which, however it may have been occasionally abused (and no human institution is free from imperfection) has been proved by the experience of ages in our native land to have well deserved that appellation. This valuable institution, in the fullest sense of the term—that is, trial by the grand and petit jury—will from this day—the first on which a Court is held in this Province—be in operation, and I congratulate you on it.'

He had at first been troubled over:

> '... the presumed difficulty of procuring in so new a colony a sufficient number of intelligent gentlemen to take upon them the highly important duties which you will have to discharge. That difficulty, however, was at once obviated in my mind after I had been a few days amongst you. And among the many interesting and novel features that the foundation of this colony presents it is not the least interesting, that within four months of the landing of the Government and the first settlers on these shores—shores hitherto untrodden by the foot of civilized man—there were found means of assembling together a number of gentlemen capable of constituting a Grand and Petit Jury, who, in point of respectability and intelligence, are, I will venture to say, not inferior to any similar body seen in the mother country.' [23]

The names of the colonists who comprised the Grand Jury are perhaps worth preserving from oblivion, for almost all of them played prominent parts in the early settlement. Colonel Light was foreman, and the others were John Brown, Captain Berkeley, Thomas Young Cotter, John Barton Hack, Young Bingham Hutchinson, George Strickland Kingston, Captain Lipson, William Henry Neale, George Ormsby, William Wyatt, Thomas Bewes Strangways, John William Stuart, and George C. Everard.

> 'We have to congratulate the Colony at this early stage of its progress'—said the Register—'on an array alike striking, whether we regard its respectability or intelligence.'

And John Barton Hack wrote in his diary (13 May 1837):

> 'The first Grand Jury to be called together in Australia met today and received the charge from the Judge. I was one of the number, and was most agreeably surprised to see that so large a number of responsible men could have been assembled at so

> early a period of the colony as that out of which the grand and petit juries were to be chosen.'

Sir John Jeffcott's address to the Grand Jury has been extravagantly praised. Loyau, for instance, said in his *Representative Men of South Australia*:

> 'He was a man of great ability and learning, as is evidenced by his speech or charge to the Grand Jury at his maiden session in 1837, which was afterwards published and re-published. It bears unmistakeable proofs of being the production of an able man.'

It is certainly a sensible and well-arranged address, which confirms the impression one receives from other sources that Jeffcott was a sound and capable lawyer, but it would be foolish to assert that it proves, in itself, that he was a very remarkable man.

Before the proceedings commenced, Mann, the Advocate-General and Public Prosecutor, was admitted as a practitioner of the Court, and in an address to the jury informed them that as prosecutor he conceived it to be his duty:

> '... without fear or favour, to bring before the Jury evidence of all the facts which might be requisite to enable them to detect and punish the guilty; but he held it to be equally clear, that he was bound in justice to the accused, to avoid all appeal to the passions, and everything which might wear the appearance of rhetorical declamation'.

Seven prisoners were presented for trial.

> 'This is not surprising'—wrote Fisher—'considering the number of sailors we have had here, of whom we have certainly had very bad specimens, which makes one more satisfied than ever as to our distance from the Port.' [24]

The original indictments, preserved in the Supreme Court files, have an added historical interest in that they are endorsed, in Colonel Light's hand, one "Not a True Bill. Wm.Light" and the remainder "True Bill. Wm.Light".

Two of the cases involved questions of law arising from the novel situation of the colonists. In one, the prisoner was charged with burglary, which by statute was defined as the breaking and entering of a dwelling house in the night-time with a felonious intent.

> 'The point at issue'—said the Judge—'is whether the huts and tents, in which the great body of our population now reside, whilst more permanent residences are getting up, are to be considered as dwelling-houses for the purposes of burglary. Upon this subject I have no hesitation in saying, that a tent or

hut, in which the owner or his family or servants resides by day and sleeps by night, and which is in fact his fixed though temporary residence, is to be considered a dwelling-house within the meaning of the law.'

The first settlement on the site of Adelaide, after Colonel Light. (AGSA)

In the other case, the prisoner was charged with having broken into a dwelling house in the night-time with intent to steal. The dwelling proved to be a store belonging to the Colonisation Commissioners, adjoining which was a tent in which a servant placed to guard the store resided by day and slept at night. It was held that the store, being detached from the tent, was not a dwelling house or part of one; and as the prisoner had not broken in but had got in through a hole previously made, he could not be convicted upon the charge on which he was indicted.[25]

Two sailors of the *Buffalo* were convicted of rioting. One was fined £1 and the other £5, both to be imprisoned until payment, Jeffcott stating that he had intended giving one imprisonment for two years, but thought it best to let the *Buffalo* take him away from the colony.

The sessions concluded with the admission of Henry Jickling and Samuel Smart as practitioners of the Court, and a presentment from the Grand Jury criticising the conduct of the marines. According to Brown, the Governor was affronted by the presentment.

> 'However he flogged 5 the day after he got it; and altho' the punishment was as hasty and as indiscriminate, as the neglect of all discipline before had been injurious, yet it was richly deserved.' [26]

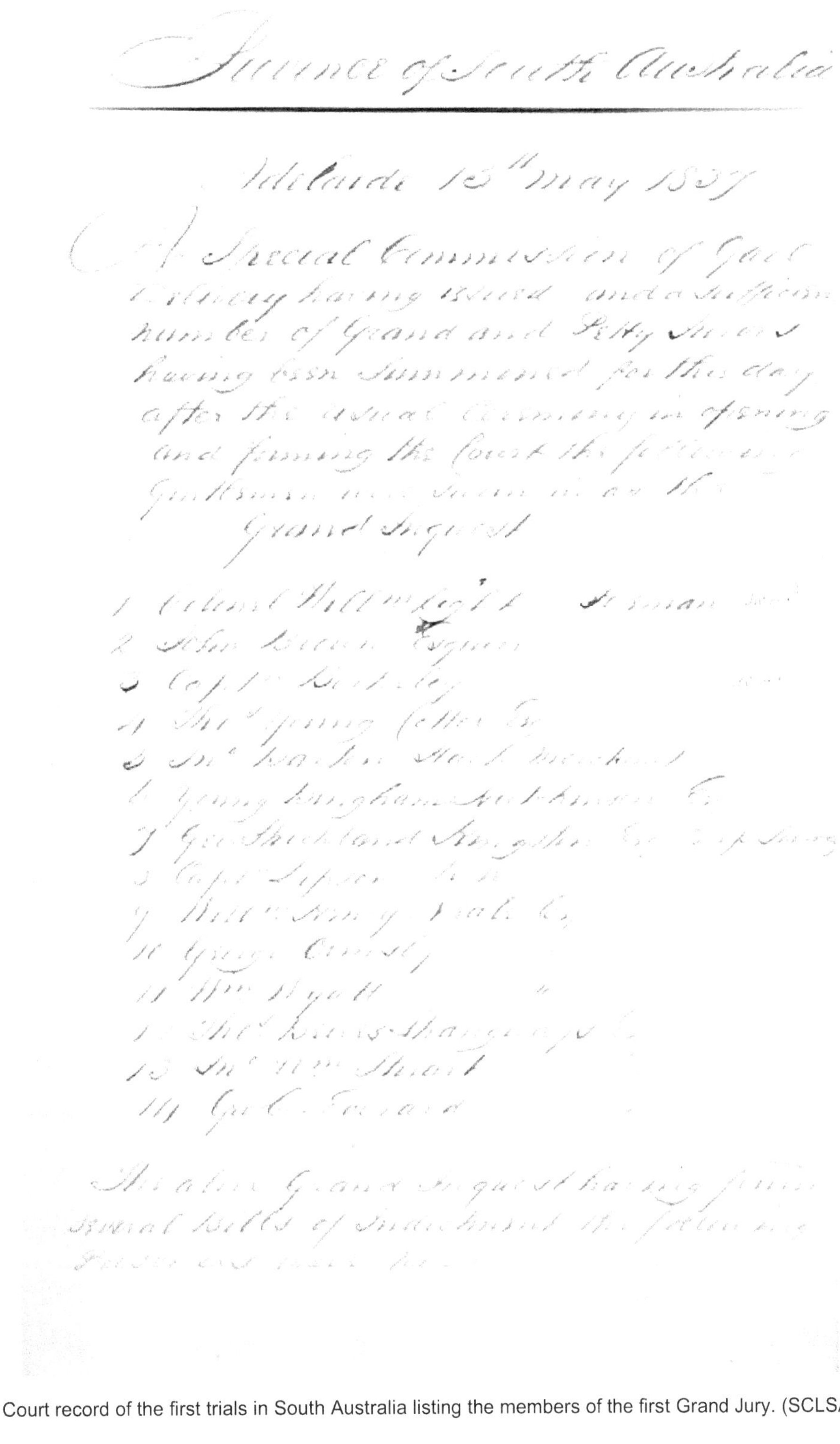

Province of South Australia

Adelaide 13th May 1837

A Special Commission of Gaol Delivery having issued and a sufficient number of Grand and Petty Jurors having been summoned for this day after the usual ceremony in opening and forming the Court the following Gentlemen were sworn in as the Grand Inquest

1 Colonel William Light Foreman
2 John Brown Esquire
3 Captn Berkeley
4 Thos Young Cotter Esq
5 [illegible]
6 [illegible]
7 Geo Strickland Kingston Esq
8 Capt Lipson RN
9 [illegible]
10 [illegible]
11 Wm [illegible]
12 [illegible]
13 Jno Wm Stuart
14 [illegible]

[illegible]

Court record of the first trials in South Australia listing the members of the first Grand Jury. (SCLSA)

Sir John Jeffcott

In the absence of the Judge

On 3 June 1837 Jeffcott left for Van Diemen's Land. He was commissioned by the Governor to buy stores for the Government at Hobart; and he did not return to the colony until 12 October.[1] For more than a month after his departure, affairs moved quietly, but the Governor then became involved in trouble. It began with "a most disgraceful pugilistic encounter" in the street between Gouger and Gilles.[2] Osmond Gilles was a man who was always quarrelling. John Brown penned a remarkable vignette of him:

> 'This man is one of the most singular compounds. An unbounded confidence in his own opinion, he yet has no courage to act upon it alone and unsupported. With a perfect contempt for anything he does not possess or cannot perform, he despises and abuses both poverty or learning; yet dreads either talent or acquirements. One of the loudest talkers and boasters, one of the most timid performers. One of the most excitable and irritable of men, one of the meanest if an insult or an insinuation be repelled with common spirit. One who quarrels or insults everyone with whom he is acquainted and yet one of a deal of kindly feeling, and who would not I believe nourish a quarrel for the world. A sensible and clever man in business matters, one may pass hours with him alone with profit upon all points he is acquainted with, but in the company of half a dozen, and with general conversation the probability is that he will treat some one so insolently or so ignorantly that you must pass over his behaviour as that of temporary insanity or knock him down if you think him in his right mind.' [3]

Osmond Gilles ca. 1865 (SLSA)

Gouger and Gilles were old enemies. Back in August 1835, Samuel Stephens had reported to Angas that Gilles:

> '... if his own statement be anything like correct, has been most shamefully used by Messrs Gouger & Co. It is, however, a great pity that he has so little command over his temper, and that he cannot express himself in sufficiently strong terms without prepetually [sic] taking the name of God in vain.' [4]

When sober, Gilles was an arrogant braggart; when drunk he became unbearable. He celebrated the Governor's landing so well that Gouger protested in Council that "owing to the disgusting and opprobious [sic] language" used by him, Gilles was not fit to be a magistrate.[5] Gouger was so offended by Gilles's exhibition that he vowed that he would have nothing to do with him, except officially; and he told the Governor after the fight that he had "invariably followed out the resolution then formed, Mr Gilles never having visited me, nor I him, excepting upon public business".

Gilles' pugilistic tendencies were the subject of this 1841 cartoon in *The Adelaide Independent And Cabinet Of Amusement* newspaper. (SLSA)

The fight arose from the wagging of Gilles's uncontrollable tongue. He conceived himself insulted by Gouger and went about bragging that "By God, if Bob Gouger does not apologize in the presence of the Governor, I will blow a hole in his ----- ----- carcase!" So far from apologising, Gouger and Mann waylaid Gilles to extract an apology from him. They were greeted with the usual torrent of abuse. "It was only on being called to my face a liar and words too loathsome to write," said Gouger, "that I felt compelled to chastise him." (The Governor reported, however, that Gouger had told him that "his friends insisted on him beating Mr Gilles whenever he saw him".) Apparently after lusty swearing all round, Gouger pulled

Gilles's nose, and a free fight followed. Gouger had the best of it, and wound up by borrowing a stick and giving Gilles a caning. Gilles's version was that it was "a ruffian-like attack on my person by Mr Gouger and his accomplices", and he asserted that he was held by Mann while Gouger attempted "to scratch my face with his nails".

To Hindmarsh it seemed a heaven-sent opportunity. He had gradually become more and more estranged from Gouger and the breach between them was completed by the Governor's discovery that Gouger consulted with Fisher and Mann upon all matters of importance, "so that in fact subjects belonging to the Executive have been discussed and others really done altogether without my knowledge". He peremptorily forbade Gouger to do this, and he now saw a chance to rid himself of this upstart Colonial Secretary. Edward Stephens having belatedly sworn an information (after the fight was over) that he feared a breach of the peace was likely to take place between Gouger and Gilles, the Governor ordered Sergeant Mew to take a sufficient force of marines and arrest them both. Gouger was accordingly arrested and marched half a mile through the town with a guard of marines with fixed bayonets. Gilles seems to have escaped this indignity, but they were both brought before Stevenson and Strangways, two Justices of the Peace, and bound over to keep the peace in their own recognisances of £500 each. An inquiry into the fracas was directed by the Governor, and held by David McLaren, Stevenson and Strangways, whose report of the evidence given before them was submitted to the Council. The fight occurred on 16 August. On 21 August the Council met, and the Governor immediately brought forward as the subject for consideration whether Gouger should not be suspended from his office. Needless to say Gouger, Fisher and Mann were unanimous in negativing this. Fisher questioned the Governor's power to suspend any officer and urged that, as the matter could be adequately dealt with in the ordinary course of the law, no further official action was needed. The Advocate-General said that the suspension or removal of any member of the Council involved questions of "the most curious legal nicety" and of equal general interest, and he wanted an adjournment to consider the points of law involved, suggesting that if a member of the Council was illegally suspended the validity of subsequent acts of the Council might be doubtful. Gouger himself said that, legal points of some difficulty having been put forward, "he thought himself peculiarly unfortunate that he had not the benefit of the advice and assistance of His Honor the Judge upon them", and he claimed the right to submit a written protest against the course which the Governor proposed to adopt.[6]

These objections Hindmarsh brushed aside. Upon all these legal points, he said, he had quite made up his mind, and was perfectly satisfied how far his powers went. If the rest of the Council would not agree with him, then he would act under the provision in his Instructions which empowered him to overrule the decision of the majority of the Council if he saw fit to differ from it. Accordingly he forthwith suspended Gouger until His Majesty's pleasure should be known, and appointed in his place Strangways, as Acting Colonial Secretary.[7]

Thomas Bewes Strangways (c1810-1859) Strangways was listed as a land proprietor on the passenger list of the *Buffalo*. His name lives on in two Adelaide streets, Bewes Street and Strangways Terrace (Strangways was on the street naming committee). He was a member of a party that traced the River Torrens to its source.

In thus "dropping the pilot", the Governor took a very hasty step and inflicted a punishment out of all proportion to the gravity of the offence, and he added to the injustice of his action by allowing Gilles to go unpunished (except by the removal of his name from the list of magistrates), although Gilles, if not the principal offender, was at least equally as guilty as Gouger, who decided to return to England to put his case. David McLaren wrote home to Angas that the Governor had made a bad mistake, for "Mr Gouger goes home full of determined opposition to the Governor and will leave no stone unturned to secure his recall".[8]

Hindmarsh, however, was delighted with his achievement. "I stood alone against all the members of the Council," he proudly told Lord Glenelg; "the whole clique assert that I have not the power to suspend an officer". He forwarded statements from Gouger, with contemptuous vice-regal annotations in the margin. When Gouger spoke of his own conduct as "courteous yet fearless", Hindmarsh noted: "uniformly overbearing and insolent"; "usual result of unexpected elevation"; "slop seller in Leadenhall Street".[9]

On 1 September, Gouger presented a written protest against his suspension on the grounds:

(1) That neither the Governor nor the Council had any power at all to suspend him.

(2) That if such a power existed in the colony its exercise must be subject to the will of a majority of the Council.[10]

His argument upon the first point was based on section II of the Foundation Act, which provided that:

> '... it shall and may be lawful for His Majesty, his heirs or successors, by any order or orders to be by him or them made, with the advice of his or their Privy Council, to make, ordain, and, subject to such conditions and restrictions as to him and them shall seem meet, to authorise and empower any one or more persons resident and being within any of the said provinces to make ordain and establish all such laws institutions or ordinances, and to constitute such courts and appoint such officers ... and to impose and levy such rates duties and taxes as may be necessary for the peace order and good government of His Majesty's subjects and others within the said province or provinces'.

Upon the strict grammatical construction of this section it appears open to some doubt whether the power of constituting courts, appointing officers and levying taxes was given to the King in Council only, or whether the King in Council was authorised to delegate this power to the Council in the colony. The latter construction was followed, apparently without any criticism, by everyone at the time; but the section affords another instance of the loose drafting which marred the Act. It was decided by the law officers in England that, under this section, the first officers of the colony and members of the Colonial Council must be appointed by an order of the King in Council, instead of following the ordinary way of appointing officers in the colonies, by issuing a warrant under the Royal Sign Manual commanding the Governor to issue Letters Patent under the public seal of the colony for the appointment of the person named in the warrant.[11] The appointment of officers by Order in Council, they said, was "entirely unknown and unprecedented", but the Foundation Act in this respect had abrogated the common law right of the King to appoint officers by virtue of his prerogative.

If, however, the officers could not be appointed by the King by virtue of his prerogative but only by an Order in Council, then, it was contended by Gouger, they could be dismissed or suspended only by an order in Privy Council and not by an act of the royal prerogative.

> 'The same power which appoints can alone suspend or remove, and the merger of the common law right in the statutable power of appointment must by parity of reasoning be held to merge the common law prerogative of suspension or removal.'

There was no doubt that at common law the Crown had the right to suspend its officers; suspension, in fact, was "probably the one effective weapon that the Governor had in the assertion of his authority".[12] But had not the Foundation Act vested this power solely in the Privy Council?

This argument was not without force; for, once admitted that the Privy Council alone could appoint, then it seemed illogical that an appointment which could only be made by what was, next to the Imperial Parliament, the most august tribunal of the Empire, could at any time be nullified by the Governor or Council of an insignificant and unimportant colony. Yet there were obvious objections to the right of suspension or removal being limited to the Privy Council in England, thousands of miles away. The *Register* was not slow to point out the extreme lengths to which the argument would have to be carried. Suppose Gouger had murdered Gilles.

> 'He must, say these wise lawyers, have continued Colonial Secretary. "The Governor has not the power to suspend him." True, His Honor the Judge might link him for the felony to a chained gang in New South Wales—but he must be transported with his character of Colonial Secretary in his pocket.'

The contentions on this point were clearly summed up by the Commissioners in their third annual report:

> 'The Governor, supported by the Chief Justice, assumed that, as immediate representative of the Crown, he possessed the

power of suspending the Government officers, and consequently the ex-officio members of the Council, until the pleasure of the Crown should be known; while a majority of the Council, with the Advocate General, maintained that as by the Act the principal officers of the Government were appointed, not by simple prerogative under the Sign Manual, but by the Sovereign with the advice of the Privy Council, such officers could be removed only by an order of the Sovereign in Council, and that, consequently, the Governor could have no power either of appointment or suspension.' [13]

It was hopeless to expect either side in the colony to admit any basis of truth in the arguments of the other. Their ideas had been formed before they reached the colony; and as Wordsworth (according to Oscar Wilde) went about finding in stones the sermons he had already hidden there, so they found in the Foundation Act and the Orders in Council what they had already made up their minds ought to be found there.

An 1833 painting of Robert Gouger by A. Stephens (AGSA)

Lord Glenelg, when Gouger's protest and the arguments of the majority of the Council reached him, took the opinion of the law officers upon the question whether, under the Foundation Act, the Governor of South Australia had the power to suspend any colonial officer appointed by an Order in Council and whether, notwithstanding an act of suspension, such officer would continue de jure to hold his appointment. Sir John Campbell (Attorney-General) and Sir R.M. Rolfe (Solicitor-General) in a joint opinion said:

'The Governor has the power of suspension, and an officer so suspended would from thenceforth cease to be entitled to exercise any of the functions or to derive any of the emoluments of his office till Her Majesty's pleasure should be known. The officer must be considered as holding during the pleasure of the Crown, and we think the Governor has the power of suspension under his commission and instructions from the Crown. This power is not conferred upon him by 4 & 5 Wm IV c.95, but there is nothing in that Act by which the prerogative of the Crown in this respect is abridged.'

In effect, their opinion amounted to this: that it is true an officer is appointed by Order in Council, but he is appointed to be an officer of the Crown and takes the position subject to all the usual incidents attaching to an office under the Crown, amongst which is the liability to suspension by the Crown.[14]

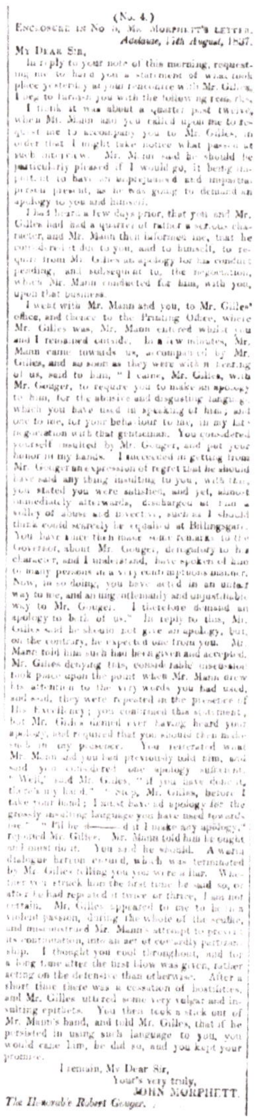

(No. 4.)

ENCLOSURE IN NO 6, MR. MORPHETT'S LETTER.

Adelaide, 15th August, 1837.

MY DEAR SIR,

In reply to your note of this morning, requesting me to hand you a statement of what took place yesterday at your rencontre with Mr. Gilles, I beg to furnish you with the following remarks.

I think it was about a quarter past twelve, when Mr. Mann and you called upon me to request me to accompany you to Mr. Gilles, in order that I might take notice what passed at such interview. Mr. Mann said he should be particularly pleased if I would go, it being important to have an unprejudiced and impartial person present, as he was going to demand an apology to you and himself.

I had heard a few days prior, that you and Mr. Gilles had had a quarrel of rather a serious character, and Mr. Mann then informed me, that he considered it due to you, and to himself, to require from Mr. Gilles an apology for his conduct pending, and subsequent to, the negociation, which Mr. Mann conducted for him, with you, upon that business.

I went with Mr. Mann and you, to Mr. Gilles' office, and thence to the Printing Office, where Mr. Gilles was, Mr. Mann entered whilst you and I remained outside. In a few minutes, Mr. Mann came towards us, accompanied by Mr. Gilles, and as soon as they were within hearing of us, said to him, "I came, Mr. Gilles, with Mr. Gouger, to require you to make an apology to him, for the abusive and disgusting language which you have used in speaking of him; and one to me, for your behaviour to me, in my late negociation with that gentleman. You considered yourself insulted by Mr. Gouger, and put your honor in my hands. I succeeded in getting from Mr. Gouger an expression of regret that he should have said any thing insulting to you, with this you stated you were satisfied, and yet, almost immediately afterwards, discharged at him a volley of abuse and invective, such as I should think could scarcely be equalled at Billingsgate. You have since then made some remarks to the Governor, about Mr. Gouger, derogatory to his character, and I understand, have spoken of him to many persons in a very contemptuous manner. Now, in so doing, you have acted in an unfair way to me, and an ungentlemanly and unjustifiable way to Mr. Gouger. I therefore demand an apology to both of us." In reply to this, Mr. Gilles said he should not give an apology, but, on the contrary, he expected one from you. Mr. Mann told him such had been given and accepted. Mr. Gilles denying this, considerable discussion took place upon the point when Mr. Mann drew his attention to the very words you had used, and said, they were repeated in the presence of His Excellency; you confirmed this statement, but Mr. Gilles denied ever having heard your apology, and required that you should then make such in my presence. You reiterated what Mr. Mann and you had previously told him, and said you considered one apology sufficient. "Well," said Mr. Gilles, "if you have done it, there's my hand." "Stop, Mr. Gilles, before I take your hand; I must have an apology for the grossly insulting language you have used towards me." "I'll be d——d if I make any apology," repeated Mr. Gilles. Mr. Mann told him he ought and must do it. You said he should. A warm dialogue hereon ensued, which was terminated by Mr. Gilles telling you you were a liar. Whether you struck him the first time he said so, or after he had repeated it twice or thrice, I am not certain. Mr. Gilles appeared to me to be in a violent passion, during the whole of the scuffle, and misconstrued Mr. Mann's attempt to prevent its continuation, into an act of cowardly partizanship. I thought you cool throughout, and for a long time after the first blow was given, rather acting on the defensive than otherwise. After a short time there was a cessation of hostilities, and Mr. Gilles uttered some very vulgar and insulting epithets. You then took a stick out of Mr. Mann's hand, and told Mr. Gilles, that if he persisted in using such language to you, you would cane him, he did so, and you kept your promise.

I remain, My Dear Sir,

Your's very truly,

JOHN MORPHETT.

The Honorable Robert Gouger.

Morphett's long and detailed letter to Gouger supporting Gouger's case regarding the altercation, as published in the *South Australian Gazette and Colonial Register* of 16 September 1837. (SLSA)

The view taken by the law officers rendered unnecessary any consideration by them of Gouger's second argument that if the power of suspension existed in the colony at all, it was vested in the Council; that the powers of the Council were "vested in an aggregate Council of Government or in a majority thereof", each member having equal rights; and that the Governor was not entitled to act in opposition to the majority of the Council. This question was soon to be raised again in the colony, and will be considered later; it is necessary now to describe briefly the bitter, though amusing, sequelae to Gouger's suspension. At first Gouger wanted to prosecute some of the witnesses at the inquiry into the affray for perjury, but Mann advised him that this was impossible, as the proceedings were extrajudicial. He then sent an angry protest to the Governor against his arrest by the marines; Hindmarsh ignored it. Another letter met the same fate. Gouger then sent Dr Wright to wait upon the Governor with copies. He could have hardly made a worse choice of an emissary, for the Governor particularly detested Wright as "a creature" of the Resident Commissioner. When Wright explained that he had come to present letters from Gouger, the Governor bundled him out, saying that if he attempted to leave the letters the servant would burn them. Wright tried again to see the Governor on the following day, but a sentry had been posted to refuse him admittance. Gouger talked loudly of bringing an action for false imprisonment against the Governor, with the damages laid at £10,000, but nothing more than talk came of it.[15]

Gilles, smarting under his caning and conscious that he had the Governor on his side, sought revenge against Mann, who, he claimed, had acted "with extreme treachery and duplicity" throughout, and "entrapped me out alone and defenceless to be the object of a planned assault, which was to be committed upon my person by the Colonial Secretary, assisted by 'my friend' Mr Mann as a second, and Mr Morphett as his 'impartial and unprejudiced witness'".[16] He urged the Governor to punish Mann as well as Gouger; and Hindmarsh, nothing loath, threatened to order an investigation into Mann's part in the fight. Mann objected to this course and questioned the legality of any such inquiry, which gave the Governor the chance to retaliate:

> 'As the order to the Magistrates to enquire into the affray between Messrs Gilles and Gouger was written under your inspection and review and the course adopted approved by you, His Excellency cannot understand the objection you now urge to follow the same course in ascertaining the part you have taken in the affair, particularly the charge made against you by Mr Gilles of being in fact the instigator of the disgraceful attack committed upon his person by Mr Gouger and of having decoyed him into a position where a breach of the peace was contemplated. His Excellency cannot avail himself of your legal advice or opinion in an affair where your personal conduct is so seriously implicated; and he considers he will act rightly in ordering the same procedure to be followed in your case as you advised and approved of in the case of Mr Gouger.' [17]

Apparently the Governor was so pleased with this retort that he forgot to take any active steps to press on with an inquiry, for none was ever held.

Mann declared that Gilles's accusations were grossly defamatory, and threatened proceedings against him in the Supreme Court as soon as the Judge returned, by indictment or action, unless they were retracted.[18] Hindmarsh, in the meantime, claimed to have discovered that upwards of £2,000 of public moneys had been left unaccounted for by Gouger; and as Gouger was about to leave for England, the Governor asked for Mann's opinion whether Gouger should not be called upon to furnish proper accounts and pay over any shortage before he was permitted to quit the colony.[19] The charge against Gouger seems to have been quite unfounded, but it gave Hindmarsh a double pleasure—it was a direct attack on Gouger, and it equally hit Mann who was torn between his duty as Advocate-General and his friendship for Gouger. Mann advised that maladministration of office in the case of high officers of government should be inquired into by the Council of Government or an indictment laid for embezzlement, but he complained that "no sufficient facts had been placed before me" to justify any proceedings.

> 'In either case the Government should come prepared with a strong array of facts to found a case so serious and I confess that to me there appears to be none such at present ... I cannot conclude this opinion, without expressing my surprise that during an interval of upwards of one month since Mr Gouger's suspension, no business-like effort should have been made to get at the facts of the case; and that now, at the very moment when it is publicly known that Mr Gouger is about to sail for Europe, the case itself should be urged. This remark is all the more forcible as I know that professional men have been engaged by the Government during my absence at Encounter Bay. I think it a duty which I owe to His Excellency to point

> out that it will be now almost impossible to satisfy the world, that a desire to embarrass Mr Gouger is not connected with the proceedings suggested, and altho' such a feeling is not one which ought for a moment to weigh when a public duty compels the adoption of any decided course of action, yet it is certainly one which ought to make the Government proceedings of such a nature as to be in no wise doubtful as to their ultimate result.' [20]

In the face of this opinion, Hindmarsh could not very well go on with the charge against Gouger, so he contented himself with directing Gilles, the Treasurer, to refuse to pay him any salary.[21]

Flushed by his apparent triumph over Gouger, the Governor attempted to dispose of Brown in the same summary way. He had never liked Brown, who, he said, treated his authority with disrespect and contempt, made speeches against the government and led every attack upon it.[22] The death of a pauper emigrant provided the excuse. Brown was ordered to have the man buried and refused to do so on the grounds that his duties were with live emigrants, not dead ones, and that he was an officer of the Commissioners and therefore subject to their orders and not those of the Governor.[23] Fisher supported him and instructed him to persist in his refusal.

> 'I do not consider the particular service required'—he informed Brown—'to be in this case within the scope of the duties of your office under the Colonization Commissioners, with regard to which you can attend to no other directions than such as you may receive from me, or the Commissioners in England.' [24]

The Governor thereupon suspended Brown, for disobedience to orders, until the pleasure of the Crown would be known, and Gilles was directed to pay Brown his salary to the date of suspension but "on no account to pay that person any wages beyond this date".[25]

Jeffcott, when he returned to the colony, was dismayed at Hindmarsh's suspension of the Emigration Agent. Brown of all people, he said, was the most dangerous to meddle with because of the anomalous character of his position.[26] Looking to the duties which he performed, the Emigration Agent seemed clearly to be an officer of the Commissioners, having no connection with the government of the colony. The Commissioners had recommended him for the appointment, but he had been actually appointed by an Order in Council which specially instructed him to be obedient to the Governor. The same argument would have been open to Brown as was put forward by Gouger, that having been appointed by Order in Council, he could be suspended only by Order in Council; but he and Fisher did not touch upon this point, which savoured too much of an appointment by the Crown, whereas they relied on the contention that Brown was an officer of the Commissioners. Brown had been angry at being appointed by Order in Council and at having his name placed by the Colonial Office in the list of their officers. "How came my name in the Colonial Office list of government officers?" he wrote to Wakefield.[27] The reason was subsequently revealed by the Colonial Office: Brown's name was specially included in the Order in Council so as to bring him under the control of the Crown, since his political views were mistrusted. This interesting sidelight was not known in the colony, and Brown declared that his appointment by Order in Council was due to a mistake. The Commissioners, he claimed, by selecting him, had appointed him pursuant to the ninth section of the Foundation Act, and the subsequent Order in Council had not made him an officer of the Government but was merely an unnecessary announcement of his appointment. The Governor's reply to this was:

> 'His Excellency has no knowledge of any appointment you hold in this Province, but in virtue of your appointment as Emigration Agent by His Majesty, contained in the Order in Council dated 13th July 1836, and as such you are clearly not an officer of the Commissioners but of the Colonial Government. His Excellency considers if any appointment by the Commissioners did in reality exist in your favour it is annulled and superseded by the subsequent order of His Majesty in Council.'

Hindmarsh had no sort of doubt about the matter. He discussed it openly with David McLaren and said that it was as clear as noonday that Brown was a government official. McLaren had doubts.

> 'The absence of the Judge'—he wrote to Angas—'is much to be regretted; his opinion would I think have had great weight in at least determining the nature of the appointment, the extent of powers &c, and thus have prevented the breach becoming so wide and irreparable.' [28]

Perhaps the Governor subsequently began to waver, for (Mann being away at Encounter Bay) he consulted Wigley, an English solicitor who had commenced practice in Adelaide. Wigley's opinion (which was subsequently approved by the Colonial Office) confirmed the Governor's views, and seems clearly right. He pointed out also the remarkable fact that, although the Emigration Agent was an officer essential to the carrying on by the Commissioners of emigration, yet the Foundation Act had omitted to give the Commissioners any power at all to appoint him. Only two sections in the Act related to the appointment of officers by them. Section XIII dealt only with the staff of the London office; section IX empowered the Commissioners to appoint:

> 'Such person or persons as they may think fit Treasurer, Assistant Surveyors, and other officers, for carrying this Act into execution respecting the disposal of the said Public Lands and the Purchase Money thereof'.

Henry Rodolph Wigley (1794-1876) Appointed the Public Prosecutor and Resident Magistrate in November 1837 Wigley continued to serve the Government until his retirement in 1856. His appointments included that of the first Commissioner of Insolvency.

But the disposal of the public lands and the purchase money was not the business of the Emigration Agent, and Brown could not be appointed under this section. De facto, therefore, Brown was the Commissioners' officer; de jure, he was not, and could not be, their officer and was an officer of the government subject to Hindmarsh's orders.[29]

Fisher would not admit the validity of the suspension and directed Brown to continue to perform the duties of the office.

> 'Having in mind the Principles (which I must ever maintain as far as I can inviolate, as essential to the fair trial of that peculiar system of Colonization upon which the success of the Colony depends) established by the Act of Parliament by virtue of which this Province is founded, and which creates an entire separation between the functions of the Government officers and those charged with the disposal of land and the arrangements of emigrants, & feeling that the course pursued in this case in assuming to suspend you from the office of Emigration Agent might be deemed a direct invasion of one of those principles, I consider it my duty the more especially to tell you that I do not consider His Excellency the Governor has the power to suspend you from the office to which you were appointed by the Colonization Commissioners.' [30]

Not content with this, Fisher issued printed handbills notifying the public that in spite of the Governor's suspension John Brown still retained the office of Emigration Agent and would continue to perform his duties as before. "I have done this," he told the Governor, "without the least intention of personal disrespect towards your Excellency, but as a matter of imperious Duty on my part." The Governor was furious at the insult. Backed by Wigley's opinion that the handbill was a seditious libel because it tended to lessen the authority of the government and to incite the people to disobey the lawful orders of the Governor, Hindmarsh issued a proclamation denouncing Fisher as seditious; and on Mann's return to Adelaide he was asked to advise whether Fisher had not been guilty of sedition, or "whether the crime is of a still more criminal nature"—Hindmarsh apparently had visions of a trial for high treason—and whether, although the Judge being absent criminal proceedings could not be taken immediately, Fisher should not be forthwith dismissed from his office of Justice of the Peace. Mann in reply endeavoured to avoid committing himself by protesting that he had not sufficient information before him to give a final opinion. Hypothetically he advised that:

> '... in case it can be proved on the part of the Crown that the Colonization Commissioners for South Australia have no right to appoint the Emigration Agent, and that they have not in fact appointed and placed him under the direction and subject to the instructions of the Resident Commissioner, then an

> indictment for a seditious libel can be sustained against Mr Fisher. On the other hand, if Mr Fisher can prove (as I have reason to believe he can) that he is appointed under the King's Sign Manual to act under the orders of the Colonization Commissioners, that he has acted in accordance with the instructions of the Commissioners and that Mr Brown is appointed by the Commissioners, and placed under the orders of the Resident Commissioner, then an indictment for a seditious libel could not be supported.'

Fisher could not with propriety, he said, be dismissed from the magistracy unless the handbill was proved to be seditious by the verdict of a jury, "which I think there is every reason to doubt", and he concluded by stating that Fisher could not be removed except by a majority of the members of the Council.[31]

Meanwhile, Fisher had threatened to prosecute Strangways, the Acting Colonial Secretary, for a libel in issuing the Governor's proclamation—"an idea", said Jeffcott, "that could only have entered into the head of a petty fogging attorney". With a curious indifference to any conflict between the duties of his official position and his private business, Mann not only proposed to conduct these proceedings on behalf of Fisher but actually accepted a retainer from Brown, and on his behalf sued Gilles, the Colonial Treasurer, for payment of Brown's salary, alleging that the suspension was void.[32] Gilles was between two fires. On the one hand, he disliked Fisher and he had peremptory orders from the Governor to pay no salary to Brown but to pay it to Hutchinson, whom the Governor had appointed to the vacant place of Emigration Agent. On the other hand, the moneys which he handled and out of which the salaries were paid belonged to the Commissioners, and Fisher, who flatly refused to take any notice of Hutchinson, tried to browbeat Gilles into paying Brown.[33]

Young Bingham Hutchinson (1806-1870)
Hutchinson was one of the earliest settlers and briefly held the office of Emigration Agent. He was the first European to climb Mount Lofty. (SLSA)

> 'It appears'—he wrote to Gilles—'that you think it necessary to apply for instructions from His Excellency the Governor as to whether you are to attend to my instructions as to the application of the monies which I place in your hands as Colonial Treasurer to the Colonization Commissioners, and with respect to the application of which, I gave you special instructions at the time of so placing the monies, and by your subsequent letter to me it appears that having received, in consequence directions to disobey my instructions in such respect you express your determination so to do. Upon this I refrain from making any observation (especially after the personal explanations I have given to you as to your line of duty) than that you must take the consequences; and that the course you have thought proper to pursue necessarily gives rise to the consideration on my part as to whether I can in future place any further sums in your hands, when by so doing I

> subject them to the control of irresponsible parties, thereby depriving the Colonization Commissioners of the control over the funds for the due application of which they alone are personally responsible.'

Placed in this unpleasant situation Gilles protested that he was only too willing to pay the salary of the Emigration Agent to the person who was legally entitled to it.

> 'My wish is to do my Duty honestly and impartially to the Government and to the Honourable Colonization Commissioners, but the position in which I am placed obliges me as the responsible Treasurer of the Commissioners ... to pay no monies belonging to them but to the proper persons.'

If he paid the wrong man, he would be personally liable to make good the deficiency, and he therefore preferred to do nothing until he got instructions from England or the question was decided by the Court.[34]

Brown's action for his salary dragged on for a long time. Mann passed it on to Johnston, another solicitor; but Johnston having accepted the office of Clerk of the Peace was promptly informed that he could not, as a government official, act in opposition to the government.[35] He handed the papers to Fisher, but before the action came to hearing Governor Gawler had arrived in the colony with instructions to reinstate Brown (who had acted under Fisher's orders and could not be held entirely responsible for the dispute) and to pay him his full salary.[36]

A Calendar of Prisoners… from the court record of the first trials (SCLSA)

Sir John Jeffcott

'of anarchy and confusion'

Jeffcott returned to Adelaide on 19 October 1837.

> 'I am sorry to tell you'—he wrote to Kermode—'I found this place politically speaking in a dreadful state, and I really do not think I shall be able to remain here with any satisfaction to myself or without compromising my present position with reference to the Colonial Office.' [1]

Mann's conduct in acting for Fisher and Brown appeared to the Judge preposterous and he felt that such improper action by the Advocate-General justified him in joining in the struggle on behalf of the Governor.

> 'I think I have diverted a part of the storm of legal annoyance which was to have been rattled off against him by Fisher and Mann by showing him how he could carry the war into the enemy's country.'

Mann's opinion that Fisher ought not to be prosecuted had been given on 23 September, and the Governor had done nothing further in the matter. Jeffcott suggested to Hindmarsh that he should direct Mann to file an ex officio information against Fisher for seditious libel in issuing the handbill. The Governor, rather humorously, wrote to Mann on 4 November that his opinion:

> '... convinces his Excellency that his view of the nature of the paper viz that it is a seditious libel, is correct, and therefore it is His Excellency's direction that you immediately take the necessary measures to file an information against Mr Fisher, so soon as the Supreme Court shall be opened'.[2]

Two days later he wrote demanding a written answer, and on 11 November, as Mann was still silent, the Governor ordered him to comply with the instructions forthwith. As Jeffcott reported:

> '... this has brought them on their marrow bones, as Mann dare not refuse without forfeiting his situation, and Fisher begins to fear the tables are turned'.[3]

Immediately on his return to Adelaide, the Judge found himself in the thick of a turbulent quarrel arising from the rivalries of the whalers at Encounter Bay. The South Australian Company objected to the appearance of another whaling ship in their waters. Blenkinsop, the captain of this vessel, suggested that they should work together, but Samuel Stephens, the company's manager, would have nothing to do with this proposal. Rival stations were established, Blenkinsop's near Granite Island and the company's at the Bluff, and a feud was carried on fiercely. Stephens complained to the Governor that the company's business was seriously injured by the operations of Blenkinsop's station and of other intruders—whalers from America and New South Wales.[4] The Advocate-General was called on to advise whether the colonists of South Australia had acquired, by the Act creating the province, an exclusive right of fishery on the shores of the colony; and if so, what steps should be taken to protect it, and, in particular, what should be done about Blenkinsop. In a long opinion, Mann set out his conclusions that the colonists had acquired a right to prevent strangers fishing along the coasts of South Australia. A difficulty arose with regard to those offenders who, like the American whalers, remained at sea and did not establish themselves on land, for the Governor had no commission as Admiral and there was no Vice-Admiralty court in the colony. Mann could only suggest that the facts should be reported to the Colonial Office for instructions; or, if matters became serious, that the Governor should ask for naval assistance from New South Wales or Van Diemen's Land. As to Blenkinsop's land station, there was no difficulty. 'I do not doubt'—Mann wrote to Gouger—'as to the right of removing Blenkinsop and his troop from the land.'

View of Encounter bay with the fisheries, attributed to Colonel Light, between 1837-39. This is the view from the Bluff with Granite Island on the far right. (ATLNZ)

Under the Foundation Act the legal estate of the land of the province was not vested in express terms in the Commissioners, but he thought it was vested in them by implication.

> 'The intent of the Act obviously is that the Commissioners should sell and pass the fee, and without the legal estate being in them this could not be effected.'

If the Commissioners were the proprietors in fee simple, then it was their duty, through their representative in the colony, not to permit any system of location on lands which were directed by the Act to be sold. Blenkinsop and his party were mere trespassers, who must take cognisance of the Act, and they should be ejected.

> 'To do this, and avoid a struggle, which would be inconvenient, I think the Buffalo should be kept that we may have the aid of her blue jackets and as many of the marines as possible.'

He recommended that Fisher should give a written notice to Blenkinsop requiring him to remove within a reasonable time. If he did not then go, Fisher should attend with a sufficient force and eject him. (Presumably Blenkinsop was to be driven to sea, as all the land belonged to the Commissioners.) 'The Colonial Commissioner should act in person, as the authority of the Colonization Commissioners is vested in him or delegated to him.'[5]

Fisher decided to go to Encounter Bay and asked for a force of marines. The Governor agreed, and suggested that Colonel Light should accompany the force in charge of them, as he had "the utmost confidence in his prudence, and his former service making him peculiarly fit for this". Blenkinsop and Fisher came to terms without a struggle, and the expedition returned to Adelaide leaving Blenkinsop still in possession.[6]

Further quarrels occurred between the two stations, and when Strangways and Stevenson visited Encounter Bay shortly afterwards, Blenkinsop seized the opportunity to lay an information against Samuel Stephens and William Wright (the master of a cutter chartered by the South Australian Company) for threatening to shoot one of Blenkinsop's men during a quarrel between rival boats. Neither Strangways nor Stevenson had any liking for Stephens and they immediately issued a warrant for the arrest of the two defendants.

Samuel Stephens (1809-1840)
The first manager of the South Australian Company arrived on Kangaroo Island in July 1836 to commence the Company's settlement on Nepean Bay (Kingscote). Stephens proved a poor choice of manager and was dismissed in November 1837 after the Company had tired of his failings, which ranged from poor accounting to drunkenness.

A Gilbertian situation followed. The chief constable was sent from Adelaide to Kangaroo Island to make the arrest. He remained on the island for a fortnight, as the guest of his prisoner Stephens, waiting for the other defendant to come to be arrested, and take them all back to Adelaide in his cutter.[7]

Mann took the view that the warrant was defective, and seized the opportunity to administer an insulting reprimand to the justices:

'The magistrates must obtain an efficient clerk to enable them to transact business with regularity, and above all to fix for them the true criteria before a warrant is issued.' [8]

On behalf of the prisoners, Fisher applied to Jeffcott on a habeas corpus for their discharge. Mann appeared for the Crown and did his best to get the prisoners released. A number of technical objections to the warrant were taken by Fisher and rejected by the Judge. One was that it purported to be in the name of the "Honourable T.B. Strangways", whereas there was no such person a magistrate of the province. Jeffcott said that the title of "Honourable" was a mere title of courtesy employed in the colonies by some officials, although they had perhaps no strict right to it, but it might be rejected as surplusage and still he remained T.B. Strangways. Blenkinsop had been summoned to attend and give evidence, but he did not appear, and it was then discovered that the constable who had served the summons had taken upon himself to insert the words "wind and weather permitting", which gave Blenkinsop considerable freedom as to when he should attend.

Edward Stephens (1811-1861)
Edward was the brother of Samuel and like him an employee of the South Australian Company. Unlike his brother he performed well in his role as manager of the Company's bank. He was active in public affairs and became a member of the Legislative Council in 1853. (SLSA)

The Judge decided that the prisoners ought not to be discharged but should be bound over to appear for trial. Samuel Stephens was released on a recognisance of £500 with two sureties of £250, Wright on a recognisance of £200 with two sureties of £100, the sureties in each case being Fisher and Edward Stephens.[9]

Jeffcott thought Mann's conduct in the affair was disgraceful. He reported to the Governor:

'There are certain features in this case and that of Wright which render it at this moment one of peculiar embarrassment; and that embarrassment I chiefly attribute to the course pursued by Mr Mann, who is, as you are aware, the retained advocate of the South Australian Company, and so much the personal friend of Mr Stephens that while nominally in custody, on being brought up here from Kangaroo Island, he slept at the house of the Advocate General, by whom every effort was subsequently made to prevent his being amenable to justice.' [10]

Mann, however, had raised the objection that, the offence having been committed on the high seas, a trial could not be had upon the ordinary commission of oyer and terminer; and the Judge had grave doubts whether he could try the case, since he had no vice-admiralty jurisdiction. Whaling and sealing were carried on extensively along the coast, and this was a matter of some importance; for if the cases could not be tried in South Australia, how were they to be disposed of? The obvious course would be to send them to Sydney or Hobart Town, where there were vice-admiralty courts, but section I of the Foundation Act said that the colonists of South Australia were not to be subject to the laws in force in the other colonies. Prosecutor, prisoners and witnesses could not be shipped to England; and

Jeffcott, unassisted by the presence of another judge and having, as he said, no confidence in the opinion of the Advocate-General, asked the Governor for leave to return to Van Diemen's Land to consult the Judges there, not only upon this case but also as to the law applicable to the Aborigines.[11]

Hindmarsh granted his request, but before Jeffcott left Adelaide he came into conflict with Mann again. Up to this time the Council had passed only five acts. Arguments had occurred as to the form in which the enacting portion of them should be expressed, the form used having been "Be it enacted by the Governor ... by and with the advice of the Legislative Council." In May 1837, when the Act to constitute the Supreme Court was passed, Hindmarsh had written to Jeffcott:

> 'The various Phraseology used yesty. to designate the Power passing our Acts has forced strongly upon my mind the propriety of our using one invariable form, that would as well suit the case contemplated in my authorities viz my having to do any act contrary to the opinion of the majority or even contrary of the whole Council, as it would when we are all of one opinion. We have, I believe, used the form The Governor &c by & with the advice of the Legislative Council. This form surely would not do were the majority or the whole to protest against the Act. It appears that the form used in India and other places would suit the case—"The Governor in Council". At all events, I will never again consent to any form that will not suit both cases. Will you do me the favour to consider this with Gouger before I have the pleasure of seeing you this morning as we may as well begin properly tomorrow.' [12]

It is clear from this that Hindmarsh had no doubt as to his power to legislate, even in opposition to the rest of his Council. Jeffcott, however, was not so sure of this and, presumably under his advice, the Governor consented to the Supreme Court Act being passed in the form "by and with the advice of the Legislative Council". No further acts were passed until November, when bills were introduced for acts regulating the constitution of juries and to establish the Resident Magistrate's Court. Mann now proposed that the words "by and with the advice of the Legislative Council of the Province" should be struck out, and in lieu thereof inserted "by and with the consent of the Council of Government of the Province, and by the authority thereof". His argument was that the authority to legislate rested in the members of the Council or any three of them (of whom the Governor must be one) and not in any individual, and that it was therefore wrong to make acts appear to emanate from the will and authority and act of the Governor, with the advice only of the Council. To make an act operative, the act must appear to come directly from the power which was the emanating cause of enactment. He further objected to the Governor sitting in the

Council at all; he could sit there only under section II of the Foundation Act, which required the members of the Council to be appointed by an order of the King in Council, whereas the Governor had been appointed by the King alone by Letters Patent.

Two days later Jeffcott delivered a long speech in reply to Mann. He began by pointing out that if Mann's contention was right, that the form of the enacting clause in the earlier acts was wrong and those acts invalid, then the Act for the constitution of the Supreme Court was ineffective and the Judge had been guilty of an illegal assumption of power. But "by and with the advice of the Council" could only mean by the authority and with the consent of that Council, for it was not to be supposed that a person would advise that to which he did not assent and, by assenting to, authorise. It was immaterial whether the Governor was appointed by Letters Patent or Order in Council, for the Order in Council appointing the officers had recognised and confirmed the Governor's appointment by directing the officers of the government "to be obedient, aiding and assisting" to the Governor in the execution of their offices. Jeffcott then answered the arguments that had been brought forward against the Governor's right to suspend Gouger. Four officers had been appointed to the Council, not by name but by virtue of their offices—the Judge, Advocate-General, Colonial Secretary and Resident Commissioner—all "for the time being", and subsequently persons had been appointed to fill those offices. The words "for the time being" showed that they were not irremovable. The Governor had power to suspend Gouger as an officer for misconduct and, as he was member of the Council only ex officio, he then forfeited his seat in the Council. If it were otherwise, and only the King in Council could remove, it would be twelve months before a refractory officer could be got out of the Council. The Governor's Instructions authorising him to dissent from the majority clearly gave him, Jeffcott thought, power to differ from the majority in an executive act such as the suspension of an officer for misconduct, but he confessed to doubts as to how far the Governor could make laws without the assent of the other members of the Council; possibly he might do so by proclamation or ordinance, but only in the case of great emergency.[13]

All these disputes as to the Governor's powers had their origin in the anomalous form of government created for the colony by the Foundation Act. In nearly all colonies the government rested on the royal prerogative, and the constitution was derived from the Commission and Instructions issued to each Governor, whereas in South Australia the constitution was fixed by statute. In those colonies where there was a representative assembly it was recognised that the Crown could not exercise powers of taxation or strict legislation without the consent of the Assembly, but the extent of the prerogative powers of the Governor was undefined and vague, and "colonial administration still presented a good many knotty problems in constitutional law". Executive and legislative functions in the colonies were often confused and, although the matter was not entirely free from doubt, it was generally agreed, at the time of the founding of South Australia, that the clause in the instructions to colonial governors empowering them to dissent from the advice of their councils related to executive acts only. In Clark's *Colonial Law,* for instance, which was published in 1834, it is said, after pointing out that the Governor was directed by his Instructions to consult his Council on most occasions:

> 'It does not appear that, in his executive capacity, he is absolutely bound to abide by their advice. It is conceived that he is competent to act, in most cases, though in the absence of any special provision for that purpose, not only without, but even against their advice; but that his power to do so is confined to cases where the Council act as part of the executive government, and not as part of the legislative government. His opposition to them in this latter character would consist of the exercise of his veto on the ordinances they might desire to pass.' [14]

In South Australia the one council was both executive and legislative; it was simply styled "the Council of Government" and no distinction was made between its executive and legislative functions. The arguments put forward by Mann and Fisher were correct so far as they applied to legislative acts of the Council, but so far as executive acts were concerned Hindmarsh was justified in acting alone.

This was the view of the law officers in England. Whether the Acts should read "with the consent" or "by the advice" of the Council they thought was an idle quarrel, since either form would be binding; the most proper form would have been "by and with the consent of the Council of the Province and by the authority of the same". They were of the opinion that the effect of the Foundation Act, the Orders in Council and the Governor's Commission and Instructions was to vest the legislative power in the Governor and Council, and that the Governor had no legislative power without the assent of the Council, although his executive power as the representative of the Crown remained unimpaired.

> 'There appears to us to be no validity in the objection of the Advocate General that the Governor cannot concur in making laws because he was not nominated by the King in Council. The Order in Council recognising that appointment is a complete answer to this objection, and the clear intention of the Act of Parliament and of the Commission was that the Governor should be an essential part of the legislature to be established in South Australia. But we think the Judge was equally wrong in contending that the Governor has vested in him a legislative power against the consent of the Council. No

such power is given him by Parliament, and it could not be conferred by the Crown. He must be confined to such executive acts as could lawfully be done by the Governor by virtue of the Crown's prerogative.' [15]

The discussion in the Council exposed more clearly than ever the hopeless disparity between the views of the Governor and the Judge on the one hand, and the Resident Commissioner and the Advocate-General on the other. The Governor made up his mind that Mann must follow Gouger and Brown. On 1 November 1837 he reported to Lord Glenelg:

> 'The strange and incomprehensible conduct of Mr Mann, the Advocate General, has placed him in direct opposition to me, and he now so openly thwarts and impedes the proceedings of the Government that I shall have no course left but to suspend him. In this opinion the Judge coincides and thinks I have no alternative.' [16]

Charles Mann, the elder (SLSA)

Mann, however, decided to retreat as gracefully as he could. On 10 November he wrote to Jeffcott:

> 'As the opinions which your Honour yesterday expressed in Council are so directly opposed to those which I am known to entertain, and to which I still adhere, with reference to the effect of the Act of the 4th and 5th Wm IV c.95, I feel my position singularly embarrassing. If I continue a member of the Council, I am conscious that a sense of imperative duty would

> probably lead to the utterance of thoughts and the adoption of measures, directly opposed to those views which your Honour yesterday expressed. The respect due to the Judge of the Supreme Court would render this collision very repugnant to my feelings, and any step by which such a result could be avoided would be pleasing to me. But for one occurrence this could easily have been effected. You are aware that in a Council held by His Excellency on the 6th of October last, His Excellency stated, 'that the recent proceedings and correspondence of the Advocate General had been of such a character, so subversive of the authority of the Government, and so opposed to the course of policy of the Governor, that it was impossible to let the matter rest where it was, and so soon as His Excellency should have had proper time to consider the course to be taken he would call a council together, and bring before it a proposition on the subject'. Now, so far from feeling abnoxious [sic] to censure, I challenge enquiry. If unremitting and laborious exertion, from the time when I arrived in the Province to the present Hour, be a test of service, that test at least I can stand; and I believe that your Honour's experience and recorded opinions are with me on that head. With reference to a want of skill in the details of my profession, or want of knowledge of its theory, I have yet to learn that I am capable of impeachment and am anxious to meet investigation.'

His opinions, he said, were given to preserve the Governor from pursuing a dangerous course. Resignation would be painful to him; 'the situation I hold was tendered to me for services performed for the colony—I left a respectable practice to accept it". Nevertheless if the Governor would certify that he had conducted himself diligently and admit his practical skill and knowledge of his profession, he was willing, if the Governor felt embarrassment from "my known views with reference to the extent of His Excellency's powers as a member of the Council of Government", to tender his resignation.'[17]

This letter Jeffcott immediately sent to the Governor, with the comment:

> 'I have for some time felt that the conduct which the Advocate General has thought proper to pursue, as well in his official capacity as legal adviser of the Government as when acting as a member of the Council, has been such as to render it impossible that the Government can go on while he retained and acted upon opinions, which, however conscientious, were such as to impede at every step the progress of the public business, and to throw doubt and discredit upon every act both legislative and executive which Your Excellency might think fit to recommend.'

The Governor briefly replied that Mann's resignation would be the most satisfactory way of ending the embarrassment and that he could have no objection to admit that Mann, whether as a member of the Council or as Advocate-General, had throughout his tenure of office acted upon a conscientious conviction that the advice which he offered from time to time was for the public service.

> 'I am equally willing to admit, that he has throughout exerted himself diligently; and I am ready to acknowledge that he has, to the best of my belief, acted with professional skill and ability.'

Jeffcott, in forwarding to Mann a copy of the Governor's answer, expressed regret that Mann should adhere to opinions which would only result in disorganisation of the public business, however conscientiously they might be entertained.

> 'You will, I am sure, give me credit for entertaining equally conscientious opinions upon the subjects upon which I have the misfortune to differ from you.' He assured Mann: '... that as a practitioner of the Court, you shall always meet from me that respect and attention to which you are entitled from your ability and legal acquirements'.[18]

Mann thereupon resigned, and the Governor, to make quite sure, accepted his resignation and at the same time suspended him. Wigley was appointed Acting Crown Solicitor and Public Prosecutor, and sent in his bill for services already rendered:[19]

> 'To daily attendance on and advising His Excellency the Governor re Mann and divers other matters; the Magistrates re Stephens and Wright and divers other matters.
> 33 days at Two guineas per day. £69:6:0'.

When the Judge had first arrived in the colony in May 1837, Brown wrote to Wakefield:

> 'I fear he has forgot all your schoolings about the colony, and I expect will not think it worth while either to support or oppose any measure that may affect its principles or its success. He is a Judge again, and having regained caste will remain, I dare say, until a better berth falls to him.' [20]

Jeffcott was not long in looking for a better berth. He applied to Lord Glenelg for appointment either as a judge or Attorney-General in Van Diemen's Land:

> 'Should Your Lordship think fit to comply with my request, I shall be happy to resign the office which I now hold, and from which, under the circumstances which will be detailed to you in Governor Hindmarsh's despatches, Your Lordship will not feel surprised that I should wish to be relieved, by a removal to some other colony.' [21]

In forwarding this application, Hindmarsh said:

> 'I do this with considerable regret as Sir John Jeffcott has supported me in the most cordial way and advised me in the most straightforward manner; but I cannot allow any wish of my own to retain him near me to stand in the way of the promotion he so eminently merits; and I therefore do not offer the slightest objection to his removal. Altho' Mr Parker's reappointment may not be consistent with usage, I confess I should be glad were he thought by Your Lordship a proper person to supply the place of Sir John Jeffcott, should his promotion take place; but I have not the slightest fear that the selection to be made by Your Lordship will be such as will gratify, by its propriety and fitness, every honest man in the colony, and I do not therefore presume to urge any suggestion of my own.' [22]

Jeffcott considered he would be justified in resigning because he had been appointed on the understanding that he should receive his salary from the Treasury and be considered strictly as an officer of the Crown, answerable only to the King or the Secretary of State, whereas he now found that his salary was to be paid by the Commissioners, who might endeavour to make him responsible to them. This he thought was a direct violation of the understanding on which he received his appointment.

A letter which he wrote to Kermode at this time paints a doleful picture of his own feelings and his opinion of the prospects of the new settlement:

> 'I wish for your advice on the propriety of my resigning at once, or at least as soon as I have held another Court, and cleared up the present arrears, which, with actions for libel, of which I have at least a dozen to try, and innumerable other actions, besides a criminal calendar of at least 20 prisoners, including the manager of the South Australian Company (Mr Samuel Stephens) for a capital felony—shooting with intent to kill—is really quite appalling; and unsupported as I am, and without the aid of another Judge, or anybody in whom I have sufficient confidence to take his opinion, my position is anything but agreeable, I can assure you ... They all have appealed to me, and as soon as my Court sits, all the questions which have been agitating this unhappy place in my absence will be brought before me in the shape of ex-officio informations, indictments, actions for libel and defamation innumerable. So that you cannot conceive the mass of misery I have to encounter; and the worst of it is, that I do not see my way at all clearly as to the course I ought to adopt. Of one thing—like every disinterested observer, in quarrels of this kind—I am certain, and that is that both parties are in the wrong. All this is disgusting and quite unsuited to my habits

and feelings, and I wish to God I was clear of them, and quietly settled with you in Van Diemen's Land, either as a humble counsel or in a situation although inferior in point of rank to that which I hold. I foresee that this Colony will be the scene of anarchy and confusion the most frightful, and a prey to the most dreadful dissensions ere long. In fact, it must necessarily be so, from the anomalous nature of the Government, and the want of protection, which the absence of any regular force, and I may add, regular authority, must induce. Vagabonds are constantly arriving here from Encounter Bay and elsewhere in the interior, who are joined by runaway sailors and escaped convicts from Van Diemen's Land, who squat on the outskirts of the town, commit constant depredations and laugh at the funny force of 20 drunken marines.

My present impression is, that I could do much better even as a Practitioner at the Bar in Van Diemen's Land than by remaining here subject myself to annoyance of which I cannot foresee the extent or termination.' [23]

View of company's fishing station and Cape Rosetta, Encounter Bay, South Australia. by J.C. Hailes 1838 (NLA)

Jeffcott left Adelaide for the last time on 19 November 1837. He went on board the *South Australian* at Encounter Bay, but the vessel was driven on shore in a gale and bilged. While waiting for another ship, he joined an expedition headed by T.B. Strangways and Y.B. Hutchinson, which was exploring the Murray mouth. Strangways and his party went by land; Blenkinsop and some of his men joined them in a whaleboat, which they safely brought in through the breakers at the mouth of the river. Jeffcott wanted to make the return to Victor Harbor by boat with Blenkinsop.

> 'I attempted to dissuade him'—wrote Hutchinson many years later—'by insisting that it was the worst surf I had ever seen, and that he would get a thorough drenching, for he was in a dress coat with suitable continuations, while we were all in rough shooting jackets. However, he would go, and borrowed my gun, flask, and shot-belt.' [24]

Imprudently, Blenkinsop loaded the boat with about 500 pounds of whalebone which he had found on the beach. In consequence the boat did not rise to the breakers and was swamped.[25]

According to an account given by Mann, who had it from one of the survivors:

> '... the boat had passed several rollers, and had run out nearly three quarters of a mile from the entrance, when a roller of fearful magnitude turned the boat on her beam-ends, and nearly filled her. She rose, however, and the Judge being alarmed, exclaimed 'The Lord have mercy on our souls, we shall all be drowned!' He had scarcely spoken before a short sea turned the head of the boat round, and a roller immediately following, she foundered. Captain Blenkinsop clung to the boat but was soon washed off. Sir John Jeffcott seized one end of an oar to which Mills was also clinging. In about three minutes Sir John relinquished his grasp, sunk, rose for a few moments, grasped at a box floating near him, missed it, and finally disappeared.' [26]

Jeffcott, Blenkinsop and two men were drowned; three others managed to reach the shore. Blenkinsop's body was found next day, buried in the sand by natives. That of Jeffcott was never recovered, but some six months later Hutchinson recognised at Adelaide the shot-belt he had given the Judge, worn by an overlander who said he had bought it from the natives.

> 'Poor John!'—wrote Kermode—'he was quite sure of being with us to take his Xmas dinner. He was an excellent hearted man, and very greatly esteemed by all here who knew him ... You will see from the whole tenor of Sir John's letters, how much he was attached to us, and how extremely urgent he was always to get rid of the place. His anxiety to leave has in a great measure been the cause of his untimely end. He had several narrow escapes before ... His life, poor fellow, has been a chapter of accidents. When he last left me, it was at Launceston, and he left with the extreme of reluctance. I told him then that something would happen to him; however he was regardless of danger and you see what has been his fate.' [27]

Jeffcott having left no will, Stevenson applied to Jickling, the Acting Judge, to be appointed administrator of Jeffcott's estate. Nothing was more natural, for the Governor had been a close friend of the Judge, and the Governor's secretary would be an appropriate person to see to the disposal of the Judge's effects. Jickling made an order as of course.[28]

Mann and Gouger, however, raised an outcry about it. Gouger was with the Kermodes when the news of Jeffcott's death arrived:

> 'The afflicting tiding reached me at Mona Vale, and spread distress around. Miss Kermode, to whom he was to have been immediately married, bore the intelligence with great firmness.'[29]

Mann arrived in Van Diemen's Land a few weeks later, and he and Gouger persuaded Kermode that Stevenson had illegally seized all the Judge's papers for some nefarious purpose of his own.[30] Stevenson acted quite legally. Even if he had not, it is difficult to see what harm he could have done with Jeffcott's papers, and there was little of any value for him to make away with. The Judge had overdrawn his salary, and the government attempted in vain to recover the amount overpaid. Kermode paid a few small debts in Van Diemen's Land. The creditors in England seem to have got nothing.

So far as can be ascertained, Jeffcott actually sat as Judge on two occasions only—at the first Criminal Sessions, and to hear the case of Stephens and Wright. He was in the colony in all only a little more than two months. The ordinary materials upon which an opinion can be formed of the ability of a judge—the reports of the cases decided by him, and the estimates of his contemporaries—are in Jeffcott's case almost entirely wanting. His character does not seem at all obscure—a young man of integrity, courage, good sense and gentlemanly bearing, whose besetting fault was a hot-headed boldness amounting to recklessness; but as to his legal attainments there is little upon which one can pronounce. His service in Sierra Leone seems to have given satisfaction and there seems no reason to doubt that he was an able and capable lawyer.

On his visit to Van Diemen's Land in June 1837, it had not been thought necessary to appoint anyone in his place, but before he left in November he informed the Governor that it would be necessary for an acting judge to be appointed to sit in chambers. He recommended Jickling, who was the only barrister in the province, and the Governor made the appointment accordingly.

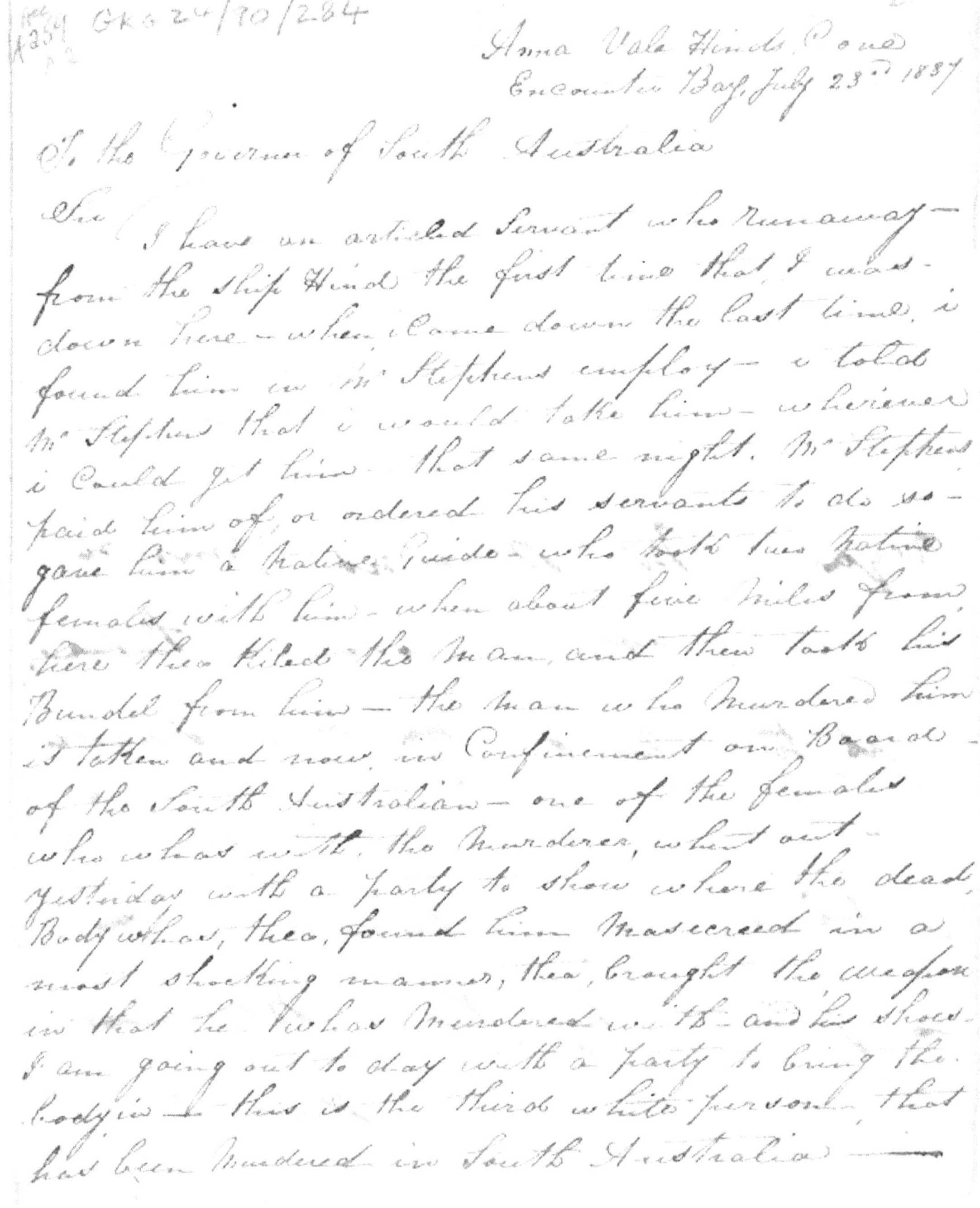

GRG 24/90/284

Anna Vale Hinds Cove
Encounter Bay, July 23rd 1837

To the Governor of South Australia

Sir
I have an articled Servant who runaway from the ship Hind the first time that I was down here – when I Came down the last time, i found him in Mr Stephens employ – i told Mr Stephens that i would take him – wherever i Could get him that same night. Mr Stephens paid him of, or ordered his servants to do so – gave him a Native Guide – who took two Native females with him – when about five miles from here they Killed the man, and then took his Bundel from him – the man who murdered him is taken and now in Confinement on Board of the South Australian – one of the females who whas with the murderer, whent out yesterday with a party to show where the dead Body whas, they found him masacreed in a most shocking manner, they brought the weapon in that he whas murdered with – and his shoes. I am going out to day with a party to bring the body in – this is the third white person, that has been murdered in South Australia —

A letter from Captain W. T. Blenkinson regarding the murder of John Driscoll. The letter continues, overleaf, "by the natives – and no notice taken of it by the authoritys, now Sir, your earliest reply to this, whether you can or will punish the murderer – will greatly oblige. Your Humble Servant WT Blenkinsop. (SR/DPC)

Chapter 3.1

Henry Jickling

Centipedes and spectacles

Henry Jickling, Judge of the Supreme Court from November 1837 to March 1839 and Master from 1850 to 1861, was an amiable but ridiculous figure, who might well have come to life, name and all, from the pages of Dickens. He will seldom be found mentioned without a reference to some of his physical oddities or eccentricities of character. A kind-hearted and studious bachelor, learned in the theory of the law but naively simple and unpractical in his ways, he made himself conspicuous by adopting a ludicrous style of dress which was peculiar to himself and remained invariable in spite of passing years and changing fashions. He wore shoes and white stockings, trousers which barely reached his ankles, and a coat with sleeves which ended a little below the elbow: over all, a large cloak. His gown in court terminated at the knees.[1] His antiquated courtesy and gentleness of manner were quite out of place in a colony at the Antipodes. He was so short-sighted that he could see only a foot or two ahead; "a pair o' patent double-million magnifyin' gas microscopes of hextra power" might have give him better vision, but the large bright-green spectacles which he used were of little service and added to the strangeness of his mien. "Phiz" would have claimed him as a model at sight, as he trotted along with a singular springy walk, peering blindly about him, and upbraiding tree stumps for their failure to return a civil answer when he addressed them politely to inquire his way.[2]

His habits were as extraordinary as his appearance. If invited out to dine, he cautiously asked first what there was for dinner, and accepted or refused according as he approved or disliked the menu. Dr Duncan preserved a story of Jickling arriving at his home on one occasion as a cheese was placed on the table at the end of dinner, and asking if he could have some. Adding mustard and vinegar, he proceeded, to the amazement of Dr Duncan, to eat the whole cheese, and then retired to a sofa and immediately went to sleep.[3]

According to another anecdote, Jickling, while staying with a friend, came to breakfast one morning with a graphic story of how he had woken up during the night, how he had seen in the moonlight a huge centipede crawling across the chair beside his bed, and how he had instantly leapt out of bed and killed it with his shoes. Curiously enough, when he got up in the morning his spectacles were missing. Upon investigation by the host, the discovery beneath the bed of some fragments of green glass and a battered spectacle frame unveiled the mystery.

The earliest record relating to him is that of his admission to Lincoln's Inn on 7 August 1818. He was then aged eighteen and was described as "of Wells, gentleman, second son of Nicholas Jickling".[4] He himself wrote:

> 'I am the son of a gentleman, who, in the character of Collector of the Customs, was during more than half a century a faithful servant of his sovereign, and whose labours, I regret to say, terminated in comparative blindness and the many evils pecuniary and otherwise incident to such a situation.' [5]

In another fragment of autobiography he mentions that his father's blindness was brought about by the composition of a book on *The Laws of the Customs*.[6]

Jickling was called to the bar on 8 June 1826. For two years he read assiduously in the chambers of Mr William Pemberton (one of the leaders of the Chancery Bar, afterwards Sir William, and Attorney-General); and in 1829 he published *A Practical Treatise on the Analogy between the Legal and Equitable Estates and Modes of Alienation*, an erudite volume of some 600 pages, upon which he must have spent several years of diligent labour. He practised his profession as an equity barrister in London for some years, but with little success. In 1834 or early in 1835 he became interested in the proposed colony of South Australia, perhaps through the medium of the Wakefields, for the testimonials which he produced in support of his application for the position of Judge in the colony included one from a Professor Henry Wakefield, who was a friend of eighteen years' standing. On 29 May 1835 Brown noted in his journal that he went with Gouger "to be introduced to Jickling at Chancery Lane". Brown had then been associated with the colonisation movement for a considerable time, so it can be inferred that Jickling was at this time a comparative newcomer to the scheme. He threw himself into it with enthusiasm. Brown patronisingly referred to him as "the industrious Jickling". He was consulted as to legal difficulties which arose about the bonds to be issued by the Colonisation Commissioners, and he lectured to the colonists on subjects so diverse as education and artesian wells.[7]

As early as February 1835 he applied to be appointed Judge.

> 'My Lord'—he wrote to Lord Aberdeen. 'It is the object of this communication to solicit of your Lordship the situation of Judge in the new Colony intended to be formed at Spencer's Gulph, under the provisions of the recent Act of Parliament. I rest my application on two grounds; first, the interest which I have ever felt in the establishment of the colony, and the desire I have of contributing my life towards the success of the undertaking; and secondly, my qualifications as a barrister of eight years standing at the bar. To these, I may be permitted to add the service of my father who during fifty years was a zealous and effective servant of His Majesty. I have merely to add, that should Your [8]Lordship think fit to entertain my application, it will not be difficult for me to furnish proofs of general and professional capacity; and (what I apprehend to be of equal importance) respectable demeanour in life.' [9]

Before any appointment had been made, there came a change of ministry, and in May 1835 Jickling wrote to Lord Glenelg, the new Secretary of State for the colonies, soliciting his patronage.[10] He furnished numerous testimonials, which spoke of his "great legal attainments, long standing at the bar, sound integrity, and high moral character". Mr Platt wrote:

> 'You are a man of strict honor and moral conduct, and distinguished by your courtesy and gentlemanly bearing';

and Mr Byles said:

> 'I heartily wish you success but almost doubt whether the post will be worth your acceptance ... If you are not a gainer by the post, I think the colony will be by your general as well as professional knowledge.'

Byles on Bills
Sir John Bernard Byles was the original author of an enduring work on bills of exchange. The book came to be known as *Byles on Bills*. A story has it that Byles had a horse called "Bills" allowing legal acquaintances to remark when he rode by, "Here comes Byles on Bills".

According to Mr A.W. Grant (a nephew of Sir William Grant MR) Mr Jickling was possessed of:

> '... a variety of information and a facility in making and communicating it not frequently met with in persons who have devoted to legal pursuits the time necessary for the professional requirements'.[11]

Jickling himself urged that if appointed he would fulfil his duties "with the honor and urbanity of a gentleman, and the zeal and integrity of a Christian", but even this assurance could not prevail upon Lord Glenelg to give him the appointment.[12]

Notwithstanding that he could not go out to the colony as Judge, Jickling was determined to try his fortune there, and he sailed on the *Buffalo* in the humble capacity of tutor to Mr Fisher's children. One glimpse of him during the voyage survives. He and Fisher were on deck talking of the advantages of establishing a public library in the colony; the Governor, however, joined in and threw cold water on their project. "It is of no use," he said; "what good will books do our colony?"[13]

The only picture of Jickling is an unflattering cartoon from *The Adelaide Independent* newspaper of 19 August 1841. (SLSA)

Henry Jickling

More squabbling

One of the first acts of the Governor on landing was to send Stevenson and Strangways, who had been appointed Justices of the Peace, to Kangaroo Island as a Commission to inquire into the truth of the rumours as to the lawless state of the island, and Jickling was appointed to act as their clerk.[1] The minutes of the proceedings of the Commission and the evidence taken by them still survive in Jickling's neat handwriting.[2]

View on the north side of Kangaroo Island by William Westall 1814 (SLV)

On his return to Glenelg, Jickling was somewhat of an outcast. He seems to have emigrated without capital or equipment. Mann allowed him a bed in a corner of his tent, and he was apparently glad to have an opportunity "to turn his, hæc, hoc, into bread and cheese, and beer", for John Barton Hack wrote:

> 'Willie (his son) has taken some lessons in French and Latin from a person named Jickling, who is a barrister by profession, and it is rather convenient, as he is not yet housed, for him to take his breakfast and tea with us.' [3]

On 30 January 1837 he was appointed a notary public by the Governor.[4]

When the city was laid out, Jickling moved there. He was admitted as a practitioner at the first Criminal Sessions and set up in practice, and on 5 July 1837 he was appointed clerk to the Bench of Magistrates, a position which carried a small salary.[5]

For a time the Governor looked on Jickling with great suspicion, as an associate of Mann and Fisher.

> 'Who friendship with a knave hath made
> Is judged a partner in the trade'.

Mann's tent, Hindmarsh reported to Lord Glenelg, was the focus of disaffection, where the "disciples of Roebuck" met—and he named specifically Fisher, Brown, Kingston, Morphett, Wright, Samuel and Edward Stephens, and Jickling.[6] After Jickling ceased to live with Mann, it became apparent that he was quite harmless, and the Governor made no objection to appointing him, on 21 November 1837, Judge pro tempore, when Jeffcott set out for Van Diemen's Land.[7] Fisher dissented from the appointment (which he and his party thought should have gone to Mann) and placed on record at the Council his opinion that Jickling was incompetent to fill the position.

> 'My dear Governor'—wrote Jeffcott from Encounter Bay a few days before his death—'I am astonished at the insolence which Mr Resident Commissioner has betrayed and the observations which he has thought proper to place upon the Minutes of Council in my absence. I mean those with reference to my absence and Mr Jickling's incapacity ... For a gentleman who is so sensitive with regard to his own character, and so fond of threatening to bring actions for libel and defamation, his attack upon Mr Jickling comes with a very bad grace.' [8]

When the news of Jeffcott's death reached Adelaide, Fisher alleged that Jickling's appointment had automatically terminated, but the Governor with a touch of grim humour, claimed that Jickling had been appointed to be Acting Judge during Jeffcott's absence and that, as Jeffcott had not returned, Jickling retained the appointment. To set any doubts about the matter at rest, the Governor, at a meeting of the Council on 26 December 1837, appointed Jickling to be Judge till Her Majesty's pleasure should be known.[9]

Almost immediately Jickling came into conflict with Mann, to whom it was no doubt galling to see a despised protégé elevated to the bench. On 29 December he attended before Jickling and wanted to go on with some legal business, which Jickling refused to take. Mann insisted and grew violent, the Judge fled, and the Resident Magistrate had to summon his constables and order them to turn Mann out of the Judge's office. Jickling retaliated by suspending Mann from practice.[10] Fisher had instructed Mann to issue a writ for libel against the *Register*, but when Mann attended on 30 December to seal the writ, the Judge refused to issue any process for him, or accept any documents bearing his name.[11]

Mann and Fisher then decided that the former should go to Van Diemen's Land to get the opinion of Mr Alfred Stephen, a leading barrister, as to the legality of the Governor's proceedings and upon various libel actions which Fisher had instituted or was about to commence. For several months Mann accordingly disappears from the scene, but his departure did not in any way lessen the violence of party feelings in the colony.[12]

Fisher had been extremely curious to find out why Jeffcott had obtained leave to go to Van Diemen's Land; the Governor was equally determined not to reveal it to him. The Council were merely informed by the Governor that "the statement he had received from Sir John Jeffcott made it imperative upon him to allow the Judge to go". Fisher asked that Jeffcott's statement should be laid before the Council, this the Governor refused.[13] On 11 January 1838 Fisher wrote asking the Governor whether the same urgent reasons still existed which had rendered it necessary for Jeffcott to obtain leave.[14] The reply was short and conclusive:

> 'The Governor desires me to say in answer to your letter of the 11th instant that as His Excellency has no confidence whatever in you, he does not think Her Majesty's service would be benefitted by any communication to you of the nature you require.' [15]

As a result of this letter, Fisher refused to attend the meetings of the Council and carried on his warfare with the Governor with renewed vigour.[16] The Governor asked to be supplied with details of the number of emigrants who had arrived in the colony; Fisher replied that the Governor had no right to the information and he would only supply it if the Governor would admit that it was conceded as a matter of grace.[17] Hindmarsh's rejoinder was:

> 'His Excellency requests me to say that as he has not hitherto experienced any instances of courtesy on your part, since his arrival in the Colony, he has no desire to ask at your hands any thing out of the course of your official duties, but considering it to be a part of that duty to furnish such reports to the Colonial Government in your official character as Resident Commissioner, and that the concealment from the public of the information these reports ought to contain, as practised by you, is not only an act of injustice to the emigrants themselves, most injurious to the colonists generally, but has in fact actually given undue advantage to persons to whom the descriptions of emigrants are privately communicated and tends directly to encourage a most improper system of favoritism, you are required forthwith to furnish to this Government for publication, and for the information of his Majesty's Government ..' [a correct report of the names and descriptions of the emigrants.]

Fisher, the Governor said, was "adopting a course of systematic concealment of the public business, exciting suspicion and distrust among the great body of the respectable colonists, as to the fair and honest administration" of the duties of the Resident Commissioner. He concluded by playing what he considered a trump card. In addition to the office of Resident Commissioner, Fisher held that of Registrar-General. So far, the latter office had been a complete sinecure, but it was an office under the Crown and not under the Commissioners. The Governor therefore ordered Fisher to make out and furnish the returns of the emigrants, as Registrar-General; and warned him that he would be held responsible for the strict performance of this duty.[18] Fisher said it was not part of the Registrar-General's duty; the Governor reiterated that it was.[19] Correspondence between officials grew heated. Fisher told the Colonial Secretary that in future he would take no notice of communications which were not addressed to him in proper language, and received an answer (probably from the pen of Stevenson and not from that of Strangways) that the Colonial Secretary treated:

> '... with profound indifference and contempt the uncalled-for observations you take the liberty of addressing to me, especially as it is evident you desire to screen yourself from the consequences of your own habitual course of improper observations by imputing to other officers that which has hitherto been exclusively your own'. [20]

Similar disputes were carried on between Fisher and Gilles. Despite their repeated threats to ignore the insults of their opponents, none of the letter writers could abstain from the personal.

It is not difficult to imagine the delays which took place in the public business while the officers of the various departments wrangled among themselves. To borrow Brown's words, already quoted: "One melancholy reflection follows all this but too closely. How is this colony to succeed with these people as leaders?"

David McLaren was thoroughly disgusted with the dilatory and incompetent ways of the government officials.

> 'I have no hesitation in saying', he wrote to Fisher after one particularly unsatisfactory episode, 'that the circumstances connected with the settlement of this transaction have been such, as to make me very careful how I commit either the South Australian Company or the Bank of South Australia again, in the possibility of being involved in so unsatisfactory and unbusinesslike a position arising out of circumstances and feelings over which they neither have nor possibly can have control'.

How anything was done at all seems amazing. Of the five original members of the Council, only the Governor and Fisher were left, and Fisher stayed away from its meetings.

> 'Here was a pretty situation for the Governor of a new colony, left in the midst of troubles and embarrassments of an

important public nature, absolutely without advisers. One counsellor contumacious—another fighting a pitched battle in the streets—a third bottle-holder to his friend—and the best and most efficient, the Judge, drowned by the upsetting of a boat. A more unpleasant situation for a Governor was never heard!' [34]

In a Council composed of the Governor, Strangways and Jickling, there was at least unanimity, although the extent of their political experience and acumen was doubtful. Hindmarsh attempted to strengthen his position by the importation of ability from abroad and offered the position of Advocate-General to George Milner Stephen, who had been clerk of the Supreme Court of Van Diemen's Land since 1830. Although this was a comparatively subordinate position, Stephen had powerful connections both in the colonies and at the Colonial Office, and he had a large share of the legal and administrative ability which has been so conspicuously displayed through successive generations of the Stephen family. He was one of the eighteen children of Mr Justice Stephen, of New South Wales. Sir Alfred Stephen, who subsequently rose to the bench of the Supreme Court of that state, was his brother.[35]

Jane Isabella Watts (1824-1894) The author of two books on early South Australian life pictured her with husband Alfred, ca. 1865 (SLSA)

In addition to being a lawyer, Stephen was a skilful miniature portrait painter and flautist, and an ardent mineralogist. Governor Gawler found him useful also as a piano tuner.[36] Mrs Watts described him brightly as:

'... a good-looking, dapper little man, with light curly hair and

> whiskers, and small in every way, who wore ladies number four's in boots (if a droll skit of that day might be relied upon) and possessed various showy accomplishments. He danced well, sang soft sentimental ditties, such as "Love's Ritornella'" "Come Away, Love", and other songs of that class, to the accompaniment of a guitar, adorned with blue ribbon, and was in fact what usually goes by the term a 'lady's man', with an abundance of small talk considered suitable to the feminine capacity'.[37]

Stephen was an ambitious man and well seized with a consciousness of his own merits, which were, indeed, very considerable. "His talents are of the very first order," said Chief Justice Pedder, of Van Diemen's Land.[38]

In offering him the post of Advocate-General, Governor Hindmarsh wrote:

> 'I am induced to do this without personal knowledge from the manner in which Sir J. Jeffcott, the Judge, has spoken of you, and from my knowledge of your relative Mr J. Stephen in the Colonial Office. I am sorry to inform you that the salary is only £300 per annum, though these are matters that we expect will mend.' [39]

Stephen accepted, and arrived in Adelaide early in February 1838. He set up his office in a small building on North Terrace, where the railway station now stands. He had brought with him a little monkey, which he frequently fastened outside his office, and:

> '... on these occasions the natives in great numbers congregated, and squatting on the ground watched the antics of the simian, whom they thought to be a little old man'.[40]

Characteristically, one of Stephen's first steps was to prepare a bill to enhance the dignity of his own position, by conferring on the Advocate-General "all the rights powers privileges and authorities as are vested in Her Majesty's Attorney General in England", but for some reason now forgotten the Bill was never passed.[41]

Hindmarsh was very satisfied with his new law officer.

> 'I have little doubt'—he informed Lord Glenelg in April 1838—'but that by his exertions we shall soon be in a condition to pass some very necessary laws that I have hitherto been unable to get brought forward.' [42]

Fisher began another quarrel over the payment of Stephen's salary. The Governor said, with sarcastic emphasis:

> 'Mr Stephen, having been appointed to offices which had been resigned by his predecessor, is of course entitled to full salary from the day of his appointment.'

Fisher refused to pay it, and said Stephen was entitled to half-pay, and that only from the date of his arrival in the colony. To support his argument he unwisely referred the Governor to the Colonial Office regulations, which laid him open to Governor's retort: 'His Excellency is gratified to perceive that you are at length disposed to acknowledge the authority of the Secretary of State.' [43]

George Milner Stephen (1812-1894) ca. 1841 One account has the position of Advocate-General being offered to Alfred Stephen – George's brother – with George taking the opportunity offered by the shared surname and connections to take the office. If true, the account is certainly typical of the colourful life of Stephen who worked, at various times, as a public servant, barrister, geologist and, in later life, faith healer. (SLSA)

The end of the Reign of Squabble, however, was approaching. The Commissioners in England, alarmed at the reports which were reaching them from South Australia, of "the intrigues, the confusion, and the approaching anarchy arising out of divided and clashing authority" prepared a series of charges against the Governor and requested his recall.[44] One or two charges were of substance; others were trivial or unfounded. Lord Glenelg reluctantly acquiesced in the Governor's recall, seeing no other way to end the feuds in the colony. At the same time, the Commissioners were dissatisfied with Fisher, and "in order to put an end to that divided and undefined authority from which so much evil has arisen" they suggested it was expedient to supersede Fisher and combine in the person of Colonel Gawler the offices of Governor and Resident Commissioner.[45] No question of the boundaries of their respective powers could then arise. With this Lord Glenelg concurred. It had been proposed by the Commissioners that after Hindmarsh was recalled the government of the colony should be administered by a commission presided over by Colonel Light until the new Governor arrived, but the Colonial Office decided to direct Hindmarsh to continue in office until his successor arrived.[47] The Governor, however, would not remain in the colony after the news of his recall arrived, to be a cockshy for the ribald taunts of his opponents, and he left on 14 July 1838 in the *Alligator*, taking the marines with him. In a final address to the colonists he made a last attack upon his opponents:

> 'The share which a Governor of South Australia possesses in conducting the new experiment in colonisation is so small that under no circumstance can he be justly responsible for its result. That responsibility rests with the Colonization Commissioners, to whom the charge of working out so peculiar a constitution is entrusted. The principle, though novel, is simple, as I believe it to be sound. Its successful application, however, depends not on the Colonial Government, but on the integrity and ability of the individuals entrusted by the Colonization Commissioners with its development and it must be to a deficiency of those qualities alone that anything approaching failure ought to be attributed.' [48]

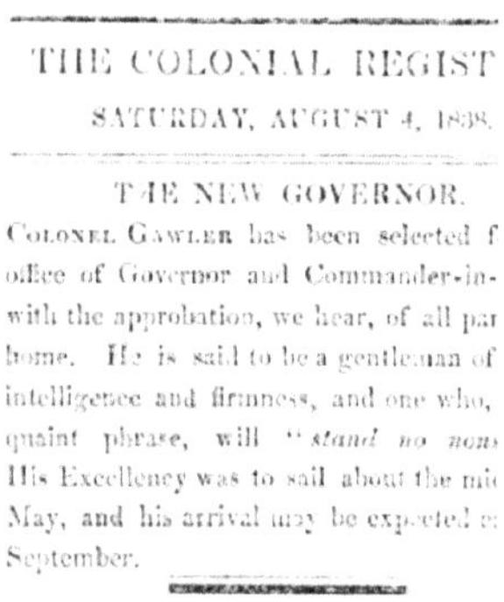
THE COLONIAL REGIST
SATURDAY, AUGUST 4, 1838.

THE NEW GOVERNOR.

COLONEL GAWLER has been selected f
office of Governor and Commander-in-
with the approbation, we hear, of all par
home. He is said to be a gentleman of
intelligence and firmness, and one who,
quaint phrase, will "*stand no non*
His Excellency was to sail about the mi
May, and his arrival may be expected
September.

The *Register's* announcement of the new Governor (SLSA)

By the Letters Patent appointing Hindmarsh it had been provided that, if upon his death or absence there should be no Lieutenant Governor appointed, the senior member of the Council should take upon him the administration of the government, and the seniority was declared as follows: the Judge, Colonial Secretary, Advocate-General, Resident Commissioner.[49] According to this, Jickling should have been appointed administrator of government, for he sat in Council as Judge, but he was passed over.

Strangways did not desire to take over the Governor's duties and resigned. Stephen was appointed Colonial Secretary and took the oaths of office as Acting Governor and Commander-in-Chief. His assumption of the latter title was loudly denounced; but as the *Register* pointed out, when the whole army of the province consisted of a single drunken Chelsea pensioner, a military coup d'état was not very probable.[50]

Fisher and Mann both made half-hearted claims to be entitled to be Acting Governor.[51] The former certainly had some grounds to be considered the senior member of the Council, upon whom the Government should devolve, for he was the only one left of the original five; but what right Mann, who had resigned, could have conceived he had to the position remains a perfect nonplus and baffle to all human understanding.

The Council was now reduced to Stephen, Jickling and Fisher, and as it was hopeless to expect that the Resident Commissioner, even if he attended, would acquiesce in anything supported by the other two, Stephen appointed Robert Bernard to be Advocate-General and Crown Solicitor and, ex officio, a member of the Council.[52] Bernard was a young Irish barrister, a cousin of Sir John Jeffcott, who had come to the colony recommended to Hindmarsh by Lord Glenelg and had been appointed in May 1838 to the schismatic post of Emigration Agent.[53]

Stephen administered the Government till Governor Gawler arrived in October 1838, and performed an "odious task" surprisingly well. With no funds in the Treasury and little assistance from Jickling and Bernard, he:

> '... carried out a heavy duty with the 'honor, zeal, intelligence and integrity' that characterized his official career. He tided over the financial difficulties, helped to support the slender police force from his own pocket, and by considerable energy and tact greatly eased the political and personal friction which existed in the colony'.[54]

Lady Hindmarsh, née Susannah Wilson Edmondes, wife of Sir John Hindmarsh. This 1840 portrait is a copy of a painting by George Milner Stephen, her son-in-law. (SLSA)

Henry Jickling

'the gentle Jickling'

It is not intended to deal with the disputes which took place during the first six months of 1838 about the progress of the surveys and the right of the government to select land for public purposes, except to mention certain legal proceedings to which they led. At the end of 1837 Colonel Light had surveyed some 60,000 acres and it was proposed that the preliminary purchasers should proceed to determine the order of selection of their land. But when a meeting of them decided that the order of selection should be determined on 1 March 1838, Strangways petitioned the Supreme Court for an injunction to restrain the Resident Commissioner from proceeding with the ballot for selection, upon the ground that the Commissioners had promised that at least 100,000 acres should be surveyed before the preliminary purchasers were required to make their choice. Jickling granted the injunction, and Fisher applied to have it dissolved, "backed with the Surveyor-General's affidavit and—his own(!)". The *Register* became hysterical; the affidavits, it said, were worthy of perusal "as exhibiting specimens of the dirty and desperate shuffling of a sinking faction", and added that:

> 'Mr Fisher entered into a long rambling commentary on the affidavits; but his speech, in so far as it was not a mere rifacimento of the affidavits, was so entirely of the radical pot-house debating society class as to be altogether unfit for our columns.' [1]

The injunction was continued, and there was general dissatisfaction at the delay in the selection and cultivation of land which was likely to be the result. A petition was presented to the Governor, claiming to be from "the majority of all landholders in the colony", protesting that the Foundation Act had expressly provided against all interference from any power whatever in the colony (except the Resident Commissioner) with the sale and disposal of land, and that they were therefore "under the necessity in a most respectful way" of informing him that the injunction was illegal, "being in direct violation of the Act".[2] B.T. Finniss wrote to the Governor more bluntly:

> 'Your Excellency allowed the great majority of the landowners to be deprived of their just rights of determining the order in which they were to select their land by permitting an injunction of the Supreme Court to have effect, contrary to the laws of England and of Equity, because one individual petitioned the Court for the same, which petition was drawn up on the advice of the Governor by the Advocate General, with the knowledge of one Captain Hindmarsh. The injunction can therefore be

said to be the joint work of the Judge and the Advocate General.'

Finniss continued:

> 'It is common knowledge that your Excellency will not allow your officers the privilege of an opinion which differs from your own. Can this be for the public good? ... Your Excellency must by now be convinced that you have not one respectable individual in the Colony who is not arraigned against you, except of course your few immediate dependents. Governors as well as private persons ought to hear the truth at times.' [3]

Boyle Travers Finniss (1807-1893)
An ex-soldier, Finniss arrived at Kangaroo Island on the *Cygnet* in September 1836 and became an influential figure in South Australia's history. A friend and business partner of Colonel Light he supported the selection of the site of Adelaide and helped in its survey. He fathered the first white girl born in South Australia (Fanny Lipson 31 December 1836) and held a great variety of government offices but is best remembered for becoming the first Premier of South Australia in 1856. (SLSA)

The difficulty was solved by a compromise between Strangways and Fisher, as a result of which the injunction was dissolved by consent.[4]

The factious disputes inevitably led to personal warfare. The *Register* savagely attacked Fisher and accused him of peculation and profiteering. He was alleged to have made large sums by privately selling the goods of the Commissioners and, in particular, a quantity of pork; and the "great pork mystery" was vindictively pursued until:

> '... the scream of indignation uttered by Mr Fisher was echoed by the whole fraternity of his followers, and a cackling ensued thereupon such as the Torrens had not heard since their wild predecessors were scared from its banks'.[5]

Challenges to duels were hurled to and fro. The Sheriff, for instance, challenged both Stevenson and Young Bingham Hutchinson;[6] and Hutchinson figured also in an amusing episode with Fisher. Hutchinson was the Emigration Agent appointed by

Hindmarsh to fill Brown's place. Fisher had refused to recognise him, and bad feeling between them was the result. At the beginning of 1838 Fisher indignantly sent to the Governor some papers which had been spread about the town, containing rude and defamatory suggestions about the Resident Commissioner. Part, he said, was in the handwriting of Hutchinson; he could not trust himself to make any observations "upon the contents of the papers or the object of the author", but was going to forward the whole of them to England for the consideration of the Secretary of State.[7] He must have been foolish indeed if he expected sympathy from Hindmarsh, who simply communicated Fisher's complaint to Hutchinson and, no doubt, was delighted with the insults. Hutchinson promptly replied to Fisher that he had been:

> '... much amused at the virtuous indignation which you so well counterfeit respecting the substance of the paper in question; but it will not impose upon those who witnessed your admirable performance at the 'Salt Pork Explanation', your tears, your invocations of pity on your family &c &c which, however, would not have saved you from the public condemnation had not your friends Messrs Gouger and Mann stepped in to your support, and that trick will not do again. I could say a great deal more, but I reserve it for another occasion, when I shall have the pleasure of seeing your name in another Gazette than the South Australian'.[8]

A few days later Hutchinson resigned his office of Emigration Agent in order, as he informed Fisher, that:

> '... disencumbered on my part of the obstacle of official inferiority of rank, we might have the mutual pleasure of communicating as private, I do not presume to say gentlemen, but individuals'.

He would be happy to meet Fisher, he said, at any time:

> '... attended only, as I generally am myself, by a trusty old walking stick; for I assure you the place is so overrun with gentlemen from the neighboring colonies, apparently of equal respectability with yourself, that I do not feel it safe to go quite alone'.[9]

Before anything could follow these insulting remarks, Stevenson laid an information that a breach of the peace was likely to happen,[10] and Fisher and Hutchinson were each bound over by the Resident Magistrate to keep the peace towards each other for 12 months, in a recognisance of £1,000, with two sureties of £500 each.

Hutchinson then amused himself by going round the town altering printed notices, which had been posted announcing a dinner to celebrate the anniversary of the establishment of Adelaide and at which Fisher was to be chairman, by scribbling "Pork and

Grindstone Blow-Out", "Pork Jobber" and similar comments after Fisher's name.[11] The grand dinner did not come off.

> 'Whether the tickets did not sell'—said the Register—'or whether there is any instinct among the bipeds of his party similar to that said to be possessed by rats, we cannot say.' [12]

Fisher, however, applied to Jickling for informations for criminal libel against Hutchinson and against the proprietors of the *Register*; both his applications were refused with costs.[13]

In March 1838 the *Register* said:

Robert Thomas
(1781-1860)
(SLSA)

> 'It has been part of the dirty trickery of Mr Fisher and his barkers to make loud complaints of the Colonial Government because of the alarming inconvenience the public were reported as suffering from the non-sitting of the Supreme Court. Nay, Mr Fisher has been in the habit of lamenting with his accustomed pathos the absolute denial of justice thereby occasioned to the numerous colonists anxious to redress their grievances and promote the general harmony by settling their disputes in a Court of law.' [14]

The fact was that only four actions had been commenced in the Supreme Court. One was by Brown against Gilles, for non-payment of his salary since the date of his suspension; the other three were actions by Fisher for libel.[15] The first of these, against Robert Thomas and George Stevenson, proprietors of the *Register*, came on for hearing before Jickling in May 1838, and the trial, which was spread over five days, proved a remarkable inauguration of the civil sittings of the Supreme Court.

> 'For most of the time the room resembled a bear garden more than a solemn Court of Justice, it being practically out of the power of the amiable Judge who was trying the cause to keep either counsel, plaintiff, or jurymen in order. The whole proceeding was of the most extraordinary character; to many new comers who were present, its want of accordance with the order, regularity and decorum of an English Court was very striking, and presented a spectacle which it is to be hoped will never again be witnessed in the Supreme Court of South Australia.' [16]

Mann, who had returned from Van Diemen's Land and had been readmitted to practice, appeared for Fisher. Trouble began early in the hearing. It was necessary for the plaintiff to prove the defendants were partners. Before the colonists had come out, Mann had acted in London as Thomas's attorney and had prepared the deed of partnership between Thomas and Stevenson. He still had it in his possession, claiming that he held it not as Thomas's solicitor but as a stakeholder between Thomas and Stevenson. Having gone through the solemn farce of issuing a subpoena to produce the deed, and serving it on himself, Mann put himself into the witness box and attempted first to put in the deed itself and then to give oral evidence of his knowledge of the fact of partnership. Stevenson, who conducted his own case, protested vehemently:

> 'I knew that neither the prosecutor nor his attorney were scrupulous'—he said—'but I did not think that so unprecedented an attempt at betrayal of professional confidence would be attempted even in this case.'

Jickling refused to admit the evidence and said it was atrocious to attempt to get it in in that way.

After this, the course of the trial was marked by constant interruptions and incessant bickering. At last, Mann having shouted that he would be compelled to teach the Judge and the jury a lesson, Stevenson groaned loudly. Mann complained that this was most indecorous, and the harassed Jickling declared that if there were any more interruptions from either party he would adjourn the Court. Almost immediately Mann interjected again, whereupon the Judge rose, called out, "I adjourn the Court and dismiss the Jury!" and left the courtroom. Confusion followed. No-one knew what was to be done. The parties were willing to go on, but upon messengers being sent to look for the Judge it was with them as with DeQuincey's Toad in the Hole—"et responsum est ab omnibus, non est inventus".

At length the Clerk of the Court came back with the sinister intelligence that the Judge had gone posthaste to Government House. The Sheriff harangued the jury on the unprecedented nature of the proceedings, and concluded by telling them that he must lock them all up. The jury got excited. Mann declared that he would stay there all night. Eventually it was decided that the jury should retire and meet again next day. "Mr Smart was about to swear them to secrecy, when he was reminded that there was no Court."

When the parties and the jury arrived next day, the Clerk of the Court informed them that he had a message from the Judge. Stephen, the Advocate-General, had been called in to act as a peacemaker and on his advice the Clerk put the message in writing and went to get the Judge's signature to it. Jickling, however, had gone, so the Clerk came back and read his message:

> 'In consequence of Mr Mann's insulting conduct the Court was adjourned by me, and the jury in the case dismissed, and I positively refuse to hear the case so long as he is present.'

Stephen went in search of the Judge and persuaded him to come back into court, where Jickling announced that he now had another ground for breaking off the hearing as he had been informed that two of the jury had made up their minds to return a verdict of guilty whatever the evidence might be. He then proposed to adjourn the Court again, but the jury objected. Angry speeches by Mann and Stevenson followed, and the Judge hastily adjourned the Court and hurried from the room. Stephen told the jury:

> 'I recommend you to go quietly to your houses. I thank God I am not in this case, and I hope I shall not be.'

Further persuasion of the Judge induced him to agree to continue the case on the following day, but it was then discovered that the foreman of the jury, disgusted with the proceedings, had gone to Port Adelaide for the day.

When the Court opened on the fifth day, Stephen intimated that he had been asked by the jury to address the Judge as to the allegation that the jury had already decided on their verdict. The jury resented this accusation, and after some discussion the Judge withdrew it, and the hearing was resumed. The verdict was guilty. Fisher thanked the jury and said he was not going to take the matter further or press for damages.[17]

"We spit upon a verdict so obtained," the *Register* informed its readers, and a new trial was moved for on various grounds, one being that two of the jury were unable to read or write.[18] This being unsuccessful, Stevenson was forced to resort to a dignified pose:

> 'Facts speak for themselves, and we rest tranquilly on the result of the judgment to be formed by those who are enabled by education and intelligence to pronounce.'

The comment of the rival paper was:

> 'What education the party alluded to has received we know not, but whatever modicum he may have imbibed, it is perfectly clear that it has not been able to remove from his mind its original taint of low-minded conceit and vulgarity.' [19]

The more violent members of the Fisher party were loud in their denunciation of Jickling's conduct of the trial, and they soon found another instance of bungling to add fuel to their imprecations. The second Criminal Sessions to be held in the colony was to have begun on 2 April 1838. By a blunder, no jurymen had been summoned to attend, and the opening of the sessions was a fiasco. It was humorously described by one spectator:

> 'The sessions opened on the 2nd of April last, when a prisoner applied to be admitted to bail or discharged; on coming to Court there was no Judge and no Jury. Shortly afterwards, however, the Judge came. It was arranged that the Court should be opened, but there was no officer to perform the duty. The Judge looks up to the ceiling, can't find him there; then down to the ground, does not see him there. The Advocate General then enacts the part of Caleb Quotem; he is crier and Clerk to the Court; the Court is opened—what then? They are still at fault—it is after all a blank day. There is no jury and it turns out that none have been summoned. The prisoner in question pleads the loss of time, and that his time is of great value, and he desires to be released by a jury. The Judge makes an agreement with the prisoner to call another

> day. The Court adjourns to nine days afterwards (observing the law regarding the sight of puppies) and is then opened.'[20]

There were thirteen convictions at this sessions, mainly upon charges of larceny and assault, and it was the first at which sentence of death had to be passed. Some desperadoes had entered the Sheriff's cottage one night and fired at him point-blank. The shot merely singed his ear. Two of the criminals were captured, tried and convicted. Both were sentenced to death, and one of them, Magee, was hanged. The hanging was shockingly managed, and the executioner (a grotesque figure, masked and padded to avoid recognition) had to complete his task by swinging on the legs of his victim as he dangled from the bough of a gum tree in the north parklands.[21]

T. Horton James, who was present at the trial of Magee, left an account of the conduct of it by "the gentle Jickling". Apparently James was of the opinion of Lessingham in the old play, that:

> 'A Judge methinks looks lovelyest when he weeps,
> Pronouncing of death's sentence'

for he describes at some length how Jickling, with great emotion:

> '... after expatiating on the enormity of the offence in the most feeling and eloquent manner, implored the prisoner not to entertain the slightest hopes of mercy or mitigation, but recommended him to make the most of his short time on earth in imploring the forgiveness of his offended Maker'.[22]

J.M. Skipper's depiction of South Australia's first execution in 1838. (SLSA)

THE

SOUTHERN AUSTRALIAN.

VOL. I — SATURDAY MORNING, JUNE 2, 1838 — No. 1

South Australian Company

Joint Stock Cattle Company.

PROSPECTUS OF THE SOUTHERN AUSTRALIAN,

Bank of South Australia

Land Office.

Immediate accommodation for a Family.

For Sale by Private Contract.

The first page of the inaugural issue of the *South Australian*. (SLSA)

Henry Jickling

The Southern Australian

On 2 June 1838 appeared the first number of the *Southern Australian*, a newspaper which had been established under Mann's editorship. Its avowed object was to oppose the *Register*—"that contemptible lickspittle production yclepted the Government paper"—and it did not hesitate to launch unbridled attacks on the rival journal and its editor.

> 'A little low and vulgar abuse, a-la-Billingsgate, mixed up with a spice of profanity, and thrown off with a domineering effrontery, fills up for the most part the outline of his polemical lucubrations'.[1]

The journalists of the colony possessed all those attributes which Pope declared to be the chief qualifications of party writers—"to stick at nothing, to delight in flinging dirt, and to slander in the dark by guess". The *Southern Australian*, unlike its reptile contemporary, was to be devoted to serving the highest interests of the public in the purest style of journalism; and as a sample of what was to come, its readers were presented, in the first number, with passages of soul-stirring rhetoric:

> 'Consider the recent administration of justice in the highest Court of the Province, and here what a scene forces itself upon our contemplation! In a Court, the Judge of which is bound to hold himself strongly aloof from the fascinations of wealth or power, we have again and again heard with deep regret and dismay, the highest executive power of the Province appealed to from the judgment seat, as a kind arbiter, whose volitions were to influence the ultimate opinion, to be thence pronounced; and this too so openly that on one occasion the very Advocate General of the Crown deprecated a course so unconstitutional. But our reasons for alarm and anxiety do not terminate. In the course of one session, the independence of the Bar and of the Jury—those buttresses of the massy fabric of English liberty, which our forefathers cemented with their blood—have been exposed to open and repeated attack. Claims of ultimate power have been insisted upon, from which we verily believe the Judges in England in the arbitrary days of the Tudors and the Stuarts of past ages would have shrunk with dismay. We have lived to hear a Judge of Oyer and Terminer in the nineteenth century insisting on an indefinite adjournment of a criminal case—and thus claiming to stand between a prisoner on his trial and a jury impanelled to pronounce on his guilt or innocence. We have lived to hear that Judge refuse to proceed with a pending trial whilst a particular Advocate (alluded to by name) carried out practically

those stern and onerous duties which are imposed upon the English barrister by virtue of his very retainer.'

"Inebriated with the exuberance of his own verbosity", the writer unfortunately could not stop to explain the precise nature of the fascinations of wealth and power which, in this small village of primitive huts, had caused the Judge to deviate from the paths of rectitude; but swept on to his comforting peroration:

> 'The high-minded and noble feeling which glowed within the breast of a Hampden, of a Sydney, of a Russell, is still too rife within our breasts to allow an invasion of rights, the overthrow of which might, in time to come, leave it in the power of a courtly parasite to snatch from merited punishment a guilty favorite or a pampered instrument of tyranny.' [2]

A public meeting at the Adelaide Tavern was called to consider the administration of the law.

> 'As it was generally understood that violent speeches were to be made against every body and everything, a number of curious and idle persons of course collected.'

Jickling was accused of incompetence. The qualities of a judge, it was said, were legal knowledge, strict impartiality, and (rather vaguely) "a freedom from those prejudices which warp and bias the mind"; and not one of these qualifications existed in Jickling. In the one breath, it was said that he was partial to Hindmarsh, and that Hindmarsh had declared him to be totally unfit for a subordinate office, that of Advocate-General. A series of resolutions were put and carried with clamour:

> That 'independence and impartiality in a Judge are essential to the due administration of justice; and that the meeting views with alarm and apprehension the avowed subjection of any person holding that office to illegitimate influence under his sole jurisdiction'.
>
> That 'the speedy administration of justice is essential to its due operation, and that unnecessary delay is in the nature of a denial of justice'.
>
> That 'freedom of speech and discussion, either in person or by counsel, is the undeniable right of every Englishman, and that the independence of the Bar is a necessary concomitant of the liberty of the subject, and that this meeting deprecates the course adopted towards certain members of the legal profession in the province'.
>
> That 'as it appears the appointment of the present Judge is merely pro tempore until Her Majesty's pleasure be known, a humble petition be prepared, praying Her Majesty to be graciously pleased to appoint to the office of Judge a properly qualified person and one in whom the colonists can repose

confidence and respect'.[3]

Having blown off steam in this way, the revolutionaries quietly settled down and left the continuation of the struggle against despotism to the columns of the *Southern Australian*, in which Mann, in a long series of controversial articles, argued at length the whole constitutional dispute over the Governor's actions. The *Register* babbled its scorn of Mann's writings—"insane drivelling", "legal fustian", "unprofitable twaddle", "insolent gabble", "distracted quiddities", "the poor attorney's crotchets", and "the idiot drivellings of a lunatic" are a few of Stevenson's epithets. It is true that the articles provide an excellent illustration of Lewis Carroll's maxims, that "a controversy may be raised about any question, and at any distance from that question", and that "a finite argument (that is, one finished and disposed of) may be produced to any extent in subsequent debates", but they are valuable because Mann put his points and argued them with vigour and ability, and it is impossible to obtain any understanding of the constitutional difficulties (and they were genuine difficulties) which followed Governor Hindmarsh's drastic suspensions, without considering Mann's views.

One cannot assert dogmatically that any particular view of the constitutional position of the Council of Government was the correct one. In default of any authoritative judicial statement, it is largely a matter of individual opinion upon a question in which the strict application of logical principles is useless. The problem is that which Professor Gray has described:

> 'The difficulties of so-called interpretation arise when the legislature had no meaning at all; when the question which is raised on the Statute never occurred to it; when what the Judges have to do, is not to determine what the legislature did mean on a point which was present to its mind, but to guess what it would have intended on a point not present to its mind, had the point been present.'

The root of Mann's opposition to the Governor lay in his belief that the Foundation Act was:

> '... not a concession of privilege, yielded of grace by the Crown to the subject—but a sacred compact, on a sufficient and ample consideration, entered into after full deliberation, and the fulfilment of the terms of which has been guaranteed to the colony by the assembled Parliament of the nation. On the one hand, the King in Parliament declares the lands of the province to be public land, applicable to a great and generous purpose, concedes legislative and executive powers, of a high and transcendent nature, to persons to be appointed by himself in Privy Council, and fixes the period when a national assembly is to supersede the exercise of the provisional powers of the Council of Government. On the other hand, the colonists

> agree to disburse every expense incident to the first formation of the colony, to pay every charge attaching to the ordinary routine of government, and to save the mother country from every expense which the colony may incur from its earliest inception.' [4]

The condition on which the founders of the colony guaranteed to secure the mother country from all expense was, according to Mann, that the colonists of South Australia should have control over their own finances, that control being secured by the existence of an independent council. He insisted over and over again that the Foundation Act was: "... a compact made in consideration of a sufficient price paid ... What it gives we are entitled to, not as a boon, but as a purchase." If that was not the meaning of the Act, "why then it is a solemn cheat and mockery".[5]

Mann may have honestly persuaded himself that the Act granted an independent Council in return for freeing England of expense and relieving her overpopulation, but it is difficult to see any basis for such a belief. The idea of a sacred compact does not seem to have been thought of until Mann, Gouger, Fisher and Brown found themselves ejected from their offices. The Colonial Office certainly had no intention of permitting an independent Council to be established and had never given the slightest cause to anyone to believe that it would be countenanced. Mann's insinuations of the motives which influenced the officials of the Colonial Office were amusing but foolish:

> 'The self-supporting principle'—he wrote—'is a bitter pill at the office of the Colonial Secretary—it is the aliquid amarum which none in that quiet dormitory can swallow, from my Lord Glenelg to the lowest subaltern. Once let it be proved that the colonies can support themselves, and my Lord Glenelg might repose with the seven sleepers, and my Lord Howick and Sir George Grey, with many a long lingering look behind, quit once and forever the quiet purlieus of Downing Street.' [6]

The *Register* more soberly pointed out that it was useless to clamour prematurely against a form of government common to the condition of all young colonies and, wisely administered, in no degree adverse to their prosperity. "The alleged concession of an Independent Council is a mere fiction—a dream without a shadow of foundation." [7]

The Charter of South Australia had fixed the period when her inhabitants should exercise a more direct control over their affairs, and to the conditions of that charter they must be content to adhere.

> 'Under the existing system, we see no reason to gear [sic] tyranny or dread misrule, so long at least as the PRESS remains unshackled and the voice of public opinion is unfettered.' [8]

Robert Thomas's hut and tent at Glenelg ca. 1836. The hut housed the Stanhope printing press (shown below) on which the Proclamation of South Australia and the *Register* were printed. (SLSA)

To Mann and his followers, however, South Australia was not the free colony for which they had hoped; "our government is not what it was intended to be".

> 'We allege'—he said—'that we have been defrauded of our rights in a manner unexampled and that we owe it to ourselves to claim of the Imperial Parliament a performance of the reciprocal contract entered into between the mother country and the Province. Our own part of that contract—the pound of flesh—has been exacted to the uttermost; can our opponents say that faith has been kept as scrupulously with us? For what did we contract to become a self-supporting colony? For what encumber ourselves with a heavy and onerous burden? We answer, that like the self-supporting colonies of North America, we entered into this contract that we might be a self-taxing and a self-legislating Province; and this vested right, this really glorious privilege, has been wrested from us, and in lieu we have offered to us the rottenness of absolute power.' [9]

They could see no difference between the rule of Governor Hindmarsh and the rule of the military governors at the convict settlements in the neighbouring colonies, and every step which Hindmarsh took they construed as another instance of his belief that high prerogative should obtain, and that there was a right divine of Governors to govern wrong. As instances of the arbitrary exercise of prerogative powers they pointed to his acting against the will of the majority of the Council, the suspension and appointment of members of Council, the transformation of "an inefficient clerk to the Magistrates into a perfect Judge", and the ordering of an Advocate-General from Van Diemen's Land.[10]

From the legal point of view, the vital question was whether the Governor had the power of suspending members of Council and of replacing them by his nominees. If so, then it was obvious that he must be supreme and able to enforce his will; and, since all the members of the Council were officials, the mere knowledge that the Governor had the power of suspension would make them subservient. The Council would be "merely a convenient means of registering the will of an autocrat".

> 'Is independence-can independence be there? Ask of the past, whether a single member who has dared, however respectfully, to differ from the Chairman of the Council of Government, holds his seat? Scrutinise the members of the present Council, and say whether the appointees of the Governor, the Jicklings, the Stephens, the Bernards of the day, can be supposed to see through any other medium than that of their master and creator. We answer fearlessly—No; and we ask—Is such a Council what we have a right to expect? ... Will any man say that an independent Council would have sanctioned the

> appointment of the military gentlemen who like locusts are now devouring our substance? Had such a Council existed, and the right to control been in them, would Lieutenant Newenham, who never saw a writ or warrant in his life, have been made Sheriff? or his son, who is about as ignorant of law as a sucking pig, have been constituted a Clerk of the Supreme Court, one of the most respectable legal situations in the colony?' [11]

To prove that the Governor's suspension of the original members of the Council was illegal, Mann advanced two lines of argument—the first, a development of the contention that since the appointments were made by the King in Council, the Privy Council alone could suspend; and the second, that the Governor could not suspend contrary to the will of a majority of the Council.

His first point was ingenious rather than substantial. The Council of Government had been established by an order of the Privy Council made on 23 February 1836. By this order, as has already been mentioned, the Governor or the officer administering the Government, the Judge, Colonial Secretary, Advocate-General and Resident Commissioner, or any three of them (of whom the Governor should be one) were given authority to make, ordain and establish all such laws, institutions and ordinances, and to constitute such courts and appoint such officers, and to impose and levy such rates, duties and taxes as might be necessary or expedient for the peace, order and good government of the inhabitants of the colony. This order referred not to individuals by name, but to offices.

> 'It is in its nature inchoate and unfinished, and if the matter had rested here, no Council could ever have existed ... It is a mere adjectival expression of qualities or conditions of persons, and not a substantive appointment of the actual individuals; a restriction, not an appointment—a series of abstractions, and not the embodying of flesh and blood councillors.'

By another order in Privy Council, made in July 1836, certain persons were appointed, by name, to the offices referred to in the first order, and Mann proceeded to expound a distinction between the person and the official, individuality as opposed to abstraction. "Persons," he said, "are independent and equal; the officer, dependent and inferior." The first order in Council could not operate without the second:

> 'It is in the nature of a condition, so operating that the person to be appointed must at the time of his claim to exercise the powers of a councillor prove that he is also entitled to fill the particular office mentioned. The office is in fact a condition precedent to his claim, but this condition once fulfilled, we contend that the nominee of the King is in as a Person, not as an Officer—is in free and not fettered—is in not merely whilst

he continues to hold office, but until the King, by appointing another person, demonstrates his intention under the Act to confer his powers on another.' [12]

The *Register* heaped scorn on the distinction drawn between the officer and the person, as an apt demonstration of a distinction without a difference.

> 'Is not an officer a person, and a person an officer? Or is Mr Mann's person in the position of the ensign of a marching regiment who, being asked if he was a soldier, answered indignantly that he was an officer and no soldier.' [13]

The answer to the argument seems to be that the use of the words "for the time being" in the Order in Council, after the reference to the various officers who were to constitute the Council, shows that the order contemplated that upon ceasing to hold the position the officer lost also his right to a seat in the Council.

Of course, if Mann were right, it followed that the Governor's suspensions and appointments were invalid, and there would be justification for Mann's repetition of Dr Parr's benediction, "Qui suspenderunt, suspendantur!" and his vehement complaints that:

> 'Governor Hindmarsh was pleased to cross the Rubicon, and of his own good will and pleasure (ex mero motu et speciali gratu) to change Thomas Bewes Strangways (who was, to use his own asseveration, the best bullock driver in the Province) into the Honourable the Colonial Secretary; Henry Jickling Esq from a very inefficient Magistrates' Clerk, into a Judge in whose hands have been, and are, the issues of life and death; and George Milner Stephen Esq, not having been previously admitted either at or under the Bar of any English court, to be barrister of the province, and Advocate General, and finally Acting Governor of South Australia; and all these gentlemen (which is the gist of the thing) into legislators and taxers, and members of a Council whose members can only, according to our theory, be legally appointed by the Sovereign for the time being.' [14]

Mann's second argument consisted of an attack on the Governor's Instructions, "under the magical influence of which an Act has been frittered away and the solemn Order of the King in Council rendered of none effect".

> 'A certain private adviser of Captain Hindmarsh (than whom a more impudent and mendacious quack is not in existence) misled his patron so far as to induce into his mind a belief that the 5th Royal Instruction enabled him to act of his own will and against the majority of the Council'.[15]

On this branch of the question, up to a certain point, Mann's reasoning was quite sound. The King, he said, by appointing five persons to the Council, had shown that individual power was not intended to obtain. By the Order in Council appointing these five persons, it was provided that any three of them, of whom the Governor was to be one, had power to act. It was clear therefore, Mann contended, that a majority of the Council was necessary to make the Acts of the Council valid and it was never anticipated that one should act alone.

> 'Such was the order of King William the Fourth; not such the order of our colonial autocrat, John the First. According to him, three meant one; and accordingly one acted in the stead of three.' [16]

Mann rightly said that the Governor's Instructions could not overrule the provisions of an Order in Council made under the authority of an Act of Parliament. The Governor's Commission, after reciting the Foundation Act and the Orders in Council, required and commanded him:

> '... to do and execute all things in due manner that shall belong to his command, and the trust reposed in him, according to the aforesaid order of the Privy Council, and according to the powers granted by the present commission and the royal instructions'.

In the recital of the Act and Orders in Council, and in the words "according to the aforesaid order of the Privy Council", Mann saw a limitation by express words of the Governor's powers and duties. The Governor's commission, he said, was sui generis.

> 'The whole Commission is guardedly worded so as to give him notice of the contract made with the people—the manner in which the sovereign has acted with reference to the statute—and the restrictions which the Act has placed alike upon the prerogative of the Crown and the acts of its representative here.' [17]

But the commission referred also to the Royal Instructions, and unless the 5th Royal Instruction was to be treated as a complete nullity, some limitation must be placed upon the language of the Order in Council requiring the consent of a majority of the Council. It was upon the question of what this limitation should be that the arguments of Mann and of the law authorities at home parted company. The law officers construed the Order in Council as applicable to the legislative acts of the Council only. To give validity to these, a majority of the Council was necessary, but in the case of executive acts the Governor was not bound to consult his Council, and the order in Council had no operation at all upon this class of acts.

To avoid this conclusion, Mann announced that the fifth Royal Instruction did not apply to the Council of Government at all, but to another Council—a Council of advice which he said the Governor was entitled at common law to summon to his assistance. Certainly no such Council was ever called into existence in South Australia, and precisely what it was (if it existed other than in Mann's imagination) it is difficult to understand. It is here that Mann seems to have gone astray. At the same time it must be admitted that the solution of the difficulty put forward by the law officers was not very satisfactory, for the boundary between executive and legislative acts was by no means clear.

The Governor himself clearly had no power to legislate or tax, and Mann argued with some force that the appointees of Hindmarsh could have no such right. In flowery language he harked back to Magna Carta to prove that there could be no taxation without representation:

> 'The claim then conceded has never from that hour been abandoned, and on the contrary the right once allowed has grown with our growth, and strengthened with our strength. Through many a dark and trying hour the banner of freedom has still been carried onward, and successively every outwork and fortification of despotic power has been overthrown, and it now floats proudly on the high places, and the innermost penetralia of absolutism. Though a world of waters intervenes between ourselves and merry England, yet we can as proudly claim exemption from taxation (save on the basis of the admitted principles of English law) as if our feet yet trod the florious shores of our father-land. A Briton has always vested in him unalienably a Briton's rights; and as one of the consequences of these rights let it never be forgotten that the Crown of England cannot of its own prerogative tax, or delegate to another the power of taxing by prerogative.' [18]

It was certainly at first sight strange that a Council composed of the Governor's nominees should have such powers, but the answer was simply that the Governor did not appoint members of Council—he merely appointed officers, and they became members of Council by operation of the order of the Privy Council.

In an attempt to remedy the difficulties of appointment which section II of the Foundation Act had created, an amending act was passed in 1838 which repealed the cumbersome system of appointment by Order in Council and provided that the appointment of officers might be made by the Queen by warrant under the Sign Manual. Mann now took a fresh stand, and contended that this power was vested in the Crown by statute and was not inherent as part of the prerogative at common law; and that, being a delegated power, "that inexorable maxim, of which the dominion is no more to be defined, than the date of its birth, or the name of its father, is to be found"—"delegatus non potest delegare"—applied and barred the Governor from acting on the power.

> 'The statutable power is in fact a bare trust, exerciseable only

by the party to whom the power is granted, and by none other; whilst on the contrary the common law prerogative being inherent in the Crown, the law of representation applies, and invests a Governor to that extent with the attributes of sovereignty.' [19]

The right of the Governor under the amending act to appoint officers arose almost immediately. It had never been satisfactory to have the Judge sitting as a member of the Council;[20] and on 8 June 1838 an Order in Council reconstituted the Council of Government, which was henceforth to consist of the Governor, Colonial Secretary, Advocate-General, Surveyor-General and Assistant Commissioner of Lands.[21] Kingston had succeeded Light as Surveyor-General but Governor Gawler did not retain him in the position, and conferred it upon Captain Sturt. Mann at once challenged the legality of the appointment. The Governor, he said, had no power to make the appointment; it was wresting a valuable privilege from the Commissioners, because the appointment lay with them under the Foundation Act, and had not been vested in the representative of the Crown by the amending act. The Foundation Act, with a curious choice of offices, authorised the Commissioners to appoint "A Treasurer, Assistant Surveyors, and other officers". The absence of the Surveyor-General from this group seemed to indicate that the appointment to that office did not lie with the Commissioners; but Colonel Light had been appointed by them, apparently under this power, without objection; and as the whole of the land of the province was vested in the Commissioners, why, asked Mann, should the appointment of the Surveyor-General be given to the Crown?[22]

Charles Sturt (1795-1869)
The unveiling of the Captain Sturt monument in Adelaide in 1916. The statue portrays Sturt in his role as explorer for which he is best remembered. Sturt also occupied a number of positions with the South Australian Government but spent his final years in England. (SLSA)

The *Register* replied scornfully:

> 'We know not the extent of our contemporary's legal erudition; but the veriest booby that ever carried a bag or dusted a bundle in the Inns of Court, knows that by law when, as in the present case, certain officers are mentioned by name, the general term 'other officers' can include only officers inferior to those specially defined';

and Blackstone was cited to the effect that "a statute which treats of things or persons of an inferior rank, cannot by any general words be extended to those of a superior".[23] Which of the two arguments was right is a matter of individual opinion.

The union of the powers of the Governor and Resident Commissioner in the person of Colonel Gawler afforded Mann another target, and he contended that the joinder of offices was illegal and void. The Foundation Act, he argued, vested the disposal of lands in the Colonisation Commissioners, who were specially made amenable to law in the event of any breach of contract by them. The Act further permitted the Commissioners to delegate their powers to a resident commissioner who, therefore, ought also to be amenable to law. But by the nomination of the Governor as Resident Commissioner, purchasers of land had been deprived of any legal remedy.

> 'The party desirous of obtaining legal relief cannot, and he is without any legal remedy whatever here, because the Resident Commissioner is also Governor, and as Governor is not amenable to law in this province. That the representative of the Commissioners should be so irresponsible is clearly contrary to the spirit of the Act of Parliament.'

It was certainly a disadvantage of this Janus-like combination of offices that the Governor could not leave Adelaide without taking the Resident Commissioner from his post, and that when Gawler added to these duties those of "principal explorer" there were necessarily considerable delays in public business. The *Register*, of course, ridiculed Mann's opinions:

> 'The legal practitioners of the opposition are certainly a very motley group—at least if their opinions are to be taken as indicative of their acquirements. Indeed, their knowledge of law resembles and almost exceeds that possessed by Sir John Falstaff of the code of honour. The fat knight held running away to be the better part of valour, and the radical attorneys think chicanery the prime beauty of the profession. If it be illegal, as these pundits maintain, for His Excellency to hold the two offices of Governor and Commissioner, it is quite clear the illegality cannot be partial and attach itself to one office only. We apprehend it must be aut Caesar aut nullus—both horns of the dilemma must be fairly occupied—the office

> of Governor must take its fate with that of Commissioner, and the unavoidable consequences are—we tremble even to hint at the portentous result, but fiat justitia ruat coelum—the blessed colony of South Australia is, at this moment, according to the opinion of Messrs Mann & Co in a state of "suave qui peut'" without either a legal Governor or a legal Commissioner, with no Council—no Secretary—no Treasurer—no clerks—and what, in the view of the same authority, is a thousand times worse than all, without an Advocate General to advise the Crown in so desperate an emergency.' [24]

Assuming Mann's objection to have been valid, the purchasers of land were not left entirely without a remedy, for they could always sue the Colonisation Commissioners in England under section XXI of the Foundation Act.

A few months after he had so decidedly alleged that the Resident Commissioner could not be sued because he was also Governor, the exigencies of his practice called upon Mann to maintain the contrary before Mr Justice Cooper in the Supreme Court. He moved, on the equity side, that a subpoena might issue against the Governor as Resident Commissioner calling upon him to appear to a bill filed by the South Australian Company to set aside a grant of land made by the Resident Commissioner. He now contended that as the Commissioners in England were amenable by statute to suits and actions, their representative in the colony must also be so amenable, and that the union of his office with another which was irresponsible did not bar this liability, although he admitted that it might be impossible to enforce remedies against the person of the Governor. A refusal to issue the subpoena would mean that all litigation with the Commissioners would have to be carried on in England, at enormous expense and great delay. The Judge did not find it necessary to decide the point, as he took the view that in any event the company had no equity, and the suit was abandoned.[25]

One of Governor Gawler's capital works projects was the building of a new Government House. This 1845 painting by S.T.Gill shows the original Government House before extensions in 1855 and 1878. (AGSA)

Colonel Gawler arrived in Adelaide on 12 October 1838, and Jickling administered the oaths of office.[1] The new Governor brought with him instructions to restore Mann and Brown to their offices. Rowland Hill, the Secretary to the Commissioners, wrote privately to Mann congratulating him on his restoration, and added:

> 'There is, however, still one difficulty to be overcome. Poor Jickling has, it is understood, declared that you shall not practice in the Supreme Court, and your appointment while this stupid disqualification exists may perhaps appear to some to be an unwarrantable attempt on the part of the authorities here to overrule those in the Colony. I had reason to believe that this difficulty was actually felt in the Colonial Office, and fearing it might stand in the way of an arrangement which I had much at heart I took on myself to assure Mr Stephen that you would remove the difficulty, if any existed, by applying to the Court—after the arrival of the new Judge, perhaps—to have the disqualification removed.' [2]

George Gawler (1795-1869) A soldier who became a "true Christian" before securing the post of Governor of the Province (and Resident Commissioner), Gawler came to a South Australia in financial crisis. He attempted to solve the crisis by accelerating the survey of land, increasing the employment and payment of public officials and through an expansive public works programme. The results of Gawler's actions remain open to debate but they led to his being replaced as Governor and suffering much criticism for his "extravagance". (SLSA)

Stephen's view was that Mann should have appealed to the Privy Council if he thought his disqualification was not justified.[3] By the time Hill's letter arrived in the colony, the disqualification from practice had long been removed, but Gawler found it impossible to take back Mann as Advocate-General.[4] The Governor's dispatches reveal his increasing exasperation at Mann's opposition. A fortnight after his landing, Gawler wrote in moderate terms:

> 'Knowing the high opinion which is entertained of Mr Mann, the late Advocate General, by the Commissioners, I at once offered to him restitution to that office. He, however, in reply having, with much candour, declared to me, both verbally and on paper, his principles of Colonial Government, and those principles being, on fundamental points, at direct opposition with those which I conceive to be embodied in His Majesty's Instructions, I was compelled to decline his assistance in the administration of the affairs of the colony. In addition to them and proceeding from them, he maintained that I could not be sworn in before the existing Council, that Council not having been legally appointed. My opinion was that my only clear course was to take the Council as I found it.' [5]

By January 1839 Gawler was reporting to the Colonial Office that Mann was the leader of a party which constantly met his efforts "with determined opposition, tinctured at times with very unprincipled misrepresentations". Mann, he said, among "other visionary theories", had proclaimed to the colony that the Council could not impose taxes and that the Governor's appointment as Resident Commissioner was illegal; "two points, I beg your Lordship to consider, as affecting property and titles to land, in the highest degree mischievous, and calculated to produce, in a society constituted as this is, the most dangerous consequences".[6] Mann's opposition, he told the Commissioners, "from the period I refused to substitute the Council of Advice recommended by him for the Council of Government ordered by Her Majesty, has amounted to absolute infatuation".[7]

Gawler had the less hesitation in getting rid of Mann because in Stephen he had a subordinate on whose ability he could rely. Within a week of his arrival in Adelaide he had formed the opinion that Stephen was "a gentleman of much talent, energy and application", and he praised "his great professional talent, very businesslike habits, and extensive colonial experience".[8]

The era of official squabbles drew to an inglorious end; the feverish condition of the body politic of the colony would not last forever. Governor Gawler had no time for rebellious civil servants. When he arrived in the colony, he said, he found: "...almost all public business was transacted through the newspapers, and every petty dispute between the government and its functionaries appeared in print".

This appeared to him preposterous, and he determined to put a stop to it. One officer of the government had even called a public meeting to discuss and justify his conduct.

> 'Any public functionary'—said the Governor—'who considers himself to be amenable to popular meetings for his official conduct knows, in this respect, nothing of his duty to the Government, to himself, or to the community at large; and they who require public officers to be so responsible show themselves utterly unacquainted with the ordinary principles of good government'. [9]

Mann found that his diatribes were of little use, and turned his energies to sheep farming and the work of his increasing practice.[10] Brown was restored to the position of Emigration Agent, but it was not long before he again offended by publicly criticising the Governor and was once more suspended.[11] This time the authorities at home turned the suspension into dismissal.[12] Gawler had been instructed to institute an inquiry into Fisher's conduct. He accordingly appointed a Commission of Enquiry, but as Fisher refused to appear before it, the most tangible results of the Commission's sittings seem to have been those disclosed in a plaintive wail from Jickling that the Commission had turned him out of doors, used his office for its meetings, and smashed his furniture.[13] Fisher, Mann and Brown having been replaced by subordinates more loyal to the Governor, the public affairs of the colony began to be transacted in peace, and when Gilles was at last removed, something approaching order was introduced into its tangled finances. The flames of old enmities had a last feeble flicker in July 1839, when several belated actions for libel by Brown and Fisher against the *Register* came on for hearing, but the juries were no longer interested in the old quarrels, and the plaintiffs recovered nominal damages only.

In the expectation that the new Judge might arrive at any time, Jickling held no further criminal sittings of the Court in 1838. As the months went by, the gaol became more and more crowded. In August 1838 there were thirteen prisoners awaiting trial and the Acting Governor suggested to Jickling that a Criminal Sessions should be held—not from any desire to afford the accused a speedy trial, but in order to save the public the expense of keeping those who might be acquitted.[14] By December there were more than twenty persons shut up in a gaol constructed to contain nine, and some dozen or more prisoners were out on bail awaiting trial. A petition was presented to the Judge, signed by all those in the gaol, praying for a Criminal Sessions to be held, and this was supported by a request from the Governor.[15] Jickling decided to hold a sessions early in February 1839, and by a blunder the jury lists were not made up in time and the sessions had to be further adjourned for a month. The insolence of the aggressor is usually proportioned to the tameness of the sufferer, and the *Southern Australian* attacked Jickling savagely:

> 'Our judgment seat is filled by a creature as useless and as pitiable as may wellbe conceived; and although the thought of one so absurd and ridiculous sitting upon the seat of judgment excites a moment's smile, yet the sad recollection comes over us, that between forty and fifty of our fellow men are pent up in a close and loathsome prison house, and that nine months have now elapsed since a judicial court has been held in the colony, and that on account of the incompetency of our judge. Let us add to all this, that manifold commercial difficulties are daily experienced, which a proper regulation of the process, pleadings and sittings of the Supreme Court would dissipate in a moment.' [16]

When the sessions began, there were thirty-five cases listed for trial, and the startling result was that every prisoner was acquitted. The lamentable failure of the Crown cases was partly due to Bernard's inexperience and lack of forensic skill; but, in some of the cases, Mann was brought in to prosecute and was equally unsuccessful. Owing to the long delay in bringing prisoners to trial, juries were sympathetic, and many of the witnesses were missing—some dead, some left the colony. Jickling himself was apparently quite satisfied with the way he had carried out his duties. "I have acted with clean hands and a pure heart," he complacently informed the Court.[17]

The *Southern Australian* naturally could not allow the opportunity to pass of attacking Bernard. One mock correspondent wrote:

> 'I am especially desirous of knowing whether you have attended at the Court House to hear any of the late trials. If you have not, do go before the Sessions are over, if it be only to hear the splendid eloquence of the talented Advocate General and Public Prosecutor, Mr Burnhard. When the deep sonorous tones of his mighty voice are first heard, Judge, counsel, jury, prisoners and lookers-on are awed into deep silence; and then the fine flow of his language and his beautifully turned periods—in short his is the ne plus ultra of forensic eloquence. Be sure to stay and hear him examine or cross-examine a witness. You will find few at this or any other bar who can equal him. He goes on until he (I was going to commit an Irishism and say the witness, when I mean the learned gentleman himself) gets so bothered he hardly knows whether he is standing on his head or his heels; and then again the High Legal Knowledge and Acumen he has shown in drawing the indictments of the prisoners is quite astonishing; and you will agree with me in thinking so when I tell you that all the prisoners that have been tried have escaped conviction—at any rate this speaks well for the kindheartedness and humanity of the learned gentleman. He is for the future to be denominated "the Prisoners' Friend".' [18]

Within a few days of the conclusion of this maiden sessions the new Judge arrived from England and Jickling returned to private practice. His tenure in office had not been a peaceful one. James, in his *Six Months in South Australia* (p.65) tells an amusing story which illustrates the Judge's tribulations. Osmond Gilles came one day into the Judge's office:

> '... where Mr Jickling was busily employed in preparing the blank forms of writs, summonses, subpoenas, commitments &c in the usual legal phraseology. He exclaimed with indignation to the learned and gentle Jickling, "What's all this, Sir?" hastily reading over the harmless words "William the Fourth, by the Grace of God, King of Great Britain and Ireland," and so forth. "Pooh, pooh! We want no nonsense of this sort here! Kings indeed! Out with it, Sir! This is South Australia". The quiet barrister was in a tremble, and getting up from his seat and rubbing his spectacles, in the simplicity of his heart assured him there was no treason in the words—that he

had merely inserted them because it was the practice of the higher courts at Westminster; but he was inflexible, and said, "Strike it out. We'll have no Kings here—if you must have a name to the papers, put in OG", meaning that active and enterprising colonist Osmond Gilles Esq.'

S.T. Gill's portrait of "OG". (SLSA)

Jickling's remuneration was miserable—£335 11s 8d for nearly 18 months in office.[19] Governor Gawler was dismayed at the niggardly salaries paid to the public officers.

> 'I am credibly informed'—he wrote home—'that the Acting Judge, upon the half salary of his office, lives without a servant, and boards with the clerk of the Court.' [20]

Jickling subsequently established himself in a little Manning cottage near the courthouse, a Manning house being a wooden structure made in England, which could be erected and taken down again at little expense.[21]

Manning Cottages
Made by the London firm of H. Manning these prefabricated houses were sent to many British Colonies and advertised as "complete for habitation in a few hours after landing".

The remainder of Jickling's colonial life may be conveniently told here. He continued to practise as a barrister and for a time, old enmities forgotten, he was in partnership with Mann. Mann then joined Edward Castres Gwynne, and Jickling thereafter practised on his own. There was scarcely any equity work in the colony and he did little more than make a living. In 1847 he was briefed as junior to the Advocate-General in the Royalty Suit, as "the gentleman most accustomed to Chancery practice".[22] When Mann resigned the position of Master of the Supreme Court at the end of 1849 to take that of Crown Solicitor, Jickling applied for it, and Mr Justice Cooper

Edward Castres Gwynne (1811-1888)
Gwynne arrived in South Australia in 1839 as a lawyer and property speculator, later adding politician and finally Supreme Court Judge to his curriculum vitae.

recommended him as being, on the whole, better qualified for the office than any practitioner in the colony who could be induced to take it.

> 'Mr Jickling'—he wrote—'has not been very successful in his endeavours for practice in his profession. This has arisen I conceive less from want of ability than from the fact that his previous habits as an English barrister have not fitted him for competition with attorneys, in whose line of practice by far the greatest amount of business is done ... His education as an Equity lawyer has been superior to that of any person likely to come into competition with him.' [26]

Jickling was accordingly appointed on 1 January 1850 at a salary of £300 per annum.

During the financial exigencies of the crisis of 1852 Jickling was temporarily appointed Police Magistrate—an office which was then combined with that of Commissioner of Police, although it was expressly agreed that he should not be called upon to perform the active duties of the latter. The *Register* poked fun at him without mercy:

> 'We understand'—it said—'that the semi-military appointment of Police Magistrate and Commissioner of Police has been conferred upon that learned and sedate functionary, Henry Jickling Esq. We trust that the peculiar nature of the functions and obligations of the Commander-in-Chief of the Police Force will not prove very uncongenial to the pacific and domestic spirit of that precise and deliberate gentleman. But we must apprize the learned civilian that it is his bounden duty forthwith to take lessons in military horsemanship and in the broadsword exercise; inasmuch as there is unfortunately some possibility that he may ere long, and more than once or twice, be called upon, like his great predecessor, the gallant Major O'Halloran, in the case of the Milmenrura murders, to head the mounted force in a desperate charge upon some insurgent tribe of blackfellows.' [24]

It was facetiously suggested that:

> '... a public examination should first take place in one of the fenced-in portions of Victoria square, of the learned gentleman's qualifications as an equestrian leader, and as to his efficiency in giving the word of command, and reviewing his gallant forces. It is said, also, that the point must first be decided at a special meeting of the Executive as to whether it may not be desirable to further signalize so very popular a promotion by requesting the learned gentleman to wear a red

> coat and a cocked hat with feathers, to cast aside his nice green spectacles, and to assume the novel appurtenances of boots and straps and spurs.'[25]

Jickling's lack of horsemanship was in contrast to a society where horse transport was vital and horse racing one of the earliest organised sports. Adelaide's first race meeting was held on 1 January 1838 with "about 800 persons" attending the first day. S.T. Gill's depiction of a subsequent meeting in 1845 shows a well-supported event. (NLA)

Jickling remained Master until September 1861. The Supreme Court office under his administration was not very efficiently managed. Jickling was appointed by the Governor; the clerks in the Master's office were appointed by the Judges; so that strictly the Master had no control over his own clerks. As Jickling said, in his stilted way:

> 'If I were to say to Mr Wilson or anybody else, will you do so-and- so, they might say (I do not say they have said, quite the contrary) "Mr Jickling, you have nothing to do with us; we derive our authority from the Judges".'[26]

The system of collecting fees was haphazard. For many proceedings, especially on the equity side, there was no fixed scale of fees, and Jickling used his own judgment as to what should be charged. Fees were not paid at the court office at all. When practitioners filed a document or had fees to pay, they were given a ticket to present and pay at the Treasury. They were then supposed to return with the receipt to the court office to show that payment had been duly made. It was convenient for a solicitor who had once lodged his documents to forget to visit the Treasury and, as the Master's office apparently kept no check on the number of tickets issued and receipts produced, documents very frequently found their way on the files without any fees being paid at all. Jickling complained that with some practitioners he had to be continually on the lookout to make sure that their fees were duly paid.[27] He cheerfully admitted the inadequacy of his system, but it never seems to have occurred to him that improvements might be made in it.

As he grew older his frail body became weaker and weaker. He suffered severely from rheumatism, and sank into a premature and tabid old age. His attendances at court became irregular and his work inefficient. Finally his fitness to hold the office was questioned in Parliament, and the Attorney-General informed the Chief Justice, in July 1861, that the Master must be told he could not be continued in employment any longer. Jickling wished to be allowed to retire at the end of the year, and Sir Charles Cooper generously supported him in this application. The Attorney-General, however, insisted on immediate resignation.[28]

Jickling asked for compensation for the sudden termination of his appointment, but this was refused. He then sought to include in his claim for retiring allowance his period of service as Acting Judge more than twenty years earlier. The Attorney-General reported that he could not count this period in assessing his retiring allowance; but Cabinet very honourably decided that in the exceptional case of this pioneer colonist the Attorney-General's opinion should be overruled, and the full amount claimed was paid—£487 10s.[29]

Soon after this, Jickling sailed for England, and he is heard of no more.[30]

Jickling's Death
Later research by Hague revealed that Jickling spent his last years on Jersey in the Channel Isles and died there in 1873.

Court record of *The Queen at the Prosecution of MacDougall v Stephen*, the first trial in the Milner Estate saga. (SCLSA)

Chapter 4.1

Sir Charles Cooper

The Mildew Estate

(Sir) Henry Ayers (1821-1897) Arriving in Adelaide in 1841 Ayers was to enjoy a very successful business career (he was a substantial share holder of the Burra mine) and a long political career (from 1857 to 1897). He became Premier in 1863 and, reflecting the instability of politics of the time, formed seven ministries in total. (SLSA)

Charles Cooper, who was the Judge appointed in England to succeed Sir John Jeffcott, was destined to remain on the bench of the Supreme Court for twenty three years—the first of a remarkable succession of four chief justices (Sir Charles Cooper, Sir Richard Hanson, Sir Samuel Way and Sir George Murray) who between them span nearly a century of legal history. The dignity of the office which he accepted had been somewhat tarnished by the appointment of a bankrupt duellist and by the interim administration of an amiable but inefficient eccentric. Cooper's irreproachable demeanour in public and private life, his punctilious attention to his duties, his unswerving honesty, restored the reputation of the Supreme Court and fully justified the tribute paid to him by J.W. Bull: "A more upright and just Judge never occupied the highly responsible seat of judgment in this or any other country." [1]

Industry and integrity, however, are not alone sufficient to ensure eminence on the bench, and, although he served the state faithfully throughout his long term, it can hardly be said that Sir Charles Cooper was a very great Judge. As a lawyer he was sound enough, but he had no exceptional grasp of legal principles, no subtlety of thought or of expression, no vigour in decision. He was a colourless man, with no dynamic force. Physically he was a "kinchin cove"—"feeble-looking and spare", Sir Henry Ayers described him.[2] He was a poor speaker, with a weak voice, and the reporters of the day more than once mentioned in the press the difficulty they had in understanding what the Judge was talking about.

'We imagine'—said the Register—'that His Honor is not himself aware how his voice drops in tone at the conclusion of his sentences. The consequence is we find ourselves with a body of introductory words before us, and the very point of the whole is wanting.' [3]

He experienced difficulty in keeping the more boisterous members of the bar in order, and in his occasional fits of petulance on the bench he was usually worsted. His timidity in coming to a conclusion, induced by overconscientiousness, frequently led to inordinate delays in the delivery of his judgments. "Oh, it's a beautiful thing to see how long and how carefully justice is considered in this country," said the innkeeper MacKitchinson to Mr Jonathan Oldbuck; but the litigants of South Australia were more impatient and grumbled at the "perpetual cur adv vult."

A "consistent and liberal Christian", Sir Charles liked to discourse to the Grand Jury upon the virtues of Sunday Schools, and to point out how the due observance of the Sabbath tended to preserve persons from crime.[4]

His merits were well summed up by the *South Australian Gazette* when the appointment of a second judge was under consideration in 1848:

> 'Though we may get a man of stronger constitution or of more portly appearance, we unquestionably will not get a gentleman who is of more unoffending, more retired, more modest and amiable habits in private life, or who is more anxious to discharge his public duties with punctuality, justice, gentleness and uprightness than Judge Cooper.'

When, at the close of his career and with failing health, he had the misfortune to be brought into conflict with the imperious Mr Justice Boothby, he could not cope with the situation. According to one account, "he was badgered and bullied and was almost sent mad by the obstructiveness of obstinacy" of his colleague.[5] By an honourable retirement on a pension he left to his more vigorous successor, Hanson, the task of endeavouring to keep Mr Justice Boothby within bounds. It is certainly no serious blemish upon Sir Charles Cooper's record that he could not handle Mr Justice Boothby, for that gentleman defied for years the united efforts of his colleagues, Parliament, the press and the public to force him from the bench.

Born at Henley-on-Thames in March 1795, Charles Cooper was entered at the Inner Temple in January 1822, called to the bar in February 1827 and went on the Oxford Circuit until his appointment as Judge in July 1838. He does not appear to have distinguished himself at the bar; the fruits and prospects of ten years' practice could not have been very great if he was willing to relinquish them for a position at £500 a year in a distant and insignificant colony. No doubt he was selected upon Lord Westbury's principle, "Look for a gentleman first, and if he knows a little law, so much the better." Leading barristers were seldom applicants for colonial judgeships.

> 'The Minister takes those whom he can get'—said Lord Brougham—'and when the place suits, rather than those who are suited to the place. A very young barrister, or a barrister who has failed to obtain practice at the bar, is thus sent out, either before he has become fit to practise at the bar (much less to decide as a Judge) or after his unfitness has been ascertained by his failure.'[6]

Lord Chancellors
Both Lord Westbury (Richard Bethel)(1800-1873) and Lord Brougham (Henry Peter Brougham) (1778-1868) became Lord Chancellors and while both were disparaging of colonial judges Westbury is noted for such cutting remarks. He once instructed a solicitor, "You will turn it over once more in what you are pleased to call your mind".

Mr Cooper's first official act was to propound a query to the Colonial Office—whether the laws made by the local legislature of the colony, constituted under 4 & 5 Wm IV c.95, had not been repealed or deprived of authority by virtue of the Act 1 and 2 Vic. c.60, which repealed the provisions of the former act relating to the constitution of the Council in the colony. Again the law officers, Sir John Campbell and Sir R.M. Rolfe (who must by now have been heartily tired of giving opinions upon the legal difficulties of South Australia) were called upon to advise. They reported that the laws made under the authority of 4 & 5 Wm IV c.95 would remain in force.[7]

The Judge, who was not married, was accompanied to the colony by his sister. He sailed in November 1838, and a few glimpses of him during the voyage are to be found in a journal kept by Henry Watson, a fellow passenger—the Judge knocked down and "drenched like a drowned rat" by a wave which came over the poop in the Bay of Biscay; and the Judge reading prayers on Sunday to a pious and attentive audience of passengers and crew, the latter having been devotionally inspired by the mate's threat, "Come, bowl up, bowl up, or I'll stop your grog."[8]

He arrived at Adelaide in March 1839 and Letters Patent under the Seal of the Province were issued constituting and appointing him Judge of the Province.[9] After the Judge had been sworn in, he was introduced to Governor Gawler in a short speech to the leading colonists. The community, the Governor said, was an orderly one; it was true that the gaol was full, but it was a very small one, and its prisoners were mostly runaway sailors and escaped convicts.

> 'With regard to the civil side'—he added—'let us hope that a tendency to frivolous and vexatious litigation will cease among us. In all possible cases let arbitration take the place of litigation. I know that some of the best friends of the colony are very anxious on this subject. I have just received a letter from Mr Angas adverting to it, and strongly urging this course. Frivolous and vexatious litigation is the bane of a new colony.'[10]

The official quarrels, as has been mentioned, faded out in a few libel actions, which were among the first cases the new Judge had to try.[11] No-one was greatly interested in them, and the vexatious litigation of which Governor Gawler complained seemed to have come to an end, when there was a fresh outburst, which to this day presents some unsolved problems. George Milner Stephen was the centre of this storm, which brought about his dismissal from public office and the ruin of his official career.

Stephen had purchased a special survey of 4,000 acres at Port Gawler, which he named the Milner Estate. This purchase seems to have turned his head. His mind became, as Governor Gawler said, "improperly engrossed" in the speculation, and he neglected his official duties in an attempt to make a fortune from the sale of his land. He was of too boastful a nature to conceal his grandiose visions, and the Milner Estate became the subject of public jest. The newspapers referred to it as "that wonderful piece of fairyland, the Mildew Estate situated at Port Brawler", and published *Rhymes to Mildew*.[12]

> 'Do purchasers keep far away?
> Like lonely Selkirk, art thou—say,
> Monarch of all thou did'st survey,
> My Mildew?'

Negotiations took place with two prospective purchasers for the sale of half of the Milner Estate for £10,000. On the night of 12 April 1839, Stephen was at a party at the residence of Rev C.B. Howard, the Colonial Chaplain. Rumours of the sale of the estate had spread, and Stephen was congratulated on the sale at £10,000. He laughingly replied that it was £20,000. Dr Woodford, one of those who heard this, took it as having been said seriously; Mr Howard said that he at first thought it was serious, but afterwards concluded it was merely said by way of joke. On the same night, Stephen went to the office of the *Register* to arrange for the insertion of a government notice. According to Mr W.K. Thomas and two compositors, he there stated that he had sold half the estate for £20,000. He then wrote, at Mr W.K. Thomas's desk, a note announcing the sale. This note was sent to Stevenson, the editor of the *Register*, who wrote a paragraph based on it for the next day's paper, stating the price of half the estate to be £20,000. The announcement aroused considerable interest, but it was soon ascertained that it was not true and that the sum was only £10,000. Stevenson persisted that he had Stephen's authority in the note for stating £20,000. If this was so, then Stephen had been guilty of a deliberate falsehood which could only have been done with the object of exaggerating the value of the remaining half of the land which he was trying to sell.

Dr John Woodforde
(c1806-1866)
The surgeon to Colonel Light's survey party of 1836 and later a practitioner in Adelaide.

The *Southern Australian* published an article stating this as a fact, and also making defamatory comments on Stephen's prior conduct in Van Diemen's Land. Stephen laid an information against MacDougall, the proprietor, for criminal libel. The trial of this action was fixed for Monday, 27 May. On Sunday, 26 May, Stephen went to Stevenson's house and insisted on having his note back, as he wanted it for the trial. Stevenson, who had refused previous requests for its return, reluctantly handed it over, having first obtained Stephen's signature to a copy. In this copy the figure was shown as £20,000. Stephen made no complaint to Stevenson at the time of any alteration, but within an hour or so afterwards he showed the original note to several persons and claimed that Stevenson had altered the figures from £10,000 to £20,000. Some alteration had clearly been made in the first figure, but whether it was a "1" changed into a "2" or vice versa, it was difficult to say.

William Kyffin Thomas
(1821-1878)
The son of Robert Thomas, proprietor of the *Register*. (AGSA)

On MacDougall's trial Stephen conducted his own case and Mann appeared for the defence. In opening, Stephen told the jury that:

> '... from the hour I set foot in this colony I have been the common pacificator; I have prevented many unpleasant collisions — in fact to such an extent have I prevented

unpleasant circumstances occurring that I have been called amicus curiae';

a statement which was hardly the truth, for since his arrival in the colony Stephen had caused more quarrels than he had settled. He gave evidence that he had written £10,000 in the note, but the note was not produced at the trial. The Judge was favourably disposed towards the prosecutor. While his house was being erected he had stayed with Stephen, and a notice in the *Southern Australian* of 1 May 1839 (only a few weeks before the trial) announced that the Judge and the Clerk of the Supreme Court would attend for the transaction of business at Mr Stephen's residence, Halifax Street, from the hours of ten to twelve on Tuesday, Wednesday, Thursday and Friday, until further notice. As he told the jury in summing up:

> 'We are living in a small community with scarcely houses over our heads. I know when I arrived in this colony I had no house to go to, but after I was introduced to Mr Stephen by the Governor, he offered me his house, and I received his kind hospitality.'

But it is hard to believe that he could have concluded, as he is reported in the *Southern Australian*, by directing the jury: "Gentlemen, I have now laid the case before you, and if you are men of common sense you will return a verdict of guilty." [13]

The Judge afterwards complained that he had been grossly misrepresented in the press, and it is to be hoped that the sentence just quoted was not correctly reported. The jury returned a verdict at midnight—of guilty. The small and ill-lit courtroom was packed with an excited crowd, and the Judge postponed sentence.

MacDougall took the next step by attending before Mr Wigley, the Resident Magistrate, to lay an information against Stephen for perjury. Upon this charge Stephen was brought before Wigley and required to give bail for his appearance at the next criminal sittings. He announced in court that he would move the Judge to have Mann, MacDougall's counsel, struck off the roll of practitioners for taking advantage of confidential communications made by him to Mann when the latter was acting as his solicitor. Mann hotly denied the assertion, and "amid the confusion which ensued Mr Stephen retired arm-in-arm with Mr Bernard, the Advocate General".[14]

When MacDougall was called up for sentence, Bernard appeared on behalf of Stephen and said Stephen did not wish a heavy punishment to be inflicted; he asked also that the punishment might be imposed in respect of that part of the libel which referred to his conduct in other colonies and not in respect of the part relating to the Milner Estate. Mann moved for a respite of judgment until after the trial of Stephen for perjury, and he put in affidavits tending to show that Stephen had given false evidence as to the note to Stevenson. Mr Justice Cooper, however, took the view—probably rightly—that since the note was never before the jury in MacDougall's case and its viability was not in issue, the affidavits showed no case of perjury, for even if Stephen had lied about the note it was not on a material part of the case. He accordingly fined MacDougall £50 and ordered him to enter into a recognisance of £300, with two sureties of £150 each, to be of good conduct for 12 months.[15]

Stephen had stirred up a hornet's nest. The *Register*, in a long article, deliberately reiterated the charges against him of altering the note and of giving false evidence in MacDougall's case, and Stephen was compelled to institute proceedings for libel against Thomas, the proprietor, claiming £4,000 damages.

Meanwhile his trial for perjury came on in July. J.W. Bull in his *Early Experiences* recorded that it was almost universally expected that on this charge he would have been found guilty, but from the start Mr Justice Cooper was strongly of opinion that there was nothing in the case. He ruled that most of the evidence tendered was inadmissible. Finally, the foreman of the jury rose and informed the Judge that the jury were so much displeased with the mode of proceedings that they wished to retire from the case altogether. This threw the court into confusion, the onlookers showing their approbation of the conduct of the jury by stamping and applauding. When the uproar had died down and one unlucky person had been committed for contempt, Mann said that as the Judge was against him on every point he would have to give up the case. Mr Justice Cooper thereupon told the jury that, there being no admissible evidence in support of the allegation of perjury, he would discharge them and direct the Clerk of the Court to enter a verdict of not guilty. The jury protested against a verdict being entered when they had not returned one, but the Judge dismissed them and a verdict of not guilty was recorded.[16]

By this time the whole community was tensely interested in the outcome of the litigation. The case of *Stephen v. Thomas* was eagerly awaited, for, as Mr Justice Cooper said, "Upon whomsoever the verdict of guilty fell, it would ruin him for life." Stephen and Mann had become bitter enemies. Mann alleged that Stephen had framed his declaration in the libel action so as to exclude evidence which he knew could be produced against him.

> 'There can be no excuse'—he said—'for keeping back one single fact. Mr Stephen has the choice of his own battlefield and as on that arena must be determined whether he can clear his character any attempt at exclusion of evidence must be fatal to him.' [17]

Stephen on the other hand replied:

> 'You may assure Mr Mann that I will take care that not the title of a fact in this case shall be withheld from the Public. I will

unweave Mr Stevenson's ingenious tale to its uttermost thread before the community. He shall not escape me, though Mr Mann's generous spirit may strive to throw a shield over him.' [18]

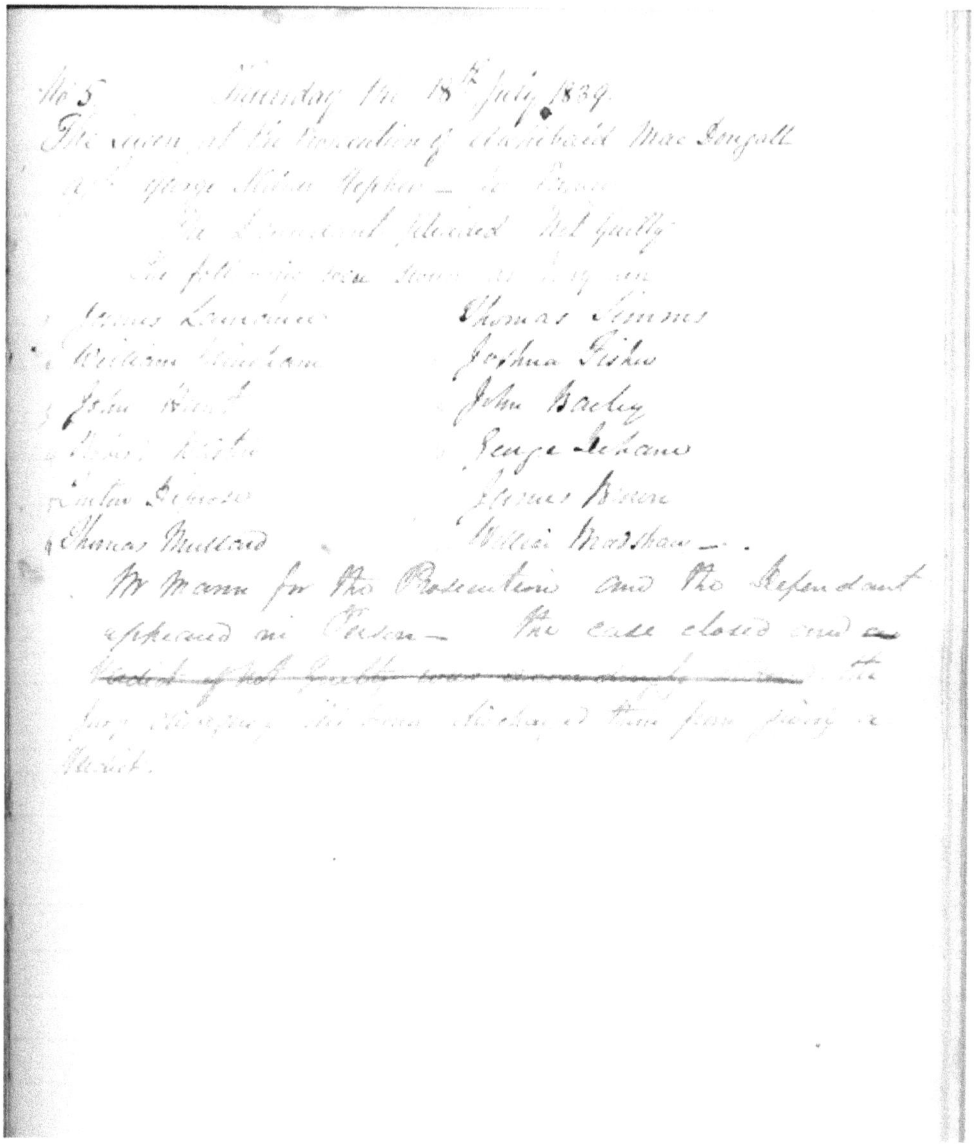

The court record for Stephen's perjury trial. The confusion of events is evident in the recording of the verdict. (SCLSA)

When the trial came on, Stephen conducted his own case and Mann the defence. The plaintiff's case consisted simply of proof of the publication of the article, which was prima facie defamatory. The defence was, in effect, justification, and rested principally on the following points:

(1) The obvious fact that, while Stevenson had no motive to falsify the note, Stephen had the greatest interest to do so.

(2) The statement by Stephen at Howard's party. Stephen did not deny this, but cross-examined to show that it was said by way of a joke.

(3) The evidence of Mr Thomas and the compositors that Stephen had said £20,000 for half the estate. This was weakened on cross-examination of the compositors by the suggestion that he might have said half the estate at the rate of £20,000, but Mr Thomas remained unshaken.

(4) The note, which became the crux of the case. Stevenson swore that the note had been altered after Stephen had taken it back, and he produced the copy certified by Stephen. He said that Stephen had admitted to him next day that £20,000 had been mentioned for the purpose of puffing. There was some rather unsatisfactory evidence of persons to whom Stevenson had shown the note before returning it to Stephen, that it was then £20,000 and showed no signs of alteration, but these witnesses were not confident that it had not been altered.

(5) Finally, the defendant proved that at an informal inquiry which the Governor had held into the matter at Government House, Stephen had proposed that this inquiry by the Governor should be a full and final one and that after the inquiry the Governor should destroy the note. This, it was suggested, showed a guilty conscience.

In answer to this case, Stephen called Governor Gawler and Captain Sturt, two witnesses whose honesty is beyond question and whose testimony is entitled to the highest weight. Both saw the note shortly after Stephen had obtained it from Stevenson, on the day before MacDougall's trial, and both expressed their opinion that the document had been altered from a "1" to a "2" and that the alteration was not recent—the inference, of course, following that Stevenson had made the alteration. The Governor further said that Stephen had told him, prior to the publication in the *Register*, that the sale was at £10,000; so that on reading £20,000 in the *Register* he was considerably surprised, and spoke to Stevenson about it on the same day, and that Stevenson had assured him that "Stephen says so".

Another witness called by Stephen was Robert Bernard, the Advocate-General. He was a personal friend of Stephen, so that where his evidence is against Stephen it is entitled to considerable weight. He was present at an interview between Stevenson and Stephen shortly after the publication of the paragraph in the *Register*, at which, he said, Stevenson taxed Stephen with having deceived him. Stephen replied with "warmth":

> '"Did I not subsequently tell you it was a mistake?" Bernard later obtained from Stevenson a copy of the note, which he gave to Stephen. His evidence on this was: 'On reading the copy I said "Have you written that note, is that your note?" He said in an excited manner, "There is more in that than meets

> the eye". I said, "What do you mean"? He said, "I will never rest until I see the original; it is not correct, and something about Mr Stevenson being a Villain.""

The rest of Stephen's witnesses were devoted to blackening Stevenson's character. Robert Gouger was called, for instance, and gave the following evidence—short but to the point: "I am acquainted with Mr George Stevenson. I would not on any account whatever believe Mr Stevenson on his oath."

In answer to the Judge he expanded this:

> 'My reason for saying I would not believe Mr Stevenson on his oath is on account of his character for want of truth in London and America as well as from particular circumstances which have occurred to myself.'

Fisher gave evidence to the same effect, though not quite so definite.

Stevenson then called further evidence in an attempt, which was not very successful, to show that he could be believed on his oath. His witnesses were Rev C.B. Howard, John Morphett, Henry Jickling, John Barton Hack and John Brown. The last-named qualified his answers to such an extent as to destroy any value his evidence might have; while Hack having been asked in examination-in-chief whether, from his knowledge of Stevenson, he would believe him on his oath and having said "Yes", was asked in cross-examination what knowledge of Stevenson's character he had, and candidly replied, "None."[19]

Reverend Charles Beaumont Howard (1807–1843)
As first colonial chaplain Howard emigrated on the *Buffalo* and earned the respect, if not the universal approval, of settlers through hard work and devotion to his calling. Howard's early death was partly due to the distress he felt at being unable to clear the debt incurred in the building of Trinity Church for which he was responsible. Howard is also noted for his part in two other deaths. He refused to see Light on his deathbed because Light was openly living with his mistress, and he effected the hanging of a bushranger by kicking the condemned man's foot into the open trap door.

The most important evidence, however, was the note itself.

> 'All who were in Court during the trial must remember how that altered document was passed from hand to hand—placed against the window, and in every other point of view—examined by the aid of eye-glasses—and how, at length, the puzzle was unriddled by the introduction of magnifiers of superior power.' [20]

In his summing up the Judge laid great stress on the note and told the jury that their verdict must rest on a decision whether the note had been first written £10,000 or £20,000. They found it was originally £20,000, and their verdict was for the defendant.[21]

This finding was not universally accepted as satisfactory. The Governor wrote that:

> 'Mr Stephen conducted his own cause and did so most inefficiently. Setting aside the general disadvantage of such a proceeding, he was physically unequal to the effort. A considerable body of evidence most important to his side was not produced or elicited.' [22]

It is certainly remarkable that two men of such unquestionable honesty and wide experience as Governor Gawler and Captain Sturt should have been strongly in Stephen's favour. Looking back on the case after the lapse of nearly a century, and without the advantage of seeing the note itself, one piece of evidence seems to stand out as particularly important—that of Bernard as to the interview between Stevenson and Stephen. There was an accusation of deceit by Stevenson, not directly denied by Stephen but met with the answer that it was a mistake. This does not necessarily involve the conclusion that Stephen wrote "£20,000" in the note, but it is, to say the least, suspicious.

The result was made more uncertain by an affidavit which was subsequently sworn by a number of the jurymen that they gave their verdict for the defendant in consequence of their examination of the figures in the note; that they did not closely observe during their examination a certain speck of ink on the altered figure; that they now believed it possible that Stephen had written the figure "2" in the first instance by mistake and immediately altered it to "1", before the ink was dry; and that in such a case Stephen might have conscientiously sworn that he had not written "£20,000" in the note.[23] This affidavit was used by Stephen on an application which he made for a new trial. Mann, appearing for Thomas, opposed this, and Mr Justice Cooper refused to grant it; but Mann said that, having obtained the opinion of the Judge, his client was willing to consent to a new trial upon payment of his costs as between attorney and client.[24] Stephen said he would avail himself of this offer, but shortly afterwards he left the colony. The verdict had damned him in public opinion. He immediately tendered his resignation of his positions as Colonial Secretary and Chairman of the Bench of Magistrates, and the Governor said that, under the circumstances of the verdict of a jury having been given against him in a case which involved "high moral offences", he was bound to accept it.[25]

> 'While so doing, His Excellency contemplates with very deep regret the unhappy circumstances in which you are placed; a sentiment which would not have been called for, had your general conduct been of the same character with that charged upon you by the verdict; but which the Governor is allowed to feel and express when he can at the same time say that your public course, as far as it came under his personal notice, without reference to the unhappy case in question, was peculiarly marked by honor, zeal, intelligence, and good feeling not only as connected with himself, but with the interests of the community at large.' [26]

This unfortunate case, which brought to a disastrous close an official career which had been marked by conspicuous ability, dogged Stephen throughout his life. Its aftermath may be briefly described.

Heligoland
Heligoland is an island of 210 hectares lying in the North Sea to the north west of Germany. Held by the British from 1801 to 1890 and then after World War II it is now part of Germany. While probably best known today for its bird life the island has been an important naval base and features in the history of European and World conflict.

After leaving the colony, Stephen went to England, and upon Captain Hindmarsh (whose daughter he had married) receiving the appointment of Governor of Heligoland, Stephen accompanied him there and acted as Secretary to the Government for some years.[27] He then returned to England and, after keeping the necessary terms, applied to be admitted to the bar. The facts concerning the libel case having been communicated to the benchers of his Inn, they held a close investigation into the matter. Stephen produced 50 testimonials to his character and eventually the benchers certified that he had fully cleared himself and that his honour and integrity were unimpaired, their certificate being based largely upon the opinions of Sir Frederick Thesiger and Sergeant Manning that the verdict in *Stephen v. Thomas* did not necessarily involve the conclusion that Stephen had committed perjury. These gentlemen pointed out that the declaration set out a libel imputing the crime of perjury in direct terms. The plea set up a justification of the allegation of perjury by setting out a statement made on oath by Stephen in MacDougall's case, and alleging that the facts contained in that statement were false—that is, that they were contrary to fact. But in negativing the truth of the statement, the plea omitted to state that those facts were untrue to the plaintiff's knowledge or that he wilfully stated them knowing them to be untrue.

> 'If therefore the plaintiff made the statement under a mistake or from forgetfulness, the issue taken upon the plea would be properly found for the defendants, provided the statement were contrary to the facts as they appeared before the jury, irrespectively of the guilt or innocence of the plaintiff in having made such statements. In this state of things (supposing the publication of the libel to be proved and the plaintiff to be therefore entitled to a verdict upon the plea of not guilty, of which there can be no doubt) he would be entitled, and is now entitled, to judgment non obstante veredicto, and a writ of inquiry to assess his damages. As the case now stands there is the finding of the jury that a statement made by the plaintiff was not founded in fact—a finding perfectly consistent with entire innocence on the part of the plaintiff.' [28]

It would appear, therefore, that Mann's bad pleading procured Stephen's admission to the bar. The opinions of Sir Frederick Thesiger and Sergeant Manning can hardly be said to clear Stephen's character. There was no doubt whatever that the figure in the note had been altered, and the finding of the jury was that it had been altered from £20,000 to £10,000. Upon this finding it seems clear that the only circumstances under which Stephen could have innocently sworn that he did not write £20,000 were those suggested by the affidavit of the jurymen. But this was an explanation which Stephen did not put forward himself, although one would have thought that if he had made a mistake in writing the figures and corrected it, that fact would have recurred to his mind when he saw the note again a short time afterwards.

Following the whitewashing in London, Colonel Gawler wrote to Stephen:

> 'However coldly I may have appeared to look upon you since the painful affair to which these things refer, I have never felt coldly concerning you. I, however, was in a position in which I was bound to show the highest respect for the decision of a Law Court; but I went altogether against my feelings and (as my evidence before that court proved) very much against my convictions. By now becoming acquainted with the ideas of those, who are most competent to form an opinion in such an affair, I am most sincerely rejoiced to be able to congratulate you heartily, on your restoration to that position in society, to which I believe you to be well entitled.' [29]

On this letter the *Register* commented (unjustly, for it is difficult to see what other attitude Gawler could have adopted):

> 'In looking coldly on a person to whom he never felt coldly—whom, therefore, he should have believed innocent—and in reserving his freezing looks for the moment when that individual was submerged beneath a most weighty and solemn verdict, arrived at chiefly by his own subordinates, Colonel Gawler enacted the part of a moral assassin.' [30]

George Milner Stephen (SLSA)

Stephen was called to the bar on 7 November 1845 and he at once applied to the Colonial Office to be restored to the position of Advocate-General in South Australia. The South Australian Company opposed this and urged the Colonial Office to make further inquiries into his past character. Lord Stanley, who was then Secretary of State, informed Stephen that he had considered his testimonials but did not find in them proof that Stephen, either in South Australia or in Van Diemen's Land, had acquired much experience as a barrister, and in England he had had none. He could not turn out the present occupant of the position, Mr Smillie, to put Stephen back.[31] He did, however, send out to Governor Robe the documents relating to the investigation and directed them to be published officially. These documents, however, had already found their way into the local newspaper and, as the Governor wrote, "had given rise to some severe comments which will doubtless be reiterated on the occasion of the official announcement".[32] The facts of the old case were revived at length, and the *Register* stigmatised Stephen's application for the position of Advocate-General by saying that "the extent of his impudence only falls short of infinity".

Stephen returned to South Australia in 1846 and commenced practice in Adelaide. More will be said later of his professional career, but to complete the story of the Stevenson note it is necessary to look forward to 1857. By that time Stephen had left South Australia and had announced himself as a candidate for election to the Victorian Parliament. The Melbourne *Argus* opposed him and alleged that Stephen, having been virtually convicted of perjury and dishonest practices, was unfit to be a member of Parliament. In a series of articles it reprinted the story of the trials eighteen years earlier. Stephen brought an action for libel against Messrs Wilson and Mackinnon, the proprietors of the *Argus*. Once again he conducted his own case, and did so very inefficiently, being frequently reprimanded by the Judge. William Hinde, the Judges' associate, was subpoenaed by the defence to produce the Supreme Court records relating to the case of *Stephen v. Thomas*, including the original note, and he took them to Melbourne. The note was put in as an exhibit, and it may be still on the files relating to the action of *Stephen v. Wilson and Mackinnon*, in the Victorian Supreme Court. Mr Evan Thomas says of the note:

> 'This document became a still more important witness than formerly, for the fading of the ink during a period of eighteen years showed clearly that the alterations were in two different inks, and that the '2' was the first figure written.' [33]

After a trial which lasted five days, and an examination of the note by microscopes, the jury found for the defendants on the ground of justification.

The concurrent findings of two juries, in different colonies and with an intervening lapse of eighteen years, cannot but make a very strong case against Stephen; and if Mr Evan Thomas's account of the revelations made by the fading of the ink is correct, then the case against him is very black indeed. There seems no doubt that Stephen was guilty of "puffing"; Gawler admitted that he thought this. But upon the question whether he wrote £10,000 or £20,000 in the note, there are certain aspects which were never satisfactorily explained. In any event, the transaction was the only blemish upon the official career of a man who rendered very considerable services to the state, and, although Stephen had a number of traits of character which do not inspire admiration, it is impossible not to feel that if he was guilty the punishment which he suffered was out of all proportion to the offence.

Charles Cooper by J.M. Crossland, ca. 1853 (AGSA)

Sir Charles Cooper

A second judge

Sir Charles Cooper's long term of office was marked by singularly few events of legal importance.

In 1840 he spent three months in New South Wales, Bernard being appointed Acting Judge during his absence.[1] On his return, the Judge settled down to an uneventful routine, punctuated only by occasional outbursts of hostility from the *Register.* It was to be regretted, said this paper, that the administration of justice in the colony did not possess the confidence of the profession nor the respect of the community. "The singularly crotchety character of His Honor, and the remarkable dicta he occasionally educes, contribute to these results." [2]

And on another occasion, after criticising the number of new trials in the Supreme Court, it gloomily speculated whether they were due to the uncertainty of the law, to the recklessness of suitors and advocates, or to a want of firmness and vigour on the part of the Judge. So unsatisfactory was the position, it was said, that representations ought to be at once made to the Colonial Office.[3]

In matters of opinion no reliance whatever can be placed upon the journalism of early days. Mr Dutton, in his *South Australia and its Mines* (published in 1846) gave a very different view.[4] "I must not omit to record"—he writes—"the very universal estimation in which our worthy and amiable Judge is held in the colony."

William Ewart Gladstone (1809-1898)
A British liberal politician who was Secretary of State from 1845 to 1846 and, more notably, Prime Minister on four occasions (1868-74, 1880-85, 1886 and 1892-94). The caricature is by Harry Furniss (NPG)

Two events call for notice during the year 1846. The first is interesting not in itself but in the comments which it evoked from Mr Gladstone, who was then Secretary of State for the colonies. An application had been made to the Supreme Court for an injunction to restrain the Government from selling certain land, in derogation, it was claimed, of the plaintiffs' title acquired under a preliminary land order. The application was resisted by the Government, and was refused. The Secretary of State sharply rebuked the Governor for the course he had taken.

> 'It is fortunate'—he said—'that such was the decision of the Court. An opposite judgment might have raised many embarrassing difficulties. But I cannot sanction the course which you followed in this case. By appearing, or permitting any officer of the Crown to appear, in defence of such a suit, you virtually acknowledged that the head of the local Government was amenable to the jurisdiction of the courts of the colony which he governs. It does not follow that because the question of jurisdiction was not discussed on this occasion, it was therefore not decided or compromised. On the contrary, the absence of any such discussion, resulting as it did from the

> absence on your part of any such objection, was a clear though tacit acknowledgment that the asserted jurisdiction really existed. I object to that acknowledgment, not on any ground of mere dignity, or usage, or precedent, but because thus to break down the barriers which separate the judicial and administrative authorities must result in great practical evils. The immunities of the Sovereign in this country, and the corresponding immunities of a Governor in the colony he rules, exist for the good of the people at large. If it were admitted that you, as Governor of South Australia, were amenable to the courts of the colony, you would of course be liable to fine, to distress, and imprisonment at their bidding. Nor can I omit to notice that a Colonial Jury might, however unconsciously, be under a strong bias against a Governor, in the character of a defendant, especially when they understood, or supposed, that the British Treasury would be really responsible. I must therefore desire that the precedent which has been established in this case be avoided in all future cases, and that no act be done (except with the express previous sanction of her Majesty's Government) from which it could be inferred that you are amenable to the jurisdiction of any court in South Australia so long as you retain her Majesty's Commission for the administration of the government of that colony.' [5]

It was, as Hodder pointed out, somewhat singular that Governor Robe should have overlooked this point, for he held the title only of Lieutenant-Governor, Governor Grey being continued formally in the office of Governor, notwithstanding his transfer to New Zealand, for the express purpose of protecting him against certain threatened proceedings arising from the dishonour of bills drawn by him in payment of government liabilities.[6]

(Sir) George Grey (1812-1898)
Only twenty-seven years old when he became Governor in 1841, Grey was driven by ambition and had no need for popular approval. This allowed him to introduce stringent, and unpopular, economies and maintain views that conflicted with those of progressive minded South Australians. Yet as the colony's fortunes improved, largely through the discoveries of copper and improving harvests, so did opinions of Grey. By the time he left for New Zealand in 1845 he was held in high regard.

At the Civil Sessions in September 1846, only one case was set down for trial, and the plaintiff did not appear. This being the first (and probably the only) maiden sittings of the Supreme Court, the old practice was observed of the sheriff presenting the Judge with a pair of white gloves.

> 'We hope the observance of this ancient custom will not be lost sight of'—said the Register—'showing as it does that our colonies are far too profitably employed to be wasting their time and substance in ruinous litigation.' [7]

Although of no great legal interest, *The Queen v. Paxton and Others* (heard in July 1848) was probably the most important decision of Mr Justice Cooper. It arose out of the attempted imposition by Governor Robe of a royalty on minerals, a step which aroused very great excitement and antagonism in the colony. Without going into the details of the protracted struggle between the Governor and the people upon this subject, it is sufficient to say that the Governor, under instructions from England, promulgated regulations securing to the Crown a royalty or seignorage of one-fifteenth upon all minerals raised from lands alienated from the Crown. The Secretary of State (Lord Stanley) and the law officers in England advised that the regulations were authorised by the Imperial Waste Lands Act.[8]

The colonists of South Australia did not agree. It was an opportunity for the local press to excel itself, and columns of vituperation streamed forth. The express non-reservation of minerals by the Crown in all land grants, it was contended, was one of the constitutional rights of the settlers, who had been induced to purchase their land at £1 per acre upon the understanding that the Crown utterly relinquished its claim to everything above or below the surface.[9] A monster public meeting was called.

> 'A DETERMINED STAND is to be made against Lord Stanley's last, greatest, and most specious attempt to rob South Australia of her boasted rights and privileges. BRITONS, STRIKE HOME!' [10]

The meeting resolved with fervour that the imposition of royalties was illegal, unjust and impolitic; and Lord Stanley and his legal advisers were the target of abuse.

> 'Oh, how I wish those lawyers would come here'—cried Mr Morphett. 'Thesiger (or the man with the hard name, as he is called) and Fitzroy Kelly! I wish they would present themselves in the Supreme Court before Judge Cooper! That respected functionary would soon send them to the right about; they would soon find they had the wrong pig by the ear.' [11]

The feeling in the colony upon the vexed question was extraordinary. At the dinner given to celebrate the return of Captain Sturt from his explorations, after honouring the loyal toasts, three hearty groans were given for Lord Stanley.[12]

In September 1846 the Governor introduced into the Legislative Council a bill to regulate and secure the collection of the mineral royalties.[13] The four non-official members opposed; the Governor and the three official members supported it. The Governor, having a casting vote, was able to sway the balance. A motion that the bill be read in six months' time having been lost on the Governor's casting vote, the four non-official members rose and walked out of the chamber, amid the cheers of the spectators, thus leaving the Council without a quorum and powerless to act.[14] A memorandum by Mr T.S. O'Halloran, one of the members, has survived, and indicates the determined stand which he and his colleagues were prepared to take:

'Proposed that:

1. All the N.O. members be present at future meetings on the Royalties Bill.
2. That we divide the Council at every stage of the Bill, and upon every point, as often as possible, by varying the form of amendments upon each and every section and paragraph so as to force a continual recourse to the Lt Governor's Casting Vote.
3. That we divide the Council on the 3rd Reading.
4. And then individually record our Protest in the Minutes of the Council.
5. Then individually retire, as before, so as to prevent the third reading from taking place.
6. To resign.' [15]

Thomas Shuldham O'Halloran (1797-1870) O'Halloran served in the British Army for over twenty years before arriving in Adelaide in 1838 and settling on the hill that bears his name. Appointed the first Commissioner for Police in 1840 he became a major protagonist in the *Maria/Milmenrura* affair. Resigning as Commissioner in 1843 he began a lengthy political career with appointment to the Legislative Council the same year. He is also noted for his farming pursuits. (SLSA)

Faced with a deadlock, the Governor wrote to Mr O'Halloran:

> 'In consequence of the very marked manner in which you yesterday, apparently by preconcerted arrangement with the other non-official members of the Legislative Council, abandoned your seat at the Council Board at a time when your services were eminently required by the Governor, in fulfilment of your duty to the Queen, His Excellency has been impelled to request that you will intimate, without loss of time, whether it be your intention to pursue the like course in reference to the Royalties Bill at the next or any subsequent meeting of Council.' [16]

Mr O'Halloran replied:

> 'Until an Act of the Imperial Parliament has been passed authorizing the levying of Royalties in South Australia, I shall consider it my duty as an independent member of the Legislature of this Province, to oppose by every constitutional means in my power any Colonial enactment having for its object the introduction of (according to my conscientious belief) an illegal, obnoxious, and most impolitic measure. From the above clear and explicit statement it will of course be understood by His Excellency that I am prepared if necessary to retire from the Council board whenever the Royalty Bill is again introduced for adoption.' [17]

Under these circumstances the Governor had no option but to give way and authorise the withdrawal of the obnoxious bill.

The regulations, however, still stood; and the proprietors of the Adelaide Mine having neglected to set aside the one-fifteenth for the Crown and refusing to give any account of minerals raised, the

Government proceeded against them in the Supreme Court to recover the royalty. The defendants contended there was no authority for the imposition of the royalty. The Advocate-General and Jickling appeared for the Government; Fisher, Gwynne and Hanson for the defendants. After a long argument, judgment was given for the defendants, the Judge expressing his relief at the knowledge that, whichever way he decided, the case would be taken to the Privy Council.[18] The Government busied themselves in starting proceedings for appeal "with every despatch";[19] but when Governor Young arrived, in August 1848, he at once reversed the policy of his predecessor and discontinued the royalty. Mr Justice Cooper's decision thus ceased to have any practical value, and the appeal was abandoned.

The year 1848 also saw the commencement of a remarkable period in South Australian history which has been distinguished by the name of the Libel Era. The scurrility of the local journalism had inevitably led to a prevalence of actions for defamation, but during 1848 and 1849 the Supreme Court was almost overwhelmed by them.[20] The greater part were launched against Mr John Stephens, the proprietor of the *Register* and *Observer*, who was sorely pressed financially by the cost of defending them. He was on the eve of suspending publication of his papers, "but his friends rallied round him, and he was tided over the difficulty". Even more bitter than the actions against Stephens were the disputes between Mr Torrens (then Collector of Customs) and George Stevenson (who was editing the *Gazette and Mining Journal*) which reached a dramatic climax when the former horsewhipped the editor.

John Stephens (1806-1850)
Brother to Edward and Samuel, John arrived in South Australia in 1843. His radical reformist views and incautious journalism, partly based on the view that "certain moral felonies were punishable only through the medium of the press", ensured his career was controversial. It was also a great strain on his health and contributed to his early death.

In few cases were the plaintiffs successful. In seven of the actions, for instance, the damages claimed totalled £12,950, while the only verdicts recovered were for one shilling, and a penny. In *Ryan v. Stephens*, in November 1848, the decision went against the *Register*, and the disappointed newspaper was not slow to express its disgruntled opinion of Mr Justice Cooper:

> 'With regard to the Judge, we feel ourselves somewhat at a loss. But we trust, that though suffering from his conduct, we shall be able to restrain ourselves within due bounds. His indecent interruption of our counsel, and his undisguised advocacy of the plaintiff's case, for his so-called summing up was throughout a speech in favour of the plaintiff, even more one-sided than that of Mr Gwynne, reflect no credit upon the administration of justice in the colony. Our readers will remember that this is the second time within the course of a little more than two months, that the Judge has availed himself of the immunities of his position to insult gentlemen who were precluded from the power of replying to him.'

After praising the noble conduct of its counsel, Mr Hanson, who had adopted "an attitude of dignified defiance", the *Register* concluded:

> 'We fear that at least when the Press is concerned, impartiality cannot be expected from Mr Justice Cooper. He has been too long in the colony alone. Oh, for a second Judge!'

The wish expressed by the *Register* had already been expressed, for more creditable reasons, on various occasions. The appointment of a second judge of the Supreme Court was first publicly mooted in July 1846 by Mr John Morphett in the Legislative Council. Governor Robe was willing for a bill to be laid before the Council for this purpose, although he stipulated that it should contain a clause suspending its operation until approved in England. He was anxious to make some change in the constitution of the Court of Appeals and thought another judge might provide a satisfactory solution by enabling a Court of Appeal to be constituted of the two judges. Mr Justice Cooper, too, had expressed a desire for the appointment of another judge to relieve him of the sole responsibility of decision.[55]

Frederick Holt Robe (1802-1871)
Governor from 1845 to 1848, Robe was a reluctant appointee whose only administrative experience was as an army officer. His Governorship was coloured by his limitations and problems arising from such issues as mineral royalties and state aid to religion.

In the following month Mr Morphett moved that the salary of Mr Justice Cooper should be raised from £800 to £1,000 a year, and that another judge should be appointed. It would be eighteen months before a judge could be sent out, and by that time the increase in the business of the Supreme Court and the probability of circuit courts being held would have rendered the assistance of a second judge necessary. Even if the work of the Court was not so great as to require a second judge, he considered it advisable that the decisions of the Judge should be subject to appeal in a more satisfactory way.[56]

A resolution embodying Mr Morphett's motion was sent to England, but the only result was that the Colonial Office sent out an Assistant Surveyor.

Nothing further was done until 1849. At the beginning of that year the Judge was seized with a severe attack of influenza which left him, as he said, "shattered" by want of sleep and in "a state of distressing nervous irritability". He applied for three months' leave of absence to recover his strength, and it became necessary for an acting judge to be appointed.[57] Public attention was thus again directed to the need of a second judge. One writer indulged himself in a mechanistic fancy:

> 'Suppose the Judge'—he said—'never ill, never tired, never needing relaxation, never longing for a moment's rest; let *him* be a sort of legal steam engine, capable of unceasing work, and constructed so that he can labour with mechanical and unerring accuracy; admit him to possess all the modern improvements; and, by way of scientifically describing him, let us say that with moderate consumption of one thousand pounds of fuel per annum, we have an engine of a dozen lawyer power, each lawyer being estimated as able to involve

> thirty-three thousand colonists in a suit a minute; suppose all this—what are we to do to meet the extending claims of fifty thousand people, increasing in litigation as the increase in wealth?' [58]

The Governor reported to the Colonial Office that the appointment of another judge would be:

> '... highly conducive to the good of the public service, and is a measure more necessary now than it was in 1846 owing to the progress of the community since that date'.

It would mean, he thought, the restoration to the Supreme Court of many important functions in the administration of justice which were given to the Resident Magistrate, whose jurisdiction he considered to be "too high and weighty".[59]

There was considerable speculation as to who should be the Acting Judge. A high-minded and capable man, said the *South Australian*, would not throw up his clients for the sake of "a transitory honor and a scanty emolument". Those few barristers who had claims for consideration were all engaged in cases about to come before the Court.

> 'Must we then descend and place a briefless barrister upon the Bench? We would sooner adopt the old form of legal fiction which required litigants to appear before the King himself at Westminster; and request Her Majesty's representative to dole out in person justice at least—if not law.' [60]

The Judge recommended Mann, the Master of the Court; no other competent practitioner, he thought, would be willing to take the position for three months on half pay. Mann had "long ceased to be connected with politics", and was "a gentleman of considerable ability and acquirements and moreover of unimpeachable honor and integrity and good moral character".[61]

Mann was accordingly appointed, and was informed by the *South Australian Gazette* that he would be successful if he curbed:

> '... his natural fondness for abstruse disquisitions—for tracing principles and remote causes—while effects and practical deductions are more germane to the matter, and at all times more fitting for the terse and commendable brevity of the Bench'. [62]

Mr Justice Cooper went to Van Diemen's Land to recuperate, and returned to his duty in August 1849. He was welcomed back to the bench by "as nice a dish of libel cases as any Judge was ever set down to"—eight of them.

> 'It is pretty clear'—said the Register (itself one of the principal offenders) — 'that the tongue of slander is as blatant and

> mischievous as ever in South Australia, and the seeds of litigation uneradicable in our little community. We are sorry to add that the only consolation the lawyers offer (cunning rogues) is, that when litigation is on the rise, there is lots of money.'[63]

Overpowered by the prospect, the Judge promptly took to his bed again, and Mann's appointment had to be continued for several months longer.

As a judge, Mann proved capable and was extremely popular. The *Adelaide Times* wrote enthusiastically:

> 'From Mr Mann's love of dealing with metaphysical abstractions, and from his known discursive flights, we confess we were not without our fears, when he first appeared as Judge Cooper's substitute; but no one supposed him capable of any littleness of mind or of any tendency to be warped in his decisions by little partialities or dislikes; and as to that about which our fears had been exercised, it seemed to be all a passing dream, so instantaneously was the close metaphysician and the ardent and glowing advocate metamorphosed into the grave, sober-minded, astute and painstaking Judge.'[64]

There was a considerable agitation that a second judge should be appointed, and that Mann should be chosen.

> 'Many of Judge Cooper's decisions'—said the Register—'would have been acquiesced in more readily, had the disappointed suitors felt assured that His Honor enjoyed a perfect freedom from all outward influence, and consequent independence of thought and action.'[65]

A better and more popular step than Mann's elevation to the bench could not be taken, said the *South Australian*: "... if there is a dissentient opinion in the province, we call upon the holder thereof now to speak or for ever to be silent".

Their call does not appear to have evoked any response.[66]

In the estimates for 1850, the Legislative Council made provision for a second judge at £800 a year and a Crown Solicitor at £500. Mr John Morphett recalled that when the resolution of 1846 had been sent home, all they had got was an Assistant Surveyor, and "in order to prevent such trifling with the wants and wishes of the colonists" he thought it would be advisable for the Governor to appoint a local barrister to be second judge, and apply to the home government for confirmation of the appointment. Since there was general satisfaction at the way in which Mann had discharged his judicial duties, he should be selected for appointment.[67]

The Governor, however, had decided that the appointment ought to be made in England. An objection to the appointment of a local practitioner was that almost of necessity he had in the colony his friends, prejudices and animosities; whereas a judge imported from England should not only be free from anything of that kind but should also be acquainted with all the latest developments in the law at home. In his *Report on Judicial Affairs at the Cape of Good Hope*, in 1826, Mr J.T. Bigge had stressed the importance of the appointment of British advocates to colonial judgeships:

> 'Without any disparagement to the gentlemen who now fill the ranks of the Bar in this colony"—he wrote—"it is not to be expected that they will suddenly relinquish the professional doctrines and opinions which all of them have learned to cherish and respect, and that however fit in other respects, they can be expected to divest themselves on the Judicial Seat of the local influence and partialities, the absence of which constitutes the brightest excellence of the English Judicial character.' [68]

Sir Henry Young had a further reason for desiring the appointment of an English barrister, inasmuch as earlier in the year G.M. Stephen had lodged an application for the office of second judge.[69] Mr Justice Cooper had no liking for the prospect of such an ebullient colleague, and the Governor reported to the Colonial Office that:

> 'Judge Cooper sought an interview with me for the express purpose of stating his opinion that the Public Service would best be promoted by the selection of an additional Judge for the Bench of South Australia being made in England, an opinion in which I entirely concur.' [70]

Sir Henry Edward Fox Young
(1803-1870)
The first civilian Governor of South Australia's record in the position is a chequered one. Assured popularity by the mineral royalty decision, which he delivered but did not make, he also approved fortuitous strategies to cope with the problems created by the Victorian gold rush, but only after considerable persuasion. In attempting to stimulate the Murray River trade he had some small successes although the Port Elliott railway project, which was part of those endeavours, was a failure. He left the province to become Governor of Tasmania in 1855. (SLT)

William Smillie (1810-1852) A devout Scottish lawyer who served as Advocate General from 1843 until his death.

Following the discussion in the Legislative Council, rumours flew round that Smillie, the Advocate-General, was to be raised to the bench and that Stephen would be given the position of Advocate-General. The *Adelaide Times* asserted that there was no truth in the rumours. It was unbelievable that the Governor could be so ill advised as to make either of these appointments.

> 'We undertake to say, that were the Colony searched through and through, two persons could hardly be found more unfitted for the offices of Puisne Judge and Advocate General. The bare mention of it, in fact, has already excited a murmur of universal discontent.'

Colonists could have no confidence in such appointments, and would meet them with "an unmistakeable demonstration of public disapprobation".

> 'The terms on which Mr Smillie has so long stood, and on which he continues to stand, with the great bulk of the colonists, must, with every right-headed man, be accounted a sufficient disqualification for the office of Judge. Caesar's wife must not only be blameless, but above suspicion. A Judge must not only be free from partialities and dislikes, and other indications of littleness of mind, in pronouncing his decisions; but to make the administration of justice palatable, he must be above the suspicion of acting under the influence of any such feelings.' [71]

On the other hand, the *Register* announced that official intimation of the elevation of the Advocate-General to the bench might be daily expected, and that it was this expectation alone which had prevented the Governor:

> '... from maintaining the credit of the ermine, doing honour to his own judgment, and an act of justice to Mr Mann, by appointing that gentleman to the office of Puisne Judge, in accordance with the general wish of the colonists and the express recommendation of the Legislative Council ... To expect that Mr Mann can 'cry content' to the appointment of another to that dignity, and fall back into the dull routine-duty of the Master of the Court, after 'his bright but brief career' upon the Bench, would be to suppose him
>
> 'Dull as that fat weed that grows on
> Lethe's banks',
>
> or dead to
>
> 'The stirrings of genius, the music of fame'.

> 'Better for the public service—better for his own reputation—that he threw up the paltry appointment, and entered anew the arena where talents such as he is known to possess will be more justly appreciated and more adequately rewarded.' [72]

Morning after morning the press came forward with conflicting predictions:

> 'With all their flippant fluency of tongue,
> Most confident, when palpably most wrong'.

Mann had proved himself "an enlightened, upright and just Judge", and a memorial in favour of his appointment as Judge was prepared, setting out that:

> '... the increased and increasing duties of this high office as at present constituted, and the perplexing and multifarious business of a court embracing in one the various jurisdictions carefully separated in the mother country, imperatively demand such a measure; no single individual, however great his talent, or whatever the strength of his powers of mental energy, being able to meet the unremitting demands upon him'. [73]

Mann himself, however, had no hopes of becoming Judge. Knowing that the judges were appointed from England, he said, he did not even apply for the position; but asked for that of Crown Solicitor, his health being sufficiently recovered to enable him to cope with general practice. Smillie reported in his favour, and he was appointed Crown Solicitor at the beginning of 1850.[74]

While the Secretary of State was agreeable to the appointment of another judge, he pointed out a legal difficulty. The original Supreme Court Act (No. 5 of 1837) had provided that the Court was to be held before "the Judge of the Supreme Court". The appointment of another judge was not contemplated.

> "It appears therefore that Her Majesty cannot regularly appoint a second Judge, unless a Charter of Justice were first issued, which I do not think it expedient to advise at present."

Either the appointment must be delayed while an act was passed by the Legislative Council providing for another judge, or a judge must be appointed provisionally, in reliance upon the local legislature passing an act immediately. He adopted the latter alternative, and appointed George John Crawford, an advocate of the courts of Ireland.[75]

Three months before the Secretary of State's dispatch was written, the Legislative Council, at Mr Justice Cooper's suggestion, had removed the difficulty by passing the Ordinance No 12 of 1849,

Dr George John Crawford (1812-1852) (SCLSA) Only two Supreme Court judges in South Australia have held LLD's. The other is John Bray (1912-1995)

providing that the Supreme Court should be held by or before one or more Judges, appointed or to be appointed by Her Majesty.[76]

Mr Justice Crawford was the third son of Rev George Crawford, Rector of Newtown Forbes and Vicar-General of the Diocese of Armagh, County Longford, Ireland, and was born at Longford in 1812. He was entered at Trinity College, Dublin at the age of 15, being, like Jeffcott, a "pensioner". He took the degree of BA in 1833, was called to the Irish bar in Hilary Term 1840, and received the degrees of LLB and LLD in 1846. He joined the Connaught bar, where he principally confined himself to the equity side. He had a powerful connection in his uncle, John Beatty West QC, who was MP for Dublin and one of the leading Irish politicians of his day. Crawford assisted his uncle in his political campaigns, notably against Daniel O'Connell for the representation of Dublin, and was himself pressed to stand as a candidate for his native county of Longford. For some years he managed his uncle's estates, near Eyre Court, so judiciously and with such kindness that the tenantry, it was said, never mentioned his name without invoking a blessing on him.

> 'For the sake of his wretched country'—said an Irish newspaper when he left for South Australia—'we regret that a gentleman who has already given so many proofs of his usefulness and his benevolence to the poor should leave Ireland.' [77]

When it was decided to appoint a second judge in South Australia, the right to nominate to the office was held by the Irish executive under a system which Crawford, by the publication of an article entitled *A Voice from the Bar*, had himself helped to bring about, whereby vacancies in colonial appointments were filled in turn from England and Ireland.

He arrived in South Australia by the *Midlothian* on 27 June 1850, with his wife and three children, and was shortly afterwards entertained at a "dejeuner a la fourchette" given to him by 24 members of the bar at the Freemason's Hotel. From this Mr Crawford retired "evidently gratified with his entertainers, a feeling which is highly reciprocated by the profession".[78]

Mr Justice Crawford's first appearance in court was at the Criminal Sessions in August 1850, when, it was reported: "... His Honor appeared in the wig judicial, which certainly added to his dignity, while it in no degree detracted from the comeliness of his appearance". [79]

This appears to be the first occasion on which a wig was worn by a South Australian Judge in the Supreme Court. In the banco sittings later in the same month, Mr Justice Cooper also appeared in a wig, and the custom has continued to the present day.

Crawford was strikingly handsome in appearance. In an age when judges' portraits were composed chiefly of shaggy eyebrows and side-whiskers, his picture shows him as clean-shaven, bright-eyed, almost boyish in appearance. Possessed of a personality of singular charm, he carried all before him in Adelaide. Mr Justice Cooper was nearly sixty years old, he had been away from England for over twelve years, and he was constitutionally timid and conservative. Mr Justice Crawford was enthusiastic and energetic, mentally and physically, and his generous tendencies of mind and natural inclinations towards law reform, fostered by his familiarity with reform at home and his practice in Ireland, where technicalities were never so rife as in England, formed a refreshing contrast to the more sedate habits of his colleague.

It was a tragedy for the colony that Crawford died, on 24 September 1852, at the early age of forty, after only two years in the colony, during the latter part of which he was incapacitated by a prolonged illness. His loss, as Sir Henry Young wrote, was "deeply and justly regretted".

> 'During his service of about two years, there was recognised in him some of the most suitable qualifications of a good Judge. Calmness, patience, firmness, diligence, quick perception, and uprightness, invariably characterised his judicial conduct. In his private and domestic relations he was full of amiability. In addition to these intrinsic merits, he possessed the adventitious but important advantage of being universally respected and esteemed.' [80]

His extraordinary popularity in the colony was shown by the attendance of thousands at his funeral—a cortege two miles long—the largest which the colony had seen; and the *Register,* in some crude but sincere "Lines suggested by the lamented death of Judge Crawford", voiced the general feeling of the community:

> 'Our country lov'd thee! In this favour'd land
> Thou hast dealt out justice with an even hand;
> And though thy sojourn with us short hath been,
> Yet have thy virtues by all men been seen,
> While many in private life have known
> The kindness by thy noble nature shown'. [81]

His untimely death was alike disastrous in that it deprived the colony of a judge whose talents and qualities were of the highest order, and in that it led to the appointment of Benjamin Boothby as his successor.

Following Mr Justice Crawford's death, Mr Hare moved in the Legislative Council that an address be presented to the Governor asking that the vacancy in the office of second judge be filled immediately from the members of the profession in the colony. The highest offices in the public service, he said, ought to be filled from among the colonists; and there were men of virtue and of the highest talents in the profession.

> 'South Australia is for South Australians, and should not be made the wash-pot of the mother country. I see gentlemen around me, who are bringing up their sons to the legal profession, and their energies ought not to be paralysed by finding closed against them the door of admission to the highest seat of justice here.'

The motion was opposed on the grounds that a second judge was not immediately necessary and that it would be an interference with the prerogative of the Crown; and it was lost.[82]

There were several local applicants for the position—Mann, Hanson and M.J. Martyn, an Irish barrister who had recently emigrated to the colony. The Governor wrote, in September 1852:

> 'The decrease of business in the Supreme Court, consequent on the great withdrawal of Population to the adjacent gold fields of Victoria, renders it unnecessary, in my opinion, that the vacancy caused by Mr Crawford's death should be supplied immediately on the spot, and therefore I do not intend to make any provisional appointment.'

By the time a judge was appointed and sent out from England, however, his services would be required. The Colonial Office selected Mr Justice Boothby, and he arrived in the colony in August 1853.[83]

A copy of correspondence regarding Paxton's Case from Justice Cooper's letter book, revealing his concern about the case. (SCLSA)

Sir Charles Cooper

Titles, salaries and pensions

Although both Sir John Jeffcott and Sir Charles Cooper were from very early days frequently styled "Chief Justice", even in Acts of Parliament, the title was not legally created until 1856. Mr Justice Cooper had asked for it in 1844, without result.[1] When Mr Justice Crawford was appointed, the Judges were styled "First Judge" and "Second Judge". In 1853, Mr Justice Boothby, with an eye to his future prospects, recommended that the senior Judge should be called Chief Justice and that his successor in that office should be nominated thereto by the Crown. The title of Chief Justice, he said, was given to the head of the Supreme Court in all the other Australian colonies, and in every British colony where there was more than one judge.[2]

A Select Committee of the Legislative Council appointed in the same year to consider the Civil List Bill also advised that the designations of Chief Justice and Puisne Judge should be substituted for First and Second Judge. The Colonial Secretary having expressed doubt whether the Council had power to alter the Judge's title, "it being the especial prerogative of Her Majesty to appoint a Chief Justice", nothing followed these recommendations.[3] Although mentioned on one or two occasions, the subject languished until the consolidating Supreme Court Act was before Parliament in 1856. Mr Hanson, the Advocate-General, had not included in the Bill any provision for the alteration of the Judge's title, partly because he was frightened of producing a hostile discussion in the House and partly because he thought that the government should not introduce a bill to give a title which the Crown had not thought fit to confer. The Legislative Council, however, inserted such a clause in the Bill, and at the next meeting of the Executive Council the Governor administered a stinging rebuke to the Advocate-General.

> 'A timid apprehension of displeasing this and that person'—he said—'soon brings a government into contempt and makes ghosts out of what when boldly approached turn out to be merely posts.'

It was quite usual, the Governor added, for the titles of judges to be conferred by colonial acts: "I believe the designation of Principal Judge of the Supreme Court of the Colony is a matter of public policy." [4]

Section 1 of the Act No 31 of 1855-56 provided that the Supreme Court should be held before one or more judges to be appointed by the Governor in Council, one of whom should have the title of Chief Justice, and that Charles Cooper Esquire should be the first Chief Justice.

Although Mr Justice Boothby had been one of the first to suggest the creation of the title of Chief Justice, and although he displayed no reluctance to assume the title of Acting Chief Justice while his colleague was on leave in 1857, yet when he failed to secure the position for himself on Sir Charles Cooper's retirement, his views suddenly altered. In his evidence before the Select Committee of the House of Assembly in August 1861 he had said:

> 'I would remark on the great mistake made by the Government and others, as to the Judges; it would seem as though the other Judges are regarded as inferior in power and functions to the Chief Justice. Correspondence goes on between the Government and the Chief Justice, and I know nothing at all about the matter, until it has been decided ... In this Colony the Chief Justice can do nothing which the other Judges cannot do. The duties are precisely the same. It is merely a title given to the headship of the Supreme Court, and the Chief Justice is simply primus inter pares.' [5]

Subsequently, however, he contended that there was no such thing as a Chief Justice at all, the Act No 31 of 1855-56 being invalid, and he attempted to take for himself the title of Senior Judge.

Mr Justice Cooper's financial position had gradually improved as the colony progressed. The original salary of £500 a year was miserably inadequate. Mr T.F. Elliott, one of the colonisation Commissioners, when giving evidence before the Select Committee of the House of Commons, was asked how the salaries in South Australia compared with those in the neighbouring colonies, and replied:

> 'Very low. Amongst the other officers I would particularly specify the Judge. It is most painful to know, as we do, how much the Judge is underpaid, and to have no means of remedying the evil.' [6]

Mr Justice Cooper complained about his salary soon after his arrival and asked for an increase. "I find it utterly inadequate"—he wrote—"in the now condition of the colony to give me a decent subsistence."

He had been induced to apply for the position, he said, by being informed that it was the intention of the Colonisation Commissioners to make a general increase in the salaries of the colonial officers. Although the Judge ranked next to the Governor, yet Lieutenant Frome, who had been sent out from England as Surveyor-General, had a salary of £800, and it was both anomalous and degrading to have an officer inferior in rank receiving nearly double the salary. He pointed out that in Van Diemen's Land the Chief Justice received £1,500 and the Puisne Judge £1,200.[7]

In forwarding the Judge's complaint to the Colonial Office, Governor Gawler wrote:

> 'So confident am I of the correctness of the statement made in it regarding the inadequacy of the salary of which His Honour is now in receipt for the clearance of his reasonable expenses, that I have had in serious contemplation the propriety of increasing it before I can receive instructions from the Commissioners. His Honour's habits are far from extravagant, he is extremely sensitive with regard to the duty of living free from debt, and it might be productive of much evil if an individual of his station were left for a twelve-month in embarrassing and doubtful circumstances.'[8]

A few months later the Governor took upon himself, without instructions, the responsibility of increasing the Judge's salary to £700.

In 1839 the Government rented, for use as a courthouse, part of the house erected by the Judge in Whitmore Square. Several years later, when he had under consideration the removal of the courthouse from Whitmore Square, Governor Grey proposed to compensate the Judge for his loss of rental by raising his salary to £800.

> 'I feel convinced'—he reported to Lord John Russell in 1841—'from the character of the Judge, from the assistance which he ever readily affords to the Government, and from the amount of remuneration which legal men obtain here in private practice, that £800 is not too high a rate of remuneration for the Judge of the Province.'[9]

This increase was sanctioned by the authorities at home in the following year, after an urgent request by the Judge that if circumstances would not permit of his salary being considerably raised, he might be appointed to one of the neighbouring colonies or to the Cape of Good Hope, should any vacancy occur.

> 'I have every reason to consider it a fortunate circumstance for the Colony'—said Grey—'that a gentleman possessing so much integrity and ability has filled the responsible post which he occupies.'[10]

Under the original Supreme Court Act, the Judge had been given, on a small scale, a right of patronage similar to that enjoyed by some of the judges in England. He had power to appoint absolutely to all offices in the Supreme Court without reference to the Government, and all such offices were held during good conduct, the Judge alone having the power of removal. Governor Grey proposed that an amendment of the Act should be made so as to bring the officers of the Supreme Court under the control of the government. Such officers, he pointed out, acted in a double capacity:

> 'In as far as relates to the collection and accounting for the fees, fines and other monies to be taken in the Court they stand to the executive government in the ordinary relation of collectors of the revenue, whilst in the capacity of officers of the Supreme Court they are occasionally required to administer to the effects of deceased persons, and are entrusted with considerable sums of money, the property of orphans and others.' [11]

It was desirable that they should give security for the due performance of their duties and for accounting for the moneys received by them, and that the executive government should have the power of instituting inquiries into their conduct. In the case of one of the clerks of the Supreme Court defalcations had been discovered, which resulted in his dismissal. The Judge said he was content to acquiesce in any legislation proposed by the Governor to restrict his right of patronage, which certainly was not then of any great value.[12]

The Supreme Court Amendment Act No 6 of 1844, which was based on the Charter of Justice in New South Wales, was accordingly passed by the Council. It provided that from and after the passing of the Act, all persons who should be appointed to the offices of Master, Registrar, Prothonotary or Keeper of Records of the Supreme Court, or to any offices whereof the duties should correspond to those performed by the Master, Registrar or Prothonotary of any of the courts of record at Westminster, should be appointed by the Crown; all persons appointed to any other office within the Supreme Court should be appointed by the Chief Justice or Judge for the time being. Those officers who were appointed by the Crown were to hold office during pleasure; those appointed by the Chief Justice or Judge were subject to removal by the Court upon reasonable cause. No new office was to be created in the Supreme Court unless the Governor for the time being first signified his approbation in writing.

In July 1846 Governor Robe informed the Legislative Council that he would like to increase the Judge's salary, and would also like to see it fixed like the Governor's and not requiring an annual vote; but he had no authority to do either.[13] Towards the end of that year, it was apparently rumoured that the authorities at home contemplated preparing a Charter of Justice for South Australia and Mr Justice Cooper wrote soliciting the position of Chief Judge if such an event happened. In forwarding this home, the Governor supported Cooper's claim and recommended and increase in his salary.[14] The Secretary of State, however, had no intention of granting a Charter of Justice to the colony.

> 'If any improvements in the Judicial System of the colony should be considered necessary'—he said—'they must be effected by Acts of the local Legislature.' [15]

In March 1848 the Judge's salary was raised to £1,000 a year.[16] Two years later he asked for an increase of another £200 a year, but the Secretary of State replied:

> 'I do not think that it would be a fitting time to increase the salary of the Chief Judge when it is proposed so immediately to call into existence a partly representative legislature, but when that body shall have assembled, I think that the question may be very properly submitted for their consideration.' [17]

Accordingly, in October 1851 a Bill to increase the Judges' salaries was introduced into the Legislative Council. By this time Mr Justice Crawford had arrived in the colony, with the same story as his predecessors—that he had come out on the understanding that his salary was to be increased. The Bill did not meet with unanimous approval. George Fife Angas said that the Legislative Council would be much better employed in cheapening legal procedure than in increasing the Judges' salaries. It was suggested that a knighthood might be appropriately conferred on Mr Justice Cooper as a mark of appreciation of his judicial services.[18] The Bill went through, and each Judge received an increase of £400, bringing Mr Justice Cooper's salary to £1,400 and Mr Justice Crawford's to £1,200. On the appointment in 1859 of a third judge, the Chief Justice's salary was raised to £1,500, the second and third judges receiving £1,300 each.

Augustus Short (1802-1883)
Bishop Short arrived in Adelaide in 1847 to commence the work of building up the Church of England in South Australia. In this he was successful although he was often at odds with members of his own church and more frequently with the Non-Conformists. He did see the Anglican Cathedral – St. Peters – built, but in North Adelaide not Victoria Square. (SLV)

In June 1855 Mr Justice Cooper tried a case, *The Bishop of Adelaide v. The Corporation of Adelaide*, which though of slight legal interest was of considerable importance to the people of Adelaide. The question at issue was whether or not Bishop Short was entitled to an acre in Victoria Square as the designated site of the Church of England Cathedral under a land grant issued to him by Governor Robe in March 1848. The existence of this grant was unknown to the public for some years. The Corporation of Adelaide had assumed control of the square, and fenced and planted it. Like a bolt from the blue came a claim from Bishop Short in 1855 that an acre in the centre of the square was vested in him. The corporation refused to recognise his claim and, after arbitration had been suggested by the bishop and refused, recourse was had to the Supreme Court, where the bishop sued the corporation for trespass. The case lasted two days and involved a detailed investigation into the laying out of the city. The jury found a special verdict that the whole of Victoria Square had been originally set apart for the use and recreation of the citizens; and upon this the Judge, holding that although the Governor could make grants of waste lands, he could not interfere with public reserves, declared the bishop's land grant to be invalid and gave judgment for the defendant.[19]

At the geographic centre of Adelaide, Victoria Square was unimproved and not particularly valuable real estate when the acre was granted to Bishop Short in 1848. In 1854 the Adelaide Council spent over a thousand pounds on the Square considerably improving its value. Still, in 1856 the *Observer* reported that gaps in fencing had the southern part becoming a "playground for truant goats". The view shown here looks south to the courts, ca. 1880. (NLA)

At the end of 1856 the Chief Justice obtained leave of absence to visit England, and his departure was the signal for eulogistic references to him in the press. Forgetful of some of its earlier comments, the *Register* declared: "His general ability and soundness as a lawyer, and his perfect uprightness and impartiality have never been called in question."

"Good jurist, bad Christian" was Martin Luther's maxim; at a farewell breakfast tendered to him at Port Adelaide, it was emphasised that the Chief Justice had been "a Christian as well as a Judge"—apparently the two qualities were still regarded as being, in general, incompatible.[20]

While in England the Chief Justice was knighted. He returned to the colony in 1858 to face during the next few years continually increasing tension with Mr Justice Boothby, whose conduct led to the appointment, in February 1859, of Mr Gwynne as third judge, in the hope that the second judge might be crushed by weight of numbers.

The Chief Justice held a dormant commission for the administration of the government in the event of the death or absence of the Governor, and in September 1860 he was sworn in as a member of the Executive Council.

> 'Although it is not desirable and it is not intended that under the present Constitution any but the responsible Ministers for the time being should take an active part at meetings of the Council as advisers of the Governor'—wrote Sir Richard MacDonnell—'I nevertheless felt it was proper that Sir Charles Cooper should be at least a member of that Council over which he may at any moment be called to preside.' [21]

The Secretary of State was annoyed and, in effect, told the Governor he was a fool.

> 'The main reason'—he said—'why the administration of the Government of the colony in the absence of the Governor has been entrusted to the present Chief Justice, is that a Judicial Officer is necessarily unconnected with political or party action.'

A place in the Executive Council could not be appropriately given as a mere honorary distinction to persons not possessing executive functions, and least of all to an officer whose duty was to hold himself pointedly aloof from politics. As the appointment was made, it could not be recalled without the appearance of a slight on Sir Charles Cooper and it would have to stand; but it must not occur again.[22]

Sir Charles held the office of Executive Councillor after his retirement from the bench, and resigned it in September 1862, when Governor Daly mentioned that he thought the appointment of the Chief Justice to the Executive Council was a step liable to great misconception, if not absolutely unconstitutional.[23]

In 1861 the Chief Justice acted as Chairman of the Commission which reported on the Real Property Act, but with his health failing him, and distressed by the conduct of Mr Justice Boothby, he sought in August 1861 an opportunity to retire on a pension. He asked for a retiring allowance of two-thirds of his salary—£1,000.

The Governor, in placing the matter before the Executive Council, referred to the Chief Justice's:

> '... high and unblemished reputation for the strictest conscientiousness, his assiduous attention to his duties, his learning and gentlemanly bearing in his varied intercourse with all classes'; and to: '... the prejudicial effect of the anxiety and wear and tear caused by his official duties on Sir Charles's constitution'.

(Sir) Richard Graves MacDonnell (1814-1881)
MacDonnell's term as Governor, from 1855 to 1862, is noted for his unsuccessful attempts to shape the Constitution along conservative lines. Reluctant to have the Governor's powers diminished and dismissive of local views and capabilities he was frequently in conflict with the reformers of South Australia.

Sir Dominick Daly (1798-1868)
Given that he was an Irish Catholic, Daly's appointment as Governor in 1861 was unusual. It was also successful as Daly had a wealth of colonial administrative experience, exercised impartiality and was supportive of the various colonial ministries and the expansion of production and immigration.

It was scarcely fair, he said, to keep the Chief Justice longer at his post:

> '... while recent occurrences impose on the Government the duty of strengthening the Supreme Court and giving it an increased weight with the Public by placing at its head some one with such a comprehensive grasp of learning and acknowledged ability combined with the requisite physical energy as might enable the Court to retrieve its position in the Public estimation. Such a task seems more than can be expected from Sir Charles Cooper in his present declining state of health, but might be reasonably expected to follow the elevation of such a person as Mr Hanson to the principal judicial office'.

Mr Hanson was then the leader of the opposition in Parliament, and the Governor was anxious that it should be known that the suggestion that Hanson should be Chief Justice was entirely his (the Governor's) own.

> 'It is a suggestion made from the necessity which, as it seems to me, exists for placing the Supreme Court at once under the most competent head. My feeling is that although Mr Hanson as leader of a respectable opposition and reputed to be the ablest member of the Legislature may be the one whose loss will be most felt, he will nevertheless be more useful just now to the public on the Bench.'

He could see no reason against the appointment except the "natural feeling of hesitation and delicacy" which the ministry might experience in putting forward a measure which would result in the removal of one of their chief political opponents.[24]

The Government concurred, and in September 1861 the Treasurer laid the matter before the House of Assembly. The Chief Justice's position, he said, had been an arduous one.

> 'He had been brought into immediate and close connection with large numbers of people in the limited society which existed in the early days of the colony, and never had the slightest stain been cast upon his character as an upright and impartial Judge.'

He moved that in view of his long service he should be permitted to retire upon an allowance of £1,000 a year. A few voices were raised to suggest that as the Supreme Court was in such an uncertain state, owing to the Boothby troubles, it might be wise for the Chief Justice to delay his resignation; but, as Mr Dutton said, "the fact of there being a row pending in the Supreme Court" was no reason why the Chief Justice should be made to endure it, especially when it was known that the Governor had the power to appoint another gentleman: "... who, from his known ability and strength of character, would, no doubt, be fully able to cope with any difficulty which might arise".

It was an open secret that Mr Hanson would be, if he chose to accept the office, the next Chief Justice, and in rising to address the House Hanson could not but refer to the embarrassing situation in which he was placed. On the one hand, too much zeal in favour of the motion might be construed as springing from a desire to take Sir Charles Cooper's place; while, on the other hand, too little would appear, in the leader of the opposition, a niggardly recognition of Sir Charles's services.

> 'No Judge who could be appointed'—he said—'would ever be called upon to go through the same difficulties which His Honor Sir Charles Cooper had done. It was not in the nature of things. They would not have to undergo the difficulties inseparable from a new settlement, or have to stand alone upon the decisions which they might give, or have to mould as it were the whole administration of justice to the requirements of a new country.' [25]

The motion was carried without a division, and an act to provide a pension of £1,000 a year was passed. (No 11 of 1861). Sir Charles Cooper at once tendered his resignation, which was accepted by the Governor and Council with expressions of: "... their esteem for him personally and their thorough appreciation of the integrity, ability and zealous assiduity displayed by him in the high office which he had so long and ably filled".

Mr Hanson was immediately appointed to succeed him as Chief Justice.[26]

> 'It had for a long time been gradually becoming more and more evident'—wrote the Governor—'that Sir Charles's physical strength was no longer equal to the cares and duties of his position. The Parliament, therefore, passed the enclosed measure with such unanimous testimony to the high character and abilities of Sir Charles as must have been most gratifying to the latter.' [27]

Mr Justice Boothby sent home a protest, asking that the Act granting the pension should be disallowed, because it did not provide pensions for the other judges and because it was part of a scheme to defeat his claims to the office of Chief Justice.[28] Sir Richard MacDonnell was disgusted with this example of "bad taste", and, with a warmth not usually to be found in official correspondence, he wrote to the Duke of Newcastle:

Duke of Newcastle (1811-1864)
Henry Pelham-Clinton, the 5th Duke of Newcastle, was an influential politician who held various public offices including Secretary of State from 1852 to 1854 and 1859 to 1864.

> 'No matter in what light Mr Justice Boothby may put his attempt to deprive an old colleague of his well earned pension, and despite of all specious pretexts of general patriotic motives, and anxiety for the security of HM Government, on which he may found so discreditable a request, and though he may thereby possibly in part deceive himself, it nevertheless stands forth prominently in my eyes as a selfish act, which would be severely stigmatized in certain social circles in England, and I am loth to admit that in this colony we should shape our conduct by a lower moral standard than that at home ... Mr Boothby seems to think he alone has discovered the wisdom of passing a general measure in reference to judicial pensions, as if the propriety of such legislation be not patent to every thinking person—though the most efficacious mode of inducing the people of this Colony to come into such views would certainly be the reverse of the coercive policy suggested by Mr Boothby.' [29]

The Secretary of State replied that the Act would be left to its operation, as a just acknowledgment of the long and eminent services of the Chief Justice.[30]

In 1862 Sir Charles Cooper returned to England. He declined a public farewell on account of his health, but was presented with a valedictory address praising his impartiality and integrity, and his "prevailing urbanity of manner". "As one of the early settlers in this province"—it was said—"you have helped to impart a healthy tone, morally and socially, by an upright, benevolent, and unostentatious example." [31]

In England he lived for many years in retirement. When his pension was under discussion, it was suggested that he might be paid a lump sum of £10,000 or £12,000 instead of an annuity of £1,000. This was rejected, for no-one expected he could survive another twelve years. The state, however, made a very bad bargain, for Sir Charles died on 24 May 1887, twenty six years after his retirement, at the age of ninety two.

An older Sir Charles Cooper. (SCLSA)

Chapter 4.4

Sir Charles Cooper

English law, Australian gums

Judges are usually meagre subjects for biography, unless they have also won their way to political distinction, or bequeathed their fame to posterity as actors in some other sphere outside the pale of their profession. "Their office," as Bacon said, "is Ius dicere, and not Ius dare: To interpret Law, and not to make Law or Give Law." It is their duty to follow, and not to lead. For the most part, the matters with which a judge deals are of evanescent importance to all except the parties immediately concerned. He must devote great talents and labour to the elucidation of questions of transitory interest. The scope of his action, when he sits alone, is limited to the particular cases which it may fall to his lot to decide, and when he sits in banco his personality must to some extent be merged with those of his colleagues. True, the more important results of his work are recorded in permanent form, but it is in a form which does not reach more than a small body of readers. The extent and value of his travail is not widely known or appreciated; nor do the reported decisions of even the ablest jurist furnish more than the scantiest of data on which to base an estimate of his mind or heart, or from which to draw any inference as to his life or achievements. "The almost monastic rules of conduct that are forced on him prevent the outside world from being informed about his views and about the conditioning elements of his behaviour." [1]

His life work is done in seclusion. He contributes his mite to the building up of a body of jurisprudence much as the coral insect adds its body to the rising atoll.

> 'Silent excellencies'—said Dr Johnson—'are soon forgotten; and those minute peculiarities which discriminate every man from all others, if they are not recorded by those whom personal knowledge enables to observe them, are irrecoverably lost.'

The biographer of Mr Justice Cooper faces all these embarrassments, and more. A new colony afforded little scope for the display of high judicial talents. Litigation was small in volume and legal interest. The range of subjects calling for adjudication was narrow, and few of his decisions, had they been ever so well reported, would now be quoted, because of the difference between the character of the questions which arose in his time and those which come before tribunals at the present day. Many of them turned upon points of practice and procedure long since obsolete; the greater part were decisions at nisi prius.

Throughout there must be remembered, also, the silent operation of the principle of "the inconspicuousness of satisfactory innovation".[2] Alterations in the practice of the Court or the habits of the profession which met with general approval passed imperceptibly into common usage. Because they worked satisfactorily, no-one's attention was specifically directed to them. Sometimes it can be said that at such-and-such a time the change was made and thenceforward observed; more often not. Paradoxically, therefore, most useful developments in the law frequently leave fewer records of their introduction than unsuccessful attempts at changes which passed quickly into the limbo of lost causes.

Mr Justice Cooper had none of the spirit of an innovator or a reformer; he was content to tread where abler feet had trod. Law developed and expanded in South Australia slowly, and almost entirely by means of legislation. Law reporters, "the troubadours of the halls of justice", were unknown during the period here dealt with, and such judicial precedents as may have been created were, for the want of any published reports, but an uncertain aid. Scarcely more than two or three of the decisions of Sir Charles Cooper can be pointed out as having distinctively moulded the development of any branch of South Australian law.

There was not, indeed, a great deal for him to do in the way of adapting English law, for the transplantation of that law had not been attended with any serious difficulties. As Adam Smith said, colonists from a civilised community taking possession of a waste or thinly inhabited country, carry out with them:

> '... the habit of subordination, some notion of the regular government which takes place in their own country, of the system of laws which support it, and of a regular administration of justice; and they naturally establish something of the same kind in the new settlement'. [3]

So, far from the pioneers of South Australia having any tendency to become lawless in their new environment, they were (like their predecessors in the American colonies) "tenacious of regulation by law and prone to litigation".[4] One landowner, on taking possession of his town acre when Adelaide was laid out, immediately erected a large "wooden falsehood" warning all and sundry that "any person found trespassing on these grounds" (an acre of unfenced shrub) "will be prosecuted with the utmost rigour of the law"—a sufficient indication that from this gentleman, at least, no relaxation of the strictness of English proprietary law was to be expected.[5]

Questions as to how far English law had been introduced into the colony of course arose, and they were necessarily sometimes confusing. "Nothing is more difficult"—said Lord Cranworth in Whicker v. Hume 7 HLC 124 at 161—"than to know which of our laws is to be regarded as imported into our colonies."

The lawyers of the 18th century saw little difficulty in the matter."Let an Englishman go where he will, he carries as much law and liberty with him as the nature of things will bear." [6]

Blackstone elaborated thus:

> 'Colonists carry with them'—he said—'only so much of the English law as is applicable to their own situation and the condition of an infant colony ... the artificial requirements and distinctions incident to the property of a great and commercial people are neither necessary nor convenient for them, and are, therefore, not in force.' [7]

But the test of applicability is by no means easy to frame with precision (if indeed it be possible to do so); it is productive occasionally of twilight phenomena presenting difficulties which might as well be resolved by the spin of a coin as by the exercise of the reasoning faculties. A colony growing from infancy to maturity is in a constant state of transition.

> 'As the code of laws, such as will be required by the colony in its mature state, would be unsuitable to its infancy, so much additions be continually made to those simple regulations which will suffice for the infant settlement.' [8]

Must the English law in force, then, be such as is applicable at the moment of the colony's foundation, to "the simple state of society of the first settlers"; or does that portion of the common law which is suited to a more advanced state of civilisation lie dormant until the circumstances of the colony are such as to require its enforcement? (See *Delohery v. Permanent Trust Co* 1 CLR 283.) This inquiry, if pursued, would lead into the thickets of conflicting theories and judgments. Fortunately, no very serious problems have ever arisen in South Australia upon the extent of the application of English law; and the investigations of doctrines academically difficult may be eluded.

South Australia was not an uninhabited country (the declaration in the Foundation Act to the contrary notwithstanding), but such Aboriginal customs as existed were from a legal point of view negligible. Thus there was no possibility of any conflict between rival systems of law, as occurred in India, Canada and South Africa. The provision in the Foundation Act that South Australians were not to be subject to the laws in force in any other part of Australia excluded any questions of the operation of the law of New South Wales. In *South Australia v. Victoria* 12 CLR 667 at 677, Chief Justice Griffith said:

> 'As this territory then formed part of the colony of New South Wales, the laws of that colony would ordinarily have continued to apply to the new Provinces when established. It was, however, provided by section 1 of the Act that those laws should not be applicable. The result was that any new Province which might be established was to be treated in law (as it was in fact) as new territory acquired by settlement, with the

consequence that the settlers would take with them the common and statute law of England so far as applicable.'

So in *White v. McLean* 24 SALR 97 at 99, Justice Boucaut said: "The view taken by Chief Justice Cooper and succeeding judges was that the laws of New South Wales, as applying to South Australia, were swept away."

Revolutionaries were not wanting who thought that the break with the old world offered a golden opportunity to remould the entire legal system.

> 'Whenever lawyers meddle with law'—wrote one enthusiast—'we are sure to have a load of long-winded rubbish on every subject in place of a dozen of plain sentences, which, divested of legal garbage, would answer the purpose quite as well, and have the additional advantage of being intelligible to everybody—except perhaps to the lawyers themselves. What we want in this colony is not the transcript of the English statute-book; but well-considered laws applicable to the state of society existing in our infant colony, unfettered by precedent, expressed simply, distinctly, and with no more words than necessary. The experiment in colonization we are making will be but half accomplished if the opportunity be omitted of obtaining and embodying the wisest laws, not of England merely, but of every other enlightened nation. So they be suited to our condition, so they be substantially just—and calculated to make law cheap and legal proceedings brief—the plea that they are not in unison with the practice of English courts ought to be thrown overboard at once.' [9]

The vast majority of South Australians, however, wanted nothing better than to adhere closely to the law of England. Motives of policy derived from local circumstances occasioned but few changes. The administration of the law in the early days of the colony, said Mr Justice Boothby: "... was so like what it was in some of the English counties, that persons coming here would hardly be able to recognise the difference between the colony and England". [10]

Men quit not easily the practices to which they have been accustomed. It was many years before the colony had a native-born and native-trained profession, and judges and lawyers educated in English ways were not likely casually to abandon their old habits and traditions. In South Australia, as in the other Australian colonies, the course of the courts was: "... to stand by the established rule of English law, and let the legislature provide for special conditions arising in the colony". [11]

Justice Holroyd in *Lyons v. Winter* 25 VLR 464 at 469 enunciated the rule upon which, for the most part, the judges acted: "We may expound the common law according to new circumstances, but we cannot go beyond the principles which British law has laid down for us."

Sir Harrison Moore has pointed out that this retention of a close connection with English law was supported by a recognition of the fact that uniformity meant increased certainty. English decisions and textbooks could be used to furnish precedents and illustrations.

> 'English experience must be richer and more complete and it was therefore a safer basis for the generalisations of legislation ... Divergence would mean uncertainty, diminishing only as costly litigation settled the law.'

> 'The conviction of the importance of access to decisions and to textbooks of repute'—he adds—'has been strong among those who have learned by experience that formal expression in abstract terms is inadequate for the full expression and the knowledge of the law; that access to a wide range of experience in its application and operation is vital, and that this the narrow limits of a small community cannot furnish.' [12]

One may doubt whether there have been many Australian lawyers who consciously formulated in their minds the principle thus put so strikingly by Sir Harrison Moore, but the obvious advantages to be derived from following English law, both substantive and procedural, could not be overlooked. Mr Justice Cooper, for instance, when drawing up rules for the Supreme Court in 1847, said that he had found in practice that the rules and manner of proceedings of the Courts of Common Law in England had generally been sufficient to control the practice of the Supreme Court.

> 'The general adoption of them has at least this advantage, that it gives the Judge and Practitioner of the Court the advantage of referring to the English books of reports and of practice. I have therefore made such Rules only as experience from time to time has shown to be necessary.'

"This advantage," he said on another occasion, "can hardly be overestimated."[13]

At a very early stage, problems arose as to how far English law was in force in South Australia. One of the first was in connection with the marriage laws. It was doubtful whether the English statute law as to marriage extended to the colony. It proscribed, for instance, the publication of banns in the parish church of the place or places where the parties resided, but where was the parish church of South Australia? If the Marriage Acts were not in force, then the earlier common law had to be resorted to, and in such a case marriage could be contracted merely per verba de praesenti. In January 1840 Governor Gawler brought this question before the Council. He considered it of the utmost importance to the community that the

Council should pass at an early period an act to regulate the mode of celebrating and registering marriages in the province, and he instructed the Advocate-General to prepare a bill for this purpose. It was more than two years, however, before an act was passed, and it was then denounced as a "mass of irreconcilable blunders" and "a monstrous abortion" of which the learned Advocate-General had been "miraculously delivered". The Governor, said the *Register*, was most unfortunate "in being saddled with intolerable nincompoops", and the Marriage Act proved "the skill of the sagacious Advocate in the art of reducing laws, as well as the administration of them, to the flattering position of public laughing-stocks". The Act was not quite as hopeless as the criticism of the *Register* suggests, and, with an occasional patching up, it remained in force and operation for a considerable period.

In February 1840 the Council attempted to get rid of all difficulties in the application of English law by passing an act (3 Vic No 10) to declare when and how far the laws and statutes of England should be deemed to be the laws of South Australia. This Act was a fiasco. At the outset it offended against the express instructions of the Crown that different subject matters must be legislated for in different acts, for in addition to declaring the law, the Act contained a number of provisions amending the law, as to juries and as to summary proceedings before justices. The only section relevant to present purposes was the first, which provided:

> 'All the laws and statutes which were in force in England on the 28th day of December 1836 so far as the same are applicable to the circumstances of this province and so far as they are not inconsistent with the Acts of the Imperial Parliament 4th and 5th William IV c.95 and 1st and 2nd Victoria c.60, or with any Order or Orders in Council made in pursuance thereof, or with any enactment made by the Legislative Council of this Province, shall be and be deemed to be part of the laws of this Province.'

At the best this section could not be very helpful; it was too loose and comprehensive.

> 'Our laws do need declaring'—said the *Southern Australian*—'but it is no good lumping together all the English laws, good bad and indifferent. They should not be brought into force in a new colony without discrimination.'

What "the circumstances of the province" might mean would depend entirely upon the whim of each particular judge.[14]

When the Act was sent home, however, it was at once disallowed on a more serious ground—that it said that English statutes should apply so far as not inconsistent with local legislation, whereas it should have read the other way about, for English statutes were not to be ousted at the pleasure of the colonial legislature.[15]

This attempt at statutory definition having ignominiously failed, the Judges were left to do as best they could by deciding in particular cases as they arose whether or not any portion of English law was in force here. Mr Justice Cooper early took the view that if a subject was covered by local legislation, he would not consider the English law.

> 'It is difficult for a Judge to declare what Acts of Parliament should apply here'—he said—'and I think we should not look further when we have local acts to refer to. The English Act may be better and more convenient, but I will not be influenced by that.' [16]

Various English statutes were from time to time specifically held to be in force—for example, 16 Charles II c.7 and such parts of 9 Anne c.19 as were not prevented from being carried into execution here by technical difficulties (gaming), 3 & 4 Wm IV c.42 (making an executor liable for costs) and 2 William and Mary c.5 (distraint for rent). With regard to the last-mentioned act, some doubts were subsequently raised by a decision of the Supreme Court of New South Wales that the Act was not in force there, and in 1862 Sir Charles Cooper recommended that an act should be passed to clarify the position. By Act 14 of 1862, therefore, it was declared that the Act of William and Mary had been, ever since the foundation of the colony, and still was, in force in the colony, and it was then declared that the Act should no longer apply and other provisions were substituted in lieu of it.[17]

In *Bank of South Australia v. Osborne*, in August 1848, the defendant pleaded the Statute of Limitations, and Mr Justice Cooper had to consider what meaning could be given to the words "beyond the seas" in the saving clauses as to parties beyond the seas, appearing in the English Acts. Was New South Wales "beyond the seas" within the meaning of the Act? He reserved his judgment and offered, if the parties wished, to take the opinion of the Judges in Sydney on the point, but the parties preferred the possibility of a speedy but inaccurate decision to that of a correct but tardy one. He held that the Statutes of Limitations (21 Jas I c.16 and 4 Anne c.16) were applicable to the colony and that the term "beyond the seas" must be construed as meaning, in effect, "out of the jurisdiction of the Supreme Court" and therefore to include New South Wales.

> 'With respect to the means of communication with New South Wales by land'—he said—'it is true that both before and since the causes of action in this case arose, persons bringing cattle from New South Wales have passed and re-passed between that colony and this, and that since the year 1846 there has been an overland mail between Adelaide and Sydney by the way of Melbourne; but, with these exceptions, the

communication between the two colonies has been by sea, and will necessarily be so for many years to come. I do not, however, rely on this circumstance, because, as it was justly observed on the part of the plaintiffs, if Sydney is not beyond the seas within the meaning of the Statutes of Limitation neither is Port Essington, nor any part, however inaccessible, of New Holland.'

Overlanders With Cattle an 1864 Frederick Grosse engraving from an original work by S.T. Gill. Joseph Hawdon, Charles Bonney and seven others were the first "overlanders" in Adelaide. In 1838 they brought cattle from the Goulburn River taking two months and earning the acclaim of Adelaide residents. (SLV)

To clear up any difficulty, he prepared and forwarded to the Governor a draft bill on the subject. It was very important, he pointed out, that these statutes should be deemed part of the law of the province. The Bill was promptly passed (No 9 of 1848) declaring that the Statutes of Limitations formed part of the law of South Australia and that the term "beyond the seas" should be construed to mean out of the jurisdiction of the Supreme Court.[18]

In the application of the common law there was less difficulty. Here, as Sir Harrison Moore has observed of Victoria: "... attempts to make the unenacted law—common law or equity—yield to special conditions in the colony have met with little judicial encouragement".[19] In at least two branches of the law, however, some departure from strict English rules was compelled.

In *Hill v. Kingsmill*, in December 1855, the Full Court had to consider whether the trees of this colony could be classed as "timber". Oak, ash and elm were the timber trees in England, with beech and birch in a few counties; to be timber the wood had to be wood used for building purposes. None of these trees were indigenous to South Australia. The Court held, with some doubt, that gum trees and similar trees were "timber", for they could be used for fences and barns, and even, if nothing better could be had, for making rough houses.

> 'With regard to the mode in which the timber is used'—the Court said—'the circumstances of the colony do not call upon us to give as strict an interpretation to the law as to the rights of the landlord against a tenant as we would in England.' [20]

Mr Justice Molesworth, in Victoria, in *Brooks v. Bedford* 1 VLT 101 seems to have been of a contrary opinion, for, after pointing out the great difference between England and Australia, "timber being here superabundant and not of value as at home", he remarked that he would have required very strong evidence to satisfy him that gum trees were trees usable for building, so as to bring them within the definition of timber trees.

Cutting Wood by J. M. Skipper, ca. 1855 (SLSA)

More difficult of solution and far more important was the application of the English law of watercourses. In *Crittenden v. Smith* (decided in June 1855) it appeared that the plaintiff was the owner of land near the present township of Smithfield. The defendant, the owner of adjoining land, subdivided it to lay out Smithfield, and to provide water for the township he diverted a creek which ran through his property in that of the plaintiff. The plaintiff sued for damages. Mr Fisher, for the defendant, submitted that there was no case to go to the jury, because the plaintiff had no right to the water. English law required twenty years user to establish such a right; the plaintiff had only been in occupation of his land for seven years and, indeed, the colony had been founded less than twenty years, so that the claim must fail. In ruling against this contention, Mr Justice Cooper said:

> 'However important the question may be, it is not so very difficult. No doubt the law cannot be precisely the same here as in England, for when a colony has not existed for 20 years, it is impossible for anyone to plead prescription for that period. We are thus obliged to go back to first principles to say what is the right which a man has to water running through his land? He is entitled to the use of the water. He may appropriate it in any way he pleases, so that he does not injure the right of any other party. Therefore if a stream is strong enough to turn a mill without wasting the water, it may be so used. In like manner the water may be used for purposes of irrigation. Now it appears to me that when a section of land has water running through it, and that section is granted to an individual, it gives him a right to use the water, and any act depriving him of that use is unlawful ... The reason why a certain period is fixed as giving prescriptive right is because it is convenient to have some time which may be deemed to give a title. In an old country it is impossible to trace rights back to their source, and consequently the evidence of a right is user; but here we can go to the beginning of every thing, and the evidence of a right such as is in dispute is the land grant.' [21]

The jury found for the plaintiff, with £30 damages. The decision was generally approved, for an uninterrupted flow of water to a section of land in South Australia very often constituted its chief value.

> 'By reason of the peculiar aridity of the climate, running water possesses a special value to the cultivators of garden and vineyards situate on the banks of creeks, as well as to the proprietors of mills worked by water-power.' (per Justice Wearing in Dunn v. Collins 1 SALR 126 at 135).

"Thou has given me a south land," said Achsah to Cael; "give me also springs of water".[22] Too often the settlers of South Australia have echoed his plaint in vain.

In 1853 the question arose whether a market overt could exist in South Australia. Mr Justice Boothby apparently thought it could, for in *Jeffries v. Field*, a case where the owner of a horse which had been stolen and sold in a public street was suing for its value, he expressed surprise that there had been a sale and purchase in market overt. Mr Fisher, who appeared for the defendant, said he hoped the Judge would reserve the point, as it was desirable it should be settled. The matter accordingly came before the Full Court, where Mr Fisher moved to have the verdict set aside, with the object of establishing whether or not a market overt was possible in the colony.

> Mr Justice Cooper: 'Where was the sale?'
>
> Fisher: 'In Rundle Street.'
>
> Mr Justice Cooper: 'Do you call that market overt? There is here a regular market, and sale in open street is prohibited.'
>
> Fisher: 'Would your Honour hold that a sale by auction in our public market is a sale in market overt?'
>
> Mr Justice Cooper: 'When you submit a case I shall decide on it.' [23]

Mr Justice Boothby does not appear to have expressed any further opinion, and the matter dropped. From some correspondence of the Advocate-General, in 1856, it would appear that the Supreme Court subsequently "more than once declared a sale in the market does not change property", from which it is to be presumed the Judges thought a market overt was not possible in the colony.[24] I have not, however, been able to find any decision to this effect.

Rundle Street in 1851 by S.T.Gill. (NLA)

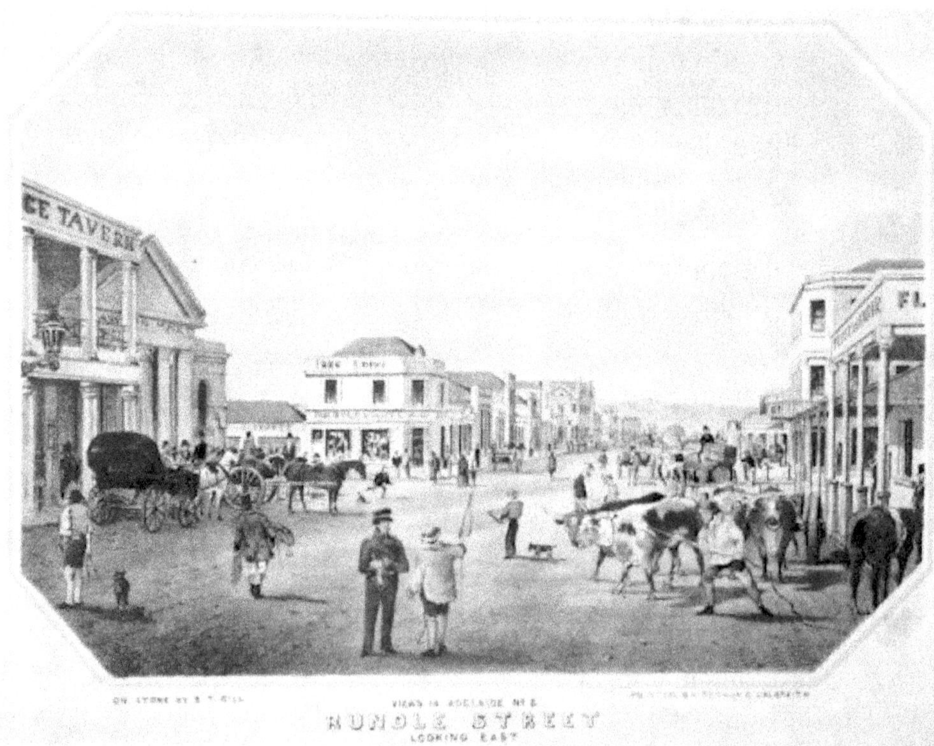

Such progress as occurred in the law during this period was due to the enacted rather than the unenacted law. In many instances English law could be modified to fit new circumstances; where it could not be stretched to cover them, the only remedy was legislation. So long, however, as the South Australian legislature was prohibited from passing legislation repugnant to the law of England, it was not possible for any very sweeping changes to be introduced.

There can be little pleasure in a recital of statutory provisions, nor is it proposed to attempt one, but a few general remarks may perhaps be here conveniently inserted upon the early legislation of the colony.

It has already been mentioned that the earliest statutes were prepared by George Stevenson. The Governor and Mann, the Advocate-General, had quarrelled before they left England. Hindmarsh had assumed that Mann was to accompany him on the *Buffalo*, and was annoyed when he found that Mann had made arrangements to go out in another vessel.

> 'The Governor complained greatly'—wrote Brown in his journal on 19 June 1836—'stating that he could not do without him, as he did not want Mann to frame laws or regulations without his seeing what was going on and suggesting what he thought best; that he wanted no rigmaroles of forms, and d--d Acts of Parliament that nobody could understand, and in fact that he wanted Mann in the Buffalo that he might get him to do as he pleased and embody his own notions; adding that he had the power and that the Commissioners had nothing to do with it. Mann got warm and they parted very sore.'

Mann had his way and sailed on the *Coromandel*, with the result that the first statutes of the colony were drawn up not by its law officer but by the Governor's secretary.

The Coromandel
Coromandel Place and *Coromandel Valley* are named after the ship *Coromandel*. The valley acquired the name through being the place where deserting sailors from the ship were captured.

Stevenson's journal contains so many entries dealing with his activities as parliamentary draughtsman that one might almost apply to him Bernard O'Dowd's words: "Not a law is a boon to the people but he has dictated its draft".

On 31 October 1836 he wrote:

> 'Drew up today the first legislative measure for His Excellency's consideration, namely, to impose certain duties on ardent spirits'; and two days later he recorded: 'Drew up an Act to regulate and settle disputes between master and servant, which I read to the Governor, who found it to be the very law he had determined to make, as he told Lord Glenelg and Mr Stephen long ago. Of course, he means to claim credit for all the legislation. I find, notwithstanding this amiable intention, that unless I do things myself, though they are not in any shape within my province, there is no chance of anything but confusion and disorder to be expected on our arrival. The Governor cannot write two sentences of grammar or common sense; that is the simple truth. But I will not allow the chance of his appropriating my labours as his own in the higher quarters to stand in the way of the good, which order and

sound legislation from the commencement are likely to ensure. In this view I am preparing the law for the constitution of the Supreme Court and the Courts of General or Quarter and Petty Sessions.'

On 21 November he was "busy with two important Acts", one for the summary determination of disputes between master and servant, the other for the prevention of imprisonment for debt, except in the case of fraud, and for the better recovery of debts. And a week later, apparently gaining confidence as he went along, he embarked upon a more ambitious venture:

> 'Drew up this morning the first sketch of a law for preventing unnecessary litigation and for the amicable settlement of all disputes by arbitration. I mentioned the subject to the Governor in London, and stated my opinion that, if we could find a means to support a Court of arbitration, it would be well to adopt it in Australia. He had never heard of the Danish practice, but said he liked the suggestion very much. So much, indeed, it appears to have taken his fancy, that, on my reading the Act to him this forenoon, I had the pleasure of being told that he had determined to introduce the Danish law into the province long before he knew me. He said also that he had consulted Lord Glenelg and Mr Stephen on the subject, both of whom approved of his intention. The latter, especially, was "in extasy" at his being "no lawyer", and therefore more fitted to make laws without any regard to form or legality. Mr Stephen, I suspect, must have amused himself with slyly quizzing the Governor, but I am quite certain that, if either Lord Glenelg or he had ever seriously listened to him for half an hour, they would have pronounced him wholly unfit for the great trust confided to his hands. The facts I record here, however, prove the quality and the moral honesty of the man.'

On 10 December:

> 'Received back from His Excellency the legislative Acts I had prepared, with his amendments in pencil. They are more curious than numerous, and I hope some of them may survive, that the higher powers may see what a clever fellow the Governor is. One instance of his ability in the science will suffice. To maintain as much as possible the faith of contracts with labourers, I had laid a heavy penalty upon anyone employing a servant knowingly during the unexpired period of his engagement with another. The Governor had interpolated the words 'or hiring', and forgot that he had done so, I

> presume, as he found mighty fault with the clause, and proceeded at great length to expound the gross injustices of punishing any man for hiring a servant under such circumstances. I agreed with him entirely but remarked that no such provision existed in the measure as I had prepared it. He maintained that it did, and, though satisfying him that the interpolation was in his own handwriting settled the dispute, he had the candour, not to acknowledge his error, oh no, (he never dreams of being wrong even in his most outrageous absurdities), but to say that his principal objection to the clause rested on a point that for the moment slipped his memory. He would, however, retain the draft until he remembered it. He did so, and I have this evening had it returned with the word 'or hiring' carefully rubbed out. The 'principal objection' remains in abeyance.'

Margaret Stevenson then took up the tale: "And now George finds that, had he not prepared these Acts, which were not within his province, they had been wholly neglected." [25]

There is a curious discrepancy between the accounts given by Gouger and Stevenson as to the date upon which the first legislation of the colony was passed. According to Gouger, a meeting of the Council was held in his tent on 30 December 1836, at which two acts were passed—one establishing Courts of General or Quarter and Petty Sessions and the other fixing the qualifications of jurors—and Magistrates were appointed. Stevenson, however, puts these happenings on 2 January 1837: "A meeting of Council at which Magistrates were appointed, and two of my laws passed without alteration."

The Acts themselves bear the date 2nd January 1837. It might be thought either that the meeting on 2 January was an adjournment or continuation of the previous meeting, or that the Governor's assent was given on that date, were it not that the same discrepancy of two days occurs again in the account of the passing of the third act. Gouger's entry is: "January 2nd—A Council was again held in my tent, then an Act was passed for the Summary Determination of Disputes between Master and Servants."

Stevenson's record is as follows:

> 'Wednesday, January 4. At a Council today the Governor proposed my law for the summary determination of disputes between master and servant, which was passed without amendment. It cost me some thought, but I hope to be repaid by seeing it produce a good effect—secure the master, on the one hand, in the labour he has paid for, and the servant, on the other, fair play and due protection.'

It would appear that Gouger is two days out in his reckoning in both cases. His diary is very circumstantial and appears on the face of it to have been contemporaneously recorded, but this error would suggest that it was written up some considerable time afterwards, when his memory of the exact days on which events had happened had become untrustworthy.[26]

The procedure adopted in the very early days of the colony when the Bill was to be brought before the Council was: "... to issue a notice 'that the said Bill could be inspected at the office of the Colonial Secretary', and affixing such notice to a tree opposite Government Hut". [27]

Once the *Government Gazette* began to be regularly issued, it became customary for abstracts of proposed legislation to be published in the *Gazetter* for the information of the public.

It is hardly surprising that the first efforts of amateur law-makers were not felicitous. Of the seven acts passed in 1837, two were disallowed, two more were marked down by the Commissioners for disallowances so soon as they could be replaced by better substitutes, but were forgotten, and a fifth proved almost useless.

In 1853 Sir Henry Young (by way of preface to a eulogy of his own merits by a comparative study of legislation) wrote:

> 'Some idea of the progress and state of the colony at respective periods of time may be gathered from noting the number and nature of the laws which were enacted during the administration of each of its several Governors.' [28]

An examination on these lines reveals that ten acts were passed by the Council under Governor Hindmarsh. While the colonial officials were divided by violent dissensions it was hopeless to expect very satisfactory legislation, and during 1838 only three acts were passed—the third being merely to amend a clerical error in the second. Early in that year, B.T. Finniss protested:

'We have held our Town land twelve months; during that time the proprietors have not had the benefit of any protecting laws, emanating from the Council and which our neighbours have obtained. We have no fencing Act to prevent disputes; no laws to protect the Gardeners from the depradations of Cattle or noxious animals which are allowed to infest the streets. We have no prison to receive felons—we have no police—no laws governing weights and measures, and no adulteration laws. These are Acts of perhaps rather much detail but none the less vital to our welfare.' [29]

Under Governor Gawler slightly better progress was made—thirty three acts being passed up to May 1841.

> 'The heavy pressure of complicated business'—wrote Gawler in April 1839—'the want of proper men, the very delicate

nature of legislative enactments, and the most deplorable character of our office accommodation, combine to retard the progress of legislation.' [30]

And at a dinner in January 1840 the Governor said:

> 'There is another difficulty which I want to obviate—the difficulty of legislation. This is truly a great difficulty. On one side some persons tell us—not without justice—we must not have hasty legislation. On the other side, we are told—not without justice—the colony wants immediate legislation. Between the two what are we to do? It is of greatest importance that we should have laws among us, but I do not wish to press them hastily.' [31]

He complained that he was unable to do as much as he could wish on account of the absence of efficient legal assistance—for Bernard, the Advocate-General, besides being inexperienced, "had a constitution so broken that he was scarcely able to bear up against the pressure of ordinary business".[32]

The newspapers were full of criticisms of the failure of the Council to attend to its business of law-making.

> 'Our bankers complain that their desire to afford legitimate credit is defeated, because the protection of the laws of England is denied them—our merchants are daily suffering serious losses from the same cause—the community is forced into unwilling distrust—unfortunate debtors are thrust, illegally, into prison—every practicable disarrangement of the monetary affairs of the colony is fostered—all this mischief is done and continued, because time cannot be found to pass two simple Acts—one to regulate the registration of titles to property, and the other a bankrupt and insolvent law.' [33]

And when acts were passed, they were met with equal hostility. The Scab in Sheep Acts, for instance, were denounced as "harassing and absurd", "elaborately mischievous", and "inefficient for any purpose beyond encouraging informers and pestering the colonists"; while the Act establishing a municipal corporation was "a mass of inexplicable confusion and incongruity, cramped with petty restrictions or dirty jealousies, and altogether insufficient for its professed object".[34]

Scab in Sheep Acts
Scab disease arrived with flocks from Van Diemen's Land and by 1845 three quarters of sheep in the colony were infected. This was despite the first Scab in Sheep Act having been passed in 1840.

A considerable portion of Gawler's legislation was disallowed on various grounds—usually because it purported to authorise expenditure which had not been sanctioned.[35]

All the Acts of the local legislature were supposed to be sent to England for the consideration of the Crown. They might be confirmed, disallowed, or (more often) left to their operation. In the last case they might at any future time be confirmed or disallowed, although of course the longer they were left the less likely it became that the right of disallowance would be exercised. When Governor Grey arrived in the colony he found that some of the statutes passed by his predecessors had never been transmitted to England at all, while of others which had been sent home no record existed of whether they had been disallowed or confirmed or left to their operation.[36]

Under Grey, from 1841 to 1845, eighty five measures were enacted. Of these, thirty three were passed up to 18 February 1843 by the official Council of the Governor and four government officers. There had been, from the earliest stages of the colony's history, an agitation for an infusion of the representative principle into the legislature. Objection was taken to the constitution of the official Council.

> 'The Legislative and Executive Departments are perfectly coincident, and all but identical, being both vested in the sole person of His Excellency; for the Members of the Legislative Council being such solely ex-officia, and their continuance in office being hourly liable to interruption, if umbrage at their conduct should be taken on the part of His Excellency, their entire legislative capacity is absorbed in his.'

Such a council, it was urged, was too small: "What are six or seven men to legislate for a growing community?" [37]

Although it would be answered that this form of government was only temporary, yet it might create faults which could not be eradicated. The time, too, was approaching when the colonists must be taxed; and there should not be taxation without representation.

> 'Let it be recollected that the necessary expenditure of the colony cannot much longer be defrayed out of the ruinous loan system; that it is unjust to take expenditure from the emigration fund; and that the Mother Country will not advance a penny in support of our local establishments ... Taxation must therefore be resorted to; and, since the burden must be borne, it is a duty the colonists owe to themselves, to prepare for the evil day.' [38]

A memorial praying for representation in the Council was presented to Governor Gawler in June 1840. He agreed that the admission of private colonists to the Council, "if prudently carried out", would conduce to the welfare of the province. He suggested four or five non-official members, the official members being also increased. The deliberations of the Council, however, he thought should not be open to the public, although an abstract report might be published; otherwise it would "assume the character of a debating society in which the representative of the Crown would appear as the leader of a party". It had been asked in the memorial that no law should come into force if it was unanimously opposed by all the non-official members, but to this Gawler objected strongly.[39]

In the same month, the Select Committee of the House of Commons appointed to consider the state of South Australia recommended that unofficial members of the Council should be added, to be elected in the province.[40]

For some time nothing further was done. The Council in the colony proceeded to pass several acts imposing taxation and duties, and in August 1842 a public meeting was held at which it was resolved that no further duties ought to be imposed until the Council was extended. When a delegation waited upon Governor Grey with this request, he very bluntly replied: "Gentlemen, I shall tax you first, and you shall be represented afterwards." [41] Up went a howl of rage from the local press. Governor Grey's recall, it was said, would be hailed with joy:" ... no Governor of a British colony ever having been so deservedly unpopular, or his measures so universally execrated". [42] A petition to the Queen for popular representation in the Council was drawn up and dispatched to England.[43]

Meanwhile the Imperial Parliament had passed the Act 5 and 6 Vic c.61, by which the Council was reconstituted. In future it was to consist of the Governor, three nominated official members and four nominated non-official members. The Secretary of State wrote to the Governor in September 1848:

> 'For the present, this form of Council has appeared to Her Majesty's Government best suited to the wants and the condition of the colony. They concur, however, in the view taken in the Report of the Committee of the House of Commons, that it may be expedient at an early period to grant to the inhabitants of the colony a certain degree of control over its revenue and expenditure, by the infusion of the element of popular representation into the local legislature. The period at which it may be desirable to introduce such a change in the constitution must depend upon the advance by the colony in wealth and population; and you will observe that the Act leaves to Her Majesty the exercise of an unfettered discretion in this respect; but I think it right to add that Her Majesty's Government concur in the opinion which seems to have been entertained by the Committee, that before taking such a step it should be made evident that the internal resources of the colony are fully adequate to provide for its own expenditure; and also that permanent provision should be made for certain fixed and definite expenses on account of the Civil Government of the colony.' [44]

A reply in similar terms was given to the colonists' petition.[45]

Very complete instructions were sent to Governor Grey for the regulation of the business of what the *Register* was pleased to term "our hermaphroditic legislature". The Governor was empowered to nominate the members, all appointments being subject to the confirmation of the Secretary of State. The Council was not competent to act in any case unless four members at least, in addition to the Governor or the member who might preside in his absence, should be present at and throughout the meeting. All questions were to be decided by a majority of votes, the Governor or presiding member to have both an original and a casting vote. All laws were to be proposed to the Council by the Governor, and no question could be debated unless it had first been proposed by him, although any member of the Council could request the Governor to bring forward a particular topic, and, if the request was refused, enter a protest upon the minutes of the Council. All ordinances were to be drawn up "in a simple and compendious form", avoiding as far as may be all "prolixity and tautology", and an annual collection of them was to be published. It was provided that the ordinances should be distinguished by titles and numbers and be divided into numbered paragraphs and clauses, with marginal summaries of the contents of each clause. In the passing of all laws, each different matter was to be provided for by a different law, "without intermixing into one and the same Act such things as have no proper relation to each other".[46]

Up to the time of the enlargement of the Legislative Council, its measures had been styled "Acts"; from 1843 to 1851 they were designated "Ordinances".[47] "I hope"—wrote R.G. Thomas—"that the colonists will leave off calling an Act of Parliament by a barbarous French word of ordonnance".[48] Upon the establishment of representative government in 1851, the title of "Act" was resumed.

During these years the Judge was frequently called upon to assist in the drafting of bills, either by preparing them himself or by settling them when drawn by others.[49] Mr Morphett, in the Legislative Council, protested against the Judge doing this work—on the grounds that it gave him too much to do, that it was unconstitutional for him to do it, and that his mind would be biased in the interpretation of such acts when subsequently he might have to consider them judicially.[50] As the Crown law officers became more efficient, less work of this nature fell on the Judges, although they continued during the 1850s to do most of the drafting of statutes connected with the reform of legal procedure and the constitution of the Supreme Court. In September 1853 Mr Angas moved in the Legislative Council that copies of all bills laid on the table of the House should be forwarded to the Judges. This he thought would be courteous, and suggestions might be obtained from them which would not occur to many of the members. The Speaker gave directions accordingly.[51]

A good deal of the legislation was simply the adoption of English statutes. Two courses were open—either to adopt them as they were passed, in toto, which led to the retention of such useless clauses as, for example, "nothing in this Act shall extend to Scotland" (see Act No 4 of 1852); or to adapt them to colonial use. The latter method was obviously preferable, but it entailed more work. A number of English acts were simply re-enacted verbatim or adopted by reference, irrespective of any incongruities and absurdities which might result. The same trouble arose in Victoria, where Sir Redmond Barry said (in *Fenton v. Day* 1 WW and A'B 64 at 65):

> 'The mode of legislation by reference from the enacting measure to other Acts may present conveniences in some respects, but it leads to the very greatest inconveniences in others—more particularly in cases of English Acts not commonly accessible in this country. Large portions of English Acts have, in some instances, been thus incorporated into our Acts by mere reference. Thus many persons are bound here by an immense mass of legislation of which they have no knowledge whatever, except by the purchase of English Acts—not readily accessible here.'

(Sir) Redmond Barry (1813-1880)
From 1852 to his death Barry was a Victorian Supreme Court judge. Noted for presiding over the trials of the Eureka rebels and Ned Kelly he was also active in many aspects of Victorian colonial life. (NLA)

So far as the criminal law was concerned, amendments in England were usually adopted fairly rapidly in South Australia. Mr Harrison, in his *Colonial Sketches* (p.107) sarcastically wrote:

> 'The law of England is adopted in the colony, with this addition, that the colonial law-makers have the privilege of passing any new enactments (not repugnant to the law of England), which leaves them a very fair margin for operations, and a perpetual subject for discussion and dissension ... Their general process has been to pass a law totally unsuited to the wants of the colony, and after the total inefficiency of the enactment has become a matter of notoriety, they set to work to patch up, amend, or consolidate it with some other enactment, until at last the statute book has swelled to that extent, that there is perhaps not a single lawyer in the colony who professes to understand it. There are some laws which the exigencies of the colony have made imperative, for the laws of England are not stringent enough to restrain the peculiar propensities of a virtuous colonial commercial community.'

Although it might perhaps be expected that in the unstable social conditions of a new colony, founded by men of radical tendencies, a liberative and regenerative spirit would be displayed in legislation, it is only very occasionally that the workings of that spirit can be discovered. So far as law reform was concerned, the pace set in

England was "hot enough to satisfy colonists deeply engaged in other tasks".

Like his predecessors, Governor Grey found himself unable to devote as much attention to legislation as he could have desired.

> 'Since I have had the honour of administering the Government'—he said at the opening of the reconstituted Council—'I have sedulously endeavoured to remedy the evils which resulted from the want of laws adapted to the novel and varying circumstances which necessarily arise in new communities.' [52]

But his time had been so taken up with financial matters that legislation perforce had been to some extent neglected.

A number of the Acts which were passed during the early years of the colony have been separately dealt with elsewhere, under various headings; and of the remainder, the greater part relate rather to economic than legal history and it is not proposed to examine their subject matter in detail.

As early as 1846 there were outcries for consolidation of the statutes. The *Register* deplored the fact that the "inextricable labyrinth of technical folly and confusion, yclepted British legislation" was being imitated on a smaller scale in the colony. Already legal gentlemen, it was said, had great trouble in ascertaining what was the law. Sweeping repeal and remodelling were urged as essential; scrappy amendments were useless.

> 'But where could a man be found with courage enough to undertake this Herculean task, even supposing that he were not be met by the determined resistance of those who batten on the Augean filth, and by its assistance force their way to the coif and the ermine, and leave to their families riches amassed from the ruin of moral peace and temporal fortunes? ... As the lawyers (the best of whom are but necessary evils) extract their largest gains from clumsy and indefinite Acts of Council, it was hardly to be expected even from the really intelligent men amongst them, that they should be at the pains of rectifying errors for official imbeciles as often as they saw them deviating from the paths of justice and common sense.' [53]

Charles Harvey Bagot (1788-1880)
The principal owner of the Kapunda mine and a pastoralist, Bagot was also a nominee in the Legislative Council (1844-51), a member in the part elective council (1851-53) and a member of the Legislative Council (1857-59, 1864-69). (SLSA)

In 1851 Mr Bagot moved in the Legislative Council that:

> '... in order to prevent the Statute Book being encumbered with several Acts bearing on the same points, it would be more expedient, as a general principle, to re-enact ordinances requiring amendment, than to introduce new amendments in separate Acts'.

In the course of the discussion which ensued, Mr Angas said that the Acts of the Council bore the character of shreds and patches, and would soon rival in complexity the statute laws of the old country. They should adopt, he thought, the model of the Code Napoleon, "so celebrated for its simplicity, clearness, and brevity". Mr Gwynne, however, pointed out that it was easier to make amendments than to reconstruct and reprint a whole act; and the Advocate-General said that the motion was either inconvenient, if it bound them always to re-enact in full, or useless, if it did not, "since no one could deny as a general principle that compactness and brevity were desirable in law-making". Nothing came of the motion.[54]

From time to time there was more talk of consolidation.

> 'Our local Acts'—said the Register, for instance, in 1856—'are fast multiplying, and we ought to take measures to obviate the necessity of having, at some future day, to grapple with such a monster difficulty as now engages the attention of law reformers at home.' [55]

John Baker
(1813-1872)
Baker settled in South Australia in 1840 after first emigrating from England to Van Diemen's Land. His business interests included pastoralism, mining, whaling and importation. A "conservative with progressive tendencies" he had a long political career that commenced in 1851.

In the following year the matter was taken up by Mr John Baker, who moved in the Legislative Council:

> '... that in terms of the Council the mode of legislation by reference is cumbrous and inconvenient, calculated to render the law upon any given subject obscure and difficult of comprehension; that it has had the effect of multiplying the number of Ordinances in our Statute Book, and is a fruitful source of litigation and expense; and that it is desirable to repeal all obsolete and unnecessary Acts, and to consolidate the laws in force in this Province'. [56]

The practice generally obtained in the province, he observed, of multiplying amendments to acts. "Instead of referring to a single Act, it was necessary to look through six or seven—a system which rendered necessary a very frequent resort to legal advisers." More than three hundred acts had been passed, many of which were obsolete, and "others were so amended as to be unintelligible". He advocated their revision and publication in a single volume.

William Henville Burford
(1807-1895) (above)
Although prominent in the religious affairs of the colony and a member of the House of Assembly (1857-59) Burford is best remembered as a soap and candle manufacturer. His business benefited from winning contracts to supply candles to the Kapunda, Burra, and Moonta mines. (SLSA)

His motion was carried and communicated to the House of Assembly, where Mr Burford subsequently moved a somewhat similar resolution, that the laws passed in the colony should be consolidated and codified. Objections having been raised on the score of the trouble and expense which would be involved, Mr Burford replied:

> 'What would be the trouble of codifying four volumes of Acts, many of which have been repealed, compared to the waggon-loads of law which were codified at Constantinople by Justinian? As to the expense, the work could be performed by

> two competent persons in twelve months, at an expense of £1000. I regret that much of the opposition to the resolution comes from members the profits of whose profession are extended by the existing state of the law.' [57]

An amendment was carried, that in future consolidation should be kept in view so far as possible, and there the matter rested. During 1859 the Attorney-General (Mr Hanson) made a useful attempt to consolidate the criminal law by a series of acts, in the drafting of which he was assisted by the Chief Justice.[58]

No attempt, however, was made to grapple with a general consolidation of the statute law. In February 1863 the Governor said, in his opening speech to Parliament:

> 'I invite your attention to the expediency of providing for the simplification and consolidation of our existing legislation. Our statute-books are becoming needlessly cumbersome and complex; and it is deserving of your consideration whether, without impairing the efficiency of our legislation, you cannot render it more simple and uniform.' [59]

William Parkin (1801-1889) An early Adelaide merchant, Parkin's success in business was such that he was able to retire with a "comfortable fortune" and devote his time to religious, philanthropic and political pursuits.

Still nothing was done. Four years later, Hon W. Parkin, in the Legislative Council, introduced the subject once more.

> 'I do not despair'—he said—'that before many years have passed away—although it may be after I have gone to dust—our laws will become reduced to a code, through the efforts of some young men of talent, endowed with sufficient mental energy and physical determination to grapple with a subject of such importance.' [60]

Later in the same year, the matter was again discussed in the Council. The Chief Secretary (Hon H. Ayers) said he had no doubt that it would be necessary in a few years to consolidate their acts, but there were great difficulties. The whole question was a large and expensive one.

> 'In the first place, it would be necessary to secure the services of a competent draftsman; and in the next place, it would involve on the part of the Legislature a great amount of care and consideration to enable them to go over all the Acts in force, with a view to their consolidation.' [61]

During 1867, also, Mr C. Lowe, a legal practitioner, published a *Tract for the Legislature* entitled: "On the Necessity for the Advantages of a Classified Consolidation of the Statute Law of the Province, the mode and facility of its preparation, and its beneficial effects on future legislation".

A complete codification of the law in force in South Australia, he pointed out, was obviously impossible; it would involve the codification of the greater part of English law. But it was within the power and means of Parliament to classify and consolidate the local statutes. He estimated that it might be done by one individual (if competent) with clerical aid, in twelve months, and passed by the legislature in another six months. It should be in the form of a code, reduced to divisions, chapters and sections, numerically arranged. Every five or ten years the amendments would be consolidated in the general code.

> 'Let Parliament, then'—he concluded—'no longer delay to provide the means for clearing the ground which is encumbered with useless carcasses or shells, which no one can complete on account of their worthlessness, and erect thereon a goodly structure, laying its foundations at a depth and strength proportioned to the longevity of a nascent empire.'

Mr Lowe's peroration fell upon deaf ears.

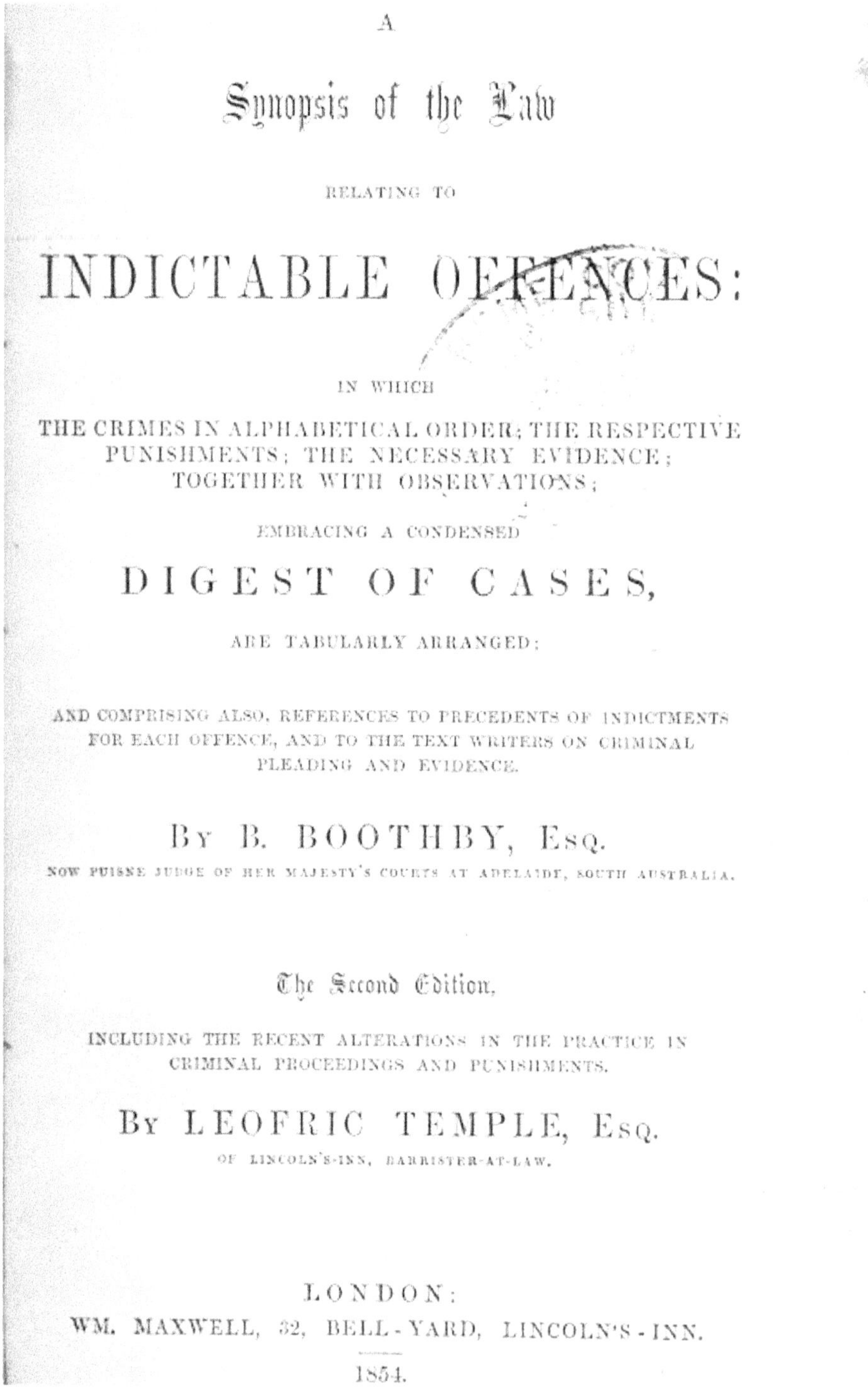

A

Synopsis of the Law

RELATING TO

INDICTABLE OFFENCES:

IN WHICH

THE CRIMES IN ALPHABETICAL ORDER; THE RESPECTIVE PUNISHMENTS; THE NECESSARY EVIDENCE; TOGETHER WITH OBSERVATIONS;

EMBRACING A CONDENSED

DIGEST OF CASES,

ARE TABULARLY ARRANGED;

AND COMPRISING ALSO, REFERENCES TO PRECEDENTS OF INDICTMENTS FOR EACH OFFENCE, AND TO THE TEXT WRITERS ON CRIMINAL PLEADING AND EVIDENCE.

BY B. BOOTHBY, ESQ.

NOW PUISNE JUDGE OF HER MAJESTY'S COURTS AT ADELAIDE, SOUTH AUSTRALIA.

The Second Edition,

INCLUDING THE RECENT ALTERATIONS IN THE PRACTICE IN CRIMINAL PROCEEDINGS AND PUNISHMENTS.

BY LEOFRIC TEMPLE, ESQ.

OF LINCOLN'S-INN, BARRISTER-AT-LAW.

LONDON:
WM. MAXWELL, 32, BELL-YARD, LINCOLN'S-INN.

1854.

Title page to Boothby's *A Synopsis of the Law Relating to Indictable Offences*. (SCLSA)

Mr Justice Boothby

Twelve hungry men

Benjamin Boothby was a man advanced in years before he entered the profession of law. Born at Doncaster, Yorkshire, on 5 February 1803, it was not until 1841 that he was called at Gray's Inn. Of his life between those two dates, all that can be ascertained is that he read in the chambers of a very eminent lawyer—Sir Thomas Wilde (afterwards Lord Truro)—who remained for many years his friend and patron.

Attaching himself to the Northern Circuit, Mr Boothby was in 1845 appointed one of the revising barristers for the West Riding of Yorkshire, and in 1849 Recorder of Pontefract, positions which he held until his departure for South Australia.[1] In 1842 he published a *Synopsis of the Law relating to Indictable Offences*, which went to a second edition in 1854, and in 1844 a pamphlet on the establishment of county courts, in which he contended for the total abolition of these courts and the provision of cheap and expeditious justice by the enlargement of the activities of the courts of common law at Westminster.[2]

While his career at the bar had not been brilliant, he had attained a respectable standing, and in many respects he was, as the Duke of Newcastle wrote, "well qualified" for the appointment of Judge of the Supreme Court of South Australia, which he received in 1853.[3]

> 'Benjamin Boothby'—said one of his friends when the appointment was announced—'is a gentleman whom I have known for thirty years, and a more dauntless advocate for high and liberal principles never pleaded for them. He is a stern defender of truth and impartial justice, and a man of no ordinary capacity, coupled with an amiable disposition.' [4]

In this eulogy there was a considerable stratum of truth. The most bitter opponent of Mr Justice Boothby could never deny that his character contained elements of great moral power. His professional and intellectual attainments were sufficient for his office; he had high ideals of the duty of a judge to the state; he had the courage to be outspoken in his opinions, and to hold fast to them regardless of criticism or abuse. His physical presence was favourable.[5] In private life he could be, when he wished, a courteous, urbane, and charming gentleman, and he was an irreproachable husband and father. To such a man the bench should have offered a term of useful and distinguished service, crowned with an honourable retirement. Yet with so many desirable attributes, Mr Justice Boothby ended his days in disappointment and disgrace.

When he came to South Australia he was fifty. Few men show much hospitality to new ideas after that age; by middle life the channels of mental activity are usually well established. "He had matured his character"—said one writer—"and settled his convictions in the stereotyped forms and stagnant atmosphere of the British judiciary." [6]

Passing by the somewhat disrespectful reference to the judges of England, it is unquestionably true that Mr Justice Boothby had an unswerving attachment to the English legal system as it existed at the time of his departure for South Australia. Colonial law, he thought, should conform to the standards established at home. Was it not monstrous impertinence of colonials—for the most part mere attorneys who had never enjoyed the inestimable privilege of eating their dinners at any of the Inns of Court—to suggest that rules formulated by the finest legal minds of England, and buttressed by the practice and traditions of centuries, should be set aside because it might be more convenient to apply another system at the Antipodes? That was not the fault of the rules; it was the fault of the Antipodes. If one of the two had to give way, he felt it his duty to see that it was not the rules of English law which he had sworn faithfully to administer.

No man holding such views could hope to be popular in Australia, and Mr Justice Boothby developed into the bogey of the Supreme Court. A Lapland wizard could not have been more successful in raising storms. While he sat on the bench, invalidity was always on tap, and freely and frequently he declared statutes of the local Parliament to be repugnant, unconstitutional and void. The rate of legislative mortality in South Australia during the years 1860 to 1867 has never been approached. The doctrine of repugnancy laid such strong hands upon the Judge that it dominated all his thinking. "A man"—said Halifax—"may dwell so long upon a thought, that it may take him prisoner."

Mr Justice Boothby ceased to hold opinions; his opinions held him. He was obsessed with them. "The intensity of his prejudices dimmed the clearness of his perception and blunted the acuteness of his intelligence."

He sought opportunities to air his notions, apparently believing, like the Bellman, that reiteration would infallibly give them the stamp of verity:

> 'Just the place for a Snark! I have said it twice:
> That alone should encourage the crew.
> Just the place for a Snark! I have said it thrice:
> What I tell you three times is true'.

His tangential style of reasoning was generally condemned, to put it bluntly, as a combination of lousy thinking, insanity and bias, but he could never be induced to admit that he was one iota in the wrong. Nor, indeed, was it easy to prove him so: he chose his own battlefield on quaggy and uncertain ground, and he slithered out of awkward corners with the elusiveness of an eel. "No man's error"—

Portrait of Judge Boothby by Nicholas Chevalier 1864 (SLV)

wrote Hobbes— "becomes his own law, nor obliges him to persist in it."

On many occasions Mr Justice Boothby could have honourably resiled from the position he had taken up—could have gracefully surrendered to superior force, marching out with colours flying—could have said, as judges have often said, "I remain convinced that my opinions are right, but I bow to those of my colleagues." Each time, however, he chose to hurl himself again into the fray. Like Amompharetus, Mr Justice Boothby never retreated. He persisted in the jactitation of his theories. He could see no flaw in his own arguments, and no merit in those of the misguided and benighted individuals who ventured to differ from him. "They are all gone out of the way, and become abominable; there is none that doth good, no, not one."

Every conciliatory approach made to him was rebuffed. Like M. Achille Quesnay he seems to have reasoned: "Toute affaire que l'on me propose est mauvaise, car si elle etait bonne, on ne me l'a proposerait pas." In truth, he was the architect of his own sorrows, and followed to destruction an ignis fatuus of his own creation.

The tenacity with which he clung to his dogmatic views, in the face of overwhelming opposition, cannot but extort admiration. It was unfortunate that his very consistency—as a rule an admirable quality in a judge—led him further and further astray. As De Quincey pointed out:

> '... the man whose error commences in a false idea of his theme, whose fault is laid in the very germ of the conception from which he starts, must be more and more erroneous in proportion as he is more and more true to himself'.

Constancy in a good cause becomes mere obstinacy in a bad one, and obstinacy eventually led him to foolish inconsistencies and obstructive tactics. His "perverse ingenuity", as Mr Justice Owen Dixon has recently said (51 Law Quarterly Review p.599), "employed itself in contriving to find some ground of invalidity in as many of the enactments of the legislature as he possibly could".

Lord Cranworth once naively remarked that: "... it would be a very dangerous thing if decrees were drawn up stating how many of the judges had taken one view and how many another". (Lord Lilford v. The Attorney General 16 LT 184 at 186).

It would be difficult to compile any statistics of dissent in the Supreme Court, but during his last few years on the bench Mr Justice Boothby disagreed with one or both of his colleagues, and rudely, on almost every possible occasion. "Those who will not be ruled by the rudder must be ruled by the rock", and soon the diapason throbbed to the cry that at all costs the Judge must be got rid of. For years he fought stoutly, but with Parliament against him, the Governor against him, his colleagues against him, the press against him, and the majority of the bar and the public against him, it was a hopeless contest. "Wise men and Gods are on the strongest side."

Mr Justice Boothby preferred to stand alone, and as the years went by it became increasingly evident that when the last brick was thrown he would be at the receiving end. The extraordinary thing is that he held out so long. Only when at last, in 1867, he was actually removed from the bench, did his confidence fail. He talked of an appeal to the Privy Council, but the reaction after this grand climacteric of his fortunes was rapid and fatal. He lost heart, retired into solitude, fretted, and died within a year.

Confident obstinacy in maintaining his idiosyncratic opinions was undoubtedly the principal factor in bringing about the Judge's ruin. "He had the quality of firmness"— it was said— "in an eminent degree, enough for three ordinary men; a bulldog obstinacy that would never yield."

Another cause, and that not of inconsiderable operation, was his singular lack of tact and insensitiveness to the feelings of others. With almost all the habits of an English gentleman, Mr Justice Boothby mingled one or two unfortunate streaks of what can only be called caddishness. He had a flair for treading on people's corns, and he rapidly earned the reputation—which was not without some foundation—of being arrogant and opinionated.

To another factor, also, reference must be made. He brought with him to South Australia his wife and twelve children, and an income of £1,200 a year did not go far when he had to maintain a respectable position in society as Judge, and, at the same time, support so many. A laudable desire to see his children well educated and established in life (three of them—Josiah, Benjamin, and William Robinson—repaid it by very valuable services to the state) meant that constant economy was necessary. He was haunted by money troubles: he even announced from the bench the difficulties he experienced "with 15 or 16 mouths to feed". His income was just too small to enable him to keep his family in the comfort which he would have desired, and for years he struggled with accumulating debts. He was not extravagant; he lived quietly and respectably; there was simply not enough money to go round, and he adopted the practice of placing the needs of his family before the satisfaction of his creditors—in short, he did not always pay his debts with promptitude. In England, he was on one occasion outlawed for failing to settle a claim against him, and his enemies did not hesitate to revive this unpleasant episode and use it against him. He came to South Australia owing money to English creditors, and during his fifteen years in the colony quite a small stream of summonses for petty debts issued out of the Adelaide Local Court against him.[7] His creditors were paid if they waited long enough, but he lived a hand-to-mouth existence which led to undignified squabbles, and undoubtedly stimulated his desperate attempts to oust Mr Hanson from the position of Chief Justice, in the hope of obtaining for himself the higher position and the higher salary. It would be unjust to say that the desire for money was the only stimulus: he genuinely believed that as a matter of law Mr Hanson had no right to the position, and that it was his duty to protest. Disappointed ambition and pecuniary needs combined to impel him to utter those views in a manner which was inconsistent with the dignity of his office.

A family group photograph of Mrs Benjamin Boothby (Maria Bradbury nee Robinson) with her children and grandchildren taken at "The Glen" in 1876. Judge Boothby's portrait is displayed next to Mrs Boothby. (Valerie Esau)

No sooner had he landed in the colony than he quarrelled with the Government over his salary. He had received notice of his appointment from the Colonial Office in February 1853, he embarked in May, and he arrived in Adelaide at the end of August. The passage money for his large family must have seriously depleted his financial resources, and he no doubt needed every penny on which he could lay his hands. The Government proposed to pay him half salary from his appointment in England to his arrival in Adelaide, and full salary from that date, when Letters Patent had been issued by the Governor constituting him Judge. Mr Justice Boothby, however, claimed he was entitled to full salary for the whole period, and, in an eighteen page letter, vehemently protested against any deduction. The Advocate-General (Mr Hanson), after conferring with the Crown Solicitor, reported that the decision of the claim must depend upon the time at which Mr Boothby became Judge. That could only be the date of the issue of the Letters Patent, and not the date of the warrant from the Colonial Office notifying him of the appointment.

> 'Although therefore I feel the force of the argument that since the date of the warrant he has given up all those sources of professional income to enable himself to discharge the duties of his office, yet unless he can show some legal authority for holding that he became Judge from the date of the Warrant I must conceive that he has no legal claim to salary prior to the date of the Letters Patent.' [8]

Much to the Judge's disgust, therefore, the Government refused his claim.

It was, perhaps, with his own debts in mind that a few months later, at the first Criminal Sessions over which he presided, Mr Justice Boothby feelingly told the jury, in a case of an assault on a debtor by a creditor who had called to collect a debt, that he hoped: "... they would show that no person could collect his debts by kicking his debtor with iron-bound shoes so as to disable him for six weeks". [9]

Soon after his arrival the Judge purchased for his home the estate known as "The Glen", at Glen Osmond, but before doing so he had become involved in an equity suit over a lease of a house which he had proposed to take. He had the mortification to have his petition dismissed by Mr Justice Cooper on the ground that he had started the wrong proceedings.[10]

For a year or two Mr Justice Boothby's performance of his duties gave general satisfaction. He sought popularity by frequently attending public meetings and dinners. He conducted the business at the Criminal Sessions in so prompt and businesslike a manner that he was thanked for the time he saved the jurors and witnesses.[11] When Mr Justice Cooper was asked to make the same improvements, he replied very tartly that he was not disposed to run a race for popularity with his learned colleague.

From the outset, however, Mr Justice Boothby deplored the abolition of the Grand Jury. It was "a most admirable institution", and by its removal "a very delicate and onerous duty" had been thrown on the Advocate-General.[12] The fall of man and the fall of grand juries, it came to be said, were regarded by Mr Justice Boothby as matters equally deplorable—the two great calamities of the human race.

The Judge early took the view that he could give directions to the Attorney-General as to what charges should be laid against persons brought before the Criminal Court. (See *R. v. Hammett* Register 12/8/59). If there had been a Grand Jury, he reasoned, he could have directed them what charge the evidence would support; the functions of the Grand Jury had been transferred to the Attorney-General; ergo, he could give such directions to the Attorney-General. When he attempted to enforce this doctrine some years later, against the will of an equally obstinate Attorney-General, a bitter quarrel was inevitable.

He liked, too, to dilate upon the great value of the institution of trial by jury, to which, in his opinion, the glory of England was attributable. The blessing ought to be preserved in all its purity, and he could hardly find words to express the horror he felt at hearing that Adelaide jurors were, in difficult cases, "guilty of the folly and wickedness of degrading themselves and their judgment by writing guilty or innocent on pieces of papers and returning a verdict as one or the other was drawn from a hat".[13] He never ceased to impress upon juries how important it was that they should do their duty, a task in which, he said, they had the inestimable advantage of hearing the arguments of counsel.

> 'Vulgar minds are disposed to regard the effort of professional gentlemen as mere hireling displays; but that is taking a very narrow and erroneous view of the subject. It is desirable and advantageous to have a class of men able by education, habit, and professional aptitude, to present every aspect merit and bearing of a case to the judgment of a jury.' [14]

The only blemish on his record during his first two years of office was one unfortunate scene in the Local Court, in which the Judges then presided on full jurisdiction days. The Judge took his seat in a bad temper and announced that he wanted it known that when he sat there he would start at ten precisely, and that all cases not ready when called on would be struck out.

> 'His Honor'—said the Register, in describing the proceedings—'was probably suffering from indisposition, as he wore his hat on the Bench, which did not seem to add much to the dignity of the Court. He was also irritable. One luckless lawyer inadvertently addressed him as "Your Worship", for which he received a reproof so sharply petulant, that he will not be likely to forget it for some time. The bystanders could not avoid wishing that His Honor would, when he next presided, bring his wig, if his head must be covered in Court, as well as a courteous feeling towards the

> Bar, even when they forget to "Your Honour" him, and a little consideration for luckless litigants whom some unforeseen accident might have detained on the road.'

Thirteen cases were disposed of in twenty minutes, most of them being struck out because they were not ready.

> 'This is celerity with a vengeance'—commented the Register—'but inasmuch as the majority of the parties will either have to recommence proceedings or forego their claims, we cannot help thinking that the law of the Local Court as administered by Mr Boothby is both roundabout and expensive.' [15]

During these years Mr Justice Boothby prepared and put forward schemes for improving the postal communication between England and Australia,[16] and for the construction of interstate railways.[17] The latter plan embraced a grand trunk railway, having three termini—Sydney, Melbourne and Adelaide. The railway was to be laid from Sydney to a point on the River Murray, whence it would branch off to Adelaide and Melbourne. At each of the three capitals enormous docks were to be constructed, to accommodate the largest ocean steamers. The capital required to finance this scheme, he estimated, would be £21,000,000. His plans were too vague and too vast to be seriously considered. The London *Times* criticised them severely as intrinsically unsound, and said the whole affair furnished "a new instance of the delusions of communities who expect to be forced into greatness by extraneous help instead of being satisfied with a steady growth".[18] The local press was politer, but agreed that the plan was hopelessly impracticable in the then state of development of the colonies

Railway History
The early history of rail in South Australia was quite different from Boothby's grand schemes. Railways were constructed in a piecemeal fashion to meet immediate needs. The first railway was built between Goolwa and Port Elliot in 1854 with a line between Adelaide and Port Adelaide completed in 1856.

> 'What Judge Boothby proposes to accomplish suddenly, in five years, will, we apprehend, be brought to pass ultimately. But it will come gradually, and as the advancing tide of civilization bears us onward.' [19]

As years went by, incidents occurred which did not tend to raise Mr Justice Boothby in the public opinion. The profession thought he was too fond of holding out to them the enormous distance which separated them from the higher standards which characterised the bar in England. He was accused of being prejudiced against Roman Catholics, and he aroused the hostility of the Irish section of the community by informing the jury, in a case in which an Irishman was charged with assault, that:

> 'It is clear that Irishmen are addicted to the use of the shillelah, and it is a kindness to themselves to teach them the guilt and danger of indulging in habits of violence or resorting to the exercise of mere brute force.' [20]

It was observed, too, that on many occasions there were differences of opinion between the two Judges.

> 'Looking at the present constitution of the Supreme Court'—it was said in the Register in August 1855—'we find that it is composed of two Judges—one certainly of great colonial experience, the other a late arrival among us—both gentlemen undoubtedly of the highest integrity of purpose and moral rectitude; but, if it may be inferred from the oft-repeated expressions of those qualified to form opinions, and from the almost universal feeling upon the subject, they are unable of themselves to create that amount of public confidence in their administrative abilities which it is indispensable every person should place in a court exercising so high a jurisdiction. This opinion partly oews [sic] its origin to the frequent different views of the law which have latterly fallen from the Bench in various cases, and partly to the fact that the interests of the colony require that the various important questions which are so frequently coming before the Court should be weighed and determined by a more sound and dignified tribunal—one which would tend to extinguish the feeling of insecurity which prevails with those before whom the prospect of a judicial determination of disputed right is at all apparent.' [21]

It was suggested that the Legislative Council should add a third judge to the Court, at a salary which would be sufficient to ensure obtaining from England a man of recognised ability. The topic was raised again in the following year, but nothing was done, and the Judges continued to differ frequently.

The passing of the Constitution Act (No 2 of 1855-56) provided Mr Justice Boothby with the first of his many grievances, real and fancied. Section 36 of the Act provided that no judge of any court of the province should be capable of being elected a Member of Parliament. This was a bitter pill to Mr Justice Boothby, who himself said openly, at a public meeting:

> 'The wisdom of the Legislature has determined that as a Judge I am ineligible to sit in Parliament, whereas a man who has just served his seven years' transportation may sit in that Parliament, from which I am excluded. There is no man so competent to sit in Parliament as a Judge—no man whose qualifications are so suitable. I confess that I had hoped to have a seat in Parliament myself, but I am excluded from a place which I believe myself fitted to fill.' [22]

Under the stimulus of this personal quarrel with the act, he had set to work to pick it to pieces, and in December 1855, when the

Constitution Bill was before the Legislative Council, he had submitted to the Governor a long memorandum setting out numerous unconstitutional provisions in the Bill. Section 32 of the Act provided that no person should hold the office of Chief Secretary, Attorney-General, Treasurer, Commissioner of Crown Lands and Immigration, or Commissioner of Public Works for a longer period than three months, unless he was a member of Parliament, and the persons for the time being holding these offices were constituted ex officio members of the Executive Council. This the Judge denounced as a restraint upon the prerogative of the Crown, unknown to the English constitution. "The Crown has always been free to choose its advisers from whatever source its will dictated."

He strenuously objected to the Attorney-General or Solicitor-General being members of the Executive Council.

> 'The Crown cannot be compelled'—he wrote—'to seek legal advice from law officers who, after the advice is given, have the power, it may be, by a casting vote to compel that advice to be adopted ... The small number of persons qualified to become Law Officers of the Crown in this Province, if the Crown were compelled to make such its Cabinet Ministers, would give to a few individuals the monopoly of always forming two out of the six members of the Executive Council of the Province ... Such a power in a very limited body would cause this Province to be virtually governed, not by the Crown, but by an Oligarchy, in which lawyers would have a predominative power ... To place the Law Officers of the Crown in such a situation would in effect be a putting up of the Judicial Office to popular election; for, as Cabinet Ministers, the Attorney and Solicitor General would be able to demand their elevation to the Judicial Bench, and the Crown would be impotent to resist ... The independence of the Judges would be endangered, for they must listen to arguments at the Bar, on great Constitutional questions arising between the Crown and the people, from the lips of men having the power of Cabinet Ministers; and who, in leaving the Court, might do so only to join a Cabinet Council to decide on the promotion to a higher rank in judicial office of the very Judge to whom the previous hour they had been addressing their arguments in behalf of the Crown.' [23]

No-one appears to have taken any notice whatever of these numerous objections.

In December 1856 Sir Charles Cooper obtained leave of absence to visit England. At a farewell breakfast given him on the morning of his departure, he paid a tribute to his colleague:

> '... to whose considerate help I am much indebted, and with whom in consequence of his kind and affectionate disposition, I have enjoyed the most fraternal intercourse. Indeed, I have looked upon him not merely as my brother in a legal sense, but also in an extended sense—that of domestic relationship'.

Mr Justice Boothby replied with similar compliments, and protestations of eternal goodwill, which in view of his later relations with Sir Charles have a very ironical flavour. "It is one thing to have a colleague on the Bench", he said, "It is another to have a friend."

> 'He put his hand upon his heart
> And swore that they should never part—
> I wonder what he would have said
> If he had put it on his head'.

It is of some significance that Mr Justice Boothby thought it necessary to make public reference to the frequency with which he had disagreed with the learned brother he loved so well.

> 'The records of our judgments in court'—he said—'show that there have been occasions when we have differed in opinion, but that difference was honestly arrived at, and was the result alone of an independent exercise of our individual judgments. This I will now attest, that we never knew of any difference in private.'

Differences of opinion often occurred in the English courts, even in the House of Lords, and "fatal, indeed, would it be to the interests of any community whose Judges should always arrive at precisely the same view".[24]

Sir Charles Cooper having departed, Mr Justice Boothby at once claimed that he should be appointed to act as Chief Justice.

> 'By various local Ordinances'—he wrote to the Governor—'and the practice of the Supreme Court, its process in some instances can only run in the name of the Chief Justice, but he being out of the jurisdiction, my name has to be substituted for that of the Chief Justice; and it becomes necessary, therefore, that a public notification should be made of the absence of the Chief Justice, and that during such absence the remaining Judge is empowered to perform the duties which would devolve on the Chief Justice were he within the Province.'

With this view the Governor concurred.

> 'Independent of the point raised by Judge Boothby'—he said—'I confess it appears to me wholly inconsistent with the usage of other colonies to have the office of Chief Justice

> vacant. It appears to me that it is a clear privilege of the next Judge to claim the acting appointment with such increase of salary as the Colonial Regulations justify viz half the difference between the salary of the Chief Justice and that of Judge Boothby, which in this instance will amount to £100 per annum.' [25]

Mr Justice Boothby was accordingly appointed Acting Chief Justice, and Mann was again appointed Acting Judge.[26]

One of the first acts of the new Chief Justice was to prescribe that the business of the Supreme Court should be opened daily with the following proclamation:

> 'All persons who have anything to do with this Civil Sittings of the Supreme Court of this Province, let them draw near and give attendance and they will be heard. God Save the Queen and this Honourable Court.'[27]

Sir Charles Cooper had left the colony only two months, when his successor provoked a tremendous public outcry, which really marks the beginning of the "Boothby question". It had its origin in sordid circumstances. Dr Popham, a medical practitioner of Glenelg, was charged with rape by a servant girl named Ann Mara, and was committed for trial. He retaliated by laying an information against her for perjury in preferring the charge against him, and she also was committed for trial at the same sessions. Mr Justice Boothby, who presided, directed that the charge of perjury should be brought on first. After hearing the evidence, he took a pronounced view against the girl, and summed up very strongly against her. The jury, however, brought in a verdict of acquittal. There was loud applause at the back of the court, and one old man was haled [sic] forward and sentenced to seven days' imprisonment for contempt of court, on the ex parte and unsworn statements of two constables who had been standing with their backs to him. Later in the day he was permitted to apologise humbly for an offence he had not committed, and was released with a severe warning not to offend again.[28]

The procedure adopted by the Judge in requiring the perjury charge to be heard first was widely criticised and denounced as "judicial perversity". Why, it was objected, should the girl be tried for perjury in respect of a charge which she declared herself ready to prove to the jury. If she proved it, then obviously she had not committed perjury. If she failed to prove it, *then* the question would arise, had she been guilty of perjury? Suppose Ann Mara, on being charged with perjury, had retorted by charging Dr Popham with conspiracy; to be consistent the Judge would have to try first the conspiracy charge, then the perjury charge, and last of all, the original charge; and it was absurd to think of justice being administered in a descending series like this.

In the course of his summing up, too, the Judge had made some incautious remarks as to discrepancies in the evidence against the girl.

> 'Discrepancies' — he said — 'are not contradictions. Discrepancies are generally taken as evidence of general truth. It is said, when people agree on every point of a story, that they each talk like a parrot. In one of the greatest works ever written in defence of the Christian religion, Paley rested on the discrepancies in the different accounts as reasons why they should be believed, being evidence of the absence of collusion and that each spoke truthfully.'

He had put his proposition too widely, and the *Register* seized on it as a target for sarcastic invective.

> 'How many discrepancies would establish truth?' -it asked scornfully- 'If no inconsistency exists, if the witnesses agree together, so far from the duty of the Jury being clear, it becomes, according to the Judge, painfully doubtful. Only when evidence is conflicting is it thoroughly trustworthy.' [29]

On the day following Ann Mara's acquittal, the charge against Dr Popham came on for hearing. Gwynne prosecuted. When he rose to open, the Judge suggested to him that it was useless to go on, and halfway through his opening, he again interrupted to inform the jury that he would direct them that it would be a dangerous thing to proceed upon the oath of the woman, and that unless satisfied upon other evidence they ought to acquit. The girl gave evidence, was cross-examined, and was closely questioned by the Judge. When her evidence was finished, he said to Gwynne, "You know the evidence that is to come—the evidence that was here yesterday," and turning to the jury, went on: "Gentlemen, it is idle to go on with this case. It is only wasting your time and the time of the public, after hearing the evidence of this woman."

Gwynne naturally said that after so decided an expression of opinion from the Judge he could have no wish to press the case.

> 'I wonder very much that you should have persisted'—was the retort—'after the intimation which I had already given. I never knew a case where counsel persisted after an intimation from a Judge that it would be most unsafe to find a prisoner guilty on the evidence.'

The Judge then fired a double-barrelled question at the jury.

"Gentlemen"—he asked—"are you dissatisfied with this woman's evidence? Do you wish the case to go on?"

Several jurors answered "No". The Judge took their negative to apply to his second question.

> 'You may go'—he told the prosecutrix—'and I believe you to be a perjured woman. Dr Popham, you may leave that box, and I consider you do so with a character unstained. How the other jury gave their decision I do not know. They will have to answer for it to their own consciences; but in my opinion no men of intelligent judgment could have come to such a decision. It was a most unwise verdict. I am of opinion that, so far as any imputation from that woman's statement goes, you leave the box with character unscathed, and you may repeat, when necessary, this my opinion. Take a formal verdict of not guilty. It is a mercy to this woman that she should not be allowed to go on with these perjuries. There is no further business before the Court. Gentlemen, you are discharged.'

The jury were hustled out of the box, and the Court adjourned, without any opportunity being given for them to explain that their "No" had been to the Judge's first question—are you dissatisfied with the woman's evidence? One juryman was deputed to interview the Judge and explain this, and say that the jury thought the case should have proceeded. He met with a warm reception from the Judge, who said he had put the question plainly, and if there was any error the fault was all theirs; but in any event, he added, the mistake, if there was one, was of little consequence, as he would have broken down the case.[30]

Mr Justice Boothby in the Popham case plainly allowed his own feelings about the credibility of the prosecutrix to sway him too far; and his remarks about the jury in the previous case were obviously improper. The result was an outcry of totally unexpected violence. Ann Mara had been victimised, was the cry; "Jeffries Boothby", who was either dishonest or a downright fool, had judicially condemned her after she had been acquitted by a jury; he had deprived her of the sacred right of stating her complaint by his deliberate and acknowledged purpose of "breaking it down". The members of the jury in the perjury case protested against the "vile imputation" which had been cast upon them; and allegations were made that the Judge was influenced by anti-Catholic bias.

> 'We say fearlessly'—said the Register—'that such a burlesque on the administration of justice as was exhibited in the Supreme Court is calculated, if not to bring the laws of the land into contempt, at least to induce the utmost want of confidence in those by whom they are administered ... The whole affair is a disgrace to the Bench of the colony and to the age in which we live. The necessity of some judicial changes is now becoming more and more apparent; and the case of Ann Mara will powerfully contribute to bring about the alterations so long and so much needed.' [31]

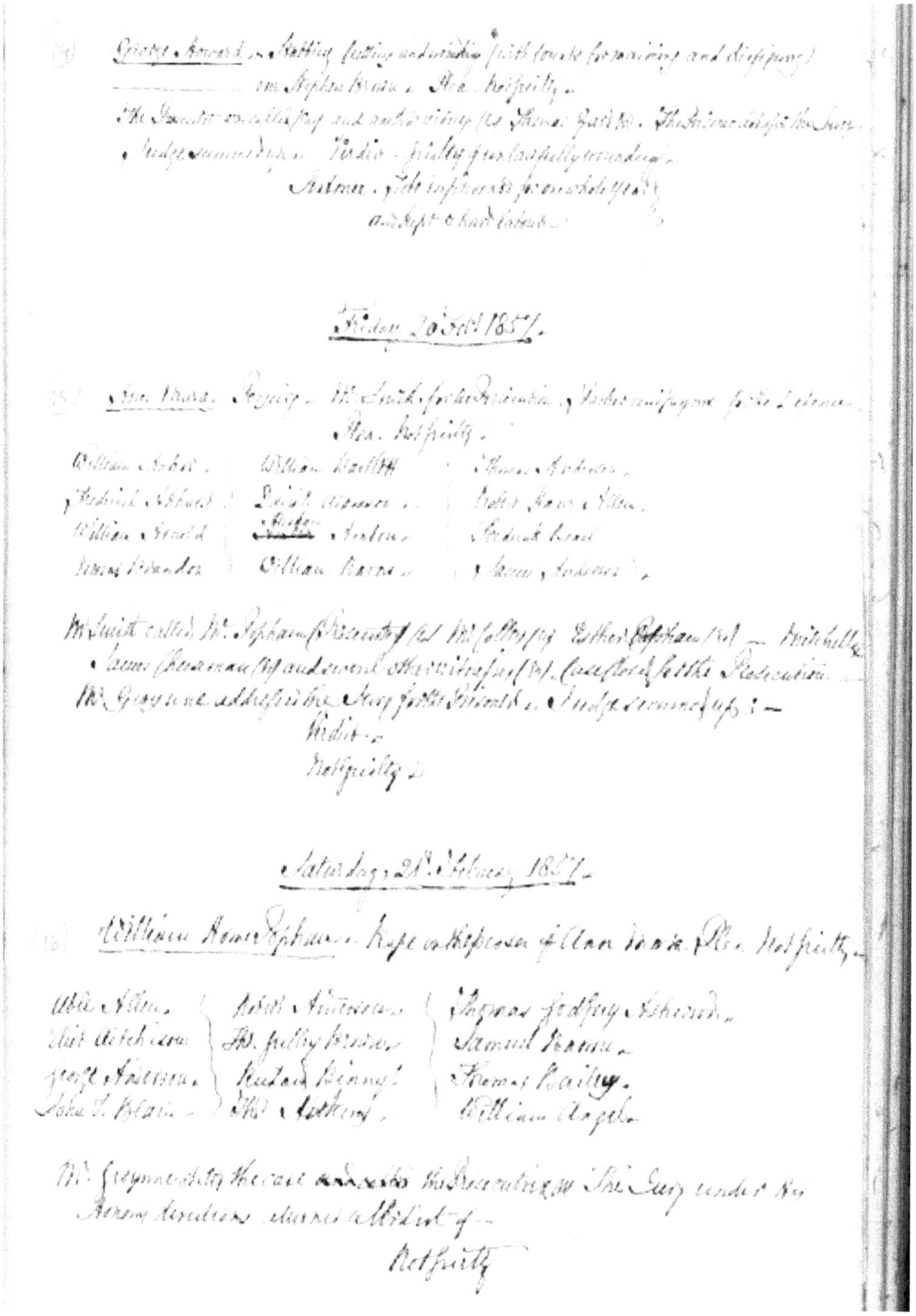

Friday 20 Feby 1857.

Saturday 21st February 1857.

Court record of the Mara and Popham trials (SCLSA)

A public meeting was called to consider the administration of criminal justice in the Supreme Court. Some fifteen hundred persons attended, and resolutions were passed deploring the conduct of the Judge.

> 'We most unhesitatingly and emphatically deprecate'—ran one—'such an unwarrantable, unjust, and arbitrary assumption of power, the which we consider it our solemn duty to resist by every constitutional means, as an insult to the feelings of men, an infraction of the liberty of the subject, a denial of justice, and a direct contravention of the right that a Briton claims of trial by jury.'

The Judge was denounced as incompetent and a liar, and as wholly unfit to be entrusted with the power which he held; he had "utterly lost the confidence of the community in his administration of the law".[32]

A memorial was drawn up for presentation to the House of Assembly, praying for the Judge's suspension or removal.[33] It was left available for public signature for some time; but enthusiasm waned, and the memorial was finally "withdrawn from the table, kicked out of doors, and afterwards set fire to on the pavement of King William Street".[34]

Mr Justice Boothby would have been more than human if he had entirely ignored the insults hurled at him. Rumours having spread that he intended to defend himself from the bench, the Court was crowded at its next sitting, but he wisely refrained from mentioning the subject.[35] Against the members of the public he could do nothing; over the profession he had a certain amount of control, and he was furious to read in the newspapers the names of a number of lawyers who had attended the meeting. On the day following the meeting a letter appeared in the *Register*, purporting to be signed by several of them, including Mr Andrews, stating that although they had been present at the meeting they had taken no part in it and did not concur in its resolutions. Another who had attended the meeting, James Penn Boucaut (then a young man just entered into practice) had not signed the letter. Andrews told Boucaut that his name had been affixed to the letter without his authority and much to his annoyance because he considered he had a right to go to any public meeting he chose without having to give an explanation. Shortly afterwards, Boucaut had to attend before the Judge on some chamber business, and he has left an interesting memorandum, written at the time, setting out their conversation. The following dialogue took place:

> Mr Justice Boothby: 'I've said the same to every member of the profession who was at that meeting, Mr Boucaut, that I consider that a professional man who was there and didn't hold up his hands against that meeting acted very improperly,

Richard Bullock Andrews (1823-1884)
Andrews left England for health reasons arriving in Adelaide in 1852 and began practising law the following year. Elected to the House of Assembly in 1857 he served as Attorney General until 1860 and later from 1863 to 1868. A Queen's Counsel from 1865 he was appointed Crown Solicitor in 1870 and in 1881 he became a Judge of the Supreme Court. (SLSA)

(Sir) James Penn Boucaut (1831-1916)
Boucaut's first employment in South Australia was as a stockman but a career in law led to him serving in Parliament for twenty-seven years. He held various ministries including Attorney General and was Premier three times (1866-67, 1875-76 and 1877-78). Appointed a Judge of the Supreme Court in 1878 he served another twenty-seven years in that role.

> and I'll hold no further communication with any man who does not disclaim it. Several members of the profession have already done so, and the same course is open to you.'
>
> Boucaut: 'Your Honour, I didn't wish to be seen. I got in amongst the chairs to avoid that, but the reporter hunted me out.'
>
> Mr Justice Boothby: 'You were there and have the same course open to you as the other gentlemen.'
>
> Boucaut: 'Your Honour takes me by surprise.'

After discussing the business on which he had attended, Boucaut said that he had been thinking about the Judge's remarks, which necessarily distracted his mind, and that he would have no objection to make a statement such as other members of the profession had made.

> Mr Justice Boothby: 'They have published it and you have the same remedy.'
>
> Boucaut: 'Mr Andrews has told me he never authorised the communication to be made.'
>
> Mr Justice Boothby: 'Very well. I want no further communication. The paper is open to you.'
>
> Boucaut: 'Good morning.' [36]

Consideration of the Judge's attitude towards him left Boucaut considerably worried, and on his return to his office he wrote asking that the Judge should state distinctly what he wanted in the way of an apology. "I cannot but feel from the tenor of your remarks"—he said—"that my prospects through life may be most seriously affected by the course I may now pursue."

Should the Judge see fit to adopt towards him in the practice of his profession the course of action so clearly implied by the Judge's manner during the conversation that morning, then the consequences would be ruinous. It was true he had attended at the meeting, but he did so merely as a spectator and took no other part in it; and he could not recognise "the right of anyone to demand any kind of disclaimer at my hands".[37]

To this letter no answer was vouchsafed; but Boucaut was convinced, from Mr Justice Boothby's manner towards him, that resentment smouldered. He thought that the Judge went out of his way to make opportunities of being rude to him in court; and the ill-feeling between them became so pronounced that several years later Hanson remarked on it, and asked Boucaut what was the cause of it.[38] The Judge had made an enemy, who, as his accuser before the

Governor and Council in 1867, was to play a leading part in the amoval proceedings.

That Mr Justice Boothby bitterly resented the attacks upon him was soon made obvious by the sarcastic dicta which from time to time he threw out from the bench. "Juries must have credit for intelligence if Judges do not," he said on one occasion; and in another case, after some bickering with counsel about a witness whose evidence the Judge thought untrustworthy, he seized the opportunity to add:

> 'Certain persons, who have more presumption than knowledge, take upon themselves to say that a Judge, sitting in this Court, is not entitled to say to a witness who gives contradictory evidence, first before a Magistrate and afterwards before himself, that in his opinion that witness is a perjured person.' [39]

On a third occasion he complained:

> 'Juries are bound to obey the direction of the Judge on points of law, and for them to refuse to do so is to disregard their oath. It is a fact that juries have been taught to disobey the Judge's direction; I do not mean by the Bar, but in other quarters they have been so instructed.' [40]

He saw in the slightest suggestion of opposition from counsel or jury an intention to insult him; and he became more and more determined to exercise his authority over them and show that he was ruler in his own court. The attacks of rheumatic gout from which he suffered were not conducive to the more genial discharge of his duties.[41] He was furious when a jury insisted on going on with a case which he thought should have been stopped. While he continually talked of upholding the dignity of the bench, he went about it in a strange way by bandying words with counsel, witnesses and jurors; and in these encounters he did not always come off best. In one case he suggested the adoption of a certain course. Mr Stow, who appeared for the defendant, was unwilling to take it.

Randolph Isham Stow (1828-1878)
One of four sons of the influential Congregational minister Thomas Quentin Stow, Randolph was a lawyer and politician who, by the time of his elevation to the Supreme Court Bench in 1875, had acquired a reputation as a brilliant lawyer and powerful speaker.

> 'It is very unusual for counsel to persist after such an intimation from the Judge as I have given'—said Mr Justice Boothby, bridling up at once at this opposition.
>
> 'Surely Your Honour will allow a counsel some discretion in conducting a cause'—was the reply.
>
> 'No experienced counsel would choose to exercise such a discretion after the expression of a reasonable opinion by the Judge.'
>
> 'That, Your Honour'—retorted Mr Stow—'leaves the counsel

> some discretion. Now, as I know the case better, perhaps, than your Honour, I may be in a position to feel that the suggestion is not a reasonable one.'

To this the Judge had no suitable answer, and fumed in silence.[42]

His particular abhorrence was the *Register* newspaper and everything connected with it. The *Adelaide Times*, until it faded out of existence in 1858, was a supporter of the Judge; through rumour, indeed, had it that those articles which praised him were written by Boothby himself.[43] The *Register*, however, was definitely and consistently opposed to him. It characterised his conduct as unwarranted and offensive.

> 'If Mr Justice Boothby'—it said—'will not permit the recent unhappy displays he has made of himself to be forgotten; if, when his opponents are willing to be silent, he persists in goading them to opposition; if he will neither study the wishes of his friends, nor the tactics of his enemies, nor the moderate counsels of temperate and disinterested advisers, all we can say is, that as His Honor makes his bed so must he lie upon it; whatever opposition he may excite will be the fruit of his own perversity.' [44]

The result was that when Mr Fisher proposed to cite to the Judge as an authority a case decided several years before and reported in the *Register*, the Judge, to use a vigorous vernacular expression, "hit the roof".

> 'God forbid'—he said—'that I should acknowledge the accuracy of reports in this Colony; God forbid that ever the Judges of this Court should have to rely upon the reports of the newspapers as to what happens in this Court.'

Not unnaturally, this annoyed the editor of the *Register*. He promptly circularised the legal profession, asking whether his law reports were satisfactory, and published triumphantly a string of replies testifying to their accuracy.[45] Mr Justice Boothby replied by launching a more venomous attack upon the paper. A libellous advertisement had been inserted in the *Register*. The person libelled sued the author of the advertisement, but, to the disappointment and annoyance of the Judge, he did not sue the newspaper. When the case came on, the Judge castigated the plaintiff severely.

> 'You have not discharged your duty to the public'—he said—'because you should have brought your action against the Register. As the action is brought against the writer only of the libel, the Jury will do right in finding for very small damages; but, if, on the other hand, it had been brought against the proprietors of the Register, I should have strenuously advised

them to give heavy damages.'

The conduct of the *Register* in inserting libels for profit he denounced as worse than hiring a man to rob another on the highway.

Roused by this, the *Register* returned to the fray with unabated vigour. Allowances must be made, it said, "for the mental infirmities of the Judge"; but his attack was obviously a vindictive and spiteful one, produced by a thirst for revenge because his conduct in the Mara case had been exposed. "Mr Justice Boothby neither forgets nor forgives, and in order to carry out his vindictiveness he disqualifies himself for the impartial administration of justice."

With a trepidation which he had good cause to feel, the editor asked: "What are we to expect at the hands of Mr Justice Boothby should we ever have the misfortune to come before him?" [46]

With amazing tactlessness, Mr Justice Boothby chose the very moment, when the public was agitated with the belief that he was endeavouring to override juries, to put into force the powers given to him by section 182 of the Supreme Court Act 1853. That section read:

> 'Upon the trial of any cause, it shall be lawful for the Judge who may try the same, to direct the jury sworn upon such cause to find the facts specially, and upon such finding, the said Supreme Court shall give such judgment in the cause, or make such order or decree, as the right and justice of the case may require.'

In the case of *Grey v. South Australian Banking Co*, heard in March 1857, Mr Justice Boothby announced that he had formed the opinion that it was important that the jury should find special facts rather than return verdicts, because "pains are taken in these days to teach jurors that they ought to treat the opinion of Judges with the greatest possible contempt". He would follow, he said, the practice of the most eminent judges, and separate the law from the facts—the jury were to decide upon the facts only, from which the law of the case would be educed by the Court.[47] In accordance with this principle, he proceeded, in a number of cases, to put a series of questions to the jury on the facts, and then delivered judgment on their answers. This led to very hostile criticism. There was always a dispute with counsel as to what form the questions should take; and it was popularly believed that he deliberately framed his questions so as to compel answers upon which he could give judgment to the side which he favoured. His power to require special findings could not be denied; but it was objected that it was a course which was dangerous and should be sparingly used.[48]

While he thus pursued a course which gave umbrage to the public and to the juries, the Judge also adopted a line of policy which placed him in frequent conflict with the bar. Following up his principle that all questions of law were for him, he would not permit the slightest reference by counsel in addressing the jury to anything except the facts of the case. As soon as a legal point was touched upon, counsel was stopped and rebuked. The construction of any document, the Judge held, was a matter of law, and he would not allow counsel to comment on it to the jury.

He was again attacked by the *Register* in a manner so outspoken that it is surprising that the Judge never attempted to punish the newspaper for contempt or libel. The conduct of Mr Justice Boothby, it said, was "unsurpassed in the records of judicial intolerance in these colonies"; he had entered upon a course which was "unconstitutional, unprecedented, and fatal"; a "more monstrous usurpation of the functions of the jury and the bar" had never been recorded in modern annals.[49]

> 'The great mass of the people, not being frequenters of the Supreme Court, can form no adequate conception of the extent to which the authority of the Judge is now made to overwhelm the freedom of the Bar, and to destroy the privileges of the Jury. We feel that our liberties are at stake—so far, at least, as our liberties are dependent upon the way in which justice is dispensed in the Supreme Court of this Province. The Acting Chief Justice is an embodiment of all the Juries and all the lawyers in the colony, nor will he allow any person's opinion to come into comparison with his own. With Mr Justice Boothby on the Bench, jurymen are ciphers and barristers are schoolboys. He dictates to the Bar the line of remark which they must adopt in their addresses to the Jury, insisting upon categorical answers to those questions, giving the verdict himself instead of allowing the Jury to give it. We enter our solemn protest against this judicial tyranny. We will be no party to the overthrow of Trial by Jury in this way. Mr Justice Boothby must have formed strange views of the people of this colony, if he supposes that they will agree to the demolition of the principal bulwark of their freedom; if he supposes that they will hand over their legal and personal security to his irresponsible custody. His Honour may contine [sic] to thwart the Bar; and the public, having no reason to doubt the ability of the Bar to defend themselves, will leave them to their own defence. But when he attempts to subvert Trial by Jury—when he, as Judge, gives that verdict which Jurors by their oath are required to give—we are perfectly satisfied that he enters upon a fatal course; we are perfectly satisfied that it is much more likely he himself will be superseded than that Trial by Jury will be abolished.' [50]

The only effect on Mr Justice Boothby of criticism was to strengthen his determination to go his own way. He persisted in the obnoxious conduct with increasing frequency, almost as though he were acting in a spirit of bravado, until his doings "formed the staple of conversation in every social circle". He complained in court that the press misrepresented him, and that the judges had a right to expect that the leading members of the profession would protect them from the imputations cast upon them. "I have been accused of acting arbitrarily"—he said—"but I appeal to the Attorney General for protection against such charges."

His appeal did not meet with an enthusiastic reception; Mr Hanson coldly replied, that, as he had been appealed to, he would venture to say that "consistency on the part of the Judges would eventually prove a sufficient answer to any comments by the press".[51]

Another point upon which fault was found with the Judge was that he exercised the powers given him by section 183 of the Supreme Court Act 1853, which enabled him, if he thought full justice could not be done to the parties on the trial of any action, to refer the cause to arbitration. He could compel the parties to adopt this course although they both objected to it. On a number of occasions during previous years both the Judges had exercised this power without protest—four times in 1854, five times in 1855, six times in 1856. In the first three terms of 1857 Mr Justice Boothby only ordered five cases to arbitration, so it could not be suggested that he was making an extended exercise of the power. A judge, he said, by judicious use of this provision, could save a great amount of litigation, and he intended to recommend the arrangement on all occasions when it appeared practicable. This attitude seems quite unobjectionable. It was urged, however, that he was thus enabled to abolish trial by jury at discretion; and that both sections 182 and 183 were "despotic in the extreme".[52]

So strong became the opposition that in October 1857 Mr Gwynne introduced into the Legislative Council a bill "to restore to South Australia the full benefit of Trial by Jury". It consisted of one short section, repealing sections 182 and 183 of the Supreme Court Act. He was warmly thanked by the *Register*; such conduct, it said, was typical of the fearless attitude of the bar when bullied by Mr Justice Boothby.[53] The Bill went through the Legislative Council with little discussion; but in the Assembly it aroused more interest. The Attorney-General (Mr Hanson) pointed out that section 182, authorising the Judge to require the jury to find on special facts, did no more than put in statutory form a right which had existed almost from the time when trial by jury was instituted; to repeal section 182, therefore, would be of little use. Another legal member, Mr Bakewell, objected to section 182 as unnecessary, and to section 183 because great evil might result from parties being compelled to go to arbitration against their will.

'I have a small opinion of Juries as they now exist'—he said.

'The institution is almost worn out. It is monstrous in civil cases that twelve ignorant, uneducated men, whose talk is of bullocks, should be put in a box to exercise powers of mind they do not possess.'

Potential jurors attending to the subject of their conversations. Bakewell may have been dismissive of bullocks and their drivers but they provided the major means of land freight transport in the 19th and early 20th centuries. This photograph was taken between 1912 and 1930 in outback South Australia. (NLA)

The lower house amended the Bill by substituting in place of the repeal of sections 182 and 183 the following provision:

> 'The power given by the said sections shall not be exercised by any Judge of the said Court unless on the application of one of the parties to the cause; and in no case shall any Judge have power to decide matters not in dispute in the cause to be referred, unless with the consent of both parties to such cause signified in open Court.' [54]

Before the Bill could be passed, the session came to an end.

In November 1857 Mr John Baker, in the Legislative Council, significantly asked the Chief Secretary whether it was the intention of the Government to introduce any measure by means of which the administration of justice might be rendered secure, and if so, what was the nature of that measure? The Chief Secretary replied that a bill was being prepared to provide for the appointment of a third judge.[55] In the following month a bill was accordingly introduced by the Attorney-General for this purpose, but it met with considerable opposition, the opinion of many members being that the appointment of another judge was a useless and unnecessary expense. Mr Bagot having made some eulogistic remarks about Mann, whom he proposed should be the new Judge, a petition was presented

John Tuthill Bagot (1819-1870) Nephew of Charles H. Bagot, a lawyer and pastoralist, Bagot was also a Member of Parliament from 1853 to 1870. He had brief stints as Solicitor General (1857) and Attorney General (1868).

to the Assembly, signed by Messrs Gwynne, Fenn, Randolph Stow, and Andrews, declaring that Mr Bagot was not the mouthpiece of the legal profession and praying that if the Actwas passed the House would accompany it with a recommendation to the Governor that he would, before making the appointment, "cause an enquiry to be made into the efficiency of any gentleman who may be proposed to fill the office". The petition was rejected as disrespectful and all reference to it was ordered to be expunged from the records of the House. The Bill passed the Assembly, but meeting with a lukewarm reception in the upper house in the last week of the session, it was withdrawn.[56]

Mr Justice Boothby, meanwhile, went merrily on his way. At the Criminal Sessions in February 1858 he had directed a jury that the evidence, in his opinion, was too weak to justify a conviction. The jury, however, desired to retire to consider their verdict. After they had been out for half an hour, he sent for them and angrily told them that after the direction he had given it was their duty to return a verdict at once. He had never known a jury in England who did not do so on the Judge's direction that the evidence was too weak; and if they found the prisoner guilty he would at once advise the Crown to discharge him. It was unconscionable of them to keep himself and the whole Court waiting after the positive direction they had had from him, and if there was one among them who was unwilling to convict, he would discharge them all. One juror announced that he was unwilling to convict, and the Judge promptly discharged the jury and released the prisoner.[57]

Next morning brought the usual attack from the *Register*:

> 'Either His Honour must be checked in his arbitrary usurpation of the functions of the jury, or the community will have to take steps for abolishing Trial by Jury altogether. As matters at present stand, Trial by Jury is a mockery, a pretence, and a sham. Twelve men are put into the box, and are sworn to give a verdict in accordance with the evidence submitted to them; but after that evidence is completed the Judge dictatorially orders what verdict must be returned, and threatens in plain language that if his mandate is not obeyed he will move the head of the Executive to reverse the verdict of the Jury. Failing to influence the Jury as a whole, His Honour invites in open Court any single juryman to adopt the views of the Bench, and this secured, he immediately dismisses the jury en masse, and refuses to allow the trial to be conducted to its proper conclusion.'

Trial by jury, it was said, had become in South Australia trial by Mr Justice Boothby; and as to his remarks as to the difference between the conduct of juries in England and in South Australia, that difference was doubtless owing to the difference in the conduct of judges in those places respectively.[58]

A few days later the Judge was in hot water again. A man was charged with obtaining a valuable security by false pretences. Mr Justice Boothby, who for some reason had a rooted dislike to this form of charge, said that there was nothing in the case and directed the jury to acquit. The jury gave no signs of acquiescence.

> 'I tell you there is no evidence in law on which to convict the defendant'—he shouted at them. 'You would not convict a man when there is no evidence, would you? If anybody advises you to do such a thing, I hope your consciences will prevent it.' [59]

A verdict of not guilty was taken; and on the morrow came the inevitable onslaught from the *Register*. This time the Judge saw fit to defend himself from the bench.

> 'I know what my duty is'—he said—'and I will discharge it according to my conscience in all cases. Unless the decent part of society interferes and puts down these attacks on the administration of justice, I am quite sure that that administration will become impossible. I suppose that the decent part of society are waiting until some rich man, or the son of some rich man, is put upon his trial in a case like this. Then the decent part of society will interfere and put down these attacks by the press on the administration of justice. But it is for the Bench to protect the poor as well as the rich, and therefore it is my duty to stop such cases whenever they come before me.' [60]

John Henry Barrow (1817-1874) A Congregational preacher, journalist and politician, Barrow proved to be influential in all his roles. He began the *Advertiser* in 1858, the same year he was first elected to the House of Assembly, and continued working in politics and newspapers until his death. (SLSA)

The psychologist would no doubt find in Mr Justice Boothby's reference (which he frequently repeated) to rich men and rich men's sons, a "poverty complex".

Not content with this, he quarrelled at a public meeting, in aid of the Indian Mutiny Relief Fund, with Mr Barrow, a newspaper proprietor, whom he accused of "traducing him every day". The *Register* did not fail to give the incident full space.

> 'The feeling in his mind is evidently assuming the character of monomania, and like every species of mental disorder, must operate most prejudicially upon the performance of his judicial functions. He seems determined to prove that he is altogether and essentially unfitted for the position of a Judge. The most essential attributes of the judicial function—imperturbable self control, calm dignity, inflexible impartiality, comprehensive survey of all the facts, cautious absence from hasty and ill-supported dicta — all these Mr Justice Boothby appears

> determined to prove that he possessed in the minimum degree. If he were anxious to destroy his judicial reputation, it would be difficult for him to accomplish his purpose more effectually than by the adoption of the course which he saw fit to pursue yesterday.'

Let Mr Justice Boothby behave himself and the public would be quiet.

> 'That serene calm which he undoubtedly was the first to disturb will again return. But let him beware lest he postpones too long the change which he must ultimately make. Public patience has been sorely tried already; and it is impossible to say how soon forbearance will become criminal. Should Mr Justice Boothby push matters to that extremity, he may rest assured that he will awaken a storm of public reprobation before which even his obstinacy must succumb.' [61]

After anxiously watching the proceedings in the Supreme Court, the *Register* could only come to the conclusion that the colony would rather be benefited than injured if the Court were abolished altogether.[62]

For a few months there was a lull; but at the Civil Sessions in October 1858, there was a further outbreak of the case of *Platt v. Stocks*. Mr Justice Boothby said there was no evidence to go to the jury, and either the plaintiff must be nonsuited or there must be a verdict for the defendant. Mr Gwynne, who appeared for the plaintiff, refused to submit to a nonsuit; and the Judge directed the jury to give a verdict for the defendant. The jury began to consult among themselves.

> 'You have nothing to do but return a verdict as I have directed'— said the Judge. 'It is the very A.B.C. of law that whenever a jury is informed by the Judge that there is no evidence for their consideration, their simple duty is to return a verdict according to his direction.'

One juror asked whether they were compelled to give a verdict. "You have the physical power to refuse to do so, but not the moral right," was the answer. After conferring for a few minutes, the jury stated that they could not on their consciences give a verdict for the defendant. "You are not required to give a verdict according to the evidence, for there is none before you"— said the Judge becoming heated at this opposition. The jury retired for half an hour and then came back into Court, and said they could not agree—ten were for the plaintiff and two for the defendant.

> 'I don't want to hear anything about numbers'— said the Judge testily. 'It is my duty to tell you that if you do not give a verdict

> as I have directed you, it will be a breach of your oath. It will be a perverse verdict. If you cannot agree, I am sorry for it, but you had better consider well what you are about.'
>
> 'We can only judge according to the evidence which has been given'—ventured one juryman.
>
> 'The evidence you have heard in that box is nothing'—replied the Judge. 'You don't know what the evidence is till you hear it from my lips.'
>
> 'As if he thought, like Otaheitan cooks,
> No food was fit to eat till he had chewed it.'

A request by the jury to be allowed refreshments was refused, and they were sent back again to chant. This time they were out from twelve o'clock till five in the evening, and the Judge again sent for them. There was not the slightest possibility of their agreeing, they said. The Judge asked counsel whether they consented to the jury being discharged; both counsel said they would leave it to the discretion of the Judge. "You are acting in direct contempt of the authority of the Court and your conduct is inexcusable"— said Mr Justice Boothby to the jury. "You will be locked up till ten o'clock, to which time I will adjourn."

The jurors again protested they could not give a verdict against their consciences and that there was no hope of their agreeing; but the Judge was inexorable. "Can we have some refreshments," piped up one bold juror. "Certainly not," said the Judge. The Attorney-General, who was appearing in the cause, humanely interposed, and said he would prefer that some arrangements should be made to relieve the jury; but the Judge would not discharge them. Once more they were locked up, and constables sworn in to keep them without refreshments and to prevent any communication with them. At ten o'clock they were not agreed, so they were locked up for the night—still without refreshments. It was not until half past ten next morning that they were called into Court and, being still unagreed, were discharged. They had been locked up twenty two hours without food or drink.[63]

In this unfortunate case, the jury were partly to blame, for there was no doubt of the power of the Judge to direct a verdict for the defendant if he was of opinion that there was no evidence fit for the jury to consider; but to keep them locked up for so long was attributed to vindictive spite on the part of the Judge. One can be fairly certain that he had added to the list of his enemies at least twelve more.

The outcry following this case led to the revival of the proposal to repeal sections 182 and 183 of the Supreme Court Act 1853, and a Bill having this object was again introduced in Parliament.[64] The Attorney-General (Mr Hanson) opposed it. The power of referring, he thought, was useful and necessary; while the judges in England frequently required the jury to find special facts. Most of the members, however, took the view that the effect of the sections was to place the judge and jury in an antagonistic position and to discredit the Supreme Court, and the Bill was passed. As the Attorney-General said, in reporting to the Governor on the act, the legislature followed public opinion and conceived that the powers had been abused and that it was necessary they should be abolished. "My individual opinion does not quite coincide with this," he added, but there was no reason why the Bill should not be assented to.[65] The Governor assented to it with regret.

> 'To me'—he wrote—'it seems that no provisions could be apparently better adapted to secure the ends of justice than those which the Act repeals. They appear to give a power of separating usefully the functions of the Judge and Jury and of enabling the former to refer to a more suitable tribunal many family disputes, and complicated accounts, which might admit of a speedier and more satisfactory settlement than is always attainable through the forms of procedure of the Supreme Court. Unfortunately, a growing dissatisfaction was for some time felt at the extensive use made of the powers by one of the Judges here, and that feeling has at last become so strong as to induce the Legislature wholly to repeal the clauses, which I think might have been made productive of great public benefit.'

He felt that an exaggerated view had been taken of many facts which led to public dissatisfaction. He could not refuse his assent to the act, but he hoped that future experience might point out "some safe mode of re-conferring on the Judges the powers now abolished, and at the same time guarding against their abuse".[66]

Henry Bull Templar Strangways (1832-1920). A nephew of Thomas Bewes Strangways, Henry settled in Adelaide in 1857 and practised as a lawyer. A member of the House of Assembly from 1858 to 1870 he held a variety of positions including Premier. His parliamentary career is noted for the passage of a land reform act – the "Strangways Act" – in 1869. (SLSA)

Mr Strangways, in the Assembly, also moved that a Select Committee should be appointed to inquire into all matters connected with the administration of law and justice in the province.

> 'Hon members'—he said—'must be aware of the constant disputes and squabbles which have taken place between the Judges of the Supreme Court, the Counsel, and the Jury. An hon. member who was in the habit of visiting the Court of Assizes, or any other courts of justice in England, must feel surprised at the scenes presented in our colonial Courts.'

The House was not willing to support a motion so vague and indefinite, and it was lost by a small majority, much to the regret of the *Register*.[67]

The House was prepared, however, to support a motion for the appointment of a third judge. Mr Barrow, the mover, expressly disclaimed any intention of reflecting upon the attainments or impartiality of the Judges of the Supreme Court, and based his motion on the fact that while the colony had only two judges, there was always a danger of a deadlock through the very conscientiousness of the Judges—one deciding one way and the other holding an opposite opinion. A third judge would also be useful in enabling circuit courts to be held. With some grumblings on the score of expense, the motion was carried, and a Bill introduced, and passed.[68] In February 1859 Mr Gwynne was appointed third judge.

The new Judge, Edward Castres Gwynne, was a man of powerful physique and blunt manners, distinguished on the bench by solid commonsense rather than subtlety of intellect. In his later years he was described as "a formidable-looking and rough-tongued Rhadamanthus" but under a rugged exterior lay an unswerving honesty which earned him also the title of "the most upright Judge ever seen on this side of the Line". He served on the bench till February 1881, when he retired on a pension of £1,300 a year, having some years previously declined a proffered knighthood.

He was born at Lewes, Sussex, in February 1811, and was a first cousin of General Gordon. He had intended to enter the army (he subsequently served as an officer in the militia in South Australia), but was induced to turn to law instead. After practising for a short time as an attorney in London, he set out for South Australia in the expectation of receiving the post of Clerk of the Supreme Court.[69] He arrived in the colony in April 1838, bringing with him a letter of introduction from Edward Gibbon Wakefield to Sir John Jeffcott.[70] He found, however, that Sir John Jeffcott was dead, and that the post of Clerk was already filled. Disappointed in his hope of an official position he set up in practice first on his own, and then in partnership successively with William Bartley, Charles Mann senior, and W.J. Lawrence.[71] He rapidly achieved prominence as a barrister, more particularly on the equity side, and during the 1850s shared with Hanson the leadership of the bar. Gwynne was not easily put out or perturbed. On one occasion, having opened a case to the jury, he was about to call his client, when he found that the client had been delayed and was not in attendance at court. Nothing daunted, he started on his opening again, and went on and on, subjecting the case to a review from every possible angle and reading long passages from *Byles on Bills* to the Judge (Mr Justice Boothby) until the belated client made his appearance, when the opening was abruptly concluded. Fortunately for Gwynne, Mr Justice Boothby had seen the same ruse to gain time adopted in England; anything done in England was to him ipso facto highly proper, and he therefore good-humouredly sanctioned it.[72]

Having taken up a large holding of land at Glynde, Gwynne carried on, as an important sideline to his practice, farming, fruit growing, and viticulture, and went in for stock and horse breeding. In 1851 he was appointed a non-official member of the Legislative

Council, in which he sat till 1854; and in 1857 he was elected to the newly constituted Legislative Council. From 21 August to 1 September 1857, he was Attorney-General in the "Ten Days Ministry" of Mr John Baker.[73]

At the time he was offered the judgeship, Gwynne had made up his mind to give up practice in Adelaide and go to Melbourne, because of rebuffs administered to him by Mr Justice Boothby. "His decisions"—he said—"whether they were good law or not, placed me in a most contemptible position as regards my clients."

The case of *The Queen v. Turner* was an instance. Turner had melted some lead and nails into ingots corresponding in bulk and weight with gold. He put these in a box of the type ordinarily used at that time for the export of gold, and lodged the pretended box of gold with the Bank of South Australia. He then procured, from the captain of a ship bound for England, a bill of lading describing the box as containing gold, and producing this document to the bank he asked for an advance upon the gold. The manager of the bank, Mr Tinline, was not to be taken in, and had the box first examined, when the fraud was discovered.

> 'I was consulted'—said Gwynne subsequently—'as to the nature of the offence that had been committed. The bankers seemed to think that the man had committed some very heinous crime—that he ought to be hung; but I considered the case more dispassionately, and advised that he had committed no offence, except the simple one of attempting to get money under false pretences—that as no money had actually been advanced, it could only be taken as an attempt to obtain money in that way. The bankers seemed disposed to doubt the ability of the Colonial Bar, as it seemed in their opinion that a greater crime had been committed. I thought differently, and I was retained to conduct the prosecution for the offence I had advised respecting. The case attracted a good deal of interest, and several bankers were present in Court. I opened the case to the jury, and Mr Justice Boothby interrupting me, said, "Has it never occurred to you, Mr Gwynne, that the higher offence has been committed in this case?" "No", I replied, "what is the higher offence?" "Forgery", said His Honour. He then snubbed me a good deal, and said he would not try the case, and that an information for forgery must be exhibited. With all deference to the Bench, I remonstrated, and trusted that my clients would not lose the remedy they had against the prisoner; but he insisted on an information for forgery being prepared, and the difficulty was how to prepare it. The only instrument upon which forgery could be alleged was the Bill of Lading, but that was a genuine document signed by the

> Captain. I had not an opportunity of conferring with the learned Judge as to the mode of charging the higher offence, but I drew an information the best way I could. The Crown Solicitor positively refused to do it, as it was so monstrously absurd, but he handed me an information in blank, and I filled it up, alleging the crime of forgery. The matter came before the Court. I felt a good deal of embarrassment in opening to the jury, but uttered a few generalities bearing on the crime of forgery, and said I would call the witnesses. Well, the man was convicted of forgery, and solemnly sentenced, although it was argued that there was no foundation for the charge. He was sent to prison, and there he remained until I became Judge ... when he was let out, the Chief Justice and myself thinking that he had suffered quite long enough a term of imprisonment for the crime he had actually committed ... Unfortunately the public attributed the matter to my ignorance. I felt that the fact of the sentence of the Court affected the question of my ability as a lawyer in advising that a trivial offence had been committed, whereas the public were led to believe that it was the grievous offence of forgery which had been committed.'

In another case, *Corporation of Adelaide v. Peryman*, the defendant was the City Surveyor. Under Gwynne's advice an action was brought against him by the corporation for negligence in the construction of certain works; but Mr Justice Boothby nonsuited the plaintiff on the extraordinary ground that the defendant had given security for the due performance of his office, and that he could not be sued until the corporation had first sued his sureties.

> 'That was very irritating to me'—said Gwynne—'for having considered the matter, I had no doubt as to the law, or as to the incorrect decision of the Judge. That I had taken so erroneous a view placed me, I felt, in a difficult position with regard to the corporation. I had led them to lay out £400 or £500 through what appeared to be gross ignorance of the ABC of law, that a man could not sue his principal until he had sued the sureties. I had authorities to support me, but it was evident that the Judge's and my law were quite distinct—either his was erroneous or mine was. I found that my reputation was suffering, that I was doing no good to anybody—that I was being degraded—and I determined to go to Melbourne.'

Gwynne actually went so far as to insert an advertisement in the daily papers that he would accept no more briefs in the Supreme Court. The offer by Hanson, the Attorney-General, of the third judgeship came very opportunely, and was accepted. "I thought that would put me above any danger of annoyance from Mr Justice Boothby. I certainly should not have practised before him any more." [74]

During the whole of 1859 there was hardly so much as a murmur against Mr Justice Boothby. The Chief Justice had returned to the colony and resumed his position; and the public felt secure now that Mr Justice Boothby was only one of three. That gentleman, indeed, behaved himself so well that by the close of the year even his archenemy the *Register* was paying him compliments.

So the first phase of the Boothby trouble came to a quiet end. It had been concerned, in the main, with squabbles between the Judge and jury, and between the Judge and counsel, and it is hard to think otherwise than that by using a little tact and assuming a conciliatory manner the Judge would have been spared most of the abuse which was freely showered upon him. While the grounds of complaint against him were often grossly exaggerated, there were faults on both sides; and he asked for much of the criticism he received.

Edward Castres Gwynne ca. 1880 (SCLSA)

Mr Justice Boothby

'the Torrens on fire'

In the next phase of the Boothby question, extending over the years 1860 and 1861 and culminating in addresses by both Houses for the Judge's removal from office, it is beyond doubt that he was in many respects very unjustly treated—in fact, scandalously so. He was assailed during this period, not for his behaviour, with which little fault could be found, but for his opinions, delivered from the bench, upon legal and constitutional questions. However distasteful those opinions were, it was never suggested that they were not genuine and bona fide. He supported them by detailed and reasoned arguments. The mere fact that he arrived at conclusions not in accordance with those popularly entertained was no ground whatever for accusing him of perfidy.

> 'Having regard to the great, complex, ever-unfolding exigencies of government much which will seem unconstitutional to one man, or body of men, may reasonably not seem so to another.'

Some of his views, scornfully derided in the colony, were pronounced by the authorities at home to be quite right. In others he went wrong, but it is hard to find the slightest justification for the drastic action which was taken against him. To heighten the injustice, his colleague Mr Justice Gwynne, who concurred with him in many of his most unpopular views, escaped scot-free.

The renewal of The People v. Mr Justice Boothby (to adopt the American phraseology) arose out of the Real Property Act. The history of that measure is narrated in a later chapter, and it is unnecessary here to say more than that the Act, passed in 1857, had met with a very hostile reception from most of the legal profession and from all the Judges. Mr Justice Gwynne and Mr Justice Boothby, in particular, detested it, and were equally outspoken in their denunciations of it. When many honest men were conscientiously convinced that the Real Property Act was a horrible blunder, it was ludicrous that Mr Justice Boothby, because he happened to share that opinion, should have been from the first selected as a scapegoat, and set up as an Aunt Sally against which it was legitimate for anyone and everyone to hurl such abuse and insults as they chose. This, however, was what happened.

The first case bearing on the Real Property Act came before the Supreme Court in April 1859—*Johnson v. Torrens*. The Act had come into force on 1 July 1858, and by section 14 all land alienated from the Crown within the province from and after the 1st day of July 1858 was to be subject to its provisions. On 21 October 1858, a land grant for a closed road was made to Johnson, whose solicitor attempted to register the grant by memorial under the old Registration of Deeds Act. Torrens, the Registrar-General, insisted

(Sir) Robert Richard Torrens (1814-1884)
Torrens was the self-proclaimed author of the system of land titles that bears his name. The son of Colonel Robert Torrens, he was Collector of Customs from 1841 to 1853 when he became the Registrar General of Deeds and began his reform of the land title system. Elected to the House of Assembly in 1857 he introduced and had passed the Bill for the Real Property Act. Later he advocated the system in other colonies and in England where he was elected an MP in 1868.

that by section 14 the land should have been granted under the provisions of the Real Property Act, and he refused to register the grant under the old system. The plaintiff then applied for a mandamus to compel him to do so. The Court held that the grant of land in question was not an alienation from the Crown within the meaning of section 14, but was an alienation from the Roads Commissioners, for whom the Governor was acting, in making the grant, in a merely ministerial capacity. On this slender distinction they held that the plaintiff had the option of bringing his land under the Real Property Act or not. If he preferred to register it under the old system, the Registrar-General must register it for him. A mandamus was accordingly granted.[1]

Another successful application for a mandamus against the Registrar-General occurred in *Hutchinson v. Torrens* in March 1860. In 1839, under a preliminary land order, the plaintiff had selected a section of land, No 121, on the Hindmarsh River. A land grant was issued to him by Governor Gawler conveying, on the face of it, 134 acres, the natural boundaries of which were precisely described. The section really contained, owing to a mistake by the surveyors, 180 acres. Having later discovered this error, the Government reclaimed 46 acres and created out of them a new section, No 144. Once again the surveyors made a mistake, and they took 56 acres from section 121, instead of 46. The new section the Government sold to one Field, who transferred to a Mrs Leeworthy, who brought it under the Real Property Act and obtained a Certificate of Title for 56 acres, which included 10 wrongly taken from Hutchinson. Mr Hutchinson, alleging that part of his land had been stolen from him, applied to the Registrar-General to inspect the application made by Mrs Leeworthy to bring her section under the Real Property Act and the title deeds on which she had based her claim. Torrens refused to produce the documents and Hutchinson applied to the Supreme Court for a mandamus, which was granted. The Chief Justice, delivering the judgment of the Court, said that the application and record of the proceedings to place land under the Act should be open to the public as the validity of a Certificate of Title depended upon the due performance of the various acts prescribed in the Act to be done. This was an important decision against the Act, section 39 of which declared that, notwithstanding any error or omission in the observance of any formality prescribed to be observed in bringing land under the operation of the Act, every Certificate of Title should absolutely vest the estate or interest described in the manner expressed in such Certificate. Upon this decision, however, noncompliance with the formalities prescribed might invalidate the Certificate of Title.[2]

In the following month the Judges went a step further. Mr Hutchinson sued Mrs Leeworthy in ejectment, claiming to be entitled to the 56 acres comprised in her Certificate of Title. This directly raised the issue whether or not the Certificate of Title was indefeasible. It was a contest between Mr Hutchinson's original land grant and the Certificate of Title. A formal verdict was entered for the defendant by agreement, the plaintiff having leave to move that the verdict should be entered for him on the ground that his land grant was a valid statutory conveyance of the land in question and that the defendant's Certificate of Title was invalid. Mr Fisher returned to the bar expressly to argue the case for the plaintiff, and Mr Hanson appeared for the defendant. The Court unanimously gave judgment for the plaintiff. The Chief Justice pointed out that the boundaries of the original section were clearly stated, but through a mistake of the surveyors more acres were included than was intended.

> 'It is a fact notorious throughout the colony'—he said—'that the sections of land marked and laid out by the Government surveyors in the early surveys were seldom of the precise size of which they were declared to be. The early settlers and purchasers took the land on the faith of the Government.'

Edward J. Snell's 1850 watercolour *Surveyors' Encampment Yorkes Peninsula* shows the conditions early surveyors worked under. It is not surprising that the work was often inaccurate. (SLSA)

The section being clearly defined by natural landmarks, he thought the whole section passed, notwithstanding that the quantity of land stated to be in it was wrong. But if the whole section had been vested in the plaintiff, then no proceedings under the Real Property Act, in his opinion, could have the effect of divesting it:

> '... for while the grant of section 121 to the plaintiff was in

> existence, any subsequent grant thereof, or of any part thereof, to another person would be void; and a Certificate of Title granted in exchange for that grant would appear to be equally so, inasmuch as it could not be founded on the original grant, which was made to the plaintiff and which seems to remain unaffected by it'.

The land grant must be surrendered for a valid Certificate of Title to issue, and if by misfortune a second grant had been made, it was the first grant and not the second which had to be surrendered to obtain a Certificate of Title.

Mr Justice Boothby agreed that the defendant's objection to the validity of the original land grant, on the ground of its conveying more than 134 acres, when only that quantity was paid for, could not be sustained, inasmuch as the boundaries were fixed by certain abutments, and did not need the aid of measurements in acres to be ascertained; under such circumstances the fee in all the land, however erroneous the description of the acreage, passed to the grantee. The second grant was therefore invalid and conferred no title; and since ex nihilo nihil fit, the Certificate of Title was equally invalid because there was nothing for it to rest on.

Mr Justice Gwynne was likewise of opinion that the original land grant was not void because of excess; for if so, he said, an excess of half an acre would void a grant, and nearly every land grant in the colony might be set aside; and he also came to the conclusion that the Certificate of Title issued to Mrs Leeworthy could not stand.[3]

This decision, that the Certificate of Title could have no greater validity than the title which was surrendered in exchange for it, was a startling one to the supporters of the Real Property Act. If the holder of a Certificate of Title was just as liable to be ejected by virtue of a prior title as he would have been had he not brought his property under that act, then by consequence all the old process of investigating title, which the Act was designed to do away with, must be still carried out.

> 'The lawyers have triumphed'—said the Register—'in their appeal to a court of lawyers, and the public must again begin de novo their toilsome efforts to obtain emancipation from a bondage which in every British community is now felt to be intolerably oppressive.' [4]

The jurisdiction of the Supreme Court to hear such actions in ejectment, it was urged, must be completely ousted.

> 'Once within the precincts of that sanctuary where the worship is casuistry, and the rank of the priests is determined by the ingenuity of their sophistry, farewell to all hope of deciding any cases on the rules of common sense and good conscience.' [5]

While the interpretation given by the Court to the Real Property Act in *Hutchinson v. Leeworthy* was of great moment to the community, it temporarily overshadowed in public opinion a question of even greater importance—that the Act might be invalid because it was repugnant to the law of England. The first difficulty could be remedied, and was, by the passing of another and clearer statute; but if the second objection was valid, then it was beyond the power of the local legislature to persist with the Act.

"Some points are so tough and so touchy," admitted that learned and doughty controversialist, Dr Isaac Barrow, "that nobody dare meddle with them." The subject of repugnancy has always been shunned, and for very good reasons—"to be wading in those deeps is the way to be drowned in them"—but since the doctrine of repugnancy must forever remain inseparably coupled with the name of Mr Justice Boothby, it is necessary to attempt some explanation of what that doctrine was understood to mean in 1860.

By the Acts establishing it, the legislature of South Australia had power to make laws for the peace, welfare and good government of the province—"Provided always, that no such law shall be repugnant to the law of England". (See 5 & 6 Vic c.76 s.29; 13 & 14 Vic c.59 s.14). But what "repugnancy: was, it was difficult to say.

> 'All words'—said De Quincey—'are suspicious, there is an odour of fraud about them, which are so base as to stretch out to four syllables. What does an honest word want with more than two?'

The exact force of this poppous [sic] quadrisyllable was "wrapped in decent obscurity".[6] When and under what circumstances did colonial legislation become repugnant to English law? How far could the colonial legislature go without exceeding the bounds of the authority given to it? By what test could be ascertained the accordance with, or repugnancy to English law, of any particular colonial statute? These were questions to which no authoritative answer could be given. Few cases had arisen, and from a quantity of vague statements and dicta no firm and luminous general principles could be elicited.

The term "repugnant to the law of England" was well established in official and legislative usage long before South Australia was thought of. Some interesting remarks upon it are to be found in a letter from the Provisional Committee of the South Australian Association to the Secretary of State, 21 February 1834, submitting a draft charter. By the charter it was proposed that the body to be incorporated should be given power to make laws, provided they were "not repugnant to the laws of that part of the United Kingdom called England". In some explanatory remarks, it was said:

> 'The expression "not repugnant to the laws of England" has been taken from the old charters. It is intended to provide, not

> that the laws made for the colony shall be the same as the laws of England, but that no law made for the colony shall supersede, or clash with, any law of England. Very many of the laws of England would be totally inapplicable to an infant colony (the Poor Laws for example), while not a few of those laws (for instance, the laws of the transfer of estates) would be very injurious to the colony, where land will continually change hands. Under the old charters, all sorts of laws, very different from the laws of England, were necessarily made; but if a law had been made in opposition to any English law (such as a law contrary to the English Navigation Laws), it would have been void, as 'repugnant to the law of England'. That term was employed on former occasions, and is here employed, to provide that no law made under the charter shall authorise the doing of any act which any law of England declares shall not be done.'[7]

In New South Wales, by the Act 4 Geo IV c.96 (1823) creating a nominee Council, the Council was given power and authority to make laws and ordinances for the peace, welfare and good government of that colony, provided that such laws and ordinances were not "repugnant to this Act, or to any charter or Letters Patent or Orders in Council issued in pursuance thereof, or to the laws of England, but consistent with such laws, so far as the circumstances of the said colony will admit". The Governor was given the exclusive right of proposing legislation to the Council, but by section 29 of the Act he was required to obtain from the Chief Justice, before presenting any proposal, to the Council, a Certificate declaring that such proposed law was not repugnant to the laws of England, but was consistent with such laws, as far as the circumstances of the colony would admit. Chief Justice Forbes and Governor Darling came into conflict as a result of the duty thus cast upon the Chief Justice.

> 'Forbes gave an interpretation to the Act which was far too rigid: he showed an inclination to ignore the phrase which gave him a very wide discretionary authority, namely that which required consistency only "so far as the circumstances of the said colony will admit".'

The disputes between the Governor and the Chief Justice were so bitter and continuous that James Stephen, when on one occasion the two officials by chance agreed, noted that it must have been "for the sake of variety". Stephen could not see any difficulty in applying the provisions of the Act of 1823, and, indeed, the express provision that the circumstances of the colony were to be considered so qualified the prohibition of repugnant legislation as to make the statute merely a reduction into writing of the long-established practice that the law of England extended to the colony so far as it was applicable to the different circumstances.

In 1828, by 9 Geo IV c.83 s.22, an attempt was made to get rid of the opposition between the Governor and the Chief Justice. Stephen was unwilling to do away completely with the provision as to "repugnancy", not because he thought it necessary in practice, but because he "feared that its omission would be noticed and give rise to an impression that a real restraint had been removed". It was accordingly provided that within seven days of the passing of any bill by the Council, the Governor should cause it to be enrolled and recorded at the Supreme Court. If within fourteen days any of the Judges transmitted to the Governor a representation that the law or ordinance was repugnant, the Governor was to suspend its operation until it had been reviewed by the Council. If the Council adhered to the Ordinance, it then came into force, notwithstanding any supposed repugnancy.

> 'This section gave expression to a compromise. The Government was anxious to make some provision for expedient and necessary variation from the laws of England, but it was also anxious to avoid repugnancy as far as possible.' [9]

The provisions of 9 Geo IV c.83 were not in force in South Australia, when the colony was founded, by reason of the express terms of section 1 of the Foundation Act, although it was subsequently contended by Mr Justice Boothby, fruitlessly, that they were introduced into South Australia by 13 & 14 Vic c.59.

Sir Roger Therry, in his *Reminiscences*, quotes a cynical letter from James Stephen to his relative Mr Justice Stephen, in New South Wales.

> 'Why bother yourself'—wrote Sir James Stephen—'with that everlasting phrase, "not repugnant to the laws of England". What does it mean? Has it any meaning? "Then why did you, Mr Counsel to the Colonial Department (you will say) bring it into the first New South Wales Act and keep it in the second?" Why, in the first place, that it might serve as a pons asinorum over which no Colonial Crown lawyer should pass without giving proof of more than asinine sagacity. Secondly, because it sounds highly constitutional and decorous. Thirdly, because it may every now and then prevent some egregious absurdity. This is indeed the correct interpretation of the phrase. Whatever is tyrannical or very foolish you may safely call 'repugnant &c'. But whatever is necessary for the comfort and good government of the colony, you may safely assume to be in perfect harmony with English law. Such, then, is my lecture about the management of your affairs. As action was the first,

> second, and third requisite in eloquence, even so is legislation with the Sydney and Van Diemen's Land Government. Take a new code wherever the old one won't suit you. Keep up the family resemblance between your law and ours as well as you can, and never think it worth while to go mad over a difficulty which an Act of His Excellency in Council can grind into powder with a blow." [10]

Stephen's attitude towards the New South Wales legislation illustrates the attitude of the Colonial Office generally towards repugnancy; the rule was preserved, as a useful device for occasionally getting rid of any colonial legislation which seemed to be making too great a break with the legal traditions of England; but so long as colonial statutes were reasonable, the Colonial Office shut its eyes to any technical repugnancies to English law.

The sole expression of English judicial opinion on "repugnancy" was to be found in *Bank of Australasia v. Nias* (1851) 16 QB 717. By an act of the legislature of New South Wales it was provided that the plaintiff company should sue and be sued in the name of its chairman and that execution on any judgment against the company might be issued against the property of any member for the time being, in like manner as if such judgment had been obtained against such member personally. Lord Campbell held that the colonial legislature had authority to pass the Act, and that there was "nothing repugnant to the law of England or to natural justice", in enacting that actions on contracts made by the company in the colony, instead of being brought against the shareholders individually, should be brought against the chairman whom they had appointed to represent them. This decision was not very helpful. If Lord Campbell meant to use "contrary to natural justice" as a synonym for "repugnant to the laws of England", it was a very inept one; a colonial law contrary to the Navigation Acts, for instance, might be quite consistent with natural justice, but it would undoubtedly be repugnant to the law of England.

Only one act passed by the South Australian legislature appears to have been expressly disallowed as "repugnant"—the Quarter Sessions Act of 1842, which attempted to abolish the Grand Jury—but, strangely, when another act was passed in 1852 having the same effect, it was left to its operation, although if the prior act was repugnant, this one must have equally been so. A number of acts were disallowed on various grounds which really amounted in effect to repugnancy, although that term was not expressly used; for instance, the Ordinance passed in 1843 to regulate the profession of law was disallowed because the Secretary of State disapproved of the power given to the Supreme Court summarily to commit to prison for twelve months any unqualified person practising as a lawyer. On the other hand, a number of acts which seem to have been repugnant, or perilously close to it, were left to their operation without comment.

Prior to 1860, the only occasion upon which the question of repugnancy was considered in any detail in the colony was in the debates in Parliament in 1857 on the Bill to legalise marriage with a deceased wife's sister.

The question whether such marriages were repugnant to the law of England was complicated by the uncertainty which existed as to whether or not they were illegal and invalid under English law. The Marriage Act of 1835 declared marriages within the prohibited degrees to be illegal, but a controversy raged as to whether a deceased wife's sister came within those degrees. In New South Wales and Victoria the Marriage Act was not in force, and there was therefore no statutory prohibition in those colonies against marrying a deceased wife's sister. It was doubtful whether the Act of 1835 was in force in South Australia, because there were no ecclesiastical courts here to enforce it. If it was not, then it was an absurd position if South Australia was left without law on the subject, and yet was unable to legislate upon it because to do so would involve repugnancy to English law.

The views of members were conflicting. The Attorney-General expressed the opinion that it was quite within the province of the Parliament to pass such a law and that it was not repugnant. Another member (Mr Burford) thought that it was repugnant, but that repugnancy was nothing for them to worry about. "We have exhibited our repugnance to English law"—he said—"in abolishing a State religion, and in the adoption of the ballot, as also in the admission of Jews to Parliament."

(Sir) John Morphett shown here as the President of the Legislative Council a post he held from 1865 to 1873. (SLV)

Mr Morphett was clear that the measure was repugnant. The very title of the Bill, he said, showed it—"An Act to amend the Law of Marriage": "The law they proposed to amend was the law of England, and in amending it they would necessarily make it repugnant to the law as it existed." The Surveyor-General could only regret that the debate had not taken higher ground: he regarded the marriages proposed to be legalised as repugnant to the law of God.[11]

That a woman should be "a wife in South Australia, and no better than a concubine in England" was certainly an awkward result, which made it difficult to escape the conclusion of repugnancy.

In a vigorous leader on repugnancy, arising from this debate, the *Register* pointed out:

> 'If the Parliament of South Australia may not pass any Acts, except those Acts are in accordance with the laws of England, we have certainly been very disloyal subjects hitherto; and, what is yet more remarkable, the Queen of England has aided and abetted our disloyalty. It is sheer trifling for hon. members to say that we cannot pass laws 'repugnant' to the laws of England; we have passed many such laws, and the Queen has ratified them. The fact is that there is not a single department of our legislative proceedings in which some 'repugnancy' may not be traced.'

The writer went on to give his views about the repugnancy proviso in the Imperial acts:

> 'We believe that the proviso, though so apparently important, has, like the learned Judge's nod, 'nothing in it'. Probably some hon. septuagenarian intimated his fear that it was just possible a New Zealand Parliament might pass an Act for decapitating the Queen, or that a Tasmanian legislature might decree the right divine of burglary. Under such circumstances, and to quiet the apprehensions of elderly ladies of both sexes, the 'united wisdom' would agree to a proviso.'

To suppose that by prohibiting repugnant legislation the Imperial Parliament intended to enforce legislative uniformity was a conclusion no rational man could come to; but if not, what did it mean? The answer he proposed was: "We believe the term 'repugnant' to refer especially to hostility to the parent country; and that the interdict is simply an interdict of treason and rebellion." [12]

This conclusion, although somewhat repugnant to the commencement of his article, clearly expresses the tenets of one of the two great groups into which the disputants about repugnancy may be classified. There were those who believed that "repugnant" was synonymous with "inconsistent", and that any variation from English law must necessarily be an inconsistency and therefore

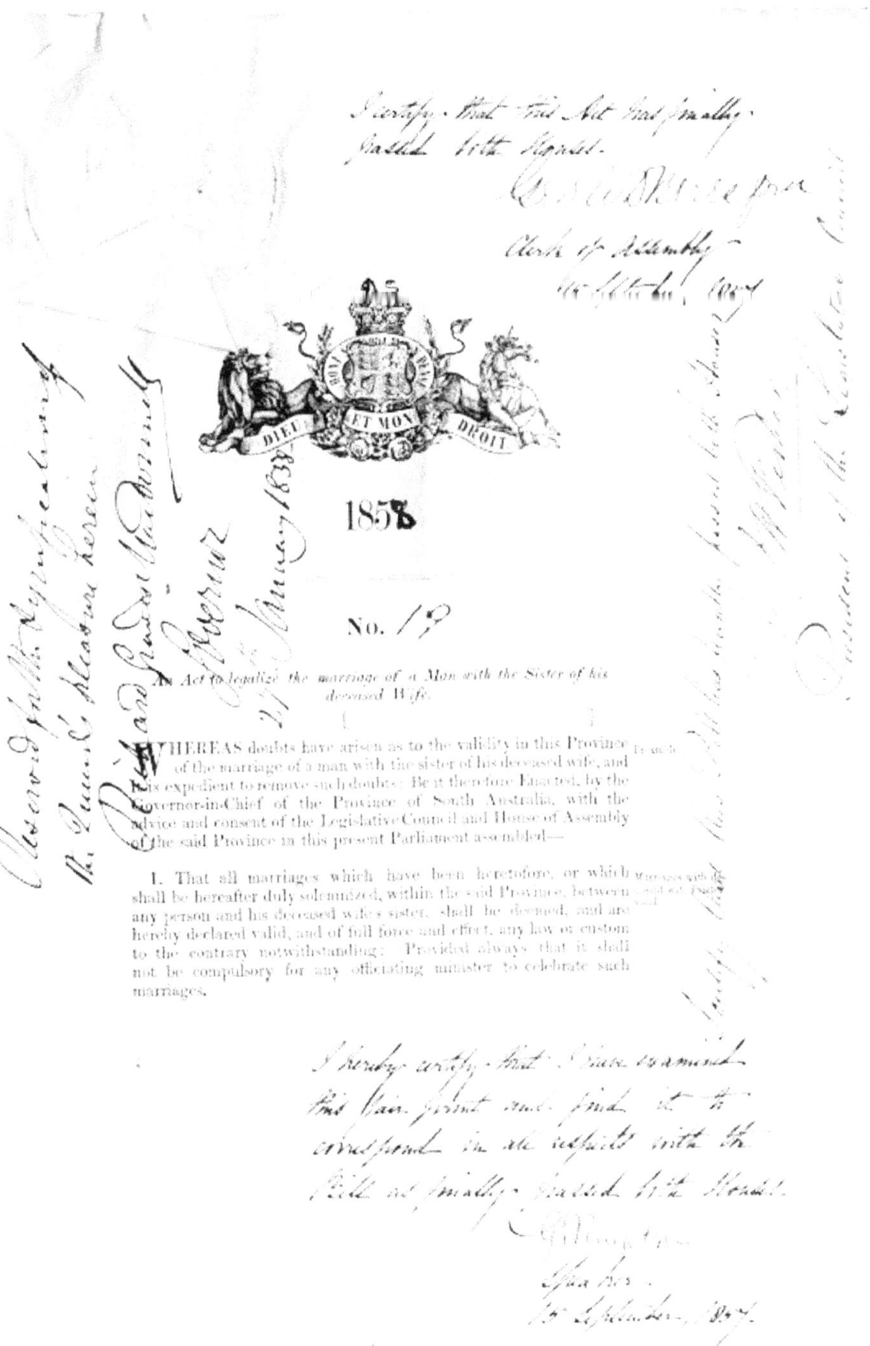

1858

No. 19

An Act to legalize the marriage of a Man with the Sister of his deceased Wife.

WHEREAS doubts have arisen as to the validity in this Province of the marriage of a man with the sister of his deceased wife, and it is expedient to remove such doubts: Be it therefore Enacted, by the Governor-in-Chief of the Province of South Australia, with the advice and consent of the Legislative Council and House of Assembly of the said Province in this present Parliament assembled—

1. That all marriages which have been heretofore, or which shall be hereafter duly solemnized, within the said Province, between any person and his deceased wife's sister, shall be deemed, and are hereby declared valid, and of full force and effect, any law or custom to the contrary notwithstanding: Provided always that it shall not be compulsory for any officiating minister to celebrate such marriages.

The "Crown Seal" copy of the Marriage Act 1858. As indicated the Act was reserved for the "signification" of the Queen but it was actually disallowed. (SCLSA) repugnant; and there were those who thought that "repugnant" implied, as its etymology indicated, not mere inconsistency but actual opposition to the law of England. Within these two groups the views of individual persons fluctuated to an almost infinite extent, but the rough classification may serve to separate the sheep from the followers of the judicial goat, Mr Justice Boothby.

In *Hutchinson v. Leeworthy* Mr Fisher boldly contended that the Real Property Act was invalid as repugnant to the law of England; it attempted to oust the jurisdiction of the Supreme Court to decide upon questions of title to land. In a book on the Real Property Act published by him in 1858, Fisher had propounded this theory of repugnancy as applied to the Act. In reviewing his book, the *Register* observed that by repugnancy:

> '... it was intended to imply something subversive of the interests of the Imperial Government, or something intended to take effect beyond the limits of the Province, in contravention of the Imperial legislation prevailing there. It never can be seriously affirmed that a law passed in the Colony which provides for something that is not provided for in the law of England, or that provides for something in a manner different from that in which it is provided for in the law of England, is repugnant to that law.' [13]

In the course of Fisher's argument, the Chief Justice mentioned that it was a common thing in the colony for men to be tried in the local courts, without a jury, for felony—a procedure quite unknown in England.

> 'As a Judge, I am ashamed to say it'—interposed Mr Justice Boothby—'this is the only dependency of the Crown, so far as I know, where such a state of things prevails. It is the only place I know where the stamp of felon may be placed on a man's brow without the intervention of a jury.'

Mr Hanson, in reply to Fisher, argued that what was meant by repugnancy was:

> '... some such thing as a prohibition of the free exercise of the Christian religion, or if any person would hang another without a trial by jury except under martial law, that would be repugnant to the law of England. It would not be repugnant to English law to do away with Trial by Jury in criminal cases, except in trials for treason; in all minor matters it would be a question for the legislature to consider and decide according to expediency.'

He considered that it was only when colonial legislation contravened fundamental principles that it became repugnant.[14]

On the question of repugnancy neither the Chief Justice nor Mr Justice Gwynne gave any judgment, deciding the case upon other grounds; but Mr Justice Boothby said that the question having been raised the plaintiff was entitled to the opinion of the Court upon it.

> 'That the validity of any legislation in excess of the powers granted to the Parliament of this province by the Imperial Parliament may be enquired into by this Court, I have no doubt'—he said. 'The fact of an Act being left to its operation by Her Majesty after the assent of the Governor having been given in Parliament, makes no difference; for the legality of an assent by the Crown, although given with the sanction of Her Privy Council, and the law officers of the Crown, must still be determined by the Courts of law, for the Privy Council and the law officers of the Crown have only the duty of advising what the law is supposed to be, but not the power of determining the law.'

The Real Property Act provided for a mode of conveyance previously unknown to English law, but upon his construction of the Act it was not repugnant; for he was of opinion that the necessary interpretation of the Act was that the decisions of the Lands Titles Commissioners in issuing Certificates of Titles might be reviewed by the Supreme Court.

> 'Had, indeed, the Legislature by express words, or necessary construction, created the Lands Titles Commissioners a tribunal to decide without review or appeal on the ownership of land, and by express words taken away the writ of ejectment—the best means known to our law of determining the title to land by the aid of a Jury in finding the facts, on which the title to land in so many cases altogether depends—I should be clearly of opinion that such provisions, without an enabling Act of the Imperial Parliament, would be altogether without legal force or validity, because repugnant to the law of England. The true construction of the Real Property Act leaves it free to work its great remedial changes in simplifying the transfer of land—an object well worthy the still further attention of the wisdom of the legislature, while the determination of title demands a more facile and summary process than our law at present admits of, as the result of careful and instructed legislation.' [15]

Mr Justice Boothby's interpretation of the Act was extremely unpalatable to the public, who preferred that construction which he said led to repugnancy. The press urged that Parliament should immediately take up the question of repugnancy, and let it be decided once and for all what was repugnant and what was not; and who were and who were not authorised to determine questions of repugnancy. A great deal of heated talk produced no tangible results. An appeal to the Court of Appeals was lodged by Mrs Leeworthy, but it was abandoned.[16] The Government paid her compensation for the loss of her land.

It may be here noticed that in 1868, in *Smith v. Bewes* 2 SALR 149, the Full Court (consisting of Chief Justice Hanson, Justice Gwynne and Justice Wearing) unanimously agreed that *Hutchinson v. Leeworthy* was wrongly decided and overruled it. They said the Full Court in the earlier case had gone wrong in upholding the validity of Hutchinson's original land grant. By the Foundation Act (4 & 5 Wm IV c.95) the Colonisation Commissioners were empowered to sell the lands of the province at a price of not less than 12 shillings per acre. Mr Smith, like Mr Hutchinson, paid the Commissioners £80 8s 0d and received a preliminary land order entitling him to select 134 acres. He duly received a grant of, as it was subsequently discovered, 220 acres. The Government, as in Hutchinson's case, reclaimed the excess and issued a grant of it to the defendant. Confidently relying on *Hutchinson v. Leeworthy*, Mr Smith brought an action to recover the land taken from him, only to prove the truth of the old saying that he who goes to law holds a wolf by the ears. To his great discomfiture the Court held that the order issued by the Colonisation Commissioners being for 134 acres, the Resident Commissioner in the colony had authority to put the plaintiff in possession of a section of that extent only, and that the grant of a block of 220 acres was therefore absolutely void; and that even had the land order been for 220 acres it would not have sustained the grant, because such a sale would have been in excess of the statutory powers of the Colonisation Commissioners, who were forbidden to sell under 12 shillings an acre.

Following the expression of Mr Justice Boothby's opinion in *Hutchinson v. Leeworthy*, the Attorney-General (Mr Strangways) was asked in the Assembly to say whether or not the Real Property Act was repugnant to the law of England. "It was right," said the questioner, "that the country should be relieved from uncertainty." In reply the Attorney-General said that he knew of no decision on the subject of repugnancy, "and in the absence of such decision I am not prepared to say I am of opinion that the Real Property Act is repugnant to the laws of England"—a cautious opinion which conveyed very little.[17]

In July 1860 a consolidating Real Property Act was introduced in the Assembly. Mr Morphett, in the course of debate, said that he had seen opinions from high legal authorities at home that the Act was repugnant, but the House paid little attention to this. A dozen cases like *Hutchinson v. Leeworthy*, it was said, could not shake the confidence of the people in the measure.[18] The Act was passed and assented to by the Governor. In forwarding it to England, he wrote to the Secretary of State:

> 'The enclosed Act is intended to consolidate the law and embody the improvements connected with the very important and interesting experiment, which has hitherto been so successfully attempted in this colony for simplifying proceedings and diminishing the expense previously attending the transfer of land. I scarcely know whether the experiment be of more consequence to this community than to the British public, where the extent and value of real property and the complications and cost attending all dealings with it, are so much greater.' [19]

A number of legal practitioners, however, had drawn up a ponderous memorial to the Secretary of State protesting against the Act and asking that it should be disallowed. Mr Harrison, in his *Colonial Sketches*, was very facetious about this:

> 'The Reform Act'—he wrote—'had such an alarming effect on the reduction of the profits of some of the conveyancers, whose talents were mainly directed to spinning out Abstracts of Title to the utmost extent that they had any chance of getting paid for at 6s 8d per sheet, that a few of them actually addressed a humble petition to His Grace the Duke of Newcastle, Secretary for the Colonies, a document so extensive and full of suppliant verbiage, that it is probable that the Honourable Secretary or his subordinates would never find time to wade through it, even if it was of some importance; and the probability is that they will get a soothing answer to their humble prayer, as they call it, for attempting to abolish the laws of common sense, and returning to a system concocted by ingenious minds from the time of the Norman Conquest, for the purpose of fleecing property holders.' [20]

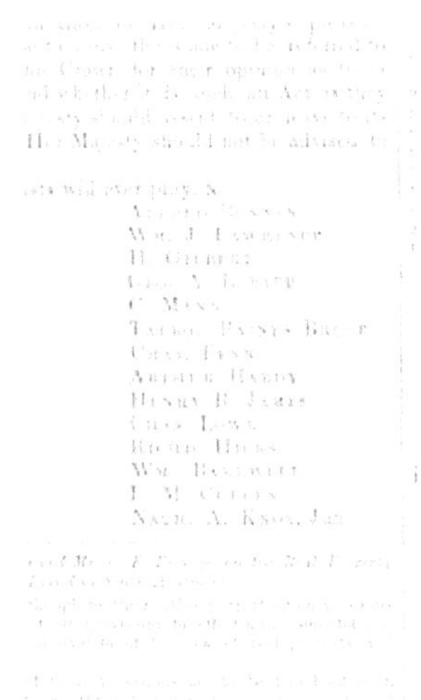

The list of memorialists from the *South Australian Government Gazette* 8th November 1860. (SCLSA)

Sir Richard MacDonnell caused the memorial to be published in full in the *Government Gazette* before transmitting it to England. It was signed, he said, by only fourteen out of forty practitioners, and four of these were young men only recently admitted. Repugnancy was the memorialists' strong point, and the Governor was at pains to set out his views with regard to this topic.

> 'It seems to me'—he said—'that the Memorialists have a very erroneous idea of what is meant by repugnancy to the law of England ... and the opinion of Mr Hayes, an eminent conveyancer, but not necessarily versed in International or Constitutional Law, rather obscures the question. A Colonial Law may be and often is wholly "different" from the English

law dealing with the same subject. Nevertheless mere "difference" does not constitute "repugnancy". English law imposes a duty of 20/- per gallon on all imported brandy, and a South Australian Act may nevertheless impose a duty of £5:0:0 or of 10/- or no duty at all on the same article—and nevertheless no one would dream of calling such legislation "illegal or void"; although if a differential duty were imposed it would be illegal, though even then not for repugnancy, but for disobedience of a positive instruction. If however the Legislative Council and Assembly were unanimously to pass, and if I were to give the Queen's assent to, an Act enabling Mr Hayes to marry two wives in Adelaide at the same time, or disabling Mr Laurence, who heads the list of the Memorialists, from receiving a Knighthood if conferred upon him by Her Majesty, I have no doubt that despite every due observance of the Standing Orders of both Houses and even if I had no Instructions forbidding my assent to such Acts—they would from the first be absolutely void—the one as utterly opposed to morality and the spirit of the English Common Law, the other as dealing with the Queen's Prerogative which is not within the class of subjects whereon Colonial Parliaments can legislate without permission. As no definition exists of what is "repugnancy" I can only explain it by illustration as above; and in like manner I would say that an Act is not necessarily repugnant to English law, because it may be clumsily drawn, as Mr Hayes hints was the case with the first Real Property Act, nor because it may "demand the greatest deliberation as well as the highest professional skill and experience to render it safe and permanent", nor because the Legislature does not "await the result of approaching discussions in the Imperial Parliament", nor because it is conceived "with a design of abrogating the system of documentary title to Real Property" and substituting "a novel and experimental system unknown to the laws of England", nor above all because it imposes "eventually upon the judicature of the parent country the duty of studying and administering that code". As for the latter extraordinary hardship Mr Hayes forgets that he commenced by observing that Bills "under Ministerial auspices were even then pending for effecting similar vital changes in the real property system of England", and therefore that the system which he deprecates would probably have to be studied by English Judges in reference to wider interests than those of South Australia. When one reflects on the encomiums

> bestowed on Mr Torrens by some English legal writers, as the author of the "experimental system" viewed with so much horror by conveyancers, and remembers that the leading principles suggested by the Royal Commission in England on Registration of Titles ... are identical with those carried out in the enclosed Act by more economical and simpler machinery, it is matter of grave surprise that it should still be a question with anyone whether such experiment, already commenced in England, would if attempted here, be "repugnant" to English law, and that Mr Hayes should doubt if this 'Colonial Legislature is vested virtually with independent competency not merely to keep pace with Imperial Legislature in all its advances, but to run ahead of its principles and policy', which last seems to me the highest compliment that could be paid to those principles—a compliment moreover entailing no risk because even attempts to develop English principles and policy here must be ever limited by the Queen's Instructions to the Governor, and also by what Mr Hayes seems to regard as a trifle, and quaintly designates as the "mere requisite of the Crown's assent".'

As the English law officers had already recommended that the previous Real Property Acts should be left to their operation, and much land had been brought under the Act, it would be disastrous if the Act was disallowed. A deputation had waited on the Governor, proposing that a counter-memorial should be prepared; but the Governor dissuaded them from this.

> 'I told the deputation that I did not see how even ten or twenty thousand yeomen or farmers signing a Memorial expressing their conviction of the excellence of the provisions of the Real Property Act, and their interest therein could either add to or subvert the weight of arguments on a mere legal question, such as whether the Act be or be not void—a question wholly independent of the merits of the Act.'

He had no doubt that many thousands would have signed a counter-memorial, for the feeling of the country in favour of the Real Property Act was extremely strong: it was shown by the enthusiastic reception given to Torrens in his lecture tours, by the large majority in Parliament in favour of it, and by the great amount of property voluntarily placed under the Act.

> 'The more the legal profession regards with disfavour such an innovation on their time-honoured and reverend usages'—the Governor concluded—'the more the country seems resolved to stand by the principles of the Act and to persist in amending

> and consolidating its provisions till opposition to it shall be fruitless. In a few years the greatest part of the land in South Australia will be brought under the Act, and then I presume the lawyers will have to follow.' [21]

The great memorial came to nothing. The petitioners had forgotten that:

> 'Great men have no great patience when they read,
> And long petitions spoil the cause they plead.'

The Duke of Newcastle simply replied that he saw nothing calling for the interference of the Crown, and the Real Property Act was left to its operation. The *Register* was delighted. The memorial, it said, was:

> '... a mere bugbear, designed to frighten naughty children in the colonies, but treated with the consideration it deserves when it makes appearance among matured legislators and statesmen. We sincerely trust that we shall hear no more of it here.' [22]

Meanwhile, during the passing of the Real Property Act of 1860 the Supreme Court had delivered another assault on the new system in the historic case of *Payne v. Dench*, which is fully described in the chapter dealing with the Court of Appeals.[23] In December 1860, Mr Justice Boothby, in *ex parte Prankerd*, gave the first indications of a new line of argument which he was developing; he suggested that the Real Property Act, notwithstanding the Governor's assent, was not in operation because the Governor should have reserved it under his Instructions.[24] This point will be considered more fully in a moment; but continuing for the present with the question of repugnancy, it is necessary next to notice a case of some importance, *Reg. v. Preston*, at the Criminal Sessions before Mr Justice Boothby in February 1861. Preston, a solicitor, had been convicted of stealing a cheque, and his counsel, Mr Lowe, moved in arrest of judgment. By the law of England, he argued, no man could be placed upon his trial for felony except upon the oath of the Grand Jury; in South Australia by Act No 10 of 1852 the Grand Jury was abolished. But the colonial legislature, he submitted, did not sufficiently consider their own powers or the probability that by their enactment the rights of colonists as subjects of the Queen were invaded; the assumed power to enable the Attorney-General to indict for felony without the intervention of the Grand Jury was in excess of the authority conferred by the Imperial statutes upon the colonial legislature; and the Act 10 of 1852 was extra vires, and void as repugnant to the law of England. In overruling this contention Mr Justice Boothby said:

> 'I think the objection a very grave one—one that deserves most serious consideration; but I should not be warranted, sitting here as a single Judge, to take a course which would

> have the effect of interrupting the administration of criminal justice in this colony. This is a question which deserved the serious consideration of those who have the preparation of the laws, and whose duty it is to make the laws of the colony consistent with the laws of England. I have frequently expressed my views upon this subject, that I consider the Grand Jury one of the noblest institutions which English men inherit from their forefathers. I am aware that a vulgar outcry has from time to time been raised against it by men more anxious to attend to their private interests than to perform their public duties. Attempts have been made to abolish that noble institution by clamours proceeding only from men who are unwilling to acknowledge any obligation but that of attention to business, or to answer any call except it proceeds from the counting house. But I believe that the great majority of the people of England will never consent to its abolition; and if they do in my time I shall most sincerely deplore such a result. I have only to repeat that this is not a question to be decided by me as a single Judge. The law as it has been administered during the last nine or ten years must be continued until the question has been decided in the Full Court or by appeal to Her Majesty in Privy Council. The sooner the question is settled the better; for, sooner or later, settled it must be. I am aware that an appeal is an expensive process; but as a single Judge, I cannot take upon myself the responsibility of putting a stop to the administration of Criminal justice in this province. It may be a question whether it is not necessary to have an Imperial Statute to give effect to the local enactment referred to; but I shall proceed to pass sentence upon the prisoner, leaving it open to Mr Lowe to carry the question before the Full Court or the Privy Council, this being a matter of error apparent upon the face of the record.' [25]

Mr Lowe did not carry the case further, and the decision passed almost unnoticed. It becomes very significant in view of Mr Justice Boothby's conduct several years later when a precisely similar point was taken before him and upheld.

In June 1861 came the case of *McEllister v. Fenn*. This was an action for slander, the plaintiff declaring that the defendant had represented him as having obtained his signature to a deed under the Real Property Act of 1858 by fraud—an offence punishable under that Act as a felony. To this the defendant had demurred, on the ground inter alia, that supposing the alleged imputation would have been slander during the time the Real Property Act of 1858 was in force, that Act had been repealed before the section had been

Edward McEllister (c1808-1866)
Arriving in South Australia in 1838 McEllister first worked as a policeman and later moved into business in Adelaide. He was a Member of Parliament from 1858 to 1866.

brought, and no action could be sustained inasmuch as no punishment could be inflicted under that Act for the offence, if any offence had been imputed. During the argument before the Full Court on the demurrer Mr Justice Boothby interposed to say:

> 'We cannot take any notice of the Real Property Act of 1860, as it has not received the assent of Her Majesty. The Governor was not empowered under his Instructions to assent to that Act.
>
> 'I am not prepared to enter upon an argument of that sort at the present moment,' said Mr Hanson, who appeared for the plaintiff, 'but supposing a doubt to arise as to the force of that Act—were a person to be put upon his trial for an offence under that Act, it might ...'
>
> 'Suppose a person charged before me,' interrupted Mr Justice Boothby, 'in reference to an alleged offence under that Act, I certainly should not allow the question to go to the Jury upon the supposition that that was law having force in this Colony.'

The Judge then brought forward his objection that the Act should have been reserved by the Governor, as being of an "extraordinary nature and importance", affecting the rights and property of subjects of the Queen not residing in the colony. The Chief Justice said it was impossible to go into the question of whether or not the Governor had obeyed his Instructions; but Mr Justice Boothby insisted on the point:

> 'How can it be argued'—he said—'that the prerogative of the Queen has not been interfered with when the Lands Titles Commissioners are constituted a tribunal to decide as to the property of subjects resident in England, without appeal? Surely the prerogative of the Queen has been invaded, supposing that there are subjects in that position in England. The effect of the Act is to erect a tribunal which shall have jurisdiction to set aside the right of appeal to Her Majesty; for that is the effect of an indefeasible title ... The Real Property Act is not only an invasion of the royal prerogative, but it is of such an extraordinary nature as is pointed to in the Royal Instructions.'
>
> Mr Hanson: 'I think we may safely leave Her Majesty and Her prerogative to vindicate themselves.'
>
> Boothby J: 'It is the duty of this Court to vindicate the Royal prerogative. I sit here a representative of Her Majesty as much as His Excellency does.'

At the conclusion of the argument, Mr Justice Boothby said that they should take time to consider the question, as the case might be the subject of an appeal to the Privy Council. The Chief Justice, however, said rather testily:

> 'I am at all events the senior Judge of this Court, and can give my opinion ... As to the question whether this was an Act or Bill which required to be reserved for the royal assent, I am decidedly of opinion that it is not our province upon the present occasion to enter into that question. Whether the Bill was of an extraordinary nature and importance or not, and whether the Queen's prerogative has or has not been invaded, are not now to be considered. I consider that those questions have been fully considered by those whose duty it was to give them consideration. If the Governor has failed in his duty in not reserving the Bill for the royal assent—and I am far from saying that it is so—but even so, I apprehend we are not entitled to say that the Act of Parliament is void. He may have transgressed his duty, but I do not mean to *insinuate* that he did so; yet it does not appear that we are to say, without having the question properly raised, that an Act of Parliament becomes thereby void. I think it would be most injudicious for us to do so. It has been said that the Royal Instructions have been published; no doubt they were required to be published, and everybody knows what they are; but it would be very difficult for Judges to discharge their duties if, upon every occasion when we are asked to put a construction upon an Act of Parliament, we had to enter upon an enquiry as to whether the Governor assented to it for the Queen in the first instance, or reserved it for the royal assent. I apprehend that it is not our duty to do so.'

He thought the words were slanderous and gave judgment for the plaintiff on the demurrer; Mr Justice Gwynne concurred.

> 'As to the question whether the Act is in force, I do not see any necessity to go into it'—he said. 'The Governor had a discretion in the matter, and that being the case, it is not a matter for this Court to enquire into.'

Mr Justice Boothby delivered his considered judgment a week later, and declared the Real Property Act of 1860 had no legal force. It was a very long judgment and an analysis of it must be tedious; but it is necessary to explain the stand he took with regard to the Governor's Instructions. His reasoning may be summarised as follows:

(1) By 13 & 14 Vic c.59 s.12 it was enacted that all the provisions of 5 & 6 Vic c.76 and 7 & 8 Vic c.74 which relate to, inter alia:

> '... the giving and withholding of Her Majesty's assent to Bills, and the reservation of Bills for the signification of Her Majesty's pleasure thereon, and the Bills so reserved; the Instructions to be conveyed to the Governor for his guidance in relation to the matters aforesaid; and the disallowance of Bills by Her Majesty, shall apply to and be in force in the colony of Victoria, and in each of the said colonies of Van Diemen's Land, South Australia, and Western Australia, in which a Legislative Council shall be established under this Act, as if all such provisions were here repeated, the name of such respective colony being substituted for the name of the Colony of New South Wales'.

The words underlined, Mr Justice Boothby contended, made the Governor's Instructions a part of the Act and gave them statutory force.

(2) Referring to 5 & 6 Vic c.76, and substituting "South Australia" for "New South Wales" it was enacted by section XL that the Queen might from time to time convey to the Governor of South Australia such Instructions as to her should seem meet for the guidance of such Governor for the exercise of the powers vested in him of assenting to, dissenting from, or reserving bills, and it was the Governor's duty to act in obedience to such Instructions; and by section XXXI that:

> '... every Bill which has been passed by the said Council ... shall be presented for Her Majesty's assent to the Governor of the said colony, and that the Governor shall declare according to his discretion, but subject nevertheless to the provisions contained in this Act and to such Instructions as may from time to time be given in that behalf by Her Majesty ... that he assents to such Bill in Her Majesty's name, or that he withholds Her Majesty's assent, or that he reserves such Bill for the signification of Her Majesty's pleasure thereon; and all Bills altering or affecting the divisions and extent of the several districts and towns which shall be represented in the Legislative Council, or establishing new and other divisions of the same ... and also all Bills altering or affecting the duties of Customs upon any goods wares, or merchandise imported to or exported from the said colony, shall in every case be so reserved, except such Bills for temporary laws as the Governor shall expressly declare necessary to be forthwith assented to by reason of some public and pressing emergency'.

It was clearly, therefore, the duty of the Governor to obey the Royal Instructions.

(3) He had no doubt that the Court was bound to take judicial notice of the Royal Instructions:

> 'They are in legal effect made a portion of the Imperial Statute which provides for their being issued; they are so connected with the Commission of every Governor that it is his duty to read and publish them on his arrival in the colony with all due solemnity, in the presence of Her Majesty's Chief Officers, and others, the principal inhabitants of the colony.'

Upon referring to the Royal Instructions it appeared that among twelve classes of bills specified, it was directed that:

> '... any Bill of an extraordinary nature and importance, whereby our prerogative, or the rights and property of our subjects not residing in the Colony, or the trade and shipping of the United Kingdom and its dependencies may be prejudiced, shall be reserved for Her Majesty's pleasure thereon'.

(4) The Real Property Act was an act of such an extraordinary nature.

> 'The number of absentee landowners and leaseholders, mortgagors and mortgagees, absentee heirs-at-law and others interested in the succession to or equitable interests in real estate, whether under wills or marriage settlements, or settlements under powers, or for family provision, or rights of dower, or any other of the various modes by which rights to real property may be created under the law of England, and under the laws in force in its various dependencies; the rights of the Banking Companies of the Province in reference to loans on deposit of deeds, or other writings creating ownership or equitable interests, and interests under leases, and the like also as to the great Land Companies of the Province, Life and Fire Insurance Companies, the great majority of whose shareholders, being absentees, are all capable of being prejudiced by the Act in question. Such a Bill, therefore, the Governor-in-Chief was erroneously advised to give his assent to; and having given it, contrary to the Royal Instructions such assent is invalid, and cannot give the force of an Act of Parliament to such a Bill.'

(5) It was true that the Queen had left the Act to its operation, but that could only mean such operation as the law would give it.

> 'Her Majesty's assent having been once given by her

representative in the Province, in violation of the Statute, or the Royal Instructions, Her Majesty has no power of remedying that mischief by an assent in England; for there is no statutory power in the Crown to give two assents—one by Her representative in the colony, and a second assent by Herself in England. The Imperial Statute gives no power to Her Majesty to remedy any error of Her Representative in giving an invalid assent to any Bill; the question of the validity of any Act so assented to, if made necessary in the suit of any of Her subjects before this Court, is a matter for its decision in such suit, subject to be reviewed by the Judicial Committee of Her Privy Council.'

(6) The contention that the Governor, in assenting to the Act, was exercising a discretion which could not be inquired into by the Court, he put aside.

'If that were so, no reason can be assigned for the Imperial Parliament having surrounded these instructions with so many restrictions and safeguards for their due observance, and would amount to a power in any Governor to dispense with those instructions when, and as he pleased. The discretion which any Governor may exercise, is limited to two sets of circumstances—one by the Imperial Statute Sec.31 of 5 and 6 Vict. c.76, which allows a discretion in reference to 'any temporary law necessary to be forthwith assented to by reason of some public and pressing emergency', and another by the Royal Instructions, which allows a discretion as to reserving a Bill in any Governor when he 'shall be of opinion that an urgent necessity exists requiring such Bill to be brought into immediate operation. Now, as the Real Property Act was neither a temporary law, nor a law which an urgent necessity required to be brought into immediate operation—for it could not be material whether such Act became a law in 1858 or 1859—it would be idle to say the provisions of the Statute, or of the Instructions, allowing of a discretion, were applicable to such Bill.'

(7) He reiterated his judgment in *Hutchinson v. Leeworthy* where he held:

(a) that the Supreme Court had the power and duty to examine into the validity of local legislation; and

(b) that the Real Property Act then in force only established a new mode of transfer of land.

But, "now that the Legislature has introduced into the last Act the provisions which I then said would destroy the validity of any such legislation, I am compelled to abide by the opinion formerly expressed".

(8) The Real Property Act of 1860, he therefore concluded, had no legal force:

> '... the assent of the Crown being given thereto contrary to the Royal Instructions, and because the Act itself proposes to deprive Her Majesty of her prerogative in deciding in Her Supreme Court, before her Judges here, on the ownership of land, subject to an appeal before the Judicial Committee of Her Privy Council. It cannot surely be proposed to set aside, by any Colonial Act, the power of appeal to Her Majesty in Privy Council as to any decision by any tribunal in this Province as to the ownership of land; and if that cannot be done, it is impossible by mere local legislation to establish what on the face of the Act of 1860 is in express words shown to be its great object—indefeasibility of title. If there is given to any Court whatever, the power of reviewing and reversing the decisions of the Lands Titles Commissioners, I cannot understand how indefeasibility can be arrived at as to any title exposed to the test of a decision as to its validity by the Judicial Committee of Her Majesty's Privy Council, if such title be indeed bad and insufficient by the laws of England.'

(9) Finally, he stated a still further point.

> 'The question as to the operation, with the force of law, of Acts of the Parliament of this Province, is of so serious importance, that I am surprised that the provisions of 5 & 6 Vict c.76 have not, in the time I have had a seat on this Bench, been brought before the Court for judicial decision. In closely examining this Statute, I am of opinion that it has been dangerously disregarded, and so risked the security of past legislation, probably to an extent that will require an Imperial Act to remove all doubts as to the validity of legislation since the coming into operation of 13 and 14 Vict c.59.'

The effect of the latter act, he considered, had been to make applicable to South Australia the provisions of 9 Geo IV c.83 s.22, which have already been referred to. No acts had ever been sent by the Governor of South Australia to the Supreme Court for the approval of the Judges as provided by that section, and, if the section was in force here, it had been flagrantly disobeyed. By section 33 of the same Act it was also provided that where any bill had been reserved for the assent of the Crown, it should not have any force or authority within the colony until the Governor signified, by speech or message to the Legislative Council or by proclamation, that the royal assent had been given; and that an entry should be made in the journals of the Legislative Council of every such speech, message, or proclamation, and a duplicate thereof, duly attested, delivered to the Registrar of the Supreme Court, or other proper officer, to be kept among the records of the colony. This provision likewise had never been followed in South Australia. Mr Justice Boothby thought both provisions were admirable.

> 'The argument of convenience and advantage, arising from such a provision of the law, is so manifest, that it must influence the inquiry whether such a regulation is still law; and I am of opinion that it is, and that it has been the duty of the Governor for the time being to obey its provisions ever since the operation of 13 and 14 Vict c.59 (1850) in this Province. It is a question of the highest importance, and needs authoritative solution by the Judicial Committee of Her Majesty's Privy Council; for if the sec. of 9 Geo IV c.83, now under consideration, was in force in New South Wales in 1850, it clearly is in operation here; and the provision that no Law or Ordinance shall take effect until it has lain fourteen days before the Judges of the Supreme Court for their consideration as to its validity, but may, after that term, if the Judges point out no objection raises doubts as to the validity of all legislation in which the provision as to recording Acts in the Supreme Court has been disregarded.
>
> I have deemed it my duty to go thus at length into the law of reservation and assent to Bills in this Province, and of their repugnancy to the law of England'—he concluded—'because of its great importance to the people of this Province; for the Legislature may deeply jeoparize [sic] the interests of the Queen's subjects they represent, by presenting to the Governor for the time being a Bill, even within his powers of assent, making important changes in the law of England. Such a Bill, although not open to objections founded on repugnancy, may, from the experience of some unforeseen mischief in the working of such a law, be disallowed by Her Majesty within two years, to the great injury, it may be, of those supposed to have acquired interests under such disallowed Act during the time it was in force. A risk of mischief of this kind undoubtedly ends with the expiry of two years; but not so with respect to any Act having an invalid assent, or being open to the objection of repugnancy, for that may go on uncontested before the Courts of Law for a number of undefined years, until some suitor of this Court raises the objection of invalidity, and which must be sustained if the law

> so provides. And it must be ever borne in mind, that the costs of setting aside invalid legislation will always fall on one or other of the suitors of this Court.'

His judgment, accordingly, was given for the defendant.[26]

The demurrer having been overruled by his colleagues, however, the action came on for trial on 27 June, unfortunately before Mr Justice Boothby. The Judge did not raise the illegality of the Real Property Act again, but he started another question which aroused just as much hostile criticism—namely, whether he was bound to follow the opinion of the majority of the Judges. The defendant's counsel urged that the words used were not slanderous. Mr Hanson, for the plaintiff, said that it had been decided otherwise by the majority of the Court on the argument on the demurrer, and that the trial judge must follow that decision. Mr Justice Boothby hinted that the case ought to be taken direct to the Privy Council from his decision, without going to the Full Court, and threw out the suggestion that he was not bound to obey a decision of the majority of the Court. Eventually he nonsuited the plaintiff on the ground that the communication was made on a privileged occasion and that there was no evidence of malice.[27]

Under the old practice, the plaintiff, when a nonsuit was to be given, was "called", although he was never intended to appear in propria persona. In this case the Judge's associate pronounced the cabalistic words of the legal fiction: "Edward McEllister, come into court and save your Writ, or you will be non-suited." To the great surprise of Judge and counsel Mr McEllister appeared, and marched forward, "a smile of good-natured bewilderment irradiating his countenance", as it was explained to him that although called, he was not wanted.[28]

The two hearings of *McEllister v. Fenn* aroused great public excitement.

> 'The subtleties of law are being exhibited with undiminished ardour in our local forum'—said the Register, calling attention to Mr Justice Boothby's: '... determined and uncompromising opposition to the Real Property Act ... A broad issue is raised between the Legislature and a member of the Bench. Everything has been done to test the validity and soundness of the Real Property Act that can reasonably be demanded.' [29]

If Mr Justice Boothby would not acknowledge an act duly passed and left to its operation after exhaustive examination, both in the colony and in England—if he felt that he could not carry it out—there was only one course open to him—resignation. The process of useful legislation was not to be impeded by the perversity of one of the Judges, whose erroneous views would encourage the legal profession to resist the Act and must lead to frightful litigation. He took "a narrow and unhealthy view of the law, opposed alike to the conveniences of the people, and the progressive tendencies of the age". No doubt it was conscientiously entertained; but seeing that his opinions were incompatible with the welfare of the colony, in the interests of the public, he should resign. If he would not, "he must be dislodged".[30]

Mr Justice Boothby paid no heed to the storm breaking over him. He remained constant and immovable, as the poet spoke of King Latinus:

> 'Ille velut pelagi rupes immota resistit:
> moved no more than rock on shore.'

In the same month as *McEllister v. Fenn* occurred two other cases which afforded him further opportunity of ventilating his opinions. In *Liebelt v. Hunt* he declared that the Parliament of the province had no power to override the common law of England.[31] The other, *Dashwood v. Cleve*, was heard before the Chief Justice and Mr Justice Boothby, Mr Justice Gwynne not sitting because he had been engaged in the case as counsel. It involved the local Customs Acts. Mr Fenn, adopting the arguments of Mr Justice Boothby, contended that the Customs Act of 1854 was repugnant, and that it was invalid through the Governor's failure to reserve it.

The Chief Justice, in giving his judgment, said that in his opinion it was a proper construction of the Imperial enactments as to the reservation of bills "to say that in every case in which the Governor has a discretion, however limited or qualified, it is not competent for this Court to enquire into its exercise". Assuming the Governor ought to have reserved the bill, his failure to do so did not make the Act invalid.

> 'A discretionary power was vested in the Governor, not that it was lawful for him to do as he pleased, but that an unwise or improper exercise of his discretion would not render his act of assent inoperative.'

Every presumption ought to be made in favour of the regularity of the Governor's proceedings, rather than declare void an act which had been acted on in countless cases for upwards of seven years.

Mr Justice Boothby was of a different opinion, but as he had lost his notebook he had to postpone giving his reasons. The notebook could not be found and he never delivered any formal judgment. It was intimated that as the two Judges could not agree, either party could appeal to the Privy Council, but neither wished to do so.[32]

In an able dispatch to the Secretary of State reviewing all this litigation, Sir Richard MacDonnell severely criticised Mr Justice Boothby's arguments, and exposed their weaknesses and fallacies. That Judge's principal objections to the Real Property Act were:

(1) That its leading feature being to render titles indefeasible, it deprived the Queen of her prerogative of deciding appeals to the Privy Council against the validity of any title.

As to this, said the Governor:

> 'It seems sufficient reply, that Her Majesty's Privy Council will no doubt determine, as heretofore, the validity of titles by the laws of the country where the property may be situated—whether in Australia or India; and that any prospective diminution of litigation, by improved legislation, will be regarded with favor, and not as an attack on the prerogative of the Crown. Indeed, there is far more reason to fear the best intentioned and best draughted Act will unfortunately leave quite sufficient room for 'appeals' to remove even the learned Judge's apprehensions on that point.'

(2) That it was invalid because the Governor assented to it contrary to his instructions.

This contention, as to some extent reflecting upon himself, the Governor subjected to an exhaustive examination. He admitted at once that the Supreme Court was necessarily and properly invested with the power of determining the validity of any local legislative provision which might appear to conflict with Imperial legislation, but he denied that colonial judges could inquire into any details connected with the Governor's dealings with acts previous to their being proclaimed and put into operation.

> 'Unless an absolute prohibition (which it is not contended was the case in this colony) had been imposed by direct Imperial authority on the Colonial Legislature's enacting, and the Governor's assenting to, any legislation on the subjects treated of in those Bills, and so long as even an infinitesimally small discretion is left in the Governor, the Colonial Courts cannot look behind the Acts placed on the Statute Book for the purpose of criticising the Governor's previous dealings therewith. They must rest satisfied with the evidence afforded by the Governor's Proclamation, that he has acted in accordance with his duty.'

(Sir) Richard Graves MacDonnell ca. 1860 (SLSA)

He referred to the case of *Rusden v. Weekes*, then recently decided in New South Wales. The Judges there, he said, had never arrogated to themselves the right claimed by Mr Justice Boothby of looking beyond the actual subject matter of the published colonial Acts, and had never disputed the authority which had placed them on the statute book.

> 'On the contrary, they contented themselves with accepting those statutes as part of the law of the land; and ... confined themselves within the strictly judicial functions of interpreting the meaning and force of the provisions of the Acts submitted for their consideration. That is a high and sacred trust, and its application is practically of far more consequence to the security and welfare of a people than the Governor's exercise of his discretion in giving the Crown's assent to Acts of the Legislature at once, or reserving them for assent in England.'

But Mr Justice Boothby went further than questioning the validity of the actual provisions of the Act, or its consistency with Imperial legislation; he said the whole Act was void because it was wrongly assented to.

> 'A greater contrast cannot be conceived than exists between the conduct of the New South Wales Judges and that of Mr Justice Boothby. The former sought only to interpret and reconcile the subject matter of the various Acts which they were bound to administer; whilst the latter, quitting his judicial functions, refused to look at all into an Act affecting a case before him, although that Act had been proclaimed and put in operation by the Governor. I may say that, whilst the former, consistently with an old legal maxim, construed the law ut stet magis quam cadat, Judge Boothby seemed to make a set at the Real Property Act, and to construe it, ut cadat magis quam stet.'

It was quite clear, said the Governor, that the Supreme Court was not in a position to review the Governor's conduct, for it had no means of knowing what his instructions were. Mr Justice Boothby was wrong in saying that those Instructions had to be published or communicated to Parliament; on the contrary, the Governor was only under orders to communicate them to his Executive Council, and even as to this he had a discretion to keep any instruction to himself if he deemed fit.

> 'It is quite impossible for the learned Judge to say what instructions I may have received ... every mail may have brought me a fresh set ... It would be a great hardship on the learned Judges to impose on them the duty of deciding the

> legality of an Act by reference to the Governor's Instructions—the most important part of which might be lying deposited in his desk, and be unknown even to his Executive Council.'

It was true that by paragraph 11 of his instructions, he was directed to reserve bills of an extraordinary nature or importance, or whereby the rights and property of subjects not residing in the colony might be prejudiced.

> 'Though possibly the first Real Property Act did not appear to me "extraordinary", and although it was also calculated, in my opinion, to benefit and "prejudice" the rights of persons interested in property here, it might, nevertheless, have been otherwise regarded by Her Majesty's advisers, because at that time it was only an experimental measure. Still it is difficult to imagine how any one—much less a Judge—can seriously affirm that the third edition of that Act, designed as it was merely to consolidate a system in actual operation, ought to have been regarded as an "extraordinary" Act within the meaning of my instructions. Still less could I have expected a Judge to have so entirely misunderstood and overlooked the first portion of the 11th section of my instructions, which plainly applies to all classes of Bills which I am directed to reserve, whether extraordinary or not, and which tells me to "reserve the same, subject to my discretion, in case I am of opinion that an urgent necessity exists, requiring that such Bills be brought into immediate operation", in which case I am authorised to assent to such Bills in the Queen's name &c. Hence it follows that the learned Judge's argument resolves into this: "The governor might have assented to the Bill, however 'extraordinary' it might have been, if he thought there was an urgent necessity for his doing so, and the assent so given is declared by his instructions, valid; but I (Judge Boothby), who had no discretion whatever in the matter, and whom no one was bound to consult, think there was no such necessity, and therefore the assent which the Governor has given is invalid." I respectfully submit that such a glaring non sequitur violates even the most rudimentary principle of logic. It would, indeed, be a most melancholy prospect for South Australians, if such doctrines were to prevail, especially as no matter at what period of time the learned Judge might fancy there had been some misapprehension by a Governor of his instructions, any Act might suddenly be declared wholly void from the first.'

The provisions of 9 Geo IV c.83 could not, in the Governor's opinion, be applicable to South Australia.

> 'The people of South Australia are told they are liable, not merely to obligations imposed by their own statutes, or by direct Imperial authority, but also to an indefinite number of provisions in the laws of other colonies, which a Judge may from time to time consider as put into operation here by the simple process of one Imperial Act naming, but not applying, another which had been framed with exclusive reference to other countries. It would almost seem as if the learned Judge, whilst tearing with one hand an Act from the statute-book of the Colonists, nevertheless feels bound with the other to proffer as compensation a fresh Act, adroitly annexed from the code of their neighbours.'

After briefly referring to the Judge's dicta that the local legislature had no power to create courts (*Payne v. Dench*), and that the validity of the Constitution Act itself was doubtful, because the Electoral Act had not been reserved the Governor added:

> 'He has, moreover, even gone the length of denying the power of this Parliament to alter the common law of England, as though any continuous legislation would be possible if no alteration suitable to the requirements of the age and of an Australian community could be made in the ancient customs of England. Nothing, however, has tended to rouse public feeling so much as the supposed reluctance of Mr Justice Boothby to be bound by the decision of the majority of the Court, because such a course is opposed to English usage and provokes unseemly litigation; whilst if the present Chief Justice be called to other duties temporarily, the Court would consist of only two, and the consequences of such a disregard, by one of the two Judges, of former rulings of the Full Court, is naturally regarded with apprehension by the general community.' [33]

Commenting on the situation, indeed, the *Register* remarked that the Supreme Court promised to become famous in the annals of jurisprudence for its arguments on the validity of laws—"edifying exhibitions of forensic gladiatorship". Mr Justice Boothby's views would involve the law in extricable confusion.

> 'It needs but a pugnacious lawyer and a narrow-minded Judge to place the whole interests of the community in jeopardy, and to make a tribunal which ought to be a protection to the rights and liberties of the people a fruitful source of oppression and of ruin.' [34]

With that singular lack of tact which characterised his judicial career, Mr Justice Boothby chose the moment when he was the target of hostile attention to give vent to an outburst from the bench against the niggardliness of the legislature in not increasing his salary. He had been thrown out of his dogcart on the way to court, which he reached half an hour late and somewhat shaken by his accident. Mr Hanson expressed the sympathy of the bar.

Dogcarts were popular light one horse carriages, mostly two wheeled. The name derives from the fact that early versions had a box for carrying dogs on hunting trips.

> 'I feel greatly obliged by what has been said by Mr Hanson, as expressing the feeling of the Bar'—replied the Judge. 'I was thrown out of the vehicle with such force that my body turned completely over in falling, making, in fact, a somersault; but I am happy to say that there was no loss of consciousness. Once before, although the fact was not made public, I was thrown out, and had to be carried to my house in a senseless condition. I really must say that I think the Legislature ought to provide the means of enabling Judges to be driven by skilful servants to Court. As it is, a Judge may, upon his way to Court, receive injuries that will disable him from the discharge of his duties. The allowance made to me, occupying my responsible office, is only £100 a year more than Judge Crawford received ten years ago, while the salary of the Governor-in-Chief has been doubled, being £4000 a year. I think I have great cause to complain, and I do so from this Bench, having thrown up my professional practice at home for the performance of judicial duties in this province on the faith of a salary, the amount of which was paid to me for two years, without a fractional deduction, but which, for the last five years, has been lessened by an amount which deprives me of the means of being driven to and from the Court in a vehicle of more than one horse and a single pair of wheels. It may be objected that there is a want of dignity in a Judge offering a public complaint of the insufficient amount of his remuneration; but I am of opinion that true dignity is less exhibited when an injustice is submitted to without remonstrance. The independence which ought to exist between the Legislature and the Judges precludes a Judge from making a petition on the subject of his salary. I am of opinion that the only course open to him for presenting a remonstrance is to do it in the way I am now doing, from my seat upon the Bench. Nothing, in my view, can be more reprehensible than private applications from a Judge to the Ministry of the day or public petition to the Legislature in respect of an increase of salary, as tending to destroy all independence between the parties.' [35]

George Marsden Waterhouse (1824-1906) Although he was the first person to hold the office of Premier in two colonies, in South Australia from 1861 to 1863 and New Zealand from 1872 to 1873, Waterhouse is perhaps best described as a capitalist. He was successful in a range of business ventures in several countries and advocated free trade and economic development. (SLSA)

On 10 July 1861, it was moved, in both the Legislative Council and the House of Assembly, that a select committee should be appointed to inquire into Mr Justice Boothby's decisions and conduct, and to report on the steps which it would be advisable to take with reference thereto.

In introducing the motion in the Legislative Council, Mr G.M. Waterhouse said that he "entertained the highest respect for Judge Boothby and all his relations with the Judge had been only those of friendship"; but the recent proceedings of the Judge had caused a feeling in the public mind that "the peculiar constitution of His Honour's mind was such that it would prevent him from giving effect to many measures beneficial to the colony at large".

> 'From the reports of recent trials it seemed that the Judge had placed himself above the Legislature of the colony, above the Governor, and even above the Queen herself. The position taken by His Honor in several cases showed a desire on his part to assume for the Supreme Court greater powers than were possessed by any Court in the British Dominions. He sought for a power as great as the Supreme Court of the United States, which was, he believed, greater than any other court of judicature in the civilized world.'

Mr Justice Boothby had no right to broadcast to the world his opinions as to the invalidity of acts not directly involved in the case before him.

> 'He had a perfect right to doubt, but not to make public those doubts. I can imagine no greater inducement to unprincipled persons to do wrong than the declaration from the Bench that the laws were illegal and of no force. If such were the opinion of the Judge, his first duty was, not to proclaim it from the Bench, but to bring it under the notice of the Government.'

> 'When a Judge'—Mr Waterhouse concluded—'assumed greater powers than the Legislature, or the Governor, or the Queen herself—when he refused to abide by the decision of the Full Court—when he threatened to thwart the operation of a useful and important measure which had been duly passed and assented to, it became highly necessary that some legislative action should be taken.' [36]

The motion was carried by a majority of eleven to two, the dissentients being Mr G.F. Angas and the Chief Secretary (Mr John Morphett). Mr Angas spoke very forcibly against the motion. It conveyed no distinct charge, he said, against the Judge; it was admittedly founded only on newspaper reports, which might be correct, but "a high functionary like a Judge was not to be convicted on press reports". Most serious charges were made, but how were they to be established? There were no lawyers in the Council, with the exception of Mr Fisher (the President); yet the motion called on them to decide what was essentially a question of law. The Judge had given extensive reasons for his decisions; for himself, Mr Angas said, he thought Mr Justice Boothby was a man of the most honourable intentions, and of great learning in matters of law. He held him in the highest respect, and thought that action should not be lightly taken against him. If the Judge was wrong, the simple, obvious and appropriate remedy was an appeal to the Privy Council to have him put right.[37]

The Council, however, was in no mood to listen to calm reason. A Committee consisting of Messrs Waterhouse, Angas, Davenport, Hall and Stirling was appointed, with power to take evidence and to call for documents and records. The Committee at once requested Mr Justice Boothby to attend before them. Very reasonably the Judge, through his associate, replied asking what were the "judicial decisions and conduct" into which the Committee proposed to inquire. One would have thought that even the worst of criminals was entitled to know what was the charge against him; but this harmless and quite proper request, made through an appropriate channel, evoked the ungracious answer: "The Committee record their disappointment at the course adopted by Mr Justice Boothby, and cannot recognize any communication through an inferior officer or third party."

This letter the Judge ignored; and the Committee, after waiting a few days, were forced to sink their pride, and to approach him more humbly, specifying the proceedings in the various cases heard by the Court in June 1861 as the subject matter of the inquiry, and also "what steps should be taken to harmonize the action of the Legislature and Judicature of this Province". The Judge then asked to be supplied with a copy of the resolution of the Legislative Council appointing the Committee. He was furnished with this, but at the same time the impatient Committee served him with a peremptory summons to attend before them and produce his commission as Judge and the form of oath administered to him on his assuming office.[38]

In a dignified reply, the Judge declined to attend, "for many weighty and sufficient reasons", amongst which he specified:

(1) The regular and proper mode of reviewing his judgments was by appeal to the Privy Council; and if they were contrary to law or unjust, they would there be reversed.

(2) As this was the constitutional provision made for the correction of erroneous decisions, a judge should not recognise any other authority as intervening between him and his duty to the Crown. To do so would be a recognition of the Committee as possessing functions which were vested in the Queen in Council.

(Sir) Samuel Davenport (1818-1906) First settling in Macclesfield in 1843 on land bought by his father, Davenport began a long involvement with the colony's political, agricultural and industrial development. His political career extended from 1846, as a nominee to the Legislative Council, through to 1866 when he resigned as an elected member of the Council. (SLSA)

George Hall (1811-1867) A merchant and pastoralist who was a Member of the Legislative Council from 1851 to 1853 and 1857 to 1867.

Edward Stirling (c1805 – 1873) Stirling had a major share in the Wallaroo and Moonta mines as well as pastoral and business interests. He was a Member of the Legislative Council from 1855 to 1865.

(3) 'The Judges of the Supreme Court have cast upon them by Imperial Statute, the functions of deciding on the validity or otherwise of all legislation by the Parliament of this Province, when any question as to such validity arises between suitors of the Queen in Her Supreme Court; and for either House of such Parliament to enquire into such judgments, by demanding the reasons thereof from any Judge, would be against natural justice, as enabling such Houses to sit as Judges in their own case, and would make every Judge liable to a danger, from which the law of England protects an often-convicted felon, if made the subject of a fresh accusation, that he shall not be required to answer to matters which shall criminate himself.'

(4) 'That if such inquiry can be constitutionally made in any case, it may be made in all, which would, on the one hand, deprive the Crown of the protection of an independent and fearless administration of the law of treason, sedition, and political libel; and on the other hand, would deprive the Queen's subjects of the like protection, in the free exercise of their right of free speech, and of a free press, whether by their representatives in Parliament, or in lawful assemblies of the people in public meeting.'

He forwarded copies of his commission and the oath taken by him, and offered to make available copies of any of his judgments not relating to any matter still sub judice. Finally, he expressed his readiness, on being asked, to give all the assistance in his power to the Committee; but he refused to do so, if it was demanded from him as a matter of right.[39]

It seems hard to find anything very offensive in this firm but courteously worded refusal; but it was construed by the Committee and most of the Legislative Council as a gross insult. The tedium of perusing the columns of the *Hansard* reports of the debates is relieved by frequent irate passages on the Judge's "rebellion", reminiscent of the Pickwick Club meetings—one from the speech of Hon G. Hall may serve as an example:

> 'The Judge was legally bound to have appeared' (Hear, Hear! and no, no!) 'and in refusing he had treated that House with contempt.' (Loud cries of "No, no!" and "Yes, yes!"). 'That was his opinion, and if any hon. member liked to be trampled on like a worm, let him.' [40]

Refusal to obey the summons of the Committee was punishable as a misdemeanour, but the House did not dare to have the Judge arrested and imprisoned, so the Committee had to do as best they could without his assistance.

Meanwhile, the similar motion introduced by Mr Moorhouse in the House of Assembly had met with a stormy passage. The introducer of the motion repeated the description of the state of alarm into which the country had been thrown by the Judge's decisions. As to the Judge's complaints about his salary, Mr Moorhouse looked upon his salary as £2,600 per annum, because they had to pay £1,300 a year to Mr Justice Gwynne to counteract the erratic conduct of his colleague. The motion was strongly opposed by three very able speakers—the Attorney-General (Mr Randolph Stow), Mr Hanson, and Mr Dutton. They contended that no case had been made out which would warrant the House in putting the Judge on his trial. The Chief Justice and Mr Justice Gwynne concurred in some of the obnoxious views—they also ought to be pilloried, if the House was to be consistent. Were they to establish a precedent, asked Mr Hanson, that Judges should hold their office only so long as they continued to carry out the law in accordance with the popular wish? And Mr Dutton, after citing authority to show that the Judge not only had the right, but was in duty bound, to examine the validity of the statutes of the local Parliament, said very forcibly:

Matthew Moorhouse (1813-1876)
Doctor Moorhouse was the first Protector of Aborigines serving in this role, with mixed success, from his arrival in 1839 until 1856. A member of the House of Assembly from 1860 to 1861 he resigned and became a pastoralist in the Mid North. (SLSA)

> 'I maintain that Judge Boothby has exercised an unquestionable right in the course he has pursued; he has given elaborate and learned written judgments on the points brought before him for decision; he has expressed his opinion in decided terms, but he has given chapter and verse for every reason he has advanced for entertaining the views he has enunciated. It is not attempted by calm argument, or legal analysis, to prove his legal decisions to be wrong; but popular excitement and popular misrepresentation and the attributing of unworthy motives in his conduct as a Judge—these are the weapons with which it is attempted to overawe his independent judgment, and to invite the sanctity and inviolobility [sic] of the judicial office. Supposing, for the sake of argument, that his judgment is erroneous, is that any reason why he should be dragged from the judgment seat? If such a doctrine is to hold good, there is not a Judge in Great Britain who would not be thrust off the Bench.'

Francis Stacker Dutton (1816-1877)
As an owner of property and the Kapunda mine Dutton was a wealthy man. But he was also a radical politician, twice a Premier, who pursued such causes as adult male suffrage and vote by ballot. (SLSA)

In opposition to these reasoned speakers was Mr McEllister, the disgruntled plaintiff in *McEllister v. Fenn*, whose words carry their own stigmata:

> 'The facts of the case were that the representatives of the people passed a law almost unanimously, and now Judge Boothby, as the champion of the legal profession, would not administer it, because it would injure the prospects of hisprofessional brethren. Was the Parliament of South Australia to be snubbed by Judge Boothby? Were they to be told that a Judge they paid would not administer the laws they

> passed? It was for the Parliament to consider whether they would stand that. The will of the people should be the will of the Government, for the people were the source of all power. If Judge Boothby was fool enough to quarrel with his bread and butter, it was his own fault.'

So little interest was displayed in the debate that the numbers present dwindled to less than the necessary quorum, and the motion came to an abrupt end by a count out of the House. It was resumed a week later, and adjourned to enable a call of the House to be made for 2 August—which meant that every member had to be present on that date. The arguments then put forward covered much the same ground as before, and the motion was finally carried by nineteen votes to fifteen, those members who voted against it being accused by the *Register* of "degrading Parliament to exalt Mr Justice Boothby".[41]

It is rather surprising that the members of the upper house (where one would have expected to find conservative tendencies protecting the independence of the judiciary) were almost unanimously against the Judge; while in the more democratic Assembly the Judge's antagonists barely outnumbered his supporters. This lends support to the view that it was the Real Property Act which was the principal cause of the agitation against Mr Justice Boothby; and that, as Hanson said, had his decisions been given on any other question, they would not have aroused such a hubbub.[42] Mr B.T. Finniss said in the Assembly:

> 'So much feeling has been excited throughout the length and breadth of the land in favour of the Real Property Act, that any one who ventures to oppose it is looked upon as an enemy to the public interests.' [43]

William Scott
(c1794-1866)
A sea captain turned farmer who sat in the Legislative Council from 1853 to 1863.

Similarly in the Legislative Council, the Hon W. Scott said of the Real Property Act:

> 'It was the Judge's opinion respecting that Act which caused the explosion that set the Torrens on fire (Laughter). That was the lever by which the cry has been raised respecting the anti-Boothby movement and the dissolution of Parliament. I would almost have thought that Paganini had been raised and was going about the country playing on his one-string fiddle to rouse the people and terrify them into the idea that their broad acres were disappearing from view, and that they would never see them more. The Real Property Act never was in danger, and that cry as to its being so is like the old cry we used to hear, "The Church is in danger."' [44]

The majority of the Legislative Council were landowners whose personal interest in the safety of their properties seems to have swamped considerations of reason and justice.

Disappointed in their attempt to compel Mr Justice Boothby to appear before them, the Legislative Council Committee fell back on his associate, Mr Hinde, and tried to get out of him what the Judge's views were. Mr Hinde was too wary to commit either himself or the Judge, and the attempt failed miserably. The Committee then sent for and examined Mr Hanson and Mr Charles Fenn. Both these gentlemen, of high standing at the bar, expressed views decidedly favourable to Mr Justice Boothby. They asserted the right of the Judges of the Supreme Court to decide whether acts of the South Australian Parliament were within the powers conferred on that Parliament by the Imperial statutes.

> 'Every court of judicature in this province'—said Mr Hanson—'having to decide questions of right depending upon the determination of the validity of Acts that this Parliament has passed, would have a right to say whether those Acts were or were not valid.'

They pointed out that many of the obnoxious doctrines of Mr Justice Boothby were merely dicta thrown out during argument and that no binding judgment had been given by him on these points. As to the Governor's assent, Mr Hanson was of opinion that a mistake by the Governor did not invalidate the Act.

> 'He has to justify himself to the Queen for violating her instructions, but it does not deprive the Colony of the benefits of a law considered by the Legislature as essential to its well being.'

With regard to repugnancy, he had no doubt that the local Parliament could alter the common law, provided it did not abrogate fundamental principles; a large proportion of the colonial statutes necessarily did so and no objection had been raised to them.

The Committee then put to him the suggestion that the local legislature should enact that until Her Majesty's pleasure should be known, all laws should be valid, any repugnancy of such law to the laws of England notwithstanding; but he refused to assent to this. "It would be inoperative: that would be assuming a power which we cannot exercise by means of any local Act." The Act would be as repugnant as the repugnancies it purported to put aside. "In whom does the power of declaring any repugnancy of colonial to English law rest?" he was asked; and he replied definitely, "It rests with the Supreme Court of the Colony, subject to appeal to Her Majesty in Privy Council."

Mr Fenn agreed that a provision such as that suggested by the Committee would be beyond the power of the South Australian

Parliament. "Can you suggest any information to this Committee," he was asked, "which would have the effect of rendering more satisfactory and stable the operation of the laws of the colony now existing?" He replied:

> 'I think if the Statutes are sent to the Judges at the Supreme Court for perusal, as suggested by His Honor Mr Justice Boothby, it would be of great advantage, both to the Legislature and to the Colony generally.'

Mr Fenn thought that 9 Geo IV c.83 s.22 was in force in South Australia; Mr Hanson disagreed with him on this point. As to the repugnancy, Mr Fenn's belief was that nothing subversive of the principles of common law was permissible.

Having called for and heard this evidence, from two experienced practitioners chosen as representing the best legal opinion of the profession in the colony, the Committee (not one of them a lawyer) drew up a report confidently laying it down that the witnesses were quite wrong. They admitted that Mr Justice Boothby was not alone in holding that it was within the sphere of his functions, as a judge of the Supreme Court, to declare that acts passed by the legislature and assented to by the Governor were illegal and invalid.

> 'If the opinions expressed on this subject by Messrs Hanson and Fenn may be considered as indicative of the opinions of the Bar generally, then the Bar, as a body, support His Honor in the assumption of the power that he claims for Judges of the Supreme Court.'

One would have expected this might well have led a committee of laymen to pause before denying it; but the Committee without hesitation said that such a power did not belong to colonial judges. Mr Justice Boothby was merely second Judge of the Supreme Court.

> 'Not only is that Court created, but its powers are defined, and its functions are from time to time prescribed by the Colonial Legislature. The Court itself being, therefore, subordinate and dependent, each of the Judges that constitute it is necessarily so likewise.'

Cheerfully the Committee conceded that judges in other colonies exercised the power claimed by Mr Justice Boothby of pronouncing on the validity of colonial acts. The widest publicity had been given to the opinions of the New South Wales Judges in *Rusden v. Weekes* (Legge p.1406) decided a few months earlier. In that case, referring to the question of judicial inquiry into the validity of colonial acts, Chief Justice Stephen had said:

> 'The power and duty of entertaining and determining that question must of necessity exist in every case where—as in the

present instance—the Act is alleged to be, in terms or in effect, in conflict with an Act of the Parliament of that Empire.'

And Justice Milford, in even plainer language, said:

> 'This Court, and every other court in the colony, is bound to regard every law which is in force in the colony; not only those enacted by the local Parliament; but those enacted by the Imperial Parliament; they form one code of laws, and where two laws are apparently inconsistent it is the province of the Court to reconcile them if possible—if not, to say which is in force and which is not ... The fundamental principle of law as applicable to powers of colonial legislature is, that they must be controlled by the Imperial Parliament, and every Court must decide whether they have been controlled or not.'

This clear authority in favour of Mr Justice Boothby's view was passed over by the Committee on the ground "that it did not appear to have been recognised by the Privy Council", although as the case had not been before the Privy Council, it is not easy to see how it could have been so recognised. The Committee based their contrary opinion on a number of authorities on the supremacy of parliament, which, applied to the English Parliament, were undoubtedly accurate, but which had nothing whatever to do with subordinate colonial legislatures.

> 'In the opinion of your Committee'—the report proceeded—'it is essential to the satisfactory administration of justice, that Acts passed by the Legislature and assented to by his Excellency, should be regarded as valid until expressly disallowed by Her Majesty. If it be otherwise, doubt must always be felt in deciding as to what are the laws under which we live, and the evils attendant upon an uncertain legislation must result.'

Admittedly the local Parliament was not competent to pass laws repugnant to those of England; but repugnancy, it was argued, must be decided by the authorities at home and it was not for a judge to say an act was repugnant after the Queen had said it was not, by leaving it to its operation. The Committee then proceeded to recommend the adoption of the very remedy which Mr Hanson and Mr Fenn had both denounced as illegal:

> 'While your Committee maintain that the Supreme Court is not possessed of the powers claimed for it by Mr Justice Boothby, yet, in the peculiar circumstances of the Colony, they consider it may be advisable, by virtue of the powers the Parliament undoubtedly possesses of providing for the administration of justice in the Colony, to enact, that in the administration of

justice in all the Law Courts of the Colony, Acts passed by the Legislature, and assented to by His Excellency, shall be received as legal and valid, until disallowed by Her Majesty.'

In conclusion, the Committee found there was no proof that Mr Justice Boothby had ever definitely refused to follow the ruling of the majority of the Supreme Court Judges, but they added a warning to him:

> 'Should any Judge refuse to administer law in accordance with the decision of the Full Court, it seems to your Committee that an address to Her Majesty, for his removal, must necessarily result.' [45]

From this report Mr Angas dissented entirely, in a manner which does great credit to his integrity and ability. The opinions expressed in it, he pointed out, were directly contrary to the evidence adduced; they were opposed to the decisions of courts in the other colonies and in England; and they were inconsistent with the recognised principles of constitutional law.

> 'The report does not set forth any one recent judicial decision of His Honor, or allege any particular act of his conduct, so as to lead the Legislative Council to any conclusion adverse to the uprightness or propriety of his judicial decisions or conduct.' [46]

George Fife Angas ca. 1855. (SLSA)

The House of Assembly Committee was more fortunate with Mr Justice Boothby than that of the upper house had been. The Judge having been applied to for his assistance in a more conciliatory manner, readily offered voluntarily what he had stoutly contended the Legislative Council Committee had no right to demand.

> 'I have no objection'—he said—'to give you my advice and opinions on such matters as may form the subject of your inquiries; but I must decline to answer any questions relating to my decisions in the Supreme Court, or relating to any cause which may be before such Court ... I claim to be regarded as coming here voluntarily to offer my advice and assistance.'

All three Judges of the Supreme Court attended before the Committee and gave evidence; and the existing legal position of the colony was thoroughly and minutely examined. It may be convenient to summarise under various headings the views of the Judges and the conclusions of the Committee on the different topics which demanded attention. The report was prepared by Hanson and was a very able and valuable document, putting forward arguments and conclusions eminently sound.[47]

(1) The first question was whether the Supreme Court had power to examine into the validity of acts passed by the legislature, assented to by the Governor, and left to their operation by the Queen.

This right and power was claimed by all the Judges. It was a duty, said Mr Justice Boothby, cast upon every court in the Empire, and every local court or magisterial authority in the province had the same duty. Mr Justice Gwynne would willingly have been relieved of the task of deciding whether local acts conformed to the provisions of Imperial statutes—"it is a function", he said, "to be exercised with great delicacy".

The Committee unhesitatingly agreed with the Judges on this point; such a power was "necessarily incident to the exercise of the duty cast upon those courts of determining the rights and liabilities of suitors and criminals". Otherwise, it was pointed out, there would be a different rule in the Supreme Court and in the Privy Council, "so that the former would be bound to pronounce a judgment which it might know was erroneous, and would be certainly reversed on appeal". But this power of the Judges "should be most cautiously and guardedly exercised".

(2) If the Supreme Court had the jurisdiction to inquire into the validity of acts, the next question was—upon what grounds could it say such acts were invalid?

Mr Justice Boothby had three main reasons for invalidity:

A. Ultra vires—excess of the powers of the local legislature.

B Repugnancy to the law of England.

C. Failure of the Governor to reserve acts for the royal assent.

Repugnancy is really a subdivision of "ultra vires", but it is convenient to consider them separately. The two questions of ultra vires and repugnancy were closely connected; any legislation which was repugnant was also ultra vires because the Imperial statutes forbade the local Parliament to pass such a law; but, on the other hand, a provision might be ultra vires, without necessarily being repugnant.

As to A.—Ultra Vires:

The principal subject upon which Mr Justice Boothby contended the South Australian Parliament had exceeded its powers was in the creation and erection of courts. The legislature, he thought, had no power to create any court. His arguments on this point are fully discussed in the chapter on the Court of Appeals, and it is unnecessary to repeat them here. In effect, the point came to this—did the powers to make laws "for the peace, welfare and good government" of the colony include a power to make laws establishing courts? Mr Justice Boothby thought it did not; Mr Justice Gwynne thought subordinate courts might be created, but that the words were not enough to give power to erect a court such as the Court of Appeals, which could override the decisions of the Supreme Court; and the Chief Justice held that there was a general power to create courts.

The Committee reported that the power conferred upon the legislature to make laws, "subject only to the limitation expressed in the Act, which limitation does not extend to Courts of Justice", necessarily included the power to make a law for the constitution, regulation or alteration of courts.

As to B.—Repugnancy:

Mr Justice Boothby, reported the Committee, understood "repugnancy":

> '... not merely in the sense of a violation of the fundamental principles of English law, such as a denial of the sovereignty of Her Majesty, or the allowance of slavery, or the prohibition of the profession of Christianity or the like—in which cases, the proposition that such laws were invalid would probably be unquestioned, and would certainly be immaterial, since no Legislature would pass, and no Governor would assent to, Acts having such a scope; nor in the sense of conflict between Acts of the Imperial Parliament expressly made applicable to the Colony, and which regulated the rights to property, or the manner in which those rights shall be acquired or evidenced (as, for instance, the Acts relating to shipping), and Acts of the Colonial Legislature relating to the same subject; but also in the sense of mere alteration of the forms of legal procedure, and

the substitution of one species of remedy for another.'

Somewhat similar views were entertained by Mr Justice Gwynne, although confined within narrower limits; this, however, was a matter of detail in the application of a common principle.

A number of acts were suggested by Mr Justice Boothby to be repugnant; for example:

(i) The Act abolishing the Grand Jury system.

"The Queen's subjects"—he said—"are exposed to that in this colony which exists in no other part of the world governed by the law of England, so far as I know."

Neither of the other Judges agreed with him on this. The Chief Justice was asked what he would do, if, after a prisoner had been tried, he objected that his case had not been before a Grand Jury? "I should sentence him," he replied. "I should do so, undoubtedly." The Act abolishing the Grand Jury was different to the law of England, but he could not see that it was repugnant to it.

(ii) The Local Courts Act.

The criminal jurisdiction exercised by the local courts was, in the opinion of Mr Justice Boothby, repugnant. It "put the brand of felony on a man in this colony without trial either by Grant or Petit Jury". Again the other Judges did not agree with him. The Chief Justice said:

'It certainly is a very great power to give to Magistrates ... I should not, however, be disposed to say that it was such a repugnancy as to make the law void; although it is contrary to the law of England as at present existing ... A mode of trial which may be adapted to the mother country may be altogether inapplicable to a colony.'

(iii) The Real Property Act.

Mr Justice Gwynne concurred with Mr Justice Boothby in holding that this Act was repugnant.

'It removes'—said the latter—'trial by jury in matters relating to the ownership of land, as provided by Magna Carta and the Bill of Rights, and so saps the fundamental principles of the constitution of the British Empire as to the security of every man's estate. It also seeks to destroy the prerogative of Her Majesty to review the decision of every court in Her Empire, as to the true ownership of land.'

Mr Justice Gwynne saw no objection to the purpose of the Act; but he objected to questions of title being submitted to the absolute decision of the Lands Titles Commission, "an irresponsible, secret tribunal".

> 'I find a body which has the power in effect of deciding absolutely on rights of property, and that without any personal summons to the persons interested to attend before them, without their investigations being conducted by sworn testimony, or in any manner analagous [sic] to that of the Courts of law as known to the English Constitution, ignoring infancy and other legal disabilities; and their judgment or decision not subject to the appeal which Her Majesty's subjects have to the Privy Council from the law Courts ... There is another principle which I think an infraction of the law of England—the taking from parties their right of ejectment ... without giving any other legal remedy.'

On the other hand, the Chief Justice could see no repugnancy in the Act at all.

In reporting upon this branch of the inquiry, the Committee pointed out that the actual differences of opinion between Mr Justice Boothby and Mr Justice Gwynne as to the application of the principle of "repugnancy", afford "a striking illustration of the doubtful nature of the principle itself, and of the uncertainty and insecurity which its adoption must necessarily introduce into the administration of justice".

> 'As the laws of England, liberal and excellent as they undoubtedly are, still bear the impress of less liberal institutions, and of usages and sentiments which are now happily obsolete, your Committee fear it may happen that Acts of this legislature, introducing those reforms which are most important and most welcome, may be just those very Acts which may be deemed to involve this element of repugnancy.'

The obvious intention of the Acts establishing the South Australian legislature, it was submitted, was to transfer to South Australia the power of passing all such laws as it might deem necessary or expedient for the peace, order and good government of the colony. Limitations were imposed to maintain the supremacy of Imperial legislation, and the integrity of Imperial interests; nevertheless it was intended to give complete powers of legislation, subject to disallowance by the Queen. Such a construction was the only one which admitted of any clear and consistent application.

> 'If repugnancy is understood in the sense of conflict, either with the fundamental principles of the English Constitution, or with Acts of Parliament affecting the colonies, then it is easy for a Court to decide whether in relation to any subject there is an Imperial Statute affecting the question which prescribes a different rule from a Colonial Act; or whether essential principles have been violated. But if repugnancy be understood

in any other sense, then what shall constitute repugnancy will, inevitably, be decided according to the peculiar views of the presiding Judge. One functionary, who may attach great value to the institution of Grand Juries, will regard the Act by which they were abolished as repugnant to the law of England; while another, who may regard these bodies as a cumbrous and unnecessary appendage to criminal procedure, and as especially unsuited to the circumstances of the Colony, will consider that Act as affirming the principles, while it departs from the forms of English jurisprudence, and, therefore, as valid. And a similar diversity would be found to exist in innumerable other cases. In fact, thus understood, repugnancy might be defined to be an alteration of the law of England which was either impolitic or unfair; the impolicy and unfairness being determined according to the opinion of the individual Judge who may be called upon to decide the question. And in this case there are very few Acts of this Legislature which it might not be contended were invalid, since almost all, in some degree, depart from the English law; and if such a question were raised, there can, in the nature of things, be no security that every such departure might not be deemed to involve the element of repugnancy; and every Act would require one or more decisions of the Supreme Court, or rather of the Judicial Committee of the Privy Council, to establish its validity.'

"Repugnant to the law of England" must therefore be construed as applying only "to such provisions of Colonial Acts as might be opposed to the fundamental principles of English law, like those already instanced, or to Imperial Acts relating to the same subject matter". It was almost inconceivable that the legislature would pass or the Governor assent to acts which were repugnant.

'To assume that an alteration in the mere details of the administration of Justice; in the appointing non-legal persons to perform quasi-judicial functions; in the manner in which a notice may be required to be given, or evidence to be taken; or the substitution of a remedy against a fund for a right to recover a particular piece of land, or any analogous matter affecting property within the limits of this Colony, could be a repugnancy within the meaning of the Act, would, in the opinion of your Committee, be to introduce a principle which would be fatal, both to the usefulness and the dignity of the Legislature, would frustrate the objects of the Imperial Parliament in conferring upon this Province the power of self-government, and would destroy all confidence in the

> enjoyment of property, and the assertion of rights founded upon Colonial Legislation.'

Another topic in connection with repugnancy which was investigated by the Committee, but upon which they expressed no finding, was whether it was proper for a judge to suggest repugnancy objections to counsel. The Chief Justice was noncommittal upon this. It might sometimes be proper for a judge to do so, he said; but he thought he ought not to be asked "any question which might tend unnecessarily to bring my learned colleague and myself into an unpleasant relative position". Mr Justice Boothby had no doubt that it was the Judge's duty to raise such a point, if it occurred to him.

> 'There seems to be an impression here'—he said—'that the Judges are limited to the examination of questions raised before them by counsel; but every practitioner must know that the reports of decided cases are full of instances in which the decisions in those cases have proceeded entirely on points of law coming from the mind of the Court, and in no way from counsel.'

In a clear case, Mr Justice Gwynne agreed, it would be the duty of the Judge to notice repugnancy, even though not raised by counsel.

As to C.—Governor's Failure to Reserve Acts for Royal Assent: Mr Justice Boothby stood alone in holding that it was the function and duty of the judges to take judicial notice of the Royal Instructions, and to refuse to recognise as valid any acts which in their opinion might have been assented to by the Governor in violation of those Instructions. The Customs Acts he considered were invalid on this ground. He was ridiculed for his solemn exposition of the consequences which might ensue from the non-reservation of this Act. The Imperial Act, he said, forbade duties being imposed by colonies contrary to any treaty.

> 'Now, the duty on spirits is 10/- a gallon in this Colony; and it is well known that, under a recent treaty with France, brandy does not pay more than 6/3d in the London Docks. Supposing duty to be charged on a cargo of French brandy, the question arises whether 10/- should be levied or not. The Emperor of the French is in amity with England; but, with a less sincere ally, it might be a false amity, waiting only for a casus belli. Here would be a casus belli if he chose to take advantage of it ... A casus belli might thus be raised and cause a European war, costing a hundred millions of money.'

Other acts which he held invalid on this ground were the Electoral Acts, which brought down with them in their fall the Constitution Act, and with it, the whole of the subsequent legislation of the province.

Both the other Judges strongly opposed this view: they considered the failure to reserve was entirely a question between the sovereign and the Governor. The Committee likewise reported that the provisions as to reserving bills were directory only, and failure to obey them did not invalidate the legislation. A judge, in claiming a right to inquire into the nature of the Governor's Instructions, overstepped the limits of his judicial duties and violated the rule "omnia praesumuntur rite esse acta".

> 'There exist no means whatever by which those instructions can be compulsorily brought before a Court of Judicature in order to enable it to decide whether or not they have been followed. At this time the Supreme Court has no judicial knowledge, and has no means whatever of obtaining any evidence of the nature of the instructions under which the Governor is or has been acting.'

This reasoning left Mr Justice Boothby unimpressed: he might well have taken as a motto the words of Antonio in *The Duchess of Malfi*:

> 'Though some o' the court hold it presumption
> To instruct Princes what they ought to doe,
> It is a noble duty to inform them
> What they ought to foresee.'

(3) The forwarding of acts to the Supreme Court.

Although the other Judges pooh-poohed the notion, Mr Justice Boothby had no doubt that the provisions of 9 Geo IV c.83 s.22 were in force in South Australia. "It is necessary that there should be an authoritative depositary provided, so that a person can ascertain where Acts of Parliament are to be found."

The omission to send the acts to the Court would have to be set right by an Imperial statute. Supposing, he was asked, the messenger carrying the act to the Supreme Court got drunk on the way and failed to deposit it at the Court—was the colony to be entirely deprived of the benefit of the act? "Oh, that is an accident, that would not be likely to occur," said the Judge, "and if it did, the entry in the journals would enable another copy to be sent." Suppose that the messenger was murdered—what then? "Such a matter would be put to rights as soon as it became known; but if no entry was made, no messenger sent at all, it is quite another state of things."

(4) Upon the question of how far a single judge was bound by the decision of the Full Court, Mr Justice Boothby's views were again at variance with those of his colleagues.

> 'There is no law that I am aware of'—said the Chief Justice—'that makes it incumbent upon a single Judge to follow the opinion of his colleagues, and I am not aware of any decisions

> on the point. But when the majority of the Court has pronounced an opinion, I believe the practice is, for the dissenting Judge to follow it.'

He was then pressed to say specifically whether, if the majority of the Judges pronounced an act invalid, it would be the duty of the dissenting Judge to give effect to that act in subsequent cases.

> 'I would rather not say whether it would be his duty or not. The inclination of my mind would be to accord with the decision of my colleagues acting with me in the same Court. Sometimes, the convictions of a single Judge may be so strong, as to make him feel justified in not doing so. I am sorry I have been asked this question.'

Mr Justice Gwynne's opinion was that the decision of a majority of the Court must be obeyed until it was shown by a higher court to be erroneous—"it would be exceedingly indecorous and inconvenient to take an opposite course".

On the other hand, Mr Justice Boothby thought a judgment of the Full Court on, say, the validity of the Real Property Act, could not bind him when sitting in a criminal court to try a man for an offence against that Act.

> 'What!'—he exclaimed. 'Is it possible for a Judge to have the death of a man on his conscience for the rest of his life, because in a civil action his brother Judges, whose judgment may be declared erroneous by a Court of Error, have expressed an opposite opinion under circumstances, where the rules of law as to construction are not the same.'

Further, he considered that a judgment of the Full Court was binding upon only in the particular case in which it was delivered, but in any other case it did not so bind him as to prevent him ruling in such a way as to compel one of the parties to take the case to a court of error. At that time a suitor dissatisfied with the Judge's ruling could obtain redress in one of two ways:

(i) He could move the Full Court for a new trial on the ground of misdirection.

(ii) He could tender a bill of exceptions, which, by the Statute of Westminster II, the Judge was bound to sign, and upon which he could go to the Privy Council, the court of error.

Mr Justice Boothby claimed that notwithstanding any decision of the Full Court, he was entitled to rule according to his own opinion in such a way as to drive one party to a bill of exceptions, and thus get the matter decided finally by a court of error.

> 'The person who contravenes the judgment of the Court, not

> unanimous on any important matter, is doing a meritorious act, because he is seeking to make the state of the law certain. The analogy is complete between these cases, and conflicting judgments of the Courts of Common Pleas and Queen's Bench ... It is easy for a Judge to say, take this matter to the Full Court—that is a very easy course; but, if a Judge considers the importance of the question is great, and the necessity of obtaining a settled state of the law, he would so rule as to compel a party to tender a Bill of Exceptions. That is my view of the state of the law. The simple contest is, whether the judgment of the Supreme Court is to be treated as conclusive as to the state of the law; to suppose it to be a Court of Error—nothing would be more injurious to suitors.'

(5) Mr Justice Boothby did not shrink from the consequences to which his opinions inevitably led; and he urged that the British Government should be asked to introduce a confirming and validating statute into the Imperial Parliament.

> 'What I say is this—where there is a doubt, the Legislature should take care that such doubt, is removed—that is what I come here for; not to say what I would do in any particular case. The interest of Her Majesty's subjects in this colony insists that all these doubts should be removed; and the only way to do so, is to ask the Imperial Parliament to pass an Act having that effect ... It would seem to me mere madness to go on for another six months without having the question placed beyond all doubt whatever.'

The other Judges agreed that an Imperial act would be advisable, "saying that the Statutes in South Australia, as they exist up to this time, are properly established as law, and that the question that such laws are repugnant should in no case be raised in the Colony; a short Act like that would be desirable". Mr Justice Gwynne was asked whether he thought the Imperial Parliament would pass a prospective as well as retrospective act.

> 'I think they would pass an Act'—he replied—'defining with more particularity what is meant by the word repugnant. I think it is due to the Judicature that there should be some more explicit definition, because, really, etymologically, anything that opposes, that fights against, is repugnant; as Polonius says, "that's an ill phrase, a vile phrase!" But, I apprehend, it means repugnant to the constitutional law of England.'

The Committee painted a gloomy picture of the state of the law in South Australia, as Mr Justice Boothby saw it.

> 'It would seem that his Honor regards as invalid the whole administration of Justice in criminal matters, whether in the Supreme Court, or in Local Courts, in consequence of the abolition of Grand Juries, and the trial of petty felonies, by Magistrates, without a jury; the whole of the Customs laws of the Colony; all Acts establishing Courts which have been passed since 1842; the Real Property Acts; all the Electoral Acts since 1851; and, especially, the Constitution Act; and, consequent upon these last, as being at least doubtful, all Acts of whatever character passed by the Parliament of South Australia. In fact, it would seem, from His Honor's evidence, that a valid Act among those assumed to be in force at the present time would be the exception, and not the rule; and that the intended boon of self-government has been, in its results, but the means of introducing elements of uncertainty and confusion into the laws and constitution of the Colony.'

Prompt action was necessary to settle these questions.

> 'At the present moment, it is impossible for any one to say whether any right which he may conceive himself to possess, founded upon an Act of the Colonial Legislature, would be recognised by the Supreme Court.'

A local act would be useless; for it was uncertain whether the Governor would feel at liberty to assent to it, and even if he assented to it, judges who thought that certain acts were invalid because they exceeded the powers of the legislature, must necessarily regard as invalid any acts passed by the same legislature to confirm them. A decision must be had either from the Privy Council or from the Imperial Parliament; and it would be more dignified, speedy, and satisfactory to apply to the latter. The Committee therefore recommended that an address should be presented to the Queen praying that she would cause the opinion of the law officers in England to be taken as to the validity of the acts of the local Parliament; and that a bill should be introduced in the Imperial Parliament declaring the validity of such acts and confirming them, and making some provision for the administration in all courts of acts of the South Australian Parliament.

In forwarding to England copies of the reports of the Committees of the Council and the Assembly, the Governor wrote:

> 'In the former document, Your Grace will find the grave error repeated of supposing that the Judges cannot impugn the validity of any Act passing by the Legislature and left to its operation by the Crown, whereas in the Report of the Select Committee of the Assembly, Your Grace will find a masterly exposition of the constitutional principles on which the validity

> of Colonial Acts depends, and a searching analysis of the various proceedings, dicta, and evidence of Mr Justice Boothby, who, as well as the other Judges of the Supreme Court, gave very full evidence before the Assembly's Committee.
>
> I confess that a very unfavorable impression is made on my mind by a perusal of Mr Boothby's evidence ... It may be true that there would always be in the distance the corrective influence of the Judicial Committee of the Privy Council, even if Mr Boothby's opinions were to be adopted by the Supreme Court. It is also possible, though apparently improbable, that Her Majesty's Government might be induced to take some such extraordinary action as that suggested in the Assembly's report, viz the introduction of a Bill into the Imperial Parliament declaring the validity of all South Australian Acts. But whatever precautions may be adopted for the future, and whatever remedies applied to the past, I entertain a profound conviction that no measures are possible which would prevent Mr Boothby's peculiar idiosyncrasies breaking out from time to time in some manner prejudicial to the interests of justice, and subversive of those conservative feelings of order and respect of law which should find in the Supreme Court their fittest rallying point. Moreover, I cannot but regard it is as somewhat derogatory to our Courts and Parliament that South Australia alone, of the group of Colonies similarly situated, should feel constrained to call on the Imperial Government to extricate her from difficulties which her neighbours do not seem to experience. Such isolated distress on the part of this Colony would rather lead to the inference that the defect lay not in the laws, but in the discretion and learning with which they are administered ... If it were possible to induce Mr Boothby to accept a retiring pension, I would gladly exert my influence to secure one for him now; but I understand that it would be premature, if not quite hopeless, to make such a suggestion—because he expects to be upheld in all his proceedings by Her Majesty's Government.' [48]

While the two Committees were taking evidence, the Attorney-General was asked in the Assembly whether he could give the House any guarantee that it would be incumbent on the Judges to administer the laws made by the legislature and assented to by the Governor. The Government were not in a position to give any such guarantee, he replied; but they were of opinion that the oaths taken by the Judges imposed upon them that duty.

> 'The Government are fully alive to the grave consequences which would result from the refusal of a single Judge to carry out the decision of the majority of the Court that an important statute has the force of law; and would regard with extreme regret and alarm such a determination on the part of a Judge, which would, in their opinion, be at variance with his duty, and would call for immediate action on their part.' [49]

The publication of the reports of the Select Committees, presenting such a gloomy picture of the uncertain state of the law in the province, aroused great excitement. They became "best sellers". The press fostered the agitation. "We want our laws administered in the colony"—said the Register—"and if the Judges we have will not administer them, we must have Judges who will." [50]

Public meetings were held and the Governor was petitioned to dissolve Parliament because of its failure to take action against the Judge.

> 'If the expediency of such a step were to be decided'—the Governor reported to the Duke of Newcastle—'by the speeches and arguments used at those meetings, by many whose speeches prove them wholly incompetent to discuss the constitutional bearing of such questions, I certainly should recoil from taking any step which might tend to the removal of the Judge. I cannot, however, disguise from myself that it is possible for a Judge, neither guilty of gross misconduct nor corruption, to exhibit nevertheless a degree of incompetency and rashness in dealing with grave constitutional questions which would render his removal a matter of simple justice to the public, whose interests he places in jeopardy. I am, moreover, compelled to admit that Mr Justice Boothby has peculiar mental idiosyncrasies which greatly impede his usefulness. I cannot, however, consent to be in any way accessory to a dissolution with a view to supporting the too prevalent opinion—that it is the bounden duty of the Supreme Court to accept under all circumstances the Acts of the Legislature as valid, whether repugnant or not to the law of England. Such a position would be tantamount to the Colony's throwing off its allegiance to the Crown.'

He sincerely hoped, he added, that Mr Justice Boothby would see reason, and:

> '... reconsider the distressing confusion in which he is involving the laws and liberties of Her Majesty's subjects here, and more especially, I hope, that he will not leave in doubt his readiness to administer the law as decided by the majority of the Court. I

fear that otherwise his continuance in office will be seriously jeopardized, as it may be then deemed incompatible with the public interests by many who would go great lengths now to avoid so noxious a precedent as the removal of a Judge, on any grounds whatsoever.' [51]

Stimulated each morning by the newspapers, the cry for Mr Justice Boothby's removal grew louder and louder; and finally, on 27 September 1861, Mr Moorhouse moved in the House of Assembly that an address should be presented to the Crown:

'... setting forth that, in consequence of the position assumed by His Honor Mr Justice Boothby, public confidence in the administration of the laws is destroyed—the validity of title thrown into doubt—ruinous litigation threatened—and the whole system of legislation in the province involved in confusion, contradiction and contempt; and praying that Her Majesty will be most graciously pleased to remove Mr Justice Boothby from his office as Judge of the Supreme Court of this Province.'

A similar motion was brought forward in the Legislative Council. The opinions of Mr Justice Boothby, it was urged, were now known and placed upon record. No longer should the country submit to the dictation of this arbitrary Judge. Public confidence in the administration of justice must be restored.

'We have no criminal law, because of the abolition of Grand Juries. It amounts to this, then, that after a man has been found guilty, no matter what his crime may be, Judge Boothby will not pronounce sentence.'

To ask for a validating act would not be consistent with their dignity as a legislature or as men; nor was there any guarantee that such an act would be a satisfactory remedy. His Honour was "fond of doubting", and he might raise other doubts.

'It was better that Judge Boothby should suffer than that the whole colony should be placed in the position His Honor's decisions were drifting it to. If His Honor was right, differing as he did from the present and late Attorney General of the colony, and from the present Lord High Chancellor of England, he might be a clever man, but he was too clever to hold the practical office of a Judge of the Supreme Court of South Australia.'

The doctrines enunciated by the Judge with regard to laws, the force and validity of which had not been previously questioned, were denounced as most monstrous and intolerable. "How many suitors in the Supreme Court had already been ruined, and how many more might be ruined if the action of Judge Boothby was not interrupted?"

It was impossible to uphold in his judicial position a judge who had openly set the laws of the country at defiance. By his interpretation of the word "repugnant" he had effectually destroyed confidence in the legislation of the colony. He interpreted their acts in an illiberal spirit; he looked on them "rather with the eye of an advocate than of a Judge". The vociferous Mr McEllister bubbled over with virtuous indignation.

> 'The Judge has said that there is no law in the colony. And yet, what is the fact? Why, that Judge has sat upon the Bench for nearly five years, administering that which he himself said does not exist. I say that no one can do this; yet this man, who says there is no law, sits there and receives £1300 a year for administering what does not, according to him, exist. I ask, why should the business of the House and the country be thrown out of order in this way, and perplexed by the action of an obstinate and determined bully? (Oh!)

Lavington Glyde (1823-1890) An accountant who sat in the House of Assembly almost continuously from 1857 to 1884, Glyde's most distinguished work was as Treasurer from 1873 to 1875 and 1881 to 1884. He was successful in business and is also noted for marrying his deceased wife's sister in 1870 before it became legal.

> Mr Glyde rose to order. 'No hon. member could call a Judge of the Supreme Court a determined bully. The Hon. member was out of order. (Oh, oh! and no, no!)
>
> The Speaker said the hon. member was not out of order (hear, hear)—but he thought such remarks had better not be made. (hear, hear).
>
> Mr McEllister: Very well. I will gain my object in another way, and say the man who assumes the championship of the legal profession' (hear, hear)—'and I say that the man who sits there and says there is no law, yet sits to administer it, has no regard to conscience. (Oh!)'

The continuance of the Judge in the Supreme Court, said another member, was quite impossible.

> 'If the Judge could make good his case, he would get an appointment elsewhere; but if he could not, he would no doubt be allowed to return to his rich practice, with a view to better his condition in life; but one thing was certain, he would never be sent back here. He had raised around himself a nest of hornets, and they would sting him so that he would be unable to remain here.' [52]

Such were the views of the Judge's opponents who had long since ceased to view the matter with the "cold neutrality" of impartial judges. They furnish but another unhappy proof of:

> '... the disregard that popular assemblies, when inflamed by

> passion, are ever apt to show for those principles of equity and moderation, by which, however the sophistry of contemporary factions may set them aside, a calm judging posterity will never fail to censure their proceedings.'

But he was not without powerful supporters, who put the case for him with ability and vigour.

The debates on the motion, indeed, produced a ministerial crisis. The Attorney-General, Mr Stow, while opposed to the views held by the Judge, could not bring himself to vote for an address for his removal. He therefore "offered himself as a sacrifice to his convictions", and resigned; and as the Chief Secretary, Mr Morphett, took the same course, the ministry broke up. The Governor sent for Mr G.M. Waterhouse to form a new ministry. After consulting with the leading men of various parties, Mr Waterhouse agreed to form a temporary ministry for the sole and express purpose of terminating the discussion on the Boothby case, and of carrying the addresses for his removal. None of the legal members being willing to support him, he was forced to go outside Parliament and appoint Mr Henry Gawler, Solicitor to the Lands Titles Commission, to be Attorney-General. The Constitution Act provided that a responsible minister might hold office for three months without a seat in Parliament. The emergency Waterhouse ministry existed only ten days, when, its object having been accomplished, it was dissolved, and a new government formed with Mr Waterhouse at the head, Mr Stow resuming the position of Attorney-General.

> 'I wish I could say'—wrote the Governor—'that the present ministry were sufficiently secure in their seats to enable them to devote their energies and time to the real business of the country. But just now they are threatened with fierce attacks by combinations formed from extreme parties, with no other object than to get into place. As I think five Ministerial crises are quite sufficient interruption of the public business in one Session, and as I regard this greed for office as the most pernicious result of responsible Government, I shall certainly not call to my Council the successful leaders of any such temporary cabal, but shall give the whole system a check by dissolving the Parliament and permitting an appeal to the general sense of the country.' [53]

There was a great deal to be said in the Judge's support. In the first place, it was a gross and patent injustice to have invited him to give evidence before the Select Committee, and then, having extracted from him in detail his opinions on the legal questions at issue, to use that evidence to incriminate him. Even the lowest criminal is entitled to be warned if it is proposed to use in evidence against him what he says in response to invitations and questionings. As Mr Randolph Stow said:

> 'It was an unprecedented course in any part of the British dominions to present an address to the Queen for the removal of a Judge for the expression of his conscientious opinions. The Committee was appointed, not for the purpose of enquiring into the conduct of Judge Boothby, or of saying whether he had been guilty of corruption but to enquire into the state of the laws. The Judge gave his evidence under the assumption that it would be used only for the purpose for which the Committee was appointed. To use that evidence now for any other purpose was unprecedented and a disgrace to the colony. He agreed that it was absurd to say the evidence could not be used, but it could only be justly used for the purpose the Committee was appointed for. He was ashamed that that evidence, given by the Judge before a Committee he knew to have been appointed for a friendly purpose should have been used to condemn him, without even giving him an opportunity to be heard in his defence. He was surprised that not one of the hon. members who supported the motion had thought it necessary to give notice of a motion that Judge Boothby should be requested to attend at the House, and be allowed to be heard there. If the address was adopted, it would be a disgrace to them. He felt it necessary to enter his protest—although he felt it would be useless—against this shameful and unprecedented proceeding.' [54]

George Tinline (1815-1895)
Tinline was only briefly a member of the Legislative Council but had made his mark on South Australian history earlier as manager of the Bank of South Australia. During the currency crisis brought about by the Victorian gold rush Tinline advocated the special assay that brought gold to South Australia and revived the colony's economy. (SLSA)

In the Legislative Council Mr Tinline said:

> 'It is not pretended that His Honor has been guilty of corruption, and though he is known not to be in affluent circumstances, his private character is unimpeached. It has not been charged against him that he is unable to administer the laws, or that he is inhumane, or immoral. He is the father of a large family, and as such, and as a citizen, his character is irreproachable. Exception has been taken more than once to the course His Honor has pursued on the Bench, but it has never been whispered that he has been guilty of partiality. He is now arraigned because he had called in question the legality of certain Acts of the Legislature.'

Then, again, all the Judges were agreed that remedial legislation by the Imperial Parliament was necessary. Instead of adopting this obvious means of redress, it was attempted to oust one of the Judges. Why should Mr Justice Boothby be singled out for attack?

> 'On the question of repugnancy'—said Mr Finniss—'all three Judges agreed in some respects; and why was it that they should try to make Mr Justice Boothby the victim? Had he exceeded his duty? No. He had only gone according to his conscience, and according to his oath.'

It was admitted that the difference between his opinions and those of Mr Justice Gwynne was only one of degree; but, said the anti-Boothbyites, look at the degree! Mr Justice Gwynne held one or two acts were repugnant, but Mr Justice Boothby, with one fell swoop, would clear away the whole legislation of ten years. Threats were indeed made that Mr Justice Gwynne had better mind what he was about, or he would share the same fate as his luckless colleague, but they were never pressed.[55]

The motion, it was urged, was a blow at judicial independence.

> 'The next step will be to elect Judges by universal suffrage and instead of honest upright and fearless Judges, the liberties and property of the colonists will be at the mercy of low political trimmers and popularity-hunting sneaks.'

Mr Justice Boothby having been singled out as the scapegoat, an inflammatory campaign against him was vigorously carried on by the newspapers. On the Boothby question, the *Advertiser* and the *Register* had joined in an "unholy alliance", and took it in turns to attack him in their leading articles on alternate days. The hunt of obloquy pursued him in full cry. He was denounced as antagonistic, blustering and bombastic, cantankerous, captious, dictatorial, egotistical, foolish, half-witted, inconsiderate and ill mannered; obstreperous, ruthless, tyrannical, and unreliable, a vain man, a wrangler, a male Xanthippe, yeasty and a zealot.[56] Equally vehement in his denunciations of the Judges who ventured to oppose the Real Property Act was Torrens himself. He addressed anti-Boothby meetings with such fervour that even the mild Sir Charles Cooper was stirred to indignant protest against the wild talk of this prominent civil servant.

Anthony Forster (1813-1897)
Forster was one of a group who purchased the *Register* in 1853. He edited the *Register* and the *Adelaide Observer* until 1864 when he returned to England. A member of the Legislative Council from 1856 to 1864 he was one of the Real Property Act's main supporters. (SLSA)

> 'I would remark'—he wrote to the Chief Secretary—'that Judges in this colony are in a peculiar situation. They are not permitted to be members of either House of Parliament; they cannot, like a private individual, address a public meeting in their own defence; and are altogether more defenceless against attacks than any other class of persons.' [57]

Torrens apologised to the Judges.

> 'Can there be any dictation more unfair and unjustifiable'—asked Mr Dutton—'than the action of the two conductors of the daily Press'—(Barrow and Forster)—'who have been for

> months past trying to overawe the refractory members of this House, who will not be dragooned by the daily press—by stirring up the country to petition for a dissolution, in order that more pliant members may be returned in the place of the old Parliamentarians—that members may be returned who will be ready to kiss the dust at the feet of Robert Richard Torrens and Mr Barrow and Mr Forster. (Uproar and cheers) ... It was susceptible of proof that Mr Torrens was all along an active fomenter of the opposition to the Judge. The whole of the tumult originated, and the ponderous machinery for keeping alive the agitation was kept at work, by the out-and-out supporters—he might say the holus-bolus supporters—of the Real Property Act. At every public meeting which had been held in the country districts the cry raised was, 'The Real Property Act is in danger!', and the key-note of all the bitter feeling which had been excited against the Judge had been his having declared that Act to be invalid.'

Sir Henry Ayers spoke to the same effect; and warned the House that they would not easily induce the Queen to dismiss "her trusty and well-beloved Benjamin Boothby".

> 'It has been said this question has nothing to do with the Real Property Act; I believe it has everything to do with the Real Property Act, and that if the Judge had said every other Act in the colony or in England was invalid, and had allowed the Real Property Act to float gently down the stream, nothing would have been said against him.' [58]

Many of Mr Justice Boothby's remarks, it was admitted, would have been better left unsaid.

> 'But they could not expect human nature to be perfect, even on the Bench; and no man could be expected to endure the perpetual abuse of public speakers, the diatribes of the press, and sometimes even the badgering of the Bar, without breaking out into some manifestation of feeling.'

Mr Glyde invited members to accompany him in imagination to Downing Street with the dispatch conveying the addresses for removal.

> 'He presumed the Secretary would hand the Despatch to the Duke of Newcastle, and would remind him—what people sometimes forgot—that South Australia was a troublesome little colony, with about 130,000 inhabitants and about equal to a fourth-rate English town. The Secretary would also remind the Duke that a Committee had been appointed to consider

> the question by each branch of the local Legislature, and that neither of them had recommended what the address prayed for, but that one report—a perfect specimen of colonial logic and bounce—signed 'G.M. Waterhouse', recommended a local Act to declare our legislation valid; and another signed 'R.D. Hanson' a name already known in the Colonial Office—recommended an Imperial Act for the same purpose. The Duke would also be reminded that the address was carried in both Houses by a narrow majority; that none of the legal members voted for it; and that the Attorney General resigned his office in consequence of the course adopted by his colleagues. The Duke would probably enquire what it was all about, and they might depend upon it that when he became acquainted with all the circumstances, and found that Judge Boothby had warned the Legislature that he feared they were trespassing on the 'supremacy of Imperial legislation and the integrity of Imperial interests', he would look with a very favourable eye upon the conduct of Judge Boothby; and that the result would be that they would get a snubbing from the Colonial Office for the impudent manner in which they had attempted to condemn Judge Boothby, before they knew whether he was wrong. If the Judge, after all, happened to be right—and he was sure he did not know his Honor was not right—what a ridiculous position they would be in. Hon. members should think of the leading articles that would appear in the 'Times' and the sarcasms that 'Punch' would indulge in at their expense, and how they would be compared to silly children who asked their mammas to turn away the doctor instead of compelling them to take the medicines prescribed for them.' [59]

As Mr Glyde mentioned, the legal members were opposed to the motion in a body. (Because, said the anti-Boothbyites, "they see a rich harvest before them, if His Honor is allowed to remain in his present position".) Mr Hanson, for instance, said:

> 'We have a Judge against whose character or integrity not one syllable is brought, and I cannot agree to punish this Judge merely because it may be that his opinions are erroneous—even though they were tenfold more so than they are at the present time. If it could be shown that any partial or corrupt judgment had been given, the case would be different, but to hold over this and every succeeding Judge the threat that, if his opinions happened to be distasteful, he would be removed from the Bench—why, such a system I can never support. If

> such a position is adopted as that indicated in this motion, it will be found that Judges are to be removed whenever their decisions chance to be distasteful to public opinion.' [60]

As for the public outcry, as shown by the numerous petitions against the Judge's conduct, petitions could be got up by the yard or by the thousand, said Sir Henry Ayers.

> 'In the district of Mitcham, where the Boothby mania was most rabid, the man who was employed to get signatures was paid by the day; and I have heard that even the hangman was so employed.'

Upper Mitcham in the early 1860's. This view looks northeast across Brownhill Creek toward St Michael's Church. (Mitcham Historical Society Collection)

The motions for an address to the Crown for the removal of the Judge were carried in the Legislative Council by a majority of nine to seven, and in the Assembly by a majority of twenty one to fourteen.

When these motions were first brought forward, Mr Justice Boothby addressed to the Governor a lengthy memorandum protesting against their unconstitutional nature, and urging that it was the Governor's duty to point out to both Houses by message that neither the Constitution Act nor any laws or usages of the British Empire warranted such proceedings, which were an unjustified interference with the independent administration of justice by Her Majesty's Judges.

The notices of motion, he said, were avowedly founded on section 31 of the Constitution Act (No 2 of 1855-56) which provided that the Queen might remove any judge from office upon the address of both Houses. But this gave no authority to either House, contended the Judge, to approve or condemn the judgment of any Judge of the Supreme Court as evidencing good behaviour or the contrary. No suggestion of mental or professional incapacity, or of personal corruption was made against him.

> 'For either House of the Legislature to enquire into the sufficiency in law of any judgment by a Judge of the Supreme Court is to usurp a function opposed to the Constitution of the British Empire, and subversive of its most valuable principles.'

No such attempt had ever been made by the Imperial Parliament. He reiterated the objections he had set forth in his protest to the Legislative Council; and continued:

> 'It is notorious that a Committee sitting in Adelaide, by an organised procedure and reckless misstatements, libelling the administration of justice for two months last past, have urged upon the Legislature a course thus opposed to the interests of the Crown and its subjects, in the independent administration of the laws; so creating an urgent necessity for the exercise of every constitutional restraint on the proposed action of the two Houses. Such organised agitation is evidenced by almost daily advertisements and leading articles in the only two daily papers of the Province, each of whose managing editors is a member of the Legislative Council. The Registrar General, an officer of the Queen's service, of high position and emolument, has also, by notorious and active interference through the said newspapers, in a flagrant instance with his own name attached, and also by speeches at public meetings, urged on the legislature the unconstitutional course proposed.'

There were numerous instances, he said, where the Imperial Parliament had been prorogued by the Crown to prevent a majority pursuing an unconstitutional course.

> 'The power of prorogation in the Crown exists as one of its main reasons for the purpose of restraining any proposed unconstitutional action by either House of Parliament or both.'

He concluded his memorandum by declaring that it was submitted as required in principle by section 23 of the Act 9 Geo IV c.83, which, for the reasons given by him in *McEllister v. Fenn*, he held was in operation in South Australia.[61]

The Governor did not see fit to act upon this protest. On the contrary, he retaliated by sending to the Judge a copy of a ruling by Lord John Russell, which he had just discovered, that the Governor's instructions "were not in the nature of legal conditions precedent, the non-observance of which would in any way affect the validity of Colonial Acts". Mr Justice Boothby ignored it.[62]

Neither of the addresses to the Queen gave any reasons. That of the Legislative Council simply stated that it was absolutely necessary the Judge should be removed; that of the Assembly requested his removal as, in consequence of the position assumed by him, public confidence in the administration of the laws of the province was destroyed. In the Legislative Council, Mr G.F. Angas stoutly protested that the accusations against the Judge should have been defined and clearly set out. The proposal of the House, he said, amounted to this: "Address the Queen for the removal of the Judge, and let Her Majesty find out the reason." [63]

The Governor, however, was of opinion that the legislature had pursued a dignified course in not giving any reasons for the request they urged:

> '... as it is not to be presumed that they would move in such a matter lightly, or till after such repeated provocation as would justify them in urging on the Sovereign the request for removal of a Judge.' [64]

The Crown law officers in England made no objection to there being separate addresses from each House, instead of a joint address; nor did they think it irregular that the addresses omitted to state any specific charges, "provided that the Crown is by any means satisfied of the reasons on which the address is founded".[65]

In his dispatch accompanying the addresses, the Governor said:

> 'There has been a vast amount of excitement on this question, to which Mr Justice Boothby has himself greatly contributed, by the arrogant tone in which he proclaimed himself right and everyone else wrong ... If I thought there was any chance whatever of the administration of justice being able to recover the great shock it has received from the injudicious conduct of Mr Boothby, I might see less objection to the Crown's interposing its protection between Mr Boothby and the Parliament. Even now I presume that some pension should be secured to him on the same scale as that accorded to Sir Charles Cooper, who is to receive a pension of £1000 per annum for twenty three years service; but I see no reason for the Crown further interposing its protection. On the contrary, the privilege which both branches of the Legislature have just

> used, in passing the enclosed Addresses, is one directly conferred on them by their Constitution Act, and is analogous to that trust which, in one of the ablest State papers ever drawn up, the great Burke declares "to be inseparable from the Commons of Great Britain in Parliament assembled, one of whose principal functions and duties it is to be observant of the Courts of Justice, and to take due care that none of them, from the lowest to the highest, shall pursue new courses unknown to the laws and constitution of this kingdom, or to equity, sound legal policy, or substantial justice".'[66]

The Governor offered the Judge an opportunity of forwarding any answer he might wish to make to the addresses, and, to ensure that he received every possible facility for putting his views of the merits of the case, said he would give him six months' leave of absence on full pay so that he might visit England. Mr Justice Boothby's reply was a somewhat discourteous refusal to take advantage of the offer.

> 'My duty to Her Majesty and the suitors of Her Majesty's Supreme Court'—he said—'forbid that I should wish or seek to absent myself from my judicial duties for any purpose not necessary to the discharge of those duties. I have completed eight years of service to Her Majesty, it is true, without a day's absence, and I thank Divine Providence for health of body and mind still to fulfil my duties.'[67]

The Judge can be excused a considerable amount of petulance. From his point of view the proceedings were a monstrous injustice from beginning to end. In a contemporary pamphlet entitled *Observations on the Report of the Committee of the House of Assembly on Judge Boothby's Case*, purporting to be by "A member of the Irish Bar of upwards of Twenty Years Standing, practising in Dublin", the pro-Boothby case is put very forcibly.

> 'If it be the duty and right of a South Australian Judge'—says the author—'to enquire whether an Act of the Colonial Legislature be valid, as being within the limited power of the Legislature, or as not being repugnant to the laws of England, then Judge Boothby has done no more than he was conscientiously bound to do. The enquiry should have stopped there—respect for the law and its officers—consideration of the immense importance and value of the independence of the Bench, and of the free and conscientious administration of justice, should have precluded the Committee and the House from going further; for all further enquiry (I mean as to Judge Boothby) is merely an enquiry whether his opinions be right or

wrong, that is, whether his law be good or bad law, an investigation for which the Committee and House are wholly incompetent and which no Judge ought to allow any lay tribunal to enter into.

It is certainly most preposterous and a dangerous symptom that an assembly of laymen should, first admitting that it is open to the Judge to discuss and decide on the validity of a Colonial Act, then proceed to criticise that judgment—to express their dissent from it—and finally to seek to punish the Judge because his law differs from theirs. There is indeed in the subsequent proceedings of the Assembly a violation of decorum and almost of good faith. When a man is summoned to give evidence before a Committee the understanding is, and the honour of Parliament demands that it should be rigidly adhered to—that he comes with a safe conduct—that he is privileged, that his evidence will not be used against him. The House is not a Star Chamber, not a Court of Visitation; its functions in this direction are simply to enquire, and when the House condescended to invite Judge Boothby to give evidence before their Committee, they must be understood to waive and abandon all proceedings of a penal nature against him. Surely they did not intend to lay a trap for him, to inveigle him into the full expression of his opinions and upon those opinions to found ulterior proceedings against him.'

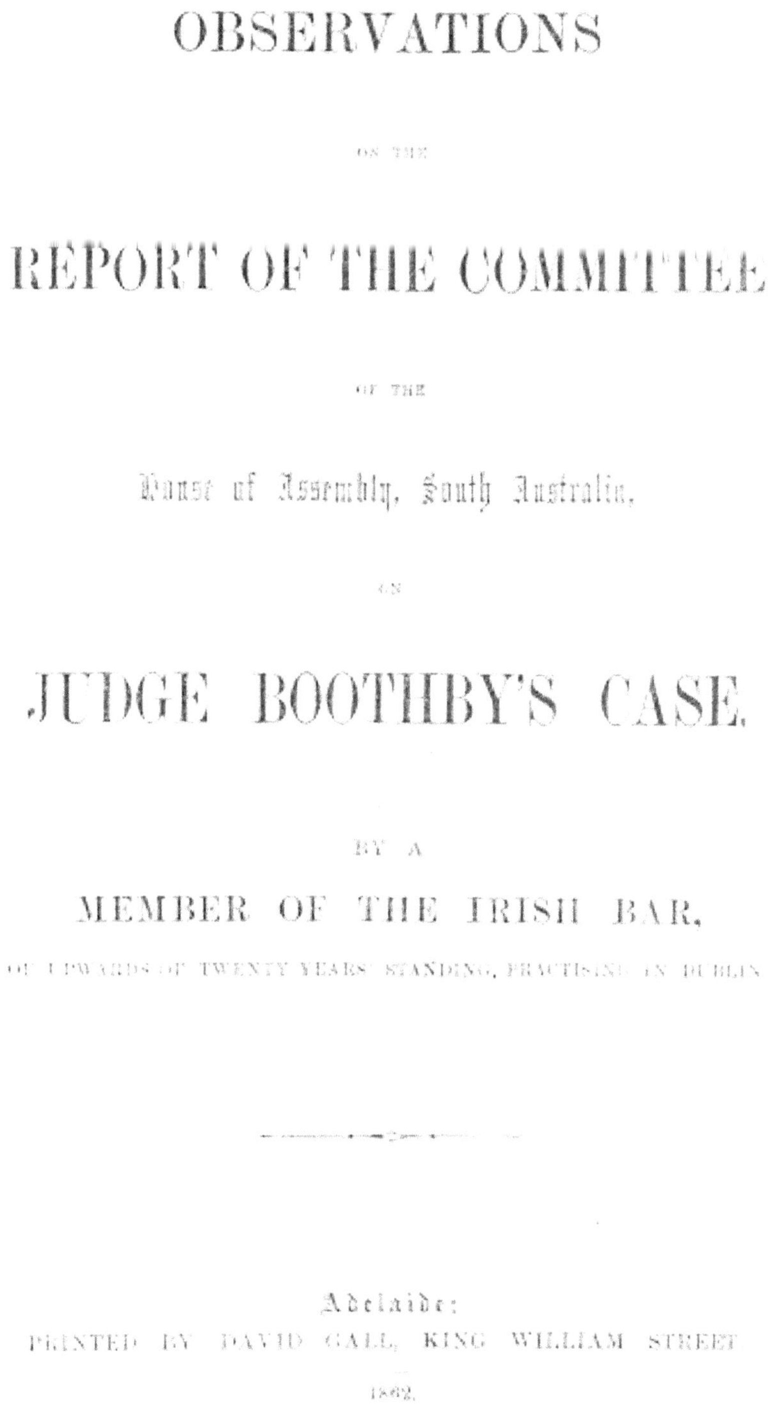

OBSERVATIONS

ON THE

REPORT OF THE COMMITTEE

OF THE

House of Assembly, South Australia,

ON

JUDGE BOOTHBY'S CASE.

BY A

MEMBER OF THE IRISH BAR,

OF UPWARDS OF TWENTY YEARS' STANDING, PRACTISING IN DUBLIN.

Adelaide:

PRINTED BY DAVID GALL, KING WILLIAM STREET

1862.

Cover of a pamphlet on the Boothby case, written apparently by a "member of the Irish Bar". (State Records)

Mr Justice Boothby

'the ablest man'

While Parliament was busy with the addresses, matters had not been improving in the conduct of the business of the Supreme Court. The Real Property Act continued to be the subject of hostile dicta. In *Ex parte Manford*, for instance, Mr Belt sought a mandamus against the Registrar-General to compel him to register certain parties claiming under a will to be proprietors of land. The applicants had a land grant and wanted to sell the land. Mr Justice Boothby at once advised them to transfer under the old system; the validity of the Real Property Act not having been determined, this would be much safer.

> 'With regard to whether or not that Act is law'—interposed the Chief Justice—'when we are solemnly asked to decide upon that, I shall be prepared to express my opinion. At present the Court has no reason to say that the Act is not valid; I know of none myself.'

Mr Justice Gwynne, however, thought that the question of the validity of the Act should be definitely decided, because it would be "undignified" to act under a statute and then when its validity was argued be compelled to say that it was not law. He had no objection to going on with the application before the court so long as it was understood that he guarded himself against admitting the validity of the Act.

> 'I have great objection'—piped up Mr Justice Boothby. 'I have given a great deal of consideration to the subject and I have not the slightest doubt upon it until I am set right by the Judicial Committee of the Privy Council—an authority to which I would gladly bow; or I may be set right by argument showing my opinion to be erroneous. Every Judge is open to be convinced.' [1]

William Bakewell (1817-1870)
Bakewell arrived in South Australia in 1839, was admitted to the bar in 1848 and served as Crown Solicitor from 1867 to 1870. He was a Member of the House of Assembly from 1857 to 1869 and again from 1862 to 1864.
(SLSA)

Again, in *Ex parte Phillis*, Mr Bakewell moved for a rule nisi for removal of a caveat lodged under the provisions of the Real Property Act. Mr Justice Boothby promptly said that he must be prepared to show the court that the Real Property Act was valid, and the following remarks ensued:

> Mr Justice Gwynne: 'You can take a rule upon the assumption that the Real Property Act is law in this colony. The question of the validity of the Act must be determined sooner or later, and it may as well be done on this motion.'

> Mr Justice Boothby: 'I ask for your assistance in the argument to show that the Act of Parliament under which you apply has

the force of law.'

Mr Bakewell: 'If the question is raised by the other side, I shall be prepared to argue it.'

Mr Justice Boothby: 'But the Court may raise it.'

The Chief Justice: 'I beg to say, that the Court may not raise it.'

Mr Justice Boothby: 'I beg the Chief Justice's pardon. I should not have said the Court, but that I shall raise it.' [2]

As the remarks just quoted indicate, the relations between the Chief Justice and Mr Justice Boothby—formerly so fraternal—had become very strained. Sir Charles Cooper had been on the bench for twenty three years and was in ill health. He was irritated and worried by the behaviour of his colleague, who was a staunch believer in the Johnsonian doctrine that treating your adversary with respect is giving him an advantage to which he is not entitled and who accordingly treated Sir Charles with thinly-veiled contempt. It can easily be imagined that to a man essentially of an ironic disposition and averse to extreme measures, this situation must have been most embarrassing and distasteful. "There is no such test of a man's superiority of character"—Sir Henry Taylor has observed—"as in the well conducting of an unavoidable quarrel." Sir Charles Cooper was very far from being the possessor of a forceful and dominating personality, and he was unable to stand up to the barrage of criticisms, sneers and insults which his colleague directed at him.

It was an open secret that Mr Justice Boothby coveted the position of Chief Justice and claimed the right of succession to it. In December 1860, in an interview with the Governor, he asserted that in the event of the death or retirement of the Chief Justice, he would be absolutely entitled to that office, and declared that he would forthwith enter on its duties. The Governor and Executive Council could not, he said, appoint anyone else to the office. Startled by this, the Governor asked him to put his reasons in writing. The Judge said he would do so. After waiting three and a half months, the Governor sent him a letter reminding him of his promise. No answer was vouchsafed to this. The Governor then brought the matter before the Executive Council. He had no wish, he said, to call attention to the personal discourtesy exhibited to himself by such conduct, but to "the very extraordinary fact that one of the Judges threatened in the event of a certain possible contingency taking place to defy the Governor and Council and to assert a right to the highest judicial office despite of the Government". This could not be done without occasioning great scandal. The Council discussed the matter at some length but could not come to any decision, although they concurred in thinking it improbable that Mr Justice Boothby would "abandon his peculiar views from a sense of their error", or would listen to any authority in the colony.[3]

In August 1861 the Chief Justice intimated to the government that he wished to retire, if he could be granted a pension of two-thirds of his salary, in order to enable him to do so. After some opposition in Parliament from members who thought that it was most dangerous for the Chief Justice to leave the bench until the Boothby troubles were settled, an act was passed authorising the payment of a pension of £1,000 a year, and in November 1861 he retired. The Governor and Council immediately appointed Mr Hanson to the position of Chief Justice.

A considerable digression is necessary to sketch even in outline the distinguished career of the new Chief Justice—"a profound thinker, an able statesman, a powerful advocate, an upright judge, an exemplary citizen, and a great man". "One of the most powerful intellects which has ever adorned the Judicial Bench of Australia", said his successor, Sir Samuel Way.[4]

Born in London on 5 or 6 December 1805 (authorities differ as to the precise date) he was the son of a noncomformist fruit merchant and importer. At seventeen he was articled to Mr John Wilks, a prominent London solicitor, a member of Parliament, and one of the Committee of the South Australian Association. Hanson was admitted as an attorney of the King's Bench on 5 April 1828 and, as has been previously mentioned, was for some time employed with the firm of Bartlett and Beddome. He reported and wrote extensively for the *Morning Post* and *Globe* newspapers—according to the *Dictionary of National Biography*, editing the latter. From 1830 on he took a prominent part on the movement for the colonisation of South Australia, and was one of those selected to address the public meeting in Exeter Hall on 30 June 1834, convened to boost the colony.

At this time John Brown, G.S. Kingston, and John Morphett were his closest friends, and it is worth noticing that three of the quartet were afterwards knighted. With Morphett he made a walking tour of the continent, a feat then very much more of an adventure than it would be at the present day.

On 31 December 1835, a number of the intending colonists gave Hanson a dinner in recognition of his services in promoting the colony "and the evening went off very well". John Brown had described in his journal on the previous evening how he had:

> '... quietly smoked a segar with Hanson downstairs. He told me that Wakefield had today had a long conversation with him in which he admitted that he was going out to the Colony at least as a visitor if not as a resident and further hinted to Hanson that there might be an opening for him too. Torrens also today asked him whether he thought his engagements would allow him to go to the colony; and if so stated that the Governor is very anxious for a private secretary in whom he could rely, to strengthen his hand and to enable him to keep his ground in

> the colony, as he already is jealous of Gouger and Parker, fearing their influence will be too great for him. We talked over the affairs of the colony, the state of parties, the character, conduct and ability of our Governor, the Company etc and I expressed my opinion that such an office would be even for Hanson a perilous and difficult task.'

S.T. Gill's depiction of John Brown, 1849 (SLSA)

The prospect of being Governor Hindmarsh's secretary had few attractions for Hanson, and when the attempts made to secure him the position of Judge in the new colony failed, he gave up his intention of emigrating to South Australia, much to the regret of his friends who had gone out to the new land.

> 'When you see Hanson'—wrote Brown to Wakefield in April 1837—'tell him we often think of him, and picture his feelings in taking a segar with his old friends. By the bye, a better opportunity for any man than he would have here as a lawyer, as a newspaper editor (for there must be an opposition paper, at whatever cost, if things continue), and as twenty other things, could not be found.' [5]

Hanson does not seem to have felt much desire for the law as a profession.

> 'His severely logical mind'—it has been said—'felt the want of any sound scientific principles at the basis of our legal system,

and doubtless he was revolted at the complicated and absurd technicalities.'

In 1837 Lord Durham made his famous visit to Canada, and Hanson was appointed to accompany him as an Assistant Commissioner of Enquiry into Crown Lands and Emigration, Charles Buller being the Chief Commissioner. Probably he was helped to this appointment by the influence of Wakefield. In 1836 he and Wakefield had both given evidence before a Select Committee of the House of Commons on "The Disposal of Lands in the British Colonies". Wakefield also went to Canada with Lord Durham, but as he could not be given an official position, it seems to have fallen to him to assist Buller and Hanson.

The Durham Report
Published in 1839, the Durham Report (*Report on the Affairs of British North America*) is a key document in Canadian history. It recommended the unification of Upper and Lower Canada, the grant of responsible government and the assimilation of French Canadians.

Very little information is available as to Hanson's part in the Durham report. Apparently he acted as private secretary to Lord Durham, and no doubt assisted in collating and digesting the evidence on which the report was based. He wrote a special supplementary report on the excessive appropriation of public lands under the name of clergy reserves. The share which Lord Durham himself had in the report has been the subject of dispute. The famous epigram, "Wakefield thought it, Buller wrote it, Durham signed it", probably sacrificed truth to incisiveness. A passage in the Greville memoirs, purporting to be based on information obtained from Hanson, supports the suggestion that Buller wrote the report, but it is generally agreed that the accuracy of the entry is doubtful. In any event, whether Durham wrote the report is not of very great importance—he approved it and took the responsibility for it. He had, says Sir Charles Lucas, the "high quality of choosing competent advisers and assistants".[6]

Hanson spent nine months in Canada. On his return to England, Lord Durham's resignation put an end to any prospects of advancement to which he might have looked from this patron, and he decided to emigrate to New Zealand. With respect to his career there, the Chief Librarian of the General Assembly Library, Wellington (Mr G.H. Scholefield) supplied the following particulars which, as they are not to be found elsewhere, are given verbatim:

> 'He arrived in Port Nicholson by the 'Cuba' on January 3, 1840 with the survey staff of the New Zealand Company. He himself was the agent of the Company for the purchase of lands. He sailed for Kawhia on February 2nd and effected the purchase of certain Waikato lands for the Company. He later visited the Chatham Islands which he also purported to have purchased for the Company, but the deed was repudiated by the British Government.
>
> Hanson was a member of the Provisional Committee of colonists for the government of Port Nicholson early in 1840, and was elected vice-president of the Committee in April.

The "Cuba" at anchor, in a NW breeze at Port Nicholson heads 1840, by Charles Heaphy, then draughtsman to the NZ Company. (ATLNZ)

Luke Nattrass's *City of Wellington, New Zealand, 1841.* (ATLNZ)

> On August 19th 1840 he was appointed with Dr Evans and Mr Moreing to present the grievances of the Port Nicholson settlers to the Governor of New South Wales.
>
> On February 15th, 1841, at a meeting of settlers called to censure Governor Hobson's policy, he opposed a resolution demanding the recall of Hobson, and proposed an amendment in favour of petitioning Parliament for redress. The amendment was rejected. On May 3rd 1841, he was appointed a Justice of the Peace and on September 3rd was appointed Crown Prosecutor.
>
> In this capacity he attended the first sitting of the court for the district of Port Nicholson on October 5th 1841. On the 27th October he was appointed a magistrate of the territory.
>
> At the first election of aldermen for the borough of Wellington on October 3, 1842, Hanson polled 126 votes. He was fourteenth out of eighteen candidates and was not elected.
>
> On discontinuance of the office of Crown Prosecutor in 1844 he was appointed Crown Solicitor and under an ordinance of that year he was appointed Commissioner of the Court of Requests on December 5th 1844.
>
> Hanson Street, Wellington, is named after him.'

Hanson came to Adelaide in 1846, at the urgent request of his friend John Brown, and commenced the practice of his profession. He at once identified himself with public matters, and became Secretary of the South Australian League for the Maintenance of Religious Freedom in the Province, which had been formed to resist Governor Robe's proposals for state aid to religion. In 1851 he was elected to the Legislative Council as a member for Yatala. A petition against his return was lodged by the unsuccessful candidate, but the Governor removed any difficulty that might have arisen by appointing Hanson to be Acting Advocate-General in the place of Smillie, who had gone to Europe. This position carried with it an official seat in the Legislative Council. Hanson accepted only on the condition that he should be allowed to vote as he thought fit on state aid to religion, and promptly voted against the government policy on this question.

On Smillie's death, Hanson's appointment became permanent, and as the law adviser of the Governor he introduced a number of measures of vast importance to the state—in particular the District Councils Act of 1852 and the Education Act of 1851, and he took a chief part in the drafting of the Constitution Acts.

Upon the coming into force of responsible government, his office of Advocate-General was abolished, a pension of £375 a year being provided for him as compensation for loss of office—the pension to merge in his salary if he obtained government office again.

He was elected for Adelaide in the House of Assembly in the first Parliament, and became Attorney-General in the Government of Mr Finniss, which went out of office on 20 August 1857. Hon J. Baker and Mr Torrens having attempted to form ministries—that of the former lasted ten days, the other twenty four days—Hanson was called upon by the Governor. His ministry—in which he was Premier and Attorney-General—lasted from 30 September 1857 to 9 May 1860.

With the details of his political career we are not now concerned although, as Miss Spence wrote:

> 'It was as a politician that Sir Richard Hanson exercised the greatest influence over the destinies of South Australia; no one man has done so much to mould the future of a colony. Of the ten years of his political life, he held office for nearly nine; six years as permanent Advocate General, and three as the head of a responsible Ministry; and during these years he was the guiding spirit of a great part of our legislation. A Liberal and a Nonconformist, he had the strongest faith in the developing power of popular institutions, and his tendency was rather to increase than diminish the people's power of self-government.' [7]

> 'In Mr Hanson, the Attorney General'—wrote a visitor to Adelaide at this time—'I am inclined to think that I recognised the ablest public man in all these Australian colonies. As private secretary to Lord Durham, and in other respects favorably situated, he has been drilled in public affairs from early youth; and he is a man of great natural capacity. With a graceful and sagacious reticence, very uncommon to our Australian politicians, he is quiet, reserved, and unobstrusive [sic] in his style of dealing with public affairs, although, when he chooses, he can dart with lion-like power upon an antagonist.' [8]

In his practice at the bar—he combined a right of private practice with his position as Advocate-General—Hanson had quickly gone to the front. In one of the first cases which he took in South Australia, in the Police Court, he appeared for a woman charged with stealing a dress. It appeared that the complainant, another woman, had made a new dress for herself. By a freak of the wind, the dress was blown out of a window and carried some distance to the house of the defendant, who found it lying under a tree. As no owner appeared to claim the dress, the finder decided to wear it herself, and set off in it for a trip to Glenelg. Unfortunately, she there met the original owner, who recognised her lost costume, and the fat was in the fire. The jay in borrowed plumage hastened to restore the dress, but the complainant would not be appeased and could not believe that it had not been deliberately stolen. She took proceedings in the Police Court, but her complaint was dismissed.[9]

Hanson's first case in the Supreme Court was one of libel—*Van Sommer v. Stephens*. The *Register*, having made some very defamatory statements about the plaintiff, Dr Van Sommer, was called on by him to retract. The paper refused in no uncertain terms: "We are prepared with the damning proofs," it said in the next issue. "Will the dirty-minded and lustful Doctor shirk us?"

The doctor was no shirker: he sued for libel. Hanson appeared for him, Stephen for the defendant. The plaintiff secured a verdict, but only one farthing damages. In view of the defendant's defiant attitude, however, the Judge gave the plaintiff costs. The *Register* hailed the verdict as a signal triumph.

> 'A common jury was found bold enough to uphold a public journalist in the honest and fearless exposure of immorality, regardless of the frowns of power, or the floating expectation of the malicious harpies who thronged around to awe them into a hostile verdict. We entertain no malice towards the unhappy plaintiff, but we pity him for his misfortune in selecting for his legal adviser a gentleman who was unwilling, though at his client's expense, to let slip the opportunity of conducting his maiden case.' [10]

Within a few years Hanson was the acknowledged leader of the bar, a position which he retained undisputed by anyone except Gwynne, until his appointment to the bench.

> 'He was, perhaps, too cold and cautious, too severely logical, to be the beau ideal of the popular advocate. His power over a jury lay not in rhetorical appeals to the passions, but in a marvellous clearness of statement, which set his case before them in the plainest, and at the same time, the most favourable light, and in an unerring eye for the defects of his opponent's cause. At times, however, when ruffled by opposition or aroused by a sense of injustice, the coldness and hesitation of his delivery disappeared, and he spoke with a force and eloquence the more effective because they were so rarely used.' [11]

> 'Fastidious in his choice of words'—said another writer—'and too wary to give his opponent any advantage by the use of an indiscreet phrase, he was cold and cautious, rather than fiery and impassioned in his addresses. Calm and equable in temperament, and with a logical faculty which enabled him to see the weak points in his own case as clearly as those in his

> opponent's, he was rarely able to identify himself with the cause of his client with that thorough earnestness of conviction which sometimes so greatly helps even a second-rate advocate.' [12]

The bench was probably more suited to his tastes than the bar or Parliament, and offered scope for the exercise of his best intellectual powers.

> 'His summings up were often masterpieces of clear and forcible statement, and seemed not only to carry conviction to the minds of a hesitating jury, but sometimes to overmaster the impressions they had already formed. There were occasions, but very rare ones, in which his strong prejudices and attachments might have influenced his opinions; and perhaps he had an undue impatience of the forms and rules of law. He was too apt to go to first principles, and seek for a solid foundation of abstract right where perhaps none existed.' [13]

B.T. Finniss said of him:

> 'Sir Richard was a man who, when seen in his proper sphere, the Supreme Court, impressed you with the idea of mental power. His broad, expansive forehead, when turned upwards in the act of addressing a jury, gave evidence of brain power within, and the deep tones of his voice ensured attention to what he uttered. He was no orator of the impassioned school, but a steady flow of carefully measured words, weighted with calm, logical reasoning, produced conviction of the sincerity and force of his argument.' [14]

In his later years he gave his leisure to the study of theology, and published a number of works expressing decidedly unorthodox and rationalistic views. He was knighted when in England in 1869.

For several years Hanson had been, by common consent, marked out as the obvious successor of Sir Charles Cooper. Of him it can be said, in reference to the rest of the profession, as was said of Papinian, "Omnes longo post se intervallo relinquerit".

> 'Mr Hanson'—the Governor wrote to the Duke of Newcastle—'is the ablest man whom I have met in these colonies, and his appointment has given general satisfaction; whilst I have no doubt his presence on the Bench will, for many reasons, including the great physical energy which he can throw into the discharge of his public duties, tend to re-establish that confidence in the administration of justice which has of late been severely shaken.
>
> I must now mention—he continued—'that I have received

(Sir) Richard Davies Hanson; a wood engraving of him as Chief Justice. (SLV)

a singular communication from Sir Charles Cooper, stating that Mr Justice Boothby had told him he (Mr Justice Boothby) had sent a communication to Your Grace, protesting against the Queen's assent being given to the Act conferring a pension to Sir Charles, on the ground, as Sir Charles believes, that the pension enabling him to retire is part of a scheme devised to deprive Mr Justice Boothby of his just claim to the office of Chief Justice. It would appear that this conduct of Mr Boothby has been the source of much pain to Sir Charles, who cannot derive from the circumstance the same relief that I experience at Mr Boothby's transfer of the bulk of his correspondence from the authorities here to Your Grace direct.'[15]

Mr Justice Boothby had, in fact, directed to the Secretary of State a long communication protesting against the unconstitutional nature of the provisions of the Act giving Sir Charles a pension, and asking that the Act should be disallowed.

'Your Grace will not fail to observe'—he said—'that while the Supreme Court has three Judges, of perfect equality in functions, powers, and authority, this Act provides a pension to Sir Charles Cooper alone, making no provision of a like nature for the other two Judges of the Court, of whom I am next in seniority to Sir Charles Cooper. The flagrantly unconstitutional nature of such legislation, I submit with great confidence to Your Grace, Her Majesty cannot be advised to sanction by leaving this Act to its operation, and so to sanction a principle which, if permitted in one case, may be followed in all—that of providing a retiring pension for a single Judge among several—so tempting the judicial mind away from its highest attribute of independence, by presenting the thought that provision for age or incapacity from loss of health is made to depend, in the case of each individual Judge, on the pleasure of a majority of the local Parliament.'

So strong was his view of "the dangerous consequences to the security of Her Majesty's Government in Her Colonial Possessions" which might follow from this act, that he proposed to ask Lord Cranworth in the House of Lords and Mr Bouverie in the House of Commons to present a petition to each House, praying that the Act might be disallowed.

'On the first print of this Bill being sent down to the House of Assembly'—he said—'I pointed out to Sir Charles Cooper the highly unconstitutional nature of its object, and that if persisted in, I should regard it as a duty to use every constitutional means of objecting to its becoming law. The passing of this Pension

> Bill, and the consequent opportunity by the resignation of Sir Charles Cooper of appointing, as is supposed, Mr Hanson to be Chief Justice—no such office existing as I confidently submit, the local Ordinance relied on, No 31 of 1855-56, having the fatal blot of not containing any words denoting by what authority it is enacted—besides the objection of its assuming to take away the prerogative of Her Majesty to appoint the Judges of Her Majesty's Supreme Court, with the advice of Her Majesty's Secretary of State for the Colonies, and substituting the advice of the Executive Council of this Province—is a part of the unconstitutional proceedings by the Legislature in reference to myself as to judgments delivered in my office as one of Her Majesty's Judges of the Supreme Court as to the validity of certain acts of the Colonial Parliament.' [16]

Mr Justice Boothby was determined not to recognise Mr Hanson as Chief Justice, and when Hanson attended at court to present his Commission, an extraordinary and ludicrous scene took place, the formal description of which, in the Master's Book, speaks for itself. Mr Hanson, the Governor thought, gave an excellent proof of his discretion by eliciting Mr Boothby's protest against the validity of his commission in the Judge's private room, instead of permitting such a protest to take place in public.[17] "By a gentle fiction", the Master of the Supreme Court recorded the proceedings as actually occurring on the bench as follows:

> 'Saturday, 23rd November 1861. Last Day of Term. Present—Mr Justice Boothby and Mr Justice Gwynne. R.D. Hanson, Esq came on to the Bench of the Court, and laid before the Judges a Commission from His Excellency the Governor-in-Chief ... The Commission referred to being read, Mr Justice Boothby made objection thereto that the same had no legal validity, and is void and of no effect, as being contrary to law. Mr Justice Gwynne declared his opinion to the contrary. Whereupon Richard Davies Hanson Esq claimed to give a judicial voice on the same question, to which Mr Justice Boothby objected, and declared his opinion to be that he was not so entitled. Mr Justice Gwynne pronounced his opinion that Richard Davies Hanson Esq was entitled to a voice in deciding on the validity of the Commission he had laid before the Court. Thereupon Richard Davies Hanson Esq: declared his opinion in agreement with Mr Justice Gwynne on both questions and in opposition to the opinion of Mr Justice Boothby, and claimed to preside over the Court by virtue of the Commission he had laid before the Court.
>
> Mr Justice Boothby gave his opinion that Richard Davies

> Hanson Esq had no right to preside. Mr Justice Gwynne declared his opinion to the contrary, and that Richard Davies Hanson Esq had such right. Mr Justice Boothby declared his intention to appeal to Her Majesty in Council on each of the several matters whereon he had declared an opinion contrary to that of Mr Justice Gwynne.
>
> Whereupon Richard Davies Hanson Esq called upon the Attorney-General to move.' [18]

The report of this fantastic scene did not immediately become public, but a few days later a copy of the Master's entry was laid on the table of the Legislative Council, and read by the clerk, while the House dissolved in laughter. The President called the members sharply to order for laughing during the reading of so serious a document, and in an unwary moment he said he was surprised that they should be guilty of such indecent conduct. At once the House rose in a body to protest against the allegation of indecent conduct. Member after member replied to the President with fervent indignation.

> 'What have we done?' asked Mr Barrow. 'A document in some parts excessively ludicrous has been read, and hon. members laughed. Is there anything in the Standing Orders prohibiting laughter or anything that declares it to be "indecent"? That there was certainly something ludicrous in the document may be inferred from the fact that the laughter was universal and simultaneous; every hon. member seemed spontaneously impressed with the self-same idea of the ludicrous. And the affair was ludicrous; so ludicrous, that if the editor of "Punch" could obtain knowledge of it, it would doubtless afford material for one of the most humorous cartoons published for many a day.'

The President finally rose "with great emotion", and after a pathetic panegyric of his services to the House, wound up in true Pickwickian style:

> 'Did he understand the House that he could withdraw the expressions without any sacrifice of the dignity of the House, or of the Chair; if so, he would withdraw them. (Loud cries of hear, hear!).' [19]

Mr Justice Boothby hastened to communicate to the Duke of Newcastle his objections to the appointment of Mr Hanson, and asked that no advice should be given to the Queen in respect of the confirmation of the appointment until he had had an opportunity of fully placing his case before the authorities at home by appeal to the Queen in Council.

> 'I shall make that appeal with entire confidence in its success, founded on legal principles necessary to be rigidly maintained for the protection of Her Majesty's prerogative of appointing the Judges of Her Supreme Court only through the advice of Her Minister, constitutionally responsible for such selection and appointment ... I shall show by my petition of appeal that Mr R.D. Hanson has not the qualification required by any usage, which has the force of law, for the office of Judge in Her Majesty's Supreme Court, inasmuch as he is not a barrister of any of the Inns of Court of London or Dublin, nor a member of the Faculty of Advocates of Scotland.' [20]

The Governor was disgusted with this "protest against the appointment of an infinitely abler man as Chief Justice because he (Mr Boothby) would have preferred that the appointment should have been given to himself".

> 'Considering that both branches of the Legislature have just sent home Addresses, praying for removal of Mr Justice Boothby from his office of Judge, he must have a very extraordinarily constituted mind to contemplate the possibility of any Ministry recommending, or any Governor complying, with such a recommendation as the promotion of Mr Justice Boothby.'

As to the Judge's argument that no-one but a barrister from the United Kingdom was capable of being promoted to the bench of the Supreme Court, the Governor scoffed at it.

> 'As there is no such law in existence, I shall content myself with observing, that all the strength of Her Majesty's Government—supposing it exerted for so pernicious an object—could not possibly prevent the leaders of the local Bars in these free Colonies looking forward to seats on the Bench of their adopted land, or, as it will soon be for most, the land of their birth. Nothing can prevent such a hope being cherished as a laudable object of ambition.'

It was strange that Mr Justice Boothby had made no objection to the appointment of Mr Justice Gwynne, though Gwynne was not an English barrister; and it was even stranger that so long as Mr Boothby received an additional £100 a year when acting as Chief Justice during the absence of Sir Charles Cooper in England, he had no doubts as to the existence of the office. "The pertinacity with which Mr Boothby insisted on the temporary precedence which he derived from it was most remarkable, and, at times, even ludicrous."

With regard to the Judge's request that the Secretary of State would withhold confirmation of Mr Hanson's appointment, the

Governor hastened to point out that no confirmation of the appointment was necessary. The Constitution Act provided for the appointment by the local Government; Mr Hanson was in office by virtue of a statutory enactment and no power of the Crown could put him out.

> 'Mr Boothby of course gets rid of that difficulty in his own peculiar way by getting rid of the Constitution Act, and declaring it null and void. But even that will not serve him, for, under my Commission, I have a power of appointing Judges ... therefore if Mr Hanson be not in by virtue of my power of appointment under the Constitution Act, he must be in by virtue of the power conferred by my Commission. I have no doubt'—the Governor concluded—'that, looking solely to the interests of this community, and to what may promote its happiness and ensure a wise and sensible administration of its laws, Your Grace, like myself, will rejoice that I have secured the services of a gentleman possessing Mr Hanson's sound judgment and abilities.' [21]

In reply to the various dispatches from the Governor and letters from Mr Justice Boothby, the Duke of Newcastle shortly wrote that he had no doubt that Mr Hanson's appointment was a wise one; that confirmation of it was not necessary and he therefore willingly acquiesced in Mr Justice Boothby's request not to confirm it; and that the Act giving a pension to Sir Charles Cooper would be left to its operation, "as a just acknowledgment of that gentleman's long and eminent services".

> 'Mr Boothby's present relations to the Legislature'—he added—'render it impossible to expect that a general Act should be passed to give retiring pensions to Judges in South Australia; but I hope, that when the present controversies are at rest, some retiring provision may be made for functionaries on whose independence not less than their integrity, capacity, and temper, the welfare of the colony so greatly depends.' [22]

This noncommittal dispatch appeared to Governor Daly (who had succeeded Sir Richard MacDonnell) "so admirably calculated to produce a favourable effect" upon Mr Justice Boothby that he immediately furnished him with a copy of it.

> 'So far, however, from moderating his tone, or apparently suggesting the slightest misgiving in his mind as to the propriety or the prudence of the course he has hitherto pursued, in reference to the appointment of Chief Justice Hanson, he called upon me on the following day (being the first interview he had sought for, in business matters, since my

arrival) and expressed himself as being highly pleased with the whole purport of Your Grace's Despatch, "as he found in it the most perfect justification of his course, that the Royal Confirmation of Mr Hanson's appointment was thereby withheld, and that Your Grace clearly acquiesced in the propriety of his intention to appeal to the Privy Council". It was to no purpose that I expressed my total dissent from his views and opinions. He persisted in asserting that there is no Chief Justice of this Province, that such an office does not and never has existed ... From a conversation which lasted for more than two hours, during which Judge Boothby deemed it necessary to read to me many documents which had been printed and form part of the long pending controversies in which he has been so disastrously involved, I find some difficulty in confining my present Despatch to such new circumstances only, as will enable Your Grace to form some idea of the disturbing influence which the sayings and doings of Mr Justice Boothby may exert upon a limited society constituted as this is. The currency which Judge Boothby has given to his opinions and assertions has had the natural effect of arousing feelings of apprehension not unmixed with curiosity.'

Townsend Duryea's 1861 portrait of Sir Dominick Daly. (NLA)

Parliament had addressed him for copies of all dispatches relating to the Judge, which he had agreed to furnish at the urgent request of the Executive Council, because he felt that the publication of them could not be productive of any consequence so injurious as the permitting of the "exaggerations and absurdities" which had obtained currency to be regarded as facts, and not contradicted.

> 'On the arrival of each mail from England I am beset by anxious enquiries as to the fate of the Petitions of the Legislature for Judge Boothby's removal, anything short of which, I much fear, will be the signal for renewed hostilities upon additional grounds, which were hitherto thought unnecessary for effecting that object, and which will but increase the injurious consequences which the conduct and temper of Judge Boothby has already occasioned.'

Although he protested his incompetence to form an opinion on the legal points involved, it appeared to the Governor most improbable that matters could ever be adjusted in such a manner as would satisfy Judge Boothby, and secure the discontinuance "of those very unseemly controversies which have done and are still effecting so much mischief in this community".[23]

The appointment of Hanson had, in fact, done little to lessen the violence of the disputes which centred round the Supreme Court. In the case of *Guthrie v. McEllister*, in December 1861, Mr Fenn moved for a new trial upon the grounds:

(1) That the Real Property Act was invalid and ultra vires.
(2) That if the Act was valid, the Certificate of Title in this particular case was void upon the ground of fraud.

Both the Chief Justice and Mr Justice Gwynne were of opinion that the verdict of the jury on the trial that there was no fraud was against the weight of the evidence, and they therefore intimated to Fenn that he could have a new trial on that ground without going into the other ground. Mr Justice Boothby could not agree to this; the question of invalidity would arise on the second trial, he said, and the Judge there should have the opinion of the Full Court on it. He wanted to go on, and urged Fenn to argue the first ground.

> 'When the majority of the Court intimate that they intend to give a decision upon one point'—said the Chief Justice—'I do not think that it is in the discretion of counsel to insist upon arguing other points. Even if it were a matter within the discretion of counsel, I would still put it to him as a useless course, and therefore not a wise one.'

Fenn acquiesced in the inevitable, and said he would take a new trial without going any further.[24]

A week later, in *R. v. Foster*, Mr Justice Boothby was afforded an opportunity of declaring another statute of the local legislature to be invalid. In 1857, alarmed at the influx into South Australia of convicts from Western Australia, Parliament had passed the Convicts Prevention Act which made it a criminal offence for any transported convict to enter South Australia. A convict conditionally pardoned in Victoria—that is, portion of his sentence remitted on condition that he did not reside in Victoria—came to South Australia and was promptly arrested and charged under the Convicts Prevention Act. He applied to the Supreme Court by habeas corpus for his release. The Judges differed in opinion. Mr Justice Gwynne thought that there might be some doubt as to the validity of the Act:

Convicts
Like South Australia, Western Australia began life as a settlement without convicts but by 1849 labour shortages lead to it becoming a penal colony. Labour shortages or not, the great dread of convicts that existed in South Australia ensured that their arrival, legally or illegally, was always vehemently opposed.

> '... but seeing the consequences of the Court annulling that Act—seeing that this Colony might thereby be made a receptacle for the convictism of Swan River and other places—seeing the inevitable effect of such a decision upon the peace of the colony and the morals of its youth, I shrink from declaring the Act invalid upon mere doubt. If the prisoner chooses to take this matter before the Queen and Privy Council he can do so, but inasmuch as I found the Act had been administered for years when I came upon the Bench, although I entertain very great doubts upon the principle, I am not disposed to invalidate the Act upon mere doubt.'

Mr Justice Boothby was of opinion that the Act was invalid and that the prisoner was entitled to his discharge. The Act had been reserved for the Queen's pleasure on 30 November 1857. The *Government Gazette* of 29 July 1858 contained a proclamation by the Governor that on 18 April 1858 the Queen in Council assented to the Act, and it was proclaimed to be in force from and after 18 August 1858. The proclamation recited that it was issued under the Imperial Acts 5 & 6 Vic c.76 s.33 and 13 & 14 Vic c.59 s.12. By section 33 of the former Act, as amended by the latter, it was provided that:

> '... no Bill which shall be reserved for the signification of Her Majesty's pleasure thereon shall have any force or authority within the colony of South Australia until the Governor of the said colony shall signify either by speech or message to the Legislative Council of the said colony, or by Proclamation that such Bill has been laid before Her Majesty in Council, and that Her Majesty has been pleased to assent to the same; and that an entry shall be made in the journals of the said Legislative Council of every such speech message or Proclamation, and a duplicate thereof, duly attested, shall be delivered to the Registrar of the Supreme Court, or other proper officer, to be

> kept among the records of the said colony; and that no Bill which shall be so reserved as aforesaid shall have any force or authority in the said colony unless Her Majesty's assent thereto shall have been so signified as aforesaid within the space of two years from the day on which such Bill shall have been presented for Her Majesty's assent to the Governor as aforesaid.'

The proclamation, in Mr Justice Boothby's view, did not pursue the requirements of this section. It did not show the date at which the Bill had been presented to the Governor for Her Majesty's assent, and it did not say when the Bill had been passed, so that there was no information given by the proclamation whether or not that assent had been given within two years. Again the proclamation said that the Act should take effect from and after 18 August 1858, but section 12 of the Convicts Prevention Act itself said that it should take effect two months from and after its passing. The passing of the Act must be when all the statutory requirements were complete. But in that case the proclamation, if otherwise valid, allowed only twenty two days instead of two months. Owing to these fatal defects Mr Justice Boothby could not regard the proclamation as one meeting the statutory requirements, and he considered that the assent of Her Majesty had never been signified within two years as required. Another fatal blot was the failure to make any entry in the journals of the Legislative Council, or to send a copy of the proclamation to the Supreme Court. Further, the Judge said:

> 'I am of opinion that the Bill presented for Her Majesty's assent contained provisions requiring an enabling Act of the Imperial Parliament before a valid assent could be given by Her Majesty in Council. To create a crime made liable to three years' penal servitude and trial without Jury, grand or petty, before only two Justices of the Peace, is so repugnant to the fundamental principles of the law of England as applied to criminal procedure, that I am very clearly of opinion the Crown as one of the estates of the Parliament of this Province, is restricted from assenting to any such legislation by the provisions of the Imperial Statutes.'

This case gave the new Chief Justice his first chance to deliver a judgment of any importance on the vexed question of repugnancy. He examined "repugnancy" in some detail, admitting the difficulty of defining it accurately. He could not see any repugnancy in the Convicts Prevention Act. A strong argument in support of it, he thought, was the fact that South Australia's original constitution provided that it was not a place to which convicts should be transported, and unless it was competent for the local legislature to pass the Act, this exception might be violated. He was of opinion that it was equally competent for New South Wales or Victoria to pass such an act:

> '... on the ground that every state—and South Australia is a state, though dependent—has a right to protect itself against the influx from other countries of criminals still under sentence'.

As to the form of the proclamation, he had to admit that part of it was beyond the Governor's powers; but there remained a clear statement that the Queen had assented to the Act, and he could not believe that an informality in the proclamation completely invalidated the whole Act. Whether there was any entry in the journals of the Legislative Council, or any copy in the records of the Supreme Court, he neither knew nor cared. He would assume there were.

> 'I cannot assume that the validity of an Act passed by both branches of the Legislature, and assented to by Her Majesty, shall be dependent upon the mistake of a Clerk of the Legislature or the failure of an officer of this Court to perform his duty.'

In the result, the validity of the Convicts Prevention Act was upheld by the majority of the Court.[25]

Woodhouse at Stirling East was Richard Hanson's home from 1863 to 1876 – this photo by Sweet is ca. 1872. Hanson purchased the property from G.M. Stephen and extended it with the help of his architect brother William. The Boy Scouts Association have owned Woodhouse since 1957 and continue to operate it as an activity centre. (SLSA)

Chapter 5.4

Mr Justice Boothby

'one of the blackest spots'

During the early months of 1862 comparative quiet reigned in the Supreme Court. All parties were content to spar for time until they saw the result of the addresses for Mr Justice Boothby's removal. The Duke of Newcastle, upon receiving those addresses, had realised the importance of the constitutional and legal questions which they involved—"questions affecting the validity of many Colonial Acts hitherto considered to be in force, the powers of every legislature, and the independence of almost every Supreme Court in Australia"—and he had referred them to the law officers of the Crown for their opinion.

> 'On some of the questions, indeed'—he wrote—'I should not myself have supposed that any doubt could exist. But, as contrary opinions have in fact been expressed by authorities entitled to deference, I thought it advisable to include those questions in the reference both for completeness' sake, and in order that my own judgment might be fortified by the highest professional authority.' [1]

In the course of their investigations into the confusion of the Boothby question, the law officers of the Crown made the astounding discovery—quite as startling as the most advanced of Mr Justice Boothby's heretical opinions—that the whole of the legislation of the South Australian Parliament from 1856 on was wholly invalid and of no effect whatever. This extraordinary situation arose in consequence of the failure of the Governor to reserve the Electoral Act (No 10 of 1855-56), under which the elections for the first and subsequent Parliaments had been held. If the Electoral Act was of no effect because it should have been reserved, then there had never been any legal elections nor a properly elected Parliament.

When the Electoral Act had been passed, Mr Hanson (the then Advocate-General) had advised the Governor that it need not be reserved, and it had been assented to accordingly. Some years later, when the Boothby arguments had provoked a closer examination of the powers of the local legislature, doubts were expressed whether the Governor had power to assent to any measure altering electoral districts or the numbers of members allotted therein, because by 5 & 6 Vic c.76 s.31, such Bills were directed to be reserved. When an Electoral Act was passed in 1861, the Governor reserved it, and in forwarding it to England called attention to these doubts. He himself was confident that the provisions of section 31 applied only to the legislation of the old Legislative Council.

> 'In all cases in which reservation of such Bills is directed'—he wrote—'it is invariably in connection with the old Constitution

of one 'Council', when there were obvious reasons for such provision, independent of the necessity of guarding against any change in the proportion of nominee and elective members. On the other hand, it is observable that, when the 32nd section of the 13th and 14th Vict c.69 has declared that the Legislatures, on compliance with certain conditions, and on obtaining the full concurrence of the Crown, shall have power to resolve the old Councils into two Houses, the language of the Act immediately changes in reference to reservation of Bills, and simply adds a proviso (section 33) that the provisions of the 6th Vict, concerning Bills reserved, shall be applicable to all Bills reserved under the 13th and 14th Vict. The provision relating to Bills reserved, and intended by that 33rd section, apply to Bills under the suggested new Constitution when actually reserved by the Governor, and are evidently those which, under any form of constitution, would necessarily be applicable to all Bills when so treated, and are contained in the 33rd section of the 5th and 6th Vict (c.76), which prescribes certain rules as to the Governor's procedure in reference to proclaiming the Crown's assent to Bills reserved, and also defines the space within which that assent must be made known. I believe the compulsory reservation of such Bills to be so inapplicable to the present Constitutions of these Colonies, that I think it very improbable it could have been intended, and as I do not gather such intention directly from the Imperial Act, but rather the reverse, I would not probably have reserved the within Bill were it not for the 9th clause in my Instructions. That clause assumes, though erroneously as I think, that all provisions of the 5th and 6th Vict as to reserving Bills under an old and dissimilar Constitution are still in force; therefore whatever I may individually think, I feel bound to admit the correctness of that assumption and reserve the Bill.' [2]

But while the doubts reported by Sir Richard MacDonnell had relation only to the question whether the provisions for the reservation of certain classes of bills, mentioned in section 32 of 13 & 14 Vic c.59, was confined in its operation to the then existing Legislative Council, or whether it extended to laws passed by the Council and Assembly subsequently established, there were two further questions which attracted the attention of the authorities in England:

(1) Whether Electoral Acts passed by the Council and Assembly ought not to be reserved for the signification of the Queen's pleasure, in virtue of section 34 of the Constitution Act, No 2 of 1855-56, which provided that the local Parliament should

have full power and authority from time to time, by any Act, to repeal, alter or vary all or any of the provisions of the Constitution Act and substitute others in lieu thereof, subject to two provisos:

(a) that it should not be lawful to present to the Governor, for the Queen's assent, any bill by which an alteration in the constitution of the Legislative Council or House of Assembly was made, unless the second and third reading of such bill should have been passed with the concurrence of an absolute majority of the whole number of the members of the Legislative Council and Assembly respectively; and

(b) that every bill so passed should be reserved for the signification of the Queen's pleasure.

(2) Whether the Electoral Act No 10 of 1855-56, which provided for the election of the first Council and Assembly, and was passed not by those bodies but by the Legislative Council, ought not to have been reserved.[3]

The opinion of the law officers was that, while the Governor was correct in his view that the Imperial Statute was not intended to apply to Electoral Bills passed by the Council and Assembly, yet those Bills ought to be reserved by virtue of section 34 of the Constitution Act. The Electoral Act of 1855-56, however, having been passed by the old Legislative Council, should have been reserved under the provisions of the Imperial Acts, and they were clearly of opinion that the non-reservation of it had the effect of vitiating the Act, and with it of rendering the constitution of the legislature and all Acts passed by it absolutely invalid.[4]

> 'I have not lost a moment'—the Duke of Newcastle hastened to inform Governor Daly—'in applying to Parliament to relieve the colony of South Australia from the embarrassments into which it would have been plunged by the public adoption of this opinion, based as it appears to be on conclusive grounds.' [5]

The Imperial Act 15 & 16 (Vic c.XI) was accordingly hurriedly passed to provide that subsequent legislation of the South Australian Parliament should not be invalidated by the mere failure to reserve an Act which should have been reserved for the consideration of the Queen.

With respect to the addresses for the removal of Mr Justice Boothby, a list of questions was framed by Sir Frederick Rogers, then Under-Secretary for the colonies, and submitted to the law officers for their opinion. His questionnaire forms an admirable precis of the questions at issue and thoroughly justifies the high opinion of his ability expressed by Sir Henry Taylor, who wrote that the Under-Secretary had "a just and penetrating judgment, and a habit of searching out every question that is before him in its whole length and breadth, and yet dealing with it conclusively and succinctly".[6]

The most convenient method of dealing with the very important opinion given by the law officers (Sir William Atherton and Sir Roundell Palmer) in reply will be to summarise it in the form of question and answer:

Sir William Atherton (1806-1864)
A lawyer and liberal politician, Atherton was Attorney-General from 1861 to 1863.

(1) Q. Is the Supreme Court of South Australia bound, and at liberty to inquire into the validity of an Act passed by the colonial legislature, and assented to, either by the Queen in Council or by the Governor in behalf of Her Majesty; and in the case of an Act assented to by the Governor, does the fact that such an Act has or has not been left to its operation by Her Majesty make any difference respecting its validity?

A. 'The powers of the Colonial Legislature being conferred by Act of the Imperial Parliament, and limited by the same enactment, and so valid or invalid, as they keep within, or transgress the prescribed limits, the Supreme Court of South Australia is, in our opinion, bound (and certainly at liberty) to satisfy itself of the legal validity of any Act of the Colonial Legislature, the provisions of which it is called upon to administer. In the case of an Act assented to by the Governor, we think that the fact of its having been left to its operation by Her Majesty would not affect the question of its validity.'

Sir Roundell Palmer (1st Earl of Selborne) (1812-1895)
At the time of the Boothby questions Palmer was Solicitor General. He succeeded Atherton as Attorney-General and in 1872 became the Lord Chancellor. In this position he undertook the task of judicature reform resulting in the Judicature Act of 1873. This act brought far reaching and much needed reform to the British court system. The portrait is from a photograph taken by the London Stereoscopic Company, ca. 1870. (RVPL)

(2) Q. Supposing the Judge at liberty to pronounce on the validity of a Colonial Act, is he to pronounce such an Act invalid if its provisions be, in his opinion, inconsistent with those of an Imperial Statute, intended by the British Parliament to extend to the colonies in general, or to South Australia in particular?

A. 'We answer this question in the affirmative, as in the case supposed an unquestionable "repugnancy" would be apparent between the English Law and the Colonial enactment; and the Colonial Legislature is debarred from the enacting of laws being thus repugnant. (13th and 14th Vict c.59 s.14).'

(3) Q. Is he to pronounce such an Act invalid if its provisions be, in his opinion, contrary to the principles of British law, which he deems fundamental—as by denying the sovereignty of Her Majesty—by allowing slavery or polygamy—by prohibiting Christianity—by authorising the infliction of punishment without trial—or the uncontrolled destruction of Aborigines et cetera?

A. Yes; 'on the same ground of an unquestionable repugnancy'.

(4) Q. Is he to pronounce such an Act invalid if its provisions be different from those which are, in fact, prescribed in respect of the same matter by British statutes in force in England, though

not properly to be described as fundamental principles of British law, for example if the Colonial Act abolished grand juries, or allowed offences to be tried by a Magistrate for which a jury is required in England, or dispensed with the unanimity of a jury, or varied the numbers of a jury, or altered the laws of evidence, or the law of primogeniture, or introduced modes of transferring real property unknown to British law?

A. No: subject to the observations to the next question.

(5) Q. If the question 3 is to be answered in the affirmative, and question 4 in the negative, can any principle be suggested which would regulate the distinction between fundamental principles of which the violation would vitiate a Colonial Act, and the non-fundamental rules or customs of legislation which a colonial legislature is at liberty to disregard?

A. 'We are unable to lay down any rule to fix the dividing line between fundamental and non-fundamental rules of English law, as referred to in questions 3 and 4, and our answers thereto. It may safely, however, be stated, that no laws which do not rest upon principles equally applicable, in the nature of things, to all Her Majesty's Christian subjects in every part of the British dominions, can be deemed to be such as would make a departure from them, by a Colonial Legislature, void on the ground of repugnancy to the principle of English law. We may add, that we can hardly anticipate any practical difficulty in the way of the Court deciding the question of repugnancy, if called on so to do. It is extremely improbable that the Colonial Legislature would pass, that the Governor would sanction, and that the Crown would leave to its operation any Act repugnant to the above sense; and we think that the tribunals should not, under those circumstances, be astute to discover such repugnancy, but ought to disaffirm existing Acts, on this ground, only in cases admitting of no reasonable legal doubt. Such cases, we think, are not likely to occur.'

(6) Q. To what extent would a single provision—invalid on account of repugnancy to English law—vitiate the rest of the Act?

A. 'We think that in an Act containing various distinct and separable provisions, one of such provisions invalid on account of repugnancy, would not vitiate the other portions of the Act, which might be free from that defect.'

(7) Q. Would a Judge be at liberty to pronounce a Colonial Act invalid, though duly assented to by the Governor, on the ground that it fell within one of the classes to which he was forbidden to assent without urgent necessity?

A. No. The Governor's Instructions are a matter between the Crown and the Governor. The Governor alone can judge of the "urgent necessity".

(8) Q. Was there any reason to doubt the validity of the South Australian Constitution Act?

A. No.

(9) Q. Having special reference to the omission of any reference to South Australia in the 29th section of the Act 13 & 14 Vic c.59, was there any reason to doubt the power of the South Australian legislature to constitute courts of justice?

A. 'We understand that the express mention of New South Wales and Van Diemen's Land in the 29th section of the 13th and 14th Vict c.59, so far as relates to Courts of Justice, was, or may have been, considered to be rendered necessary by Imperial Legislation on the subject of the Courts of Justice of those colonies previous to the passing of that Act, and that no similar legislation had taken place with respect to Courts of Justice in South Australia. Under these circumstances, we see no reason to doubt the power of the South Australian Legislature to constitute Courts of Justice.'

(10) Q. Was there anything objectionable in Mr Boothby's view of his own obligation to conform his own judgment to the decisions of the Supreme Court of which he was a member?

A. 'We deem it to be the duty of a single Judge, in any particular case, generally speaking, to conform his own judgment to the decision, on the same point, of the Supreme Court of which he is a member. Such is the practice of single Judges in the United Kingdom; and a departure from it, unless under extraordinary circumstances, would, as it seems to us, be highly inconvenient.'

With regard to the Judge's removal, the following questions were put to the law officers:

(1) Has Her Majesty, under the 31st clause of the Constitution Act, the legal power to dismiss Mr Boothby on such addresses as were now presented to her by the two Houses of the South Australian legislature?
(2) Has she the legal power to refuse to dismiss Mr Boothby?
(3) If the Queen has a discretion in the matter, can Her Majesty be properly advised to dismiss Mr Boothby, in conformity with these addresses?
(4) If so, should removal be grounded upon the supposition that the Crown is bound to take for granted that the legislature has not acted without reason, and to lend its authority to give effect to their decision; or upon the merits of the case, as disclosed in Mr Boothby's reported judgment, in the evidence taken before

the Committees of the two Houses of the legislature, and in the reports of those Committees?

(5) If on the latter, what acts or opinions of Mr Boothby have necessitated or justified his removal?

(6) Will any appeal lie to the Privy Council, or Judicial Committee of Privy Council, against such decision?

(7) If Mr Boothby cannot properly be dismissed in conformity with the addresses now forwarded, is that refusal to be justified by the technical objection (if it be one) that two addresses have been presented instead of one; or by the absence of any specific charge in those addresses, or by the inadequacy of the charges which may be extracted from other sources?

(8) If the mode of procedure adopted by the legislature is irregular or insufficient, what course of procedure or mode of address ought to be adopted by them in order to bring the question of Mr Boothby's dismissal properly under Her Majesty's cognisance? and:

(9) What course of proceedings would be, or has ever been adopted in order to procure the removal of an English Judge, under the second clause of the Act 22 Geo III c.75?

Their reply was as follows:

'We have to observe, that, although Mr Boothby has in some instances, as it appears to us, mistaken the law (as, for example, with reference to the Real Property Act, which we think not invalid, on the ground on which he rests its invalidity, of the Governor's assent being contrary to the Royal Instructions) yet, in some other respects, he has been right; and the fault has been with the Governor, in not reserving Acts for the Royal assent which were expressly required by Statute to be so reserved. Moreover, the Houses of Parliament in the Addresses by which Her Majesty is prayed to remove the Judge were not, in strictness, when they so addressed the Crown, a lawful Parliament, although they either have been, or shortly will be, legalized as from the beginning; and, under these circumstances, we think that the Crown would not be well advised to accede to the Addresses.

We see no objection to a separate address to this effect being presented by each House, or to the absence on the face of such Address of a statement of specific charges, provided that the Crown is by any means satisfied of the reasons on which the Address is founded. We think that the Crown is invested always with a discretion as to compliance or non-compliance with such an Address. But we entertain no doubt that the Crown might properly remove a Judge on the address of both Houses, if satisfied that owing to his perversity or

> habitual disregard of judicial propriety, the administration of justice might be practically obstructed by his continuance in office. No appeal to the Privy Council or any other Court or tribunal, would lie against such a removal of a Judge by the Crown.
>
> No instance of the removal of an English Judge by the Crown on the Address of both Houses of Parliament has occurred since the passing of the 22 Geo III c.75.' [7]

The last statement in this opinion was not correct (see Todd's *Parliamentary Government in England*, 2nd edition, volume II, p.908), but otherwise the questions and answers form an admirable resume of the legal difficulties raised by Mr Justice Boothby.

Acting upon these opinions, the Secretary of State refused to recommend that Mr Justice Boothby should be removed in compliance with the prayer of the addresses.

> 'I think it advisable, however'—the Duke of Newcastle informed the Governor—'to take this opportunity of defining the position which I conceive the Sovereign to occupy in respect to this matter. I hold the practical independence of the Supreme Courts of a Colony to be, with the appointment of the Governor, the right of exercising a veto upon Colonial enactments, and the right of appeal to Her Majesty in Council, among the links which bind together the Colonial Empire of Great Britain. It is of vital importance, not only to the Colonies but to all those who have dealings with them, of whatever kind, and to the Imperial Government itself, that these Courts should exercise their functions in entire independence, not only of the local Executive, but of the popular feelings which are from time to time reflected in the Legislature, or of any political party which may happen to be in the ascendant. And I consider that the principal guarantee of this independence is to be found in the assurance that a Judge once appointed will not be displaced without the reasonable concurrence of an authority wholly removed from all local or temporary influences. By the existing law of South Australia, I consider such an authority to be entrusted, and very properly entrusted, to Her Majesty acting on the advice of Her Ministers in Great Britain; and I hold that, in dismissing a Judge in compliance with addresses from a local Legislature, and in conformity with that law, the Queen is not performing a mere Ministerial Act, but adopting a grave responsibility which Her Majesty cannot be advised to incur without satisfactory evidence that the dismissal is proper. On the other hand, I am far from denying that, in estimating such evidence, great deference is due to the

> judgment of the two branches of a Colonial Legislature, expressed after full inquiry and debate, in the course of which full opportunity for defence has been given to the Judge inculpated. I concur in the opinion of the Law Officers, that Her Majesty might properly be advised to "remove a Judge on the Address of both Houses of the South Australian Parliament, if satisfied that, owing to his perversity, or habitual disregard of judicial propriety, the administration of justice might be practically obstructed by his continuance in office"; and I am not prepared to deny that sufficient proof of such perversity might be afforded by his inflexible enforcement of opinions which are inconsistent with the beneficial performance of his duties, and which, after mature deliberation, the other Members of the Court of which he is a Member, the Legislature of the Colony in which he exercises his functions, and the ordinary advisers of Her Majesty's Government in this country, deem to be incorrect in point of law.' [8]

The news that the Judge was not to be removed reached the colony in June 1862, and was received with mixed feelings; but the publication of the report of the law officers gave rise to hopes that Mr Justice Boothby would make peace with honour, and gracefully bow to the views of the Secretary of State. A very favourable impression was manifest, wrote the Governor; and he had hopes that the Colonial Office would not again be troubled on the subject.

> 'Your Grace will not fail to understand'—he cautiously added—'that I of course presume that Judge Boothby has sufficient sagacity to avail himself of this opportunity, which I believe there are very few who are not well pleased is afforded to him, to withdraw from the position he has assumed and to work harmoniously with his colleagues. In justice to Mr Boothby, I may further add that I am not aware there has been anything questionable in that gentleman's judicial conduct since my assumption of this Government. I have more than once assured him that any influence I may possess shall be cheerfully directed to consigning past differences to oblivion, if he will only permit me to do so, by avoiding for the future the causes of those controversies in which he has unhappily been so long engaged. Up to the arrival of the last mail, on which day I last saw him, he adhered to his opinion in regard to his right to the position and salary of First Judge of the Supreme Court.' [9]

Mr Justice Boothby had, indeed, but a poor opinion of the opinions delivered by the law officers of the Crown.

> 'I was for years'—he said—'as a law student in the chambers of the late Lord Truro, when he was Sir Thomas Wilde, and during all the time he was Attorney General—than whom no law officer of the Crown ever devoted more of learning and ability to the duties of his office; I saw how those opinions are asked and prepared. When a question arises, the Counsel to the Colonial Office first considers it, and he decides whether it is worth while to send it to the Attorney and Solicitor General. Both these distinguished men are so engrossed by the business of their private clients, and the numerous and various public duties they have to perform, that they have not time to go into these things, so it is vain and preposterous for any in this province to suppose that such opinions are offered as being more than advice of what the law is supposed to be, or anything more than opinions formed without the responsibility of judicial decision.' [10]

At this stage of the Boothby question it may be said that the honours were equal. The anti-Boothbyites had succeeded in obtaining a declaration from England that some of the most unpopular views of the Judge were wrong; but on the other hand, the Judge himself was seated on the bench as firmly as ever and his right to examine into the validity of local legislation had been conclusively established. Those members of Parliament who had voted against the Judge's removal were cock-a-hoop, and could not resist taunting their opponents.

> 'I am sure'—Mr Duffield told the Assembly—'that our children and our children's children will regard that era as one of the blackest spots in the history of South Australia; but I remember with pride that there were fourteen men in the colony who will be ensured in after ages the fame they deserve for having stood up, against the will of the majority, against the opposition of the Press, and of White's rooms assemblages, to defend and maintain order and peace, and uphold the Bench. And if they have one thing to be proud of more than another, it is that, although the Senate of the Colony rejected the views of that minority, the British Parliament had carried the very resolution they proposed in this House, and they have a right to take some credit to themselves for the course they pursued, and the position it had resulted in placing the colony in. (Hear, hear). For if it had not been for that stand, the Parliament of South Australia, at this moment, would have had no legal

existence any more than it had had previously. (Oh!) It will be a brighter line in the history of the colony which will record the action of that minority than that which will tell how a Ministry was appointed under the Constitution of the land for the sole purpose of removing a Judge from his position—without—but perhaps I had better say no more on the subject. (Hear, hear).' [11]

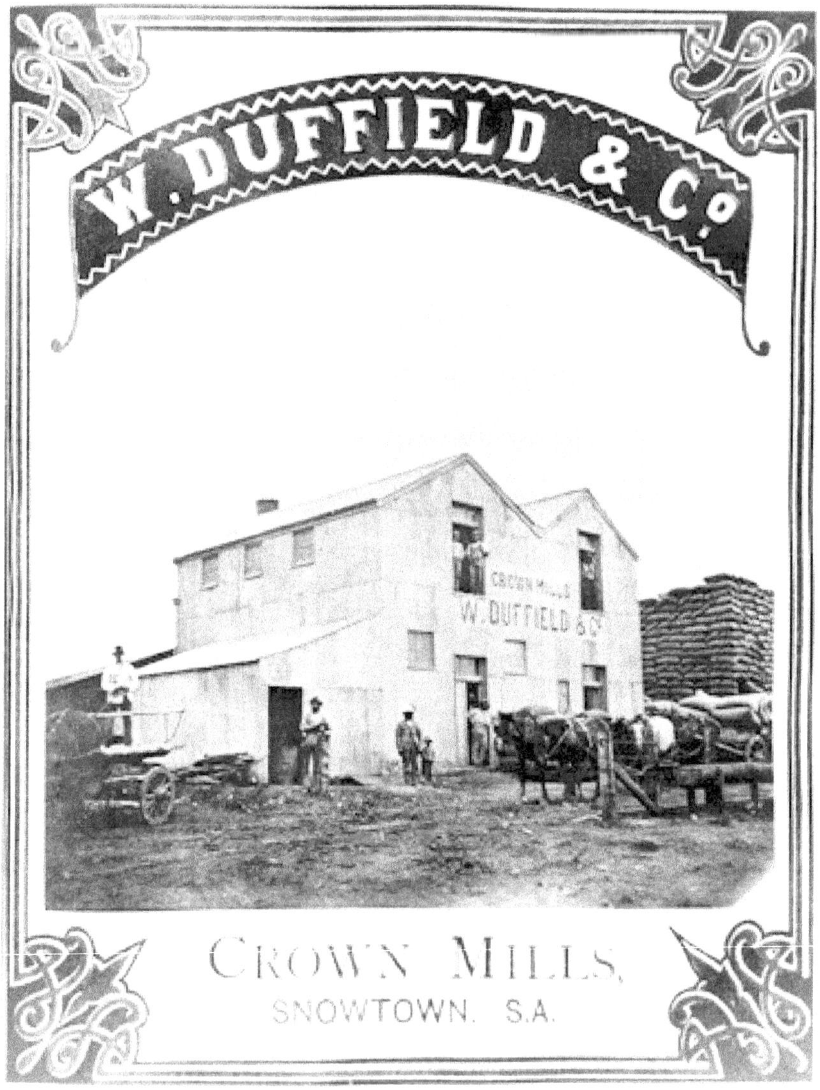

Walter Duffield (1816-1882) Duffield may have been a poor judge of history but his business acumen could not be questioned. Beginning as a tenant farmer at Echunga in 1839 his interests expanded to include flour mills at Gawler, Wallaroo, Snowtown and Port Pirie and pastoral lands across the colony. He was a Member of the House of Assembly (1857-68 and 1870-71) and a Member of the Legislative Council (1873-80). The picture of his mill at Snowtown is one in a series of his mills. (SLSA)

Henry Clinton, 5th Duke of Newcastle, an 1848 portrait by Frederick Say. (NPG)

Chapter 5.5

Mr Justice Boothby

'grave questions'

Meanwhile Mr Justice Boothby had been leisurely preparing that petition, which, as he had intimated to the Duke of Newcastle in 1861, he proposed to present to the Queen against the appointment of Mr Hanson as Chief Justice. He laboured at it for a year. In its final form, as signed by him in November 1862, it was a voluminous document of fifty-three paragraphs, containing some ten thousand words.

After reciting the scene which took place when Mr Hanson presented his Commission as Chief Justice, the petitioner complained that by the determination of the several questions in the manner set forth in the Master's entry:

> 'Your Majesty's Royal Prerogative is invaded, the administration of justice denied, impeded, and endangered, and Your Petitioner aggrieved and deprived of his just and legal rights, his rank and precedence in the Court, and the emoluments of his office, secured to him by law.'

His grounds of objection were as plentiful as blackberries and they form a curious and ingenious medley. Briefly, the more important were:

(1) The form of the instrument appointing Mr Hanson was not supported by any precedent.

> 'A Judge's Commission of any Supreme Court is always by Letters Patent, the form of which is established by precedent ... The Governor and Executive Council of the Province have no authority to appoint a Judge by an instrument unknown to the law, and any new form of appointment can only be created by legislative authority.'

(2) The Imperial Act 22 Geo III c.75 was disregarded by the omission of any clause binding Mr Hanson to reside in the colony.

(3) The Constitution Act was invalid.

(4) If the Constitution Act was valid, the words of section 29 of that Act, vesting the appointment "to all public offices under the Government" in the Governor and Executive Council, could not be construed to include the office of Judge of the Supreme Court.

> 'A Judge of Your Majesty's Supreme Court is not an officer under the Government of this Province, but a representative of Your Majesty in the administration of justice in Your Majesty's Courts of Law, whose decisions are subject to be

reviewed only by Your Majesty in Council ... The section cannot be construed to take away, in the absence of express words, Your Majesty's undoubted prerogative of appointing the Judges of the Supreme Court ... Moreover, such Act does not contain any words conferring the power of appointment, and the mode of its exercise, by any and what form of instrument; and such omissions, Your Petitioner submits, cannot be supplied without legislative authority.'

(5) The opposite construction of the clause would be in effect to repeal the provision of 22 Geo III c.75 passed to regulate the granting of patent offices in colonies, which by section 3 authorised the Governor and Council of any colony to appoint to any vacancy in any patent office, occasioned by death or amotion until the King's pleasure be known.

'The Council mentioned is the Council of any Colony as known to the law at the date of such Statute, all the members of which were appointed by the Royal Prerogative, and cannot be held to include an Executive Council in which members sit, ex officio, as the holders of certain offices under the provisions of the Constitution Act of this Province, No 2 1855-6, section 2, such Act never having received the sanction of the Imperial Parliament.'

(6) That by Ordinance 5 of 1837 the appointment of judges was vested in the Crown, and that this Ordinance had in legal effect the authority of an Imperial Statute, being confirmed by 5 & 6 Vic c.61 s.2, and its provisions therefore not being capable of repeal by a provincial statute.

(7) By Ordinance No 12 of 1849, which made provision for a second Judge, it was enacted that the Supreme Court should be held before one or more Judges to be appointed by Her Majesty.

(8) 'That by a supposed Ordinance, No 31, 1855-6, the then Legislative Council assumed to create the title of Chief Justice of the Supreme Court; but such Ordinance Your Petitioner submits is a nullity, having no words to denote by what authority its provisions are enacted, the usual and necessary words after 'Be it therefore enacted' by the Governor-in-Chief of the Province of South Australia with the advice and consent of the Legislative Council being altogether omitted from such Ordinance.'

(9) That the supposed Ordinance No 31 of 1855-6 was invalid:

'... from assuming a power in the then Legislative Council of the Province, with only the assent of the Governor-in-Chief, to take away Your Majesty's undoubted prerogative to appoint the Judges of the Supreme Court of this Province, with the advice of the Secretary of State for the Colonies, and substituting the appointment by the Governor, with the advice of the Executive Council of the Province, practically limited by section 32 of the Constitution Act to ex officio members, elected to the present Provincial Parliament by popular election, so making the appointment of Judges of Your Majesty's Supreme Court but slightly removed from the direct action of election by universal suffrage'.

(10) The Ordinance spoke only of the *title* of Chief Justice.

'The office of Chief Justice is no where provided for by any charter or statute, and such title is given by the assumed Ordinance to the then Senior Judge, by his name Charles Cooper, Esquire; and Your Majesty's petitioner is by name mentioned as the only other Judge of the Court. And, if such Ordinance could be construed as valid, Your petitioner submits that, as one of the two Judges named therein, the provision of section 1—that one of the Judges of the Supreme Court shall have the title of Chief Justice, and that Charles Cooper, Esquire, should be the first Chief Justice—did, by necessary construction give to your petitioner an incohate [sic] right to the title of Chief Justice, had Charles Cooper, Esquire, died the next day after receiving such title.'

(11) That as the supposed Ordinance had no force, the title of Chief Justice did not, and never had, lawfully existed. The Judges were equal in powers and functions; and the question of precedence and headship of the Court was to be determined by the priority of each Judge's appointment. The title of Chief Justice, if lawfully conferred, would only be another name for Senior Judge—denoting that, as such, he was primus inter pares.

(12) That no charter, ordinance, act, or any authority was to be found for the existence, even in name, of the office of "First Judge and Chief Justice", as described in the Commission laid before the Court by Mr Hanson.

(13) That the office of "First Judge" was not mentioned in any act, ordinance or charter. The terms First Judge and Second Judge were to be found only in the schedule to Ordinance No 3 of 1851, providing for the salaries to be paid to each of the two Judges, and providing a higher salary for the then Senior Judge. The necessary constructions of "First Judge" was that it was synonymous with Senior Judge; and Second Judge

denoted the Judge next in seniority to the first. No salary was anywhere provided for a Chief Justice.

(14) That the Letters Patent and Commission under which he had been appointed conferred on him all the rights, profits, privileges and advantages belonging and pertaining to his office, and:

> '... one of such rights, profits, and advantages was his right to become, by force of seniority and as a legal incident of his appointment, the First or Senior Judge, along with the accompanying right to the higher salary'.

(15) That the headship of the Supreme Courts in the other Australian colonies had always been arrived at by seniority. And he had accepted his position, under the expectation, grounded on a knowledge of this fact, that succession to the headship of the Court was one of the rights and advantages incident to his office, and guaranteed to him by his patent.

(16) That by custom and usage the exercise of the Royal Prerogative in the appointment of Judges of the Supreme Courts of colonies had been restricted to barristers of England or Ireland, and members of the Faculty of Advocates of Scotland.

> 'Such rule is never departed from unless in a case of temporary necessity, to which every rule of law must yield, and until the circumstances which created such necessity have passed away.'

Mr Hanson was only an attorney, admitted as a practitioner of the South Australian Supreme Court. "The local right of audience conferred on the attorneys of the Supreme Court of this Province cannot bring with it a qualification for the office of Judge."

(17) 'Grave questions of public policy, affecting the security of and prosperity of Your Majesty's Colonial Empire are necessary to be considered in ascertaining and determining the legal qualifications and lawful appointment of Judges, inasmuch as the due administration of justice in any Colony cannot be viewed as a matter of merely local concern; and because the practical independence of the Supreme Court of a Colony, together with the appointment of the Governor, the right of exercising a veto upon Colonial enactments, and the right of appeal to Your Majesty in Council, are the links which bind together Your Majesty's Colonial Empire.'

(18) Further, he submitted:

> 'It is of vital importance, not only to the Colonies but to all who have dealings with them of whatever kind, and to Your Majesty's Imperial Government itself, that all Judges of the

Supreme Courts should exercise their functions in entire independence, not only of the local executive but of the popular feelings from time to time reflected in the Legislature, or of any party which may happen to be in the ascendant.'

If Judges could be lawfully appointed by the Governor with the advice of his Executive Council only, it would be, in effect, to elect Judges by popular voice through the medium of universal suffrage. To give the nomination of all Judges to the Ministry of the day would be an innovation which ought not to be permitted.

'Political and party objects in such appointments in a limited community must always prevail. Election to Parliament would become a necessary stepping-stone to judicial appointment. Political friends and opponents would unite in approval of an appointment as Judge, which removed from one party a leader whose influence excited at once the jealousy of his followers and the fears of his opponents.'

The Attorney-General of the day would be able to demand his own elevation to the bench, or that of some political or professional rival or friend, and the Governor would be impotent to resist.

'If the promotion of a Judge to the headship of the Court is declared to be a subject for local executive interference, irrespective of seniority, the independence of the Judges must be endangered, and become practically a mockery. The Judges, under such circumstances, must listen to arguments at the Bar on constitutional questions, arising between the Crown and the people; from the lips of an Attorney-General, having the power of a Cabinet Minister; and who, on leaving the Court, might do so to join an Executive Council, assembled to decide on the promotion to higher rank in judicial office of one among the Judges to whom, in the previous hour he had addressed his arguments in behalf of the Crown. The anomaly of one attorney filling the office of Attorney General, advising the appointment of another attorney to the office of Judge of the Supreme Court, necessarily presents the temptation to regard professional and political interest in such advice. Your petitioner does not suggest that such motives actuated the Attorney General as one of the Executive Council which advised the Governor in the appointment of Mr Hanson, but the fact exists that the Attorney General ex officio, a member of the Executive Council, who advised the appointment, was then by twenty years the junior in age, and by many years also a junior in practice, to Mr Hanson as an attorney of the Supreme Court; and by such appointment one of the attorneys in largest practice was removed from the Court, and a leading member of a political party from the House of Assembly.'

(19) That Mr Hanson was not entitled to give a voice in the determination of the validity of the instrument appointing him Chief Justice.

(20) That Mr Gwynne, who took part in the determination, was gazetted a Judge in 1859, and had acted as such Judge from that time: "... but by what form of instrument, or whether by any, Your petitioner has no knowledge". His objection to Mr Hanson applied equally to Mr Gwynne who also was only an attorney; and Gwynne likewise had no right to be on the bench.

His petition, Mr Justice Boothby concluded, raised such grave questions of constitutional and public law, necessary to be decided for the safe and secure administration of justice, that he confidently relied upon them being decided without "onerous cost" to him. He prayed that the instrument by which Mr Hanson claimed to act and preside as Chief Justice should be declared null and void, as being unjust and contrary to law.[1]

This extraordinary document was duly forwarded to the Secretary of State by the Governor, with the comment:

> 'It is scarcely necessary I should observe, what must have been long apparent to Your Grace, that the State of feeling upon the Bench of this Colony, which is but too well known to the whole community, is calculated to destroy those sentiments of respect and confidence with which the administration of justice ought to be regarded, and that it is very desirable that questions like those raised in the accompanying Petition should be set at rest as speedily as possible.' [2]

Edward Cardwell (Viscount Cardwell) (1813-1886)
Cardwell succeeded Newcastle as Secretary of State in 1864 and served in that role until 1866. As Secretary of War (1868-74) he performed his most noted work bringing about the reform of the British army including the abolition of the purchase of commissions, shortened terms of service and the creation of a reserve. (NPG)

In due course the appeal was referred to the Privy Council for hearing, and Mr Justice Boothby advised that he must proceed in the matter like any other appellant. Months went by and the Judge did nothing, for the very good reason that he did not intend to spend any money on the appeal. As had been said long before, in *Hudibras*:

> 'Lawyers have more sober sense
> Than t'argue at their own expense'.

Later, in December 1864, the Judge forwarded a long submission to the Secretary of State, praying that his appeal might be determined without cost to himself on the ground that the questions raised by his petition were of vast public importance.

> 'I very humbly submit that in the strict fulfilment of my office as Judge, I have directed the attention of Her Majesty's

> Government to serious legislative errors by the Parliament of this Province ... I hope I may be excused urging the extreme importance of the subject matter of this communication, now before the Colonial Office for three years. If my view of the law is correct, the result of the delay deprives me of salary to the amount of two hundred pounds per annum; a total arrear has now accrued of six hundred pounds. What is worse to bear, however, is the sense of an injustice done in the deprivation of a legal right to the headship of the Court in which I have held her Majesty's Commission as Judge for twelve years.' [3]

The Secretary of State shortly replied that he could not see any reason why the Imperial Treasury should pay for the appeal, and if the Judge still desired to pursue his complaint, he must do it at his own expense.[4] The appeal therefore lay dormant; but thenceforth the Judge spared no effort to induce some litigant to take a case to the Privy Council, involving the points which he had raised. As was subsequently said by Mr Way:

> 'Any apathy on His Honor's part in prosecuting his appeal at his own expense has been amply compensated by his endeavours—making use of his judicial position for the purpose—to get the question litigated between private suitors.' [5]

Boothby's seventh child Joshua (1837-1916) distinguished himself as the government statist, in particular on census work. Unfortunately he was forced to resign in 1880 over unauthorised personal expenses drawn while he was at the Paris Exhibition. He returned to the civil service in 1891 but without the esteem he once enjoyed. (SLSA)

Chapter 5.6

Mr Justice Boothby

'A most horrible stew'

For a few months there was a tacit truce. Mr Justice Boothby was the first to break the suave harmony of things and was early in the field for the next campaign. It opened with preliminary skirmishing between the Governor and the Judge. In accordance with the view of the majority of the Judges, the Government had decided that the time had arrived for circuit courts in the South East. Mr Justice Boothby loudly protested that the Act empowering the holding of circuit courts was of doubtful validity, and declared that any such court would be illegal.[1]

He next annoyed the Governor by styling himself "Senior Judge", an innovation which elicited a sharp rebuke from Sir Dominick Daly, who wrote that he was prepared to recognise the Judge's position as Second Judge of the Supreme Court, but saw no reason whatever for the assumption of the title of Senior Judge, "an official designation unknown to the law of the Province".[2]

The serious renewal of hostilities, however, was provoked by the inquisitiveness of Sir J.H. Fisher, the President of the Legislative Council, who apparently had not changed from the days when Sir John Jeffcott described him as a hair-splitter. When Sir Dominick Daly was appointed Governor, Sir James originated a rumour that the Acts of the incumbent Governor ceased to be valid upon the appointment of his successor, although it would necessarily be several months before that successor could arrive in the colony. This disquieting problem was duly reported to the Colonial Office, and a reply was received citing 9 & 10 Vic c.91—"An Act to continue Patent Commissioners until the exhibition of the Commissions revoking them"—as a sufficient answer.[3] The Secretary of State seems to have been not quite so confident as he pretended, for he proceeded to apply to the Imperial Parliament to place the matter beyond doubt. The Act 26 & 27 Vic c.76, therefore, after reciting that doubts were entertained respecting the period at which letters patent took effect within colonies and possessions beyond the seas, enacted that no existing letters patent should be deemed to have taken effect in any colony until they were there publicly made known or acted upon, and that no future letters patent should take effect until the making of them had been signified in the colony by proclamation or other public notice.

Not content with thus troubling the Governor and the Colonial Office, Sir James pursued his inquiries, and made the interesting discovery that the Electoral Act of 1861 was invalid—as invalid as that of 1855-56 had been—and with it all the subsequent legislation of the local Parliament. Officiously he communicated his find to the dismayed Governor, who tartly reported to the Secretary of State that Fisher was "one of those gentlemen who are said to devote much time and research to the discovery of defects in legislation".[4] Governor Daly's asperity may be pardoned. No sooner had the Imperial Parliament relieved the colony from the frightful potential consequences of six years of invalid legislation, following the failure to reserve the Electoral Act of 1855-56, than up bobbed Sir James Fisher and proclaimed to the world that the Electoral Act of 1861 was also bad, and all acts passed since 1861 of no effect. "Shall we come out of it all," the Governor doubtless asked himself, "some day, as one does from a tunnel?"

The grounds of Fisher's opinion were that the Electoral Act of 1861 was an act which altered the constitution of Parliament, because it varied certain electoral districts and altered the number of members returnable for some of them. It therefore fell within the provisions of section 34 of the Constitution Act; and accordingly the Bill should have been:

(1) passed on the second and third hearings by an absolute majority in each house; and
(2) reserved for the Queen's assent.

It had been reserved and assented to by the Queen, that assent being given on the assumption that the Act would not have been reserved and forwarded for assent unless it had been properly passed. But in fact it had not been passed by an absolute majority of each house.

Sir James Hurtle Fisher, by Simon Calvert 1875. (SLV)

'It seems clear, therefore'—said Fisher—'that it must be invalid and void, as, under the section referred to, it was not

> lawful to present the Act to Sir R.G. McDonnell for Her Majesty's assent; and, therefore, he had no authority to receive it for reservation, much less to reserve it—in fact, there was nothing to reserve; and, consequently, there would be no Act which could be properly submitted for Her Majesty's assent, or to which Her Majesty could assent with any effect. This matter is one of vast importance, as, of course, if the Electoral Act is invalid, all the elections which have recently taken place, and those in progress under it, will be equally so; and, as our Parliament is now dissolved, it would, I imagine, be necessary to apply for an Act of the Imperial Parliament to supply a remedy; unless it should be feasible, and considered more desirable, to have fresh elections under the Acts which that in question professes to repeal, and which would, of course, be still in force if that is invalid.' [5]

At the same time as Sir James Fisher was expounding to the Governor his discovery about the Electoral Act, a similar point with regard to another act was being put to a practical test before the Full Court in the case of *Driffield v. Torrens*, which was heard in November and December 1862. In a laudable attempt to put an end to the dual system of land registration which had existed in the colony since 1857—under the Registration of Deeds Act and under the Real Property Act—Parliament in October 1862 passed an Act (No 27 of 1862) repealing the Registration of Deeds Act abolishing the General Registry Office, and providing that all future registrations of dealings with land must be made in accordance with the provisions of the Real Property Act. The legal advisers of Mr Driffield told him that the Act was invalid, and he applied to the Court for a mandamus to compel the Registrar-General to register a deed of conveyance under the Registration Act No 8 of 1841. The Registrar-General, who had closed the General Registry Office, stoutly refused to register except under the Real Property Act.

The argument that the Deeds Registration Act of 1862 was invalid was an ingenious one. It rested upon the contention that the Deeds Registration Act was an amendment of the Constitution Act. This result was arrived at in a roundabout way. Section 6 of the Constitution Act prescribed the qualifications of electors for the Legislative Council; and, inter alia, any adult male, having a leasehold estate in possession, situate within the province, of the clear annual value of £20, "the lease thereof having been registered in the General Registry Office for the registration of deeds", was declared to be entitled to vote at the election of members for the Council. Registration of the lease was essential to give the leaseholder a right to vote. But if the General Registry Office was abolished, then no leaseholder could register his lease there, and a class of persons was thereby prevented from voting. This, it was said, was an alteration in the constitution of the Legislative Council, within section 34 of the Constitution Act; and therefore the Deeds Registration Act should have been passed by an absolute majority in each House and reserved for the royal assent—formalities which had not been complied with.

This argument found favour in the eyes of both Mr Justice Boothby and Mr Justice Gwynne, the Chief Justice dissenting; and the Deeds Registration Act No 27 of 1862 was pronounced invalid.

Mr Justice Gwynne said it was clear that the provision as to registration in the Constitution Act meant registration in the General Registry Office, which had then been in operation for many years, and that registration under the provisions of the Real Property Act was not an equivalent. It was Act No 8 of 1841 that the legislature had in view when the Constitution Act was passed, and they intended that the lease, in order to confer political rights, should be registered under the provisions of that act.

> 'This view is confirmed by the course of practice from the passing of the Constitution Act up to the present time. I never till now heard it questioned that registration of a lease under the provisions of 5 Vict No 8 was not a compliance with the requirements of the Constitution Act, or that any other mode of registration would satisfy that requirement, or even was possible. Then comes the Act upon which the question is raised, namely, the Act of the last session No 27. This Act repeals No 8 of 5 Vict, and consequently sweeps away the whole system of registration established by it. And it not only does not provide any substituted means by which a lease of land can be registered, but studiously provides that instruments relating to chattels real (which leases are) or freehold estate shall not be registered under its provisions. It appears, therefore, to me, that the Act No 27 of 1862, if upheld, would have the effect of depriving all leaseholders, who acquired their leases after it came into operation, and others, of their right of voting at the election of members of the Legislative Council, by reason that such leases could not be registered, as required by the Constitution Act.'

Mr Justice Gwynne had no doubt that this was an alteration of the Constitution Act which required the due performance of the formalities prescribed by section 34 of that Act; and he threw out in addition the suggestion that section 34 might be ultra vires and invalid. The reasoning which led him to this last opinion may be summarised as follows:

(1) The Act 5 & 6 Vic c.76 gave the then Legislative Council power to make laws for the peace, welfare and good

government of the colony, but the Council had no power to alter the qualification either of the elective members or of the electors.

(2) It was contended that the South Australian legislature acquired this right of altering the qualification of electors by the effect of section 32 of 13 & 14 Vic c.59, which gave power to the Governor and Legislative Council:

> '... from time to time, by any Act or Acts, to alter the provisions or laws for the time being in force ... concerning the election of the elective members of such Legislative Council, the qualification of electors and elective members, or to establish ... instead of the Legislative Council, a Council and a House of Representatives, or other separate Legislative Houses, to consist of such members to be appointed or elected respectively by such persons and in such manner as by such Act or Acts shall be determined, and to vest in such Council or House of Representatives or other separate Legislative Houses the powers and functions of the Legislative Council for which the same may be substituted'.

(3) But the only power of altering the qualification of electors given by this section was given to the old Legislative Council, and was exercisable over the old mixed Council only: the qualification to be altered was the qualification of the elective members of the mixed Council; and the power of alteration, being peculiar to that Council, had passed away with it.

(4) It was doubtful, therefore, whether the mixed Council which passed the Constitution Act had the power to vest in the legislature thereby created the power or function of altering from time to time the qualification of the electors of the present Legislative Council.

Mr Justice Boothby cordially agreed that the Deeds Registration Act was invalid as an attempt to alter the constitution of the Legislative Council without complying with the provisions of section 34 of the Constitution Act.

> 'There exist grounds for very grave doubt'—he added—'whether the repeal of the Registration Act of 1841 can be made by any statutory authority but that of the Imperial Parliament, inasmuch as it received the confirmation of the Imperial Act 5 & 6 Vict c.61 s.2 and as such, I am of opinion, is in legal effect of the same force as an Imperial Statute made expressly applicable to this Province.'

He hinted that the Constitution Act itself was invalid, and concluded his judgment by urging that the case should be taken to the Privy Council, to obtain "a definitive declaration of the law".

The Chief Justice completely dissented from the opinion of the majority. He could not see that the Deeds Registration Act affected the Constitution Act and even if it did, he was not prepared to admit it was invalid. He took the opportunity to refute from the bench the "prevalent idea" that: "... in entertaining the question of repugnancy this Court is assuming novel functions instead of applying well-known principles of English jurisprudence".[6]

But he also added to the confusion by putting forward the view that the restrictions purported to be imposed by section 34 of the Constitution Act were quite inoperative.

> 'It is not pretended'—he said—'and, so far as I am aware, there is no pretence for saying, that any power was conferred upon the old Legislative Council, established by authority of the Act 13 and 14 Vic c.59, to limit the exercise of the powers of the new Legislature which they were empowered to establish.'

The judgment in *Driffield v. Torrens* aroused a fresh outburst of popular fury. The attack on the Deeds Registration Act was attributed to the malice of those lawyers who had opposed the Real Property Act, to which the later Act was an adjunct.

> 'The decision must be set aside'—said the Register—'because it is an outrage on common sense to say that the new law does in any way amend the Constitution Act. Let the case be taken to the Court of Appeals at once to be reversed; if necessary let it be taken to the Privy Council to settle the matter; and let the Imperial Parliament legislate once and for all to get rid of the difficulties continually arising between the legislature and the bench.'[7]

The Governor called upon the Attorney-General (Mr Randolph Stow) to furnish a report upon the objections made by Sir James Fisher, and upon the case of *Driffield v. Torrens*. Mr Stow pointed out that, assuming an absolute majority of members was necessary to pass the Electoral Act or the Deeds Registration Act, there might be difficulties in proving on any legal investigation whether or not a majority was present. On referring to the journals of Parliament, he found that no record was kept of the number of members present when the Acts were passed.

> 'Assuming that, on an inquiry into the validity of an enactment actually passed, presented for assent, and assented to, a Court would receive the records of the Legislature as evidence of the non-concurrence of the required number of members, I cannot conceive that any tribunal would look beyond those records, or regard evidence which either contradicted the records or proved facts upon which they were silent—a course of procedure which would render the rights, the fortunes, the

liberties, and even the lives of the Queen's subjects, dependent in many cases upon the memory or honesty of persons present on the occasion, who might depose to the exact number of persons who were in the House at the particular moment at which the reading of a Bill took place. It is the duty of the Houses to present to the Governor such Bills only as are rightly passed; and his duty to refuse for assent any Bill not passed according to law is equally clear. The Electoral Act 1861 was presented to the Governor for the Queen's assent, was reserved for and received that assent; and, on the principle that everything which the law requires to be done will be presumed to have been rightly done until the contrary is proved, it would, I apprehend, be presumed that the Electoral Act was properly presented and reserved for assent, in the absence of proof to the contrary; and principles of public policy and convenience would seem to dictate that, when the records of Parliament are silent as to the performance of anything necessary by law to the validity of any Act which has passed the Parliament, the presumption that the necessary preliminaries have been performed is incontrovertible; and, consequently, it would be incompetent on any trial in which the validity of the Electoral Act may be questioned, to give extrinsic evidence that the required number of members had not concurred in the Act ... If such evidence should be allowed in cases where an absolute majority is required, it must similarly be admitted in all cases; and Acts which for years have been considered as part of the law of the land—Acts on the validity of which vast interests, public and private, may depend—may be declared inoperative and void upon the evidence of some person who may testify that on the first, second or third reading, or some other stage of the Bill, the majority present did not vote in favour of the measure, or that a quorum was not present. In the present case it is possible that Sir James Fisher or some one else may testify that an absolute majority was not present and concurring in the Act; but as the journals are silent on this point, I consider that such evidence could not be received on any legal investigation—the fact of the Bill having been passed and presented to the Governor for the Royal assent, and the silence of the Journals as to any irregularity, being conclusive evidence of the propriety and legality of all proceedings preliminary to the presentation of the Bill to the Governor.'

In view of the immense importance of the questions involved, and the doubts expressed by highly qualified lawyers, Mr Stow urged that the Governor should apply to the home authorities to obtain the opinion of the law officers in England; and also to obtain an act of the Imperial Parliament declaring the present Constitution and Electoral Acts, and all former Electoral Acts, and all legislation dependent on them to have been valid.

> 'At present the legality of the Electoral Act, under which the whole House of Assembly have been recently elected, is doubted by one of our Judges, and by others whose opinions are worthy of consideration. The power of our Legislature to effect any alteration in the Constitution, in either House, even with the assent of the Queen, is authoritatively denied; and a general feeling of uncertainty as to the validity of our Legislation is consequently prevalent. I know of no means which would satisfactorily remove those difficulties, and restore public confidence in the powers of our Legislature, short of an Imperial Act; and if in that Act provisions were inserted, under which any Act passed by the Parliament of this Province, and having the sanction of the Royal Assent, should be excluded from criticism by any Court in the Colony, on the ground of its not being within the powers conferred on Parliament, and whereby every such Act should be declared valid when assented to by the Governor, until disapproved of by the Queen, the relations of the Courts of the Colony to the Parliament would be assimilated to the relations which exist between the Queen's Courts in the United Kingdom, and the Imperial Parliament those questions which are now continually agitated, as to the validity of the Acts of the Local Parliament would be at an end, and a fruitful source of discord between the Parliament and the people on the one hand, and the Courts on the other, would be removed. At the same time I would suggest, that any Act, of the nature above indicated, should confirm all the provisions of the Constitution Act of the Province—power being given to make alterations in manner pointed out by that Act, and that it should be declared, that in all cases a copy of an Act of the Local Legislature, filed in the Supreme Court or other public office, with certificates of the President and Speaker, that the necessary majorities had concurred in its first, second and third reading—should be conclusive evidence that the Act had properly passed through both Houses.' [8]

In reporting this new development of the invalidity problem, the Governor wrote to the Secretary of State:

> 'Whatever may be the legal rights on either side, and whatever

> causes may have brought about the present unsatisfactory state of these matters, the public welfare demands that some effectual remedy be at once applied.'

He asked for an Imperial Act declaring all legislation in the colony subsequent to the constitution to be, and to have been, valid and effectual, ab initio.[9]

The Duke of Newcastle flatly refused to submit "so sweeping a proposal" to the Imperial Parliament.[10] To extract the colony from the legislative morass in which it was struggling, however, he procured the passing of the Act 26 & 27 Vic c.84, which, after reciting that "doubts are entertained respecting the validity of divers Acts passed by the Legislature of South Australia for the purpose of altering the Constitution of the Legislative Council and House of Assembly of the said Colony, and respecting the power of Colonial Legislatures to make laws for the above purpose", enacted in section II:

> 'All laws heretofore passed or purporting to have been passed by any Colonial Legislature with the object of declaring or altering the Constitution of such Legislature, or any branch thereof, or the mode of appointing or electing the members of the same, shall have and be deemed to have had, from the date at which the same shall have received the assent of Her Majesty or of the Governor of the Colony on behalf of Her Majesty, the same force and effect for all purposes whatever as if the said Legislature had possessed full power of enacting laws for the objects aforesaid, and as if all formalities and conditions by Act of Parliament or otherwise prescribed in respect of the passing of such laws had been duly observed.'

Although he had obtained this Act for the colony, the Duke of Newcastle was weary of the continual appeals from South Australia for legislative assistance; and in transmitting the Act to the Governor, he administered a rebuke to the slipshod colonials:

> 'I think it necessary to observe'—he said—'that although the Parliament of the United Kingdom may properly be called upon to remove complications which are the result of Imperial Legislation it is not at all proper or desirable that the Statute Book of this country should be encumbered with enactments which are only required to extricate Colonial Governments and Legislatures from the consequences of their own irregularity or inadvertence, especially when this irregularity consists in an omission on the part of the Legislature to conform to rules of their own making. Your Government must therefore clearly understand that it is their province to see that the rules

> required by law in the process of legislation are constantly kept in view and carefully observed, and, if those rules are found to be productive of inconvenience, to submit to the Legislature measures for their amendment.' [11]

The Validating Act was passed in July 1863, and was not received in the colony for some weeks. In the meantime the local Government had been pitifully shillyshallying about what should be done. The General Registry Office was hastily reopened for business. An appeal to the Privy Council was decided on, and then abandoned. When Parliament met in February 1863, the Governor laid before it the Attorney-General's opinion and announced that the Imperial Parliament had been asked for validating legislation.[12] In March 1863 the Attorney-General obtained leave to introduce a bill to amend the registration law in the hope of settling the vexed question of invalidity;[13] the Bill was referred to a Select Committee which, after consideration of it had dragged on for months, reported in October 1863 that the opinion of the Privy Council should be obtained as early as possible and that the Registration of Deeds Act No 27 of 1862 should be repealed on the ground of its inconvenience, though without any admission that it was invalid.[14] At this stage the Validating Act arrived from England; but after perusal of it the Government had to admit that it was doubtful whether or not the Registration of Deeds Act had been validated. They announced that they would assume it had been, and would give the public another opportunity of testing it in the Supreme Court—a course vehemently denounced by the press as merely affording the Judges another opportunity of exercising their ingenuity in discussing constitutional problems.[15]

The opportunity was not long in coming. *Auld v. Murray*, which came on for hearing before the Full Court in November 1863, was a claim for specific performance of an agreement to purchase certain land. The land was under the Real Property Act, and the agreement to purchase was contained in a memorandum of lease under that Act. The archenemy of the Real Property Act, Mr Fenn, appeared for the defendant, and contended, on grounds similar to those successfully taken in *Driffield v. Torrens*, that the Real Property Act was void. The effect of section 41 of the Real Property Act of 1861, he argued, was to prevent leases of land being registered under the Registration of Deeds Act No 8 of 1841; and leaseholders were thereby deprived of voting for the Legislative Council elections. By a majority the Court upheld the validity of the Real Property Act, the dissentient, of course, being Mr Justice Boothby. Any hopes that the Validating Act might have set at rest the constitutional problems which had so long vexed the colony were speedily dissipated, for the judgments delivered in *Auld v. Murray* made confusion worse confounded.[16]

Patrick Auld
(1855-1911)
Auld was a pioneer vigneron who started the Auldana vineyard in the early 1850s. He was one of the earliest promoters and exporters of South Australian wine. His son, William Patrick (1840-1912) succeeded him as manager of Auldana and had a similar career in wines and spirits but is also noted for his being charged with the murder of an Aboriginal whilst on an expedition. He was acquitted after a lengthy trial. The picture is of Auldana winery, ca. 1900. (SLSA)

Mr Justice Gwynne embarked upon an investigation of the question whether the legislature of South Australia had any power at all to alter the constitution of the Legislative Council, and concluded that it had not; and that section 34 of the Constitution Act was absolutely void. The then existing legislature, he said, was the creation of 13 & 14 Vic c.59. At the time that Act was passed, the legislature consisted wholly of nominees of the Crown. Section 7 of the Act empowered this nominee Council to establish a partly nominated, partly elective Legislative Council, but:

> '... although the nominee Legislature were empowered to divide the Province into convenient electoral districts, and to

> make other provisions for ensuring the orderly, effective, and impartial conduct of elections, no power was conferred on it to fix or alter the qualification either of the elective members or their constituents. These delicate matters were defined by 5 and 6 Vict c.76 and 7 & 8 Vict c.74.'

After seven or eight years of the mixed Council, section 32 of the Act of 13 & 14 Vic was resorted to; and the mixed Council, assuming to exercise the power thereby given, passed the Constitution Act No 2 of 1855-56.

> 'There can be no doubt'—said the Judge—'that the present Legislature has vested in it the powers and functions of the late mixed Council—that is, it has authority to make laws "for the peace, welfare, and good government of the Province" but I deny that it has powers of the same description as those conferred on the late mixed Council by the 32nd section of 13 and 14 Vict, or powers analagous [sic] to them; those powers were peculiar to and inseparable from the mixed Council. By that section the late mixed Council was authorised to amend and patch itself up from time to time, or in the alternative to duplicate its Houses of Legislature. They eventually acted on the latter alternative, and thereupon the whole power and authority contained in that section became extinguished. It would be very absurd to contend that the present Legislature has power to double the now existing Legislative Houses, or to reduce them to one, and again to substitute two; and it appears to me it would be equally absurd to contend that it has power to alter the qualification of the electors and elective members of the defunct mixed Council, or even of two-thirds only of its own members and electors, or of two-thirds of either House of Legislature. What I understand to have been the intention of the Imperial Legislature was to confer on the present Legislature, when established, all the general and ordinary powers or functions of the Legislative Council for which it was substituted, and those only; thus excluding the special and extraordinary powers of the 32nd section, which are not of a transferable nature, and extinguishable.'

The power to alter the qualification of electors was a power conferred upon the mixed Council, to be exercised upon itself; and both Council and power ceased to exist at the same instant of time. Section 34 of the Constitution Act, he therefore concluded, was ultra vires and a nullity.

Section 41 of the Real Property Act 1861, upon the construction of it contended for by Mr Fenn, the Judge thought would have the effect of altering the constitution of the Legislative Council. Leases, to come within section 6 of the Constitution Act, must be registered in the General Registry Office and nowhere else.

> 'What was the object of the legislature in requiring the lease to be registered? To prevent spurious votes—to adopt means whereby the title to real property might be more certainly known; and these safeguards were afforded by the provisions of the 5th Vict No 8. To my mind the matter is too clear for argument.'

If, therefore, Fenn was right in his construction of section 41, that section (at least) was void and ultra vires, unless it had been confirmed by the Validating Act 26 & 27 Vic c.84. But the Validating Act only touched statutes passed "*with the object* of declaring or altering the Constitution of the Legislature ... or the mode of appointing or electing the members of the same". How could it be said that the Real Property Act of 1861 was passed with such an object? There was nothing in the Act to suggest it; and it was transparently obvious that in fact no-one at that time ever suspected that the Act affected the Constitution at all. Had the Imperial Statute meant to confirm all acts which *in effect* did alter the constitution, then why, asked Mr Justice Gwynne, had it not said so? It had used the words "for the purpose of" and "with the object of", and effect must be given to those words. They must have been used to distinguish between what was done knowingly and designedly, and what was done unwittingly and unintentionally. Section 41 of the Real Property Act, therefore, could not be validated by the English Act.

But the Judge was of opinion that Mr Fenn's construction of section 41 was wrong, and that it did not prevent a lease of land under the Real Property Act from being registered in the General Registry Office under the old system; thereby giving the leaseholder his vote under the Constitution Act section 6. The Real Property Act, therefore, in his opinion could not be successfully challenged on this ground.

Mr Justice Boothby, in his judgment, excelled himself in the vigour with which he attacked the Real Property Act. He repeated the opinion which he had expressed in *McEllister v. Fenn*, in 1860:

> '... having seen no reason to alter that opinion ... and which I must retain until better taught by a judgment of the Judicial Committee of Her Majesty's Privy Council, or by the provisions of Imperial Legislation'.

He thoroughly concurred in Mr Fenn's construction of section 41, and agreed with him that if section 34 of the Constitution Act was valid, then it operated to render void section 41 of the Real Property Act, if not the whole of that Act. But it was his duty, he said, to declare that further grounds existed for the invalidity of the Real Property Act. It had been passed by an unlawful Parliament.

The tortuous chain of reasoning by which he arrived at this opinion is at first sight not easy to follow, but it may be summarised as follows:

(1) The old nominee Council had established the mixed Council by Ordinance No 1 of 1851.

(2) By the Electoral Act No 10 of 1855-56, Ordinance No 1 of 1851 was absolutely and unconditionally repealed without any qualification, and the Act working the repeal was declared to come into operation at the same moment as the Constitution Act No 2 of 1855-56.

(3) By section 41 of the Constitution Act, that Act took effect from proclamation of it, and it was proclaimed in the *Government Gazette* of 24 October 1856.

(4) By section 42 of the Constitution Act it was provided that:

> '... anything herein contained to the contrary notwithstanding, the Legislative Council now subsisting shall continue and exist until the issue of the first writs for the election of Members of the Parliament hereby constituted'.

Those writs were issued on 2 February 1857.

(5) Ordinance 1 of 1851 of the nominee Council therefore stood absolutely repealed, without any qualifying words, either on 24 October 1856 or on 2 February 1857.

> 'The question therefore arises whether at the latest on and after 2nd February 1857 there was in legal operation any Statute which warranted the election of a Legislature composed of two Houses as proposed by the Constitution Act No 2 of 1856, and this will depend on whether the legal effect of repealing No 1 of 1851, the Act of the nominee Council establishing the mixed Council of one House, was not also to hinder the legal operation of any Acts passed by the Mixed Council for any purpose after the date that its existence as a mixed Council ceased, by the words of absolute repeal in the 53rd section of No 10 of 1856.'

Powers of legislation conferred by statute cannot have any further operation after the absolute repeal of the statute conferring such powers.

> 'The mixed Council of 1851 had power to pass the Constitution Act, but it had no power to give effect to its enactments, except by so providing by express words that such should be the case, notwithstanding and after the absolute repeal of its own authority. The omission, therefore, of any

> such proviso, worked a repeal in legal effect of the Constitution Act at the very same moment that the Legislature which passed it became itself defunct by absolute, unqualified, and unconditional repeal.'

Mr Justice Boothby therefore announced with pride that his opinion was that there never had been in the colony a lawful Parliament of two Houses and that all its purported legislation was illusory. He apologetically added that "this defect" had not been present to his mind when he gave his judgment in *McEllister v. Fenn*.

The Chief Justice hastened to refute this staggering pronouncement of his colleague; and he did so conclusively. Mr Justice Boothby's objection, in a nutshell, was this—the Electoral Act of 1855-56 repealed Ordinance 1 of 1851, without making any provision for keeping in force the Acts passed by that legislature, and in the absence of such provision all those Acts, including the Constitution Act and Electoral Act, lost their force, and there was therefore no legal parliament.

> 'I am quite aware'—said the Chief Justice—'that consequences can never bar a conclusion; but consequences so startling may well induce us to pause before adopting the reasons upon which they are founded.'

Mr Justice Boothby's argument, he pointed out, was self-destructive:

> 'Such reasoning falls like an inverted cone,
> Wanting its proper base to stand upon'.

For if the Electoral Act of 1855-56 had no operation, then Ordinance 1 of 1851 was not repealed, since it was only that Electoral Act which repealed it; and if it was not repealed, then all the legislation of the mixed Council, including the Electoral Act itself was valid.

> 'It is, in fact, only by assuming that the Electoral Act is a valid and subsisting Act that the consequences deduced from the repeal of the Ordinance No 1 of 1851 can be supported, and if it is valid and subsisting for that purpose it must be for others also. The inference, in fact, is reached by assuming something in the premises which is denied in the conclusion, and I need hardly say that this is not a valid form of syllogism.'

In addition, the legislature which passed the Electoral Act of 1855 and that which then existed derived all their power from the Act 13 & 14 Vic, and the validity of their enactments must depend upon the provisions of that Act.

> 'So long as that Act is unrepealed, the powers which it confers subsist, and the effect which it gives to laws made by the

> Legislatures which it originates or sanctions continues unimpaired.'

But while the Chief Justice agreed with Mr Justice Gwynne in upholding the validity of the Real Property Act, he did so on a different ground. Mr Justice Gwynne thought section 6 of the Constitution Act required registration of the lease in the General Registry Office but that Real Property Act leases could be so registered; the Chief Justice, however, considered that section 6 was satisfied by registration of the lease in the ordinary way under the provisions of the Real Property Act—a conclusion which seems open to doubt.

It is easy to imagine the excitement caused in the colony by the publication of the judgments in *Auld v. Murray*. The anti-Boothby outcry was renewed with fervour, and it was not diminished when, a few days later, that Judge took the opportunity, in the case of *Martin v. Elliott*, to have another fling at the Real Property Act.

> 'It would be monstrous'—he said—'to suppose, if a case went before the Judicial Committee of the Privy Council, that the mere production of the Certificate of Title given under the Act of a local Legislature would bar further enquiry into the title. Certainly, if such a decision were given, I should bow to it, although I should greatly wonder at it.' [17]

The *Register* commented rather sourly that Mr Justice Boothby was determined to be in the public eye. "His learned colleagues may have the best of the argument, but he always carries off the laurels in his desperate leaps and astounding tumbles." [18]

The Supreme Court, it declared, as a result of the lack of confidence in the Judges, was being left without business. Cases were settled or taken to the Local Courts. Some of the Civil Sessions were almost maiden ones.

> 'The Judge comes on to the Bench, as his duty requires, listens to a few tame words from some half-interested advocate, in the presence of a few sleepy auditors, says a word or two himself, praises the jury, dismisses the jury, and all is over. The Supreme Court presents the appearance of an effete institution which is lagging behind the age. Persistent frequenters of its precincts sigh for the good old times when many a pretty quarrel was got up before the Judges for the special delectation of belligerent citizens, who went to watch the administration of justice as they would go to witness the performance of a sensation drama. "O, what a falling off is there!" No lawyers' jokes; no expert fencing; no fierce onslaughts on timid witnesses; no insidious cajoling of "honest" jurymen. The glory has departed. All the interest is transferred to the Local Courts where it is

> believed if there is sometimes less law there is quite as much justice, and at a much more reasonable cost. Cases which a few months ago would have been tried before the supreme tribunal are now submitted to the inferior courts, and judging from all we have seen of the decided tendency of litigation to run at the present time in the minor channels, it would appear that at a not very distant period our Judges will have to close the Supreme Court, in reference at any rate to civil causes.' [19]

This gloomy lament was doubtless considerably exaggerated; but unquestionably the administration of justice in the Supreme Court was rapidly becoming a scandal.

Following *Auld v. Murray*, the Chief Justice called the Governor's attention to the general uncertainty which existed as to the validity of local legislation, in order that the subject might again be brought under the notice of the Secretary of State. There were two main grounds, he pointed out, upon which the validity of the Acts of the South Australian Parliament might be questioned:

(1) That the Governor had not reserved them for the signification of the Queen's pleasure, as he was bound by law to do with regard to certain classes of acts.

(2) That the Acts themselves were repugnant to the law of England.

As to the Governor's assent being wrongfully given, the Chief Justice wrote:

> 'It is undoubtedly true that such assent is given in conformity with the advice of the principal law officers of the Crown in the Colony, and that, consequently, it is in a sense the Colony which is responsible for the error. But it is, nevertheless, a matter worthy of consideration, whether the validity of important laws should be made to depend upon the soundness or otherwise of the view taken by a Colonial Attorney-General, as to the class to which any particular Act belongs. Of course, I must not be understood as offering any opinion as to the soundness of any objection to the validity of an Act upon this ground, but it is an objection which has been made in this Colony, and which has been upheld by one of the Judges of this Court. I would suggest, therefore, whether it might not be worth while, if an opportunity offers, to define the effect of any such mistake on the part of the Governor. The only effect of his assenting to the Act, instead of reserving it when such reservation is required, is, in cases when Her Majesty's assent would have been given, that it operates from the time at which the Governor's assent is given in the Colony, instead of from the time when it would have received Her Majesty's assent

in England; and, in cases where it would not be so assented to, then that it has the force of law during the interval between the Governor's assent and its disallowance. In the former case it would appear that no inconvenience would result from the mistake, and in the latter the inconvenience would be but slight. Such, however, as it is, it might be provided against by an enactment to the effect that in cases where a Governor had assented to an Act which he was by law required to reserve for the signification of Her Majesty's pleasure, such assent should not be invalid, in case her Majesty should be pleased to leave the Act to its operation, but that in cases in which any Act so assented to, should be disallowed by Her Majesty, then the assent should be held to have had no force or effect whatever. I need hardly say that I do not contemplate by this, that there should be any relaxation of the duty at present imposed upon Governors to reserve Bills for the signification of Her Majesty's pleasure, but merely to remove what has been a fertile source of doubt and cavil in this Colony, and may at any moment equally prove to be so in any other Colony similarly circumstanced.'

With regard to repugnancy, the Chief Justice said, the difficulty arose from the utterly indefinite nature of the restriction.

'So far as I am aware, it has never received any judicial interpretation, and I think it would be difficult to frame one. In a vague general way our Legislature and the Law Officers of the Crown may know what it means, and it is not perhaps probable that any Act could be passed which really violated it. But in the meantime it exists as a possible ground of objection which may be brought forward at any moment. It has already been urged once in the Court of Queen's Bench, and once before the Judicial Committee of the Privy Council (though in each unsuccessfully) as a ground of objection to two Acts of the Legislature of New South Wales, and it is always impossible to say when it may arise. It is true that, in all probability, it would prove unsuccessful; but there is, nevertheless, a possibility that in some unexpected quarter it might meet with success, and the existence of such a possibility weakens confidence in our laws, and tends to encourage litigation. It must be observed that in this respect the Legislatures of these Colonies, and I believe of the Cape also, are differently circumstanced from the North American and I believe the West Indian Colonies. In the latter the restriction is, that they shall not pass any law repugnant to any Imperial Act made applicable to those Colonies—(I have not the Acts at hand to refer to the precise language, but this is the substance)—and this would seem to be all that is required in view of Imperial interests. Such a restriction is clear and intelligible, and no doubt can arise with regard to its interpretation; and coupled with the power of disallowance vested in Her Majesty during a period of two years, would seem to give all the security against perverse or mistaken legislation which can be required. It may, consequently, be worthy of consideration whether, in this respect also, some Imperial enactment would not be expedient. I ought not to conclude without saying that, individually, I do not consider any legislation necessary to alter the present state of the law. I think that the real effect of the law, as it exists, is substantially the same as it would be if the enactments I have suggested were made. But such enactments would remove doubts which are widely entertained in this Colony, and which may at any moment arise in the neighbouring Colonies, and they would allay the irritation which has sprung up on the subject in this Colony by removing the causes of apparent conflict between the Bench and the Legislature.' [20]

Sir Robert Porrett Collier (Lord Monkswell) (1817-1886)
In his early legal career Collier had spectacular success defending Brazilian pirates. They were condemned to death but Collier's representations to the Government resulted in a grant of free pardon. By 1863 he had become Solicitor General and went on to become a judge on the Privy Council. The portrait is by Alfred Thompson (1870). (NPG)

The Governor also called for a report from the Attorney-General and Crown Solicitor upon the judgments in *Auld v. Murray*. These gentlemen entirely dissented from the views of Mr Justice Boothby, but were inclined to agree with Mr Justice Gwynne's argument that section 34 of the Constitution Act was invalid. They advised that Imperial legislation should again be sought, and especially "a comprehensive measure validating the whole of the provisions of the Constitution Act".[21]

In accordance with these suggestions, Sir Dominick Daly asked the Secretary of State to apply once more the legislative remedy for the difficulty in which the state was involved. "It is at present", he said, "the most fruitful source of uneasiness in the Colony."[22]

The English law officers (on this occasion Sir Roundell Palmer and Sir Robert Collier) reported that it was advisable that the extent of the legislative powers of colonial Parliaments should be defined by Imperial legislation.

> 'We think it expedient'—they said—'to declare, by Imperial legislation, that any general instructions which may have been, or may be, given by Her Majesty to any of the Governors of Her Colonial Possessions, to reserve any particular class or classes of Bills passed by the Colonial Legislatures for the signification of Her Majesty's pleasure thereon, shall not have, or be deemed to have had, the effect of suspending or rendering void any assent which may have been, or may be,

> given by such Governors to any such Bills, in the name or on behalf of Her Majesty, without reserving the same for the signification of Her Majesty's pleasure thereon, unless it shall have been, or shall be, required of any Act by the Imperial Parliament or of the Colonial Legislature in force for the time being, that such Bills should be so reserved. But we do not think it advisable to enact that, if any such Bills required by law (ie by Act of Parliament or local statute) to be reserved, should have been assented to by the Governor without reservation, the subsequent assent thereto of Her Majesty should have a retrospective operation so as to make the Act good ab initio. The reasons against such legislation (assuming it to be necessary or desirable, in some cases, to require by law that a Bill should be reserved) appear to us to preponderate over the arguments in its favour.'

If an act which ought to have been reserved was not reserved, or if an act which ought to have been passed by a certain majority was not passed by that majority, they were of opinion that it would be void in toto.

> 'The difference between these cases and the case of repugnancy is, that in the latter the subject-matter of the invalid part of the legislation is wholly ultra vires; and, so far as the Act dealt with matter which was intra vires, all necessary conditions for the due exercise of the legislative power have been fulfilled ... When the power of legislation with regard to a particular subject is given, not to a simple majority, but to certain specified majorities in one or both branches of the Legislature, it is evident that such majorities are a condition sine qua non to its exercise; and, consequently, that the Judges are not at liberty to treat any law on that subject as valid if it appears, either on the face of the law itself or by other proper evidence, that it was not in fact passed by the required majorities. We do not, however, think that it is absolutely necessary that it should appear on the face of the law itself that it was passed by the requisite majorities (if that fact can be otherwise proved) in order to authorise the Judges to act upon such legislation as valid and effectual; and we incline to think (although this point may perhaps admit of some doubt) that the Judges ought to presume, until the contrary is proved, that every Act which has passed the Legislature, and which is authenticated as an Act of the Legislature in the ordinary way, was passed by such a majority as would be necessary according to law to give it effect.'

They dissented from the view expressed by Mr Justice Gwynne in *Auld v. Murray* that the Validating Act would not have validated the Real Property Act, because the Real Property Act had not been passed "with the object of" altering the constitution.

> 'It must be presumed, that a legislative body intends that which is the necessary effect of its enactment; the object, the purpose, and the intention, of the enactment, is the same; it need not be expressed in any recital or preamble; and it is not (as we conceive) competent for any Court, judicially, to ascribe any part of the legal operation of a Statute to inadvertence ... We think, therefore, that (if the Colonial Registration Act was indeed invalid on the ground suggested) the Imperial Statute 26 and 27 Vict c.84 was effectual for giving it validity.'

At the same time, they added, their opinion was that the Real Property Act did not affect section 6 of the Constitution Act and was therefore not in any way ultra vires or invalid.

> 'Having in view'—they continued—'the unfortunate disposition manifested upon the Bench of South Australia to favour technical objections against the validity of Acts of the Colonial Legislature, and the confusion and general sense of insecurity which it must be the tendency of such a state of things to produce, we think it will be very expedient to pass an Imperial Act, for the purpose of empowering the Legislature of that Colony (and of any other Colonies or Colony which may be in like circumstances) to alter its own constitution; and, at the same time, to confirm absolutely all South Australian Acts, which down to this time have received the assent of Her Majesty, or of the Governor in Her Majesty's behalf.'

Mr Justice Boothby's opinion, in *Auld v. Murray*, that there was no lawful Parliament, they denounced as unsound and erroneous.

> 'Without inquiring whether, on general principles, all the Acts of a Legislature ought to be held annulled by a simple repeal of a prior Act which constituted that Legislature, it is, at all events certain that no such effect would follow if it were apparent on the face of the repealing statute that the Acts of the abolished Legislature were meant to remain in force. And, upon the face of the Act No 10 of 1855-56 which repeals the Ordinance No 1 of 1851, it is apparent that the Constitution Act No 2 of 1855-56, was intended to remain in force; because it is expressly provided (we quote the words of Mr Justice Boothby himself) that the Repealing Act shall "come into operation so soon as the Act No 2, 1856, to establish a Constitution for

> South Australia, shall, come into operation". The two Acts, therefore, were both to operate simultaneously, and from one and the same instant of time. If the Constitution Act could be held repealed by this statute, it follows that it never came into operation at all; and if it never came into operation, it follows that the Ordinance No 1 of 1851 itself (as was pointed out by the Chief Justice in the cause of Auld v. Murray) was never repealed. The reasoning, therefore, of Mr Justice Boothby travels in a vicious circle, and results in repugnant and absurd conclusions. But we think if it were better founded it would be properly and sufficiently met by such legislation as that which we have had the honour to recommend.' [23]

This opinion of the law officers was not given until September 1864; and it is necessary to return to the progress of affairs in the colony in the meantime.

In November 1863, on the last day of term, Mr Archibald Michie, a well-known Melbourne barrister, applied for admission as a practitioner of the South Australian Supreme Court. By a remarkable chance, Mr Justice Boothby, who as a rule was punctuality personified, was on this morning delayed on his way to the Court and arrived ten minutes late. When he came on to the bench, he found that his two colleagues had already made an order for Mr Michie's admission. He immediately announced that he did not agree to the order; and complained that they had not waited for his arrival before commencing business. He had grave objections to Mr Michie being admitted.

> 'It would involve a great injustice to the South Australian Bar, the members of which could not go into other colonies and be heard upon ordinary motions. Those gentlemen had expended their time, and prepared by a costly education for admissions as practitioners in that Court, and if persons from the neighbouring colonies could be introduced under such circumstances it would be a great injustice to the Bar of this colony ... The present case was open also to the very grave objection that it gave facilities to rich men which poor men could not compass. The very name of Mr Michie, the Minister of Justice for Victoria, might influence a Jury, but that was an advantage which could only be purchased by a rich suitor, and they ought to be careful how they made in practice one law for the rich and another law for the poor.'

Anything more foolish than his last reason it would be hard to imagine.

(Sir) Archibald Michie (1813-1899)
Michie was one of the barristers who defended the Eureka rebels in 1855 as part of a long and successful legal career. He was also a long serving politician and a newspaper correspondent. (SLV)

The Chief Justice said it was a great pity that statements of that sort should be thrown out without that consideration which he felt certain would induce his colleague to greatly modify his opinions; and Mr Justice Gwynne said that to have Mr Michie on the roll would be an honour and not a disadvantage to the bar. He was a Queen's Counsel and Minister of Justice in Victoria—a gentleman of long standing and great eminence in the profession.

> 'In fact, for any lawyer in these colonies not to know Mr Michie would be to argue that he was himself unknown ... As to the danger of Mr Michie tending to make one law for the rich and another law for the proof [sic], that had always been the case in England. It was only the wealthy who were able to retain the services of men eminent for legal skill and forensic talent, and this was an advantage incident to wealth all over the world.' [24]

Mr Justice Boothby, however, remained dissatisfied, and a month later he delivered a long written judgment dissenting from the order. Some of his reasons bordered on the ludicrous. For instance, he said:

> 'The affidavits before the Court describe the applicant as a Cabinet Minister, holding the office of Minister of Justice in the province of Victoria. If the professional eminence of the applicant could at all affect the law which regulates the admission of the practitioners of this Court, for myself, from

> personal knowledge of that eminence, I should at once say, let him be admitted. But I must look at the consequences of admitting a principle, and enquire what are the results of admitting an applicant so circumstanced in all cases. Practising barristers—anomalous and strange as it undoubtedly is, as compared with the practice of constitutional and responsible government of Her Majesty's United Kingdom—are in all the Australian colonies made Cabinet Ministers. I have yet to learn that a practising barrister, while such, was ever made a Cabinet Minister of England. In questions of treason, sedition, or political libel, is a Cabinet Minister of a neighbouring colony to have the right of audience in the Court of this colony, or in case of a trial in this Court of a charge of murder against a Victorian officer of Customs from a death occurring in the attempted levy of Victorian customs on the boundary-line between the two Provinces, is a Victorian Cabinet Minister, after advising a seizure, the legality of which is to determine the position of the accused as whether guilty of murder or manslaughter, or whether the facts show a justifiable homicide, to appear as of right in this Court to defend the accused?'[25]

Whatever Mr Justice Boothby's shortcomings, lack of imagination was not one of them.

Mr Michie never seems to have appeared in any case here. It was rumoured that he sought admission in order to appear for the claimants in the great Moonta Mines case—to which reference will be made at some length—but he was not engaged as counsel in that cause.

In *R. v. Hart*, heard before Mr Justice Boothby at the Criminal Sessions in February 1864, the unexpected spectacle was witnessed of that truculent and independent Judge bowing to the authority of the Chief Justice, the legality of whose appointment he persisted in denying. The prisoner, an insolvent, was charged with embezzlement. Mr Stow, who appeared for him, objected to certain evidence taken before the Commissioner of Insolvency being put in, on the ground that there was no Insolvency Court. That Court, he said, was established by an Act passed by a Parliament which, according to Mr Justice Boothby's judgment in *Auld v. Murray*, had no lawful existence.

The Judge said that that judgment had been prepared by him after much consideration, but the opinion he expressed went for nothing, as it was overruled; for although Mr Justice Gwynne said nothing on the point, the Chief Justice was against him. The question would have to be settled by the Privy Council, and if Mr Stow took the case there, he would be conferring a great service on the legislation of the colony. It is not surprising that Mr Stow was not anxious to take to the Privy Council the case of an insolvent prisoner.[26]

This case aroused little attention at the time, but it may be said to mark the watershed in the Boothby troubles. Up to this time, there be little doubt that the Judge, though he may have been cantankerous and wrong, had not very far exceeded the limits of proper judicial conduct. If he honestly held the views he announced from the bench, it was his bounden duty to maintain them. If he believed that the Chief Justice and Mr Justice Gwynne were not legally appointed Judges, it was his duty to say so; and having said so, there was nothing inconsistent in his continuing to sit on the bench with them, under protest. It could not be expected that he, a lawfully appointed Judge, would sacrifice his livelihood and retire from the bench because the other Judges were unlawfully appointed. But if he genuinely considered that the Chief Justice was not duly appointed and had no right to sit on the bench, then it was a dereliction of duty for him to surrender his judgment to that of the usurper, as he did in *R. v. Hart.* He could not blow hot and cold. Having thus acknowledged the lawfulness of the Chief Justice's appointment, it is impossible not to feel that he was inconsistent and insincere when he reverted, as he did at a later stage, to his contention that the Chief Justice was not lawfully appointed. He allowed passion to get the better of his good sense. From this time on, he proceeded to stray further and further from the right path; and his aberrations eventually became so wilful and eccentric as to be destitute of a semblance of justification. His terrible propensities developed until he sat apart in the Supreme Court like Giant Despair in Doubting Castle, watching for stray legislators who might wander into his inextricable meshes, and dispatching them with all the horrors of repugnancy and ultra vires.

Captain William Bloomfield Douglas (1822-1906)
Douglas was appointed the Harbour Master and Collector of Customs at Port Adelaide in 1858.

Meanwhile he continued his excursions into the realms of invalidity. In *Humberstone v. Douglas* in March 1864, he said that all the Customs Acts passed in the colony, with the exception of the first, were invalid because they had not been reserved for the Queen's assent.[27] In the following month, in *Hall v. Commissioner of Crown Land*, he announced that the Northern Territory Act No 23 of 1863 was invalid, because it was passed by an unlawful Parliament—inconsistently reverting to his argument in *Auld v. Murray* which, he had admitted in *R. v. Hart*, he must consider as overruled by the opinion of the Chief Justice.[28]

A case of some importance, *R. v. Nethery*, came before Mr Justice Gwynne at the Criminal Sessions in May 1864. The prisoner was charged with perjury. His counsel, Mr Boucaut, objected that the information was in the name of Richard Bullock Andrews, Attorney-General of the province, whereas there was no such officer. The information purported to be laid under Act 10 of 1852, by which any person might be put upon trial by information in the name and by the authority of Her Majesty's Advocate or Attorney-General; but that had not been complied with. Her Majesty's Attorney-General was an officer well known to the law—the gentleman who then held the office was Sir Roundell Palmer. The Act did not say the Attorney-General of South Australia and in fact there was no such person. Mr Boucaut also objected that the Act 10 of 1852 was ultra vires and repugnant to the law of England—the same objection as that overruled by Mr Justice Boothby in *R. v. Preston* in February 1861.

Mr Justice Gwynne held against the objections, which, he pointed out, might have been taken many years before. "Sir Charles Cooper sat here for years and heard informations filed by a gentleman who at any rate was generally reputed to be Attorney General of the Province."

He would follow the established practice of the Court. Although there might be something in the objections, he would not upset the practice of his predecessor. He offered to reserve the points for the consideration of the Full Court, but the case was not taken further.[29]

In *Re Ware: ex parte Bayne* (June 1864) the effect of the Validating Act (26 & 27 Vic c.84) was again considered. The question was, whether Act 27 of 1862, which the Court had held in *Driffield v. Torrens* to be invalid, had been validated. The Chief Justice expressed the same view as that later taken by the law officers in England, and held that it had been validated. What was the meaning of "passed with the object of", he inquired?

> 'It may have either a popular or legal meaning—that is, it may either mean what we may conceive to be the intention or object of the makers, apart from those considerations which guide us in interpreting the language of the statute, or it may mean that which is assumed to be the intention or object of the Act, because it is the meaning and effect of the language which the makers of that law have employed; and I am of opinion that the latter is the true construction. In construing a Statute, we have to discover and to give effect to the intention of the Legislature; but we gather this intention from the language they employ.'

It was impossible, he thought, to distinguish between the object of the legislature and the effect of their legislation.

Mr Justice Gwynne, on the contrary (and Mr Justice Boothby agreed with him) maintained his previously expressed opinion.

> 'It appears to me that to say a Legislature cannot effect objects by legislation which it did not design or intend is to beg the whole question. I think the local Legislature did so by the Act No 27 of 1862. They did not design by that Act to alter the Constitution, but they have in effect done so.'

He therefore thought the Act was not validated.[30]

Inspired by these controversies, one of the journalists of the day burst into rhyme:[31]

> 'Oh, here's a to-do,
> A most horrible stew!
> Cooked up, Justice Gwynne, by Judge Boothby and you!
>
> So keen your avidity,
> And such your rapidity
> In riddling our laws
> With repugnance and flaws,
> That there's nothing left valid except invalidity.
>
> O, Boothby and Gwynne,
> How outsiders must grin,
> To see a whole province perplexed by your quiddity;
>
> Don Quixote was queer,
> Had a tile loose, I fear;
> But, oh—rum-ti-iddity!
> The Don never matched your absurd invalidity'.

The continuance of the invalidity arguments proved too much for the patience of Parliament, and in June 1864 both Houses appointed Select Committees to prepare addresses to the Queen setting forth the "serious evils" and "weighty grievances" which had arisen from the doubts as to the validity of local legislation. The Committees worked together in collating evidence, but prepared separate addresses. That of the Assembly reminded the Queen that it had ever been the proud boast of Englishmen that their laws were certain and well defined. But no longer could South Australians so boast—uncertainty was now the rule rather than the exception.

> 'The uncertainty of the laws affecting life and liberty in this Province may best be illustrated by the fact that one of the Judges (Mr Justice Boothby) has repeatedly given it as his opinion that the Act passed by the Legislative Council of the Province, No 10, 1852, abolishing the Grand Jury system, and establishing in lieu thereof a Public Prosecutor, is repugnant to the law of England, and therefore invalid, and consequently that all criminals convicted since that date before the Supreme Court have been illegally tried and condemned. He has pointed out that although, owing to the general poverty of the criminals hitherto tried and condemned, an arrest of judgment has not yet been moved, it may some day happen that a criminal of wealth (or whose friends are wealthy) may cause the question to be tried; when, should his opinion of the law be upheld, it will turn out that judicial murder has been

> committed, in the matter of those unfortunate criminals (happily few in number) who have thus suffered death illegally in the absence of trial before a Grand Jury. What may be the consequences to the prosecutors and officers of justice in the more numerous cases of others thus illegally imprisoned and condemned to hard labour, and who may be still living and in a position to commence actions for such wrongs, deserves serious consideration.'

If Mr Justice Boothby was right in maintaining there was no lawful Parliament, then it was quite impossible for the difficulties to be remedied locally. Imperial legislation was essential.

> 'We trust Your Majesty will graciously relieve us'—the address concluded—'from further suffering under this enormous evil unknown to English law, to wit, the power claimed by our Judges to declare laws passed by the Parliament of this province illegal.'

The address of the Legislative Council was in a similar strain.

> 'For several years past'—it said—'the validity of the laws passed by the Parliament of South Australia has been questioned or denied by the Judges of the Supreme Court, or by one or more of them; such questioning or denial of the validity of the laws has led to frequent and painful differences between the Legislature and Judicature; the objections to the Acts of the South Australian Parliament are of such a nature, that the Legislature cannot frame their measures so as to avoid these objections, unless by surrendering what they believe to be their rightful privileges as a Parliament; and the objections urged against the Acts of the Colonial Legislature often rest upon considerations and involve difficulties wholly beyond the power of this Parliament to rectify or remove, even were it conceded that such objections are themselves well founded ... The local circumstances of this Colony in many respects differ so widely from those of the mother-country, that a corresponding divergence in legislation is unavoidable; Acts applicable to society in England are not in all cases applicable here; and the advantages derivable from local legislation would be to a great extent lost, if it were to be held that simple diversity of enactment amounted to 'repugnancy', and that no laws are valid that are different in principle from the laws of England.' [32]

As an appendix to the addresses, a draft of an act was submitted, which it was requested might be laid before Parliament in England.

> 'I have no hesitation'—wrote Mr Stow, the Attorney-General—'in advising His Excellency to recommend this Act to the favourable consideration of the Rt Honourable Secretary of State with a view that in substance it may be passed into law by the Imperial Parliament. Should this take place the Act will, I apprehend, free the local Parliament from the embarrassing restrictions and conditions imposed upon them and be a means of relieving the colony from the troubles occasioned by the continual litigation as to the powers of Parliament.' [33]

In forwarding the addresses, the Governor emphasised the importance attached to a speedy termination of these proceedings, so injurious and discreditable to the colony.

> 'I cannot omit the occasion to express a fervent hope that some means may be open to Her Majesty's Government by which the pretensions of Mr Justice Boothby may be finally set at rest, and a decorous state of things restored to the Bench of the Supreme Court of this Province.' [34]

To the Honorable the HOUSE of ASSEMBLY of the Province of South Australia, in Parliament assembled.

The Memorial of the undersigned Inhabitants of the Province of South Australia.

Respectfully Sheweth---

THAT your Memorialists have viewed with surprise and regret the line of conduct pursued by His Honor the Acting Chief Justice as Judge at the Criminal Sittings held on Friday and Saturday, the 20th and 21st days of February, one thousand eight hundred and fifty seven.

THAT your Memorialists feel it their solemn duty to resist by every constitutional means such an unwarrantable, unjust, and arbitrary assumption of power, as an insult to the feelings of men, an infraction of the liberty of the subject, a denial of justice, and a direct contravention of the right that every Briton claims of Trial by Jury.

THAT your Memorialists are of opinion that His Honor the Acting Chief Justice has utterly lost the confidence of the community in his administration of the law in the Courts of this Province.

YOUR MEMORIALISTS therefore pray that your Honorable House will be pleased to address Her Majesty the Queen, praying Her Majesty to remove Benjamin Boothby, Esquire, from his office of Judge, and also to address His Excellency the Governor, requesting His Excellency to suspend His Honor the Acting Chief Justice from his Judgeship until Her Majesty's pleasure be known, and in the meantime to make such other provision as may be necessary for the due administration of the laws.

And your Memorialists will ever pray, &c.

Memorial – a petition asking for the removal of Boothby. (SR/SC)

While these addresses were in course of preparation some very remarkable proceedings were taking place in the Supreme Court. The story of the great legal fight for the Moonta Mines is too long to be told in any detail here, and only an outline of it can be given.

In 1861 copper was discovered by a drunken shepherd named Ryan, in the employ of Mr W.W. Hughes, at Tiparra. Ryan could not get a mining lease himself, nor for a long time could he get anyone to take any interest in his tale about his find. Eventually a small syndicate was formed in Adelaide, with a man named Mills as the head of it. Ryan signed an agreement with the syndicate by which he was to receive a fifth share in the mine. Owing to lack of definite data as to the site, the syndicate were unable to get a lease, and they sent a party up to the site to peg out a proper claim. In the meantime, Hughes had got wind of the syndicate and realised that a valuable find had been made. He at once lodged an application in the name of a dummy and falsely claimed to be authorised to do so by the discoverer. Owing to vagueness as to the site, this application was void. He hurried to the Wallaroo district to get more precise information and found that Ryan had already shown the site to the syndicate party, who had left on their return journey to Adelaide. By offering Ryan the tempting bait of an immediate payment of £6 a week, with a share of the mine, Hughes induced him to desert the syndicate, and he obtained from him the necessary details as to the site of the find. These he sent to Adelaide by a man named Horn, who, by a famous Paul Revere-like ride on horseback, overtook the syndicate party. The Mills party arrived at the door of the Land Office at 8.30 am and had to wait until 10 am for the office to open for business. At 10 am Mr Taylor of Elder Stirling and Co, Hughes's representatives, arrived. The Chief Clerk did not arrive till 10.15, when, knowing Mr Taylor, he attended to him first and took his application for a mining lease. When the turn of the Mills party came, they found that they had been forestalled, and their application was too late. They did not tamely submit, but pestered the Government with complaints until in 1863 a Select Committee was appointed to inquire into the whole question of the Tiparra leases. The Committee reported in favour of the Mills party, but left the matter to be decided in the courts.[1]

Walter Watson Hughes (1803-1887)
Hughes was a sea captain involved in the opium trade before settling in South Australia in the 1840s. Before Ryan's find at Moonta another of Hughes' shepherds had found copper at what was to become the Wallaroo mine. Through ownership of the mines Hughes became wealthy and, subsequently, a public benefactor. His most noted donation being that of 20,000 pounds to start the University of Adelaide. Hughes is pictured here with his wife, Sophia, the daughter of Adelaide solicitor James Henry Richman. (Pamela Oborn)

The claimants therefore began proceedings in the Supreme Court seeking by writ of scire facias the revocation of the leases granted to Hughes and Stirling. Thus began a desperate forensic struggle, which was prolonged over several years. The case was taken to the Privy Council and, after an adverse judgment there,[2] the claimants began fresh proceedings in the colony, which were finally compromised by payment to them of £10,000.

It is important to notice two points in connection with this litigation. First, Mr Justice Boothby was suspected, and subsequently accused, of favouring the defendants; and very stringent comments were made upon the way in which he invariably upheld the defendants' objections and passed rude remarks about those of the plaintiffs. Secondly, one of the counsel for the claimants was James Penn Boucaut. Boucaut had a considerable pecuniary interest in the syndicate formed to fight the claim, and his dislike of Mr Justice Boothby was inflamed by the opposition which the claimants experienced from the Judge during the progress of the case.

The Moonta case (as it was known) first came into open court in May 1864, when the defendants Hughes and Stirling moved to quash the writ of scire facias. The bar reaped a rich harvest, four counsel appearing on one side, and three on the other. There is little pleasure in wading through the pages of technicalities upon which the arguments turned. Shortly the defendants' main points were:

(1) That the mining leases were Crown grants and the Supreme Court had no jurisdiction to issue a writ of scire facias for annulling a Crown grant.

The exclusive right of issuing writs of scire facias, it was contended, had belonged in England to the common law side of the Court of Chancery, in a department called the Petty Bag Office. No other court at Westminster possessed the power to issue such writs. But the common law jurisdiction of the Court of Chancery had not been conferred upon the Supreme Court—only the equitable jurisdiction of that Court—ergo, the Supreme Court could not issue writs of scire facias.

(2) That the writ lay only for the revocation of a record, and there was no record in the Supreme Court on which to found such a writ.

(3) That it did not appear from the records of the Court that the authority of Her Majesty's Attorney-General of England had been obtained prior to the issue of the writ. It was upon this last point that Mr Justice Boothby had most to say. His heart warmed at such a congenial topic. Mr Bakewell, for the defendants, said the question was, had the Attorney-General of South Australia any right to represent the Crown or to give authority to use the Queen's name?

'Is there not a prior question?'—said Mr Justice Boothby—'as to whether there is any Attorney-General in the Colony?'

Mr Bakewell: 'There is a person having that name; but it is merely a name.'

Mr Justice Boothby: 'Neither by Statute nor by patent is there such a person ...'

Mr Justice Gwynne: 'Previously the principal law officer of the

Crown was called the Advocate General. What that meant as distinguished from Attorney-General, I don't know. From the time of the passing the new Constitution Act he has been called the Attorney-General; I don't think he was called so previously.'

Mr Bakewell: 'Yes; the Constitution Act speaks of an officer called the Attorney General, but without defining his powers; and it is of the utmost importance that the writ should be set aside, unless the power rested with him to allow the Queen's name to be used, because the Crown might not choose to be bound by the judgment of this Court unless the process were properly set in motion.'

Mr Justice Boothby: 'The whole expense of the prosecution of the suit might be proved to have been thrown away on an appeal being made to the Judicial Committee of the Privy Council.'" [3]

A rule nisi was granted, but, upon the rule absolute being moved, Mr Bagot for the plaintiff raised a preliminary objection that the rule nisi was informal and without effect. It was headed: "In the Supreme Court: Regina on the prosecution of Samuel Mills against Walter Watson Hughes and others".

'Now, by the 26th chap. of 4 Geo II'—said Mr Bagot—'it is enacted that all legal proceedings in English Courts shall be in the English language.'

Mr Justice Gwynne: 'And not in the Latin?'

Mr Bagot: 'Yes; and if I recollect my schoolboy days right, "Regina" is Latin and not English.'

Greatly taken aback by this ridiculous technicality, the counsel for the defendants struggled to meet it.

'The first question'—said Mr Bakewell—'is whether the Statute to which Mr Bagot refers is applicable to this colony.'

Mr Justice Gwynne: 'Why, could you file proceedings here in Norman-French or Latin?'

Mr Bakewell: 'If the Court permitted. My friends rely on a certain Statute, and I would ask whether that is applicable here.'

The Chief Justice: 'Is not that part of the Statute applicable to the circumstances of the colony? Might the proceedings have been in Chinese?'

In spite of Mr Bakewell's submissions that the word "Regina" had become an English word, that the Queen so signed herself, and that the use of a solitary word was not an infringement of the statute, the Chief Justice and Mr Justice Gwynne upheld the objection and discharged the rule nisi.

Mr Justice Boothby strongly dissented, contending that if it was an infringement of the statute the defendants should be permitted to amend such a trivial slip, but this sensible attitude was taken as proof that he was biased in favour of the defendants.[4]

Mr Bakewell moved again for another rule nisi, which was granted, and this time correctly intituled. Upon the second motion for the rule absolute, Mr Justice Boothby renewed his assertions that there was no Attorney-General in the province. Further, he said, there was no Chief Justice in the province, and there never had been.

> Mr Boucaut: 'The other side have not taken that ground.'
>
> Boothby J: 'I only mention it as a matter that will be brought forward.'
>
> Mr Boucaut: 'If there is no Chief Justice there is no Justice in this Court.'
>
> Boothby J: 'There is no charter or commission under which the Chief Justice holds office. In a case involving some £20,000 or £30,000 the judgment might be invalidated on account of this.'
>
> Mr Justice Gwynne: 'I always abstain from making remarks when a point of this kind is raised, because my learned colleague has publicly and privately stated that I am no Judge at all' ...
>
> Mr Justice Boothby: 'The office of Attorney General has been assumed all along. It is the same with the Chief Justice, who is referred to as the Judge or the Chief Justice. Something is spoken of as the office of the Attorney-General; the first mention of such an officer being in the Constitution Act, which referred to him as one of the officers who should be a member of Parliament. There is nothing to show what the office has to do with that of Advocate General, or that the duties formerly performed by the Advocate General should be performed by the Attorney General. It was simply a statement that the Attorney General should be a member of Parliament ... It was the statute of William IV which appointed the Advocate General, and it will have to be shown how the old office has been got rid of before it is shown how the new one was established.'

By a majority (the Chief Justice dissenting) the rule was made absolute and the writ of scire facias quashed, on the ground that the leases sought to be annulled were not records of the Court so as to lay the necessary foundation for the writ.[5]

As the case was being taken to the Privy Council, Mr Justice Boothby seized the opportunity to add a resume of his opinions upon the invalidity of the Constitution Act and of all subsequent legislation, and upon the non-existence of any Chief Justice or Attorney-General. His judgment, said the *Register*, would have made the colonists tremble, had they not already become familiar with his sweeping objections to the laws of the province; and gloomy doubts were expressed whether any extent of legislation, imperial or otherwise, or any decision of any court, could prevent Mr Justice Boothby from discovering invalidity and repugnancy.[6]

The Moonta and Wallaroo mines were to produce more than twelve million tons of crude ore and have a major influence on South Australia's economic and social history. This photograph, ca. 1870, shows Wallaroo and its smelters. (SLSA)

That learned Judge went on his way regardless of criticism:

> 'Like the irregular crab,
> Which though it goes backward,
> thinks that it goes right,
> Because it goes its own way'.

Every now and again he erupted from the bench some comment upon the illegality of the proceedings before the Court. In *In re Baigent*, for example, he revived his objection that copies of acts had not been sent to be recorded in the Supreme Court.

> 'The Court has been proceeding very loosely'—he said—'but when a knowledge of the error is arrived at, it should not be persisted in. We were blinded before by ignorance; but our eyes being opened, we must not transgress again—at least, I cannot.'[7]

The other Judges ignored the point.

In December 1864 he tried a case which, in justice to him, deserves mention because it gave rise to rather unfair misrepresentations of his decision. He has been ridiculed for deciding that a man who went into his neighbour's paddock, took a bullock, killed it and concealed the hide, was not guilty of an offence, inasmuch as a custom existed in country districts entitling neighbours so to deal with one another's cattle.[8] In fact, the case (*R. v. Manning*) was a charge of sheep-stealing, in the course of which the Judge said: "It is a common practice, an understanding among sheepfarmers, to take and destroy a strange sheep coming into their flocks lest it should lead others astray."

"I never heard of such a rule," said the Crown Solicitor. The Judge reiterated that he had heard of it, and he expressed doubt whether it would be safe to convict.

> 'One stray sheep in a flock might cause great annoyance and trouble, and it was a common arrangement for sheep-farmer A to kill a sheep of sheep-farmer B's one day, and sheepfarmer B to do the same with regard to sheep-farmer A's the next day. I have heard it stated on oath this is so, and indeed sheepfarming could not be carried on in the colony unless some such practice existed.'

Finally he directed a verdict of not guilty, genuinely feeling, apparently, that there might not have been any criminal intent on the part of the prisoner. The case when examined hardly justifies the sarcasms based on it which were subsequently levelled at him.[9]

Nevertheless, the frequent disclosure by the Judge of his peculiar opinions continued to damage the credit of the Supreme Court, and the year 1864 closed with a further appeal by the Governor for action by the authorities at home:

> 'I have so frequently had occasion'—he wrote—'to allude to the very discreditable want of harmony and dignity so frequently exhibited on the Bench of the Supreme Court in this colony, that it can scarcely be necessary for me to observe that a better state of things cannot be expected until the points raised by Mr Boothby shall have been disposed of, and his pretensions (which I have never myself believed to be well founded) set at rest.' [10]

The Colonial Office received with resignation the addresses for Parliament and the news of the latest developments in the Boothby struggle. "I have just returned from holiday"—wrote Sir Frederick Rogers to the Governor in November 1864—"and so am not quite master of your mail of this month, but I see Boothby is at it again." [11]

(Sir) Frederic Rogers (Baron Blachford) (1811-1889) From 1860 to 1871 Rogers was undersecretary of State for the Colonies. He also served as a Privy Councillor and was one of the founders of the Guardian newspaper.

This time it was decided to make an attempt to settle the matter once and for all and to carry out the recommendations of the law officers. A draft of the act which subsequently became so well known as the Colonial Laws Validity Act was accordingly prepared and forwarded to South Australia for the consideration of the Governor. He was instructed also to obtain the views of his Government and of the Chief Justice upon the Bill. The Governor hastened to reply that he was delighted with the Bill and that the Chief Justice approved of it.

> 'It is, of course, not likely that Boothby will be satisfied with anything that may be done. I hope there need not be much delay or difficulty in putting him to silence in regard to his personal pretensions, for otherwise the Bench must continue to be a scandal and a reproach to this Community.'

The Attorney-General (Mr Stow) in a report on the Bill, pointed out the difficulty arising in the colony from the power claimed to look behind the records of colonial parliaments to inquire whether all requirements of the law as to legislation had been fulfilled; and an additional section was included in the Act to overcome this.[12]

Boothby family tree. Boothby's many descendants include the novelist Guy Boothby.
(Valerie Esau)

Chapter 5.8

Mr Justice Boothby

'invalidity trouble'

In March 1865 Mr Justice Boothby presided at the civil sittings, and aroused hostile comment by the manner in which he regulated the proceedings according to his own ideas of what was proper.

> 'What do litigants go to the Supreme Court for?'—grumbled the Register. 'Is it to obtain trial by Jury, or to see Mr Justice Boothby sitting like the "fabled Jove", with the fate of every man in the palm of his hand? ... Some of the clients are told that they had better go to arbitration; others are advised not to listen to their lawyers, but agree to a non-suit; whilst in not a few instances the counsel are sent back to 'mend their nets', with a recommendation to come again next session, when they will probably be able to catch a few fishes, either large or small.'

The old complaint was brought forward, that the Judge was usurping the functions of the jury. When he was on the bench, the jury was not wanted.

> 'Their important duties then cease. All that they have to do is to sit from morn to night listening to the more favoured actors on the scene. The lawyer pleads, the witness gives his evidence, and the Judge decides; but as to the time-honoured 'British Juror'—the champion of our liberties and the protector of our freedom—he is no more thought of than Gog and Magog. He sits in the box as a mere form, whilst his work is done by the Bench.' [1]

Nevertheless, except for these complaints, the Supreme Court for some months faded out of the public gaze.

In June 1865 the temporary lull was rudely shattered by the decision of the Court, in *R. v. Neville*, that the criminal jurisdiction of the Local Courts, which magistrates had exercised for many years without question, was illegal because it was repugnant to the law of England. Neville was a gentleman who had first become known to the public by pretending that he had discovered the remains of the ill-fated explorer Leichhardt. He was later convicted before Mr Justice Gwynne of horse-stealing, a count in the indictment charging him with having been previously convicted on a charge of felony. The previous conviction was one made by the Local Court of Willunga for stealing a rug of the value of thirty shillings. The Judge deferred sentence and reserved three questions for the consideration of the Full Court:

(1) Whether there was such a court as the Local Court of Willunga.
(2) Whether the power assumed to be given by the legislature to courts of full jurisdiction to try all cases of felony up to a certain amount was repugnant to the law of England.
(3) Whether a conviction by the Local Court for stealing a rug valued at thirty shillings was a conviction for felony.

Founded in 1839, Willunga was one of South Australia's first villages. The Southern Vales area, now noted for its wine production, was first a major wheat growing region with the mining of slate also providing economic impetus. The view here (ca. 1870) is of the township looking toward Victor Harbor with the Police Station on the left and Post Office on the right. (SLSA)

Mr Stow QC appeared for the prisoner and, relying on the decisions in *Payne v. Dench* and *McEllister v. Fenn*, contended that the legislature of South Australia had no power to create courts of law, and that the power conferred by the Local Courts Act on a Special Magistrate and two Justices of the Peace to hear and determine certain felonies "in a summary way, according to equity and good conscience, and the substantial merits of the case ... without a jury", and to impose sentence of imprisonment, was repugnant to the law of England.

The majority of the Court were content to decide the case upon the latter ground alone. Such part of the Act as conferred this criminal jurisdiction, said Mr Justice Gwynne, was repugnant and void. Mr Justice Boothby concurred. In a long dissenting judgment, the Chief Justice said that, in view of the frequent doubts expressed by Mr Justice Boothby as to the power of Parliament to create courts, he had hoped that the question would have been at last definitely decided.

> 'If from any reason the Legislature of this Colony alone of all the Australian Legislatures has been left without the power to constitute courts, and to make provision for the better

> administration of justice, any delay in the judicial declaration of this fact can have no other effect than that of adding to the inconveniences which have been already occasioned, and of prolonging a state of uncertainty already too protracted.'

He regretted that the other Judges had avoided giving judgment on this point; he himself had no doubt that the power to make laws for the peace, order and good government of the colony gave power to constitute courts.

With regard to the repugnancy point, he said:

> 'I have never met with a definition of repugnancy which seemed to me to throw any light upon the subject, and I have never been able to frame a definition which satisfied myself. The nearest definition I can give is that an Act is repugnant to the law of England, not when it alters forms or rules, but when it contradicts the substance and principle of the law of England.'

He pointed out that in England, when death and forfeiture of property followed a conviction for felony, it was no doubt necessary that the safeguard should exist requiring all trials for felony to be before a jury, but he could not see that this should be so in minor cases where the maximum penalty which the Court could impose was imprisonment for six months. To say that, because some of the offences cognisable by the Local Courts were still called by the name of felony, the criminal jurisdiction of those Courts was repugnant seemed to him to be "putting words in the place of things" and to be making the question depend upon a mere matter of nomenclature. Repugnancy as thus interpreted would prevent any improvement or simplification in the procedure of the law.[2]

The decision was a staggering one. Was South Australia doomed never to hear the last of this monstrous "repugnancy"? "The fatal word has been written on the walls of the Supreme Court, and no hand can rub it out."

Mr Justice Gwynne's secession from the right path was deplored as catastrophic.

> 'If year after year it is found'—said the Register—'that a portion of the Bench do their utmost to neutralize local legislation; that they declare every law containing new principles repugnant, as they did the Real Property Act; and that suitors in the other colonies are allowed to proceed quietly under similar laws, whilst suitors here are stopped and embarrassed by the Bench, why, then, the result will be that the Supreme Court will be regarded as a curse to the colony.' [3]

As for Mr Stow, who had taken the objections, words could not be found strong enough to denounce the way in which he had "strutted in borrowed plumes ... picking up the worn-out objections of Mr Justice Boothby, and giving them all the force of his own eloquence". Stow had been Attorney-General in the Parliament which passed the Local Courts Act of 1861; he had introduced the Bill; he had advised the Governor to assent to it; and for him now to contend that the Act was invalid was looked upon as the lowest degree of treachery. The Government were strongly criticised for not being better represented by counsel on the arguments in *R. v Neville*; the best counsel should have been briefed from the other colonies to argue such an important question. "It had been said that one of the Judges, at least was open to conviction, and some attempt should have been made to convince him." [4]

The Government were indeed faced with a serious situation. Hasty arrangements were made that in future all prisoners should be committed to the Supreme Court for trial. But what of those prisoners in the gaol and the stockade who had been convicted and sentenced by illegal tribunals? And what of the hundreds who had paid their fines or served their sentences, and who now had the opportunity of revenging themselves by actions for wrongful imprisonment or illegal extortion? The depth to which the reputation of the Supreme Court had sunk is shown by the course the Government took. Those prisoners who were serving sentences imposed by Local Courts were kept in gaol, notwithstanding that their imprisonment had been declared unlawful, whilst a bill was immediately introduced into Parliament to protect Special Magistrates, Justices of the Peace, and persons acting under them, from actions in consequence of the exercise of the criminal jurisdiction of the Local Courts. The Magistrates Indemnity Bill was severely criticised in the Assembly by Mr Boucaut, who pointed out that if the Judges were right in their opinion that the criminal jurisdiction of the Local Courts was illegal because it was repugnant, then any attempt retrospectively to legalise what had been done in the exercise of that jurisdiction must equally be repugnant.

> 'The time has arrived'—he said—'when the Government should grapple with the whole question and if they are afraid to do so it is the more necessary for this House to take it up. A difficulty has overshadowed our legislation for many years, and it is monstrous to have country members leaving their private business and attending here to make laws which are set aside as soon as questioned.' [5]

Neville Blyth (1825-1890) The Blyth family emigrated to Adelaide in 1839 and Neville and brother Arthur (1823-1891), after working in the family merchant business, set up as ironmongers. In this they were successful, as they were with land investment. Both brothers entered politics with Arthur becoming Premier twice (1871-72, 1873-75). (SLSA)

When the second reading of the Bill was moved, Mr N. Blyth proposed as an amendment a resolution that:

> 'This House protests against the decision of the Supreme Court of this Province that the 8th division of the Local Courts Act is beyond the powers of the legislature of this colony to pass; but being in expectation of receiving at an early

> date an Imperial Act removing all doubts as to the validity of South Australian legislation, suspends all action in the matter till next session.'

What, he asked, was the use of passing another act? The Judges would not treat it with a whit more respect than the other acts they had condemned.

> 'Has not our legislation been treated contumeliously? Has not a Judge, when referring to another measure, said: 'I treated it with all the respect it deserved: that is, I took no notice of it'?'

As for the base conduct of Mr Stow, the speaker was unable to trust himself to characterise it. "Let him never come back to us," he cried.

> 'Let him never come back to us,
> There would be doubt, hesitation, and pain,
> Forced praise on our part, the glimmer of twilight,
> Never glad confidant morning again. (Hear, hear!)'

> 'What is repugnancy?' he continued. 'There never has been anything like an exact or mathematical definition. It is a mistake to suppose that when a Judge speaks of repugnancy, it is some thing as obvious as the leak in a ship or a crack in a vessel—something tangible to the senses, a thing that can be felt or seen. It is nothing of the sort; it is a matter of opinion ... The only rational rule is to regard repugnancy as something opposed to natural justice; such as interference with the right to get married, the exercise of the Christian religion, or anything which it is against common sense to suppose we would attempt to enact.' [6]

While Mr Blyth's amendment was being eagerly debated, the Supreme Court fired an even more devastating broadside by its judgment in the case of *Dawes v. Quarrell*. *R. v Neville* had decided that the Local Courts had no criminal jurisdiction; *Dawes v. Quarrell* went a step further, and decided that there were no Local Courts at all.[7]

Mr Justice Boothby and Mr Justice Gwynne agreed in holding that the omission from 13 & 14 Vic c.59 of the provision enabling the erection of courts, which had been expressly set out in the earlier Acts relating to South Australia, had left the local legislature without power to create local courts, and that the Local Courts Act of 1861 was therefore invalid. Their opinion was not without a plausible foundation. In the Acts 4 & 5 Wm IV c.95 and 1 & 2 Vic c.60, as well as in the Swan River Colony Act (10 Geo IV c.22), in addition to the power "to make laws for the peace, welfare and good government" of the colony, the words "and to constitute such courts etc." were used. Obviously, the power to make laws for the peace, welfare and good government did not include the power to create courts, or the additional words so carefully inserted would have been unnecessary. The Act 13 & 14 Vic was in pari materia with the earlier Acts, and there was no reason why the words "peace welfare and good government" should be given a wider construction than that attaching to them as used in the earlier Acts. If, therefore, the provision as to erecting courts was deliberately omitted from the Imperial Statute, the colonial legislature had no such power.

The Chief Justice dissented at length. He denied that the Act was repugnant and he considered that the power to establish courts had not been taken from the South Australian Parliament.

Mr Justice Gwynne also said the Local Courts Act was repugnant and invalid because it introduced a procedure unknown to English law; and he added some more curious reasons:

> 'It appears to me'—he said—'that the Local Courts Act of 1861 was not within the competency of the Local Legislature of South Australia, inasmuch as it abolishes pro tanto the Supreme Court, this Court being founded not immediately though mediately on Imperial legislation. I am also of opinion that it is opposed to the Constitution Act. The 30th and 31st sections of that Act provide that the Judges shall hold their office during good behaviour, and shall be removable only by the Queen, upon the address of both Houses of Parliament. Thus is the independence of the Judges secured for the public good; but of what avail is this provision to the public if the great mass of the current business of the Supreme Court is removed from the Judges and conferred upon gentlemen dependent for their offices upon—not to say the Attorney General—but the Ministry of the day. And surely the Judge is practically, so far as the public is concerned, as much removed by taking the business from his Court and jurisdiction as he would be by taking him from that business and jurisdiction.'

The second of these reasons lends some support to the opinion openly expressed by the *Register* that the Judges were jealous of the Local Courts because they took most of the business and the Supreme Court was falling into the background. "Under these circumstances there is a tangible reason for the dead-set which has lately been made at our Local Courts." [8]

The Insolvency Court necessarily fell with the Local Court; and if Mr Justice Gwynne was consistent, it appeared that he must commit a species of legal suicide and hold that the Third Judge and District Courts Acts, to which he owed his appointment, was invalid. The prospects of litigation and confusion were frightful. During the previous six years, for instance, nearly 50,000 summonses had been issued from Local Courts; every one of these processes was, according to *Dawes v. Quarrell*, invalid. Since the passing of the Local

Courts Act of 1861, 430 persons had been convicted in Local Courts and sentenced to imprisonment: every one, apparently, had been unlawfully confined. In the Insolvency Court from 1859 to 1865, 765 adjudications had been made: every one of no legal effect.[9]

This Townsend Duryea photograph (ca. 1866) of Victoria Square looking north shows the old Local Court building (left with small tower) and the Town Hall (with high tower). The Insolvency Court and the Local Court relocated temporarily to the Town Hall in 1866 to allow the GPO to be built before ultimately moving to Victoria Square. (NLA)

The immediate question was—what were the Local Courts to do? Some closed their doors; others carried on in defiance of the Supreme Court's decision that they had no legal existence. Magistrates who wrote to the Government for instructions to sit or not to sit were told that they must decide according to law, of which they were the sole judges.[10] Accordingly, some heard cases as usual; others refused to do any business at all; others again made an effectual compromise by adjourning the cases before them sine die. In the Adelaide Local Court, on the day following the judgment in *Dawes v. Quarrell*, Mr Bruce, appearing for one defendant, contended the Court had no jurisdiction. Mr Bonney SM, who presided on the bench, said the Court would continue to sit until there was an official intimation there was no such Court. What was an official intimation? asked Mr Bruce; there were no law reports in the colony, and the proceedings of the Supreme Court were only known through newspapers. He pressed his objection and threatened quo warranto proceedings; Mr Boucaut joined in and read cases to the bench where magistrates had been indicted for illegally holding courts. Undeterred, the bench decided they were still a court and that the case must go on, but at Bruce's request adjourned it to the following day.

Next day another solicitor, Mr Wigley, took the objection there was no court and, when the bench overruled this, he put on his hat, wished them good morning and walked out of the courtroom. The case was dealt with in his absence. Bruce's case was then called on again, and that gentleman said that, as the Court had intimated it had had no official notice of the decision in *Dawes v. Quarrell*, he would prove it by evidence. He called Mr Boucaut, who, after demanding and exacting payment of a witness fee before he would speak, gave evidence that he had been present in court and heard the judgments delivered by the Judges. After considering the objection for half an hour, the bench ruled they had jurisdiction to hear the case, which was proceeded with. The decision of the Adelaide Local Court to ignore the ruling of the Supreme Court was speedily followed by the country courts, and the absurd situation arose of inferior courts, which had been pronounced by the Supreme Court to be legally non-existent, continuing to function as usual.

Cabinet met and deplored the delay in obtaining Imperial legislation to extricate the colony from this morass.[11] In a long dispatch the Governor poured out a tale of woe to the Secretary of State. Mr Justice Boothby's opinions, he said, that the legislature had not since 1842 possessed the power to erect courts or to appoint judges had long been known; and it was suspected that Mr Justice Gwynne to some extent participated in the doubts of his colleague.

> 'It was however supposed'—said the Governor—'that Mr Justice Gwynne, who owed his appointment to an Act of the Legislature, and who had a high reputation for prudence and good sense, must have entertained substantially different views from his colleague and at any rate that he would take care to avoid as far as possible any action which might have the effect of stirring the question. These expectations have been falsified by the event.'

After giving details of the judgments in *Dawes v. Quarrell*, the Governor went on:

> 'The decision is sufficiently embarrassing even if it was confined to the Local Courts, since it would affect most materially the administration of justice throughout the Colony, but the same principle of course extends to every Court, and in fact Mr Gwynne, who has been temporarily acting as Commissioner of Insolvency, has desired to be relieved from acting any longer on the ground that the decision of the Supreme Court necessarily involves the invalidity of the Act under which the Court of Insolvency was constituted. And I am advised that the same reasoning would show not merely that every Act passed for the better administration of justice during the last twenty years is invalid, but also that this is the case with two of the most popular and useful measures of the

Legislature, the Real Property Act and the District Councils Act. In fact, no one seems at present to be able to say how far the effects of these two principles of invalidity may extend. I need hardly say that this decision and its apprehended consequences have caused a very general feeling of irritation and alarm, and are doing much to weaken public confidence in the administration of justice by means of the Supreme Court. It is said, and not altogether unreasonably, that no one can tell under what laws he is living, or what will in any given instance be the decision of the Supreme Court, for after a series of years during which certain laws have been reputed to be valid, acted upon as valid by the Supreme Court, and made the foundation of their proceedings in innumerable cases, with a full knowledge on the part of the individual Judges of the existence of certain objections, these Judges may turn round and declare that they have been giving effect to assumed laws which they knew all the time had no validity. It is asked where this is to stop, and to this question no one is prepared to give an answer. Of course, there can be no doubt in the mind of any dispassionate person of the sincere desire of the majority of the Court to discharge their duty conscientiously. But in a conjecture like the present it is not easy for everyone to be dispassionate, and feelings of anger and distrust prevail, I am informed, to a considerable extent. These however will I trust soon fade away, but in the meantime they somewhat add to the difficulty in which the Government is placed, and I confess I feel that position to be very difficult and embarrassing. On the one hand I am anxious not to take any step which may trench upon the independence of the Judges of the Supreme Court, which I would by all proper means maintain and protect, and on the other I am desirous to put an end in any practicable way to the state of, I may almost say, anarchy, which these decisions, if carried out to their legitimate consequences, will as I fear inevitably produce. The difficulty is increased by the fact that if the majority of the Supreme Court are consistent with their former judgments, as I presume they will be, the remedial action whatever it is must be taken by the Government itself, it having been already decided by the Supreme Court to be beyond the power of the Legislature—so that I anticipate that ultimately there will be no alternative but either to wait the arrival of some Act confirming the local legislation, leaving the Colony (if the Act is not already on its way, as I trust may be the case) to remain practically without laws for many months,

> or to assert the power of the Local Court of Appeal, and in our Executive capacity give effect to its decision notwithstanding my great reluctance individually to sit as President of the Court, and notwithstanding the suggestion, I might almost say the threat, from the tone in which it has been urged by some persons, that in that case the Executive would be brought into collision with the Judges.' [12]

The ministry decided to resort to the latter alternative. But the amount at stake in *Dawes v. Quarrell* was only £20, whereas there was no right of appeal to the Court of Appeals unless at least £100 was involved. To overcome this, a bill was introduced into Parliament to amend the provisions of the Supreme Court Act relating to the Court of Appeals by giving a right of appeal irrespective of the amount involved. By suspending the standing orders, the Bill was rushed through both Houses in a few days, and assented to by the Governor before Parliament was prorogued, on 1 August 1865.

The majority of the Supreme Court proceeded to make it clear that they were not going to be overawed by popular clamour into resiling from their opinion. On 29 July, Mr Daly moved the Full Court for a rule calling on the Magistrate at Port Adelaide (who, in obedience to *Dawes v. Quarrell*, had refused to perform any judicial acts) to show cause why he should not issue execution at the request of a judgment creditor. He rose and said he moved for the rule under the Local Courts Act.

> 'There is no such Court,' said Mr Justice Gwynne.
>
> 'With your Honor's permission, I shall read an affidavit and make my application,' said Mr Daly.
>
> 'Certainly not,' said the Judge.
>
> 'I imagine,' said the Chief Justice, 'that any counsel has the right in the interest of his client to address any argument to the Court with a view to appeal.'
>
> 'According to that ruling,' replied Mr Justice Gwynne, 'we may go on for ever and be discussing the question of the Local Courts until Doomsday. When the Court solemnly decided that there are no such Courts the question was settled; and for my part I will hear no argument which assumes the existence of Local Courts.'

Mr Justice Boothby supported him.

> 'There has been a decision on this point'—he said—'and counsel should remember that they are practitioners of this Court, and that this Court has power to strike off the rolls any practitioner who treats the decisions of the Court with disrespect. For my own part, I am quite prepared to act on that

> principle. If any counsel is told to hold his tongue, he is bound to submit and be silent.'

After further discussion, Mr Daly submitted that he was entitled at least to make his application and have it refused, with a view to the matter being taken on appeal to a higher court.

> 'If your motion is founded upon the assumption that the Local Courts exist'—said Mr Justice Gwynne—'I cannot hear you, for I have, after careful consideration, arrived at the conclusion that there are no Local Courts. I do not say that my judgment is right, but that is the conclusion to which my intellect leads me. It is my duty to express my opinion, erroneous or otherwise, and I say that it is not proper for counsel to address the Court on the assumption that it is erroneous until it has been proved so.'

Mr Daly then made his application, which was promptly refused. The Magistrate was quite right, said Mr Justice Gwynne: "The decisions of this Court must be upheld by him and by the Government, otherwise we will have nothing but anarchy."

> 'I am of the same opinion'—said Mr Justice Boothby. 'If any of the invalid Courts assume to exercise jurisdiction it is to be hoped that the practitioners of this Court will not countenance them. By doing so they are liable to be struck off the rolls. The Attorney General should himself remember that he is only a practitioner of this Court.'

The Chief Justice said he was bound by the decision of the majority, and would have said no more had it not been for Mr Justice Boothby's remarks, with which he entirely disagreed. The following squabble ensued:

> The Chief Justice: 'I can conceive nothing more at variance with the spirit in which justice ought to be administered in this Court than an attempt to impose silence upon practitioners under the threat of their being removed from the roll. I can only say that such is not the view which I take of the position of this Court or the duty of practitioners.'
>
> Mr Justice Boothby: 'I distinctly wish to be understood that I object to counsel demanding to be heard upon the same grounds over and over again, not for the purpose of appeal. It is a clear contempt of this Court, and I consider this motion is intended to serve some object out of doors.'
>
> Mr Daly: 'My only object is to appeal in this case.'
>
> Mr Justice Gwynne: 'It is a great pity that you did not say so in

> the first instance, nor until it had been suggested by my colleague the Chief Justice.'
>
> The Chief Justice: 'I do not think that there was anything in my remarks to justify a suggestion that a false pretence has been put forth in support of the motion.'
>
> Mr Justice Gwynne: 'I beg to say that that is a most unfounded remark.'
>
> The Chief Justice: 'It is what I understood you to say.'
>
> Mr Justice Gwynne: 'Then you grossly misunderstood me.'

At this stage Mr Daly incautiously announced that he was going to appeal to the Court of Appeals and asked the Court to put in writing their reasons for refusing his application. "There is no such Court," said Mr Justice Boothby. Mr Daly submitted it was not competent for the Supreme Court to question the existence of a court superior to it.

> Mr Justice Boothby: 'We cannot hear you. This Court has decided that there is no Local Court of Appeals, and the question cannot be raised on a motion of this kind.'
>
> The Chief Justice: 'Then how can it be raised? If I sit alone, I shall hear you or any other practitioner argue as to the existence of the Court of Appeals. I can only say that a more outrageous decision was never given, and that no precedent can be found for an inferior court setting aside a superior court. I repeat that if I sit alone I shall hear any practitioner argue the question.'
>
> Mr Justice Gwynne: 'And if I sit alone I am prepared to hear any argument tending to settle the question of the Local Court of Appeals. I do not, however, agree with my colleague in the opinions he has expressed with regard to the decision of this Court on the question. I think that no honest-minded lawyer could come to any other decision. Perhaps it would have been better if I had not followed the example of my learned colleague. It is sufficient for me to say these are my opinions; it is below my dignity to defend them. Whether in the opinion of my colleague they are unprecedented, I neither know nor care.'

Unseemly discussions like this could not but degrade the Supreme Court in the eyes of the public. The *Register* openly said that the Governor should suspend one or two of the Judges in order that the law might be properly administered.

An appeal was immediately instituted in *Dawes v. Quarrell*, provoking Mr Justice Boothby to say that the question could be settled only by the Privy Council, and that to think to get it settled by the Executive of the colony was "a most extraordinary hallucination".

Meanwhile, as a result of the Supreme Court's decision, a crop of actions for damages was springing up, the first of which, *Thompson v. Simpson*, came before the Full Court on a demurrer on 4 August 1865. It was an action for false imprisonment. The plaintiff had been arrested by the Sheriff on a ca. sa. on a judgment obtained in the Local Court and removed into the Supreme Court. The plaintiff's contention was that as the Local Court judgment had no effect in law, the ca sa was also invalid, and his arrest therefore unlawful. The case was treated as a test case, and Mr Justice Boothby was well satisfied to hear that it was likely to be taken to the Privy Council. "It will be a matter of the highest gratification to me to see this done," he assured counsel, and he seized the opportunity to urge upon them the importance of seeing that the question of the testing of writs issued out of the Supreme Court was brought before the notice of the Judicial Committee. "I have looked at the records of the Court"—he said—"and I have not found one valid writ issued from this Court since the retirement of Sir Charles Cooper." [13]

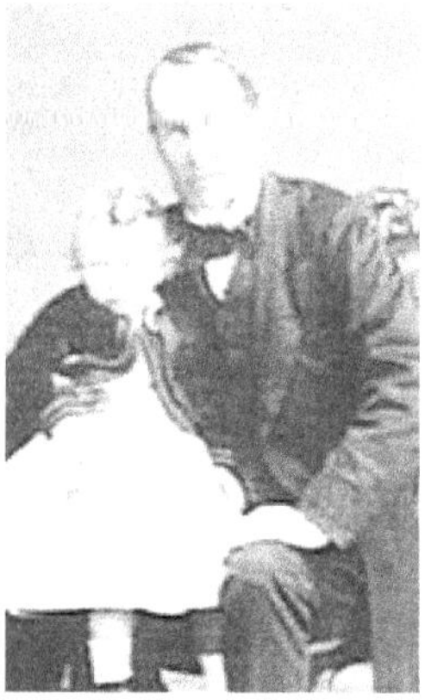

Rupert Ingleby (1820-1881) Ingleby's legal career extended beyond private practice to include service as the City Coroner, a Magistrate and as the Crown Solicitor. Appointed a QC in 1875 he was also a keen gardener and three times an unsuccessful political candidate. He is pictured with his son Rupert (1869-1930) who was appointed a QC in 1927. (SLSA)

On the same day, in another case before the Full Court (*Harrald v. Carruthers*), the question was raised whether the Insolvency Court was also a court with no legal existence. Mr Ingleby was for the plaintiff, Mr Mann for the defendant; and Mr Justice Boothby started the proceedings by addressing Mr Mann as follows:

> 'I think it a kindness to you, Mr Mann, to refer you to what I said the other day. You are, I believe, the Clerk of what is called the Local Court of Appeals, and I say that any one who recognises that Court by appearing before it in any way would be removed from the rolls of the Supreme Court. I would remind you that this can be done without any of the profession moving in the matter; for it is the duty of every Judge who sits here to protect her Majesty's prerogative in her own appointed Courts. She has the sole power of establishing them, except so far as she has committed her prerogative to Statute; and it is an insult to her to go to another Court and say, "Don't take any notice of what is said in the Supreme Court—it is all nonsense." If any practitioner did this, and yet was allowed to remain on the rolls, that would be a course of conduct which the Courts of Westminster would not allow for an hour. I give you this advice as you are in a position which may render such proceedings possible; and the right to do it, if it was carried to the Privy Council, would be upheld, for I am sure the Judges would protect Her Majesty from insult, for the insult was to Her and not to the Court. In a case where the Sheriff of Kent was fined £500 by the Court of Queen's Bench, it was held

that Her Majesty in legal estimation was present in all Her Courts, and that any contempt of the Judges would be contempt to Herself.'

Mr Mann: 'With regard to my being Clerk of the Court of Appeals, I may say that I have been drawing certain sums as salary on account of that situation; but hitherto I have not been required to do anything else. If I am called upon to act in my capacity as Clerk, I shall give Your Honour's remarks every consideration.'

Mr Justice Boothby: 'My regard for you has led me to give you this advice. I do not wish you to be in a position which will necessitate the Court striking you from the rolls.'

Mr Mann: 'I am obliged to Your Honour.'

The Chief Justice: 'Before anything could be done by this Court with regard to striking a practitioner from the rolls some argument must be submitted on both sides, and when the question is brought forward I shall give my best attention to those arguments, and do all I can to maintain unimpaired the dignity of Her Majesty—not that I think I would have great power in that respect—while at the same time endeavouring to uphold the independence of the profession of which I was one.'

Mr Justice Boothby: 'My remarks were made with the same view. I have always held the opinion that I have expressed, but I am prepared to bow to English authorities. I considered it wise, seeing the situation which Mr Mann occupied, to make the remarks I have given utterance to.'

Charles Mann Jnr. (1838-1889) The eldest son of Charles Mann was admitted in 1860. He entered Parliament in 1870 and was Attorney-General (1871–72 and 1873–75) and Crown Solicitor (1881-89). A QC from 1875 he refused a position on the Supreme Court bench in 1884. (SLSA)

Mr Randolph Stow (with whom Mr Justice Boothby was soon after to have a memorable rencontre) was sitting at the bar table, and at this stage he intervened in the proceedings.

'Do Your Honour's remarks apply to the profession generally?' he asked Mr Justice Boothby.

'Yes,' replied the Judge.

'Then I may say for myself,' stoutly retorted Mr Stow, 'and I think I can do so for the majority of the profession, that I shall practise before any Court where I think the interests of my client requires that I should do so.'

Mr Justice Boothby: 'And I as a Judge shall not recognise you if you think fit to practise in Courts which have been declared to have no existence. I shall never hear your voice in the Court,

> nor take any notice of legal proceedings in which your name appears as attorney on the record. The Court has a clear power of doing this if sufficient ground is shown; and this I should look upon as sufficient. I am only surprised that such a state of things should possibly exist, namely, that a practitioner should practise before a Court which has been declared to have been unlawful and to have no existence. Such a notion would never be entertained anywhere else.'
>
> Mr Ingleby: 'Things are reversed here.'
>
> Mr Justice Boothby: 'They are reversed indeed.'

Mr Justice Gwynne said he thought the Insolvency Court fell with the Local Courts and was equally invalid.

> 'I will be happy to hear reasons stated to show that my judgment is erroneous'—he added. 'If, therefore, you can bring topics to pursue this argument you may try it—not that I think you can convince me, but I am willing to let you make the experiment.' [14]

It was decided that the experiment should be tried, and the matter was adjourned to the following week to be argued. When counsel then rose to address the Court, however, Mr Justice Boothby stopped him with a new objection. "I do not think cases of this sort can be taken out of Term," he said.

> Mr Ingleby: 'There is an Act on the Statute Book giving power to hear out of Term.'
>
> Mr Justice Boothby: 'The words are merely permissive, and it will be destructive of all the rules of law and the practice of the Courts to take cases of this kind out of Term. There will be endless difficulty and litigation to settle the new practice, whereas if the old rule is adhered to we have the benefit of the whole of the decisions of the Court as a guide.'

The Chief Justice read from clause 30 of Act No 3 of 1862, as follows:

> 'The Court shall have and exercise out of Term all the powers and authorities it now has and may exercise in Term.'
>
> Mr Justice Boothby: '"Shall" and "may" are convertible terms. We have power if we choose to exercise it. The old law and the practice of the Courts of Westminster, which in many cases is as much law as the printed Statutes, clearly show that there are some cases which cannot be taken out of Term.'
>
> The Chief Justice: 'There is no rule of Court, is there?'

The Master replied in the negative.

> Mr Justice Boothby: 'But the rules in England are applicable here ... Colonial Legislation has always surprised me ... The rule and the practice which have been in force are plainly consistent with reason and common sense, and absolutely necessary for the proper dispensing of justice. Where particular duties are assigned to separate periods, those who have business belonging to any particular class will take care to be in Court; but if the Court may take any kind of business on any day there is a necessity for the attendance of attorneys every time it sits, and one effect of this will be to put hundreds of pounds into their pockets. Such a state of things is frightful. The practice in England is so strict in this respect that the Courts fix particular business for the several days in term; and thus the parties, knowing when to be present, are able to save costs, for attorneys are entitled to charge for attendance. Any other practice introduced here will produce frightful results.'

> The Chief Justice: 'I can understand this appeal to the practice and rules of Court, but when we are told that frightful consequences will follow from a particular course, I consider that the first result of adopting that course will be that parties who have come down by appointment to argue a particular demurrer will have to return without doing anything, and that the Court which has met for little other than for the special purpose of hearing that argument will find itself without other business. I confess I am unable to appreciate the force of what has been said. I can quite understand that in England, where there is a division of the profession, and the class of persons who practise are distinguished from attorneys—a division of labour which cannot exist here—such a rule as has been alluded to may be found very useful, but so far as my experience goes, it would in this Colony be found inconvenient in every way. The rules of this Court were established when there was very little legal business in the colony, and Term time was not merely made to include the sittings of the Full Court, but also those for the trial of causes. It has happened repeatedly, and it may happen again that the second and third weeks may be taken up by the sittings, and then there are only eight weeks in the year left for Banco business. This circumstance, I think, justified the Legislature in passing this Act; and legislation having taken place to empower the Court to do Term business, at any time they choose, I think the convenience of suitors will be very much served by exercising

this power.'

Mr Justice Boothby: 'This defect will appear on the record and I will draw the attention of the Privy Council to it. The point has only occurred to me just now. It is an exceedingly important one.'

Mr Ingleby: 'We came down understanding that the Court had fixed today for the argument.'

Mr Justice Boothby: 'Inadvertently so far as I am concerned.'

The Chief Justice: 'We consider that having the power to go on, and without deciding the general principle which may be subject to argument, that the parties having by appointment come here we should proceed.'

Mr Justice Boothby: 'As this is a particular case, and we have made the appointment, I will say nothing more, except that the point may be taken before the Privy Council, the consequences of which the parties will have to bear. I know that in England a case brought forward in this way would be at once sent back, that being the only check on irregular proceedings.'

The Chief Justice: 'No doubt that is so, but I regret that not a single instance of the kind has found its way into the books.'

Mr Justice Boothby: 'When children have learned their ABC it is not necessary to bring it before them over and over again.'

The Chief Justice: 'Go on, Mr Mann.'

Mr Mann then proceeded to argue that there was a distinction between the powers necessary to create Local Courts and those necessary to create an Insolvency Court; and that the non-existence of the latter Court did not necessarily follow as a corollary to *Dawes v. Quarrell*. In the course of discussion as to the power of creating courts, Mr Justice Boothby announced:

'There are a great many Courts which may be created here tomorrow, and if any person applies to this Court to call them together, it would be bound to issue its decree, and that decree would have to be obeyed.'

The Chief Justice: 'I should be sorry to express an opinion of that sort without argument.'

Mr Justice Boothby: 'I have no doubt in the world upon the subject. The Resident Magistrate's Court is still in existence, and it is idle for people to say that there are no means of collecting debts. It would be the plainest duty of this Court to put in force the Acts of the Legislature. Mr Mann in his earliest readings—while sitting upon a clerk's stool in a legal office—must have seen that one of the functions of the Queen's Bench—all of which were possessed by the Supreme Court—was to cause Courts to pursue their jurisdiction.'

The Chief Justice: 'I trust we shall confine ourselves to the question before us.'

Mr Justice Boothby: 'I must claim my right to shortly address counsel ... The Chief Justice has a right to express his opinion and so have I; and I think it very desirable that suitors out of doors should be informed of what they could secure by coming to this Court. I hear statements to the effect that traders are unable to collect their debts, and I tell the public generally that they are entitled to have their rights determined before the Resident Magistrate's Court. Complaints are made that we are without law; but the parties should come to this Court, and ask what the law is.'

The Chief Justice: 'Go on, Mr Mann.' [15]

These specimens of the bickering which continually went on will serve to show that the temper of the Chief Justice was becoming sorely tried by the aberrations of his colleague Mr Justice Boothby.

In both *Thompson v. Simpson* and *Harrald v. Carruthers* judgment was reserved, but neither case is again heard of, for a few days later news arrived in the colony of the passing of the Colonial Laws Validity Act, and the litigation which had sprung from *Dawes v. Quarrell* seems to have been abandoned by mutual consent without more ado.

The Colonial Laws Validity Act—"the charter of colonial legislative independence"—had passed the Imperial Parliament on 29 June 1865.

In his dispatch forwarding the Act to the Governor, the Secretary of State, after mentioning that it had been passed to set at rest the questions raised in the Supreme Court respecting the validity of colonial laws, added:

'It is intended, as far as possible, to obviate doubts and litigation on this most important subject by declaring that no Colonial law shall be void for repugnancy to the law of England, unless it is inconsistent with an Imperial Act intended by Parliament to extend to the Colony in which such law is passed, nor because it is at variance with the Governor's Instructions. It also establishes the power of Colonial Legislatures to regulate the administration of justice, on which doubts had been thrown, and the power of every

> representative legislature to alter its own constitution.'

Upon the principle applied by Mrs Squeers in distributing her brimstone and treacle—that if a boy was not ill one morning, he might be the next, so the remedy had to be taken in advance—the Act was given general application to all colonies.

The provisions of the Colonial Laws Validity Act are too familiar to require repetition here.

The passing of the Act was hailed with joy in Adelaide.

> 'As cold water to a thirsty soul, so is good news from a far country.'

The publication of it in the newspapers, wrote the Governor: "... had the effect of immediately checking the litigation to which what I must call the reckless conduct of the puisne Judges had given occasion."[16]The press was jubilant: the Judges had been put right, and Mr Justice Boothby's nonsense exposed. "The invalidity quarrel is at an end"—announced the Register.[17]

The timely arrival of the Act had, in fact, prevented a serious disaster. The Government and the Supreme Court were on the brink of a bitter dispute, for the puisne judges hotly resented the revival of the Court of Appeals for the express purpose of overruling them; and had not the Validating Act arrived in time they would have been little inclined to recognise the existence of such a court or to take any notice of its decrees.

As it was, the rejoicings of the newspapers were premature. Although news of the passing of the Act was published in the press on 14 August 1865, no official intimation that it was in force was received for another month. During the interim, more trouble arose. Two cases involving the same point, *Murray v. Varley* and *Murray v. Ridpath*, came before the Full Court—consisting of the Chief Justice and Mr Justice Boothby—on 29 August 1865. The plaintiff had been the defendant in certain Local Court actions and had paid money into Court in respect of them. When *Dawes v. Quarrell* decided that there were no Local Courts, he demanded his money back, and, upon the Clerks of the Courts refusing to return it, he sued them for money had and received. The defendants' main plea was section 218 of the Local Courts Act 1861, which provided that actions against any person for anything done in pursuance of that Act should be commenced within three months, and that one month's notice of action should be given to the defendant. To this plea the plaintiff demurred. If there were no legal local courts at all, he argued, section 218 was a nullity and could have no application.

The Chief Justice and Mr Justice Boothby disagreed in opinion and the case had to be reargued before the full bench which, on 5 September, held the plea was bad. Mr Justice Gwynne said that, as there were no legal Local Courts or officers of such courts, the plea amounted to nothing. "It sets forth a state of things no doubt intended to exist by the Legislature, but which really has no legal existence."

Mr Justice Boothby agreed.

> 'To support this plea'—he said—'would be to uphold the preposterous principle that while the Legislature could not create a jurisdiction beyond its powers, yet that it could set up an authority in officers which would enable the maintenance of that jurisdiction.'

The Chief Justice dissented, and thought that the plea could be supported, but had to bow to the decision of the majority of the Court.[18]

The two cases came on for trial at the civil sittings on 12 September, before the Chief Justice; and the defendants, their principal plea having been disallowed, had, of necessity almost, to confess judgment for the amount claimed. "I am bound by the opinion of the majority of the Court," the Chief Justice told the jury, "to say that there was no Local Court of Adelaide, and that there never has been such a Court"; and he directed them accordingly to find for the plaintiff. Mr Ingleby for the defendants tendered a bill of exceptions to the ruling, which the Chief Justice willingly signed.[19]

Up to this time, although it was known that the Colonial Laws Validity Act was passed, official copies of it were still lacking, and in *Murray v. Varley* and *Murray v. Ridpath* the argument had therefore proceeded on the assumption that there was no such act. A few days later, the Governor's copies of it arrived, and were at once published in a *Gazette Extraordinary*.

> 'The beneficial effects of the new Imperial Validating Act'—wrote the Register a few days later—'are already manifesting themselves, and no doubt points which previously would have been seized upon with avidity will by virtue of its invalidity-dispelling charm rest in unhonoured oblivion.' [20]

Magistrates and Justices of the Peace were circularised by the Attorney-General and advised that all doubts as to their jurisdiction, both civil and criminal, having been removed, they could continue their judicial functions without danger.

The Governor reported that the Chief Justice assured him that the Act was sufficient in every respect to meet all the difficulties that had been raised.

> 'It is rumoured'—added the Governor—'that Judge Boothby is of a different opinion, but it remains to be seen upon what grounds, and I would fain hope that I may ere long be enabled to report a better state of feeling in reference to the Supreme Court than I have yet had the satisfaction of witnessing in this colony.' [21]

Upon the official publication of the Colonial Laws Validity Act, Mr Ingleby at once moved for a new trial in *Murray v. Ridpath* and *Murray v. Varley* on the ground that the Chief Justice had misdirected the jury. The point was, when was the Act to take effect—when it was passed in England or when it was proclaimed in South Australia? The Court declined to hold that there had been any misdirection and refused the application.[22]

Mr Justice Boothby lost no time in making public his views upon the effect of the Colonial Laws Validity Act. The *Register* of 25 September 1865, in a leader headed "The First Nibble", began:

> 'On Saturday Mr Justice Boothby commenced operations against the new Validating Act. Let not legislators, imperial or colonial, think they are going to escape the clutches of this astute Judge. He is always ready. He lies in wait for them as Colonel Quagg did for the 'grace-walking brethren', and he ill-treats them for the same reason—because he can, because he likes, and because it "does 'em good".'

The case which provoked this criticism was *Walsh v. Goodall*, an action for damages for trespass. The defendant pleaded he had entered under a lease from one Farrell; the plaintiff replied by pleading a prior lease by Farrell; and the defendant rejoined that his lease had been registered in the General Registry Office under Act 8 of 1841, and had thereby gained priority over that of the plaintiff. To this the plaintiff demurred, and the question arose, had the Colonial Laws Validity Act validated the Registration of Deeds Act No 27 of 1862, which the Supreme Court had held to be invalid? If so, then the defendant's lease, which had been registered in the General Registry Office after the passing of Act 27 of 1862, had been registered under a repealed statute and the registration was ineffective.[23] Mr Justice Boothby expressed the opinion that the Validating Act did not extend to validate measures unconstitutionally passed in Parliament.

> 'The repealing Act'—he said—'was held not to have been passed by absolute majorities of both Houses, although required to be. Measures so passed are not made valid by the new Act.'

The Full Court directed that the demurrer should be argued before them.

> 'Here, then'—said the Register—'is the beginning of more litigation. At the next sitting there will be a field-day, at which it is very clear that Mr Justice Boothby will give the Imperial Act no quarter.'

The conduct of the Government with regard to the General Registry Office had been characterised by vacillation and indecision throughout. Upon the passing of Act 27 of 1862 the General Registry Office had been shut up; when Act 27 of 1862 was declared invalid the General Registry Office was hastily reopened. If the Imperial Act had validated the Local Courts Act, then had it not also validated the Registration of Deeds Act?

> 'In accordance with this the portals of the Registration Office ought to close themselves up again with a bang until another tap from the judicial wand makes them fly open once more like the magic doors in a Christmas pantomime.'

But public opinion had by now veered to the view that Act 27 of 1862 had been a blunder. A Committee of the House of Assembly had recommended several years before that it should be repealed, but nothing had been done. By now enforcing the Imperial Act in one direction and letting it lie idle in another, the Government were almost inviting more "invalidity trouble".[24]

'invalidity trouble'

When the judgments in *Walsh v. Goodall* were delivered, in October 1865, the two puisne judges agreed that the Colonial Laws Validity Act had not validated the Registration of Deeds Act 1862. The Court had already held that the latter Act had altered the constitution. Section 5 of the Colonial Laws Validity Act gave power to colonial legislatures to make laws changing their constitutions, but only if such laws were passed in the manner and form required by the then existing law. Mr Justice Gwynne thought that this provision, reading the Act as a whole, modified the construction which ought to be given to section 7, which validated South Australian legislation.

> 'The seventh clause established all laws passed under the General power of the Legislature, but as to such powers as were specially vested in the Legislature for altering its constitution, and which were only to be exercised sub modo, it appears to me it was not the intention of the Imperial Parliament to establish, where the local Ordinance prescribing the mode of exercising their powers had not been observed.'

Mr Justice Boothby agreed. The Chief Justice dissented and said there was no reason for narrowing clause 7 by importing into it the proviso to clause 5. In accordance with the decision of the majority of the Court the demurrer was upheld. Mr Stow said it was probable that the plaintiff would appeal to the Court of Appeal. "I wonder that any advocate in this Court should avow such an intention"—said Mr Justice Boothby—"after our solemn judgment that there is no such Court of Appeal."[25]

Notwithstanding this rebuke, Mr Stow successfully persisted in his appeal, the majority of the Supreme Court Judges having held, in *Murray v. Ridpath* (2 March 1866) that the existence of the Court of Appeals had been placed beyond doubt by the Colonial Laws Validity Act.

ANNO VICESIMO OCTAVO & VICESIMO NONO

VICTORIÆ REGINÆ.

C A P. LXIII.

An Act to remove Doubts as to the Validity of Colonial Laws. [29th *June* 1865.]

WHEREAS Doubts have been entertained respecting the Validity of divers Laws enacted or purporting to have been enacted by the Legislatures of certain of Her Majesty's Colonies, and respecting the Powers of such Legislatures, and it is expedient that such Doubts should be removed:

Be it hereby enacted by the Queen's most Excellent Majesty, by and with the Advice and Consent of the Lords Spiritual and Temporal, and Commons, in this present Parliament assembled, and by the Authority of the same, as follows:

Definitions: "Colony:"

1\. The Term "Colony" shall in this Act include all of Her Majesty's Possessions abroad in which there shall exist a Legislature, as herein-after defined, except the Channel Islands, the *Isle of Man*, and such Territories as may for the Time being be vested in Her Majesty under or by virtue of any Act of Parliament for the Government of *India*:

"Legislature," "Colonial Legislature:"

The Terms "Legislature" and "Colonial Legislature" shall severally signify the Authority, other than the Imperial Parliament or Her Majesty in Council, competent to make Laws for any Colony:

7 D The

566 28° & 29° VICTORIÆ. Cap. 63.

Colonial Laws Validity.

"Representative Legislature." The Term "Representative Legislature" shall signify any Colonial Legislature which shall comprise a Legislative Body of which One Half are elected by Inhabitants of the Colony:

"Colonial Law." The Term "Colonial Law" shall include Laws made for any Colony either by such Legislature as aforesaid or by Her Majesty in Council:

Act of Parliament, &c. to extend to Colony when made applicable to such Colony. An Act of Parliament, or any Provision thereof, shall, in construing this Act, be said to extend to any Colony when it is made applicable to such Colony by the express Words or necessary Intendment of any Act of Parliament:

"Governor." The Term "Governor" shall mean the Officer lawfully administering the Government of any Colony:

"Letters Patent." The Term "Letters Patent" shall mean Letters Patent under the Great Seal of the United Kingdom of *Great Britain* and *Ireland*.

Colonial Law when void for Repugnancy. **2.** Any Colonial Law which is or shall be in any respect repugnant to the Provisions of any Act of Parliament extending to the Colony to which such Law may relate, or repugnant to any Order or Regulation made under Authority of such Act of Parliament, or having in the Colony the Force and Effect of such Act, shall be read subject to such Act, Order, or Regulation, and shall, to the Extent of such Repugnancy, but not otherwise, be and remain absolutely void and inoperative.

Colonial Law when not void for Repugnancy. **3.** No Colonial Law shall be or be deemed to have been void or inoperative on the Ground of Repugnancy to the Law of *England*, unless the same shall be repugnant to the Provisions of some such Act of Parliament, Order, or Regulation as aforesaid.

Colonial Law not void for Inconsistency with Instructions. **4.** No Colonial Law, passed with the Concurrence of or assented to by the Governor of any Colony, or to be hereafter so passed or assented to, shall be or be deemed to have been void or inoperative by reason only of any Instructions with reference to such Law or the Subject thereof which may have been given to such Governor by or on behalf of Her Majesty, by any Instrument other than the Letters Patent or Instrument authorizing such Governor to concur in passing or to assent to Laws for the Peace, Order, and good Government of such Colony, even though such Instructions may be referred to in such Letters Patent or last-mentioned Instrument.

Colonial Legislature may establish, &c. Courts of Law. **5.** Every Colonial Legislature shall have, and be deemed at all Times to have had, full Power within its Jurisdiction to establish Courts of Judicature, and to abolish and reconstitute the same, and to alter the Constitution thereof, and to make Provision for the Administration of Justice therein; and every Representative

Legislature

Colonial Laws Validity.

Legislature shall, in respect to the Colony under its Jurisdiction, have, and be deemed at all Times to have had, full Power to make Laws respecting the Constitution, Powers, and Procedure of such Legislature; provided that such Laws shall have been passed in such Manner and Form as may from Time to Time be required by any Act of Parliament, Letters Patent, Order in Council, or Colonial Law for the Time being in force in the said Colony. Representative Legislature may alter Constitution.

6. The Certificate of the Clerk or other proper Officer of a Legislative Body in any Colony to the Effect that the Document to which it is attached is a true Copy of any Colonial Law assented to by the Governor of such Colony, or of any Bill reserved for the Signification of Her Majesty's Pleasure by the said Governor, shall be *primâ facie* Evidence that the Document so certified is a true Copy of such Law or Bill, and, as the Case may be, that such Law has been duly and properly passed and assented to, or that such Bill has been duly and properly passed and presented to the Governor; and any Proclamation purporting to be published by Authority of the Governor in any Newspaper in the Colony to which such Law or Bill shall relate, and signifying Her Majesty's Disallowance of any such Colonial Law, or Her Majesty's Assent to any such reserved Bill as aforesaid, shall be primâ facie Evidence of such Disallowance or Assent. Certified Copies of Laws to be Evidence that they are properly passed. Proclamation to be Evidence of Assent and Disallowance.

And whereas Doubts are entertained respecting the Validity of certain Acts enacted or reputed to be enacted by the Legislature of *South Australia*: Be it further enacted as follows:

7. All Laws or reputed Laws enacted or purporting to have been enacted by the said Legislature, or by Persons or Bodies of Persons for the Time being acting as such Legislature, which have received the Assent of Her Majesty in Council, or which have received the Assent of the Governor of the said Colony in the Name and on behalf of Her Majesty, shall be and be deemed to have been valid and effectual from the Date of such Assent for all Purposes whatever; provided that nothing herein contained shall be deemed to give Effect to any Law or reputed Law which has been disallowed by Her Majesty, or has expired, or has been lawfully repealed, or to prevent the lawful Disallowance or Repeal of any Law. Certain Acts enacted by Legislature of South Australia to be valid.

LONDON:
Printed by GEORGE EDWARD EYRE and WILLIAM SPOTTISWOODE,
Printers to the Queen's most Excellent Majesty. 1865.

The eastern entrance to what is now the Supreme Court was built in 1875. See also page 574.

Chapter 5.9

Mr Justice Boothby

Stow v Boothby

A fresh stage of the Boothby question was reached in the criminal sittings held before that Judge during the month of May 1866. The sessions commenced on 8 May, and for a few days proceeded without serious interruption, although the Judge had been put in a bad temper by the noise of drays rumbling past the courthouse and had ordered the Sheriff immediately to spread "manure or some other suitable material" on the roadway to deaden the sound.[1]

On Friday, 11 May, Mr Stow QC appeared for one Hibbart, who was charged with rape. He annoyed the Judge by mentioning to the jury the law relating to the offence. Mr Justice Boothby interrupted him at once; Mr Stow claimed he had a right to state the law of the case to the jury as well as the judge.

> 'I have never known an instance in all my English experience'—replied the Judge—'of a counsel venturing to state the law of the case in a criminal prosecution without first appealing to the learned Judge by whom it was being tried ... It will be my duty to tell the jury that they must dismiss the opinions of counsel from their minds, and take the law from the presiding Judge.'

The prisoner was acquitted, the jury stating, in reply to the Judge, that they considered the girl to have been a consenting party. The Judge ordered the prisoner to be removed but not to be discharged, and said he would consider as to whether it was not his duty to order another information to be laid against him. On the rising of the Court, he directed the Crown Solicitor (Mr Wearing) to inform the Attorney-General (Mr Boucaut) that he considered it to be the duty of that officer to lay an information against the prisoner for an indecent assault, with another court charging him with a common assault. The prisoner had been on bail, and the Judge said he would enlarge the bail till the following Friday. Mr Stow submitted that if the bail was extended to the following Tuesday, the Attorney-General would have ample time for considering the Judge's suggestion.

> His Honour: 'The Attorney General has no discretion in the matter when instructed by a Judge.'
>
> Mr Stow: 'I conceive the Attorney General is himself the Judge in such cases.'
>
> His Honour: 'Oh dear no. He is bound to obey the instructions of the Judge. This has been ruled in England over and over again.'

The prisoner was accordingly bound over to appear on the following Friday.

On the next day, 12 May, Mr Stow obtained from the Court of Appeals a peremptory order directing Mr Justice Boothby to transmit a copy of the proceedings in *Copeland v. Wentzel*; and it was surmised that Mr Justice Boothby's antagonism to Mr Stow was due to this order, which he no doubt knew on Friday was to be applied for on the following day.

After considering Hibbart's case, the Attorney-General decided that it was not his duty to lay another information against him, because:

> '1st. It would be very hard, even if not unjust, to put Hibbart again on his trial after an acquittal, on the express ground of consent by the female, which was found by the jury in answer to his Honour, and to do so would be substantially, if not absolutely illegal, for nemo pro eadem causa bis vexari debet.
>
> 2nd. His Honour had no power to give me such an order, or to take away my discretion, and it is the Crown, and not the Judge, that is to decide upon the institution of prosecutions, and obeying the order of the Judge in the manner directed, under the circumstances, would be admitting that the Attorney General was a mere machine, and would have introduced a precedent, not only derogatory to the office, but much more objectionable, as one that would hereafter become dangerous to the liberties of the people.
>
> 3rd. It appeared to me that the order of His Honour was given inconsiderately, and out of hostile feeling to the prisoner's counsel.'

On Tuesday, 15 May, Mr Stow accordingly applied to the Judge to discharge Hibbart as the Attorney-General would not indict the prisoner.

> His Honour: 'Oh, no; I shall not do that. It will be strange if a practitioner of this Court is to decide whether a prisoner is to be prosecuted, and the property and persons of Her Majesty's subjects protected. There were sworn depositions against Hibbart. The jury acquitted the prisoner of rape, and I directed the Attorney General to indict him for another offence, and he was bound to do it. I, as Judge of the Supreme Court, have so directed him. In England, I have seen numbers of cases in which Judges have ordered fresh bills to be presented to the Grand Jury. The Attorney General here is the same as the

> Grand Jury in England, and I direct the Attorney General as the Grand Jury. If that is contrary to law it can be shown. I shall be glad to hear the Attorney General come into Court and argue that he is not obliged to obey my instructions.'

The Crown Solicitor said that the Attorney-General had considered the case but had decided not to indict Hibbart again.

> His Honour: 'The Attorney General is public prosecutor and is bound to be here. The Crown Solicitor is not Public Prosecutor, he simply appears for the convenience of the Attorney General. I consider the Crown Solicitor is very unfairly treated; he is doing the work the Attorney General receives a large salary for doing—that is, acting as public prosecutor.'

> The Crown Solicitor: 'It would be indelicate for me to argue that point. The Crown Solicitor is mentioned as the public prosecutor in the schedule to the Constitution Act.'

> His Honour: 'That does not matter at all; calling him the public prosecutor does not make him so. Calling a man Attorney General does not make him Attorney General. You will please communicate to the Attorney General that I request him to appear and explain why he does not indict Hibbart.'

Next day, the case of *R. v. Green*, a charge of murder, was called on. The Judge, before the jury were sworn, asked the Crown Solicitor whether the Attorney-General was coming down that morning.

> 'In cases of murder'—he said—'it is the duty of the Attorney General to be in attendance; not that I am at all disparaging the ability of the Crown Solicitor to conduct the case, but all the assistance available should be had in cases of this kind.'

The Crown Solicitor said that the Attorney-General was not coming, and in view of the Judge's remarks suggested that some other case be taken. Accordingly the case of one John Baker, charged with horse-stealing, was called on, and an extraordinary scene ensued. Mr Stow QC said he appeared for the prisoner.

> His Honour: 'Have you a licence to appear against the Crown?'

> Mr Stow: 'That is a matter entirely between myself and the Crown.'

> His Honour: 'Oh, no! I must uphold the law, and cannot allow you to address the Court without a licence. There is no power to appoint a Queen's Counsel in the Colony.'

Mr Stow: 'Then I do not require a licence.'

His Honour: 'Yes, if you call yourself a Queen's Counsel you must obey the law.'

Mr Stow: 'The appointment of Queen's Counsel is a retainer for the Crown, and without doubt it would be most improper for me to appear against the Crown unless I had proper authority, but that is a matter purely between myself and the Crown; and it is not competent for a Judge on the Bench to interfere.'

His Honour: 'Oh yes; I must see that you have the proper authority, and will adjourn the case for half an hour to give you an opportunity to produce it.'

Mr Stow: 'I don't think I could obtain the authority in half an hour.'

His Honour: 'I shall see that the prisoner is not injured, and will adjourn the case till Mr Stow obtains the authority, or till the prisoner can secure the services of another counsel.'

Addressing the prisoner, the Judge told him that Mr Stow was not in a position to defend him, and the case would be postponed until he placed himself in a proper position or until the prisoner could employ another counsel. Mr Stow remained seated, and said nothing. The Judge asked him what he intended to do. "Surely I can retain my seat until I see whether the case is adjourned," replied Mr Stow. After a few further remarks, the case was adjourned to 12 o'clock. At that hour the Judge resumed his seat on the bench, to find the Court crowded with spectators attracted by the report of a row between the Judge and Mr Stow. As Mr Stow took his seat, his clerk put a document in his hands.

His Honour: 'I do not with to see your licence, Mr Stow; if you state you have it it will be sufficient.'

Mr Stow: 'That was not my licence. I understand, Your Honour, on the ground that I am a Queen's Counsel, requests me to state whether I have a licence to appear against the Crown. I decline to answer the question. And I have understood your Honour to say there are no Queen's Counsel in this Colony.'

His Honour: 'No; certainly there are not.'

Mr Stow: 'Then I do not require a licence.'

His Honour: 'But you have appeared in robes you are not entitled to wear.'

> Mr Stow: 'That question was not raised.'
>
> His Honour: 'Have you taken the oaths?'
>
> Mr Stow: 'I shall decline to answer that question. My position here as counsel for the prisoner has nothing to do with my being a Queen's Counsel; it is entirely a matter between the Crown and myself whether I have a licence to appear or not. Sitting after sitting I have appeared against the Crown, and no question has been raised; there has been no objection, either by Your Honour, or by any other Judge.'
>
> His Honour: 'But you appeared in a costume to which you are not entitled.'
>
> Mr Stow: 'I have appeared in this costume all the sittings.'
>
> His Honour: 'But not to defend prisoners.'
>
> Mr Stow: 'Yes, to defend prisoners. I understood Your Honour alluded to an order of the Governor, naming me as Queen's Counsel.'
>
> His Honour: 'Yes, there is an order of the Governor to that effect.'

The Judge left the bench, and on resuming his seat read from the peremptory order to himself to forward his notes in *Copeland v. Wentzel*, in which Stow was referred to as a Queen's Counsel, and said:

> 'So you are presented to me as Queen's Counsel, and I shall expect you to say whether you have a licence to appear in the case or not.'
>
> Mr Stow: 'And I protest against the demand, and I should ill perform my duty to other Queen's Counsel were I to accede to your Honour's request. I consider it a gross personal affront that Your Honour should insinuate that I appear here without proper authority.'
>
> His Honour: 'Oh, no; nothing of the sort. You have never sat in Courts in England; I have for a series of years, and it was customary to ask whether Queen's Counsel had licence to appear. The other day, when you were doing as you were now, I made up my mind to instruct the Bar as to the practice. These things do not appear in books; it is not necessary to go into the ABC of things; it is the plainest matter possible. I

Randolph Isham Stow, ca. 1870. (SCLSA)

think, however, that it would be well if some one would write an elementary work on the law, to instruct the Bar of this Colony. In England, a Queen's Counsel would not even accept a brief till his clerk assured him that his licence was obtained.'

Mr Stow: 'I do not dispute that; but the Judge has no power to compel a Queen's Counsel to say whether he has a licence or not.'

His Honour: 'I shall adjourn this case till the prisoner can obtain the services of another counsel.'

Mr Stow: 'And I shall advise my client not to engage another counsel; and I shall also advise him to take no part in the proceedings; and I shall attend on the day to which the case is adjourned, and appear for the prisoner.'

His Honour: 'Very well; you know the consequences.'

Mr Stow: 'Your Honour can do what you think your duty as Judge, and I shall perform my duty.'

His Honour: 'Have you taken the oaths?'

Mr Stow: 'If I have not I am not a Queen's Counsel; I submit that this course, if persevered in, must prejudice the case of the prisoner. Unless a Judge is informed to the contrary, the usual practice is to infer that licence, and I refuse to answer Your Honour's question as to whether I have a licence or not. It is not suggested by the Crown that I have no licence, and the Crown Solicitor appears for the Crown, and does not object to my defending the prisoner.

His Honour: 'Judges do not ask for the licences in England, because they rely on the knowledge of the Queen's Counsel that they require a licence, but this is the first time of your appearance.'

Mr Stow: 'I have appeared several sittings, and defended prisoners.'

His Honour: 'Not before me.'

Mr Stow: 'Yes, before your Honour. It appears to me so inconsistent on the part of Your Honour to say that I am not a Queen's Counsel and then ask for my licence. It seem that your Honour's attention was first called to my being a Queen's Counsel by the peremptory order in the appeal case of Copeland and Wentzel.'

His Honour (to the prisoner): 'You had better employ another counsel. Mr Stow will not defend you.

Mr Stow: 'I beg your Honour's pardon; I insist upon defending the prisoner.'

His Honour: 'Then I shall order you into custody.'

Mr Stow: 'Then I will wait till the time arrives. Your Honour can take your own course, but I am not to be threatened beforehand.'

His Honour: 'I am not sure whether there is a properly appointed tipstaff. If this contest between you and the Court is to continue, I shall see what course to adopt. The case is adjourned to Saturday.'

The Crown Solicitor now rose and said that the Attorney-General did not propose to attend the criminal sittings.

His Honour: 'Is the Attorney General aware that his position as Attorney General and the sufficiency of the indictments is to be argued?'

The Crown Solicitor: 'Oh yes, your Honour, he is quite aware of that.'

His Honour: 'Then I shall communicate with His Excellency on the matter. The interests of the public and the Crown are entitled to the best assistance, and the Attorney General should be here. I shall feel it my duty to communicate with the Secretary of State, in order that he may be acquainted with the position of affairs here.'

The adjourned case of *R. v. Green* came on for trial on Friday, 18 May, and Mr Strangways, who appeared for the prisoner, took an objection to the indictment, which was signed "by one J.P. Boucaut, a person calling himself Attorney General". He submitted that there was no Attorney-General.

'Such office could not be created by implication, but only by an enactment defining his powers and receiving the direct assent of all the estates of the realm. In the enacting clauses of the Constitution Act, the only mention of the Attorney General was, that after the first election under the new Constitution Act, no person should hold any one of certain offices mentioned—the Attorney General being among the number—for more than three months without being elected to one of the Houses of Parliament. The Attorney General was once mentioned in Schedule A—and that was the most important matter connected with the office—where it stated

> that when he was appointed he should have £1,000 per year. The 32nd clause of the Act did not appoint an Attorney General; it anticipated his appointment, and his lawful appointment was still necessary. It was contemplated by the Act that an Attorney General would be appointed, but not that he would be appointed by implication ... The only ground of recognizing the Attorney General was that a salary was set apart for the office; but simply providing a salary for an officer to be appointed was not to be taken as a proof that he was appointed.'

The Crown Solicitor objected to discussing at nisi prius questions of such a character and of such magnitude, and in which such vast consequences were involved. Suppose the Judge decided there was no Attorney-General. If that decision were acted upon, every prisoner in the stockade would have to be released.

> His Honour: 'Oh, no; I have read of such foolish things in the public prints, but such results would not follow.'
>
> The Crown Solicitor: 'I respectfully submit that such a result would necessarily follow from a decision that there was no Attorney General.'
>
> His Honour: 'We should have the assistance of the Attorney General; he is not justified in being absent when questions of such vast importance are being discussed. I am in the position of being assisted by only one counsel. In England it was a different thing; the counsel there are all men entitled to be called men learned in the law. A late Governor held that he could appoint a layman as Attorney General. Most extraordinary views were held in the Colony on those subjects ... The position of the Governor is seriously affected, because no opinion of Judges can free him from his responsibility. By the Royal Instructions, when the question of carrying a capital sentence into consideration, he is bound to summon the Judge who passed sentence to the Executive Council. Even if the majority of the Full Court decided that there was an Attorney General, I should advise the Governor to consider the grave doubts upon this subject. I shall adjourn the consideration of the argument till Tuesday morning. Whenever a local ordinance conflicts with an Imperial enactment, it is void. Hitherto I have left prisoners to object to the indictments and carry their cases to the Privy Council; but, considering the enormous expense of such proceedings, I think they should be protected by the law here.'

He reserved his decision on the point raised by Strangways. Similar objections were promptly taken by other counsel in succeeding cases, and judgment had to be postponed in these also.

It will be remembered that the point as to the lawful existence of the office of Attorney-General had been taken and overruled before Mr Justice Gwynne in *R. v. Nethery* in 1864 and before Mr Justice Boothby himself in *R. v. Preston* in 1861. On Tuesday, 22 May, however, the Judge announced his decision that the informations must be quashed, on the grounds:

(1) That there was no Attorney-General.

(2) Assuming there was an Attorney-General, there was no warrant in law for putting any man on his trial for any crime at all without the intervention of a Grand Jury.

> 'This is the decided opinion I have expressed for five or six years'—he said—'and now that there are two or three lives at stake, it is time the matter should be settled. I have consequently given my decision, and the Crown will be able to move the Full Court that my order to quash be taken off. I cannot state a case for the opinion of the Full Court in a criminal matter, as that can only be done after conviction; but the counsel for the prisoner having wisely and properly raised the point before me, I as a Judge am bound by my oath to state the law as it stands. I declare the information to be bad in law; but for the purpose of the Crown applying to the Full Court in this matter, I am glad to know that Term commences on Monday next, for it is only during Term that an application of this kind can be lawfully made. The case cannot be brought on at the present sitting; but that is the fault of this information, which is bad, in spite of what is said by an uninstructed press, or any one else who chooses to talk on subjects without knowing what he is talking of. The only means of setting the matter right, is to repeal the Act professing to take away trial by Grand Jury. I hope it will never in my lifetime be deliberately decided to destroy this glorious institution of our forefathers; and I would call attention to the fact, that the first Judge who sat in the position I now occupy, referred to it as constituting a glorious distinction between South Australia and the other colonies, tainted as they were with convictism. So large an element of convictism was there, that it was found necessary to take it away, although the Imperial legislation gave power to re-establish it. But the boast of this province has been, that it has kept free from the convict taint; and when I came here and found what the state of the law was, I expressed my opinion respecting it in all quarters,

> namely, that it was utterly illegal to destroy the institution of Grand Jury. So long as what was called nomineeism prevailed in South Australia, such a thing was never attempted. It was attempted in respect of trials at Quarter Sessions, but even that was not entertained at home. But when another Parliament was created, with a representative element consisting of two thirds of its members, it took the first opportunity to destroy the great boast of their forefathers—founded on Magna Carta—which had existed for generations, and which Englishmen would never part with, knowing that if they did so they might have been reduced to the state of subjects in the country of Italy. I point this out; and I would say, that by simply repealing the Act No 10 of 1852, which professes to give the Attorney General the power which he now claims, the Parliament would restore the Grand Jury, and the administration of the criminal law would proceed as in the old country. And if afterwards the deliberate view of the people was in favour of having crime inquired into without the intervention of Grand Jury—the boast of their forefathers—their view would have to be carried out. I think, however, that honest and wise persons in England would not bring their families out to a place where the laws of their mother country were so abandoned and disregarded.'

If an indictment was presented to the Court of Queen's Bench in England, he said, found by the Attorney-General of England, the judges "would simply tear it in pieces and throw it on the floor".

In view of the attitude taken by the Judge, it was useless for the sittings to continue. The prisoners' counsel would all take the same objection, and where they were not represented by counsel the Judge would take it for them. The Crown Solicitor therefore intimated that he could go no further with the cases. Before the sittings closed, however, another scene occurred between the Judge and Mr Stow.[ii]

Over the weekend the Judge had seen the Crown Solicitor at the Court and had spoken to him about the course he proposed to take of quashing the indictments, and he then referred to the conduct of Mr Stow.

> 'His Honour'—said the Crown Solicitor, subsequently describing the interview—'used considerable gesture and spoke with great indignation of the way Mr Stow had conducted himself in Court when he refused to produce his licence. His Honour said he had charged him with corrupt motives as a Judge. Then he rehearsed what he should say to Mr Stow when the Court met again. He used precisely the same words, and so far as I could judge, the same attitudes and

> intonations afterwards on the Bench. At the interview, he imagined Mr Stow feeling contrition for the offence he had committed, and he assumed what Mr Stow would say expressive of that contrition. Then His Honour rehearsed to me the form of absolution he would pronounce under the circumstances. He alluded to Mr Stow's youth, and the heated circumstances under which he made the statement, saying that after such a very ample apology had been made, he would dismiss the whole occurrence from his mind. After this, I was going to leave, when His Honour observed to me, "Stow's friends should talk to him about this." I mention this as I have heard, and seen in print, that Mr Justice Boothby states that I agreed to make a representation to Mr Stow, and broke my promise. I may say that I gave no promise whatever to make a communication to Mr Stow, but after I left the Court House, I saw him in the street, and went with him and told him all that had passed in the Court House. Mr Stow, I may say, did not receive this communication very favourably, and I left, having discharged, as I thought, a duty.' [iii]

So far from Mr Stow quietly receiving absolution and a judicial blessing, however, events happened in a very different way. Addressing the Crown Solicitor, the Judge said:

> 'You had better move that the cases be adjourned until next sitting.'
>
> The Crown Solicitor: 'I do not take that position. The public are inconvenienced by adjournment, and particularly the witnesses. So far as they are concerned, I desire to go on with the cases immediately; but after the intimation of your Honour that the indictments are bad, it would only be consuming time to proceed.'
>
> His Honour: 'Then it is your duty to make a motion to me to postpone the trials till next sittings.'
>
> Mr Stow QC: 'Appearing as I do for two or three of the prisoners, I strongly object to their trials being postponed till next sitting.'
>
> His Honour: 'That raises the question whether as Queen's Counsel you can act for a prisoner without leave. If you have been instructed by a prisoner, it is his duty, through his attorney, to obtain for you a licence to appear. In all cases that this is done, I will listen to you.'
>
> Mr Stow: 'I have already intimated my objection to the

William Alfred Wearing
(1816-1875)
In 1856 Wearing was appointed Crown Solicitor and Public Prosecutor with the right to continue private practice in which he had been engaged since arriving in the colony in 1850. A QC from 1865, Wearing was made the third judge of the Supreme Court in 1867. In 1875 he conducted the first circuit court at Darwin (then Palmerston) but drowned whilst returning to Adelaide when the ship he was travelling on, the *Gothenburg*, was wrecked on the Great Barrier Reef. (SLSA)

production of any licence, and I persist in it.'

His Honour: 'And I persist in my refusal to hear you. I believe it is capable of proof that clerks in your office have stated in public that they had been instructed to obtain a licence for you. I adjourned the Court to enable you to ascertain whether your clerks had done so or not, and I will not now allow you to go on without knowing if you have it. I would even subpoena your clerks to ascertain the fact.'

Mr Stow: 'I beg your Honour's pardon. Did I understand your Honour to say that you would subpoena my clerks?'

His Honour: 'Yes.'

Mr Stow: 'I would object strongly to such a course, and I would submit most respectfully that your Honour has no power to do so.'

His Honour: 'And I respectfully say that you are wrong. If you object to my ruling, you must go to the Full Court or the Privy Council, and if you do not do so, but persist in your conduct, and remain standing up, I shall treat you the same as I should treat any person in that gallery, and order you into custody, which I would do in two minutes.'

Mr Stow: 'Your Honour did not order me to sit down.'

His Honour: 'No, I did not, but I will. I must call your attention to the fact that in public you imputed to me—Her Majesty's Judge, sitting here as I do in the stead of the Queen herself—and thought it consistent with your duty as one of Her Majesty's Council as you claim to be, to say that my mind was operated upon in a matter of this sort by the circumstance that you had been compelled to serve upon me an order of the Court of Appeals.'

Mr Stow: 'I deny having said so.'

His Honour: 'I certainly heard it, and it is capable of proof by others, and unless you deny it or make an apology, you deserve to be scouted while walking in the streets by any honourable or honest man. It is not a question of whether you insult a Judge, but whether honourable men and gentlemen will recognize you as belonging to their order if you do not make an apology.'

Mr Stow: 'I trust your Honour will allow me to say a few words.'

His Honour: 'If you deny it I will accept your denial.'

Mr Stow: 'No; I will not allow it to be put so. I certainly alluded to the case of Copeland v. Wentzel, but only in the way that your Honour alluded to it. You said that you had received no official notice of my being Queen's Counsel, until you received the order served upon you, in which I was named as Queen's Counsel.'

His Honour: 'That was afterwards.'

Mr Stow: 'No; at ten o'clock your Honour alluded to that order. At twelve o'clock, you brought the order out of your room, read so much of it as allowed that I was named as one of Her Majesty's Counsel, and holding it out to the jury, stated that I claimed to be such—'

His Honour: 'I did not address the jury, who had nothing to do with the matter. I addressed the whole body of the Court.'

Mr Stow: 'I will take it in that way then.'

His Honour: 'My objection still stands. If you state that you did not say what I have repeated—'

Mr Stow: 'In Court?'

His Honour: 'In open Court. I adjourned the Court, as you said that I was actuated by motives connected with the case of Copeland v. Wentzel.'

Mr Stow: 'I never said a word above [sic] motives.'

His Honour: 'You did.'

Mr Stow: 'No. Your Honour said your attention had been called to the proceedings in Copeland v. Wentzel and I said that Your Honour's course of procedure appeared to arise from that case.'

His Honour: 'That was a very improper thing to say. Do you repeat it?'

Mr Stow: 'I am not to be caught in that way.'

His Honour: 'Your conduct is utterly unworthy. To say nothing of the relation which should subsist between Bench and Bar, your conduct is dishonourable and should excite disgust in the mind of every honourable man.'

Mr Stow: 'Will Your Honour allow me to say—'

His Honour: 'No, I will not hear you.'

Mr Stow: 'I object most strongly to having such insults cast on

> me; but I feel sure, when I go out of this Court, that no one will think the stigma rests on me. It is not likely to injure me, but the person who gave the insult.'
>
> His Honour: 'I would have made short work of this before now if it were not for the honourable name which you bear. I consider that your conduct is a contempt of Court, and that you might, therefore, be committed; but I leave you to the contempt of every honest man who knows the facts of the case.'
>
> Mr Stow: 'I know of no—'
>
> His Honour: 'I won't hear you, Mr Stow. Sit down!'

The prisoners were then placed in the dock, and the Judge addressing them, said:

> 'In consequence of the decision of the Court upon objections raised on points of law your cases will be adjourned until next sittings.'
>
> Mr Stow: 'On behalf of the prisoners for whom I appear I beg to object—'
>
> His Honour: 'I can't hear you. You must sit down unless you show me, or allow your clerks to show me, whether you have a licence or not. The clerks have been speaking aloud in public places and telling the fact, and it is well known to you that they have the licence.'
>
> Mr Stow: 'Will Your Honour allow me to speak?'
>
> His Honour: 'No.'
>
> Mr Stow: 'Your Honour has no right to make me responsible for gossip out of doors.'
>
> His Honour: 'What I have stated is capable of proof upon oath here. It resolves itself into a dispute between you and me. Sit down, Sir!'

The Judge then proceeded to adjourn all the cases to the next criminal sittings. In one case, the Crown Solicitor tendered a certificate of the Attorney-General that he declined to proceed, but the Judge took no notice of it. "There is no authority to issue a certificate"—he said."There is no Attorney General. There are sworn depositions before me, upon which he can be tried." [iv]

The close of this remarkable sessions thus saw Mr Justice Boothby at open war with the Court of Appeals, with the Attorney-General, and with the leading member of the profession. The *Register* ruefully remarked:

(Sir) James Penn Boucaut, ca. 1880. (SLSA)

> 'They are all at cross purposes, and nobody will do what he is ordered to do. His Honour must refuse to obey the order of the Court of Appeals; then the Attorney General refuses to come into the Supreme Court in order to argue that he is Attorney General or to conduct prosecutions; and lastly, Mr Stow refuses to say whether or not he has obtained a licence enabling him as Queen's Counsel to appear against the Crown.' [v]

Mr Stow's conduct was admitted to be defiant and provocative, but justifiable in the circumstances.

> 'When a Judge commences by intimating that the gentlemen who appear before him as Queen's Counsel are only sham Queen's Counsel—something like the unqualified homeopathists amongst the doctors—and when he follows this up by requesting that the licence to practice in the particular case before the Court should be produced in the same way as a hawker's licence, it is not strange that the counsel thus attacked should resent the insult.'

Why was it, it was asked, that scenes occurred only when Mr Justice Boothby was on the bench? "All goes well until Mr Justice Boothby appears on the scene, and then it is 'battle, murder and sudden death'." [vi]

Scenes in the Supreme Court when he presided were becoming too common to require special notice, but his language on this occasion had been exceptionally vituperative.

In a voluminous report upon the proceedings, the Crown Solicitor wrote:

> 'Mr Justice Boothby indulged in a torrent of invective such as, so far as my experience serves me, was never before uttered by any Judge in any of Her Majesty's Courts of Justice. I can only express my opinion respecting it by stating that it was a grievous scandal to the administration of justice, and highly derogatory to the Judge. His Honour's threat to subpoena Mr Stow's clerks to prove Mr Stow guilty of falsehood was, in my opinion, most discreditable. I consider that Mr Stow exhibited throughout a most extraordinary and commendable self-control. His Honour's language was coarse and insulting in the extreme, his tone and gestures had that effect. As I listened, I marvelled at Mr Stow's great forbearance.
>
> His Honour also acted, I think'—continued the Crown Solicitor—'in a way most unbecoming a Judge, when he denied the right of the Governor to create Queen's Counsel. If His Honour considered that those appointments were made in

> excess of His Excellency's authority, there was a means of remedying such an error, if it existed, more decorous than that adopted by the Judge. His Honour was pleased to express himself in somewhat contemptuous terms respecting the legal attainments of the members of our Colonial Bar. After stating that certain matters were the ABC of law, he declared a wish that some one would write a treatise upon the elements of English law, for the use of practitioners in our Supreme Court. From an experience of upwards of sixteen years in the Supreme Court of this Province, and with the advantage of having practised, not so long as His Honour, but for the limited period of two years in Westminster Hall, I am induced to consider the reproach of His Honour was not merited. It is possible that our Colonial Practitioners may not have reached that ideal standard of excellence which His Honour, during his career at the English bar, probably had in view; tested, however, by the more moderate exigencies of Colonial life, in my opinion these gentlemen do not deserve the severe censure passed upon them by His Honour. A censure so sweeping, proceeding from a Judge, may tend, I fear, to depress the energies of our Colonial practitioners; and these observations, therefore, seem to me to have been uttered by His Honour unwisely.' [vii]

The only thing to be done was to see whether the Full Court could remedy the chaos which would follow an enforcement of Mr Justice Boothby's opinions. That he should now think so highly of the Full Court, though at other times he rudely asserted there was no legally constituted Full Court at all except himself, was an amazing inconsistency." But what is the use of looking for consistency in Judge Boothby's proceedings? His rule of conduct on the Bench is inscrutable; it passes all understanding." [viii]

The Government were in a quandary. The Attorney-General, the Crown Solicitor and Mr Ingleby conferred as to the best mode of dealing with the difficulties raised by the quashing of the informations by Mr Justice Boothby, but they had grave doubts whether the Full Court had power to do anything at all. In a joint opinion, the Crown Solicitor and Mr Ingleby reported:

'1 That by the constitution of the Supreme Court the Judge sitting in criminal matters in fact forms the Court, and that, therefore, as the Judge has not reserved a question for the consideration of the Full Court, there is no mode of correcting a judgment given by the Judge presiding at criminal sittings by appeal to the other Judges. The case of the Queen v. Wilson, in 6 Vol of QB Rep 620, is conclusive.

2. That we are of opinion, that an attempt to obtain leave to appeal to the Judicial Committee of the Privy Council would be of very doubtful success ... It may be the Privy Council would, in a question involving the status of the Attorney General, allow an appeal—but the attempt would only be an experiment. We would advise the Crown to issue a special commission to try the prisoners who remain untried under the Act No 13 of 1858.' [ix]

The Attorney General concurred in this opinion, but thought he should bring the matter before the Full Court, which he did, on 28 May. Mr Justice Boothby, he said, had intimated that the Crown could move to have the order to quash taken off, and also that the matter might be referred to the Privy Council. The Attorney-General, however, admitted he saw no means whatever of doing one or the other. The Crown Solicitor mentioned the possibility of a special commission being issued.

> 'The suggestion which has fallen from the Crown Solicitor'—said Mr Justice Boothby—'is a piece of advice which the Governor will act wisely in not listening to. The sittings of the Supreme Court are regulated by Statute, and there is no power to interfere with them.'

Mr Justice Gwynne also raised a difficulty as to the issuing of a special commission. The Act No 10 of 1852, abolishing grand juries, limited the hearing of informations found by the Attorney-General to sessions of the Supreme Court. This would appear to refer, he thought, to ordinary established sessions and to exclude the idea that the Attorney-General could discharge the functions of the Grand Jury at any extraordinary sitting. "I have felt a little twinge of conscience on that subject when upon circuit," he added. Mr Justice Boothby welcomed his colleagues doubts as a peg on which to hang another attack on South Australian laws.

> 'The whole anomaly of present proceedings is such'—he said—'that I believe it to be capable of proof in a Court of Justice, that informations have been sent down by the Attorney General of the day in blank, and then filled up from the depositions in Court, and men have been tried and convicted, and have served long periods of confinement in the Dry Creek Prison. It is only one instance to show what a frightful amount of injustice may be perpetrated under the present system. In some cases the Attorney General cannot possibly have seen the depositions, on account of the distance from which they had to be sent.'

The Court not being able to suggest any remedy to get over the quashed indictment, matters remained at a standstill.

This 1877 sketch by an inmate of the Yatala (Dry Creek) Prison depicts "smoko" in the Yatala quarry. (SLSA)

The case of the man Hibbart, who was out on bail waiting for another charge to be laid against him, was then mentioned to the Court. The Attorney-General said the Crown had no intention of again prosecuting the man, and he consented to the bail being discharged. Mr Justice Boothby was very annoyed.

> 'Under the present system'—he said—'a person in practice may appoint a Judge, and then a week afterwards come in and practise before him. He is His Excellency's responsible adviser, and has a right to take this course; and moreover he has a right to send his clerk to practise before that Judge. Such proceedings destroy entirely the rights of the profession. In this Court no law clerk or articled clerk would be heard for a moment. The privilege is confined to practitioners by Statute, and I only mention this matter now to show the frightful anomalies which these departures from the law of England introduce. It must strike the mind of every thinking man.'
>
> The Attorney General: 'I cannot argue the question, nor do I acquiesce in the statements His Honour has thought fit to make. I feel it will be more respectful to the Court and more becoming in me not to argue the matter.'
>
> Mr Justice Boothby: 'I go by the reports of the public prints, and I see by them that these anomalies exist. A person elected by universal suffrage is placed in office, and if the legislation

> suffering such a thing is valid, he being a practising attorney is authorised to perform acts which would not be deemed possible in any community but South Australia.'

The Chief Justice and Mr Justice Gwynne agreed that the Attorney-General had exercised a wise discretion in refusing to prosecute Hibbart again, and they discharged him, Mr Justice Boothby vigorously protesting:

> 'I think that a most frightful state of affairs was presented by the evidence'—he said. 'My only surprise is that twelve men, accustomed to the law of England, could have found as they did. And in my experience in the English courts, I have known scores of instances in which Judges have, after prisoners have been acquitted by Juries, ordered them to be detained on the possibility of other charges being preferred against them. That is precisely the course here. I have known instances in which the punishment of death has been inflicted in cases of this kind; and I have had occasion when trying prisoners charged with like offences to ask for pity to be extended to me, owing to my having had to sit in a kind of pool of moral iniquity. And in this matter, after finding that the Jury had so grievously overlooked their duty, and after deciding that the indictment had been in fact so much waste paper, I thought it well to detain the prisoner with a view to his being again placed on his trial. This is the first time in which a Judge has been interfered with in a matter of this sort; but I cannot help it. Things are constantly occurring here which are contrary to all my ideas of what is right.'

During the proceedings, Hibbart's counsel had read and tendered an affidavit as to what took place on the trial. Mr Justice Boothby denied the accuracy of it, and demanded that it should be removed from the file.

> 'I think the Court have not been regardful of my dignity'—he said—'in allowing the affidavit to be read, and to remain upon the files of the Court where persons who wish to prove whatever they can against me will be able to peruse it. I have no doubt it will be attempted hereafter to prove me a monster in human shape, and I think, out of regard for my reputation as a Judge, it should not be placed upon the files.'

The affidavit was accordingly withdrawn.[x]

The Government now faced a serious and pressing problem. Mr Justice Boothby had declared all the informations against prisoners to be so much waste paper, and the Full Court had pronounced itself powerless to intervene. It is not surprising that it was decided to make another attempt to end the whole problem by removing the obnoxious Judge from the bench. The Attorney-General (Mr Boucaut) in a long and outspoken memorandum to the Governor reviewed the whole of Mr Justice Boothby's turbulent career in the colony. He cited the Judge's own decision in *R. v. Preston* in 1861, refusing to quash the indictment, where he said: "As a single Judge, I cannot take upon myself the responsibility of putting a stop to the administration of criminal justice in this colony." Yet five years later this was the very thing he had done.

> 'I should be at a loss'—wrote the Attorney-General—'how to account for His Honour's quashing the informations for the reasons given—especially after His Honour himself had so powerfully exposed the danger and impropriety of a single Judge deciding such a point—except that a consideration of his entire judicial career in this Province renders it impossible for any other conclusion to be arrived at than that His Honour was influenced by the desire of expressing a deliberate contempt for the Colonial Legislature which passed the Act, No 10, referred to, and this conclusion is further strengthened by the difficulty of otherwise accounting for His Honour's inconsistency, in first ordering me as Attorney General to file informations, and then immediately quashing those I had already filed.
>
> It is needless for me to point out to your Excellency'—he continued—'the great excitement existing in the public mind by reason of the proceedings of His Honour; but I may remark that such excitement is not unnatural, when it is recollected what a great expense is thereby caused to the Colony, as well as great delay, confusion, and uncertainty in the execution of the laws. If His Honour had now attracted to himself public attention and reprobation for the first time, I might not have felt it necessary to address your Excellency, but when I recollect that, from an early period after His Honour's arrival to the present sittings, His Honour's proceedings have constantly brought scandal on the administration of justice, and have been overbearing and unbecoming a Judge in a very high degree, I feel that no alternative is left me but to point this out. It is with great pain I feel it my bounden duty to state that His Honour is obnoxious to many grave charges—of arrogance, ignorance of law, infirmity of temper, want of respect to the other Judges, want of judgment, and constant and wilful contempt of all things Colonial.
>
> His Honour's want of consideration for the dignity of his position in small matters has been frequently and publicly

exhibited by His Honour's frequent reference to the remarks of the press ... The manner in which His Honour overrules counsel is often as much to be objected to as the ruling itself. His Honour's arrogance and want of respect for the feelings of the Bar has been uniform, there being scarcely any counsel, of any eminence, that has not suffered therefrom. Often, when any argument is urged opposed to His Honour's views, His Honour replies in a most offensive manner, frequently hinting and often stating that because the Bar here has not had His Honour's experience at Westminster Hall they are ignorant of the duties of their profession.

His Honour's want of consideration for his colleagues has been frequently shown. On one occasion he demanded on the Bench that Sir C. Cooper should show his Commission; and His Honour was constantly in the habit of interrupting him, and treating him also with disrespect. On the 23rd March last, His Honour, in open Court, stated that the late Chief Justice had brought the Bench into contempt—a most unjust and unfounded aspersion, which induced the present Chief Justice to say, he had always had a very different estimate of Sir Charles. His Honour's conduct to the present Chief Justice, Mr Hanson, has also been most unseemly from the first ... In fact, his assumption of authority over the other Judges, and his refusal to defer to their judgment, had not only become notorious and a public scandal, but entirely incompatible with the just administration of the laws.

Even if His Honour, during the recent sittings, had first given occasion for the bar and the people of this Colony to complain, I respectfully submit that there would be enough to warrant Parliament praying Her Majesty for His Honour's removal, on the ground that His Honour's longer remaining on the judgment-seat was fraught with peril. Not only does His Honour's conduct show a want of the decorum expected in a Judge, and exhibit a marked want of respect towards the Bar and the Parliament, but it is such, that if still permitted, there must be an end to all security for liberty, all power of legislation, and all confidence in the administration of justice. The Bar here has always been most respectful to the Bench—in truth, submissive; but if a Judge is to be at liberty, day after day, to lay down such doctrines as His Honour has laid down, and to carry them out in the manner His Honour carries them out, there is also an end to all advocacy. The Supreme Court has become a place to which the public every now and then flock to enjoy an anticipated scene, in which it is expected His Honour will prominently figure, and speak of a good house, as in speaking of a theatre. It would be bad if such a state of things were believed of a Judge, though undeserved; but when justified, it becomes deplorable, for such an example not only shakes present confidence, but becomes a most dangerous precedent, and its injurious effects are necessarily felt through all society. I believe it is possible the public may think that the outspoken contempt of His Honour for our Local Acts and institutions is of all His Honour's proceedings the most dangerous and subversive of good government; but I cannot help thinking that far more really dangerous is the general conduct of His Honour, not so much noticed or seen by the general public, in which His Honour shows day by day, his indifference to legal precedent and constitutional usage, and his determination to set at nought everything opposed to the view His Honour for the moment may entertain.

I am fully sensible of the serious responsibility I incur in writing this report'—the Attorney-General concluded -'I know well the strong conservative feeling really animating the people of this Colony, and their great reluctance to do or permit anything to weaken the position of the Judges; I know how all our greatest statesmen and writers have looked upon the absolute independence of the Judges as the mainstay of liberty and good government; and I acknowledge the contempt which should be visited upon any man that would rashly, or without good grounds do anything to weaken that independence. But I believe this independence is valued in England because it is deserved; and I know that, if not deserved, it would not only not be valuable, but would become a curse instead of a blessing; and I should look upon myself as guilty of criminal neglect towards the position I hold, and towards Your Excellency and the people you govern, were I from any fear of personal consequences, to refrain from pointing out the unfitness of a Judge, when, after most serious and anxious reflection I believe, in my present position, it is my bounden duty to do so. If I saw any hope of improvement in His Honour, I might hesitate. I believe that such a hope has prevented a report of this nature reaching Your Excellency before; but no reasonable man can any longer expect improvement. The proceedings of His Honour during the recent criminal sittings show this, and prove that neither judicious conduct, nor equal justice, nor legal decisions are to be expected from His Honour. I have therefore humbly to submit to Your Excellency, that it is against the public interests that His Honour should remain longer on the Bench, for so long as His Honour continues a Judge, neither the Bar nor the public can have any confidence whatever in the administration of justice.' [xi]

This report was supported by an opinion of the Crown Solicitor and Mr Ingleby that they thought the ministry had no other course open to them but to advise the Governor that Parliament should be asked to petition the Queen for the removal of the Judge.

Cabinet accordingly met and, "in consequence of the perseverance of Mr Justice Boothby in a course of action which obstructs the due administration of justice", recommended the Governor to summon Parliament immediately, although it had been prorogued to 29 June.[xii] The Governor, considering that the case could be effectually dealt with only through Parliament, summoned the legislature to meet on 15 June. In reporting his action to the Secretary of State, he wrote:

> 'I very much regret that I am compelled again to bring the conduct of Mr Justice Boothby under your notice. It has often been my duty to address the Secretary of State upon this subject; but, until now, I have not wholly ceased to hope that Mr Boothby might possibly avail himself of the opportunity that was afforded to him by the Imperial Legislation (28 and 29 Vic c.63), to the necessity for which his alleged doubts had so largely contributed, and that he might adopt a line of conduct suited to the position of a Judge of the Supreme Court. His recent conduct, however, forbids the indulgence of any such expectation, and has brought matters to such a point that decisive measures must be adopted to save the administration of justice from further injury at his hands ... Public feeling is so unanimous in desiring that an end should speedily be put to the present state of things, and that the administration of justice should be restored to a position meriting the confidence of the community, that I have not hesitated, with the advice of my Council, to take the course which I believe to be best calculated for the attainment of the desired object. Indeed, I am not aware that there is any other course open to me; for to suspend Mr Boothby from office would but complicate a difficulty which must ultimately be submitted to the action of Parliament. It has become but too apparent that nothing short of his removal from the Bench can meet the requirements of the case. Nearly all those who, like myself, have long believed in the possibility of his

improvement, have arrived at the same conclusion.'

The publication of the proclamation for assembling Parliament, the Governor added, had the effect of calming the excitement:

> '... which was general and increasing ... and was succeeded by a general expression of approval of that measure, as the only means of dealing satisfactorily with the difficulties which Mr Boothby had occasioned'.[xiii]

During the interval which elapsed before Parliament met, the Attorney General worked at preparing the case against the Judge, and busied himself in obtaining the views and support of the profession. Mr Ingleby reported that he knew of cases in which he suspected the Judge's decisions were influenced by extraneous considerations, and that he had two cases in his own office in which he thought Mr Justice Boothby had shown gross partiality towards Mr Elder.

> 'I believe the result must prove'—he said—'1st. That Mr Justice Boothby is ignorant of the elements of his profession; or 2ndly. That his judgment is influenced by his feelings and he thus abuses his judicial position.
>
> As a member of a small Bar in a small community'—he cautiously added—'I must request that this or any future report will not find its way into print ... Should the efforts now being made to remove Mr Justice Boothby prove abortive, my position at the Bar would be seriously compromised.' [xiv]

Mr Wearing, the Crown Solicitor, also forwarded a confidential memorandum:

> 'Extensive experience and observation have convinced me that Mr Justice Boothby's decisions are usually determined by his personal sympathies and private interests, and not by an honest intention to administer right between man and man. I believe that a feeling of distrust in His Honour's administration of the law is all but universal, not only amongst lawyers, but also with those who although not members of the profession are yet accustomed to take an intelligent interest in the proceedings of the Supreme Court. This feeling has gone on increasing from the time when His Honour first became a Judge amongst us. I express the above views to you upon the distinct understanding that this letter shall not be used otherwise than for the information of the Colonial Government or the Secretary of State for the colonies, and that under no circumstances it shall be published.' [xv]

Another member of the profession, Mr James Brook, wrote in a similar strain that the removal of the Judge was absolutely necessary.

> 'The refusal of the Judge to recognise the Court of Appeal, his efforts to frustrate its authority and to destroy the respect which should naturally attach to the highest court of the Province, his contemptuous references thereto and his utter disregard of the deliberate action of the Legislature, appear to me your strong points, and which treated properly, and I may say as you can treat them if you like, will prove sufficient to attain the desired end. His decision on the question of the Attorney General and of the Criminal Informations are subsidiary, and may be of service, but are not the main points on which to rely—whilst his personal quarrel with Stow requires delicate handling and might be injurious to your cause. He has—after all—as many friends in the profession as Stow, and there are other reasons.' [xvi]

James Brook
(1840 –1872)
A one-time partner of Samuel Way and the editor of volume 1 of the South Australian Law Reports. (SLSA)

Mr Parker was asked by the Government to advise whether the objection raised by Mr Justice Gwynne, that the Act 10 of 1852 only allowed the Attorney-General to prefer informations for felony at the ordinary sessions of the Supreme Court and not at a special sessions, was fatal to a special commission, or whether there was any other way of meeting the difficulties raised by the quashing of the indictments. His opinion was that the Governor could issue a special commission for the trial of prisoners, addressed to the Judges of the Supreme Court, which would make the special sessions a sessions of the Supreme Court within the meaning of the Act 10 of 1852, but he added an unwelcome rider to the effect that prisoners whose cases had been summarily disposed of in May might, if placed on their trial again, plead autrefois acquit.

> 'The informations quashed by Mr Justice Boothby may be pleaded at the next trial of the prisoners, in all cases wherein the prisoners were arraigned and pleaded to the informations.'

The Attorney-General hastily noted on the opinion:"It would never do to put this opinion before the House and thus show prisoners a defence"—and although the opinions of the Crown Solicitor and Mr Ingleby and the reports of the Crown Solicitor and the Attorney-General were laid before Parliament and printed, Mr Parker's opinion was discreetly concealed.[xvii]

A further case was also submitted to Mr Parker for an opinion upon the Judge's removal. The questions put to him and his answers were as follows:

> '1. Has His Honour Mr Justice Boothby so captiously or persistently set up his individual opinions against the decisions of the other Judges of the Court, and so

captiously and persistently refused to submit to, or be guided by such decisions, as to have misbehaved himself in his office?

I think he has.

2. Has His Honour, in Mr Parker's opinion, in the exercise of His Honour's functions, or by his conduct, so maintained his individual opinion factiously, or by his conduct wilfully obstructed or delayed the administration of justice in a Court of higher jurisdiction as to have been guilty of such misbehaviour in his office as to justify his Honour's amotion?

I think he has. See 22 Geo III c.75.

3. Has His Honour, in Mr Parker's opinion, improperly disregarded the orders of a Court to which appeal lies from His Honour's decision?

I am of opinion that he has.

4. Has His Honour improperly assumed that the Acts of the Court of Appeal are illegal, or proceed upon mistake or error of judgment?

I think His Honour has improperly assumed that the Acts of the Court of Appeal are illegal. Seeing that His Honour has power to appeal against his amotion, and looking at the decision upon the construction of the Statute to which I have above referred (22 Geo III c.75) that the Court of Queen's Bench in the case Ex parte Ramshay 18 QB Rep p.173, intimated that where inquiry had taken place, and opportunity had been afforded the County Court Judge of replying to charges, the Court would not inquire into the discretion of the Chancellor of the Duchy of Lancaster, who had removed the Judge, I think inquiry and an opportunity of answering the complaint must precede amotion. If there be no inquiry, or an inquiry without the opportunity offered of replying to the charges, I think the amotion will be hard to be had upon appeal to the Privy Council.' [xviii]

Although Mr Parker advocated removal of the Judge at once by the Governor and Council, the Attorney-General was not prepared to take the responsibility of advising this, and preferred putting the matter before Parliament.[xix]

Parliament met on 15 June, and in his opening speech the Governor said:

'I have called you together for the dispatch of business at the present time, not for the purpose of inviting your attention to the general business of the country, but solely on account of the unforeseen exigency occasioned by recent proceedings in connection with the administration of justice in this colony, which appears to my Government and to myself to require your immediate consideration'—and he invited the members to adopt such measures as might seem best calculated 'to remove existing obstacles to the efficient administration of justice, and to secure, as far as practicable, respect and obedience to the law.'[xx]

In moving the adoption of the address in reply in the Assembly, Mr Rounsevell voiced the sentiments of the majority of the members.

'I have always looked up to our Judges'—he said—'with the highest respect ... But I consider that our judgment-seat has been lowered in the view of the world; that our Government has been degraded and our legislation trampled on.'

Now the Naval & Military Club, the residence of John Rounsevell (1836-1902) on the corner of Hutt and Angas Streets, ca. 1872. A pastoralist who began his working life in his father's coaching business, Rounsevell was first elected to the House of Assembly in 1865. He continued, intermittently, as a MHA until 1884. His half brother, William Benjamin Rounsevell (1843-1923), was also a politician. (SLSA)

He admitted that Mr Justice Boothby was a thorough lawyer; a gentleman of high talent and ability; and that he was conscientious in the line of action he had taken. But why, if they had no valid laws, did he continue to administer their imaginary ones?

'If it is true that we have no Attorney General, no valid legislation, no anything except the Judge, why does not that

> Judge take some rational and constitutional means of pointing out his doubts to the Government instead of allowing matters to reach the present crisis? Sitting, as he does, to try men for their lives, why turn the solemn temple of justice into a theatre of ridicule against the Government, the laws, and those who administered them?' [xxi]

Mr Strangways moved as an amendment, that:

> '... the House regretted that the Governor should have been advised to call Parliament together for the avowed purpose of removing Mr Justice Boothby from his office as a Judge of the Supreme Court before any steps were taken to ascertain the opinions of the other Judges on the point of law raised by Mr Justice Boothby.'

In a long speech he argued that the Judge was right in his opinion, that the Court of Appeals was illegal and that the Grand Jury had never been abolished, and he attacked the Crown law officers for failure to argue the matter before the Full Court.

> 'What course did they adopt?'—he asked. 'On the first day of the present Law Term three learned gentlemen went down to the Supreme Court with the avowed object of telling the Court—and it took three of them to do it, namely James Penn Boucaut (Attorney General), William Alfred Wearing (Crown Solicitor) and Rupert Ingleby, a specially retained counsel—that after careful consideration they had arrived at the conclusion that they could do nothing else than go to the Supreme Court, and inform the Court that they could do nothing. Not only that the counsel could do nothing, but they gave the Bench a gratuitous piece of information, which more properly ought to have been given by the Bench to the Bar than by the Bar to the Bench—that the Court had no jurisdiction in the matter, and as a thing of course when asked what they intended to do, they all three one after the other said they intended to do—nothing. It was a repetition of the old story—"What are you doing Jemmy? Nothing. What are you doing Billy? Helping Jemmy. What are you doing Rupert? Helping Billy and Jemmy."'

He protested against the Judge's removal.

> 'The result would be to hold the same grounds of accusation in terrorem over the other Judges so as to intimidate them against holding opinions objected to in Mr Justice Boothby's case. It was pretty generally understood that had the question of the position of the Attorney General been brought before the Full

Court Mr Justice Gwynne would have coincided in opinion with Mr Justice Boothby.'

Mr Strangways' amendment was negatived without a division;[xxii] and on 22 June the Chief Secretary moved in the Assembly that an address be presented to the Queen praying for the removal of Mr Justice Boothby from his office:

> '... because he persistently refuses to administer laws duly enacted by the Parliament of South Australia; declines to give effect to the Imperial Statute known as the Validating Act; is accustomed from the Bench to impugn the validity of the Local Court of Appeals; refuses to conform his judgments to the decisions of the Supreme Court; obstructs the course of justice by perversity and an habitual disregard of judicial propriety; and has delivered judgments and dicta not in accordance with law.'

A similar address was moved in the Legislative Council on 26 June.[xxiii]

The Judge still had a few supporters. In the Assembly Mr Reynolds urged that the Judge should be given time to consider the "rambling charges" brought against him; and Mr Andrews said:

> 'A Judge should not have less than justice because he was a Judge. That which was granted to the merest felon they ought not to deny to His Honour. He ought not to be condemned unheard.' [xxiv]

Thomas Reynolds
(1818-1875)
"Teapot Tommy" – so called for his support of the temperance movement – was a grocer and jam maker whose success in business allowed his involvement in politics. A devout dissenter and a reformer his political career extended from 1854 to 1873 and included two periods as Premier. After politics he settled in Darwin but, like Wearing, died in the wreck of the *Gothenburg* whilst returning to Adelaide. Simon Calvert's *Loss of the Steamship Gothenburg* (1875) is pictured. (SLV)

In the upper house the Hon J. Baker moved that, instead of an address, a Select Committee should be appointed to inquire and report. They had only a one-sided statement to go on, he said; and as for the Attorney-General's report: "I can hardly conceive that a paper less creditable to a gentleman in his position could be written."

Stow, he thought, had provoked and deserved any abuse he received, and even if the Judge's opinion were wrong he should not be removed: he should be retired with a pension. Mr G.F. Angas seconded his amendment. "I have no favour for Judge Boothby"——he said—"but I always thought him to be a conscientious man who would do his duty faithfully."

The pro-Boothbyites, however, were a very small minority. Most of the members said the Judge was mad, or corrupt, or both, and described his attitude on the bench as being: "Don't you believe my colleagues. I am the man from England. I have practised before the Courts at Westminster, and am the only Judge acquainted with the law." [xxv]

The addresses were carried in each House by an overwhelming majority, and were forwarded to England. The Judge had been supplied with copies of the proceedings and of the addresses, but he was not offered any opportunity to make a defence before Parliament, if he so desired.

In his dispatch accompanying the addresses the Governor wrote:

> 'The feeling in both Houses has been all but unanimous for the removal of the Judge; and indeed I am not aware that opinion in and out of Parliament has ever been less divided on any important subject. It is felt universally, and by no one more strongly than myself, that the presence of Mr Justice Boothby on the Bench is detrimental to the best interests of the Colony.'

He had for a long time hoped that the Imperial Legislation, and especially the Colonial Laws Validity Act, would have put an end to Mr Justice Boothby's objections.

> 'Unhappily, however, this natural expectation has been falsified by his conduct; and I doubt if there has been any period since Mr Justice Boothby was appointed in which he has been so fertile in objections, and certainly there has been none in which he has been so reckless in giving effect to them, as since the arrival of that Act.
>
> It is noticeable'—he continued—'that there was no one in either House who appeared to dissent from the opinion that the removal of the Judge would be advantageous to the Colony, though, upon other grounds some few dissented from the Address; and, from all I have been able to learn, the opinion of the people is at least as decided as that of their

representatives. No voice has been raised in his favour—no intimation even has been given of any dissatisfaction with the conduct of my Government. On the contrary, the press, which is a tolerable index of popular feeling, has been unanimous on the subject. I do not attempt to account for Judge Boothby's conduct by any reference to various motives that are attributed to him. It would afford me the greatest satisfaction if I could regard it as prompted solely or even principally by a sense of duty; but it is not, perhaps, a matter of much importance as far as the immediate action of Her Majesty's Government is concerned ... I deeply regret that a person holding so high an office, who under many aspects is estimable, and who has reached an age at which it will be impossible for him to commence any other course, should be exposed to the loss of an appointment he has held for so many years ... But notwithstanding all these, and the other considerations which would lead me to desire that so extreme a measure as his removal should not be adopted, I am compelled to state my conviction that it is in the highest degree important to the peace, order, and good government of the Colony, that Her Majesty should be advised to comply with the prayer of the Addresses.' [xxvi]

Edward Preston.

Judge's Note Book (Judge Boothby) February 1861 (R v Preston) (Supreme Court Library of South Australia)

The addresses having been dispatched to England, there was comparative quiet in the colony. The outcry on this occasion had not been so great as in 1861; the uselessness of mere vociferation had been realised. It was decided by the Government to let the prisoners remaining untried from the May Criminal Sessions wait until August, when the Chief Justice was due to hold a Criminal Sessions; and their causes were then disposed of without any trouble. The Governor reported, on 28 August 1866:

> 'At this moment the Chief Justice is engaged in delivering the gaol of an unusual number of prisoners, including those left untried by the course of proceedings adopted by Judge Boothby at the last Criminal Sessions; and the orderly and efficient manner in which the business of the sessions now proceeds, forms a very favorable contrast to the last, in which Judge Boothby presided, and renders the desire of the whole community more intense to see the administration of justice saved from further interruption as speedily as possible. By the established tour of duty of the Judges of the Supreme Court, it will be Judge Boothby's turn to preside at the Criminal Sessions early in February, and a repetition of the conduct that has already occasioned so much embarrassment, is to be apprehended from his having another opportunity to display the indifference with which I understand he professes to regard the proceedings that have been adopted for his removal.' [1]

A few days later, the Attorney-General introduced in the Assembly a bill to amend the Third Judge and District Courts Act by providing for the issue of Special Commissions by the Governor, and to enable the Attorney-General to file informations at circuit courts. He admitted that the object of the Bill was to provide a means of preventing Mr Justice Boothby from taking another Criminal Sessions when his turn arrived. The Bill met with considerable opposition, it being forcibly urged that to give the executive power to say which judge should try a cause was dangerous; and the Act (No 11 of 1866-7) was not passed till the end of the year. It provided that the Governor, with the advice and consent of the Executive Council, might issue a Commission directed to any one of the judges of the Supreme Court, authorising and requiring such judge to hold and preside at any criminal or civil sittings of the Supreme Court; and that persons might be put upon trial for any crime or offence before such courts in the same manner as at the Criminal Sessions of the Supreme Court, upon an information presented in the name and by the authority of the Attorney-General of the province.

Henry Howard Molyneux Herbert, Fourth Earl of Carnarvon (1831-1890)
A liberal leaning conservative politician, Carnarvon became Secretary of State in June 1866 holding the office until March the next year. In this short time, while he did not solve the Boothby problem, he did introduce the British North America Bill that led to the confederation of Canada. Later in his career his work dealing with South African and Irish issues was less fruitful. (NPG

The Act did not meet with favour in England. The Secretary of State wrote that he could understand that the Act had been thought necessary to meet exigencies.

> 'But in proportion as the emergency is special, so must the remedial Act be special in its character, and especial care should be taken that it shall not go beyond what is absolutely needed to provide against the anticipated danger of a failure of Justice. In these respects the Act is, I think, open to two objections: first, it is made perpetual instead of temporary; secondly, it appears to go beyond what the circumstances of the case require in that it allows the issue of Special Commissions to any one Judge to hold Civil as well as Criminal Sittings.'

For the time being, he neither approved nor disapproved of the Act, but advised that it should be amended to meet his objections. In any event, Special Commissioners should be appointed only if absolutely necessary to prevent a failure of justice.[2]

Mr Justice Boothby had drawn up and forwarded to the Secretary of State a protest against the addresses for his removal. The Governor, he said, had placed himself in the position of a prosecutor before the two Houses of Parliament, with his Executive Council sitting in those Houses. He therefore refused to transmit his protest, as the official practice required, through the hands of the Governor.

> 'I submit very confidently that it would be contrary to natural justice, and to all analogy in, to say the least, quasi-judicial proceedings of a penal nature, that I should place in the hands of the Governor-in-Chief, and by consequence in the hands of his Executive Council, my joint accusers, the answer I have to make to the statements and accusations of these Addresses, and the grounds on which I protest against the legality and justice of all their proceedings. As my prosecutors, they have obtained against me, from the two Houses respectively, a reference for trial on a highly penal charge, which, if established, brings, as a consequence, loss of property, and what is far worse, the stigma of being an incompetent and unjust Judge while representing Her Majesty in her Supreme Court of this Colony. Having done this they cannot on any principle of justice, or analogy to judicial procedure, require that I should inform them what is the nature of the answer I have to make.'

He submitted that there were no grounds at all for his removal and that the opposition to him was due to his enforcement of Imperial legislation.

> 'The motive to these Addresses is so transparent that it cannot be concealed—to get rid of these Imperial restraints, or failing that to get rid of every Judge who ventures to enforce them. Coupled with the Addresses for my removal in 1861, both instances may be justly regarded as the beginning of a legislative agitation, to bring about a repeal of these restraints; and the Imperial Parliament is thus shot at, through the sides of a Judge. It is manifest also, that if the removal of a Judge is made to depend on Addresses such as these, from Colonial Parliaments, on grounds like the present, that Judges who enforce Colonial legislation, at the cost of Imperial, are secure in their office, and need not fear any Addresses to remove, and the Crown helpless, as to any remedy, in the absence of such Addresses.' [3]

With his letter he forwarded a "Memorandum of Topics" intended to form the basis of his reply to the charges against him, containing ninety three heads, in which he reiterated all his objections to the legislation of the colony, to the Court of Appeals, to the existence of the Attorney-General and to the legality of the appointment of the Chief Justice. A copy of this was forwarded by the Colonial Office to the Governor for his information, and Mr Boucaut, the Attorney-General, proceeded to add ninety three criticisms of the Judge's topics. Summarising them, he said:

> 'Mr Boothby's memorandum shows in itself how ready he is to throw contempt on everything Colonial—whether his colleagues, the press, the Parliament, or the people. The frequent attacks on Mr Hanson go far to prove that that gentlemen's appointment to the office of Chief Justice is in truth the cause of Mr Boothby's renewed outbreak against the Colony's well-being. A careful consideration of this document is alone sufficient to prove how fatal to the administration of justice is Mr Boothby's presence on the Bench, and what just cause the Legislature and people of the Colony have to complain of his perversity, and of any action of Her Majesty's Government that prolongs such a state of insecurity.' [4]

Mr Boucaut's labours were wasted, however, for the Secretary of State curtly replied that in forwarding Mr Boothby's list of topics he had no desire to receive any explanation of the statements they contained. "It is quite clear that no good can be done by this kind of irregular controversy." [5]

In addition to Mr Justice Boothby's protest, the Secretary of State received a lengthy communication from Mr H.C. Palmer, a local barrister, who seems to have been almost the only adherent the Judge had among the profession.

Hamilton Charles Palmer (?-1880)
Palmer led, apparently, a peripatetic life as a lawyer working, variously, from Riverton, Kapunda, Adelaide and Port Pirie.

> 'The outcry against Mr Justice Boothby'—wrote Mr Palmer—'is a clamour of a clique and its followers, and not the healthy expression of public opinion; the public generally are satisfied that Mr Justice Boothby has done good service to the Colony by checking and correcting the errors of a loose and over-hasty course of legislation, notwithstanding a frequent dissent and probably a warrantable dissent from some of His Honor's opinions. Speaking as a Barrister practising before His Honor, I may be allowed to add that His Honor has uniformly reciprocated such courtesy as he has received from the Bar, that he has commanded, as far as my experience goes, the respect and deferential confidence of juries, that on the occasion above referred to (the quarrel with Stow as to his license to appear against the Crown) his Honor's temper was tried more than on any other occasion that it has been my lot to witness, and if His Honor was in any wanting in the dignity inseparable from his position, in my humble opinion it was in exposing himself to conduct and language unsuited to the relative propositions of the parties, by not sooner quitting the judgment seat.'

Mr Palmer's reputation among the profession, however, was such that his statements cannot be accepted as very reliable testimony.

British Guiana
British Guiana in northeastern South America was a colony based on a plantation economy that first used African slaves and then, from the 1840s, indentured labour, mostly from India. Accordingly, the indigenous Amerindians now form a minority in a multicultural country that gained independence as Guyana in 1966.

A curious pamphlet was anonymously printed and published at this time in Adelaide, consisting of a reprint of certain judgments delivered in the Supreme Court of British Guiana, the Chief Justice of which had been suspended by the Governor but restored to office by the Secretary of State. The judgments were supposed to support the case of Mr Justice Boothby, and the more relevant passages were printed in italics. That Mr Justice Boothby was aware of the judgments is shown by the fact that he several times referred to them in court. An index to the contents of the pamphlet shows its trend and the object of its publication, and the style of this index seems to stamp it conclusively as being the work of Mr Justice Boothby himself. A few examples will illustrate this, the language being typical of the Judge:

> 'Illegal directions to Clerk of Supreme Court by Executive Government, leading to lamentable proceedings against the Judges.
>
> Judges entitled to expect from law officers of the Crown more than they claim from private advocates.
>
> Contempt of the authority of a Court presided over by Her Majesty's judges is a contempt of the sovereign's authority.
>
> An Act not clearly legal for a Judge to perform he must deem

> illegal until his difficulty be removed.
>
> Pecuniary consequences for illegal acts to Great Officers of Government, in a recent instance.
>
> Officers of a Court of Justice not at liberty to take directions from the Executive Government.
>
> Public opinion, so called, will not deter Courts or Judges from doing their duty.'

The very peculiar construction of these sentences is identical with that used throughout the memorandum of ninety three topics which the Judge prepared at the same time. Aut Boothby, aut diabolus.

After his short "Reign of Terror" in May 1866, little opportunity was given to Mr Justice Boothby during the rest of the year to show his terrible propensities. He continued to sit on the bench as usual, both in the Full Court and for the trial of civil causes, and in a few instances showed that he had not at all resiled from any of his opinions. On 1 June 1866, for instance, Mr Stow, provoked by the quarrel about his licence, brought before the Full Court the question of the position of Queen's Counsel in the colony and asked for a ruling as to their precedence and as to their holding briefs against the Crown. Mr Justice Boothby intervened at once.

> 'There is an important preliminary question'—he said—'and that is whether Queen's Counsel exist here, or whether they can be appointed here. It is quite obvious that what is wanted is for the Court to express an opinion which may have a bearing on proceedings which are to be taken hereafter.'
>
> Mr Stow: 'No. If Your Honor thinks that, I will sit down at once.'
>
> Mr Justice Boothby: 'I have no doubt in the world that it is the case.'
>
> Mr Stow: 'Your Honor, it is rather with a contrary view.'
>
> Mr Justice Boothby: 'The object is to obtain from the Court an expression of opinion as to matters that are past.'
>
> Mr Stow: 'I simply ask that the rule for the future may be known.'
>
> Mr Justice Boothby: 'I think the Judges will see that this is a matter which they should not entertain now.'
>
> Mr Stow: 'When a Counsel disclaims an intention imputed to him, and states most solemnly—'
>
> Mr Justice Boothby: 'I accept the disclaimer for yourself

> personally; but there are others who have motives for taking the matter up.'

Mr Stow then said that he would stop at once, if Mr Justice Boothby thought the application would have some effect other than that which he had expressed. "I most decidedly think so", said the Judge. "Indeed, there can be little doubt of it from the present tone of public discussion." The matter was therefore allowed to drop.[6]

In *R. v. Johnes*, in September 1866, Mr Stow moved for a rule nisi to arrest judgment in the case of a man found guilty of misdemeanour, on the ground that no offence was disclosed by the indictment; or for a new trial on the ground of misdirection. Mr Justice Boothby asked to see the record, and once [sic] announced that it was merely waste paper.

> Mr Stow: 'What ground does Your Honor take?'
>
> Mr Justice Boothby: 'The ground that there is no Attorney General, and that if there is, there is no Grand Jury.'
>
> Mr Stow: 'I am not instructed to take that point.'
>
> Mr Justice Boothby: 'You should take every point whether you are instructed or not, supposing you think them to be good in law.'

Mr Stow said he thought it a waste of time to take a point which could only postpone his client's fate; he preferred to rely upon the substantial grounds of his application. A rule nisi was granted, Mr Justice Boothby saying that he expected the Crown to consider the objections he had mentioned.[7] Mr Ingleby appeared to show cause for the Crown against the rule being made absolute, and Mr Justice Boothby promptly asked him to argue the question whether the indictment was not bad because signed by the Attorney-General.

> Mr Ingleby: 'I am not instructed to do so.'
>
> Mr Justice Boothby: 'You ought to have been. It is known very well that I hold that opinion, and I gave notice that I should go upon it in this case, and I ought to have been assisted.'

It was eventually decided, upon other grounds, that the prisoner must be discharged; Mr Justice Boothby mentioning that the Act professing to do away with grand juries was invalid, and that he should give a written judgment on this question on another day. That day never came.[8]

The only other matters which came before the Supreme Court up to the last weeks in 1866 which call for notice in connection with Mr Justice Boothby are the cases of *Galbraith v. Elder* and *MacDonald v. Galbraith*. Mr Justice Boothby was accused of displaying, throughout the protracted litigation of these actions, gross partiality towards Mr

Thomas Elder, his next-door neighbour at Glen Osmond, who was the defendant in the first action and the real plaintiff in the second.

Galbraith v. Elder began as a simple claim for damages for libel and wrongful dismissal, but it developed into a maze of technicalities—motions for new trials and in arrest of judgment, attempts by the plaintiff to abandon demurrers and attempts by the defendant to have them argued, rules to set aside a ca sa wrongfully issued, and rules to set aside a "nolle prosequi" on the ground that a "remittitur damna" should have been entered instead. These bewildering proceedings gave rise to loud complaints by the plaintiff and his advisers that Mr Justice Boothby took up the cudgels for Mr Elder, suggested points to his counsel, advised an appeal to the Privy Council and wilfully delayed giving judgment, in order to prevent the plaintiff from exercising his just rights; but they are otherwise of no particular interest, and it would be futile to go into them in detail.[9] It is necessary to turn instead to the fate of the addresses for the Judge's removal.

(Sir) Thomas Elder (1818-1897)
A businessman and pastoralist whose name lives on thanks to the success in business and his philanthropy. Elder's business interests included the Wallaroo and Moonta mines, wool selling and huge pastoral holdings. He supported much exploration and was responsible for the introduction of camels and their Afghan drivers to the outback. He was a member of the Legislative Council from 1863 to 1869 and 1871 to 1878.

Upon receiving them, the Secretary of State was of opinion that, the matter being of such importance and its decision involving numerous and disputed questions of law, the addresses must be referred to the Judicial Committee of the Privy Council for advice as to what course ought to be pursued. The Governor in one of his dispatches had thrown out a suggestion that Mr Justice Boothby might be got rid of by being pensioned off, and the Secretary of State replied that if the question could be disposed of in this way it would be the means of saving expense, delay and anxiety, both to the Judge and to the colony.

When the Governor communicated to the Executive Council the news from England, it met with unqualified disapproval. The Secretary of State was told, in effect, to mind his own business and not come interfering with suggestions about giving a pension to the Judge. Let him clearly understand that the local Government had no intention of even considering a pension until some decisive action on the addresses was taken in England. As for referring the matter to the Privy Council, it was said bluntly that his Lordship had blundered. If a decision of the Privy Council had been wanted, that could have been obtained easily enough by taking proceedings in the colony for the Judge's removal under 22 Geo III c.75, leaving it to the Judge to appeal against his amotion if he wished to do so.

> 'By the course, however, which has been followed by Her Majesty's Government, the Colony has been placed in a much worse position than if action had been taken under the Statute of George III, intended for Colonies with Constitutions. In this respect, therefore, the possession of a constitution by South Australia is only a disadvantage, and it cannot be that this was the intention either of Her Majesty's Government or of the Imperial Parliament.'

The Council were of opinion a serious blow had been dealt at colonial responsible government.

> 'The proceeding of His Lordship tends to diminish the reliance hitherto placed on Her Majesty's Government, by appearing to show a disregard of, and indifference to, the urgent prayer of the Colonial Parliament, in what they feel to be a great and pressing emergency; and it may lead the public mind to think that it would be better altogether to dispense with conservative safeguards, than to encounter the vexation, obstacles and delays, which they occasion. However much such arguments are to be deprecated, it is impossible not to fear that they may be urged and find popular acceptance if the decision of the question should be long delayed. There is no feeling more unanimous and deep-seated in the Colony than that of distrust and alarm at Mr Boothby's administration of justice; and nothing but the confidence expressed by the Colonial Government in Her Majesty's immediate attention to the petitions of the two Houses, has prevented serious and dangerous public excitement ... The Colonial Parliament always cheerfully submit their enactments to Her Majesty's Government, and the Colonial Government will always gladly submit to the Judicial Committee, in due course of law; but against such an unusual and extraordinary course as that which His Lordship has adopted, the Council feel that it is the duty of the Colonial Government respectfully, but most firmly, to protest.' [10]

In forwarding a minute of these views, on 28 December 1866, the Governor wrote:

> 'There can be no doubt that the sentiments of my Council on this subject are the reflex of public opinion and feeling to so great an extent that it is most desirable that the case should be speedily disposed of.' [11]

Shortly afterwards, however, further information arrived from England, setting out that the Privy Council had decided that details of the charges against Mr Justice Boothby must be framed with precision and embodied in a case, that a legal agent must be appointed in London to conduct the proceedings and that particulars of the charges must be communicated to the Judge, who could then put in an answer to them. The Executive Council now bubbled over with rage. They replied point-blank that they were not going to go before the Privy Council.

> 'The course which His Lordship recommends to the Government of South Australia is one which they are not able

to follow without the sanction of the Legislature, and one which they would certainly not recommend the Legislature to adopt. For the Government to follow the course suggested, would not only involve a large expense, for which the Legislature must be asked to make provision, but it would be to acknowledge that His Lordship was right in declining to exercise a duty belonging to his office; and also that the Addresses of the Parliament of South Australia, which are by law made a sufficient ground for the removal of a Judge, may be rightly passed over as having no force whatever—and the latter consideration must forbid their recommending such a course to Parliament. If His Lordship declines to advise Her Majesty, and practically shows that he attaches no importance to the laws or the Parliament of South Australia it becomes the duty of the latter, on behalf of those whom they represent, to vindicate their position by some other steps. Without, however, pretending to indicate the course which the Legislature of South Australia may think it right to pursue, it is enough to report that the Government can neither adopt nor recommend that one which His Lordship suggests. It is with very great regret that this Government have received the intimation of the course which the Right Honourable the Secretary of State has thought proper to take on this occasion. They are most desirous to preserve unimpaired all the ties which connect South Australia with the Mother Country, and not only to acknowledge that they are subjects of the British Crown, but to cherish and deepen the feelings of loyal attachment to Her Majesty; still they cannot but fear that these ties must be loosened, and these feelings diminished, unless Her Majesty's Advisers are prepared to recognise the rights of the Colony, and to pay attention to the respectful demands of its Parliament. In the present instance, it appears that these have been disregarded; and the Government cannot but anticipate a considerable degree of regret and apprehension at the result of such action, if persevered in.' [12]

This was strong language, and the Governor apologetically wrote, on 26 February 1867:

> 'It is a matter of sincere regret to me that the views of my Council are so much at variance with those of Her Majesty's Government ... It has not been in my power to prevail upon my Advisers to modify those views in any respect; and in truth I am bound to assure your Lordship that, in my own opinion, my Ministers would not be sustained by the Parliament or by

the great majority of the community in any other course than that which, after the fullest consideration, they have determined to pursue in this matter, which has long been the source of deep anxiety and injury to the colony.' [13]

The Privy Council Chamber as it exists today. Designed in 1828 by Sir John Soane the Chamber has seen only minor changes since coming into use. (Privy Council Office).

On the same day the Secretary of State had replied to the first protest, explaining the reasons for referring the matter to the Privy Council. Before acceding to such a serious demand as that for the dismissal of a judge, he said, Her Majesty's advisers were bound to require satisfactory evidence that the dismissal was proper.

'If such a dismissal were called for on the ground of drunkenness, dishonesty, or any other grave and unequivocal delinquency, and if the proof of that delinquency, with the defence of the accused person, and the observations of the Governor upon that defence, were duly forwarded to the Secretary of State, the question would be reduced to one of moral guilt and of the effect of evidence on which a minister would probably find it possible to form a clear judgment with no other legal advice than that which is ordinarily at his command, and, if the case had been sent home in a proper shape, this would have been in some degree, the case with Mr Boothby—against whom charges are brought of gross impropriety of language and behaviour on the Bench.

But these charges are subsidiary to that of "perversity"; that is to say, of obstinate adherence to opinions which are erroneous in point of law. The leading accusation against Mr Boothby, with which the others are connected, and from which they in a great measure derive their weight, is that of habitually obstructing the administration of justice by decisions which he ought to know to be wrong in their legal aspect. It is thus impossible, in my judgment, to deal separately with the question of conduct and the question of law: and, having regard to the nature of Mr Boothby's disputed decisions, the manner in which they are laid before me, the absence of any appeal against them to the Privy Council, and the fact that, on a former very important occasion, it was discovered that Mr Boothby's technical objections were well founded, I do not think that the question of law could be properly disposed of, and a Judge of the Supreme Court pronounced to be perversely erroneous, except on the advice of a tribunal whose legal authority is superior to his own. If this is so, it will hardly be disputed that the Judicial Committee is the tribunal whose advice should be sought for such a purpose.

Your Ministers appear to consider'—he continued, with a tinge of sarcasm—'that a different course would have been pursued in England. What would have been done in England must be more or less a matter of conjecture, as no English Judge has yet been removed on Addresses from the Houses of Parliament; but, assuming that Her Majesty would be advised to accede, as a matter of course, to the prayer of Parliament, it must be remembered that the circumstances of the two cases are very dissimilar. It is probable that the charges against an English Judge would have been stated with a precision which is wanting in the Addresses transmitted to me from South Australia—that they would have been supported in detail by

> authentic evidence—that the Judge would have had every opportunity for defence—that the legal questions at issue would have been debated within the walls of Parliament by some of the greatest lawyers of the day—and that in cases of doubt, the advice of the most eminent Judges would have been obtained. Indeed, it is impossible to say what precautions might have been devised to secure Parliament against any misapprehension of law. In this novel proceeding, the course of which Her Majesty is now called upon to determine, it is incumbent upon the Crown to secure to Colonial Judges a protection against exaggeration and misunderstanding, from whatever quarter it may proceed, as effectual as that which their English brethren might be expected to obtain from the deliberations of such an assembly as the British Parliament. And I must add, that the circumstances of the present case illustrate the necessity of such an intervention. For I do not even see that Mr Boothby has been called on to answer the charges against him. The only answer on his part, of which I am aware, is that contained in his recent letters, which in the opinion of your advisers, I ought not to have read or to have communicated to the Council Office. I scarcely know whether I am right in understanding that they expected me to advise that the Queen should dismiss Mr Boothby without perusing this, or any other defence of his conduct. If such were their expectations, it would be wholly impossible for me to accede to them. So long as Her Majesty's Government have any part in such a transaction, the question must be decided by a procedure, which will ensure that entire justice is done, and I must add, at the expense of the parties interested—the Judge and the Colony. I should be wholly departing from my duty, as I understand it, to the Colony, not less than to the Crown, if I were to allow any argument to be drawn from the vehemence with which Mr Boothby's dismissal is called for. No urgency on the part of the Colonial Parliament or people, can justify Her Majesty's Government in becoming a consenting party to that dismissal, without having first ascertained that it was in itself justifiable.'

On one point, however, he was able to agree with the local Government—that it would have been far better for them to have commenced proceedings under the authority of 22 Geo III c.75 and taken the responsibility of removing the Judge themselves, instead of transmitting an ex parte case to be dealt with on the other side of the world:

> '... with the evident probability that the first step would be to put Mr Boothby on his defence, and with the possibility of calculating the delays to which this necessary step might lead. I am inclined to think that even now'—concluded Lord Carnarvon—'your Government would act most wisely by commencing proceedings under that Act. But they will do well to bear in mind, that in that case, their decision will be subject to an Appeal to the Privy Council, and that with a view to that Appeal, their charges must be adequate and precise, that the evidence of facts must be sufficient, and that Mr Boothby must be fully heard in his defence.' [14]

This important dispatch reached the colony in April 1867. In acknowledging it, the Governor wrote:

> 'I confess that I cannot but feel some degree of regret at the view which your Lordship has thus felt compelled to take; and I trust that Your Lordship will believe that I feel very strongly the importance of maintaining the independence of the judicial office, and I am assured that the same feeling is experienced by both branches of the Legislature of the colony. And, if the Legislature has addressed Her Majesty praying her to remove a Judge; and if I have ventured to recommend compliance with that Address, it is only because a long experience of the conduct of Mr Boothby has convinced them and me that his continuance in office was incompatible with the tranquil and orderly, and even with the fair and equal administration of justice. And though I fully admit that the present question should be decided upon its merits, and uninfluenced by any vehemence on the part of the Colonial Parliament, yet the fact, that in a community habitually so temperate and peaceful as that of South Australia, so strong a feeling should have been excited in the people and the Legislature upon this subject, might, I would venture to suggest, be relied upon as showing the urgency of the occasion, and even the expediency of examining, and possibly of deciding the case apart from the purely legal questions with which alone the Judicial Committee of the Privy Council would deal.' [15]

The extraordinary conduct of Mr Justice Boothby during the early months of 1867 brought about a crisis in the administration of the law; and the Government, following the suggestion so plainly thrown out by the Secretary of State, decided to take proceedings in the colony, under the Act of George III, to remove the Judge from his office.

Justice Benjamin Boothby, ca 1860s. (NLA)

Mr Justice Boothby

'the desert rose'

The last phase of Mr Justice Boothby's eccentric career began just before Christmas 1866, when he decided to revive in open court his old objection that his learned brothers were not judges at all.

> 'According to the argument of my learned colleague Mr Justice Boothby'—retorted Mr Justice Gwynne—'there is only one Judge upon the Bench. It reminds me of the story of a gentleman in the stocks, who was told by his friend that they could not put him in the stocks; but, said he, "Here I am."'
>
> 'I see no use in discussing the question'—said the Chief Justice. 'The more Acts we are establishing in the Colonial Legislation the more confident my learned colleague is that it is all invalid. I must confess, however that I am sitting here, and I can hardly refrain from exercising the power of the office.' [1]

Mr Justice Boothby, quite unimpressed by the opposite and hostile views of his pseudo colleagues, remained as independent as the Miller of Dee.

> 'And this the burden of his song
> For ever us'd to be—
> I care for nobody, not I,
> If no one cares for me'.

When the February Criminal Sessions came round, which it was the turn of Mr Justice Boothby to take, the Governor issued a Special Commission to the Chief Justice to hold them. On the first day of the sessions the Court was crowded, for the rumour spread that Mr Justice Boothby intended to offer some obstruction to the proceedings going on under the Chief Justice. Sure enough, when the Chief Justice took his seat on the bench, entering from one side of the Court, Mr Justice Boothby entered from the other and also took his seat on the bench. The Commission was read. Mr Justice Boothby then intervened and delivered a protest.

> 'I am here to-day'—he said—'ready to fulfil my duties as the Judge of our Lady the Queen, authorised and entitled to preside at the Criminal Sittings of the Supreme Court now to be held at this hour in due course of law. Such authority, however, so vested in me, is sought to be set aside by a document just read to the Court, and to be filed on record. I protest hereby against its validity and declare my judicial opinion to be that such document is wholly inoperative and void, as contravening Imperial Statutes founding the

jurisdiction of this Court. It professes to take the power to preside at this hour from out of me, and to vest such power in another. A coercive and punitive power is thus sought to be exercised over me, which, if not warranted by law, amounts to a civil trespass, as restraining my personal freedom and depriving me of the power to attend to my duties to the Queen, by presiding in Her Court at this hour. A continuance of such restraint I shall regard as manifested after this protest by a continuance to occupy the place accorded to the presiding Judge, coupled with any interference in the Court Proceedings, by any expression of judicial interference. If such conduct is manifested I shall forthwith retire, and so leave the responsibility of exercising the coercive powers of a Criminal Court not lawfully constituted to those who choose to enter upon such experiments, and having secured to myself the means of pecuniary compensation and redress through the process of Her Majesty's Courts in Westminster Hall against all who have shared in the making and service of the illegal documents against which I protest for the contumely and indignity this day put upon me, if the vindication of my judicial character and office shall so require. I am content with the objection founded on the absolute illegality of the document, but guard myself from being supposed to have passed by unnoticed the many objections upon its face.'

The Chief Justice simply told the associate to call the jury. "In pursuance of what I have stated in my protest I now retire from the Bench"—said Mr Justice Boothby, and he left the Court.[2]

At the risk of tiresome repetition, it is perhaps worthwhile to reproduce the amusing description of this scene in the short-lived *Pasquin*, which flourished at this time. A "Stranger" writes to say that he had paid a visit to the Supreme Court. "Shortly after ten had sounded, a side door opened and a Judge entered, bowed to the assembled bar, and took the centre of three seats under the regal canopy."

While the stranger was meditating on the majesty and dignity of the law, thus transplanted to a distant colony, another Judge, "of venerable aspect", entered and took his seat by the side of the first.

> 'This struck me as singular, but no more; but no sooner had the official read the Commission for trying the criminal prisoners, than the venerable Judge who had last entered claimed the attention of the Court, and commenced reading a most remarkable protest against the legal proceedings then and there about to ensue. Amidst profound silence, in a low voice and with a slightly perturbed demeanour, he denounced in

THE BEST OF FRIENDS MUST PART.

"BROTHER! BROTHER! WE WERE BOTH IN THE WRONG."

An 1869 *Adelaide Punch* cartoon of Gwynne and Hanson showing them in a state which Boothby would have wished. (SLSA)

> calm and dignified language some gross and peculiar irregularity relating to the position of the Chief Justice then upon the Bench, which being concluded he arose and retired from the Court. A low murmur of suppressed approbation and sympathy for the courage and consistency of the venerable old man ran through the Court at the conclusion of the protest.
>
> As a stranger, the whole proceeding was to me an enigma. The experience of years in many lands had never made me acquainted with anything so strange, so disreputable, and so damaging to the dignity of the Bench in any English Court of Justice.
>
> Turning to one nigh at hand, I enquired the meaning of these strange proceedings. "Sir," said he, "this is a Judge who upholds the observance of all the great principles of English Jurisprudence, the practice of which in their integrity has been found extremely prejudicial to a people who do not so much seek after impartial justice, inasmuch as justice did aforetime occasionally seek after them! ... At last, the Parliament incensed beyond measure at the determination of the Home Government not to sanction their desperately invalid acts and illegal proceedings, adopt the measures you have this day seen, and South Australia has exhibited before all the world the most gross and vulgar insult to a justice on the bench that the history of lawless times and of dishonest people has yet recorded."'[3]

Pasquin, it may be added, was strongly pro-Boothby.

> 'The wonderful judge'—it said—'has been smashed or "smiflicated" regularly every month for the last four years, and yet blooms on like the desert rose, stronger and firmer for the ill-usage and coarse invective so freely lavished.'[4]

Finding his protest was ignored, Mr Justice Boothby proceeded to heave another spanner into the works. Parliament had just passed the Equity Act (No 20 of 1866-67) which consolidated all the various provisions relating to the jurisdiction and procedure of the Supreme Court in Equity. The Act required the Attorney-General to present his Commission as such to the Supreme Court in order that it might be recorded. On 25 February 1867, the Attorney-General duly attended before the Court with his Commission. Mr Justice Boothby looked at it and immediately said that it was a piece of waste parchment.

> 'There is no power given by the Imperial Statute for the Governor to make the appointment'—he said.

> Mr Justice Gwynne: 'There is a local Statute requires it, I believe.'
>
> Mr Justice Boothby: 'Oh yes; but the Parliament has no power to authorize the appointment. It is a prerogative of the Queen of England, and by the present commission the only office of the kind is that of Advocate General established by Imperial Act. It is provided in express terms that any Act of the Local Parliament which contravenes Imperial Legislation shall be inoperative. I declare this piece of parchment to be illegal and inoperative.'
>
> The Chief Justice: 'I hardly know what power one Judge has to declare a document illegal; he may express his opinion—'
>
> Mr Justice Boothby: 'Of course that is my opinion. I declared so far as my opinion.'
>
> The Chief Justice: 'I understand my learned colleague to declare the Commission illegal. The Court orders the Master to make a note of it in the records of the Court.'
>
> Mr Justice Gwynne: 'That can do no harm that I see and if any point of law is raised it may be preserved, notwithstanding its being recorded in the book.'
>
> Mr Justice Boothby: 'I quite agree that it can do no harm, and it is equally clear it can do no good, so far as any legal results founded upon it. Only it is deluding the public in the meantime, leading to most expensive litigation, which will fall upon some suitor in the Court some day.'

Describing the scene, the *Register* said that the effect of the Attorney-General's presentation of his Commission was at once sudden and alarming.

> 'If he had been a Spanish picador brandishing a red flag aloft, and if he had stepped into a ring devoted to bull fights instead of a Court of law, he could not have been more suddenly charged upon.' [5]

A few days later the Judge followed this up with another attack on the Equity Act. Mr Way moved, in *In re Rodgers*, for the attachment of a party under that Act for failure to obey an order of the Court for payment of costs. The majority of the Court thought the order should be made, but Mr Justice Boothby desired the Master to record his dissent.

> 'I shall take care I am entirely free from being concerned in putting into force unlawful legislation by the assumed

> Parliament of this Province. Those who choose to incur the risk can do it. I have no more doubt that the Equity Act is beyond the powers of the Parliament than that I have a seat on this Bench. It was an attempt to alter the Equitable Jurisdiction of the Court as defined by Imperial Statute, which was expressly declared by the validating Act should not be.'

(Sir) Samuel James Way (1836-1916)
A dominant figure in South Australian legal history, Way was admitted to the bar in 1861, made a QC in 1871, served as Attorney-General in 1875 and appointed Chief Justice the following year. He served as Chief Justice for forty years during which time he was also made Lieutenant-Governor (1890), a Judge of the Privy Council and offered a seat on the High Court (1906). (SCLSA)

The Chief Justice then suggested to Mr Stow, who was in Court, that he might act as assigned counsel for the party moved against so that the question of the validity of the Equity Act might be argued.

> 'I should be very happy'—said the Chief Justice—'to hear any gentleman on behalf of the plaintiff, and perhaps I might then understand the argument of my learned colleagues. I confess I am unable at the present moment.'
>
> Mr Justice Gwynne: 'I quite agree ... and if Mr Stow would allow us to assign him to argue the matter at the next sitting it would be more agreeable.'
>
> Mr Stow: 'I don't know who Your Honor means it would be more agreeable to.'
>
> The Chief Justice: 'I am anxious to learn if possible the ground of my learned colleague's suggestion.'
>
> Mr Justice Boothby: 'I merely throw out the proposition. The time for reasons has not come yet, but I have taken care to

guard myself against the liability of exercising coercive measures.'

The Chief Justice: 'I understand my learned colleague's conclusions very clearly, but he has never given any reasons, and I am anxious to see whether there are such reasons as to recommend those conclusions to my mind. He says the time has not come, and that was the reason he had not given reasons. I can only say I have never yet heard any reasons upon the subject from him or anybody else, and it is very desirable the matter should be put in such a shape before the Court, as that my learned colleague might pronounce his reasons on which his conclusion is founded in a judicial decision. In the absence of any argument, it appears to me that the Legislature of this Colony has power to regulate the proceedings of Courts in the Colony, and that this Court is bound to obey its laws.' [6]

On 5 March, Mr Justice Boothby, in *Wright v. Lindsay*, drew attention to the fact that the bill in the proceedings was attested in the name of the Chief Justice.

'I am of opinion'—he said—'that no proceedings so attested are legal, and I shall take care that I do not expose myself to the consequences of assuming an authority which is unwarranted.'

He promised to give reasons on the following day. When succeeding cases were called on, he proceeded to warn counsel that the Court had no power to make orders on proceedings commenced by bill in equity, attested by the Chief Justice; that counsel, attorney and everyone else concerned would be liable to serious consequences; and that counsel would take an order from the majority of the Court at their peril. "Every attempt"—he said—"to alter the law established in the Colony by English legislation is void." [7]

Next day he gave his judgment in *Wright v. Lindsay*.

'I am of opinion that the plaintiff's bill is absolutely void, and, as such, this Court is without jurisdiction to make any coercive order upon it; and this opinion is founded on reasons many times judicially stated by me, and which it is now unnecessary to repeat—among others, my judgment in the appeal case of The Queen v. Hughes and Others, transmitted to the Judicial Committee of the Privy Council—that the only lawful teste of any process of this Court, running in the Queen's name, is by a Judge appointed under her royal sign manual in the manner well known to the law; and if there be more than one Judge so appointed, that a lawful teste of such process can only be in the

> name of the senior among such Judges. This objection, as it renders the plaintiff's bill of complaint absolutely void, deprives the Court of any jurisdiction to make any order upon it of a coercive nature, and so hinders any order of costs to the defendant, to which he would be otherwise most clearly entitled. The defendant, however, has his remedy in a right of action for damages against all parties implicating in the serving and issuing and pretended and unlawful process of this Court, such as this plaintiff's bill of Complaint. In addition to the reasons on the merits that would entitle the defendant to a decree in his favor on grounds disclosed to the Court, the records of this Court show that the plaintiff relies on probate of the will of Richard Hicks, granted by Richard Davies Hanson CJ, who is not a lawfully appointed Judge of this Court. Probate of any will granted by him is therefore void and without legal effect, to the grievous injury of those who are interested in the property of the testator, whether real or personal, in cases wherein probate of such will is necessarily relied on.' [8]

On 8 March one of the numerous applications in the litigation between Messrs Elder and Galbraith came on for hearing. Mr Justice Boothby reiterated his warning that the proceedings were void.

> 'I would advise you, Mr Belt'—he said—'to take case [sic] that you do not void proceedings instituted by you in this Court, through the teste of the Chief Justice. I, being the senior Judge, will test your Bills for you any day.'
>
> Mr Justice Gwynne: 'I think that would be the better plan—that it would be better for the teste to be in the name of my learned colleague; for there being no other Judge, of course, his teste would be held correct.'
>
> The Chief Justice: 'If there is no other Judge.'
>
> Mr Justice Gwynne: 'It is part of my learned Colleague's argument that he is the sole Judge; and if the teste is in the name of the sole Judge it must be right. Being sole, he is senior Judge.'
>
> Mr Justice Boothby: 'It is a matter in which suitors are more interested than I am, namely the security of their litigation, and their being saved from expenditure of thousands of pounds in the way of costs. The rights of parties are the same, however small the sum involved may be; but when such immense amounts are litigated it is quite time that the legality of the

constitution of the Court should be set at rest. I protested against its present constitution from the very hour that those sitting with me became my colleagues.' [9]

William Charles Belt (?-1899)
Belt arrived in Adelaide in 1851 but his practice of law was delayed by the lack of business occasioned by the gold rushes. He lived at Mitcham and then Walkerville where he was chairman of the council in 1859 and 1863. The Belt Fountain, pictured, in Walkerville was presented to the district by his daughter in his memory. (Tony Kimberlin)

When he again raised the same objection in the next case called on, Mr Bakewell, the counsel concerned, protested rather ruefully:

> 'I am afraid I am in the same boat with all the rest of the suitors.'
>
> Mr Justice Boothby: 'Oh yes, that can't be helped. But the question might have been settled, as it has been before the Government and the country for five years. It is my duty simply to declare to suitors what their rights are, and every one should listen. Parties may submit to the unlawful decision of the Court—that I have nothing to do with. I have only to declare what are their rights and what they are exposed to from future litigation.'
>
> Mr Justice Gwynne: 'According to the same argument every writ of summons, and every summons or order from a Judge in Chambers, excepting my learned colleague, has no validity whatever.'
>
> Mr Justice Boothby: 'Nothing is lawful that is done by an unlawful Judge. I merely point out the matter to suitors; and if they venture to act on illegal authority I can't help it. I only point out to suitors the position in which they are placed, and the litigation which may arise.'

> The Chief Justice: 'I understand that my learned colleague has done, and still does, more than that. Although more than one decision of the Court had affirmed the validity of the Supreme Court Procedure Act of 1855-56, he has given his judgment that the bills filed are absolutely void, and that no proceedings can be taken under them because they are tested in the name of the Chief Justice, and not in the name of himself. He has given a judicial decision to that effect, and has not contented himself with simply pointing out the matter to suitors.'
>
> Mr Justice Boothby: 'I point out to all concerned—assumed Judges and suitors—the position in which they are placed.'
>
> The Chief Justice: 'My learned colleague delivers a judgment that the bill filed is bad on the ground he has mentioned, and requests the Master to enter his protest. That is more than pointing out a matter to suitors.'
>
> Mr Justice Boothby: 'I shall continue to do so in every case until the Judicial Committee of the Privy Council have decided that I am wrong. But I am not stopping the business of the Court, although if Judges appointed as they have been choose to run the risk, and suitors choose to act upon their decisions, I can't help it ... Every judgment of this Court that has my assent is valid; my dissent does not stop the business of the Court, but has only reference to the legality of the decisions.' [10]

Again and again he raised the objection, until, when in one instance he failed to do so, his colleagues were incredulous:

> 'As those that long have dwelt in noisome rooms
> Swoon presently if they but scent perfumes'.

There was method in his madness, however, and he proceeded to point out that in this case the petition was addressed to the Hon R.D. Hanson, Hon Benjamin Boothby, and Hon E.C. Gwynne. It could, therefore, be accepted as valid. "The words 'Hon Benjamin Boothby' being there, all the rest is surplusage. That is how I take it. That is a good legal maxim." [11]

During the latter part of March 1867, Mr Justice Gwynne was away on circuit in the South East, having received a Commission to take the place of Mr Justice Boothby, whose turn it was to preside at the circuit courts. A number of applications in equity came before the other two Judges, but they all had to stand over because the Judges could not agree on any order.

"Things seem to be rapidly approaching a dead-lock," the Attorney-General reported to the Governor: the business of the Supreme Court would soon be brought to a total stop.[12] A memorial was drawn up by a number of practitioner s and presented to the

Attorney-General, urging the necessity for the appointment of a primary judge in equity who would have power to deal alone with much of the business which then had to be brought before the Full Court.[13] The Attorney-General was in a quandary.

> 'It is clear'—he wrote—'that the position assumed by Mr Justice Boothby renders the administration of justice on the Equity side of the Court a complete lottery. If one of the other Judges be absent there is a total stoppage of business as was shown on the last sitting of the Court. If the other Judge should differ, then no plaintiff could recover judgment, and this unfortunate position is felt throughout the whole progress of a cause. I feel strongly that it is not to be expected—nor indeed justified—that the two learned Judges should continue to have the extra work thrown on them which is caused by the present unfortunate state of affairs—still less to have any increase of that work. Under ordinary circumstances the Primary Judge in Equity would be relieved of Nisi Prius Sittings and Criminal cases, because although the Equity business is more quiet and less exciting than Jury trials it is nevertheless more laborious. But it is evident that while His Honor Mr Justice Boothby continues to uphold his views as to invalidity, no arrangement can be made to withdraw one of the other Judges from the general business of the Court.'

One of the Judges, he thought, might consent to act as Primary Judge as a temporary arrangement: "... and so aid in preventing the inconvenience and discredit that must otherwise inevitably follow".[14]

The matter was placed before the Chief Justice and Mr Justice Gwynne for their consideration, but before any decision had been reached Mr Justice Boothby's conduct had brought their patience to breaking point.

On Mr Justice Gwynne's return from circuit, the Full Court resumed its sittings (12 April 1867). The first case called on was *Englebrecht v. Sutherland*, which had been tried before Mr Justice Gwynne at the Mount Gambier circuit court. Mr Andrews moved for a new trial. Mr Justice Boothby was away at once.

> 'There is a very important question to be raised, Mr Andrews'—he said—'whether or not the Governor has power to alter the rotation of the Judges. I have complained to Her Majesty at home that I have been most arbitrarily and unlawfully set aside, but we cannot hear anything respecting it at present; still, it is a question of excessive importance. I should like the thing to go on that that question may be argued, and it may be seen whether I am wrong in supposing that I am most arbitrarily and unjustly set aside from my office; and the

worst is, when I am so treated, with the consent and approval of those who call themselves my colleagues, though they have no more pretence in law to being such than you who stand on the floor of the Court.'

Mr Justice Gwynne: 'If my learned colleague continues to be constantly telling me I have no right to sit, I shall not sit here, and shall make a representation to that effect. I have stood it for many weeks, and it has been reiterated on motion after motion. I suppose my learned colleague does not mean to be offensive—'

Mr Justice Boothby: 'Certainly not.'

Mr Justice Gwynne: 'Immediately when I come here I am attempted to be set aside on the ground that I am sitting under the pretended authority of those who call themselves the Executive Council ... I claim my right to sit here.'

Mr Justice Boothby having made some remark to him, Mr Justice Gwynne continued:

'I do not wish to go into that now, only it is extremely offensive to me, and, I have no doubt, to my learned colleague, the Chief Justice, to have this constantly thrown in my face. I claim to sit here by virtue of an Act of the local Parliament, authorising the Governor, with the consent of the Executive Council, to appoint a fit and proper person as Third Judge. Under that I was appointed, with the approval of the Executive Council, and that appointment was confirmed by the Queen in the London Gazette—'

Mr Justice Boothby: 'Is there any evidence of that?'

Mr Justice Gwynne: 'The Queen assented to my appointment; but, however, that is not of any importance here. I know, too, that my learned colleague holds his appointment by virtue of an Act providing for the appointment of a Second Judge upon precisely the same authority as I hold mine, and I am not aware that there is any defect in the Legislature which vested power in the Local Government to make such appointments. But even if there were, it is healed by the Validating Act, which expressly declares that all laws made up to that period shall be valid and effectual; so I hold my appointment by virtue of the Act of the Imperial Parliament. My learned colleague says he is anxious to uphold the actions of the Imperial Parliament, but in this case he is putting it aside and degrading it. My right to sit here amounts to as clear a certainty as a mathematical demonstration, and therefore it is extremely offensive for my learned colleague every time I sit here to throw such objections in my face. I feel it very offensive.'

Mr Justice Boothby: 'I feel it offensive that a Judge should consent to a mere Executive authority, without ever the question being submitted to this Court for decision—that he should consent to sit here, and so supersede my authority. I am not giving a judgment now. I have given my reasons over and over again. It is said that the Validating Act provides for the appointment of Judges by the Executive; but on the contrary it provides, in distinct words, that every Act of this Parliament which sets aside Orders in Council or contravenes Imperial legislation shall be treated as void. And the first Act says that Judges shall be appointed by His Majesty, and that is further confirmed by Imperial enactment, without which Judges cannot have power to sit; but the Legislature here profess to set aside this, and say—No: the appointment of Judges shall not be by the Queen, but by the executive.'

Mr Justice Gwynne: 'I was only going to add, as my learned colleague made these remarks, that I consider the business of this Court very important. I consider the rights of parties which we decide here require the whole of my attention and what little law I may possess; and frequently I come here with a desire to perform what I have to do to the best of my ability, when my mind is ruffled, and what little power I have is very seriously diminished. I have stood it now for some months—not to say years; and I can only say if it is continued I shall make an application to the Governor to relieve me of my appointment.'

Mr Justice Boothby: 'It would be very wise for your own sake if you did.'

Mr Justice Gwynne: 'This is a continuation of similar insulting remarks.'

The Chief Justice: 'I may say the remarks of my learned colleague, Mr Justice Boothby, have ceased to annoy or affect me in any way, because I feel, especially on this point, that by constantly dwelling upon his fancied rights and fancied wrongs, he has incapacitated himself judicially from forming any reliable conclusion upon the subject, and therefore I look upon them as I should any other utterance founded upon mental or moral illusion.' [15]

An 1870 photograph of the Mount Gambier courthouse which was completed in 1865 and used for the Supreme Court on its South East circuit. (SLSA)

On 15 April, in *England v. Coulthard*, Mr Justice Boothby was brimming over with objections and reverted to his favourite topic—the Privy Council.

> 'The great object'—he said—'is to have the proceedings properly conducted, and any suitor may go to the Privy Council, and get the whole of them set aside as illegal, unless they are so conducted. Quite irrespective of any decision of the Court, the Queen's subjects can go to the Privy Council and point out the illegality of matters from which they receive detriment.'

Mr Justice Gwynne, however, was more matter-of-fact in his views. He recognised the force of Pope Leo I's maxim, "Longinquity of region doth cause the examination of Truth to become over-dilatory."

> 'I hear a great deal about the Privy Council'—he said—'but I think that Her Majesty's subjects here practically think as much of going there as to the Great Mogul. I don't hear of any great desire on the part of the Bar to go to the Privy Council.'
>
> Mr Stow: 'If we went to the Great Mogul we should have to take expensive presents, and the expense of going to the Privy Council would be about as great.'
>
> Mr Justice Gwynne: 'Practically I think one tribunal as available as the other.'

The case concluded with a warning by Mr Justice Boothby:

> 'If the plaintiff takes any relief, it will be at the peril of having to bear endless costs, which, in my opinion, will ultimately follow from the writ being unlawfully attested in the name of the Chief Justice. I think it necessary to warn suitors of the risk to which they are exposed in suits in which there was absence of jurisdiction. If I should concur in any coercive jurisdiction of the Court, where it has no jurisdiction, or if I acted without jurisdiction, or in excess of my jurisdiction, I should be personally liable. There is no doubt of it; it has been decided over and over again. Whatever may be done by those who claim to be my colleagues, I shall protest on every question, and will not expose myself to an action for having exceeded my jurisdiction.' [16]

"Call on the next case," said the Chief Justice; but the next case proved no better. Mr Justice Boothby informed Mr Stow, who was appearing, that the teste of the bill was unlawful.

> Mr Justice Gwynne: 'What is the teste?'
>
> Mr Justice Boothby: '"His Honor Richard Davies Hanson Esq, Chief Justice".'
>
> Mr Justice Gwynne: 'What should it be?'
>
> Mr Justice Boothby: 'It should be in the name of the Senior Judge, whoever he is. That is clearly what is required by the law.' ...
>
> Mr Justice Gwynne: 'I may say with regard to this that Mr Justice Boothby seems to be the victim of a fallacy. Mr Justice Boothby says it is improperly tested, inasmuch as it has not been done in his name. Now it appears to me that if there is no Chief Justice there is no senior Judge. In the King's Bench at home there is a Lord Chief Justice and four Puisne Judges, and in the absence of the Lord Chief Justice No 1 Puisne Judge is the senior Judge; but here there are no Puisne Judges, and only on the hypothesis that there is a Chief Justice can there be a Senior Judge. In the same sense as a wrangler is called a senior wrangler, not meaning he is the eldest man or the longest at college, but that he holds a higher degree. Therefore if my learned colleague is not technically entitled he would still be the Senior Judge; but surely Mr Justice Boothby would not claim to be senior Judge because his patent confers upon him the office of Second Judge, and my patent gives me the office of Third Judge. Suppose Mr Justice Boothby were to die—which God

grant may not occur—I should not be the Second Judge; I should require a new patent, and should not ipso facto become Second Judge; it is a separate office. There is no such person as Senior Judge, unless it be the person who occupies the centre seat, receiving the larger salary, and certainly is treated as such by the local Legislature.'

Mr Justice Boothby: 'It will be required of my learned colleague probably some day to put the patent of which he speaks in the form of a plea, so it can be ascertained whether it has the effect he says or not. If it is as he says, he must apparently remain Third Judge to the end of his life.' ...

Mr Stow: 'Perhaps I may be allowed to say, as suitors have been warned against the costs likely to accrue to clients accepting relief on writs tested in the name of the Chief Justice, that having been in office at the time when this question was first suggested, I believe Mr Justice Boothby never had his patent till 1862, but acted under a warrant.'

Mr Justice Boothby: 'You are mistaken. I had a patent delivered to me within a very few days of my entering the Colony, that being in pursuance of a warrant of Her Majesty. If my learned colleagues have anything of that sort, it would settle the matter, but a patent would not. I have yet to learn that this Parliament here has power to confer titles. We shall have them soon making Baron this and Lord that. There is a difference in law between titles and offices. I believe the very first year, or, at all events, soon after he arrived, Sir Charles Cooper wished to take the title of Chief Justice. There is a public document which shows he was very anxious from the first to take up the title; but it was not done till 1856, when Sir Richard MacDonnell took upon himself, without reserving the question for the consideration of Her Majesty, to take from her the power of appointing Judges, and also, with the advice of His Executive Council, to confer a title. If all that can be done without the Home Authorities, I am greatly mistaken, but I shall be very much astonished, if when the Privy Council is appealed to they find that it is right; and if they do not, the questions affecting property and title that have been decided here will be upset. The real question is the security of litigation as to the determination of suits.'"[17]

"Now we will go on again, please," said the Chief Justice; but the next case was even worse—it was the revival of the great Moonta case. The previous decision of the Supreme

Court had been upheld by the Privy Council (*The Queen v. Hughes* LR1 PC 81). Not a whit disheartened, the Mills claimants returned to the fray and commenced fresh proceedings under the new Equity Act.

> 'We may now safely regard the Moonta law-suit as an institution'—said Pasquin. 'It has passed from its primitive erratic state into a distinct organised existence ... The strongest point in Mills's favour is that although his legal advisers do not understand a single point of his case, the Moonta lawyers are evidently in the same destitute condition, and the consequent confusion of facts and complication of localities, is just as likely to put Mr Mills on the throne of China as into the Moonta property.' [18]

The same paper gave a detailed description of the "Mills's Equity and Legal Practitioners' Mining Company":

> 'The main shaft is under the Supreme Court. The mine is worked entirely by lawyers. It was discovered by an Attorney General, and pays a handsome dividend every time the Judges put on their wigs.' [19]

The Moonta case was only before the Court for a short time on 15 April, but Mr Justice Boothby was able triumphantly to declare that the writ was "a piece of waste parchment", before passing on to the next case, *Stone v. Stone*, in which a more serious outbreak occurred. This was an application for a decree for judicial separation in a case which has been heard by the Chief Justice and a jury at the preceding Civil Sessions. The Chief Justice said he thought there ought to be a decree in favour of the plaintiff.

> Mr Justice Boothby: 'No doubt. I am only sorry she cannot have it with any security, inasmuch as the Judge who tried it was a person not having legal authority to sit as a Judge.' ...

> Mr Justice Gwynne: 'I do not wish to enter into discussions with my learned colleague Mr Justice Boothby. Again he has repeated that offensive line of observation. He says neither the Chief Justice nor myself are Judges of this Court, and that his opinion was expressed, and I knew it years ago. Now, if Mr Justice Boothby in a gentlemanly manner had mentioned that to me, I should respect him and his motives for doing so; but when every five minutes we have these insulting observations, it completely disqualifies me from performing the duties of my office. It ruffles my mind, and though I ought to maintain my temper, it is very difficult to do so.'

> Mr Justice Boothby: 'I am not responsible for that when I declare my inability to acquiesce in a decree. It is necessary for me to judge each individual case in order to protect myself

from most severe consequences. It is for that reason I do it. If the litigants are satisfied they must go on. I merely point it out in order to shield myself. I have pointed out over and over again what is the result of unlawful interference.'

The Chief Justice: 'I feel very great difficulty either in remaining silent under the perpetual statements of His Honor the Second Judge, or of stating my feelings upon the subject; but I think that under the circumstances the latter course is desirable. When I was appointed Chief Justice of this Court His Honor the Second Judge raised objection to my appointment, and it was then agreed that there should be a formal entry upon the book of the Court of the objection taken by him to my taking my seat; of the opinion given by my colleague Mr Justice Gwynne, and of the opinion given by myself claiming to be Chief Justice. Then these opinions having been given, His Honor the Second Judge acquiesced for the time in the decision, preserving his right as clearly he was entitled to do to petition the Queen on the subject, and from that time until comparatively a short time since the proceedings of the Court have gone on without any interruption from His Honor. His Honor did take the course that he spoke of doing. He sent home a petition to the Queen, and I have the best authority, I have his own admission, that the petition was referred by the Queen to the Judicial Committee of the Privy Council, and that he was informed such had been the case, and was told that if he chose to prosecute an appeal against the order of the Court admitting me to sit as Chief Justice at his own expense he might do so. But he has not chosen to do that, and finding representations made by him to influential persons in England were not successful in leading to a litigation of the decision, he has within the last year and a half, or about that time, as it appears to me, taken every step that could suggest itself to his imagination by obstructing the course of business here, to compel the Government of this Colony to try the question of the constitution of the Court not at his own expense—as the Imperial Government said he was bound to do—but at the expense of the Colony. I may say I have felt this long, and regret it, but I feel that his proceedings have been dictated by no other motive than that of compelling the Government of this Colony, or some individual—by obstructing the business, throwing out suggestions or recommendations—to try the question of the constitution of the Court at their expense instead of his.'

Mr Justice Boothby: 'Undoubtedly I have been told that I could bring this before the Privy Council at my own expense. But I answer that it is a most unreasonable thing to suppose that I, with my salary, should go before the Judicial Committee of the Privy Council to ascertain the validity of the laws of the Colony, and the practice of the Judges of this Court. It is a subject in which the whole of the suitors of the Colony and every subject of the Queen is interested my own individual interest is a trivial, incidental matter, but the security of the liberty and property of suitors in this Court is a matter which must be brought to a judicial decision.' [20]

This altercation proved the last straw. When the Court sat on the following day, the Chief Justice read the following statement:

'After the rising of the Court yesterday, I conferred with my learned colleague, Mr Justice Gwynne, as to the course which it was expedient for us to adopt, in view of the line of conduct of His Honor the Second Judge. We both felt that a repetition of such proceedings as marked the sittings of the Court yesterday and Friday could not but lower the dignity of this Court, and weaken the confidence of suitors and the public in the administration of justice. And at the same time we felt that, however painful and in some sense degrading such scenes might be, we must be prepared to encounter them if no means could be devised for the purpose of peculiar views—in the hope that something might be agreed upon to prevent the time of the preventing their recurrence. We have had already under our notice a representation, addressed by some members of the profession to the Hon the Attorney General, calling his attention to the necessity of taking some steps to enable the Court to exercise more satisfactorily its Equity Jurisdiction, and we had invited His Honor the Second Judge to meet us for the purpose of considering the reply that we should give to that communication. It seemed therefore to us that the same opportunity might be taken of bringing under his notice the effects of the mode which he had adopted of enforcing his Court and the Bar being wasted, and the respect due to this Court being diminished or destroyed. Until such an attempt at least was made, it, however, appears to us expedient to discontinue the sittings of the Court, and they will therefore be adjourned until the first day of Term.

'I dissent from that order, and shall still continue to sit here as

> the Full Court'—said Mr Justice Boothby.'

The Chief Justice then directed the Master to adjourn the Court, and he and Mr Justice Gwynne left the bench.

> Mr Justice Boothby (addressing counsel): 'You will understand I still sit here, and any suitor is at liberty to make any application. Mr Belt, do you move in any matter?'
>
> Mr Belt: 'No.'
>
> Mr Justice Boothby: 'Do you move, Mr Baker?'
>
> Mr Baker: 'No.'
>
> Mr Justice Boothby: 'Mr Way, do you move?'
>
> Mr Way: 'No.'
>
> Mr Justice Boothby: 'Make a note, Mr Hinde, that I called upon Mr Belt, Mr Baker and Mr Way to move.'

The Master having made the entry, the Judge continued: "Make an entry Mr Hinde, that I adjourn the Court till the first day of Term." The Judge then waited till the entry was made and read over to him, and then left the Court.[21]

This abrupt and extraordinary interruption of the business of the Supreme Court naturally produced a profound sensation. *Pasquin* wrote indignantly:

> 'How have the public offended their Honors the Judges that they refuse to administer justice? We are not conscious of any impropriety or malpractice that has laid us open to the deprivation of legal rights. The Supreme Court is still our refuge in case of injury; we yet look to that tribunal for comfort and protection whenever our liberties or properties are assailed or invaded. Why, we humbly ask, has justice laid aside her bandage and scales, closed her temple, and left her votaries lamenting the heavy pressure of suffering without the consolation of law.' [22]

There was a deal of angry discussion in Parliament. Mr Strangways denounced the feeling of personal antipathy which, he said, was so openly displayed towards Mr Justice Boothby by the other two Judges. They had no right to stop work because they disliked Mr Justice Boothby.

> 'It seems to me'—he said—'that the action of the other Judges was to force the Government to decide against His Honor, which perhaps otherwise they might not have done.'

There were only three ways to settle the difficulty, in his opinion:

> 'One, to get rid of one Judge; secondly to get rid of two; and lastly, to get rid of the three—and it was difficult to say which would be the most popular of the three.' [23]

In the Legislative Council, Hon J. Baker urged that there was a great deal to be said in favour of Mr Justice Boothby.

> 'Apart from his legal decisions, his conduct on the Bench was not more reprehensible than that of the other Judges towards him. He had watched the conduct of the Judges narrowly for some weeks past, and he had seen a degree of animosity displayed by the other two Judges towards Mr Justice Boothby which he had never shown towards them. No remarks of his were ever so gross and personal as those of the other Judges. He had never heard him accuse them of corruption, though they were not loth to charge him with that offence. Any attorney who might be so disposed could get up quite as serious charges against the other Judges, and could make out as strong a case as that urged against Mr Justice Boothby.'

Mr Baker then indulged in some comments which may have been understood by his hearers but which now remain mysterious. In 1862, he said, two subjects were deeply exciting the public mind. One was the Moonta case.

> 'The other question referred to a social matter which he would not particularly specify. He found on one side, and holding very strong views on that matter, the Bishop, the former and present Presidents of the Legislative Council, the late and present Speakers of the House of Assembly, and other gentlemen of influence ... These two questions had had much to do with their subsequent political action. An undercurrent was at work, which had a marked effect on their political life. Neither of those questions was yet settled, for the feeling with reference to each still existed. Mr Justice Boothby was on one side and the Chief Justice was on the other, and the result was that there was no cordiality on the Bench.'

He had to admit that it was impossible for the three Judges to sit together harmoniously; but that was no reason for treating Mr Justice Boothby unfairly.

> 'I think I am not wrong'—Mr Baker said—'in supposing that the Chief Justice was consulted in all the steps which have been taken against Judge Boothby. My impression is that the Executive have been looking through the Chief Justice's spectacles.' [24]

The majority of the Council agreed with Mr Parkin, that the Supreme Court had become "a by-word, a mockery, and a reproach". Schoolboys in England, said Mr Parkin, would be taught:

> '... that in South Australia there was a 'bogy' whose name was Boothby that troubled everybody. This bogy was a frightful thing. It said that nothing was legal in the Colony—that they had no Parliament, no laws. Whenever a case came before him the bogy declared it repugnant. This bogy had nearly frightened the Government to death.'
>
> 'That is what will be said of this colony'—concluded Mr Parkin—'and I say this bogy must not be suffered longer to exist.' [25]

The general feeling of the public was one of relief that the Boothby question had been brought to a crisis and must be disposed of at last.

On 24 April the Chief Justice and Mr Justice Gwynne addressed to the Governor a letter of complaint about their colleague.

> 'It will not be necessary'—they said—'to recapitulate the various methods in which he has endeavoured to assert his claim to be the sole rightful Judge, as Your Excellency will probably have been made aware of them from the Honourable the Attorney General. It is sufficient to say that not merely are his remarks personally' offensive and insulting to ourselves, intended to lower us in the public opinion, and calculated to produce that effect, but the position he has assumed is inconsistent with the equal administration of justice, since it would lead him in every case, irrespective of the merits of the question, to decide in favor of the defendant—and it would in the event of any circumstances preventing the attendance of either of ourselves, put a stop to the exercise of the functions of the Court. We felt this so strongly, that having to meet His Honor to confer upon one subject submitted to us by the Honorable the Attorney General, we adjourned the Court in order that we might take the same opportunity of endeavouring to come to some understanding that should enable the business of the Court to be carried on without a repetition of the proceedings of which we complained. Unhappily, however, that interview failed to produce any result, as Mr Justice Boothby refused even to discuss the proposal to make other arrangements with a view to the more satisfactory administration of justice on the equity side of the Court, and expressed his determination, in every case that he might deem of sufficient importance, to repeat his warnings

> and protests. We feel that we have no right on the ground of personal annoyance, or of difficulties in the administration of justice caused by an obstruction which unitedly we can overrule, to close the Court against suitors, which would practically be the result of our declining to sit with Mr Boothby, and, therefore, we have no alternative but to bring the matter under the notice of Your Excellency with a view to the adoption of such remedial measures as it may be in the power of Your Excellency's Government to apply.' [26]

Cabinet met and decided that proceedings must be taken for the removal of the Judge under the Act 22 Geo III c.75. But who was to bell the cat? Mr Boucaut, the "Robespierre of South Australia", obligingly undertook the distasteful task.[27] He had resigned his position as Attorney-General on account of his interest in the Moonta case, and he consented to lay a series of charges against the Judge.

> 'During my tenure of office as Attorney General'—he wrote to the Chief Secretary—'it became my duty to inquire into the causes of the universal distrust of His Honor Mr Justice Boothby's administration of the office of Judge of the Supreme Court. Upon such inquiry it appeared to me that His Honor had laid himself open to the following charges:
>
> I. Conduct and language contumacious and disrespectful to the Court of Appeals, and obstructive of the said Court in the performance of its duties.
>
> II. Perverse refusal to recognise the authority of Parliament and to administer the laws of the Province.
>
> III. Expressions on the Bench disparaging and insulting the Legislature, the Government, and the Institutions of the Province; and language and behaviour on the Bench calculated to bring the administration of justice into contempt.
>
> IV. Language on the Bench offensive and irritating to the other Judges, and public denial of their authority.
>
> V. Allowing private and personal feeling to interfere with the fair and impartial administration of justice.
>
> I have the honor to submit that an investigation before His Excellency and the Executive Council ought at once to be held concerning the above charges, with a view (should it appear that they are well founded) of His Honor's amoval from office under the Imperial Statute 22 Geo III c.75; or of such other action as His Excellency and the Executive Council should deem expedient and proper.' [28]

Mr Way was instructed by the Government to act as solicitor in the conduct of the proceedings, and Messrs Parker, Ingleby and Downer were briefed as counsel. The Governor directed an inquiry as asked by Mr Boucaut, and notice of it was given to the Judge on 6 June.

The *Adelaide Punch's* take on Boucaut's elevation to the bench in 1878. (SLSA)

Pasquin rushed to the Judge's support. The charges, it said, should have been sent at once to the Chief Secretary:

> '... that the offending barrister might be dealt with according to such form of proceeding as may be usual or appropriate when a member of the profession is guilty of gross insolence and insubordination to the Bench'.

But instead the ministry had disgraced themselves by taking part with:

> '... the turbulent and insulting barrister ... a very young practitioner, who, it is said, has only as yet distinguished himself by a series of weak and palpable errors in the management of a very important case'.[29]

In the meantime more scenes had been taking place in the Supreme Court. The first day of term, to which the Court had been adjourned, was 27 May; but the Chief Justice and Mr Justice Gwynne decided to sit earlier for the disposal of urgent business. Mr Justice Boothby, however, would not take any notice of them and refused to come into court, persisting that the Court stood adjourned until 27 May. On that day the Court sat, but, Mr Justice Gwynne being absent, all equity matters had to be adjourned. "It is idle to mention anything in Equity," said the Chief Justice. "As a matter of course they will stand over."[30]

On 31 May, the new Attorney-General (Mr Andrews) presented his Commission and asked that it should be recorded. Mr Justice Boothby was away to a flying start.

> 'I am of opinion'—he said at once—'that this is an entirely unlawful document, that it is inoperative and void, as His Excellency the Governor-in Chief has no power to give such a commission, and if it be acted upon it exposes all those acting under it to serious results in cases where the coercive jurisdiction of this Court may be sought to be exercised.'

The Act merely required the Commission to be "noted", and not entered in extenso in the records of the court.

> 'The word "note" is a strange phrase to be used'—said Mr Justice Boothby. 'It seems as if there were an object in using it—to shut out enquiry as to the lawfulness of the document. ... This has been issued at the peril of those who issued it, and it is at their peril and on their responsibility that those who act upon it do so, whether it be the gentleman at the head of the Government, or those who put in force any coercive power of this Court against the persons or liberty of any of Her Majesty's subjects. If the Court does not order this to be entered in full

> in the book I shall detain them till I have made a copy of it. Give me a sheet of paper.'

He then proceeded to copy the Commission, while the other Judges went on with the business before the Court.[31]

On 3 June, judgment was given by the Chief Justice and Mr Justice Gwynne in a case which they had heard on 10 May. Mr Justice Boothby said:

> 'I regard this judgment as relating to a case heard at a sitting of the Court when the Judges had no jurisdiction, and consequently the proceedings are entirely illegal. I understand that it proceeds on the consideration of an argument heard on the 10th May. Previous to that, by the act of the Judges, and also by my own act, the Court had been adjourned until the First Day of Term, and I shall contend hereafter probably that mine was the only lawful adjournment. But taking it that there was a lawful adjournment ordered by the other Judges, the reassembling by their own authority earlier than the day fixed without consulting me is clearly unlawful. I certainly received a note from the Master that my colleagues had determined to sit on an early day, but of that I took no notice. I should have surrendered all my self-respect if I had at all taken notice of such a document; and, what would have been far worse, I should have reduced myself a party to the unlawful proceedings of the Court sitting before the day to which it was adjourned. That such is the state of the law I have no doubt whatever.' [32]

The sempiternal Moonta case was now called on again—this time affording occupation to no less than ten counsel. Mr Justice Boothby demanded to know what was the position with regard to the old sci fa proceedings—had the costs been paid?

> 'There is no entry in the records or statement that the costs have been paid, and it is the duty of this Court not to allow a suitor to be harassed by other proceedings until those of the former have been satisfied ...'
>
> The Chief Justice: 'We had better go on.'
>
> Mr Justice Boothby: 'I must have a record made, and I call upon the parties concerned to state what has become of the former proceedings.'
>
> The Chief Justice: 'Go on, Mr Bagot.'
>
> Mr Justice Boothby (to the Master):'Mr Hinde, have there been any costs taxed in the case of the appeal to the Privy Council?'

The Chief Justice: 'Are we to proceed or not?'

Mr Justice Boothby: 'We must know whether the costs have been paid. Have they been taxed, Mr Hinde?'

Mr Hinde: 'Not that I am aware of. I know nothing about it."...

William Hinde
The third Master of the Supreme Court, Hinde served in that role from 1861 to 1878.

Mr Justice Boothby: 'I must have a decision of the Court on the point.'

The Chief Justice: 'You are not counsel for the defendants on the brief, surely?'

Mr Justice Boothby: 'No; but I am bound to see the law administered according to law.'

The Chief Justice: 'Will you go on, Mr Bagot?'

Mr Justice Boothby: 'Enter, Mr Hinde, that I objected to this being proceeded with until I knew that the costs of the former suit were satisfied.'

Mr Justice Gwynne: 'I consider it is just as much my duty to know whether these costs have been satisfied as it is to concern myself to know what the learned counsel had for breakfast this morning. The one has just as much pertinency to the case as the other. It is not the place of the Court to hunt up the records to see whether former costs have been paid or not. It is no business of mine to be satisfied that they have been paid, and I don't care whether they have or not.'

Mr Justice Boothby: 'It is the duty of the Court to see if their officers have done their duty.'

The Chief Justice: 'I venture to say that in the annals of British jurisprudence never has such an objection been taken at the commencement of a case as has been taken in this matter and I only ask the counsel to go on because I cannot trust myself to characterize such interruptions. Go on, Mr Bagot.'

Mr Justice Boothby: 'That I suppose is to be taken as altogether unanswerable. I do not desire to bandy observations backwards and forwards with the other Judges, but I require my objection to be recorded in order that the point may be taken before the Privy Council.'

The Chief Justice: 'The decision of the Court is that it be not recorded.'

Mr Justice Boothby: 'Then enter my dissent, Mr Hinde.'

> The Chief Justice: 'No; there will be no entry at all.'
>
> Mr Justice Boothby: 'I suppose by the united action of my colleagues I am to be put down; but it remains to be seen whether their law or mine is correct.'

The argument in the Moonta case went on for days, with frequent interjections and interruptions by Mr Justice Boothby. Invariably these were in favour of the defendants, and the Chief Justice was finally moved to say:

> 'I cannot understand the motive which can influence Mr Justice Boothby in taking upon himself the character of a partisan in the case.'
>
> 'I am a partisan only in behalf of the law'—retorted the Judge. 'I despise the suggestion of any other kind of partisanship, which can only emanate from a mind capable itself of acting as partisan.' [33]

During the proceedings reference was made to the shorthand notes of the argument on the hearing before the Privy Council. Mr Justice Boothby immediately complained that he had not been permitted to see them.

> Mr Justice Gwynne: 'I may explain that I did not encourage Mr Justice Boothby to read the notes, because they showed that he was made a butt of. I did not press them on him, not wishing to hurt his feelings.'
>
> Mr Justice Boothby: 'I should like to have seen the terms and manner in which I was made a butt of before the Privy Council.'
>
> Mr Justice Gwynne: 'Those who have read the notes will know that in the references made to Mr Justice Boothby by counsel his name was received with bursts of laughter.'
>
> Mr Justice Boothby: 'That might be the case with the remarks of counsel; for the remarks of counsel here are often indecent and improper.'

The investigation of the charges against the Judge was fixed to begin on 24 June. Notice was given to him that counsel would be heard either in support of or in answer to the charges, and he was furnished with a list of the principal cases which would be relied upon as evidence against him.

When the Full Court sat on 21 June some discussion took place as to the arrangement of business.

'I have a serious occupation in reference to my services to Her Majesty'—said Mr Justice Boothby. 'I shall defend her rights in this Court, and I must have as much time as I can possibly get. According to the doctrine of Lord Mansfield, in the case of Burrowes, to assault or seek to destroy Her Majesty's authority in the Courts of Law, or to deny her right to reign there, is as great an offence as to deny her right to reign anywhere else. I have therefore a serious duty to perform in reference to Her Majesty, and I ought to be freed from attendance on the Court; although, at the same time, I should be wanting in my duty to Her Majesty and to suitors wishing to try their rights here if I did not sit when the Court sits. Under the circumstances, I think the Court is bound not to require me to come here.'

'I may say'—said the Chief Justice—'there is a feeling that the position the Second Judge is placed in is one which renders it inconvenient that business should be taken, or that the Court should sit at present, and ... without agreeing as to the object or result of the proceedings which have been referred to, I quite agree that it will be better that the Court should be adjourned. We must sit tomorrow, being the last day of Term. We had better adjourn until these proceedings are terminated.'

Mr Justice Boothby was so cantankerous, however, as to show no gratitude for the consideration shown him. After some formal business had been disposed of on the following day, and the Court was about to adjourn, he announced that he would be in attendance at Court on the following Tuesday morning, when he would call on the Moonta case.

'The Court is constituted by a single Judge, and there is no warrant for postponing that case for a single day. I am desirous, when the case goes elsewhere, to have it on record that the Judges have adjourned the Court—'

Mr Belt: 'His Honor Mr Justice Gwynne fixed Tuesday next for a motion to dissolve an injunction.'

Mr Justice Boothby: 'He may come into Court, but I shall also come, and declare my readiness to hear the Moonta case. I give this notice to all parties, and if those who resist the bill do not come in they will fail in their duty to their clients, and must take the consequences both as to their reputation and legal responsibility. I look upon it that the unlawful interference with this Court by the Executive authority is the first case of the kind in any courts under the Sovereigns of England since the days of Charles the First and Charles the Second.'

The Chief Justice: 'I stated yesterday that the majority of theJudges of the Court felt that, having understood that proceedings were being taken before the Governor and Council for the purpose of considering charges which have been brought against His Honor the Second Judge, and recognising the authority of the Governor and Council, under the Imperial Act by virtue of which they assume to act, there would be an unseemliness in sitting while those proceedings were going on. If the sittings of this Court are continued during that time, His Honor could either give it as an excuse to the Executive for refusing to be present before the Governor and Council in the course of the enquiry that he had to attend to the business of the Court; or if he felt the position he was placed in to be one where his individual interest required his presence, if the Court sat it involved the necessity of taking proceedings in the Court while he was absent. The majority of the Court did not wish to appear to take one or the other position ... The Court should be adjourned to Monday week.'

Mr Justice Boothby: 'I could understand very well the object of the other Judges before, but now it is expressed in clear language that they wish to give expression before the world, and of course before His Excellency and those advising him, that the opinion of the Judges is that they have lawful authority. The whole object of my going is to show that they have not, and if I fail in doing that here I shall not elsewhere; and, undoubtedly, I must also show that the Counsel who supports this Bill—the attorney I should call him—is the person who makes these charges. Another extraordinary circumstance is that charges are made by the other Judges. I have good reason to believe that the Attorney General of the day has not, and I cannot think that he has taken the matter on himself. I am told that counsel are to be heard and evidence taken, and the object is to set the counsel at liberty from the Moonta case in order that they may go before the Executive Council in support of these charges—charges which go altogether to the question of whether or not I propound erroneous law. That is a question which the Constitution has provided another tribunal to try, and though there can be no entry made I shall be present here, as I said, on Tuesday morning. Make an entry in your book, Mr Hinde, that I shall be here on Tuesday, and call on the Moonta case.'

The Chief Justice: 'As I consider that I am the Chief Justice, and as I know I am expressing the opinion of the Third Judge, who is not present, I state that the Court will be adjourned till Monday, the 1st July.'

Mr Justice Boothby: 'You will enter, Mr Hinde, that I declare the Court adjourned till Tuesday next.'

Mr Hinde: 'I will do so.'

Mr Justice Boothby: 'Or perhaps that will be a short notice to the parties—so you may say Wednesday. On that day I shall be in attendance to hear the Moonta case. The Court is constituted legally by one Judge.'

The Chief Justice: 'Will you read the entry, Mr Hinde?'

Mr Hinde (reading): 'Mr Justice Boothby stated that he adjourned the Court until Wednesday, the 26th of June instant, when he should attend and call on the case of the Attorney General v. Hughes.'

The Chief Justice: 'Then, that the Court adjourn till Monday week.'

Mr Justice Boothby: 'That "the Chief Justice said that the Court was adjourned till Monday week".

Mr Hinde: 'I have made the entry that the Court adjourned till Monday, the 1st July.' [34]

The Court rose with the date of its next sitting left in this somewhat ambiguous state. On the following Tuesday, Mr Justice Gwynne sat. In answer to an inquiry from Mr Stow, he said that he did not intend to be present next day, when Mr Justice Boothby had threatened to call on the Moonta case.

'I observed'—he said—'that on Saturday some disagreement took place. I was coming in, but I thought, upon reflection, that I should thereby subject myself to be drawn into some such unseemly contest as those we have witnessed; on which occasions, though one may try to exercise patience, one cannot always commend his temper, and I purposely abstained from attending on that account. What I expected took place, and I somewhat rejoice that I had no part in it.'[35]

Next day Mr Justice Boothby entered, true to his promise, and took his set upon the bench. Mr Palmer and Mr Strangways—two counsel who had always been strong supporters of the Judge—appeared at the bar.

His Honor: 'Will you read the cases which are undisposed of, Mr Hinde?'

> The Master: 'Attorney General v. Hughes and others—'
>
> His Honor: 'That is the adjourned case. Does either party appear. Does any one appear either for the plaintiff or the defendants?' (No one answered.)
>
> 'I order it to be struck out, Mr Hinde; but I give the parties permission to come in hereafter and ask for it to be suspended until the Full Court sits. I do this in order that the circumstances may be put upon record. Of course, it will be restored upon application to the Court, but it will be necessary that the application shall be made.'

He then directed the Master to call the list of cases, some twenty in all. No-one attended in any of them, and the Judge ordered them all to be struck out.

Mr Palmer then brought forward a ludicrous matter. A few days earlier he had had occasion to quote from a copy of a warrant of a Local Court and, amidst loud laughter from the Court and especially Mr Justice Gwynne, had interpreted the words "L.S." as meaning "Large Seal". He now wished to explain that the error had been made "through inadvertence and not ignorance".

> 'There is a very great excuse for your misapprehension'—gravely said the Judge—'because it is customary for Magistrates to use a wafer. Locus sigilli must mean the seal of the Court, and it could never be supposed that you did not know the meaning of the Latin term denoted by L.S. when you have obtained the degree of Bachelor of Laws in the London University; that that should be suggested by a Judge of this Court or any one else is unreasonable. You must have passed an examination that has been passed through by very few of the practitioners of this Court, who, I observe took pleasure in the remarks which fell from one of the Judges on the Bench, and which I certainly regret. There is nothing at all reflecting upon either your learning, Mr Palmer, or your position, because when I know that you are a Bachelor of Laws in the University of London, certainly it is quite impossible that you can have attained that distinction without a full knowledge of the Latin language. I understood at the time what you meant to point out to the Bench was that the seal of the Court was used, which was proper only for the Court, and was not a proper seal to be used by the Magistrate to his own name. It was a gross impropriety on the part of those who did so. Your excuse is very satisfactory, and I think that you were called upon to make it, Mr Palmer.'

The Judge proceeded to read a statement as to the constitution of the Court:

> 'I have greatly to deplore the absence of my colleagues on this occasion, especially as I see that pains have been taken to show what is the cause of that absence. I have expressed very freely my opinion in public, and have also been before His Excellency in Executive Council to show him how unlawfully he is acting in summoning me or in listening to evidence of my judgments or judicial conduct in the present mode.'

He quoted from the judgments in the British Guiana case, to which reference has been previously made, and continued:

> 'All who throw contempt upon or deny the power of the Queen's Judges, or seek to interfere with their lawful jurisdiction as much as in them lies, seek to deny her right to reign, because she reigns in her Courts of Justice in the administration of one of her prerogative powers just as completely as she does in her Parliament or Privy Council in respect of the civil and political affairs of the Government ... I should have made no allusion to the subject only it is publicly announced that my colleagues thought right to express an opinion in law as to what His Excellency was advised to do in reference to certain well-known circumstances now existing. I also take the opportunity of saying from this Bench what are my views. The matter must be carried elsewhere, and I certainly sleep on a bed of roses in reference to its being carried there. Has any gentleman any further motion to make?'

No-one moving, he adjourned the Court to the following Monday.[36]

"The Glen", Justice Boothby's home, was located near what is now the beginning of Adelaide's south eastern freeway. It was sold in 1896 by Boothby's sister for 2500 pounds to the Passionist Fathers, who have since used it as a monastery, naming it "St Paul's Retreat".

As the Judge's remarks showed, the inquiry into his conduct had been commenced. The Executive Council met at Government House on 24 June 1867. Mr Parker, Mr Ingleby and Mr Way appeared as counsel to support the charges; and Mr Justice Boothby and his son were in attendance. In accordance with the maxim that attack is the best defence, the Judge lost no time in starting the proceedings.

> 'Your Excellency'—he began.
>
> His Excellency: 'I beg your pardon for one moment. I have a few words to say to the Council before you commence.'
>
> Mr Justice Boothby: 'I shall not remain in the presence of any Attorney of the Court.'
>
> His Excellency: 'I merely wish to state the object for which we have assembled.'
>
> Mr Justice Boothby: 'I am quite aware, Your Excellency.'
>
> His Excellency: 'Certain grave charges—'
>
> Mr Justice Boothby: 'I do not recognize the charges at all. If Your Excellency insists upon reading them, I shall retire whilst they are being read.'
>
> His Excellency: 'I am not going to read them; I am merely about to open the proceedings.'
>
> Mr Justice Boothby: 'I have a preliminary objection to make before any charges are read, and I must make that first. In a Criminal Court any objection to the indictment might be taken before it is read.'
>
> His Excellency: 'I am not going to read any indictment.'

The Judge then read a long document, asking for copies of all dispatches relating to the addresses for his removal, so that he could show the Governor the dangerous course on which he had been advised to enter.

> 'I put in this document before Your Excellency'—he went on—'and I claim that it may be noted on the proceedings. Of course, Your Excellency, I do not ask for an immediate answer to my request for the Despatches, but I shall certainly decline to proceed until I have an answer to it.'
>
> His Excellency: 'Decline to what?'

> Mr Justice Boothby: 'I shall decline to proceed until I have an answer in respect of it. I shall be glad to attend here tomorrow morning.'
>
> Mr Parker: 'I propose to your Excellency to go on.'
>
> Mr Justice Boothby: 'Who is this person?'
>
> Mr Parker: 'I am your Honor's senior at the English bar by nearly ten years.'
>
> Mr Justice Boothby: 'By whom is he instructed? He has no locus standi unless he is instructed, and I have a right to know by whom he has been instructed.'
>
> Mr Parker: 'I am instructed by Mr Way.'
>
> Mr Justice Boothby: 'And who is he instructed by?'
>
> Mr Parker: 'I cannot answer these questions.'
>
> Mr Justice Boothby: 'But I must know, and have it noted on the proceedings.'
>
> Mr Parker: 'I am properly instructed as counsel in this case, and I will not permit any one—'
>
> Mr Justice Boothby: 'I shall not enter into discussions. I shall retire but I shall be glad to have an answer to my request, and will attend upon your Excellency again.'
>
> His Excellency: 'Certain grave charges having been preferred—'
>
> Mr Justice Boothby: 'I shall not listen to any charges.'

The Judge retired and the Governor managed to finish his remarks.

Mr Parker opened the case.

> 'We remember very well, most of us'—he said—'the time when Mr Justice Boothby arrived in this Colony. He succeeded a Judge who had been universally popular—Judge Crawford, whose sudden demise was deplored by all persons. The same good feeling Judge Crawford inspired would have been extended to Judge Boothby, if His Honor's manners and demeanor [sic], and conduct had been equally courteous; but his behaviour has disappointed the Bar, the public, and also suitors ... We come to the time that Mr Justice Boothby ceased to be Acting Chief Justice. I may say that from that moment he has shown a disposition—I hardly know how to characterize it—to abstain from administering the law, and to advance his own grievances and feelings. These grievances—these fancied

wrongs, I may call them—appear to me to arise from a morbid imagination. I cannot conceive how they arise, unless from a jealousy towards the present Chief Justice; because from the moment he ascended the Bench attacks were made upon him, and Mr Justice Boothby claimed the appointment which had been conferred on a former attorney General of this Province, and an able member of the Bar.'

After adverting shortly to the charges, Mr Parker concluded his opening by saying:

> 'If Mr Justice Boothby is to rule the whole Court, and prevent the administration of justice going on in its usual current, injustice will be produced instead of the benefit which should result from the operations of the laws ... If Mr Justice Boothby had observed the quiet and courteous demeanour his predecessor had adopted, we should not have been here now to bring charges against His Honor. If his career had been usefully directed to the administration of justice, and the fair and impartial interpretation of the laws, I am sure we should have cheerfully submitted to any decisions he might give. If we could have seen that no morbid views had actuated him in his course of procedure, we should have been glad to entertain his opinions and even have rejoiced to find a Judge differing from the other Judges in judgments put forward with proper language and in a proper spirit. We should have felt then some confidence in his judgment, but, as we found that a different spirit animated him—that the benefits we expected would flow from his decisions were not derived from them—when we found that, instead of upholding the dignity of the Bench, he had succeeded in alienating all good feeling from him, I submit that the good will of the Legislature, the Bench, the Bar, and the public has been removed from through his own misconduct.'

Boothby's Son
Boothby was accompanied by Joseph Gilbert Boothby (1832-1892) a manager of an insurance company and sometime Consul for Italy in South Australia. Another son, George (1834-1883), came under consideration at the inquiry. He was a clerk at Elder Smith and Co. and one who benefited from ownership of shares in the Moonta mine, acquired via Elder. This information was presented as a possible reason for Boothby's allegedly preferential treatment of Elder.

After some formal evidence had been given, the Council adjourned to the following day, it having been decided to allow the Judges a copy of the dispatches demanded by him.[1]

Next morning Mr Justice Boothby appeared, again accompanied by his son, and on entering the room where the Governor and Council were sitting, said:

> "If you Excellency is at liberty I propose to read this document.'
>
> His Excellency: 'I suppose the Council have no objection to your reading it.'

Messrs Parker, Ingleby and Way then entered the room.

> Mr Justice Boothby: 'I shall not allow counsel to interfere until

> the question of jurisdiction is decided. I shall certainly retire if they do.'
>
> His Excellency: 'Just so: you can do that. I do not think you can dissent from the course we think proper to take.'
>
> Mr Justice Boothby: 'Oh, no! But they cannot interfere until the question of jurisdiction is decided. They have no locus standi unless there is jurisdiction.'

The Judge proceeded to read a statement thanking the Governor for furnishing the dispatches, but asking for a week within which to prepare a written objection to the jurisdiction which the Governor and Council proposed to exercise.

> 'I leave this document with your Excellency'—he added—'and pray that it may be entered on the proceedings. Of course I do not ask for an immediate answer, but—'
>
> His Excellency: 'If Judge Boothby will retire for a few minutes, we will, perhaps, be able to give our answer at once.'
>
> Mr Justice Boothby: 'I hope your Excellency will allow me to be shown into a separate room from the practitioners of the Court. Yesterday I was asked to go into the same room.'
>
> His Excellency: 'Show His Honor into the drawing room, or any available room that there is. I cannot make the house larger than it is.'
>
> Mr Justice Boothby: 'Oh, no.'

After a short consultation the Council determined to proceed with the investigation of the charges, and, when the evidence had been given, if the Judge required further time for his defence, any application he might make would be considered. On this being communicated to the Judge, he forthwith sat down and wrote a protest against the decision:

> '... as contrary to the procedure of all legal tribunals, to proceed in the hearing of evidence until the question of jurisdiction is decided. And further, that it is not competent to your Excellency to hear or be advised on any question of law, save by your responsible law advisers, the chief of whom now sits with your Excellency, and whose advise [sic] alone it is your constitutional duty to follow, unless you see cause to the contrary. I repeat my protest that I do not appear as a defendant, but only to ask your Excellency for a decision as to your legal rights to institute these proceedings'.[2]

The Judge then withdrew; the taking of evidence was continued; and Mr Randolph Stow and Mr Wearing (the Crown Solicitor) were examined. The latter was asked:

> 'Have you observed His Honor during his career as Judge in the Colony?'
>
> 'I certainly have.'
>
> 'What opinion have you formed: have you confidence in his legal attainments?'
>
> 'I should say, that my confidence is rather limited.'
>
> 'Do you think, from what you have observed, that he is usually influenced by the merits of the case before him or by personal bias?'
>
> 'Well, in particular cases, I have remarked, I think, very considerable personal bias. I won't say that he can never act with a view to the merits of the case, but on frequent occasions I have observed a strong bias.'
>
> 'Has your attention been drawn to His Honor's conduct in the case of the Attorney General v. Hughes & Others?'
>
> 'Yes; I may say that I am not engaged as counsel in the case, and therefore I have not been in attendance at the Court during the whole progress of it; but I have been at times a spectator, and I believe I have read all the proceedings reported in the newspapers. From these sources of information, I should certainly form a decided opinion that Mr Justice Boothby was not impartial ... It seems to me that he has acted from the first as a strong partisan on the side of the present owners of the mine ...'
>
> 'Have you noticed the conduct of His Honor in reference to the Legislature of the Province?'
>
> 'Yes; on frequent occasions I have noticed a disposition on his part to go out of his way to offer disparaging remarks on the Legislature of the Province; and as to particular officers—especially the Attorney General—his observations have been very offensive.'
>
> 'Have you observed his conduct with regard to the other Judges?'
>
> 'Yes; I have noticed a constant course of conduct on Mr Justice Boothby's part, now for a long time, calculated to produce a chronic state of irritation in the minds of the other two Judges.

He has seemed to take every opportunity to dissent from them. In fact, I think a person could generally predict the result of any proceedings—finding the Chief Justice and Mr Justice Gwynne on the one side, the necessary inference would be that Mr Justice Boothby would be on the other side.'

'What has been the effect on the business when a Judge has been absent, leaving one Judge with Mr Justice Boothby?'

'To paralyze the action of the Court.' [3]

A police trooper (Robert W. Ewens) in winter dress, 1860. (SAPHS)

At each adjournment a police trooper was dispatched to serve notice of the adjournment upon Mr Justice Boothby, and formal proof of the service of the notice was given each morning before the inquiry was resumed.

The most important evidence was given on the third day when the Chief Justice and Mr Justice Gwynne attended. The former spoke of the complete interruption of business on the equity side owing to Mr Justice Boothby's refusal to recognise the authority of the Equity Act.

'Will your Honor inform the Council'—he was asked—'the state of the contentious business of the Supreme Court?'

'It is in a very unsatisfactory state, and independently of these questions there has always been a very great difficulty to keep up the business. There has been a great difficulty in preventing arrears of business from accumulating, because Mr Justice Boothby always desired to adjourn the Court—to sit as short a time and as seldom as possible ... There are large arrears of business at the present time—I think I may say entirely in consequence of the position taken by Mr Justice Boothby.'

'Has your Honor noticed anything remarkable in His Honor Mr Justice Boothby's conduct in the course of arguments?'

'Yes. Unquestionably there have been interruptions of a sort that do not often occur, so far as my experience has gone, in other Courts. Suggestions are made to counsel on one side of any particular case to urge points which they have not suggested, and which, as a general rule, when they are suggested, they have not thought it necessary to argue, and then they have been argued by Mr Justice Boothby from the Bench in many cases. There have been personal attacks upon counsel of a very unseemly nature, as it appears to me. Remarks are made as to their position, or to their assuming to hold offices which they have no right to hold—no right to suppose they hold—and manifestations of feeling which are

> not quite consistent with the impartial administration of justice—personal feeling, at any rate, on the part of Mr Justice Boothby, towards the counsel appearing in the case. It is impossible not to have noticed that on many occasions.'
>
> 'Has your Honor noticed remarks as to the status of the Bar here?'
>
> 'Yes; no doubt there have been. Not merely as to the status of the bar, but as to the state of legal knowledge in the Colony possessed by attorneys and Judges—and in fact every one but Mr Justice Boothby—implying that no one in the Colony knows even the ABC of the profession except himself. These are things to which I have referred as rendering the administration of justice, and keeping the mind in an unbiassed and impartial state, so difficult.'

In the Chief Justice's opinion, it was impossible to describe Mr Justice Boothby's conduct in the Moonta case and in *Galbraith v. Elder* as anything but that of a partisan.[4]

Mr Justice Gwynne was asked to say what had induced him to join with the Chief Justice in the letter to the Governor of 4 April 1867, and replied:

> 'It was from the continuous insulting expressions made use of by Mr Justice Boothby. I may say, that until I went down under a Commission from his Excellency, to Mount Gambier, out of my turn he never was personally offensive to me. The remarks which were made to the Chief Justice, were equally applicable to me, but up to this period, I was a sort of logical victim. They only applied to me by inference; but when I came back from Mount Gambier I found that it was a very improper act that he conceived I had done. I thought it was my duty to go, because if Mr Justice Boothby had gone, and was at all consistent, he would have decided every information invalid, and the prisoners would have been set at large. I went, and on my return he began to be personally offensive to me. He continues to say on every available occasion that I am not a Judge, and that my learned colleague is not a Judge—that, in fact, we have no pretence to the office.'
>
> His Excellency: 'That has been since your return?'
>
> Mr Justice Gwynne: 'Since my return. He was not directly offensive to me before that, unless that the remarks he applied to the Chief Justice applied to me, but then, there was the inference to be drawn first, and in that shape they were not so offensive. Since then, he is constantly making observations of

this sort, "I told you when you were appointed that you were not a Judge—that the Governor could not appoint a Judge, that you have no pretence for being a Judge, and that I warned you." I told him that amongst gentlemen advice unasked was considered impertinence, and that I did not want his advice, but upon every occasion it has been intruded upon me; the bar and the public have been warned against acting on coercive processes proceeding from myself and the Chief Justice, and we have been advised that we are liable in our persons and estates for every coercive process in our names. This he has done, not once, but daily, and two or three times a day, not only in Court, but in Chambers, and offensively too. It is impossible to try to reconcile him. I would have been happy to let bygones be bygones, if he had met myself and the Chief Justice, and promised to behave himself in future, but he would not do so, but re-echoes this cuckoo insult on every occasion that arises. I have tried remonstrance with him—I have pointed out the number of years that I have been here, and that it was selfish of him to suggest that actions should be brought against me. I have said to him, "It is very selfish of you, for in the first instance it is not defending yourself to point me out as the victim, and altogether I think it is highly offensive of you. I should not object to your Honor saying once that I was not a Judge, but every time I open my mouth upon the Bench to tell me that I have no business there—that I have no business to speak as a Judge, is another affair." And yet it is so every time the Court sits. It is useless to specify all the times, for it takes place on all occasions in Court and in Chambers. Mr Justice Boothby expressed to me great regard for purity in the administration of justice, and he told me in the presence of the Chief Justice, that if ever I tried an action of ejectment, and there should be a single deed in the link of title, which had the name of Gwynne & Lawrence on it, it was my duty to leave the Bench and send for him, and he would try the cause—for, said he, that would be interest enough to lead me to cease to try the cause. He also pointed out the monstrous injustice of appointing a practitioner a Judge of the Province. With regard to the judgments of the Court, very often matters, which in my humble opinion and in the opinion of the Chief Justice, are very simple, and in which we are prepared to give our decisions at once, have to be delayed. He says "it is very discourteous of you to attempt to give an opinion where a Judge differs and wishes for time, you have not had the benefit of my experience in Westminster Hall, or you would see the impropriety of it." We adjourn the judgment, and the thing goes on for weeks and weeks and months, because he is not prepared, and we cannot deliver ours, because he says it would be discourteous of us, knowing his opinion to be different.'

His Excellency: 'Do suitors never object to these proceedings?'

'They do delicately.'

'It has a tendency to increase arrears of business, I suppose.'

'Of course it has. The Chief Justice and myself have always had a delicacy in attributing the delay to its real cause. If we stated the real cause, it would be, that Mr Justice Boothby will not permit us to give our judgments, and will not write his own. I may say, that in every instance where he says he intends to give a written judgment, he gives a verbal judgment with us. If we are opposed to him, he promises a written judgment at a future time, which is never given. His verbal judgment is to the effect that the opinions we have expressed are monstrous—are opposed to all law—that if we had the experience in Westminster Hall that he has had, we would never think of delivering such erroneous judgments, but he would take an opportunity of setting us right by a written judgment, which he never delivers.'

Westminster Hall
Westminster Hall dates back to 1097-1099 when it was the largest hall in Europe and helped Westminster become the administrative, judicial and ceremonial centre of the Kingdom. The first English Parliament met in the Hall in 1265 and in later centuries it housed the law courts.

He had heard Mr Justice Boothby's remarks so often, said Mr Justice Gwynne, that they ceased to be amusing and became offensive.

'I must say that Mr Justice Boothby is a subject not altogether devoid of amusement to a person taking a light view of matters, but in the serious discharge of duties fun is out of place very often.'

By Mr Parker: 'I think he recommended you to resign?'

'Well, I explained to him that where serious rights were concerned, and grave duties were performed, I got sick of being constantly told that I was not a Judge. I found that these statements got into the papers and I fancied affected the behaviour of people towards me, besides lowering the dignity of the Court. I got sick of it and said, if he thought it necessary and it was his view, I had no objection to his asserting that I was not a Judge, and having done so once, he should take action upon it, and not at every opportunity use this insulting line of observations. As I say, I got sick of it, and I did seriously think of sending in my resignation; but I have determined not to sit with him any longer. I found that I was doing no good to the Colony, that the Court was being degraded, and business arrested; and that while in one view it was absurd that it yet acted very seriously. I felt that I was compromising myself in submitting to it—not that I personally cared, but because the interests of the Colony and of suitors, and the dignity of the Judicial Office were suffering, and I determined to make a stand. I may say that I have been associated with Mr Justice Boothby longer than my learned colleague has. I was on the Bench in Sir Charles Cooper's time, and I am bound to say that never in any consultation in Chambers did Mr Justice Boothby ever quote a case, or throw the slightest light upon any subject of discussion. He would declare, "It is monstrously absurd to hold as you hold. There are thousand cases against your position"; but when asked to show one case—Sir Charles Cooper would say, "Well, show us one case, and we will agree with you"—but he would shift his ground and say, "It is too simple a proposition; there is no case in the books, for it is so well-known a principle of law that it is foolish to expect a case upon it." And that has been the way ever since I have been associated with the present Chief Justice. Mr Justice Boothby has never thrown any light upon a case, or called attention to any book, but he has simply said—"That is my opinion and you must act upon it, and if you don't, I shall in my judgment tell them so and so, and do so and so," the effect of his statement being this—"I shall do everything to degrade your opinion if you don't coincide in mine." Sir Charles Cooper felt annoyed by it, and I felt that the object seemed to be to delay and put off judgment; and when he told his opinion if you did not agree with him, he would threaten to tell the Bar and the Colony this that and the other ... Mr Justice Boothby seems to attach great importance to being called to the English Bar. If that has some talismanic effect, I could never detect it myself; but Mr Justice Boothby is pleased to insult the Bar here by calling them attorneys.'

'I may say'—continued Mr Justice Gwynne—'that I don't know that he ever agreed with the Chief Justice in any important case since he has been upon the Bench. In every case of moment he has always violently opposed the Chief Justice's opinion whatever that might be.'

It was impossible, he said, to sit any longer with Mr Justice Boothby.

> 'I feel that so strongly that I think I should not serve the country or my own interest to remain a member of the Bench if Mr Justice Boothby is there.' [5]

The Council proceeded to take the evidence of Mr Ingleby, Mr Downer and Mr Galbraith as to *Galbraith v. Elder*; and a number of practitioners (Messrs Belt, Bagot, Moulden, Thrupp and Boucaut) and the Master of the Supreme Court were examined as to the delays and obstructions caused by Mr Justice Boothby. Mr Way then summed up, on 4 July 1867, and the Council adjourned to 13 July, the Judge being given due notice of the adjournment.

That irrepressible gentleman, however, not at all abashed by the proceedings in course against him, continued to be a centre of trouble. On 1 July the Full Court sat. The Attorney-General asked the Court to allow matters in which he was engaged to stand over, in order that he might attend at the inquiry. The Chief Justice said there was no objection.

> 'Let me give you a word of advice'—said Mr Justice Boothby—'in relation to proceedings to be taken hereafter, that you may be found assisting an unlawful Court. I shall hold all parties responsible; they may rely upon it.'

The Chief Justice and Mr Justice Gwynne decided to adjourn, but Mr Justice Boothby dissented.

> 'The Court stands adjourned'—said the Master.

> 'I shall continue to sit'—said Mr Justice Boothby—'and shall be glad to hear any suitor who has any business, either in his own person— '

> The Chief Justice: 'It is understood that the Court is adjourned by the majority of the Court. If Mr Justice Boothby, as an individual Judge, chooses to sit, and thinks he has power to do so, of course—'

> Mr Justice Boothby: 'I can't be prevented, of course.'

> The Chief Justice: 'No doubt he will act as consistently with his idea of his duty as of his dignity.'

> Mr Justice Boothby: 'I do it in order that the law may be carried out, and that there may be no excuse for saying that I closed the Court—that I obstructed the business of the Court.'

> The Master: 'The Court stands adjourned till Tuesday the 9th inst.'

The Chief Justice and Mr Justice Gwynne then left the bench, Mr Justice Boothby continuing to sit.

Joseph Eldin Moulden (1812-1891)
The law firm Joseph founded still operates in Adelaide today under the name of 'Mouldens'. Joseph began practice in Adelaide in 1851, later being joined in practice by two of his sons, Beaumont and Bayfield. (Mouldens)

> 'The Court does not stand adjourned'—he said—'notwithstanding what the Master pleases to say. I am ready to hear any application from any suitor, by himself in person, by his Attorney or by counsel.'

The members of the bar, however, withdrew; and after vainly inviting motions, the Judge directed the Master to adjourn the Court to Friday the 5th inst.

On 11 July the Court sat again to hear a criminal case—*R. v. Seller*—a question of law having been reserved for the consideration of the Full Court.

> 'I see the Attorney General is here'—said Mr Justice Boothby. 'I shall have something to say about this information, which professes to be a criminal information signed by him; and if he can support it in law, I shall be most glad to hear it. You hear what I point out'—he warned the Attorney-General—'because I think it is a question of very serious importance to you personally, for if this is no information which you have jurisdiction to issue, there are serious responsibilities attaching to you in reference to this person who has been brought under it, and it seems improperly and unlawfully tried. Therefore I point this out to you in order that you may consider the absolute necessity of getting this matter settled, for the protection of yourself and the officers of the Government. I daresay it will be said "Oh, we will go on, and when the thing is brought before the Court, we will pass a Bill to protect you"; but that cannot go on for ever.'

The Attorney-General merely said that he was not prepared to discuss the subject.

Eventually the conviction of the prisoner was quashed, Mr Justice Boothby adding that the information was bad, and he pointed out to the prisoner that he had a remedy for the great wrong which had been done to him.

The next case called on was a petition under the Real Property Act, but upon a Certificate of Title being produced Mr Justice Boothby said that he would treat it as waste paper, because there was no jurisdiction in anybody to grant such a document.[6]

On 16 July Mr Stow mentioned the Moonta case to the Court. This, it will be remembered, Mr Justice Boothby had struck out because no counsel had attended on the day of what might be called his private sessions. Stow asked that it should be reinstated.

Mr Justice Boothby: 'What ground have you, Mr Stow, for not being present in Court when it was called on: In my experience a cause is never reinstated without some reasons for the absence of the party being shown.'

> Mr Justice Gwynne: 'In this case, Mr Stow, you need not trouble yourself, for I regard the case as still being on the list, considering the act of striking it out a mere nullity, upon the ground that the day on which it was done was not one appointed for the Court to meet.'
>
> The Chief Justice: 'I agree.'
>
> Mr Justice Boothby: 'I think quite the contrary. The purpose of my sitting in Court was to claim my authority to do so, as no doubt I have it in law. My object was served, namely, to escape the imputation that any delay in the administration of justice in this Court was occasioned by me. I am quite willing for it to be restored, as I stated at the time.'
>
> The Chief Justice: 'It will not be restored—it is not struck out.'

It was idle to go on with business, said the Chief Justice, until the inquiry had terminated; but Mr Justice Boothby protested.

> 'Throughout the civilised world'—he said—'it should be known that in the midst of a cause in which the Crown is a party, a Judge—one of three trying the cause—should be sought to be removed by mere executive authority during the progress of the cause, and that on the complaint of an attorney of the Court who is interested not only in his position as an attorney and his position as an advocate, but according to the affidavits upon the files of the Court in a much more important matter.'
>
> The Chief Justice: 'The Court will adjourn for a fortnight.'
>
> Mr Justice Boothby: 'I am not a consenting party to that, and you will also place it in your book, Mr Hinde, that I dissent from any adjournment. I am ready to go on sitting to hear any business that suitors may bring before me.' ...
>
> The Chief Justice: 'Mr Hinde, you will adjourn the Court, if you please.'
>
> Mr Justice Boothby: 'You may make an entry in the book Mr Hinde, that I requested such an entry by you, and the other Judges dissented.'
>
> The Chief Justice: 'The Master is in a certain dignified position as an officer of the Court, and has certain duties of his office to perform, and I should think it is no part of them to be an amanuensis of Mr Justice Boothby.'

Mr Justice Gwynne concurred and the Master therefore refused to make an entry in his book as requested.

> Mr Justice Boothby: 'Who do you intend to obey.'
>
> The Master: 'The majority of the Court, your Honor.'
>
> The Chief Justice: 'You will enter that the Court adjourned on the 30th inst., Boothby Judge dissenting.'
>
> Mr Justice Boothby: 'Enter that I dissent from the adjournment of the Court.'
>
> The Chief Justice: 'Mr Hinde would not put "I dissent", for he probably would not dissent.'

The Master then adjourned the Court.

> 'I inform all suitors present'—said Mr Justice Boothby—'that I will remain here, and am ready to hear any matter they may bring forward, either in their own person or by their attorney or counsel.'

The Chief Justice, Mr Justice Gwynne and all the practitioners left the Court, and the Master was also going when he was called back by Mr Justice Boothby. The Master hesitated at the door, torn between two fires. "Do you say you won't?" called out the Judge in a threatening tone. "I think your Honor is placing on me more than you should," replied Mr Hinde, and disappeared. A few minutes later he came back into Court without his gown, to get some papers.

> Mr Justice Boothby: 'Don't take off your gown. If you have it on when the other Judges are here, I require that you should when in my presence here.'
>
> The Master: 'The Court is adjourned.'

The Judge said the Court was not adjourned, and he asked the Master to make an entry that he had remained on the bench and called upon any suitors to bring their business before him if they wished to do so. He handed the Master a slip of paper with the entry he wanted written on it.

> The Master: 'I can't read it, Your Honor.'

The Judge read it to him.

> The Master: 'Your Honor, I can't enter it.'
>
> Mr Justice Boothby: 'Don't say you can't. Will you obey my orders?'
>
> The Master: 'I will obey the Court.'
>
> Mr Justice Boothby: 'Will you obey my orders?'

The Master: 'I shall not, your Honor.'

Mr Justice Boothby: 'Very well.'

The Master: 'I have obeyed the Court, your Honor, and I have said so several times.'

Mr Hinde then walked out of the Court. The Judge read his entry to the reporters present and gave them a copy of it, and then sent a messenger to ask the Master to come into Court. Mr Hinde refused to come and, after sitting in Court for about twenty minutes, the Judge left the bench.[7]

The *Register* humorously described the incident under the appropriate heading of "The Hinde and the Panther".

William Hinde (SCLSA)

On 13 July the Judge had attended before the Governor and Council and had once more read a long memorandum refusing to furnish any evidence in reply but asking for further time to consider what answer to the proceedings he should make. His request was granted and the hearing further adjourned to 29 July. On that day he again attended.

'He drew from his pocket a foolscap epistle
As calmly as if 'twere a nine-barrelled pistol,
And threatened them all with the judgment to come'.

The Governor and Council, he said, had no jurisdiction whatever. His principal grounds of objection were:

(1) That the words "Governor and Council" as used in 22 Geo III c.75 referred only to colonies having a Governor and Council possessing the combined functions of a legislature and executive.

(2) That to apply the provisions of that Act to the circumstances of the province "involved infractions of natural justice, by allowing a tribunal with positive powers to be composed of persons who are at once prosecutors, judges, and jurors, and all of whom, in another tribunal, have, in the same several capacities, each given a judgment and opinion on accusations substantially the same as those now before them".

(3) That the Government was paying the expenses of the inquiry and the costs of the prosecuting counsel.

'I am entitled to regard your Excellency and Executive Council as prosecutors of the present proceedings, and as providing funds for carrying on the same out of the Public Treasury.'

(4) That all the members of the Council, by their votes and speeches in Parliament, had expressed opinions hostile to him.

'Such expressions of opinion on the part of any person called as juror to try an oft-convicted felon, would entitle the accused to object successfully as being a person who had already prejudged the case.'

(5) That his office, being held during pleasure of the Crown, did not come within the terms of 22 Geo III c.75.

He concluded by giving notice that if his objection was not upheld he would appeal to the Privy Council.

After a few minutes' consideration, the Council decided to proceed.

> Mr Justice Boothby: 'Then my appeal, of which notice appears on the proceedings, goes on, and my appearance before your Excellency is ended. I will only express the hope, that if your Excellency ventures upon going to the extent of a motion, you will place me in a situation that I shall be able to defend my rights in another proceeding—that there may be nothing unseemly—that the manner of securing those rights be carried out under seemly circumstances; for I shall certainly go to the Court and enter my protest, and require to be taken off the Bench by the tipstaff of the Court, or some one else. That is necessary in order to secure my rights. Of course, I don't anticipate anything; but I think it right to suggest to your Excellency that I shall certainly go to the Court, and require to

> be removed by what in law would constitute force, so as to make it an act of trespass on my person.'

The Judge then withdrew and the Council proceeded to find the charges established and proved and, by reason of the Judge's misbehaviour in his office, ordered his amotion from that office. The order was forthwith drawn up and served upon him. It was published in a *Gazette Extraordinary* the same evening, and the judicial career of Mr Justice Boothby was at an end.

The result of the inquiry was a foregone conclusion. In many respects it was a most unsatisfactory form of proceedings. It was not in accordance with normal ideas of propriety, to say the least, that Mr Justice Boothby should be prosecuted, before a body of judges who had already publicly announced their opinion he was guilty, by counsel retained and paid by those judges, upon charges laid by an avowed enemy—an enemy, too, who had a considerable pecuniary interest at stake in the removal of judicial opposition to the success of the Moonta claimants. Upon the first four charges there was undoubtedly evidence upon which the Council could properly find misbehaviour, and that his removal was necessary can hardly be questioned. But the charge most serious to the Judge's honour and reputation—that of allowing private and personal feelings to influence him on the bench—seems to have failed miserably, although he was found guilty of it. It was admitted that the only allegations against him in this respect were favouring his neighbour, Mr Elder, in the Moonta case and in *Galbraith v. Elder.* That the Judge took a strong view in favour of the defendants in these cases could not be denied, but that he was influenced by any unworthy motives in so doing was certainly not proved. The attempt to show that he was biased by pecuniary interests because some years earlier some shares in the Moonta mine had been given to one of his sons was unworthy and disgraceful, and all the accusations against him on this head were ex parte statements founded on unreliable gossip. Mr Elder himself said, and there is no reason to doubt him, that Mr Justice Boothby had never asked or received any benefits at his hands.

> 'Ever since the Moonta case and Galbraith's case appeared in the Court, His Honor studiously avoided me. It is perfectly true that our houses are contiguous, but Mr Justice Boothby had not been in my house nor I in his for a very long period; in fact there has been a suspension of our friendly relations since these actions commenced.' [8]

When the cost of the inquiry became known, there was an outcry in Parliament. The total sum paid to Mr Way to cover his charges, counsel fees and disbursements was more than £2,500. It was denounced as "a scandalous and profligate waste of public money", and "daylight robbery of the public". The Government replied that it was useless to cry over spilt milk—the charges had been agreed and paid. They were high because "it was difficult at the time to get a respectable member of the legal profession to undertake the duty". The case was an important one which would probably get to the Privy Council, and it demanded the best legal assistance obtainable; and it was also a disagreeable one and, if the charges had failed, it might have resulted in serious loss of practice to those engaged as counsel.[9]

In spite of his threat that he would not leave the bench until ejected by force, the Judge quietly acquiesced in the order for his removal, contenting himself with the prospects of a successful appeal to the Privy Council.

> 'Now that the Rubicon has been crossed, and no convulsions of nature have followed the removal of Judge Boothby'—the Register wrote—'people wonder why there should have been so much excitement beforehand. The fact is the Executive did at last so unexpectedly what had been talked about so long, that Judge Boothby ceased to be Judge Boothby almost before anyone was aware of it.' [10]

The Governor, in reporting the result of the inquiry, said:

> 'I believe that I am fully justified in stating that the action my Government have taken in this case has given very general satisfaction, both to the legal profession and also the public, and the silence of Parliament although in full possession of the proceedings shows that there is no disposition in any quarter to criticise unfavorably the action of my Government in this important matter.'[11]

Mr Wearing, who had been Crown Solicitor since 1856, was appointed to the vacancy on the bench—"a gentleman every way qualified", said the Governor, "to uphold the efficiency and dignity of the Supreme Court"—and Mr Justice Gwynne, having been appointed Primary Judge in Equity, set out to overtake the arrears of equity work. These had accumulated not only on account of the obstructive tactics of Mr Justice Boothby but because of the difficulties in the conduct of work in that jurisdiction by all the Judges.

> 'It was found practically that the administration of the Equity jurisdiction concurrently with that of the Common Law by the same Judges, greatly interfered with the conduct of business in both branches; either matters on the Common Law side were postponed in order that the Equity business might not be interrupted, or vice versa, and when this was not done, the hearing of cases was necessarily broken off in the middle and only resumed after the lapse of many days or perhaps weeks,

> when the argument had been resumed to the disadvantage both of the Bar and the Court.'[12]

So far as Mr Justice Boothby himself was concerned, he had never been able to bring himself seriously to contemplate the possibility of removal, and the actual amotion came as a tremendous blow, from which he never recovered. His health failed rapidly and he retired into seclusion, rarely leaving his home. He intended to appeal to the Privy Council, and he was not without friends to assist him. Mr Palmer started a fund to defray the expenses of an appeal against the "illegal and unconstitutional proceedings of the Governor and Council", and an address was presented, signed by a number of colonists, assuring the Judge of their:

> '... firm conviction that in the exercise of your high and responsible duties as one of the Judges of the Supreme Court of this province you have been actuated solely by a conscientious desire to do your duty; and that all imputations of your having been influenced by other or personal motives are utterly without foundation in fact'.[13]

The Judge maintained that he was still legally in office and applied to the Governor for leave of absence to go to England to prosecute his appeal. Hon J. Baker, in the Legislative Council, made an eloquent appeal for the granting of such leave to the Judge on salary. He admitted that, whatever the result of the appeal might be, it would be impossible for Mr Justice Boothby to return to the South Australian Supreme Court. But great animus had been shown and great injustice done.

> 'The Judge has given way to infirmities of temper and shown unamiability of disposition, but for that is he to be dismissed in his old age, to spend his remaining years dishonoured and in poverty? ... I for one can say that when I see that feeble old man with bent form walking the streets I rejoice that I took no part against him.'[14]

His motion failed. The Government answered that the Judge had been given an opportunity to defend himself at the inquiry, and if he wanted to go to England no-one would stop him. His removal had been absolutely necessary.

> 'The complaints against him were not the result of some sudden and temporary excitement, but had existed for years. His mind was evidently too crotchety, his tendencies to be obstructive were too deep-seated, and his feelings of personal authority and importance too strong to allow him to administer the laws in a satisfactory manner.'[15]

The Judge's request for leave of absence was referred to the home authorities by the Governor, and the Secretary of State replied that he could see no objection to it, provided Mr Boothby was informed that it was given to him merely to avoid any question being raised as to the breach of a condition as to his original appointment, and upon his distinct undertaking that the fact of such leave being given should not in any way be relied upon by him as an admission that he was still a judge or as throwing any doubt upon the validity of the proceedings. The leave of absence, he said, should be given to "B. Boothby Esq" without any title.[16]

Steps had been taken by the Government to resist the proposed appeal to the Privy Council, and Sir Roundell Palmer and Mr Coleridge QC were retained.[17] But on 21 June 1868, a stormy period in South Australian history was brought to a close by the Judge's death.

> 'Little more than a year ago'—wrote the Register in announcing it—'the Boothby question was agitating the colony from end to end; now it has been settled for ever by the cold hand of death. Boothbyites and anti-Boothbyites may now renounce their differences, and forswear their animosities over the corpse of their champion and bugbear. The denouement has been as painful as the struggle itself was desperate.' [18]

Boothby and many of his family are buried in the North Road cemetery at Nailsworth. The towering monument is inscribed: "Sacred to the memory of Benjamin Boothby Second Judge of the Supreme Court Died June 21st 1868 aged 65 years – Also his wife Maria Bradbury Died June 18th 1888 aged 82 years." (Helen Whitington)

While Boothby's amoval from office captivated Adelaide's attention for most of 1867, the highlight of the year was Prince Alfred's visit. He was received with "the utmost enthusiasm" as illustrated by Frederick Grosse's engraving. (SLV)

Although the colonists could bring with them to South Australia the law of England, they could not bring the courts by which that law was administered at home; and during 1837 the legislation of the Council of Government was concerned mainly with the institution in the colony of a hierarchy of courts, patterned as nearly as possible upon those existing in England.

In accordance with the usual principles of judicial architecture, the pyramidical system was followed, and the courts comprised:

(1) A Court of Appeals.
(2) A Supreme Court.
(3) Courts of Quarter Sessions.
(4) Courts of Petty Sessions.
(5) Courts of Resident Magistrates.

The Court of Appeals and the minor courts are the subject of separate chapters; it is here proposed to deal with the Supreme Court, under the following heads:

(1) The jurisdiction of the Supreme Court.
(2) The procedure of the Supreme Court.
(3) The officers of the Supreme Court.
(4) The site of the Supreme Court.
(5) The Supreme Court Library.
(6) Circuit Courts.

The Jurisdiction of the Supreme Court

> 'With respect to Courts of Justice'—said a contemporary authority on colonial law—'though their establishment is usually directed in general terms by the King's Commission and Instructions to the Governor, their denomination, quality, number, and particular constitution are for the most part left to be settled by the legislature of the colony.' [1]

Presumably it had been decided in a general way, before the colonists sailed, what form their courts should take, but the earliest reference to be found to the Supreme Court is in Stevenson's journal where he notes on 2 November 1836, on the *Buffalo*, that he has been engaged in drawing up laws for the constitution of the Supreme Court and Courts of Quarter and Petty Sessions. The Supreme Court Act was left in abeyance until the Judge arrived in the colony and could give his approval of it. There was, of course, a quarrel about it in the Council. The Governor had inserted a provision reserving to the Crown the right of appointing future judges of the Supreme Court. "This was done"—he said—"to counteract the exorbitant pretensions of the members of the Council, particularly those of the Resident Commissioner and of his clique out of doors."

Fisher contended that the Council, having been given power to appoint officers for the peace, order and good government of the colony, could and should appoint the judges. The Governor argued that the Crown could not be divested, without express words, of its prerogative right of nominating judges. Gouger and Mann both thought the Governor was wrong but, rather than have any trouble over it, they were willing to leave the appointment to the Crown.[2]

The Act was passed on 31 May 1837 (7 Wm IV No 5) and gave the Supreme Court:

(a) The jurisdiction exercised by the Courts of King's Bench, Common Pleas, and Exchequer at Westminster;
(b) The equitable jurisdiction of the Lord Chancellor;
(c) Ecclesiastical jurisdiction in request of the granting of probates and letters of administration;
(d) Power to appoint guardians and keepers of the persons and estates of infants, and of "natural fools, and of such as are or shall be deprived of their understanding or reason by the Act of God so as to be unable to govern themselves and their estates, which the said Court is hereby authorised and empowered to inquire, hear and determine by inspection of the person or such other ways and means by which the truth may be best discovered and known".

The Court was to be held before the Judge of the Supreme Court, appointed and removable by the Crown "and by no other authority". In the case of the absence, resignation, sickness or death of the Judge, the Governor and Council were empowered to appoint a temporary judge.

This Act remained in force, with only minor amendments, until 1855 when it was re-enacted in the consolidating Supreme Court Act of that year. The jurisdiction conferred on the Supreme Court comprised all that commonly exercised by the superior courts at Westminster, and it was only in a few instances that the Court was found to be lacking in any requisite jurisdiction. Cases of incest, for example, were cognisable in England by the ecclesiastical courts only. No such courts existed in South Australia and offences of this nature therefore had to be ignored.[3]

Again the Chancellor exercised in England a certain restricted common law jurisdiction. Only his equitable jurisdiction had been conferred on the Supreme Court, and in the Moonta case it was contended that there was no jurisdiction for the Court to issue writs of scire facias, which were proceedings restricted to the Chancellor's common law jurisdiction. So also in 1865 proceedings were taken in *The Queen v. Baker* against certain lessees of Crown lands by writ of intrusion to eject them, but the Supreme Court held it had no jurisdiction to hear the actions—a defeat which was remedied by a statute introduced in the following year.

Certain subsidiary jurisdictions conferred upon the Supreme Court may be separately noticed:

(a) Vice-Admiralty Jurisdiction.

The necessity for a Court of Vice-Admiralty had been among the subjects canvassed by the Converzatione Club, which the intending colonists of South Australia had formed in London, and an opinion had been obtained from H.W. Parker as to how the Court should be constituted. This was forwarded to the Colonial Office, but James Stephen did not think very highly of it. "Mr Parker"—he said—"writes on a subject with which it is evident he is not very familiar." [4]

Nothing further was done, and the colony was founded without any provision being made for a Court of Admiralty. Two instances have been mentioned when the absence of such a court gave rise to difficulties—the presence of whalers in South Australian waters and the case of Stephens and Wright.[5]

Townsend Duryea's picture of the wharves at Port Adelaide ca. 1866. (NLA)

After a long delay the Governor received, in 1841, a Commission empowering him to establish a Vice-Admiralty Court.[6] The Judge, however, asked for time to obtain from England books relating to the law and practice in admiralty, of which he had had no experience; on their arrival, he said, he would feel "more at ease" in undertaking such work.[7]

In December 1842, E.C. Gwynne wrote to the Governor complaining of the failure to establish the Vice-Admiralty Court. The Governor replied that there were "obstacles" which prevented the opening of the Court, but promised that it would be brought into operation as soon as possible. Mr Gwynne persisted, and wanted to know what were the obstacles—an embarrassing question as it would have been hardly seemly to have admitted publicly that the only obstacle was the Judge's ignorance.[8] Evading a direct answer, the Governor wrote to the Judge asking him to hurry up the books from England. Gwynne said he had himself been consulted on two cases, and knew that there were others, which required an application to a Court of Admiralty. His clients had to languish unsatisfied for a further eighteen months. At the beginning of 1844, Mr Matthew Smith asked the Judge in court when the Vice-Admiralty Court was likely to be opened, as business was accumulating.[9] He was told that "the matter was under serious consideration", but it was not until May 1844 that sufficient books arrived to give the Judge confidence. The Governor then issued Letters Patent appointing Mr Justice Cooper and the Judge of the Supreme Court for the time being to be commissary in the Vice-Admiralty Court. The Letters Patent further gave to Mr Justice Cooper specifically the power of appointing a deputy.

Mann was made Registrar, and the opening of the Court was carried out in style. Eleven barristers were sworn in as advocates and proctors, and entertained the Registrar at a professional lunch.

> 'These gentlemen'—said the Register—'are now privileged to take cognizance of offences on the high seas, and to inquire into nautical matters; but we have not heard that any of them ventured, on the first day of their new practice, to be even half-seas over.' [10]

No salary was attached to the positions of Judge and Registrar: they were to be remunerated by the fees taken, which never exceeded a few pounds a year.[11] Successive masters have always held the appointment of Registrar [12]

In 1849, when Mann was acting as Judge during Mr Justice Cooper's absence, Jickling raised the question whether he had any power to sit in the Vice-Admiralty jurisdiction. Mann confessed that he did not know. "The truth is"—he said—"we are all very ignorant of the law of that court, and the less we have to do with it, the better." [13] Upon consulting the Letters Patent, it was found that he was ex officio, empowered to execute the duties of Commissary; but the Advocate-General being doubtful whether Mann could be both Commissary and Registrar, Mr Wilson, the Acting Master, was temporarily appointed Registrar.[14]

The Vice-Admiralty Court as constituted in South Australia was an instance court only and could not take cognisance of criminal offences. In one case a steward was charged with stealing on a ship while it was voyaging to Adelaide. The case against him was clear but the jury having found that the offence was committed more than three miles from South Australian shores, the Judge, after some hesitation, ordered the prisoner to be discharged on the ground that there was no jurisdiction in the courts of the colony to try him.[15] A similar question arose again in cases at Port Adelaide before Captain

George Frederick Dashwood (1806-1881) Dashwood was a former naval officer who sought government employ after farming unsuccessfully at Echunga. He served as, variously, Commissioner of Police, a Magistrate, Collector of Customs and Emigration Agent. He was also a Member of the Legislative Council before responsible government. (SLSA)

Dashwood, the Magistrate there, and he, following the Judge's ruling held that he could not try the offenders.[16] He asked the Government to take steps to enable such crimes to be punished, and the Judge supported the recommendation. "The want of a power to try offences committed upon the sea is certainly felt here"—he wrote.[17] But he did not think that the South Australian legislature had any power to pass an ordinance giving jurisdiction to the Supreme Court to try cases of crimes committed on the high seas. In the first place its powers were limited by the Act 5 and 6 Vic c.61 s.5 to the making of laws for the peace, order and good government of the colony; and secondly, the Colonial Office had several years before, after consultation with the English law officers, laid down certain rules upon the enacting of laws in colonies for the regulation or punishment of acts done on the high seas.

> 'When the operation of a Colonial Act is confined to a range not exceeding one League from the shore, and relates to matters of local interest, the regulation of which by local enactment is indispensable to the welfare of the colony, no objection will be made to such an Act on the ground of the local range and extent of its operation exceeding the limits of the jurisdiction of the Colonial Legislature; examples of such Acts are those relating to Pilotage, to Quarantine, to Customs duties, and to Fisheries.
>
> But if a Colonial Enactment be made to take effect on the High Seas at a distance exceeding three miles from the shores of the Colony—that is, if it shall purport to regulate, to prevent, or to punish any acts done on shipboard beyond those limits, such enactment will be null and void. In what manner Acts of that kind may be disposed of by Her Majesty is a question on which no inflexible rule can be laid down. But it may be stated, as a general rule that the Queen will, in no case, be advised to confirm or sanction any such enactment.' [18]

The difficulty was removed by the arrival of the Imperial Act 12 and 13 Vic c.96 which gave the required jurisdiction to colonial courts. The steward had a lucky escape, for this Act had been passed at the time of his trial but its existence was unknown in South Australia.

In 1856, Mr Justice Cooper, exercising the power given to him by the Letters Patent, nominated Mr Justice Boothby as his deputy. When he resigned his position as Chief Justice in December 1860, Sir Charles Cooper forgot all about the Vice-Admiralty Court, and it was not until a year later that it suddenly occurred to him that Mr Justice Boothby's deputation might have ceased upon his retirement. He hastily wrote to the Governor that it was advisable that a new commission should issue at once, and he suggested it should issue not in the name of Mr Justice Boothby but in that of the new Chief Justice.[19] This was done, and another grievance added to Mr Justice Boothby's long list. He complained to the Secretary of State of his eviction from a position which he claimed to be his by right of succession, but was told in reply that it was customary to appoint the Chief Justice of a colony to be the Judge in Admiralty, and that no exception could be made in his case.[20]

(b) Matrimonial Causes Jurisdiction.

Upon the passing in England of the Matrimonial Causes Act 1857, the Secretary of State forwarded a copy of the Act to the Governor, calling his attention to the importance of the subject and directing him to propose a measure to the local parliament incorporating the provisions of the English Act so far as possible.

> 'Her Majesty's Government'—wrote Lord Stanley—'regard this subject as within the general class of internal affairs which the duty and right of regulating belong to the Colonial Legislatures under free institutions. But they are at the same time fully sensible of the great importance of uniformity of legislation on this head ... and the danger as well to public morality as to family interests, which might arise from the law of the Colonies on the subject of marriage and divorce differing materially from that of the mother country and of each other.' [21]

The Governor consulted the Chief Justice, who wrote that he had long been sensible of the want of such a law, and that the colony was so far advanced as to make it expedient to invest the Supreme Court with such a jurisdiction.[22]

A bill was accordingly introduced into the Legislative Council in September 1858 by the Chief Secretary, who said:

> 'Under the existing law, I am aware of no remedy, but the injured party is obliged to pass his or her life in misery and torment, and their earthly career is probably terminated by some act of brutal violence. The only course of procedure under the present state of things is to apply to Parliament by petition for a private Bill, and this Bill, after passing through the usual formalities, and going through both Houses of the Legislature, cannot be assented to by the Governor, but must obtain the assent of the Queen before it can become of any value.' [23]

There was considerable opposition to the Bill from a number of members who professed to fear that it would let in a flood of immorality, but it was passed by a small majority. It was practically a transcript of the English statute, conferring on the Supreme Court the jurisdiction given in England to the Divorce Court, but it provided that condonation of adultery should be a discretionary bar only and not an absolute bar, as in England. "In this respect"—wrote the Governor—"the Act is perhaps an improvement on the English Act." [24]

The alteration was not regarded with favour by the authorities at home. They saw no reason why there should be a variation from the English Act. The colonial Act might be more wisely framed, but it was vitally important to maintain uniformity of legislation in matters of social and domestic interest, and the advance of uniformity: "... would far overbalance that which could be attained in the better workmanship (if the fact be so) of the colonial provision".[25] The Act, however, was left to its operation, and the first cause in the matrimonial jurisdiction was heard on 29 August 1859.[26]

(c) Jurisdiction in Insolvency.

During his term of office as Judge, Jickling delivered one ruling which did credit to his humanity but aroused a considerable stir amongst the small legal profession and trading community: he held that the law of England relating to the arrest of debtors by creditors was not in force in the colony. The disappointed creditor concerned at once intimated to the Governor that he intended to appeal to the Court of Appeals. The Governor wrote to Jickling that he was anxious "to avoid the inconvenience and delay to the course of public business attendant upon a solemn appeal to the Council", announced it as his opinion that the law of arrest was in force in South Australia, and demanded an explanation from the Judge why he refused to grant process to the creditor. This seems to have startled Jickling into reversing his decision, for nothing further is heard of the appeal, and shortly afterwards debtors are found being arrested and lodged in gaol.[27] Their plight was an unenviable one, for the gaol was small, crowded and insanitary, and there were no bankruptcy or insolvency laws available in the colony by which they could secure their discharge. "People do not emigrate to become insolvent," said Mr Justice Gwynne, referring to the original failure to confer any insolvency jurisdiction on the Supreme Court.[28] In August 1840 the imprisoned debtors petitioned the Governor to enact an insolvency law. Three months later another memorial followed, but without result. The Governor was compelled, however, to issue rations to the debtors at the cost of ten shillings a week, a step which was freely criticised as imposing on the state a debt solely for the benefit of a few creditors.[29]

The Judge suggested that speedy relief might be given by the passing of a short act adopting the essential features of the English Bankruptcy Acts, to be superseded by a longer and more detailed act later, but the Governor considered that the Royal Instructions that no act was to be of less duration than two years offered a serious objection to this plan.[30] A bill was slowly prepared, the position of the debtors in the gaol becoming steadily worse. The Act was passed at last in June 1841. The Supreme Court was constituted a Court of

Insolvency, and its insolvency jurisdiction was to be exercised by the Judge or Judges of the Supreme Court, or by a Commissioner or Commissioners to be appointed by the Crown. Provision was made for the appointment of Commissioners for country districts. An official assignee and other ministerial officers were to be appointed by the Judge. All proceedings were commenced by petition to the Judge, who authorised the prosecution of the proceedings either before him or before a Commissioner. The Supreme Court was to be a court of review. Practitioners might practise in insolvency before the Judge or Commissioner, "but no other person shall be allowed to practice except in districts or places where there shall not be a number of enrolled practitioners sufficient for that purpose".

Any person in gaol for debt or for contempt of court for non-payment of money might apply by petition requesting his release, and the presenting of the petition was deemed to be an act of insolvency. If any such prisoner did not within twenty-one days of his committal to gaol pay or satisfy the debit, he was deemed to have committed an act of insolvency upon which the detaining creditor could petition for an order vesting the real and personal estate of the debtor in the Official Assignee. Other acts of insolvency upon which a creditor might petition for a sequestration order were specified in the Act. One or two now appear rather curious: for instance, the debtor committed an act of insolvency if being in prison or in custody for debt he escaped; or if he remained in prison twenty-one days consecutively charged with a debt, although the original cause of his imprisonment might not have been for debt.

Upon a sequestration order being made, the estate of the debtor was administered by the Official Assignee in the same manner as in bankruptcy in England, and the court could discharge the prisoner from custody. An appeal lay from the Supreme Court in its insolvency jurisdiction to the Court of Appeals.

This Act gradually brought about the release of those confined for debt. In February 1843, the Sheriff was able to report that there were no debtors in the gaol—a circumstance which had not occurred since February 1839.[31] While this was very satisfactory to the debtors, the Act brought no relief to creditors, who received very little after the debtors' estates had been realised and distributed. This was due to a number of causes, principally the sudden depreciation in the values of property. Most of the debtors had mortgaged their land and, with the great fall in values during 1841-42, there was usually only enough to cover the secured creditors. Frequently the debtor was unable to collect money due to him because his debtors were all insolvent. In the twelve months following the passing of the Act, the estates of fifty persons were dealt with, and the figures relating to them are remarkable. Their total assets when they contracted the earliest debts in their schedules were £11,000—that is, the average sum possessed by each was £220. Their total debts were £151,700—that is, an average of £3,034 owing by each. This gives an insight into the extent to which speculation was rampant in the colony. "No care on the part of the Government"—wrote Grey—"could have prevented extensive insolvencies." Apart from a few fortunate investors, the lawyers, who "reaped a rich harvest from the rapid succession of conveyances", were the only class who benefited.

From the passing of the Act in June 1841 to September 1842, the total debts of the bankrupts were £168,467. The total assets realised were £1,079 7s 9d—an almost incredible figure; much less than one per cent of the total. The cost to the Government was fortunately as small as the amount realised, and the insolvency department paid its own way from the fees taken.[32]

With the passing of the crisis, business in insolvency fell off. The improvement in the financial condition of the colony is shown in the following figures of the numbers of fiats of insolvency granted from 1841 to 1844.

	1841	1842	1843	1844
Creditors petition	2	15	10	2
Debtors petitions	34	22	14	8
	36	37	24	10

A similar story is told in the figures as to the numbers of writs which passed through the hands of the Sheriff.[33]

1839	1840	1841	1842	1843	1844
47	154	140	136	82	46

One of the most extraordinary inmates of the debtors' prison was Richard Lyon Milne, an eccentric (to put it mildly) who for many years bombarded the Governor, Parliament and the press with fantastic schemes on every subject under the sun. In a letter to the Governor in June 1841 from the "Queen's Palace", as he called the "petty Bastille" where he was incarcerated, he poured forth a long tale of woe, concluding:

> 'To crown the tender mercies of the tyrannical democrats with which this Eldorado swarms, the solemn mockery of religion is added. A beast will not defile its lair; but the inmates of Her Majesty's Menagerie after being doomed to a segregation which sinks them lower than brutes, are called upon to attend prayers on the Sabbath. Reckoned lower than beasts six days of the week and men on the seventh!' [34]

Ulrich Hubbe (1805-1892)
Hubbe arrived in 1842 as one of Angas's German migrants. Land dealings in the Barossa led to his insolvency. But he recovered from this situation and went on to establish schools, teach and interpret, and play an active role in the Lutheran Church. More importantly, he played a vital role in the creation and passage of the Real Property Act.

Another prisoner of some note was Dr Ulrich Hubbe, who was confined for debt in June 1843 and went insolvent. His father having sent him £25 from Germany, his creditors consented to his retaining it for himself. The Official Assignee claimed it for payment of court fees. Hubbe petitioned the Governor to remit the fees, and the Judge recommended that this should be done. Governor Grey refused the request.

> 'To assent to such a repayment'—he said—'would be to establish a very dangerous precedent. It would be to say that the Law requires the Government to demand certain fees and payments, but that these will only be demanded from such persons as are not poor. The Government would thus have in every case to ascertain whether or not the person was so poor, as to be exempted from the operation of the law.' [35]

In April 1844 the Judge was relieved of his insolvency duties by the appointment of Mr Wigley as Commissioner of Insolvency and, from this time on, although the jurisdiction exercised was strictly that of the Supreme Court, the Insolvency Court became a separate court entirely.[36] Mr Wigley retired in 1856 and was succeeded as Commissioner by Mann.

By Act No 14 of 1857-58, legislative approval was given to what had in fact existed for many years, and a separate Court of Insolvency was created, with jurisdiction in all matters of insolvency, subject to an appeal to the Supreme Court. In forwarding this Act home, the Governor took the opportunity to urge that there should be imperial legislation on the subject.

> 'The general and rapidly increasing facilities of communication between the various distant portions of Her Majesty's dominions'—he wrote—'would seem to indicate the expediency, whilst they render practicable the policy, of aiming at a more complete unity of legislation than was formerly attainable, throughout those dominions. This applies to most of those portions of our civil and criminal law, which involve only general principles of Equity, and to which some great natural Moral Standard of right or wrong can be applied, unmodified by any peculiar local considerations.' [37]

The Secretary of State took objection to a provision in the Act which enabled the Court of Insolvency to compel an insolvent to convey to the Official Assignee any real property of which he was possessed in other parts of the world, and directed that this clause should be repealed.[38] An amending act was accordingly passed in 1859, which also provided that the Commissioner of Insolvency should hold office during good behaviour, subject to removal by the Governor upon the address of both Houses of Parliament.[39]

A ruling was given by the Attorney-General in 1858 that the Commissioner of Insolvency should be addressed by the title of "His Honour", in accordance with the practice in England.[40]

Mann held the office until his death in 1860. During the period he was Acting Judge in 1857, Mr Matthew Smith was Acting Commissioner, and Mr H.W. Parker also acted as Commissioner for a few months in 1860.[41] In the latter year, however, a consolidating Insolvency Act was passed, by which Mr J.W. MacDonald was

Henry Edward Downer (1836-1905)
Downer was also Member of the House of Assembly for Encounter Bay (1881-1896) and served as Attorney-General in 1890.

appointed Commissioner, with power to appoint a deputy in case of absence or illness. Under this power, Mr MacDonald in 1865, having met with a serious accident, appointed Mr Justice Gwynne to act for him, the Judge being a close friend.[42] Mr MacDonald died shortly afterwards, and the Government had considerable difficulty in finding anyone sufficiently experienced to replace him. The Attorney-General suggested that the Judges of the Supreme Court should act as Commissioners, with £200 a year each extra.[43] This was not acceptable to the Judges. Finally, Mr H.E. Downer, a young practitioner, was appointed. He had to face at first a considerable outcry on account of his youth and inexperience, but he survived it and held the position for fifteen years.[44]

Architect's drawing of the Customs House at Port Adelaide. The building was completed in 1861 and combined the Police Station, Customs House and the Local Court house. (SR/DAIS)

The Procedure of the Supreme Court

The Supreme Court Act of 1837 empowered the Judge to make Rules of Court to regulate forms and procedure. The first Rules were drawn up by Sir John Jeffcott and are dated 18 November 1837.[1] They provided:

(1) That the Supreme Court should be held "at and in the City of Adelaide" at times to be appointed.

(2) That "until further order all the business of the said Supreme Court in all its various branches shall be conducted in the office of the Judge for the present, but in its several and respective jurisdictions shall be commenced and continued in a distinct and separate form, and that all the paper writings delivered by the Attorneys or Solicitors for the purpose of being filed or used in any cause or proceeding depending or otherwise in the said Court shall be written in a clear legible hand and no paper shall be received unless the same is written as aforesaid".

(3) That the office hours should be from eleven to two.

(4) That all writs should be issued under the official seal, and that all affidavits should be sworn before the Judge.

(5) That the Sheriff or his under-Sheriff should personally attend the Court in all its sittings, and not depart without leave.

(6) That the business of the Court should be conducted by practitioners to be admitted by the Judge, "and who are individually to act in the several capacities of Barrister, Attorney, Solicitor, and Proctor".

(7) That the following should be admitted to practice until the last day of the next term when they and all others thereafter admitted would be required to conform to such rules as should be made in that behalf:

Henry Jickling, Barrister
Charles Mann and Henry Rodolph Wigley, Attorneys admitted in England
Charles Johnson, Attorney admitted in Dublin

(8) That there should be three terms in each year, consisting of fourteen days each.

(9) That the rules and orders, forms and manner of proceedings of the English courts should apply so far as possible; but in any case of hardship the Judge might dispense with any English rule of practice.

With only a few minor amendments and additions, these Rules regulated the procedure of the Court until 1850.

On his arrival in the colony, Mr Justice Cooper framed a Rule of Court to provide for the holding of a Court of Oyer and Terminer and Gaol Delivery in May, July and November 1839, and in every succeeding year on the second day of each term and at such other times as the Court might appoint, and in May 1844 he divided the legal year into four terms instead of three.[2]

In a report to the Governor on the Court's procedure in January 1847 he wrote:

> 'So far as respects the Common Law jurisdiction of the Court, I have found that the rules and manner of proceeding of the Superior Courts at Westminster have been generally sufficient guides in the practice of the Supreme Court; and the general adoption of them has at least this advantage that it gives the Judge and practitioners of the Court the advantage of referring to the English books of Reports and of practice. I have therefore made such rules only as experience from time to time has shown to be necessary.' [3]

On the equity side there had been little business, but it had been very difficult to follow the English Chancery practice. Suits in equity seemed to be on the increase, and in *Tilt v. Rutland*, in January 1848, the Judge said that it would be necessary for him to settle some rules to provide for them. He had sent for books of practice and copies of the rules in force in England, and he would either adopt these generally or draft from them "a brief and useful set of local rules".[4]

A copy of the existing Rules of Court was sent home by the Governor.

> 'These Rules and Orders'—said the Secretary of State in reply—'embrace a large variety of questions to the just appreciation of which a corresponding extent of minute local information is indispensable. They are questions on which it is of the utmost importance that no conflict of opinion or collision of authority should arise between the Court and the local Legislature.'

Henry George, (3rd Earl Grey)
(1802-1894)
Colonial Secretary from 1846 to 1852

Hence the practice had been established that such rules should be submitted to the local legislature for confirmation and were not to be of force unless so confirmed. "Before this practice was established the Courts of Justice exercised a kind of legislative power of which the limits were ill-defined and the results not seldom inconvenient."

The Governor was therefore directed to propose an act to the Legislative Council to render the validity of Rules of Court made and to be made dependent on confirmation by the Council.[5] He accordingly asked the Judge to make such alterations of the Rules as he might think fit, as a preliminary to the introduction into the Legislative Council of an ordinance in pursuance of these instructions.[6] The Judge agreed, but did nothing, and the Ordinance was introduced and passed (No 5 of 1848) providing that the Rules then in force should continue until 1 September 1849, after which date their validity was to depend on their ratification by the Legislative Council.

Illness prevented the Judge from revising the Rules before the date fixed by the Ordinance, and he asked the Governor to introduce a short ordinance further continuing the time within which the existing Rules were to be in force. The Advocate-General recommended that this course should be adopted, rather than that the Rules should be confirmed in what might be found to be an imperfect state, and he suggested that they should be printed for the information of the profession—a suggestion with which the Governor agreed.[7] By Ordinance No 10 of 1849 the Rules of Court were continued in force until 1 March 1850, when they were to cease to have effect unless previously confirmed.

New Rules were framed by the Judge in 1850, replacing those made by Jeffcott.

> 'These rules'-he wrote-'do not in themselves form a complete system of practice, nor do I conceive it necessary that they should do so, because it is provided by the third rule that the English rules of practice of the superior courts at Westminster shall be adopted so far as the circumstances of the colony will permit and so far as they are not at variance with the expressed rules of the court or with any local ordinance. I conceive it to be very desirable to adopt the English practice generally because it gives the Judge and practitioners of this Court the advantage of the English books of practice and reports. This advantage can hardly be over-estimated.' [8]

Mr Smillie, the Advocate-General, in an article published in the *Law Review*, had dealt with some of the difficulties of practice in colonial courts.

> 'It might be supposed'—he wrote—'that a fairer opportunity for simplifying cumbrous and inapplicable forms could hardly be offered. Not certainly on the principle of 'Fiat experimentum in corpore vili', but because time has not yet reared on the spot a structure of vested interests to oppose improvement, nor can there be any conflict of rival authority, where all power is in the same undivided hands, and because there is a mixed population actively engaged, more inclined to get through business readily, than to go a roundabout way from excessive deference to legal antiquities. In such favorable circumstances no doubt considerable relaxation has already been achieved to disarm the terrors of sharp practice. Yet it is often disconcerting to see how many difficulties arise, and how frequently parties are turned round on mere points of practice. In the absence of consolidated rules of procedure ... where no

> express provision can be pointed to, the question always recurs, "What is the practice at home?", and litigants and lawyers are alike launched on a sea of doubts all the wider and more perilous by its involving the moot points of all the Courts of England.'[9]

The Rules of 1850 provided that the business of the Court should be carried on at the courthouse in Waymouth Street, until the courthouse then in course of building (the present Police Court) was ready for occupation. Little attempt was made to lay down any new local procedure, the English Rules (as has been mentioned) applying generally so far as circumstances admitted. The Judge had power to dispense with any English rule in case of hardship. There were to be four terms, and Civil and Criminal Sessions were each to be held four times a year. These Rules were in due course confirmed by Ordinance No 2 of 1850.

No improvements had been made in equity procedure, which remained obscure and haphazard. In August 1850 the Judge announced that he would not willingly introduce all the tortuous English Chancery practice into the Supreme Court, and that he would deal leniently with deviations from strict English practice.[10] He was still toying with the idea of framing rules to simplify equity practice and had postponed doing so until the arrival of Mr Justice Crawford. That gentleman was a more energetic reformer than his older colleague, and within three months of his arrival in the colony a bill to regulate proceedings in equity had been drafted, modelled on a recent Irish statute, with forms copied from English practice. This combination of the English and Irish system the judges thought the best that could be devised as an experiment in reform.[11] This Bill was introduced into the Legislative Council, but allowed to lapse on account of expected semi-revolutionary reforms in Chancery practice in England, and a draft bill for the consolidating and amendment of the various Supreme Court Acts, submitted by the Judges in November 1852, was also shelved.[12]

The influence of that great period of law reform in England, which began in 1850, was now being felt in the colony. In October 1852 the Legislative Council resolved on an address to the Governor recommending him to appoint a commission to inquire into the present law of the province, with a view to the introduction of reformatory additions and alterations.[13] The proposal met with general public support, and it was suggested that the commission should communicate and cooperate with the other colonies.

> 'It is certain'—said the Register—'that on no other subject could all the colonies more cordially join than on a proposed investigation of the laws which have been hastily adopted from the mother-country, and are frequently most inapplicable to our state ... When we contemplate the wide and extensive

prospect opened out to our view by the Law Commission, we observe a region abiding in thorns and brambles, such as in former days grew up, stubborn and obstructive, in the luxuriant soil of England until the gentle hand of the law reformer partially removed these time-honoured impediments to improvement ... If the Commissioners succeed in presenting to us a well digested and skilfully arranged code of Statute law, the gratitude of the present generation, and of future colonists for centuries to come, will be their meed. Then may each of our benefactors exclaim—"exegi monumentum aere perennius". In what mode this enduring monument is to be constructed, remains the subject of future anxious and deliberate consideration.' [14]

The Governor had no intention of appointing "a vague and costly commission" which the colony could not afford; but although he did not think it expedient to accede to the Legislative Council's request, he asked Mr Justice Cooper and the law officers to report any plans or suggestions of reform which they might think desirable. In particular, he asked them to consider:

> '... the expediency of abolishing the technical forms which distinguish Equity from Law, and of providing for the fusion of Law and Equity into one and the same system and mode of procedure; the Court in Equity deciding the questions before it, without the delays and costs of reference to the Master, and the Court in Common Law exercising its jurisdiction as freed from antiquated forms and technicalities, as are now the County Courts in England'.

He hoped it would be possible in South Australia:

> '... during its infancy, and consequently before the prescription of age and usage shall be pleaded against reforms'—to become free of the expense, delays, and technicalities of England—'and that here we will be able to do what they would fain do in England—make the language of litigation as the language used in the public and private business of ordinary life, and as open to the comprehension of clients, as it ought to be to their advocates, although the latter must necessarily continue to be the agents for procuring for individuals the benefit of the law. In proportion as cheap and speedy justice is obtainable from the Supreme Court of the Colony, will the desire to confer jurisdiction on inferior courts of unprofessional Judges diminish, and there can be no doubt that the Supreme Court with professional Judges and a learned Bar will be always

> preferred by the Public, provided its processes be simplified and cheapened to the level of the inferior courts now becoming so popular.'

A consolidation or codification of the laws of the province, he thought, might perhaps be opportunely entered upon after the receipt of these reports.[15]

Both the Judge and the law officers slept on the matter for six months, but in May 1853, after a reminder from the Governor, the Advocate-General (Mr Hanson) sent in a lengthy report. The division of the Court into legal and equitable sides seemed to him to be "indefensible in principle and cumbrous and inconvenient in practice".

> 'It is difficult to imagine that a system can be either wise or just under which the same individual acting as Judge in the same Court at the same time and in reference to the same subject-matter applies a different rule according as the proceedings before him are or are not entitled "Equitable jurisdiction". Either the rules of equity or those of law should prevail, and at any rate the practical absurdity should no longer be permitted to exist of allowing one party to enforce a claim or the other to avail himself of a defence on one side of the Court of which the same Judge sitting upon the other side restrains him by injunction from reaping the fruit. I think, therefore, that one principal object of legislation as regards procedure should be to abolish the distinction between courts of law and equity, substituting for the two inconsistent and conflicting rules which at present exist one rule which shall be enforced in the same Court and by the same method of proceeding. If this step be taken, then it would be important to simplify the form of procedure. The success of a party, plaintiff or defendant, depends at present upon many points beside the real merits of the case. His lawyer may in the opinion of the Judge have mistaken the form of action or he may have stated his case in a manner which the Judge imagines is not borne out by the evidence, and in either case he may be defeated though his right to a verdict upon the real facts of the case is undoubted even by the Judge himself, and would if the matter were untrammelled by technical considerations be practically recognized. Add to this that the proceedings are needlessly complicated and protracted.'

As a remedy Mr Hanson suggested a form of procedure analogous to that of the Local Courts, though with some alteration. Actions would be commenced by a summons accompanied by a complete but untechnical statement of the plaintiff's claim or demand, the defendant being required to appear on a given day before an officer of the Court to be appointed for that purpose. It would then be the duty of this officer to make up the issue from the viva voce allegations of the respective parties, and in accordance with rules to be prescribed by the Judge for securing the materiality of the points put in issue. If the issue was a question of fact, or so far as it was a question of fact, it should be tried by a jury or perhaps by three assessors under the direction of a judge, giving either party, however, the right of demanding a jury. If it was a question of law, then it would be decided by the Court, which would give judgment according to the respective rights of the parties upon the facts admitted by the record or proved in evidence. There should be ample powers of amendment and of reference either to an officer of the Court or to other parties.[16]

The Judge in his report referred to the recent remedial statutes in England—the Common Law Procedure Act and the Chancery Amendment Act of 1852—which he hoped to see adopted as soon as possible in the colony.

> 'It appears to me'—he said—'very desirable for a colony to avail itself as much as possible of the improvements made from time to time in the mother country. These improvements are in England prepared by able lawyers well versed in the several branches of the law to which they have devoted themselves, and they are discussed in the two Houses of Parliament by learned and practical men. The laws of the colony are founded on those of England, and there is irrespective of their excellence one especial advantage in retaining them and adopting the English improvements as far as possible, that the opinions of the learned Judges of England thereon become authorities and guides to the colonial Judges.'

With regard to improving proceedings at law, in South Australia as in England on trials of actions, questions of fact were for the jury and questions of law for the Judge.

> 'I conceive it will be necessary to continue this method of trial, unless the whole system of pleading be altered. Without venturing to discuss the advantages of this system of trial at length, I may observe that it obliges the presiding Judge in every case to call the attention of the jury to all the leading facts and to express openly his opinion upon the law bearing upon them, whilst the jury generally deal with the facts of the case according to the dictates of plain good sense. I cannot say that this is always the case—sometimes they appear to act under some bias caused perhaps by a knowledge of the parties

> or by the influence of popular feeling. This is an evil which it is impossible entirely to remedy in a small community, and the instances in which I have observed its presence are not numerous.'

Despite its defects, the Judge thought, trial by jury was still the best system that existed, and it had the collateral advantage that:

> '... it causes a large portion of the community to take a part and an interest in the administration of justice, and thereby to acquire a knowledge of and a respect for the law, which is unknown where trial by jury does not exist'.

Trial by jury in the early digging days, an 1886 engraving that depicts community interest in the administration of justice operating through the jury system. Whether the jurors had much respect for the law is open to question. (SLV)

He did not consider it necessary, however, that there should always be a jury of twelve. In civil cases four or six would do as well, and the state of the colony required a diminution, owing to the numbers of persons who had left the colony. The Sheriff had great difficulty in finding the requisite number required for jury panels, and there would be considerable relief in this respect if the number necessary to serve on the jury was reduced. He suggested the introduction of the system in force in New South Wales, of a jury of four in civil cases, with leave to either party to call for a jury of twelve. If after six hours the jury were not unanimous, three-quarters could give a verdict; but if three-quarters could not agree, the jury might be discharged.[17]

In his opening speech to the Legislative Council at the beginning of the session 1853-54, the Governor said:

> 'Although I did not deem it expedient to comply with the recommendation of the Council for the appointment of a commission, with a view to the general amendment and codification of the law, believing such measure to be at the least premature until the result of the corresponding enquiries instituted in England shall have been made public, I have not been unmindful of the importance of some legislation upon this subject. I have with this object directed to be laid before you a Bill for the more effectual administration of justice by means of the Supreme Court, founded for the most part upon an Imperial Statute of last year.' [18]

A bill based on the Common Law Procedure Act of 1852 was accordingly introduced and passed with little opposition (No 5 of 1853). It introduced one provision not in the English Act—it enabled a defendant to plead an equitable defence in a court of law. Hesitation was expressed by a few members at the colonial parliament thus going ahead of England, but the Advocate-General said the provision had been introduced by him because he wished to put an end "to the anomaly and absurdity of the present system, whereby the same Judge decided the same case on two different principles, according as his face was turned in the legal or equitable direction".[19]

> 'I am glad to find'—said Mr Gwynne—'that the cobwebs of antiquity in legal matters are to be swept away, and the proceedings in Courts of law adapted to the measure of common sense. I congratulate the profession on getting rid of their ancient friends, Richard Roe and John Doe, and all the antiquated rubbish that impeded the high road to justice.' [20]

Mr Gwynne called attention, however, to the system of equity in vogue in the colony—"nothing was more monstrous", he said. Following up this criticism, Mr Fisher a few days later moved that an address should be presented to the Governor, representing the necessity for a legislative measure to simplify and regulate proceedings in equity. The equity rules so long ago promised by Mr Justice Cooper had never been forthcoming. In defence of the Judge, Mr Waterhouse said that no doubt the rules had not been made because of the Judge's time being occupied with professional duties.[21] This remark led to a long and critical letter to the *Register* from a person who signed himself "Aliquis".[22]

> 'So far from its being the fact'—said this writer—'that His Honor's time is wholly absorbed in professional avocations, I venture to assert without fear of contradiction, just the contrary is the truth; and I will say further, that there is no individual in this colony, whether in or out of office, whose

> income is earned more easily than Judge Cooper's. His labours on the Common Law side of his Court are the lightest imaginable; and indeed how can they be otherwise when the whole business of litigation is at present handed over to the Local Courts?'

Civil causes took up about twenty days a year, criminal causes about the same, and business at chambers was negligible. So far as chamber work was concerned:

> 'His Honor attends three times a week; frequently there is hardly anything for him to do, and when there is anything, it may generally be transacted in an hour at the utmost. If one were not speaking of so dignified a person, one would be disposed to say that the exercise required of him in his judicial duties is not more than sufficient to keep him in health.'

Stimulated by these proceedings, the Judge prepared and forwarded a draft bill for the amendment of proceedings in equity, adopting the recent improvements made in England. "I have no doubt"—he wrote—"that its effect will be very beneficial." [23] Mr Justice Boothby concurred[24] and it was passed in December 1853 (Act No 14 of 1853). "I confess"—said Mr Hanson, when moving the second reading of the Bill—"that I despair of seeing any very great improvement being effected in the procedure in equity at the Supreme Court." [25]

Early in 1854 a meeting of the legal profession was called to assist the Judges in framing new Rules under the acts passed in 1853, so that the proceedings might be simplified to the greatest possible extent, "without ruinously reducing the emoluments of the gentleman of the long robe".[26] The new Rules came into force in February 1854, and equity rules followed shortly afterwards.[27]

A bill to consolidate the various ordinances relating to the Supreme Court had been prepared in November 1853, but it was not introduced into the Legislative Council until August 1854. It met with a very hostile reception, and was said to contain inaccuracies in every line. The Advocate-General hastened to give the Judges the credit for drawing the Bill and, as the opinion of the House was so definitely expressed, he withdrew the Bill to save it being thrown out.[28]

Interest in law reform continued strong, and the press diligently urged upon the Government the necessity of adapting the jurisprudence of the colony to the new phases and conditions of social life.

> 'Under the old regime'—said the Register—'law was a thing of precedent, and quibbles upon terms, of constructions and objections, of facts outraged and technicalities made paramount, of horsehair and etiquette; of dry routine and dull pomp. Law was dreadful, occult, voracious. The gloomiest

> region best suited the barrister's chamber; and the seat of justice recalled the Inferno of the poet ... In consolidating the social order of a new community, and in properly arranging the multifarious liabilities of so much newly acquired property, there will long continue in this province a noble sphere for the energies of a profession many of whose members constitute the brightest adornments of our national history.' [29]

The consolidating Supreme Court Bill was reintroduced in 1855 in an amended form, and this time passed the House without much opposition (No 31 of 1855-56). During the same session the Supreme Court Procedure Amendment Act (No 24 of 1855-56) was passed, giving the Court power to direct arbitration before trial, to try questions of fact submitted by consent of the parties, and to hear and determine cases stated.

For several years the only important alteration in Supreme Court procedure was the repeal of sections 182 and 183 of the Supreme Court Procedure Act of 1854, which was brought about by the anti-Boothby agitation.[30] The Supreme Court was far from giving satisfaction, however. Some of the criticisms of it have been referred to in the chapter dealing with Mr Justice Boothby, and to these may be added a statement by Mr Mildred in the House of Assembly in May 1860:

Henry Mildred (1795-1877) A farmer and miller, Mildred was an early colonist who arrived in 1837 to work for the South Australian Company. He later became the Commissioner of Main Roads, a Special Magistrate and a Member of the House of Assembly (1857-65) and the Legislative Council (1866-73).

> 'The very heavy expenses connected with trials in the Supreme Court have long been a matter of complaint, and it has been remarked that new trials are frequently granted, and under many circumstances these are brought about by what gentlemen of the legal profession describe as misdirection to the Jury by the Judge, or that the Judge has not summed up according to the evidence. In some instances no doubt this is to be attributed to the character of the Jury system of the present day, but the Supreme Court has for many years been regarded as a sort of Pandora's box with hope at the bottom, but constant disappointment in the interim.' [31]

The Attorney-General (Mr Stow) promised a measure to simplify the proceedings in the Supreme Court, and a bill to amend the Supreme Court Procedure Act was introduced in May 1862. The principal points of this Bill, which was based on Imperial legislation, were:

(a) the regulation of interpleader proceedings;
(b) the giving of power to the Court to give relief by a summary process against forfeiture for non-payment of rent or non-insuring;
(c) joinder of too many plaintiffs was no longer fatal to an action, but judgment might be given in favour of such plaintiffs as were entitled to recover.[32]

Later in the same session a bill was brought forward by Mr Boucaut to improve equity procedure by enabling the judges to hear evidence in any suit on the equity side, thus saving the expense and inconvenience attending the old practice of taking the evidence before a master and reducing it into writing. Both Acts were passed without opposition.[33]

No further amendments of substance were made until 1866. In April of that year Mr Charles Mann junior, who had been employed by the Government drafting bills, wrote to the Attorney-General suggesting the preparation of a comprehensive measure revising and consolidating the law relating to the jurisdiction and procedure of the Supreme Court, nearly every branch of which, he said, required amendment.[34] Mr Boucaut, the then Attorney-General, did not think it expedient to go so far as asked by Mr Mann, but during the year he introduced a series of amending measures—relating to matrimonial and testamentary causes, lunacy, revenue jurisdiction and equity jurisdiction—which made extensive reforms.

In the Equity Act of 1866 provision was made for the appointment of a Primary Judge in Equity.[35] It was thought that probably in time one judge would devote his attention to common law matters, one to equity and the third to probate and matrimonial jurisdiction, while the three judges together would form a Court of Appeal.[36] Owing to trouble with Mr Justice Boothby, no appointment of a primary judge could be made until 1867, when the position was allotted to Mr Justice Gwynne.[37]

It will be convenient, before leaving this branch, to give some account of trial by jury in South Australia, which was the only Australian colony to enjoy from its earliest days the full right of trial by jury as known to the law of England. The Act 7 Wm IV No 2 passed on 2 January 1837, provided that no person should be qualified to serve upon the grand or petit jury unless he was between the ages of 21 and 60, and was possessed of real estate to the value of £50 or personal property to the value of £100. A more extensive act was passed in November 1837 (1 Vic No 1) which regulated the preparation and revision of jury lists by the justices of the province, from which lists jurors were to be summoned in turn by the Sheriff. All issues of fact, whether in civil or criminal proceedings, were to be tried and damages assessed by a jury of twelve. In civil cases parties could apply for a special jury if they wished. Special jurors comprised those described in the jury lists "as an esquire or person of higher degree, or as a Justice of the Peace, or as a merchant (such merchant not keeping a general retail shop) or as a Bank Director", or possessing real estate of the value of £500 or personal estate of the value of £1,000. They received one guinea for each case they heard. Common jurors were less fortunate; they received only one shilling for every jury on which they were actually called to sit. Their qualifications were those already mentioned as prescribed by the Act 7 Wm IV No 2. Section XXXII of the Act 1 Vic No 1 provided:

> 'No person shall be put on trial on any indictment at any criminal sessions of the Supreme Court unless the bill of such indictment shall first have been presented to a Grand Jury and shall have been returned by them a true Bill.'

The Grand Jury was to consist of not more than twenty three men nor less than thirteen, between the ages of 21 and 60, and of good fame and condition.

It can hardly be said that the jury system worked very satisfactorily. The lists were inefficiently compiled and service on the jury was often evaded. In January 1839, out of a population of some 5,000, only 102 men could be found fit to be put on the list of special jurors, and 113 on the list of common jurors—figures which indicate radical errors somewhere. In some cases the lists gave no Christian names, but as there was no requirement in the Act that names should be given, many refused to give them when asked.[38]

No provision had been made in the Jury Acts for any exemptions from service, and by the Act 3 Vic No 10 an attempt was made to amend some defects of the earlier acts and to provide that those classes of persons exempted in England should also be exempt in South Australia. This amending Act, however, was disallowed. In 1843 another try was made at amendment by the Act 6 and 7 Vic No 12, which contained a general provision that trials by jury in South Australia, whether in civil or criminal proceedings, should be subject to the same incidents and rules of proceedings as were observed upon trials by jury before the judges of the superior courts of record in England. In forwarding this Act home, Governor Grey wrote that the Act 1 Vic No 1 was "faulty in many respects and positively incorrect in some". No record copy of it had been kept and it was therefore impossible to ascertain whether the errors were errors on the part of the printer or errors in the original enactment.

> 'Subsequently to my arrival in the Province'—he said—'it was discovered in Your Lordship's Department that none of the colonial enactments for the first year of her present Majesty had been transmitted for the purpose of being laid before the Queen. Her Majesty's pleasure had therefore never been taken upon this Act.'

The earlier act had contained a provision that after recovering any debt or damages in the Supreme Court the successful party should pay the Court two per cent on the amount received. This proved inoperative because after parties obtained a verdict they came to private arrangements with the defendant, and judgment was not entered up. Payment of the percentage was thus in most cases evaded.[39]

The police were required to serve summonses on common jurors, while the Sheriff had to arrange for the attendances of special jurors. In 1844 the Sheriff tried to throw upon the police the duty of summoning special jurors, but the Commissioner of Police objected that his men were already fully employed. The service of summonses on 48 individuals residing over every part of the colony, as often as it might become the interest of litigants to require special juries, would be attended, he said, with "great wear and tear on horses", and would occupy too much time, especially as the police would have to attend at court to prove service if those summoned did not attend.

> 'I am by no means satisfied'—commented the Governor—'that it is desirable to encourage the practice of applying for special juries by the Government defraying the greater portion of the expense of such a proceeding.' [40]

As settlers spread out into the country, it became more and more irksome for them to come long distances, without remuneration, to spend days or perhaps weeks in Adelaide in attendance on the Court. It was also increasingly difficult for the Sheriff and the police to find them and to serve them with precepts to attend as jurors.

To compel a country settler to serve on a jury at Adelaide was in most cases to impose a very severe punishment on him. Sidney Smith had many years earlier in his inimitable style put the objections to trial by jury in a new colony. The colonists, he wrote in his essay on Botany Bay:

> '... are too young, too few, and too deficient for such civilized machinery at present. "I cannot come to serve upon the jury—the waters of the Hawksbury [sic] are out, and I have a mile to swim—the kangaroos will break into my corn—the convicts have robbed me—my little boy has been bitten by an ornithorynchus [sic] paradoxus—I have sent a man fifty miles with a sack of flour to buy a pair of breeches for the assizes, and he is not returned." These are the excuses which, in new colonies, always prevent Trial by Jury; and make it desirable, for the first half century of their existence, that they should live under the simplicity and convenience of despotism.'

George Charles Hawker (1818-1895)
Hawker is best remembered as a successful pioneer grazier of the Barossa Valley and the Mid North. He was also a long serving Member of the House of Assembly. (SLSA)

In similar fashion Mr Justice Cooper wrote of the farmers of South Australia:

> 'They are altogether of a different class from the country gentlemen of England who come half-yearly to the Assizes, and to whom an absence from home of two or three days is seldom a matter of great inconvenience. Here a settler would often find it better to submit to a fine than to leave his sowing or harvest or shearing.' [41]

As an instance may be cited a memorial presented to the Governor in 1844 by Mr G.C. Hawker and fourteen others, who all lived seventy to one hundred and twenty miles from Adelaide, begging to be relieved of the harassing and expensive duties of jury service. When summoned to sit on a Grand Jury, they complained, they were compelled to be absent from their homes for eight to fourteen days and, when required for a special jury, the period might be longer.[42]

S.T. Gill's *December* depicts farmhands at work during harvest time. (NLA)

When on one occasion the Judge fined a number of jurors for non-attendance, the *Observer* remarked that it was not before it was necessary.

> 'Indifference had reached such a pitch that many persons actually treated a summons as a matter of no importance. It was no unusual thing to reply to the serving officer, with a laugh, "Oh, there'll be enough without me." The result was that those who attended had double duty to do, while those who chose to do so, evaded the annoyance altogether.' [43]

But even when the jurymen were got to court, matters were scarcely improved. In one case a man in the dock on a criminal charge was acquitted and, within an hour, he was serving on a jury on the trial of another case—illustrating, no doubt, Angelo's dictum in *Measure for Measure* that "the jury may, in the sworn twelve, have a thief or two guiltier than him they try".[44] In another case, the *Observer* wrote that the jury requested leave to withdraw to consider their verdict.

> 'They were accordingly locked up; but as they were not denied candle our reporter caught a glimpse of the locus in quo at a

> late hour last evening. Mr Bulpitt (from whom a pocket pistol had been taken by an officer of the Court) was looking more than usually solemn; and whilst several jurymen were laying down the law, two or three were laying down their heads upon the table, and some others were smoking snuffing or chewing the cud. At length a surreptitious message being conveyed to them that the Judge was on the eve of retiring for the night, they grew unanimous at once, and returned a verdict of 'Not Guilty', which was received with no small satisfaction by the prisoner's friends.' [45]

The standard of intelligence of some of the jurors may be measured by a rule laid down by Mr Justice Crawford in June 1851 that only those who could read would be permitted to sit in the jury box; a precaution which was shortly afterwards shown not to be unnecessary, when the foreman of a jury announced that they found a verdict for the "affidavit", which was construed to mean the plaintiff. [46]

In 1847 Governor Robe contemplated some alterations in the jury law, but, rendered cautious by previous disallowals of acts, he sent home a draft of his proposed measure for consideration. The Secretary of State refused to discuss it. Legislation, he said, ought to be initiated in the colony and would then be considered by the Queen's advisers. Exceptions to this rule might occur where uniformity of proceedings throughout the colonies, or a number of them, was desirable. "But Jury Trial is not such a subject. It admits and even requires, much flexibility in the treatment of it, according to the varying circumstances of different colonies." [47]

Mr Justice Crawford was largely responsible for the abolition of the Grand Jury. An act passed in 1842 to abolish the Grand Jury had been promptly disallowed as being repugnant to the law of England.

> 'But the local authorities persevered. In 1843 they pushed aside, without abolishing, Grand Juries, by an ordinance which ordered that 'no person should be put upon trial ... unless the bill shall first have been presented to a Grand Jury on the prosecution of her Majesty's Attorney or Advocate General and shall have been returned by them a true bill, reserving always nevertheless to her Majesty's Attorney or Advocate General the right of filing informations ex officio, and to the Supreme Court the right of permitting informations to be filed'.' [48]

At the Criminal Sessions in February 1852 Mr Justice Crawford launched an attack on the Grand Jury system, which he said was very generally considered useless.

> 'It was advantageously dispensed with in the other colonies,

and it may be worth consideration whether it would not be desirable to petition the Legislative Council to abolish it here also.' [49]

In accordance with this suggestion, the Grand Jury prepared a petition to the Council. Mr Justice Cooper, at the criminal sittings in May 1852, supported his colleague. The difficulty the Sheriff experienced in getting the Grand Jury together, he thought, showed that some reform was needed, and he considered the Grand Jury might safely be done away with, although he was not prepared to admit that it was wholly useless. The system did spread a knowledge of the law and court procedure.[50]

Mr Justice Crawford gave a further push to the abolition movement at the August sessions,[51] and in November by Act No 10 of 1852, grand juries were done away with. In their place was substituted the information of the Advocate or Attorney-General. This measure did not meet with unqualified approval. For many years attempts were made to have it repealed. In the Legislative Council in 1857, for instance, Mr Gwynne advocated the restoration of the Grand Jury,[52] and in 1859 Mr Mildred moved in the Assembly for leave to bring in a bill to repeal Act No 10 of 1852. He was induced to bring the motion forward, he said: "... in consequence of having observed for a long time past the very unsatisfactory manner in which trial by jury has been conducted in South Australia".

He objected to the absence of any stepping stone between committal by a Justice of the Peace and placing the accused in the dock.

John Bentham Neales (1806-1873)
Raised by his uncle, the famous political philosopher Jeremy Bentham, Neales arrived in Adelaide in 1838 and launched into business. He was an entertaining and successful auctioneer, profited from shares in the Glen Osmond, Montacute and Burra mines and had a long political career. (SLSA)

> 'In England the magistrates are formed of different material from what they are in this colony, where there are such limited means of selection. Some of the Justices in this colony have been shepherds who can scarcely write their own names, yet the liberty, character and honor of their fellow-men is placed in their hands.' [53]

The motion, however, was strongly opposed and had to be withdrawn. "Crablike legislation would never do for this country'—said Mr Neales—'and this measure if passed would not be one but two steps backward." [54]

> 'In my opinion'—Sir Charles Cooper wrote to the Chief Secretary—'trial of offences upon an information by the Attorney General preceded by a magisterial inquiry is better suited to the state of this Colony than trial upon an indictment found by a Grand Jury.' [55]

With this opinion may be compared that of a great Victorian judge upon the same question:

> 'Without entering into any arguments respecting the relative

> merits of these two modes of initiatory scrutiny'—said Sir Redmond Barry—'an experience of several years satisfies me that, irrespective of other considerations, the system which obtains with us is that best adapted to the circumstances of a country in which the population is in some districts thinly distributed, and where it would be exceedingly difficult to assemble a sufficient number of persons qualified and competent to act as Grand and Petty Jurors.' [56]

The position of a juryman was not one to be coveted. It was no uncommon thing for members of a jury, if they disagreed, to be locked up in the jury room all night with nothing to eat. On one occasion a juror wanted to send for an overcoat to keep him warm while sitting up in this fashion; Mr Justice Boothby was scandalised at the request and threatened him with instant committal for contempt if he delayed entering the jury room.[57] In return for their services, special jurors still received £1 1s 0d per case and common jurors the magnificent remuneration of one shilling a case.[58] A proposal in Parliament in 1860 that jurors should be paid fell through on account of expense. The Attorney-General said that payment at six shillings a day and sixpence a mile for travelling expenses would run the Government into an outlay of £2,000, which could not be afforded.[59] Sir Charles Cooper did his best to get payment for jurors.

> 'The property qualification for jurors is very small'—he wrote to the Chief Secretary—'and brings within it persons of a very low station in life—little farmers cultivating their own land, and labourers, whose absence from home involves the loss not only of time but of the means of earning subsistence for themselves and families.'

All jurymen, he urged, should be paid at a fixed rate per day and, to lessen the expense, common juries in civil cases should be composed of four men, while a limited circle should be drawn round Adelaide, beyond which jurors should not be summoned.[60]

Nothing was done until 1862 when by Act No 1 of that year, all jurymen in civil cases were given ten shillings a day for every day on which they should be "present and punctual in their attendance". Many aspired to be special jurors who were not really possessed of the necessary property qualifications.

> 'It was difficult to imagine'—said the Chief Secretary—'how these persons valued their personal property so high as £1,000 unless they reckoned their wives and children.' [61]

A fund for payment of the jurors was raised by levying fees from the suitors.

A motion that jurors in criminal cases should be paid was defeated.

> 'Every man summoned as a juror on such cases'—it was said—'should hold it to be equally his duty to himself and to the community to attend and give his services for the good of the country.'

The Government agreed, however, to pay jurors sixpence a mile for travelling expenses, and to pay witnesses 3s 6d per day.[62] In 1865 the Government decided to pay jurors in criminal cases 3s 6d a day, like the witnesses. When the matter was being discussed in Parliament, some members suggested that 3s 6d a day was too little, but Mr Boucaut having uttered a direful warning that if too high a payment was fixed the Justices of the Peace would be given an increased jurisdiction to lessen the number of trials in the criminal court, the opposition was hastily abandoned.[63]

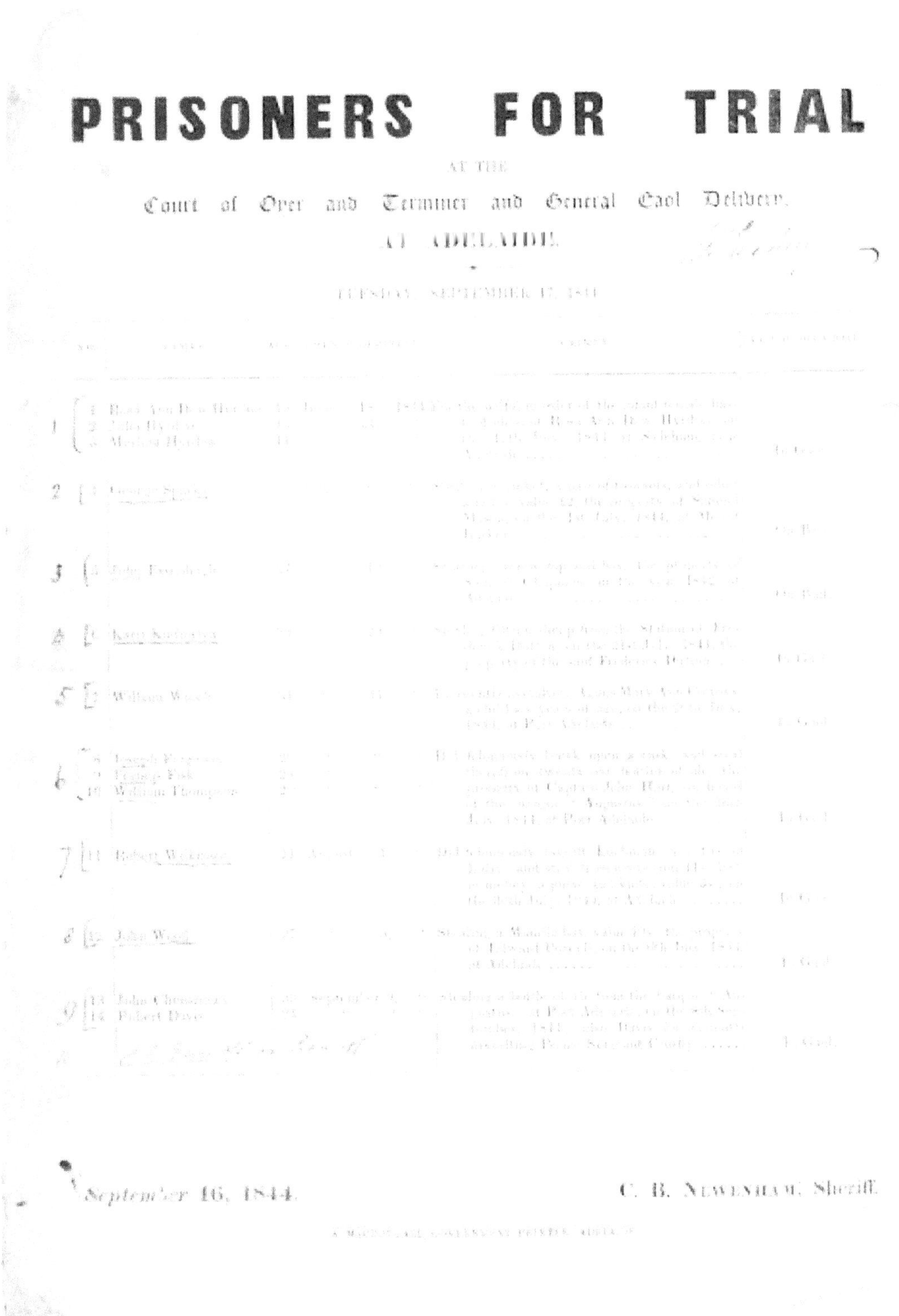

PRISONERS FOR TRIAL

AT THE

Court of Oyer and Terminer and General Gaol Delivery,

AT ADELAIDE.

TUESDAY, SEPTEMBER 17, 1844.

September 16, 1844.

C. B. Newenham, Sheriff.

Criminal cause list 1844 (SCLSA))

By the Supreme Court Act of 1837 it was provided that the Court should have such ministerial and other officers as might be necessary for the administration of justice in the Court, and for the due execution of its judgments, decrees, orders and processes. The numbers, names, duties and salaries of such officers were from time to time to be fixed by the Judge, with the consent of the Governor in Council, and the appointment and removal of officers was vested in the Judge.

Until 1844 the only officers of the Court were the Sheriff, the Clerk and a messenger.

The first Sheriff was Samuel Smart, who has already been mentioned as having been admitted as a practitioner of the Court at the first Criminal Sessions held by Jeffcott in May 1837.[1] He was a solicitor who had accompanied Jeffcott to Adelaide from Van Diemen's Land. Fisher described him as "a very clever and gentlemanly man".[2] He was appointed Clerk of Arraigns and Sheriff for a year; according to Loyau "to facilitate the arrest of several Vandemonian convicts who had escaped to this colony and committed outrages, and who were known to Smart".[3] For his services at the first Criminal Sessions, Mr Smart received £20, but it does not appear whether he had any other salary.[4] He was apparently a close friend of Sir John Jeffcott, and went back to Van Diemen's Land with him for two months in 1837.[5] The most exciting experience of his term of office was the attempt made to murder him by Magee and two other ruffians who entered his cottage one night and fired a gun at him from the door. The distance was only a few feet but the bullet missed him, merely singeing his ear and leaving powder marks on his face. The men escaped into the darkness but he had recognised them, and next day volunteers were sworn in by the Governor to pursue them. Two were captured, and their trial before Jickling has already been referred to. One was hung and the other transported. The execution proved a ghastly spectacle. There was no executioner, and up to the morning of the execution the Sheriff had not been able to find anyone to undertake the duty. He was almost distracted with the fear that he would have to do the hanging himself which, as he was the person whose life had been attempted, would have been particularly unseemly. On the morning of the execution, a crowd gathered at the appointed spot—a gum tree on the parklands near Montefiore Hill. The marines were marched up and formed a guard; the prisoner was brought up in a cart, and the executioner then rode up on horseback, a grotesque figure masked and disguised by padding on his back and chest in order to avoid recognition.

'With one filthy hand the monster greased the rope, and the

> cap was adjusted over the prisoner's face, the noose set about his neck, and at the flick of the whip, the horses dragged the cart from beneath him. The hangman immediately rode off, but he had bungled his job. The noose slipped, and Magee was left suspended by the neck in mid-air, revolving slowly like a carcase on a spit and uttering the most lamentable groans and entreaties.'

The crowd was horrified; some called out for him to be cut down, others for the marines to shoot him. Women fainted. The Sheriff was completely unnerved and unable to do anything. The hangman was chased and brought back and, jumping off his horse, he grasped the dangling figure by the legs and hung there till the man had ceased to struggle.[6]

J.M. Skipper's pencil sketch shows the execution of George Hughes and Henry Curran on 16 March 1840. Arrangements had improved by that time to the extent of the creation of portable gallows. However, Hughes was able to escape briefly and then abuse the hangman, and his execution required Reverend Howard kicking his feet into the open drop and the hangman hanging on to his legs until he was dead. (AGSA)

When his term expired, Smart was succeeded as Sheriff by C.C. Dutton, who held the office from May 1838 to January 1839, when Charles Burton Newenham was appointed. Apparently Smart was a candidate for the position in this year, for the *Southern Australian* said Newenham was appointed because Smart was "not smart enough to take his hat off as quick as he ought, to the Governor".[7] For many years Smart was in practice as a solicitor in Adelaide, first in partnership with Thomas Wilson, then as Smart, Wilson and Bayne, and finally as Smart and Bayne. In 1860 he went to Melbourne, where he died in March 1865.[8]

Charles Christian Dutton, the second Sheriff, settled at Port Lincoln in 1839, but the Aborigines were so troublesome that he had to give up his station, and he and a party of men with drays and cattle set out overland for Adelaide. Nothing further was ever seen of them. Search parties under Inspector Tolmer and Edward John Eyre went out but found nothing. A few of the cattle wandered back to Port Lincoln and, some years later, one of the drays was found; and there is little doubt that the whole party were killed by the natives.[9]

Attack on store dray by S.T. Gill (NLA)

Newenham was reappointed Sheriff annually, and held the position until 1856. In 1840 his reappointment was, by an oversight, not notified in the *Government Gazette*, and as doubts were expressed as to the validity of acts done by him, an act was passed (3 Vic No 12) to declare his appointment to have been regularly made and to indemnify him for anything done in the execution of his office. In March 1842 an ordinance was passed regulating his appointment and duties. He was declared to be an officer of the Supreme Court:

> '... and shall be attendant thereon and be obedient to all the rules and orders thereof and shall execute all such process civil and criminal as shall be directed to him from the said Court for that purpose'.

The Court was empowered to fix certain limits beyond which the Sheriff should not be compellable to go in person or by his deputies, and under this power a Rule of Court was made by Mr Justice Cooper in 1850, fixing the limits of the Sheriff's bailiwick at: "... one hundred and twenty miles from the Supreme Courthouse now in the course of erection in the City of Adelaide". (i.e., the present Police Court.)[10] This rule still remains in force, and any process to be executed beyond that distance must be executed by a special bailiff appointed by the Court for that purpose.

The Sheriff's Act also provided that the Sheriff was to have the charge and superintendence of all gaols, and the custody of all imprisoned debtors and criminals, but he was not to be liable for any escape unless it happened through his wilful default or neglect (section IV). Provision was also made for replevin (section VI), and the first replevin action was heard by the Court in 1845.

A schedule of fees to be taken by the Sheriff was directed by the Act to be drawn up. Prior to this the Sheriff had fixed the amount of the fees as he chose, following as nearly as he could the charges made in the other colonies and in England. Poundage fees went into his own pocket, under an arrangement made when he took office that he should be allowed these sums:

> '... to make amends for the great risque I ran, and the constant liabilities I incurred in having actions brought against me for acts done, over which I may be said to have little or no control'.[11]

His salary was only £200 a year, with an allowance of £30 a year for an office, and his expenses were so heavy that he said unless he was allowed poundage he could not carry on. Under the Sheriff's Act, however, all poundage had to be paid into the general revenue. The Sheriff applied urgently for an increase of salary.

> 'The office of Sheriff'—he said—'is acknowledged on all sides to be one of extreme danger, and I can safely say, that were it not for the great caution which I have hitherto exercised, would long since have plunged me into ruin.' [12]

The Judge recommended that he should receive £350, and Governor Gray approved of this.[13]

The Sheriff's position, however, was not very satisfactory, for his appointment had to be renewed each year. He solicited the Secretary of State to make it permanent, but without success.[14] In June 1849 he applied for a further increase of salary, stating that he had no clerk and did all the office work himself, but only received the answer that his office being annual he should consider himself lucky to have had it for so many years.[15] At the end of 1854 he obtained leave of absence to visit England, and William Robinson Boothby, who had come to South Australia in the previous year with his father Mr Justice Boothby, was appointed Deputy Sheriff and Returning Officer for the colony. Newenham did not return to office and Boothby, at the age of twenty seven, was in 1856 appointed Sheriff. As Returning Officer he conducted all the elections for fifty years after the establishment of responsible government.

'Naturally interested in election methods, he prepared both the clauses of the Act of 1856 that instituted voting by ballot, and those of the Act of 1858 that substituted for deletion of the names of unfavoured candidates the placing of a cross against the name of the favoured candidate.'

William Robinson Boothby (1829-1903)
An exemplary public servant, William Robinson Boothby held multiple positions and performed with distinction in them all. The electorate of Boothby is named after him. (SLSA)

The olive plantations, which still exist around the Adelaide Gaol, were planted under his direction in an attempt to utilise the prison labour in the production of olive oil. Samples of olive oil made at the gaol secured prizes at exhibitions both in Adelaide and abroad, but this industry seems to have shared the usual fate of all attempts to make use of convict labour.[16]

The first permanent Clerk of the Supreme Court appears to have been W. Newenham, a son of the Sheriff, "about as ignorant of law as a sucking pig", said the *South Australian.* He received a salary of £160 per year, raised in 1841 to £200. Newenham continued till 1844, when the first Master was appointed.

Governor Grey, when he arrived in the colony, was amazed to find Mr William Bartley, a solicitor who had been appointed by Governor Gawler to the office of Registrar-General, contentedly drawing his salary of £400 a year, although there was no registry office and nothing to register. The office was as nice a sinecure as could be imagined, and the holder of it added to his income by private practice as a solicitor. Grey at once suspended him and demanded an explanation of what he had done to earn his salary. Mr

Bartley replied in a dignified strain. He was appointed, he said, on the understanding that he should not do any professional work during the hours due to the registry and this condition he had scrupulously observed. (As the hours of government civil servants were very short, this still left him a considerable time for his private practice.) He had kept himself always ready to act, "not knowing the day when I should be called upon to do so". A registration bill had been twice prepared, the first one having been burnt in the fire at old Government House, but it was not yet passed.

> 'Though owing to the non-passing of the Bill I have not been engaged in Registration business, I have ever been ready to attend to it, and have attended whenever called upon—which I have been—to assist in any Government business in conferring with His Honor the Judge, or the Advocate General, upon any Bill or other matter when my opinion has been desired.' [17]

Governor Grey, however, though that £400 per year was too high a retainer for this gentleman's services, and he indicated that they were dispensed with, although he proposed at some time in the near future to pass a Registration Act. Bartley then suggested that he should be appointed to the offices of Registrar-General and Master of the Supreme Court, but he asked for a salary of £700 a year, claiming that he could make more than this in practice.[18] The Judge was inclined to favour the suggestion.

William Bartley (1801-1885) Bartley commenced practice on arrival in Adelaide in 1839. He was, at various times, a partner of Mann, Gwynne, Stow and Bakewell. Appointed Senior Solicitor in the Land Titles Office in 1857 he held the position until 1881.

> 'I feel the want of a person on whom I can rely for the fair and fearless taxation of costs, and to whom I can occasionally refer matters of importance arising in the Court. I can only hope to get a competent person by allowing him a liberal salary: and I do not know how this can be accomplished except by adding another office to it.' [19]

He did not consider Bartley's demand unreasonable, as he might obtain a much larger income by private practice, but he could not recommend that he should be allowed a fixed salary of £700 while the salaries of the Governor and other officers were at such a low figure, or while the salary of the Judge remained at £600. He suggested he should be offered £400 a year, with a right to sit as a member of the Board of Advice of the South Australian Company and to practise as a notary public. Nothing came of this suggestion, and the establishment of the Supreme Court remained on a "very moderate scale".[20] In 1844 Newenham departed, and Charles Mann was appointed Master Prothonotary and Clerk, at a salary of £300 per annum.[21] "A clever, agreeable man"—said Mrs Watts—"and brimfull of information on innumerable topics." [22]

After his suspension by Governor Hindmarsh, it will be recalled that Mann departed for Van Diemen's Land, at the request of Fisher, to take the opinion of Mr Alfred Stephen (the brother of G.M.

Stephen and subsequently Sir Alfred Stephen, Chief Justice of New South Wales) upon the legality of the council appointments and upon the libel actions which Fisher had commenced. He reached Hobart in December 1837 and remained there until the end of March. Nearly four years later, Captain Sturt, who was then Assistant Commissioner, was astounded to receive a bill from Mann for £270 for his remuneration and expenses incurred in this voyage to Hobart. Mann's bill originally was for £403 16s 3d; Fisher had paid him £200 before Governor Gawler arrived, and he claimed the balance plus interest at ten per cent. He said that as he had received his instructions from the Resident Commissioner, the Colonisation Commissioners were liable to pay, and that he had sacrificed his personal interests to public duty.

> 'At that time I had the leading business of the place. There was not another man at that time who could have put the legal points of the very intricate subject at issue in sufficient form before counsel.'

As a result, he had (so he alleged) lost much of his practice and connection at Adelaide. Governor Grey flatly refused to pay a penny of this very stale demand, and his refusal was confirmed by the Commissioners at home, who said Mann's claim was quite inadmissible.

> 'He was not even in the public service when he went to Van Diemen's Land, nor, had it been otherwise, would it have been allowable to detach a person at the public expense to other colonies to seek law opinions on the contentions that had prevailed in South Australia or on libel cases affecting Mr Fisher.' [23]

Any business that Mann may have lost by his absence, he soon regained, and he practised for some years with considerable success as a barrister. He subsequently said that immediately prior to his appointment as Master he was earning £1,300 a year. An attack of paralysis put a sudden stop to his business, and upon medical advice that any attempt at active practice might terminate in disorganisation of the brain, he accepted the quiet but poorly paid position of Master. The title of Master had been added, and the salary raised from £200 to £300 in the hope of obtaining the services of a competent person.[24]

> 'With respect to salary'—wrote the Judge—'I beg to say that I consider £300 per annum a very moderate salary for a person competent to perform the duties of Master &c both in the Common Law and Equity Jurisdiction of the Supreme Court, and I hope that this sum will not be considered unreasonable by His Majesty's Secretary of State.' [25]

The duties of the Master were extended by Ordinance No 14 of 1845, passed to provide for the performance of certain duties by the Master during the occasional absence of the Judge. The Master was empowered to issue writs for the arrest of persons about to leave the province, to order particulars or amendment of pleadings, to give time to plead, to issue summonses, to order taxation of costs, and to make other similar orders of an interlocutory nature. A party aggrieved by any such order of the Master could apply to the Judge on his return to review it.

Charles Algernon Wilson
(c1818- 1884)
A ca. 1843 watercolour by Martha Berkeley
(AGSA)

At first Mann had to discharge the duties of both Master and Clerk. This was frequently found inconvenient, for when he was in court there was no-one to look after the court office; and in 1846 Charles Algernon Wilson (a son of the Thomas Wilson who has been mentioned as practising in partnership with Samuel Smart) was appointed as Clerk.[26] Wilson, who was described as a "kindly unassuming man", remained Clerk on a miserable salary for many years, and acted as Master when Mann was Acting Judge in 1848. In 1858 he became Registrar of Probates and Commissioner of Inland Revenue, and in 1876 Chief Clerk at the Supreme Court. He was a keen naturalist and entomologist and wrote articles for the local papers on natural history.[27]

Governor Robe in 1846 put forward a proposal to abolish the office of Registrar-General, give the Deputy Registrar the title of Registrar, and place his office under the control of the Supreme Court. The Colonial Office put a stop to this.

> 'In general'—he was told by the Secretary of State—'it is to be desired that the legal tribunals and the Judges presiding in them should be confined exclusively to Judicial business, and the control of the office of the Registrar of Deeds does not therefore seem to me to fall within their appropriate province.' [28]

In July 1849 Mann submitted to the Colonial Secretary a long memorandum of the duties which he performed, and asked that his salary should be increased. As Master in Equity, he said, he exercised independent though subordinate judicial functions. In the majority of decrees the Court referred inquiries to him which involved the taking of evidence and consideration and reporting upon accounts. As the Master had to approve of the titles to estates in which the funds of infants, creditors or legatees might be invested, he had to have a full knowledge of conveyancing. On the common law side, his duties were not so responsible. He attended in court, noted the orders, and drew them up; this required an intimate knowledge of the theory of pleading and the practice of the courts of common law—"a practice multifarious in its nature and a theory so extensive that the acquisition of it pre-supposes the individual attention of the officers (five in number) who are in England appointed to this single section of the law". Little assistance was to be derived from English works of practice which, without practical experience, were "too often but blind leaders of the blind". He was responsible for the taxation of bills of costs, and "costs involve a knowledge of the minutiae and proper price of every legal proceeding taken—a knowledge which is absolutely unobtainable except by experience". In addition, he checked the books of account, superintended the duties of the office, and acted as Clerk of Arraigns. For all of these duties he received only £300 a year.

> 'It is submitted that although such a salary would be taken by many persons to whom want of practice would render the salary desirable, it is not quite so clear that such want of practice would make it desirable for the Government to confer the appointment.' [29]

The answer to his long memorandum was disappointing:

> 'However high His Excellency's estimate of your personal qualifications may be, he regrets that it does not appear to him that the office of Master requires a higher remuneration than that at present assigned to it.' [30]

A few months later Mann applied for and obtained the position of Crown Solicitor, which had for the first time been severed from that of Advocate-General, and he was succeeded by Jickling, who remained Master until his removal in 1861. His duties were prescribed by the Rules of Court made by Mr Justice Cooper in 1850 to be such as were performed by the masters of the respective courts at Westminster and in Chancery, and he had also to be Registrar on the ecclesiastical side, Clerk of Arraigns, and to perform the duties assigned to him by Ordinance No 11 of 1843.[31]

In May 1850 the Judge reported that, the business of the Court having steadily increased, a second clerk was required. The fees received during the previous five years had been:[32]

1845	£429 9s 4d
1846	£303 13s 3d
1847	£374 4s 2d
1848	£488 17s 0d
1849	£617 14s 2d
1850 (first quarter)	£259 11s 3d

The Government would not sanction the extra expense. In the following year Mr Justice Cooper again applied for the appointment of further assistance, and recommended the appointment of another clerk to act as Clerk of Arraigns and associate, "that is to say, to attend in Court during its sittings, to arraign prisoners on their trial, record verdicts and other proceedings, and also to act as Judges' Clerk". Business in the Supreme Court office got into arrears when it was left with only one clerk to attend to everything, owing to the Master being engaged in court.[33]

All thought of a second clerk was temporarily banished by the depression of 1852 and the rush to the diggings. The Government circularised all its departments, asking what reductions could be made. The Judges replied that, although "nothing but the present gloomy aspect of affairs" would have induced them to suggest a reduction in the Supreme Court establishment, yet if absolutely necessary the services of Jickling could be dispensed with. In that event the judges would do part of his work, "anticipating that the business of the Supreme Court will be hereafter considerably diminished in consequence of the general depression".[34] Jickling was for a short time transferred from the Court and employed as a magistrate, but with the passing of the depression he returned to his place as Master.

S.T. Gill's *The new rush* c. 1852 (NLA)

A curious light upon the emigration to the diggings is to be found in a letter from the Clerk of the Court to Mr Justice Cooper stating that:

> '... on account of the present extensive emigration to Victoria, writ of Capias are constantly required; to sign which and take the customary previous affidavits I have on several occasions had to attend out of office hours—an hour or more before ten, and an hour or two after three pm'.

Plaintiffs, he said, were willing to pay extra fees for writs issued after office hours, and as "in the present reduction of Salaries any additional amount would be acceptable to me", he asked the Judge to fix an opening fee and approve his taking it as an addition to his salary. As a precedent, he stated that in the time of his predecessor

Newenham, the office was always closed on Saturdays, and only opened on payment of a fee of 10s 6d. Whether or not his application was granted and fees fixed by the Judge cannot be discovered.[35]

By 1853 the depression was passing and the Government approved of the appointment of an associate and Clerk of Arraigns at a salary of £150 a year. Mr Justice Cooper appointed William Hinde, an English solicitor who had recently arrived in the colony and who had, besides practising in England, been clerk of a county court there for four years.[36] Hinde succeeded Jickling as Master in 1861, and his place as judge's associate was taken by Lionel J. Pelham, who edited the first volume of *South Australian Law Reports*, and was drowned with Mr Justice Wearing in the wreck of the *Gothenburg* on the Great Barrier Reef (24 February 1875) while returning from holding the first Circuit Court at Palmerston.

Lionel J. Pelham (1808-1875) ca. 1867 (SLSA)

A few words may be added as to the administration of the Supreme Court office. During the first years chaos reigned supreme. Jeffcott had drawn up a table of fees to be charged, but when Jickling took over, this had been lost and fees were taken in a haphazard manner.[37] The financial records of the first years are very fragmentary, but the total revenue derived from the Supreme Court from May 1837 to March 1838 was £8 7s 6d from fees and £26 0s 0d from fines.[38] After this, fees all went into general revenue and are lumped together indistinguishably in the accounts. The Governor, in October 1838, thinking that the amount derived from fees was remarkably small, wrote to Jickling asking what fees were prescribed. Several letters produced no answer, but pressure finally wrung from the Acting Judge the admission that he did not know. Gawler thereupon directed him to make out a new scale of fees, at higher rates, so as to increase the court receipts. Jickling refused to do it, contending that it was a matter for the Governor in Council, who alone had power to raise taxes.[39]

The next record of any fixation of fees is in 1844 when, after the appointment of Mann as Master, Mr Justice Cooper made rules prescribing the fees to be taken on the common law side.[40] On the equity side the fees remained for many years in the discretion of the Master, who followed as best he could the scales applied in Chancery. All writs and summonses had previously been signed by the Judge himself, but it was now directed that writs should be signed by the Master and sealed with the Supreme Court seal. This seal had been bought by Jeffcott in Van Diemen's Land for £3,[41] but it was adapted only for use with sealing wax. A supply of candles had to be kept, and every time a document was presented for sealing, an impressive ceremony—in more senses than one—had to be gone through. A candle was lit, and wax melted, and the seal impressed. Mann soon got rid of this cumbrous method and bought a new seal which could be inked and documents stamped, as is done at present.[42]

The hours of attendance were short. By a rule made 8 January 1847, the Master and Clerk and were required to attend from ten to three, the office being open from eleven to three, and a similar rule was made in the General Rules of 1850.

In the early days the proceedings were commenced and carried on in a motley form—varying from scraps of paper a few inches in size to huge engrossments on parchment measuring about four feet square. It is hardly possible to conceive how the Judges and counsel ever managed to read and comprehend the crabbed, closely packed lines running for two or three feet across an unwieldy sheet of stiff and crinkly parchment. When the eye reaches the end of the line, and travels back to the other side of the parchment, it is an almost hopeless task to find the next line to read, unless a yardstick is used to mark the place. Jeffcott's rules in 1837 had prescribed that all documents filed should be legibly written, but they said nothing as to size and shape. The General Rules of 1850 provided that "all paper writings" filed to be used in any proceedings were to be written in a clear legible hand and were to be of a convenient form and size. A curious and annoying feature of the practice of the office was that all documents were classified not according to the case to which they related but according to their nature; thus all bills in equity were filed in one bundle, all affidavits in another, all writs in a third, all judgments in a fourth, and so on.

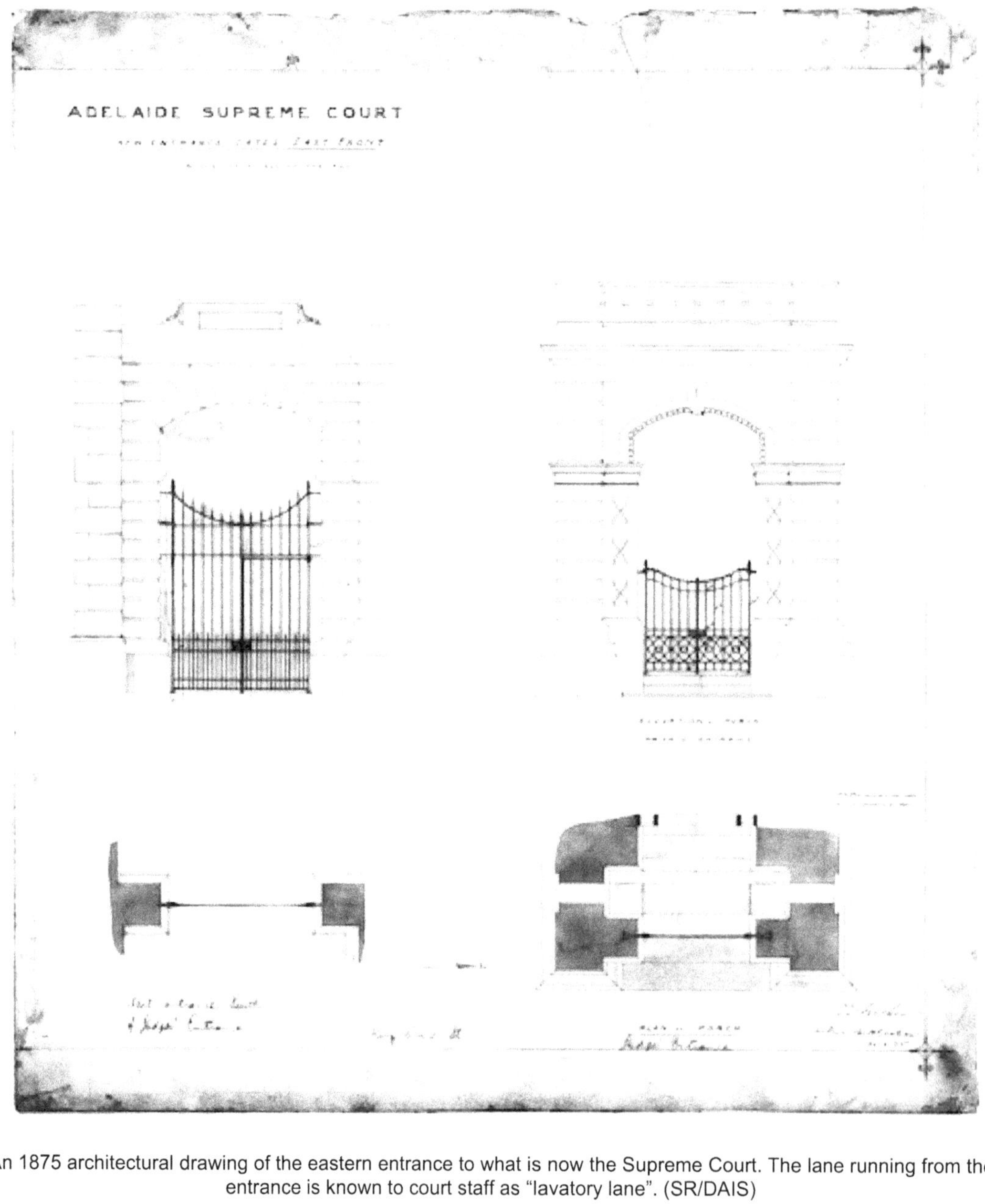

An 1875 architectural drawing of the eastern entrance to what is now the Supreme Court. The lane running from the entrance is known to court staff as "lavatory lane". (SR/DAIS)

The Supreme Court

The Site of the Supreme Court

The first sitting of the Supreme Court was held in May 1837 in the Resident Commissioner's office. Later in the same year an office for the Supreme Court was erected in Victoria Square, although its exact site is uncertain. Sir John Jeffcott wrote to the Governor on 13 October 1837:

> 'Finding on my return yesterday from Van Diemen's Land that no office has as yet been put up for the Judge, although ordered some months ago by a vote of the Council, and it being absolutely indispensable to the due performance of my duties that such an office should be erected forthwith, I beg to propose to your Excellency that a small frame house which I have brought with me, consisting of two rooms and a closet, and just calculated for the purpose, be purchased by the Colonial Government for such sum as it may by the valuation of a competent person be considered worth, and put up without delay on some part of the public land, either in Victoria Square, the place appropriated for the public offices, or elsewhere.' [1]

The Government purchased the house, and as Victoria Square was still scrub intersected by a few paths, the Resident Commissioner was asked to send a surveyor to find the acre on which the office might be erected.[2]

In October 1837 it was proposed that an iron store of the Commissioners, on the north side of the river near the foot of Montefiore Hill, should be made available for the purpose of the Judge holding a court, and Fisher consented.[3] Nothing came of this, and the earliest reference to a courthouse is found in a memorandum of agreement made on 19 January 1838 between T.B. Strangways (Colonial Secretary) on behalf of the Government and Osmond Gilles, by which Gilles agreed to let "all those newly erected premises situate and being on the west side of Gilles Arcade" and "known as the Court House", for a term of three years from 1 January 1838 at a yearly rental of £50.[4] Although the premises were already called the "Court-house", there is no evidence that the Supreme Court had held any sittings there; they may probably have been occupied by the Resident Magistrate's Court. Mrs Mary Thomas described the courthouse as "a wooden building not roofed then except by a few boards which could afford but little protection in rough weather",[5] and according to T.H. James it was the busiest place in the town, "being at once the Bow Street, Old Bailey, Westminster Hall, and Lincoln's Inn of the Colony".[6]

Here Jickling held the second and subsequent sittings of the Supreme Court, and it continued in use until the arrival of Mr Justice Cooper in 1839. He brought out with him some large wooden Manning buildings, which he erected on acre No 614 in the south-eastern corner of Whitmore Square, facing north.[7] It was arranged that the Government should rent portion of these buildings as a temporary Supreme Court, the Judge living in the rest of the house. A few days before he landed in the colony, the *Southern Australian* had said:

> 'We cannot but express our wonder that a Court House should not be at once erected. The solemnities of justice should on all occasions be reverently upheld—and we do not think it decorous that the Judge should hold his court like a Druid, or be compelled to oust the Resident Magistrate. We trust that this will be attended to, and that at our next session, we shall find a 'new house swept and garnished'; and new heads to grace the new walls.' [8]

Nothing was done for several months, but the *Government Gazette* of 12 September 1839 contains a notice that the office of the Clerk of the Supreme Court in Whitmore Square would open for the transaction of business on Monday, 16 September, the hours of attendance being from ten to one, Saturdays excepted. The first sittings of the Supreme Court to be held there appear to have been in February 1840.

> 'Although some inconvenience will be experienced by the majority of the public from the distant situation of the new courthouse'—said the Southern Australian—'yet in other respects it is decidedly preferable to the old one. We hope, however, that ere long a proper Court House will be erected in its proper place—Victoria Square.' [9]

Apart from the actual courtroom, the only facilities provided for the public at the Whitmore Square courthouse were a shed for stabling horses and a narrow verandah on the north side. There were continual complaints about the inadequate accommodation, especially from the ladies; the men, it appears, could take their ease at a handy hotel where there was an attractive barmaid.[10] An excellent impression of the courtroom is to be obtained from the amusing story told by Tolmer. In November 1840, Joseph Stagg was being tried for the murder of a man named Gofton.

> 'The preliminaries having been duly gone into, the prisoner, who was defended by Mr Charles Mann, pleaded "Not Guilty". Being the first witness called in the case, I was proceeding to give my evidence, when an unparalleled and ridiculous incident occurred, which I will endeavor to describe.

> The room used as the court contained two French windows, which opened into the garden, the judge's elevated seat being between the two. On the judge's left hand, along the side-wall, were the jury. On his right, fronting the jury-box, was the prisoner in the dock, with Mr Ashton, the governor of the gaol, standing on his left hand, and opposite the witness-box, immediately under the bench, at a large table covered with law books, briefs, etc sat the Sheriff, Mr Newenham, the officers of the Court, the Advocate-General, Mr Charles Mann, the Counsel for the prisoner, the late Sir James Fisher, Messrs Poulden, Nicholls, and others, and on the floor at the right of the bench were several chairs occupied by Miss Cooper (now Mrs Newenham), Mrs Walker, and several other ladies. Suddenly, a sharp report was heard like that of a pistol or rifle, followed by the repeated cries of "He's shot at"; whereupon I drew my sword and said, "Where is he?", and in an instant the foreman of the jury, followed by the other eleven, dashed through one glass window into the garden, and the judge, the lawyers, and ladies went pell-mell through the other! One lady, indeed, in the eagerness to effect an exit, was unceremoniously jostled, and fell sprawling on the floor, and doubtless retains a vivid remembrance of the occurrence to this day. The people, who occupied every available space in the body of the court, being equally panic-stricken, rushed out into the street tumultuously, and in less than five seconds there only remained myself, the prisoner, and Mr Ashton, who I noted immediately locked the prisoner's left arm within his, and with the left hand held a pistol at his head, who, the while, laughingly looked on. Never was such a scene witnessed! It was, at the moment of the alarm, generally believed that, being the principal witness in the case, a confederate of Stagg's had fired a shot at me to prevent my giving further evidence. The actual cause of the commotion and terror after all, was simply the snapping of a defective beam through the overcrowded state of the room, which was over a cellar. The break, however, was quickly made safe by means of supports under the flooring, when confidence was restored, and the trial was proceeded with.' [11]

For the use of this building as a courthouse, the Judge received a rental of £200 a year, and he further had the advantage that the court messenger and caretaker (who lived on the premises and received a salary of £1 per week) acted as his servant.

When Governor Grey arrived he considered that the situation of the courthouse was "not well adapted for business", and he at once marked down the payment of £200 a year rent as an extravagance.

He looked round for some building which might be used as a substitute. For a time he toyed with the idea of converting the chapel at the gaol into a courtroom, which struck him as being a very satisfactory economy, since with a slight weekly rearrangement of the furniture it could still be used for divine service on Sundays, and it would save any expense in bringing prisoners to and from the gaol to court.[12] For some reason—presumably the inconvenient situation of the gaol, which was certainly not "well adapted for business"—he gave up this idea and thought instead of transferring the Court to the schoolhouse on North Terrace.[13] When confronted with an estimate of £1,088 10s 6d for the necessary alterations and repairs which would be involved in the move, he hastily abandoned the scheme and decided that the existing arrangements would have to continue.

The courthouse remained at Whitmore Square until 1843. In 1842 a slight unpleasantness occurred between the Governor and the Judge about it. The Governor decided, in March 1842, to give up the lease on 30 June, as the rent was too high. When Mr Justice Cooper was informed, he replied that the Government's tenancy had commenced at Christmas and consequently the notice to quit should determine at that period, and he would therefore consider it as a notice to quit at Christmas next. This displeased the Governor, and the Judge, "rather than have any difference of opinion", agreed to let it for another year at the reduced rental of £100, on condition that the Government would at the end of the period replace the floor with one suitable for a private house.[14] The floor of the Court was apparently of a primitive nature, and strewn with sawdust. A requisition by the Sheriff for some bags of sawdust to be supplied to the Court produced a characteristic memorandum from Governor Grey, who never allowed a suggestion of waste or extravagance to slip past him.

> 'The Government'—he said—'cannot afford to pay for sawdust for the Supreme Court. It would be no great exertion for the messenger to put a sack upon his back and walk down to the Parklands and fill it up at the saw pits.' [15]

This seems a very trivial item, but a chip shows which way the stream is flowing. "Rare as epic song," said Meredith, "is the man who is thorough in what he does." Every penny of the Government expenditure passed before the vigilant scrutiny of Governor Grey, and over and over again the official dockets are endorsed by him with the same curt phrase—"The Government cannot afford ..."—followed by stimulating and strongly worded remarks, well calculated to stir the drowsiest of civil servants into startled economy and activity.

> 'I can conscientiously declare'—said Governor Grey to the Legislative Council in July 1843—'that I have, during the past two years, been engaged in a constant warfare against

> expenditure. I am convinced that the government of a young community cannot exercise too cautious circumspection against being led into unnecessary expenditure. I believe that the evil effects of such an expenditure, both upon the prosperity and morality of the country, are generally very much underrated. It must ultimately be met by increased taxation; and unless this is most judiciously imposed, it will obstruct the complete development of the productive powers of a country, and must consequently produce a want of wealth, comfort and contentment amongst the bulk of the population, whose poverty preventing them from indulging in any remission from their habitual toil will leave them little leisure for the improvement of their moral and intellectual faculties.'

The effect of his ruthless economies is shown by startling figures. In 1840 the Government expenditure in South Australia was £169,966. It fell to £104,471 in 1841; to £54,444 in 1842; to £29,842 in 1843; and although even Grey had to admit that this was almost the irreducible minimum, he got it down in 1844 to £29,453. It would perhaps be no bad thing if every Member of Parliament had to learn these figures by heart.[16]

At some time in 1841 the office of the Supreme Court was moved to Victoria Square. In October of that year a notice was published by the Judge, requesting that all letters and papers on business should be directed to him at the Supreme Court office in Victoria Square, and not to his private residence. The courthouse, however, remained at Whitmore Square and in hot weather the Judge was accustomed to transact all business at his home, which he found much cooler than the office.[17]

In 1843 the Government began to look about for a building to house both the Supreme Court and the Resident Magistrate's Court. They were approached with an ingenuous offer by Mr Emanuel Solomon, a gentleman who some years before had started business in Adelaide in partnership with his brother. Mr Solomon had an exceedingly fertile brain.

> 'His speculating tendencies found abundant scope in the sphere in which his lot was cast, for houses of all kinds were few and far between, and the style of architecture was of the most primitive kind, more worthy the aboriginal designers of wurleys than of builders acquainted with the Tuscan, Doric, Ionic, or Corinthian orders. By Mr Solomon's spirited endeavours respectable and commodious blocks of city residences were erected, and a theatre, which rose on the ruins of the first wooden structure devoted to Momus, was established by him in what was then, and is still known to colonists as "Gilles' Arcade".'[18]

The Queen's Theatre, site of the Supreme Court from 1843 to 1850, as it stands today. The building was first used as a theatre in 1841 (the first performance was of *Othello*) and has been used as auction rooms, a tavern, horse bazaar, car garage and a car park. Renovated in the 1990s it is now available for hire for functions and exhibitions or as a theatre. (Tony Kimberlin)

It was this theatre which Mr Solomon now offered to the Government—free. In addition, he offered to do all the necessary work of converting it into courtrooms, and rooms for judge, jury, witnesses, and so on—all for nothing. The Government could take the building, converted into a modern courthouse, for seven years at a peppercorn rent. All that Mr Solomon asked in return was that no more licences for public houses should be granted in the neighbourhood than were then in existence. Mr Solomon calculated that the exclusive privilege which his hotel (situated next to the theatre) would have, of supplying all the thirsty who had business in Her Majesty's courts of justice, would more than compensate him for the absence of any rental.[19]

Governor Grey replied that the Government did not conduct business on those terms, but if Mr Solomon was willing to rent his theatre, without any undertaking as to public houses, the Government would take it. The Judge had inspected the site and the buildings, and was very much opposed to it; possibly the loss of his own annual rental prejudiced him a little.

> 'The situation of the buildings is bad'—he wrote. 'They form part of the same building as Mr Solomon's public-house, and the north end is very near another public-house and billiard-room; and they are therefore an unsafe depositary for public records.'

The lighting was poor, and there was great annoyance caused by noise from the neighbouring taverns. Altogether he could see nothing to make the offer of Messrs Solomon desirable except cheapness.[20]

The profession did not agree with the Judge. On 3 April 1843, a meeting of the South Australian Law Society was held at Messrs Smart and Co's offices. There were present Henry Jickling (Chairman), J.H. Fisher, Taylor, Mann, Morphett, Gwynne, Smith, Skipper, MacDonald, Bayne, and Johnson; and it was resolved that "the Theatre is a fit and commodious building for the Law Courts and offices, and would be convenient to the profession".[21] A copy of this resolution was forwarded to the Colonial Secretary and, after some negotiations as to terms, the Government took a lease of the theatre from Mr Solomon.

Mr Solomon proceeded forthwith with the necessary alterations. "When finished"—the South Australian proudly announced—"the Courts will, for extent, convenience, and number of rooms, be probably unsurpassed in these colonies." [22]

The Supreme Court room measured 32 feet by 38 feet, the Resident Magistrate's Court room 32 feet by 50 feet, and connected with the courtrooms were no less than 18 apartments for the Judge, Resident Magistrate, Sheriff, Advocate-General, Registrar-General, and court offices [sic], together with a fireproof room for deeds and documents. By September 1843 the alterations were sufficiently advanced for the citizens of Adelaide to realise the grandeur of the new Courts. The "Seat of Justice" was surmounted by a crimson canopy, and the Resident Magistrate's Court, being surrounded by the boxes of the old theatre, looked "altogether grand and unique".[23]

The Judge took possession of the new Court in November 1843, and he found his worst fears realised; not even a crimson canopy could compensate for the fact that the enterprising Mr Solomon had promptly opened a low-class taproom in connection with his adjoining tavern.[24]

A description of the remarkable spectacle which the Courts presented is to be found in the *South Australian Almanack* of 1847:

> 'The stage is now the Supreme Court; of the green rooms, one is appropriately turned into a robing-room for counsel, and another makes a very decent cell in which to lock up a refractory jury. More appropriately still, a lower dungeon which formerly served for ghosts and wizards to rise from or sink into, in the melodrama or pantomime, is made a temporary prison for the rough and rugged old convicts from Sydney and Van Diemen's Land, who form the staple of our criminals. The pit is our Police Court, and is still surrounded with the tiers of boxes which occasionally, as if in member of olden times, are tenanted by an inquisitive audience. What were once the lobbies are now the offices respectively of the Police

> Commissioner and his clerks. The Resident Magistrate and the Official Assignee occupy the saloon, while the Ladies Cloak Room is claimed by the Sheriff.' [25]

It is distressing to be compelled to relate that Mr Solomon's workmanship was more pretentious than substantial. Within a year or two the gaudiness had worn off, and rain began to come through the roof. The Judge now realised, with thankfulness, the blessings of a crimson canopy, for he alone was dry while the body of the Court received a sprinkling with every passing shower.[26]

In 1846 the Legislative Council voted £4,000 for a Supreme Court house.[27] The Registrar-General described the theatre building as "disreputable and insecure", but as there was nowhere else to go while the new courthouse was building, the Government renewed the lease of the theatre for a further two years at £250 per annum. When Mr Solomon found that the Government had decided to leave his desirable premises, he was at first downcast. But not so for long. The exuberant fertility of his invention soon asserted itself and he burst upon the astonished public with a proposal to dispose of all those buildings, "built for a Theatre and now occupied by the Supreme Court and Law offices", by a grand lottery—1,000 tickets at £6 10s 0d each, to be paid, if desired, in monthly instalments of 10 shillings. I regret that I have not been able to discover the fate of the grand lottery.[28]

A year went by, and the Governor then intimated to the Legislative Council that nothing had been done with regard to the new courthouse. The sum voted had been found to be insufficient for the designs, and he had therefore contracted for one of smaller size and had changed its site.

> 'Were it on either of the acres to the North of Victoria Square, it could not be made of anything like uniform appearance with the present public offices; but as there would no doubt before long be a new Council Chamber required, it was thought better to have that on the one acre, and the court on the other, at the southern end. They could be built uniformly, and the Post Office, with Police and Magistrate's Court, might form one building on the acre opposite the Government Offices, like them, in the Grecian style.' [29]

Since the sum of £4,000 had proved insufficient and a smaller courthouse was necessary, it is rather startling to find that the tender accepted was for a price of £6,780; the original plans must have been on a truly grand scale. Under the contract, work was to be commenced on 10 November 1847 and completed on 10 August 1849.[30] It is perhaps hardly necessary to say that the work, being a government contract, was neither completed within the time specified nor for the contract price. The building (including additional work for a strongroom which had been overlooked in the plans) cost over £8,000, and it was not ready for partial occupation until July 1850, nor completely finished till February 1851. In the meantime, successive renewals of the lease of Mr Solomon's theatre were necessary, and those premises became steadily more and more dilapidated and decrepit. The Government, with the prospect of shifting to a new courthouse, spent no money on painting, cleaning or repairs; Mr Solomon, with the prospect of losing the last tenant his ramshackle building was likely to have, did likewise. The Court which had been lauded as the best in the Australian colonies sank into a "wretched ruin" and a "rookery". Parts of it, said the *Adelaide Times*, were "thorough receptacles of every description of filth". Sanitary conveniences appear to have been overlooked in the admiration of the crimson canopy.

> 'No Person with anything of a decent coat will now venture in these localities unless he feels a fancy to a fairy dive into interminable labyrinths of cobwebs and dust, with various other compositions, said to possess wondrous virtue in fertilising lands. It is high time something was done in the shape of purification of these beastly dust holes, and similar other nuisances throughout the building.' [31]

Squabbles amongst the staff of the offices as to whose duty it was to clean the premises had resulted in a satisfactory state of deadlock, in which everyone did as little as he possibly could. When the Government vacated the building and Mr Solomon inspected it, his protests were loud and of a pecuniary nature. He engaged G.S. Kingston to examine the place and make an estimate of the sum needed to place it in a habitable state. "Dirt and filth in every room," reported Kingston: "I never saw any building given up by the tenant in such a disgracefully dirty and dilapidated state." Beneath the stage, which formed the Supreme Court room, there had previously been some dressing rooms which had not been required when the Government took over the theatre. One of the interesting discoveries made by Kingston was that the person who gave the Supreme Court what little cleaning it received had for the past seven years saved the Government any expense in dustbins by simply sweeping all the dirt and rubbish through a hole in the floor into the dressing room beneath. The renovations necessary to put the building in a state of habitancy were estimated by Kingston at £150. The Colonial Engineer, having checked the estimate, was forced to admit that it was not a penny too much, and Mr Solomon had to be paid.[32]

The Government had some difficulty in obtaining possession of the new Supreme Court house. The contractor had been given an extension of time to complete the building, and he refused to give possession to the Government before the date fixed, partly because he had not been paid and partly because he was liable, until that date, for any damage done by fire. But the Government were determined not to wait and had one of the windows smashed open. Entrance once effected, the doors were opened and the court furniture hastily carried in. The annoyed contractor threatened legal proceedings against those who had broken in, but confronted with a fait accompli he could do nothing but acquiesce.[33]

Supreme Courthouse ca. 1870. This building, now part of the Adelaide Magistrates' Courthouse, was designed by Colonial Engineer Edward C. Frome and his successor Richard Lambeth. The builders had trouble obtaining the large blocks of stone that are a feature of the building eventually obtaining supplies from a number of different quarries including those at Beaumont, Mitcham and the Finniss River. (SCLSA)

When the new Court was opened to the public and sittings commenced, it was found to be very inconvenient and badly arranged. The courtroom itself was "large and lofty", but in the centre of it was placed a very high dock, and the seats for spectators were ranged behind it, amphitheatre fashion, in such a way that only those in certain positions had a view of the proceedings. The Judges complained that the public, in their anxiety to see over the dock and hear what was going on, climbed up on the back of it and thus kept up a constant disturbance. The acoustics of the building were bad; justice it was said, was not only blind but deaf. No-one at the back could hear what was said on the bench. According to the *South Australian*, the judge, jury, prisoner, and counsel formed "a snug little party, and had all the fun to themselves"[34] The slightest noise or movement echoed through the room. The decorations were criticised as being too gay for a court of justice. The Court proved extremely cold and draughty, and the profession complained bitterly that "the current of air which rises up through the floor from the passage to the dock tends very much to injure their health". The Judges said that the bench was so constructed that they could not sit at it to take notes without turning their backs to the jury, and they were unable to communicate with the Master except by standing up and leaning over. In the Judges' chambers the fireplaces were so built that, when a fire was burning, the windows had to be kept open to let the smoke out. It was lamentable, the *Register* said, that after the great expense the courthouse should be so deficient.

> 'It is extremely difficult to catch the purport of any observation made by the Bench or the Bar. Every motion of the people assembled echoes through the lofty hall like the murmur of a forest breeze, or the roar of troubled water. The loudest voice becomes confused with its own reverberations, and the incessant clink of hammers, and the banging of doors increases the dissonance like the din of distant artillery.' [35]

In addition to the sins of misfeasance were those of nonfeasance. There was no robing room for counsel and, as Mr Justice Crawford said, "there is a great want of decorum in the Members of the Bar being obliged to put on the Court costume in open Court." Nor were there any rooms for the grand or petit jury; and on one occasion a jury had to be hastily sent to the Judge's room "to prevent the public witnessing an unseemly discussion in the jury box".[36]

Mr Justice Crawford was worried also about a problem of some delicacy.

> 'When jurymen required to retire for natural purposes, they were obliged to go out into the yard in charge of a policeman. Such things are unseemly and tend to bring the administration of justice into contempt. Moreover a question might arise whether such accomodation could be afforded to a juror without the consent of the prisoner on trial.'

Fortunately the Court never seems to have been called upon to decide this difficult point. Presumably it would have been resolved by the application of the maxim, "Necessitas facit licitum quod alias non est licitum."

These numerous defects were gradually remedied. The dock was altered and the seating accommodation changed; the cells were converted into Judges' chambers, and new cells erected, and rooms were provided for the jury and for counsel to robe in—the latter being appropriately entituled Robing Room by a whimsical painter.

This courthouse, which is now the Police Court, was occupied by the Supreme Court until January 1873. For a good many years before that date it had been found inadequate. With three Judges and only one courtroom, there were bound to be difficulties, especially when a lengthy Criminal Sessions monopolised the courtroom for days. A room upstairs was used occasionally for holding a second court, but it was very inconvenient and unfit for use in the summer months. In 1867 the present Supreme Court buildings were erected, the intention being that they should house the Local and Insolvency Courts. The latter Courts had for some time past been situated where the post office now stands, and the proposed alteration in their site did not pass without criticism. The advocates of the new site argued that, if all the Courts were at the south end of Victoria Square, the legal profession would gather round there and all legal business would be centralised.

> 'If it is at all likely'—commented the Register—'that the south side of Victoria Square will, at no distant period, become the Lincoln's Inn of South Australia, then it might be wise policy to concentrate all the Courts of law there. But this is a mere assumption. It has been felt by many persons that the erection of the Supreme Court on the site it now occupies was a mistake at first, as it increases the inconvenience of the public, and adds to the cost of administering the law; and that it is just as likely that some day the Supreme Court may be removed to a more eligible situation as that the whole of the Courts for the administration of justice will be concentrated in its neighbourhood.'

One of the reasons given against the removal of the Local Courts was:

> 'Lawyers and witnesses do not feel inclined to tramp across the Square in all weathers, and cabs and coaches would be in requisition ... Witnesses and lawyers would not walk, and they would have to ride at the expense of hapless clients.'

The Police Courts, too, it was contended, should be in the heart of the city.

> 'Quiet citizens and nurses with their interesting charges, accustomed to seek pure air and refreshment in Victoria Square, would indeed have the monotony of the scene sometimes varied by seeing a drunken Jezebel dragged to the Court through one of the 'lungs of the city', or hearing the foul-mouthed utterances of a blackguard on his way to an interview with Mr Beddoms.' [37]

The Police Court building was completed in 1867 (shown here ca. 1870) later it became part of the Supreme Court complex. (SLSA)

The Supreme Court Judges, when they saw the completed building across the road, were consumed with envy and decided they would much prefer it to the one they were occupying. "It is scarcely possible"—they said—"that the business of the Supreme Court should continue to be conducted in the present building."

They accordingly appropriated the new building although, they said, they had no intention of permanently ousting the Local and Insolvency Courts.

> 'The new building is not such as they would have recommended had it been originally intended for the use of the Supreme Court, but it provides superior accommodation to that furnished by the present building; and their Honors would, therefore, propose that it should be occupied by the Supreme Court until the resources of the Colony may enable the Government to erect one more suitable.' [38]

Even after it had been altered and enlarged to meet the wishes, they declared that: "... the building is not suited for the Supreme Courthouse of the Colony".[39] Nevertheless, there the Supreme Court has remained ever since, and prospects of the Government erecting a more suitable building are at present remote.

The Supreme Court building was completed in 1869 and until 1873 housed the Local and Insolvency Courts. Built of Tea Tree Gully sandstone it was designed by Robert G. Thomas and William Minn. (SLSA)

In the preparations for the founding of the new colony of South Australia, a supply of legal literature was not overlooked. Mr Butterworth, the law bookseller, was called upon to supply the Statutes at Large, and after several years of patient pressure he managed to exact payment for them. Governor Hindmarsh demanded to be furnished with Blackstone's Commentaries, the Code Napoleon, and works on parliamentary practice and procedure.[1] From his subsequent conduct in the colony it would seem doubtful whether the Governor's reading in any of the last-mentioned works was very extensive, while what use he thought he could make of the Code Napoleon it is difficult to imagine. The Judge, Sir John Jeffcott, also brought with him a collection of law books, but lost them all in the wreck of the *Isabella*. The Governor granted him £150 to replace them, on condition that the books should be the property of the Crown and be kept at the Supreme Court, and the books which the Judge bought in Van Diemen's Land with this sum formed the nucleus of the Supreme Court Library.[2]

With singular obtuseness, the Colonial Office refused to send out to the colony copies of the English statutes as they were passed. G.M. Stephen complained of this when he was Acting Governor, in August 1838, but no notice was taken of him.[3] A fire in 1841 destroyed Mr Butterworth's set of statutes and a number of other books in the Legislative Council Library, but a request by Governor Gawler that they should be replaced and that the new Acts of Parliament should be sent out as passed met with a flat refusal from Downing Street.[4] One is not surprised to find the Advocate-General, Mr Smillie, full of complaints of the inconvenience felt by the Judge and himself from the want of statutes, for as late as 1848, although odd copies of statutes had drifted out to the colony from England and some had even been adopted by the local legislature, there was no complete copy in the colony of the Imperial Acts for the years 1834-1843, nor had any volumes of statutes been received from the other Australian colonies since 1838. The Supreme Court had managed to secure a set of English Acts coming down to 1833, and the Legislative Council had purchased those from 1844 on, but in between was a legislative hiatus of ten years.[5] The library at the court was for the use of the Judge only; practitioners relied on their own resources and on what they could borrow from their fellow lawyers.[6] Gradually it accumulated accessions; a catalogue prepared by the Master in 1844 shows that the library then numbered 204 volumes.[7] In the same year Governor Grey cast covetous eyes upon it and contemplated appropriating it for the use of the Legislative Council; he had been given to understand, he said, that the books had been purchased for the use of the Legislative Council. A perusal of the

Colonial Secretary's records would have shown him he was quite wrong in this assumption, for the money advanced by Governor Hindmarsh for the purchase of books was distinctly earmarked by him as being "for the use of the Judge's office".[8] Before he could carry out his threat, Governor Grey was transferred to New Zealand.

By Act No 6 of 1845, regulating the profession of the law, an annual fee of £5 was levied from every practitioner. The sum derived by the Government in this way had grown by June 1848 to £345, and it was suggested that this should be expended in the establishment of a law library to belong to the Crown and to be under the control of an officer of the Supreme Court, but to be available to the profession. The Governor laid the proposition before the Legislative Council, but it met with a very hostile reception.

> 'The profession of the law has become a lucrative one in this province'—said Mr Jacob Hagen, one of the nominated councillors—'and I see no reason why the members of it should have a library at the public expense.'

Even Captain Bagot, a lawyer, turned blackleg and voted against the appropriation as setting a bad precedent. The money was therefore added to the general revenue.[9]

The rejection of this proposal was severely criticised in the press. It was useless, it was said, to expect every practitioner to have his own library, for in most cases the cost would be prohibitive. The lawyers would get no pecuniary benefit from a library but, on the other hand, the loss of it would be felt by the public.

> 'All lawyers know'—said the South Australian Gazette—'that their difficulty is to prevent their clients from rushing into litigation; and when the client with his feelings excited and suffering under a supposed injury, instructs his solicitor to institute a suit, nothing but authority as decisive as the latest case in point will drive him from his purpose; and the solicitor, not having a perfect library to refer to, goes on with the proceedings at a cost of £50, or £100, or £500 (as the case may be) until the matter comes before the Court, when the Judge—having the advantage of a good library—informs the unfortunate suitor that he is mistaken altogether in his law, and he has only the satisfaction of paying his own and his opponent's large bills; whereas could his solicitor have consulted the authorities, he would have informed his client, at the cost of a guinea or two, that his case was hopeless.' [10]

Nothing further was heard of the suggestion until Mr Justice Crawford arrived in 1851, and at once urged the necessity for establishing a library. He was "strongly impressed with the necessity which exists for such an establishment". If the Government provided a suitable room and accommodation, he had no doubt that a library would be soon established by the profession, and he made a handsome offer to supply a large number of reports to give the library a start.[11] The Government took this under consideration, and while they were still dozing over it, the Judges followed it up in December 1851 with a joint request on behalf of the profession that £500 should be placed upon the estimates for the purchase of books for the library. It was intended that the library should be used by all practitioners paying the annual practising fee, and they would pay in addition an entrance fee and annual subscription to be fixed by a committee, of which the Judges would be members. In other colonies, the Judges pointed out, there was no tax upon the legal profession, and in South Australia the tax had been originally proposed as a means of providing a law library, although the Legislative Council had availed themselves of the proceeds of it to increase the general revenue.[12]

This request came too late for it to be complied with in the estimates for 1852, but the Governor promised to bear it in mind when preparing those of 1853.

Some months later Mr Rupert Ingleby offered his library of common law and admiralty reports to the Government for £225.

> 'I make this offer with greater confidence'—he said rather bitterly—'as these reports have for a period of several years been gratuitously consulted by the Profession and used in the Courts of this Province, and are therefore well known to the Acting Attorney General and Crown Solicitor.'

The Governor got as far as inquiring the balance of unexpended revenue, but the answer to this question was not favourable and Mr Ingleby's offer was declined on the ground of poverty.[13]

In 1854 the members of the profession petitioned the Legislative Council, setting out the "urgent want of a Library of Reference of legal works, both English and American, in the prosecution of their professional pursuits". Such a library would be of extensive public utility, "as ensuring greater certainty and uniformity in the decisions of our Courts, and rendering them more fully in accordance with the decisions of other tribunals". Since the expense would exceed the means of individual practitioners, they asked that practising fees should be appropriated to the founding of a law library, accessible to all members of the profession on payment only of such annual sum as might be necessary to meet its expenses.[14] The petition was favourably received, and the Council voted an address to the Governor asking him to accede to it; and a committee was appointed, consisting of Messrs Hanson, Gwynne, Fisher, Fenn and Bagot, to consider the best means of providing for the reception of books intended for the law library. The committee went diligently about their task and, after obtaining an extension of time, brought up their report, which must stand as one of the most inane parliamentary papers ever printed. After prolonged thought, the committee solemnly recommended that the books should be placed in a room near the courthouse and that a librarian should be appointed to look after them.[15]

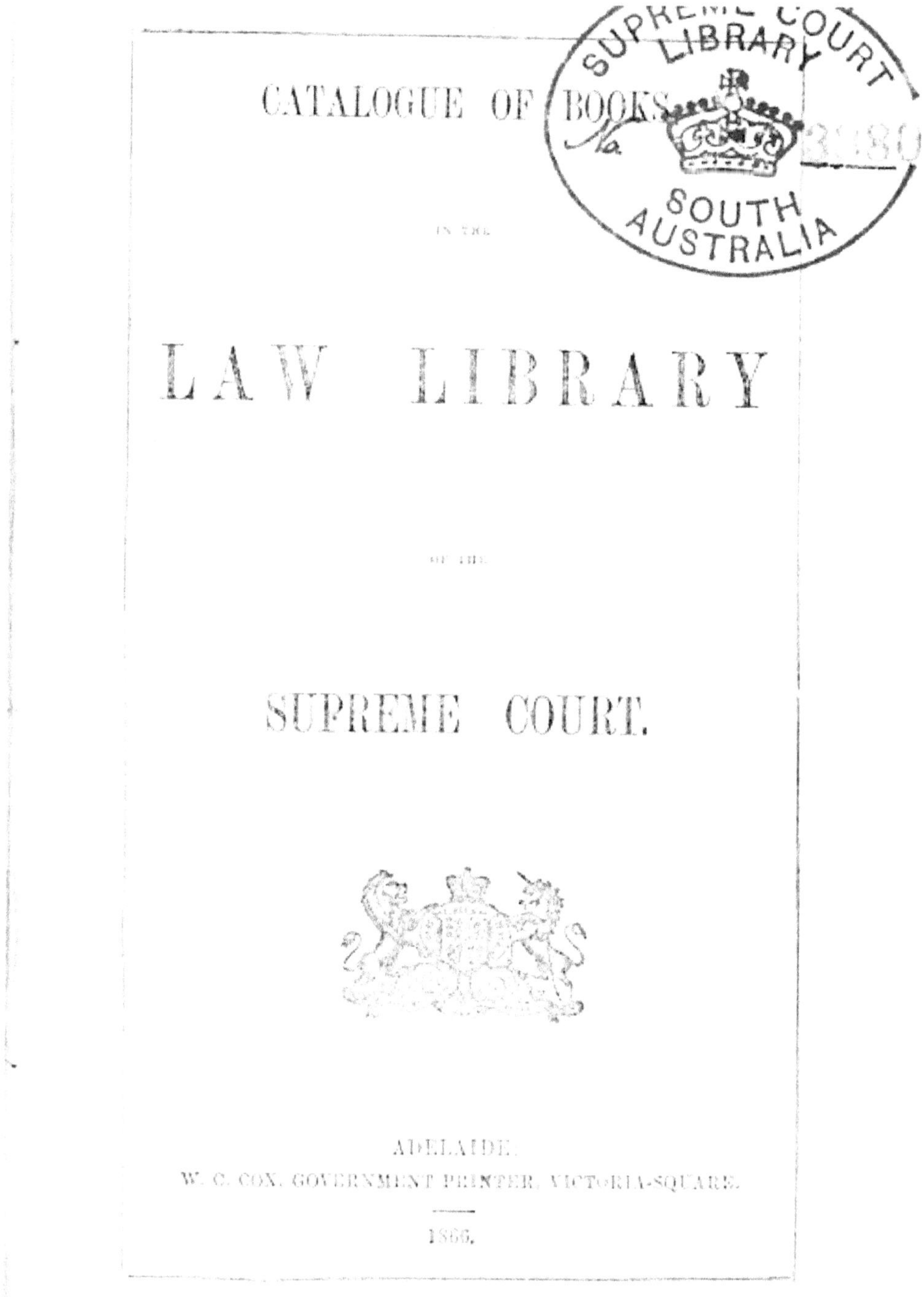

CATALOGUE OF BOOKS

IN THE

LAW LIBRARY

OF THE

SUPREME COURT.

ADELAIDE:
W. C. COX, GOVERNMENT PRINTER, VICTORIA-SQUARE.

1866.

The title page from the Library's first catalogue of 1866. (SCLSA)

The request for a parliamentary vote again missed the estimates for the current year 1854 but it was included in the following year, and Mr Finniss, the Colonial Secretary, gave directions that in future estimates the amount of the legal practitioners' fees was to be set aside for the law library.[16] A list of books was drawn up by the Judges and the law officers and in due course, in April 1856, they arrived from England. They were placed in a room at the courthouse which was occupied by Mr Cleland, the Registrar of Births, Deaths and Marriages, and he was appointed to look after them, with a small additional remuneration.[17] Once more the library had a narrow escape from vice regal appropriation, for the Governor disapproved of Mr Cleland spending his time looking after law books. He considered the practitioners should find someone to take charge of the books and, if they did not do so, he proposed to remove the books to the Legislative Council Library.[18] How the library was preserved from this fate does not appear, but Mr Cleland continued to superintend it, and in 1858 he was formally appointed to the newly created post of Law Librarian, with the princely addition of £30 per annum to his salary.[19]

A committee consisting of the Chief Justice and several practitioners prepared rules for regulating the library, and advised upon the selection of new books.[20] The Attorney-General, in answer to an inquiry in 1860, said that a practitioner had no right to use of the law library—it was merely a privilege conceded to him, subject to such rules and regulations as might be in force from time to time. "The Library", he said, drawing a peculiar distinction, "is one of reference and is not for the purpose of study."[21]

There were occasional parliamentary grumblings at the sum appearing annually in the estimates for the law library. The most heated discussion occurred in 1860. The legal members contended that the library was for the benefit of the people; "a good library would save inexperienced lawyers rushing their clients into ruin". Mr Dutton also supported them, pointing out that:

> '... the great cost of a law library would preclude individual members of the legal profession from supplying themselves with private libraries, and it was right that the Legislature should provide, and keep in one place, all the recent law works and legal decisions. The public interests would be injured if these legal works and decisions were not available in the administration of justice.'

There were, however, a good many members who thought, with Mr Glyde, that the £5 practising fee paid by the lawyers was a "sort of premium on obtaining a legal game certificate, authorising them to sport on the public", and these insisted loudly that lawyers should buy their own books. The Government, it was said, might as well buy agricultural books for farmers. After an angry debate, the tide was turned in favour of the lawyers by the amusement created at finding a ponderous quotation from Plowden in an opinion given by the then Attorney-General, Mr Strangways, a gentleman who was not remarkable for the profundity of his legal knowledge. In that "celebrated opinion", it was said, the works of the "antient Plowden" were referred to; if those works were to be found in the library, then by all means let the library be maintained; indeed, if all the books in it only contained information equal to that in the opinion of the learned Attorney-General, money should be lavished upon their protection. Goethe very truly remarked that an angry man is easily appeased if he can be once made to smile and, under the genial influence of a little satire, the opposition was relaxed and the estimates passed.[22]

A minor disturbance in the affairs of the library was created in 1861 by Mr Justice Boothby, who removed a number of books and refused to return them when the Librarian asked for them. The library regulations did not apply to him, he said, and he would return them at his leisure. The Librarian complained to the Attorney-General, who complained to the Chief Secretary, who in turn complained to Judge Boothby, and also instructed the Librarian to refuse to let the Judge have any more books until he returned those already borrowed. The Judge's only answer was to make another visit to the library and, ignoring the agitated opposition of the Librarian, he marched off with another book as a prize. Once more the complaints went the round to the Government offices, and this time Mr Justice Boothby was peremptorily informed that in future he was forbidden to borrow any book from the library without the Governor's permission being first had in writing. This drastic step appears to have put an end to the Judge's predatory habits.[23]

The library remained in the office of Mr Cleland until 1865. In that year the practitioners combined to draw up a memorial to the Chief Justice, representing the great inconvenience accruing from this arrangement. The space available for the library was very cramped and the business of the Registrar, it was said, necessitated "a flow of conversation between him and the persons who register (chiefly females) which is not favourable to the perusal of legal literature".[24] A rearrangement of rooms was made, which resulted in Mr Cleland being ousted and replaced as librarian by one of the clerks in the Supreme Court office. Mr Cleland promptly demanded compensation for loss of office. His claims were quieted by an increase in his salary; placidly, he resumed in his new quarters his platonic discourses with registering females, and legal literature was thenceforth perused in peace.[25]

Chief Justice Sir Samuel Way bequeathed his legal collection of 2300 volumes on his death in 1916. His bookplate is shown here. (SCLSA)

The institution of circuits courts was urged as early as 1846 by Mr Morphett in the Legislative Council, and it was one of the chief reasons put forward for the appointment of Mr Justice Crawford as Second Judge that one of the Judges would then have time to make a tour of the country districts.

From time to time the suggestion was revived.[1] In August 1853, for instance, an indignant correspondent wrote to the *Register*:

> 'Why should two Judges be always enjoying their etium cum dignitate at Adelaide, when they might be rendering good service to the State by travelling constantly circuits through the colony, administering a code of laws which would at least have the merit which does not attach to the decisions of the rural sages who are now employed viz that of being sanctioned by high legal authority? Why do these forensic luminaries linger in the south when they should be serving their Sovereign in the north? And why do they hide the light of their countenances in their urban retreats when they might impart a wholesome moral influence through the length and breadth of the land, and at the same time acquire for themselves information relative to the people in the country districts and respecting rural affairs, which would prove highly useful to them in their judicial duties afterwards ... The people would not then be dissatisfied at paying high salaries to their Judges, because the latter would have duties to perform beside those merely of going to the Bank and receiving their salaries. Their position in the State would be recognised by public opinion, and a higher utility than that of wearing horse-hair would be theirs.' [2]

No further steps were taken by the Government, however, until 1855. In June of that year the Commissioner of Police drew up a memorandum, pointing out the extreme inconvenience and pecuniary loss to which in many instances witnesses were subjected at the Supreme Court. At the last sessions, he said, witnesses had come from Mount Remarkable and Tatiara. They were obliged to start early and be in attendance on the first day of the sessions, although the case in which they were interested might not come on for some days. The subject, he thought, urgently required the attention of the Government.

> 'People are becoming so alarmed at the injury and inconvenience entailed upon them by their being witnesses in any case, that if some remedy be not adopted, the

administration of justice will be seriously impeded, and the perpetration of crime will be concealed in order to escape the inconvenience of giving evidence against the criminals.'

The Sheriff backed up the Commissioner of Police. "The altered circumstances of the colony as to the value of daily labour", he said, rendered it just and reasonable that some addition should be made to the amount of compensation allowed to witnesses.[3]

The Colonial Secretary (Mr Finniss) admitted that both the points raised—inconvenience from distance and insufficiency of the allowance by reason of the increase in cost of food and travelling—were felt as difficulties by the Government. The only remedy he could suggest was that the Judges should hold Circuit Courts—to begin with, at Kooringa and Penola. Considering that the grievance was "one of serious import to the cause of good government", the Governor asked the Advocate-General to consider and report upon it. In reply Mr Hanson wrote:

> 'I think there would be insuperable difficulties in organising Courts of Quarter Sessions here, since there is not any such class of men in the province as that from which, in the Mother Country, County Magistrates are selected. And the same difficulty would exist in the way of any increase to the power of the Local Courts, since the salaries given to the Special Magistrates are not such as to secure the services of a person of competent legal attainments. The establishment of Circuit Courts to be presided over by the Judges could form the only appropriate and adequate remedy, but this would require an augmentation of the number of Judges. Possibly the time may be considered to have arrived for this, and such a proposal might receive the sanction of the Legislature.'

Kooringa is one of the townships that collectively make up "The Burra". By 1851 the copper mines of Burra had attracted a population of 5,000 compared with Adelaide's 18,000 so the suggestion that a circuit court be held there is not surprising. The 1996 photograph shows the Paxton Square cottages that were built between 1849 and 1852 as accommodation for miners and their families. (NLA)

In the meantime, he suggested, the Court might be given a discretion to make an extra allowance to witnesses in special circumstances of hardship.

> 'I agree with the Advocate General'—noted the Governor—'that the most satisfactory remedy would be an additional Judge and Circuit Courts—both for civil and criminal business. The reception of such a Bill by the Council as yet must be doubtful. I propose therefore that the Advocate General be instructed to prepare a bill authorising the Supreme Court to vary from time to time, according to circumstances, the scale of payment to witnesses. 2ndly, I propose that the Governor be authorised to issue Commissions of oyer and terminer and all other commissions issued to Judges of Assize in England, and to direct courts to be holden in any place and at any time he may deem expedient, one of the present Judges presiding at such Court assisted by two or more of the country Magistrates. Mere Circuit Courts would at first be a delusion—but I would then be in a position to ask for money to build Court houses and country jails, and by and by for additional judicial assistance. I think there is no doubt the time has already arrived for some such step being taken, and the change in the law which I recommend would prepare the Public Mind for it.' 4

The Advocate-General was instructed by the Colonial Secretary to prepare a bill accordingly. He asked for further instructions on several points—were the two Magistrates, for instance, to act as a jury, or should provision be made for the summoning of ordinary juries?

> 'I never meant that the Advocate General should adopt only the suggestions enumerated in the Colonial Secretary's letter'—replied the Governor—'but rather that he should embody my own hints in a measure sufficiently full and comprehensive to carry into the country districts the full powers of the Supreme Court to settle questions of civil and criminal law arising there. If I were to write down suggestions for each section of such a bill I might as well settle the draught of it myself. I do not understand what the Advocate General means by Justices acting as jurors—I never heard of such a proposition being acted on—but the idea might I think be carefully worked out in civil proceedings.'

The procedure should be simplified as much as possible, and the Judges should be requested to assist in preparing a bill as would enable them "simply, cheaply, and frequently as possible to dispense justice in remote country districts as fully and completely as they now can in the courthouse at Adelaide".[5]

At the opening of the Legislative Council in November 1855, the Governor said:

> 'The period for carrying justice nearer to every man's door, by the establishment of Circuit Courts, seeming now to have arrived, a measure with that object will be proposed, as the rapid progress and increased means of the colony no longer justify the ends of justice being frequently defeated by imposing on witnesses and prosecutors the necessity of long and expensive journeys from the remotest ends of the Province.' [6]

The Chief Justice, however, was lukewarm in his opinion upon the proposal. The Supreme Court, he wrote, was by statute a court of Oyer and Terminer and, to bring circuit courts into operation, it was only necessary to give the Governor power to declare where they should be held and how often, and to appoint such officers as might be necessary. As to the expediency of establishing circuit courts throughout the colony, however, he doubted whether the time had arrived when this could be done with general advantage. Inconvenience had not been very great except in a few cases. Although with circuit courts parties and witnesses would not have far to travel, counsel would have to come from Adelaide at considerable expense for a few cases. "And I am fully persuaded that without the attendance of counsel justice will not be satisfactorily administered in the Circuit Courts."

If there were only a few cases for trial, the travelling expenses of the Judge, officers, and counsel—

> '... the difficulty of getting to and from remote places, the bad accomodation [sic] in many inns, and the small dignity which attends a court which has habitually little or nothing to do, are matters which appear to me worthy of consideration'.

Further, jurors were drawn from the whole province. It would be difficult to prepare separate jury lists for separate districts, so that who had served on a jury at the Circuit Court should not be called on again to serve at Adelaide, and it might be hard to get a fair and unprejudiced jury out of the small population in the neighbourhood of the circuit town.[7]

While the opinion of the Chief Justice deserved great weight, said the Governor, he could not agree with him.

> 'I cannot believe that it tends to the progress of justice, or even of civilization, that a question of a disputed right to an acre of land at Port Lincoln or Mount Gambier should entail the expense and the personal annoyance and the difficulties which

> must follow the decision of such dispute being fixed at Adelaide ... I have strong reason for supposing that the Judge underrates the inconvenience—amounting to a denial of justice—experienced frequently in those places through the want of the Supreme Judicial authority being close at hand to settle vexed questions of real property. I also believe that there may be found methods of finding at each place quite sufficient legal knowledge and ability to conduct cases so as to insure the Judge directing the jury, or in cases of demurrer, himself deciding rightly ... I believe that distant parts of the country are now sufficiently settled to require that their interest in a ready administration of justice be no longer overlooked—although at present and for many years to come the 'dignity' of Circuit Courts visiting these localities must depend much more on the reputation they may import with themselves than on the amount of business they will find, or the conveniences which travel-fatigued Judges can count on.'

After all, it was a question of time, concluded the Governor. Had the time come for circuit courts? "I think it has. Others think it has not." [8]

The want of enthusiasm on the part of the Judges, however, led to a temporary abandonment of the proposal, and it was not until October 1857 that it was again brought forward when, during the discussion on the estimates in the House of Assembly, Mr J.B. Neales ingeniously argued that the establishment of circuit courts would be productive of a great advantage to the country—namely, the adequate maintenance of the roads. "Travelling Judges"—he said—"will surely see that the roads are properly attended to; in fact, it will be a Road Bill in itself." [9]

At a later stage in the same session the Attorney-General introduced a bill to establish circuit courts and to provide for the appointment of a third judge. As drafted, the Bill provided for juries of four in both criminal and civil cases tried on circuit. This was so objectionable to members that it was amended, but the House could not come to any agreement on the subject. Some thought circuit courts and another judge were an absolute necessity; some wanted circuit courts but thought a third judge was unnecessary; others again thought both were an extravagant luxury. In support of circuit courts, Mr Hay ingenuously urged that it would contribute to the health of the Judges to travel about. After struggling through the Assembly, the Bill was withdrawn by the Government.[10]

Alexander Hay (1820-1898) Starting life in South Australia in 1839 as a "warfer and packer" Hay went on to become a successful merchant and pastoralist and long serving Member of Parliament. (SLSA)

It was reintroduced in December 1858 in an improved form, and passed.

The Act (No 13 of 1858) empowered the Governor to appoint "a fit and proper person" to be Judge of the Supreme Court at the same salary as the Second Judge and, with the advice of Executive Council, to issue commissions to the Judges to hold Courts of Oyer and Terminer and Gaol Delivery at times and places to be named in the commissions, for the trial of both civil and criminal cases.

> 'Such Court so holden shall stand to the Supreme Court in the same relation as Courts of Oyer and Terminer and General Gaol Delivery, and Nisi Prius, in England, stand to Her Majesty's Court at Westminster.'

In the Legislative Council, Mr Forster made an iconoclastic protest.

> 'It is clear'—he said—'that the Supreme Court of the Colony, as administered, is of no benefit to the community. It would be far better for the interests of the community if it were swept away, and some other means of obtaining justice determined upon. I am surprised that the Government, instead of proposing to appoint a third Judge, do not suggest that some other Court should be established to secure justice to suitors. If they had proposed to sweep away the Supreme Court on the civil side, and to appoint a Court of Arbitration where suitors could obtain justice, I should have supported them in the proposition, but I cannot support them when they come to this House simply because two Judges cannot agree, and ask the House to go to the enormous expense of appointing a third judge as umpire.' [11]

The Attorney-General, in advising the Governor to assent to the Act, pointed out that it was designed to remove two defects—the frequent differences of opinion in the Supreme Court and the great cost to litigants and prosecutors residing in the country.[12] In forwarding the Act to England, the Governor wrote:

> 'The necessity for making justice easily accessible—though often felt in older and more densely populated countries—is strikingly obvious in a newly settled country like this, where the inhabitants are few in proportion to the extent of territory occupied, an the distances to be traversed to the metropolis are disproportionately long and difficult. The consequence is that much inconvenience and loss is necessarily endured to avoid yet greater inconvenience and loss in journeying to Adelaide, and much crime is likewise supposed to go unpunished from the natural dread which prosecutors and witnesses entertain of a summons to Adelaide to the great detriment of their business and sacrifice of their time.' [13]

The first Circuit Court was not held until early in 1862, when Mr Justice Gwynne visited the South-East in the steamer *Ant.*[14] For several years Courts were held at irregular intervals at Mount Gambier and Robe. In 1867 the Government considered holding a circuit court four times a year in the South-East, but the Crown Solicitor (Mr Wearing) reported that twice a year would be often enough. Mr Justice Gwynne agreed, and added:

> "At a time not far distant I have no doubt it will be thought expedient by the Government to appoint a competent person to the office of Judge of the Supreme Court to be resident at Mount Gambier. He would preside in their Insolvency Court, in their Local Court, and could give them a sitting in their Circuit Court twelve times a year if they wished it. The offices of Judge's Associate, Clerk of the Local Court, and of the Insolvency Court, and Deputy Sheriff could also be concentrated in one intelligent well-paid officer.'

Samuel Calvert's *Travelling in a dust storm in South Australia* (1867) illustrates the difficulty of travel in colonial times. (SLV)

A point of some difficulty which Mr Justice Gwynne thought might arise was the extent of the territorial jurisdiction of the Circuit Court—from what places, for instance, were prisoners to be committed for trial at circuit courts? "Is the extent of the Judge's Jurisdiction (territorial) to be determined by the stupidity of the community JP?" [15]

At one time it appeared possible that questions of venue might become an important branch of South Australian law (see for example *Cherry v. Colton* 2 SALR 17, *Leake v. Sutherland* ib 72, *McCaull v. Clarke* ib 204) but civil business at the Circuit Courts, instead of growing in proportion to the increase in population, decreased proportionately to the improvement of the means of transport and communication, and has now for very many years been negligible.

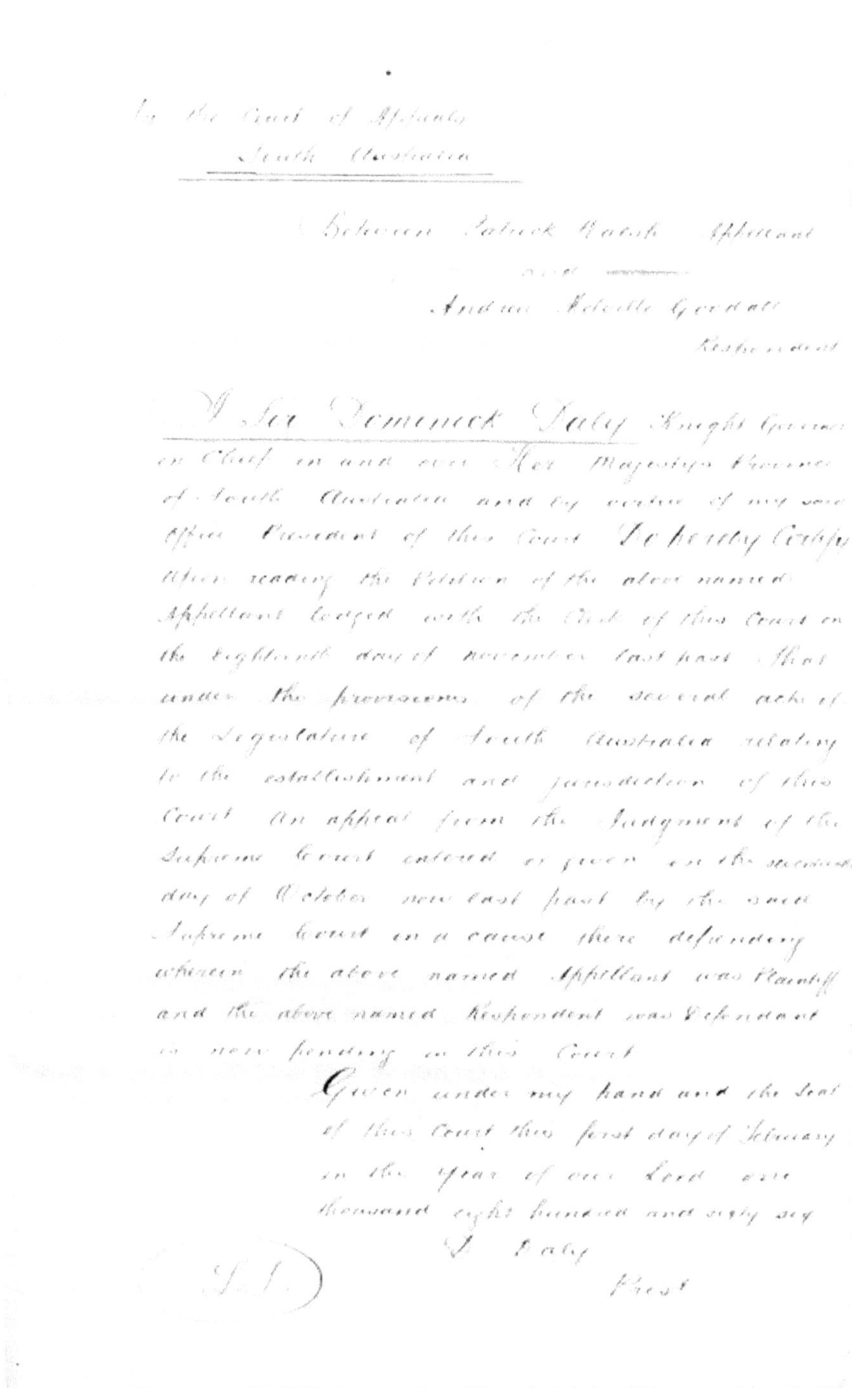

In the Court of Appeals
South Australia

Between Patrick Walsh Appellant
and
Andrew Melville Goodall
Respondent

I Sir Dominick Daly Knight Governor in Chief in and over Her Majesty's Province of South Australia and by virtue of my said Office President of this Court Do hereby Certify after reading the Petition of the above named Appellant lodged with the Clerk of this Court on the eighteenth day of November last past That under the provisions of the several acts of the Legislature of South Australia relating to the establishment and jurisdiction of this Court An appeal from the Judgment of the Supreme Court entered or given on the second day of October now last past by the said Supreme Court in a cause there depending wherein the above named Appellant was Plaintiff and the above named Respondent was Defendant is now pending in this Court

Given under my hand and the Seal of this Court this first day of February in the year of our Lord one thousand eight hundred and sixty six

D Daly
Prest

(L.S.)

Certificate of appeal pending in Walsh v Goodall. Note the use of "LS" – the device which Henry Palmer suffered confusion over. (SR/SC)

Chapter 7

The Court of Appeals

'intricate and subtle questions'

After an "adventurous and chequered career" during the first thirty years of its existence, the Court of Appeals slumbered peacefully for over half a century. Its jurisdiction was last invoked in 1882. The various Acts establishing and regulating the Court were all repealed by the Supreme Court Act 1935, which omits all mention of the Court of Appeals, and (subject to a possible contrary contention to be hereafter mentioned) the Court has presumably ceased to exist.

It was established by the Supreme Court Act 1837 (7 Wm IV No 5) section XVI, which provided that the Governor and Council of the Province (with the exception of the Advocate-General and Crown Solicitor) should constitute a Court to be called "the Court of Appeals of the Province of South Australia". Jurisdiction was given to the Court to receive and hear appeals from the judgments, decrees, orders and sentences of the Supreme Court in cases where the sum at issue amounted to £100, but subject to an important proviso that, on any appeal brought from a judgment of the Supreme Court founded upon the verdict of a jury of twelve men, the Court of Appeals should not reverse, alter or inquire into the judgment except for error of law apparent upon the record.

The constitution of this Court was for many reasons unsatisfactory, but in a new colony with only one judge there was no other way of providing for a review of his decisions. The delay and expense of an appeal to the Privy Council was almost prohibitive. Similar courts had been common in the American colonies and in the West Indies. Alexander Hamilton, in *The Federalist* (No LXXXI), put the obvious objections to them in forcible and convincing language:

> 'There is an absurdity in referring the determination of causes, in the first instance, to judges of permanent standing; in the last, to those of a temporary and mutable constitution. And there is a still greater absurdity in subjecting the decisions of men, selected for their knowledge of the laws, acquired by long and laborious study, to the revision and control of men who, for want of the same advantage, cannot but be deficient in that knowledge. The members of the legislature will rarely be chosen with a view to those qualifications which fit men for the stations of judges; and as, on this account, there will be great reason to apprehend all the ill consequences of defective information, so, on account of the natural propensity of such bodies to party divisions, there will be no less reason to fear that the pestilential breach of faction may poison the fountains of justice. The habit of being continually marshalled on opposite sides will be too apt to stifle the voice both of law and

of equity.'

The Commissioners who inquired into the administration of justice in the West Indies some ten years before the founding of South Australia had roundly condemned the system of placing judicial appellate power in the hands of executive and legislative councils.

> 'In consequence of this arrangement'—they said—'the decision of a regular bred lawyer comes upon appeal before a military officer and a small number of gentlemen, who, though highly honourable and intelligent, labour under the disadvantage of the want of a professional education. The result is a want of confidence among the colonists as to the uniform administration of the rules of justice. The Commissioners, in every instance, recommend that this practice should be altered.' [1]

In the case of South Australia, the Court was perhaps slightly less offensive in its original constitution, because:

(1) At that time, the Judge was a member of the Council. The advantage of having in the Court of Appeals at least one qualified lawyer, however, was offset by the fact that the Judge was required to sit in judgment on his own decisions. It was further undesirable for two reasons that the Judge should be a member of the Council: first, the administration of justice should be kept free from any suggestion of political influence and, secondly, judicial habits and training are not usually conducive to the proper performance of administrative functions.

(2) The members of the Council were all officers of the government, appointed and removed at the pleasure of the Crown. Political influence was not likely to be strong. "There was no such thing as Ministers going to the country, or being engaged in party warfare." [2]

(Sir) George Strickland Kingston ca. 1838 by S.T.Gill (SLSA)

When, in July 1838, the Council of Government was reconstituted by Order in Council, the Judge was omitted from it and the Surveyor-General (G.S. Kingston) included in his stead. The only other legal member of the Council, the Advocate-General, was of course excluded from the Court of Appeals for the reason that he would be interested, as counsel, in many of the causes which came before the Court.

The first attempt made by a party to avail himself of the right of appeal in October 1838 met with an unsympathetic reception from Governor Gawler. With a humanity which was a little in advance of his time, Jickling, the Acting Judge, had held that the right to arrest a debtor on mesne process had not been brought out to South Australia with the common law. The creditor announced his intention of appealing. The Governor, who was sufficiently busy without adding judicial work to his duties, wrote to Jickling protesting against "the inconvenience and delay to the course of public business which the forms attendant upon a solemn appeal to the Council would occasion". He could see no reason why the law of arrest should not be in force in the colony, and he demanded Jickling's reasons for holding the contrary in so decided a tone that the timorous Judge seems to have been overawed into reversing his decision, for the appeal is heard of no more and in a short time the gaol begins to be packed with debtors in as miserable a plight as any in the Marshalsea or the Fleet.[3]

The first appeal to come before the Court arose out of extraordinary and ridiculous circumstances. The *Ville de Bordeaux* was a French ship which had been illegally sold at Sydney. It came to South Australia in January 1841, ostensibly to load sheep for Bourbon, but Torrens, the Collector of Customs, had his suspicions aroused about the vessel by a number of peculiar circumstances and formed the opinion that it was being used in contravention of the Navigation Acts, which prohibited a foreign ship from trading between British ports. Pending a further investigation, he obtained authority from the Governor to have the vessel removed from Glenelg, where it was anchored, to Port Adelaide and two customs officers were placed on board for this purpose. Instead of heading for Port Adelaide, the vessel put out to sea, taking the customs officials with it and leaving Torrens dancing with rage on the beach. He sent post-haste to Adelaide for the police and Alexander Tolmer (then Inspector of Police) has told in his *Reminiscences* the amusing story of what followed. He and his men were at a Sunday morning church parade when, about the middle of the service, Torrens's messenger arrived. The sensation in the church, as the whole body of police hastily seized their caps and swords and hurried out, may easily be imagined. The congregation, with visions of the town being sacked by bushrangers or attacked by hordes of wild blackfellows, probably prayed more fervently than they had done for a long time past. Galloping to Glenelg, the police found the *Ville de Bordeaux* still in sight about seven miles down the Gulf. Torrens had seized a flock of some 2,000 sheep as they were about to be taken on board the vessel, and he was busily engaged in having the struggling animals branded with a broad arrow in black tar. Piling into a whaleboat, the enthusiastic and excited party set out to row after the escaping ship. As there was a strong wind and a heavy sea, they soon tired of this and realised the absurdity of hoping to catch up with it. Returning to the beach, they set out on a helter-skelter ride through the swamps of the reed beds on a short cut to Port Adelaide, which they reached with their white Sunday uniforms covered with black mud. The *Courier*, a small paddle-wheel steamer belonging to the Government, was requisitioned and all hands turned to stacking firewood and coal

Alexander Tolmer (1815-1890)
The title to Tolmer's autobiography - *Reminiscences of an Adventurous and Chequered Career at Home and at the Antipodes* - is as good a summation of his life as any. A man of action he rose to the position of Commissioner of Police in 1852 only to be demoted the following year. Perhaps best known for devising and implementing the gold escort service he is also noted for being part of the Maria/Milmenrura episode. (SLSA)

on board. In the hurry of getting some provisions, a cask of brandy was staved in.

> 'An empty cask was then quickly procured, and what was saved of the brandy was put into it. This exciting part of the proceedings had to be performed with ladles and dippers, and probably owing to the fumes of the spirits, and nips imbibed on the sly, speedily stupefied the men and rendered them helpless.'

Amid great confusion and cheers from a crowd which had gathered on the wharf, the *Courier*, with its decks loaded with police and firewood, cast off. All went well for a few hundred yards and then the engines stopped.

> 'Captain Lipson requested me'—writes Tolmer—'to let the police jump up on the paddle-boxes, and start the wheels by shoving them round with their feet. This novel expedient had the desired effect, and once more we proceeded rapidly on our way, but alas! only for a short distance, as the vessel came to a standstill altogether.'

The *Ville de Bordeaux* at Port Adelaide by J.M. Skipper (AGSA)

Once more, the police had to be called upon. The crowd on the shore were in hysterics at the sight of perspiring and brandy-excited policemen frantically labouring at this new species of treadmill. At length, the *Courier* got out into the Gulf and for several days steamed up and down searching in vain for the *Ville de Bordeaux*. When shortage of fuel compelled a return to Glenelg, it was found that the French ship was safely secured at Port Adelaide, the crew having mutinied and brought it back. "Lipson's horse marines" had been out on a wild-goose chase.

> 'In the attempt I have made'—wrote Tolmer, in describing the foregoing mad and quixotic proceedings—'I confess my utter inability as a writer, as it requires the pen of Dickens, a Lever or other such talented writers to convey to the reader the absurdity and folly of the whole thing.' [4]

A confused series of prosecutions and actions followed, almost as silly as the previous proceedings. The ship not having been claimed within a month from its seizure, Torrens claimed that it was forfeited to the Crown, but the Judge refused to make a declaration of forfeiture and ordered a writ of appraisement and delivery to issue.[5] It was against this order that the appeal to the Court of Appeals was brought by the Advocate-General on behalf of the Collector of Customs.

To make the necessary preparations for constituting the Court, Mr Thomas Wilson, a solicitor, was appointed to be its clerk. He was a man of very considerable talents, who traced his pedigree to Oliver Cromwell, and was a claimant for the dormant peerage of Annandale. Educated in Germany, he spoke several modern languages fluently and was a good classical scholar. He had practised in London with great success, having the good fortune to obtain the lucrative position of agent for Lord Portman's extensive London properties, and had travelled round the Continent gathering a magnificent collection of engravings. Alfred Russell Wallace, the naturalist, was his nephew and in his autobiography *My Life* Wallace describes a visit to his uncle's home at Dulwich. "I remember"—he says—"being much impressed with the large house, and especially with the beautiful grounds, with lawns, trees and shrubs such as I had never seen before." [6]

Mr Wilson later gratified his artistic leanings by purchasing a large estate in Radnorshire, where he rebuilt to his own luxurious designs a ruined abbey. He published books on art, *The Catalogue of an Amateur* and an *Illustrated Catalogue of the Works of Rembrandt.* His *Shakespeare Illustrated*, we are told, was valued at 1,000 guineas, but whether he published it or illustrated it or merely owned it does not now appear. An accomplished musician, he was also a practical organ-builder and designed and named a new stop, the "Clarabella".[7]

In 1834, disaster overtook this connoisseur of the fine arts.

> 'Owing to a series of events which we were only very imperfectly acquainted with'—wrote Wallace—'he became bankrupt in this year, and his own wife and large family were at once reduced from a condition of comfort and even affluence to poverty almost as great as our own. But we children also

> suffered, for legacies of £100 each to my father's family to be paid to us as we came of age, together with a considerable sum that had reverted to my mother on the death of her stepmother in 1828, had remained in Mr Wilson's hands as trustee, and was all involved in the bankruptcy. He did all he possibly could for us, and ultimately, I believe, repaid a considerable part of the money, but while the legal proceedings were in progress, and they lasted full three years, it was necessary for us to reduce expenses as much as possible.' [8]

As soon as the bankruptcy proceedings were finished, Mr Wilson set out with his family to start life afresh in South Australia, which he reached in 1838. He remained in practice in Adelaide till his death in 1863, at the age of seventy -six, and managed to make a comfortable living for his family. No salary was attached to the position of Clerk of the Court of Appeals, but he was allowed to take as remuneration any fees received. The Governor airily talked of Mr Wilson paying into the Treasury all fees received in excess of £400 a year.[9] The amount received annually was much nearer 400 pence. After holding the position for fifteen years, Mr Wilson estimated his remuneration had averaged over that period less than five shillings a week.[10] In 1841, however, he was no doubt glad to take the appointment in the hope of adding a little to his shattered fortune.

He prepared rules to regulate the procedure of the Court. Under these, the appeal was instituted by a petition, stating the general grounds of appeal. The respondent had to appear by his solicitor within fifteen days, and an order was then made setting down the appeal for hearing. Each party could be heard by two counsel.[11]

A preliminary objection was taken in the *Ville de Bordeaux* appeal that the order appealed from was not a final but an interlocutory order and was not appealable. This objection was upheld or, as the *Register* chose to put it, "the appeal was kicked out of Court".[12] The newspapers had taken sides on the question with their accustomed acerbity, "who peppered the highest was surest to please", was the motto of early South Australian journalism. Every step Torrens had taken, declared the *Register*, was flagrantly illegal and it characterised the appeal as a crowning act of folly on the part of Smillie, the Advocate-General.

> 'The total smash thus given to the Collector's practical and theoretical knowledge of his duty, and the really melancholy exhibition of downright incapacity on the part of his legal adviser and abettor, dispose us for the present to refrain from administering any additional corrective to these foolish and ignorant young persons, believing that the public breeching they have just undergone may be sufficient for at least one week.' [13]

The Court of Appeals itself the *Register* described as "a new tribunal of exceedingly doubtful utility", and it questioned the legality of an appeal on behalf of the Crown from the Supreme Court to the Governor and Council.

> 'Its impropriety is sufficiently apparent, as bringing the Crown into the invidious position of judging in its own case. The idea of an appeal—on a strict point of law, too—from the decision of the highest legal tribunal of the Province is, under the circumstances, a positive farce. Of the Governor and Council, it is neither discreditable nor disrespectful to assert that they can know no more of the law of England, and are no better qualified to review the decisions of Chief Justice Cooper founded upon that law, than the Advocate General himself.' [14]

In November 1841 the Judge declared the *Ville de Bordeaux* to be forfeited to the Crown for a breach of the Navigation Acts (though on totally different grounds from those upon which the ship had been seized),[15] and the *Southern Australian* was now able to reply to the *Register*. The prosecution had triumphed, it was said:

> '... in spite of all the misdeeds concocted by the native virulence and long-fostered venom of a hyper-hypocritical bawler who made it his boast that he could direct public opinion on the subject through a corrupt and prostitute press'. [16]

The squabble over the ship went on for many years, until in 1852 the British Government paid its French owner £4,000 to settle his claims. The *Ville de Bordeaux* itself rotted away as a hulk on the Port River. To disentangle the whole of this confused and complicated story would take a volume in itself and could reveal little that was creditable to anyone concerned in it. The only person who seems to have profited from the whole affair was Charles Mann, who acted for the ship's captain. A local poet composed a song to him, to the air of *Charlie is my Darling*, beginning:

> 'Come Charlie! dinna look sae glum,
> Villa-de-Bordeaux we've lost, not won,
> But still we'll try anither turn,
> Before we lose our fee'. [17]

In 1842 the constitution of the Council of Government was altered and the Executive Council became a separate body from the Legislative Council, which thenceforth comprised the Governor, three official members and four non-official appointed members. This change left it open to question whether the Court of Appeals still existed, for neither the new Legislative Council nor the new Executive Council could be considered as the "Council of the Province" referred to in the Act of 1837. The Judge wrote to Governor Grey in February 1844: "As at present constituted it does not appear to me to be such a Court as is contemplated by the Supreme Court Act—supposing the Appeal Court to be in present existence"—which, considering that the Judge was no longer a member of the Council and the Council itself was much changed in character, he thought was doubtful.[18] The Governor accordingly directed a bill to be introduced into the Legislative Council to amend the Supreme Court Act, as he considered that the doubts about the Court of Appeals should be settled without delay.[19] Section 3 of the Supreme Court Act Amendment Act (No 6 of 1844) provided that, wherever in the previous Act the term "Governor and Council" was used, it should be construed to mean "the person lawfully acting as Governor of the Province for the time being and the Council of Government or the Executive Council thereof".

Shortly after this reconstitution of the Court, two appeals were brought to it.
The first, *Angas and Others (trustees of the South Australian Company) v. Duff*, arose out of an action for damages brought by the former parties for an alleged rescue of goods distrained for rent. The jury gave a verdict for £180 damages, contrary to the direction of the Judge, who considered the plaintiffs were not entitled to recover, and he subsequently made an order setting aside this verdict and directed that the plaintiffs should be non-suited.[20] The plaintiffs appealed on the ground that the Judge had no power to set aside the verdict of a jury and direct the plaintiffs to be non-suited without their consent. When the appeal came on for hearing, it was objected that the Court of Appeals was a Court of Error and possessed jurisdiction only in cases where error appeared on the face of the record. After several hearings, the Court of Appeals sent the parties back to the Judge with a request that he would reconsider his decision.[21] The Governor said the Court was very doubtful whether it had any jurisdiction.

> 'It having been argued for the appellants in this case that the constitution of this Court is peculiar, without analogy to the jurisdiction of any Court of Error known in England, and that it derives a portion of its powers from prerogative, we think it right to observe, that no appeal from an inferior court lies to this Court in its character of the Council of Government, for it possesses no powers as such Council, except those which have been conferred upon it by Her Majesty in the Royal Instructions; and no power of hearing such appeals as might be made to the Queen in Council is, by those Instructions, given to the Council of Government. In all questions, therefore, relating to the jurisdiction of this Court, we shall have to consider solely the powers which have been conferred upon the Court of Appeals by the Local Act 7 William 4th c.5.' [22]

The Judge refused to alter his previous decision, and the parties returned to the Court of Appeals where, after further hearing, it was held that there was no jurisdiction to entertain the appeal. In delivering the judgment of the Court, the Governor referred to the Supreme Court Act of 1837 and continued:

> 'The powers conferred upon this Court by that Act are large, and in this respect correspond with the powers which are, by the same enactment, conferred upon the Supreme Court of this Province. They appear also to us to have reference to the different branches of jurisdiction of the Supreme Court, as in Equity, Ecclesiastical Law, and so forth, thus enabling this Court, upon appeal from the Court below, to regard the practice observed in England in reference to those respective jurisdictions. The decision in the case of Powell v. Washbourne appears to us to show, that when the constitution and practice prevailing in the local courts in British Colonies are after the Common Law Courts at Westminster, which is the case in this Province, error alone is the subject of appeal; and we therefore entertain strong doubts whether, in a cause from the common law side of the Supreme Court, we are not restrained by the practice of Courts of Error in England; and these doubts are much increased in the present case, as, even assuming that the Court had jurisdiction in it, we are unable to see how we could properly give effect to that jurisdiction.' [23]

In the second appeal, *Archer v. Thoume Moulin and Co*, the Judge had made an order in chambers for a new trial of an action between the parties. Mr Fisher for the respondent took the objection that this was an interlocutory order from which no appeal lay and the Court, agreeing with him, said they had no jurisdiction to entertain the appeal.[24]

In each of these cases, the result was very unsatisfactory to everybody concerned. Each of the parties was left to pay his own costs, estimated in *Angas v. Duff* to be £250 to £300. "An appeal from the decision of a Resident Judge to a Governor in Council is now pretty generally understood to be of little value"—remarked the *Register*.[25] Mr Wilson, the Clerk of the Court, was placed in an unfortunate position. In *Archer v. Thoume*, the fees due to him were £12, but he had neglected to make sure of them in advance and the appellant now refused to pay, alleging—with some logic—that if the Court had no jurisdiction to hear his appeal then it had no jurisdiction to take fees from him. Mr Wilson could ill afford to lose the amount, and he complained to the Colonial Secretary. The Government rather generously agreed to pay him but, to prevent it happening again, he was instructed to prepare a rule that fees should be paid at every step of the proceedings and that no member of the profession should be allowed to practise in the Court in any way so long as fees due by him were unpaid.[26]

In 1846 Governor Robe tried to alter and improve the constitution of the Court.[27] It then consisted of the Governor, Colonial Secretary and Surveyor-General, all three of them military officers with no legal training at all. The Governor reported to the Secretary of State:

> 'In the case of appeal on account of error in law I need not say that such a Court composed as I have stated is not the most competent to expound that law. I am aware that in the earlier stages of the progress of a colony, when means are wanting for the payment of salaries to Judges professionally educated, resort must be had to Courts of the nature of the Appeal Court of this Province, but that it is viewed as a mere temporary arrangement I conclude from the circumstances of her Majesty's confirmation of the Ordinance 7 William IV No 5 and of an amending Ordinance No 6 of 1844 having been withheld.' [28]

He had consulted the Judge, who suggested three methods of relieving the Governor and Council from the duty of hearing appeals:

(1) By referring the appeals to a judge of one of the neighbouring colonies.
(2) By diminishing the amount in respect of which an appeal could be had to the Privy Council.
(3) By an increase in the number of judges of the Supreme Court.

The Governor thought the second proposal might be practicable. By lowering the minimum appealable amount to £300, as at Gibraltar, "substantial though from the great distance tardy justice would be obtained". The third suggestion, however, would be more acceptable to himself, to the Legislative Council and to the colonists.

Nothing followed his suggestions, and during the next few years occasional appeals were brought, one in 1846, another in 1849 and a third in 1850. In the last-mentioned, *Saunders v. Newenham*, the two Judges (Cooper and Crawford) attended and read written opinions. The Governor was in favour of allowing the appeal, but was overruled by the majority of the Court.[29] No more appeals occurred until 1856.

In 1853 Sir Henry Fox Young, the Governor, called on the Advocate-General (Mr Hanson) for a report on the Court of Appeals and, in particular, directed his attention to "the absurdity of the present constitution of that Court". He suggested that cases for appeal should be stated by consent of appellants and respondents, authenticated by the Judge and Registrar of the Supreme Court and then sent in that state for the decision of the Court of one of the neighbouring colonies, the appellate court having the power to return the case for further evidence or explanation, if required, before coming to a final conclusion.[30] Hanson does not seem to have furnished any written report, but in the following year, when the

Judges proposed that an amending Supreme Court Act should be introduced into the Legislative Council, Finniss (the Colonial Secretary) suggested a separate bill to deal with the Court of Appeals. Hanson then prepared a memorandum, which was considered and approved by the Executive Council. After criticising the constitution of the Court, "which is not selected with any reference to its knowledge of law, while in what probably would be by far the most numerous class of cases it is confined to matters of law solely as the ground of its judgment", he said:

> 'It has occurred to me that the materials for constituting a Court of Appeals for the various colonies might be found in their respective Supreme Courts. The separate Courts might for this purpose form one Court, analagous to that of the Exchequer Chamber, for the hearing of appeals from any of the Supreme Courts, those Judges only giving an opinion in each case who are not members of the Court whose judgment is appealed against. In this way, if the four Australasian colonies, including Van Diemen's Land, should join, there would be three courts to revise the decision of any one, or if Van Diemen's Land should not be included, then there would be two such Courts.' [31]

John Alexander Jackson (c1809-1885)
Jackson was Colonial Treasurer from 1839 to 1841 and Colonial Secretary from 1841 to 1843. He resigned from the latter position as a result of questions of conflict of interest and his accounting performance relating to his time as Treasurer. He returned to Tasmania and then to London resurrecting his career by acting as an agent for colonial interests, including those of South Australia. (SLSA)

The suggestion of a Court of Appeal for all the Australian colonies was not new, although it does not seem to have been previously put forward in the way proposed by Hanson. In 1849 a Committee of the Privy Council had been appointed to inquire into the constitutional changes which it might be advisable to make in the government of the Australian colonies. The Committee had recommended the establishment of a general assembly of delegates elected by the legislatures of the colonies, the range of the legislative authority of the general assembly being limited to ten topics, which included "the establishment of a General Supreme Court, to be a Court of Original Jurisdiction or a Court of Appeal for any of the inferior Courts of the Separate Provinces" and "the determining of the extent of the jurisdiction and the forms and manner of proceedings of such Supreme Court".[32] J.A. Jackson, who had succeeded Osmond Gilles as Colonial Treasurer in South Australia, in a memorandum to Lord Grey in the same year, wrote:

> 'The establishment of a General Supreme Court of Appeals from the separate provinces would not, I have a very strong persuasion, be in any respect desirable. In the great majority of instances the ordinary administration of the law by the superior Courts in each colony, with their powers of granting new trials, and their equitable jurisdiction, would be quite satisfactory. But if a formal appellate jurisdiction is required, I should submit the necessity of its distinct establishment in each colony; so that

> each colony would have its complete system of judicial procedure. To send an appellant from Adelaide to Sydney or Melbourne would be a grievance really not very much inferior to that of sending him before the Judicial Committee of Her Majesty's Privy Council.' [33]

The *South Australian Gazette* denounced the idea of a general Supreme Court as "equally preposterous and impracticable".

> 'There is nothing known here favourably'—it said—'of the wisdom, discretion, or legal knowledge of the Courts of Van Diemen's Land or New South Wales that would tempt anyone but desperate suitors to have recourse to them for final decisions. The power of doing so would certainly increase inducements to litigation, and delays of justice might become more practicable than they are at present ... but we must rather put up with a little occasional and unintentional injustice from our own countrymen, than trust foreigners who have no claim whatever to confidence or respect.' [34]

Wentworth's Constitutional Committee of 1853 advocated a general Colonial Court of Appeal,[35] and it was included in the memorial of the General Association for the Australian Colonies submitted to the Secretary of State in 1857.[36]

No action was taken on Hanson's memorandum by Sir Henry Young, but Sir Richard MacDonnell, his successor—who had formerly been Chief Justice at Gambier—became interested in it and strongly advocated a federal court. In January 1856 he proposed to the governments of the other colonies that steps should be taken to form a "highly qualified and impartial tribunal having adequate jurisdiction to determine within each colony appeals from the courts of each". His idea was an appellate Circuit Court, composed from "the materials supplied by the proximity of the colonies to one another, and the ability which distinguishes the Judicial Bench of each". A central court in one state would not be supported by the others, but some of the Judges of the existing Courts could at certain periods of the year visit the neighbouring colonies. It might be left to the Judges themselves to arrange the division of the circuit each year amongst themselves, but they should be able to visit each colony twice a year.

> 'For the increased duties and expenses thus thrown on the Judges, a general fund might be established by contribution of the several colonies benefitted by the proposed arrangement, and the Judges whilst engaged in such duties ought to receive liberal pay and travelling allowances for themselves and necessary attendants.'

If the present Judges could not manage this, then it might be advisable to establish a separate Circuit Court of appellate jurisdiction, but he estimated that probably not more than one month in each year of the Judge's time would be taken up in the Circuit Court work.

> 'Such a Court, combining as it would the judicial knowledge and ability of all these colonies with a complete apparent as well as real absence of all local prejudice or bias, would ere long so completely secure the confidence of the public as to diminish, if not entirely put an end to appeals to the Privy Council—appeals in general unsatisfactory in the issue, expensive and tedious.'

In addition, it would improve federal action in the laws of Australia and the interchange of views between the Judges would be very beneficial. "The facility of appealing to an impartial and highly competent tribunal on the spot would lead to a more extended confidence in the administration of justice." [37]

Sir Richard MacDonnell's proposal proved as abortive as those which had preceded it.

Later in the same year the Supreme Court Procedure Act was passed (No 24 of 1855-56). Inter alia, this contained a series of sections designed to extend the jurisdiction of the Court of Appeals which, it will be remembered, was narrowly restricted by:

(1) The proviso to the section creating the Court in the Supreme Court Act of 1837; and

(2) The rulings of the Court that appeal lay only in the case of:
  (a) final judgments or orders; and
  (b) error apparent on the face of the record.

Section 22 of this Act enabled an appeal to be brought upon a judgment upon a special case; in all cases of rules to enter a verdict or non-suit upon a point reserved at the trial, if the rule to show cause was refused or granted and then discharged or made absolute, the party decided against could appeal (section 24); and similarly in all cases of motions for a new trial upon the ground that the Judge had not ruled according to law, provided that where the application for a new trial was upon "matter of discretion only, as on the ground that the verdict was against the weight of evidence or otherwise", no such appeal should be allowed (section 25). The appeal was to be upon a case stated by the parties and, if necessary, settled by the Supreme Court, setting out so much of the pleadings, evidence and judgment objected to as would raise the question for the decision of the Court of Appeal (section 28). When the appeal was from the refusal of the Court below to grant a rule to show cause, and the Court of Appeal granted such rule, the rule was to be argued and disposed of in the Court of Appeal (section 29). By section 30, the Court of Appeal was required in all cases to give such judgment as ought to have been given in the Court below, and proceedings might be taken thereupon as if the judgment had been given by the Court in which the record originated. Section 31 gave the Court of Appeal power to order costs.

The object of these sections, which were copied from sections 32 to 43 of the Common Law Procedure Act (17 & 18 Vic c.125) was very laudable, but they were drafted on the pre-existing legislation without any thought of the confusion which might result. "The English Act has been adopted"—said Mr Justice Boothby some years later—"by striking out the word 'error' and inserting the word 'appeal' without considering the effect of the alteration." [38]

It was doubtful whether the procedure of the appeal by case stated was to apply to all appeals or only to those under the provisions of this Act. If the latter, it introduced an inconvenient anomaly, for the rules provided for appeal by petition. It was held in *Wood v. Lowe*, a case heard by the Court in 1860, that an appeal lay in the cases specified in the Supreme Court Procedure Act irrespective of the amount involved, although otherwise an appeal only lay if £100 at least was at stake—another anomaly.[39] Further, although the Supreme Court Act of 1837 had given the Court of Appeals a definite statutory title—"the Court of Appeals of the Province of South Australia"—the section just referred to and spoke only of the "Court of Appeal". There can be no doubt that the same Court was intended, but Mr Justice Boothby seized upon the distinction and said it was apparent that the sections could not apply to the "Court of Appeals", which was a different Court.

Later, in 1856, the Supreme Court Act (No 31 of 1855-56) was passed. It repealed the Supreme Court Act of 1837, but preserved the existence of what was described, with a reversion to the original name, as "The Court of Appeals of the Province of South Australia". Completely ignoring the provisions made in the Supreme Court Procedure Act, the Supreme Court Act simply repeated the provisions of the 1837 Act as to the jurisdiction of the Court of Appeals.

During the debate in the Legislative Council on the Supreme Court Act, the Court of Appeals was characterised as "totally worthless", but the Advocate-General said he could see "no more efficient materials at present in Adelaide from which it could be composed" and, in default of any better appellate tribunal, the Council was not prepared to abolish it.[40]

Mr Justice Boothby's opinion was that the model of appeal might be allowed to remain unchanged until the formation of a second legislative chamber "should have created a machinery for the working of a system of appeal analogous in principle to the House of Lords in England".[41]

In November 1856, in the case of *Bruce v. Hagen*, the Court showed that an appeal to it was no mere formality. Encouraged by an admission by the Chief Justice to the Governor that he thought he had made a mistake in the judgment he had delivered, the Court of

Appeals decisively reversed it.[42] Perhaps litigants disappointed in the Supreme Court took heart from this decision, for business now began to press upon the Court of Appeals. There were three appeals in 1857, four in 1859 and one in 1860.

Stimulated by this revival of the Court's active functions, Mr Wilson, its Clerk, put in a claim to a fixed salary. He had charge of the books and papers of the Court, but he had no Court office and nowhere to keep them. The Government had grudgingly supplied him with a little tin box and told him to find a niche for it in the registry office strongroom but, upon applying there, he was refused accommodation.[43] He submitted that, for transacting the business of the highest legal court of the province, he should be given an office and £150 a year. He also put forward a plan for amending the anomalous constitution of the Court by adding to it the Judge or Judges who had taken no part in the Supreme Court proceedings and one or more barristers who had not been concerned in the litigation.

> 'Thus a tribunal would be formed'—he said—'where legal acumen, educated common sense, and adequate notions of general justice, would be combined; and, presuming the legal members to agree, the decision of the majority of such a Court, would, except in very obstinate cases perhaps, preclude all desire to push the matter in dispute to the expensive ultimate tribunal.' [44]

His scheme, which would have made the constitution of the Court even more peculiar than it already was, did not meet with favour, but it was decided in 1858 to pay him a fixed salary of £120 a year, thus creating an office which was as near a sinecure as anyone could reasonably expect.

In *In re Longson*, which came before the Court in 1859, the point arose whether there was a right of appeal in insolvency matters. The first Insolvency Act (5 Vic No 1) had expressly given an appeal to the Court of Appeals because the Judge of the Supreme Court acted as Commissioner of Insolvency but, this Act having been repealed and a separate Commissioner appointed, a right of appeal to the Supreme Court had been given instead. The appellant Longson had been sentenced to twelve months' imprisonment by the Commissioner. He appealed to the Full Court, which affirmed the sentence. He now claimed a further right of appeal to the Court of Appeals under the general provision allowing an appeal from judgments or decrees of the Supreme Court. The majority of the Court held there was no such right of appeal. They considered that the "legal intendment" of the general words giving an appeal from the judgments of the Supreme Court must be confined to matters in which the Supreme Court had an original jurisdiction, and it had no original jurisdiction in insolvency. The Governor cautiously refrained from assenting to this opinion but said that, whether it was right or wrong, it was unwise and unnecessary to have a double right of appeal.[45] He accordingly gave instructions for the introduction into the Insolvency Act of 1860 of a provision that the decision of the Supreme Court on appeal from the Insolvency Court should be final and conclusive and that no appeal should be allowed therefrom to the Court of Appeals.[46]

A point was raised in *Wood v. Lowe* in February 1860 that, as the Court of Appeals was constituted of the Governor and Executive Council, every member of the Council must be present on the hearing of an appeal. The Court ruled that a quorum was sufficient, as in any other case where the Executive Council performed its functions.[47]

Meanwhile, the plan for a general Colonial Court of Appeal had not been entirely lost sight of. Mr Bagot had urged it in the Legislative Council in 1856,[48] and in June 1860 the question was again taken up by Parliament. The Chief Secretary moved in the Legislative Council that an address should be presented to the Governor representing the necessity that existed for the establishment of a general Court of Appeal constituted of judges appointed by the government of each of the adjacent colonies, the Court possessing full and final powers of adjudicating upon all cases referred to it. He stressed the unsatisfactory nature of the local Court of Appeals and referred to the difficulty which arose in the case of *Lloyd v. Kelly*, which was part-heard before the Court in 1860 when a change of ministry occurred and the case had to be commenced de novo before the new Executive Council.

> 'If the members of the Court of Appeal were selected for their mental qualities'—he said—'and because of their aptitude for arbitration, there would be less objection than at present, where members of a Ministry might possibly be required to sit to decide on a question having political tendency, in which they must to a certain extent be biassed ... As the Court of Appeal was at present constituted, if a decision were given in accordance with the opinion of the legal adviser (the Attorney General) the members would lie under the imputation of being influenced by this opinion; while if the decision were contrary to his advice, they would be suspected of giving a verdict for fear of being considered biassed ... It was inconsistent that while perhaps every member of the Cabinet might be ignorant of the principles on which law was founded, they should sit to adjudicate upon cases in which their own legal adviser should appear as an advocate.' [49]

He thought one judge from each colony would be sufficient to constitute the Court. Mr G.F. Angas spoke against the notion. Such a court, he considered, would be impracticable owing to its expense and the indifference of the other colonies, nor was there any reason for it when their own Court of Appeals was presided over by a former chief justice. The resolution was carried, with an amendment that the Court ought to be composed of the Chief Justice of the State Supreme Courts.[50]

A similar resolution was moved by Mr Strangways (Attorney-General) in the House of Assembly, where Mr Finniss raised the same objection as that taken by Mr Angas—the great expense—"for the Judges will not travel in so humble a way as ordinary people, and if such costs fall on the suitors it will be fearful". The resolution, however, was carried in the lower house also,[51] and the Governor accordingly communicated with the Governments of New South Wales, Victoria and Tasmania suggesting the establishment of such a Court.[52] New South Wales and Tasmania did not trouble to reply. Victoria displayed some interest in the proposal and offered to assist in forming an ambulatory Court, making a circuit once or twice a year in each colony.

> 'To give some permanence and certainty to this Court'—reported Mr R.D. Ireland, the then Attorney-General of Victoria 'perhaps it might be an advantage if one permanent Judge were appointed to sit with the Chief Justices. He might be called the Judge Assessor, and his functions would be analogous to those of a similar member of the Judicial Committee of the Privy Council, where the office is always filled by a retired Colonial Judge.' [53]

The failure of the other colonies to cooperate made further progress with the scheme impossible.

A few months later there arrived from England an Order in Council making provision for appeals from the Supreme Court of South Australia to the Privy Council.[54] To understand the effect of this document, it is necessary to consider in some detail the provisions which had been previously made by the local legislature for appeals to the Privy Council.

Section XVII of the Supreme Court Act of 1837 (re-enacted as section 19 of the Supreme Court Act of 1855-56) purported to give an appeal to the Privy Council from the Supreme Court under certain conditions. As a matter of strict law, the local legislature does not seem to have had any power to give or restrict such a right of appeal. In *British Coal Corporation v. The King* (1935) AC 500 at 511, it was pointed out that:

> '... the practice had grown up that the colonies under the authority either of Orders in Council or of Acts of Parliament should provide for appeals as of right from their Courts to the King in Council and should fix the conditions in which such appeals should be permitted.'

In the case of South Australia, no statute or Order in Council gave such authority, but it was nearly thirty years before any appeal was taken from the Supreme Court to the Privy Council. By that time, the order Council just referred to had been promulgated.

The language of section XVII is extremely difficult to construe. Section XVI had given the Court of Appeals jurisdiction to hear appeals from "the judgments decrees orders and sentences" of the Supreme Court in all cases where the sum or matter in issue amounted to £100, and the Court of Appeals could "affirm, alter or reverse the said judgments, decrees, orders or sentences, in whole or in part, or dismiss the said appeal with costs, as may be just". Following this, section XVII provided that any person might appeal to the Privy Council "in case *any such judgment decree order or sentence* shall be given or pronounced for or in respect of any sum or matter at issue" above the amount of £500. So far this seems quite clear. The only "judgments decrees &c" referred to previously are those of the Supreme Court and therefore "any *such* judgment &c" must be the judgment of the Supreme Court referred to in section XVI. But section XVII then goes on:

> 'Or in case the said Court of Appeals should, by any such judgment decree order or sentence reverse, alter or vary any judgment decree order or sentence of the Supreme Court, the person or persons feeling aggrieved by any such judgment decree order or sentence of the said Court of Appeal may ... apply to the said Court of Appeals, by petition, for leave to appeal therefrom to the Privy Council.'

It will be observed that here there is no mention of any minimum amount of £500 and the words "any such judgment &c" are applied to the judgments of the Court of Appeals. The only mention of the Supreme Court in the whole section is that just given above, when it is merely referred to as descriptive of the judgments of the Court of Appeal from which an appeal is given. It is the Court of Appeals to which application is to be made for leave to appeal; it is the Court of Appeals which is to stay proceedings or order security; it is the Court of Appeals which is to forward a certified copy of the proceedings to the Privy Council. Altogether, the only reasonable conclusion to be drawn from the section seems to be that an appeal could be had to the Privy Council from the Court of Appeals:

(1) Where the amount involved was over £500; or

(2) If the amount involved was over £100 and below £500 and the Court of Appeals reversed, altered or varied the judgment of the Supreme Court and that it was not intended to give any right of appeal direct from the Supreme Court to the Privy Council.

The general understanding of the profession from the earliest days was that an appeal lay direct under this Act from the Supreme Court to the Privy Council, but the more section XVII is looked at the harder it seems to discover how any such interpretation can be placed on it.

The Order in Council of 9 June 1860 made confusion worse confounded. Some doubt as to its value arose at once from the fact that it ignored the Supreme Court Procedure Act and the Supreme Court Act of 1855-56 and solemnly recited the Supreme Court Act of 1837, which had been repealed four years earlier. It then provided that any person might appeal to the Privy Council from the Supreme Court where the sum involved amounted to over £500. The procedure laid down was that the appellant should within fourteen days of the judgment complained of apply to the Supreme Court for leave to appeal to the Privy Council. The Supreme Court could at its discretion grant leave to appeal to the Privy Council against any interlocutory judgment or order and could either direct judgment to be stayed or execution to issue but, if the latter, then security must be given to abide the result of the appeal. If the Judges disagreed and there was no majority, the judgment of the Chief Justice or Senior Puisne Judge was to be entered as the judgment of the Court. The right of the Privy Council itself to give leave to appeal in any case was expressly reserved.

A peculiar feature of this Order in Council was that it entirely overlooked the possibility of appeals to the Privy Council from the Court of Appeals, which had been provided for both in the Supreme Court Act of 1837 and in that of 1855-56. It was now clear enough that an appeal lay direct from the Supreme Court to the Privy Council where £500 was involved, but what about appeals from the Court of Appeals? Would the Privy Council consent to recognise the right of appeal purported to be given by the local statute, which (bearing in mind that in cases falling within the Supreme Court Procedure Act there was no restriction as to the amount at issue) might result in attempted appeals in petty matters? Again, there was the singular anomaly that if a man in a case involving, say, £250 lost in the Supreme Court, appealed to the Court of Appeals and lost again, he would have no further remedy. On the other hand, if he won in the Supreme Court, was taken to the Court of Appeals by his adversary and there lost, he could appeal to the Privy Council from the order reversing the decision of the Supreme Court. This appears to be clearly the result of section XVII, although *Lowe v. Wood*, decided by the Court of Appeals in 1860, seems to deny it. In this case, Mr Hanson petitioned for leave to appeal from the decision of the Court to the Privy Council. The amount at stake was only forty shillings, but it was regarded as a test case. An appeal to the Court of Appeals had been allowed on the ground that the case was one within the Supreme Court Procedure Act and, therefore, the amount involved was immaterial. Leave to appeal to the Privy Council, however, was refused, the President (Sir Richard MacDonnell) saying: "It is clear that there is no appeal given by the Statute to the Privy Council unless in matters where the value in question exceeds

£500."[55] The correctness of this construction of the Act seems to be very much open to question.

No case has ever been taken from the Court of Appeals to the Privy Council, and the question whether there is such a right of appeal must now be merely an academic speculation.

In a dispatch to the Secretary of State on 19 December 1860, the Governor pointed out some of these discrepancies in the Supreme Court Act itself and between the Act and the Order in Council. He came to the conclusion that, in matters of £100 to £500, appeal lay only to the Court of Appeals. Where the right or property at issue was over £500, the parties could go from the Supreme Court either to the Privy Council under the order or to the Court of Appeals under the Act. As to whether an appeal lay from the Court of Appeals to the Privy Council—and, if so, under what circumstances—he was silent. The whole position was so uncertain that he took the opportunity to urge his scheme for a Federal Appellate Court.

> 'I have long regarded as obviously objectionable"—he said—"the appeal given in this colony from a professional to an unprofessional tribunal, though there are and have always been many precedents for it elsewhere in Her Majesty's Colonial dominions.'

He recapitulated the steps he had taken to induce the other colonies to consider the matter and commented adversely upon the proposals that the general Court of Appeal should consist of the chief justices of the Supreme Court and should have final powers of adjudication:

> '... restrictions which apparently are injudicious, as any limit to the number of Judges from whom the Court might be formed would render it all the more difficult and in practice frequently impossible to constitute the Court at all, whilst it is also not within the power of a Colonial Legislature to annul the right of a final appeal by Her Majesty's subjects to the Queen in Council.'

In conclusion, he asked for support from the Home Government, as the subject was one of general federal importance.[56]

A sympathetic reply was received from Lord Newcastle, who concurred in thinking that the appeal from the Supreme Court to the Executive Council was "quite unfitted" for the circumstances of South Australia. He would learn with satisfaction, he said, that the Australian colonies had succeeded in establishing an effective Court of Appeal, but he had no desire to be thought a busybody by prescribing to them the course they should take. If they could agree upon any plan, and it could not be carried out without Imperial legislation, he would give any assistance required.[57]

Two days after Sir Richard MacDonnell had sent off his dispatch about the Court of Appeals, he had to sit down and hastily write another one announcing that the Judges of the Supreme Court were giving it as their opinion that there was no longer any Court of Appeals in existence and that, notwithstanding that the Court for several years had been pretending to sit, it had been extinguished by the Constitution Act of 1856.[58] Most of the odium attached to this judicial discovery fell upon Mr Justice Boothby but, in justice to him, it may be pointed out that the doubt as to the existence of the Court of Appeals was first given currency not by him but by Sir Charles Cooper in the case of *Lloyd v. Kelly* earlier in the year. The Court of Appeals had heard an appeal in this case and, reversing the decision of the Supreme Court, ordered judgment to be entered for the plaintiff, who then moved the Supreme Court for leave to issue execution, but the Judges raised the question which Court was to carry out the judgment. Section 24 of the Supreme Court Procedure Act said that the Court of Appeals should give such judgment as ought to have been given in the Court below "and all such further proceedings may be taken thereupon as if the judgment had been given by the Court in which the record originated", but should the proceedings be taken in the Court of Appeals or in the Supreme Court? The Court of Appeals had no machinery or officers to enforce its judgments and Hanson contended that it was clear from the books of practice that execution must issue from the Court where the record originated. Mr Justice Boothby having thrown out some remarks that he did not think the Court of Appeals had had jurisdiction to hear the appeal, the Chief Justice added that there was another question worthy of consideration:

> 'When the Court of Appeals was established it consisted of the Governor and a differently appointed Executive Council. As that had been altered by the Constitution Act, had not the Court of Appeal been abolished?'

The following remarks ensued:

> Mr Justice Boothby: 'The former Court consisted of persons who might be taken as selected for the peculiar duties they had to perform. Now the Court consists of the Executive, ex officio.'
>
> Mr Hanson: 'The Court of Appeal always consisted of the Executive, who were its members ex officio.'
>
> Mr Justice Boothby: 'But then they were appointed by the Royal Prerogative and not dependent upon representing a constituency ... I think it is very doubtful whether the Crown had power to assent to the Constitution Act without the consent of the Imperial Parliament. If the question was raised I

> have little doubt that the Constitution Act would be found to be not worth the paper it is printed on.'

It was finally agreed that, if the Court of Appeal sent down an official record of its judgment to be filed in the Supreme Court, the latter Court could act upon it.[60]

Very little notice seems to have been taken of the dicta of the Chief Justice and Mr Justice Boothby, but later in the year they ripened into a unanimous judgment of the Full Court in the case of *Payne v. Dench.* From the gravity of the issues involved, the labour spent on the elaborate arguments and judgments, the number of times that it came before the Court and the public excitement it aroused, *Payne v. Dench* must be considered one of the most important cases ever decided in the Supreme Court.

It took its origin in a contract for the sale and purchase of some land, which had been brought under the provisions of the Real Property Act. The defendant failed to complete the purchase according to his contract and, when sued, raised the defence that the Certificate of Title tendered by the plaintiff was not such a sufficient title to the land as he was bound to accept. The action came on for hearing before Mr Justice Boothby and a jury in October 1860.

Evidence was given by Torrens, Registrar-General, that a Certificate of Title was issued to Payne pursuant to his application to bring the land under the Real Property Act, as purchased from one Coulthard, whose written consent was annexed to the application. It was not suggested that Coulthard's title was bad, but it was argued for the defendant that there was no evidence of any transfer of his estate to Payne. Torrens was subjected to a very bitter and hostile cross-examination, which developed into a personal attack on his qualifications to be an authority on land law, but he stood up to it stoutly. When it was sneeringly suggested to him by counsel that in law "a little learning is a dangerous thing", he smartly retorted, "Yes, as your clients have no doubt discovered."

After considerable argument, it was arranged that there should be a judgment for the plaintiff, subject to the opinion of the Full Court on points of law reserved. The case was duly argued before the Full Court at great length and judgment was reserved. While the Judges were considering the matter, the Real Property Act of 1860 was passed and the case was argued a second time before the Full Court, ostensibly upon the point whether the Act of 1860 had any retrospective effect, although in fact the second argument was even fuller than the first. The whole object of the Real Property Act, of course, was that the Certificate of Title should be conclusive evidence of title. If this was not achieved, then it was hardly worthwhile to have passed the Act. Mr Justice Boothby was strongly of opinion that the legislature had no power to pass an act ousting the jurisdiction of the Supreme Court to inquire into the title to land. It was monstrous, he said, that the Lands Titles Commissioners, three persons sitting in a back room at Adelaide, should be empowered to give a title which could not be inquired into by the Court. Mr Justice Gwynne was equally roused to indignation by the thought that, if he went to England for a holiday and came back to find someone had obtained a Certificate of Title to his property at Payneham, he could not bring an action for ejectment.

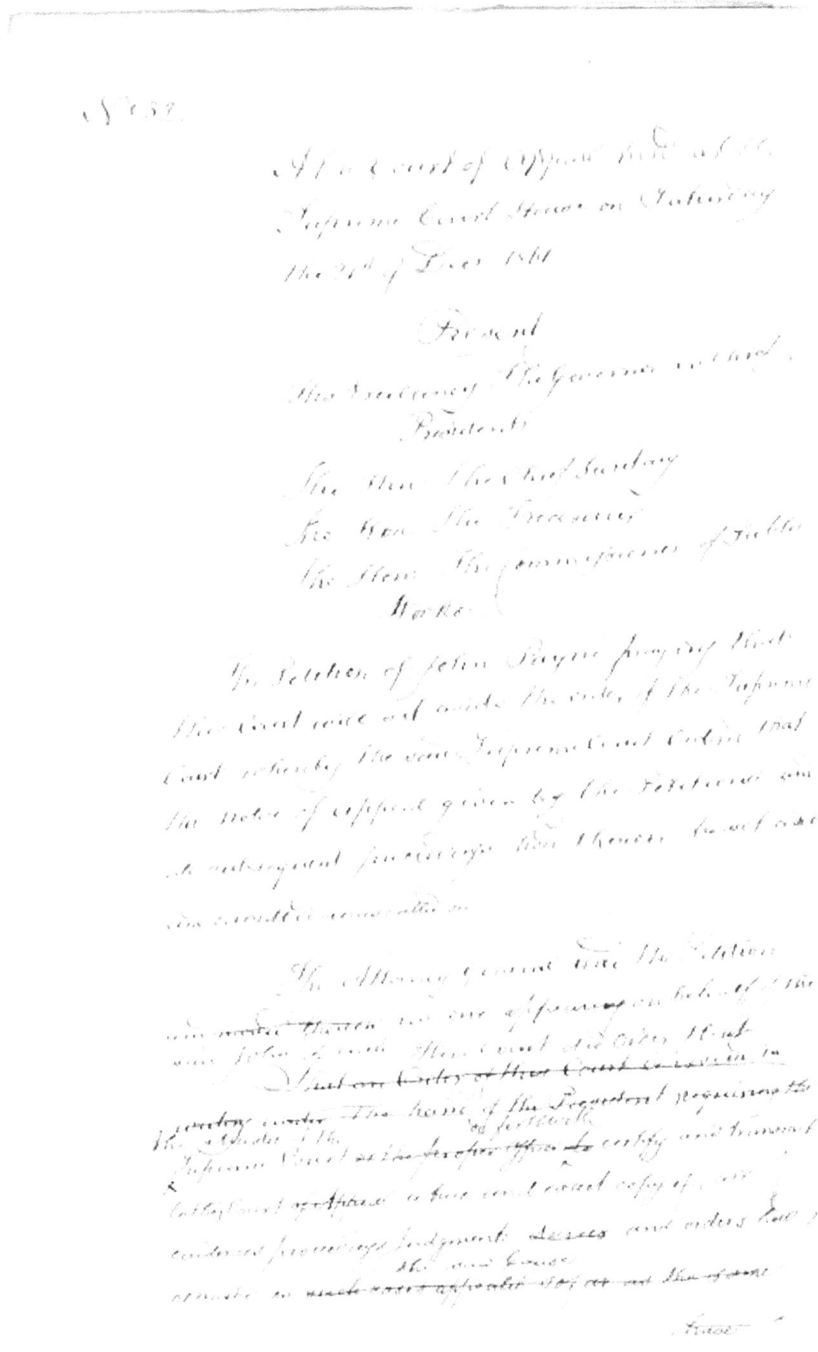

Court document from the *Payne v Dench* case. (SR/SC)

The three Judges were unanimously of opinion that judgment should be entered for the defendant.[61]

The decision was received with a howl of rage from the partisans of the Real Property Act. The Judges were accused of usurping legislative functions and of straining every point against the Real Property Act with the zeal of professional antagonism. Mr Justice Gwynne was said to "palpably biassed" and Mr Justice Boothby "avowedly hostile" to the Act. It afforded conclusive evidence, said the *Register*, that the principle of law reform embodied in the Real Property Act would never meet with fair play in the Courts of law.

> 'The biassing influences of professional feeling, the force of habits engendered by a special training and made irresistible by lifelong devotion, and the authority of maxims which custom has rendered sacred irrespective of their intrinsic character, all tend to make our Judges the worst possible expositors of a popular reform that violates time-honoured prejudices and cuts out the root of professional profits.'

"Of course", it added, "this is a decision which must be reversed on appeal." [62]

Notice of appeal to the Court of Appeals was given for the plaintiff. The defendant took out a summons that the notice of appeal should be struck out on two grounds:

(1) That the plaintiff had become a lunatic and was confined to an asylum; that he was therefore incapable of authorising an appeal; and that the appeal was in fact being carried on by Torrens, who was providing the funds, for the purpose of defending the Real Property Act. Affidavits were filed in support of these contentions.

(2) That there was no Court of Appeals in existence.

The summons came on for hearing before Mr Justice Boothby in chambers, but he considered it of such importance that he referred it to the Full Court. The Full Court decided that it could not hear the matter out of term and sent it back to Mr Justice Boothby in chambers but, before doing so, there was a sufficient discussion of the question whether the Court of Appeals existed to show the trend of judicial opinion. Mr Fenn, who was the leader of the diehard opponents of the Real Property Act, appeared to argue that there was no Court of Appeals:

> 'By clause 18 of the Act 31 of 1855-56, the Court was to be constituted of the Executive Council, appointed by the Queen; but by the Constitution Act it was provided that certain persons, dependent, not upon the Queen, but the will of the people for their offices, should be the Executive Council. That was a Court altogether different from the Court to which jurisdiction had been given by the previous enactments.'

The constitution of the Council was altered by the Constitution Act. The offices of Colonial Secretary, Advocate-General and Colonial Treasurer were done away with and their holders granted retiring allowances as compensation for loss of office. By section 32 of the Constitution Act:

> 'After the first general election of the said Parliament no person shall hold any of the offices following, that is to say; Chief Secretary, Attorney General, Treasurer, Commissioner of Crown Lands and Immigration, and Commissioner of Public Works, for any longer period than three calendar months, unless he shall be a member of the Legislative Council or the House of Assembly for the time being; and the persons for the time being holding such offices shall ex officio be members of the Executive Council.'

The old Executive Council which formed the Court of Appeals, Fenn contended, was gone and with it had gone the Court of Appeals. Mr Justice Gwynne concurred with this view. "The officers"—he said—"owe their origin to a different source; they are distinguished by different names and have different powers."

Mr Justice Boothby thought that there was no power in the Crown to appoint as judges persons who were not educated to the law and who were chosen by popular election. Both these Judges said there was no Court of Appeal. The Chief Justice did not express any opinion on the point.[63]

After further argument in chambers, Mr Justice Boothby made an order dismissing the notice of appeal on the ground that the plaintiff, being a lunatic, was incapable of giving any retainer to his solicitor to prosecute the appeal. He added that he had grave doubts whether there was a Court of Appeals at all.[64]

The plaintiff's counsel Mr Stow then obtained from the Full Court a rule nisi calling upon the defendant to show cause why Mr Justice Boothby's order should not be set aside. Mr Fenn appeared to show cause and wanted to argue the non-existence of the Court of Appeals. Mr Justice Boothby supported him, but the other two Judges were of opinion that the argument must be confined to the point which formed the ground of the order sought to be set aside, namely the plaintiff's lunacy. The Chief Justice and Mr Justice Gwynne being of opinion that a sufficient retainer had been shown to justify the appeal, the rule was made absolute. Mr Justice Boothby adhered to his former opinion. The Chief Justice again said nothing about the Court of Appeals, but Mr Justice Gwynne reiterated his opinion that the Court of Appeals had been swept away by the Constitution Act and said that Fenn could move again on this point.[65] Fenn thereupon immediately applied for and obtained a rule nisi calling upon the plaintiff to show cause why the proceedings in appeal should not be set aside on the grounds:

(1) That there was no Court of Appeals in the province; and
(2) That, if there was such a Court, it was not competent to entertain the question at issue in *Payne v. Dench.*

At last the legality of the Court of Appeals had to be decided, and a full-dress argument followed on the motion for the rule absolute, Mr Hanson and Mr Stow appearing for the plaintiff, Mr Fenn and Mr Belt for the defendant; probably the four ablest men then at the bar.[66]

The principal point to be determined turned upon the construction of three Acts—the Constitution Act (No 2 of 1855-56), the Supreme Court Procedure Act (No 24 of 1855-56) and the Supreme Court Act (No 31 of 1855-56)—and it is important to notice that, although passed in this order, these Acts *came into operation in the reverse order*. Thus:

(1) The Constitution Act (No 2 of 1855-56) was reserved for assent on 4 January 1856, the royal assent was given in England on 24 June 1856 and, by virtue of a proclamation under section 41 of the Act, it came into operation on 14 October 1856.
(2) The Supreme Court Procedure Act (No 24 of 1855-56) was assented to on 18 June 1856 and came into operation on 1 August 1856.
(3) The Supreme Court Act (No 31 of 1855-56) was assented to on 19 June 1856 and came into operation on 1 July 1856.

This explains what at first sight appears extraordinary; that it should have been held that a Court, the existence of which was affirmed by an Act numbered 31, was destroyed by the Act No 2 of the same session.

The three Judges concurred in holding that there was no longer any Court of Appeals.[67]

Mr Justice Gwynne based his decision on the fact that the Supreme Court Act came into force before the Constitution Act. The Executive Council referred to in the Supreme Court had been abrogated by the Constitution Act and another and different Executive Council substituted, to which the Supreme Court Act did not apply. After referring to the establishment of the Court of Appeals in 1837, he said:

> 'The Council of the Province at the time it was invested with appellate jurisdiction consisted of the Colonial Secretary, the Treasurer, and the Surveyor General. These officers were all appointed by the Crown, and held office during its pleasure. They were not the leaders of any political party, and were not likely to have any violent political opponents; and seeing that the Council had continuity and permanency beyond any other body then existing in the province, it would seem to have been the most appropriate depository of the supreme judicial power ... Now the question is raised, and is before the Court for its

decision—does the appellate jurisdiction which belonged to the old Council attach to the present Executive Council of the Province? It seems to me that it does not. I cannot agree with the assertion that the present Executive Council is nothing but a continuation of the Council of the Province established by 7 William IV No 5. It may have the same name, but its organisation is entirely different. The present Executive Council is composed of the Ministry of the day—gentlemen having particular political opinions, the leaders of a particular political party, and necessarily having violent political opponents. The present Council is liable to frequent and often rapid changes, in the case of the retirement of one administration and the coming in of another. It is, moreover, liable to absolute though temporary suspension, as in the case of a dissolution of the Parliament. Through the happening of any such contingencies much of the business of the Court, however nearly completed, must be commenced de novo. What a waste of time and money would a Court subject to such casualties inflict upon its suitors; Again, the Judges of this high Court would, contrary to the general principles of the British constitution, be really and practically elected by the people instead of, as in the case of the old Council, nominated by the Crown. The present Council, as it appears to me, has many characteristics, some of which I have pointed out, which distinguish it from and prevent my recognising it as a mere continuation of the old Council. If, therefore, it is not such a continuation of that Council, how does it come by an appellate jurisdiction? No doubt it has all the appropriate powers, duties and functions of other Executive Councils, and consequently of its predecessors; but judicial functions are not essential to an Executive Council, and I am not aware of any legislative enactment attributing those functions to the present Executive Council.'

He was supported in his opinion by section 36 of the Constitution Act, which provided:

> 'No Judge of any Court of the said Province ... shall be capable of being elected a member of the said Legislative Council or House of Assembly.'
>
> 'I confess I am unable'—he continued—'to reconcile the hypothesis, that the Ministers of the Government for the time being are Judges of the highest Court of the Province, with the express provision of an Act which says that no Judge of any

> Court of the said Province shall hold a seat in its legislature. On the whole, it appears to me that 'the Court of Appeal' referred to in the 24th Section of the Supreme Court Procedure Act 1855, and 'the Court of Appeals of the Province of South Australia' referred to in the 18th section of No 31, 1855-56, is one and the same Court, and can be no other than the one established by the 7th William IV No 5, and that this Court having died out, and none other having been established in its place, we are at present without a local Court of Appeal in this province.'

Mr Justice Boothby agreed with this view. The defendant, he said, contended that, since the Constitution Act came into operation, the Court of Appeals had become defunct by reason of the change in the constituent members of the Executive Council which the Constitution Act introduced. The plaintiff argued that the name "Executive Council" was the same and that whatever body existed under that name would have appellate jurisdiction over the Supreme Court, but "to call two entirely distinct and separate bodies by the same name is surely not sufficient to make them the same body". Formerly the Executive Council had been the creation of the royal prerogative alone. Now the Crown could not choose its executive from the whole body of its subjects, but was limited to such as might succeed in obtaining seats in Parliament and who, on appointment to their offices, became by statute ex officio members of the Executive Council. In the old Council legislative, executive and judicial functions had all been combined, but it was not so in the new one. He too relied upon section 36 of the Constitution Act.

> 'The Executive Council'—he said—'as constituted before the Constitution Act, were undoubtedly Judges of the then Court of Appeal: Is the same body meant in the Constitution Act, which provides that all the official members of the Executive Council shall be members of Parliament; and which also provides that any Judge in any Court shall become incapable to sit or vote, and may be sued for the penalty of £500, to be paid to him who brings the suit? Such a construction would render inoperative the plainest words of the Act, which provide that 'no Judge or any Court' shall sit in either House.'

In *Payne v. Dench*, there could be an appeal only by virtue of the extended jurisdiction given by the Supreme Court Procedure Act, but that Act was assented to on 18 July 1856. The Queen had assented to the Constitution Act nearly a month earlier and it was, therefore, quite impossible to contend that the Queen had assented to an Executive Council so altered in its constitution as a body to possess and exercise the judicial functions given by the Supreme Court

Procedure Act, because she must have been quite unaware of the existence of that Act.

From the point of view of policy, there were obvious objections to the ministry of the day being judges, perhaps in cases of political libel. The Executive Council, as now constituted, was a body always subject to sudden fluctuations in its composition.

> 'Practitioners of this Court may form part of the Executive Council. Is such a practitioner to be heard before this Court as counsel or attorney one day, and on the next be found sitting as a member of a judicial tribunal to reverse, it may be, its decisions?'

He had additional grounds for his judgment. He was of opinion that there was no prerogative in the Crown, since the introduction of constitutional government, to appoint to the exercise of judicial functions in the Supreme Court or any higher court any person not educated by the practice and administration of the law. Further:

> 'In my judgment'—he said—'there is nothing more clear than this, that until the existing Imperial Statutes for the better government of the Australian colonies are repealed, there is no power in Her Majesty to assent to any legislation by the Parliament of this Province which shall seek to override or extinguish the power of Her Majesty through Her Justices of Her Supreme Court of deciding on all matters relating to the lives, liberties, and properties of Her subjects, such decisions to be reviewed only by Herself in Her Privy Council.'

Finally, Mr Justice Boothby said that the Order in Council of 9 June 1860 had superseded and deprived the Court of Appeals of its functions. The absence of any mention of the Court of Appeals in the Order in Council showed that it was the opinion of the Privy Council that the Court of Appeals no longer existed.

> 'The effect of this Order in Council is to limit the right of appeal from decisions of this Court to Her Majesty in her Privy Council only, which right is extended to all cases. Were it otherwise, on a decision by this Court in any action or suit on some point in favour of the plaintiff, and on others in favour of the defendant, and both dissatisfied, the plaintiff might be found appealing to one court and the defendant to another'—

which he thought absurd.

As if he had not already a sufficient quiverful of arguments, a few months later still another ground was announced by Mr Justice Boothby which he had overlooked. He reasoned as follows:

(1) The first Act creating South Australia into a Province (4 & 5 Wm IV c.95 s.2) had provided for the constitution of "such Courts" as might be necessary and it was under this power that the Supreme Court Act of 1837 had been passed. The Imperial Act 1 and 2 Vic c.60 also empowered the Queen, by means therein provided, to establish all such laws and to constitute *"such Courts"* as might be necessary for the peace, order and good government of her subjects.

(2) The Imperial Act to provide for the better government of South Australia (5 & 6 Vic c.61) repealed 4 & 5 Wm IV c.95 and 1 & 2 Vic c.60. It confirmed all laws passed under those Acts and, by section 5, constituted a Legislative Council with authority "to make laws for the peace, order, and good government of the said Colony" but, while this Act thus confirmed all existing Courts, it gave no power to create Courts; a power given by express words in each of the two former Imperial Acts.

(3) The Legislative Council of 1844 had no power to put such a construction on the words "Council of the said Province" used in the Supreme Court Act of 1837 when creating the Court of Appeal, as to make that Court consist of the Executive Council alone, for that would be to create a new and different court from that which the Imperial Act had confirmed. The "Council of the Province" had legislative and executive functions; the "Executive Council" had executive functions only.

(4) The Legislative Council established by 5 & 6 Vic c.61, which had not been given any power to create Courts, continued till 1850, when a new Legislative Council was established by 13 & 14 Vic c.59. Section 25 of that Act provided that all existing laws in South Australia should remain in force. In section 29, the legislatures of New South Wales, Van Diemen's Land and Victoria were expressly given power to make further provisions for the administration of justice, but the name of South Australia was significantly omitted and no such power had been given by any Imperial statute to the South Australian legislature.

(5) The Legislative Council of 1856, therefore, had no power to constitute a Court of Appeals to consist of the Executive Council, as it purported to do by Act No 31 of that year, for to do so was to alter the effect of Imperial legislation, which had confirmed a Court of Appeals consisting of the "Governor and Council of the Province".

But even if a Court of Appeals did still exist, Mr Justice Boothby thought it had no jurisdiction in this case, which was that of a judgment upon a rule to enter a verdict upon points reserved at the trial. It was not a case of error apparent on the record, and therefore the appeal could only be brought under the Supreme Court Procedure Act 1855-56, but he was of opinion that this Act had not given an extended jurisdiction to the Court of Appeals. The legislature, in passing the Act 24 of 1856, he said, seemed to have assumed that there was a Court of Appeal having such jurisdiction, but it was not so, owing to the proviso in the section of the Supreme Court Act creating the Court of Appeals. Although the Act 24 of 1855-56 said, for example, in section 24 that "in all cases of rules to enter a verdict upon a point reserved at the trial ... the party decided against may appeal to the Court of Appeal", it did not say what Court was meant by the "Court of Appeal" or that any Court within the province should have jurisdiction to hear an appeal in respect of a rule granted or discharged to enter a verdict upon a point reserved. "Such a jurisdiction, I am of opinion, can only be created by express words; it cannot be founded on mere inference and implication."

The Act 24 of 1855-56 should have repealed the proviso in the Supreme Court Act or should have enacted that, notwithstanding that proviso, an appeal should be allowed. On this ground alone, therefore, he thought the rule should be made absolute.

The Chief Justice (Sir Charles Cooper) delivered a very wavering judgment. He said he was substantially in agreement with his colleagues. He disagreed, however, with the contention that it was not competent for the local legislature to establish a Court of Appeal within the province. He did not think that the ex officio members of the Executive Council were "Judges" within the meaning of section 36 of the Constitution Act, but, strangely, in the next sentences he contradicted this by saying that section 36 afforded strong ground for the opinion that the members of the Executive Council were never intended to sit as a Court of Appeals. If the section did not touch them at all, it is difficult to see why it should do anything of the sort. Similarly, he thought that the Order in Council dealt only with the Supreme Court and was never intended to affect the Court of Appeals, but then swung round the other way again and said that it favoured the idea that the Privy Council were of opinion that there was no existing Court of Appeals in the province. He was vague on the second point raised by the rule, merely saying that he thought the observations of Mr Justice Boothby were of great force. As a final wobble, he announced that, although he agreed with his colleagues, he did not think the rule should be made absolute:

> '... for I do not feel so confident in my opinion as to say there is no doubt on the question; and after having permitted several cases of appeal to go from this Court to the Governor and Executive Council appointed by him under the power given to him by the 29th section of the Constitution Act, I am not disposed to stop the progress of an appeal which has been so long commenced. I think the better course will be to call the attention of the Governor and Executive Council to the peculiar circumstances of the case rather than to decide it ourselves in the first instance; but my learned colleagues being

of a different opinion, the rule must be made absolute.'

For a Judge to hold that there was no Court of Appeals, and then say that he was not disposed to act upon that opinion because he thought he had gone wrong several times before in thinking that there was such a court and he would like someone else to shoulder the responsibility of straightening out the tangle, strikes one as unusual.

The outcry at the decision in *Payne v. Dench* was tremendous. It was alleged to be part of a deep-laid plot by the legal profession to frustrate the working of the Real Property Act, which would be left hopelessly at the mercy of a hostile tribunal. It was impossible to believe that a court which had existed for twenty four years was to be suddenly annihilated.

> 'There is something most extraordinary, almost astounding'—said the Register—'in the mere fact of an inferior Court sweeping out of existence a superior Court, established especially to revise its judgments, and in the cool ease with which the feat has been accomplished.' [68]

What next? Would the Judges proceed to abolish the Supreme Court and establish a triumvirate of dictators?

The Governor was alarmed at the position which might arise if some party persisted in petitioning the Court of Appeals, and he and the Executive Council could not conscientiously yield their convictions to the opinion of the Supreme Court:

> '... or believe that, for several years, we have been actually hearing cases referred to us from the Supreme Court and delivering judgments therein, whilst, nevertheless, we were all the time a non-existing body.'

A collision with the Supreme Court ought to be avoided at all cost, and yet he was afraid it might come about for he was convinced that the Judges were quite wrong. The arguments which he put forward against the decision are indeed powerful.[69]

> 'When the Governor and Executive Council were first constituted a Court of Appeal'—he explained to the Secretary of State—'all the members of the Executive Council were either nominated by the Crown, or in accordance with instructions from the Crown. No change is made therein by the Constitution Act, beyond that of adding to the nominees of the Crown or of the Governor under Instructions from the Queen, five office-holders in the Colony. The Executive Council does not necessarily consist of those individuals only—they might be a small minority of the Council, for a hundred members might be added to it at any moment, as well now as before the passing of the Constitution Act. It therefore

> seems a gratuitous begging of the question to assert that such a change affects the judicial powers of the Council as a Court of Appeal, seeing that those powers spring not from the general positive enactment, and not from the personal 'status' of individual members, still less from their individual merit or professional education.'

The appellate jurisdiction of the Executive Council was entirely statutory, and any objections to its members on the ground of ignorance of law must have applied just as strongly to the members of the old Executive Council. He was surprised to find it maintained that:

> '... although the Executive Council exercises all other functions and powers entrusted to it by a long series of statutes previous to the Constitution Act, and signifies its constant exercise of the same by my public notices and proclamations, it can nevertheless no longer hear appeals; yet what greater right has it to proclaim a District Council than to hear an appeal? Both rights depend on the statutes of the colony; and if a change in the personnel of the Executive Council by the Constitution Act be sufficient to abrogate any one of its previous powers, it must equally annul all.'

The Constitution Act was admittedly not intended to abolish the Court of Appeal and he could not agree that such was its necessary affect. It referred to the Governor and Executive Council and the appellate jurisdiction created by the Supreme Court Act attached to them.

> 'What makes such idle discussion still more inexcusable is, that the last named Act, when declaring the Governor and Executive Council to be a Court of Appeal, excepts from that Court the law officers for the time being, in the following words: "With the exception of the Attorney or Advocate-General and Crown Solicitor." This is conclusive; for, previous to the Constitution Act, the principal law officer of the Crown in South Australia was designated and known only as the Advocate-General. The Act No 5, 7th Wm IV, which first constitutes a Court of Appeal, consisting of the Governor and Council, excepts therefrom only "the Advocate-General and Crown Solicitor". That exception would not, however, have been sufficient in June 1856, when the Queen's confirmation of the Constitution Act, appointing an Attorney General, and making no mention of an Advocate-General, was daily expected. Hence the words "Attorney or Advocate-General" are naturally and pointedly

> used in the later Act, to ensure there being a Court of Appeal, in either case, whether there was still to be an Advocate-General under the old, or an Attorney-General under the new Constitution. It is, moreover, to be noted that no officer ever sat or could sit in Executive Council as "Attorney-General" till appointed thereto "ex officio" by the Constitution Act, which it is now asserted abolished the Court of Appeal.'

The Governor certainly demonstrates by this last argument that any abrogation of the Court of Appeals by the Constitution Act was fortuitous and quite unforeseen by the legislature, but it may be doubted whether it goes any further. He had accused the Judges of begging the question. In the reply which he made to the argument based on section 36 of the Constitution Act, he himself seems to have fallen head over heels into the same fallacy.

> 'I believe that the 32nd section of the Act meets this difficulty when it enacts, in ONE sentence, that those five persons are to be members of Parliament, and also to be members, ex officio, of the Executive Council; for it seems inconsistent with the rules of legal construction to suppose that the same Act can appoint certain members of Parliament to a Council having judicial powers, and nevertheless forbid them to exercise the powers with which such an office invests them. It is surely sounder law to hold that so direct an enactment operates as an exception to the general rule against Judges being members of Parliament, laid down in the 36th section.'

But he here assumed that the Executive Council to which these persons were appointed *had* judicial powers, whereas the whole question at issue was whether it had such powers or whether, because it was an altered and different Executive Council, it had lost them.

In a passage which was discreetly censored before the dispatch was made public, he said:

> 'As there is a very strong feeling in the colony relative to what too many regard as the hasty and indecorous eagerness with which opinions on so important a subject have been put forward by two of the Judges, I feel it the more desirable that as Governor I should if possible avoid all questions likely to bring me as President of the Court of Appeal into collision with the Supreme Court, where at present the Chief Justice appears to be in a minority. I am more particularly anxious therefore to have the assistance of such legal advice from Her Majesty's law officers as Your Grace can procure for me. I am especially aware that there is afloat an unpleasant idea as to the

> Bench being biassed in reference to the Real Property Act, and an apprehension that such an idea may lead during the next session to some very radical change in the constitution of the Supreme Court. That feeling would be enhanced by any judgment of myself in Council, opposed to the decision of the Supreme Court on the points adverted to in this despatch.'

He hoped to be able to stave off further discussion of the question till he could receive instructions from England, but concluded gloomily that: "... altogether, circumstances are tending to and may end in a crisis requiring much firmness and prudence on the part of the Executive here".

This dispatch was sent before the final judgments in *Payne v. Dench* were given. Immediately after delivery of his judgment, the Chief Justice wrote to the Governor calling attention to the momentous importance of the decision.

> 'I can only say for myself'—said Sir Charles Cooper—'that if it is determined that a Local Court of Appeals now exists, or if such a Court is erected by competent authority, I shall be prepared to render it all deference and respect.' [70]

In sending this letter to the Secretary of State, the Governor commented:

> 'So far as my own opinion is concerned, I am quite unable to see any force in the argument of the Judges, and am only surprised that the policy and expediency of continuing a Court such as that which is now established could not be separated in the reasoning of the Bench from the very different question of its actual legal existence.'

He also added an objection to the argument founded on section 36 of the Constitution Act much sounder than the one he had previously taken. That section simply declared that "no judge of any Court of the Province shall be capable of being elected" a member of Parliament. The Judges had assumed this to be a prohibition against judges sitting in Parliament but, on the strict language of the section, a member of Parliament who was constituted a Judge subsequent to his election might legally hold his seat until the term of his parliamentary service had expired. Mr Justice Gwynne had been a member of the Legislative Council at the time of his appointment as a Judge and he had immediately resigned his seat, but it would appear that he could have retained it till the end of the term for which he had been elected.

> 'I cannot but think—and I believe such was the case—that the language of that section was framed expressly in reference to the other provisions of the Act, which, by appointing certain

> members of Parliament to be ex officio members of the Executive Council, and therefore Judges of a Court of Appeal, left them capable of sitting in Parliament without requiring them to be elected.' [71]

Sir Richard Bethel (Lord Westbury) by Michele Gordigiani. (NPG)

No time was lost in England in obtaining the opinion of the law officers, Sir Richard Bethel and Sir William Atherton, whether the Executive Council established under the Constitution Act was competent and entitled to act as the Court of Appeals. They had before them only the statutes and the remarks made by the Judges on the motion which they sent back to Mr Justice Boothby in chambers and, therefore, their opinion cannot have as much weight as it would have carried had they been possessed of all the arguments which were later brought to bear upon the point. Unfortunately, also, they followed Lord Mansfield's maxim, "Decide promptly, but never give any reasons. Your decisions may be right, but your reasons are sure to be wrong." They simply reported:

> 'We observe, with regret, the opinion expressed by the Supreme Court in South Australia, in the case of Payne v. Dench, as to the Local Court of Appeal. We have read with surprise the dicta attributed to some of the Judges of the Court, in the report of that case. In our judgment, that opinion is altogether erroneous. The legal continuance, jurisdiction and authority of the Local Court of Appeal, as established by the 18th section of the Colonial Act (assented to on 19th June 1856), are not at all affected by the Constitution Act, or anything done under it. There cannot be any reasonable doubt as to that Court being still in existence, with undiminished authority.' [72]

Meanwhile, in the colony the judgment of the Full Court was received with the utmost disfavour. It was impossible, said the *Register*, for "even the most careless reader or the most incoherent thinker" to coincide in it. Several members of Parliament and "other gentlemen of influence" met at the offices of Messrs Elder Stirling and Co to consider the position in which the colony was placed by the decision, and it was decided to convene a public meeting.[73] This was done, and the following resolutions submitted:

(1) "That the recent decision in the Supreme Court, ignoring the existence of the Court of Appeals, places the machinery for the administration of justice in this colony in an unsatisfactory state, by impeding access to the only channel through which, without ruinous expense, redress may be sought in the event of error influencing any decision of the Supreme Court."

(2) "That in order to bring this question to issue it is desirable the decision in Payne v. Dench be submitted to the Court of

Appeals without loss of time", and that a committee should be appointed to collect the necessary funds.

(3) "One of the Judges having denied the power of the legislature of this colony to create any Courts with appellate jurisdiction from the decisions of the Supreme Court it is expedient this question should receive the attention of the Parliament at an early date."

The tone of the speeches made at the meeting may be illustrated by a sentence from that of Mr Barrow, the proprietor of the *Advertiser*, who declaimed: "The question is, are we to have a Court knocked upon the head by the fiat of two out of three Judges?"

The resolutions were carried with enthusiasm, together with an additional one put forward by Mr G.M. Waterhouse that a memorial should be presented to the Governor praying for a bill to be introduced to remove the doubts that had arisen as to the existence of the Court of Appeals and to create machinery to enable the Court to give effect to its decisions.[74]

Had the question before the meeting been considered more soberly, it would have been seen that there were difficulties in the way of both the remedies which were proposed, continuing the appeal and passing an act. How was the appeal to be got before the Court of Appeals? There was no procedure for doing this without the active concurrence of the Supreme Court. The Court of Appeals might claim to have some inherent powers, as a court, but how would it compel the Supreme Court to forward the necessary documents relating to the case? Then again, if the decision was reversed by the Court of Appeals, the Supreme Court must ignore it because they said there was no such court. The Court of Appeals itself had no means of enforcing its decision.

> 'Its discussions'—said the Register—'can have no greater influence than those of an extremely respectable debating club. They may have moral force but they are destitute of judicial authority.'

The Court of Appeals was in fact guarded front and rear by the Supreme Court. The Judges held the keys to it, and neither ingress nor egress could be obtained except with their permission.

It does not seem to have occurred to anyone that to carry on the appeal with public funds might be rather unfair to the unfortunate respondent, who had to pay his own costs.

Then, as to passing an act to put the Court of Appeals in an independent position with means to enforce its judgments, this would make the Court an antagonist of the Supreme Court rather than its superior, and there might be a clash of authority. If an appeal court could not derive its authority from its unquestioned superiority, it was hardly worth having at all.

The *Register* did not hesitate to put forward the removal of Mr Justice Boothby as the only sure remedy.

> 'The law administrators are but individuals, high in personal character and official dignity, and sacred so long as they reverently and truly administer the law, but still only individuals, chosen for the performance of a special function, and subject to removal when they cease to perform that function rightly.' [75]

Parliament had not been sitting at the time judgment was given in *Payne v. Dench*, but it met shortly afterwards, on 30 April 1861. The existence or non-existence of the Court of Appeals was, of course, a subject very prominently before the legislators. In his speech when opening Parliament, the Governor mentioned that he had communicated with the other colonies on the subject of a general Court of Appeals, but (following his policy of keeping the matter dormant until instructions came from England) he made no reference to *Payne v. Dench*.[76] The decision was too important, however, to be silently passed over; and in the reply to the Governor's speech, the Legislative Council said:

> 'We feel that the position of this colony, as recently manifested by judicial decisions, is most unsettled and unsatisfactory; and we think that speedy legislation for the establishment of a Court of Appeal within the Province is desirable.' [77]

The House of Assembly was also of opinion that "the present position of the Court of Appeal should at an early date be made the subject of Parliamentary action".[78] The Chief Secretary promised that legislative action would be taken. The Government "were prepared to go with the Parliament in providing the country with an efficient Court of Appeal".[79]

It soon became imperative that an immediate decision be made whether there was to be a Court of Appeals or not. On the one hand, the Governor and Executive Council were firmly convinced that the Court still existed and that they could not, even if they wished, divest themselves of the judicial duties cast upon them, although they fully realised that, as they had no officers to carry out their orders, the Supreme Court, by refusing to take notice of them, might render all their proceedings nugatory. On the other hand, application was made to the Supreme Court to take the decision in *Payne v. Dench* a step further by treating as absolute nullities the judgments and proceedings of the Court of Appeals since the passing of the Constitution Act. *Bruce v. Hagen*, which was heard by the Court of Appeals in November 1856, has already been referred to. It was an action for ejectment, heard before the Chief Justice, in which the verdict had been given for the plaintiff. The defendant tendered a bill of exceptions to the Chief Justice's ruling and, upon it, appeal was made to the Court of Appeals, which reversed the judgment below. Mr Fenn now wanted to issue execution on the original judgment of the plaintiff, as it had been decided that there was not, and had not been, at the time *Bruce v. Hagen* was heard any Court of Appeals in existence. Mr Justice Boothby agreed with him, but the Chief Justice was very hesitant. Mr Justice Gwynne, having been engaged in the case as counsel, would not sit. After argument, the motion was adjourned, and it was intimated to Mr Fenn that he should move again for a rule calling upon the defendant to show cause why he did not follow up his bill of exceptions.[80] This was not what Fenn wanted, and he abandoned his application, but it was quite possible that other applications of a similar nature would be made which could not be sidetracked in this way.

> 'Your Grace can easily imagine'—the Governor reported to the Duke of Newcastle—'the disturbance of property and vested interests, held for several years under decisions whose validity had not previously been doubted, which would be occasioned if the Supreme Court were to follow up to its logical conclusion their decision of the non-existence of the Appeal Court.' [81]

The Governor laid the problem before the Executive Council, pointing out that there seemed to be only two courses open:

(1) To acquiesce in the abolition of the Court of Appeals altogether and repeal the provisions purporting to establish it; or

(2) To pass an act affirming its existence and investing it with adequate powers to give effect to its judgments.

He had no liking for the anomalous Court, but he felt that the abolition of it was a measure to which Parliament could not be induced to assent.[82] A bill was therefore prepared and introduced in the House of Assembly by the Attorney-General (Mr Randolph Stow) declaring that the Governor and Executive Council were, and had been from the passing of Act No 31 of 1855-56, the Court of Appeals. The recent appointment by the Governor of the Chief Justice as a member of the Executive Council occasioned a vigorous debate upon the question whether he should be excluded from the Court of Appeals, along with the Attorney-General and Crown Solicitor. On the one side, it was urged that it was against human nature that, if the Chief Justice were to sit in appeal on one of his own judgments, he could be altogether impartial and that his influence might be so great as to lead the non-legal members of the Court to subordinate their opinions to his. On the other, it was said that, if the Court of Appeals was to try questions of law, it was eminently desirable that a professional judge should sit. To add a provision expressly excluding the Chief Justice, said Mr Hanson, would be an insult to him; an expression by the House that it had no confidence in his opinion or impartiality.

'Surely they would not say that knowledge was a disqualifica-

> -tion for a gentleman to sit in this Court? The knowledge of the laws possessed by the Chief Justice would be of great benefit to the members of the Court of Appeal in arriving at a correct decision on the question of law which would be brought before them.'

It was decided to make no specific mention of the Chief Justice in the Act, leaving it open to him to sit in the Court of Appeals in his capacity of a member of the Executive Council if he thought fit to do so.[83]

The Act passed both Houses with little opposition, although in the Legislative Council the President (Sir J.H. Fisher) expressed some doubt whether the Parliament could pass an act declaring what the law was before its passing, so as to bind the Supreme Court. It was only evidence of the sense of the legislature as to the pre-existing law, he said, and upon that law in this case the Supreme Court had already given its judgment.[84]

By this Act (No 5 of 1861), an attempt was made to put the Court of Appeals on a sound legal basis. It was declared a Court of Record and the Governor was given the title of President. The President and two or more members of the Executive Council formed a quorum. To enable the Court of Appeals to exert its superior authority over the Supreme Court, section 3 provided that whenever an appeal was pending the Supreme Court or its proper officer should forward a copy of all proceedings, evidence and orders, together with the Judge's reasons for judgment, if any were given. By section 4, whenever an appeal was pending under the Supreme Court Procedure Act 1855-56 against a decision of the Supreme Court on the common law side, the presiding Judge or any other Judge should, on being so required by writing under the hand of the President, transmit a certified copy of the notes made by the Judge at the trial and of all evidence and documents connected with the case. Section 6 empowered the Court of Appeals to do "all things necessary to carry its decision into effect" and the officers of the Supreme Court, the Sheriff and all persons in the Government service were required, under penalty of summary dismissal, to carry into effect any writ, rule or order of the Court.

In reporting that there was no objection to the Governor giving his assent to the Act, Mr Stow (the Attorney-General) remarked:

> 'It has been maintained that the legislature of this Province has no power to constitute a Court of this nature, but I have no doubt that the provisions of the Imperial Statute to make any laws for the peace, order, and good government of the Province, which are not repugnant to the laws of England, clearly confer the power to constitute such Courts as may be considered necessary for carrying these laws into effect and that this Court is not in its Constitution, nor are any of the

powers conferred upon it, repugnant to the law of England.' [85]

The Act had just passed the legislature when an important dispatch from the Duke of Newcastle arrived, in which he warned the Governor that the opinions of the law officers in England had no binding authority on colonial Judges, whose duty it was to frame their decisions in accordance with their own notions of law and whose judgments must be treated by the Executive as correct, unless and until they were reviewed by a higher tribunal.

> 'How to bring those judgments under the cognizance of such a tribunal is a matter to be considered, first, by the suitors who may consider themselves aggrieved, and next, if the matter is of sufficient political importance, by the Colonial Government. But I cannot help observing that even should the law as laid down by the Judges be incorrect, it would seem at first sight inexpedient to incur the expense and trouble of an appeal to England, in order to establish the existence of a Court which, whether legally constituted or not, is certainly of a most anomalous character, and which therefore it would seem far better to abolish by Act of the Colonial Legislature, than to maintain by a judgment of the Privy Council.' [86]

The Governor, in his reply, supported the action taken by the colonial Parliament.

> 'I confess'—he said—'I see some strong reasons why the colonists should be reluctant to abolish the protection which they suppose is in some cases afforded them by the Court of Appeal. While the soundest legal opinions in the Colony and the conduct of Her Majesty's Government lead to the inference that the persevering attempts made by the Legislature of this Province to improve, simplify, and cheapen the law and practice connected with the transfer of land are both praiseworthy in their tendency and within the scope and power of the legislature of the Province, it is natural that the settlers here should feel alarmed at the attitude assumed and the opinions expressed by a majority of the Judges in reference to the Real Property Act.' [87]

The Secretary of State left the Act to its operation, but expressed his regret that the legislature should have found it necessary to sanction and perpetuate a Court "which in its present shape exists only by accident and of which the composition is such as to be wholly indefensible on any constitutional principle".

> 'To separate the functions of a Judge from those of a Governor'—he pointed out—'is one of the first precautions

> which Society adopts in order to secure itself from injustice, when it becomes capable of political and judicial organisation. But by this Act the decisions of Judges educated to the knowledge of the law, trained to impartiality in its administration, and raised by their tenure of office beyond the reach of external influences, will continue to be brought under the review of the Executive of the day—a body of gentlemen not accustomed to study the intricate and subtle questions which will be brought under their cognizance—whose very capacity for party conflict is in some degree adverse to the judicial habit of mind—who must necessarily act in questions of public interest, under the pressure of political necessities, and whose decisions, whether good or bad, are almost certain to be treated as matters for political attack or defence. It is impossible to hope that such a Court of Appeal will for any length of time escape the suspicion of deciding questions of personal right with some reference to politics, and I need hardly add that no institution is safe in a country where the administration of justice does not command confidence. I do not imagine that thinking persons in South Australia are blind to these considerations. If the Legislature is unwilling to alter the constitution of the present Court of Appeal, I presume it is influenced by that distrust of the Supreme Court which has arisen out of recent controversies.'

It was to be hoped, he added, that the Court would be only a temporary expedient and:

> '... as the due administration of justice in any Colony cannot be viewed as a matter of merely local concern, I feel no hesitation in instructing you not to lose any fitting opportunity of causing the propriety of its removal to be brought under the notice of the Legislature'. [88]

Content with the passing of the Act No 5 of 1861, public opinion ceased to worry about *Payne v. Dench*. The Real Property Act was amended to overcome the adverse decision. The appellant remained non compos for some time. He then obtained an order from the Court of Appeals in December 1861 that the Supreme Court should send up a certified copy of the proceedings and the judgments, but no-one was anxious to press on with the appeal and it was abandoned. In the following year, Mr Payne petitioned Parliament to pay the costs incurred by him in his unsuccessful action, on the ground that the colony had greatly benefited from the experience gained through his litigation. His petition met with a sympathetic hearing and a sum was voted sufficient to pay his legal expenses, which amounted to £329 14s 11d.[89]

The question soon arose whether or not the Judges would consent to recognise the attempted validation of the Court of Appeals by Act 5 of 1861. In September 1861 Fenn applied for a rule, in the case of *McEllister v. Fenn*, calling upon the plaintiff to show cause why a notice of appeal given by him should not be set aside, on the ground there was no Court of Appeals. The Chief Justice had resiled from his opinion in *Payne v. Dench* and, with some misgivings because he was acting against a decision of the majority of the Court, had taken the recognisances for the appeal.

> 'When the judgment with respect to the Court of Appeal was given'—he said—'I was not aware of the actual state of the facts as they are known to me now. I had not then referred to the Governor's Commission, nor to the Royal Instructions to the Governor. Upon looking at these documents I am of opinion that the Court of Appeal is still in existence. Therefore, although I have announced an opinion in unison with that given by my colleagues, I hold the contrary opinion now.'

He optimistically expressed the view that his learned brothers might also be of a different opinion when they perused those documents, although he should by now have known his colleagues better.[90]

Mr Justice Gwynne adhered to his opinion in *Payne v. Dench* that the Court of Appeals had died out, and he declared that no competent authority had established a new one. With some asperity, he remarked that it was unseemly on the part of the Governor to have given his assent to a bill which was in direct opposition to the judgment of the Supreme Court.[91]

Mr Justice Boothby brushed aside the Act of 1861 with contempt. It has obvious, he said, that the legislature had no power to create such a court without an enabling act of the Imperial Parliament.

> 'If this Parliament had absolute power they might create such a Court; but having only limited power, can they pass an Act to constitute laymen judges of this Court? Would such an Act, when assented to by the Queen, be valid? A more monstrous proposition could not be submitted to the Judicial Committee of the Privy Council.'

He scouted the idea that the Act had validated the Court of Appeals.

> 'It would be idle to suppose for a moment that the legislature which has not power to create a Court, should have power to say that what a Court did was valid. It amounts to saying "we have the power because we say we have the power".'

He had, too, several entirely fresh objections. With unholy glee, he had discovered that the enacting portion of the Supreme Court

Act of 1855-56, instead of reading, "Be it enacted by His Excellency the Governor-in-Chief of South Australia, with the advice and consent of the Legislative Council thereof," simply read, "Be it enacted as is hereinafter set forth." He hastened to Parliament House to peruse the original Act. It was not a misprint, it was an omission in the Act as passed. No-one had noticed it before.

> 'The blot is, however, now hit, and the question arises for determination what is the legal effect of such omission. I am of opinion that the omission of these words is fatal to any legal operation of the supposed Statute. The authority of the Parliament of this Province rests only and entirely on Imperial Statutes. The enactment of every law made under such authority must be in a manner known to the law, and by words which show jurisdiction to legislate.'

A further fatal objection was that the alleged Act assumed to take the Queen's prerogative of appointing the Judges of her superior court with the advice of the Secretary of State. Her Majesty, according to Mr Justice Boothby, could not assent to such a deprivation of her prerogative without the assent of the Imperial Parliament.

> 'For this reason, the Royal Instructions accompanying the Commission of the Governor-in-Chief, and which in legal effect form a part of that Commission, and have a statutory force, require that all Bills whereby Her Majesty's prerogative may be affected shall be reserved for Her Majesty's consideration.'

This Bill, therefore, should have been reserved, and the failure to do so rendered it of no effect.[92]

The Chief Justice said he was too unwell to write out his judgment, but gave it extempore. On reconsideration, he had altered his opinion. The foundation of his opinion in *Payne v. Dench* had been that the Court of Appeals was substantially different or composed of persons altogether different from those mentioned in the Act of 1837, but seeing that the Queen had reserved the power to appoint members of the Executive Council and that, by the Commission issued to the Governor subsequent to the passing of the Constitution Act, she declared who were to be the Executive Council—that there were to be certain members ex officio, as mentioned in the Constitution Act, and others appointed by the Governor—it appeared to him that a mere alteration in the personnel of the Executive Council did not do away with the Court and it was still in existence. He might possibly be mistaken, he concluded. He would be glad to find that he was mistaken, but he believed it would be found that he was not mistaken.[93]

The order of the majority of the Court was again that no Court of Appeals existed but, curiously, this decision—apparently a flagrant defiance of Parliament—aroused little comment. Petitions by both Houses for the removal of Mr Justice Boothby had been dispatched to England, and apparently no-one wished to take up the quarrel of the Court of Appeals again until it was seen what was the result of those petitions.

Augustine Stow (1833-1903)
A brother to Randolph, and for a time his associate at the Supreme Court, Augustine Stow held a number of government positions including Registrar of Probates and Chief Clerk of the Supreme Court, Public Trustee and Deputy Registrar of Companies. He was an MP, variously, from 1862 to 1871 and continuously active in the Congregational Church. (SLSA)

For several years the Court of Appeals languished without business. In May 1862 the Attorney-General was asked in the Assembly whether it was intended to take steps to abolish the Court, in accordance with the instructions of the Secretary of State, but the reply was that the Government did not consider it a suitable time. In the following year Mr Augustine Stow introduced a bill for this purpose. Owing to his ill health, it became the "will-o'-the-wisp" of the session, and was finally withdrawn. There was little chance of it meeting with the favour of the legislature.[94] At the intercolonial conference in Melbourne in the same year, the South Australian delegates raised the question of a general Court of Appeal. The other states, however, were quite satisfied with their system of appeal direct from the Supreme Court to the Privy Council. Their representatives laughed at the South Australians and advised them to abolish their funny Court of Appeals as soon as they got home.[95]

In July 1865, however, the Court of Appeals was suddenly reinvigorated. The majority of the Supreme Court held, in *Dawes v. Quarrell*, that the colonial legislature had no power to establish courts and that the Local Courts Act of 1861 was therefore invalid. To overcome this disastrous decision, the Government bethought themselves of recourse to the Court of Appeals. The amount involved in the case, however, was only £20 and there was no right of appeal. A bill was accordingly introduced into Parliament by the Attorney-General to provide for appeals being had from the Supreme Court to the Court of Appeals irrespective of the amount involved. It was strongly opposed by Mr Boucaut in the Assembly. He contended that for Parliament to extend the jurisdiction of the Court of Appeals openly and avowedly for the sole purpose of enabling a particular decision of the Supreme Court to be overruled was to establish a most dangerous precedent. And what use would the Act be when passed, for the Supreme Court had already in *McEllister v. Fenn* decided that the Court of Appeals did not exist and, indeed, this followed as a necessary consequence of their decision in *Dawes v. Quarrell.* The Judges would simply ignore any proceedings of the purported Court of Appeals. What could be accomplished, he said, by "this miserable abortion of a Bill". "What we want is a comprehensive dealing with the subject; whereas we are discussing our position in driblets, and trying to make piecemeal amendments." [96]

In the Legislative Council, Mr G.F. Angas, while giving the Government credit for their effort to meet the emergency, urged that the Bill would only have the effect of involving suitors in interminable difficulties. The Supreme Court had pronounced there was no such court as the Court of Appeals and that opinion had been respected, since there had been no court held for several years. The Act could only result in a collision between the Supreme Court and the Court of Appeals and then an appeal would have to be made to England.[97]

Notwithstanding considerable opposition, the Bill was rapidly pushed through both Houses, most members thinking that the Court of Appeals was now their only hope.

> 'Some of the Judges'-it was said-'are wanting in that breadth of mind and judgment which is essential to an occupant of the judicial bench. They weave a web of technicalities about themselves when they take up a subject, and argue entirely in a vicious circle. Such a course may be creditable at the Bar, but it is a frame of mind altogether unbecoming in a Judge.' [98]

In proroguing Parliament on 4 August, the Governor said:

> 'My Government have witnessed with great regret a recent judgment of the Supreme Court in which it has been decided that the Legislature has no power to constitute Courts of Justice. The effect of this decision, if upheld, will be at once to invalidate every judgment heretofore given in the Insolvent Court and every Local Court—in one of which upwards of twenty thousand cases may be affected—and to render every officer presiding at or engaged in carrying out any decision of either of these Courts liable to actions for damages; to put a stop to the proceedings of all the Local Courts throughout the province, and of the Insolvent Court; and thus to deprive creditors of an easy means of recovering their debts, and of procuring a fair and equal distribution of the estates of their debtors. Impressed with the importance of the crisis thus occasioned, and desirous that any measures adopted might leave unimpaired the independence of the Judges—which I would by all proper means maintain—a Bill has been introduced, which has received your sanction, to enlarge the powers of the Local Court of Appeal, and to facilitate proceedings before it. You may be assured that, in the discharge of the responsible duties thus imposed upon myself and all the members of the Executive Council, the most scrupulous care will be exercised to protect the rights of individual litigants.' [99]

The Act as passed (No 15 of 1865) provided that the Court of Appeals should have power and authority to receive and hear appeals from the judgments, decrees, orders and sentences of the Supreme Court in all cases, although the sum or matter in issue should not amount to £100. Section 2 provided that, within three weeks from the passing of the Act, any person might appeal to the Court of Appeals from any judgment of the Supreme Court, by giving fourteen days' notice in writing to the opposite party or his attorney and to the Master of the Supreme Court, and such notice should be a stay of proceedings, provided a recognisance was entered into in the same manner as was provided for giving bail on appeal under the Supreme Court Procedure Act 1855. This section was necessary, because the time for appealing in *Dawes v. Quarrell* had long gone by. In case the Judges might refuse to take the recognisance on appeal, section 3 provided that the Clerk of the Court of Appeals might take them and the recognisances so taken should have the same effect as if taken before a judge of the Supreme Court.

In reporting that he had assented to the Act, the Governor wrote:

> 'I am not ignorant of the objections which may be urged against it, but after careful consideration have decided to assent to it. I do not refer to the objection which has been raised by some persons in the legislature on the ground that the Bill interferes with the independence of the Judges or interrupts the due administration of justice. If the Court of Appeals exists, and it is constituted by precisely the same authority as the Supreme Court, then the independence of the Judges is no more affected by any appeal to it than it would be by an appeal to Her Majesty in Council, which is provided for by the same authority; and as to obstructing the administration of justice it appears to me a mere matter of common sense that it is the majority of the Judges of the Supreme Court who do this when they as members of an inferior court assume to determine that a court of superior authority no longer exists. But the objections which I feel are that all laws affecting the administration of justice should have regard only to permanent objects, and should not be directed to the removal of merely temporary inconveniences, that they ought to be desirable for their own sake, and I feel that this is not the case with the proposed Act.'

He regarded the measure as a temporary one which, arising out of a particular emergency, ought to be repealed as soon as that emergency was past.

> 'It is not a speculative question, of however high importance, nor even a practical question affecting only isolated individuals, but is one which affects all the existing relations of the numerous classes of the colony, depriving them in effect of all the advantages of law.'

He could see no other way out of the difficulty. It was suggested that the Supreme Court might suspend judgment until an appeal to the Privy Council could be had, but this would hang up innumerable cases in the colony in the meantime and would exaggerate the difficulty. With great reluctance, the Governor therefore gave his assent to the Act.[100]

The revival of the Court of Appeals in order to counteract the decision of the Supreme Court was generally approved.

> 'Things have just come to this pass'—said the Register—'that if the Supreme Court will not administer justice, some other Court must administer justice. The colony is not to stand still; the functions of government are not to be suspended at the whim of one or two of the Judges.'

Admittedly, the constitution of the Court was anomalous. Nevertheless, if its constitution was ten times more incongruous, the Government ought to set it in motion rather than "see all our laws shipwrecked and destroyed by legal technicalities".[101]

As soon as the Act came into force, notice of appeal was given in *Dawes v. Quarrell*, the Government indemnifying the appellant. By the end of 1865, there were three other appeals lodged; *Varley v. Murray, Ridpath v. Murray* and *Walsh v. Goodall.* Like *Dawes v. Quarrell*, the first two of these were brought against the decision of the Supreme Court that the legislature had no power to create local courts. The third was an ordinary appeal by a dissatisfied party, which involved the question of the invalidity of the Registration of Deeds Act No 27 of 1862.[102]

Mr Wilson, the Clerk of the Court of Appeals, had died in 1863 and had been succeeded by Charles Mann junior.[103] For two years Mann had enjoyed a very snug little sinecure, drawing £120 a year for doing nothing. In the estimates for 1866, his salary was actually raised to £150 a year, an increase which was allowed by Parliament only after considerable grumbling and inquiry. What did the clerk do? What were his hours—the Attorney-General was asked—and was it not ridiculous to give a man a bonus for doing nothing except draw his salary? The Government defended the increase on the ground that a superior man was necessary for the post and no such man ought to be offered less than a fifth-class clerk's salary. Besides, said the Attorney-General: "... the gentleman found an office for doing the work of the Court of Appeals in. His private offices were the offices of the Court. (Loud laughter)" [104]

When, for the first time, he was called upon actively to exercise the duties of his office, Mann was disgusted with the Court's rules of procedure, which were still those drawn up and gazetted in 1841. He advised that they should be repealed and replaced by fresh rules.

> 'The Rules, in my opinion'—he wrote—'are entirely unsuited to the requirements of the Court, and no provision is made for

carrying out or enforcing its decrees. The rules were made when no doubt existed as to the jurisdiction of the Court, and when the practice of the Supreme Court had not been reduced to its present simple state and consequently they are extremely cumbersome, dilatory, and almost unworkable.' [105]

He accordingly framed new rules, which were gazetted in February 1866, and provided for appeal by petition supported by affidavit. Notice of appeal was to be given to the respondent and, if he failed to enter an appearance within seven days, the appeal could proceed ex parte. Each party filed a case and parties could be heard in person or by counsel, but only two counsel on each side were allowed. All petitions and cases were required to be on parchment.[106]

Notwithstanding the Act amending and enlarging the jurisdiction of the Court, the puisne Judges of the Supreme Court soon made it clear that their opinions were still decidedly against the existence of a Court of Appeals. When an application which he had made in the Supreme Court failed, Mr Daly intimated to the Court that he was going to appeal to the Court of Appeals and he asked the Court to put in writing their reasons for rejecting his application. "There is no such court", promptly said Mr Justice Boothby. It was not competent for the Supreme Court, Mr Daly submitted, to question the existence of a court superior to it. The submission, as previously related (Chapter 5 8), gave the Judges another occasion to state their opinions on the existence of the Court of Appeals.

Again, in *Harrald v. Carruthers*, heard on 4 August 1865, Mr Justice Boothby uttered dire threats that any member of the profession appearing before the Court of Appeals would be struck off the rolls for contempt of court. Similarly, he rebuked Mr Stow in *Walsh v. Goodall* for announcing that the defeated party would appeal to the Court of Appeals. "I wonder that any advocate in this Court should avow such an intention," said the Judge.[107]

When notice of appeal was given in *Murray v. Ridpath*, the respondent moved the Full Court to have the notice of appeal set aside and removed from the files of the Supreme Court upon the grounds:

(1) That notice of appeal had not been given within the time prescribed.
(2) That no lawfully constituted Court of Appeal had ever existed in the colony.
(3) That, if such a Court of Appeal did ever exist, it had—since the passing of the Constitution Act—become extinguished or died out in consequence of the change of the composition of the Court as originally constituted.

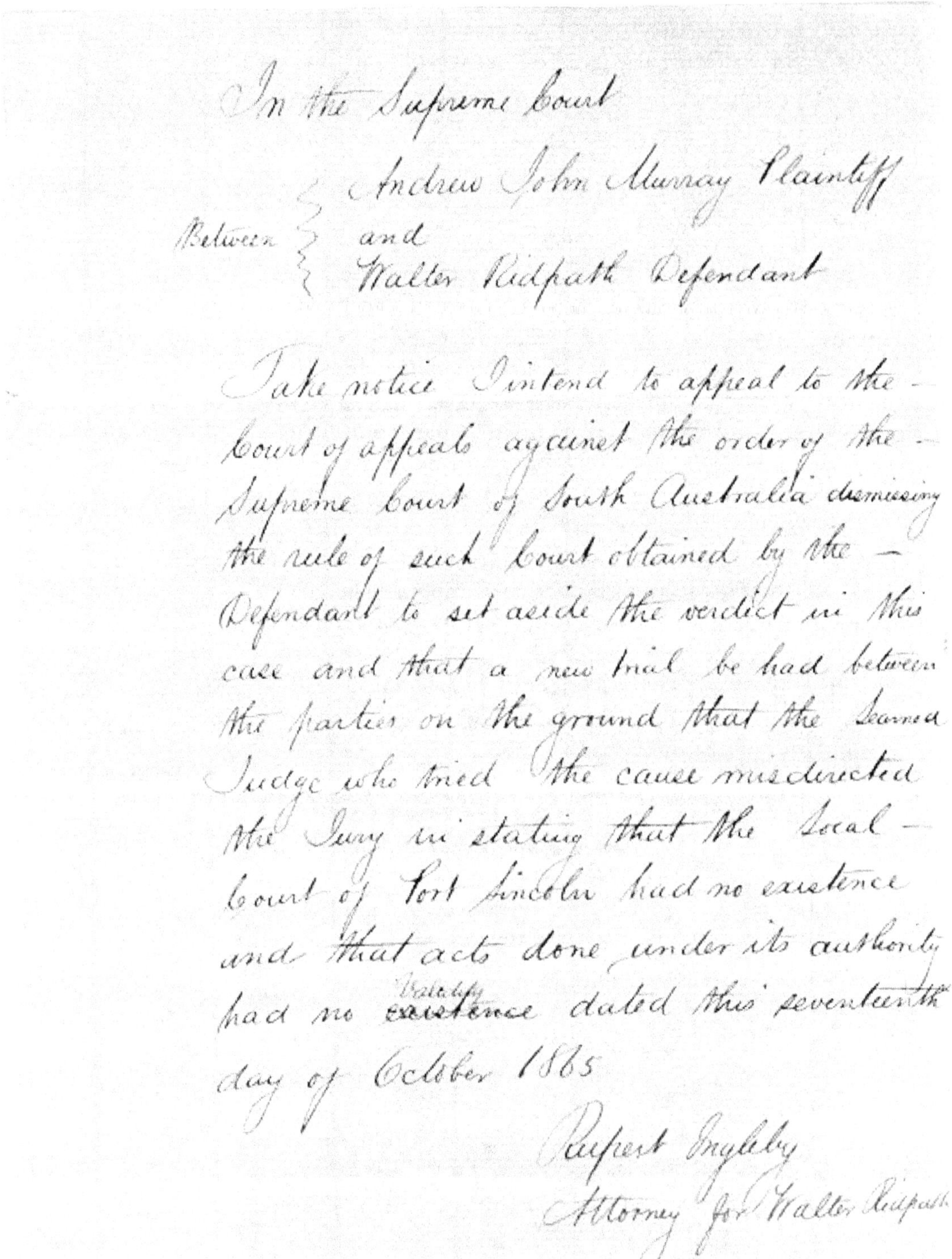

In the Supreme Court

Between { Andrew John Murray Plaintiff
and
Walter Ridpath Defendant }

Take notice I intend to appeal to the Court of appeals against the order of the Supreme Court of South Australia dismissing the rule of such Court obtained by the Defendant to set aside the verdict in this case and that a new trial be had between the parties on the ground that the learned Judge who tried the cause misdirected the Jury in stating that the Local Court of Port Lincoln had no existence and that acts done under its authority had no ~~existence~~ validity dated this seventeenth day of October 1865

Rupert Ingleby
Attorney for Walter Ridpath

Rupert Ingleby's notice to the Supreme Court of his intention to appeal to the Court of Appeals in *Murray v Ridpath.* (SR/SC)

A rule nisi was granted on 3 November 1865 and, when the action was argued before the Full Court, Mr Belt for the plaintiff contended that there was no Court of Appeals because the legislature of South Australia had exceeded its powers by interfering with the Judicial Committee of the Privy Council. The Act creating the Court of Appeals, he said, could not stand with the order of the Privy Council made in 1860, which had ignored the existence of the Court of Appeals. No local act could interfere with the right of the Queen in Council to receive appeals.[108]

The Court reserved judgment and, perturbed by the persistence of these doubts as to the existence and jurisdiction of the Court of Appeals, the Governor sought the advice of the Attorney-General, who reported that the Court of Appeals existed and that the Governor and Council must sit.[109] By good fortune or design, the Court of Appeals did not meet until after the Supreme Court had delivered judgment in *Murray v. Ridpath*, upholding by a majority the lawful existence of the Court of Appeals.[110]

Mr Justice Gwynne thought that the effect of the Colonial Laws Validity Act was to affirm the existence of the Court of Appeals, and his former doubts were thus removed. He doubted, however, whether there was any right of appeal from the Court of Appeals to the Privy Council. No such right was given by the Order in Council of 1860, which referred only to appeals from the Supreme Court.

> 'The Act of our Legislature has given in such cases a further right to appeal to the Privy Council'—he said—'but I do not think that such right is valid, as the Orders in Council specify that all other appeals, except those therein mentioned, shall only be by leave of Her Majesty, in exercise of Her Royal Prerogative, as the Supreme Court of Appeal.'

He could not see, however, that the Orders in Council in any way operated to defeat the present appeal, and he thought the notice of appeal was good.

The Chief Justice could see no conflict between the Order in Council and the local Act, and the Validating Act seemed to him to have removed all doubt as to the existence of the Court of Appeals.

Mr Justice Boothby dissented. Referring to the Order in Council, he said:

> 'It has been argued that this Order does not repeal the Court of Appeal in this Province. True, no express words of repeal are used; but the question is, do the provisions of the Order in legal effect work such repeal? and I am of opinion they do. The plain words are that, although (which has the same legal meaning as notwithstanding) there may be a Court of Appeal within this Province, it is desirable provision should be made to enable parties to appeal from the decision of the Supreme

> Court to Her Majesty in Council, and then provides regulations under which such appeals shall be made. Looking at the whole document in the light of well-settled rules of construction, and mindful that it is passed by the only and highest tribunal, having the duty of ultimately construing Imperial Acts relating to the Colonies, and of reviewing the decisions of this Court as the Court of first resort in construing such Acts, it would be to set at nought all such rules of construction if this Court were to hold that there is not a plain intention on the face of this Order to pass by, to ignore, to treat as non-existing any authority in any Court whatever to receive or hear appeals from the decisions of the Supreme Court of the Colony, save only the Court of Her Majesty in Council. To take away authority from any Court it is not necessary to repeal the Court; it is enough to provide that its jurisdiction shall be possessed by some other specified and defined Court.'

He thought that the plaintiff's rule should be made absolute and he reiterated and adhered to his opinions, expressed in *Payne v. Dench* and *McEllister v. Fenn*, that there was no lawful Court of Appeals in existence.

This judgment was given on 2 March 1866. Two days later the Court of Appeals sat to hear *Walsh v. Goodall*. It was argued for the respondent that the right of appeal in cases of over £500 had been taken away by implication, since the Order in Council directed that such appeals should be taken to the Privy Council. Without giving any reasons, the Court held that its jurisdiction was not confined to cases under £500, that the Registration of Deeds Act No 27 of 1862 was valid, and operated to repeal Act No 8 of 1841, and that the judgment of the Supreme Court must be reversed.[111]

The decision met with public approval.

> 'Our present objectionable Court of Appeals is a necessary evil'—said the Register. 'It is not an institution that we have never been proud of or satisfied with. Secretaries of State have advised us to get rid of such an anomalous Court, unless we had so great a want of confidence in the Supreme Court as to make the retention of the higher tribunal a necessity; and it was really this which causes the Parliament to be so sensitive on the subject. We retained the objectionable court because there was a feeling that the other Court was hostile to local legislation, and that an emergency might arise when it would be safer to take the law from the Governor and the Ministry than from the majority of the Judges.'

Now that much of apprehension had been removed, it was suggested, the Court of Appeals had served its purpose and it would be an appropriate time to bring forward again the project for an intercolonial Court of Appeals.[112]

The judgment of the Court of Appeals in *Walsh v. Goodall* was not, however, received with much favour in the Supreme Court. Mr Stow moved that the order of the Court of Appeals should be made a rule of the Supreme Court or that the proper officer should be directed to enter it in the record of the Court.

> 'The Court of Appeals'—said Mr Justice Boothby—'has reversed the judgment in the face of an Order of Her Majesty in Council, that all appeals from this Court are to be direct to herself; and I cannot undertake the risk of allowing such a judgment to be entered.'

Mr Justice Gwynne curtly said that the Court of Appeals had power to enforce its own orders; let it do so. More mildly, the Chief Justice pointed out that the application was a novel one and he would like to hear argument on it. Mr Stow then abandoned his application and said that the order would be enforced by the higher court. Mr Justice Boothby gave him a parting warning: "Parties who enforce illegal proceedings under the Act of 1861 must expect to take the consequences of theirs acts." [113]

The *Register* was up in arms at once at the "unseemly display of temper by two of the Judges". The Court of Appeals had been held to have a legal existence; why then did Mr Justice Boothby continue to speak of it as if it had no existence? "Is it to be a legal court as long as it upholds the decisions of the Judges, and an illegal court as soon as it reverses those decisions?" [114]

It seemed obvious that Mr Justice Boothby was determined not to yield and that he wanted to provoke a conflict between the two courts; nor was it long before an opportunity arrived for Mr Justice Boothby to have the conflict which he sought. An appeal had been instituted in the case of *Copeland v. Wentzel.* This had originated in the Supreme Court as an action for damages for negligence. Mr Justice Boothby non-suited the plaintiff, who moved for a new trial. The rule was discharged, and the plaintiff then appealed to the Court of Appeals. Section 4 of the Act No 5 of 1861 provided that, upon an appeal being made, the Judge who presided on the trial of the case should, on being required so to do by the President of the Court of Appeals, transmit a copy, certified to be correct, of the notes made by him on the trial and of all documents put in evidence. On 10 April 1866 a requisition under this section was served upon Mr Justice Boothby, requiring him to send up copies of the proceedings in *Copeland v. Wentzel.*[115] He did not do so. Mr Stow, who appeared for the plaintiff, tried to persuade the Chief Justice to get over the difficulty by stating a special case. The Chief Justice, however, said that the statute was clear; it was the trial Judge who must send up the copy of the proceedings.[116]

In *Copeland v Wentzel* the plaintiff had his hands and arms cut and permanently injured by a sawmill. Pictured is a sawmill at Williamstown ca. 1890 (SLSA)

The Court of Appeals sat on 12 May 1866 and, as there were no papers before it, it made a peremptory order that Mr Justice Boothby should transmit the necessary documents to the President of the Court on or before 25 May and adjourned to 26 May.[117] On the last day mentioned in the order, Mr Justice Boothby forwarded to the Governor a letter, which the *Register* characterised, not without reason, as "rude and evasive", saying that he had been too busy to attend to the matter but would furnish a reply to the requisition and have it handed to the Governor when the Court of Appeals sat next day. He put forward the excuse that the order directed the transmission of documents in the custody of the Supreme Court over which the Full Court alone had control and that the documents would require the seal of the Supreme Court to be affixed, whereas no single judge had power to order this. There was no substance in those points, for the order only required him to forward copies and to certify them as being correct.[118]

On the following day the Court of Appeals met, but neither the requisitioned documents nor the promised reply from Mr Justice Boothby came to hand. Mr Stow for the appellant said that, as the Judge had not forwarded his notes, he could not carry the case any further. The respondent's counsel then applied to have the petition of appeal dismissed, but the Court ruled that, under the peculiar circumstances, the further hearing of the case must be adjourned sine die.[119]

After the Court had adjourned and its members were dispersing, the Judges' Associate delivered to the Governor the promised communication from Mr Justice Boothby, which consisted of a long memorandum of sixteen reasons intended to show that the Judge was not by law bound to comply with the peremptory order served upon him. Among his reasons were:

(1) 'On the assumption that Ordinance No 31, 1855-56 and Act No 5 1861, are in lawful operation—the latter Act having, by section 2, declared the Court of Appeals a Court of Record—the legal incident attaches that all its Judges must be sworn as such by an oath of office. No such oath is provided by the Statute, and the Judges cannot prescribe an oath for themselves.'

(2) 'The Judges of the Court are all declared by the Government Gazette to be members of Parliament, and ex officio members of the Executive Council; judicial notice must therefore be taken that all the existing members of the Executive Council are members of Parliament, while the Constitution Act provides that such cannot be Judges of any Court.'

(3) 'The President of the Court being required by the Statute to be His Excellency the Governor-in-Chief, who by his Commission, under Statutory Regulations, is also the representative of the Crown in Parliament, introduces an anomaly so patent, that it cannot be law. Her Majesty could not sit in person. It is a legal incident of the prerogative that She can only sit by Her Judges, whom the law requires to be men learned in the law—a want of qualification attaching to every member of the Court.'

(4) 'Even if the Judges were lawfully constituted, they could not sit to determine the lawfulness of their own acts in passing Statutes contrary to the provisions of Imperial Statutes, and in deciding for themselves whether they have jurisdiction or not.'

(5) 'The facts disclosed in the case of *Copeland v. Wentzel* show what hardship and injustice would be worked by the establishment in law of a Local Court of Appeal, having the power to deprive a defendant of the security which the unanimous judgment of the Supreme Court has thrown around him, so that he shall not be exposed to be again dragged by the Plaintiff into another Court, who has already caused to the defendant an outlay in costs necessary to defend himself from litigation never founded in law to the extent, in my judgment, of not less than £100, and which he may never be able to recover from the plaintiff from his want of ability to pay either his own or defendant's costs.'

(6) 'Suitors in a Court of so doubtful legality to say the least, have no security that any litigation therein will permanently protect their rights.'

He reiterated his opinion expressed in *Murray v. Ridpath* that the Court of Appeals was without jurisdiction and annexed to his memorandum a copy of his judgment in that case, ignoring the fact that the other two Judges had disagreed with him.

> 'At an early sitting of the Full Court, on the first day of term'—he concluded—'I shall read in open Court the above reasons, and seek the advice and opinion of the other Judges, and act thereupon as my judgment directs.' [120]

The belated delivery of this letter after the Court of Appeals had adjourned seems to have been due to accident, but it had the unfortunate result that the newspapers, not knowing of the letter, published only an account of the adjournment of the proceedings and openly accused the Judge of deceit and failure to keep his promise. In consequence, when Mr Justice Boothby took his seat on the bench on 28 May, he said: "I have to inform the Court of important circumstances connected with my position as a Judge, which have occurred since the last day of its meeting."

He then recapitulated the events which had taken place with regard to the appeal in *Copeland v. Wentzel* and his promise to let the Governor have a reply before the Court sat.

> 'I came down to my Chamber on Saturday under the impression that the Court of Appeals did not sit until 11 o'clock; but to my surprise on looking through the door at five minutes past ten, I saw in the Court the Clerk and two or three members of the profession. I immediately put the document containing my reasons in the hands of Mr Pelham (the Associate), and at a quarter past ten he stated that he had delivered it to the Clerk. How, then, a statement could have got abroad respecting the nonfulfilment of the promise made in my letter of the 25th I cannot understand.'

The Judge then read the memorandum he had forwarded, and continued:

> 'This memorandum was certainly delivered at a quarter past ten, or within a few minutes of that time; for the Associate informed me in my room that he had handed it to the President or the Clerk. I directed him to give it to the Clerk. To say, therefore, that the Court sat on the 26th without having my reasons forwarded to it is a misstatement on the part of those who take pleasure in such misstatements, and one which cannot be justified. The fact must have been known to everybody present, and the Associate and myself are in a position to prove it. And, on going into the Court, I could not help seeing that His Excellency and the Ministers were in the room of the Chief Justice, the former having in his hand the paper I had forwarded, which he was engaged in reading. I therefore say, this being a matter upon which my learned colleagues' opinion should be taken, that I shall, upon the first

> sitting of the Court after Wednesday next, bring the matter forward. I will allow two days for either party to come in and move in the matter; for, as I have already said in Chambers, I have no power to do what is required of me, for I have no control over a rule of Court, whatever I may over my notes; and besides there is the question of the affixture of the seal of the Court. For the documents may be forwarded to the Judicial Committee of the Privy Council, and there, by a positive rule, no document can be looked at that has not the seal of the Court below attached. As I said, I shall on Thursday morning, introduce this matter to the notice of my brother Judges, and ask for their opinion.'

Despite this statement, Mr Justice Boothby never did seek the advice of his brothers on the matter. It is a remarkable instance of blind inconsistency that he should even have proposed to take the opinion of Judges whom he still maintained were not Judges at all.

While he was making his personal explanation from the bench, he was annoyed by someone talking in court and stopped to say, rather petulantly: "The Clerk of the Attorney General should not interrupt a Judge during the delivery of a solemn judgment."

When he had finished, the Attorney-General (Mr Boucaut) rose and said that, in fairness to his clerk, he wished to point out that the clerk had not spoken at all.

> Mr Justice Boothby: 'I heard a voice, and, looking round the Court, I saw it proceeded from your clerk. It is a matter of surprise to me that judgments of this Court are treated as they are by the Bar during their delivery, and I shall not permit a clerk to confer with his employer while I am reading mine. True, this is not a judgment, but it is a matter of importance for the Court.'
>
> The Attorney General: 'I do not say there was no sound in the Court. I only state that it did not proceed from my clerk.'
>
> Mr Justice Boothby: 'I saw the motion of his lips.'
>
> The Attorney General: 'I think your Honor is now doing me an injustice. I repeat that my clerk was not speaking to me; and your Honor's remarks are calculated to hurt his feelings. There were several around me talking, but your Honor is not justified in saying that what I have stated is not correct. My statement should be sufficient.'
>
> Mr Justice Boothby: 'I was interrupted by the voice of your clerk.'
>
> The Crown Solicitor: 'I think it is only just for me to say that I

was sitting close to the Attorney General and did not hear any voice. I think your Honor must be mistaken.'

Mr Justice Boothby: 'I may be mistaken, and I accept the apology at once; but clerks of attorneys should not interrupt by talking to their masters during the proceedings.' [121]

As a result of the Judge's defiance of the order of the Court of Appeals, the proceedings in *Copeland v. Wentzel* came to a stop. Nothing further could be done.

'It is utterly impossible'—said the Advertiser—'that the Court of Appeals established by law and validated by an Imperial Act, can allow itself to be coolly extinguished by an inferior officer of State, and therefore we presume that His Honor's contumacy will be followed by suspension.' [122]

The Governor hesitated to take the drastic step of suspension, which he feared might lead to more trouble, but the Judge's conduct, both with regard to the Court of Appeals and at the May Criminal Sessions, led him to call Parliament together a fortnight earlier than had been originally proposed in order to deal with the crisis which had arisen in the administration of justice. He felt himself in duty bound to maintain the authority of the Court of Appeals.

'There is no portion of my public duty which is more irksome to me'—he wrote—'than that of President of the Court of Appeal, feeling, as I have always done, the full force of the objections that are urged against its composition; and I would gladly avail myself of any opportunity to have the present law repealed; but, so long as the law remains in its present state, I am bound to cause it to be administered to the best of my ability. And the prospect of its repeal is, I regret to think, daily rendered more remote, chiefly by the conduct of Mr Boothby himself, in reference to the Legislation of the Colony generally.' [123]

A further argument as to the jurisdiction of the Court of Appeals arose in June 1866, when Mr Belt moved the Supreme Court, on behalf of the unsuccessful respondent in *Walsh v. Goodall*, that so much of the judgment of the Court of Appeals as gave costs to the appellant should be struck out.

'Have we any power to order part of the judgment of a superior court to be struck out?'—asked Mr Justice Gwynne.

'Not so far as the judgment itself is concerned'—replied Mr Belt 'but I submit that the Court of Appeals has no power to order costs.'

Meanwhile, Mr Justice Boothby had pricked up his ears.

> 'Something was said about a superior court'—he interjected. 'This Court by Imperial Statute is called the Supreme Court, and it is out of the question to talk of a thing superior to what is supreme.'

The majority of the Judges being of opinion that they had no power whatever to interfere with the judgment of a higher court, the application was refused.[124]

> 'The thought of there being a "superior" court'—commented the Register—'is wormwood and gall to Mr Justice Boothby—a court, too, assuming to exist by Statute, and merely by Statute, like the other two Judges, and not like our 'well-beloved Benjamin Boothby', who was created by Commission under the Sign Manual of Her Majesty the Queen of England! Can such things be, his Honor wants to know, or can they exist anywhere except in miserable South Australia.' [125]

The cases remaining to be dealt with by the Court of Appeals were *Dawes v. Quarrell, Ridpath v. Murray* and *Varley v. Murray*. The first of these was settled and abandoned. In *Ridpath v. Murray*, the respondent petitioned to have the appeal dismissed. The appellant, a clerk of a Local Court, had been indemnified by the Government, who were conducting the proceedings, and it was argued that the Government being the real plaintiff in the action, the members of the Government who composed the Court of Appeals were disqualified from adjudicating upon the matter because of their interest in the result. The Court, however, refused to be persuaded that the Executive Council had any interest in the matter beyond that of any other citizen and the application was dismissed. No reasons were given and, when reasons in writing were asked for, with a view to appeal to the Privy Council, the request was refused.[126] The Government was not anxious to press on with the appeals, but they had to be disposed of and, after a number of adjournments (partly on account of the Governor's gout), they at last came on for hearing in November 1866. In both *Varley v. Murray* and *Ridpath v. Murray*, the judgment of the Supreme Court was reversed, but again no reasons were given.[127]

During the debates in Parliament in June 1866, upon the address for the removal of Mr Justice Boothby, the Court of Appeals came in for a deal of scathing criticism. It was generally agreed that it was an anomaly which ought to have been long before knocked on the head but, having survived and proved of some utility in a time of crisis, it was thought that such protection as it offered ought not to be cast aside until the fate of the Judge had been definitely decided.

The disfavour with which the Court was regarded was increased when a person named Hyrdess, a Currie Street ostler, commenced actions for penalties against the Chief Secretary and the Commissioner of Crown Lands. Section 36 of the Constitution Act provided that "no Judge of any Court of the said Province" should be capable of being elected a member of Parliament. Hyrdess alleged that the Chief Secretary and Commissioner of Crown Lands had been elected members of Parliament during the time they, as members of the Executive Council, were sitting as Judges of the Court of Appeals and that they were, therefore, ineligible to sit in Parliament. An Act (No 2 of 1866) was hastily passed to protect the Executive from actions upon this ground. It provided that any such actions should, on the application of the defendant to the Supreme Court, be ordered to be discontinued without costs.[128]

In December 1866 the Hon J. Baker introduced in the Legislative Council a Bill to abolish the Court of Appeals, which he stigmatised as "an abominable anomaly".

> 'We are now arrived at a period when it may be abolished'—he said—'and if I succeed in this attempt, I shall give my undivided attention to the establishment of a better tribunal in its stead. We could not establish a worse, for, so far as I am concerned, I would rather go into the streets and take the first four bullock drivers or car men I met with to whom to appeal from the decision of the Supreme Court than to take a case before the Court as at present constituted, for the Executive are necessarily so mixed up with political matters that it is absurd to expect that they would give an impartial judgment.'

A 1906 photograph of four bullock drivers awaiting the opportunity to replace the Court of Appeals. (SLSA)

He stressed the fact that members of the Court gave no reasons for their judgments, obviously because they knew nothing of law. A good name for the Court, he said, would be "A Court to Reverse the Decisions of the Supreme Court". Mr Baker's efforts, however, were fruitless. A motion that the Bill should be read a second time six months thence was carried without a division, the general opinion of the House being that the Court of Appeals was still of some use as a possible safety valve in the case of further trouble with Mr Justice Boothby.[129]

Early in 1867 Mr Boucaut (the then Attorney-General) prepared a detailed memorandum to be submitted to an approaching intercolonial conference, in favour of the establishment of a general Court of Appeals for the colonies. He submitted the following reasons in favour of such a court:

> 'First: The delay caused at present by the appeal to the Judicial Committee of the Privy Council. True in South Australia there is the Local Court of Appeals, composed of the Governor and Executive Council; but that is an unsatisfactory tribunal, and only just one degree better than no Court of Appeal at all, and would be gladly abolished in favor of an Intercolonial Court on a more Satisfactory basis. This delay is brought about:
>
> I. By the distance from England of these colonies, which necessarily causes very considerable delay in the mere transmission of appeals and the decisions thereon.
>
> II. By the press of business upon the Judicial Committee, in that it has to decide appeals from all the forty or fifty British Colonies, in all parts of the world; to administer on appeal almost every known civilized code; and also to hear appeals from the Admiralty and Ecclesiastical Courts, besides various other appeals, in England.
>
> III. By the pressure of other calls on the individual members of the Judicial Committee, each one of whom is almost invariably a member of some other Court, requiring his more particular attention.
>
> These various causes operate to bring about the delays constantly complained of, and which are in the highest degree unsatisfactory.
>
> Second: The expense of an appeal to England; for although the expenses have been considerably diminished of late, it would seem certain that they must of necessity be much less if an appeal could be heard at our own doors instead of at our antipodes.
>
> Third: The tendency of such a Court to bring the various Colonies nearer together, or certainly to prevent a gradually

> increasing dissimilarity that must be disadvantageous to communities bordering upon one another, and closely connected. And the establishment of such a Court would, I apprehend, be either a step towards federation, or one that would tend to make federation easier hereafter when it becomes a necessity. In short, such a Court would prevent delay, would save costs, and would tend to a closer and more intimate relationship between these various colonies that must be advantageous to all of them, and more especially, I think, to Victoria and New South Wales.'

He thought that the local interests and feelings of the various colonies would prevent a fixed court and he inclined towards an ambulatory court visiting each colony perhaps twice or four times a year. As to the personnel of the court, was it to be formed:

> '1. Of entirely distinct Judges.
> 2. Of the Chief Justices of the various colonies, and an assessor, as the Attorney General of Victoria (Mr Ireland) had suggested.
> 3. Of the Judges of the various colonies to be appointed by the various governments, with such an Assessor.'
>
> 'Of these various modes'—wrote Mr Boucaut—'the first is entitled to great consideration, and the expenses to the combined Colonies of a Court of Appeal of three high class Judges would be comparatively trifling. But if it should be determined that the Court should consist of Judges from the various Colonies, then, I think, the third plan, as being less restrictive is better than the second. It might happen at times that it would be most injurious to the public interests to have the Chief Justice absent from a particular colony, nor is it well entirely to overlook the contingency that it might be undesirable to have a Chief Justice, as of course, a member of the Court of Appeals. Political influence might hereafter appoint Chief Justices, whom all would regret to see permanent members of such a Court. Further, the Chief Justices, by virtue of their office have considerable authority and influence; and it would be hardly fair to the other Judges, and hardly well for the public interests, so greatly to increase this authority and influence, as would follow from making them such permanent members. I think it would be wiser not to restrict the Colonial Governments too greatly in this but to leave them the power year by year to fix the particular Judge to represent the Colony in the Court. If the Court sits for one year in a particular colony, then the Judge once named could

> sit for that year. If it be objected that it gives too much power to the Governments to allow them to nominate the particular Judge, then the Judges might sit year by year in rotation. Many reasons could be adduced to show that either of these plans is preferable to permanently fixing it in the Chief Justices alone.' [130]

The proposals thus revived by Mr Boucaut proved abortive and a year or two later, it is interesting to note, he had considerably modified his view. The greater attention given to colonial matters in England, he said, caused him to be less strongly in favour of an intercolonial court than he was at the time of his minute in 1867.

> 'No Colonial Court could expect for many years to attain to the authority of the Judicial Committee, which also furnishes a strong bond between the colonists and the mother country.' [131]

When the Boothby troubles were finally disposed of, by the death of the Judge, another effort was made to get rid of the Court of Appeals. Mr Andrews, the Attorney-General, introduced a Bill for its abolition in August 1868.

> 'The Court'—he said—'has been stigmatized by persons holding all shades of political opinions as a most inconvenient institution. It has been made use of; but I believe its utility will be found to exist more in idea than in reality. The questions brought before it chiefly related to the validity of Acts said to be ultra vires; but these doubts have been determined by Imperial Legislation ... I do not say that no moral influence has been exercised by it, but as a Court of law it is hollow, rotten, unsatisfactory and useless.'

It had been created originally because the colony had at first to avail itself of the best material at hand, but it now formed only an expensive halfway house to the Privy Council, of no use except to the lawyers. "To filter the decisions of the Judges through a political institution like the Court of Appeals is to keep the ball rolling and heap up costs."

In an able speech in reply, Mr Boucaut agreed that, from a purely legal point of view, the Court of Appeals should be swept away, but if once abolished it might be difficult ever to constitute such a court again if it was needed.

> 'I know what has happened in South Australia'—he said—'and I know what might happen again. It is said Mr Justice Boothby is not a Judge of the Supreme Court now. Granted; but there might be other Judges worse than Judge Boothby. We wanted it urgently once and we may want it again.'

Sir Dominick Daly, he said, had told him that he thought the Judges in all the colonies were prone to assume a position of superiority over the other powers that would never be dreamed of in England and that it was desirable there should be some check upon them. No harm could be done by the Court and it might still be of some use.

Once more, however, the attempt to get rid of the Court of Appeals was defeated by a large majority. The recollections of the Boothby troubles were still too vivid,[132] but the Court had fallen into a decline. A few more cases were brought before it, at gradually increasing intervals, the last being in 1882.

When the Commonwealth Constitution Act was framed, provision had to be made, in section 74, to give the High Court of Australia jurisdiction to hear and determine appeals from the Court of Appeals.[133]

The Acts establishing the Court were all repealed by the Supreme Court Act 1935, and their provisions were not re-enacted. The intention obviously was that the Court should be abolished, but section 3(a) of the Supreme Court Act 1935 provides that:

> 'The repeal shall not affect any principle or rule of law, or any established jurisdiction, notwithstanding that the same may have been affirmed by, or derived from, any of the repealed enactments.'

It could hardly be denied that the Court of Appeals exercised an "established jurisdiction", affirmed by and derived from the statutes repealed. "Jurisdiction" is defined in section 5 to *"include"* certain powers and authorities of the Judges of the Supreme Court, but this definition is by way of enlargement and not of exclusion. It might possibly be contended, therefore, that the jurisdiction of the Court of Appeals—an "established jurisdiction"—has been expressly saved by section 3(a) and that the Court still exists. It is not likely, however, that any dissatisfied suitor will wish to attempt to set in motion the rusty machinery of this anachronism.

Two views of Adelaide that span the life of the Court of Appeals. The top one is Anne Gildon's 1839 view of North Terrace (NLA). Below is a photograph taken around 1930 looking east.

Chapter 8

Courts of Inferior Jurisdiction

'cheap, summary and expeditious'

On 2 January 1837 the first Act of Council was passed, to establish Courts of General or Quarter and Petty Sessions.[1] The Act provided:

1. *Courts of General or Quarter Sessions* for the province, or for districts thereof, should be held at such times and places as the Governor in Council by proclamation appointed.

   These Courts were empowered to take cognisance:

   (a) "Of all matters and things cognizable in Courts of General or Quarter Sessions in England, so far as the circumstances and condition of the Province shall require and admit".

   (b) "Of such matters and things as may be necessary to give effect to any future Acts of the Council".

   (c) "In a summary way of all crimes and misdemeanours and felonies of whatever description not punishable with death" which might be committed within the province.

   All Magistrates or Justices of the Peace for the province were appointed members of and Judges in the Courts of General and Quarter Sessions.

2. *Courts of Petty Sessions* should be held at such times and places as might be necessary before two or more Justices of the Peace for the province, or for the district in which such courts might be held.

   Petty Sessions were given jurisdiction over all misdemeanours and offences not punishable with death or transportation, with power to punish by fine not exceeding £12 and imprisonment in solitary confinement, or otherwise at the direction of the magistrates, for any term not exceeding three calendar months.

Section VII of the Act provided that the Courts of General or Quarter Sessions should settle rules of practice and procedure for the conduct of dispatch of business and the fees to be taken, both in the Courts of General or Quarter and Petty Sessions; the rules to be approved by the Governor in Council.

With regard to the titles of the Courts thus created, it may be noted:

(a) The distinction between General and Quarter Sessions was frequently confused. In England, according to Holdsworth:

> '... the Courts of Quarter Sessions for the whole county have always been held four times a year at times prescribed by Statute. At times other than those fixed by statute Courts of General Sessions can be held'. [2]

In South Australia the Courts were referred to indiscriminately as Courts of Quarter Sessions, General Sessions, or General Quarter Sessions.

(b) The use of the term "Petty Sessions" is surprising, for in England "even in 1849 it was hardly a technical expression".[3]

The jurisdiction of quarter sessions in England was wide, but that conferred on quarter sessions by this Act was very much wider. To empower them to take cognisance "*in a summary way*" of any crime not punishable with death was to give them a jurisdiction both "unconstitutional and dangerous", while their jurisdiction over "such matters and things as may be necessary to give effect to any future Acts of the Council" was vague and almost unlimited.

Equally extraordinary was the jurisdiction given to the Courts of Petty Sessions. While they could hear and determine a number of misdemeanours of a very grave nature, which cried out for trial by jury, they could not try cases of petty larceny or pilfering, which were the very offences which it was most desirable should be dealt with summarily in a minor court.

Owing to these anomalies the Act proved of little use. What was apparently the only sittings of Quarter Sessions under this Act, as a criminal Court, was held on the day after it was passed, for the purpose of swearing in constables; while so far as can be ascertained no Court of Petty Sessions ever sat at all.[4] From time to time the Justices of the Peace dealt with minor offences such as drunkenness and fighting, but they seem to have derived their jurisdiction not from the Act but from their general powers as justices.[5]

On 7 January 1837 Gouger noted in his journal that he was: "... called upon as Magistrate, to decide the first case which had arisen in the colony, but which was dismissed with costs".

And on 17 January he wrote:

> 'On Saturday last I decided two cases of quarrel between Master and Servant, according to the Act passed by the Legislative Council, on the 2nd ultimo, without which enactment the long process of a civil action would have been required to procure redress.' [6]

Governor Hindmarsh had been instructed to appoint, on his arrival in the colony, a Police magistrate to exercise summary jurisdiction over petty offences; but he was restricted in the salary to be paid to £100 a year. If a professional man was to be appointed the salary was absurdly low, even allowing for the right of private practice which the magistrate was to be permitted at first, and the Governor had difficulty in finding anyone in the colony qualified to occupy a judicial office who would accept the position. "Where shall I get a Gentleman fit to do such duty who would give up his time for so small a sum?"—he complained.

He urged Lord Glenelg to increase the salary to £200.[7] Months went by without anything being done, although the failure of the proposed Courts of Quarter and Petty Sessions made the establishment of a tribunal for the summary trial of small offences a pressing need. The justices did the best they could in the absence of any efficient police to bring offenders before them, and of any gaol in which the guilty could be imprisoned.

During the first year, also, the settlers suffered from the lack of any provision for the recovery of small debts. Complaints about the defective state of the law in this respect were numerous, and in August 1837 Jickling made a formal protest to the Colonial Secretary.[8]

In an attempt to remedy these deficiencies the Council passed, on 17 November 1837, an act: "... to establish Courts of Resident Magistrates and to provide for the recovery of small debts and the punishment of certain offences".

This Act is of considerable importance, for it remained in force and operation until the establishment of Local Courts in 1850. Mann, the Advocate-General, who drafted it, based it on similar legislation in force at the Cape of Good Hope. It authorised the Governor from time to time to define certain parts of the province and to constitute them into districts, within each of which a court (to be a court of record and called the Court of the Resident Magistrate) was to be established. A Resident Magistrate and a Clerk of the Peace were to be appointed for each district, and until the proclamation of districts any two or more Justices of the Peace might hold such courts and exercise the authority of a Resident Magistrate.

The jurisdiction conferred on the Courts may be summarised as follows:

A. Civil

(1) The Courts had jurisdiction to hear and determine in a summary way all actions, plaints and suits for the payment of any debt, damages or matter not exceeding £20, and to award costs; but they could not determine any actions relating to the title to land or where rights in future might be bound.

(2) Their decision was final and conclusive and could be enforced by execution, the Magistrate being empowered to order payment by instalments if he thought fit.

(3) To prevent matters within the jurisdiction of the Resident Magistrates Court being taken to the Supreme Court, the defendant in an action in the Supreme Court, if the Judge certified that the action should have been brought in the lower court, was to get costs in any event, and double costs if the successful party.

(4) Defendants were to be sued in the Court for the district where they resided or where the cause of action accrued and, until districts were marked out, the Court at Adelaide was given general jurisdiction over all suits cognisable under the Act.

B. Criminal

The Resident Magistrate had jurisdiction without appeal in all cases of offences not amounting to felony committed within his district, and could punish by fine up to £10 or by imprisonment with or without hard labour for any term up to three months.

C. General

By section XXI the Courts of Resident Magistrates were given jurisdiction "to hear and determine all cases where one or more Magistrates or Justices of the Peace are empowered to act".

In pursuance of this Act, the whole of the province, except Kangaroo Island, was proclaimed as one district—the District of Adelaide. A Court was constituted at Adelaide, and Henry Rodolph Wigley, an English solicitor, was appointed Resident Magistrate.[9] When not engaged in his own Court, he continued his private practice.

> 'After all is over'—wrote James in his Six Months in South Australia—'he acts, when the Supreme Court is sitting, as barrister and solicitor; and in this distracted colony, where the vile spirit of party, led by those pests of the place, Mr ----- and Mr -----, is tearing the colony to pieces, it is no small praise to Mr Wigley, the Resident Magistrate, to say that all men concur in speaking well of him. His important and daily duties are the best executed and worst paid in the colony, for all these honours and offices only bring him in a salary of £100 a year, which, when potatoes are £50 a ton, is exactly a remuneration of two tons of potatoes per annum.' [10]

Rules and regulations for the procedure of the court having been drawn up by Jickling, the Acting Judge, the first sitting was held on 20 December 1837.[11]

For a year or two the Court functioned without arousing any active opposition. Mann was well satisfied with his handiwork.

> 'The Court of Resident Magistrates'—he wrote—'which sits weekly to try all cases not attended with aggravation, and which do not amount to felony, operates very powerfully to repress the more trifling misdemeanours, that obtain in every community. I proposed this species of jurisdiction, and take credit to myself for doing so.' [12]

The Act was not regarded with favour, however, by the Commissioners in England, who recommended that it should be disallowed after sufficient notice had been given to enable a new act to be prepared, but their recommendation was shelved and forgotten.[13]

On the civil side, an immediate and beneficial result of the establishment of the Resident Magistrates Court was to diminish the quantity of petty business brought before the Supreme Court (or at least so Jickling said,[14] although as the business which had to that date been brought before the Supreme Court was trifling, it is not easy to see how it could have made much difference); and on the criminal side it provided a tribunal more fitted to dispense justice than the haphazard administration of police law by justices. There were, nevertheless, serious defects, first in the constitution and jurisdiction of the Court, and next in its procedure and administration, which militated against its successful working.

I. The Constitution and Jurisdiction of the Court

The whole jurisdiction of the Court, civil and criminal, in matters of law and of fact, was vested in a single individual without any right of appeal or review."This is a power"—reported the Advocate-General in 1843—"which has not been conferred on the Judge of the Supreme Court ... and ought not to be enjoyed by any single functionary whatever." [15]

No such unfettered power was given to any magistrate in England. Further, with respect to the civil jurisdiction of the Court, there was a strong popular feeling (not shared in official circles) that £20 was too low a maximum and that the jurisdiction should be extended; while on the criminal side the jurisdiction was inconvenient because:

(1) All felonies being excluded, a variety of petty larcenies and other small offences had to be sent to the Supreme Court for trial.

(2) On the other hand, all misdemeanours being within the cognisance of the Resident Magistrate, many serious offences might be disposed of summarily by him which ought to have been sent to the Supreme Court for trial by jury.

II. The Procedure and Administration of the Court

It is probable that the Court was intended to be a court of conscience, the determination being "in a summary way"—words similar to those which had been used in New South Wales in establishing Courts of Requests (3 Wm IV No 2). But Wigley, the Resident Magistrate, early decided that as the words "according to equity and good conscience" did not appear in the Act, the Court must be administered strictly as a court of common law. All the technical forms of action, as in assumpsit, debt, trespass, or case, were observed, and the rules of pleading and evidence strictly adhered to. The rules drawn up by Jickling, for instance, merely required the plaintiff to furnish in writing two copies of his claim or demand, one for the court and one for service. Wigley held that this statement in writing must be a proper pleading. Similarly he required the defendant to plead with all the accuracy necessary in an action in the Supreme Court. In one case, a defendant who produced a written receipt signed by the plaintiff, for the sum demanded, was precluded from proving it because he had not alleged payment but had, in his defence, only said that he did not owe the money; and the result was a verdict by which he had to pay the same debt a second time. In 1843 the Advocate-General reported that by strict adherence to these rules the Court had become:

> '... an arena of petty litigation, a large portion of the decisions proceeding on points of form alone, by which from the necessity of employing attorneys in every case how trifling soever, encouragement has been given to discreditable professional quibbling, such as ought now-a-days to be deemed out of place in any Court, above all in a Court for the suits of the poor'. [16]

In addition, the procedure had been complicated by a multiplicity of incidental steps which gradually crept in—summonses for particulars, for rules nisi, and for a variety of interlocutory orders. Since it was essential for a party to a suit to employ an attorney, costs were high. The solicitors who frequented the Court rapidly developed habits of pettifogging, and a custom arose amongst some of them of remunerating their clerks by permitting them a right of private practice, in their master's name, in the Resident Magistrates Court. This was condemned by a majority of the profession, but its existence indicates that the business of the Court passed too often through the hands of attorneys of the Dodson and Fogg type, and that already there were in South Australia some of: "... those anomalous practitioners in the lower depths of law who on prudential reasons deny themselves all indulgence in the luxury of too delicate a conscience". [17]

Dodson and Fogg
"Dodson and Fogg" were disreputable lawyers in Charles Dickens' *The Pickwick Papers*.

The Court was hampered, too, by inefficient and indolent clerks. Proper books of account were not kept, moneys disappeared, records were lost, and the work was behindhand.[18] One of the clerks had a running account with some of the solicitors, giving them credit for fees, and reimbursing the Government out of the costs if and when they came through the Court. At an inquiry which Governor Grey ordered to be held into this "systematic trafficking", the other clerk stated that he was frequently upbraided by the solicitors and considered very discourteous because he refused to allow them credit.[19]

Among the public, these various disadvantages aroused gradually increasing dissatisfaction, to which the Grand Jury gave vent in March 1839. They objected to their time being wasted over trivial offences which should have been tried before a minor court which had to be brought before the Supreme Court because of the anomalous jurisdictions of the inferior courts.[20] Governor Gawler replied to their protest:

> 'Under the very heavy pressure of complicated business, with the most inconvenient accommodation for transacting it, I have hitherto been compelled to allow many questionable public arrangements to remain as I found them. Among these

> are the proceedings connected with the administration of justice.'

A difficulty had arisen, however, against putting the Courts of Quarter Sessions into operation:

> 'In the present very active state of private business, I doubt if the Magistrates of the Province could, without too great a sacrifice, give their time to the duties of Quarter Sessions. This consideration alone prevents me from immediately constituting such Courts. In the meantime the Resident Magistrate's Court is, to a great extent, a substitute for them.' [21]

It proved a poor substitute, and in March 1841 the Grand Jury again complained that nothing had been done to provide for the trial of minor offences. The Judge agreed that there should be a more summary way of trial of such offences. Although he himself was not so busy, he said, that he could not afford time to hear the case, the attendance of jurors was a great inconvenience to them. He suggested the substitution of the information of the Advocate-General for the presentment of a Grand Jury in cases of small felonies, and the trial of these cases by a jury of six instead of twelve. For this purpose the Court of Quarter Sessions should be revived, a certain number of justices being required to attend; but the jurisdiction of Quarter Sessions should be limited to cases where the punishment could not exceed seven years' transportation or imprisonment for two years, with or without hard labour or a whipping. Difficult cases should be referred to the Supreme Court. The original Quarter Sessions Act, he thought, should not be acted upon: it was passed at a very early period, conferred powers not usually exercised by such courts in England, was objected to at the time, and had since remained in abeyance.[22]

In May 1841 Governor Gawler was recalled and the matter was again dropped.

During 1840 the Judge paid a visit to Sydney, and he returned with the idea of amending the jurisdiction of the Resident Magistrates Court to bring it into line with the Courts of Request in New South Wales. He prepared a draft of an amending bill and forwarded it to the Governor in November 1841. He proposed to reduce the civil jurisdiction to £10, which he said was quite enough for the summary and uncontrolled decision of a magistrate where a superior tribunal existed which could be invoked.

> 'The cheap and speedy recovery of small debts above that amount'—he wrote—'must, I think, be provided for by stringent rules directed to that object, and I propose to make such as I trust will give general satisfaction.'

He also introduced, from the New South Wales Courts of Requests Acts, provisions empowering the examination of the parties on oath, and providing that attorneys or agents should not be allowed to conduct cases except under cases of unavoidable necessity. The criminal jurisdiction was proposed to be amended by a proviso that nothing in the Act should be construed to give any magistrate jurisdiction to determine in a summary way any perjury, embezzlement, obtaining goods by false pretences, unlawfully receiving goods so obtained, abduction of women or children, attempt to commit rape, conspiracy, libel or slander.[23]

The amending Bill was very unpopular. There was general agreement that the attainment of cheap and expeditious justice was defeated by the delays and expense of the Resident Magistrates Court and that some form of a court of requests ought to be introduced, but the proposal to reduce the jurisdiction to £10 raised a storm of opposition. It was urged that to force a creditor to sue in the Supreme Court for £15 was a rank injustice, for the delays there would be worse and the costs could not be less than £20. The general opinion was that the jurisdiction should be extended to £30, and the *Register* advocated an unlimited jurisdiction by consent. One suggestion was the substitution for the Resident Magistrate of a board of commissioners composed of respectable townsmen, with a permanent chairman, to sit as a court of requests, the legal profession being totally excluded, and imprisonment for debt abolished except where fraud or concealment of property was concerned. To cut down the criminal jurisdiction of the Resident Magistrates Court, it was said, could only lead to swelling the calendar at the Criminal Sessions with cases fit for the Police Court.[24] Memorials were addressed to the Governor objecting to the Bill, and in March 1842 a public meeting was held, at which a resolution in the nature of a compromise between various views was carried, recommending:

(a) In civil cases, that a roster of fifty assessors be drawn up, and that the Resident Magistrate should sit with two assessors once a week to hear and determine causes, without appeal. Cases under £10 to be determined according to the equity of the claim and without solicitors; in claims from £10 to £20, solicitors to be allowed to practise at a moderate rate of fees.

(b) In criminal cases, that the Resident Magistrate have jurisdiction in cases of assault; and power to impose a fine of £5 or a month's imprisonment in all cases short of felony; to be assisted by two assessors in more serious cases.[25]

Mr Justice Cooper seems to have been annoyed at the opposition to his Bill, and addressed the Grand Jury at length and rather testily at the Criminal Sessions in March 1842, in an attempt to persuade them to his view that £10 should be the limit of the Resident Magistrate's jurisdiction.[26] As a result of the agitation against it, the Bill lapsed.

In August 1842 the City Council decided that their dignity demanded that they should have a court and a sheriff.[27] The Court was to be styled the Corporation Court and was to have power to take cognisance of minor offences and punish by fine not exceeding

£5 or by imprisonment not exceeding six months. It was also to be available for the recovery of debts under £20. At that time the Council and the Governor were at loggerheads. The Council had just passed a resolution censuring the Governor's administration of the affairs of the colony, and could hardly have chosen a more inauspicious moment to come before him with a request that their powers be enlarged.[28] The Governor refused to give effect to their proposals, so the Mayor and aldermen decided to constitute themselves a court by their own resolution. They held one sitting and fined a man twenty shillings for selling a beast within the city limits without a licence.

> 'The fine was not enforced—in fact it was remitted. Whether the act of grace came from the Governor because the Corporation had gone beyond their powers, or from the Corporation because they could not carry them out, is unknown.' [29]

The first attempt of the corporation to usurp judicial functions thus failed ignominiously, and a few weeks later the Council ceased to exist. "Mayor, aldermen, councillors and all, vanished into thin air, and the chairs and tables were seized by the landlord of the premises, under a distraint for rent." [30]

The Court of Quarter Sessions, while it had lapsed as a criminal court of original jurisdiction, had been kept alive as an appellate body. Under numerous acts provision was made for appeals from summary convictions by justices to a Court of Quarter sessions. There was little consistency in the provisions regulating the right of appeal under different acts, and in November 1842 it was found advisable to establish a uniform practice. Section 5 of Ordinance No 6 of 1842 provided that in all cases where a right of appeal had been given the appellant should pay into the hands of the justices the amount of the penalty or costs, or, if there was no pecuniary penalty, should enter into a recognisance to duly prosecute his appeal to the next general sessions of the peace, whose judgment was final and conclusive. Costs of the appeal, not exceeding in the whole £10, could be allowed to either party.

An attempt was also made to revive Quarter Sessions as an available criminal court. Ordinance No 7 of 1842 repealed 7 Wm IV No.1 and instituted Courts of General Sessions of the Peace. Its objects were to limit the extensive powers which had been conferred on the Courts of Quarter Sessions and, as Governor Grey wrote: "... to create a machinery which was both inexpensive and adapted to the present circumstances of the colony".

Jurisdiction was given to the Courts of General Sessions over:

(1) All crimes and misdemeanours cognisable before quarter sessions in England (except such as were by law punishable with death or transportation for a term exceeding fifteen years).

(2) All such appeals and other matters as might be assigned to them by a local ordinance.

Every Judge of the Supreme Court was ex officio a justice of the Court, and the Governor was to appoint a chairman possessing competent knowledge of the law. In order to dispense with the attendance of the Grand Jury, all criminal proceedings before the Courts were to be by information in the name of the Advocate-General.

Governor Grey appointed Mr Justice Cooper to be chairman.

> 'Such appointment' he said—'will be in accordance with the present state of this Province, and with the amount of judicial business which the Judge has to transact. It will also enable me'—he added, with his usual thought for economy—'to avoid entailing on the Province any expense for defraying the salary of the Chairman of Quarter Sessions.' [31]

The Judge accepted the office at the Governor's request, although he said it was undesirable that the two offices should be permanently combined.[32] He drew up rules for the procedure of the Court—apparently none had been made under 7 Wm IV No 1. These provided for the form of information to be used by the Advocate-General; that no justice was to vote on the decision of an appeal unless he was present at the whole hearing of it; that justices could not take part in appeals from their own judgments or decisions; and fixed a scale of fees, not overlooking two shillings to the court crier for each appeal heard.[33]

The Governor had intended to bring before the Council, at the same time as the General Sessions Act, a Jury Act in which provision would be made as to the persons who should be qualified and liable to serve as jurors at the General Sessions, but, owing to the pressure of business, the Jury Act was put aside and a short act to provide for trial by jury at the General Sessions had to be hastily passed.[34]

During 1843 the Court of General Sessions sat three times, but there were only a few cases brought before it. The total number of convictions for the year was five.[35] A timetable was drawn up by the Judge which provided for:

(1) Three General Sessions of the Peace—in January, May and September.

(2) Three criminal sittings of the Supreme Court—in March, July and November.

(3) Four civil sittings of the Supreme Court—in February, May, August and September.[36]

The General Sessions, however, came to an abrupt end with the disallowance of the Ordinance on the ground that the dispensation with the Grand Jury was repugnant to the law of England.

> 'The short experience which was had of the working of this

Ordinance'—reported the Advocate-General—'gives no cause for regret that it should have been discontinued. With the exception of the absence of the Grand Jury the proceedings were more cumbrous than in the Supreme Court. The same attendance of Common Jurors was required, and His Honor the Judge, presiding over a less extensive jurisdiction than in his own Court, was assisted by an indefinite number of Justices of the Peace who had no voice, except after verdict when consulted as to the sentence.' [37]

Matters now reverted to their former state and the Act 7 Wm IV No 1 revived. Governor Grey consulted the Judge as to whether any further attempt to make Quarter Sessions an available criminal jurisdiction was advisable; but the Judge was disposed to let it drop. The number of cases for trial at the Sessions had been very small, and if a Grand Jury was necessary the inconvenience to the jurors would far outweigh any other advantage that might result from a continuance of the Sessions. Members of the Grand Jury were now scattered through the country.

There were only 136 on the list of grand jurors. Of these, 26 should be summoned for each of the three sittings of the Supreme Court, and the same number for each of the three General Sessions of the Peace. Allowing for the number who from various causes would be unable to attend at court, probably each of the others would be called on twice a year, which the Judge thought would be very burdensome to them. Similarly, there were 725 names on the list of common jurors, of whom 324 ought to be summoned for the criminal and civil sittings and the General Sessions. This left 401 from whom it might be thought that grand jurors could be taken for the General Sessions. But the Sheriff had the greatest difficulty in finding more than the 324, owing principally to the great movement of people from town to country and the difficulty of keeping trace of them. To be certain of procuring 24 jurors the Sheriff had to issue summonses to 40.[38]

As a result, the criminal jurisdiction of the Sessions was abandoned. The Criminal Court sat four times a year instead of three. Courts of Quarter Sessions were again proclaimed under the old act and sat to hear appeals, when there were any, meeting on the day when the quarterly meeting of the Bench of Magistrates was held, so that there was usually a good attendance of justices.

The Resident Magistrates Court had been badly hit by the severe economies which Governor Grey ruthlessly enforced. The Court had two clerks, one on the civil and one on the criminal side. Grey decided one must be dismissed. Wigley wrote to point out the inconvenience which would follow, as no-one could attend to the public in the office while the Court was sitting. If it was essential to economise, he suggested both clerks should be retained at reduced salaries. All his letter produced was the grimly humorous reply:

> 'Mr Wigley must carry on the duties of his Court as well as he can with one clerk. The state of the public finance does not admit the employment of a greater number of persons in that Court. I cannot sanction the employment of two clerks at a reduced rate. I do not conceive that the Clerk will be too highly paid for the duties he has to perform at his present rate of remuneration. Should such, however, prove to be the case, his salary must be reduced to such a sum as he ought to receive.' [39]

One clerk was accordingly dismissed. Similarly, when Wigley wrote that there were no books of reference in the court and that he had an opportunity of buying a copy of Chitty's *Burns Justice* for the use of himself and the justices, the Governor curtly replied that there were no funds in the Treasury to pay for it.[40] Economy, however, could be carried too far. To save the rent of the courthouse, Wigley was ordered to remove his court to two rooms in the offices of the Commissioner of Police, which were then situated on the parklands, near the site of the present railway station. He obeyed his instructions and wrote in a tone of subdued triumph to say that half of the furniture could not be got in and was standing in the open yard. The room to be used as a court was only ten feet by seven, and by the time a table and chairs, magistrate, clerk and solicitors were in, there was no room for anyone else—parties, police, witnesses or spectators.[41] Grey had to give way and promise that better accommodation would be found.

The effects of the financial depression were felt not only in the Governor's severe economies but in a general falling off in the business of the court, which is clearly shown in the following table covering the years 1840 to 1843.[42]

	1840	1841	1842	1843
Information under Acts of Council	84	171	88	132
Cases sent to the Supreme Court	71	66	60	45
Trials on the criminal side	67	10	4	-
Cases sent to the Commissioner of Police	6	-	1	-
Drunkenness	288	240	255	108
Various	117	64	176	66
Causes on the civil side	1,082	1,413	763	499

In May 1843 the Governor called for a report from the Advocate-General upon the Resident Magistrates Court. The Advocate-General having rather pompously pointed out that the objects of the Court had been to release:

> '... from the more cumbrous trappings of legal from, the machinery of courts designed for determining small debts, the disputes principally of the poor, where precedent is of less importance, where judicial discretion is least likely to be

> dangerous, and where the imposition of heavy costs amounts to a denial of justice'—

Grey noted:

> 'Might not all these ends be obtained by putting beyond the pale of the law debts under £10 or £20? Are not these courts for the recovery of small debts positive nuisances—and would it not be better to prevent the contraction of small debts, than to multiply means for enforcing the payment of them?' [43]

Improvements which the Advocate-General suggested were.

(1) New rules prescribing simpler forms and procedure.
(2) Wide discretionary powers of amendment to meet technical objections.
(3) The exclusion of legal practitioners, whom he classed as "an encumbrance of the practice of small debts courts". In the long run he considered this would benefit the profession by putting an end to much pettifogging.

He did not agree with the suggestion which had been made, that a jury of four should decide on the facts. It was objectionable, he thought, on many grounds.

> 'In economy, it can come little in advance of ordinary jury trials, while it is subject to the same complexity as regards the distinct provinces of the judge and jury, gives rise to the same incidents of error for which the law provides new trials or other modes of review, and after all is only a jury trial in name, having neither the solemnity nor the solid advantages of that august form of judicature.'

Nor did he favour the allowance of an appeal to Quarter Sessions or the Supreme Court. While it would have some advantages, it would deprive the public of a cheap, speedy and final decision.

> 'An appeal is virtually a second suit, involving expense and delay, towards which the prior decision generally goes for nothing. I think therefore substantial justice is best attained by such causes being heard fully and determined finally, but at once if possible.'

The best mode of trial, he considered, would be to associate several minds in the hearing and decision, "to such a number as may best ensure correctness without dividing responsibility"; this might be attained by having two justices sit with the Resident Magistrate as assessors, to decide according to equity and good conscience, the award of the majority being final and conclusive.[44]

Upon this report being referred to Mr Justice Cooper, he wrote to the Governor in reply: "I have long been of opinion that the constitution of the Resident Magistrate's Court is defective"— [45] and he undertook to draw up new rules to improve its procedure. These were promulgated in September 1843, superseding those made by Jickling in 1837. Under the new rules, the parties might be examined on oath, no plaintiff or defendant was to be defeated for defect of form or variance in evidence in support of his claim, and wide powers of amendment were given. No person was to appear or act for the parties in any suit under £10, except in cases of necessity or for sufficient cause, and then no costs were to be allowed for professional assistance—a provision well calculated to keep professional interference to a minimum. In cases above £10 attorneys might be employed, on the following scale of fees:

£10 to £15........................... £0 13s 4d
Above £15................................ £1 0s 0d [46]

These rules were not welcomed. It was a great hardship to people living some distance from Adelaide to have to come to court in person to recover a debt of a few shillings; and the fact that the rules permitted a party merely to enter an appearance without indicating his ground of defence, for which the plaintiff might be unprepared at the trial, was objected to. This last point was amended in May 1845, by requiring the defendant to disclose the grounds of his defence, but the other remained a grievance for years.[47] All processes had to be served by an officer of the Court, no matter where the defendant lived, and mileage fees to places in the country frequently were prohibitive. Nor was the attempt to oust the attorneys very successful. Litigants continued to learn by bitter experience the truth of the maxim:

> 'The law decides questions of meum and tuum,
> By kindly arranging to make the things suum'.

One suitor in 1846 complained that:

> '... this court, instead of helping a creditor to recover a small debt by a cheap and easy process, realises the old tale of the lawyer and the oyster—the plaintiff and the defendant are left to luxuriate upon the empty shell, while the whole matter in dispute goes to the lawyer'.[48]

In 1845 the *Register* said that since the introduction of the new rules there had been nothing but complaints of their inconvenience, and in the following year it declared that the Resident Magistrates Court stood in need of radical reform. "Its constitution is anomalous, its working dilatory and expensive, and its results uncertain and usually unsatisfactory." [49]

Governor Grey decided in May 1843 that, in view of the great reductions he had made in the Police Department, the time of the Commissioner of Police would not be fully occupied with police administration, and he therefore directed him that he was to sit as a Police Magistrate to hear and determine cases of minor offences.

Major O'Halloran, the Commissioner, refused to do this, and resigned.[50] B.T. Finniss was appointed in his place, the first of a series of magistrates appointed not for their knowledge of law but because they had served their country well as soldiers. At first the Police Magistrate's duties were confined to cases arising under the Police Acts, but he gradually undertook, sitting with other Justices of the Peace, more and more of the work on the criminal side of the Resident Magistrates Court, Wigley being given instead the position of Commissioner in Insolvency.[51]

Finniss laboured under the same difficulties as Wigley with regard to want of books of reference. He asked to be supplied with Chitty's *Burns Justice*, Archbold's *Peel's Act*, and Archbold's *Pleadings*. These he said were essential. "Not even legally qualified gentlemen ever attempt to practice without having books of this description to refer to."

Once again the Governor's reply was there were no funds; but with a sneer at Smillie, whom he did not like, he added that he considered Finniss's claim to be far stronger than a similar one recently made by the Advocate-General, "as that officer is supposed to be a gentleman in extensive legal practice".[52]

The powers of the Police Magistrate were to some extent regulated by Ordinance No 19 of 1844, which dealt with the police force. It empowered the Governor to appoint a Commissioner of Police for the Province, and for the City of Adelaide, and such other towns and districts as might be declared by proclamation. By section LXX all offences which were punishable on summary conviction before Justices of the Peace could be heard and determined by the Police Magistrate in a summary way. An appeal to Quarter Sessions from his decisions was given.

Finniss had not been acting as Police Magistrate very long before a quarrel took place between himself and Wigley over the distribution of the work. In many cases it was necessary that Finniss should obtain another Justice of the Peace to sit with him. Frequently he was unable to go on with cases because he could not find another magistrate, and the cases would either have to go before Wigley (who as Resident Magistrate exercised the jurisdiction of two justices) or be adjourned. Wigley refused to help him and their relations became so strained that in 1845 the Advocate-General was called upon by the Governor to report about the matter. His sympathies were with Finniss, who, he said, had met with opposition from Wigley from the time the police duties had been transferred.

> 'A cordial co-operation between these two magistrates might be very advantageous in the administration of justice. The obstructions which Mr Finniss has had to contend with from a class of practitioners, could be effectually put down by Mr Wigley, who, not only by his kindred education, but by the influence which his civil jurisdiction gives him, knows well the

language with which to silence the fraternity.'

The state of the Resident Magistrates Court was such that the Advocate-General concluded by saying: "While other tribunals are open, I shall never willingly resort to the Resident Magistrate's Court, as at present administered." He urged that its objectionable criminal jurisdiction should be abolished or revised, and the Court remodelled in a form similar to the Courts of Requests established in New South Wales in 1842, which would give a satisfactory jurisdiction for the recovery of small debts.[53]

Charles Bonney (1813-1897)
Part time work as a magistrate was but one of many roles Bonney fulfilled – from overlander to politician. This portrait is from a painting in the Norwood Town Hall, Bonney having served as Mayor of Norwood for three consecutive terms. (SLSA/City of Norwood, St Peters & Payneham)

Finniss continued to have difficulty in getting another magistrate to sit with him. Mr Bonney, the Commissioner of Lands, was frequently requisitioned to sit in the Police Court, with the result, said the *Register*, that: "... complaints both loud and deep proceed from people attending at the Crown Lands Office, at the delays consequent on the Commissioner's absence in the Police Court".[54]

At length Finniss applied to the Governor, asking that either the powers of two justices be conferred upon him, or another Police Magistrate be appointed to sit with him.[55] The Governor directed Wigley that he must hear all cases which required the presence of two justices,[56] but no sooner had Wigley reluctantly embarked upon these, than doubts were expressed by Mr Justice Cooper as to the legality of the Resident Magistrate exercising the jurisdiction of two justices, except where that jurisdiction was expressly given to him. The Advocate-General accordingly advised Wigley to abstain from exercising those powers, and the old trouble arose again.[57]

In reply to an annoyed inquiry from the Governor, Smillie said that his own opinion was that the jurisdiction so exercised by the Resident Magistrate was quite proper; the Resident Magistrates Act was not worded in the clearest manner, but it could not be doubted that:

> '... the legislature intended the powers of two Justices of the Peace to be conferred on the Resident Magistrate as well with regard to future ordinances, as to the very few then in operation'.

But he had advised Wigley to desist solely in deference to the view expressed by the Judge.[58]

On this report, the Governor ordered Wigley to resume hearing cases where two justices were required; but the Judge having again expressed a strong view that it was illegal, an act was introduced and passed to settle the matter by amending the Resident Magistrates Court Act of 1837.[59]

Finniss was succeeded as Commissioner of Police by Captain Dashwood, and the difficulties which they both experienced in legal matters were accentuated when, in 1849, Alexander Tolmer was appointed acting Commissioner of Police and Police Magistrate. While he was an excellent and dashing officer, of undoubted courage and resource, Tolmer was ignorant of law and temperamentally unfitted for a judicial position. Even his best friends would admit, the *Register* said, that:

> '... many of the qualities which render him valuable as an officer of police are incompatible with the habits of grave deliberation requisite for the dignified discharge of magisterial duties'. [60]

His first official acts were to direct the mounted police to cultivate the moustache; and to issue a general order to the foot police that any of the mounted police found drunk or misbehaving themselves were to be taken into custody and brought before the Police Magistrate.[61] Dignity and decorum were conspicuous by their absence from his Court. Spectators stood where they liked and crowded around the counsel table in the centre of the Court:

> ' ...obstructing the officers in attendance, and breaking the backs of counsel and others doomed to sit at the table. Of old they were limited to the space outside the rails on either side of the Court; but covering, as they sometimes do, in a thick mass, the whole body of the office, it now frequently resembles rather a bit taproom or a bear garden than a Court of Justice.' [62]

Tolmer's own story of his troubles makes pathetic reading.

Matthew Smith (c1794-1858) Smith arrived in the colony in November 1836 and served as a Resident Magistrate and as the Commissioner of Insolvency. (SCLSA)

> 'By diligent application and hard study of the various statute laws and acts of Council I mastered the situation ... No one knows but myself how my faculties were strained and how I spent hours burning the midnight oil poring over and studying Roscoe's "Law of Evidence" and other legal authorities.'

Indignant at legal technicalities, he struggled with his "herculean task", which was:

> '... rendered more embarrasing [sic] in consequence of the array of eminent legal functionaries, such as His Honour Judge Gwynne, the late Sir R. Hanson, Sir J. Fisher, Messrs Parker, Ingleby, Smith and others, who in defending their clients, endeavoured by every ingenuity to puzzle and make me believe that black was white'.

On one occasion he threatened to commit Hanson for contempt of court, and he firmly believed that Hanson thereafter became his deadly enemy and thwarted his promotion. As Police Commissioner, he would direct a prosecution; and he was unable as Police Magistrate to conceal his anger when from some flaw in the evidence or information a prisoner, whom he knew to be clearly guilty from his previous perusal of the statements of the police, had to be acquitted.[63]

It is necessary now to turn to the development of the inferior courts other than those at Adelaide.

On 11 July 1838 a Resident Magistrate's Court at Kangaroo Island was proclaimed and William Giles, the South Australian Company's manager, was appointed Resident Magistrate.[64] In October 1839 the District of Kangaroo Island was amalgamated with that of Adelaide, and a Resident Magistrate's Court established for the District of Port Lincoln, with Mr Matthew Smith as Resident Magistrate. Mr Smith remained there for eighteen months and then resigned, as he found Port Lincoln did not make the progress he had expected. Dr James Macdonald succeeded him, but resigned a year later, and the position of Resident Magistrate was not filled again, although a Government Resident was stationed there.[65]

William Giles (1791-1862) Giles was placed in charge of the South Australian Company's business on Kangaroo Island in 1837; a thank-ess task for the Island community was in decline. He moved to Adelaide in 1841 to take McLaren's place as the colonial manager of the company. He remained manager until his retire-ment in 1861 proving to be a hard working and enterprising employee who did much to further the progress of the colony, not least by fathering twenty-one children.

In May 1838 the Bench of Magistrates had arranged for a Justice of the Peace to attend regularly at Port Adelaide for the purpose of hearing complaints made either by masters of vessels or seamen about matters arising on board vessels in the harbour.[66] For many years the Port had no court other than those held by justices on occasional visits there to deal with minor offences. Most of this judicial business eventually fell to Torrens, the Collector of Customs, and Captain Lipson, the Harbour Master, who were, of course, constantly at the Port; but it was not at first excessive. In 1845, for instance, in three months they sat only three times and heard half a dozen cases of assault and fighting.[67] As shipping increased, however, so did the number of cases to be tried. Most of the cases occurred when there was a great deal of shipping in the Port, which was precisely the time when the Harbour Master and Collector of Customs were busiest at their own duties.[68] Dr Handasyde Duncan, the Health Officer, was made a Justice of the Peace to assist them; but they could do little. The Court had no clerk, and all cases except those of drunkenness and offences against the Merchant Seamen's Act or Port Regulations were sent to Adelaide.[69]

Dr Handasyde Duncan (1811-1878) (above) Duncan came to South Australia for health reasons in 1839. He tried farming but was unsuccessful and so returned to his profession. In 1849 he was appointed health officer and colonial surgeon at Port Adelaide and, later that year, Immigration Agent. In this role he worked vigorously to ensure that the health and "quality" of immigrants was improved. (SLSA)

In December 1848 the Police Magistrate (Captain Dashwood) was told he would have to hold a court at Adelaide and at Port Adelaide on alternate days. He protested very loudly: "Independent of the injurious effects to my health consequent upon a journey on horseback of 26 miles"—(he lived in the foothills—Dashwood's Gully is named after him)—

> 'every other day, under the influence of a scorching sun, and smothering dust, so frequent at this season of the year, which indeed has on one or two occasions almost prevented me from taking my seat on the Bench, I find myself in the disagreeable position of filling an office, the duties of which I am unable efficiently to discharge for want of time.' [70]

The Governor had to agree that sitting one day at Adelaide and the next at the Port left Dashwood little time for his work as Commissioner of Police, and he promised to bring the matter before the Council with a view of relieving him of "the incessant exercise of magisterial duties" by making provision for a paid Resident Magistrate at Port Adelaide.[71] In August 1849 Dashwood himself was appointed a Stipendiary Magistrate at the Port, at a salary of £350 a year.[72] He held the position for a little more than a year, becoming with his colleague Dr Duncan the target for very acrid newspaper comments, arising from some doubtful decisions with they gave.

> 'These Port Solons'—said the Register—'are neither gifted with the wisdom of Solomon, nor the dignity of a Lycurgus. Their arbitrary decisions savour more of an iron Jeffries than of a mild and judicious Hale. Is it possible, after this, that the Queen's representative can approve the judgment of this brace of learned nincompoops?'

Dashwood was said to have brought to the bench a strong military flavour; he was "notoriously arbitrary, overbearing and insulting". At Adelaide, the *Register* claimed, he had been kept in check by fear of its reports, but: "... at the Port he indulged the natural tendencies of his arbitrary decision and his acquired perspicuity and promptitude lapsed into crude hasty and despotic decisions".[73]

Eatanswill
Eatanswill was a fictional village in *The Pickwick Papers.* The villagers were divided between two political parties with the parties each supported by newspapers inclined to use invective.

The newspapers took sides, and a stream of Eatanswillian journalism flowed from the pens of the respective editors. The lofty comments of the *Register* on the rival paper conducted by Stevenson may serve as an illustration:

> 'When you expose a perverse construction of law, and denounce an oppressive magisterial decision'—wrote the virtuously indignant editor of the former paper—'you may well, from former experience, calculate upon encountering, in addition to the ire of the accused parties, the plausible apologies, the Jesuitical casuistries, the malignant insinuations of the Joseph Surface of the Adelaide Press. But the turpitude of his special pleading (artful as it undoubtedly is) becomes apparent when touched by the Ithuriel spear of truth.'[74]

In October 1850 Dashwood thankfully returned to his old position of Commissioner of Police and was succeeded as Magistrate at the Port by Mr R.F. Newland.[75]

In the country districts, throughout the 1840s, the position of the minor courts was very unsatisfactory. After Port Lincoln had ceased to have a Resident Magistrate's Court, the only Resident Magistrate outside Adelaide, until 1847, was Edward John Eyre at Moorunde, on the Murray. His work there was almost entirely among the Aborigines, and his judicial functions were very limited. The demand and necessity for courts followed the trend of population. Gawler was settled very early, and from 1843 onwards local Justices held courts at regular intervals.[76] North of that town there was for a long time only a single magistrate—Mr G.C. Hawker of Bungaree. In 1844 Mr Hawker complained to the Government of the want of magistrates in the north—a want which was being felt more and more as the population increased. The two Acts which were most frequently required to be invoked by people in the country were the Master and Servant Act and the Scab in Sheep Act. "These are both, comparatively speaking, null and void up here"—wrote Mr Hawker—"owing to the time and expense necessary before a case can be brought forward for adjudication." Offences under both of these acts had to be tried before a Resident Magistrate or two Justices, but, to find a court so constituted, settlers had to go from 60 to 100 miles or more.[77]

Edward John Eyre
(1815-1901)
Famous for his exploration of Australia and lauded for his work with Aboriginals at Moorunde Eyre's career was more chequered once he left South Australia. Appointed Lieutenant Governor of New Zealand in 1846 he clashed with Governor Grey and while Governor of Jamaica in the 1860s his handling of a rebellion led to his recall and a lengthy investigation of his actions. Simon Calvert's 1891 *Eyre's Journey to Albany* depicts his epic trek across the Nullarbor with the Aboriginal "Wylie". (SLV)

With a similar complaint that there was only one Justice of the Peace in the district, a petition was presented in 1845 by the inhabitants of the Encounter Bay area, asking for the establishment of a court.

> 'Innocent and Respectable Settlers'—it said, with all the dignified emphasis of capitals—'have been seized by the Police, and dragged as Felons before an Adelaide Tribunal on groundless charges, subjected to Ignominy, Serious Expense, and Loss of Time.' [78]

The discovery of the Burra mines and the sudden rush of population to Kooringa compelled the establishment there first of a police station (September 1846) and then of a Police Magistrate (November 1847).[79] The mines inevitably became a refuge for a considerable number of bad characters and runaway sailors, and it became quite impossible for prisoners and witnesses to be brought all the way to Adelaide for trial. A Resident Magistrate's district—the District of the Murray, but why so called is not clear—was created with its headquarters at Kooringa, and Mr William Lang was appointed Resident Magistrate at a salary of £300 a year.[80] He had come out from England with a direction from the Secretary of State that he should be given some official position, and had been appointed to succeed Eyre at Moorunde. He was then transferred to the Burra, and Moorunde was abandoned.[81] Mr Lang's tenure of office at the Burra was short and unsatisfactory. The conditions under which he administered the law were deplorable, the courthouse consisting of a hut ten feet by six.

> 'In a rapidly rising town like Kooringa'—said the Register in July 1849—'such a mockery of sacred justice—by holding courts in private houses, or in wattle-and-daub huts—is abominable; and unless something be speedily done for the comfort and convenience of the suitors and the public, we can assure the Viceroy that he shall be ever and anon awakened from his apathetic slumbers.' [82]

Cornish miners at Burra ca. 1870 (SLSA)

In the opinion of many of the inhabitants of the district, Mr Lang's administration of the law was equally unsatisfactory. There were continual complaints of his inefficiency and bias, and eventually, in 1851, he was transferred to Willunga. There he fared no better, and in 1852 he was removed from office for incapacity, being succeeded by Mr G. Worthington, an English solicitor and the author of *Worthington on Wills*, a textbook of some repute in its day.[83]

At the end of 1848 a new Resident Magistrate's district was created—the South-Eastern District—and Captain G.V. Butler was appointed Resident Magistrate, with his Court at Robe.[84] This alleviated conditions in that district, but petitions flowed in to the Government from various towns seeking the establishment of courts—Gawler, Mount Gambier, Mount Barker, Clare.[85]

At the time of his transfer to New Zealand, in 1845, Governor Grey had been considering making the Resident Magistrate go on circuit, and towards the end of 1848 Governor Young revived this proposal. Mr Wigley, the Resident Magistrate, did not receive it very kindly and suggested a number of objections—he was too occupied by his other duties as Commissioner of Insolvency and Visiting Justice of the Gaol; he was doubtful whether he could hold a court elsewhere than in the courtroom for the district; it would interfere with the work of the Court at Adelaide; where were proceedings to be issued from—Adelaide or Mount Barker or wherever the Court was to go?[86]

The Governor saw no merit in the objections as to overwork. The importance of the matter, he said, was too great to be "obstructed by the attention necessary to the Insolvency Court and the visiting of the Gaol"; and, in any event, the business in the Adelaide Court would probably be diminished by that heard elsewhere.[87] On the question of law, whether more than one Resident Magistrate's Court could be established in any one district, he sought the opinion of the Judge, who said that Wigley could adjourn his Court from Adelaide to Mount Barker, Gawler, or wherever required.[88]

Mr Wigley now fell back on his second line of defence, and raised the question of expense. He asked for a travelling allowance of £2 2s 0d a day for himself and 25 shillings for his clerk. Since he had "not much time for walking", he sarcastically added, he would expect also a yearly allowance for a horse. He admitted that his calculations of the expenses of going on circuit might not be accurate. "I have only been in one Tavern in the country since I have been in the colony and am therefore wholly unable from my own experience to estimate the exact expense."[89]

The Governor retorted that he saw no reason why Mr Wigley's expenses should be so much more than those of his clerk, and that they would not be allowed more than 21 shillings a day each while away from Adelaide.[90]

Mr Wigley replied that he had his dignity to consider; his clerk could travel in the public conveyance with the parties and witnesses, and could eat and board with them at the hotel, but the Resident

Magistrate must hold himself apart. The Governor was not impressed, but in order to do away with one of Wigley's objections he wrote to the Judge suggesting that Wigley should be relieved of the duties of Commissioner of Insolvency, and the Master (Mann) appointed to sit in insolvency. The Judge replied that Mann could not be spared from the Supreme Court "while his duties are so multifarious as at present", and that in his opinion it was more important that Wigley should carry out his duties in insolvency, than go touring the country.[91]

The Governor therefore decided to postpone taking any action until he could bring the matter before the Legislative Council. This he did in July 1849, explaining that he proposed to relieve the Commissioner of Police of "that incessant attention to judicial functions" which had "completely frustrated" the main object of his office—the superintendence of the police.

> 'I propose, also, that all paid magistrates exercising a summary jurisdiction shall, at times and places to be notified, hold Circuit Courts in the country; and, in order to this arrangement, much of the civil Judicial Business which has so occupied the time of the Special Magistrate in the City of Adelaide as to necessitate the employment there of the Police Commissioner also, shall be disposed of by a Judge of the Supreme Court, presiding in an inferior Court of Civil Justice, in a manner quite as summary and inexpensive as that hitherto in use under the Special Magistrate.'

With this object in view he had requested the Secretary of State to agree to the appointment of a second judge of the Supreme Court.[92]

The Resident Magistrates Court certainly called for reform.

> 'This farce of a Court of Law does not keep pace with the Colony'—it was said in 1849. 'It is now retrograding; ten years ago, it was a boon to the colony, and worked well; now it is a positive mockery.'[93]

According to a timetable prepared in 1847, the Court was open on weekdays from ten to three, as follows:[94]

Monday and Tuesday	Entering plaints and other business
Wednesday	Trial of Cases
Thursday	Return day of summonses
Friday	Paying money out of Court
Saturday	Entering plaints and other business

In 1849 this was amended by a rule that no summonses would be issued "except on Monday and Saturday between the hours of eleven and two"; and by 1850 the issue of summonses had been restricted to Saturdays only.[95]

The Governor was encouraged by the obviously unsatisfactory condition of the minor courts to embark upon a plan of general reform, with the object of introducing so far as possible local self-government throughout the colony.[96] In a valuable dispatch he set out clearly the objects at which he aimed:

> 'Reforms to be accurately judged of'—he wrote—'require that the point at which they commenced should be observed, for although in the progress of the future, improvements will be surpassed in number and importance, the earliest beneficial changes are at least entitled to be distinguished as precedents. In glancing therefore at the administrative changes which have taken place in the local government since 1848 it is necessary to bear in mind some general idea of the less popular system which previously prevailed. This may be most concisely but exactly expressed by saying that nothing could be done, or even projected, whether insignificant and local, or great and important to the Public at large, without the personal intervention of the Governor. Had he been ubiquitous, omniscient, and unerring, there would no doubt still have been no stint in the use of the privilege to censure and grumble which is more or less characteristic of all free men. As, however, at least the ordinary deficiencies in these superhuman qualities were inherent in his nature, it was of personal, not less than of public importance, that the office of Governor should be relieved of detail duties throughout the entire Colony, the efficient performance of which it were vain to expect from any one individual; even if other appropriate functions of a different and more comprehensive kind had not sufficiently monopolised the time and attention of the Head of the General Government. Since 1848 therefore the aim has been gradually, as opportunities offered, to adopt the constitutional principle that the control executive should not attempt to engross to itself all the powers of the state, great and small, but that they should be distributed among local authorities, and that even in matters appertaining properly and exclusively to the general government, the votes of the popular representatives in the legislature should be allowed a paramount influence. Very much is yet required to be done to carry out this principle to its due extent in the Rural Districts; nor in those instances in which it has been adopted, could it be suddenly or easily

> introduced and applied. The difficulties and occasional failures of the early trials of this principle; the disinclination to levy local assessments even for local objects; the suspicions which were expressed that the Executive resorted to local authorities as an escape from responsibility and as a relief of its own proper labours, are petty details not worth being saved from oblivion. But the policy of creating local Courts for the recovery of small debts and trial and punishment of minor offences; the usefulness of admitting the taxpayers in District Councils to exercise a control over their own local affairs, of making the burthen of expenditure to be locally felt, and its application to be locally regulated, and thereby imparting to the Districts benefitted by the expenditure a lively interest in keeping it within economical bounds, is an ancient and an inherited policy, which not only remaining unimpaired by time, but receiving from it fresh applications and developments may be perhaps remembered in the future annals of South Australia as having assumed a permanent character under the administration which commenced in 1848. It is to be hoped that here, as elsewhere, this principle will eventually prove the means of calling into healthful activity all those popular and local instincts and attachments—that invigorating yet amicable rivalry—that diffusion of power which prevents central dominion from becoming despotic, and that habit of local self government which there is experience to prove is the perfection of Civil Society.' [97]

We are concerned here only with that portion of the Governor's far-sighted policy which pertained to the minor courts. Conscious of "their total inadequacy to the growing wants of the country", he directed a series of statutes to be prepared by the Advocate-General, which completely remodelled the inferior courts and introduced the system still in force. Quarter and Petty Sessions were done away with entirely and replaced by courts presided over mainly by Stipendiary Magistrates, who were necessary because Justices of the Peace were generally slow to take on themselves the responsibilities of the bench, and it was hard to induce sufficient of them to act as magistrates.[98] Mr Justice Cooper was not enthusiastic over the proposed alteration, which he thought would be productive of mingled good and evil:

> 'On the one hand the law will in all probability be administered with greater impartiality, and on the whole with greater accuracy; but on the other hand the superseding voluntary by stipendiary magistrates will have the effect of preventing persons from qualifying themselves to act as Justices of the Peace by endeavouring to gain some knowledge of law and

> thus in the course of a few years it will be found that the class of person from amongst whom Justices of the Peace are now commonly taken will be less informed upon matters respecting the rights and liabilities of persons than they would probably be if they were likely to be called upon to act in a judicial capacity. In fine, a general system of stipendiary magistrates will have a tendency to prevent the gradual growth of such a class of gentry as now forms the boast and ornament of England.' [99]

The program of reform sponsored by the Governor consisted of the following statutes:

(1) Ordinance No 3 of 1849, "to provide a better mode than that now in use of deciding any difficult question of law that may arise in criminal trials", by enabling them to be reserved for the consideration of the Judges of the Supreme Court.

(2) Ordinance No 9 of 1849, to protect Justices of the Peace from vexatious actions for acts done by them in the execution of their duties.

(3) Ordinance No 15 of 1849, "to facilitate the performance of the duties of Justices of the Peace out of Sessions, with respect to persons charged with indictable offences"—an adaptation of 11 & 12 Vic c.42.

(4) Ordinance No 5 of 1850, establishing Local Courts.

(5) Ordinance No 6 of 1850 (based on Jervis's Act 11 and 12 Vic c.43) regulating the summary jurisdiction of Justices of the Peace.

(6) Ordinance No 7 of 1850, regulating the office of Coroner.

In introducing Ordinance No 5 of 1850 in the Legislative Council the Advocate-General pointed out that the Resident Magistrates Court at Adelaide, despite its defects, had been of some use.

> 'But beyond the district of Adelaide the benefits, such as they were, of a Resident Magistrate's Court had not been extended because it was difficult to find persons who could safely be entrusted with the large powers conferred by the Act ... Under the present system the Justices of the Peace throughout the colony could not assist the colonists in the recovery of their just demands to the extent of even one shilling. The Resident Magistrate was the only person who could do so, but that Court was a perfect anomaly and far from giving general satisfaction.' [100]

So far as the Resident Magistrate was concerned:

> '... his power was summary in cases of assault and breaches of agreement under particular acts: but, in cases of the most trifling felony, he had no jurisdiction whatever; he could not even punish a boy for stealing a cabbage from a greengrocer's

shop'.[101]

With regard to Quarter Sessions, the bench of justices sat only to hear appeals:

> '... but this was solely from the self-regulation of the Bench, for if criminal charges had been brought before then, there was nothing to prevent their assuming the extreme jurisdiction I have referred to and, without the intervention of a jury, convicting a prisoner and sentencing him to transportation'.[102]

It was undesirable, the Advocate-General considered, that the criminal jurisdiction of Quarter Sessions should be revived.

> 'Although the Chairman was really the responsible party on points of law, still being surrounded and interfered with by the other members of the Bench, the decision could not be expected to be based upon that wise and just spirit of legislation that characterised the higher courts where the Judge was uncontrolled by any power but that of the jury and unshackled in the deliberate dispensing of the law in its true meaning by the interference of equals in power on the bench who knew little or nothing of that law.'[103]

In short, the colonists had:

> '... a Court of General and Quarter Sessions doing nothing beyond the hearing of appeals; they had the power of proclaiming a Court of Petty Sessions which had never been called into existence; and they had a Resident Magistrate's Court unsatisfactory to the people, with irresponsible power in some matters and helpless in others'.[104]

Under the new system these courts were abolished. In their place the Governor was empowered to establish by proclamation Local Courts for the recovery of small debts and for the trial and punishment of minor offences, to be held at times and places specified in the proclamation.

> 'The Local Courts'—wrote the Governor—'bear as close, albeit humble, affinity to the English County Courts as the present circumstances of the Colony render desirable or feasible. They are probably destined by the example of their cheap, summary, and simple mode of procedure, eventually to being about the adoption in the higher legal tribunals of the Colony of a language as to process, pleading, and practice which shall have the convenience of being universally intelligible and be an acceptable substitute for the fictions and technicalities which are now only to be unriddled by lawyers,

and that slowly and expensively.'[105]

The jurisdiction of the Local Courts was as follows:

A. Civil

All pleas of personal actions where the debt or damage claimed was not more than £30, excluding actions:

(1) of ejectment;
(2) involving title to any corporeal or incorporeal hereditaments or easement, toll, fair, market or franchise;
(3) in which the validity of any devise, bequest, or limitation under any will or settlement may be disputed;
(4) for malicious prosecution;
(5) for libel or slander;
(6) for criminal conversation, seduction or breach of promise of marriage.

The claims were to be "heard and determined in a summary way, according to equity and good conscience, and the substantial merits of the case".

Substantially the procedure was the same as that now in force. Practitioners had no right to receive any fees in claims less than £5 or more than 10 shillings unless the claim was over £10 or more than at the rate of five per cent of the claim. This scale had been adopted after some discussion in the Legislative Council, where the Advocate-General had put forward a scheme for payment of attorneys by a flat rate of ten per cent on the amount recovered.

> 'I consider it would work most advantageously'—he said—'in restricting vexatious litigation and suppressing the malpractices of petty lawyers, who are constantly running about the Courts and offices pretending to be engaged on necessary business, when in fact they are only solicitous to find pretexts for swelling their bills of costs.'

A percentage, he thought, would be better than a tariff of minute fees which might be accumulated by the ingenuity of the profession. The Governor thought a percentage would be an inducement to a speedy termination of litigation, but Mr Bagot threw cold water on the scheme, holding that it would not pay in small cases and would amount to too much in large cases.[106]

B. Criminal

Local Courts were given power to hear and determine summarily any of the following offences:

(1) All simple larcenies of property to the value of £5 (not being larcenies of sheep, horses or cattle, and not being by law punishable with transportation).
(2) All other felonies having no greater punishment than for simple larceny.
(3) All misdemeanours and minor offences, except:

(a) abduction, assaults on women and children, conspiracy, embezzlement, forgery, perjury, libel and slander;

(b) all such offences as by statute should be declared to be not triable by Courts of General or Quarter Sessions of the Peace in England.

The punishments which could be imposed were, in the case of felony, imprisonment for not exceeding six months; and in the case of misdemeanours, a fine not exceeding £20 or imprisonment not exceeding six months. In a case of an aggravated character, the Court could commit the prisoner for trial before the Supreme Court or remand him until the Advocate-General should have elected whether he would have the case decided in the Local Court or in the Supreme Court.

The Courts were divided into courts of limited jurisdiction or full jurisdiction. The jurisdiction of the former could be exercised by a Justice of the Peace alone or by two or more Justices of the Peace, in civil cases where the claim was under £5, and in the case of petty offences, where the punishment was not more than a fine of £5 or imprisonment for fourteen days. In all other cases civil and criminal cognisable under the Ordinance, the trial had to be before a Special Magistrate and two Justices of the Peace, the decision of the majority prevailing if there was a disagreement.

The Ordinance No 6 of 1850 was the forerunner of the present Justices Act and established the procedure now familiar in the Police Court.

With the abolition of Quarter Sessions, it became necessary for some arrangement to be made respecting the mode of appeal from summary convictions by magistrates.[107] The Judge was very doubtful of the propriety of an appeal being given to the Supreme Court. It certainly ought not to be allowed, he thought, in cases less than £10.

> 'I feel a doubt'—he added—'whether this kind of jurisdiction will not tend to lower the Supreme Court unless the appeal is in all cases confined to questions of law ... I am strongly of opinion that an appeal from one person to another person on matters of fact is undesirable. Even if there were two or more Judges of the Supreme Court I am of opinion they would not be beneficially employed in deciding on matters of fact in appeal cases.' [108]

It was decided to give a right of appeal to a Local Court of full jurisdiction, the appeals to be heard and determined in a summary way.

The Resident Magistrates Court held its last sitting in Adelaide on 1 May 1850.[109]

No account of the Resident Magistrates Court could be complete without mention of the extraordinary gentleman who was its clerk from 1839 to 1850—John Bond Phipson. Arriving in the colony in 1838 at the age of seventeen, Phipson (who came from an old and wealthy English family) developed into one of the "characters" of the colony. Becoming hopelessly addicted to drink, he committed wild eccentricities which would have resulted in the social ostracism of a man of less brilliant abilities. In 1850 a dispute arose between him and the Governor, who, he claimed, had promised him the post of Government Resident at Guichen Bay, and had then taken it back again because of Phipson's unfortunate marriage with a servant girl. Phipson departed to England and pressed his grievance, without success, upon the Secretary of State. While there he came into a substantial legacy on the death of his father, went out to South Africa in 1851 to join his brother, who was a Sheriff of Natal, and lost all his money in a newspaper venture. Back in Australia in 1852, he took part in the rush to the Victorian goldfields, and then joined the staff of the Melbourne *Argus*, on which he was the chief law reporter and leader writer. After some years, his habits led him astray again and, after losing another small fortune which he received on his mother's death, he turned his hand to the most varied occupations. By turns he was orange-vendor, shepherd, gunpowder magazine keeper, knockabout hand on a station, sailor, contractor for cutting thistles and spreading gravel on footpaths at North Adelaide, and (most remarkable of all) temperance lecturer. Returning to South Australia in 1865, he was in and out of the inebriates' retreat, the lunatic asylum and the gaol. In a petition, in that year, for remission of a sentence of two months' imprisonment for using abusive language, he admitted "with shame and sorrow" repeated convictions for drunkenness; "but in extenuation would urge that I have suffered reverses of fortune unparalleled, I believe, in the history of any man in this colony". On one occasion his friends in Adelaide clubbed together and sent him to the Northern Territory. In a short time he turned up again, having been provided with a return passage by public subscription. Having recovered his health, he was received back into the public service as a clerk in the Local Court at Port Adelaide. He died on 4 May 1880, after a life crowded with the most varied colonial experiences it would be possible to imagine.[110]

Local Courts were proclaimed in June 1850 and from this time on, their working became largely a matter of routine, calling for little comment.

In November 1850 the Governor approached the Judges with the suggestion that the inferior court of civil jurisdiction in Adelaide should be held before one of them, under a special commission to be issued for that purpose. The Judges replied that, although they were not overworked, they had objections to undertaking this duty. By placing them on the level of a special magistrate, who might not have had any legal training, the dignity of the Supreme Court was lowered in the estimation of the public, and its usefulness as a court of appeal would be materially affected. The Governor allowed the matter to drop.[111]

In August 1851, however, Mr Wigley complained that he was unable to cope with the work of the Adelaide Local Court. On one day seventy six cases were listed for trial. He disposed of twenty, and the remainder had to stand over for some days, as he was engaged in insolvency work. When he resumed in the Local Court he found thirty six new cases added to the list. The Governor replied that he must adjourn some of the insolvency work, and at the same time he also wrote to Mr Justice Cooper asking him to accept a special commission as special magistrate to deal with some of the Local Court arrears. The Judge declined, on the ground that it would be beneath his dignity, but Mr Justice Crawford volunteered to sit in the Insolvency Court in order to relieve Mr Wigley.[112]

The Governor's next step was to bring before the Legislative Council a bill requiring the Judges to sit in Local Courts both in Adelaide and on circuit. The Bill was passed, but the Judges strongly protested against it and requested the Governor not to assent to it. It was more objectionable, they said, than the original proposition that the inferior court of civil jurisdiction at Adelaide should be held before one of them, with Wigley taking the criminal work. This Act would impose upon them an inferior duty and would have the effect of "degrading them as Judges of the Supreme Court in the estimation of the public". They were willing, however, to do any extra work in the Supreme Court which might be imposed on them by the alteration of the machinery of the Supreme Court with reference to civil actions for small sums.[113]

The Adelaide Town Hall, shown here ca. 1866, is where the Local Court heard civil cases from 1866 to 1869 and criminal cases from 1866 to 1867. (ACCA)

Upon further representations having been made by the Governor of the necessity for such an act, the Judges reluctantly replied that their opinions remained unchanged:

> '... nevertheless if His Excellency should be of opinion that such an emergency exists as requires the Judges to depart from what they conceive to be their legitimate sphere of duties they will sacrifice their own opinions so far as to withdraw their remonstrance against the passing of the ordinance in question, on the assurance of His Excellency that he will submit to the legislature early in the next session an Act repealing it'.

Otherwise they must persist in requesting the Governor not to assent to it.[114]

Somewhat taken aback by this opposition, the Governor gave way, and informed the Council that he deemed it expedient to withhold his assent to the Act, but he persisted in arguing the matter with the Judges. They agreed with him that:

> '... there is nothing degrading to the dignity of any one however exalted his station to be empowered and enabled to exercise judicial functions concurrently with gentlemen holding Her Majesty's Special Commission of the Peace, and certainly they would not wish their former observations to receive a construction inconsistent with this opinion'.

But they feared that the Judges of the Supreme Court, by sitting in an inferior court and having as part of their ordinary duties cognisance of small matters such as petty assaults and complaints under the Impounding Acts or Master and Servants Acts: "... would lose a portion of that respect which attaches to courts of Superior Jurisdiction, part of whose duty it is to correct and control inferior courts".

If the Governor insisted, they would accept the work he wished them to do, although it had a degrading tendency: "... inasmuch as it places them in a lower scale of magistracy and a somewhat anomalous position".

They suggested that a special commission as Special Magistrate should be issued to Mr Justice Cooper, and a commission appointing Mr Justice Crawford a Commissioner of the Court of Insolvency. They were very reluctant to do this:

> '... but I believe'—wrote Mr Justice Cooper—'there is an absolute necessity for a temporary arrangement, and I feel that this is a time of anxiety and distress in which I may be fairly expected to give up any scruples, not of an unsurmountable character, in the way of carrying it out, and I the more readily do so in consequence of the very gracious conduct of His Excellency in withholding his assent to Ordinance No 21 of

1851 in deference to the opinion of my colleague and myself'.

During 1852, therefore, Mr Justice Cooper sat in the Local Court and Mr Justice Crawford in the Insolvency Court, and the latter also acted for six weeks as Master, Jickling having temporarily been appointed Police Magistrate.[115]

In October 1852 it was decided to separate the incongruous offices of Police Magistrate and Commissioner of Police. There was too much work for the one man properly to carry out the duties of both positions, and it had always been very undesirable that the Commissioner of Police should sit in a court where the witnesses were chiefly men under his own command, who had acted under his instructions in getting up the case.

> 'It was hardly to be expected that while sitting as Judge he could divest himself entirely of those feelings, or throw aside that knowledge, which belonged more properly to the executive branch of his functions, or that he could wholly avoid a leaning, however unintentional, towards the men who formed the force over which he presided'. [116]

The separation of duties was accordingly effected by Act No 3 of 1852.

At the end of 1852, Mr Justice Cooper wished to resign his Commission as a Special Magistrate, but at the request of the Governor he did not press his resignation. In October 1853, however, he again renewed his application to be relieved of his duties as a magistrate.

> 'I am particularly desirous of being freed from this office'—he wrote—'because I find that it occasionally places me in a very unpleasant position. Whilst acting under my commission I have no greater authority than either of the two Magistrates who may be sitting with me, so that their joint opinion will over-rule mine on a point of law.' [117]

Sir Henry Young referred this letter to the Advocate-General for an opinion whether legislation might not be introduced to attend the jurisdiction of the Local Courts.

> 'My view has always been'—he said—'that the present jurisdiction of £30 is sufficiently large for the present courts; but that each Judge might singly exercise the full jurisdiction of those Local Courts increased to £50.'

In reply Mr Hanson wrote that he thought the Judge's resignation should be accepted.

> 'I confess'—he said—'that I still retain a very decided objection to conferring upon any person so great an extent of

irresponsible power as to place in his hands the sole and uncontrolled decision of all matters up to £50.' [118]

In December 1853 an act was passed conferring on the Judges of the Supreme Court all the powers given by the Local Courts Act to a Special Magistrate and two Justices so far as related to the holding of pleas of personal actions, and the Governor requested the Judges to sit in the Local Court in pursuance of this Act. Under it, eleven sittings of the Local Court were held by Mr Justice Cooper up to August 1856, and twenty-six by Mr Justice Boothby up to January 1857, after which the Act fell into abeyance.[119]

The Local Court system was rapidly extended throughout the country. In 1855 there were fifteen courts, and by 1861 the number had risen to twenty-nine, with two courts of limited jurisdiction only sitting at Glynde and Magill.[120] The *Register* wrote that:

> '... the scientific nonsense, the wire-woven refinements, the dilatoriness, the pedantry, the mystery, the verbosity, the glorious uncertainty, and the ruinous costs and expenses of Westminster Hall are being exchanged for the celerity, certainty, economy and common sense of the County Courts'—and that the local courts in South Australia would do what the county courts were doing in England, and provide: '.. cheap, summary and expeditious justice; without subtlety, dialectic accuracy, hair-splitting distinctions, and obstructive technicalities'.

It saw an advantage in the Local Courts attracting the legal business of the colony inasmuch as this would drive the Supreme Court to reform its procedure.

> 'In an infant colony'—it was said—'it is unwisely servile and timid to rear and propagate the artificial restrictions and the pedantry of pseudo-science, by which both the transfer of property and the investigation of truth in Courts of Law have become encumbered in the course of ages in the mother country; and to engraft on our local jurisprudence that hyper-technical canon of interpretation from which the administration of justice in England is at the present moment hastening to be emancipated.' [121]

At Adelaide difficulties arose at first from the understaffing of the Local Court: it was "most painful", said Wigley, "to hear the numerous complaints of process paid for and not issued". In view of the financial exigencies of 1851 to 1852, the Governor was very unwilling to make any addition to the staff of the Court. The revenue of the Court must be made to cover its expenses, he said, and if another clerk was appointed, the fees would have to be raised. He at last agreed to appoint J.M. Skipper—the artist—as an additional clerk.[122]

> 'We understand'—wrote the Register—'that the appointment has been made with singularly bad grace, His Excellency having expressed his opinion, that, without further evidence, he could not believe the necessity for the appointment, after the unmistakable expression of opinion on the subject by the Stipendiary Magistrate and several gentlemen of the Bar. This is strange—very.' [123]

John Michael Skipper (1815-1883)
Although he spent most of his working life in law Skipper is known today through his work as an artist. He was one of few who recorded images of early South Australian life and these works are now of great historical interest. Skipper was one to whom the law relating to the marrying of a deceased wife's sister applied for he married Robert Thomas's eldest daughter, Frances Amelia, in 1839 and after her death he married her younger sister Mary in 1856. (SLSA)

On the whole, however, the Local Courts were a satisfactory innovation. In 1861 their jurisdiction was extended to £100, with jurisdiction by consent beyond that amount; they were enabled to hear actions of ejectment, false imprisonment, and libel and slander; in cases between £30 and £100 a right of appeal to the Supreme Court on questions of law was given; and the limited jurisdiction was raised from £5 to £20.

In March 1864 the Government proposed that as the business in the Local Courts had greatly increased since the jurisdiction was raised, and important legal questions frequently had to be decided, it would benefit the public if one of the Judges would consent to hear some of the more important of the Local Court cases. The Judges unanimously refused the suggestion, as being inconsistent with their position, and impairing the usefulness of the Supreme Court as the ultimate court of appeal.[124]

A scheme for the establishment of circuit courts in connection with Local courts was then formulated by the Government and submitted to the Judges in May 1864, and in opening Parliament a few days later the Governor said:

> 'Since the passing of the Local Court Act 1861, by which the jurisdiction of the Local Court was extended, questions involving important points of law have frequently arisen which Stipendiary Magistrates and Justices of the Peace can scarcely be expected satisfactorily to determine. My Government are therefore of opinion that the assistance of the Judges of the Supreme Court would be of great advantage in deciding such cases, and to accomplish that object, it is proposed to introduce a measure to establish, in connection with Local Courts, circuit Courts to be presided over by the Judges of the Supreme Court.' [125]

The Judges still refused, however, to sit in Local Courts, where on circuit or not, and in October 1864 the Attorney-General tried to meet this objection by bringing in a bill to provide for sittings of the Supreme Court in country districts, at Local Court charges—in fact, Local Courts in all but name. Nothing came of the measure.

The decisions in *The Queen v. Neville* and *Dawes v. Quarrell*, in 1865, that the criminal jurisdiction of the Local Courts was illegal and that there were no Local Courts at all, have been fully described in the chapter dealing with Mr Justice Boothby. The Local Courts survived *Dawes v. Quarrell*, but their criminal jurisdiction was never again exercised.

There remains to be mentioned a singular anomaly—the Mayors Court, which flourished between 1856 and 1860. How and by what right the Court was established remains a mystery. Under Ordinance 11 of 1849, establishing the municipal corporation, the Mayor for the time being was ex officio made a Justice of the Peace, but that was his only claim to judicial power.

> 'It was stated'—said Mr Worsnop in his History of Adelaide—'that it was done under the advice of the Police Magistrate, though how he could authorise the establishment of such a tribunal does not appear. Its first sitting—at least the first recorded—was held on the 2nd April 1856, when a person was fined for removing sand from the river without a licence. In reference to this Court the Mayor states: "The establishment of the Mayor's Court has, I believe, given satisfaction to the citizens generally."' [126]

As well as being the source of illegal sand the Torrens supplied Adelaide's water until 1860. It was also a resource in a number of other endeavours as this ca. 1870 photograph of a wool scouring plant at Thebarton shows. (SLSA)

For several years the Mayor held his Court in the City Council chamber, imposing fines for nuisances, driving on the footpaths and similar offences against corporation by-laws. Practitioners enjoyed a right of audience, and the penalties went into the coffers of the corporation. A more flagrantly illegal usurpation of judicial power, it seems hard to imagine, but no-one objected to it. The Mayor even sat in appeal on his own decisions. In February 1859 a public meeting was held and a resolution passed that the Court ought to be abolished—on the score of inconvenience, not of illegality—and shortly afterwards its sittings were discontinued. A proposal in 1860 by some members of the Council that the Court should be revived met with strong opposition from the press and was abandoned.[127]

In conclusion, some notes may be added on the various courthouses occupied by the Resident Magistrates Court, the Police Court and the Local Court.[128]

In 1838 the site of the Resident Magistrates Court was on the north side of Currie Street, opposite Gilles Arcade. Here the town gossips gathered, to exchange news and listen to the cases:

> '... and then come away praising the mildness, suavity, and justice of the Magistrate's decision ... The town being such a wilderness, it always looks like Sunday—nothing stirring but stagnation; and the only place where anything is going on is the Courthouse of the Resident Magistrate'. [129]

In 1840 the Court was transferred to Gilles Arcade, and at the beginning of 1841 Captain Lipson's house on the north side of Currie Street (near Peel Street) was rented by the Government for the Resident Magistrate. Governor Grey's attempt to economise by sending Wigley to occupy rooms in the office of the Commissioner of Police on North Terrace has been referred to. Captain Lipson refused to release the Government from their agreement with him, and successfully sued the Colonial Secretary for the rent for the balance of the term for which the house had been taken. With the house thus thrown back on their hands, the Government transferred the Commissioner of Police to it, until the lease ran out, in 1845.[130]

From North Terrace the Resident Magistrates Court was moved in July 1843, to Gilles Arcade, and in about November 1843 into the old theatre which had been converted to provide premises for the courts. A new building was started in May 1848, on the corner of King William Street and Franklin Street, to house the Resident Magistrates and Police Courts, and the post office, but it was not completed until August 1851. The lease of the theatre had expired in 1850, at the same time as the Resident Magistrates Court ceased to exist, and the Local Court of Adelaide had to hold its first sittings when and where it could, either in the new Supreme Court house in Angas Street or in a nearby hotel, where rooms were hired by the day.[131]

> 'This Court'—wrote the *Register* in February 1851—'seems to have a roving commission; for when held under the roof of the Supreme Court House there were scarcely two consecutive weeks that it was to be found located in the same room ... It has always been thought bad enough that the public should

> thus have to play at hide-and-seek with the Court; but this morning the dozens in attendance, after roaming all over the building, walking into all the rooms, up-stairs and down, prying into cupboards, and peeping through keyholes of doors which refused to turn on their hinges, were astounded to hear that the Court would be held at the Prince of Wales public house.' [132]

The Prince of Wales
The Prince of Wales Hotel operated in Angas Street from 1848 to 1922 on a site that is destined, again, to be used for court business as part of the land on which the new Federal Courthouse is being built.

Until the post office building was ready, the Police Magistrate was moved to the former location of the old native school, near Kintore Avenue, where the Colonial Engineer had accomplished:

> '... an apparently impossible feat by having found a temporary domicile for the Magistrate and his myrmidons, possessing even less accomodation [sic] than that which they are quitting'. [133]

The Local and Police Courts remained at the GPO corner until 1866, when the building was pulled down and the present post office erected. The Courts moved to rooms in the town hall for three years, while new premises were erected—the present Supreme and Local Court buildings. The Police Court occupied what is now the Local Court, and the Local and Insolvency Courts took the present Supreme Court building, which they occupied from July 1869 to January 1873. It was then surrendered to the Supreme Court, and the Local and Insolvency Courts went over to the Angas Street courthouse. There they remained until 1891, when they changed places with the Police Court.

Although built and originally occupied by Arthur Hardy (see p. 711), "Birksgate" at Glen Osmond is best known as the home of Thomas Elder. Among other endeavours on the property, Elder built a gas plant, a zoo and a tower used to signal to his yachts in St Vincent's Gulf. (SLSA)

Chapter 9

The Law Officers of the Crown

'in the service of the colony'

Charles Mann, who was appointed in England to be Advocate-General, Crown Solicitor and Public Prosecutor in the new colony, was a London solicitor, aged thirty six at the time of his appointment, and had been for some years a keen supporter of the colonisation movement.[1] He was to receive a salary of £300 a year. His suspension by Governor Hindmarsh, the appointment of Wigley to act as Crown Solicitor pro tem, the arrival and administration of G.M. Stephen and the appointment of Robert Bernard have already been described. Governor Gawler had anticipated that upon the return of Gouger to the position of Colonial Secretary, Stephen would revert to his former position of Advocate-General. Stephen's resignation, following the verdict in the Milner estate libel action, meant that the Governor had to continue the inexperienced Bernard as Advocate-General and, for lack of any other suitable candidate in the colony, he recommended that Bernard's appointment should be confirmed. Bernard was a young man, his health was not strong, and his practice had been limited from that cause: "... but his general reading and information are sound, his judgment is good, and his character highly honourable". [2] Before any reply could be received from England, Bernard's state of health compelled him to take the sinecure position of Registrar-General.

Mr Hawker, in his *Reminiscences*, has preserved an amusing story about him. Government House in those days was a very rude structure, and a lantern was hung out at night to guide people through the scrub which surrounded it. On one occasion, the Governor was giving a dinner party. The Crown Solicitor was invited, but did not make an appearance, and dinner proceeded without him. Afterwards the Governor and his guests went outside to saunter round on the cleared ground in front of Government House, facing the Torrens.

> 'In our perambulations we became aware of an extraordinary sound, which apparently proceeded from somewhere in the ground. A lantern was procured, and a search revealed a hole—evidently partly sunk for a well—about nine feet deep, and standing in it, nearly up to knees in limestone mud and water was the unfortunate Crown Solicitor, who had missed the guiding light to Government House. When he was extricated from his unpleasant position, it was difficult for us to repress laughter. His appearance was comical. The white mud had completely obliterated the black colour of his silk stockings and part of his dress-coat, so that he was black nearly one-half and dirty white the other half.' [3]

For three months in 1840 Bernard acted as Judge while Mr Justice Cooper was on a visit to New South Wales, but he died shortly after the Judge's return.[4] Owing to his illness the business of the Advocate-General's office had fallen into arrears and Governor Gawler was compelled to appoint another Advocate-General immediately, without referring the matter to England. He chose William Smillie, a young Scottish lawyer who had come to South Australia with his father Matthew Smillie in 1839, and had been successively a clerk in the Land Office, and Emigration Agent. His father was also a solicitor, and they had practised in partnership for some years at Leith. The son had been admitted as a practitioner in Scotland in May 1833, at the age of twenty three. His attention having been drawn to the colony of South Australia, he wrote a series of articles pointing out the advantages of emigration there, which were published in the *Stirling Observer* and reprinted in 1838 as a pamphlet under the title *The Great South Land.* The family came to South Australia shortly afterwards and his father settled as a farmer on land which he took up at Nairne, which was named by him after his wife.[5]

A 1931 photograph of the monument in the Nairne cemetery to the Smillie family. (SLSA)

In reporting that he had promoted Smillie to be Advocate-General, Governor Gawler wrote:

'He is not an English barrister, but there is no person of this

> class in the colony possessing suitable talent and character; and the business connected with the Advocate General's Office has fallen so much into arrears and it is of so important a description that serious evil would have attended a delay in referring it again to England.'

He commended Smillie as a "very devoted, intelligent, and honourable young man" whose deficiency in experience would be offset by his talent and industry.[6]

Governor Gawler laboured throughout his term in the colony under the disadvantage of not having a reliable legal adviser, and this prevented him from carrying out very much in the way of legislation or improvements in the administration of justice. He reported to the Commissioners in June 1840:

> 'During the year and a half referred to, setting aside all other hindrances, I had virtually, as to practical legislation, that of not being able to procure one working legal adviser. The late acting Advocate General, for whose memory, as regards his character and general judgment, I have very great respect, was unfortunately extremely inexperienced in practice, and had a constitution so broken that he was scarcely able to bear up against the pressure of ordinary business. The want of sound and efficient legal practitioners is an unspeakable disadvantage in a new community under a new system, which springs at once into a large population with its multifarious legal and legislative requirements, and in which, in opposition, every man is disposed to be a lawyer.' [7]

Arthur Hardy
(1817-1909)
Hardy arrived in South Australia in 1839 with considerable capital and hoping to escape the worst effects of his tuberculosis. A politician, barrister, pastoralist and quarry owner he became one of the richest men in Adelaide. His wealth allowed him to build Birksgate at Glen Osmond and, later, Mount Lofty House. However the bank collapse of 1886 left him heavily indebted and with greatly reduced means for the rest of his life. (SLSA)

After the extraordinary scene at the Criminal Sessions in March 1839 when every prisoner was acquitted, the Governor decided that the Crown Law Office must be strengthened, and he offered the position of Clerk of the Peace to Arthur Hardy, a young English solicitor who had come to the colony with the intention of taking up land and farming.[8]

Provision for the appointment of a Clerk of the Peace had been made in the Resident Magistrates Courts Act 1837, and originally the offices of Clerk of the Peace and Clerk of the Resident Magistrates Court were united in the person of the same person. When the Resident Magistrates Court acquired two clerks, the clerk on the criminal side performed the duties of the Clerk of the Peace, which were to manage the prosecution of small cases; to prepare indictments, issue subpoenas and arrange for the attendance of witnesses; to prefer bills to the Grand Jury; and to attend before the Judge on applications for bail. With increasing business, the duties of clerk on the criminal side of the Resident Magistrates Court were allotted to a separate officer; and the Clerk of the Peace, when Hardy took the position, really acted as an assistant to the

Advocate-General, his duties being very similar to those performed by the modern Crown law clerk. He interviewed and took proofs from witnesses and arranged for their attendance at court, reported on criminal cases, prosecuted in small cases, and drafted indictments. The more important briefs were frequently sent to outside practitioners to be prepared.[9]

Smillie and Hardy carried on the legal work of the Government more efficiently than Bernard, but they by no means escaped criticism. At the Criminal Sessions in March 1841, for instance, half the accused were acquitted, and the newspapers raised a clamour that the moral condition of the colony was endangered by the incapacity of the legal functionaries of the Government. The sessions, it was said, proved one of two things—either many innocent persons had been wrongly accused of crimes which they had never committed or, through mismanagement by the Public Prosecutor in getting up the cases, guilt was allowed to go unpunished.[10] This was nothing, however, to the execrations which were showered upon the unfortunate Smillie over the *Ville de Bordeaux* case, and the journalists of the day were, to say the least, outspoken. The *Adelaide Chronicle*, for instance, said:

> 'The miserable incapacity of the Advocate General—his total unfitness for the position he occupies—have long been acknowledged. The imbecility, trifling and mismanagement exhibited day after day, in this responsible department, cannot much longer be endured, either by His Excellency or by the public; and for the sake of the best interests of the colony we earnestly hope that some gentleman with a smattering, at least, of English law and commonsense will be found to fill the office, previous to the ensuing assizes.' [11]

The *Register* was equally violent in its denunciations of the Advocate-General:

> 'Ignorance the grossest and imbecility the most pitiable have been the distinguishing marks of his career in his new capacity. He was a hard-working Emigration Agent, and in his private circle, there is nothing to object to. In any subordinate office of the local Government, in which dull plodding and official subservience only were required, he might have done well enough; but as Advocate General—as the head of the legal profession—as the legal adviser of the Crown—the legislator for a great community—to place a young man who was a member of no recognised Court of Law in England, Ireland or Scotland—who possessed neither knowledge nor experience, nor judgment, nor discretion—who was palpably deficient in the most ordinary requirements of his office—was a joke

> which the great Governor Gawler only could have gravely perpetrated, or the indulgent colonists of South Australia tolerated. Justice can neither be done to the colony, nor the wrongs of the injured parties vindicated, while an incubus so useless and so oppressive as the present Advocate General is allowed to obstruct the free movements and to suffocate the healthier aspirations of the Government.' [12]

Smillie wrote in reply that he scorned to take any notice of the attacks. But he found a doughty champion in the editor of the *Southern Australian*, and the annals of Eatanswill can hardly parallel the onslaught which this gentleman delivered upon his brother of the *Register*. Mr Smillie, he said, had been maliciously attacked with savage ferocity.

> 'In every important case in which his professional skill has been called into existence, he has thoroughly smashed the clumsily sophisticated theories of his opponents, and has thus walked triumphantly over the course [sic], the pompous and oft-reiterated predictions of the enemies of good order to the contrary notwithstanding.' [13]

Would the colonists suffer "a miserable poltroon to pursue this reckless course of extravagant and ferocious vituperation"? No, no, a thousand times—no! For who would then be safe from "the fangs of this literary assassin", from the "vile tergiversation" or "the gross apostacy [sic] of this pitiful scribbler", whose attacks were "the offspring of motives as remarkable for their innate malignity, as for their base and filthy turpitude"?

The early colonists may have suffered many hardships unknown to this degenerate age, but at least their morning reading was lively and entertaining.

Hardy resigned his position in April 1841, and the office of Clerk of the Peace was abolished, that of Assistant Crown Solicitor being substituted in its place.[14] To this, William Bernard was appointed. He was a brother of the former Advocate-General and had been admitted as an attorney of the Court of Exchequer in Ireland in 1835. Like his brother he suffered from ill health—both were apparently consumptive—and he died in 1843. The salary placed on the estimates for the Assistant Crown Solicitor was £200 a year, and this was sanctioned by the authorities at home. But when Governor Grey began his campaign of economy the legal members of the civil service suffered with the others. The Advocate-General had been paid a fixed salary of £300 a year, and an allowance of £3 3s 0d per case in the Criminal Court. Altogether his salary averaged about £540 to £550. "The system of giving an uncertain remuneration in the form of fees" appeared to Governor Grey to be "for many reasons objectionable", and he therefore stopped the allowances and placed

Smillie on a salary of £540 to compensate him for the loss of fees. Shortly afterwards, however, he cut the salary down to £400. On account of his failing health, William Bernard had to obtain leave of absence in December 1842, and J.H. Richman, a solicitor who had been clerk to the Bench of Magistrates, was appointed as Acting Assistant Crown Solicitor, but at half-salary only. On Bernard's death, Governor Grey did not want to appoint a successor—he said a clerk should be sufficient—but, as Smillie contended that he could not get through the work alone, Richman was offered the position at £100 a year and took it.[15]

Grey had a poor opinion of Smillie's merits; the Advocate-General was not vigorous enough in his work to satisfy the Governor's requirements. He offered the position to W.H. Mackie, a solicitor whom he had met in Perth. Mackie's reply refusing the offer miscarried, and Grey waited a long time for an answer which never arrived.[16] Smillie's appointment had never been confirmed in England, and in November 1844 he applied to the Secretary of State to be placed on the permanent list. In forwarding this application, Grey reported on it in a very unfavourable tone:

> 'The fact is I apprehend Mr Smillie's object in desiring to obtain a formal notification of his appointment really is that in the event of the population and public business of the colony continuing to increase as rapidly as it is at present, Her Majesty's Government may be precluded from sending out from England an experienced English barrister as the chief Law Officer of the Crown, at the same time leaving Mr Smillie in the position of Crown Solicitor. Mr Smillie, for whom I have in many respects a most sincere esteem, was only admitted to practice in Scotland as an agent or solicitor before the courts of that country, and for some time after his arrival in this colony he did not practice the legal profession at all, but was in the first instance a clerk in the Land Office, and subsequently Emigration Agent, and I am constrained to state that the Government has, in many cases, suffered severely from Mr Smillie's want of legal knowledge and experience.' [17]

Frederick Holt Robe ca. 1890 (SLSA)

He had informed Smillie that it would be his duty to recommend that an English barrister should be sent out, and he suggested that this should be done when the financial condition of the colony warranted it. Governor Robe, however, formed a very favourable opinion of Smillie and was genuinely sorry that he had the task of communicating to him the refusal of the Colonial Office to confirm his appointment. "The intelligence," Robe said in his laconic style, "was far from welcome to him."[18]

In 1846 Smillie's salary was raised to £500 but, to offset this, Richman resigned because the Government would not give him more than £2 a week, and Smillie was left to carry on alone.[19] He had put forward a suggestion that fines recovered from revenue prosecutions should be used to pay the expenses of an increased law establishment, but Governor Grey would not listen to this.

Smillie seems to have steadily improved in ability as he gained more experience. Both Governor Robe and Sir Henry Fox Young found him very capable. The newspaper criticisms gradually died away, with one or two mild outbursts now and then, such as to say that the law officers of the Government, if consulted upon any question, were likely:

> '... to adopt the petty quirks and paltry subtleties which generally distinguish lawyers of feeble intellect and small acquirements—men unable to grasp a difficult question, but who take much pains of mistifying [sic] plain ones'.[20]

Just as Smillie's position was becoming firm, however, a new danger arrived, in the person of G.M. Stephen. Stephen landed in Adelaide again in 1846, glowing with virtue from his recent whitewashing, and determined, if possible, to regain his post of Advocate-General. The Secretary of State had said he would leave the matter to Governor Robe's discretion. But "a dapper little legist" like Stephen was not of a character calculated to appeal to that unemotional governor, and there was no doubt, also, that his reappointment would have provoked a terrible tirade from the newspapers. The *Observer* cynically suggested that if Stephen were:

> '... to go the circuit of the Australian colonies, he might find a settlement more congenial to his views, and affording a wider scope for the exercise of his professional talents'. [21]

The Judge too had been antagonised by Stephen, who, full of his newborn authority as an English barrister (the Judge and Jickling being the only other barristers in the colony) attempted to "bounce" the local practitioners and put them in their place. He offended both the Judge and Smillie by insolently remarking in court that he had heard in England, and it was notorious, that it was his Honour's constant habit to conduct the prosecution for the Advocate-General. The Judge indignantly disclaimed this, but it probably rested on a substratum of truth, for no doubt in Smillie's early years of office the Judge was accustomed to intervene and assist the prosecutor rather than see justice defeated by a lamentable breakdown of the case for the Crown.[22]

Governor Robe was a man of few words. "Il faut avouer que ce Monsieur a un grand talent pour le silence." He had a "Port" in the full Meredithian sense of the word—"something unsympathetically impressive". But beneath an austere and unattractive exterior he concealed a droll wit and more shrewdness than he was usually credited with. He was, however, no diplomatist, and his utterances, few though they were, almost invariably gave offence to someone. As an instance of his tact, take his reply to a deputation of Methodists who came to petition for a portion of the cemetery to be appropriated for Methodist use alone. The Governor simply said, "Surely, Gentlemen, you don't intend to continue your quarrels underground," and bowed them out.

He handled Stephen, however, with dexterity. He had no intention whatever of appointing him Advocate-General.

> 'In the existing state of feeling on the part of the colonists of this province towards Mr G.M. Stephen'-he wrote-'however unmerited such prejudice may be on his part, I very much question whether I would be promoting the true interests of Her Majesty's service by entrusting the Crown advocacy into the hands of one, against whom it is not unreasonable to suppose the prejudices of juries would be arrayed.' [23]

Without expressing this opinion to Stephen, however, he neatly told him that, being by profession a soldier, he could not decide which was the better qualified—Smillie or Stephen—to be Advocate-General and that, as he had had no cause to be dissatisfied with Smillie during the short experience he had had of his work, he did not think he could recommend any change. Stephen waited a few months and then renewed his application in a long letter to the Governor, which, even allowing for the circumstances of embittered disappointment in which it was probably composed, reflects no credit upon the character of its writer. He commenced by a panegyric upon his own merits. His practice at the bar, he claimed, was four times as extensive as that of any other practitioner, and his chamber business far superior to that of any barrister in Adelaide. He said that he had returned to South Australia understanding that he was to have been restored as Advocate-General (which was an understanding in no way warranted by the noncommittal attitude of the Secretary of State).

> 'With this sole object I abandoned an enviable home in my native land, where I enjoyed the society of a circle of distinguished friends. For this I declined the practice there of my profession; which might have led to far higher honours than I can obtain here.'

He modestly suggested that if the Governor found any difficulty in deciding between the respective merits of himself and Smillie, the matter should be solved by having two officers—he being appointed to the higher rank of Advocate-General and Smillie put in the subordinate place of Crown Solicitor. He charitably added:

> 'Should such decision be approved, perhaps the Government at home (which I believe in no instance ever appointed a Gentleman of Mr Smillie's station in the profession to a law office) might consider that his want of professional rank, and

> of an English law education, did not disqualify him for holding the office of Crown Solicitor, in which position were I appointed Advocate General, I should work with him cordially.' [24]

In all this talk about the high qualities necessary for an Advocate-General, Stephen completely ignored the fact that he was lifted to that position, without any forensic experience, from the very subordinate place of clerk of the Supreme Court at Hobart.

Governor Robe realised that by this "Modest Proposal" couched in such conceited and arrogant terms, Stephen had played into his hands. Confident that such a document would be regarded with the utmost disfavour at the Colonial Office, he at once wrote to Stephen saying that he would be pleased to forward the letter to England to enable the Secretary of State to decide which of the candidates was best fitted for the office. Whatever his own opinion might be, he added, as to the advantage to be derived from a second law adviser to the Crown in the colony, he could not in justice to Smillie, who had now for some years been the only one, recommend that Stephen should be allowed to supersede him.[25]

To this letter, Stephen, who no doubt realised the error he had made, did not reply. The Governor followed up his advantage by pressing for an answer whether Stephen would like his letter sent home, or whether he abandoned his application, and the result is found in a note by Robe, endorsed on Stephen's letter, that Stephen had verbally intimated to him that "he did not wish a copy of this letter to be sent to the Secretary of State".

In the following year Robe wrote home recommending that Smillie's appointment should be confirmed. He had had consistent support from the Advocate-General during the troublous times with the non-official members of the Council over the mineral royalties question.

> 'He speaks with fluency; in general he takes a clear and comprehensive view of the question under discussion, not permitting himself to be strayed from his purpose by popular clamour.' [26]

The recommendation was approved, and the confirmation communicated to Smillie in December 1848.[27] It came too late to be enjoyed.

> 'Since February 1845'—Smillie wrote—'I have had single-handed to cope with the whole law business of the Government, including the preparation of Bills for the local Legislature, the conducting the trials in criminal and civil cases in which the Crown or officers of Government have been concerned, and advising on all references, and the drawing of all pleadings and public deeds and instruments. Though the

> emoluments of my office were fixed on the assumption that I was entitled to engage in private professional practice, my public duties have been such as to render this next to impossible.' [28]

His health was broken. He took three months' leave of absence in 1849 to recuperate, but it effected little improvement.[29] He had asked for an Assistant Crown Solicitor, but only obtained a grudging answer that if assistance became urgently necessary in any particular case he might apply to be authorised to engage an outside practitioner's assistance. In July 1849 the Legislative Council decided, not without some dissent, to vote a sum for the appointment of a Crown Solicitor. It was urged that the Advocate-General, with his duties of attending the Council, preparing acts and conducting the cases in the Supreme Court, was unable to give proper attention to minor proceedings, which "frequently fell to the ground". Mr Morphett, on the other hand, said that "the generally felt and not mildly expressed opinion was that the post of Advocate General was not only a good but an easy one", and that if a Crown Solicitor was appointed he should not be subordinate to Smillie, but of equal rank.[30]

The appointment of Crown Solicitor went to Mann, who appears to have taken it with the view that he was to be, as Morphett had suggested, on an equality with Smillie and that each would be head of a separate department. He asked Smillie how the duties should be divided and suggested that he should write to the other colonies to ascertain what were the duties performed by the Crown Solicitor there. Smillie, who had anticipated Mann would be his subordinate, was taken aback at this attitude, and hastily wrote to the Colonial Secretary objecting to any division of the work or any definition of Mann's duties. "Omnis definitio periculosa est," he said in a classical outburst.[31] Mann was accordingly informed by the Government that he and the Advocate-General were to be jointly the law advisers of the Crown, that they could not have separate departments, that the Advocate-General was to be superior, and that all references and correspondence to and from the department must be made through him. As to division of duties within the department, they must arrange that between themselves.[32]

Smillie's health, however, now gave way completely. He obtained eighteen months' leave of absence from Governor Young, who reported:

> 'I have found the favourable opinion which my predecessor entertained of his merits has been fully realised by the zeal and efficiency with which Mr Smillie has discharged every duty of his important office.' [33]

He travelled to England on an extended voyage by way of Peru, Panama, West Indies and the United States; visited Scotland; and was on his way to Italy, when he died suddenly at Paris on 11 December 1852.[34] The newspapers which ten years earlier had slated him unmercifully now tried to make amends. "He wore himself out in the service of the colony"—said the Register—"and in the end absolutely died the victim of the drudgery to which he had been subjected." [35]

Upon Smillie's departure, Mann for about a month was Acting Advocate-General. G.M. Stephen (who, despite his boasted practice, had been for a while in somewhat precarious financial circumstances and had even been paid visits by the Sheriff's officers) applied to be appointed Acting Crown Solicitor.[36] "I am conscious," he said, "of having passed through an arduous professional career of five years at this bar with integrity, zeal and honor"—a consciousness which many citizens of Adelaide did not share. Any hope he might have had of obtaining the appointment he solicited was ended by the Governor's appointment of Richard Davies Hanson to be Acting Advocate-General, whereupon Mann reverted to his post of Crown Solicitor.

Hanson had come to the colony in 1846 and had immediately become one of the leaders of the bar. In 1851 when the partially elective Legislative Council came into being, Hanson was elected for the District of Yatala, but a petition was lodged against his return upon the ground that the Government had opened a polling place in the district without giving the required notice. The Governor solved any necessity for a trial of the petition by appointing Hanson Advocate-General which meant that he had, ex officio, a seat in the Council, and he thereupon resigned his disputed seat for Yatala.[37]

At the end of 1851 the Governor recommended that should Smillie be unable to return to his position, Hanson should be permanently appointed:

> 'Mr Hanson's management of the Government Legislative business, and his assistance to the general business of the Government in Council, have been such as to lead me to the conclusion that the satisfactory working of the local administration is greatly promoted by the skill and influence which he is able to exercise, and that his confirmation in the office of Advocate General in the event of any casualty occurring to prevent Mr Smillie's resumption of the office would be very conducive to the continued advantage of Her Majesty's service.' [38]

Upon Smillie's death Hanson succeeded to the position, which he held until the opening of the first Parliament under responsible government. In that Parliament he was returned to the House of Assembly for Adelaide and was Attorney-General in Mr Finniss's ministry.

Mann remained Crown Solicitor until 1856, when he was appointed Commissioner of Insolvency. He was succeeded as Crown

Solicitor by William Alfred Wearing, who held the position until his appointment as third judge in 1867—"the wittiest Judge", according to Mr Justice Bundey, "that ever sat on the South Australian Bench".

With the change to responsible government the title of the Chief Law Officer was altered to Attorney-General. The title of Advocate-General had given rise to some quibbling. In *The Queen v. Paxton* (the mineral royalties suit), for instance, in 1848, Mr Fisher had objected to the Advocate-General laying ex officio information—only an attorney-general could do that, he said. Mr Justice Cooper held against the objection.

> 'I am of opinion that as the Advocate General has been always recognised as Her Majesty's Law Officer, particularly in the Jury Ordinance No 12 of 1843, and as he is the only law officer of the Crown in the colony, I cannot properly reject an information filed by him on Her Majesty's behalf.' [39]

Mr Justice Boothby subsequently contended very strenuously for many years that there was no such thing as an attorney-general in the colony. The Privy Council, he said, would have to decide whether the prerogative of the Crown could be restricted by a provision that the Queen should not have law advisers except from among men who had previously obtained election to Parliament. What was the Crown to do if there should be no lawyer in Parliament? [40] But even assuming this provision of the Constitution Act was valid, there was a further objection. There had never, he said, been any express legislative alteration of the office of Advocate-General to that of Attorney-General. The latter title was admittedly mentioned in the Constitution Act, but that, he thought, was not sufficient.

> 'It might lead to a very undesirable state of things in the administration of justice. So long as poor men only were convicted the convictions might stand unquestioned; but let a rich man's son be convicted say of rape, and they might have the authority of the whole proceeding questioned, and a failure of jurisdiction. It was not enough that the new office was referred to; there should have been an authoritative abolition of one office and a constitution of the other office by statute.' [41]

And on another occasion he said:

> 'I know of no Statute creating the office of Attorney General in this colony, it is merely spoken of as a name ... an objection will some day be raised on a criminal information that it is bad, for that such office has never been created, which must be judicially determined, and may be carried to the Privy Council.' [42]

The attempts by the Judge to maintain this view have already been touched on in the chapter dealing with him.

In the Constitution Act of 1853, which was disallowed, the office of Solicitor-General was mentioned. All reference to it was dropped out of the Constitution Act of 1855-56. When, in August 1858, the Finniss ministry resigned, Hon J. Baker formed a ministry in which E.C. Gwynne was Attorney-General. Gwynne held a seat in the Legislative Council and, in order to strengthen his very insecure government in the lower house, Mr Baker created the office of Solicitor-General, which was accepted by Mr J.T. Bagot, without salary. As soon as Mr Bagot appeared in the House in his official capacity a question of privilege was raised. Mr Hanson called attention to the fact that there was a stranger in the House. Section 17 of the Constitution Act provided that if any member accepted an office of profit or pension from the Crown, during pleasure, except such offices as were by the Act required to be held by members of Parliament, his seat should thereupon become vacant. Section 32 provided that no person should hold the offices of Chief Secretary, Attorney-General, Treasurer, Commissioner of Crown Lands and Immigration or Commissioner of Public Works, for any longer period than three months, unless he was a member of Parliament. Mr Hanson contended that the fact that Mr Bagot received no salary did not prevent the office being one of profit.

> 'This is a new appointment and I do not know on what authority it was made. Even Her Majesty can create no new office, excepting by the sanction of the Legislature. This appointment of Solicitor General must, therefore, have been made in accordance with a custom established in England. The appointment as Solicitor General imposes certain duties which involve the receipt of certain fees; and there is no doubt that the office is one of considerable profit.' [43]

Mr Bagot replied that he would not receive a sixpence from his appointment, and a somewhat acrimonious debate followed, which was still in progress when the House adjourned. Next day a motion of want of confidence in Mr Baker's administration was carried by a majority of twenty-four to seven. The ministry resigned, having held office for ten days, and to Mr Bagot belongs the unique distinction of being the only Solicitor-General the state has ever had.

Mr Baker's Government was succeeded by one formed by Mr. Torrens, in which R.B. Andrews was Attorney-General. This survived for a month before being ousted by Mr Hanson, who remained in office as Premier and Attorney-General from September 1857 to May 1860.

In January 1858, when the Circuit Courts Bill was under consideration, Mr Torrens moved in the Assembly for the insertion of a clause that "the title and emoluments of Chief Justice shall be held by the Judge who shall have had his commission for the longer period".

> 'I cannot shut my ears'—he said—'to what is talked of all through the town. That the Bench is not what it should be, is not only the opinion of professional men but of many others. The position of the Attorney General, as a practitioner of the Supreme Court, is believed to be injurious to other practitioners.'

Mr Hanson opposed the amendment:

> 'I should say that neither emoluments nor position would ever induce any Attorney General to accept a puisne Judgship [sic] in this colony. By this clause, a man placed at the head of his profession would be exposed to the bar of exclusion, under the pretence of leaving open to all others the highest post, the highest honours, it had to award.'

Other members objected to the introduction of a system whereby any gentleman, however old, however incompetent, however deficient in legal acquirements, if made a puisne judge must, if he outlived the others on the bench, become Chief Justice; and the motion was rejected.[44]

Subsequently the question was several times raised in Parliament whether the Attorney-General had a pre-emptive right to a seat on the Supreme Court bench if a vacancy occurred during his tenure of office, but on each occasion the then Attorney-General repudiated any such right.[45]

The relations between the Judges and the Attorney-General were not always of the most amicable nature. In October 1856 the Chief Justice and the Master had been requested by a circular letter to correspond officially with the Government through the Attorney-General. Sir Charles Cooper indignantly objected to this attempt to make him a subordinate official in the department of the Attorney-General and said that he would continue to correspond as previously with the Governor and the Chief Secretary. The Master had to obey, and the Judges resented this subordination of an officer of the court to an outside authority. In January 1859, when Jickling applied for leave of absence, the Chief Justice urged that the power of granting leave should be with the Judges (subject to their reporting it to the Governor and obtaining his approval) and not with the Attorney-General.

> 'The Attorney General is a practitioner of the Supreme Court and appears as such not only before the Judges, but before the Master from time to time, and it is obvious that this direct power of granting favours places him in a different position from any other practitioner.'[46]

The control gained by the Attorney-General, however, could not be got rid of, and this rankled with the Judges. In 1866 Sir Richard Hanson and the then Attorney-General (Mr Boucaut) came to grips upon the question of the administration of the Supreme Court. A deadlock seems to have been reached after some heated correspondence, which terminated in a sarcastic request by the Chief Justice to be informed: "... whether the Supreme Court is to be a branch of the Attorney General's Department in everything but deciding cases." [47]

The requirement of the Constitution Act that the Attorney-General should be a member of Parliament gave rise to debates which occupied the attention of Parliament at intervals of fifteen years. With a barrister in such active practice as Mr Hanson, it was soon found that his private and political work very often clashed. Questions were frequently postponed in the House because the Attorney-General was engaged in court. Mr Hanson himself announced that he did not propose to let the attorney-generalship ruin his private practice.[48]

Summarising from many debates the principal objections raised to the Attorney-General being a member of Parliament and of the Ministry, they were:

(1) The inconvenience which necessarily arose from "the casual transfer of the office whenever a change of ministry took place".

(2) The difficulty experienced by those forming an administration in finding an attorney-general among the few legal members of Parliament. "It was not every lawyer who could take the position of Attorney General."

(3) The Attorney-General could not give proper attention both to the duties of his office and to his private practice.

(4) He had incompatible functions. As minister he controlled the courts; as barrister he practised in them.

(5) He had the duty of filing criminal informations—a dangerous power to give to a party man.

(6) "The Attorney General should not compose a part of the Ministry, for from the character of his training and education, he was a scientific and professional man, and could not therefore occupy a position in the Ministry without being out of place. He was only qualified to act as a subordinate officer under the Government to which he was attached."

(7) Men of talent in the profession were precluded from becoming the law advisers of the Crown unless they chose to go into Parliament.

(8) "The office of Attorney General should be filled not from the limited circle of legal gentlemen in the House but from the entire bar of the Supreme Court, and the appointment should not depend on the ins and outs of any Ministry."

(9) Bills had to be prepared. The Attorney-General was too busy to attend to this, although it was his proper duty, and considerable expenses had to be incurred in engaging outside counsel to draft and settle them. If the Attorney-General was a permanent official only, he would be able to do this work.

(10) In a small legislature a person possessing great influence, such as the then Attorney-General (Mr Hanson)—"an influence arising from his argumentative ability and legal acquirements"—was sufficient to counterbalance the advantages of representative government."He possessed a power far greater than it was safe to entrust in the hands of an individual."

(11) The administration of justice would be improved and facilitated by having a permanent minister of justice.

(12) "The Legal profession had an absolute monopoly on one of the five offices of the Government, and an equal chance of all the others."

(13) If the Attorney-General was not a private practitioner or a party man, he could consult with the Judges upon amendments of the law.

(14) The attorney-generalship, being a stepping stone to the bench, should not be a party position or restricted to a few members of Parliament.

To all these arguments (of varying weight) the answer of the Government was that questions of law continually arose which rendered it absolutely necessary to have in the Cabinet a man of the highest legal attainments, who was in harmony with the Government policy and who could state that policy to the House.

The first attack was made by Mr Burford, who moved in the House of Assembly in September 1858:

> '... that the practice hitherto observed, rendering it necessary to unite in one person the two offices of Attorney General and Member of the Administration is highly inexpedient and objectionable, and that it is expedient to appoint a Parliamentary Draughtsman'. [49]

The motion failed, but the Reynolds Government, which succeeded that of Mr Hanson in May 1860, announced its intention of making the Attorney-General a non-political officer. Nevertheless, nothing was done to carry out this undertaking.

In October 1861 attention was again called to the position of the Attorney-General by the fact that when Mr Waterhouse formed his emergency ministry for the purpose of passing addresses for the removal of Mr Justice Boothby, he was unable to find any lawyer in Parliament who would take the position of Attorney-General. He was therefore obliged to go outside, and the office was conferred on Mr Henry Gawler, one of the solicitors to the Lands Titles Commissioners. The appointment caused amusement because it was patently a stopgap, intended to last (as in fact it did) for only a few days. In the Legislative Council, Hon H. Ayers demanded to know whether, in the event of the retirement of the Chief Justice, Mr Gawler would, virtute officii, be entitled to succeed him; the Government was bombarded with legal questions and complaints that the Attorney-General was not in his place in the House to answer them; and there were sarcastic references to the fact that Mr Gawler, unmoved by his sudden access of dignity, had placidly gone on with his work at the Lands Titles Office.[50]

Next year Mr Magarey was successful in having a motion carried in the Assembly to the effect that it was desirable the Attorney-General should not be a political man, but once more nothing was done. Mr John Hart tried again with a similar motion in 1863, but this time the debate developed into a heated argument whether lawyers ought to be permitted to sit in Parliament at all, and the motion was lost. Nothing daunted, Mr Hart brought the matter forward again in 1865, and again failed.

In December 1865, however, an amending Constitution Bill was introduced by the Government, in which it was proposed to increase the number of ministers from five to seven, including a minister of justice; while the Attorney-General was to be retained, he might or might not be a responsible minister and member of Parliament, the clause relating to him being permissive. The Bill did not get past the second hearing.[51]

In spite of a resolution in the House in 1871 that it was desirable that the Attorney-General should not necessarily be a member of Parliament, it was not until 1873 that the requirement to this effect in the Constitution Act was repealed.[52]

John Hart
(1809-1873)
At sea from the age of twelve, Hart first visited South Australia before European settlement on ships that traded with sealers on Kangaroo Island. His maritime association with South Australia continued and culminated in his running a whaling station at Encounter Bay from 1844 to 1846. He then engaged in land based business pursuits including pastoralism, mining, smelting and milling. A long political career saw him serve as Premier on three occasions (1865-66, 1868 and 1870-71).

Thomas Magarey
(1825-1902)
The name Magarey is now most readily associated with the footballers' medal named after a grandson of Thomas. Football, however, would have been far from the thoughts of Thomas who was an intensely religious man. His time in Parliament, from 1860 to 1865, was often devoted to religious issues and he was one of the founders of the first Church of Christ in Australia in 1849. In his later years he took to astronomy and installed a telescope in his Enfield home. (SLSA)

Mt Lofty House, pictured here as it exists today, was built by ArthurHardy between 1852 and 1858 and used as his summer residence. Its various owners added to the original structure but the Ash Wednesday fires of 1983 destroyed all but the stone walls of the property. It has since been fully restored and operates as a deluxe hotel and restaurant. (Mt Lofty House website)

Chapter 10

The Legal Profession

A hunger for horsehair

"In a newly founded colony," wrote the satiric Mr Harrison in his *Colonial Sketches*, "it is amusing, but not surprising, to see with what velocity a few representatives of the interesting tribe called lawyers make their appearance thirsting after spoil and exulting in a new field of enterprise." [1]

Within a year of the founding of the colony, there were five solicitors practising in Adelaide, one of whom wrote in January 1838: "I am in full practice, and well employed. I consider my own success as certain, as I get more business than I can do." [2]

The Rules of Court made by Sir John Jeffcott in 1837 provided that Henry Jickling (barrister), Charles Mann and Henry Rodolph Wigley (English solicitors) and Charles Johnson (an Irish solicitor) should be admitted to practice until the last day of the next term, when they, and all others thereafter admitted, would be required to conform to such rules as might be made in that behalf. Sir John's death occurred before he had framed any further rules. In March 1838 Wigley, Johnson, Samuel Smart and G.M. Stephen were admitted as practitioners by Jickling; later in the same year Robert Bernard and E.C. Gwynne; and in March 1839 J.W. Nicholls.[3]

John Warner Nicholls (c1798-1880) Nicholls was to serve as the Coroner and the Clerk of the Adelaide Local Court.

Jickling made a Rule of Court requiring every person seeking admission as a practitioner to affix a notice on the outside of the courthouse or give notice in the Government Gazette, and stipulating for a residence of six months in the colony before admission. In July 1839 Mr Justice Cooper rescinded this rule, abolished the residential qualification and ordered that any barrister or solicitor of the superior courts of England, Ireland or Scotland might be admitted on production of satisfactory evidence of his status.[4]

During the early years of the colony speculation in land was rife. Properties changed hands with rapidity, and the conveyancers reaped a rich harvest. They complained, however, that unqualified persons were in many cases drawing conveyances and mortgages and stealing their work. A meeting of the profession was held in 1839 to consider this important topic, and representations were made to the Governor, which resulted in the introduction into the Legislative Council, in December 1840, of a bill to restrain unqualified persons from doing legal work. The practitioners virtuously claimed that their object was not to protect themselves from opposition but to save the community from the confusion which must result if invalid titles and conveyances were put into circulation, an evil which was "very seriously and deeply felt in the colony at this moment". The "Attorneys' Monopoly Act", as it was stigmatised, met with a very unfavourable reception and had to be withdrawn. It had been proposed to allow the Judge to determine the rate of payments to be made by the public to the profession for business done, but this was denounced as certain to lead to high fees.[5]

A bill to regulate the profession of the law was again brought forward in 1843 and was passed in November of that year. It was promptly disallowed by the Secretary of State, to the annoyance of the Judge, who wrote that some of the parts objected to had been copied by him verbatim from an English statute.[6] The Governor was instructed to propose to the Legislative Council the re-enactment of the measure, with the offensive portions omitted.[7] This was done, and the Ordinance passed in July 1845 remains the principal Act regulating the profession in this state.

It is of some interest to compare the provisions of the two Acts of 1843 and 1845. Both provided that no person should thereafter be qualified to practise the profession of law in the province unless he should have been duly admitted as a practitioner of the Supreme Court, and a penalty of £50 was imposed upon anyone who, without being so admitted, drew or prepared for fee or reward "any conveyance lease or other deed relating to any real or personal estate or any proceedings in Law or Equity". The 1843 Act also referred to an anomalous class of practitioners—persons not duly admitted as practitioners of the Supreme Court but permitted to practise by virtue of a certificate upon examination, signed by the Judge, the Advocate-General and the Crown Solicitor, of their being sufficiently qualified to practise. This provision was introduced by the Governor because he thought the time might come when at places like Port Lincoln or Rivoli Bay, on the outskirts of the colony, it would be necessary to have someone competent to do legal work, and it was not to be expected that fully-fledged practitioners would open up offices in the outback.[8] Similarly, in the Insolvent Act of 1841 (5 Vic No 1 s.VII) provision had been made for permitting unqualified persons to appear before the Commissioner of Insolvency in country districts where there was not a sufficient number of qualified practitioners. These powers were never exercised. No objection was taken in England, but the clause was dropped out of the 1845 Act.

Both Acts contained a clause exempting notaries from the penalty for doing legal work, and also "persons acting only as Law-Stationers or as Clerks". Exactly what the word "clerk" might cover it is difficult to say.

The principal objection to the Act of 1843 was in respect of the second clause, which provided that if any admitted practitioner permitted an unqualified person to practise in his name, the practitioner should be struck off the roll and forever disabled from practice, and the Court could commit the unqualified person to the debtors' prison for any time not exceeding one year. This power of committing to prison in a summary way, without a trial, the Secretary of State said was "a needless and harsh encroachment on the general principle that no man is to be imprisoned by way of punishment except it be on the verdict of a jury". He also objected to the fourth section which empowered the Court to punish in a summary way any practitioner for any misconduct in any business in which he might have been engaged as a legal practitioner. "To this"—he said—"there are many obvious objections, and there is no very obvious argument in its favour." Both of these sections were omitted from the later Act.[9]

This 1844 painting of Port Lincoln by George French Angas suggests a settlement a long way from being able to support a "fully fledged" practitioner (SLSA)

The Acts also declared the power of the Supreme Court to tax practitioners' bills of costs, and provided that no action should be brought by a practitioner for his costs until after the expiration of one month from the delivery of a proper signed bill. An annual fee of £5 was imposed upon each practitioner.

The 1845 Act was concluded with a proviso that it should not be construed:

> '... so as to prevent the separation of the Practitioners of the Supreme Court into the two distinct classes of Barristers or Advocates, and Attorneys Solicitors and Proctors, when it shall seem to the said Court convenient that such separation should be made: And provided also that from and after such separation the term Practitioners in this Ordinance shall be deemed to include only persons acting as Attorneys Solicitors or Proctors'.

The division of the profession was a subject which had come up for discussion at a very early stage in the colony's legal history. There was no general rule in the colonies as to separation of barristers and solicitors; in some it existed, in others not.[10] In August 1841, a meeting of the profession presided over by the Advocate-General was held for the purpose of deciding:

> '... whether, from the advanced state of the colony and the great increase of legal business, it was not expedient to separate the practice of a barrister from that of a solicitor or attorney'.

A resolution in favour of dividing the profession was agreed to by sixteen out of twenty one lawyers present. Two would not vote and three dissented unless their right to appear in court as a barrister, though without any further fee, was reserved—a proviso which the majority considered improper. A committee waited on the Judge and recommended that the change should be made, and Messrs Smillie (Advocate-General), Mann, Fisher, Nicholls, George Morphett and Poulden expressed their determination to be barristers.[11] Nothing was ever done to carry out their recommendation, probably because the Judge felt that it would be idle to start a class of barristers in the province when there were only one or two members of the profession who really had been trained to that branch of the law. Until the arrival of G.M. Stephen from England in 1846, Jickling and Nicholls seem to have been the only English barristers in the colony.

The Act of 1845, however, clearly contemplated a division of the profession in the near future. That it was, in fact, to some extent so divided in operation may perhaps be inferred from a letter by Mr Nicholls which appeared in the *Southern Australian* in January 1845, indignantly protesting against having been described as a solicitor. He was, he said, a barrister of ten years' standing and had confined his practice to that branch of the profession so far as the circumstances of the province would admit.[12]

In the Legislative Council in June 1845 the Advocate-General said:

> 'A very general wish for such a division has been expressed by the members of the profession, one or two of whom only objected to it. The division of labour has been usually found a convenience, and has worked well in the legal profession, in particular.'

Mr Morphett thought that division was unnecessary in a small community. The Governor said it was not required immediately, although he hoped that before long it would be necessary.[13]

In 1849, however, the *Register* wrote:

> 'We believe there is but one gentleman here who strictly confines himself to the practice of a barrister, the profession not caring to act as counsel unless also employed as attorney, the brief fees not being near so profitable as the solicitor's pickings.'

The Judge, to discountenance this "twofold exercise of legal trading", refused to allow counsel fees to solicitors appearing as counsel in cases from their own office.

> 'In order to evade this rule of court, considering it fair that, if their clients wished them not only to act as counsel, but to prepare the pleadings, they ought to be paid for doing double duty, the old lawyers put their heads together (for in South Australia they are not allowed to wear wigs) and agreed to make use of dummies, or as His Honor has justly characterised them, "subterfuges", the practice now being for a less fortunate brother to lend his name as the 'attorney in the cause' to his more fortunate professional friend. By this arrangement, the barrister, who covertly brings the action, on taxation, not only pockets his own fees, but the nominal solicitor's also, although the whole business has been done in his own office.'

This scheme, which was strongly disapproved of by the Judge, was brought to light by a case in the Resident Magistrates Court. One lawyer, Mr Matthew Smith, had started an action in the name of another, Mr Wotherspoon, who was in fact a mere dummy. Mr Smith engaged a valuer to do work qualifying as a witness, but would not pay his fee. The costs were taxed in Wotherspoon's name, showed the amount of the valuer's bill as a disbursement, and this sum was recovered from the other side. The Sheriff paid the whole of the judgment and costs to Mr Smith, showing that he knew it was only a sham to have brought the action under Wotherspoon's name. The valuer now sued Mr Smith for his fee, but the very shabby defence was that he was not liable because he was not the solicitor on the record—he had only acted as counsel. This piece of sharp practice was upheld by the Magistrate on technical grounds, but the exposure of the system seems to have given it a death blow. It is not necessary to be so uncharitable as to assume that similar schemes were practised by all the members of the profession.[14]

The question of costs where the same person appeared as both attorney and counsel, or where one partner feed another as counsel, remained (and still remains) troublesome. In 1851 Mr Justice Cooper said that where a solicitor acted also as counsel, he did not think it necessary to have a brief prepared such as was used in England. Gentlemen were aware of the whole case because it went through their office. The Admiralty rule of practice forbade the same person to charge as advocate and proctor, and he thought that was a fair principle. "As for the charge 'attending counsel with brief', why should a gentleman charge for attending himself in his own office?"[15]

Mr Justice Crawford agreed, and added that he thought that counsel fees on nisi prius cases should be about £6 6s 0d for the first day and £2 2s 0d refreshers—figures which will not be read without a shudder by those lawyers who think that the importance of questions is in this ratio: "first, costs; second, pleadings; and third, very far behind, the merits of the case". (See per James LJ in *Hall v. Eve* 4 ChD 341)

From time to time the agitation for division of the profession was revived. In June 1865 the Attorney-General was asked in the Assembly whether he had considered the propriety of introducing a bill to define the position of barristers in the colony, and whether the Government intended doing so. He replied that the Government had no intention of introducing any bill on the subject, as they considered the position of barristers in the colony was sufficiently defined.[16]

Although in theory all members of the profession were alike, and all had the same rights and could perform the same duties, in fact the functions of barrister and solicitor always diverged to a considerable extent. The leading members of the bar almost of necessity had to limit themselves to forensic practice. Of course, a large nondescript class also existed of solicitors who went into court occasionally and succeeded in wasting the time of the court and the money of their clients.

The joinder of the two branches of the profession was anathema to Mr Justice Boothby. In 1864, in one of the numerous letters with which he bombarded the Colonial Office, he called attention to the provision in Ordinance No 6 of 1845 enabling the Court to separate the profession into two classes.[17]

> 'I submit'—he wrote—'that if attorneys are placed on the Bench of the Supreme Court, this power of separation conferred on the Judges of the Supreme Court will be indefinitely postponed, so continuing all the mischiefs which the union of the two offices in the same person necessarily create.'

The number of practitioners in the colony increased steadily. In 1844 there were twenty; in 1847, twenty four; and by 1866 the number had grown to sixty.[18] At first the Judge examined into the credentials and qualifications of any person applying for admission. For the first six or seven years all those admitted had previously been called to the bar or admitted as attorneys in Great Britain. After that the admissions were increasingly of men whose legal knowledge was based on private and undirected study in the colony, and on practical experience gained by clerkship. By Rules of Court made in February 1851, regulations were prescribed as to the service and knowledge required from articled clerks, and the Master of the Supreme Court and Messrs J.H. Fisher and Arthur Hardy were appointed examiners to inquire into the fitness of persons applying for admission.[19] Surprise had previously been expressed at the facility with which admission to the profession could be obtained in Adelaide.

'The mere production of a certificate of practice'—said the Register—'or of admission to the Inns of Court, is sufficient to

> entitle any legal gentleman to practice in colonial chambers, or to assume the functions of a full-blown barrister. No question is asked as to character, and the candidate's legal abilities are not subjected to any test or analysis. Some unprincipled practitioner, all but unknown in the colony, may readily acquire a licence which he may use as a means of victimising unsuspecting clients, or a status enabling him to plunder the public—a grossly unskilful or uncouth pleader may make his way to the Bar without the necessity of being called, as in England, to the exercise of that honourable profession—and an uncertificated bankrupt or a felonious absconder, who may touch upon our shores in his flight from justice, may make his nest in full feather, and crow self-applaudingly to the echo which shall applaud again, until the final accomplishment of another career of ingenious fraud, legal insincerity, or flagrant crime.' [20]

It must be admitted that from a very early date in the colony's history, a few scoundrels managed to make their way into the profession of the law; and very many more who had no conception of that profession in its true light, as a scholarly profession giving service to society. To a certain extent this was no doubt inevitable. With his usual good sense, Sir Walter Scott wrote:

> 'In a profession where unbounded trust is necessarily reposed, there is nothing surprising that fools should neglect it in their idleness, and tricksters abuse it in their knowledge. But'—he continued—'it is the more to the honour of those, and I will vouch for many, who with integrity, with skill and attention, walk honourably upright where there are so many pitfalls and stumbling-blocks for those of a different character. To such men their fellow-citizens may safely entrust the care of protecting their patrimonial rights, and this country the most sacred charge of her laws and privileges.'

More searching inquiry as to the character and suitability of applicants for admission to the profession was vitally necessary. The appointment of a board of examiners served to impose some barrier to indiscriminate admissions and, to borrow the words of Sir Redmond Barry in *In re Spensley* 1 WW and A'B (L) 173 at 183, it may be said to have:

> '... formed as near an approach to the establishment of a body of benchers as the circumstances of the country would admit of at the time the rules were framed, and was certainly a great advance on the system which previously existed, when the Judges alone were the persons to decide upon the legal

proficiency and social standing of candidates for admission to the bar'.

By 1865 Mr Harrison was able to write, in his usual vitriolic style:

> "In addition to the regular importation of English practitioners we have also colonial-fledged lawyers, and some specimens of this alarming race combine all the trickery of the colony with the least possible amount of the true spirit of English law. Our village is therefore inundated with two species—English and colonial—who nearly all combine to bleed their fellow colonists with a pertinacity worthy of a better cause.' [21]

The records of two efforts by the profession to form a law society or bar association survive. In 1843 a "South Australian Law Society" was in existence. It has already been mentioned in connection with transfer of the Supreme Court to Mr Solomon's theatre—a resolution being then passed by the society approving the theatre as suitable for a courthouse. Another resolution passed by the society was that:

> '... the Act of Council 6th Victoria No 12 is injurious in its tendency and has the effect of impeding if not of preventing the transfer of Real Property and imposes restrictions which so far as this meeting has the means of judging are unusual and undesirable'.

This resolution was forwarded to Governor Grey, and it bears an endorsement by him that he had seen Jickling (the chairman of the meeting) and pointed out to him that the resolution was informal and disrespectful, and that Mr Jickling had thereupon apologised for it.[22]

Whether or not this rebuff damped the ardour of the members of the society it is impossible to say, but no further trace of that body is to be found.

Mr Justice Crawford, on his arrival in Adelaide in June 1850, was tendered a professional breakfast, at which Mr Justice Cooper took the opportunity of urging the formation of a law society. He was supported by Fisher and Jickling and, after the Judges had retired, it was resolved that a law institute or society should be established. Smillie, Mann, Hanson, Gwynne, Maguire, Bartley and Parker were appointed as a committee to make the necessary preliminary arrangements.[23] "The great importance of the proposed institution must be apparent"—said the Register—"when we state that one of its objects will be the formation of a complete law library." [24]

Some weeks later a meeting of practitioners was held in Smillie's chambers to consider a set of rules which had been drawn up for the proposed society. There was general agreement that the subscription should be so moderate as not to deter any respectable practitioner from joining, but unanimity could not be arrived at as to the rules, which were referred back to the committee for revision. Nothing further seems to have been done for a year, when the proposal was revived. More than thirty members of the profession met at dinner and a new committee was appointed. Mann was elected president of the society. Members were to dine together on the first day of each term. Gwynne offered the use of his chambers for committee meetings, the committee consisting of Messrs Mann, Fisher, Parker, Gwynne, Worthington, Fenn and Smith, with Hardy as treasurer and Maguire as secretary. Admission fee was fixed at £1 1s 0d and the annual subscription at £2 2s 0d. Admission to the club was by election, and one practitioner, who attended the meeting uninvited, was thrown out.[25]

The formation of this "select law club" was generally approved. "It seems likely to be effectual"—said the *South Australian Gazette*—"not merely in weeding out the pettifoggers, but in securing to the public more protection against their rogueries." [26]

The bar should justify itself, the *Register* urged. "The companionship of a sickly sheep will infest a healthy flock; and to tolerate or countenance a dishonest lawyer will entail odium on every member of an honourable profession."

The profession ought to constitute itself a court of inquiry and if misconduct was proved the Judges should be called upon "to perform an act of salutary expurgation".[27]

One of the society's first acts was to caveat a candidate for admission to the bar, who had been guilty of discreditable conduct in England before coming to the colony. Gwynne and Fisher appeared on behalf of the society to oppose his admission and said that the society intended to make an effort to preserve the respectability of the profession.[28]

Apparently the enthusiasm with which the Law Society had been founded soon ebbed away, for in the *Register* of 31 January 1856 a correspondent writes recommending the revival of "an institution which has unfortunately ceased to exist—the Law Association".

> 'I am persuaded'—he said—'that this Society might be the means of effecting great good by collecting information on subjects connected with the law, and devising remedies suggested by the experience of the various members of the association; aided also by the liberal support of the Council in appropriating the annual tax upon solicitors to the formation of a law library, a high standard of learning might be maintained amongst us, which would, while liberalising the profession, tend greatly to the public advantage. Such an Association during the short time it existed, was also found to have a tendency to cement the connection which, for the general welfare, should always exist between the bench and the bar. The Association might become affiliated with the Law

> Amendment Society of London, and thus acquire a mass of information, and receive suggestions most useful for the amelioration of our legal institutions.'

There was little difference between the modern practitioner and those of the early days of the state. Then, as now, barristers were known "to wrest from reluctant juries triumphant verdicts of acquittal for their clients, even when those clients, as often happens, were clearly and unmistakeably innocent". Then, as now, there were the usual justified complaints of the law's expense, delays, inanities and inconsistencies. Forensic habits were of a not unfamiliar type. At the opening of the Civil Sessions in September 1842 Mr Justice Cooper expressed his hope that counsel would observe more decorum and not contradict one another so much, nor colloquise, as he was sorry to say had been the case the previous sessions.[29]

Conditions of practice were, of course, at first crude. Take, for instance, the following little anecdote from the *Southern Australian*:

> 'A dog having come into the Resident Magistrate's Court and created disturbance, the Clerk of the Court gave it a kick, as a broad hint for him to depart, but he would not go, and the proprietor seemed to be very much amused at the proceedings. The Magistrate having found out the latter said he would fine him 5/- for contempt of court. The owner alleged that the dog had made a noise only in consequence of the kick; but at this crisis, one of the learned counsel having his olfactory nerves rudely assaulted from something underneath the table, and having announced that interesting fact, the Magistrate made the rule absolute, two days being allowed the dog's master to pay the fine.' [30]

The Supreme Court did not sit very frequently but it made up for this by sitting long and late. When Mr Justice Cooper arrived in the colony, the time for commencing the day's proceedings was 9.30 am. He continued this practice for some years.

> 'I thought'—he said—'in this climate, where people can, if they please, assemble at an earlier hour, that such was not an unreasonable time to fix for the commencement of the business.' [31]

Somewhere about 1850 the starting time seems to have been delayed until ten o'clock. In civil cases, the Court usually adjourned late in the afternoon, but in criminal cases it often sat on into the night. In a case in 1848, for instance, the *Register* records: "It being now ten o'clock the Judge asked the Jury whether they would like him to sum up then or in the morning."

The jury elected to proceed, and a verdict was returned at midnight. In criminal cases, too, the Court sat on without any adjournment for refreshments. There was no need for the jury to adjourn to a tavern, said Mr Justice Cooper; they could bring something with them. Similarly, Mr Justice Crawford used to tell jurors who felt inconvenienced by long fasting to bring some sandwiches with them, and munch them as the case proceeded.[32]

On the civil side it was customary to adjourn for half an hour for lunch, but apparently counsel could not always rely upon this. In a case in 1845, for instance:

> 'It being now 3 o'clock, Mr Fisher applied for the usual adjournment for lunch, which His Honor refused, but ordered in some refreshment for himself, which he ate on the bench, being anxious to proceed with the evidence of the next witness.' [33]

During the first decade, the most prominent members of the profession were Mann, Jickling, Fisher, Stephen, Bartley and Poulden. Most of the lawyers congregated in Stephens Place and Gawler Place and, when the courthouse was at Whitmore Square, generally rode to and fro on horseback.[34]

Mr Fisher seems to have carried into practice the same hair-splitting methods which distinguished him elsewhere. A prisoner was charged with stealing a tether-rope from a policeman. Mr Fisher, who represented him, objected to the form of the indictment. The word "tether", he said, was a substantive, not an adjective, and one tether-rope was therefore incorrect. A tether was the thing itself, and there was no such word as "tether-rope". "It appears to me"—said the Judge—"it would be difficult to describe this rope more properly. The meaning of the word 'tether-rope' is a rope to tether." [35]

Mr Fisher, however, was responsible for one witticism. He was addressing the Judge in a case involving a dispute between landlord and tenant, when a nail in the bench on which counsel sat caught his gown and tore it. He complained that on a previous occasion his trousers had been caught on the nail and torn. "They are rents in a rear," said the Judge. "Yes," replied Fisher, amid laughter, "and a distress to me." [36]

G.M. Stephen's return to South Australia in 1846 distinctly enlivened the bar. His conduct towards the Judge was denounced as "ill-bred, vulgar, and insolent",[37] but in spite (or perhaps because) of this he quickly acquired a considerable practice, especially in the Criminal Court. Being thrown out of a dogcart laid him up for some time, but in March 1850 the *Register* reported that Stephen had returned:

> '... to his wonted avocations at the criminal bar of which he is certainly the Clarkson or Adolphus of South Australia. The thieving fraternity have now " good time coming", for if anybody in the colony can get them off, 'twill be he.' [38]

At that sessions he was employed in nineteen cases, and in thirteen of them managed to secure an acquittal or a reduction of the charge to a simple offence. He was apparently more fortunate than Mr Walker (the gatecrasher who had been thrown out of the Law Society), for Mr Walker sued for damages for libel for a paragraph published in the daily press, reading as follows:

> 'It is said that the friends of some of the lately convicted criminals who had been defended by Mr Walker, were so exasperated at the lame manner in which those defences were conducted, that they summarily smashed every pane of glass in that gentleman's house.'[39]

He obtained a verdict, with one shilling damages.

Stephen was also the plaintiff in two libel actions against his old enemy Stevenson. In the first of these, bitter personalities were raked up and Stevenson, who conducted his own case, alleged that Stephen's methods of practice were condemned by all the responsible members of the profession. Stephen indignantly denied this, and made the astounding statement:

> 'To show the confidence entertained by the profession in my probity, many practitioners employ me to draw up pleadings in cases in which they know I am engaged in opposition to them.'

His years in the colony, he pathetically told the jury, had been years of unremitting labour, relieved only by the endearments of his home and the society of his children. The jury remained adamant and returned a verdict for the defendant.

In the second case, Stephen's complaint was that he had been called a "pettifogger", and Stevenson, not inappropriately, engaged Mr Fisher to explain what "pettifogger" meant. It was not, said Mr Fisher, as the plaintiff alleged, "a low and disreputable practitioner". "It was derived from the French words 'petit voguer'—a seeker of small cases, and it could not be applied to a barrister of the Supreme Court." The jury returned a verdict for the plaintiff, with one farthing damages.[40]

Perhaps disappointed with this fruitless litigation, Stephen turned his attention to other fields, and in December 1851 he wrote excitedly to the Governor to announce that he had obtained information, "from a certain party who is moving in a respectable sphere of life", of the existence of two, if not three, goldfields. They would sacrifice their private interests to those of the colony, and disclose the existence of these fields of untold wealth, upon condition that the discoverer should be appointed inspector of gold licences, with an adequate salary, and should be allowed the first ten licences.

> 'For myself I intended to solicit the appointment of Commissioner of granting licenses, as created in the adjoining colonies. But I am quite contented to let Your Excellency

> decide whether my self denial and services to the public can in any other way be rewarded, or more beneficially employed in the Public Service.'

He wound up with the "gratifying intelligence" that he also had in his possession samples of "coal of great purity found in the colony".[41] The Governor refused these public-spirited proposals. Shortly afterwards Stephen departed for Victoria.

In May 1849 Mr H.W. Parker arrived in the colony. It will be remembered that Mr Parker was the gentleman first selected for the position of Judge and that he resigned, with gloomy predictions of strife in the colony. "Who does not feel some satisfaction at the fulfilment of a foreboding, even when it is a mournful one?" asked Goethe; "all presentiments, when confirmed by the event, give a man a higher opinion of himself." Mr Parker's success as a prophet may perhaps be considered too remote an influence, but he certainly came to the colony imbued with a strong sensibility of his own importance. He at once began to criticise, and to inform the Judge and the profession generally how things were managed in England.

> 'The learned gentleman takes great pleasure'—said the Advocate-General in 1849, in a case in which Parker was opposed to him—'in referring to his recent English experience; but, before long, he will find that many things that go smoothly in England, do not work well here.' [42]

In the following month Mr Justice Cooper became so annoyed by Mr Parker's bumptious conduct when addressing him that he told him to sit down, or he would be made to do so. "I am sure"—Mr Parker blandly announced to the Court—"that all must regret such an undignified exhibition of irritability on the Bench."

A few rude remarks having been exchanged, Mr Parker claimed that the Judge was treating him disrespectfully. The Judge retorted:

> "As for your experience, Sir, I really know nothing of it. I think I do remember you were called to the Bar before I left England, and I have heard nothing of your standing, which may be high, or your experience, which may be great. But as you have only recently been admitted here, of course you are a junior counsel.'

Mr Parker was not to be put down, and replied with a clever piece of insolence:

> 'Your Honour might remember that I was with you for some years in the Court of Queen's Bench. I then reported the proceedings of that Court and of course knew you were in practice, but I never had the pleasure of hearing your Honour address the Court.'

The Judge had apparently been touched upon a vulnerable point and he flared up at once:

> 'What do you mean by that observation? I will not allow you to address me in that manner. Let it be understood that in future you will conduct yourself with proper courtesy towards me.' [43]

Mr Parker soon settled down to local ways, and was for many years a leading member of the bar. In England he had been for some years an assistant Poor Law Commissioner, and just before leaving for Australia had published "an exhaustive and very valuable work"—*A digest of the Law relating to the Relief of the Poor.*[44] He came to Adelaide primarily not as a lawyer but as director and local manager of the "Adelaide City and Port Railway Company", which had been formed in England with the intention of building and operating the first railway in South Australia. Mr Parker claimed to have had great experience in railway matters. "I have been before Select Committees of the House of Commons"—he said—"and for 5 years of my life I travelled 200 miles a day on railways." [45]

Adelaide's first reservoir at Thorndon Park was completed in 1860. The photograph is of the reservoir in 1875. (SLSA)

An Act was passed by the Legislative Council (No 1 of 1850) authorising the company to construct the proposed railway, but the plan fell through, and Mr Parker, after dabbling in schemes for building a reservoir to supply Adelaide with water, and a railway from Melbourne to Geelong, resigned himself to the practice of the law.

In 1855 he had an unpleasant experience. After a dispute with his managing clerk as to moneys alleged to have been received and not accounted for, Parker charged him with stealing some £200. The clerk was tried, acquitted and sued for £4,000 damages for malicious prosecution. He was non-suited, the non-suit was set aside by the Full Court, and on the second hearing he obtained a verdict for £500 damages.[46]

During the period 1850 to 1860 the ascendancy at the bar was gained by Mr Hanson and Mr Gwynne, their nearest competitors being Mr Fenn, Mr Bakewell, Mr Parker and Mr Belt, and the next few years saw the rapid rise of two able young men—J.P. Boucaut and Randolph Stow.

On the whole, however, the bar of South Australia was not remarkable for brilliance. It seldom, if ever, said the *Register*, displayed "that shining eloquence which haloes justice and makes vice detestable".[47] While popular distrust of the legal profession was not carried to the point of prohibiting lawyers from practising, as was done in some of the early American colonies (see 24 California Law Review p.11), "the tribe", as they were often called, were continually subjected to vociferous belittlement. Their general opposition to the Real Property Act undoubtedly gave rise to very genuine feelings of hostility. In 1869 Mr Bagot optimistically said:

> 'Since 1858 there has been a down upon lawyers, but they have been able to outlive a great deal of it, and they will go on being fairly paid till the end of time.' [48]

Mr Harrison's pen was moved to its most facetious efforts when he considered the lawyers of South Australia. The celebrated firms of Quirk Gammon and Snap, and Dodson and Fogg had branch establishments in the colony, he said; and there were numerous descendants, too, of that old-established firm I. Catchem and U. Cheatem.

Quirk Gammon and Snap The firm of "Quirk Gammon and Snap" was a creation of the political economist Henry George (1839-1897) used in his 1877 *Progress and Poverty* as an example of an unscrupulous law firm.

> 'I. Catchem's talents were of that description that are sure to lead to some solid advantages in a colony where trickery, subserviency, shrewdness, pretence, and unscrupulousness have always asserted their prerogatives, and been the foundation of success in the legal profession ... Cheatem had long embraced the principles of total abstinence from all intoxicating liquors, being moved thereto by the great expense and deleterious quality of the compounds sold in the colony, and also by the conviction that weak tea was more conducive to the clearness of his intellect, the exercise of his legal acumen, and extending a bill of costs to the extreme limit that human ingenuity can make verbiage to be paid for. Cheatem devoted all the energies of his mighty mind to law; general literature he knew nothing of, evidently considering it a trivial mode of spending time, which could be much more profitably employed by studying the nature of legal impositions. The only relaxation he allowed himself from severer studies was looking up law points, to see with what ingenuity common sense can be distorted by those who are paid for the purpose, and Harrison's Digest, with its hundred thousand precedents on small points,

> was his favourite compilation; and nothing delighted him so much as to see with what exceeding nicety a hair can be split by scientific authorities, or to see what Judge Browbeat decided some sixty years ago.' [49]

Edward Klingender ca. 1865 (SLSA)

With regard to legal costume, barristers and judges appear to have worn at first a gown, but no wig. The earliest reference upon this topic which has been found is contained in a letter written by Mr Edward Klingender (an Adelaide solicitor) in May 1844, in which (referring to E.C. Gwynne) he said:

> 'Mr Gwynne made his first appearance in a gown on Wednesday, and I need hardly say obtained a verdict for his fortunate client, for if he could not get a verdict I should like to see the fellow that could.' [50]

It is not clear whether this relates to Gwynne's first appearance in court as a barrister or literally to his first appearance in a gown—probably the latter, for he had then been in practice for several years.

In May 1846 there was a stir in legal circles when two newly arrived barristers, Messrs Wilkin and G.M. Stephen:

> '... appeared in the full costume of the London Bar, including the wig, which, though it certainly reminds us of the Courts at home, being dispensed with by His Honor and the Colonial Bar, it is hardly perhaps in the best of taste to wear'.

Wigs, it appears, were not entirely unknown in South Australia, but had been worn on very rare and special occasions only. The Judge took no notice of the wigs until, some months later, Mr Nicholls also appeared in one. Mr Justice Cooper then inquired whether he wore the wig supposing it to be a necessary part of his costume as a barrister. Mr Nicholls said he had worn it as a mark of respect. The Judge remarked that members of the English bar were admitted in South Australia as general practitioners and he did not think it was fair to the other lawyers in Adelaide who could not obtain wigs to make an invidious distinction.

> 'As long as only one gentleman thought fit to make himself ridiculous by dressing in that which was not the costume of the Court, I did not say anything about it, but when I find others following his example, I think it necessary to do so.'

Mr Nicholls disclaimed any intention of giving offence. He said he had not worn a wig when there was little business in the Supreme Court, but matters were now changed and he thought a wig would be appropriate.

G.M. Stephen then interposed and said that when he had first appeared in a wig and saw the Judge without one, he felt uncomfortable, knowing that his own appearance was in consequence peculiar. In England, however, he would not have been permitted to plead without a wig, and the omission to wear it might have been construed as a mark of disrespect for the judge here. Sooner than appear guilty of disrespectful conduct, he said with his usual flamboyancy, he would tear off his wig and throw it on the floor. The Judge dryly said it was not necessary for him to do that. He had used the word "ridiculous" because Stephen had been in the colony before and must have known that the wig was dispensed with. The use of the wig, too, was not consistent with the climate of South Australia.

> 'If indeed anybody is justified in wearing a wig'—he said rather ruefully—'it is myself; for in summer time I am tormented with the flies settling on my bare head. But I fear that if I were to adopt it, I should be still more fatigued than I am already by the long sittings which I have frequently to endure. At the same time, I do not say that I may not make a change in the costume of the Court, and adopt that to which I had long been accustomed in England, when we have a more convenient Court-house, should the contemplated division be made in the profession, and should gentlemen be able to procure wigs.'

In Sydney, he added, wigs were worn, but nearly all the barristers there had brought their wigs with them from England. It was impossible for wigs to be obtained in Australia.

> 'As regards respect to the Court, there is an established dress worn both by me and all the gentlemen of the Bar, which everyone can procure—a black gown, white neckcloth, and white bands.'

Messrs Stephen and Nicholls then retired, and: "... in a few minutes returned with no other head-dress than that for which they are respectively indebted to nature". [51]

The "Battle of the Wigs" was a nine-days wonder in Adelaide, and there were not a few who agreed with Jefferson: "For Heaven's sake, discard the monstrous wig which makes the English Judges look like rats peeping through bunches of oakum."

Oakum
Oakum is old rope that has been picked apart to be used for caulking in boat repair.

The Rules of Court made by Mr Justice Cooper in 1850 prescribe the barrister's costume as follows: "The costume of the gentlemen attending the Court as Barristers shall be as heretofore—a black cloth (sic - ? coat) and waistcoat, a white neck-cloth, and banns (sic)."

The rule is reminiscent of the ambiguous chapter heading to one of the letters in P.G. Hamerton's *The Intellectual Life*—"To a Young Man who had firmly resolved never to wear anything but a grey coat". As "Q" has remarked, Mr Hamerton could hardly have meant that. Similarly Mr Justice Cooper can hardly have meant that the rule should be strictly complied with. It remains the only written rule regulating the barrister's costume in South Australia, although the wearing of the ridiculous wig has become obligatory by custom.

The Judges first began to wear wigs when Mr Justice Crawford arrived, and continued to do so thereafter. In hot weather Mr Justice Gwynne would sometimes discard both wig and gown. The profession, or some of them, "hungered for horsehair", and in the *Register* of 14 March 1877 the following note appears:

> 'The growing tendency of the present age is to discard useless forms and customs, that have either little significance or have lost that which they once possessed; but a move in a contrary direction has been made by their Honors the Judges, who recently issued a request that in future legal gentlemen when practising in the Supreme Court would wear wigs. In accordance with this intimation, several of the lawyers engaged at the Criminal Sittings on Tuesday morning appeared in these sometimes becoming but rather uncomfortable coverings.'

The innovation gave rise to varied comment. The wig, said one journal, was a very gentlemanlike institution. "Now that the Old World is getting Radical, and disrespectful things are being said about the wig, it is refreshing to find South Australia is becoming conservative." [52]

On the other hand, the *Australasian* was very cynical about it:

> 'We may assume that up to this time the practitioners of this Court have been so insensible of the dignity of their profession as to omit the use of so essential a portion of forensic costume. To any correctly regulated mind such a disclosure is painful in the last degree. It comes to us like one of those appalling social revelations which at times show us how much of benighted ignorance and primitive savagery still lurk in the fabric of civilized society. Here, in the nineteenth century, in a British colony, is a Supreme Court which has gone on for years administering justice founded on the arguments and contentions and cited cases of wigless counsel. The fact comes to us with the effect of a mental earthquake, and renders our most fixed ideas and venerated traditions insecure. Of course we are aware that on occasions of great emergency, such as days of intense and overpowering heat, our own Judges have graciously given permission to counsel to lay aside for a short time the head covering of horsehair which gives dignity to their aspect, but it was always felt that the concession was a perilous one, and that it savoured of tampering with the springs of justice. Possibly it was only granted from the Court being able to see its way to validating and confirming in a later

sitting any decisions which might be regarded as vitiated from the absence of an essential requirement. Between such a state of things and the wretched demoralising spectacle of a Court where wigs were unknown it is evident there is an awful chasm. What makes the Adelaide case the more insidious and dangerous is the fact that as far as is known it does not appear that the administration of justice was rendered in any way less satisfactory by the miserable, we may say indecent, condition in which counsel appeared in Court.' [53]

Mr Ebenezer Ward, a politician whose exploits with bailiffs form the subject of an amusing libel action reported in the early South Australian Law Reports, started a campaign in 1889 to do away with lawyers' wigs, but he only evoked merriment. One poet twitted him:

'Oust the gown and hirsute gearing!
Ebenezer, you are daft!
You would break the cherished idols
Of the learned legal craft.

Ebenezer, old traditions
Must be followed by the law;
Sticklers are they for old usage,
All those men of tireless jaw'. [54]

Ebenezer Ward (1837-1917)
A sometime adulterer and bankrupt, Ward was also a politician whose parliamentary career stretched from 1870 to 1900. Even longer was his involvement with newspapers. At age twelve he started as a proofreaders' boy and was involved with papers as a journalist, editor and proprietor for the rest of his life. (SLSA)

The Judges appear to have restricted themselves to black gowns until Sir Samuel Way introduced a change in July 1877, when the *Register* wrote:

'The forms of the judicial tribunals of the mother-country are being gradually introduced into the Courts of this colony. The latest innovation on previous practice is the wearing of time-honoured distinctive costumes by some of the Judges. The Chief Justice, in presiding at the trial of the libel case in the Supreme Court, appeared in the scarlet robes trimmed with ermine which had been for centuries the dress worn by Judges when presiding in Criminal Sessions. Without wishing to be personal we cannot refrain from saying that they were very becoming to his Honor.' [55]

In 1849 there was talk in the colonies of colonial Judges being addressed as "My Lord", and Mr James inquired of Mann, the Acting Judge, in what way he would wish the bar to address him—as "Your Worship, Your Honor, or Your Lordship?" Mann laughed and said he preferred the old style of "Your Honor".[56]

King's Counsel were first appointed in the colony in 1865. They had been appointed in Victoria two years earlier by Mr Higinbotham, who was then Attorney-General, thinking that the appointments would be beneficial to the bar by bringing it into closer correspondence with the state of the profession at home; although he issued a warning that if Queen's Counsel were introduced they must exist in reality as well as in name and accept all the conditions which applied in England by professional usage forbidding them to do the work of the junior bar.[57]

The regulations drawn up in Victoria to govern the office were copied in South Australia. They provided:

'1. No barrister shall be appointed Her Majesty's Counsel except on the recommendation of the Chief Justice to the Governor.
2. On every such appointment a fee of three guineas shall be paid for the patent at the office of the Chief Secretary.
3. For every licence to appear against the Crown in cases in which the services of any of Her Majesty's Counsel may be dispensed with, a fee of one guinea shall be paid at the same time.' [58]

Messrs Randolph Stow, R.B. Andrews and W.A. Wearing were the first Queen's Council, and their appointment came as a surprise to the public. "What are QCs for?—and why are three of these dignitaries appointed at the present moment? are questions which the public ask and which nobody answers." It was said to be anomalous where there was no division of the profession; if the new appointments were a step towards that division, then there was some meaning in them, although it would be putting the cart before the horse.[59]

Mr Justice Boothby, of course, was opposed to the appointments. In his disjointed schedule of 93 topics, one complaint read:

> 'The rank of Queen's Counsel, created by His Excellency, without any warrant in law that I am acquainted with, or communication to, or any knowledge by me until I saw by an announcement in the 'Government Gazette' that three practitioners of the Court had, on recommendation of the Chief Justice, been appointed Queen's Counsel. The union of the office of Queen's Counsel with that of a practising attorney has, I apprehend, never before been known of in any Court of Her Majesty, where only the law and practice of the Superior Courts of Her Majesty at Westminster is administered.' [60]

Hon J. Baker brought the matter forward in the Legislative Council, wanting to know by whose authority the appointments had been made.

> 'The subject'—he said—'involves important questions in reference to the Supreme Court, which sooner or later must be taken into consideration by the Parliament. In every part of the British dominions barristers are distinguished from attorneys, and I do not see why the same distinction should not be made here. The time will soon arise when this distinction must be

> made here, as has been done in the other Australian colonies, and I therefore maintain that the appointment as Queen's Counsel of Attorneys will lead to serious difficulties. There will be very little inducement to persons educating their sons to the profession of law if on their attaining to the position of barristers they are to be set aside by the appointment of attorneys as Queen's Counsel. It is true that in this colony we have appointed attorneys as Judges of the Supreme Court; but this is no reason why such a state of things should be continued, or why we should not look forward to the time when there will be a proper distinction made in regard to the members of the legal profession. Any one who has read the discussions upon the subject which have taken place in the mother country will see the importance which attaches to it, and the necessity that a distinction in the members of the legal profession should be recognised in this colony.'

The Chief Secretary replied that the Governor had power to make the appointments.

> 'Queen's Counsel'—he said—'possess no peculiar advantages over other members of the Bar. They are simply retained to defend the Government. It is true that they thereby acquire a certain status.' [61]

Shortly after the founding of the colony, Governor Hindmarsh began to appoint solicitors to be notaries public. In August 1835 notice was given that:

> '... in appointing persons to be Notaries Public, who have grounded their applications to be admitted to practice as such upon the claim that they have acted in that capacity in Great Britain, His Excellency must reserve to himself the power of cancelling any such appointments in cases in which great misconduct shall subsequently distinctly appear to have accompanied the exercise of that office in the Mother Country.' [62]

In 1841 Mr William James arrived in the colony. Previous to leaving England, he said, he applied to the Faculty Office at Doctors Common for a faculty as a notary. He was informed that no persons, unless they were possessed of authority from that office, were competent to act as notaries public in South Australia when a functionary who was so provided was practising there. Sir John Campbell, the Attorney-General, was said to have given an opinion to this effect. To avoid incurring any expense which might prove useless, Mr James applied to Lord John Russell for confirmation of the opinion. After a considerable delay he received a reply that the application not having been made to him by the Governor of South Australia, the Secretary of State should decline giving an answer to the question. "The cautious tone" of this reply induced Mr James to believe the information he had received was correct, and he spent £50 in procuring the faculty. But when he reached the colony he found a dozen or more notaries in Adelaide. He complained that all these persons had been illegally appointed, but his complaints were unsympathetically received by the Governor.[63] The Advocate-General advised that the Governor had power to appoint notaries, and that notaries admitted under the English Acts had no exclusive right to practise in the colonies and no right to object to other qualified individuals acting as notaries there.

> 'It appears to me'—wrote the Colonial Secretary (Gouger)—'that if anybody has power to appoint Notaries Public in Colonies, it is the Governor, especially as he represents in many cases the Royal Prerogative.'

The Judge was consulted and agreed that the local notaries were not illegally appointed.

> 'I cannot enter'—he said—"into all the mysteries of the power which lies in Governors to make Notaries Public, but it appears to me to be convenient and is certainly practised in some colonies." [64]

To the mortification of Mr James, notaries therefore continued to be appointed in the colony without question until Governor Young in 1850 questioned the legality of this procedure. The law officers then reported:

> 'It has been customary for the Governor of the Colony to appoint Notaries Public. It is conceived that this is the general practice in the Colonies and that this practice is based upon the Governor's right to exercise the ordinary prerogatives of the Crown. There can be no doubt that every notarial act of a Notary Public so appointed would be recognised in the Courts of this Province, and most probably elsewhere, although no decision on this head appears as yet to have been made, the point having never been judicially raised.'

The Governor had a discretion in making appointments, and there was no right to appointment incident on admission to practice as a barrister and attorney of the Supreme Court.[65] This satisfied Sir Henry Young, but his successor Sir Richard MacDonnell refused to make any appointments, considering he had no power to do so. An Act was accordingly introduced and passed (No 14 of 1859) legalising all former appointments by previous Governors and providing that applications to be admitted to practice as a notary should in future be made to the Supreme Court.

In the same year another act was passed providing for the appointment of commissioners for taking affidavits and for the administration of oaths. It was agreed that the oath was usually administered in an unbecoming manner; the only portion which could be heard was, "So help you God, where's the shilling?"[66]

Finally, a few words may be added upon the subject of law reports, without which there could be small hope of any distinctive local developments in the law.

> 'While former decisions rest only on the memory of the Judge, overburthened in the term, and perplexed with a multiplicity of causes; or in the memory of counsel frequently under powerful bias, in the recollection and statement, little assistance in establishing uniform principles can be expected from precedents.' [67]

Apart from the newspapers, there were no reports at all in the colony until 1867. Reporters must depend upon the profession for subscription and support and, with a very small number of practitioners, publication of reports could only take place at a prohibitive cost. In June 1865, Mr Boucaut moved in the Assembly for a grant of an amount not exceeding £150 for the purpose of procuring the publication of reports of the cases heard and determined by the Judges of the Supreme Court. The Attorney-General said the Government would support the motion, for the publication of reports would be of advantage to the profession, the magistracy and the public.[68] Mr L.J. Pelham, the Judges' associate, was appointed to prepare and revise the reports, at a remuneration of £1 per week, and the first volume of South Australian Reports (now generally known by his name, or as Volume 0) appeared in 1867.[69] The series of South Australian Law Reports began shortly afterwards, the volumes being edited by various practitioners. An ambitious attempt in 1884 to establish a "South Australian Law Journal" failed after publication of one number.

John Michael Crossland's *Portrait of Nannultera, a Young Poonindie Cricketer* 1854. Poonindie was a mission established in 1850 near Port Lincoln to convert Aboriginals away from "barbarism" and toward a Christian European life. The portrait was painted as "proof" of the success of the mission and the "progress" of the Aboriginals. The view of successful assimilation conveyed by the painting was, of course, belied by the reality of Aboriginal contact with Europeans. Indeed, Poonindie's Aboriginals suffered a very high mortality rate through the 1850s. (NLA)

Chapter 11

The Aborigines and the Law

'bone of your bone'

One of the numerous deficiencies of the Foundation Act was its failure to make any provisions for the Aborigines. The preamble having gloomily recited that the proposed province consisted of "waste and unoccupied lands which are supposed to be fit for the purposes of colonization", the Act went on to declare that the whole of the land should be open to purchase by British subjects.

After the Act was passed, however, the Colonial Office (according to Brown, in order "to satisfy the Saints in the House of Commons") decided that they could not authorise the continuance of the colonisation scheme unless some satisfactory arrangements were made for the protection of the natives. Lord Glenelg therefore proposed that the settlers should occupy only a small district, which was not already in the occupation of the natives. The colonists were up in arms at once. Robert Thomas wrote to Lord Glenelg accusing him of having thrown "a causeless impediment" in their way, "thereby constraining their energies and disappointing their most sanguine views and expectations". It was well known, he said, that the natives wandered from place to place without any fixed location, and these wandering propensities of the Aboriginal tribes were a sufficient reason:

> '... why the millions of fertile acres over which they tread, like the beasts of the earth, unconscious of their value and ignorant of their use, may be taken possession of by a colony of civilized people, without doing them the smallest injury ... I confess myself at a loss to comprehend how a few strolling savages, entirely ignorant of the arts of civilized life, and not only without the means, but absolutely averse to cultivating the land, and who, if they may be said to possess a small portion of it today by erecting their crude huts, will abandon it tomorrow, can be called its actual proprietors, or what wrong it can do them if others till that which they know not the use of'.[1]

John Brown wrote indignantly in his journal:

> 'That measures should be devised and enforced for their protection and civilization as far as possible is not only just and humane, but politic; but that a legislature should authorize the sale of land and the formation of a colony in a part expressly declared by them for the purpose, and then as soon as people have embarked their money and spent their time on such an assurance, suddenly find out that there are natives and native rights which they ought to have first enquired about is beginning at the wrong end, and, if just to the Aborigines, is

> unjust to the Colonists. At least, this ought to have been foreseen and prepared for, and we not delayed by their oversight.' [2]

And in another entry he has some sensible and pointed remarks:

> 'What is to be the interpretation of the word 'occupy' is the question. The Act itself declares the ground to be waste and unoccupied, and this question, if raised at all, ought to have raised before it was past (Sic). But it is not occupied according to any law regulating possession which is recognized by civilized people. I believe it is now only started to record by correspondence the opinion of Government upon a point which they may think will be hereafter moted by the Quakers or others upon the grounds of supposed Humanity and Abstract Rights. I say the supposed Humanity for the idea of buying the land by a few hatchets or old clothes, may be a purchase in one sense, but is decidedly a Jew's bargain. The mind it can reconcile must be as blunt to the real feeling of strict honesty as it is squeamish upon Humanity. Because a Native is ignorant of its value it is no excuse for a false price. If you buy at all, it is quite clear the seller ought to have what is given for it; and this with us is easily ascertained viz 12/- per acre.' [3]

A compromise was reached by which the Commissioners undertook that all native rights should be respected and that a protector of the Aborigines should be appointed.

Alexander Schramm's *Civilisation versus Nature* ca. 1859. (NLA)

The views of the Commissioners were set out in their first report (1836). The due observance of justice to the natives and the preservation of native rights, they said, could not but be regarded as of the first importance in the formation of the new settlement. The natives should be guarded against personal violence and outrage, they should be protected in the undisturbed enjoyment of their proprietary right to the soil wherever such right might be found to exist, and it should be an invariable and cardinal condition in all bargains and treaties made with the natives for the cession of lands possessed by them that a permanent subsistence should be supplied to them from some other source. Many of the native tribes had been exposed to injustice and cruelty in their previous intercourse with Europeans.

> 'The Colonization of South Australia by industrious and virtuous settlers, so far from being an invasion of the rights of the Aborigines, is a necessary preliminary to the displacement of the lawless squatters, the abandoned sailors, the runaway convicts, the pirates, the worse than savages that now infest the coasts and islands along that extensive portion of New Holland, and perpetrate against the defenceless natives crimes at which humanity revolts.'

No portion of the land of the province was to be offered for sale until it had been ascertained by the Protector of the Aborigines whether it was occupied or enjoyed by the natives; if so, it must first be acquired by surrender or cession from its native proprietors. The Protector's duty was to see that all bargains or treaties made with the natives were faithfully executed, and to call upon the executive government of the colony to protect the Aborigines in the undisturbed enjoyment of the lands which they were not disposed to transfer to the settlers.

Cessions of territory by natives were not only to be voluntary but involved a stipulation that the natives should be permanently supplied with subsistence and with moral and religious instruction. To create a permanent fund for this purpose it was proposed that lands ceded by the natives to the Colonisation Commissioners should be sold under the condition that for every 80 acres conveyed the party to whom the conveyance was made should pay for four-fifths, or 64 acres only, the conveyance being subject to a stipulation that at the expiration of a term of years the lands so conveyed should be divided into five equal parts. One of these parts would be resumed as a reserve for the use of the Aborigines; the remainder would remain with the proprietor as his freehold. In determining which of the five parts should be resumed, the proprietor was allowed first choice of two of the five parts and the Protector was then to select the reserve out of the remaining three parts. By this ingenious arrangement, the proprietor would get the gratuitous use of 16 acres for a term of years sufficient to yield him a remuneration for clearing and improving and, as he would be doubtful which parts he would ultimately get, he would have to distribute a certain amount of labour upon each of the last three blocks. The reserves would then be worth considerably more than their unimproved value and could be used as a fund for the benefit of the Aboriginals.

> 'Thus conducted, the colonisation of Southern Australia will be an advent of mercy to the native tribes. They are now exposed to every species of outrage, and treated like cattle of the field; they will in future be placed under the protection of British laws, and invested with the rights of British Subjects.'

Following up this plan, the Commissioners directed Colonel Light that in surveying land he was to use the utmost caution to prevent collisions with the natives.

> 'You will consider the wild animals as the property of the natives, of whom any which may be desired as food should be purchased. You will therefore discourage sporting and in inhabited districts prevent it altogether.' [4]

The Commissioners' schemes as to the purchase of land from the natives were never put into force, and thus perhaps a legal difficulty was avoided which might have otherwise arisen, namely whether the Commissioners had any powers under the Foundation Act to promulgate such a plan. The Act did not recognise the existence of Aborigines. It empowered the Commissioners to declare that all the land of the province was public land open to purchase by British subjects, and provided that the lands must be sold for ready money. Nowhere did it give the Commissioners any right to reserve part of the land for the benefit of the natives. George Fife Angas, giving evidence before the House of Commons Committee in 1841, contended that the setting aside by Governor Gawler of Aboriginal reserves at Adelaide and at Encounter Bay was illegal and that the natives could not purchase or hold lands. He urged that the natives should be acknowledged and naturalised as British subjects and should have the power of buying and selling land. Additional laws should be made for them. "A valuable code of laws" for the natives, drawn up by Mr Standish Motte, a barrister of the Middle Temple, was placed before the Committee but unfortunately was not printed.[5]

Correspondence later took place between a number of colonists who held preliminary land orders, and Captain Sturt, the Assistant Commissioner, about the withdrawal of certain sections of land in favour of the Aborigines. Sturt's reply was that prior to the landing of the colonists the Aborigines possessed "well understood and distinctly defined proprietary rights over the whole of the available lands in the province" and that their rights must be respected. Apparently this was considered to be sufficiently secured by reserving a few sections for them. No person was sufficiently interested or litigious to challenge in the courts the legality of the reservations.[6]

Intending colonists were assured, before leaving England, that the protection of their lives and property had not been overlooked.

> 'No danger is to be apprehended from the natives'—it was stated in the first number of the Register—'for it is well ascertained that they are a tractable and inoffensive race when treated with kindness. Pains have already been taken to establish a friendly intercourse with them, and they will be treated in every respect with forbearance and consideration.'

Rapid Bay, encampment of Yankalilla blacks by George French Angas ca. 1840s (NLA)

Governor Hindmarsh had particular instructions from the Colonial Office that he was to give proper protection also to the natives, and one of his first steps was to issue a proclamation apprising the colonists of his resolution:

> '... to take every lawful means of extending the same protection to the Native Population as to the rest of His Majesty's subjects, and of my firm determination to punish with exemplary severity all acts of violence or injustice which may in any manner be practised or attempted against the natives, who are to be considered as much under the safeguard of the law as the Colonists themselves and equally entitled to the privileges of British subjects. I trust therefore with confidence to the exercise of moderation and forbearance by all classes in their

intercourse with the native inhabitants and that they will omit no opportunity of assisting me to fulfil His Majesty's most gracious and benevolent intentions towards them by promoting their advancement in civilization and ultimately under the Blessing of Divine Providence, their conversion to the Christian Faith.' [7]

At first the natives proved friendly and inoffensive. "They have committed some depredations, such as spearing a few sheep and such like"—wrote Mrs Mary Thomas—"otherwise their conduct has hitherto been peaceable and orderly." [8]

The Governor himself wrote home:

> 'My preconceived notions were quite opposed to fact as regards these people, they being as good looking blacks as I ever saw and much more apt and intelligent than any account of the New Hollanders I had read led me to expect.' [9]

Their numbers were too small to give any cause for apprehension; it was rather the natives who needed protection from the white settlers. At a dinner given to him before leaving England, Governor Hindmarsh had called upon the colonists above all things: "... to prevent the aborigines from imbibing from them a taste for that bane of humanity—spirituous liquors". [10] The most effective way the colonists could do this, he said, was by setting them an example "in forming one vast temperance society". The Governor's premonitions were fulfilled, for some of the colonists lost no time in giving liquor to natives. While the first settlers were living in tents at Glenelg, the Government had to issue a proclamation prohibiting the supply of ardent spirits to natives, and offering a reward for the conviction of any person committing this offence.

> 'One of the first things we noticed on entering the settlement"—wrote one pioneer—"was the truly English custom: I mean several printed bills—one a caution, the other a reward. The caution was a high fine on any person giving spirits or wine to the blacks; the reward was £5 for the discovery of a person who had already transgressed the orders.' [11]

At the first Criminal Sessions in May 1837 two white men were charged with stealing spears and waddies from some natives. In addressing the Grand Jury, Sir John Jeffcott said:

> 'There is one offence to which, although it is the last upon the list, I shall first advert, because it is one upon which I consider it of paramount importance that I should offer a few observations, and I trust the observations which I consider it my duty to offer, may make a due impression upon those for

whom they are intended.'

After referring to the Commissioners' expressions of the policy to be pursued towards the natives and to the Governor's proclamation, the Judge continued:

> 'They have been declared British subjects. As such they are entitled to the full protection of British law, and that protection, while I have the honor of filling the situation which His Majesty has been pleased to confer upon me, shall be fully and effectually afforded them. I will go further, and say, that any aggression upon the natives, or any infringement of their rights, shall be visited with greater severity of punishment than would similar offences committed upon white men.' [12]

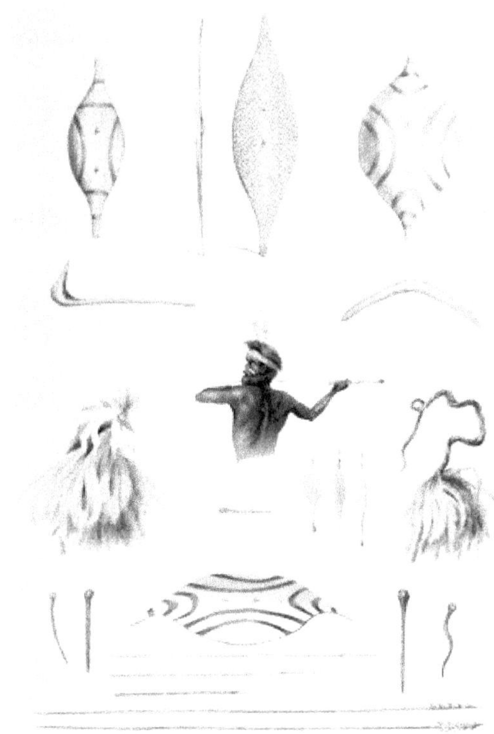

Native weapons and implements by George French Angas ca. 1840s (NLA)

The prisoners were acquitted, but the Judge, in an address through an interpreter, attempted to explain to the natives whose weapons were supposed to have been stolen the nature of private property; that as their property would be held sacred, they must in return respect the property of the white men; and that all acts of aggression on either side would be severely visited. "To all of which, when explained by the interpreter, they nodded or rather laughed assent, for they seemed evidently pleased in the interest taken in them." [13]

In Adelaide itself the natives never gave any very serious trouble. There were complaints of minor nuisances such as begging, petty pilfering of melons and potatoes, or camping on the acres which the colonists had bought, and taking wood for their fires; the Protector had occasional trouble with them when they refused to eat their porridge and insisted on having biscuits supplied to them; and a problem which was not solved for several years was that of their wandering about the streets naked. In 1841 the Governor issued an order:

> 'The Police will prevent any of the Natives from appearing in the town who are not clothed with tolerable decency. If any of the native male adults should persevere in resisting this order they will be taken before a Magistrate and committed to prison on the charge of indecent exposure.'

The local blacks soon acquired a few rags of cast-off clothing, but from time to time strange natives from the country wandered into the town and unwittingly offending against this Ordinance, were seized and locked up for twenty-four hours without food. What they thought they were being punished for, it would be vain to speculate. As settlement spread, offences of this nature rapidly disappeared.[14]

Murder
The murder at Encounter Bay was the subject of Blenkinsop's letter (reproduced in Chapter 2.5). The Aboriginal was called Reppindjeri and for a time he suffered incarceration in a barrel while on a ship to

In June 1837 a white man was killed by the blacks at Encounter Bay and the first serious legal problem as to the punishment of natives arose. The Advocate-General visited Encounter Bay to make inquiries, and one native, supposed to be the murderer, was captured and brought back to Adelaide. It had now to be decided whether he was to be tried and, if so, how. The Judge was away in Van Diemen's Land, and Mann said that he thought the matter was so important as to call for the special consideration of the Governor and Council:

> 'I feel that the habits of the civilized and uncivilized man differ so widely and the uncertainty of evidence arising out of our ignorance of the language of the natives is so great that a serious responsibility will attach to the adoption of any application of the strict rules of English law to cases similar to the present. On the other hand, it seems equally impolitic, nay even impossible, to leave the subjects of His Majesty unprotected and their lives and property exposed to the vindictive passions or cupidity of the aborigines.'

He was inclined to suggest that those natives who were known to the Protector and who had acquired a reputation for trustworthiness should be allowed to give evidence.[15]

The Governor wrote to Mr Angas with reference to the prisoner:

> 'We are not yet decided how to proceed with him, but evidence is being collected. It would, however, be worse than useless to bring him before a Jury unless there is almost a certainty of his conviction. To release him under any circumstances (his tribe knowing him to be guilty) would be naturally ascribed by the natives to fear ... As to this prisoner,

> had the whites knocked him on the head, on discovering his guilt, I believe his relatives would have considered it quite in the way of business, and then thought no more about it. Not so, I fear, should a regular process condemn him. And yet the bull must be taken by the horns. The colonists must be protected, and we must do all that we can to show these poor people that justice is equal between us.' [16]

The accused solved the immediate difficulty by escaping, but the problem remained, and one of the objects of Sir John Jeffcott's intended visit to Van Diemen's Land in December 1837 was to consult with the Judges there as to what course he should adopt upon the trial of native prisoners.

As settlement extended, conflicts with the natives became more numerous. In March 1838, Governor Hindmarsh issued a proclamation stating that there was reason to believe that many of the outrages by blacks had been induced by the previous aggression of the settlers. The colonists were commanded to abstain from hostile measures, or the use of firearms against natives, and:

> '... to remember at all times that the native population are under equal protection of the laws, and are to be regarded and treated, and are liable to the same punishment in all respects as Her Majesty's other subjects. The advantages which may be derived by treating the aborigines with kindness, notwithstanding what has recently occurred, must be evident; for, by retaliating injuries upon a race of being who never discriminate when seeking revenge, the unoffending may suffer for the wrongdoer'.

Every instance of an Aboriginal committing "a fault or any act of impropriety" was to be reported in order that measures could be taken to prevent the repetition of such conduct "by an uniform system of punishment".[17]

Governor Gawler, when he arrived in the colony, also urged forbearance, but it is not likely that a homily which he delivered to the colonists was very much appreciated by them.

> 'Remember'—he admonished them—'that we are descended from the same first parents; they are bone of your bone and flesh of your flesh; you are brothers—the colour of your skin is no excuse for you. They are children in understanding; you bear with the ignorance of children—bear with theirs; so shall we have the gratification, under God's blessing, of making them happy and useful members of society.' [18]

About two hundred natives, with their lubras and children, were entertained by the Governor at a dinner in the parklands. With the help of an interpreter, he delivered a speech to the Assembly and, in conclusion, waved his plumed white hat, which caused a native with a sense of humour to call out, "Berry good cockatoo, Gubner"; and as the "Cockatoo Gubner" Gawler was known amongst the natives for many years.

> 'A few days after this feast, which gave new wants to a harmless race of beings, they relished roast beef and roast mutton so well, that they immediately commenced operations to supply themselves with those luxuries which neither they nor their forefathers had ever tasted before.' [19]

Governor Gawler's dinner for Aboriginals in the parklands (AGSA)

In spearing sheep, the natives were not without justification. The white man came and killed their kangaroos; why should not they kill "the white man's kangaroo". The *Southern Australian* was at pains to show by an ingenious distinction that, while it was a most heinous offence for a blackfellow to spear a sheep, it was no offence at all for a white man to shoot kangaroos.

> 'The latter animal'—it said—'traverses the waste owning no guide or master, but its own free will, until it becomes property to him who has pursued and succeeded in killing it. The former, on the contrary, is in all stages of its existence the property of an individual, or of successive individuals; an equivalent has been given for it, and it is fed and protected at the expense of its owner.' [20]

In March 1839 the first native was brought to trial before the Supreme Court. He was accused of wilfully and maliciously setting fire to grass. It was a common practice, and in the opinion of the natives a laudable one, to burn off the withered grass to hasten the growth of new grass. Obviously this was dangerous and would have to be stopped, but how far could it be said to be wilful and malicious?

> 'I shall require very satisfactory evidence'—said Jickling—'that the native knew he was committing a serious crime before I shall consent to inflict upon a native of the country what in the case of a white man I should conceive to be a punishment proportioned to the offence.' [21]

Like every other prisoner at this sessions, the native was acquitted and the Grand Jury drew up a presentment deprecating the strong feeling among many of the colonists against the Aborigines. Governor Gawler replied:

> 'I have seen with deep regret that petty offences and depredations have been increasing among the aborigines, and that these evils have been accompanied by a corresponding increase of impatience and anomosity [sic] against them by some of the settlers. Every friend of morality must see with deep concern that that vice which brutalises man—or rather which degrades him lower than the brute—drunkenness—that vice which especially renders man a burden to himself and a pest to society, is through the example or at the instigation of thoughtless and abandoned persons, gaining ground among the natives. As one of the leading points of hope for them, its progress must be steadily and universally discountenanced by us. The aborigines have been brought under British law. To the utmost of my power, when they are guilty of crimes, I will not from any mistaken sympathy towards them, suffer those laws to be evaded; but, at the same time, as aborigines may be punished by our laws, by those laws they must also be protected, and I look to the juries of the colony for steadfast support in defending them, according to the full scope and power of British statutes, against every lawless aggression. It must also be remembered that, if (on?) the one hand we have set before them the blessings of Christianity and civilisation, we have, on the other, received from them the beautiful country, of which, until our arrival, they were undisputed possessors.'

It had been suggested that no native carrying weapons should be allowed to enter any town or settlement, but the Governor did not approve of this:

> 'I do not at present see that the disarming of the natives when they enter towns would offer advantages sufficient to counterbalance the expense and trouble which would be required to carry it into effect, and the evil feelings which it might excite. It is not in town that their arms can often be made instruments of mischief, nor indeed can they often be formidable in the rural districts if settlers take, as they should, ordinary precautions against them.' [22]

In April 1839 one of Osmond Gilles's shepherds was killed by natives. A proclamation was issued stating that for the purpose of inducing the Aborigines to give up the offenders, the Government had resolved to withhold from them the usual provisions.[23] This was very widely condemned as a harsh and short-sighted measure which punished the innocent for the guilty. A colonist who signed himself "W.B." (perhaps Mr William Bartley) contributed to the *Southern Australian* a sensible letter which placed the relations between the settlers and the Aborigines in their true light. The proclamation depriving them from food, he said, was not so much unjust as unwise. The food was given to them purely as a gift and there was no reason why it should not be discontinued, but to do so was impolitic, for it confused in the minds of the natives the ideas of right and wrong by punishing the innocent, and it confirmed them in their practice of taking vengeance on the first white man they met for any injury done to them. Further, if they had not provided food for themselves, the Government would have had to rescind its order rather than see them all starve to death, which would have been a confession of weakness. It was useless for sentimental settlers to talk about the right to appropriate land or injustice in dispossessing natives. "Let every sincere objector on this ground prove his sincerity by at once leaving the colony, which he thinks he has so unjustly taken from another."

The plain fact was that the natives *must* conform to the laws and customs of the settlers, because might was right and there were only two ways of dealing with them:

(1) Driving them away to other parts of the colony by the use of physical force.

(2) Attempting to educate and civilise them.

The latter was obviously the proper course, and the one to which the colonists should turn their attention.[24]

A public meeting was held to consider the relations of the colonists and the Aborigines, and it was agreed that a crisis had arrived. Prompt measures were urged."A decision as summary as the forms and spirit of justice will admit of, should be adopted. [25]

Three natives were caught and charged with the murder of the shepherd. The public outcry against them was prodigious and the Government, impressed with a consciousness of the danger of error which, as Mr Justice Bundey has remarked, always exists "when a community, especially a limited one, is excited by the prevalence of any particular class of crime, and jurymen are called upon to enquire into charges of similar character during such excitement",[26] postponed their trial in the hope that the agitation would subside.

Mann was instructed to defend them. The Advocate-General and Mr Matthew Smith appeared to prosecute. In opening the case the Advocate-General said:

> 'If they find equal justice administered to them as well as to ourselves—if they find we treat them as we treat each other, they will soon learn to respect our laws. When a murder is committed amongst themselves, I am led to understand they require blood for blood, but amongst them as amongst all other uncivilized nations, the friends of the deceased are the parties who administer justice ... They, therefore, cannot wonder if we should punish them for committing that crime upon us.' [27]

One native was found guilty and sentenced to death.

At the same sessions three other natives were also charged with murder, and again one was found guilty and sentenced to death. These latter prisoners were defended by Jickling. It was his first appearance as a barrister on the criminal side and, from the uncomplimentary remarks made about his efforts, it was probably as well for the prisoners that they were unable to appreciate the ability of their counsel.

Both the condemned natives were hanged. Their execution did not pass without criticism. It was denounced as "judicial butchery". The evidence to some extent consisted of admissions said to have been made by the accused in words and manifestations of feelings, but it was doubtful, to say the least, whether they had any idea of what was going on. The Judge himself said:

> 'It is a painful feature of the present case that, however desirable it may be to make the prisoners thoroughly understand the proceedings, this can only be done through the medium of interpretation, in a broken language, of which the interpreters themselves have only a limited knowledge.'

No evidence was called for the defence; the Aborigines did not know how to give it; and it would have made no difference if they had. Fifty native witnesses to prove a watertight alibi could not have been heard without being sworn, and they were quite ignorant of the nature of an oath. The counsel assigned to defend no doubt did their best in the addresses they made to the jury, but, as it was said, it was:

> '... just as if a learned gentleman had been assigned to plead for two dogs upon trial, for the purpose of inducing the jury to

> take a favourable view of certain reported barks, howls, and motions of the tail'. [28]

The Colonisation Commissioners in their fourth annual report were at pains to justify the executions:

> 'To subject savage tribes to the penalties of laws with which they are unacquainted, for offences which they may possibly regard as acts of justifiable retaliation for invaded rights, is a proceeding indefensible except under circumstances of urgent and extreme necessity. Such circumstances had unhappily occurred in the case under consideration ... If the murderers had not been tried, convicted, and legally punished, the settlers unprotected by the governing authorities would have been compelled to take the law into their own hands, and in their fear and rage might have commenced an exterminating warfare against the natives. The necessities of the case left but a choice of evils, and the authorities chose the least. In establishing a new colony, it is one of the first and most sacred duties of the legal government to protect the native races; but to protect the native against the colonist, without at the same time protecting the colonist against the native, would be impracticable. The aborigines cannot have the protection of British law without being made amenable to British law. If the European and native races are to live together in amity, they must live under equal laws; to place them under different codes would be to place them in hostility to each other. Were a system established inflicting punishment upon the colonists for offences against the natives, and not inflicting equal punishments upon the natives for offences against the colonists, the colonists debarred from equal justice and protection by the constituted authorities, would speedily adjust the balance by taking the law into their own hands. If it be necessary to inflict the punishment of death for the murder of a native by a settler, it is equally necessary to inflict that punishment for the murder of a settler by a native. It might, perhaps, be practicable to abolish capital punishment in both cases, but it would not be practicable to abolish it in one case and to retain it in the other without producing a state of lawless and vindictive hostility between the races ... It is only by equal laws, impartially administered, that the heathen savage can be brought within the pale of Christian civilization. In order to accomplish this most desirable end, we must treat our less favoured fellow man with a kindness too enduring and real to allow impunity to crime, and we must constrain him to obey the law of England

while we teach him the law of God.'[29]

The difficulties in the application of British law to uncivilised Aborigines were forcibly demonstrated in July 1840, when the Ship *Maria* was wrecked on the Coorong and its crew and passengers were brutally murdered by the natives of the Milmenrura or Big Murray tribe. Some steps had to be taken to punish the guilty. The Governor consulted the Judge and the Advocate-General, who both expressed the opinion that the law could not be brought into effect at all.

> 'I feel it impossible'—said the former—'to try according to the forms of English law people of a wild and savage tribe, whose country, although within the limits of the Province of South Australia has never been occupied by settlers, who have never submitted themselves to our dominion, and between whom and the colonists there has been no social intercourse.'[30]

This opinion he subsequently elaborated in next addressing the Grand Jury.

> 'Let me disclaim all idea of conceding rights to the native population at one time and withholding them at another'—he said. 'My objection to try the natives of the Big Murray tribe is founded not on any supposed defect of right on their part, but on my want of jurisdiction. It is founded on the opinion that such only of the native population as have in some degree acquiesced in our dominion can be considered subject to our laws, and that with regard to all others, we must be considered as much strangers as Governor Hindmarsh and the first settlers were to the whole native population, when they raised the British standard on their landing at Glenelg. And as I apprehend, no one would have thought of trying according to the forms of English law, any of the native population who might have attacked the British settlement the day after its establishment, so I conceive that, by the same reasoning, it would be impossible to try, according to these forms, people who are now almost as much strangers to us as the whole native population were to the first settlers—a people, towards a political union with whom, no approach has been made. I will not attempt to define with accuracy the circumstances which bring one class of natives within and leave another without the pale of our laws ... I must content myself with saying, that to bring them within the pale there must be some submission or acquiescence on their part, or at least, some intercourse between us and them.'

The natives executed in 1839 had been in friendly intercourse with the settlers. Jickling had objected that they were not cognisant of, nor amenable to, English law; but in summing up the Judge had told the jury that as the natives seemed to have acquiesced in the dominion exercised by the settlers and as the crime was one against the law of nature, which even amongst themselves would have been punished with death, he overruled the objection.

> 'I felt I was taking a fearful responsibility on myself on that occasion; but I also felt, as I still feel, that it is for the general benefit of the native population that the crimes of any of its members should, whenever practicable, be enquired into and punished according to the forms of English law, rather than by any other means, for by thus proceeding all pretext is taken away for settlers taking the law into their own hands, as they might otherwise be too apt to do, and they at the same time receive forcible warning that the natives are under the protection of the same laws as themselves.'

But the Murray blacks were wild: "there had been no exercise of dominion over, no intercourse with them; they owed no obedience to English law".

> 'Cases may arise in which it will be difficult for the Judge to decide to which of the two classes they properly belong; still it is his duty at least to endeavour to keep in view the English law as his guide.' [31]

Upon these views having been expressed by the Judge and Advocate-General, the Governor called a special meeting of the Council at which it was decided to dispatch Major O'Halloran, the Commissioner of Police, with a strong party, to apprehend and bring to summary justice the murderers.

> 'To this end'—Major O'Halloran was instructed—'your first object should be, if possible, to make prisoners the whole number congregated with the murderers. It is of very great importance that, if possible, in effecting this portion of the duty, no blood should be shed, or violence shown or encountered. The future effect of the expedition on the minds and conduct of the natives, will certainly be much more beneficial if the murderers can be captured without bloodshed. This, however, will probably be the most difficult part of your duty, and if, in the execution of it, you are really compelled to abandon temperate measures, and to resort to those of extreme force against the whole tribe, you will not be held blamable. Your duty is to capture the murderers, and this object must be effected if they fall within your reach ... When

> the prisoners are taken, you will proceed deliberately and with all suitable form to discover who were the persons actually concerned in the murder. You will take every reasonable method of exhibiting to your own party and to all the blacks present, that your inquiry is deliberate, and conducted on principles of the strictest justice ... Should your mind become satisfied of the guilt as to actual participation in the murder of any number not exceeding three, you will, if possible, move the whole tribe in your power to the spot at which the murder was committed. You will there explain to the blacks the nature of your conduct, and the orders you have received from the Governor, and you will deliberately and formally cause sentence of death to be executed by shooting or hanging, upon the convicted murderers not exceeding three, as above described ... For so doing this shall be your sufficient warrant.' [32] (Tolmer I 180-1)

The punitive expedition succeeded in capturing a number of natives, two of whom were given up by their tribe as being among the actual murderers. A drumhead court martial was held, the two natives found guilty, taken to the beach and hanged, in the presence of their tribe.[33]

This painting, by Edward C. Frome, depicts the hanging of the two Aboriginals by O'Halloran's expedition. (AGSA)

When their summary execution became known at Adelaide there was a furious outburst of controversy as to whether it could be justified.[34] The officials of the Colonial Office in England were horrified when they heard of it, and wrote out in great alarm to the Governor that the law officers had advised that the murders with which the natives were charged having been committed within the limits of the province defined under the authority of an Act of Parliament, the Aborigines might have been brought to trial in the ordinary legal tribunals, that their summary execution was contrary to law, that Major O'Halloran and those assisting him were guilty of murder as principals and that Governor Gawler was guilty of murder as an accessory before the fact. They could only be indemnified by an Act of Parliament or a pardon under the Great Seal. As a matter of policy and to keep the matter as quiet as possible, the Secretary of State thought it advisable not to do anything to give the officials concerned protection until someone actually prosecuted them—a step which it never occurred to anyone to take.[35]

Although the officials of Downing Street might put their consciences to rest by pretending that to confer upon all natives within the province the benefits of British citizenship was all that was necessary to solve any judicial doubts as to jurisdiction to try Aborigines, and that the courts could then proceed without more ado to administer justice according to the established forms of English law, yet Mr Justice Cooper could not bring himself to agree and persisted in maintaining that it was impossible for him to try prisoners who were quite unacquainted with Europeans.

> 'My opinion rests upon the ground that wild and savage people whose country although within the limits of the colony has never been occupied by settlers, people between whom and the settlers there has been no social intercourse, and who until the moment of the commission of their alleged offence have never been known, cannot reasonably be deemed cognizant of our assumed dominion over their country and themselves.' [36]

In a case in 1846, for instance, where two natives were charged with murder, it was found that they belonged to a strange tribe whose language was not known.

> 'If it be admitted'—said the Judge—'that the aborigines came for the first time into contact with Europeans when the offence with which they are charged was committed I do not think them fit subjects for trial in our Criminal Court.' [37]

In another case in the same year he laid it down that "a person wholly uncivilized ought not to be prosecuted".

In Governor Grey the colony received a man who had had experience with native tribes and who had formed conclusions upon the best methods of improving their social and moral condition. The natives, he pointed out, were generally treated upon the principle that although they should, as far as the persons and property of Europeans were concerned, be made amenable to British laws, yet so long as they only exercised their own customs amongst themselves and not too immediately in the presence of Europeans, they should be allowed to do so with impunity. This principle was due to philanthropical motives and ignorance of the peculiar traditional laws of the savage and uncivilised natives.

> 'It is necessary, from the moment the aborigines of this country are declared British subjects, that they should, as far as possible, be taught that the British laws are to supersede their own ... I do not hesitate to assert my full convictions that while those tribes that are in communication with Europeans are allowed to execute their barbarous laws and customs upon one another, so long will they remain hopelessly immersed in their present state, and, however unjust such a proceeding might at first sight appear, I believe that the course pointed out by true humanity would be to make them, from the commencement, amenable to British laws, both as regards themselves and Europeans; for I hold it to involve a contradiction to suppose that individuals subject to savage and barbarous laws can rise to a state of civilization, which those laws have a manifest tendency to destroy and overturn ... To punish the aborigines severely for the violation of laws of the existence of which they are ignorant, would be manifestly cruel and unjust, but to punish them in the first instance slightly for the violation of these laws would inflict no great injury on them, whilst always punishing them when guilty of a crime, without reference to the length of time that had elapsed between its perpetration and their apprehension, at the same time fully explaining to them the measure of punishment that would await them in the event of a second commission of the same fault, would gradually teach them the laws to which they were henceforth to be amenable, and would show them that crime was always eventually (although it might be remotely) followed by punishment.'

If the Aborigines were allowed to rob and murder one another under their own laws, they would get the idea that wrongfulness consisted not in the acts but only in their being done to white men. It would be easy near the towns to enforce an observance of English laws, but:

> '... to attain this object in remote districts, it is necessary that each colony should possess an efficient mounted police ... No

> objection to this force on account of expense can hold good, it being absolutely necessary for the cause of humanity and good order that such a force should exist; for, so long as distant settlers are left unprotected, and are compelled to take care of and avenge themselves, so long must great barbarities be necessarily committed'.[38]

In a minute on these views of Grey, Sir George Gipps said:

> 'It is only the more obvious offences against society that can, with any degree of justice, be visited against the savages with extreme severity—such as murder, rape, violence against the persons, and other offences which there can be no doubt should be regarded alike by the savage and civilized man as deserving of punishment.'[39]

Mr Justice Cooper used to say that he always looked with dread on cases in which natives were concerned, because of the difficulty experienced in communicating with them—a difficulty which may be illustrated by the fact that in 1843 there were at one time four natives in the gaol who spoke four languages which appeared to be as distinct from each other as English and German and for which no interpreters could be found. The Judge occasionally remanded natives in the hope that an interpreter might be discovered, but more often they had to be released and sent back to their tribe.[40]

Even when a conversation could be carried on with natives, it was seldom of much use. The natives had no conception at all of the abstract idea of truth although it could be impressed upon some of them, in a negative way, that if they told a lie they would be punished. The missionaries taught them a few phrases, which they learnt to repeat, but whether they understood them was another question. One native confidently asserted in the witness box that if he did evil on earth, he would be sure to go to heaven when he died.

An almost insuperable obstacle to the application of British law to the Aborigines was the fact that a native from his ignorance of the nature of an oath was not competent to give evidence.

> 'To him'—as Mr Justice Angas Parsons has said—'an oath meant nothing. He had his own ideas of devil-worship and nature worship; but the kissing of a Book which he could not read, and the swearing by one God, when he professed acquaintance with many, made the administering of an ordinary oath a farce, if not an impossibility.'[41]

It was speciously argued that the inadmissibility of their evidence would operate to their advantage because the hardship of it was always urged on the jury by their counsel and by the Judge and was taken into consideration by the executive in carrying into effect the judgment of the Court. Edward John Eyre, who for several years did remarkable work amongst the natives at Moorunde, wrote more soundly:

> 'Can it be deemed surprising that a rude, uncivilized being, driven from his home, deprived of all his ordinary means of subsistence, and pressed perhaps by a hostile tribe from behind, should occasionally be guilty of aggressions or injuries towards his oppressors? The wonder rather is, not that these things do sometimes occur, but that they occur so rarely. In addition to the many other inconsistencies in our conduct towards the aborigines, not the least extraordinary is that of placing them, on the plea of protection, under the influence of our laws, and of making them British subjects. Strange anomaly, which by the former makes them amenable to penalties they are ignorant of, for crimes which they do not consider as such, or which they may even have been driven to commit by our own injustice, and by the latter but mocks them with an empty sound, since the very laws under which we profess to place them, by their nature and constitution, are inoperative in affording redress to the injured ... In declaring the natives British subjects and making them amenable to British laws, they have been placed in the anomalous position of being made amenable to laws of which they are quite ignorant, and which, at the same time, do not afford to them the slightest redress from any injuries which they may sustain at the hands of Europeans. This arises from their being unable legally to give evidence in a Court of Justice, and from its rarely happening that any aggressions upon them take place in the presence of other Europeans, who might appear as witnesses for them. During the past year, two such cases have come before me, of complaint on the part of the natives against Europeans, and several others have been brought under my notice by natives, in which I could take no steps to redress them from my inability to receive their evidence, and from the impossibility of procuring any other than native evidence. This very great disadvantage under which the aborigines labour, must until remedied tend materially to prevent the full development of those good results which might otherwise be expected to accrue from their intercourse with Europeans. It is impossible to explain to the natives the reason of their being unable to give evidence; they only see that their own people are always punished for offences, that the Europeans almost always escape, and they naturally deduce an inference unfavorable to the justice of the white man.'

Edward John Eyre ca. 1860 (SLSA)

No permanent improvement in their character or conduct, he thought, could be expected until some way was devised by means of which the evidence of the natives could be received, both in cases where they themselves only were concerned, as well as in those where Europeans were concerned. This was a vitally important subject, he concluded: "... one upon which all our connections with the aborigines principally hinge". [42]

In 1843 the Imperial Parliament passed the Act 6 & 7 Vic c.22 which enabled colonial legislatures to make provision for the reception in courts of law of the testimony of Aborigines, and Governor Grey was directed to introduce an act for this purpose into the Legislative Council.[43] An Act (No 8 of 1844) was accordingly passed, providing:

(1) Any Justice of the Peace might receive the information of an Aboriginal or half-caste upon his affirmation or declaration to tell the truth, the whole truth and nothing but the truth, without administering the usual form of oath.

(2) The evidence of Aboriginals and half-castes might be taken upon their affirmation to tell the truth, the whole truth and nothing but the truth, provided that in preliminary proceedings the substance of the evidence was to be reduced into writing and signed by a mark of the person giving it, and verified by the Justice of the Peace.

(3) Before taking evidence, the Court was required to caution the Aboriginal that he would be liable to incur punishment if he did not tell the truth, and wilful falsehood was made punishable as for perjury.

(4) The degree of weight and credibility to be attached to such evidence was to be left to the Justice or Judge, or to the jury under the direction of the Judge.

(5) The Act further provided that, "No person whether aboriginal or other shall be convicted of any offence upon the sole testimony of such uncivilized persons", but it was not necessary to such conviction that any particular fact affirmed by such uncivilised person should be corroborated by other evidence; two clauses which appear to be contradictory.

Two years later the words "No person ..." et cetera quoted above were repealed and it was enacted that no person, whether Aboriginal or white, should be adjudged to suffer death or sentenced to transportation upon conviction of any offence upon the sole testimony of uncivilised persons.

These Acts were not conspicuously successful. Few natives had any idea of "the truth, the whole truth, and nothing but the truth". More often than not they were bewildered and had no idea why they were being questioned, or if they did they endeavoured to guess what the Judge and the questioners would like them to say and answered accordingly. They were blissfully unconcerned with consistency, and contented themselves with trying to satisfy whoever happened at the moment to be interrogating them. Some of them had a superstitious fear of mentioning the name of an acquaintance who had died, which made them extremely reluctant to give any evidence at all in cases of murder.[44] Sometimes the only available interpreter was another native who could not be sworn; or, if he could be sworn, the accuracy of his interpretations was often doubtful.

> 'I consider it a matter of the greatest moment'—said Mr Justice Cooper—'that the Court and Jury should be able to place full reliance on the ability and fidelity of the Interpreter and this can seldom be the case with uncivilized natives. When the testimony of any of these poor people is given through the medium of an educated and intelligent interpreter the Judge and Jury may at least feel satisfied that they know what the witness has said, but how can they have this satisfaction if they cannot rely upon the correctness of the interpretation?' [45]

In 1848 the Judge drafted an Aboriginal Evidence Ordinance (No 3 of 1848) superseding the earlier legislation, and providing:

(1) That in all proceedings in the administration of justice, whether civil or criminal, wherein the testimony of uncivilised persons was required, the court, (coroner?) or Justice, might receive such evidence without administering any oath and without any formality, except that it should be first explained to the Aboriginal that he was required to tell what he knew about the matter.

(2) Such testimony, upon being reduced to writing, might be received in evidence when under like circumstances evidence of a civilised person would have been admissible.

(3) Any Aboriginal might make an information or complaint before a Justice of the Peace without any oath being taken.

(4) In preliminary proceedings the unsworn testimony was to be reduced to writing and certified by the magistrate.

(5) The weight to be attached to the evidence was a matter for the Court or jury.

(6) Unsworn native interpreters might be used provided the Court was satisfied of their ability to interpret.

> 'I would strongly impress upon you"—wrote the Secretary of State to the Governor when the Act was sent home—"the importance of the consideration that no such Ordinance, however carefully drawn up, will be found to work satisfactorily, unless those who are charged with the administration of the law anxiously endeavour to discourage the evasion of its spirit and substance by the unnecessary introduction of technical refinements.' [46]

In 1846 occurred the first instance of an Aboriginal being charged with an offence against another Aboriginal. A preliminary discussion took place as to the jurisdiction of the Court. Mr Justice Cooper (presumably facetiously) remarked, "At present I do not know that the party murdered was an aboriginal native, as the indictment does not so term him." "It calls him Ballooloolyoo," replied Mr Hartley. "Surely that is not an English name!" "How can I know that?" said Mr Justice Cooper.

The Judge held he had jurisdiction and the native was tried, convicted and sentenced to death—a sentence which was afterwards commuted by the Governor. A report of the proceedings was forwarded to the Secretary of State, who approved of the course adopted.[47]

A similar case arose in 1851, when three natives were charged with the murder of another Aboriginal. Mr Justice Cooper told the Grand Jury:

> 'I have on former occasions felt bound to say that if the aborigines were amenable for offences committed against Her Majesty's civilized subjects, I could not point to any law by which they could escape the consequences of crimes committed among themselves ... I feel it is my duty to treat the charge of murder between aborigines the same way as I would between any other subjects of Her Majesty, regard being had to the rules of the law which regulate evidence in such cases.'

The Grand Jury, in reporting that in accordance with the Judge's direction as to the law they had found a true bill against the Aboriginals, added a long protest:

> 'That in so doing many of the Grand Jurors have done violence to their own natural feelings of equity and justice; since, without entering upon the abstract question of the rights which, possession once obtained, the superior and more powerful people may justly exercise over those subjected to them, the Grand Jurors conceive that if the subjugated tribes be uncivilized men, it is morally incumbent on the superior people, in the first instance, to confine their interference to the mutual protection of both races in their intercourse with each other, and not to meddle with laws or usages having the force of laws among savages, in their conduct towards their own race.'

They believed that the slaying of the natives was in accordance with a law common among the native tribes, that the man killed knew that law, and that he knew the risk he ran if he violated it. Prior to the occupation of the country by the colonists, the native tribes admittedly had power to make their own laws and usages for their own protection and government.

'It can scarcely be assumed that the limited intercourse which has yet subsisted between the colonists and the aborigines, especially on the confines of the province, should have sufficed to impart such information to those uncivilized men as would justify us in breaking up their own internal system for the punishment of offences to which all their previous traditions and habits give force and sanction.'

While the jury relied on the wisdom and humanity of the Judges and the Government to extend mercy to the natives, they considered:

'... that a system which only nominally denounces severe penalties, and from the very fact of their injustice, declines to enforce them, is a system which fosters rather than prevents the evils which it professes to punish and designs to remove'—

and they asked the Judges to consider the law with a view to defining the limits within which it should be the province of British law to interfere between Aboriginal natives in their own social relations, since the Grand Jury could not but feel that, if manslaying were an offence to be recognised, other infractions of the law such as adultery or even polygamy might become equally cognisable by the Courts. If so: "... a whole train of anomalous proceedings, repugnant to every feeling of right and justice, would be presented for the adjudication of our tribunals".

This protest took the Judge by surprise. He replied that it was a subject to which, from its difficulties and importance, he had from his earliest arrival in the colony devoted much patient attention. Europeans could not be punished for crimes against natives without apparent injustice if natives were not to be punished when they injured Europeans, although he had always endeavoured to secure justice to the natives by looking after their interests and by assigning them counsel.

'I am not aware of the unreasonableness of trying persons who are not cognizant of the law by which they are to be tried. I have therefore made it a rule that I will not try persons by our mode of trial who were not cognizant of our existence as a nation.'

With regard to offences by natives amongst themselves, if the Court had jurisdiction to try them for offences against white men, he thought it must necessarily have jurisdiction over their own quarrels and wrongs. What was considered crime by civilised people was, no doubt, in many instances not considered as a crime at all amongst the Aborigines.

'They, however, as I have learned from diligent enquiry, are accustomed to punish deeds of violence; and for a life taken

> away by violence to inflict on the man who had taken away that life the penalty of the sacrifice of his own life.'

In summing up to the jury, the Judge repeated that he had no doubt at all as to his jurisdiction, but: "... the question of the guilt or innocence of the parties, arising from the degree of ignorance in which they might be of our laws, is not so easy to decide".

A verdict of guilty having been returned, the prisoners were asked through an interpreter whether they had anything to say why they should not be condemned to be hanged, to which they replied, very naturally, that they did not like to be hanged. They were sentenced to death, but reprieved by the Governor.[48]

The *Register*, commenting upon the case, pointed out that as a matter of policy the colonists were compelled to interfere in the disputes of the Aborigines. "The principle which would exempt us from all inter-meddling would soon give the strongest tribe the undisputed mastery of the whole country." [49]

Charged with Murder
Thomas Donelly was tried on 13 and 15 March 1847 "For the wilful murder of an aboriginal native named 'Billy' on 1 September 1846 at Rivoli Bay".

The first white man to be charged with the murder of an Aboriginal was tried in March 1847, convicted, and hanged.[50]

> 'Whatever question may be raised as to the right to try any of the aborigines for aggressions upon settlers or others'—said Mr Justice Cooper—'no question can arise as to the right to try British subjects for aggression upon the aborigines, and I hope the law will never be found wanting in strength to avenge their wrongs.' [51]

Cases in which natives were involved were not very numerous, but from time to time dissatisfaction was expressed at the prosecution and trial of uncivilised Aboriginals.

> 'When a native is charged with a crime of the nature of which he is ignorant, before a Court of whose jurisdiction he knows as little, the solemn forms and legal paraphernalia of the trial look painfully like a farce, and the sentence, inevitable according to law, is preposterous according to common sense.' [52]

No person of common humanity could look indifferently upon a scene such as that described in the following extract from the *Register*, relating to a native brought from Rivoli Bay to stand his trial in the Supreme Court on a charge of sheep stealing:

> 'The prisoner wore a wild and scared appearance. The adventures of the last few days must have been strange to him indeed. The firearms of the white men—the chain with which he was bound—the sea-voyage—the buildings at the port and city—and now the justice-room, on every object of which he gazed with looks of wonder; and handcuffs, too, annoyed him

> exceedingly, and he incessantly endeavoured to remove them. He several times spoke and seemed most desirous of an answer, but his language was wholly unintelligible to Mr Moorhouse and the black policeman Jimmy, who addressed him in various dialects. When brought to the bar he was alarmed, and evidently thought summary punishment was to be inflicted on him.' [53]

Eventually this poor creature had to be released and taken back to the South East, as no-one was able to communicate with him.

In 1860 a Select Committee recommended that a protector of Aborigines should be appointed with power to visit native tribes periodically for the purpose of holding courts and dispensing justice, in all except capital cases. To drag natives to the Supreme Court for trial was denounced as an "expensive mockery"—a waste of public money, the time of the Court and the labour of the police. A black man was left to his savage habits, it was said:

> '... he is an outcast until he does something wrong; and then he is instantly a privileged British subject—privileged to be tried by twelve men sitting in a box, and to be sentenced by a Judge whose words are incomprehensible'. [54]

Not only did the Aboriginal prisoners suffer but, if any native witnesses were required to attend the Court, the only way to get them there was to use force. As soon as a native found himself in the custody of a policeman, he moved heaven and earth to escape, and almost invariably native witnesses had to be put in irons and handcuffs to prevent them from running away. The natural result was that by the time they were called on to give evidence they were frightened out of their wits and thought they were about to be punished for some offence they had unwittingly committed.

The recommendations of the Committee were ignored and the native problem was left slowly to solve itself. The Aboriginals were never very numerous, and their numbers diminished owing to the encroachments on their hunting grounds and consequent reduction of their natural food resources, the effects of disease and vices contracted from white men, and the disintegration of tribal life. Those who survived became hangers-on on the outskirts of civilisation, broken in spirit, who were seldom guilty of any serious offences.

John Upton's portrait of Sir Robert Torrens ca. 1880 (NLA)

Chapter 12

Registration of Deeds and the Real Property Act

"A virgin country," it has been pointed out, "offers unusual opportunities for the installation of a land register. No elaborate searching of titles is required, and registration is cheap and effective."[1]

One of the first measures of the South Australian Commissioners was to require Mr Fisher, the Resident Commissioner, to prepare, in conjunction with the two conveyancing counsel, a registration code under which, it was hoped, the fees upon the transfer of property, while less than the cost of a deed of conveyance in England, would become an important source of public revenue. Before leaving England, Fisher published a pamphlet entitled "A Sketch of three Colonial Acts suggested for adoption in the new province of South Australia, with a view to ensure the most perfect security of title to property, to simplify and facilitate the mode, and moderate the expense of its transfer: with proposed forms of Deeds". The Acts he proposed were: first to establish a general register of titles, secondly to facilitate the transfer of property by deed, and thirdly to provide for the registration of births, deaths and marriages.[2]

Mr Fisher was appointed Registrar-General and his plan was to have been put in force as soon as possible in the colony.

> 'The importance of proper regulations on these subjects'—it was said in the first number of the Register, published in England—'cannot be too highly estimated, particularly as we believe they combine the greatest simplicity with perfect security.' [3]

The unhappy differences which arose between the Governor and the Resident Commissioner proved an obstacle to bringing the registration scheme into force. In June 1837 Fisher reported to the Commissioners that the Registration Bill would be passed in a few days.[4] To the Governor, however, nothing in which Fisher had a hand could by any stretch of imagination be acceptable. Sir John Jeffcott, it was said, had laughed at the idea of Fisher's Act being passed, and Mann, the Advocate-General, had adversely criticised it. The *Register* denounced the scheme as useless except to provide Fisher with a salary. (It should be added, however, that Mr Justice Cooper later said that Mr Fisher's Bill was drawn "with great care and ingenuity".) [5]

At the end of the year Fisher complained that he had done all he could to get the Registration Bill through the Council, but without success.[6]

Upon the office of Resident Commissioner being vested in Governor Gawler, Mr Fisher found his occupation gone, and the matter was pigeonholed.

Dealings in land in the colony in each case of course began with a land grant, in the name of the Commissioners. Some objection was taken to this and it was urged that, since there was no clause in the Foundation Act vesting the land of the colony in the Commissioners, the grants ought to run in the name of the Crown.[7] The proper view seems to be that the Foundation Act by necessary implication vested the land of the province in the Commissioners in fee. The Commissioners were empowered to sell and transfer the land, and they could not do this unless they had the title to it. The original system appears to have been that a single land grant was issued to the purchaser. In October 1839 it was prescribed that in future duplicate land grants would be made, one to be given to the purchaser and the other to be retained by the Commissioner.[8]

Henry Gawler (1827-1894)
Henry was the son of Governor Gawler and after being admitted to the Bar in England in 1852 returned to Australia in 1858. He worked as solicitor in the Land Titles Office – apart from four days as Attorney General as his part in the Boothby saga – from 1858 to 1884. (SLSA)

Transactions in real property were carried on under the same system as was in force in England. During the first years of the colony, land speculation was rife and properties underwent rapid and remarkable transitions from hand to hand—so sudden in many cases that the preparation of the tedious formal conveyances could not keep pace with the requirements of purchasers.

The vital necessity of establishing a registry office was over and over again urged, both in the colony and by the Commissioners at home. The latter instructed Governor Gawler in July 1839 to adopt a system of registration of title with the least possible delay, and in December 1840 they are found still urging that if an act has not been passed, Mr Fisher's scheme, "with such modifications as experience and the actual circumstances which have arisen may suggest", should be forthwith proposed by the Governor to the Council.[9]

Perhaps the only subject upon which the press of South Australia in those days was unanimous was the importance of a registration system. It could not be overrated said the *South Australian*. Of the measures expected from the Council:

> '... the first in magnitude as in urgency are certainly the Registration Laws"—wrote the Register. "The confusion which has already arisen, from the minute divisions into which town allotments have been subjected, is almost entirely to be attributed to the want of a proper law enforcing the registration of sales of real property. Were a system organised by which registry could confer perfect security on all such titles and transfers, the public would surely never murmur because they paid a reasonable sum for it.'

And the *Adelaide Chronicle* added:

> 'It will be very difficult to repair the mischief inflicted upon the colony since the time of its establishment from the want of a

> Registration Act, or to extricate the titles to real property from the lamentable confusion into which they have fallen by any legislative enactment.' [10]

In May 1839 Mr W.A. Poulden, an Adelaide solicitor, wrote to Mr Justice Cooper:

> 'In investigating the titles, I find that a system of transfer has been adopted alike ruinous to the Purchaser or Lessee, or even to a Mortgagee. I do not mean to advance for one moment that such has invariably been the case, but in a new colony like this, where a complete mania at present exists for land speculation, I think for the security of all parties concerned some beneficial legislative enactment may be framed by the Council for the establishment, say, of a Registration or Enrolment Office ... I would suggest the passing of a Legislative Act creating a Registration or Enrolment Office, where the Original Grants of all lands, from the Crown, with plans, should be deposited, or copies of them; and I would made it imperative, that every transfer of land in this Province, be the same by Conveyance, Lease, Assignment, or Mortgage, should be registered or inrolled within a certain period after sale &c upon payment of a certain fee, or else to be void. Let the fee for each transfer already effected be very trifling, and let the fees for all future transfers be fixed at such a rate as would remunerate the officer appointed to be Registrar. Thus the Colonial Government would be indemnified against all expenses incident to the creation of such an office, and every holder of property rendered more secure, and I would venture to assert that no dissentient voice could be raised against a system so manifestly for the benefit of all; or, should the Colonial Government think it right to receive the fees with a view to the increase of the Colonial Revenue, let them do so, and appoint an Officer or Officers at stated salaries.' [11]

Still the Government slept. Bernard, the Advocate-General, drafted a bill, but it was not until January 1840 that it was introduced into the Council.[12] There it stuck at the second reading. Petitions were lodged against it, alleging that registration by memorial instead of by deposit of the original documents, or copies of them, was ineffectual because it did not disclose enough of the contents of the document to enable anyone to judge accurately of the effect of the document. Registration of original documents or duplicates, on the contrary, would:

(a) dispense with the necessity of covenants for the production of title deeds; and

(b) preserve complete evidence of title, although the owner might lose by fire or accident documents in his possession; while
(c) official copies could be obtained where necessary to transmit titles to England.[13]

The matter was referred to the Judge, who prepared an amended bill, framed on the Registration Act for the North West Riding of Yorkshire. In one important feature, namely the effect of an unregistered deed as against a subsequent purchaser having previous notice of it, the Bill differed from its model.

> 'According to the construction put on the English Registration Acts'—the Judge wrote—'which are silent respecting notice and which the former Draft followed in this respect, a purchaser would be bound in Equity by a Deed of which he had notice although such Deed would not bind him in law. It is certainly against conscience for anyone to take advantage of an omission to register a deed of which he has actual previous notice, because he cannot be prejudiced by the omission, but notice is sometimes presumed from circumstances, and questions may arise as to what circumstances are sufficient to create the presumption. As I think it peculiarly inconvenient that such questions should be raised here, where the same Judge sits at law and in Equity, I have endeavoured to provide against litigation on this point by providing that no notice shall have effect unless it be by an instrument to which the subsequent purchaser is a party.'

Upon the question of enrolment, by memorial or at length, he canvassed the pros and cons at great length. The latter would be more important, he thought, if there were means of making enrolments of deeds on parchment. Parchment skins, however, were scarce in South Australia and he doubted whether the advantage to be gained:

> '... by enrolling on so perishable a material as paper would counter-balance the additional expense which would be occasioned by it to individuals and to Government, which would be very considerable, arising from the necessity of having a distinct set of books and indices and additional clerks at a high rate of wages'.

After a certain amount of characteristic weathercock wavering, he "ventured to recommend" registration by memorial in preference to deposit of the original deeds.

> 'Assuming that the first object of every system of registration is to prevent fraud, I think the next ought to be to effect this with as little interference with private rights and prejudices and

with as little costs and inconvenience to parties as possible, and taking these two objects together I am of opinion that they can be better obtained by registering a memorial of every deed as proposed in the present Draft Bill than by the other method. The Memorial gives such information as is necessary to prevent fraud, without disclosing more. It gives sufficient notice of the nature and extent of every conveyance and incumbrance affecting property to put persons on their guard against fraud whilst the title deeds are left in the custody of the owners. I do not see that a deposit of the title deeds gives protection against fraud, but it may be said in its favour that deeds are not likely to be lost and will always be forthcoming. This is true if the office be very well arranged and always very well managed, but if otherwise persons are more likely to be injured by the misplacing of documents in a public office than by the loss of them if left in private custody. They will at all events in ordinary cases be much less accessible; for persons wanting to see them must go to the office for that purpose and be kept waiting till it is convenient for the Registrar or his Clerk to attend to them; they must then peruse them with much less convenience than they could if they were in private custody; and after they are perused some one must take care that they are restored to their proper place. Besides being more inconvenient it would also be more expensive. This is not very obvious at first sight; for a registration by deposit seems more simple and inexpensive, but it is only necessary to look at Schedule No 2 of the Registration Bill prepared by Mr Fisher to see that besides the mere deposit it would be necessary to have indexes of reference and entries almost as lengthy as the Memorials now proposed to be used; indeed to be useful they must be quite as lengthy for they should contain what that Schedule omits vizt [sic] a description of the property affected by the document indexed, or the document itself must be referred to in every case. Nor would these entries supersede the necessity for copies of the title deeds either in the first instance or whenever a professional opinion might be required as to title; and moreover as it would be improper to remove the deeds themselves from their place of custody, it would be necessary to have office copies of any deeds required to be produced in evidence. I think it will be obvious from what I have said above that the plan of registration by deposit of the deeds will generally be more expensive and troublesome to parties than a registration by a Memorial. It must also in the

> first instance be more expensive to Government; it will require a much larger building and much more costly fitting up. It will also be more difficult for the registering clerks; for whereas the professional man who prepares a conveyance can at the same time easily make a memorial of it which any person who can write may copy into the Register Books, it will take a person, even if he be conversant with deeds, a considerable time to make the necessary abstracts from documents which he has never before seen. There is, moreover, one disadvantage peculiar to this Province which registration by deposit of deeds has in comparison with registration by memorial. Almost every conveyance I have seen has been on paper; and as it will be impossible to find and take out any one document from a bundle without in some degree rubbing others, the wear and tear of deeds in searching will be considerable. On the whole it appears to me that the advantage arising from a deposit of title deeds is not so great as to compensate for the expense and inconvenience it would occasion.'

A further objection to deposit of the original deeds was that to provide for the safe custody and easy reference of the instruments, which would be of all kinds, shapes and sizes, would require a more complex and costly arrangement than the custody of and reference to mere memorials.

> 'After the best consideration I can give to this subject I cannot recommend a general system of registration by deposit either of original or duplicate deeds. I am, however, not at all wedded to the plan of registration by memorial, and if I could hope that deeds could be uniformly so much shortened as to make the copying them as little troublesome as copying memorials, I should prefer the plan of registering at full length as the most simple, altho' not in all respects the most convenient.'

He could not, however, recommend relying upon an Act of Parliament to shorten the language of deeds. "Many occasions will arise rendering special covenants and provisions necessary"—and, he added sarcastically—"many more in which professional men will think them so."

He therefore advised the adoption as a general system of the method of registering deeds by depositing memorials of them at the Registry Office, with the exception of:

(1) Original land grants and land orders which were short and could be lodged or copies in full.

(2) Judgments, which could be registered by a mere index containing the names of plaintiffs and defendants, and the date and amount of the judgment.

(3) Wills, of which duplicates on parchment could be lodged, filed in consecutive order and indexed.[14]

At length, in October 1841, an Act to provide for the Registration of Deeds, wills, judgments, conveyances and other instruments was passed (5 Vic No 8). It established a registration office and provided for registration by memorial. The Act remained in force until it was repealed and substantially re-enacted by the Registration of Deeds Act 1935, and its provisions are too familiar to require any detailed examination.

When the Act was sent home, the Secretary of State took objection to a provision which gave precedence to a deed executed and registered in the colony over an earlier deed executed out of the colony but enrolled later, and he required the Act to be amended in this respect. This caused the passing of the Act 6 Vic No 12.[15]

The essential point to be noted with regard to the Registration Act is that it was not an act to establish the validity of titles. Registration was optional and did not validate a bad title. In the case of conflicting deeds, however, that which was first registered prevailed.

By the neglect to establish a system of compulsory registration of dealing with land at the founding of the colony, a unique opportunity of providing a complete record of transactions in real property had been forever lost. When the Registration Act came into force, transactions had been far too numerous and too confused for it to be made retrospective.

> 'There seems to have been in this Province, from the first of its establishment'—remarked the Observer in 1843—'a system of transfer from hand to hand of incomplete purchase deeds and ineffectual securities prepared by parties not legally educated; and we can only suppose that the original low price of the land and the novelty of their position rendered the colonists careless of legal consequences in their first bargains. Lawyers were looked upon as necessary evils to be endured as little as possible; cheap law obtained from unqualified persons who offered it, at the time was perhaps thought good enough law; and the dispensers of it good enough lawyers.' [16]

Many of the titles to estates in the colony, freehold and leasehold, were indeed unsafe and imperfect. "Look to your titles and to your title deeds" was a piece of advice very frequently pressed upon the colonists. In addressing the Grand Jury in March 1846, Mr Justice Cooper said:

> 'A man may buy and pay for land, have his deeds registered, and years hence the title may prove insufficient. I have seen many deeds which would come under this remark. There is another thing about which a mistake exists. It is thought that

> when a conveyance is signed and registered, all is done which is necessary; but the most important thing is to examine the title of the seller. Registration does not, as some fancy, make a bad title good.' [17]

With the object of providing "for such defects in existing titles to land as must necessarily have resulted from the difficulty of procuring, in a young and unsettled community, the assistance of duly educated legal practitioners and conveyancers" Governor Grey procured the insertion into the Ordinance 6 and 7 Vic No 15 ("To Facilitate Conveyances of Real Estate") of a section providing that:

> '... whereas many conveyances of lands and hereditaments have been heretofore made in this Province by means of deeds of feoffment and deeds of release without any accompanying livery of seisin having been made in the case of such conveyances by way of feoffment and without any previous actual entry or deed of bargain and sale or lease in the case of such deeds of release and it is apprehended that great difficulty will hereafter arise in the establishing a good title to lands and hereditaments so conveyed by either of the means aforesaid and it is therefore deemed expedient to provide against such an evil'—

all such imperfect conveyances should be deemed to have been properly made and executed.[18]

The Registration Act, once in operation, worked smoothly and the gradual but steady progress made is revealed in the following return of registrations for the years 1842 to 1850:[19]

Number of	**1842**	**1843**	**1844**	**1845**	**1846**	**1847**	**1848**	**1849**	**1850**
Mortgages	78	64	52	50	56	88	175	355	634
Land grants	-	-	31	74	83	188	245	343	643
Conveyances and other instruments	777	356	405	558	778	971	1,260	2,113	3,288
Bills of sale	36	63	67	51	57	45	65	58	84
Judgments	17	21	4	3	2	4	2	8	14
Warrants of attorney	32	43	25	14	14	7	10	23	19

During the same period the fees received annually rose from £588 10s 0d to £3,347 2s 3d.

Early in the 1850s, however, the question of improving the registration system came to the fore. Mr Justice Cooper, in a letter to Mr Worthington (an Adelaide solicitor) in February 1852, came directly to the great stumbling block in the way of further progress.

> 'After all the simplification which can be made in the forms of security upon real property"—he wrote—"there will remain the never ending difficulty of title. It will still be necessary as a

matter of prudence to have the advice of a professional man, upon every advance of money on a bill of land, or in a transfer of it. In short, in order to render a mortgage or a bill of land as easy of transfer as a Bill of Exchange and at the same time retaining the security of a mortgage of real property, it will be necessary to alter the law of real property, and to assimilate it to that of personal property. This is a very extensive and intricate subject which I cannot pretend to discuss within the space of a letter. It is one of great interest especially in a young and almost a new settlement.' [20]

From this time on, the columns of the newspapers were filled with lengthy articles and correspondence upon the registration question, which was agitated for several years before it was resolved by the passing of the Real Property Act in 1857.

Amendment of the registration system was advocated by a committee of the Legislative Council in 1851 and Mr Hanson was instructed to prepare a bill. He promised to do his best, although, he wrote:

> '... I am by no means confident of my ability to execute the task thus imposed upon me. The improvement of the law of registration involves many of the most difficult and doubtful points of English law.' [21]

He prepared a bill accordingly which was submitted to the Governor and to Mr Justice Cooper in December 1852. The old issue as to the merits of registration by memorial or registration of the originals or copies was revived and debated once more. The Judge preferred the former because:

(1) Owners of land were generally unwilling to part with the custody of their title deeds.
(2) Greater responsibility was imposed on the government officers if they had to look after original deeds.
(3) The original deeds would occasionally have to be produced in court, which would be inconvenient if the deeds were bound in volumes.

> 'Undoubtedly the present system of registration is defective'—he said—'but I think the principal defect is in the indexes and in the want of subdivisions in the register into districts, so that searches are very difficult and laborious and are daily becoming more so.' [22]

Mr Hanson was not an enthusiast upon registration. He was convinced, he said, that any system of registration must at an earlier or more remote period "break down by its own weight".

> 'The Transfers of landed property are so frequent and the

> manner in which the different titles become united and afterwards diverge and become united with others is so various and complicated, that I despair of seeing any system adopted which shall for more than a few years possess the requisites of clearness and simplicity, and which will not ultimately cause greater expense and insecurity than it prevents.'

If deeds were registered by deposit of the originals, then copies should be provided or kept by the owners.

> 'If not, is not the risk of annihilating the evidence of perhaps half the titles in the Colony by a fire in the Registry Office too great to be incurred by the Government?' [23]

In another report, in May 1853, Mr Hanson wrote:

> 'That the present system requires amendment is unquestionable ... I do not think that the English law with all its incidents derived from the feudal system and still bearing evident marks of its origin is adapted to the circumstances of a colony such as South Australia. I am unable to discover any valid reason for drawing a distinction between land and other property as regards the law according to which they are to be held, descend, and be distributed ... I think if the principle of requiring the registration of deeds is adopted, the direction of the legislature should be to make the Register the sole evidence of title, and to provide that no deed shall have any validity for any purpose until registered.' [24]

Here Mr Hanson was heading towards the great reform of the Real Property Act—the establishment of validity of title by registration.

No steps were taken by the Government, but registration remained one of the prominent topics of the day. In May 1856 Mr Anthony Forster moved in the Legislative Council that an address should be presented to the Governor requesting him to call the attention of the Crown law officers to the state of the law with regard to the conveyance of real property, with a view of simplifying and cheapening the transfer of land. The Advocate-General (Mr Hanson) said he did not oppose such a step, although he despaired of finding a measure at once simple and effectual by which the transfer of real property could be regulated.

> 'The simplification of the present system"—he said—"would require more time and deliberation than any other subject connected with the alteration of the law. The mere conveyances are as simple as they can be, but the complications of the system arise out of the necessity of deducing the title, which involves a great deal of careful investigation and consequent expense.' [25]

Mr Forster, who was the editor of the *Register*, followed up his motion by a series of articles in that paper in July 1856 advocating real property reform.

There has from time to time been discussion as to the precise share which Sir Richard Torrens had in the introduction of the measure of reform which bears his name.

> 'Torrens' fame'—wrote Dr Kerr—'has suffered from two detractions, the one contemporary, that of a charge of plagiarism on the score of the similarity of his measure with the report presented by the Commissioners on Registration of Title on 15th May 1857; the other, posthumous, that the real author of his system was not Torrens, but a Dr Hubbe, who wrote a pamphlet in his support.' [26]

Ulrich Hubbe ca. 1880 (SLSA)

Both of these charges Dr Kerr, after a careful examination of the report, unhesitatingly rejected as entirely unwarranted, and any further discussion of Torrens's right to have his name attached to the Real Property Act system is perhaps merely killing the slain. The true position cannot be open to any serious doubt and, to knock the opposing theories on the head once more, the leading facts may be summarised as follows:

(1) From the earliest days of the colony (and in particular during the years 1850 to 1856) the topic of registration had been thoroughly canvassed in Parliament, in the press and amongst the legal profession. The possibility of making validity of title dependent upon registration had, as we have seen, been recognised, as is shown by the comments of Mr Justice Cooper and Mr Hanson quoted above.

(2) Mr Forster, in the articles in the *Register* in July 1856, of which he afterwards claimed the authorship, advocated:

(a) The establishment of a registry office through which all titles must pass and which would have authority to authenticate and declare the validity of titles. (The genesis of this suggestion in the colony can be traced back to at least as early as 1843, in which year a correspondent in the *Southern Australian* suggested the adoption of the old feudal system of surrender to the lord and re-grant by him; the method of transfer of all land would be by handing in the grant to the Registrar-General, who would cancel it and issue a new grant to the transferee.)[27]

(b) Titles having been issued from a central tribunal with the stamp of validity should be transferred, when intact, by endorsement; and when divided, by a reissue for each particular part.

(c) He discussed the Merchant Shipping Act and its provisions as to transfer of title of ships, and recommended it as the groundwork of a code.

These articles, Mr Forster claimed, "struck a sympathetic chord" in the mind of Mr Torrens, who came forward:

> '... and professed his willingness, if supported by persons equally earnest with himself, to propound a scheme to meet the necessities of the case, and to free the colonists from the evils attendant upon the old system of transferring real property'. [28]

Torrens himself, in the pamphlet which he published in 1859, declared that he had had his attention:

> '... painfully drawn to the grievous injury and injustice inflicted under the English law of real property, by the misery and ruin which fell upon a relation and dear friend, who was drawn into the maelstrom of the Court of Chancery'—and that he then resolved:'...some day to strike a blow at that iniquitous institution'.

It would be absurd to attempt to restrict the stimulus which impelled Torrens along the path of reform to any particular incident, for he must have had the whole subject prominently brought before him in Parliament and in the press for many years. Probably the inadequacies of the old system were strikingly brought home to him by his own purchase of a piece of land at Brighton. He bought it from Mr Bartley, and before that it had belonged to Mr Justice Cooper and to Mr E.C. Gwynne. Yet notwithstanding that the property had thus been through the hands of three of the best lawyers in the colony, it was found that the title to part of it was defective.[29] (Perhaps the previous owners had discovered the defect and were anxious to pass on the land, like a bad half-crown.)

(3) The Prussian system of registration was known to him. It had been described, for instance, in the *Register* in August 1856 by a Tanunda correspondent who, after giving details of the code, sarcastically added that continental legislation was not likely to be followed:

'It is chargeable with the gross impropriety of admitting into its text the full stop—that low character so nicely eschewed by Brittania [sic] in her statutes. Good Gracious! John Bull to plot treason against the time-honoured, illegible, and ungrammatical sheepskin! to think scorn of an indenture and other sacred mysteries! to cast away his Lares and Penates, barrister, solicitor, agent, and all whom he had carried hither so tenderly, like Aeneas from burning Troy! to clear his dwelling of those dangerous cobwebs, permeable to big flies but wherein the little ones stick! and all this for the sake of a stranger creed, promulgated among the vassals of Brandenburg, and redolent of old Fritz's tabatiere.' [30]

In addition, information upon the working of the German code and of the registration system of the Hanse town was supplied to Torrens by Dr Hubbe.

(4) Torrens thus had ample material upon which to draw. His long service as Collector of Customs must have made him thoroughly conversant with the Merchant Shipping Act, while his experience as Registrar-General had familiarised him with the practice of registration. Making use of all the information derived from these various sources, he prepared a draft bill. In introducing the Bill in the Legislative Council in November 1856 he is reported to have said:

"I had thought of the subject for some time and submitted the draft of the Bill to several gentlemen in whose judgment I had confidence; but I did not call in a large number. I have been benefited by their advice and have altered many parts of the

> Bill ... I am happy to say that all approved of the principle, and I am preparing a fresh copy embodying their suggestions with regard to details. I have also had the assistance of a high legal authority—one who has devoted much time to that branch of law.' [31]

> There is no reason to doubt the accuracy of this contemporary statement. The real services rendered by Torrens were not that he was the actual inventor or first discoverer of the principles of the Real Property Act but that he took the matter in hand when others shrank from it, that he went to considerable trouble to embody the principles in a bill, and that he persisted with the Bill in the face of great opposition until he forced it through Parliament. He had assistance all the way through—he could not have succeeded without it, nor did he ever attempt to conceal it. Dr Hubbe sat just outside the bar of the House during the consideration of the Bill and was frequently consulted by Torrens.

In a letter to Mr W.H. Burford many years later, Torrens recalled that Burford had supported him by rounding up members when it appeared likely that the Bill would lapse through want of a quorum.

> 'I had laboured arduously'—he said—'devoting my best powers and my leisure hours to the project that is embodied in that Act, and which you state, and as all except a few professional bigots admit, has proved an immense boon to the landed interest in Australia and throughout the Colonial Empire, as it is now all but universally adopted. When I perceived that the tactics of the Government and the profession were to refuse me even a hearing on the subject, and that the representatives of the people were allowing themselves to be made instrumental to a 'Count out', I certainly had made up my mind to cease from wasting labour and energy on a cause that was so little appreciated.' [32]

In his dispatches the Governor (Sir Richard MacDonnell) uniformly gave the credit for the Act to Torrens. He spoke of it as "Mr Torrens's Act". In February 1858, when forwarding the original Real Property Act, he referred to the: "... indomitable perseverance, industry, and energy with which Mr Torrens has conducted the Act through all its various stages".

In July 1858 he wrote: "It cannot be denied that Mr Torrens has exhibited marked ability, industry and enduring courage in carrying his measure to a successful issue."

And in May 1859:

> 'I believe no Public man in this colony or elsewhere ever worked out a legal reform or engaged in a self-imposed public

task with more disinterested perseverance than has been shown by Mr Torrens in all his labours connected with the Real Property Act.'[33]

Finally, it may be observed that Torrens at the time claimed the credit for the measure—acknowledging, of course, that he had assistance—and that this claim was not disputed until many years later, when perverse ingenuity attempted to deprive him of an honour which he had undoubtedly earned.

The system of land transfer introduced by the Real Property Act is so well known and has been so thoroughly considered in works of authority that any examination of its details here would be superfluous. It is proposed only to add a few remarks upon the difficulties experienced by Torrens in putting his measure into operation, after he had forced it through Parliament. A good deal has already been said as to this in the chapter dealing with Mr Justice Boothby, and what follows is merely supplementary.

The objects of the Act according to Torrens were fourfold—to introduce into the law of real property Certainty, Economy, Simplicity and Facility. To the achievement of these desirable ends the legal profession was opposed almost en masse. Their opposition was universally attributed to their fear of losing the profits of the old system of conveyancing. This no doubt had some influence upon them, but it was rather a conservative mistrust of such a sweeping change in the law which actuated them. The shrewder members of the profession were not much afraid of their purses growing thinner as a result of the Act. In January 1858 a young articled clerk, Samuel James Way, destined to become Chief Justice, wrote to a relative in England:

> 'The present Cabinet is a strong one, and our legislators have settled down to work in right earnest. They are passing measures, of the last importance and the utmost intricacy, through both Houses at railway speed. Inter alia is Torrens's Bill (prepared by a non-professional man) which essays to alter the whole law relating to the transfer of real property. Its supporters innocently imagine that it would do away with almost all the emoluments of the conveyancers. The initiated see in it the seeds of interminable litigation, and a gold mine for the present generation of lawyers. I have not taken the trouble to read the Bill yet. It will be time eno' to do that when it becomes law. If there are no costs to be extracted from it, it will be an ingenious scheme indeed.'[34]

The hostility of the profession, however, was only slowly overcome. Mr Gwynne went so far as to assert in Parliament that his firm would advise their clients not to advance moneys on mortgage on properties under the Real Property Act. A large proportion of the deeds of title were in the hands of the legal profession, who were enabled to exercise an influence over landholders inimical to the working of the Act and to dissuade them from bringing their land under it.[35] A step had been taken, however, which could not be retraced and it was impossible that the old system could be reverted to once the new one was under way.

It was soon discovered that the first Real Property Act had many practical and technical deficiencies.

> 'It may however be admitted'—pointed out Sir Richard MacDonnell—'that in opening out a path so novel, many obstacles and many difficulties must be expected to arise during the progress of so extensive a change, and it is no discredit that all those difficulties and objections had not been earlier foreseen.'[36]

An Act introducing numerous amendments was hurriedly passed in 1859, upon which the Governor commented:

> 'I would be sorry to think that the Act of the Session 1857-58, and the enclosed Act were to terminate the legislation intended to effect such sweeping changes in the law and tenure of real property. On the contrary I feel that an Act like the enclosed—which in its second section repeals upwards of fifty sections of the Act which it is intended to amend—and which nevertheless is also by its 3rd section declared to be a part of, and to be read and construed as one with the Act of which it repeals so considerable a portion, is obviously a measure, which though suitable if merely intended temporarily to meet certain objections and make certain amendments not admitting of postponement, cannot be considered as properly entitled to occupy a permanent position in the Statute Law of the colony. It still remains to collect all the amendments to the enclosed Act, and those which further experience may suggest, and consolidate them into one comprehensive Real Property Act—worthy of the reform contemplated and already in a great measure accomplished.'[37]

The consolidating measure for which he wished was passed in 1860, embodying the changes which several years' experience had suggested.

> 'Despite a very active and persistent opposition on the part of some members of the legal profession'—the Governor then reported—'the measure continues to hold a high place in public estimation.'[38]

A further amending Act in 1861 followed the report of the Real Property Act Commission appointed in that year and, in sending the Act home, the Governor said that it showed there was:

> '... a keen and laudable spirit of perseverance in this legislature and this people, which will assuredly succeed despite of any opposition, even from quarters which ought to set the foremost example of willing obedience to the laws, and of readiness to promote their operation'. [39]

The Real Property Act system was by this time so firmly established as to place out of the question all further hope of ousting it, and the legal profession had to make the best of it. In parting with this topic, it may not be out of place to give an extract (the length of which will be excused by the amusing vigour of its language) from Mr Harrison's *Colonial Sketches*, published in 1862:

> 'It is not improbable'—he wrote—'that the days of the majority of the colonial lawyers are numbered. About four years ago they were advancing so swimmingly in the plundering line, that a legal millenium [sic] in South Australia might be supposed to have arrived, when unfortunately for their peace of mind a Goliath appeared in the shape of a civilian of no legal training whatever, who undertook to bring their mysteries to the scrutiny of common sense, and produced a Bill entirely upsetting the old system of conveyancing, and by a public registration of title made the transfer of land as cheap and expeditious as any other commercial transaction, and in fact sounded the death knell of slow conveyancing in the colony of South Australia. A discordant wail broke forth from the despairing hair-splitters, who first smiled contentedly at the folly of an ignoramus attempting to understand and explode their favourite amusements connected with their profession; but when the people almost unanimously determined to have the reformation, they exhibited, in many cases, an illustration of the external appearance of the knight with the sorrowful countenance, and tried humility as an interesting change from their former pretensions. A correspondent to one of the papers advised some of the slow conveyancers to look out for reputable employment, but this was hardly compatible with their precedents, for they are distinguished for a preugnance [sic] to hard work ... I am convinced that respectable members of the legal profession in England have no conception of the greed and meanness displayed by many of their brethren in South Australia, which are too often compelled to be made known to the initiated by the existence of a Public Registry

Office for Deeds of all transactions connected with land, and consequently any person on paying a fee can go and search against any property and ascertain what position it is in ... The colonial lawyers have literally brought about their own destruction by an obstinate adherence to old forms and expensive and tedious processes, which are obnoxious in England, and much more so in a new place, where the land is of so little value, and cut up into innumerable allotments and distributed among a much poorer class of people than in England, and where, in consequence, the people demand a speedy and mercantile system of transfer lease and mortgage; and as the lawyers, blind in their own avarice and conceit, would not make gradual concessions to the wants of the age, they have ultimately induced a civilian to lay the axe to the root of the whole system, and by making the Registration Office a government institution, do away with their services almost altogether.' [40]

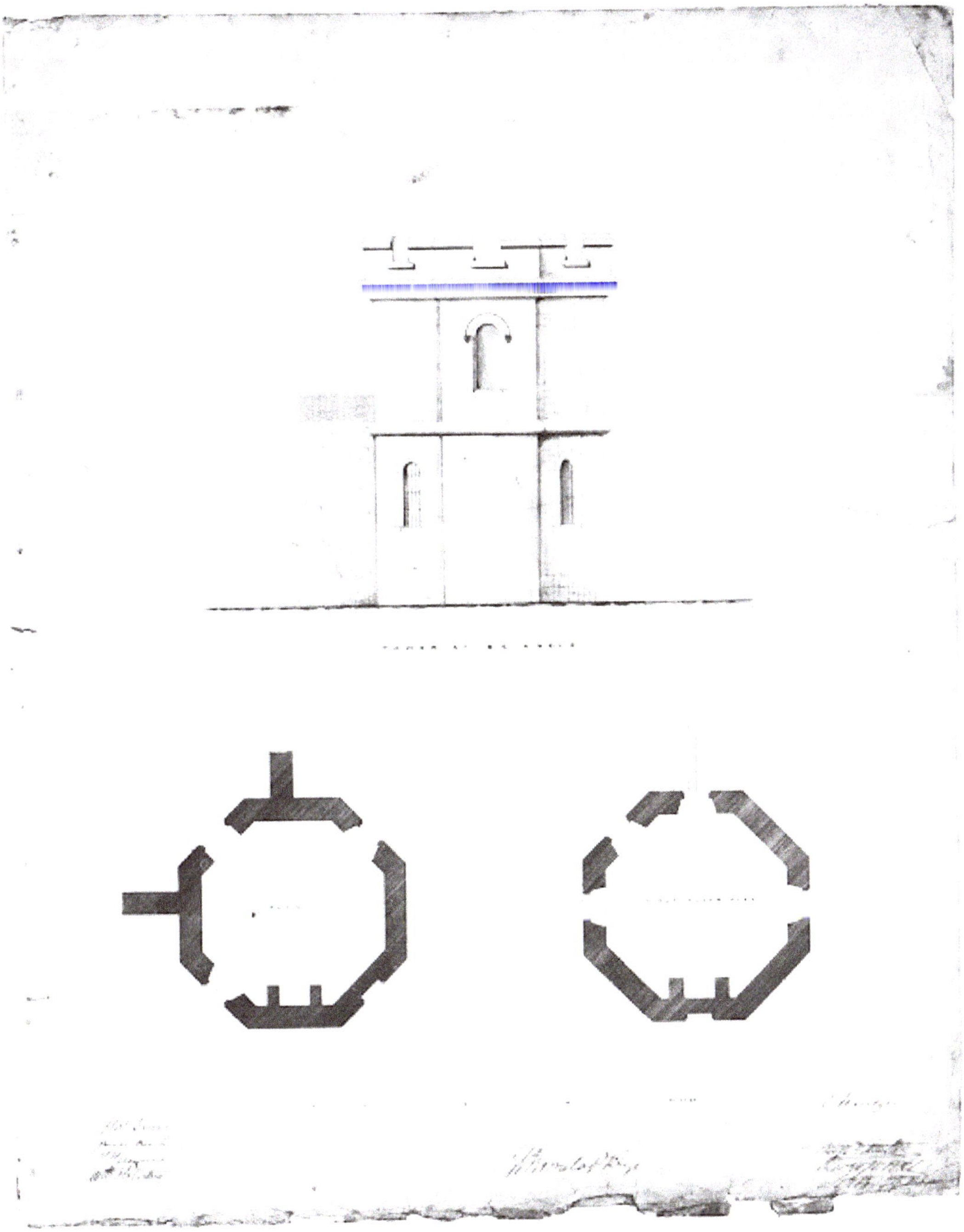

Architectural drawing of a Gaol tower. Five towers were originally planned but because of their high cost only two were built and only one completed. (SR/ DAIS)

Chapter 13

The Gaol

'high walls and strong doors'

Within a few weeks of the proclamation of the colony a firm of builders was tendering for the erection of a wooden gaol at Adelaide, at an estimated cost of £250.[1] Apparently the price was too high, for nothing came of the proposal, nor was an offer some months later to construct a prison for £168 any more successful.[2] Prisoners were kept in irons on board the *Buffalo* until the vessel sailed in June 1837, when another place of confinement had to be found.[3] The Council, as usual, disagreed. Gouger wanted a lockup onshore; Mann proposed that the captain of the *Tam O'Shanter* be contracted with to take prisoners on board.[4] Two prisoners who were on the *Buffalo* were temporarily transferred to the *Tam O'Shanter*, and the *Buffalo* took away a few of the most scoundrelly marines.[5]

The next step, shortly afterwards, was the erection of a structure which, as Sir Henry Ayers afterwards said, "was certainly not adapted to the end in view—the safe keeping of prisoners".[6] It consisted of a tent, "with an airing ground in front enclosed with a rope, round which one of the turnkeys patrolled with a Brown Bess musket". Owing to the facilities for escape, the prisoners were kept heavily ironed and allowed little exercise. They slept on the bare ground, without even a blanket to cover them. A petition for relief which they sent to Governor Hindmarsh bears an endorsement by him that he was "daily shocked at seeing the miserable condition in which these unfortunate men are placed, for even the Marines who are well clothed and have both greatcoats and blankets suffer considerably".[7]

T. Horton James, in his *Six Months in South Australia*, wrote of the state of things at this time:

> 'As there is no jail in the place, the prison being nothing but a canvas tent, of course there cannot be expected to be so much of terror excited in the criminal as there might be; and a notion had almost got abroad that the laws are powerless—the Judges weak—and that any offence might be committed with impunity.' [8]

Early in 1838 the tent was replaced by a wooden lockup house of two small compartments each nine feet by ten, ventilated by means of loopholes eighteen inches deep and four inches wide, played outwards. Other buildings were subsequently added, and the whole was surrounded by a pine fence, with a wicket gate at which a sentry was stationed.[9] W.B. Ashton was appointed Governor of the Gaol,[10] Sergeant Mew was Gaoler, and marines acted as warders. Escapes were frequent. "No reliance whatever can be placed on the vigilance of the Marines," complained the Sheriff.[11]

In July 1838 Sergeant Mew was replaced as Gaoler by James Hately, and the escapes became less frequent. Hately's methods were effective but rough. In October 1838, when Hately was fined £5 for ill-treating a prisoner who had escaped and had been recaptured, the Sheriff asked that the fine should be remitted.

> 'Since Hately has had charge of the Gaol, I have every reason to be pleased with his management, as before he was appointed Gaoler, prisoners were constantly escaping and the Gaol presented a scene of confusion forming a striking contrast to the present order and regularity of this department.'

Hately having promised not to use unnecessary violence again, his fine was remitted by Stephen, the Acting Governor, who requested the Sheriff to impress upon the Gaoler "the absolute necessity, while holding his present office, of restraining any petulance of temper".[12]

Governor and staff at Adelaide Gaol by H. Glover shows William Bake Ashton, his son A.J. Ashton and staff in the interior of the gaol ca. 1850. (SLSA)

The Sheriff (Mr C.C. Dutton) reported in November 1838:

> 'The present insecure state of Her Majesty's Gaol for the Province renders it highly necessary for me to call the attention of His Excellency the Governor to the necessity of erecting a new and suitable building. The value of a well-regulated Gaol to a young colony must be very great; for not only will it do away with the necessity of sending our convicts to the neighbouring colonies, but in securing to this Province the benefit of their labour (which even the Mother Country has now found to be desirable) Public Buildings may be erected at a small expense, thereby conferring a lasting benefit on the community.'

He recommended that a site should be chosen where plenty of stone could be quarried on the spot and a substantial wall of at least twenty feet high built enclosing a square within which buildings could be erected from time to time as required. Governor Gawler approved of his plan and undertook to fix the site at an early date.[13]

Nothing was done for eighteen months. Meanwhile the condition of the prisoners was deplorable. They were herded together in an ill-ventilated and insanitary hut. In August 1838 there were thirteen prisoners in a gaol built to hold nine, and it was suggested to Mr Jickling, the Acting Judge, (but without avail) that he should hold a Session of Gaol Delivery to make more room and to save the public the expense of keeping any who might be acquitted.[14] By December 1838 the number had grown to twenty, of whom fourteen or fifteen were awaiting trial, the next sessions being four months ahead.[15] Many were sick, and the Sheriff complained that the Colonial Surgeon never went near the Gaol.[16] The amenities of the prisoners may be imagined from the following inventory of all the articles in charge of the Gaoler for the use of the Gaol:

> '4 pair shackle handcuffs, 3 iron bars, 15 iron shackles, 1 small padlock, 7 pair cross irons, 3 iron pots, 1 frying pan, set of iron work for stocks, 1 water cask, 2 washing tubs. Bedding: 8 beds; 15 rugs; 5 stretchers. Tools: 2 shovels, 1 cross cut saw, 2 axes, 1 bullock chain.' [17]

The prisoners, however, had a few alleviations. Solitary confinement was an impossibility. Those sentenced to hard labour had nothing to do. An attempt to make them work at the Port proved abortive.[18]

Negrohead
A strong black tobacco.

> 'Unless the sentences passed by his Honour the Judge are enforced with the utmost vigour'—wrote the Sheriff—'they become ridiculous and the community will at last begin to look upon the proceedings in the Supreme Court as a pleasant farce performed for their amusement, and the Gaol as a place of recreation where O.P. Rum and figs of Negrohead may be obtained ad libitum. In order to keep those prisoners sentenced to hard labour at work, tools are absolutely necessary, and as a few falling axes &c can be purchased at a small expense, I beg to urge the necessity of their being provided for the use of the Gaol; for if funds are wanting for all other purposes surely the requisite expenses attending the due administration of the law must be provided by the Legislature, or all security of life and property is at an end. Considering the numerous public buildings and other necessary works required by the Government, and there being no means of keeping prisoners in solitary confinement at

> present, it would be better that all the prisoners ... should be required to labour, and a ration allowed them accordingly.' [19]

The inmates of the Gaol chatted with their friends over the five-foot fence which surrounded it.

> 'It was quite usual for the prisoners to convert the prison into a drinking shop, and they had not the least difficulty in procuring liquor and enjoying it with their visitors.' [20]

Mr Ashton having posted upon the front of the Gaol a notice forbidding persons to bring spirits to the prisoners, the amount of liquor consumed within the Gaol was limited to the quantity which could be smuggled across the back fence when the sentry was not looking.[21]

Altogether the building was, as Governor Gawler wrote to Rowland Hill, "the most deplorable contrivance for confinement that can be imagined".[22]

> 'Prisoners are only detained in the old building called the "gaol"'—wrote the Governor on another occasion—'by a degree of excited attention on the part of the governor, gaoler, turnkeys and sentries, which could not be permanently maintained, and which has been only supported thus far by the prospect of relief from the erection of a proper edifice.' [23]

The local press denounced the Gaol as "a wretched and filthy hovel".[24]

During 1839 conditions were improved. A more efficient gaol guard was recruited.[25] "We do not hear now"—it was said—"as on former occasions, when a prisoner has been called for to take his trial, 'Your Honour, he has escaped.'" [26]

The Act 2 Vic No 1, regulating the retailing of liquor, contained stringent provisions forbidding the introduction of liquor into the Gaol (sections XLI to XLIV). What was perhaps the most unfortunate defect in the system remained unremedied. Owing to the crowded state of the Gaol, no separation between various classes of prisoners—convicted felons, debtors, men awaiting trial—was possible, and they were all herded together. The Grand Jury, in a presentment at the Criminal Sessions of March 1840, described the Gaol as:

> '... altogether inefficient as regards the proper accommodation and the safe custody of the prisoners ... The prisoners are in a fearfully crowded state, and no classification of them can be effected. The debtor cannot be kept apart from the felon: and the unhappy men condemned to die do not enjoy that decent solitude befitting their awful condition'.[27]

In May of that year the Governor brought the question before the Legislative Council. Respectable persons imprisoned for debt, he pointed out, were confined with criminals of the worst description—most of them runaway convicts and sailors—and all were kept in "not by walls, but by a multiplication of sentries, creating a very expensive gaol establishment".[28]

The number of debtors in gaol steadily increased. In May 1840 there were seventy to eighty persons confined on various charges.[29] As there was no other gaol in the province, all prisoners from country districts had to be committed to Adelaide. The Act 4 Vic No 1, passed in June 1840, authorised and directed magistrates in country districts thus to commit prisoners. The Commissioners in England criticised the Act for making no provision that whenever a gaol should be erected in any district, the power of committing to Adelaide from that district should cease.[30]

A site for a new gaol was selected in July 1840, but it was not until March 1841 that the buildings were so far completed as to permit of prisoners being removed to it.[31] The Grand Jury visited the old Gaol and found it to be "a most miserable, insecure and filthy prison". In the new Gaol, on the other hand, "the security and comfort of the prisoners confined therein appears to have been judiciously attended to".[32] The Sheriff's report on the state of the old Gaol when it was vacated presented a squalid picture:

> 'It consists of one stone building for twelve prisoners, the rear wall of which is in so bad a state that were it not for the building immediately behind it, it would fall out. One wooden building, the outer part of which (together with the stone foundation) is totally out of repair, so much so that we have lately been obliged to place an extra guard outside for the security of the prisoners. A wooden building for Females, also in want of repair ... These buildings are surrounded by the common five foot fence, with spikes on the top, the whole of which, with the gates, are crumbling down, and afford little or no security for the safe keeping of prisoners, seven of whom made their escape from Gaol during the past year in consequence of the insecurity of these buildings and this fence.' [33]

At the time of transfer, the number of prisoners had fallen to 44.[34]

No item of Governor Gawler's expenditure has been so seriously criticised as the Gaol, and it was undoubtedly an extravagant building. According to Mr Dutton (*South Australia and its Mines* pp.121-122) the Gaol was "a libel on our free, industrious and well-disposed population: it is a libel on a colony proverbial for the security of both life and property". Mr Harrison, in his amusing but unreliable *Colonial Sketches*, wrote:

> 'The most striking architectural object on entering Adelaide, by the railway from the Port, is an immense prison, which cannot fail to give the newly-arrived emigrants a wholesome idea of the necessities and tendencies of the colony. This large jail was planned by a somewhat facetious Governor, who, in reply to the urgent demands of the colonists for the distribution of the public money in reproductive works, commenced this establishment, much to the indignation of some worthy colonists, who could not see prophetically that this large building would soon be too small for the prospective wants of the colony.' [35]

An architectural drawing of the front of the gaol. (SR/ DAIS)

It was a long time before the Gaol was found too small. It was constructed to hold 48 male felons, 12 female felons and 58 debtors—in all, 116 prisoners, with room for another 25 in case of necessity. The passing of the Insolvent Act rendered the provision for so many debtors quite unnecessary. During 1842 the average number of prisoners was about forty. In the following year it dropped to about thirty. In February 1843 the Sheriff was able proudly to report that there were no debtors at all in the Gaol—an event which had not happened for four years.[36] Governor Gawler was undoubtedly right in contending that "it would have been folly to have built a gaol too small",[37] but he should have foreseen the reductions in the number of debtor prisoners which the passing of an Insolvent Act would bring about.

The Council having approved the Governor's recommendations that a new gaol should be built, the Colonial Architect prepared plans and specifications, and the tender of Messrs Borrow and Goodiar, a respectable firm of builders, was accepted. The actual contract with them was later lost in a fire and it became a matter of dispute as to what its provisions were. According to Governor Gawler, the contract price (only one-half of the building being erected at first) was £18,000. As work progressed, considerable departures from the original plans and estimates were made without any authority, and carelessly acquiesced by the government officials supposed to be superintending operations. The most wasteful expenditure was on the towers of the Gaol. "Which of you," says Scripture, "intending to build a tower, sitteth not down first and counteth the cost, whether he have sufficient to finish it?"[38] The answer appears to be Governor Gawler, for one. From a memorandum left by Captain Sturt, it seems that the Governor passed the plans for the towers without particularly examining them, as he was busy when they were submitted to him.[39]

> 'High walls and strong doors were doubtless necessary'—remarked Sir Henry Ayers, many years later—'but not angle towers, surmounted with cut-stone battlements, the stone alone costing 42s per cube foot to work, while for other services artisans were paid from £3/18/- to £4/4/- per week, and the cost generally was so greatly enhanced from the high price of labour and unforeseen contingencies that it brought ruin upon a most respectable firm of contractors, and involved the colony in debt for years afterwards.' [40]

Governor Gawler does not seem to have been dissatisfied with the progress of the work.

> 'Errors have been committed in the course of its construction by the Architect'—he said—'but as a whole it is a well designed and admirably built edifice. Its proportions are large, as being a portion of a large model, but its accommodations are not greater than the colony in an increasing state requires.' [41]

Governor Grey, however, took a very different view. An adequate gaol could in his opinion have been erected for £4,000 to £5,000, whereas when he arrived in the colony Messrs Borrow and Goodiar had already received £13,800 and the building was only partly finished. "It has been in portions very carelessly executed, and for years to come there is no chance of its being even half filled with prisoners." [42] He promptly put a stop to the work. The contractors claimed a further £6,000 was due to them, and the celebrated case of Borrow and Goodiar against the local Government began its long career. The Colonial Architect inspected the works and valued them at £16,423. Then he valued them again, at £16,762. Then the contractors valued them and made it come to £19,713. Then the Government and the contractors agreed that the question should be referred to arbitration, and the arbitrator, setting aside the valuations of both parties, decided the true value of the whole work to be £32,022. Governor Grey went back on his submission and refused to accept the award.

S.T. Gill's sketch of Adelaide Gaol ca. 1850 (NLA)

Meanwhile the buildings had received a few finishing touches, and the Colonial Architect went and valued them again, this time at £19,647. After further argument the Government proposed that the matter should be taken before the Supreme Court, but, the Advocate-General having advised that there was no hope of obtaining a jury who would not give a verdict against the Government, this plan was hastily dropped. After long negotiations the contractors were paid another £6,132 and £600 expenses of arbitration, and another old account for work done by them at the Port was paid, and Governor Grey seems to have regarded the matter as settled.[43] But, in company with Ella Wheeler Wilcox, Messrs Borrow and Goodiar (or rather their creditors, for their estate had been assigned) believed that no question was ever settled until it was settled right. For years they pushed their claim without success. In 1852 the Claimants Relief Act was passed, enabling them to sue the Government. This they promptly did, and eventually the action was listed for trial. Torrens was named by the Governor as nominal defendant and in April 1856 the Advocate-General applied, on his behalf, for an injunction to restrain the claimants from proceeding to trial. The injunction was refused.[44] In July 1856 the trial came on before Mr Justice Cooper and after a hearing lasting several days the jury returned a verdict for the plaintiffs for £35,405 1s 5d, being a judgment for £15,735 11s 9d, with interest at 10 per cent for 12½ years.[45]

The Government obtained an order for a new trial and threatened to fight the case to the Privy Council.[46] The claimants were unable to finance the ruinous contest and they petitioned the Legislative Council for relief. Their petition was debated with acrimony, Mr Duffield declaring that the non-settlement of the Borrow and Goodiar claim was "the blackest spot in the history of South Australia".[47] Finally, £10,000 was paid to the assignee to settle the matter.[48] Disputes then arose amongst the creditors. Messrs Borrow and Goodiar, in 1842, had mortgaged the debt to the South Australian Banking Company, which now claimed the whole sum and sued the assignees in the Supreme Court to recover it. The assignees contended that the money had been voted by Parliament for Borrow and Goodiar's creditors in general and should be rateably distributed amongst them all, and they came back to Parliament in 1858 for a decision whether or not the money was so paid. The House refused to interfere in the matter and left them to their remedy in the courts, and with this the case of Borrow and Goodiar against the local Government disappears from human ken, after an existence of seventeen years.[49]

The Act 4 Vic No 7, to legalise the new Gaol, had a curious history. The Act was burned in the fire at old Government House in 1841, and not a single copy is known to exist. All that is known of the Act is its number and title. It was formally repealed in 1842.

In March 1840 it was decided that some use should be made of prison labour. The Judge had advised that without a special act prisoners could not be set to work outside the Gaol. By Act 3 Vic No 13 it was provided that all male persons sentenced to hard labour might be employed in labour upon such public roads or other public works within the province as the Governor in Council should direct. This step was generally approved.

> 'Hitherto'—said the Register—'the hard labour of the prisoners has been confined to smoking, sleeping, and devouring comfortable rations, occasionally varied by the privilege of assisting the drawing of a barrel of water from the river to the Gaol.' [50]

Chain gangs were formed, dressed in a conspicuous uniform of red cap, grey jacket with a number on the back, and red trousers, and these colourful squads were set to work roadmaking at North Adelaide.[51] The work was supposed to be from sunrise to sunset, and the men were allowed threepence a day as a gratuity for good work.[52] The working parties, however, were not very successful. Friends came to look on, and brought refreshments, and sometimes the whole gang—guards included—staggered back to the gaol intoxicated.[53]

In the following year, reduction in the number of guards made by Governor Grey in his economy campaign caused the working parties to be discontinued, as warders could not be spared to look after them.[54] The Governor complained that the great size of the Gaol made it impossible for him to make so great a reduction in the establishment there as he would have wished; capable of holding 140, the average number confined had only been about 40.[55]

Shortly afterwards a dispatch arrived from England disallowing the Act for the employment of prisoners on the ground that it increased the establishment of the colony without the sanction of the home authorities, and the inmates of the Gaol were again free from any necessity of working.[56]

Conditions within the Gaol were slightly improved. A rough classification was made into separate divisions for felons, debtors, and females. Each prisoner was allowed a mattress and a rug. The scale of rations was not luxurious. A debtor, for instance, was allowed, per week, seven pounds of bread, five pounds of meat, four ounces of tea, one pound of sugar and a quarter of a pound of rice.[57]

In October 1841 the Sheriff wrote calling attention to trouble which was being experienced with the female felons "owing to the impossibility of keeping them separate from the Guards who are on duty during the day between the walls and unavoidably in company with the female prisoners who may be confined in this space", and he asked that a separate enclosure should be made for women prisoners. The Colonial Secretary (Gouger) sent the complaint to the Governor, remarking that a proper classification of prisoners was a most important consideration in the construction of gaols, but it had been overlooked in the construction of the Adelaide Gaol. This evoked a reply from Governor Grey typical of his vigorous and economical methods:

> 'These alterations would require a considerable outlay. We have no money at present. Like other desirable objects they must therefore necessarily be postponed. I confess it appears to me to but ill accord with the Sheriff's usual discernment that he should keep such immoral Guards, at a time when so many men of excellent character are out of employment. I conceive the Sheriff is bound by his duty to the public instantly to dismiss any man whom he suspects of such conduct—in a case of this kind no feelings of kindness should be indulged. It would appear to me to be a much cheaper plan to dismiss immoral men, than to build separate enclosures to keep them from the female prisoners. You can hint something of this kind to Mr Newenham; I have perhaps put it too broadly.' [58]

By the Act 6 Vic No 4 (passed in October 1842) an attempt was made to regulate gaols and prisons within the colony. The Act shows, as Mr Justice Angas Parsons said: "... an early desire that those who had offended against the law should be fairly and humanely treated while subject to compulsory incarceration".[59]

The Governor was directed to appoint visiting justices, the Judge of the Supreme Court also having power to visit and examine any gaol at any time. Rules and regulations were to be drawn up for the good management of the gaol, the right to make regulations with regard to imprisoned debtors being reserved to the Supreme Court. Persons imprisoned but not sentenced to hard labour were to be set to light work by the Sheriff or visiting justices. With a view to economy, the Act stipulated that no prisoner who had the means of maintaining himself should have any claim to be kept at the public expense.

Great difficulty was experienced with native prisoners. The Sheriff complained that they ate the rations given them "with voracious haste" and were still hungry, and he had been reduced to feeding them to a large extent on rice, which was cheap, took a longer time to eat and left them better satisfied. To sentence natives to long terms of imprisonment was to sentence them to a lingering death; if shut up for any length of time they invariably pined and became ill, and had to be released.

> 'The punishment of death is neither so terrible to themselves or their fellows as that of imprisonment'—wrote Governor Grey to Lord John Russell in 1841. 'From their earliest days they have been accustomed to view death under a variety of forms and circumstances, so that they have become in some degree habituated to it; and to face death or danger in a daring manner is considered by them an act of heroic virtue worthy of emulation. But the idea of imprisonment is to them novel and frightful in the extreme. The imprisonment of a civilized man, considered relatively to punishment, bears no comparison whatever with that of a savage; to the former it presents but slight terrors; to the latter the loss of liberty is an almost inconceivable idea. He has never heard of such a thing; and so contrary is it to their habits, that it is almost impossible he can even have imagined it.' [60]

A curious legal question arose from the escape of a prisoner, who was recaptured after being at large for eighteen days. The Sheriff wanted to add eighteen days onto the man's term of imprisonment, but the Advocate-General advised this could not be done. The prisoner could not be legally confined beyond the term specified in his sentence; the escape must be separately charged against him.[61]

For several years there was little alteration in the condition of prisoners, who were employed within the walls making tents, corn sacks and ore bags, and in picking oakum.[62] The Judge, in September 1845, drew attention to the defective state of classification of prisoners. Those in gaol for failure to pay fines on summary convictions were put in the felons' ward. This, he thought, was wrong, but the only other place was the debtors' ward or with the lunatics, a number of whom were confined in the empty wards.[63] Nothing seems to have followed from his representations. The prisoners went on picking oakum until the stores of oakum became a problem. In September 1848 three cells were filled with a ton and a half of it, waiting for removal, and the prisoners were picking far more than could be disposed of.[64] It was therefore decided that a treadmill for grinding flour should be installed at the Gaol. Eight prisoners at a time worked on it and ground three to four bushels of wheat per hour.

The innovation was opposed both within and without the Gaol. Major O'Halloran, in the Legislative Council, said that he was at a loss to know what advantage would follow the introduction "of that criminally useless torture, which destroys the physical man, while it invariably increases his depravity". The prisoners complained that the work was too strenuous; though accustomed to hard labour when at liberty and on a liberal diet, they could not do the work on gaol rations. The Colonial Surgeon investigated and found that the daily rations were: bread, one pound; meat, half a pound; rice, a quarter of a pound; tea, a quarter of an ounce; sugar, half an ounce; salt and vinegar. This cost the Government fourpence per day per head. He recommended an increase in rations to those engaged on the treadmill, which brought the cost to Government to fivepence and three-farthings per man per day. The prisoners went on strike and refused to work.

Mr Wigley, the Visiting Justice, took the view that the use of the treadmill was not proper until rules had been made to bring it under the term "hard labour" and he was disinclined to order any punishment to the men, but the law officers were of opinion that the use of the treadmill was legal and that if the prisoners refused to work they must be compelled to do so. The men were accordingly driven back to the wheel.[65] When this species of punishment ceased to be in operation has not been discovered—it certainly went on for several years.[66]

An aerial view of Adelaide Gaol in the 1980s – essentially how it existed when it was decommissioned in 1988. The original radial plan is still evident in the photograph, but equally, so are the many additions and alterations that were made to the Gaol. Most notable of those, perhaps, is the building in the foreground that was added in 1879. (Adelaide Gaol)

Ralph Meyrick Hague

Biography
by
Helen Whitington

Prologue

In autumn 1936 an unassuming and studious young lawyer submitted a thesis outline entitled *The Early Legal History of South Australia, 1837-1867* for consideration by the University of Adelaide's Law Faculty. The thesis was the culmination of years of diligent, original research carried out during the Great Depression. Not only was it a work of meticulous scholarship it was also one of the first in its field of Australian legal history. Despite this the subject was not approved by the University Council and no written reason was given.

The Council's rejection reflected the belief held by the legal profession, the University and, indeed, many Australians that Australia, its people and its history merited little scholarly attention. Their worldview was constrained and Anglo-centric. To the bright, hopeful young man accustomed to academic accolades at school and university the rejection was a huge setback and was to echo throughout his life.

It was to be a source of bitterness that was never fully compensated by a career as a highly regarded government lawyer, editor of the *South Australian State Reports* and *Law Society Judgment Scheme* and esteemed sage for the wider legal profession. Those close to him consider this rebuff as pivotal, contributing to a lifelong habit of self-effacement, retiring ways and an extreme reluctance to put his name to any further writing. Such was his aggrievement that in the 1990s he resolutely resisted the attempts of important people, including Dame Roma Mitchell, and Professor Alex Castles to resubmit his thesis for a L.L.D. (Doctor of Laws) or even to publish the entire work.

Never again did he offer the entire manuscript for critical scrutiny. But although daunted and, perhaps, his ambitions dashed, his interest in the topic remained. Throughout the 1930s, 1940s, 1950s and 1960s, he continued to research and write about the law in the infant colony. It was important to him that someone tackle this immense task, that a record be made and the early growth of an independent colonial legal system be recognized. Perhaps he knew that one day his endeavours would find an audience. That has proven to be the case for his thesis, retitled *History of the Law in South Australia 1837-1867*, has endured in manuscript form to become the pre-eminent reference for students of South Australia's early legal history.

This publication project recognises both the significance of his pioneering work on our legal history and the fact that Australia's intellectual culture has radically altered. It is now a country ready to embrace its unique past, present and future.

What follows is a brief account of our scholar, Ralph Meyrick Hague, a glimpse of him in boyhood, at university, in his father's legal firm, during the Second World War, as public servant and editor of law reports, as neighbour, friend and relative. From it can be gleaned some understanding of why Hague looked beyond the prevailing mindset of his class and profession and painstakingly brought to our attention South Australia's very early legal history representing it with accurate and often entertaining clarity.

Ralph Hague the gardener and cat owner upon the steps of his front verandah in 1987. (Kate Brown)

Beginnings

On Saturday October the 12th 1907, the day Ralph Meyrick Hague was born to solicitor Percy Hague and retired school teacher Magdalen Hague, in the South Australian coastal town of Port Pirie, the local newspaper, the *Port Pirie Recorder and North West Mail* unwittingly but appropriately gave prominence to legal matters in particular to the illness of an Adelaide Supreme Court Judge. It was reported under the "Latest City News" that his Honour Mr Justice Gordon "is suffering from appendicitis (sic)" which caused the postponement of a shipping damages case. Noted too was the busy bar practice of Percy Hague's partner Henry Barwell who represented the bulk of the plaintiffs before the Port Pirie Local Court. The firm of Barwell and Hague also featured twice on the newspaper's advertisement cluttered front page. Among this jumble of promotional material for stables, dentists, sewing machines and cough cures, Barwell and Hague boldly offered "Money to lend on freehold security". They appeared again on the same page more formally and with alphabetic advantage, almost at the top of the newspaper's, "Professional & Business Directory" as "Barwell & Hague, Solicitors, Queen's Chambers, Ellen Street". It was an inkling of the professional world the new born babe would inhabit as a man and one quite different to the noisy, industrial world and busy port he knew as a boy.

At the turn of the twentieth century, around the time of Ralph Hague's birth, Port Pirie was a boomtown, being the international seaport for the famed silver, zinc and lead mines of the Silver City, Broken Hill. From the late 1880s, following the discovery of silver and minerals in the Barrier Ranges and the subsequent erection of ore refining and smelting plant, Port Pirie rapidly became the site of the world's largest smelting works. For decades a special ore train clanked, rattled and hissed its way Monday to Friday through summer and winter, from Broken Hill to Port Pirie, carrying concentrates to the ceaseless smelters. Back to the mines travelled freight loads of trimmed Scandinavian and North American timber and other requirements of BHP. At Port Pirie's many wharves in the mangrove protected inlet, called "Taparrie" by the local Nungunu aborigines, berthed the ships, both steam and sail, of many nations. For at least fifty years after 1900 Port Pirie was among the four busiest seaports in Australia, outranking Port Adelaide. Not only was the inland harbour a despatch point for lead (and later zinc) concentrates and silver ingots but also huge shipments of wheat, barley, sheep and other agricultural product left Australia's shores via Port Pirie. Up to twenty ships were in port at any one time, including big overseas coal burning steamships, small coastal sailing ketches and the regular and most essential local steamers or "tea and sugar boats", servicing Port Pirie shopkeepers and merchants until well after the Second World War.

Smelters operating twenty-four hours a day and the attendant improvement in Port Pirie's prosperity attracted many immigrants from across the world and Australia including recent law graduates Percy Hague and ambitious Henry Barwell. It was in the town centre with its skyline of ship masts and smoke stacks and its low street scapes of single and two storeyed Victorian buildings that these two young men set up in practice in 1900. They took over from D.C. Scott, solicitor to the Port Pirie Council, founding the firm that is now known as Kelly & Co. Such was the success of the fledgling firm of Barwell & Hague that within two years both men evidently considered themselves financially secure enough to embark upon the state of holy matrimony, Barwell with Anne, the daughter of Canon Webb, Rector of Clare and Percy with Magdalen, schoolteacher and daughter of David Meyrick, miller and potter of Port Pirie and his wife Elizabeth.

Intending bridegroom Percy Hague's forebears hailed from Manchester, which in mid Victorian England, was intellectually and culturally vibrant, a politically progressive city, as well as being the commercial and financial hub of the Empire's cotton trade. One would have supposed that the grammar school educated sons of a Congregational clergyman, might have encountered career opportunities a plenty in a place where the Victorian middle classes thrived. However the Reverend William Hague, Percy's grandfather remarried after the death of his wife Ellen and it is a Hague family tradition that the six children of the first marriage were displeased. Two sons had already left home. Of those remaining, two, James and Edward booked passages on the *Time and Truth* and sailed away to South Australia in 1855 to escape the stepmother experience. Others from the family were to follow, including the younger children Thomas, Percy's father and his sister Frances Mary.

Thomas Hague, father of Percy, who left England with his sister Frances in 1856 and joined his elder brother James and Edward in the Barossa Valley. He died through misadventure aged forty-seven in 1885 when Percy was twelve. (Erica Micklem)

The young Hagues were attracted to the Barossa, just why is unknown, and they arrived bearing letters of introduction to residents of that valley. Following a five-year stint in the employ of Angaston storekeepers, Radford Bros, James opened his own store in Penrice to be later joined by brother Edward who had already dabbled in market gardening, ironmongery and matrimony. Eventually their successful business venture expanded to include general stores in Angaston and Truro and upon the death of James in 1916, Hague & Co was sold to the Eudunda Farmers Co-operative.

Later immigrant and younger brother Thomas took a different career path. After initially reuniting with his brothers in Angaston where the *Adelaide Almanac and Directory for South Australia* notes him as mail carrier and carpenter, he married Elizabeth Watson, daughter of George Watson, ship builder and carpenter. In 1874 the *Adelaide Almanac* finds him elsewhere, in Moonta where he still reports as carpenter. Moonta and Kadina at that time were the largest and fastest growing towns in the colony, outside Adelaide. They were the focus of eager immigrants, especially industrious Cornishmen, keen to work in the newly opened copper mines. Doubtless as the government laid out the new townships to cope with the influx of immigrants, there were commissions a plenty for enthusiastic artisans like Thomas. Just as South Australia's "little Cornwall" and copper mines drew Thomas, so Port Pirie's boom times would attract his son Percy some twenty or so years later.

Thomas' business prospered and when he died unexpectedly aged forty-seven in 1885 his widow Elizabeth, now with six children, inherited a flourishing hardware store and undertaking business. Undertaking was a particularly lucrative trade since the lack of clean drinking water, inadequate sanitation and consequent epidemics in the Copper Triangle sent countless souls to an untimely demise as the many mounds in Moonta's graveyard attest. Although Elizabeth reportedly left a substantial sum to her six children, at the time of her widowhood, the business was not sufficiently profitable to send Percy, after some years at Moonta State School, to Prince Alfred College as a boarder. He attended the College but as a day student while staying with an Adelaide aunt. Moreover, Percy's legal education was funded by generous Uncles James and Edward. According to information given by Ralph Hague to the writer of *On a Handshake – the History of Kelly & Co.*, Percy undertook the lesser legal qualification, open to country students articled to country practitioners. Articled clerks, working twenty-five or more miles outside Adelaide were not required to attend lectures, only to pass examinations. From the offices of H.W. Uffindell who practised in Moonta and Kadina, and later P. McMahon Glynn, Percy then went on to practice to his own account with Henry Barwell in Port Pirie.

Percy's fiancée, Magdalen, was also the descendant of a 1850s immigrant. Her grandfather Morgan Meyrick sailed to the Great South Land from Cardiff in Wales where he had plied the trade of potter. In the Adelaide foothills suburb of Magill, Meyrick established another pottery and his son David, Magdalen's father, apparently adopted the same calling, although on Magdalen's marriage certificate he is just described as miller.

In the afternoon of the 25th of June 1902, Percy, a twenty nine year old handsome high cheek boned groom with the wide, carefully clipped moustache wed twenty four year old Magdalen in a tiny Anglican Church of England, St Barnabas, Solomontown. The *Port Pirie Recorder* reports a very quiet ceremony, "with only a few very intimate friends and relatives". Whether the young couple had a honeymoon is unknown. But ten months later, on the 16th of April 1903 Percy and Magdalen were blessed with their arrival of their first born, John Meyrick, to be followed by Ralph Meyrick after an interval of four and a half years.

Schooling, Country and City

Port Pirie Primary

Little pictorial record, let alone written evidence remains of the juvenescence of either Ralph or Jack. Alas for the peering eyes of posterity, Magdalen, grieving and depressed after the death in 1951 of her beloved husband of forty-nine years, burnt most of the family photographs. There is however an appealing photo portrait of Ralph or Jack in the safekeeping of the Barr Smith Library Special Collections. The boy child gazes at us with large expressive eyes, a slightly puzzled look upon his preschool face. He wears a puffy white sailor suit shirt with a knotted scarf under the broad stiff collar. Another photograph from those tender years, now in the bulky Hague family album of Erica Micklem, has been positively identified as our subject. The face in the latter photograph is of a smiling tousled haired toddler dressed like a girl (as was the fashion) in a side buttoned frock coat, knee high socks and sandals. The face is an eerie echo of Ralph's visage in old age.

Despite the paucity of family documentation about the two brothers early years there are records elsewhere, albeit scant ones, in the public domain. Ralph like his brother attended Port Pirie School, in Ralph's case from 1912 until 1918. Renamed Port Pirie West Primary School around 1978 and situated opposite the Recreation Grounds on a long straight street called, "The Terrace" running from south to north through the town past the shelters, it is the city's oldest school and was officially opened in 1876. Remarkably the original building, recently restored and repainted in heritage colours, is still standing and in use amid the prefabricated, transportable classrooms on the site. Hague would therefore easily recognise this, his first alma mater with its attractive stone walls, decorative brick quoins, steeply pitched roof line, and odd sets of narrow front windows.

Ralph's first official attendance on the 21st of October 1912 was dutifully noted in a grey board Admission Register for Boys. Written in a teacher's careful blue ink copperplate, Ralph's name appears among the nineteen other boys and twenty girls also stepping on this initial rung of the educational ladder. A closer examination of the relevant Register pages discloses that Ralph the solicitor's son was, in his primary schooling, mingling largely with the children of the blue-collar parents. Of the forty new faces in the school grounds that spring Monday, nineteen were the progeny of labourers. Other manual trades recorded in the "occupation of the father" column are those of boilermaker, smelter worker, painter, fisherman and turner, with a sprinkling of white collar and small business jobs: time keeper, boot importer, insurance agent, store keeper, merchant, draper and tailor. One father, Charles Anderson is even curiously described as occupied with "home duties", perhaps a polite euphemism for unemployed. Apart from the influx of more "orthodox" immigrants, as many as two hundred sailors a year deserted their sailing ships or steamers, looking for employment in Pirie's smelters and farming hinterland. Therefore it is not surprising that the School Admissions Register included names redolent of exotic cultures and remote places: Pavlich, Ziepos, Horemburg, Speck, Brusnahan, Merlino. Already Ralph was meeting representatives of the non Anglo Saxon world. It was a hint of the multi cultural country Australia would eventually be.

Like the rest of his class, Ralph most probably walked or bicycled to school. The Hagues lived on Government Road (a generic name once given to new thoroughfares), Port Pirie West, which intersected with "the Terrace" so school was no great distance away for the young student. Perhaps he dawdled his way along with other five year olds, Lancelot Morgan, the draper's son or Ronald Knight, the merchant's son, also residents of Government Road, with older siblings in charge. Ninety years ago Government or Goode Road as it is now called, was a mixture of small cottages and grander dwellings and the Hagues owned one of the latter. Nevertheless the rest of Port Pirie West was definitely a blue-collar community, and in the days before the predominance of cars, conveniently close to the smelters, wharves, railway, and city centre. The boys and girls trudging to and from school along unmade roads, dusty in summer and often muddy in winter would have been all too aware of the raw face of the town's primary industry. Often the sky was streaked black with thick scuds of smoke from the town's smelters stacks or hazy yellow with sulphur fumes. Such was pollution that pupils' eyes frequently streamed with tears and coughing was endemic. In summer when the Northerlies blew the poisonous smoke over the city, the air contamination was worse.

The close proximity of Port Pirie West to the smelters meant the children (and indeed adults) whether at home, play or in class heard the sound of the air horn siren, signalling the change in shifts. Then there was the noise from the wharves, of ships loading and unloading, as well as the ever-present racket from steam trains rumbling down Pirie's gently curving main thoroughfare, Ellen Street. Spot fires were not infrequent at the smelters furnaces and elsewhere so the alarm bells and the fire brigade racing engine added to the general cacophony.

Dwelling as he did in the heart of Port Pirie, young Ralph was surely grounded in the realities of working class Australia as few children of middle class professionals in Adelaide were. Until his eleventh year he lived against a background of union unrest and industrial tensions. In 1909, there was a grim five month long lockout when most of the smelter workers and their families were without wages. After 1914 of course in a town geared to the crucial production of lead, and where two thousand five hundred men and women had enlisted, work and war were inextricably linked. In 1916 and 1917 Port Pirie was wracked by further industrial difficulties and there were tense negotiations over whether workers would form national stoppages over wages and conditions and in doing so endanger lives at the battlefront, jeopardise munition production and damage Digger morale. The decision to avert or join a national strike in 1917 depended on Port Pirie and Australia watched while this country town decided. Women demonstrated in the streets, the pubs were closed and there were turbulent angry mass meetings and open fighting between service men and strike supporters

Hague's ability to relate to people of all classes possibly found its origins in his early acquaintance with working class people. Whether a person was a humble cleaning woman or a high status Lieutenant Governor, Ralph Hague cared not a jot. Further more he knew from first hand experience that Australia was not just an island of Anglo culture but a molten emerging society, developing new ways and new traditions in the face of quite different antipodean circumstances.

Outside school, how the innocent and not so innocent idle hours of Jack and Ralph's childhood were spent is largely guesswork apart from brief allusions in the local newspapers. Theirs, most likely, were the pursuits of country children accustomed to daylong freedom, with the coast and town as their playground. Presumably, the two boys played with the four children of Percy's partner Henry Barwell who were of similar age. In contrast to the Hagues who were housed in working class Port Pirie West, the Barwell family resided at "St Vincent", a large and beautiful return verandah villa two miles outside the smoke haze and clangour of Pirie's industries. Did the older John take his little brother on distant all day adventures exploring the mud flats north of Pirie or the mangrove swamps, breeding grounds for prawns, mosquitoes, crabs and fish opposite the town? Maybe there was fun, messing about with other boys in boats, fishing from the local wharves and jetties, crabbing out past the smelters in the shallows or dab netting, knee deep at Telowie Beach or rocky Weeroona Island? Almost certainly they could not resist the endless opportunities for sliding and sky larking on the unfenced fine gravely piles of black slag down by wharves adjacent to the lead smelters. Then there were those other meccas for energetic children: the swimming mud flat beach at the Solomontown end of the river and the deep dock water where older boys swam. Did the wandering children strike up dockside conversations with sailors speaking strange foreign tongues and broken English from faraway lands? Since both boys' fathers were at various times vice consuls for Sweden and the firm had extensive shipping connections, it is highly probable that John and Ralph were taken aboard the many graceful four masted vessels that berthed in the regularly dredged channel that served as the town's harbour.

Saturday was invariably devoted to sport in Port Pirie so the Hague boys were likely participants in some organised physical activity on that day, perhaps summer's tennis and cricket or winter's football and hockey. Percy was an active sportsman whose interests included tennis, cycling and shooting. Of course most of the usual leisure time activities, both sporting and social, were affected by the Great War which began in Ralph's seventh year and ceased in his eleventh and took so many young men away to distant battles. Ralph and Jack's parents were prominent members of the Port Pirie community and significant and enthusiastic players in the town's efforts towards "helping the man who is fighting for you". Every opportunity and occasion was used for fundraising for the defence of Australia and the Empire. Mrs Percy Hague was from 1914 until indifferent health in 1917, the prudent and much appreciated treasurer of the Red Cross Society.

Apparently the Hague children were impressed by their parent's philanthropy and followed suit, as did many of their age group. Master Jack was one of those who sent Christmas billycans to homesick soldiers stationed in Egypt and received, along with others, a letter from the Abbassia Camp expressing gratitude. Both boys probably took part in the popular 1915 Australia Day procession, when two thousand five hundred of Port Pirie's school children joined military units and a float with women dressed as Britannia and Red Cross nurses on the streets of the town. In April 1916 the *Port Pirie Advertiser* noted Jack and nine year old Ralph's youthful contribution, listing their five shillings – among the cholera belts, socks, scarves and mittens sent to the Red Cross Society. When casualty lists began to tell the terrible story on the front lines and not surprisingly morale dropped, perhaps the Hagues were among the audience at the distracting and popular benefit picture show evenings run by their mother and others in conjunction with the "Cooee and Casino Picture Managements". During the war screenings at the cinema included "war topicals" to incite patriotic fervour. Silent motion pictures in those early days of film had melodramatic and emotive titles like "Drawn into Quicksand", "The Song of the Wage Slave" and "If the Huns came to Melbourne".

A month after Armistice Day in late 1918 Ralph completed his primary education and was one of the few students to be awarded a QC or qualifying certificate. The other two boys from Government/Goode Road, Ronald Knight and Lancelot Morgan also passed the "compulsory" standard. The spidery handwriting in the "Brief Remarks" column of the Admission Register indicates destinies for the rest of Ralph's classmates as varied as their beginnings. Some went on to high school or transferred to different primary schools. The draper's son Lancelot enrolled at Scotch College and Ronald completed his secondary schooling at St Peter's College ahead of Ralph. Another boy was dispatched to a reformatory and as many girls as boys were simply described as "over age".

St Peters College

Brother Jack followed his father footsteps by completing his later high school years in Adelaide though as a student of St Peter's rather than Prince Alfred College, as in Percy's case. According to Erica Micklem, Jack was a very homesick and unhappy boarder, who wrote beseeching letters to Port Pirie, begging his parents to let him leave the hated school. Percy meanwhile had his professional as well as personal dilemmas. In 1915 Percy's partner Henry Barwell began a career in politics as Member for Stanley in the House of Assembly. He was rapidly promoted to various ministries and around this time Barwell and his family moved to Adelaide, the seat of power in state politics. Francis Kelly joined Barwell in his new Adelaide chambers and so began the firm of Barwell & Kelly. Barwell eventually served as Premier from 1920 to 1924.

Percy must have felt some sympathy with his partner's aspirations. Two of his close relations, Great Uncle James Hague, the Angaston storekeeper and his son William were likewise politicians as Members for Barossa. Indeed Barwell as Premier would eventually appoint William Hague to important ministries. Peter Howell in the *Australian Dictionary of Biography* views William Hague as a humane politician, resisting racially discriminatory legislation against Australians of German extraction during the First World War and similarly shameful legislation against Aborigines. His oft remarked theme was that "pioneers had succeeded through energy and industry, not through strikes and go slow policy". Later, Ralph Hague, his first cousin, would march to much the same life themes.

By 1918, responding in part to his eldest son's pleas, his partner's change in location and possibly influenced by the end of Ralph's primary schooling, Percy transferred his family to Adelaide, firstly into temporary accommodation at 39 Oxford Terrace, New Parkside, according to the *Sands & McDougall Directory* and then if St Peter's College register is accurate, to Audley House, Prospect Road, Prospect. Percy, still Vice Consul for Sweden oscillated between Adelaide and Port Pirie, continuing to practice in both places. In keeping with the volatility of teenagers, Jack Hague modified his views and was now not too pleased to be a dayboy. Perhaps he felt more settled with his brother attending the same school and undoubtedly the passage of time softened his initial impressions.

St Peter's College, Ralph's new school with its architectural echoes of England's Oxbridge and vast green and shady grounds was a sharp contrast to the basic simplicity of Port Pirie Primary in the heart of polluted, working class Port Pirie West. However the two schools do share educational milestones and are both significant in the history of education in South Australia. Ralph's primary school is the oldest in Port Pirie while St Peter's is the oldest in the State, opening its doors in 1847.

To a rural lad of twelve the visual difference and standard of facilities must have been quite amazing. Then as now St Peter's College gave the impression of being set in the country, perhaps even another country, with its views of the faintly blue Adelaide Hills, absence of city and traffic noise and fifty acres of green hedges, tennis courts, ovals and gracious avenues of trees. The dignified sandstone buildings with their steep roofs of slate and grey corrugated iron were intended to resemble the original Cistercian St John's College, Oxford.

After the deep water of Port Pirie's docks and the tidal mud flat beach of Solomontown, there was now the opportunity to plunge in a "swimming bath" of some one hundred feet with dry towels provided and an attendant always present. Another modern facility the 1920 school prospectus emphasized, was the deep drainage system, which, to parents Magdalen and Percy must have seemed a blessing after the primitive single pan and cesspit sewage of much of Port Pirie, a town where typhoid fever epidemics intermittently raged. Then there was the large ninety feet gymnasium and accompanying instructor, a stone chapel the size of a church with beautiful stained glass windows, black and white floor tiles, two libraries one for masters and the other for students, specific laboratories for chemistry, physics and biology, a boat house for the boat club and even a miniature rifle range.

St Peter's College, like Oxford and Cambridge was and is clearly intended for training leaders, and leaders including Royal visitors, generals, bishops, politicians and governors regularly came and went, doubtless to inspire and affirm. Numbered among its old boys were premiers, judges and other notables from South Australia's establishment. It was a whole world away from the humble school where the segregated sons and daughters of labourers heard the smelters siren indicate the change of shifts. At St Peter's College, the ringing of the school bell close by Big Quad and the reverberations of the chimes from the lofty clock tower alone marked the passing of time.

When Ralph entered the purlieu of St Peter's in 1919, it was a school and a world on the brink of change. Following the carnage and conflict of the Great War people everywhere were intent upon creating a better, wiser world. In January 1919 the Paris Peace Conference opened shortly before the school year began. 1919 was also the last year of the wartime stewardship of the Acting Headmaster, Mr T.A. Caterer. Freed by the cessation of fighting, the school's Council of Governors was now able to seek out the best candidates to replace him, since those most able, were no longer at the front. A peacetime headmaster, epitomizing the English public school tradition was appointed in the person of the Reverend Kenneth Julian Faithfull Bickersteth, M.A., M.C. In anticipation of the new head, the September issue of the *St Peter's School Magazine* warned its readers, "Tremble ye slackers", for Bickersteth was schooled at "Rugby" known for its devotion to close organization and hard work and had received honours in modern history at Christ Church Oxford, England's oldest university.

As a clergyman, Bickersteth, upon his assumption of the post of Headmaster, immediately and understandably placed "additional emphasis on the chapel as the centre of school life" as well as allotting an extra hour's Scripture to a large number of forms. It was reported that, elsewhere "boys who passed through his hands could not well escape the influence of his own absolute, devotion and intensely virile Christianity". Hague appears not to have responded to such fervour and although confirmed in the school chapel, by the Lord Bishop of Adelaide along with forty eight other boys in November 1922, was not apparently throughout his life an active or even intermittent churchgoer.

After touring a number of English schools with a "reputation … in the maintenance of public school ideals or the adoption of the latest teaching methods", the new Headmaster substituted the unsatisfactory "district system" of organizing boys and sports with the house system in the manner of Melbourne Grammar and Clifton. Under the altered regime of school organization every boy was compelled to attend games, at least one day a week unless physically unable, so presumably Hague played football in winter and cricket in summer as well as tennis, at which he excelled. The new system was also a combination of pastoral care with mentoring, as each boy remained with the same house for the rest of his school days. John and Ralph Hague belonged to "Irwin's House" in the charge of the Reverend W.H. Irwin, as well as a tutor, a House Captain and sundry prefects. "Irwin's House" was one of four houses for dayboys, apart from three for boarders, and five for the Preparatory School. Until 1924 these houses were named after the supervising master; after 1924 Irwin became "Hawkes" after the founder and early governor of the school, George Wright Hawkes.

The 1920s saw much building activity at St Peters. Not only was the physical landscape of the school changing in young Hague's first years there but also the school's academic focus. St Peter's had been founded in 1847 to provide a good classical and mathematical education on Church of England principles; however it was anticipated that a new literary Head would stress "English literature and kindred subjects", giving them as much emphasis as mathematics, classics and sciences enjoyed in the past. The forecast proved accurate for Bickersteth quickly initiated the upgrading of the boys and masters libraries. By means of a Council of Governors grant, the foundations of a really good student library were laid in the Tower Room of the new classrooms. The College magazine for May 1920 noted approvingly of the encouraged widening of interests with new societies springing up everywhere, including the camera and wireless clubs and the revamped (former Charles Jury) Literary Society, as enthusiastic boys took advantage of the high tide of change. There was also an amazing growth in Form newspapers, especially in the upper part of the school, where "such effusions as the 'Weekly Wowser' and 'Higher Truth' wage their wordy combats. Keenness and energy [were] in the air".

Moreover under Bickersteth, with his English sense of tradition, there was renewed pride in consciousness about the school's past, which in many ways was inextricably entwined with the early days of the colony. From August 1921 all through the rest of Hague's school years and beyond, there were regular articles in a series entitled "History of the School 1847-1921", published in the College magazine. These chronicled the founding of St Peter's in the simple straggly country village that was Adelaide and subsequent tales associated with its evolution into a leading college of six hundred students. Articles included sketches of important pioneers and figures in the school's beginnings such as Bishop Short and Sir James Hurtle Fisher. The College magazine also launched an appeal for the restoration of the derelict schoolroom behind the State's oldest church, Holy Trinity. The schoolroom "was an object of great interest as one of the earliest brick erections remaining and dear to the school as the birthplace of their alma mater". There was a request too in the August magazine of 1922 for information and photographs about any of the school early proprietors, many of whom were notable settlers. This was the very territory to be explored later by Hague in his legal history writing. It was gleam of green and gold in a school curriculum and worldview that was largely Empire red. Maybe St Peter's, in celebrating its past, alerted the young scholar to the treasure chest of South Australian history, awaiting discovery?

All of the elements which were to characterise Ralph Hague's intellectual life in adulthood, an emphasis on literature (and poetry), libraries, respect for and interest in the past were upper most and fostered during his six years at St Peter's. Furthermore the man at the helm of the change, Bickersteth had taken a master's degree in modern history and was said to draw the best from boys, by the force of his belief in them. And it is obvious from school reports and letters sent home that Bickersteth had faith in Hague.

Hague was definitely one of the many boys and masters who helped the new Headmaster effect the school's transformation. His 1925 "Valete" records him belonging to the Library Society for 1922-25, the Library Committee in 1923-25 and Magazine Committee for 1925. As to the reasons for his very literary choice of co-curricular activities, they must remain conjecture. Perhaps Hague's bent was nurtured by his mother, a former teacher who had two brothers who worked in the print media: Charles as part owner of the *Port Pirie Recorder* and Morgan as Sir Langdon Bonython's youngest sub editor at the *Advertiser.*

From July 1922 onwards when Hague was elected Secretary of Junior Literary Society we can see him, albeit sketchily, through the eyes of the school magazine's boy reporters at the evening meetings held in the homes of Masters Henderson, Gordon, McDonnell and later Bickersteth. Members and masters read aloud excerpts from the poetry, plays and prose of exclusively English speaking writers such as Twain, Shakespeare, Carroll, Sassoon, Sheridan and Goldsmith. Papers were also given, (some conscientiously typed, some not) on the life, literature and times of selected members. High standards were not always maintained and Hague drew fire for "a rather scrappy paper on journalism". Afterwards he "hastened to cover up his delinquencies by reading … copious extracts from Sir Phillip Gibb".

Hague's other principal co-curricular activity was as committee member for the Library housed in the Tower Room of the new building. A glance through the "Library Notes" for Hague's years at school makes amusing light reading. Despite its initial increase in funding in 1920, the student library was far from the ideal haven for sober research and in August 1922 an exasperated committee expressed some satisfaction that pianos had been removed and at last quietness reigned and because the doors are regularly locked, books are no longer "used as aerial missiles". Perhaps a Tower Room was not the most suitable accommodation for a boys' school library?

1923, the year Hague joined the committee, started with "a considerable bank balance" because in the previous year, the school had introduced a library levy of one shilling per student per term. The optimistic "Library Notes" continue with mention of pleasing augmentation of the drama and science sections, comment on well received subscriptions to several illustrated papers and magazine and the presentation of three etchings by the Headmaster Bickersteth "which will improve the appearance of our library". Then follows an observation that "boys are beginning to realise that books should be treated as friends and not as missiles". However not all was satisfactory. Preparatory school readers newly admitted to the library precincts were chided for favouring light "literature" and older boys chastened for leaving books on the floor and the library untidy. In mid 1923 there is an unforeseen calamity and the committee laments the forced sharing of library rooms with the Wireless Club and consequential shelving of plans for a lunchtime periodicals reading room. By December 1923 the "Library Notes" speak of a new and evidently successful system "by which all books but fiction are for reference purposes only", to aid in study for scholarships and public examinations. In 1924 the wry commentary continues though the magazine does report pleasing progress. All books were renumbered and re-catalogued and many rebound and a Yale lock installed to prevent the "leakage of books, hitherto unpreventable". Boys anxious not to be forgotten in the annals of school history were urged to present a book to the library instead of carving names inches deep in desks.

By the end of 1925, (and Hague's final year) it was clear that our subject and the other committee members had made a remarkable contribution. It was reported that regular consignments of books shipped out from faraway England had brought most noticeable changes in school reading habits. The library opening daily instead of thrice weekly was now crowded, had a complete card index system and was user friendly too. So busy was the energetic and inspired committee that members found it difficult to manage when yet another batch of new books arrived. The "Library Notes" conclude with some hand wringing, rueing the loss of Wreford the Librarian and Hague as Secretary, given "their splendid work". "We hope to find others, equally keen to replace them". The experience was an invaluable one, being a practice run for the creation of Hague's own extraordinary book collection.

Hague in his final two years also juggled other school responsibilities, probably made easier by the fact the Leaving Honours was then accomplished over three years. One of them was in 1925 as a member of the Magazine Committee, firstly involved as "School News" sub-editor and then as Literary Editor. The latter was not an easy task in a very masculine school with a high sports profile, where year after year many "literary" contributions were deemed second-rate by a despairing, rather censorial committee. In the "Answers to Correspondents" column in the College magazine such withering criticism appeared, "you seem to have had a bad attack of sonneteering of late …". The rejected verse is too mediocre for publication …". "Your association with the 'Monthly Murmur' appears to have been your downfall". Even Hague's one and only detected attempt at verse in 1923 was passed over with the remark, "Do you think we are a home for lost sonnets?"

Hague upon becoming Literary Editor, after a mid year magazine committee shuffle, proved generally more tactful than previous editors, offering gentle criticism and useful suggestions. However he was capable of censure softened with schoolboy wit, "Now we understand why the dustman failed to remove it". And he was insistent on standards asking the loyal supporters of the "Literary Pages": "to write legibly, and not to send in contributions on pieces of paper that look suspiciously like that piece we saw blowing around the quadrangle the other day". After an outburst of sonneteering, artificially stimulated by a member of staff, he observed: "the sonnet form the finest in the language", was treated too carelessly and not respectfully enough; "an attempt at humour in the form is not likely to succeed". Despite the ineptness and mediocrity of contributors, Hague was not daunted and bravely introduced his readers to an unfamiliar category of writing, that of literary criticism, with an adulatory article entitled "Oscar Wilde, the Artist", from the pen of "H.B." By way of enticing further such essays, he tellingly says: "Good prose is always welcome, especially that dealing with Australian subjects".

Ten years hence he kept faith with the Australian focus and submitted his own unique contribution to critical scrutiny. After a further decade he would again take the role of editor but in the specialist area of legal reporting, checking the writing of learned judges, not the scribblings of schoolboys. Hague's effective use and love of language and careful attention to detail first nourished and exercised at St Peter's, were attributes for which he would eventually and most deservedly be acclaimed.

- oooOooo -

St Peters speech day, held in the school grounds, marked the end of the school year and, in 1925, the end of Hague's secondary schooling. Hague must have felt some measure of satisfaction mingled with inevitable nervousness as he stood to receive his prizes for English and History from His Excellency the Governor, Sir Tom Bridges. He had crowned the latter years of his secondary schooling with very visible success. As early as 1921 he had anticipated what was to come by winning the McDonald Scholarship for English. Apart from being a leading figure in the literacy co-curricular activities of the school, he represented Hawkes House in tennis along with R.H. "Bob" Barwell and others for 1923-1924 and "played very well indeed". Like Barwell and Ronald Knight, also Port Pirie boys, he was a House Prefect and like Barwell, a School Prefect too. The school acknowledged his exemplary efforts by making him Vice Captain of St Peter's in 1925 with C.B. Sangster as Captain. Did the youth speak easily to that densely packed eager audience? As a man, Hague would try to avoid public speaking in court or elsewhere. He also eschewed large gatherings, active participation in clubs and societies. Then there is the question of how the kindly, gentle Hague manage his leadership role in a school led by a strict disciplinarian who frequently wielded the cane, flinging his weapon into the corner of the room after a flogging and trembling as he said, "It hurts me more than it hurts you". Not surprisingly prefects in the Bickersteth era were encouraged to employ the cane and beatings were used to exert authority as well as to inflict punishment.

Although Hague did not know his public examination results, as he shook the Vice Regal hand and walked away with his prizes, he had already passed some Leaving Honours subjects in 1924, gaining a place on the Special Honours List, coming third in the State in French as well as modern history. He shared the distinction in French with J.N. McEwin, the son of one of the founding partners of "Baker McEwin" and later a distinguished lawyer himself. When the 1925 public examinations results were finally released Hague came twenty-first in the General Honours List in South Australia and took fifth place with a credit in modern history. As some inattentive Supreme Court Judges were later to discover, Hague was an able Latin scholar for he also sat and passed the subject at the Leaving Honours level.

On that warm summer's morning, Hague and other senior students were poised at an important juncture. The school gates of South Australia's oldest and most pre-eminent college were about to close behind them. Speech Day was launching them into the adult world. Attentively or otherwise they had listened year after year to long speeches delivered by Speech Day dignitaries and other important school visitors. Such homilies were heavily laden with precepts for life and examples of great and mighty men apparently doing their best. The value of teamwork was always emphasised, that glory is not to be found in the prize but in the effort made to obtain it, that men were best ruled by example. On Hague's last Speech Day the Right Reverend Arthur Nutter Thomas, the Lord Bishop of Adelaide, urged the assembled school to, "Grease the wheels thoroughly if you can't drive the train."

The Governor then added his pennyworth of moral instruction when he spoke of the duty an individual owed to the community and to make it and the world a better place. They were all maxims of which Hague took careful heed. Indeed his life was to be an exemplar of many of them.

Certainly St Peter's boys knew their place in the grand scheme of things, as leaders upholding the red mantle and authority of Empire. That success ahead was very likely, given the living evidence and often presence of old scholars such as Sir Henry Barwell, Premier of South Australia and Mr Justice Poole who in 1922 was made Administrator and Acting Chief Justice of South Australia. In these inter-war years connections with and thoughts of England were still foremost in Australian life. The Antipodean private school boy was told that the ideals of peace and democracy flourished best under a British flag, while the frequent presence of leaders of British society, including this or that lord and the Governor of the State made tangible the links with the Motherland and Royalty. England's official cricket team came and practised at the school nets in 1924. The Prince of Wales and heir to title of Emperor was, in the winter term of 1920, not three hours in Adelaide before he enquired about St Peter's Squash (Fives) Court where, eager for exercise after arduous official duties, he played games on two separate occasions and thrashed all comers. The Headmaster's own father, the Reverend Samuel Bickersteth who had visited St Peter's in 1922, was chaplain to His Majesty the King. Many staff, including Bickersteth, almost inevitably had English public school and university educations and took their leave in England. If Australian institutions and culture were considered of interest it was only be a few.

Hague and his fellows were ushered out into the waiting world with the concluding words of the Venerable John Moyes the Archdeacon of Adelaide enjoining one and all to face the challenges of public service with a spirit of adventure. However Hague's principal contribution to society was not to be in the service of the Empire but in the creation of a new postcolonial world. Long before his elders and others of his generation, he quietly broke free.

Whither Now? – Journalism, Law, Academia and War

Journalism

1926 was an important and pivotal year in the life of Ralph Hague. In that year he and his family moved to the Gilberton house, which was to be his home until death claimed him seventy -one years later; and he began a career in journalism, which, though brief, shaped his future. Hague was then eighteen and had just left school; and his brother, John, at nearly twenty -three, was a newly admitted solicitor.

Until 1919, home in Port Pirie had been principally 77 Goode Road, a large return verandah villa built of stone with an eye catching iron roof and tall slender chimneys crowned with terracotta pots; it was, and still is, set on a substantial block at the rear of which once ran a private lane, a feature shared by Percy's subsequent homes.

After his family's relocation to Adelaide, and a year or so in temporary quarters, Percy bought, in April 1920, another home at 140 Grant Avenue Toorak Gardens. This house was an art nouveau influenced two-storey, tiled residence with dainty small paned leadlight windows and cream pebbledash walls. Most likely, given the timing, this acquisition was financed by the sale of Goode Road to Barrington John Knight, a Pirie brewer and publican. 140 Grant Avenue is at the eastern end of a long thoroughfare rising to meet busy Portrush Road. Its height and scale are unusual in a street of single-storey dwellings. This and the fact that the house is blessed with a wide north facing balcony with sweeping views from the Gulf across the Adelaide Plains was probably appealing to the Hagues. At the back of the property there is still a twenties era grass tennis court with apparently original posts and fencing. Given Percy and Ralph's prowess with the racquet, it is possible to surmise the Hague family were either regular users of the court or authors of its installation. Nevertheless in old age, Hague the avid raconteur spoke not of the physical charms of his virginia creeper covered home but about Sir Robert Helpmann, then fifteen who actually danced in his street. Helpmann, fresh from six months in Melbourne with Anna Pavlova's Ballet Company, lived not far from Hague at number 123.

After Toorak Gardens the Hagues next permanent address was 6 Frederick Street Walkerville. It is said that Percy chose the house while Magdalen was in hospital and that she never really liked the home. Be that mere hearsay, true or false, it was Magdalen's and Percy's last home. For the elegant villa with its ornately carved wooden verandah balcony, marble fireplaces and vast cellar, Percy paid £1,885. Like Grant Avenue, the Frederick Street home was on high ground with a raised verandah from which one could contemplate the Adelaide Hills and at closer quarters, the to-ings and fro-ings in the street below. At the time Magdalen was nearly fifty and Percy fifty-three. Both their boys had recently embarked upon careers and perhaps the smaller Frederick Street was more suitable. If the usual course of life events occurred, the two young men soon would be leaving home. While John was obviously attracted to law and pursued the calling of his father, Ralph evinced an early interest in journalism. His hankering was for a role in the realm of creative writing. That he enjoyed the output of other wordsmiths is evident from his school reports and choice of school co-curricular activities.

Hague's keenness and ability must have impressed St Peter's headmaster for Bickersteth wrote to Sir Langdon Bonython on the 6th of August 1923, about "three quite able boys", Hague among them "anxious to take up journalistic work". The man Hague would see was Sir John Langdon Bonython, pre-eminent in the Australian press world as proprietor and editor of the *Advertiser*, which was an Adelaide daily with a reputation for liberally progressive policies, reflecting the aspirations and ideas of South Australia's middle classes.

Between five and six o'clock one weekday evening Hague went as arranged to the Advertiser and saw Sir Langdon who had an open door policy. Doubtless the slight, dark haired fifteen year old felt a little apprehensive in the presence of such an august and important man, a knight, made C.M.C and K.C.M.G., with a reputation for independent views, plain speaking, being stern, strict even with his own eight children. Apparently Bonython counselled Hague to first obtain a "degree if circumstances permit". It was not advice Hague wished to hear though his zeal was undampened by the seventy five year old former Parliamentarian who had joined the *Advertiser* as a sixteen-year-old journalist in 1864. Long ago Bonython wished to proceed to higher education but had been impeded by his parents' lack of funds. Maybe he recommended to Hague the course he once wanted for himself.

When Hague's school days came to a close two and half years later in 1925, he was still enthused with the idea of a career in the Fourth Estate. Indeed, it will be recalled he delivered "a scrappy paper" on that very topic to the Literary Society in 1924. He could, however, hardly apply for a place at the *Advertiser* given the outcome of his discussions with Bonython; but fate and close relations favoured him.

A newcomer to Adelaide's very competitive print media scene provided an answer to the young man's dilemma. The *News* was the brainchild of James Edward Davidson an intrepid, honest, professional journalist and astute businessman whose career in newspaper ownership began with Broken Hill's *Barrier Miner* and in 1919 included the *Port Pirie Recorder*. Amid calamities such as paper breaks, mechanical and power failures, the first edition of the paper rolled off the presses on the 24th of July 1923 to crowds who queued for hours to buy one shilling souvenir copies. Initially the afternoon tabloid was a broad sheet appearing in two editions. It supplanted, by agreement, two other afternoon papers the *Express and Telegraph* and the *Journal*. Davidson bought them and Adelaide's weekly the "Mail' to begin his venture. The *News* was quickly embraced by the public who liked its "boisterous campaigning" nature.

From a sepia photograph of the original editorial staff, including editor, Stanley Kingsbury and Davidson, it is plain to see that the early days of the *News* were exhilarating, albeit challenging times. There is a special energy and alertness about the mostly smiling, mostly young assembled throng who posed for the photograph. Undoubtedly in the eyes of a stripling eager to begin his career in such a situation, it was an exciting and promising opportunity. And he had connections among the staff. His cousin, Reece Hague, escaping a life in politics prescribed by the expectations of his father, William, and grandfather, James, was employed there as a journalist. Maybe Hague's entrée was also facilitated by another family wordsmith, his mother's brother, Charles Meyrick, one time owner of the *Port Pirie Recorder*, now a Davidson publication.

Reece, it seems, helped his young cousin to settle in. Hague began as a cadet journalist and cadets under the award served four years before they became journalists. According to friends and relatives, Ralph covered sporting events, specifically tennis and golf and despite his later protestations that he knew very little about these activities, in fact the compulsory nature of sport at St Peter's and his skill at tennis, meant he was not the novice he claimed to be. Moreover his work seemed to satisfy his employers. Among his work colleagues were journalists who eventually became household names. There was Lionel Coventry, the well-known caricaturist and cartoonist and Lawrie Jervis senior, the football columnist, who also lived at Gilberton and caught the same train as young Hague.

Midway through his cadetship Ralph decided newspaper work was not his milieu. He liked "the inside work" but disliked the interviewing. Perhaps he realised he lacked the brash, inquisitive boldness necessary for reporting. Almost certainly sport and sporting events did not fire his imagination. Nonetheless those in charge, hoping to keep the young cadet, offered, by way of enticement, a job assisting the cable sub editor, but he was not deterred, his mind made up, his eyes on another métier, the profession of his brother and father.

His stint, though short in Adelaide's afternoon tabloid, had an indelible life-shaping legacy. Specifically it equipped him with important skills, that is shorthand and typing which he maintained and used throughout his life to great effect especially in his editing of legal reports. Typing certainly made him self-sufficient enabled him to do his editing and organise his material without secretarial staff. He understood the process of publishing because of his newspaper experience and could communicate efficiently with printers through cryptic notes. Maybe and most importantly journalism taught him the discipline of writing simply which according to Professor Castles gave Hague "a facility, an ability to write [his legal histories] without academic challenge in the clarity that was rarely … found amongst people like him at the time". Thus, at the Crown Law Office he was famous for the brevity of his opinions. One wonders too if his delight in telling stories, and he told them well, was in part attributable to journalism. Indeed anecdotes were used by him to explain the world, to make a point but unlike the press, never maliciously. A number of onlookers have observed, as did Hague himself, that his ability to type probably spared his life during the Second World War, keeping him away from actual combat and in army administration.

Law: University

Adelaide University's Law School, like St Peter's College, was intended to be an educational outpost of the British Empire, to teach English-style law as a university discipline in the English manner. In fact, South Australia's oldest university was, in the nineteenth century, among the very few tertiary institutions, both here and abroad, to place legal education in a university setting. Not unexpectedly, teaching in the English manner often meant that there was an English focus and often English content in the curriculum. Nevertheless, this was in keeping with the tenets and culture of the time and attune to the ambition of one of the prime movers of the Law School, Sir Samuel Way CJ.

When Hague first entered the Law School's Mitchell Building in 1928, aged twenty, older and probably a little wiser than most of his fellow students, Australia and the world was sliding towards the Great Depression. After the exuberance and high capital investment of the earlier 1920s, Australia's delicately balanced, tariff-protected economy was very vulnerable to shifts in overseas trade.

The Law School in 1925 had experienced its own crisis when the Professor of Law, Coleman Phillipson, compromised his academic integrity and indeed the Law School's reputation, by offering private tuition to allegedly struggling law students. He was replaced, rather controversially, after an inquiry found that there was an obvious conflict of interest between Phillipson's two roles, that of examiner and that of coach. His successor was the urbane Arthur Campbell from the New South Wales Bar, an able linguist, brilliant honours arts graduate and engineer, and former associate to Sir George Rich of the High Court. Needless to say, his non-degree legal qualifications provoked some criticism upon his appointment to the professorship. In some senses, Campbell was a little like Hague was to become in his later years: a good administrator, convivial, friendly and unassuming, considerate of others; a portly bachelor gentleman who loved bridge. Until his unforeseen death in 1949 he was the only full-time member of the teaching staff and was important in reasserting the School's good name and reassuring the ruffled student body after the Phillipson scandal.

Campbell's highly regarded teaching in elements, constitutional law, contracts and wrongs (torts and criminal law) was complimented by dedicated part-time lecturers, mostly city practitioners who covered the rest of the English-orientated curriculum. Hague was lectured to by an all male cast, a variety of lawyers including aloof, upright and rigorous property lecturer Teddy Benham, who delighted in the esoterics of feudal land law; popular lecturer in evidence, procedure and private international law Geoffrey Reed, who was later elevated to the Supreme Court Bench; Herbert Mayo, who taught jurisprudence and also became a Supreme Court judge. And then there was Charles Brebner for Roman law. Brebner sought to engage his students' interest in the obscure antiquities and events of Ancient Rome by means of an imaginary parrot belonging to the jurist Gaius. Latin, too, was part of the curriculum. To enter Law one required a matriculation pass in Latin; and to pass Law, a pass in Latin was essential. Such a stipulation did not pose a problem for star Latin student Ralph Hague. The only legal history taught was *English* legal history.

Reflecting on those times Alex Castles, who was lecturer and Professor of Law at Adelaide University from 1958 until 1967, roundly condemned the absence of Australian content in the topic of constitutional law. Apparently, prior to the 1960s, students were basically instructed in the English legal system until the late nineteenth century and then told that the Australian system was but a branch of England's. According to Castles, "nothing much about the Australian legal system was taught", not even colonial advances on the English Judicature Acts, and scant consideration was given to the Australian Constitution. There was certainly no indication that Australia's systems had different and distinctive beginnings and had developed in their own individual ways. Any application of English law in Australia was dealt with via the Colonial Laws Validity Acts, which were to frustrate Boothby and fascinate Hague in his investigation of early Australian legal history. Such was the education of the Adelaide lawyer; and elsewhere in Australia it was largely the same. A redeeming feature of the undergraduate law degree was the compulsory inclusion of two arts units. Hague heroically managed somehow to go beyond this requirement, taking seven arts subjects as well as persevering with law. These embraced subject areas in which he had shone at school: British and European history, English language and literature, economics and geography.

The students who attended in the 1920s were, like Hague, mostly from private schools and many among them did not regard the legal qualification as their means to a livelihood. In the 1930s, a higher proportion of the undergraduates were the product of state education and saw matters differently. Not a few experienced difficulties paying the fees and expenses associated with their course because of prevailing economic adversity.

Hague's early undergraduate years witnessed an increase in the numbers of women among the student body. This trend continued into the beginning of the 1930s when Roma Mitchell began her legal studies. She joined sixteen other female law students in 1931, and together they faced some discrimination on the part of the mostly male, and probably jealous, student population. Excluded from the Law Students Society (L.S.S), the scene of essential mooting and debating activities, on the grounds of gender, these irate but determined women formed their own association, cannily under the presidency of Professor Campbell. Hague admired feisty intelligent females and was supportive of women facing discrimination or employment difficulties and this may have stemmed from this period. Or perhaps his feminist sympathies resulted from knowing how his mother's career in teaching was stymied by the Education Department's practice in relation to married women?

Whatever the case, undoubtedly the uniquely small, intimate environment of the Law School in the 1920s and 1930s and the easy exchange of ideas therein were influential in the moulding of young, vigorous minds. Apart from the numbers being only about sixty or seventy with everyone knowing everyone else, there was the fact of their physical isolation from the rest of the student population. After their first year, passed entirely at the university, law students worked as articled clerks in legal offices, coming only to the Mitchell Building for lectures. Hague was articled to his father at Smith, Kelly, Hague and Travers in 1929. The outcome of this enforced segregation was a group of students who largely kept to themselves, organised their own social events and by and large related well to each other.

They had surmounted the difficulties attendant upon the Phillipson scandal, the appointment of an engineer, Arthur Campbell, to head the Faculty, and the exigencies of the Depression, to produce "not only an intellectual climate but also a camaraderie within the student body which has probably never been equalled", according to Andrew Ligertwood (Dean of the Faculty of Law 1981-1982) In this situation, Hague the hard working scholar thrived. He was among remarkable and often enlightened young men and women who would go on to judicial office and illuminate the annals of our State's legal history. Among them were John Bray, Roma Mitchell, David Hogarth and John Ewins. Other impressive intellects were to enrol and graduate in law later in the 1930s: Howard Zelling, Andrew Wells, Elliot Johnson and Don Williams.

It should not be thought that life for these law students was all work and no play. From the tales recalled in *Law on North Terrace*, there is plenty of evidence of extra curricular fun, a good deal of heavy drinking, late nights and the usual undergraduate pranks. Of Hague's part in all this we know but little. Fortuitously, a small window was opened on his otherwise obscure student days by John Tregenza who interviewed Hague in 1972 about his role in keeping order during a water workers' strike in 1928. 'When asked about his social life at University, Hague darkly said, "Well, there wasn't a great deal of it ... When I started there was no university union [building]. You saw more of your legal acquaintances in the Law School down at the courts than you did in the university". Of the extent of his participation in debates, public meetings and societies, he commented, "Oh no, not very many". He was a different lad from the one who was a dedicated committeeman at school. Perhaps undergraduate societies were not geared to his enthusiasms? Could it be that Hague was already exploring legal history?

All the same, he did tell Tregenza about one noteworthy episode when in 1928 he and many other undergraduates responded to advertisements calling for strike breakers during the waterside workers strike at Port Adelaide. Presumably Hague's participation was possible because his first undergraduate year was free from work constraints. Hague's account of his and others adventures with the "Citizens Defence Brigade" is characteristically amusing.

After the preliminaries associated with recruitment at the Adelaide Railway Station, Hague and the other volunteers were issued with bayonets and rifles at the Torrens Parade Ground. Hague only ever used his "bayonet for opening tins of jam and condensed milk ... at the wharf", and there was no ammunition given for the rifles. After a dismal and damp winter's night in an underground room at Fort Largs with several hundreds huddled under overcoats and blankets and "packed in like sardines", Hague spent the first day of strike breaking in typical Hague fashion in "quite the warmest and most comfortable place …" around the fire with the cooks who were "making tea and soup …". Then in complete darkness, "... in the dead of night we rolled across to Port Adelaide" by train, but "... they'd forgotten to tell anybody there so they could open the gates to let us in". So the student strikebreakers, with cumbersome rifles and heavy overcoats and blankets, crawled over six feet of galvanised fencing protected with rows of barbed wire. The next three days and nights were idled away in drizzling rain, playing cards and talking. "When the booze began to trickle in, those who drank proceeded to get drunk." Bedding was, at first, bales of wool, then blankets, and finally bunks on a deserted gulf steamer. "I can remember living on jam and bread and condensed milk", and by the end of it the volunteers, without washing or shaving, and sleeping in their clothes, looked as disreputable as the strikers were supposed to be. If Hague reflected upon his boyhood memories of Port Pirie's industrial troubles during those long hours of enforced inactivity, it does not emerge from the Tregenza interview.

In 1931 Hague was again on the sidelines of a threatened riot situation. He witnessed the aftermath of the infamous Beef Riots, in the depths of the Depression. In the same conversation with Tregenza he spoke of jarrah truncheons the size of baseball bats being used in crowd control by horse-mounted policemen.

Hague finished his law course in 1931 as he finished his school days, with much deserved success, and his efforts were rewarded by official acknowledgment. Because his work was of a consistently high standard throughout and he "demonstrated ability to undertake advanced work and original investigation", he gained three David Murray scholarships in Roman law (1929), private international law (1930) and jurisprudence (1931). There were even greater honours bestowed upon him. Four times from 1928 until 1931 he won the coveted Stow Prize, which was awarded to law students "who show exceptional merit in not less than two subjects in any year of their course". This made him easily eligible for the Stow scholarship, (which required three Stow prizes) gold medal and to be styled "the Stow Scholar". Reportedly, he carried the medal, which resembled a large gold coin with a raised and gilded likeness of Stow upon it, with him wherever he went. Only very few knew of this academic triumph, for Hague rarely spoke of it, but his close keeping of medal, nestled in cream velvet in a small brown calf case, suggests a measure of pride. Later in life, Hague modestly accounted for his academic achievements by saying that he was older than other students.

The Stow awards were created in memory of Randolph Isham Stow, an outstanding barrister and one of the first three to be appointed Q.C. in South Australia, whose brief presence in the judicial firmament was ended by his death from liver atrophy in 1878. Sir Samuel Way considered him to be "one of the greatest judges Australia ever had whose gifts would have gained him distinction in any part of the world". His career at the Bar paralleled Mr Justice Boothby's on the bench. Perhaps Hague, the ex reporter and budding scholar, upon winning the Stow prize, did some investigation and read of his benefactor's courageous struggles with Boothby and was drawn deeper into this chaotic period in South Australia's legal history.

Law: Practice

When Hague's Bachelor of Laws degree was conferred on 29 April 1932 by Sir George Murray CJ, in his role as Chancellor of Adelaide University, most Australians were still deeply troubled by the Depression. The same was still true upon Hague's admission to practice on the 17th of December of the same year. During these hard years, the incomes of the partners at Smith, Kelly Hague & Travers were sliced in half and most likely it was the same situation in other firms. There was, however, "an abundance of bankruptcy work" which kept Hague's father's firm afloat. For many articled clerks, debt collecting burdened their days and dominated their workloads. It is almost certain that Hague, given his kindly nature, would have baulked at such a grim and confrontational duty.

Because of the shortage of legal work, the slow economy and high unemployment, many graduates, after admission, never found jobs in the law and took work wherever it was available, often drifting to fields of endeavour such as the government and the press, some never to return to practice. Fortunately, Hague was able to continue at his father's firm where he began as a clerk after leaving the *News* in 1927. From 1928 until 1938 much of his time was employed in assisting the firm's senior and junior barristers, Frank Villeneuve Smith KC and John Leo Travers prepare their cases. This entailed chamber appointments, interviewing witnesses and getting pleadings in order. In a way, it was not unlike cadet journalism.

Working for such outstanding and ambitious barristers was surely excellent training for young Hague. It was an age when clerkship with eminent counsel was deemed an auspicious and important element in a legal career, offering as it did familiarity with court procedure and an apprenticeship in great advocacy. And if those who worked with Frank Villeneuve Smith are to be believed, he was, despite his superlative intellect and lofty status, a considerate and loyal leader who acknowledged a junior's work in court. Hague has described Villeneuve Smith as a "flamboyant but brilliant barrister who was a legend in the legal community ... the nearest approach to a genius that I've had anything to do with". He saw Villeneuve Smith and Edward Erskine Cleland as easily the two outstanding lawyers of his time. Villeneuve Smith at thirty five was the youngest KC ever appointed, a distinction he shared with his good friend R.G. Menzies, another great lawyer and later Prime Minister. He practised exclusively as a barrister and for most of his professional life he was the only one to do so. Tall, dark and handsome, with a penetrating gaze and large pince nez attached to a long black silk ribbon round his neck, with an exceptional command of language, a ready wit and a knowledge of law said to put *Halsbury's Laws of England* in the shade, Villeneuve Smith dominated Law School, court rooms, national and international legal conferences, in fact any company in which he found himself.

Villeneuve Smith's capacity for work was, not surprisingly, enormous. Reputedly his was a sixteen-hour day, six-day week, often concluding well after midnight, anticipating by half a century the legal work loads of our times. In this pre-war office environment, which Hague saw as "easy going", with no one being overtaxed, Villeneuve Smith was a man to admire and emulate. But perhaps his was not a path that everyone could or would have wished to pursue.

Taking into account Hague's own interests, character and background, one has the feeling that South Australia's most eminent counsel was a factor in turning Hague away from bar work and even private practice. While Villeneuve Smith sprang from a thrusting, individualistic family, including great grandsire Admiral Villeneuve, Emperor Napoleon's commander in chief at the Battle of Trafalgar, and a sprinkling of controversial, even iconoclastic lawyers, Hague's great grandsire was a Manchester clergyman, his grandfather a carpenter and his father a solicitor who preferred paperwork to court, a jovial, low-key gentleman who enjoyed home life and outdoor activities. From watching Smith and Travers, Hague was privy to the best and worst of a barrister's life, which by its very nature demands a huge commitment in time and does not allow an easy separation between home and office. Hague wanted something different, to leave the professional sphere behind while exploring other realms at home. He noted, too, the toll imposed by a heavy case load, that barristers were perpetually immersed in solving the problems and personal affairs of strangers.

While it soon became clear that bar work was a difficult, knife-edge and stressful existence, which did not suit Hague's mild and modest temperament, even the responsibility of handling others' affairs as a solicitor worried Hague. "If you make a mistake in private practice, you've ruined someone's life or fortune. It's quite serious." That he was vacillating over his ultimate destiny, his place in the law, is evident from the now faint handwritten card records in the University of Adelaide's archives. Having completed four years of legal and art studies, with accolades aplenty, he could not resist the call of further scholarship, and started a combined History and English honours degree in 1932. Although the course requirements were fulfilled in 1932, something distracted him in 1933, for there is no examination result recorded. As if an honours degree and private practice were not enough, he commenced a Diploma in Public Administration in the same year. Was he even then thinking of a career in government? It too was left in limbo, although temporarily resumed in 1936. What brought the abandonment of two academic courses by an individual renowned for hard work and constancy to the task in hand? It is most likely that another more absorbing project waylaid our scholar, and this was simply the research and writing for his *The Early Legal History of South Australia.*

Academia: The Thesis

Hague explained his involvement in what was undoubtedly in this mammoth undertaking in his usual understated way. Apparently, in the lean days of the Great Depression, Hague, then twenty six years old and still a bachelor living at home, had time to do the huge amount of original research his project necessitated.

Hague may have been inspired by the Law School's previous history of erudition. There was Professor John William Salmond, whose authorship of *The Law of Torts* in 1902 and *Jurisprudence* in 1907 first brought the School an international reputation. His successors to the professorship, Jethro Brown and Coleman Phillipson, were also distinguished legal scholars with many influential publications to their credit. Apart from professorial scholarship, there was evidence of high quality post-graduate legal research: Donald Kerr's L.L.D. thesis on *Judicial Interpretation of Australia's Constitution* published in 1925; Thomas Hewitson's 1922 doctoral thesis on *The Origin and History of Suretyship*; and William Anstey Wynes' L.L.D. thesis, published later and in many editions as *Legislative Executive and Judicial Powers in Australia.* One wonders if Hague was aware that Australian legal history was already being tentatively explored across the border by another scholar, Dr C.H. Currey with his 1929 L.L.D. thesis, *Chapters on the Legal History of New South Wales.* According to Dr John Bennett, legal historian and author, Hague and Currey were the first to venture into the field, aside from works on constitutional law by men such as Sweetman, Melbourne and Evatt.

What prompted Hague to commit himself to the project, which eventually became a lifelong quest, of collecting and recording "such information as can now be found relating to the establishment and development of the law in South Australia, the Courts ... Judges and ... Legal Profession from the founding of the Colony to the removal ... of Mr Justice Boothby"?

Hague was a curious person who, aided by his exceptional memory, relished the gathering of stories, titbits about incidents and people, whether from the past or from his own immediate milieu, be it his suburb or work. G.H. Pitt, the legendary Principal Librarian of the Public Library of South Australia, who was acquainted with Hague for over 20 years, wrote in 1949 that:

> 'It was not long before I became impressed by [his] love of historical research, not for the sake of any kudos to be gained … but for its own sake ... he never begrudged the time or effort necessary ... I came to realise that he possessed, to an unusual degree, the patience, enthusiasm, honesty and freedom from bias necessary for sound historical work.'

And Hague took pleasure in relating what he found to those interested, whether in print or in conversation. In the approach to the celebration of South Australia's Centenary in 1936, there was surely heightened interest in the pioneering days and much excavation of details, which had long lain dormant.

The production of Centenary books and Centenary stories leading up to 1936 was undoubtedly a pre-occupation of not a few upright citizens and establishment figures, as was the case in Australia's Bicentenary and South Australia's Sesquicentary. To a man of Hague's investigative inclinations in this climate of enquiry, it must have been fairly clear that there was little written about South Australia's legal history, apart from what was already in primary records, potted biographies and brief summaries. No attempt had been made before Hague to survey the genesis and early growth of South Australia's legal institutions in any detailed way.

It has been suggested that there was a nicely mischievous and slightly irreverent side to Hague's nature, that he liked doing what others would not, and that he dared, in his own quiet way, to be original. And given the usual intentions of organisers associated with historic occasions, the objective in 1936 was probably to represent South Australia's pioneers in all their solemn glory. Hague, after some preliminary digging in dusty records, became aware that the glorious past was mostly inglorious, and he decided to chronicle the history just as it was, including the foibles and frailties of the major, and some minor players. Abetted by his delight in the quirky, and his impish streak, Hague immersed himself in what was a huge undertaking, which surely consumed many of his waking hours over a number of years, and although the period covered was only small, the final manuscript amounted to about 1,500 double-spaced typescript pages.

Hague's own past had been preparing him for the project. His childhood away from the well-heeled, leafy suburbs of Adelaide and the Anglo orientation therein, afforded him the privilege of seeing the beginnings of our national identity in the frank, unabashed rawness of country life. He saw Australian reality without pretence, and valued it regardless. St Peter' College, where he spent "six happy years", in its search for its own unique traditions, apart from those adopted from great English public schools, honoured the early days of the colony when it too was new. Many of the College's original benefactors were significant in the young colony's first years. Some of these men gazed, grim-faced, in weathered stone from the heights of Old School House and regularly appeared in the school magazine as part of its "History of the School 1847-1921". The series continued throughout Hague's secondary schooling.

Then there was the influence of St Peter's dynamic headmaster, the Reverend Bickersteth, a graduate in modern history from Cambridge University, who impelled the school along new academic paths, both literary and historical. He personally encouraged Hague to develop his aptitude for English and history, urging his parents to allow him to remain longer at school "for the opportunity of learning perhaps the best that a school like ours can give". He also recommended that Hague obtain a university degree in whatever career he chose. What we see in *The Early Legal History* is an expression of Hague's principal pleasures: the law, research and writing, made possible by his training at the *News* and his academic study which gave him the skills to accomplish the labour of love he had set himself.

Although hearsay has it that Hague submitted his treatise for an L.L.D (a higher Doctorate of Laws), in fact he offered *The Early Legal History* as a possible thesis subject for the Bonython Prize. The sum of money, originally £100, is still awarded by the Council of the University of Adelaide in memory of Sir Langdon Bonython who endowed the Chair of Law, and is intended to foster "significant contributions to the science of Law". The subject material for the thesis must be approved by both the Faculty and the Council.

Hague first approached the Faculty of Law on the 9th of March 1936. Subsequent to the submissions of his proposal, he was interviewed by the Dean sometime in May regarding the scope of the thesis. The Faculty then consulted their Honours Sir George Murray and Sir Angas Parsons, Chief Justice and Justice respectively of the Supreme Court, over suitability. After that, the Dean reported to the Education Committee, which said, "If the subject is treated critically, the Faculty is prepared to approve it". In a typed report of the Faculty of Law there first emerges some doubt with the qualification, "whether the subject maybe treated merely historically or critically and philosophically". Alas the use of the word "merely" was a harbinger of the eventual outcome. It is indicative of a now outdated viewpoint that an historical approach to the law was of small moment.

On the 2nd of June 1936, Hague received, presumably by post, a cold and formal five-line letter from the University's Registrar: "Dear Sir, I have with regret to inform you that the Council at its meeting was unable to approve...". No reason was given for the rejection of the thesis. How stunned the young scholar must have been! Something of the shock, pain and incredulity he felt comes to us through the choice of language used by various witnesses to Hague's life when describing his response to the rejection. Words and phrases such as "bitter", "aggrieved", "hurt", "taken aback", "one of his greatest disappointments" surface in their testimony. Years of exhaustive and most revealing research and writing were cast into oblivion by blinkered academics and judges, heedless of the significance of what had been submitted. Professor Castles attributed the rejection to "the sheer parochialism and narrow mindedness of an incredibly inward looking ... people that ran the law in South Australia in the 1930s". He described such people as "snobs, [who] never regarded Australians as first rate lawyers". Furthermore, for them, legal history was English legal history and of course was best written by English academics. In their opinion, and they were arbiters of a legal prize, legal history, including Australian legal history, was history, not law. Professor Castles damned their decision on another ground. He considered that Hague's magnum opus was "far in excess in quality of the other L.L.Ds ... awarded by the University of Adelaide in the 1930s … I'm probably the only person who's seen them all." Hague himself was extremely reticent on the subject, although he did imply to close friends, including the Brown family, that the University considered his thesis too long.

During or even before the negotiations with the University, Hague arranged for a private printing by Hassells, a scholarly press in Currie Street, of a small biographical portion of the thesis. It was entitled *Sir John Jeffcott*, an appropriate choice, he being the first judge of the infant colony. Other excepts were to follow: *The Gentle Jickling* in 1939, *The Court of Appeals* in 1940 and another on a topic and character not in the thesis by the name of *General Bacon* also in 1940. Whatever Hague's motives were in arranging the private printing they demonstrate that he was "down but not out" and that his interest in the South Australian legal history was undiminished.

Several important and revealing letters connecting the pamphlet about *Sir John Jeffcott* and the thesis were found in Hague's private papers after his death. Two of them are in the sloping, easy to read hand of Sir Angas Parsons who advised the Faculty over the thesis. In the first, dated the 20th of May 1936, he thanks Hague for sending him *Sir John Jeffcott*, describing the small work as "very interesting".

His concluding remark to the short note is telling: "What a quarrelsome lot some of the pioneers were." It is almost as if he is bothered, even annoyed by Hague's findings. In the second letter, dated the 9th of June, when the judge surely knew of Hague's rebuff, Angas Parsons enclosed a vice regal note. It was from the then Governor Sir Winston Dugan. Apparently, Dugan borrowed Angas Parsons' copy of *Sir John Jeffcott*, which he reported as giving him "a very pleasant hour over the fire". Did the judge communicate the second time with Hague to console? Or was he not in agreement with the final decision over the thesis?

The third significant letter is from Sir George Murray CJ, written from his home at Murray Park, Magill, on his personal stationery. This letter is even more illuminating. Murray, like Angas Parsons, was a party to the fate of the thesis. He begins by thanking Hague for sending him *Sir John Jeffcott* and suggests that the absence of authorship on the pamphlet's title page was because:

> 'you were afraid the revelations you had to make would throw a dampener on our Centenary and perhaps put a stop to Glenelg's ambitions for a monument to our pioneers. A little later there will be no danger of these consequences.'

There are well-substantiated grounds, in hindsight, for disagreeing with the Chief Justice's reasoning. Hague always had a hard to shake habit of not assigning authorship to his intellectual efforts. Moreover, he would not have trawled through South Australia's colonial past if he had not wanted the results of his labours to be known. Indeed, he deposited his thesis at the Public Library in January 1937, just six months after its rejection. I rather believe, given Murray's observation, that the nature of Hague's revelations was yet another negative in the eyes of the establishment, militating against the acceptance of the thesis, particularly ill-timed in the Centenary year. South Australia was applauding one version of a segment of its history and Hague was presenting another rather disturbing and different picture. It is likely that this unruly portrait challenged Bench and Gown, especially as it came from one of their own and not somebody outside of the establishment.

Herbert Mayo was far less cautious in his reaction to the Jeffcott pamphlet from either the older Sir Angas Parsons or Sir George Murray. His letter of thanks, dated the 22nd of May 1936 is full of compliments and, as befits an academic, he takes a long and wider view of what Hague was offering. Presciently he says:

> 'I think it is high time that a commencement was made to place on record something of the early history of the Bench and Bar … so that we may know what the Bench had to suffer and the Bar had to put up with in those early days. You … are eminently fitted to grapple with the task and I hope that since you have made a start you will continue your good work'.

Mayo concluded his letter by placing an order for the rest of the pamphlets. Little did Mayo realise the work he desired was under consideration at that very time at his place of part-time employment, Adelaide University. The Jurisprudence Lecturer's encouragement demonstrates that some in Adelaide were receptive to Hague's endeavours. Nevertheless Hague waited another twenty-five years, for a world war to be fought and the gradual disintegration of Britain's Empire, before there was mainstream and even academic acceptance.

From letters he received in the 1940s, 1950s and 1960s we know he was unremitting in his search for new material for his chosen area, sending English correspondents on difficult errands as he expanded chapters from the original thesis to create individual titles. *Sir John Jeffcott, Mr Justice Crawford, Mr Justice Boothby* and *The Gentle Jickling.* These he distributed along with his shorter pamphlets.

Throughout the month of March 1957 many judicial personages such as Sir Herbert Mayo, Sir George Ligertwood, Sir Geoffrey Reid, the President of the Industrial Court, E.W.R. Morgan and senior members of the profession including John Bray, Harry Alderman, David Hogarth, Charles Bright as well as the Law Society and curiously, the "Adelaide Club" were presented with specially printed copies of *Mr Justice Crawford.* All expressed pleasure, gratitude and enthusiasm for yet another of Hague's local histories. Sir George Ligertwood was so enthralled that he requested a copy of the Boothby manuscript. Not a few readers urged Hague to publish so that a broader audience would benefit from his invaluable research.

Some years later, in 1962, Sir Herbert Mayo, ever Hague's champion, tried to do what the readers of *Mr Justice Crawford* suggested and press Hague into print. Mayo attempted to persuade the Libraries Board and the Law Society to jointly publish *The Early Legal History.* His efforts bore no fruit. Gerald Fischer acting on behalf of the Public Library wanted to do much the same with the *Sir John Jeffcott* manuscript. These well-intentioned gestures were met with the same resistance and unwillingness that Castles and Dame Roma encountered when Hague was asked, "to resubmit his thesis", for an LLD in the 1990s. Fischer alludes to Hague's reaction in a letter dated the 21st of May 1962:

'I can understand your reluctance to undertake the labour and (rather unlikely) critical consequences of publication. These considerations could make a tedious bore out of what has been an enjoyable excursion at your own inclination'.

There was recognition too beyond Hague's own small circle of legal colleagues and acquaintances. In 1960 Geoffrey Sawer, Professor of Law at the Australian National University proposed a short term fellowship so that Hague could finish his Boothby manuscript. He had heard of it from Alex Castles, then a young lecturer at the

Adelaide Law School brought over from Melbourne by the provocative new Professor of Law, Norval Morris in 1958.

Castles was trained in constitutional and legal history at the University of Chicago and so had an interest in the evolution of "native legal systems". When he started at Adelaide's Law School very little on Australian legal history had been published and Australian legal history hardly featured in University law courses. Not surprisingly Hague's unpublished histories attracted him and after "tremendous fights in the faculty", Australian law was introduced into constitutional law. Hague's manuscript was placed in the Law School Library and students began using his material. These were moves, which brought about the eventual demise of the outdated notions that legal history only meant English history and that legal history was history not law.

That Australia possessed a unique and distinctive legal system from colonial times was at last gaining acceptance and wider currency was in part due to other scholars writing in the same area: S.H.Z. Woinarski with his *History of Legal Institutions in Victoria* in 1941; Dr T.P. Fry of Brisbane with his *Australian Courts and Administrative Tribunals*, and Enid Russell who in 1950 completed a thesis concerning Western Australian's legal history.

Castles' connection with interstate academia and fascination with the controversial, ever intriguing Boothby inspired an approach to Hague by Melbourne University Press (M.U.P.) in 1962. Geoffrey Sawer had spoken to that press's director, Peter Ryan of Hague's "polished style which applied to so rich a subject and would make a splendid book". He wondered if Hague would favour them "with an opportunity to see the ms". Hague sent Ryan instead his *Mr Justice Crawford* and then the expanded *Sir John Jeffcott* which Ryan saw as "a prelude to Boothby and other works". He wrote thus to Hague: "I detect a wide latent interest in the old judges and lawyers, a readiness to read about them if someone does the research and makes it easy".

His anticipation of the ready reception of *Sir John Jeffcott, Portrait of a Colonial Judge* proved accurate and the work received gratifying reviews and enjoyed pleasing sales in 1963 and beyond. One Adelaide reviewer, John Tregenza, hoped that Hague's next publication will be his general legal history "which has the merits of this biography (Jeffcott) with a good deal of substance". Another reviewer Sir John Barry described *Sir John Jeffcott* as having the quality of entertaining scholarship and looked forward to publication of Hague's biography of that judicial maverick, Boothby.

There was clearly a market for legal history but Hague, despite negotiations with M.U.P. over *Boothby* and *Jickling*, did not publish again. Was he disaffected by Melbourne University history Professor John La Nauze's rather critical assessment on of his Boothby manuscript or had the process of publication become too arduous for one who took delight in research and writing for its own sake?

Hague's legal histories were likewise acknowledged for their usefulness in litigation by both Bar and Bench. Tony Bishop recalled the *Early Legal History* … and *Court of Appeals* residing in the Crown Solicitor's Library and being used by Brian Cox in preparing cases to do with fisheries and the jurisdictional limits of the states. "In some of those key cases, the history is cited and certainly it was always on our list of authorities". Both Bray CJ and Zelling J used Hague's thesis and *Court of Appeals* to clarify discussion regarding the effect of the Colonial Laws Validity Acts on local legislation in, Gilbertson v SA, 15 SASR, 81 and 104. King CJ, some ten years later in August 1987 corroborated the fact of the history's importance in determining early law when he wrote to Hague on the occasion of his retirement as SASR editor:

'It is still the principal source readily available to us of the early history of the law and is frequently resorted to when judges and others wish to acquaint themselves with some point … of our early history'.

Such usage by the Bray and King Benches of Hague's text is strong refutation of the University's apparent implication in 1936 that the thesis was merely history.

Post-war academics, Dr J.M. Bennett and Professor Alex Castles in contrast to their predecessors had no doubt about the value of Hague's pioneering work. In the forward to his *Law Makers and Wayward Wigs* in 1987, Castles wrote: "… it remains a vital repository of research, scholarship, wit and wisdom which may never be equalled".

Academia: Lecturing

Ultimately, having decided bar work was not his bent, Hague probably cherished the dream of a niche in academia, and his thesis may have been intended in part at least as a means to this end. Without the necessary postgraduate qualifications, entry to the halls of learning was, of course, much harder. But being a patient scholar accustomed to the hurdles posed in research, he was not one to abandon his ambition easily, and in 1938 joined the galaxy of new part-time lecturers at the Law School, replacing those departing for the bench, firstly as an examiner in Roman law and real and personal property, and then as a lecturer in jurisprudence (including Roman law) in 1939. These "able and pleasant" enthusiastic young men included Martin Kriewaldt, Anthony Pickering, Frank Piper, Kevin Ward, Earnest Phillips and Lou Whitington.

Hague's capacity for relating stories, for lucid explanation, for illumination by means of his lively wit and his thorough enjoyment of the law gave him a distinct advantage over other less skilful lecturers. Kevin Ward KC of Ward, Mollison Litchfield & Ward, wrote in 1949, after speaking with students whom Hague had lectured, that he treats his subject "... often regarded as dull, with a freshness which stimulates interest and provokes thought". Alex Castles had another interpretation of Hague's lecturing when interviewed in 2003. He spoke of Hague's originality of approach to his subject, which was not tied down to the simplistic thinking of jurisprudence, as being perceived as a threat just as his work on Boothby was to those who espoused the view that Australian law was a branch of the English legal system.

Certainly Hague's irreverent "cock a snook attitude" permitted a certain laxity and casualness among the law student population. According to Brian Magarey, a returned services student whom Hague lectured, "It was well known that Hague had a low opinion of Roman law and that no-one would fail". Magarey himself presented a dubious paper, which was returned with the pass mark of 50 per cent. The next year Dr Bray lectured in jurisprudence and Roman law and half the class failed. Bray clearly took the subject quite seriously, believing a grounding in Roman law was essential for Australian law students.

Yet Hague was sufficiently adept and ambivalent not to engender disrespect; in fact to inspire admiration from all quarters. One former student recalled him in the *Law on North Terrace* as "the genial Ralph Hague who showed students the houses where the legal philosophers lived". Another, Gwenneth Stokes (née Woodger) at Law School in the late 1930s commented, "Lectures were always stimulating, always taxing. I remember especially Professor Campbell, of whom I was terrified, Earnie Phillips with his vast knowledge, John Bray and Ralph Hague". Again Hague is in fine company. Even Dr Bray, who filled Hague's post during the war years, held Hague in the highest regard, according to Tony Bishop. In the long term, though, Hague, with his subtly couched challenges, proved to be the nemesis of Bray and those who thought like him.

The experience of lecturing in 1939 and in the immediate post-war period evidently confirmed in Hague's mind that academia was where he wished to be. His chance came unexpectedly in 1949. The opportunity to combine his love of scholarship with a career was brought about when portly Arthur Campbell, Professor of Law since 1926 and the longest serving Dean in the Law School's first one hundred years, was found dead on the floor of his Walkerville home, still only in his fifties.

Kevin Ward KC canvassed the feelings of prominent members of the legal procession who it seems shared his view that Hague was the ideal man for the position, and he urged Hague to apply. Apart from lobbying discreetly in the right quarters, Ward provided Hague with an extraordinary reference eulogising his many virtues as a scholar, lecturer, legal practitioner and administrator. Interestingly, Ward emphasised the advantages of appointing an experienced practitioner to the professorship. G.H. Pitt, Principal Librarian from the Public Library of South Australia, also wrote a paeon of praise.

"In the course of many years as Archivist I have known no other student with the same combination of ripe scholarship, clear thinking, tireless energy and literary brilliance." Villeneuve Smith KC likewise supported Hague, writing to him: "How pleased I am to know that you are an applicant ... I know of no-one better qualified." He too used his considerable influence. Alas, a life Villeneuve Smith saw as more congenial to Hague than the Bar was not to be. Neither were Ward's hopes for a Law School more attuned to the realities of practice fulfilled.

Adelaide University replaced Campbell with a man who embodied their idea of legal scholarship: thirty two year old Richard Arthur Blackburn, a St Peter's old boy, a first-class Arts graduate and Rhodes scholar with a B.C.L. degree from Oxford where he was named Eldon Scholar in 1949. The University possibly envisaged Blackburn, a younger man by eleven years, as more responsive to the changing expectations for law schools in the post-war world. Perhaps Blackburn's English tertiary education was a critical factor in a community still strongly Anglo-centric after the military and emotional alliances forged during the war. Hague's academic glories were, after all, home grown and he lacked what Blackburn had, those outstanding postgraduate qualifications, those glittering prizes. Perhaps his failure to claim the professorship, to win in yet another joust with academia in part explains the depths of his lingering bitterness over the Bonython prize? A door to a place in the realm of scholarship for which he had long and quietly yearned finally swung shut.

John Meyrick Hague, Ralph's elder brother, was associate to Sir George Murray CJ from 1926 to 1928. This snapshot shows him in full legal attire behind the buildings along the eastern aspect of the Supreme Court complex. (Rob and Marilyn Brown)

War

On the 10th of August 1939, three weeks prior to the outbreak of the Second World War, before a single Australian solider enlisted or suffered under fire, Magdalen and Percy Hague lost their first-born son and Ralph's only brother, aged thirty six years. He was buried far from Adelaide in a lonely grave near Mount Magnet, Western Australia, under the vast arch of the inland sky. A simple marble plaque, broken cement slab and low askew metal railings encrusted with mud and almost engulfed with weeds, now mark the remains of a young man whose career began with much promise and hope.

Bearing the requisite L.L.B. and admission to practice in 1926, John, lean, good looking and obviously able, sought a position at the Supreme Court and was appointed as clerk of arraigns and first associate to Sir George Murray. Then as now, such a situation is considered desirable and augurs well for the young people so selected. John remained with the Chief Justice for two and a half years and in a farewell letter to his associate signed "ever your sincere friend", Sir George wrote:

> 'We have been so happy together that it would be idle to pretend that I do not part with you with regret, but I want to

see you succeed in the profession and the next step is to break away from here.'

During his associateship John was attracted to government legal services, and inspired with a spirit of adventure, wrote away for a Crown Law job in faraway Rabaul in Papua New Guinea and another in Adelaide. Finally he settled upon private practice with Joseph Nelligan at Scottish House, Waymouth Street.

It seems that John Hague was dogged with ill health. By 1934 he is no longer in the Australian Legal Directory, and in 1936 Murray CJ is writing to John in the country, presumably on the Western Australian station owned by his friend Hector Brooks, where he went to recover from suspected tuberculosis. Hague liked bush life and determined to settle in the area, three hundred kilometres east of Geraldton, starting a practice in the small mining town of Mount Magnet. Alas, his hopes for a return to good health and private practice among new friends in new surroundings were short-lived.

Ralph Hague rarely alluded to his brother John and the little that is recollected comes to us from an interview with Erica Micklem and from various black and white photographs of John: in full barrister's regalia by himself, behind the Supreme Court building, and with other associates similarly kitted; painfully thin, lean, tanned and moustached, he is also depicted with a camel in a bush stockyard and astride a horse, presumably in Western Australia. Yet he was clearly missed by his own family, and indeed by friends from his new life, for a letter surviving from nearby Meekatharra indicates that his father Percy, with the assistance of willing hands, made sure the grave was tended for many years. Then there are the telltale photographs both recent and old of John's burial place, found in his brother's house after he too had died.

On the 27th of December 1940, Hague, aged thirty-three, enlisted for service at Keswick, South Australia's wartime army headquarters. His prime motivation for doing so is not recorded but one may assume he believed, as many of his peers did, that he too must shoulder the burden of defending Australia and the Empire. It was the start of a largely unremarkable six years, first in the Citizens Military Forces until June 1942 and then in the Australian Imperial Forces (A.I.F.) until January 1946. His was a quiet war, away from the vicissitudes of fighting and the front line. Initially he was at Keswick as a sergeant in the 2/3rd Machine Gun Battalion and "someone came through ... fairly high up" and said "I could use you in my unit", and he was transferred. His previous machine gun unit then went overseas and reportedly most perished somewhere on a Pacific island. "Hague always felt a bit bad about that because he felt he should have been with them."

However, in the light of his age, education and legal career, the Army saw Hague as more valuable in an administrative rather than combative role. Hague himself would later joke that his ability to type kept him from actual fighting. Indeed, as Kevin Ward K.C. wrote in

1949, "It was commonplace among legal men that the best way to procure a satisfactory treatment of any matter with the military at Keswick was to communicate with Mr Hague"; so it seems the Army correctly judged his capabilities.

Rapid promotion accompanied Hague's characteristic diligence and he went from sergeant to lieutenant in six months, and by December 1942 he was appointed a captain in the C.M.F.. Keswick Headquarters continued to view Hague as administrative and legal support, even after his transfer to the A.I.F. in 1942, where he was groomed for officer duties. He performed well in the officer courses, and come 1943, in "confidential reports" Hague is described "as an exceptionally brilliant officer, showing definite suitability for senior staff officer duties" and "with his extensive knowledge of legal matters ... better employed in a legal capacity".

It was because of this legal acumen that for the first and only time Hague travelled overseas in early 1945. He was posted to Lae in New Guinea's lushly forested Eastern Highlands. Lois Schmidt remembers Hague speaking of his involvement in court martials there, not defending or prosecuting, but advising. Two other stories emanate from Hague's year in Papua New Guinea. Erica Micklem is the source of one of these. On his way to another town north east of Lae, Hague sat next to an American from Jersey City who regarded him with the greatest suspicion upon learning his name. It seems the Mayor of that city was a great scoundrel and when he died, a local newspaper published his photo with the caption "Mayor Hague, may God have mercy upon his sinful soul". This story much amused that Mayor's Australian namesake. The other is much briefer and perfectly illustrates Hague's placid, no fuss nature and his ability to find himself a comfortable spot. Hague's cousin "Ned" (Edwin) Scales, totally unaware of his presence in Lae, or indeed in Papua New Guinea, remarkably ran into Hague emerging "from this lovely tent". Without so much as a "fancy meeting you here" comment, Hague greeted his cousin with a smile and said, "Hello, Ned".

Hague left the Army in January 1946, four months after the Japanese surrender on 2 September 1945, as a major in the Officers Reserve. He liked to say, when speaking of his one thousand eight hundred and sixty days of continuous full time war service, that he enlisted in the Air Force, served in the Army and was demobbed by the Navy.

How was Hague affected by his war service? Reportedly he loved Army food, especially bully beef, and may be his predilection for nourishment from tin cans, especially Kraft's braised steak and onions, after the death of his mother in 1960, was a consequence of his time in uniform. It is possible too that the Army was another major factor in modifying Hague's writing style and ability to communicate effectively. In his capacity as Staff Captain, Directorate of Organization Hague received in May 1944, along with other like officers, a letter from the Adjutant-General at Victoria Barracks,

Major General H.W. Lloyd. "I address you with the sole object of improving both the standard of military writing and English … and doing some thing about the dreadful state of our files". Attached was a short paper on military writing. A further paper came to hand in September 1944 on the same topic. The instructions forwarded could almost be a manual for legal reporting and editorial work and the fact that Hague kept them suggests he deems their content significant. "Form … The best is the simplest … Remember that tired men, surrounded by … the distracting circumstances of … battle may have to read orders, instructions …". These words could easily apply to busy, weary judges or barristers in the midst of trials or judgment writing. Hague as editor excelled in the clarity and brevity of his headnotes.

Upon the cessation of hostilities in the Pacific and in Europe and the return to civilian life, Hague, like many men and women who served, had the unsettling feeling that he was a changed person and no longer fitted into the pre-war past, or even the private practice he had left behind in Adelaide; and he looked for another niche in the law to suit the man he had become.

Hague's only recorded romance happened sometime between 1940 and 1946. With a twinkle in his eye, he mentioned to Lois Schmidt an attachment to an Army nurse "which didn't work out"; so Hague in one respect at least left the war as he entered it, as a bachelor, but according to Army records, with a tropical tan!

Hague as a Captain during the Second World War. (Rob and Marilyn Brown)

"Well done, good and faithful servant"

After demobilisation in January 1946, Hague found himself back in Adelaide and feeling like a "misplaced person". Presumably over the six years in army service he carefully considered his future in post-war Australia, so when a job at the Crown Solicitor's Office was in the offing, it was not hard for him to turn his back on partnership in Kelly, Hague and Travers and private practice which he "never liked very much". Hague applied for the position with Reginald Kearnan another ex-serviceman who was in similar circumstances, his practice having disintegrated during the war. "Although there was only one job, they kindly took the both of us. Made an extra job and we both started there almost simultaneously".

The two-storey building at 24 Flinders Street accommodated the Crown Solicitor's Office on the first floor and the Attorney General's office and the Registrar of Births, Deaths and Marriages on the ground floor until the early 1970s. It is an important element in a complex of historic buildings that comprises the "A listed" rare Gothic Revival Pilgrim Church, the Old Assembly Hall north of the church, the Treasury buildings and the General Post Office. These form a pleasing visual link with other heritage buildings bordering Victoria Square, and despite the infiltration of post-war high-rise, give a distinctive character to Adelaide's premier square.

Countless times over the next twenty four years from 1946 until his retirement Hague walked up the worn marble steps on his way to his office on the first floor. It was said that you could set your clock on his arrival and departure times, so precisely punctual was he. Keeping "good public service hours", and doing a good day's work, Hague walked in through the door at nine o'clock and out again at five to five. And I have the impression that he was happy there, in that almost Dickensian rabbit warren, pleased to have a job which was stimulating but not too exacting, allowing him the freedom to do what he especially loved outside of office hours: reading and research. Elliot Johnston astutely commented that it gave him the opportunity to be interested in the law without the pressure of being a notable person.

In the 1940s, 1950s and 1960s, the number of solicitors and support staff at the Crown Solicitor's Office was small. Certainly there were eight legal staff and probably four clerical when Hague and Kearnan commenced work. Among the most memorable solicitors were the Crown Solicitor, Albert J. Hannan K.C. C.M.B. M.A. L.L.B. and Roderick St Clair Chamberlain L.L.B. as Crown Prosecutor. "Tace"(pronounced "Tacky") Hannan, like Hague, was a Port Pirie boy, although hailing from a farming family. In personality the two men differed completely but there was common ground in scholarship. Hannan was twice a Stow prizewinner and a recipient of a David Murray Scholarship. After a long occupancy of the position of Crown Solicitor, from 1927 until 1952, he made history in 1954 as the first Catholic to be appointed (acting) Supreme Court judge. Joe Chamberlain, another farmer's son, was also destined for the Supreme Court Bench.

Reginald Kearnan, who like Hague entered government employ as a temporary solicitor, was quickly promoted, becoming Crown Prosecutor in 1948. After that there was a long wait until Chamberlain's ascent to the Bench in 1959 when Kearnan was made Crown Solicitor and Q.C. the next year. It could be said that Kearnan, a Catholic of Irish descent with a fondness for the bottle, impeded Hague's career. In those orderly times headway from below depended on the progression of those above; and Kearnan's decade long and often inadequate occupancy of the post of Crown Solicitor effectively blocked any real advancement for Hague.

Another bright young man who joined the Crown Solicitor's Office in 1948 not long after Kearnan and Hague, and whose name now, as then, figures in the folklore of legal history was Elwyn Bewell Scarfe or "Eb". He had the reputation for being "under the weather" after lunchtime and apparently his tippling brought him trouble with the police. It is said that Hague observed of his colleague, "That man's going to come to a violent end". This is, indeed, what happened as Scarfe was killed in a car accident near his home at Yankalilla in 1970. Until his death Scarfe remained in the Crown Solicitor's Office, doing principally bar work, specialising in criminal matters. After an extended spell as first Assistant Prosecutor he served as Crown Prosecutor from 1952 until 1970.

During his early years at the Crown Solicitor's Office, Hague was often away in the countryside north of Adelaide, including Gawler and the Barossa Valley, busy with Builders Licensing Court work. He was assigned a driver and the two men would take lunch at a convenient local hotel. Hague would abstain from liquor but the other man "used to drink quite a bit".

Minor courts did not worry Hague but according to Lois Schmidt (née Brown), who worked at the Crown Solicitor's Office from 1948 to 1952, he was most reluctant to appear higher up the court hierarchy. In 1947 his role as prosecutor before sitting magistrate Mr L.E. Clarke came to the notice of the *Adelaide Truth* and his name and photograph were emblazoned across the top of page 6 amid bold headlines "Osteopath in court: new act challenged". The *Adelaide Truth* was a scurrilous newspaper, which specialised in muckraking and reporting seedy divorces. Hague kept a cutting of the case as a memento, so his brief association with sensation probably amused him. For its own sake, the case may have been intriguing. Hague was a man who liked legal principles and this particular case devolved upon an inadequate definition of physiotherapy, which had been hurriedly devised by a late night Parliament.

After some years, Hague's job evolved into that of opinion writer, essentially a solicitor who represented the interests and solved the problems of the bigger government departments, "but not the kind of problems that were going to worry you personally". This suited Hague, who found the stress and responsibility of private practice onerous. He was, according to Tony Bishop, close to certain heads of departments and would always attend personally to their work. One of these people was Leo Doyle, Commissioner of Stamps, who was at Law School with Hague.

Iris Stevens, another junior solicitor at the Crown Solicitor's Office, related to me Hague's cardinal principles in tackling the opinion work of government departments:

> 'Include a clear direction whether or not a particular course could or should be taken and preferably that it not be in Latin nor too abstruse for the recipient to follow.'

It was an approach, which contrasted with that of Andrew Wells, Assistant Crown Prosecutor and Assistant Crown Solicitor from 1953 to 1956, who reportedly clouded his opinion work at times with arcane legal history. Clive Brooks, who was a Crown Law solicitor of some thirty-three years standing and having perused the Crown Solicitor's opinion books on many occasions reflected thus on Hague's work:

> 'It is quite evident the Crown Solicitor's opinions became much more detailed and better researched during the post World War Two period. Mr Hague was a positive influence in that trend.'

Brian Cox, a former colleague of Hague's from 1955 and a Supreme Court judge from 1979 to 1999, summed up the quality of Hague's solicitorial work: "His legal opinions were a model of directness and clarity and commonsense and he was held in high regard". Very seldom did his opinion extend over a page, almost to the extent that sometimes the answer was either yes or not because he shrewdly believed that that was what busy departments basically wanted. One notable example of this was illustrative of the humour he brought to his work and it was mentioned in Hague's Law Society obituary.

> 'He prepared an opinion for a government department notorious for posing questions to which the answer was obvious. Hague forwarded his response to the Deputy Crown Solicitor … for settling before it was returned to the department. The Deputy was nicknamed "Joe" (Chamberlain) and Ralph's opinion simply read "Ho! Ho! Ho! No, no … Joe".'

Two other instances of his highly developed sense of fun in relation to opinion writing particularly impressed Sam Jacobs, a Justice of the Supreme Court from 1973 to 1990, who in his youth was lectured at Law School by Hague.

> 'A man sued the Royal Adelaide Hospital after losing a testicle during an operation. When the case was presented to Hague, he opined that the R.A.H. should deny liability on the grounds that

> "testicles should be weighed and not counted", which is a play on the Latin phrase "testes (witnesses) ponderantur, non numerantur".'

The second anecdote is even more daring, especially since it comes from Hague's days as a very junior solicitor and Hannan K.C. was the most senior person in the office, in fact the Crown Solicitor, and a very religious man.

> 'A case in the Magistrates Court was completed with costs ordered against the Crown. There was some difficulty with this and the firm involved ended up sending a procuration order to the Crown. The typist who prepared the documentation misspelt procuration as "procreation". When Hague noticed this he declared that it should be sent for the personal attention of Mr Hannan.'

Hague, not unexpectedly, given the quality of his work, was esteemed by others, apart from his professional colleagues and support staff. It is reported that Sir Thomas Playford had a direct line to him and frequently sought his advice, bypassing Hague's superior, Kearnan. Hague quickly realised that a wise public servant never incurred the Premier's displeasure and he apparently succeeded.

But the admiration was not all one sided. Hague appreciated in others the qualities and goals he set for himself. According to Stewart Cockburn in his biography *Playford the Benevolent Despot*, Ralph Hague, like most other senior public servants, was unstinting in his respect for Playford's sheer ability. To his cousins John Scales, Caroline Milne (née Scales) and Elizabeth Ormsby (née Scales) Hague voiced the common conviction that Playford was South Australia's best ever Labor Premier. Hague, though, was not himself a political animal, never waving a banner or exhibiting a party bias in his life.

The management style that Hague fostered and practised in his own milieu and he effectively ran the Crown Solicitor's Office for many years was quite different from Playford's. While Playford was dictatorial, Hague by contrast was considerate, consultative and encouraging and always cheerful. There was not a hint of the autocrat; never was he demanding and neither was he aloof. And in part, because of his nature and in part because of long experience, he was imperturbable; no matter what the crisis was, he maintained a calm demeanour. Hague held to the view that most situations resolve themselves.

Former colleagues, both administrative and professional, speak of the Crown Solicitor's Office during Hague's sway there, as a happy little place, where animosity was rare, though gossip was rife. Everyone was polite and protective of young girls like Joan Guerin and Lois Brown. Hague mingled quite informally with the staff, especially the secretarial support staff, in the large room near where his office was in the early years, also at lunchtime in the small lunch room, where people relaxed or played table tennis in the library and

"… there was always lots of laughter and Ralph's was the loudest". At one stage during a burst of keeping fit, coincidentally at the time he purchased a new black Hillman Minx, Hague invited Joan Guerin to walk part of the way home with him, she living at Prospect and he at Gilbertson. In spite of their age and professional differences, he would keep her happily amused for most of that journey.

Yet there was a certain detachment. He did not make particular friends among the solicitors until the arrival of L.K. "Toby" Gordon in 1953 and reportedly ate his cheese sandwich, bought by the office junior, on the plate in his room. He never joined the solicitors, including Chamberlain and Kevin Healey, in the Flinders Street "Gibbs" shop where they ate their lunch, nor did he participate in official functions at Christmas time, invariably using annual leave on that day. As to why he withdrew on these occasions, it has been suggested that he did not think much of some professional colleagues and certain public servants, considering them to be "lightweights", though he never stated it. In his own quiet way he held to the opinion that various individuals did not deserve the respect they demanded, and he ignored them.

Part of his management style – and he was officially Deputy Crown Solicitor from 1960, though in practice much earlier – entailed doing a daily circuit round the office to say hello, to hand out the dockets and to allow staff to discuss problems they encountered and because he was liked and easy going, the "modus operandi" was most effective. Iris Stevens explained to me that she "… found these little visits extremely helpful as he offered a great deal of practical advice" and a little gentle probing here and there on his part, gave him an idea of how each employee was coping. One day his kindly inquisitiveness led to the discovery that Iris Stevens and another solicitor were writing divergent opinions about the same issue for the same department, though having been allocated separate dockets. He amiably pointed out the desirability of referring to a previous file, which dealt with a similar issue to ensure consistency.

Apart from Tony Bishop, it is from women like Iris Stevens who was ultimately appointed to the District Court Bench after time with the Public Service Board as the first female Commissioner, that we have the clearest portrait of Hague in his professional setting. Indeed, these women, including Joan Morris and Lois Schmidt, remained in contact and close long after he retired and they went on to employment elsewhere. Their accounts of the Crown Solicitor's Office include many of his random acts of kindness and empathy: a garden working bee for the Chief Clerk on sick leave for twelve months; arranging wedding presents for former employees; and being especially supportive of younger people and articled clerks at the beginning of their careers. Joan Morris remembered with gratitude the time he took to coach her in shorthand when she was seeking to further her career.

> 'Every morning tea break he would mark out 'Hansard' and read it to myself and another girl who wanted to get her 120 wpm … Thanks to Ralph, I secured the position of stenographer to Parliamentary Counsel Dr Anstey Wynes.'

Lois Schmidt told another Good Samaritan story:

> 'His shorthand was better than mine. Albert Hannan used to give me a lot of shorthand. It was stuff I really didn't understand, Socrates, Plato, the Vatican … that as a teenager was really beyond me … Sometimes I couldn't read it back so I would go to him. He would read it back for me and often make a much better job of it than "Tace" Hannan had in the first place!'

Yet it should not be thought Hague was an office angel. He could be stubborn but never unreasonable and his mischievous streak was ever present. At times he used his impishness as an agent of change and to make a point. Iris Stevens first met Hague at a bus stop in Walkerville, where he and she caught public transport to town. Initially, just desultory remarks about the weather and similar pleasantries passed between them; but gradually over the months Iris Stevens grasped that her bus stop acquaintance was a mine of information about the people and place of Walkerville. She did not offer her name, nor he his.

A little later, around mid 1966, Iris Stevens applied for the position of solicitor at the Crown but "was not overly optimistic as a prior application to the Commonwealth Crown … met a degree of incredulity that a female should make such an application". At the interview, she was shown into an office where she saw her bus stop acquaintance seated. "I blurted out, 'You're the man from the bus stop'. 'Yes', he admitted, 'I'm the man from the bus stop'." He explained that he was acting Crown Solicitor in the absence of Mr Kearnan, who in his capacity as solicitor for the railways was on a lengthy railway enquiry. After her appointment, and she was the first female solicitor in the South Australian Crown, and possibly anywhere in Australia, Iris Stevens soon realised that if Kearnan had been involved in the selection process, he, like many others at the time, would not have chosen her, and Hague knew that. Iris Stevens was allocated an office overlooking Flinders Street and when Kearnan resumed his usual duties, she became aware her office was next to his and again "suspected a mischievous mind at work". Kearnan did not speak to her for nearly five months.

Tony Bishop and Malcolm Gray also benefited from Kearnan's prolonged absence and came to the Crown in the same lot of interviews. A bemused and grateful Tony Bishop occasionally wonders what Kearnan would have done with him. He knew Kearnan was most discouraged, despite protestation, at the initial interview by "the vagabond beard" he had been proudly growing since visiting

Moscow. At the time the only other bearded solicitor in Adelaide was Blind Jack Davey!

Hague had been previously instrumental in breaking down the barriers to married women's employment in the case of Joan Morris. In 1960, when Joan returned from England, as wife to Les Morris, a former Registrar of the District Court, and mother of a daughter, she was invited by Hague to return to the Crown. After much haggling and outright opposition from the Public Service Board, which had not been employing married women, Joan Morris resumed her old job at 24 Flinders Street. Gordon Tillett who "made decisions about hiring and firing" and deemed by many a titch tyrannical was mostly very amenable to Hague and frequently sought his advice. Perhaps therein lies the explanation for Hague's victories for women. He is an unlikely hero for women's liberation but Hague was in his own curious way a quiet "revolutionary".

Hague formally assumed the role of Deputy Crown Solicitor in 1960. His remaining years at the Crown were a mixed bag for Hague. Among the blessings were the close friendships that developed between him and "Toby" Gordon, Assistant Crown Solicitor, and Edward Ludovoci, the meticulous Parliamentary Draftsman who succeeded Dr Anstey Wynes. Ludovici introduced Hague to the exotic delights of hot curries in an attempt to widen his narrow diet, and Hague, in his turn, helped Ludovici with "sticky legal points", including the draft he was preparing for the new Companies Bill.

Then there were the pleasures of participation in the variously titled "Land and Business Agents Board" based at 24 Flinders Street. Apart from opinion writing, Hague was reputedly an expert conveyancer, a skill at which his father Percy also excelled. Large departments like Highways, in possession of substantial portfolios of property, were inevitably either buying or selling or compulsorily acquiring real estate, and required such expertise. Hague was the person to whom difficult matters in conveyancing were referred by the conveyancing clerks. Almost certainly Hague's deep knowledge of property transactions led to membership of the "Land and Business Agents Board". Some of the other members in the 1960s and 1970s were Bill Bruce, a land agent, Douglas McLeod, a solicitor at Lempriere, Abbott, McGovern, McLeod, "Toby" Gordon and W.C. "Bill" Langcake, secretary to the Attorney-General, and they met once a month to deal with complaints by the public about land agents. On those occasions a bottle or two was shared over lunch, which not infrequently lingered into the afternoon, the gentlemen, usually "the souls of discretion in their professional roles", enjoying a leisurely gossip as well as the clearly convivial company. Hague, according to Iris Stevens, "though a kindly man .... displayed a sharp eye for the idiosyncrasies of others". After his retirement from the Board in 1967 Hague continued to attend these gatherings, which for the men involved, became quasi-social events.

Hague had a rude shock and a rebuff from the incoming Liberal Government under Steele Hall. In 1968 Reginald Kearnan retired due to ill health and the post of Crown Solicitor was advertised in the Government Notices. No one applied. The short-lived Labour administration had just relinquished the Treasury benches and there was a new Attorney General, Robin Millhouse, in Dunstan's place. Millhouse approached Hague and said, "Ralph, you haven't applied?" and Hague answered, "I'm aware of that". Then Millhouse said, "Well, I'd like you to apply" and believing that he had been "given the nod", Hague tendered his application. Unbeknown to him, Millhouse had also gone to Andrew Wells, who was an Assistant Crown Solicitor with "Toby" Gordon. Wells had not applied either, allegedly because he was "pretty absentminded". In the end, both men applied but, alas, Hague was overlooked for the man some twelve years his junior and who was the office barrister, not a solicitor which the post required.

It was the only occasion when Wells noticed Hague visibly annoyed, almost surly, in seventeen years of working together. Six months later in February 1969, the Government parsimoniously tried to combine the role of Crown Solicitor with that of Solicitor-General (the latter being new to South Australia, though present elsewhere in Australia) in the person of Andrew Wells. It was quickly comprehended that the two positions were not compatible and the way was cleared for the realisation of Hague's rightful claim. In February 1969 he was made Crown Solicitor and Wells Solicitor-General. The very next year the rapidly rising star of the inaugural Solicitor-General took him even further to the Supreme Court Bench as acting puisne judge and then puisne judge, specialising in the Land and Valuation Division.

Behind Hague's discomposure there were deeper reasons than most knew. The whole clumsy, inept affair must have seemed like a nasty replay of his application almost twenty years earlier for Professorship of Law at Adelaide University. Then as now, he was urged to put in for a job on the understanding that it was very likely, only to be knocked back. In both instances it was by much younger men with analogous qualifications. Wells, like Richard Blackburn, was a St Peter's old scholar, and like Hague, a David Murray Scholarship winner and Stow medallist. Both Blackburn and Wells were Rhodes scholars who carried off an eerily identical English accolade, each being named the Eldon Law scholar in 1949 after completing their B.C.L. degrees at Magdalen College, Oxford. Both men were admitted to the English bar and belonged to Inner Temple. Clearly it was still an Antipodes that worshipped the glittering trophies of the Mother Country, rather than homegrown glories. Hague understood he lacked what Blackburn and Wells possessed in fine degree, the all-important postgraduate qualifications. Failure to claim the Bonython Prize in 1936 had unanticipated, far-reaching ramifications.

When Hague formally assumed the mantle of Crown Solicitor, the post in which he had long acted must have seemed like a lesser thing and he was loathe to stay. He was sixty-two and close to retirement and he was in fact Crown Solicitor by default. There might have been other considerations bearing upon Hague's decision to retire early. Though he "maintained a detached approach to politics and he never expressed his convictions, he was well aware of current events". In May 1970 the Labor Government was returned to power, beginning the so-called "Dunstan decade". Emerging from the political radicalism and turmoil of the 1960s, it espoused different values and priorities. Dunstan as Premier and Attorney General saw himself as a catalyst for change, not only for South Australia but elsewhere. If Hague were to remain, he would be working within new parameters and new codes of behaviour. A courtly, old-fashioned gentleman such as he might have been uncomfortable as the raw winds of change swept through the public service and felt the new era was not for him. He had been part of the long reign of Sir Thomas Playford and was accustomed to different people and procedures. Moreover, if he had known the government's initial intention to revamp the role of Crown Solicitor, he would not have applied. He was, after all, a government solicitor, not a barrister. Understandably, therefore, when Professor Castles and Dame Roma Mitchell, some twenty years later, offered him an L.L.D. for his *Early Legal History* he shrugged off their well-meant gesture. To accept an honour in such circumstances, in another race not truly run, would surely diminish it.

Hague remained as Crown Solicitor for just over a year and a half. The Government's mishandling sullied his incumbency of the post, long ago occupied by some of the lively characters in his history: Charles Mann, the unfortunate William Wearing, William Bakewell and William Smillie. When he retired on the 29th of June 1970 his good friend and colleague "Toby" Gordon succeeded him, and Brian Cox, Assistant Crown Solicitor replaced Andrew Wells as Solicitor-General. Hague reportedly never occupied the handsome Crown Solicitor's Office with beautiful windows and French doors overlooking Flinders Street. He remained, perhaps as a small protest, in his old Deputy's office across the way.

Kerwin Maegraith's 1928 caricatures of "legal and court luminaries". Among those depicted are people significant in Ralph Hague's career: Roderick Chamberlain, in the first year of his time as Crown Prosecutor, Frank Villeneuve Smith, who had just become a partner in Percy Hague's firm, and Mr Justice Napier at the start of his forty three year tenure on the Supreme Court bench. Also brother John Hague at the bottom. (News Corporation)

"To our great benefit"; Forty Four Years of Law Reporting

A brief letter from The Law Book Company of Australasia dated 27th of May 1947 launched the start of Ralph Hague's forty year engagement as editor of the *South Australian State Reports* (SASRs). He was to begin with the volume for 1947 and "the fee to be paid" [was] £200 per annum. A postscript indicates the Law Book Company were "willing to remit £50 on publication of each part if you so desire". It was a professional relationship that would endure until 1987. Previous notable editors of the series were the politician, High Court aspirant, lawyer and supporter of women's rights, Sir John Downer; Thomas Hewitson, Law School lecturer and R.N. Finlayson, founder of "Finlayson & Co". Hague's immediate predecessor was Earnest Phillips.

Hague edited the SASRs for half his lifetime. Aged forty years, a junior solicitor of the Crown when he began, Hague was a bachelor without the usual calls of family upon his time, steady, of sober habits, punctual, hard working and utterly reliable in temperament, having an ability to think clearly and to express himself concisely. He had the necessary experience too. Certainly his time at the *News* gave him a facility and economy with written language and accustomed him to the practices of publishing while his years in the "rough and tumble" of private practice meant he was well apprised with both Bench and Bar. Then there was the exacting discipline of military writing during the Second World War. Hague was by preference a solicitor and therefore free from the disruptive caseloads inevitable in the profession of barrister.

Law reporting is an often unremarked but crucial element of the legal system because it gives coherence in the working of the courts. Upon it depends the realisation of "one of the cardinal principles of justice, that like cases should be decided alike". And Ralph Hague was the lynchpin of that process in South Australia.

Eventually Hague was entrusted with the editorship of both types of reports, that is, the judge authorised law reports, the SASRs and from 1971 until 1991 the so-called "irregular non-selective reports" that are the *Law Society Judgment Scheme* (LSJS). Professor Castles explained the significance of the "Judgment Scheme" lay in its non-selectivity, covering as it did, all the work of the court, and because it was not subject to judicial influences or charges of manipulation. Non-selective reports often had the advantage too of appearing more promptly, ahead of the authorised reports.

From the testimony of a few we have a picture of Hague at work as reporter and editor of both the SASRs and the LSJS. The judgments came to him in a form released by the judges and the Brown girls, Jo and Kate, young neighbours of his in Frederick Street, remember the bulky deliveries arriving and watching wide-eyed and fascinated, as the piles grew ever bigger on his kitchen table.

According to Elliot Johnston and Chief Magistrate Kelvyn Prescott who in 2000 followed him as editor, dealing with so many judgments was an immense "and time consuming task… It's a job which can be done a little bit here and a little bit there … you read most of the judgments by the Supreme Court". Moreover the work grew as the bench increased in size. When Hague started in 1947 there were five judges. By 1987 and his retirement from the SASRs, fourteen sat in judgment.

The task in his charge involved choosing those cases that were worth reporting, correcting printing or other errors and then to make catchwords and headnotes. Professor Alex Castles commented thus, "The real role for a law reporter is the headnotes … and he [Hague] had a real capacity for writing good headnotes". In the days of Sir Mellis Napier, the *South Australian State Reports* were especially hard to edit because Napier "was very difficult to pin down, as to what he was really doing or why he was really reaching a decision … it was very time consuming": and Castles himself had great difficulty so "I gave up writing him in the ALJ".

Elliot Johnston as a justice on the Supreme Court Bench from 1983-1988 was well aware how thoroughly Hague checked the judgments and was like other judges, a recipient of proofs, suggesting emendation. One instance he never forgot was in relation to his judgment in *Waiata Pty Ltd v Lane & Other,* (39 SASR 290). Apart from indicating some minor corrections on the proof, Hague penned an incidental note pointing out that he (Johnston) used the word "quadrant" thirty two times. Johnston J realised he was being lightly chastened and took the comment good humouredly as Hague intended and of course did not effect any changes. Flawed Latin quotations, problematic passages, and faulty grammar were similarly targeted and returned to any erring judicial author. Neighbour and friend, Marilyn Brown, said of Hague's eagle eye for judicial slips or indeed of any mistakes in written language he discovered, "He enjoyed and gained satisfaction from correcting grammatical errors in work placed before him. He cherished the written word as an artist loves form, shape and colour on canvas". As editor Hague was not being critical. He was striving, wordsmith that he was, for the best possible outcome on the page.

Hague was, with his trilby and old-fashioned briefcase, a familiar sight in the Supreme Court, Law Society and Crown Law Libraries, which he visited in order to do his editing work. He was always congenial company for the librarians and the practitioners he met there, enjoying a word or two, inevitably gathering some interesting legal gossip or re-telling tales for which Hague had an exceptional memory. After he retired in 1970 as Crown Solicitor the revising and editing took on a new meaning for him, separated as he was from the daily practice of law. From behind his old Remington and L.C. Smith typewriters (which he never upgraded) and during his circuit of legal libraries, he maintained his relationship with the legal fraternity and kept abreast of developments in the law.

For Hague there were other benefits. His careful reading of judgments for nigh on half a century gave him an extraordinary breadth of acquaintance with the judiciary as well as unique insights into the working of many a judicial mind. His cousin, John Scales, remembered that Hague "loved doing the SASRs and he loved talking about what he thought of the judges". He had "a great deal of time for Roma's commonsense and for King's conciseness" and also a high regard of John Bray's intellect.

It was in fact Bray's elevation to the bench in 1967, which briefly caused trouble between Hague and the Law Book Company. About the time of Bray's appointment, the numbers of reportable cases significantly escalated and there loomed the possibility of more than one volume of the SASRs per year. Given the quality of the Bray Bench Hague surely saw the consequences for himself. Since he was only paid per year the outcome would be more work for less remuneration. The Law Book Company nevertheless wished to abide by the original agreement as stated in 1947. Hague being stubborn and undoubtedly correct in his prediction gave notice and the job of law reporter for the SASRs passed to a replacement for the year 1967. Such was the decline in the standard of reporting and editing that by 1968 Hague's name was restored to the title page of the SASRs. "LBC came knocking on Ralph's door. Do you want your job back? We'll pay you by the volume"; and so Tony Bishop reported, "he continued on his merry way" for the next nineteen years until his retirement from editing in 1987 aged eighty, receiving towards the end in August 1984 praise from the bench.

Unexpectedly but most deservedly Hague's unsung but exemplary role as editor and law reporter received special commendation at the sitting to mark the end of Wells J's fourteen years of judicial service. Evidently Wells felt much obliged to him and said:

'Ralph Hague has presided over the law reports for a long, long time. He has a fund of scholarship and an infinite capacity for taking pains. I would wish to record my deep sense of gratitude … his work has raised the *South Australian State Reports* to a point where … they are at least the equal of any other reports in Australia and they are probably the best. I only hope that we can replace him'.

Tony Bishop provided a postscript to this story, which illustrates the modesty of our subject. Once it was a tradition that important moments in legal history to wit the special sittings of the Supreme Court were recorded by way of preface in the reports. Tony Bishop being present in Courtroom One to see Wells J officially step down, expected to read his allusion to Hague's work. When the appropriate part of the law report was published, he realised Hague had cut out the words of commendation; so he rang Hague saying: "Ralph, there's something missing from that farewell speech". Hague replied, "Oh yes, I know that … we can't have any errors in the state reports, ha ha!"

Many others too expressed equally laudatory opinions of his editorial style, its simplicity, precision and economy that brought the SASRs undisputed acclaim. Mitchell J wrote in June 1971 that Hague's law reporting was "to our great benefit". Another woman, Gwenda Fischer, former librarian at Adelaide's Law School and New South Wales Law Society and editor of the "Current Index to Australian and New Zealand Legal Literature", who was also a friend of Hague's put the librarian's point of view. She believed "he was far beyond anyone else in Australia in terms of the production of those law reports" and she appreciated the speed at which the reports invariably appeared.

Hague's fine reputation travelled across the Tasman Sea and in July 1978, the New Zealand Council of Law Reporting despatched their new editor, Ms Frances Wilson, after several months with the Incorporated Council of Law Reporting and Butterworths in London, to Adelaide and Mr Hague for tutoring. The SASRs were regarded as "shining examples of law reports, while their New Zealand equivalents were in "a parlous state" and had "hardly ever been worse". It seems the young woman and the seventy one year old editor discussed "the gruesome topic of law reporting over the fire", at Frederick Street.

Hague continued editing the *Law Society Judgment Scheme* until 1991, when on the cusp of the computer age approach to publishing, he was made an honorary member of the Law Society. There is little evidence of that long twenty-year association save for one letter from the President of the Law Society, David Wicks, regarding payment. In it the Society proposed to increase the fee, as from July 1978, to $2,000 per annum. Clearly the discussions between Hague and the Law Book Company were again repeated with the Law Society but on this occasion Hague was not the winner, for the letter concludes, "We have considered further the question of making the fee payable on a per volume basis but at the present … propose to continue making payment on an annual basis".

I am sure Kelvyn Prescott thought quite differently about the value of Hague's work when he became editor of the Judgment Scheme in addition to the SASRs;

> 'I immediately realised the amazing extent of the knowledge Ralph has accumulated and the extent of his indexing system.' Given the amount of remuneration 'he worked in a voluntary capacity for the profession and the public … dedicated to the profession he loved'.

It amused Hague not a little that teams of reporters and the latest technology should take over the task managed by one old man and his elderly typewriter.

Six Frederick Street, which was Hague's home from 1926. It was one of four similar houses built in close proximity. Apparently a builder erected them to accommodate his four daughters. (Rob and Marilyn Brown)

Retirement: "Among your books and treasures"

One fine but chilly June winter's morning, a year after his retirement, Ralph Hague arose to find himself reported in the Saturday *Advertiser* tossed over his brush fence. And there were also important telegrams delivered that day, one from the Prime Minister William McMahon and another from the Premier Donald Dunstan. Hague was among eleven men and three women named in the State list for the Queen's Birthday Honours announced that Saturday, the 12th of June 1971. Both State and Commonwealth Honours were front-page stories and featured prominently elsewhere in the *Advertiser.* In keeping with his customary low profile and retiring disposition, Hague as one of the few South Australians so mentioned without a photograph.

The Queen, upon the recommendation of the Dunstan Labour Government, made Hague and another South Australian, Raymond Turner, "Commanders of the Order of the British Empire". Hague's C.B.E. was "for services to the legal profession". Justice Roma Mitchell, a fellow student at law school from 1931, was also distinguished with a C.B.E. for her "services to law" but acknowledged in the Commonwealth list. In keeping with her usual high profile, Mitchell J, in full-bottomed wig, stiffened bands and wing collar smiled at *Advertiser* readers from behind heavy rimmed glasses, fashionable at the time.

Hague's insignia for "The Most Excellent Order of the British Empire" was established in wartime England by George V for meritorious services other than military and was the first British order, apart from the Crown of India, to "afford the ladies their rightful places in the field of decorations". Considering his support for women's equality of opportunity in employment, it is to be imagined Hague was pleased to have this particular decoration which entitled him to place initials C.B.E. after his name and that Mitchell J, the exemplar of successful career women, was among those so honoured.

But it is doubtful whether he ever used the initials; certainly he spurned the publishers of *Who's Who in Australia* year after year, throwing their letter requesting his inclusion in the wastepaper basket. Almost certainly Hague was not among the well groomed men wearing medals and tails and the elegant women in shimmering silken gowns at the Government House Reception given in the Queen's honour that evening by Sir James Harrison. The *Advertiser's* social editor did note Mitchell J in her oyster crepe dress and green jewelled author's cape collar and Hague's former colleague at the Crown, Sir Roderic Chamberlain accompanied by Lady Chamberlain mingling in the crowded reception rooms with "urns of flowers and glowing fires".

There is a lighthearted tale that Hague loved to tell about his C.B.E. Two months later, in August 1971, a letter came bearing the Queen's coat of arms and inviting Hague, along with Justice Mitchell and other recipients of the Honours to a Government House Investiture on Friday the 1st of October 1971. Sir Mellis Napier, now retired from the Bench and in his vice regal role as Lieutenant Governor, presented the insignias in the Grand Ballroom where guests and recipients were seated. Somehow Sir Mellis, aged eighty nine, managed to slightly muddle arrangements as Hague received Justice Mitchell's insignia instead. Over refreshments afterwards Hague and Mitchell exchanged "badges".

In the days that followed the postman was busy delivering letters from well wishers to 6 Frederick Street. Mitchell J wrote:

> 'I was delighted to see your tremendous services to the law recognised. I hope … you are enjoying yourself among your books and treasures and that you will continue to edit the SASRs'.

The Anglican Bishop the Right Reverend T.T. Reed and Justices Walter and Zelling expressed their felicitations. Two further correspondents wrote rather perceptively. Sir Mellis Napier, having observed Hague's career from his unequalled forty-three years on the Bench offered his congratulations writing, "It is always to me a great satisfaction when I know that these things go to those who really earned them". Zelling J said: "You are always so unassuming that I feared your great services and your learning would pass unrecognised". Hague must have felt some pride in this imperial tribute, for the badge, with its light blue enamel cross, each arm in the shape of a "fleur de lys", did not lie neglected in its black leather case. Upon close inspection the insignia appears well handled and the gold backing worn away.

As enjoined by the Governor Sir Tom Bridges at his last St Peter's Speech Day, Hague had indeed gone out into the adult world and "interested himself in the work of the State or country". He had not however, taken to heart the rest of the vice regal message, to keep loyal to the Empire, putting it first. Hague the independent thinker decided his loyalties very early, carrying a different flag for the Australia that was to be, long before the old Imperial orders were swept aside for new Australian honours in 1975.

- oooOooo –

Hague's retirement from the legal community in 1970 although partial, for he remained editor of the SASRs and became editor of the *Law Society Judgment Scheme*, gave him opportunities in his own neighbourhood community of Frederick Street to form relationships and strengthen old friendships which were vital for the next twenty seven years of his life. And he continued researching South Australian legal history in the midst of his immense and always growing library, ceaseless in his quest for greater understanding and new information. Sales of his published book *Sir John Jeffcott* slowly but steadily increased in the 1970s, reflecting the new national pride in things Australian.

Frederick Street was, and is still is, quite a small street with a dozen or so houses ranging from the modest to the grand mansion once owned by the pastoralist McLachlan family. It was in their youth, according to the Scales siblings, Pamela, John and his twin sister, Caroline, a very family orientated street. The Scales household, headed by Millicent "Mim" and Edwin "Ned" Scales, lived at number 8 from roughly 1935 until 1952 when they all moved to a larger home and an acre garden close by in Buckingham Street. Blood ties between "Mim" Scales and Magdalen linked the two families. Mim was a Barton Hack which Hague must have liked, given that family's importance in early South Australian colonial history.

The intimacy of Frederick Street was in part due to size and in part an outcome of a strong sense of community, shaped in the difficult days of World War Two, when the men were away, the women supported each other and their children played together, on traffic spare open spaces, running in and out of the houses. Mrs "Mim" Scales was very community minded and people gravitated towards her conversation and cups of tea and the Hagues were part of that circle. To the children of Frederick Street and top end of James Street the Hagues at number 6, were "Cousin" Percy, "Cousin" Lena (Magdalen) and "Cousin" Ralph.

Percy reminded young John Scales of the red nosed character "Punch" on the front page of the English magazine of that name, rotund and jovial like his son Ralph was to be. Lena is spoken of as loving, "a considerable person", with a sunny nature, who towards the end of her life was mostly bedridden but enjoyed visitors, even when very ill, stoically consoling herself with the thought that someone else was worse off. It seems Lena was a bit of a wit like her second son and told this story against herself. She had a very chatty friend and wished to end an overly long telephone conversation but was caught out with what seemed like a bright and cheery concluding remark "Must go, the telephone is ringing".

The young Scales watched Ralph's devotion to both his parents, noted how pleased and proud he was of his upbringing, commending his able nursing of ailing Lena almost till death's door. They remember even now, seeing the light shining in the Hague kitchen on dark cold mornings and smelling the aroma of sizzling sausages and bacon wafting across the lane as Ralph fried breakfast for his parents. The three of them, father, mother and son went on country drives over the weekend with a thermos of tea and their beautiful red setters, who sipped the tea from a saucer.

There were other expeditions in the car. Miss McLaren, a single teacher who courageously adopted a baby in the days when it was rare and ran the local kindergarten from the back of her home at number 12, was driven to the beach with her daughter and Lena. (One of the pupils at her kindergarten was Francis Villeneuve Smith, only child of barrister Frank Villeneuve Smith QC by his second wife). For many years, even after the Scales shifted to Buckingham Street, Hague would back his dusty black Hillman Minx down the private lane to collect their Friday meat and Saturday vegetable orders, telephoned through to local shopkeepers by Mrs Scales. He stayed afterwards for a cup of tea and a chat. This routine was repeated weekly for the next thirty-four years, reaching beyond the first Mrs Scales' death in 1968 when it changed to simply a cup of tea with Marjorie Priddle the new Mrs Scales. Hague was undeniably and absolutely a creature of habit.

Over time, after "Mim" and her family moved to Buckingham Street, Hague gradually developed a special relationship with the children of his little community. He became a sort of father figure, a low key pied piper and whenever the cry went up amongst the various parents "where are the children?", they were most often at "Cousin" Ralph's. Apparently he sat in the front room reading but all the while keeping an eye on the street below and would welcome any young person. Caroline Scales went there every afternoon for "whisky cordial" and peppermints. Upon seeing each other she would curtsey and he would bow. The whisky cordial routine shocked sedate matrons and delighted small children who enjoyed the naughtiness of it. Hague himself was undeterred. Apart from the impromptu visits, the Scales children looked forward to Christmas when it was a tradition to visit number 6, after church and before lunch. While the adults were being convivial inside, they sat in cane chairs along the back verandah, enjoying the wicked whisky and presents brought on trays.

Hague possessed an affinity with children, an ability to relate to them in a serious but humorous way and he was always courteous and never rushed. Joan Morris' daughter Christine, was intrigued with his grandmother's clock in the Frederick Street hall and he would greet her with, "Have you come to see Grandmother?", which delighted the little girl.

As the Scales' grew up, Hague remained a much-loved figure in their adult lives. His utter dependability pleased them. After his parents died, Percy aged seventy-eight in 1951 and Magdalen aged eighty-two in 1969, their rituals became his. The Scales family knew exactly where to find him, how he would react and what he was likely to do and say and that they were always welcome. His honesty and plain speaking never bothered them, in fact they respected it. When he said what he meant, it made interpersonal relations easier. If he preferred not to join their Christmas celebrations, they understood.

On the occasions Hague did leave Frederick Street, whatever the weather, he invariably wore a hat, a sports jacket, white shirt and tie and the overall impression was grey. For the Scales and for others his hat was a symbol, both of his total consistency and slight eccentricity, an anachronism from the post war years when it was normal for older public servants to wear hats, usually of the Royal Stetson pattern.

Hague's understated sense of humour now geared to their adult lives, remained appealing. As a people watcher with a marvellous recall of events, he regaled them with quirky tales of others idiosyncrasies, though never to big note himself, be unkind or boast. To his cousins, Hague was a lovable, "vivid character in a low key way", who underpinned their existence. In his eulogy at Hague's cremation, John Scales said, "He was always there … a rock in my life, no matter what … When he went somehow part of your foundation disappeared. He was so constant that part of our lives disappeared too".

In the mid 1960s and early 1970s several new families with young children bought homes in the small community of Frederick Street. Each was representative of the type of friendships enjoyed by Hague in his retirement. There was Mrs Valerie Esau, with her husband and two boys, Mark and William, who described herself as peripheral in Hague's life and then there were the Browns, Marilyn, Rob and their two girls, Katrina and Jo for whom Hague meant much more, becoming over twenty five years a dear friend and virtual grandfather to the children.

The Frederick Street Mrs Esau encountered, when she moved then in 1965, initially to number 9 and then upside to number 12 after the death of her husband, still offered the friendliness and intimacy fondly remembered by the Scales family but probably in a different way, for it was a changed and faster world. Friendliness between neighbours often included invitations to drinks. Tea seemed to be off the menu in the sophisticated latter half of the twentieth century. Mrs

Esau said, "We all knew each other and he [Hague] knew the Boothbys and my mother".

Valerie Esau is a direct descendant of Justice Boothby, a living connection in Hague's own street with the obstinate judge who bedevilled the Supreme Court Bench, enraged Parliament and the populace in colonial South Australia and who held Hague enthralled for most of his adult life. Hague gave Valerie Esau a signed copy of his Boothby manuscript. Obviously she read it because she expressed the view that Hague "was a bit harsh on Boothby" and in the interview offered her family's perspective on the judge. They believed he should not have sent to South Australia, being a stickler for British law, which clearly was not adapting well to the new colony. Boothby was, it seems, two people, a totally different character away from the law, a wonderful loving family man who alas could not bend in his professional life.

Valerie Esau's relationship with Hague was casual, not close. She was more an observer than a friend. Their meetings were most often in the street and they talked about gardening, a mutual interest. To her he was the gentleman in the crumpled suits who gallantly smiled and tipped his hat when he sighted her on his frequent walks. She noticed his distance from the world, his old-fashioned ways and measured steps, his use of humour to make a point, to rail a little against life or so she believed. She watched perhaps a little wonderingly at the extraordinary rapport developing between the two young Brown girls and the elderly gentleman she knew to be very private. Then there were the regular visits of an unknown woman, who proved to be Lois Schmidt, and close to him like the Brown family.

Marilyn and Rob Brown and their daughters Kate and Jo entered Hague's life two and a half years after he retired when in December 1972 they purchased the semi bungalow at number 3 Frederick Street. Acting upon the suggestion of Graham Prior who was then Senior Solicitor at the Crown, Hague introduced himself. Over time a strong attachment would grow between Hague and the Browns. Hague was ideally placed to be the two young girls' Frederick Street grandfather. Initially though his very difference, his touch of eccentricity, excited their childish imaginations and innate curiosity. In the sun heedless 1970s Hague wore a hat in the street, drove his "ancient" black car just on Saturdays, fed the fish in the garden pond with scrambled egg and "had the largest collection of books we had ever seen".

Of course, the inevitable happened as it had with the young Scales. Jo and Kate's acquaintance with Mr Hague opened the door to a child's wonderland just across the street, a place of fun things to do and treats a plenty; bon bons, tim tams, peppermints and ice cream. Soon Kate and Jo brought their friends after school and Mr Hague became known as "the ice-cream man". How amazed they must have been to find an adult who responded intuitively to their young hearts and understood them, happily participating in their simple pleasures.

Perhaps Hague himself rediscovered the familial intimacy he lost long ago with the deaths of his parents.

In this unexpectedly perfect child's playground there were treasure hunts in the garden and travel agent games in the house. Hague, who only ventured once out of the State when compelled by war, was dispatched to "exotic destinations". The children played shops in his well-stocked pantry and learnt card games including auction bridge at the kitchen table. Under his guidance Kate and Jo were allowed to roam freely in number 6 and naturally became curious about his past. He eluded their probing questions and one in particular about the name of his father, whom he ingeniously called "Marmaduke Montague Ouja Kapivy". From this incident he too was rechristened but as "Monsieur Ouja Kapivy".

Ralph Hague upon the occasion of his eightieth birthday in 1987, celebrated with friends at number three Frederick Street. (Rob and Marilyn Brown)

Hague delighted in their company as much as they delighted in his. One little episode, which he often recalled especially entertained him. Jo and Kate stumbled upon a dead lizard in the street and wished, as children do, to bury it. Hague suggested they sing a funeral march which they did not know and instead they sang a song little girls learn early, "here comes the bride …".

The friendship between the girls and Mr Hague deepened as the years of their youth flew by. They often tackled their homework on his kitchen table and he listened to Kate on clear summer days practice her cello and piano across the way. It all seemed to make sense, having Mr Hague with his vast knowledge, love of language and literature and his veritable "State Library" on their very doorstep. He encouraged both girls in their chosen fields, Kate with music and Jo with arts and law, helping them build libraries to match their interests, assisting with tuition fees and corresponding with them overseas when they studied in England. Hague, though missing "his girls" kept his letters lively and amusing. Always his humour was apparent.

'In my extreme old age, I am so slow in replying … that I am considering another change of name, from Ouja Kapivy to Snail. I think Mr R.M. Snail, 6 Frederick Street would look quite well as an address'.

Hague started collecting stray cats and they also figured in the correspondence. Often he addressed his letters with "Cat Cottage, 6 Frederick Street" and began with "miaow, miaow, miaow".

As the ties grew close between Kate and Jo and Hague so gradually too did the bonds of friendship formed between their parents and Hague. There were Sunday drinks, shared birthday parties and a friend's day once a year to show appreciation of his contribution to their girls. Hague came over too for Christmas morning drinks before Pam Reid, his cousin, picked him up for Christmas dinner at her house. Later with greater infirmity, he remained at the Browns for Christmas Day.

Pamela Reid descends from two of the various Hagues who immigrated to Australia from Manchester and it was at her table he relished the company of other intellectuals, academics and writers like John Playford, Robert Reid, Pamela Reid's husband was a lecturer in politics at Adelaide University and Mrs Reid worked at Flinders University. Through the Reids Hague kept in touch with Alex Castles. After Robert Reid's death in 1976, Hague seemed to fill a gap at the Reid Family table on Christmas Day.

Others sought Mr Hague's company for different reasons. Some like Brendan Burley (a neighbour from the mid-seventies to the mid-eighties) and Tony Bishop called intermittently for a chat over whisky, imparting to their host the latest legal gossip. Joan Morris continued the tradition of her family's Christmas Eve visits. Iris Stevens brought her husband and there were regular monthly lunches near Melbourne Street with old friends, Toby Gordon, Colin Moody and Sir Walter Crocker. Sir Walter, a retired diplomat and Lieutenant Governor surprised and flattered Hague with his attention. In a self-effacing comment to Lois Schmidt he explained away the visits of Sir Walter and Colin Moody who drove him. "He [Crocker] had a very busy life and when he retired he was still doing the rounds … visiting to fill in his time". The pleasure that Crocker evidently gained from Hague's company never occurred to one such as he.

People also came seeking scholarly advice. More wrote for the same reason and Hague was invariably pleased to give of his erudition and expertise. His correspondence throughout the 1970s and 1980s is indicative of his undiminished enthusiasm for South Australian legal history.

Behind all these peripheral figures and friendships, though important, there was as Valerie Esau accurately observed, another sustaining relationship besides the Browns, which stretched far back to 1948 and Hague's first years at the Crown. After the death of her husband in 1984 Hague and Lois Schmidt saw each other more frequently. Weekly she stopped at Frederick Street after work on Fridays and then Tuesday, helped him with his shopping and appointments after he ceased driving and became a fond companion who shared his memories and supported him in his last years.

How highly he was esteemed by his friends is clear from the extremely generous contribution made to the research for this project by all Hague's neighbours, relatives and friends, especially the Brown family, Lois Schmidt, Tony Bishop, Erica Micklem, Pamela Reid, John Scales, Elizabeth Ormsby, and Caroline Milne. It is a rare sort of accolade, which, though won during Hague's lifetime, endures beyond it in the minds of those whom Hague loved and who loved him in return.

Bibliophile Extraordinaire

Ralph Hague was a bibliophile, a man smitten with a love of books and reading, a man who found stimulation, entertainment and solace in a personal library of remarkable size. Hague bequeathed some thirty thousand hardback books to the Barr Smith Library of the University of Adelaide. It was the largest bequest the Barr Smith had ever received and a complete surprise. Not even Sir Samuel Way's substantial gift of some sixteen thousand volumes approached it. Susan Woodburn spoke to the Book Collectors Society "of the immensity of the library", "only fully appreciated when more than thirty thousand volumes were boxed for removal". The subsequent processing and checking against existing Barr Smith holdings absorbed a project team of seven university students and staff, working from August 1997 to April 1998.

First-time visitors to number 6 were always taken aback by the sheer quantity of books it contained. There was shelving, often double or triple stacked, in all of the seven principal rooms of Frederick Street, including the three bedrooms, every one of which had been converted into library space. His parents' twin single beds in the major bedroom were literally bowed by the weight of books, and their wardrobes filled to overflowing. Hague himself slept in a south-facing sleep-out and it, too, was overrun. Dozens of boxes occupied the large cellar and crammed the sunroom, obscuring the view through the French doors into the dining room. Only the simple bachelor kitchen and garden laundry were without books. Michael Treloar of Rare and Antiquarian Books described Hague's home as "a most agreeable place for a bookman", a book "hermitage" and "a user-friendly book place". It was, to his eyes, well organised, very library fashion, with steel and wooden shelving in several of the small bedrooms and Hague had reinforced the flooring with special joists to cope with the colossal weight.

As to organisation, Susan Woodburn, former Barr Smith Special Collections Librarian, remembers the various rooms being assigned certain categories of books. There were sets and series in the low shelves in the front hallway and drawing room. The floor to ceiling bookshelves in the study contained biographies, while on the floor were boxes of gardening books and catalogues. The rare and bibliophilic material was kept in the tightly packed shelves of number 3 bedroom.

In the sleep-out were two undressed pine plywood chests of drawers, bought in 1970 or 1971, as if in anticipation of the delightful possibilities of retirement, with an idea of bringing order to the collection and sundry papers. In them, Hague set up an alphabetical catalogue of his holdings, typing, as librarians do, title, author, date, publisher etc on the slips of paper recycled from Law Society

Judgment Schemes. The fronts of these drawers are grey with the finger marks of years of use. Hague's good habits of order and economy are evident elsewhere in the chest of drawers. Cuttings, mainly from newspapers, were stored in recycled envelopes, arranged alphabetically and marked with the relevant topic or person's name. There are hundreds of such yellowing envelopes with folded frail papers inside. Coverage in this manner started in the 1940s. Previously cuttings were stuck in exercise books, some dating back to the 1920s and earlier. Also stored in the bottom of one of the chests are spare typed manuscripts of *Justice Crawford* and *The Gentle Jickling*. The contents of these chests complemented what was already in the books on the shelves, many of which themselves held pertinent information inserted by Hague: "newspapers cuttings, articles about authors, prices paid for and subsequently fetched by works and Hague's own cryptic notes on his reading of the work". It was not the plan of the Barr Smith to assume possession of these chests but the removalists thought otherwise, and they now stand in the Special Collection stacks, in odd contrast to the regiments of shelving, as testimony to Hague's disciplined approach to reading and research, speaking volumes about the time he expended in pursuit of his hobby and that he valued ease of access to his collection and papers.

Hague's home was dominated by his enormous book collection with all rooms save the kitchen overflowing with titles. This is a partial view of bedroom three from the central hall. (Rob and Marilyn Brown)

What were Hague's intentions in amassing such a considerable library? Treloar explains that it clearly was not an investment library. He did not chase the great prizes of book collecting, for example, first and signed editions. Hague wanted reading material, which is not the best in terms of investment. Rather than selling, he preferred donating to institutions, especially since he was dissatisfied with attempts at selling. Culling and giving were his way of creating space and he aimed at collection building with a view to breadth rather than depth. His were "beer or middle order tastes" and according to Treloar, he spent no more on books than others spend on more typical amusements. He bought thematically for entertainment as well as education. Treloar further observed about Hague's motivation, "I liked him for being alive, he was enjoying life, and books were clearly a major source of enjoyment". They were his way of engaging with the world, of exploring the best and most interesting intellects. The modern means of keeping up to date with news and ideas did not appeal. He disliked noise, and television and radio were the epitome of noisemakers. The Brown family gave him a brand new television and after his death it was wheeled back across Frederick Street in virtually mint condition, barely used.

Hague, despite being a serious buyer of serious books, was not beyond the pleasures of fiction, but he acquired nostalgia and vintage fiction, rather than the Mills and Boon escapist variety, of which the works of author Guy Boothby, a descendant of the irascible judge, are an example.

In her talk to the "Book Collectors Society" in 1999, Susan Woodburn outlined the educational aspect of Hague's book acquisition. His tastes were "broad ... wide-ranging content with particular interest in history", especially British, American and South Australian biographies of politicians and statesmen. In the category of literature, biography again figures. Poetry was emphasised with notable collections of Christopher Morley, Edmund Blunden, to whom he was undoubtedly introduced by Headmaster Bickersteth, Roy Campbell, and decadent poet and critic of 1890s England, Arthur Symons. Of his favourite authors, only Vita Sackville West would be readily identified by the reading public of today. Susan Woodburn noted the presence of a considerable number of items in the category of limited editions, private presses and fine printings and bindings, but felt these were acquired for their content rather than physical attributes.

Not surprisingly, with the bequest came Hague's own manuscript biographies: *The Gentle Jickling, Mr Justice Boothby, Mr Justice Crawford* and *Sir John Jeffcott* and the controversial *Early Legal History*. And still in the category of law the lives of early and contemporary legal luminaries, both British and American, were a predominant theme.

Hague's other area of special focus was "books about books". His collection comprised many American offerings on the topic. "Hundreds ... [of books] on great books, best books, book collecting ... the book trade, clubs and plates, on printing, bibliography" and book-mad people like he. These form the basis of the Hague Memorial Library, which features with other "bijou" libraries in the Reading Room of Barr Smith Special Collections. Most of the rest of the bequest, for reasons of scale, variation in age and content was integrated, into the University's main collection.

There had been an earlier and much smaller gift in 1983. Hague's collection of pre-1800 imprints valued at $17,000 was donated to the Barr Smith under a tax incentive scheme for the arts scheme. In response to the librarian's suggestion of a handing over ceremony, Hague replied with the following:

'To me anything of that kind would be a most unpleasant ordeal and I respectfully beg to be excused ... If anyone is to be a guest of honour ... should it not be the Deputy Commissioner of Taxation?'

Three years later in 1986 Allan Brissenden, chairman of the University Department of English Literature, wrote to Hague asking if he minded being mentioned in a title *Early Printed Books in South Australia* and then delicately posed the question: "Is it ... I wonder presumptuous of me to ask if you have ever considered presenting your magnificent post-1800 collection to the library as well?" Perhaps Hague was prompted by this suggestion at the time he visited Perpetual Trustees to dictate his final will and testament in 1993?

When asked to reflect on the overall nature and content of Hague's "magnificent" library - and apparently Hague never used the word library in relation to his collection - Susan Woodburn commented that his was essentially a "nineteenth century gentleman's library therefore scholarly ... not a lot on law and when compared with what is now collected, shows how tastes have changed".

The medium, by which Hague made his book purchases, particularly towards the latter half of his life, when his health was declining, is in a sense a forerunner of on-line shopping. Book dealers at home and abroad sent catalogues to him because his name was on their mailing list. These suppliers included "Oak Knole" in the United States, Peter Arnold and Ken Hince from Victoria, Michael Logie, a remainders man in Pirie Street and names once familiar in the Adelaide book trade scene, Harry and Marcia Muir at "Becks", "Preeces", the "Argonauts Bookshop" and "Rigbys". Friends Gerald and Gerald Fischer suggested additional dealers. "Serendipity Books" in Western Australia and "ABC Books and Curios" in Sydney, with whom they had dealt successfully, being ardent collectors themselves. Michael Treloar, who in 1976 set up his first antiquarian bookshop in College Park, not far from Gilberton, recalls Hague being on his early mailing lists. Tony Bishop remembers something of Hague's book buying habits from his days at the Crown in the late 1960s. It seems he subscribed to an airmailed edition of the *Times Literary Supplement*, selected books from its pages, and when the orders arrived from England, made the short trip down to the GPO from 24 Flinders Street to collect them.

> 'A common last sighting of Ralph at night was to see him walking down the little stairs carrying in both arms parcels of books in string. That was when he was building up his magnificent collection ... very much a life pursuit.'

Book buying offered Hague rewards apart from the satisfactions of ownership and reading. He found another community beyond the law and beyond Frederick Street, a further possibility for intellectual stimulation and friendship. He was reportedly close to Harry and Marcia Muir at "Becks" in Pulteney Street and received a Christmas book bonus from them. Other suppliers deemed his regular patronage worthy of Christmas cards and small gifts. Long distance relationships evolved in the exchange of correspondence between him and book agents - an arm's length familiarity, which suited Hague. Most weeks book deliveries came to his door and the postal delivery woman and Hague were beyond the nodding stage of acquaintance.

One book trade relationship gave singular pleasure to both parties. As a courtesy, Michael Treloar would drop off Hague's order on his way home and very soon a business acquaintance was transformed into something more personal. Hague invited the bearded and longhaired Treloar inside for a whisky or tea at the kitchen table or in the drawing room and their conversation would always shift to book trade personalities.

'What, as bookmen, are the other bookmen doing? ... My role in his life was to [transmit] book trade intelligence ... It was a joy to go there because it was full of things I enjoy ... My fondest recollection would be the sheer enjoyment we both got from talking about mutual knowledge of the book trade.'

Outside the book trade, other relationships arose out of the bond of book collecting. Tony Bishop believed this was true of Hague's attachment to him, and Gwenda and Gerald Fischer fall into this category, although Fischer's first contact with Hague derived from his days as Assistant Archivist at the Public Library. Bishop, the Fischers, Treloar and Hague belonged to the Book Collectors Society of South Australia. Hague was even an inaugural member when it started in 1981 and most civilly forwarded a cheque for $29 in 1990 for members' pre-dinner drinks but never attended a meeting. It was the same with every other society or club to which he belonged and there were a number: the Returned Services League, St Peter's Collegians' Association, Bibliographic Society and Friends of the Special Collections of the Barr Smith Library.

His books also helped him stay connected with young people, bringing the new generation whom he so liked to his very door and as he gently instilled in them the delights of reading and book acquisition, he made a difference to their lives. Without a doubt this was true of Kate and Jo Brown and to a lesser extent myself. Through his bequest to the Barr Smith Library his great collection is available to many more, both young and old, beyond his own immediate circle of bookmen, personal friends and legal colleagues and neighbours, spreading the knowledge he so valued.

What Hague would feel about the specially designed bookplates intended for insertion in all the volumes retained by the Barr Smith Library, invites discussion. In life, Hague stoutly resisted signing any of his own books or writing dedications in gifts for friends. Tony Bishop is of the opinion the "Ralph Meyrick Hague C.B.E." alluded to in the bookplate, would be turning in his grave.

- oooOooo -

Hague the long-term bookman was also a modest collector and connoisseur of other things of intellectual interest and visual beauty, "objets d'art" which contributed much to the charm and grace of his home, especially the drawing room. As the parameters of Hague's physical world progressively shrank over the next twenty-seven years the pleasant sanctuary that was Frederick Street was surely important for his psychological well-being.

In every room except the bathroom, paintings, mainly watercolours, hung on the walls, even the ends of book shelves did service as hanging space. As with books, Hague chose thematically and with considered criteria, liking particularly landscapes and decorative imagery. David Dridan, an artist well known to post-war

South Australians, visited number 6 once and observed to Hague of his paintings, "Do you realise there's a bit of water in all of them?" The criteria, which guided his purchases, were: affordability, the artist must be listed and bought by our State Gallery and Hague must be really enamoured by the work. All save two paintings in his keeping were by Australian artists and fittingly so in the light of Hague's enduring commitment to his country.

It was not an adventurous collection, rather safe, given the criterion that the artist must be represented in a national gallery but in hindsight Hague's taste and discrimination guided him well for most of the artists are still celebrated for their painting skill and their names not unfamiliar to today's gallery visitors: Kenneth Jack, Mervyn Smith, Hans Heysen, John Rowell, Alan D. Baker, William Knox, Gwen Barringer, William Ashton, D'Auverge Boxall, Louis McCubbin, Sydney Long, John Goodchild, Reshid Bay, Napier Waller and Jack McDonagh. Some exceptions to the watercolour rule were Dorrit Black's fine coloured linocut "The Castle, Taormina" and some elegant etchings by Henri Van Raalte.

Hague had the reputation among his relatives for supporting struggling artists but this was not generally so except perhaps with Carlyle Jackson represented twice in the Frederick Street kitchen where five paintings hung. Friends were told Jackson sold his "oeuvre" to support his alcoholic habit. Hague was thoroughly informed about his chosen artists and enjoyed discussing his collection.

In the dim light of the dining room of number 6, away from general view, was a head and shoulders portrait of Hague, in characteristic regulation grey, painted in the 1950s by Louise Cornwall. His cousin and neighbour "Mim" Scales, who had commissioned Cornwall to paint portraits of her children, introduced Cornwall to Hague. Reportedly he was taken with attractive Louise Cornwall's happy, teasing manner and she "visited a lot for glasses of sherry".

Hague found it hard to resist the mail order catalogue from Franklin Mint, so around the house were displayed some fine special edition plates. Persian rugs figured on his shopping list from time to time and were laid upon the carpeted floors of Frederick Street.

His other diversion was gardening, and in the early days of their acquaintance with Hague, the Brown girls knew if they could not find him in the house, he would be at the compost heap, "extracting good things for his pot plants." And there were many little pots with much the same in them because it seems Hague had a talent for propagation. There wasn't a vegetable plot in sight for the man who dined largely from tins, and well shaped shrubs and trees were a feature rather than annuals. Not all visitors to number 6 were welcome. Magpies took delight in purloining goldfish from his two ponds, which caused Hague much vexation.

Hague's interest in gardening went beyond the practical side of that outdoor activity and his library included a collection of general gardening books, years of the British *House and Garden*, kept by the Barr Smith Library for their landscape architecture students, as well as a valuable set of gardening titles by Vita Sackville-West. The latter were added to the rare books at the Barr Smith because of their "likely enduring interest".

Gradually, gardening and visits to galleries and bookshops ceased. Hague was seen struggling down Stephen Terrace to the shops, resting upon fences, there and back. He told Pamela Reid that he fell over in the garden "like a turtle on its back, with his legs in the air". In September 1989 he wrote thus to Gerald Fisher:

'The tranquil serenity of life in this establishment was recently disturbed by my being hurried into the Memorial Hospital for a couple of weeks [for bladder stone and prostate gland removal] ... As I have never been a patient in a hospital before, it was quite an experience; but I am not seeking repetition.'

Alas, constant good health proved elusive. Hague went from being a man of rounded features to one much thinner. He declined Pamela Reid's hospitality at Christmas because of Parkinson's disease, for it embarrassed him that he could not hold a teacup without rattling it. As always, his good humour prevailed and he assured her that the doctor assured him, "he didn't need to worry about being too debilitated [by Parkinson's] because you will be dead by then". Soon his eyes, so vital for his close reading, started to deteriorate and there was painful laser treatment with Dr David Crompton and the use of big magnifying glasses to help. Age had taken away both of his two cleaning women. Unbelievably one had worked for his parents as well, and was retained at number 6 principally to keep his brass and silver bright.

In the last few months of his life, Hague no longer slept in his simple iron bedstead. Repose only came with difficulty and he slept instead in a comfortable armchair in the study. To the Brown family, upon whom he was utterly reliant, it was becoming obvious that the challenges of remaining independent were proving too much for their friend and neighbour. Tony Bishop telephoned about this time, probably to keep in touch with his friend of some thirty years. What followed was a remark he will never forget. "How are you, Ralph?" he enquired. "Orr", Hague replied with the characteristic tremor in his voice, "tottering on the brink of eternity".

On the morning of the 10th of March 1997, Rob Brown noticed Hague's front door, invariably open by half past eight, was still closed. Neither was his rubbish bin ready awaiting collection on the footpath. Alarmed, Marilyn Brown and a neighbour frantically looked through all the windows of number six and the police were called. Somewhere between midnight and early morning, Hague suffered a heart attack in his study. A book was found by his side. He was reading to the very last, as he himself slipped into history.

Telling their daughters, the cherished companions of Hague's retirement years, about his passing, was the hardest thing Rob and Marilyn Brown have ever had to do. Kate and Jo flew home from London and Leeds where they were studying and organised the service. At a viewing, the two young women bade their friend and erstwhile "grandfather" farewell. "He looked fantastic ... at peace, with almost a cheeky smile on his face ... the usual white shirt, grey trousers and, as Jo insisted, grey socks."

The few who attended the private funeral at Centennial Park on that early autumn Saturday of the 1st of March listened to Kate playing J.S. Bach's Partita No 1 on the piano and L. Couperin's Suite in F on the harpsichord, as Hague had loved to do from the verandah of his home at Frederick Street.

A plaque placed on Hague's last resting place simply reads:

> Ralph Meyrick Hague
> 1907 - 1997
> Bibliophile Extraordinaire

It is but one of the reasons for which he is a remarkable, albeit little known, South Australian.

Epilogue

Hague lived for nearly the entire span of the twentieth century and died close to the excitement of preparations for the new Millennium. He was a bystander in the ebb and flow of national feelings, as well as agent for change in the creation of our own identity, part of us growing up and growing away from the Old World. Over eighty nine years he watched the map of the world metamorphose from its predominant mantle of empire red to a Jacob's coat of many colours with individual nations appearing, each with its own unique history, Australia among them.

As a small boy in industrial Port Pirie he saw a glimpse of the Australia that was to be, a place of prosperity, energy and new immigrants. It was then a country asserting and readjusting itself to the idea of Federation before the serious strains of the cataclysmic Great War. The outbreak of conflict saw a resurgence of the imperial ties, a dilution of national sentiment and after the Peace Treaty of Versailles, it was clear the bonds linking us to Great Britain had not been weakened, particularly in an institution like St Peter's College, with its English headmaster and English orientated culture. However, St Peter's gave its gifted students the freedom to think, to take advantage of their privileged position, to explore and consider their world.

Hague, with his Australian focus first evident in his intellectual activities at St Peter's and his deep love of history, chose to investigate the background to his professional life, the law. Most probably he began the research for his magnum opus at the start of the Depression when briefs were scarce and people modified their entertainment to suit their pinched pockets. Certainly, scratching around in musty files was cheap and a preoccupation suited to Hague's semi-reclusive nature. Douglas Pike wrote in 1964 of those "years of patient research" which continued through the 1940s, 1950s and 1960s and "made Hague's studies the best reference sources on South Australian judges".

What he did was controversial, a new view of the colonial past, and in effect therefore a way of severing old ties and casting aside inappropriate perspectives. This challenged those who critically assessed his History, for what Hague revealed was a legal system that had its own beginnings and developed separately from English law. Boothby J tried to put a stop to that; hence Hague's interest in him. Alex Castles ranks Hague with S.H.Z. Woinarski and Doctors Currey and J.M. Bennett as the people "who really began to lay the basis for acceptance of Australian legal history". He helped banish the ignorance of both Bench and Bar about their past, in particular he depicted, according to Sir John Barry writing in "Meanjin" in 1963, the colonial judges who were "potent influences for good or evil; whenever it happened that there was a competent and receptive government and an able and constructively minded judge the combination was socially fruitful". Hague's pioneering efforts alerted others that there was still valuable work to be done. Some of that work has been done and much of it is informed by Hague's efforts. Yet despite this later work Hague's study endures because of its primacy and its detailed original research.

Another contribution of considerable moment to his profession was as law reporter and editor of the *South Australian State Reports* and *Law Society Judgment Scheme*. For over forty years his editorial style set the standard which similar publications at home and abroad attempted to emulate. King CJ, upon learning of Hague's retirement as editor, wrote this to Hague:

> 'I was asked to convey on behalf of all the judges our lively appreciation of the debt which all connected with the law owe to you in consequence of your devoted and skilful editorial work.'

Both Bench and Bar were fully aware, though not always appreciative, of how much better the system of justice worked because of the high standard of law reporting and how much easier it was for them as individuals to play their part in the system.

The Law Book Company similarly recognised the importance of Hague's editorship and tried to include a valedictory memorandum in the SASRs. Hague refused to co-operate. Alas, therefore, to readers of our reports beyond Hague's own time, he will be just another name in the procession of editors. Hague liked the cover of anonymity. His reward was in the work itself and doing it well, be it law reporting or legal history.

And what of the value of Hague's bequest to the Barr Smith Library? It was his contribution to another community, the community of scholars. The University and South Australia have benefited from his bequest, which is notable for its early imprints and for its "books about books" which are now held in the Hague. Memorial Library.

To those whose hearts he won and to those he gave in ways great and small, Ralph Meyrick Hague will be remembered as the erudite, old-fashioned gentleman whose selfless generosity, charming and witty companionship and utter constancy are irreplaceable.

> 'Men make their own history more wisely when they know what that history has been about.'

These words of Manning Clark could also be Hague's epitaph and perhaps his aspiration for the legal profession.

Illustrations

Chapter 2.2

- *Montefiore*, ca. 1895 (State Library of South Australia – B 25130)
- *Sir John George Shaw-Lefevre* by Carlo Pellegrini, 1871 (National Portrait Gallery, London – NPG 2741)
- *Mona Vale, the residence of William Kermode Esq., Van Diemen's Land* (Allport Library and Museum of Fine Arts, State Library of Tasmania)
- The courthouse where Jeffcott was tried in Exeter as it stands today, 2003 (Jane Stephenson)

Chapter 2.3

- *David McLaren*, 1830 (State Library of South Australia – B 7333)
- *A view of J. Barton Hack esqrs. Farm, Echunga Springs, Mount Barker, South Australia* from a sketch by Col. Gawler by J. Hitchen, ca. 1840 (National Library of Australia - nla.pic-an7837302-v)
- *The new port, Adelaide, South Australia* by J. Hitchin, 1841 (National Library of Australia - nla.pci-an6016283-v)
- *The first settlement on the site of Adelaide*, (after Colonel Light – unknown artist) watercolour on paper, 22.9 x 45.7 cm (Art Gallery of South Australia, Adelaide, Gift of Mrs Simpson Newland 1926, 0.596)
- Court record of the first trials in South Australia listing the members of the first grand jury (Supreme Court Library of South Australia)

Chapter 2.4

- *Osmond Gilles*, 1865 (State Library of South Australia – B 7030)
- Cartoon from *The Adelaide Independent and Cabinet of Amusement*, Volume 1 Number 5 2/9/1841 (State Library of South Australia – B 15998/5)
- *Portrait of Robert Gouger* by A. Stephens (working 19th century) 1833, 12.7 x 10.1 cm (Art Gallery of South Australia, Adelaide, Gift of the Adelaide Gouger 1913, 0.682)
- Morphett's letter *South Australian Gazette and Colonial Register* 16/9/1837 (State Library of South Australia)
- *Young Bingham Hutchinson* by Townsend Duryea, ca.1860 (State Library of South Australia – B 11177)
- A calendar of prisoners… from the court record of the first Supreme Court trials (Supreme Court Library of South Australia)

Chapter 2.5

- *View of Encounter Bay with the fisheries* attributed to William Light, between 1837 and 1839 (Alexander Turnbull Library, National Library of New Zealand, Te Puna Matauranga o Aotearoa – A-096-047)
- *Edward Stephens*, 1865 (State Library of South Australia – B 9502)
- *Charles Mann, the elder*, ca. 1870 (State Library of South Australia – B 6620)
- *View of Company's fishing station and Cape Rosetta, Encounter Bay, South Australia, taken from the beach*, 1838 (National Library of Australia - nla.pic-an6016320-v)
- Letter from Captain Blenkinsop (State Records/Department of the Premier and Cabinet - GRG 24/90/284)

Chapter 3.1

- *Dick Ling* from *The Adelaide Independent and Cabinet of Amusement* 19/8/1841 (State Library of South Australia - B 15998/1)

Chapter 3.2

- *View on the north side of Kangaroo Island* by William Westall, 1814 (La Trobe Pictures Collection, State Library of Victoria – pb00061)
- *Mr and Mrs Alfred Watts* by the Adelaide Photographic Company, 1865 (State Library of South Australia – B 7966)
- *George Milner Stephen*, 1841 (State Library of South Australia – B 7011)
- The *Register* 4/8/1838 (State Library of South Australia)
- *Lady Hindmarsh* by George Milner Stephen, 1840 (State Library of South Australia - B 7010)

Chapter 3.3

- *Boyle Travers Finniss* by Hammer and Co. photographers, 1882 (State Library of South Australia B 11204)
- *Robert Thomas*, 1850 (State Library of South Australia - B 6019)
- *Execution of Michael Magee* by John Michael Skipper, 1838 (State Library of South Australia - B 7797)
- *Southern Australian* 2/6/1838 (State Library of South Australia)

Chapter 3.4

- *Robert Thomas' tent and rush hut Glenelg* by John Michael Skipper, 1836 (State Library of South Australia – B 2128)
- Stanhope printing press by Henry Krischock photographer, 1936 (State Library of South Australia – B 9390)
- Charles Sturt monument, 1916 (State Library of South Australia - B 39842)
- *Government House, North terrace, Adelaide 1845* by S.T. Gill (Australia 1818-1880) 1845, watercolour on paper, 27.1 x 39.7 cm (Art Gallery of South Australia, Adelaide, Gift of the South Australian Company 1931, 0.34)

Chapter 3.5

- *Colonel George Gawler* by Samuel Laurence, photographer, 1843 (State Library of South Australia B 14428)
- *Osmond Gilles* by S.T. Gill, 1850 (State Library of South Australia - B 347)
- *Adelaide race course '45* by S.T. Gill, 1845 (National Library of Australia - nla.pic-an2377127-v)
- Court record of the first trial in the Milner Estate saga (Supreme Court Library of South Australia)

Chapter 4.1

- *Sir Henry Ayers* by J. Hubert Newman, photographer, 1873 (State Library of South Australia - B 10161)
- *Portrait of William Kyffin Thomas* (unknown artist) oil on canvas, 59.7 x 49.5 cm (Art Gallery of South Australia, Adelaide. Gift of Mr Evan Kyffin Thomas 1931, 0.778)
- The court record for G. M. Stephen's perjury trial (Supreme Court Library of South Australia)
- *George Milner Stephen*, 1886 (State Library of South Australia - B 24984)
- *Charles Cooper* by J.M. Crossland (Australia 1800-1858) ca. 1853, oil on canvas, 127.0 x 101.2 cm (Art Gallery of South Australia, Adelaide. Gift of the legatees of Mrs W. Bartley 1895, 0.636)

Chapter 4.2

- *William Ewart Gladstone* by Harry Furniss (National Portrait Gallery, London – NPG 3385)
- *Thomas Shuldham O'Halloran* by Government Photolithographer, photographer, 1865 (State Library of South Australia – B 447)
- *Sir Henry E. Fox Young, Knt, C.B. Governor-in-Chief* (Allport Library and Museum of Fine Arts, State Library of Tasmania)
- George John Crawford (Supreme Court Library of South Australia)
- Justice Cooper's Letter Book, letter on Paxton's Case (Supreme Court Library of South Australia)

Chapter 4.3

- *The Right Reverend Augustus Short, D. D., Bishop of Adelaide* by Samuel Calvert, 1872 (La Trobe Pictures Collection, State Library of Victoria – IAN13/08/72/168)
- *Adelaide, Victoria Square, looking north* [actually it is looking south], ca.1880 (National Library of Australia - nla.pic-an10608594-82-v)
- Sir Charles Cooper (Supreme Court Library of South Australia)

Chapter 4.4

- *Overlanders with cattle* by Frederick Grosse after S.T. Gill, 1864 (La Trobe Pictures Collection, State Library of Victoria – IAN 24/03/64/9)
- *Rundle Street looking east* by S.T. Gill, 1851 (National Library of Australia - nla.pic-an75666601-v)
- *Cutting wood* by J.M. Skipper, ca. 1855 (State Library of South Australia – B 5553)
- *In his habit as he lived; Sir Redmond Barry on horseback near Public Library*, ca. 1880 (National Library of Australia - nla.pic-an23621420-v)
- *Charles Harvey Bagot* by S.T. Gill, 1849 (State Library of South Australia – B 329)
- *William Henville Burford* ca. 1890 (State Library of South Australia – B 7109)
- Title page to Boothby's *A Synopsis of the Law Relating to Indictable Offences* (Supreme Court Library of South Australia)

Chapter 5.1

- *Portrait of Judge Boothby* by Nicholas Chevalier from a photograph by the Adelaide Photographic Company, 1864 (La Trobe Pictures Collection, State Library of Victoria – IAN 25/10/64/13
- Family group of Mrs Benjamin Boothby (Valerie Esau)
- Court record of the Mara and Popham trials, Criminal Sessions Record Book 13/8/1855 to 14/8/1863 (Supreme Court Library of South Australia)
- *Richard Bullock Andrews* by Hammer & Co., photographers, 1870 (State Library of South Australia – B 7014)
- *Two unidentified men attending to a bullock's hoof*, ca. 1912-1930 (National Library of Australia - nla.pic-an24295339-v)
- *John Henry Barrow* by Johnstone O'Shannessey & Co. Photographers, 1870 (State Library of South Australia – B 8760)
- *Henry Bull Templar Strangways*, ca. 1875 (State Library of South Australia – B 11138)
- *Edward Castres Gwynne* by Hammer & Co, photographers, 1880 (State Library of South Australia – B 7015)

Chapter 5.2

- *Surveyors' Encampment Yorkes Peninsula* by Edward J. Snell, 1850 (State Library of South Australia – B 55782)
- *The Hon. J. Morphett, President of the Legislative Council, S.A.* by Samuel Calvert, 1866 (La Trobe Pictures Collection, State Library of Victoria – IMP27/07/66/300)
- The "Crown Seal" copy of the Marriage Act 1858 (Supreme Court Library of South Australia)
- *South Australian Government Gazette* 8/11/1860 p. 1000 (Supreme Court Library of South Australia)
- *Sir R. G. MacDonnell*, ca. 1860 (State Library of South Australia – B 5975)
- *George Marsden Waterhouse* by Stump & Co. photographers, ca. 1890 (State Library of South Australia – B 11140)
- *Sir Samuel Davenport*, ca. 1870 (State Library of South Australia – B 17481)
- *S.A. Northern Pioneers; Matthew Moorhouse*, ca. 1870 (State Library of South Australia – B 6912/K10)
- *Francis Stacker Dutton*, ca. 1885 (State Library of South Australia – B 3657)
- *George Fife Angas*, ca. 1855 (State Library of South Australia – B 9501)
- *George Tinline* by Vianelli, photographer ca. 1880 (State Library of South Australia – B 7110)
- *Anthony Forster*, ca. 1880 (State Library of South Australia – B 53194)
- Upper Mitcham in the early 1860's. (Mitcham Historical Society)
- *Observations on the Report of the Committee of the House of Assembly on Judge Boothby's Case* by "A member of the Irish Bar…"(State Records/Supreme Court – GRG 36/37)

Chapter 5.3

- *William Bakewell* by Hammer & Co., photographers, ca. 1860 (State Library of South Australia – B 11303)
- *John Brown* by S.T. Gill, 1849 (State Library of South Australia – B 333)
- *The "Cuba" at anchor, in a NW breeze, at Port Nicholson heads* by Charles Heaphy, 1840 (Alexander Turnbull Library, National Library of New Zealand, Te Puna Matauranga o Aotearoa – A-144-003)
- *City of Wellington, New Zealand* by Luke Nattrass, 1841 (Alexander Turnbull Library, National Library of New Zealand, Te Puna Matauranga o Aotearoa – C-029-004-2-3)
- *The Late Sir R.D. Hanson, Chief Justice of South Australia, 1876* (La Trobe Pictures Collection, State Library of Victoria – IAN18/04/76/53)
- *Portrait of Sir Dominick Daly* by Townsend Duryea, ca. 1861 (National Library of Australia - nla.pic-an10673556-v)
- *"Woodhouse", Summertown* by Samuel White Sweet, ca. 1872 (State Library of South Australia – B 10648)

Chapter 5.4

- Sir Roundell Palmer by the London Stereoscopic Co. photographers (Roger Vaughan Picture Library)
- *Crown Mills, Snowtown*, 1882 (State Library of South Australia – B 47833)
- *Henry Clinton, 5th Duke of Newcastle* by Frederick Richard Say, 1848 (National Portrait Gallery, London – NPG 4576)

Chapter 5.5

- *Edward Cardwell, Viscount Cardwell* by Carlo Pellegrini, 1869 (National Portrait Gallery, London – NPG 2569)
- *Josiah Boothby* by the Adelaide Photographic Co., ca. 1870 (State Library of South Australia – B 7001)

Chapter 5.6

- *The Late Sir James Hurtle Fisher* by Samuel Calvert, 1875 (La Trobe Pictures Collection, State Library of Victoria IAN24/02/75/21)
- *Unloading grapes at Auldana winery, ca. 1900* (State Library of South Australia – B 12194)
- *Robert Collier, 1st Baron Monkswell* by Alfred Thompson, 1870 (National Portrait Gallery, London – NPG 2734)
- *Hon. Archibald Michie, Minister of Justice* by Samuel Calvert, 1863 (La Trobe Pictures Collection, State Library of Victoria – IAN/25/08/63/8)
- Memorial re removal of Judge Boothby (State Records/Supreme Court - GRG 36/61/00)

Chapter 5.7

- Walter Watson and Sophia Hughes (Pamela Oborn)
- *Wallaroo* by Samuel Sweet photographer, ca. 1870 (State Library of South Australia – B 10630)
- Boothby family tree (Valerie Esau)

Chapter 5.8

- *Willunga* by Townsend Duryea, ca. 1870 (State Library of South Australia – B 7193)
- *Neville Blyth*, ca 1865 (State Library of South Australia – B 3650)
- *Part of Victoria Square, looking north, ca. 1866* by Townsend Duryea (National Library of Australia - nla.pic-an24189475-v)
- *Charles Mann, Junior*, ca. 1880 (State Library of South Australia – B 3651)
- *Rupert Ingleby* by Townsend Duryea, ca 1870 (State Library of South Australia – B 6994)
- The Colonial Laws Validity Act (28 &29 Vic. C. 63) (Supreme Court Library of South Australia)

Chapter 5.9

- *Randolph Isham Stow*, ca. 1870 (Supreme Court Library of South Australia)
- William Alfred Wearing (Supreme Court Library of South Australia)
- *Sir James Penn Boucaut* by Charles H. Manning, ca. 1880 (State Library of South Australia – B 7000)
- *"Smoko" in the Quarries, Yatala by an inmate*, ca. 1877 (State Library of South Australia – B 21925/8)
- *James Brook*, 1880 (State Library of South Australia – B 13252)
- *Hutt Street* by Samuel Sweet, 1872 (State Library of South Australia – B 10761)
- *Loss of the Steamship Gothenburg* by Samuel Calvert, 1875 (La Trobe Pictures Collection, State Library of Victoria – IAN24/03/75/41)
- Judge's Note Book (Judge Boothby) February 1861 (R v Preston) (Supreme Court Library of South Australia)

Chapter 5.10

- *Henry Howard Molyneux Herbert, 4th Earl of Carnarvon*, 1878 (National Portrait Gallery, London – NPG D9525)

- *Sir Thomas Elder*, ca. 1890 (State Library of South Australia – B 34517)
- The Privy Council Chamber (Privy Council Office)
- *Portrait of Judge Benjamin Boothby*, ca. 186? (National Library of Australia - nla.pic-an12884004-v)

Chapter 5.11

- *The best of friends must part*, cartoon *Adelaide Punch*, 30/1/1869 (State Library of South Australia)
- *Sir Samuel James Way*, ca. 1870 (State Library of South Australia – B 5970)
- The Belt Fountain, Walkerville (Tony Kimberlin)
- *Court House, Mt. Gambier* by Richard E. Collett, 1870 (State Library of South Australia – B 46434)
- *A (nearly) full dress rehearsal*, cartoon, *Adelaide Punch*, 28/9/1878 (State Library of South Australia)
- The "Glen" (The Passionist Monastery)

Chapter 5.12

- *Police Trooper Robert W. Ewens in winter dress, 1860* (South Australian Police Historical Society)
- *Joseph Eldin Moulden* (Mouldens Solicitors)
- William Hinde (Supreme Court Library of South Australia)
- Boothby grave (Helen Whitington)

Chapter 6.1

- *Part of the wharves of Port Adelaide, fronting the Bonding Warehouses, 7 miles from Adelaide* by Townsend Duryea, ca. 1866 (National Library of Australia - nla.pic-an24190014-v)
- *George Frederick Dashwood*, ca. 1850 (State Library of South Australia – B 31064)
- Custom house etc Port Adelaide (State Records/Department of Administrative and Information Services, Building Management - GRG 38/58 12/4)

Chapter 6.2

- *Trial by jury in the early digging days* by Thomas Carrington, 1886 (La Trobe Pictures Collection, State Library of Victoria – mp009914)
- *December* by S.T. Gill, ca. 1847 (National Library of Australia - nla.pic-an2377111)
- *George Charles Hawker*, ca. 1870 (State Library of South Australia – B 3712)
- *John Bentham Neales*, ca. 1840 (State Library of South Australia – B 15386)
- Criminal Cause List 16/9/1844 (Supreme Court Library of South Australia)

Chapter 6.3

- *Execution of George Hughes and Henry Curran, Adelaide, 16 March 1840* by J.M. Skipper (Australia 1815-1883) 1840, pencil on card, 15.0 x 20.1 cm (Art Gallery of South Australia, Adelaide. Morgan Thomas Bequest 1936)
- *Attack on store dray* by S.T. Gill, 1865 (National Library of Australia - nla.pic-an7149191-v)
- *William Robinson Boothby*, ca. 1914 (State Library of South Australia – B 8073)
- *Charles Algernon Wilson* by Martha Berkeley (Australia 1813-1899) ca. 1843, Adelaide, watercolour on card, 15.5 x 12.5 cm (Art Gallery of South Australia, Adelaide. Gift of Miss Emily Watson 1950, 0.1474)
- *The new rush* by S.T. Gill, 1865 (National Library of Australia - nla.pic-an7149201-v)
- *L.J. Pelham*, 1867 (State Library of South Australia – B 22979)

- Eastern entrance to Supreme Court (State Records/Department of Administrative and Information Services, Building Management – GRG 38/58)

Chapter 6.4

- The Queen's Theatre (Tony Kimberlin)
- Supreme Courthouse, ca. 1870 (Supreme Court Library of South Australia)
- *King William Street* [Police Court], 1870 (State Library of South Australia – B 1928)
- *King William Street* [Supreme Court] ca. 1870 (State Library of South Australia – B 4668)

Chapter 6.5

- Supreme Court Library catalogue, 1866 (Supreme Court Library of South Australia)
- Sir Samuel Way's bookplate (Supreme Court Library of South Australia)

Chapter 6.6

- *Paxton Square cottages, Burra, 1849 (in old township of Kooringa)* by Brendon Kelson 1996 (National Library of Australia - nla.pic-an13233522-6)
- *Alexander Hay*, ca. 1885 (State Library of South Australia – B 50607)
- *Travelling in a dust storm* by William Anderson Cawthorne and Samuel Calvert, 1867 (La Trobe Pictures Collection, State Library of Victoria – IMP24/01/67/13)
- Certificate of appeal pending in *Walsh v Goodall.* (State Records/ Supreme Court - GRG 36/37)

Chapter 7

- *George Strickland Kingston* by S.T. Gill, ca. 1838 (State Library of South Australia – B 350)
- *Alexander Tolmer* by Government Photolithographer, ca. 1860 (State Library of South Australia – B 449)
- *The 'Ville de Bordeaux' at Port Adelaide* by J.M. Skipper (Australia 1815-1883) 1841, Adelaide, watercolour on paper 10.8 x 16.2 cm (Art Gallery of South Australia, Adelaide. Morgan Thomas Bequest Fund 1942, 0.1199)
- *John Alexander Jackson* by J.A. Jackson, 1845 (State Library of South Australia – B 7152)
- Dench document (State Records/ Supreme Court – GRG 36/37)
- *Richard Bethel, 1st Baron Westbury* by Michele Gordigiani (National Portrait Gallery, London – NPG 1941)
- *Augustine Stow*, ca. 1890 (State Library of South Australia – B 3835)
- Notice of appeal *Murray v Ridpath* (State Records/Supreme Court – GRG 36/37)
- *Arliegh Gosden's Saw-mill* by Thomas Sladdin, ca. 1890 (State Library of South Australia – B 18921)
- *Bullock team*, 1906 (State Library of South Australia – B 9856)
- *Adelaide, South Australia* by J. Hitchen, ca.1841 (National Library of Australia - nla.pic-an7832564-v)
- *North Terrace looking east*, ca, 1920s-30s (Adelaide City Council Archives – HP 1603)

Chapter 8

- *Charles Bonney*, ca. 1900 (State Library of South Australia – B 7390)
- Matthew Smith (Supreme Court Library of South Australia)
- *Handasyde Duncan*, ca 1835 (State Library of South Australia – B 10471)
- *Eyre's journey to Albany* by Samuel Calvert and J. MacFarlane, 1891 (La Trobe Pictures Collection, State Library of Victoria – IAN01/01/91SUPP/12)
- *Cornish miners, Burra*, ca. 1870 (State Library of South Australia – B 46012)
- *Adelaide Town Hall*, ca. 1866 (Adelaide City Council Archives – 44T.A. 203)

- *John Michael Skipper*, 1863 (State Library of South Australia – B 7028)
- *Wool scouring plant*, ca 1870 (State Library of South Australia – B 542)
- *Glen Osmond [Birksgate]* by Samuel White Sweet, ca. 1872 (State Library of South Australia – B 10632)

Chapter 9

- *Monument in Nairne cemetery*, 1931 (State Library of South Australia – B 6036)
- *Arthur Hardy*, ca. 1858 (State Library of South Australia – B 18681)
- *Frederick Holt Robe*, ca. 1890 (State Library of South Australia – B 5976)
- *Thomas Magarey*, ca. 1840 (State Library of South Australia – B 56079)
- Mount Lofty House (Tony Kimberlin/Mount Lofty House)

Chapter 10

- *Port Lincoln* by George French Angas, ca. 1844 (State Library of South Australia – B 15276/13)
- *Thorndon Park Reservoir* by H. Davis, 1875 (State Library of South Australia – B 7349)
- *Edward Klingender*, ca. 1865 (State Library of South Australia – B 26753)
- *Ebenezer Ward* by Pyn, ca. 1870 (State Library of South Australia – B 6981)
- *Portrait of Nannultera, a young Poonindie cricketer* by John Michael Crossland, 1854 (National Library of Australia - nla.pic-an2242510-v)

Chapter 11

- *Civilisation versus Nature* by Alexander Schramm, ca. 1859 (National Library of Australia - nla.pic-an9308949-v)
- *Rapid Bay, encampment of Yankallila blacks* by George French Angas, James William Giles, 1847 (National Library of Australia - nla.pic-7322212-v)
- *Native weapons and implements* by George French Angas, James William Giles, 1846 (National Library of Australia - nla.pic-7342542-v)
- *First dinner given to the Aborigines, 1838* by Martha Berkeley (Australia/Great Britain 1813-1899) 1838, Adelaide, watercolour on paper, 37.5 x 49.5 cm (Art Gallery of South Australia, Adelaide. Gift of J.P. Tonkin 1922, 0.692)
- *"Pilgaru" – two natives hung for murder, September 1840* by E.C. Frome (Australia 1802-1890) 1840, Adelaide, watercolour on paper, 11.1 x 19.0 cm (Art Gallery of South Australia, Adelaide. South Australian Government Grant, Adelaide City Council & Public Donations Fund 1970, 709HP43)
- *Edward John Eyre*, ca. 1860 (State Library of South Australia – B 5880)
- *Portrait of Sir Robert Torrens* by John Upton, ca. 1880 (National Library of Australia - nla.pic-an2284297-v)

Chapter 12

- *Henry Gawler*, ca. 1860 (State Library of South Australia – B 22868)
- *Ulrich Hubbe*, ca.1880 (State Library of South Australia – B 9042)
- Adelaide Gaol [tower] (State Records/Department of Administrative and Information Services, Building Management – GRG 38/58, 5/9)

Chapter 13

- *Governor and staff at Adelaide Gaol* by H. Glover, 1850 (State Library of South Australia – B 17790)
- Adelaide Gaol [front of gaol] (State Records/Department of Administrative and Information Services, Building Management – GRG 38/58, 5/8)

- *Adelaide Gaol, park lands facing south…* by S.T. Gill, ca. 1850 (National Library of Australia - nla.pic-an2376678-v)
- Adelaide Gaol, ca. 1980s(Adelaide Gaol)

Endnotes

Presumably when Hague completed his manuscript in 1936 he had a complete (or very near complete) set of endnotes. Unfortunately, with the passage of time, a significant number of those references have been lost. The listing presented here was compiled from existing copies of the manuscript. Where practicable additions have been made but the notes remain incomplete.

The abbreviations used in the endnotes are as follows:
AGL – Attorney-General's letter books (Archives)
AGP – Attorney-General's papers (Archives)
CLCO
CLO – Colonization Commissioners' letters to officers in S.A. (Archives)
CO – Colonial Office records (Records Office, London)
CRJ
CRSA – Correspondence relative to S.A., published by the House of Commons, 1841
CS – Colonial Secretary
CSL – Colonial Secretary's letter books (Archives)
CSMisc
CSP – Colonial Secretary's papers (Archives)
ECM – Executive Council minutes
GHD
PRSA – Public Records of S.A.
RC – Resident Commissioner
RCL – Resident Commissioner's letter books (Archives)
RSC
RSCD
RSCE

Chapter 1.1

1. 4 & 5 Wm IV c.95 (referred to as the Foundation Act)
2. RSC, 1841, p.ix
3. Quoted A.G. Price, *Advertiser*, 15/8/1934
4. *Register*, 11/1/1840
5. South Australia v. Victoria, transcript of proceedings in High Court, p.14
6. A.G. Price, *Founders and Pioneers*, (Adelaide: Preece, 1929) p.11
7. E.G. Wakefield. *A View of the Art of Colonization …* (London: Parker, 1849) p.49
8. *Register*, 25/3/1876
9. Price, p.11
10. See A.G. Price, *The Foundation & Settlement of South Australia, 1829-1845* (Adelaide: Preece, 1924)
11. Price, *Foundation*, pp.219-220
12. CRSA, p.1;Price, *Foundation*, pp.221-222
13. RSCD, p.1
14. RSCD, p.1; Rudall, Thesis
15. RSCD, p.19
16. RSCD, pp.19-22
17. RSCD, p.21
18. CRSA, p.34

19. Rudall, Thesis
20. Wakefield p.47
21. Price, *Foundation,* p.229

Chapter 1.2

1. Rudall's classification

Chapter 1.3

1. Rudall, Thesis, p.62; SA Commissioners to Colonial Office, 8/12/1835
2. For the letters patent see South Australia v. Victoria (1914) AC 283 at p.291
3. Brown, Journal, 14/1/1836
4. Rudall, Thesis, p.105
5. Ditto, p.106
6. Rudall, An.X, Law Officers to CO
7. RSC, p.xxx iv
8. RSCD, p.49
9. RSCD, p.50
10. Brown, Journal, 26/3/1835
11. RSCD, p.51
12. *Register,* 18/6/1836
13. Rudall, An.III
14. Brown, Journal, 12/1/1836
15. RSCD, p.66
16. Rudall, An.IV
17. RSCD, p.68
18. RSCD, pp.72, 75-76
19. CSL, 30/3/1838 (to Resident Commissioner)
20. RSCE, p.223
21. RSC, p.iv
22. T.H. James, *Six Months in South Australia* (London: J. Cross, 1838) p.65
23. Rudall, An.IV, Stevenson to Colonial Office, 17/2/1837
24. Angas Papers, Rowland Hill to Angas, 8/6/1835
25. Brown, Journal, 13/11/1835, 30/12/1835
26. Rudall, An.IV, Hindmarsh to CO, 24/12/1839
27. Ibid
28. Brown, Journal, 12/4/1836

Chapter 1.4

1. Stevenson's Journal, printed in *Proceedings of the Royal Geographical Society of Aust (SA Branch),* vol.XXX, pp.21-73
2. Angas Papers, Hindmarsh to Angas, 11/10/1836
3. Ibid
4. Stevenson, Journal, 19/8/1836
5. Ditto, 30/8/1836
6. Angas Papers, Stevenson to Angas, 10/10/1836
7. Ibid
8. Stevenson, Journal, 25/10/1836
9. Ditto, 9/12/1836
10. Angas Papers, Hindmarsh to Angas, 11/4/1837
11. Stevenson, Journal, 25/12/1836

12. M. Thomas, *The Diary and Letters of Mary Thomas (1836-1866)*, (Adelaide: W.K. Thomas, 1925) 3rd ed.pp.62-63
13. Rudall, Thesis, p.100
14. J. Allen, *History of Australia* (Melbourne: Mason, Firth & MacCutcheon, 1882) p.135
15. Angas Papers, Hindmarsh to Angas, 12/6/1838
16. J.D. Lang, *Historical Account of New South Wales* 2nd Ed (1837), vol.I, p.152
17. E. Hodder, *The History of South Australia…* (London: Sampson Low, Marston, 1893) vol.I, p.104
18. Jeffcott, Letter to Kermode
19. CSL, 8/12/1937 [sic], 13/12/37 (to Resident Commissioner)
20. Rudall, An.IV, Stevenson to CO, 25/11/1837
21. *Southern Australian*, 16/3/1847, 19/3/1847
22. Rudall, An.IV, SA Commissioners to CO, 23/4/1838; CLO, 4/8/1837, 19/8/1837, 14/10/1837 (to Fisher); ditto, Rowland Hill to Gawler, 27/9/1838
23. CLO, 15/9/1837, 21/2/1838 (to Fisher); 17/9/1837 (to Light)
24. Stevenson, Journal, 9/12/1836
25. Rudall, An.II
26. Archives, A355/B5, Fisher to SA Commissioners, 1/6/1837
27. Rudall, An.I, Hindmarsh to CO, 6/1/1837
28. Angas Papers, Hindmarsh to Angas, 5/1/1837
29. Rudall, An.I, Hindmarsh to CO, 1/2/1837
30. Third Annual Report of SA Commissioners 1838
31. Rudall, An.V, Gouger to CO, 1/8/1838
32. Rudall, An.I, Hindmarsh to CO, 11/2/1837
33. Angas Papers, Hindmarsh to Angas, 15/2/1837
34. J.B. Hack, Diary, 16/3/1837
35. Brown Papers, Brown to Wakefield, 8/5/1837
36. Rudall, An.II, Fisher to SA Commissioners, April 1837
37. Brown Papers, Brown to Wakefield, 8/5/1837
38. CSL, 10/4/1837 (to Resident Commissioner)
39. CSL, 15/4/1837 (to Resident Commissioner)
40. Rudall, An.II, Hindmarsh to CO, 12/4/1837
41. Angas Papers, Gouger to Angas, 5/3/1837
42. Rudall, An.I, Hindmarsh to CO, 12/4/1837
43. Angas Papers, Hindmarsh to Angas, 15/2/1837
44. Ibid
45. Ditto, 11/4/1837
46. Ditto, 4/6/1837
47. CLO, 18/11/1839 (to Gawler); Archives, 895/86, Government circular (May 1840) that trafficking must cease
48. Rudall, An.I, Hindmarsh to CO, 12/4/1837
49. Brown Papers, Brown to Wakefield, 10/4/1837
50. Ditto, 8/5/1837
51. Archives, A355/B5, Fisher to SA Commissioners, 1/6/1837
52. Ibid
53. Second Report of Colonization Commissioners 1837, App.No.4
54. Brown Papers, Brown to Wakefield, 10/4/1837
55. CSL, 15/4/1837 (to Resident Commissioner)
56. CSMisc`, 12/4/1837
57. Rudall, An.I, Hindmarsh to CO, 22/4/1837
58. CSL, 17/4/1837, 24/4/1837 (to Advocate-General) and 25/4/1837 (to Resident Commissioner)

Chapter 2.1

1. A.M. Rowan, *Distinguished Kerry Men*; Archives, Notes on Sir J.W. Jeffcott
2. Information from Librarian, Trinity College, Dublin; and Acting Chief Justice, Sierra Leone, 1935
3. C. Clark, *A Summary of Colonial Law*, (London: Sweet & Maxwell, 1834) pp.494-495
4. Annual Register 1833, App. to *Chronicle*, p.193
5. Annual Register 1833, *Chronicle*, p.105 ff., *Law Magazine and Review*, August 1833, p.367 ff. (Available in Supreme Court Library, Adelaide)
6. *Law Magazine and Review*, August 1833, W.C. Townsend, *Modern State Trials* (1850), p.163
7. *Law Magazine and Review*, August 1833
8. Archives, 516/B7, Notes on Jeffcott by J.W. Wallace
9. Gouger, Journal, p.124

Chapter 2.2

1. SA Commissioners to Lord Glenelg, 23/7/1835, 18/8/1835
2. CRJ
3. R. Garnett, *Edward Gibbon Wakefield*, (London: T. Fisher Unwin, 1898) p.109
4. Gouger, Journal, pp.171, 173; Brown, Journal, 23/2/1835
5. Parker to Lord Glenelg, 15/2/1836
6. *Advertiser*, 17/3/1874
7. CRJ, Parker to Lord Glenelg, 15/3/1836
8. Ditto, 29/3/1836
9. Ditto, Hindmarsh to Lord Glenelg, 31/3/1836
10. Brown, Journal, 3/4/1836
11. CRJ, Jickling to Lord Glenelg, 11/4/1836
12. I. O'Connor, *E.G. Wakefield*, (London: Selwyn & Blount) p.118
13. Brown Papers, p.45; Brown, Journal, 14/4/1836, 16/4/1836
14. Brown, Journal, 15/4/1836, 18/4/1836, 19/4/1836, 20/4/1836, 21/4/1836
15. CRJ, Hindmarsh to Lord Glenelg, 21/4/1836
16. Brown, Journal, 25/4/1836
17. CRJ, Jeffcott to James Stephen, 19/4/1836
18. Brown, Journal, 28/4/1836, 4/5/1836
19. CRJ, SA Commissioners to CO, 6/5/1836 and reply 11/5/1836
20. CRJ, Rundle to Grey, 29/9/1836
21. CRJ, Rundle to James Stephen, 10/10/1836
22. CRJ Grey to Jeffcott, 27/5/1836,
23. CRJ, Charles Milford to Glenelg, 2/6/1836
24. CRJ, T. Skelton to Grey, 11/7/1836
25. Rudall, An.III, SA Commissioners to CO, 3/9/1836CRJ, Jeffcott to James Stephen, 9/6/1836.
26. J.B. Hack, Autobiography
27. Ibid

Chapter 2.3

1. For dates of the Judge's arrivals and departures from the colony, see RCL I.p.126
2. Archives, A355/B5, Fisher to SA Commissioners, 1/6/1837
3. Rudall, An.I, Hindmarsh to CO, 19/5/1837
4. Brown Papers 67, Brown to Wakefield, 8/5/1837
5. Angas Papers, Hindmarsh to Angas, 24/2/1837
6. Angas Papers, Hindmarsh to Angas, 11/4/1837

7. Rudall, An.IV, Stevenson to CO, 25/11/1837
8. Angas Papers, Stevenson to Angas, 9/12/1837
9. Rudall, An.II, Fisher to SA Commissioners, April 1837
10. CSL, 24/3/1837 (to John Morphett)
11. Angas Papers, McLaren to Angas, 22/6/1838
12. Angas Papers, Hindmarsh to Angas, 24/2/1837
13. Rev W. Norris, *Annals of the Diocese of Adelaide* (London: Society for the Propagation of the Gospel, 1852), p.2
14. J.B. Hack, Diary, 25/4/1837
15. Norris, p.2
16. Angas Papers, Gouger to Angas, 5/3/1837
17. Brown Papers, Brown to Wakefield, 8/5/1837; Angas Papers, Hindmarsh to Angas, 4/6/1837
18. Brown Papers 67; J. Blacket, *History of South Australia* (Adelaide: Hussey & Gillingham, 1911) p.137
19. Brown Papers 68, Memorial dated 16/5/1837
20. Brown Papers 71, Brown to CO, 31/5/1837; Brown Papers 67
21. Blacket, p.138
22. Brown Papers 67
23. *Register*, 3/6/1837
24. Archives, A355/B5, Fisher to SA Commissioners, 1/6/1837
25. *Register*, 3/6/1837
26. Brown Papers 67, Brown to Wakefield, 8/5/1837

Chapter 2.4

1. CS, 185/1837; Gouger to Gilles, 2/5/1837
2. See details in *Register* 16/9/1837
3. Brown, Journal, 16/1/1836
4. Angas Papers, Samuel Stephens to Angas, 3/8/1835
5. Stevenson, Journal, 28/12/1836
6. *Register*, 16/9/1837
7. Ibid
8. Angas Papers, MacLaren to Angas, 22/9/1837
9. Rudall, An.I
10. Brown Papers 78, Protest of Robert Gouger, 1/9/1837
11. Rudall, An.V, Law Officers to CO, 21/8/1838
12. C. Clark, *A Summary of Colonial Law*, (London: Sweet & Maxwell, 1834) p.28; Manning, *British Colonial Government after the American Revolution* (1933), p.117
13. Third Annual Report of SA Commissioners 1838
14. W. Forsyth, *Cases and Opinions on Constitutional law,* (London: Stevens & Haynes, 1869) p.70
15. *Register*, 16/9/1837; Rudall, An.V, Gouger to CO, 1/8/1838
16. CS, 298/1837 (Gilles to Hindmarsh, 23/8/1837)
17. CSMisc, Stevenson to Mann, 27/9/1837
18. CSMisc, Mann to Stevenson, 23/9/1837; Mann to Gilles, 23/10/1837
19. CSL, 23/9/1837 (to Advocate-General)
20. CSMisc, Opinion of Charles Mann "in the matter of the Colonial Secretary in suspension", 26/9/1837
21. CSL, 2/10/1837 (to Colonial Treasurer)
22. Rudall, An.I, Hindmarsh to CO, 30/5/1837
23. CSL, 8/9/1837 (to Brown) and replies
24. CSMisc, Fisher to Brown, 9/9/1837
25. CSL, 11/9/1837 (to Brown); ditto (to Colonial Treasurer)

26. Jeffcott, Letter to Kermode
27. Brown Papers, Brown to Wakefield, 10/4/1837; CSL, 13/9/1837 (to Brown)
28. Angas Papers, MacLaren to Angas, 13/9/1837
29. CSMisc, Opinion of H.R. Wigley, 21/9/1837; Rudall, An.V, SA Commissioners to CO, 26/4/1838, and reply 11/5/18383
30. CSMisc, Fisher to Brown, 12/9/1837
31. CSL, 13/9/1837 (Fisher to Hindmarsh with copy of notice); *Register*, 16/9/1837; CS, 370/1837; *Register*, 14/10/1837; CSL, 23/9/1837 (to Advocate-General); CSMisc, Opinion of Advocate-General, 28/9/1837
32. CSMisc, Mann to Gilles, 23/10/1837
33. CSMisc, Instructions to Hutchinson; CSL, 3/10/1837 (to Colonial Treasurer); RCL, 5/1/1838 (Colonial Secretary to Colonial Treasurer); CSL, 13/9/1837 (Fisher to Colonial Secretary); RCL, 4/1/1838 (Resident Commissioner to Colonial Treasurer); RCL, 5/1/1838 (Colonial Treasurer to Colonial Secretary)
34. RCL, 8/1/1838 (Resident Commissioner to Gilles); 6/1/1838 and 9/1/1838 (Gilles to Resident Commissioner)
35. RCL, C. Johnston to Fisher, 10/2/1838
36. Rudall, An.V, CO to SA Commissioners, 11/5/1838

Chapter 2.5

1. Jeffcott, Letter to Kermode
2. CSL, 4/11/1837 (to Advocate-General)
3. Ditto, 6/11/1837 and 11/11/1837; Jeffcott, Letter to Kermode
4. Angas Papers, Blenkinsop to Angas, November 1837; Stevenson to Angas, 25/11/1837 ("Blenkinsop has been represented to be a sort of Pirate. There is no trusty evidence on this head, and it is not believed here in any degree.")
5. CSL, 6/6/1837 (to Advocate-General); CSMisc, Opinion of Advocate-General, 8/6/1837; CSMisc, Mann to Gouger (undated) and 6/7/1837
6. CSL, 14/6/1837 (to Resident Commissioner)
7. *Southern Australian*, 22/9/1838
8. CSMisc, Opinion by Mann, 17/10/1837
9. *Register*, 11/11/1838
10. *Register*, 7/4/1838
11. Jeffcott to Hindmarsh, 16/11/1837 (quoted R. 18/8/1838)
12. Brown Papers 70, Hindmarsh to Jeffcott, 28/5/1837
13. *Register*, 1/6/1838
14. C. Clark, *A Summary of Colonial Law*, (London: Sweet & Maxwell, 1834) p.36
15. Rudall, An.V, Law Officers to CO, 8/8/1838
16. GHDSuppVol, Hindmarsh to CO, 1/11/1837
17. CSMisc, Mann to Jeffcott, 16/11/1837
18. *Southern Australian*, 22/9/1838; *Register*, 7/4/1838
19. CSMisc, December 1837
20. Brown Papers, Brown to Wakefield, 8/5/1837
21. Jeffcott to Lord Glenelg, 1/11/1837 (in GHDSuppVol)
22. GHDSuppVol, Hindmarsh to Glenelg, 1/11/1837
23. Jeffcott, Letter to Kermode
24. Reminiscences of Y.B. Hutchinson, *Observer*, 7/7/1866
25. *The Land of Promise by one who is going* (1839), p.128, J.B. Hack, Autobiography; R. 6/1/1838.
26. R. Gouger, *South Australia in 1837* (London: Harvey & Darton, 1838)
27. Archives, Notes on Jeffcott
28. Supreme Court files, Affidavits 1837
29. Gouger, Journal, p.219
30. Archives, Notes on Jeffcott

Chapter 3.1

1. Hawker, *Reminiscences*, I.p.14; J. Blacket, *History of South Australia* (Adelaide: Hussey & Gillingham, 1911) p.87
2. Hawker, I.p.13; Mrs Napier Sturt, *Life of Charles Sturt* (London: Smith Elder, 1899), p.158
3. Archives, Reminiscences of Miss Annie Duncan, p.21
4. Information supplied by Librarian, Lincoln's Inn
5. CSP, 1930/1849
6. CRJ, Jickling to Glenelg, 25/7/1835
7. Rudall, Analysis X
8. CRJ, Jickling to Lord Aberdeen, 9/2/1835
9. CRJ, Jickling to Lord Glenelg, 8/5/1835
10. CRJ, Testimonials to Jickling
11. CRJ, Jickling to Lord Glenelg, 25/7/1835
12. Stevenson, Journal, 13/9/1836

Chapter 3.2

1. Stevenson, Journal, 7/1/1837
2. Archives, A331/B4; Angas Papers, Report by Stevenson and Strangways
3. J.B. Hack, *Reminiscences*; Diary, 20/4/1837
4. *Register*, 3/6/1837
5. CSMisc, Minutes of meeting of Magistrates held 5/7/1837
6. Rudall, An.I
7. *Register*, 6/1/1838
8. Jeffcott to Hindmarsh, 1/12/1837, printed in R. 29/9/1838
9. *Register*, 6/1/1838; RCLI, Certificate by Stevenson, 6/1/1838
10. *Register*, 20/1/1838
11. RC Letters Inwards, Mann to Fisher, 4/1/1838
12. Gouger, Journal, p.219
13. *Register*, 18/8/1838
14. RCL, 11/1/1838, Resident Commissioner to Governor
15. Hindmarsh to Fisher, 12/1/1838, printed in R. 18/8/1838
16. RCL, 29/1/1838, Fisher to Stevenson
17. CSL, 8/12/1837 (to Resident Commissioner)
18. CSL, 13/12/1837 (to Resident Commissioner)
19. CSL, 10/1/1838 (to Resident Commissioner)
20. RCL, 10/1/1838 (Resident Commissioner to Colonial Secretary); ditto, 12/1/1838 (Strangways to Resident Commissioner)
21. RCL, 2/2/1838 (MacLaren to Resident Commissioner)
22. T.H. James, *Six Months in South Australia* (London: J. Cross, 1838) p.66
23. Fred Johns, *Australian Biographical Dictionary* (Melbourne: MacMillan & Co., 1934)
24. Archives, Letter from Mrs Gawler, 7/12/1838
25. J.I. Watts, *Memories of Early Days*, (Adelaide: Advertiser General Printing Office, 1882) p.22
26. See documents with GHD, 15/12/1845 (CO to Robe)
27. Ibid
28. Hawker, *Reminiscences*, I.p.10
29. *Register*, 17/3/1838
30. GHD, 15/12/1845 (CO to Robe)
31. CSL, 31/3/1838, 3/4/1838, 6/4/1838 (to Resident Commissioner)
32. Rudall, An.IV, SA Commissioners to CO, 22/12/1837; ditto, An.V, SA Commissioners to CO, 26/4/1838
33. Rudall, An.V, SA Commissioners to CO, 13/4/1838

34. Rudall. An.V. CO to SA Commissioners 21/4/1838
35. CLO, 4/1/1839 (to Gawler)
36. Rudall, An.VIII
37. Proclamation by Hindmarsh, 14/7/1838; R. 14/7/1838
38. *Register*, 4/8/1838
39. Ibid
40. *Register*, 14/7/1838; Rudall, An.VIII (Stephen to CO, 24/7/1838)
41. GHD, Stephen to CO, 24/7/1838; R. 16/6/1838; Rowan, *Distinguished Kerry Men*
42. A. G. Price, *Foundation and Settlement, 1829-1845,* (Adelaide: Preece, 1924) p.130

Chapter 3.3

1. *Register*, 3/3/1838, 10/3/1838
2. Copy of petition in possession of C. Travers Borrow
3. Finniss to Hindmarsh (undated). Copy in possession of C. Travers Borrow. (There is no proof that this letter was sent, but it expresses Finniss's sentiments.)
4. *Register*, 24/3/1838
5. *Register*, 17/2/1838
6. Supreme Court, Criminal Files 1838; R. 24/3/1838
7. RCL, Fisher to Hindmarsh, 14/1/1838
8. RCL, Hutchinson to Fisher, 19/1/1838
9. *Register*, 12/2/1838; RCL, Hutchinson to Fisher, 3/2/1838
10. RCL, Wigley to Fisher, 5/2/1838
11. *Register*, 7/4/1838
12. *Register*, 28/4/1838
13. *Register*, 17/3/1838
14. *Register*, 24/3/1838
15. Ibid
16. T.H. James, *Six Months in South Australia* (London: J. Cross, 1838) p.67
17. *Register*, 19/5/1838
18. Ibid
19. *Southern Australian*, 2/6/1838
20. *Southern Australian*, 9/6/1838
21. *Register*, 28/4/1838
22. James, p.55

Chapter 3.4

1. *Southern Australian*, 9/6/1840
2. *Southern Australian*, 2/6/1838
3. *Southern Australian*, 9/6/1838; *Register* 16/6/1838
4. *Southern Australian*, 27/10/1838
5. *Southern Australian*, 9/1/1839
6. *Southern Australian*, 16/1/1839
7. *Register*, 26/1/1839
8. *Register*, 20/10/1838
9. *Southern Australian*, 3/4/1839
10. *Southern Australian*, 23/6/1838
11. *Southern Australian*, 9/1/1839
12. *Southern Australian*, 9/1/1839
13. *Register*, 22/12/1838
14. *Southern Australian*, 29/12/1838
15. *Southern Australian*, 28/7/1838
16. *Southern Australian*, 9/1/1839

17. *Southern Australian*, 29/12/1838
18. *Register*, 3/11/1838
19. J. Bentham, *Principles of Legislation*, I.p.23
20. *Southern Australian*, 17/4/1839
21. Rudall, An.V, S.A. Commissioners to CO, 23/6/1838
22. *South Australian Gazette* Extraordinary, 5/12/1838
23. *Southern Australian*, 10/4/1839, 17/4/1839
24. *Register*, 13/4/1839
25. *Register*, 10/11/1838
26. *Southern Australian*, 11/5/1839, 15/5/1839

Chapter 3.5

1. Hawker, *Reminiscences*, I.p.8
2. CLO, Hill to Mann, 4/9/1838
3. Rudall, An.V, SA Commissioners to CO, 4/8/1838
4. *Register*, 5/1/1839; SA, 9/1/1839
5. GHD, Gawler to CO, 26/10/1838
6. Ditto, 22/1/1839
7. Gawler to SA Commissioners, 16/2/1839
8. GHD, Gawler to CO, 20/18/1838, 14/2/1839
9. *South Australian Gazette*, 4/7/1839
10. *Adelaide Stock and Station Journal*, 18/5/1927, p.4
11. Land Office Letters Out 1838-1842, 24/10/1838 (to Brown); *South Australian Gazette*, 11/7/1839
12. CLO, 23/5/1840 (to Gawler)
13. CSL, 28/3/1839 (to Jickling)
14. CS, 162/1838
15. *Southern Australian,* 1/12/1838
16. *Southern Australian,* 6/2/1839
17. *Register*, 6/3/1839; SA, 13/3/1839
18. *Southern Australian*, 13/3/1839
19. SA Blue Book 1840, p.27
20. CRSA, p.136
21. Hawker, I.p.16
22. CSP, Advocate-General to Colonial Secretary, 13/11/1847
23. CSP, 1931/1849 (Cooper to CS, 25/10/1849)
24. *Register*, 19/2/1852
25. *Register*, 20/2/1852
26. Parliamentary Papers 1855-56, No 158K, p.266
27. Ibid
28. 1860 Hansard 540; 1861 Hansard 432; AGL, 13/7/1861 and 18/7/1861 (to Chief Justice); AGP, 400/1861
29. AGP, 447/1861 and 474/1861
30. J. Blacket, *History of South Australia* (Adelaide: Hussey & Gillingham, 1911) p.87

Chapter 4.1

1. J.W. Bull, *Early Experiences of Colonial Life in South Australia*, (Adelaide: Advertiser, Chronicle and Express, 1878) p.86
2. *Observer*, 28/5/1887
3. *Register*, 20/5/1851
4. *Register*,11/3/1846
5. 1866, Hansard 85

6. Quoted *Adelaide Times*, 20/8/1849
7. Rudall, An.V, Cooper to CO, 31/7/1839; Law Officers to CO, 22/8/1838; W. Forsyth, *Cases and Opinions on Constitutional law,* (London: Stevens & Haynes, 1869) p.8
8. Henry Watson, Log Book of Voyage to South Australia 1838-39, 2/11/1838 and 5/11/1838 (Archives)
9. *Southern Australian*, 3/4/1839
10. *Register*, 6/4/1839
11. *Southern Australian*, 17/7/1839 (Brown v. Thomas, verdict for plaintiff, 40/- damages); *Southern Australian*, 24/7/1839 (Fisher v. Thomas, verdict for plaintiff, 40/- damages); *Southern Australian*, 14/8/1839 (Fisher v. Thomas, verdict for plaintiff, 1/- damages)
12. *Southern Australian*, 24/2/1839, 22/5/1839
13. *Southern Australian*, 29/5/1839
14. *Southern Australian*, 5/6/1839
15. *Southern Australian*, 3/7/1839
16. *Southern Australian*, 17/7/1839
17. Supreme Court Misc Papers (Archives)
18. Supreme Court files
19. Supreme Court files, Stephen v. Thomas, Judge's notes of evidence
20. *Register*, 4/2/1846
21. *Southern Australian*, 11/9/1839
22. GHD, Gawler to CO, 25/9/1839
23. Supreme Court files
24. *Adelaide Guardian*, 28/9/1839; R. 28/9/1839, 5/10/1839
25. *Register*, 14/9/1839
26. CSL, 12/9/1839 (to Stephen)
27. See documents accompanying GHD, 15/12/1845, CO to Robe
28. *Observer*, 31/1/1845
29. *Register*, 12/7/1845
30. *Register*, 31/1/1846
31. GHD, 15/12/1845, CO to Robe
32. GHD, 5/7/1845, CO to Robe; 20/2/1846, Robe to CO
33. M. Thomas, *The Diary and Letters of Mary Thomas (1836-1866),* (Adelaide: W.K. Thomas, 1925) 3rd ed. pp.142-146

Chapter 4.2

1. *Register*, 27/6/1840
2. *Register*, 6/9/1845
3. *Register*, 6/11/1844
4. F. Dutton, *South Australia and Its Mines*, (London:T. & W. Boone, 1846) p.181
5. GHD, CO to Robe, 13/6/1846; E. Hodder, *The History of South Australia…* (London: Sampson Low, Marston, 1893) I.p.213
6. Hodder, I.p.214
7. *Register*, 28/10/1846
8. Hodder, I.p.216
9. *Observer*, 24/5/1845, 7/3/1846
10. *Observer*, 21/3/1846
11. *Observer*, 28/3/1846
12. *Observer*, 28/2/1846
13. Brown Papers 108
14. Hodder, I.p.220
15. Brown Papers 109
16. Brown Papers 110
17. Brown Papers 111

18. *Register*, 15/7/1848, 29/7/1848; Finniss, pp.53-54
19. AGL, 11/1/1849 (to Colonial Secretary)
20. *Southern Australian*, 11/11/1842 (Cooper J to Grand Jury); Hodder, II.p.180
21. *Register*, 8/11/1848
22. *Observer*, 11/7/1846; *Register*, 11/7/1846
23. *Register*, 22/8/1846
24. CSP, 356/1849, 377/1849, 393/1849
25. *SA Gazette*, 20/9/1849
26. GHD, Young to CO, 4/3/1849
27. *Southern Australian*, 20/2/1849
28. CSP, 382/1849
29. *SA Gazette*, 22/2/1849
30. *Register*, 22/8/1849
31. *Adelaide Times*, 3/9/1849
32. *Register*, 6/4/1850
33. *Southern Australian*, 13/3/1849
34. *Register*, 21/7/1849
35. C. Graham Botha, *The Early Influence of the English Law upon the Roman Dutch Law in South Africa* (*South African Law Journal*, November 1923 - reprinted, p.7)
36. CSP, 614/1849
37. GHD, Young to CO, 28/3/1849
38. *Adelaide Times*, 13/8/1849, 20/8/1849, 3/9/1849, 10/9/1849
39. *Register*, 18/8/1849
40. *Register*, 13/10/1849; *Adelaide Times*, 4/10/1849
41. CSP, 1369/1849
42. GHD, CO to Young, 16/1/1850
43. GHD, Young to CO, 18/9/1849
44. *Honorary Magistrate*, January 1910, p.281; *Register*, 28/9/1852; Information from Librarian, Trinity College, Dublin; Southern Australian, 8/8/1850
45. *Register*, 27/6/1850, 9/7/1850; *Southern Australian*, 9/7/1850
46. *Register*, 13/8/1850
47. GHD, Young to CO, 25/9/1852
48. *Register*, 27/9/1852
49. *Register*, 9/10/1852
50. GHD, Young to CO, 25/9/1852, 30/9/1852 and 2/10/1852

Chapter 4.3

1. CSL, 10/4/1844 (to Judge)
2. CSP, 2966/1853; CSL, 1/11/1853 and 26/11/1853 (to Boothby J)
3. *Register*, 16/9/1853
4. *Register*, 18/6/1856, 18/6/1856; ECM, 21/6/1856
5. Parliamentary Papers 1861, No 154
6. RSCE 70
7. CS, 392/1842 (Judge to Governor, 26/2/1840)
8. Despatches to Colonisation Commissioners, 29/2/1840
9. GHD, Grey to CO, 13/8/1841; CS, 10/11/1841, memo
10. GHD, Grey to CO, 27/5/1842
11. Ditto, 5/3/1844
12. CS, 24/2/1844 (Judge to Governor)
13. *Register*, 1/7/1846
14. GHD, Robe to CO, 20/10/1846
15. GHD, CO to Robe, 10/6/1847
16. CSL, 7/3/1848 (to Judge)

17. GHD, CO to Young, 30/6/1850
18. *Register*, 3/10/1851
19. T. Worsnop, *History of Adelaide*, (Adelaide: J. Williams, 1878) pp.117-126; *Register*, 29/6/1855, 30/6/1855; F. Johns in *A Journalist's Jottings*, (Adelaide: Hassell Press, 1922) p.123, made the surprising statement that the verdict established "the principle that a grant of land to a religious body was ultra vires".
20. *Register*, 23/12/1856, 24/12/1856
21. GHD, MacDonnell to CO, 24/9/1860
22. GHD, CO to MacDonnell, 22/1/1861
23. ECM, 2/9/1862
24. ECM, 20/8/1861
25. 1861 Hansard, 747-752
26. ECM, 20/11/1861
27. GHD, MacDonnell to CO, 26/11/1861
28. Parliamentary Papers 1861, No 63
29. GHD, MacDonnell to CO, 26/11/1861
30. GHD, CO to MacDonnell, 17/3/1862
31. *Register*, 31/1/1862

Chapter 4.4

1. 35 Columbia Law Review, p.958
2. 34 Columbia Law Review, p.871
3. *Wealth of Nations* (Everyman edition), II.63
4. Journal Soc Comp Legislation, November 1934, p.333
5. J.W. Bull, *Early Experiences of Colonial Life in South Australia*, (Adelaide: Advertiser, 1878) p.53
6. W. Forsyth, *Cases and Opinions on Constitutional law,* (London: Stevens & Haynes, 1869) p.1
7. Blackstone, *Commentaries*, I.p.107
8. CRSA 26
9. *Register*, 12/8/1837
10. Proceedings, p.? [sic]
11. Journal Soc Comp Legislation, November 1934, p.182
12. Ditto, pp.182-183
13. CSP, 53½/1847, 213/1850
14. *Register*, 15/2/1840;*Southern Australian*, 20/4/1840
15. Rudall, An.VI, CO to Gawler, 13/9/1841
16. Mitchell v. Finniss, *Observer*, 30/8/1845
17. *Register*, 30/8/1848, 20/9/1848, 27/9/1848
18. CSP, 1667/1848 (Judge to Colonial Secretary 25/10/1848)
19. Journal Soc Comp Legislation, November 1934, p.181
20. *Register*, 4/11/1855
21. *Register*, 20/6/1855, 22/6/1855
22. Joshua XV 19
23. *Register*, 17/11/1853, 28/11/1853
24. AGL, 29/1/1856 (to Clerk, Local Court, Mount Barker)
25. Stevenson, Journal
26. Gouger, Journal; Stevenson, Journal
27. Langham, p.13
28. GHD, Supp Young to CO, 14/3/1953
29. Letter to Hindmarsh. Copy in possession of T.C. Borrow.
30. RSCD 244
31. *Register*, 16/1/840
32. RSCD 297

33. *Register*, 14/11/1840
34. *Register*, 23/1/1841, 3/7/1841
35. See eg GHD, CO to Gawler, 31/12/1840
36. GHD, Grey to CO, 16/7/1842, 3/11/1843
37. *Southern Australian*, 12/12/1839
38. *Register*, 21/9/1839
39. GHD, Gawler to CO, 27/6/1840; *Register*, 18/12/1841
40. RSC, p.xx
41. *Register*, 27/8/1842, 10/9/1842
42. *Register*, 1/10/1842
43. *Register*, 11/11/1842
44. PRSA 190
45. *Register*, 5/1/1844
46. PRSA 192
47. AGL, 5/6/1851
48. *Register*, 5/1/1854
49. See eg CSP, 28/9/1843, 29/9/1843 (Judge to CS)
50. *Register*, 6/7/1846; *Observer*, 11/7/1846
51. *Register*, 15/9/1853
52. *Observer*, 1/7/1843
53. *Register*, 6/2/1846, 18/2/1846
54. *Register*, 30/10/1851
55. *Register*, 12/6/1856
56. 1857 Hansard 102
57. 1857 Hansard 404
58. 1859 Hansard 31,100
59. *Register*, 28/2/1863
60. 1867 Hansard 1435
61. 1867 Hansard 489

Chapter 5 – no surviving endnotes

Chapter 6.1

1. C. Clark, *A Summary of Colonial Law*, (London: Sweet & Maxwell, 1834) p.52
2. Rudall, An.I
3. AGL (to H.P. Minchin JP, 24/1/1859)
4. Rudall, An.X, SA Commissioners to CO, 8/12/1835; CO to SA Commissioners, 15/12/1835
5. ?
6. *Adelaide Chronicle*, 10/6/1841; *Register*, 9/9/1841
7. CSP, 973/1942 (Judge to CS, 8/12/1842)
8. CSP, 1030/1842, 6/1843
9. *Register*, 2/2/1844
10. *Register*, 11/5/1844
11. Judges Letter Book, 1847-1859 (Mann AJ to Admiralty, 21/4/1847 and 1/10/1847)
12. Supreme Court Files - Vice-Admiralty
13. *Adelaide Times*, 9/4/1849
14. AGL, 9/5/1849 (to CS)
15. *Register*, 15/3/1848
16. CSL, 5/12/1849 (to Judge)
17. CSP, 2264/1849
18. Despatches, CO to Grey, 16/12/1842
19. Supreme Court Misc (Cooper CJ to Governor, 4/12/1861)

20. Parliamentary Papers, 1862, No 86
21. Despatches, CO to MacDonnell, 12/4/1858
22. Judges Letter Book, 18/8/1858
23. Footnotes 23 to 44 are missing

Chapter 6.2

1. Supreme Court Files
2. Ditto, Rules of Court, 6/5/1839 and 9/5/1844
3. CSP, 53½/1847
4. *Register*, 19/1/1848
5. Despatches, CO to Young, 17/9/1847
6. CSL, 7/3/1848 (to Cooper J)
7. CSP, 1465/1849; CSL, 17/8/1849 (to Cooper J)
8. CSP, 213/1850
9. Civil Procedure in England, America and Scotland Collated, in the *Law Review and Quarterly Journal of British and Foreign Jurisprudence*, February 1853
10. *Register*, 27/8/1850
11. Judges Letter Book, Cooper J to CS, 8/9/1852
12. CSP, 3108/1852
13. *Register*, 13/10/1852
14. *Register*, 7/12/1852, 9/12/1852, 20/12/1852
15. CSL, 10/11/1852 (to Cooper J) and 8/12/1852 (to law officers)
16. AGL, May 1853
17. Judges Letter Book, June 1853 (Cooper J to CS)
18. *Register*, 22/7/1853
19. *Register*, 3/8/1853, 21/9/1853
20. *Register*, 3/8/1853
21. *Register*, 18/8/1853
22. *Register*, 23/8/1853
23. CSP, 2284/1853
24. CSP, 2858/1853
25. *Register*, 30/11/1853
26. *Register*, 2/1/1854
27. CSP, 71/1854 and 639/1854
28. *Register*, 9/8/1854 and 24/8/1854; AGL, 23/9/1854 (to CS)
29. *Register*, 6/2/1855 and 9/2/1855
30. ?
31. 1860, Hansard, 70
32. 1862, Hansard, 153
33. 1862, Hansard, 890, 1006; AGL 17/10/1862 (report on Equity Act)
34. AGP, 215/1866
35. Act No 20 of 1866-67
36. 1867, Hansard, 1435
37. ?
38. *Southern Australian*, 30/1/1839; *Register*, 23/2/1839; CSP, 1051/1844
39. Despatches, Grey to CO, 3/11/1843 and 7/9/1844
40. CSP, 1202/1844
41. ?
42. CSP, 1407/1844
43. *Observer*, 7/3/1846
44. *Register*, 9/10/1844
45. *Observer*, 30/11/1844
46. Despatches, CO to Robe, 17/7/1847

47. *SA Gazette*, 26/6/1851; *Register*, 9/9/1851
48. E. Hodder, *The History of South Australia…* (London: Sampson Low, Marston, 1893) vol 1, p.
49. *Register*, 10/2/1852, 12/2/1852, 18/2/1852
50. *Register*, 11/5/1852
51. *Register*, 10/8/1852
52. 1857, Hansard, 75,625, 684
53. 1859, Hansard, 105
54. 1859, Hansard, 110
55. Judges Letter Book (Cooper to CS, 11/4/1859)
56. See 1, *Victorian Law Times*, 161
57. *Register*, 20/3/1856, 21/3/1856
58. *Register*, 7/7/1857
59. 1860, Hansard, 97
60. CSP, 1376/1860
61. 1862, Hansard, 577
62. 1862, Hansard, 159, 246, 358, 425
63. 1865, Hansard, 173, 175

Chapter 6.3

1. *Register*, 3/6/1837
2. Archives, A355/B5, Fisher to Colonisation Commissioners, 1/6/1837
3. G.E. Loyau, *The Representative Men of South Australia,* (Adelaide: George Howell, 1883)
4. CSL, 22/5/1837 (to Colonial Treasurer)
5. CS, 139A/1837
6. ?
7. *Southern Australian*, 9/1/1839
8. Loyau
9. ?
10. Rule of Court, 11/2/1850; *Register*, 11/6/1850
11. CSP, 26/1/1842 (Sheriff to CS)
12. CSP, 715/1842
13. CSP, 1214/1843
14. CSP, 19/12/1843
15. CSP, 1128/1849
16. *Australian Encyclopedia*
17. CSP, 282/1841
18. CSP, 485A/1841
19. CSP, 526A/1841
20. *Register*, 31/7/1841
21. *Observer*, 13/4/1844
22. J.I. Watts, *Memories of Early Days*, (Adelaide: Advertiser General Printing Office, 1882) p.16
23. CSP, Mann to Sturt, December 1841; CLO, 13/8/1842 (to Grey)
24. *Register*, 24/8/1844
25. Supreme Court Misc, Cooper J to Governor, 12/4/1844
26. CSP, 13/1846 (Judge to CS, 7/1/1846)
27. G.E. Loyau, *Notable South Australians, or, Colonists – Past and Present*, (Adelaide: Loyau, 1885)?
28. Despatches, CO to Robe, 8/12/1846
29. CSP, 1257/1849
30. CSL, 11/7/1849 (to Mann)
31. CSP, 556/1850

32. CSP, 1158/1850 (Judge to CS, 31/5/1850)
33. CSP, 310/1851
34. Judges Letter Book, 19/1/1852 (Cooper to CS)
35. Supreme Court Files, T. Wilson to Cooper J, 26/1/1852 (in bundle of Rules of Court)
36. CSP, 3088/1851; Judges Letter Book, 1847-1859, Cooper to CS, 24/1/1853 and 1/2/1853
37. Supreme Court Misc
38. CS Misc, Memo of Internal Revenue, May 1837-March 1838
39. CSL, 25/10/1838 (to Judge); CSP, 206/1838 (Jickling to CS, 26/10/1838)
40. *Observer*, 13/7/1844
41. CSL, 22/5/1837 (to Colonial Treasurer)
42. CSP, 486/1844

Chapter 6.4

1. CSP, 412/1837
2. CSO, Drafts of Outgoing Letters, 1837-1839 (to Resident Commissioner, 2/10/1837)
3. CSL, 21/10/1837 (to Resident Commissioner); CSP, 421/1837
4. Archives, A666
5. M. Thomas, *The Diary and Letters of Mary Thomas (1836-1866),* (Adelaide: W.K. Thomas, 1925) 3rd ed.p.67
6. T.H. James, *Six Months in South Australia* (London: J. Cross, 1838)
7. Hawker, *Reminiscences* I.p.43
8. *Southern Australian*, 27/3/1839
9. *Southern Australian*, 16/1/1840
10. Hawker, II.p.16
11. A. Tolmer, *Reminiscences of an Adventurous and Chequered Career at Home and at the Antipodes,* (London: Sampson Low, Marston, Searle & Rivington, 1882)
12. CSP, 635/1841
13. Supreme Court Misc
14. CSP, 56/1842
15. CSP, 932½/1842
16. G.C. Henderson, *Sir George Grey*; (London: J.M. Dent, 1907), *Observer*, 1/7/1843
17. CSP, 122/1841
18. G. E. Loyau, *The Representative Men of South Australia,* (Adelaide: George Howell, 1883) p.223
19. *Southern Australian*, 10/3/1843
20. CSP, 441/1843
21. Supreme Court Misc
22. *Southern Australian*, 4/8/1843
23. *Southern Australian*, 12/9/1843
24. CSP, 1053½/1843
25. *SA Almanack*, 1847, p.77
26. *Register*, 27/5/1846
27. *Observer*, 22/8/1846; *Register*, 1/4/1846
28. *Observer*, 20/6/1846
29. *Southern Australian*, 2/7/1847
30. Archives, A877, p.1
31. *Adelaide Times*, 1/1/1849; *Register*, 1/4/1850
32. CSP, 1467/1850
33. *Southern Australian*, 2/7/1850
34. *Southern Australian*, 23/4/1850
35. *Register*, 9/8/1850
36. CSP, 2206/1850; *Register*, 27/9/1850, 13/11/1850; *Southern Australian*, 2/7/1850

37. *Register*, 24/3/1866
38. Parliamentary Papers, 1868-69, No 89
39. Parliamentary Papers, 1868-69, No 96

Chapter 6.5

1. Rudall, An.
2. CSL, 22/5/1837 (to Jeffcott)
3. Despatches, Stephen to CO, 6/8/1838
4. Despatches, Gawler to CO, 14/1/1841; CSL, 28/9/1842 (to Advocate-General)
5. CSP, 695/42, 71/1848, 2264/1849
6. *Register*, 30/9/1846
7. CSP, 11/7/1844
8. CSP, 10/7/1844; Memo by Grey on letter from Advocate-General to Clerk of Council
9. *Register*, 21/6/1848
10. *SA Gazette*, 1/7/1848
11. CSP, 1487/1851
12. CSP, 3681/1851
13. CSP, 2742/1852; CSL, 25/9/1852 (to R. Ingleby)
14. Parliamentary Papers, 1854, No 1
15. Parliamentary Papers, 1854, No 97
16. CSP, 1201/1855
17. AGL, 18/4/1855, 9/4/1856 (to CS)
18. CSL, 14/4/1856 (to Advocate-General)
19. CSP, 336/1858
20. AGL, 7/5/1858 and 21/7/1859 (to CS)
21. AGL, 10/8/1860 (to H.C. Palmer)
22. 1860, Hansard, 548, 669
23. AGL, 25/10/1861 and 13/12/1861 (to CS) and 12/11/1861 and 25/11/1861 (to Law Librarian); CSL, 25/10/1861 and 17/12/1861 (to Boothby J); AGP, 656/1861
24. Memorial in possession of Law Librarian, Supreme Court
25. AGP, 429/1865, 461/1865 and 505/1865

Chapter 6.6

1. *Register*, 30/7/1853
2. *Register*, 23/8/1853
3. CSP, 1719/1855
4. Ibid
5. CSL, 17/7/1855 (to AG); CSP, 2272/1855
6. *Register*, 2/11/1855
7. CSP, 3750/1855
8. Ibid
9. 1857, Hansard, 570
10. 1857, Hansard, 694, 740, 750, 711
11. 1858, Hansard, ?
12. AGL, 23/12/1858
13. Despatches, MacDonnell to CO, 13/1/1859
14. *Register*, 18/2/1862
15. AGP, 418/1867

Chapter 7 (Incomplete on Hague's typescript)

1. C. Clark, *A Summary of Colonial Law*, (London: Sweet & Maxwell, 1834) p.33
2.
3. CSL, Colonial Secretary to Jickling 25/10/1838
4. Alexander Tolmer, *Reminiscences of an Adventurous and Chequered Career at Home and at the Antipodes,* (London: Sampson Low, Marston, Searle & Rivington, 1882), pp.209-212, Chronicle, 10/1/1935, p.14
5. *Southern Australian*, 8/6/1841
6.
7.
8.
9.
10.
11. *Southern Australian*, 13/8/1841
12.
13. *Register*, 19/6/1841
14. *Register*, 14,28/8/1841
15. *Southern Australian,* 24/12/1841
16.
17.
18.
19.
20.
21.
22.
23.
24. *Southern Australian*, 13/9/1841
25. *Register*, 20/11/1844
26. CSP
27.
28.
29. *Register*, 7/9/1850
30.
31. CSL, Colonial Secretary to Advocate General, 26/5/1853, CSP 1726/1854
32.
33. Quick and Garran, *Annotated Constitution of the Australian Commonwealth*, pp.82-85
34. *South Australian Gazette*, 29/9/1849
35.
36.
37. CSL, Colonial Secretary to Colonial Secretary, NSW, 9/1/1856
38. *Register*, 28/8/1860 Lloyd v Kelly
39. *Register*, 2/2/1860
40. *Register*, 29/11/1855, 8/2/1856
41. CSP, 2966/1853
42. *Register*, 24/11/1856
43.
44.

45.
46. CSP, 1263/1859
47. *Register*, 2/2/1860
48. *Register*, 8/2/1856
49.
50.
51.
52.
53.
54.
55. *Register*, 10/7/1860
56. Despatches, MacDonnell to Colonial Office 19/12/1860
57. Despatches, Colonial Office to MacDonnell 8/3/1861
58. Despatches, MacDonnell to Colonial Office 21/12/1860, Proceedings, Appendix vi
59. Footnote number 59 is not indicated in the text
60. *Register*, 28/8/1860
61.
62. *Register*, 27 & 29/11/1860, 1/12/1860
63. *Register*, 12/12/1860
64. *Register*, 26/12/1860
65.
66.
67.
68.
69.
70. Cooper CJ to Sir R MacDonnell 24/4/1861, Proceedings Appendix x
71. Despatches, MacDonnell to Colonial Office 26/4/1861, Proceedings, Appendix x
72. Despatches, Colonial Office to MacDonnell 26/4/1861, Proceedings Appendix xi
73.
74.
75.
76.
77.
78.
79.
80.
81. Despatches, MacDonnell to Colonial Office 15/6/1861, Parliamentary Papers 1861, No. 171
82. ECM, 11/6/1861
83.
84.
85. AGL, 30/8/1861
86. Despatches, Colonial Office to MacDonnell 10/7/1861
87. Despatches, MacDonnell to Colonial Office 16/10/1861
88. Despatches, Colonial Office to MacDonnell 20/1/1862
89.
90.
91.

92.
93. *Register*, 7/9/1861; 9/11/1861
94.
95.
96.
97. 1865, Hansard, 953
98.
99. 1865, Hansard, 1030
100. Despatches, Daly to Colonial Office 26/7/1865
101. *Register*, 20/7/1865
102. AGL, 19/1/1866 (Report on Court of Appeals)
103. AGL, 25/4/1863
104. 1866, Hansard, 727-728
105. AGP, 601/1865 (Mann to Attorney-General, 2/11/1865)
106. *South Australian Government Gazette*, 22/2/1866
107.
108.
109.
110.
111. *Register*, 5/3/1866
112. *Register*, 12/3/1866
113. *Register*, 26/3/1866
114. *Register*, 4/4/1866
115.
116.
117.
118.
119.
120. Proceedings, p.8, ibid Appendix pp.xix-xxii
121.
122. Proceedings, Appendix p. xliii
123. Despatches, Daly to Colonial Office, 28/5/1866
124. *Register*, 2/6/1866
125. *Register*, 4/6/1866
126.
127.
128. 1866, Hansard, 241, 255-263, 328
129. 1866, Hansard, 1207
130.
131. AGP, 9/1867 Boucaut Papers 132/21 (Archives)
132. 1868-69, *Hansard*, 102,270,413,435
133.

Chapter 8

1. 7 Wm IV No 1
2. Holdsworth, *History of English Law*, I.p.292
3. Ibid, I.pp.293-294

4. Stevenson, Journal, 3/1/1837; CSL, 3/1/1837 (to Samuel Stephens)
5. Record Book of Cases heard by Justices of the Peace, January-May 1837 (Archives)
6. Gouger, Journal, pp.204-205
7. Angas Papers, Hindmarsh to Angas, 15/2/1837; Despatches, Hindmarsh to CO, 7/2/1837
8. CSP, 305/1837
9. *Register*, 6/1/1838
10. T.H. James, *Six Months in South Australia* (London: J. Cross, 1838) p.53
11. CSMisc, Rules dated 28/11/1837; *Register*, 6/1/1838; Archives, 546, Record of Suits in Resident Magistrate's Court, November 1837 to October 1839
12. *Adelaide Chronicle*, 17/3/1840
13. Rudall, An.V, SA Commissioners to CO, 31/8/1838
14. *Register*, 28/4/1838
15. CSP, Opinion of Advocate-General, 15/5/1843
16. Ibid
17. Ibid; AGL, 28/3/1850 (Memo on Local Courts)
18. *Register*, 9/5/1840
19. CSL, 2/5/1843, Report on charges against clerk of Resident Magistrate's Court
20. *Southern Australian*, 13/3/1839
21. *Southern Australian*, 3/4/1839
22. CSP, 126/1841 (Cooper J to Governor, 23/3/1841); CSP, 405A/1841 (Ditto, 13/7/1841)
23. CSP, Cooper J to Governor, 10/11/1841; *South Australian Government Gazette*, 24/2/1842
24. *Adelaide Chronicle*, 2/3/1842; *Southern Australian*, 25/2/1842, 4/3/1842; *Register*, 26/2/1842, 8/4/1842; CSP, 23/12/1841, Memorial from Adelaide Corporation; CSP, 10/3/1842, 8/4/1842 (petitions)
25. *Southern Australian*, 8/3/1842, 22/3/1842
26. *Southern Australian*, 11/3/1842
27. T. Worsnop, *History of Adelaide*, (Adelaide: J. Williams, 1878) p.53
28. CSP, 567/1842
29. Worsnop, p.54
30. F. Dutton, *South Australia and Its Mines*, (London: T. & W. Boone, 1846)
31. Despatches, Grey to CO, 3/11/1842
32. CSP, 928/1842 (Judge to CS, 26/11/1842)
33. CSP, 45½/1843
34. Despatches, Grey to CO, 18/2/1843
35. *Southern Australian*, 13/10/1843
36. CSP, 1226/1843
37. AGL, 28/3/1850 (Memo on local courts)
38. CSP, 2/2/1844 (Judge to Governor), 27/7/1844 (Ditto)
39. CSP, 153/1843, 307/1843
40. CSP, 969/1842
41. CSP, 280/1843

42. CSP, 28/3/1844
43. CSP, 15/5/1843 (Opinion of Advocate-General)
44. Ibid
45. Ibid
46. *Observer*, 16/9/1843
47. *Observer*, 7/10/1843; *Register*, 24/5/1845, 31/5/1845; Judges Letter Book 1847-1859 (Cooper J to H. Gilbert, 16/1/1849)
48. *Register*, 21/8/1844
49. *Register*, 19/2/1846
50. Despatches, Grey to CO, 15/4/1843
51. CSP, 10/4/1844, Police Commissioner's Quarterly Report
52. CSP, 1412/1844
53. CSP, 1139/1845
54. *Register*, 18/8/1849
55. CSP, 834/1845, 640/1846
56. CSL, 21/4/1847 (to Resident Magistrate)
57. CSP, 1171/1847
58. CSP, 1228/1847
59. CSL, 1/10/1847, 9/11/1847 (to Resident Magistrate)
60. Register, 18/8/1849
61. *Register*, 26/9/1849
62. *Register*, 26/9/1849
63. A. Tolmer, *Reminiscences of an Adventurous and Chequered Career at Home and at the Antipodes,* (London: Sampson Low, Marston, Searle & Rivington, 1882)
64. *Register*, 14/8/1838. For Giles, see J.I. Watts, *Early Reminiscences*, (Adelaide, Advertiser, 1882) p.25
65. Government Gazette, 3/10/1839; CSP, 59/1841 (Smith to CS, 17/2/1841); *Adelaide Chronicle*, 7/4/1841; Government Gazette, 10/3/184?
66. *Register*, 1?/5/1838
67. CSP, 755.5/1845
68. CSP, 1?45/1846 (Torrens to CS)
69. CSP, 1310/1846, 1340/1847
70. CSL, 4/12/1848 (to Police Magistrate); CSP, 238/1849 (Police Commissioner's Quarterly Report)
71. CSL, 3/2/1849 (to Commissioner of Police)
72. CSL, 9/8/1849 (to Dashwood)
73. *Register*, 31/1/1850, 2/2/1850
74. *Register*, 2/2/1850
75. CSL, 28/10/1850 (to Dashwood)
76. *Southern Australian*, 18/7/1843; CSP, 30/1844
77. CSP, 443/1844 (G.C. Hawker to CS, 25/4/1844)
78. CSP, 379/1845
79. CSL, 18/9/1846 (to Commissioner of Police; CSP, 1420/1846 (Police Commissioner's

Quarterly Report)

80. CSP, 1442/1847 (Advocate-General to CS, 13/11/1847); CSL, 9/8/1847 (to Lang), 5/11/1847 (to Advocate-General); *Southern Australian*, 19/11/1847
81. *Register*, 21/7/1849
82. *Register*, 14/7/1849
83. *Register*, 17/11/1851, 2/7/1852; Despatches, CO to Young, 14/12/1852, 15/12/1852
84. CSL, 28/11/1848 (to Advocate-General), 29/1/1848 (to Butler)
85. CSP, 15?3/1847, 2133/1849, 1440/1850, 1508/1850; *Register*, 12/7/1848; *Southern Australian*, 20/4/1847
86. CSP, 1658/1848 (Wigley to CS, 24/10/1848)
87. Ibid, Memo by Governor
88. CSL, 15/11/1848 (to Judge)
89. CSP, 1948/1849 (Wigley to CS, 16/12/1848)
90. CSL, 11/1/1849 (to Wigley)
91. CSP, 100/1849 (Wigley to CS, 12/1/1849; Judge to CS, 10/1/1849)
92. CSL, 23/1/1849 (to Wigley); *Register*, 11/7/1849
93. *Register*, 14/12/1849
94. SA Almanack 1849, p.87
95. *Register*, 14/12/1849, 22/1/1850, 4/2/1850; CSP, 2327/1849
96. AGL, Memo of 28/3/1850
97. Despatches, Young to CO, 14/3/1853
98. *Southern Australian*, 16/7/1847
99. Judges Letter Book 1847-1859 (Cooper J to Advocate-General, 15/12/1849)
100. *Southern Australian*, 21/12/1849
101. *Southern Australian*, 18/12/1849
102. *Southern Australian*, 21/12/1849
103. *Adelaide Times*, 20/12/1849
104. *Southern Australian*, 21/12/1849
105. Despatches, Young to CO, 14/3/1853
106. *Register*, 21/2/1850
107. AGL, 1/2/1850 (to Judge)
108. Judges Letter Book 1847-1859 (Cooper to CS, 17/12/1849 and to Advocate-General, 2/2/1850)
109. *Register*, 2/5/1850
110. *Observer*, 8/5/1880, p.766; CSP, 770/1865; Archives, 585/A4 (Letter from Phipson to Howell, 16/11/1879)
111. CSP, 2456/1850
112. CSP, 2415/1851, 2451/1851, 2504/1851
113. CSP, 1349/1852
114. CSP, 1350/1852
115. *Register*, 3/1/1852; CSP, 104/1852; CSL (to Jickling, 16/1/1852, 16/2/1852, 25/2/1852; and to Wigley, 17/1/1852)
116. *Register*, 22/9/1852

117. CSL, 22/11/1852 (to Cooper J); CSP, 2736/1853
118. CSP, 2736/1853
119. Act No 21 of 1853; CSL, 13/12/1853 (to Cooper J); Parliamentary Papers 1861, No 54; Register, 13/9/1861
120. Parliamentary Papers 1855-56, No 158L, p.19; Schedule to Act No 15 of 1861
121. *Register*, 12/2/1852
122. *Register*, 9/8/1850; CSP, 976/1851, 1033/1851, 1052/1851
123. *Register*, 11/7/1850
124. CSL, 26/3/1864 (to Hanson CJ); CSP, 617/1864
125. CSL, 26/5/1864 (to Judges Associate); *Register*, 28/5/1864
126. Worsnop, p.131
127. *Register*, 10/4/1856 et ff.; *Register*, 23/2/1859, 17/12/1860 and 20/12/1860; Worsnop, p.171
128. See generally notes in Archives by G.H. Pitt
129. James, p.54
130. *Southern Australian*, 13/6/1843, 16/9/1843
131. Archives, A877, p.43
132. *Register*, 11/2/1851
133. *Southern Australian*, 28/6/1850

Chapter 9

1. G. E. Loyau, *The Representative Men of South Australia,* (Adelaide: George Howell, 1883), SA Stock & Station Journal (?)
2. Despatches, Gawler to CO, 20/11/1839
3. Hawker, *Reminiscences,* I.p.9
4. Blue Book 1840, p.80
5. Archives, A678/A1 (Notes on Smillie family)
6. Despatches, Gawler to CO, 6/4/1840
7. RSCD, 297
8. *Honorary Magistrate*, October 1906, p.120
9. CSP, 542B/1840; 122/1841; 21/5/1845 (Advocate-General to Governor)
10. *Adelaide Chronicle*, 17/3/1841
11. *Adelaide Chronicle*, 13/10/1841
12. *Register*, 11/12/1841
13. *Southern Australian*, 17/12/1841
14. *Adelaide Chronicle*, 14/4/1841
15. CSL, 23/2/1842 (to Advocate-General); PRSA, 205; AGL 1848-1857, p.25
16. CSP, 288/1843
17. CSP, 8/11/1844 (Smillie to Lord Stanley); Despatches, Grey to CO, 27/12/1844
18. Despatches, Robe to CO, 19/3/1846
19. CSP, 126/1845, 172/1845
20. *Register*, 6/9/1845
21. *Observer*, 23/5/1846

22. *Observer*, 20/6/1846
23. Despatches, Robe to CO, 18/5/1846
24. CSP, 1276½/1846
25. CSL, 20/10/1846 (to Stephen)
26. Despatches, Robe to CO, 11/11/1847
27. CSL, 13/12/1848 (to Smillie)
28. AGL 1848-57, p.25
29. CSP, 7/1849
30. *Register*, 21/7/1849
31. CSP, 203/1850
32. CSL, 1/2/1850 (to Mann)
33. Despatches, Young to CO, 29/5/1851
34. Despatches, CO to Young, 14/10/1851, 17/5/1852, 26/6/1852, 22/12/1852
35. *Register*, 3/5/1853, 12/9/1853
36. CSP, 1676/1851
37. CSL, 18/7/1851 (to Hanson)
38. Despatches, Young to CO, 11/12/1851
39. *Register*, 29/7/1848
40. Parliamentary Papers 1861, No 154
41. *Register*, 26/12/1860; *Payne v. Dench*
42. Parliamentary Papers 1861, No 154
43. 1857 Hansard 493
44. 1857 Hansard 741
45. See for example 1860 Hansard 60
46. CSP, 140/1859
47. AGP, 590/1866; AGL, 7/8/1866 (to Chief Secretary)
48. 1858 Hansard 326
49. 1858 Hansard 34
50. 1861 Hansard 989, 995, 1023, 1030
51. 1865-66 Hansard 445, 668
52. Act No 5 of 1873

Chapter 10

1. R. Harrison, *Colonial Sketches*, (London: Hall, Virtue & Co., 1862) p.107
2. J. Stephens, *The Land of Promise* (1839), p.118
3. Supreme Court files, Roll of practitioners and practitioners' oaths
4. *South Australian Gazette*, 18/7/1839; *Register*, 16/11/1839
5. *Southern Australian*, 22/12/1840, 8/1/1841; *Register*, 2/1/1841
6. CSP, Judge to Governor, 15/10/1844
7. Despatches, CO to Grey, 27/4/1844
8. *Observer*, 18/11/1843
9. Despatches, CO to Grey, 27/4/1844
10. C. Clark, *A Summary of Colonial Law*, (London: Sweet & Maxwell, 1834) p.55

11. *Southern Australian*, 3/8/1841
12. *Southern Australian*, 21/1/1845
13. *Register*, 28/6/1845; *Observer*, 28/6/1845
14. *Register*, 18/8/1849
15. *Register*, 8/4/1851; *Southern Australian*, 8/5/1851
16. 1865 Hansard 481
17. Proceedings, App.xp.ccxliii
18. *Observer*, 24/2/1844; SA Almanack 1847, p.89; *South Australian Government Gazette* 1866 (List of practitioners)
19. *Register*, 7/3/1851; Judges Letter Book, 24/2/1851
20. *Register*, 25/2/1850
21. Harrison, p.107
22. CSP, 489/1843 (Resolution of 11/4/1843)
23. *Southern Australian*, 9/7/1850
24. *Register*, 9/7/1850
25. *Register*, 30/7/1850, 9/6/1851, 10/6/1851; *SA Gazette*, 7/6/1851
26. *SA Gazette*, 7/6/1851
27. *Register*, 27/11/1850
28. *Southern Australian*, 24/6/1851
29. *Southern Australian*, 6/9/1842
30. *Southern Australian*, 22/12/1843
31. *Register*, 18/8/1854
32. *Register*, 18/3/1848, 14/8/1851, 18/8/1854
33. *Register*, 30/8/1845
34. *Observer*, 28/5/1887, p.32
35. *Observer*, 14/3/1846
36. *Observer*, 5/9/1846
37. *Register*, 17/6/1846
38. *Register*, 25/3/1850
39. *Register*, 3/10/1849
40. *Register*, 11/9/1851, 13/9/1851
41. CSP, 3779½/1851 (G.M. Stephen to Governor, 15/12/1851)
42. *Register*, 19/9/1849
43. *Register*, 17/10/1849 (*Younghusband v. Gilles*)
44. *Register*, 16/5/1849; *Advertiser*, 17/3/1874
45. Parliamentary Papers, 1851, No 17, p.6
46. *Register*, 25/6/1855 (*Sandford v. Parker*)
47. *Register*, 22/1/1850
48. 1868-69 Hansard 1337
49. Harrison, pp.108-111
50. Letter from Edward Klingender, 31/5/1844 (in possession of Mr C. Travers Borrow)
51. *Observer*, 5/9/1846
52. *Register*, 28/7/1877

53. Quoted, *Register*, 27/3/1877
54. *Observer*, 17/8/1889
55. *Register*, 12/7/1877
56. *Southern Australian*, 29/5/1849
57. E.E. Morris, *Memoir of George Higinbotham* (London: Macmillan, 1895), pp.81-82
58. *South Australian Government Gazette*, 16/3/1865
59. *Register*, 16/3/1865
60. Proceedings, App.p.xliii
61. 1865 Hansard 290, 713-715
62. *South Australian Gazette*, 22/8/1839
63. CSP, 313/1841 (James to CS, 15/6/1841); CSP, 547/1841
64. CSP, 2/11/1841, Petition by J.H. Richman for appointment as notary
65. CSP, 812/1850
66. 1859 Hansard 540-542
67. *Great American Lawyers* (1907), V.p.8
68. Hansard, 20/6/1865
69. AGL, 26/3/1866

Chapter 11

1. M. Thomas, *The Diary and Letters of Mary Thomas (1836-1866),* (Adelaide: W.K. Thomas, 1925) 3rd ed.p.185
2. John Brown, Journal, 4/1/1836
3. Ditto, 16/12/1835
4. First Report of Colonisation Commissioners 1836, App.No.9
5. RSCE, 210.218/
6. *Register* 25/8/1840
7. Thomas, p.62
8. Ditto, p.123
9. Rudall, An.I
10. J. Blacket, *History of South Australia* (Adelaide: Hussey & Gillingham, 1911) p.46
11. Ditto, p.73
12. *Register*, 3/6/1837
13. *Register*, 8/7/1837
14. CS, 246/1847, 1251½/1843; CS, 14/6/1843, Memo filed from book formerly kept at Government House; CS, 39/1842, 414/1843, 490/1843; SA, 5/9/1843
15. CS, 259/1837 (Mann to CS, 28/7/1837)
16. E. Hodder, *The History of South Australia...* (London: Sampson Low, Marston, 1893) I.p.89
17. *Register*, 17/3/1838
18. *Register*, 20/10/1838, 3/11/1838
19. W. Mann, *Six Years Residence in the Australian Provinces*, (1839) p.291
20. *Southern Australian*, ?/5/1839
21. *Register*, 9/3/1839
22. *Southern Australian*, 3/4/183?

23. *Southern Australian*, 24/4/183?, 27/?/183?
24. *Southern Australian*, 8/5/1839
25. *Southern Australian*, 10/5/1839
26. W.H. Bundey, *Conviction of Innocent Men*, (Adelaide: Wigg, 1900) p.6
27. *Southern Australian*, 29/5/1839
28. *Adelaide Chronicle*, 24/3/1804
29. Fourth Annual Report of Colonisation Commissioners, p.9
30. CS, 511/1840 (Judge to CS, 12/8/1840)
31. *Adelaide Chronicle*, 24/3/1840
32. A. Tolmer, *Reminiscences of an Adventurous and Chequered Career at Home and at the Antipodes,* (London: Sampson Low, Marston, Searle & Rivington, 1882 I.pp.180-181
33. Ditto, I.pp.188-189
34. See, for example, *Register*, 19/9/1840; Thomas, pp.164, 168
35. GHD, CO to Grey, 14/12/1841
36. CSP, 383½/1847 (Judge to Governor)
37. Supreme Court Misc Papers (Archives) (Advocate-General to Colonial Secretary, 16/10/1846, and memo by Judge)
38. "Suggestions with reference to the practicability of improving the moral and social condition of the aboriginal inhabitants of Australia" by Captain George Grey, quoted *Register, 18*/4/1840
39. *Southern Australian*, 12/10/1841
40. PRSA, Report from Cooper J to Governor, 11/11/184?; SA, 10/3/1843; R. 18/3/1848
41. *Honorary Magistrate*, October 1905, p.58
42. Hodder, I.p.133; SA, 10/2/1843
43. GHD, CO to Grey, 5/7/1843
44. Kathleen Hassell, *The Relations between the Settlers and Aborigines in South Australia 1836-1860* (Adelaide: Libraries Board of S.A., 1966)
45. Judges Letter Book, Cooper J to Governor, 1/4/1848
46. GHD, CO to Young, 29/11/1848
47. *Register*, 25/11/1846, 28/11/1846
48. *Register*, 13/5/1851, 16/5/1851, 20/5/1851
49. *Register*, 17/5/1851
50. *Southern Australian*, 16/3/1847
51. *Adelaide Chronicle*, 4/11/1840
52. *Register*, 28/5/1853
53. *Register*, 18/5/1845
54. *Register*, 18/3/1865

Chapter 12

1. Encyclopaedia of the Social Sciences, IX.p.130
2. *Register*, 23/7/1856
3. *Register*, 18/6/1836
4. A355/B5, Fisher to Colonisation Commissioners, 1/6/1837

5. CS, 5530/1841
6. CS, 464/1837, Fisher to Hindmarsh, 19/12/1837
7. *Register*, 29/12/1838
8. Government Gazette, 10/10/1839
9. CLO, 6/7/1839 (to Gawler); CRSA, SA Commissioners to CO, 11/12/1840
10. *Register*, 14/9/1839, 9/11/1839; *Adelaide Chronicle*, 19/8/1840
11. Supreme Court Misc Papers (Archives), W.A. Poulden to Cooper J, 2/5/1839
12. *Southern Australian*, 23/1/1840; R. 25/1/1840
13. CS, 1/1841, 68/1841
14. CS, 385/1841, 5530/1841
15. GHD, Grey to CO, 15/11/1843
16. *Observer*, 15/7/1843
17. *Observer*, 14/3/1846
18. GHD, Grey to CO, 15/11/1843
19. CSP, 1213½/1851
20. Judges Letter Book, 2/2/1852 (in reply to scheme put forward by Worthington—see Supreme Court Misc Papers, Archives)
21. CSP, 1130/1852, Hanson to Colonial Secretary
22. Judges Letter Book, Cooper to Governor, 7/12/1852
23. AGL, 8/6/1853 (to Colonial Secretary)
24. AGL, 16/5/1863 (to Colonial Secretary)
25. *Register*, 8/5/1856
26. D. Kerr, *The Principles of the Australian Land Titles (Torrens) System*, 1 (Sydney: Law Book Co., 1927)
27. *Southern Australian*, 17/10/1843
28. A. Forster, *South Australia*, (London: Sampson Low & Marston, 1866) p.219
29. *Register*, 1/6/1857
30. *Register*, 16/8/1856
31. *Register*, 21/11/1856
32. Archives 93, Letter from R.R. Torrens to W.H. Burford, 17/9/1875
33. GHD, MacDonnell to CO, 11/2/1858, 9/7/1858, 17/5/1859
34. Way Papers (Archives), 308/7, S.A. Way to Wenman, January 1858
35. *Register*, 29/1/1858, 2/2/1858; GHD, MacDonnell to CO, 17/1/1860
36. GHD, MacDonnell to CO, 17/1/1859
37. Ibid
38. GHD, MacDonnell to CO, 19/6/1860
39. GHD, MacDonnell to CO, 18/12/1861
40. Harrison, pp.114-116

Chapter 13

1. CS, ?/1837
2. CSMisc, Tender of 10/6/1837
3. Archives, A542/B8 (Colour Sergeant of Marines to Finance Committee, 31/5/1837,

seeking extra pay for looking after prisoners on the *Buffalo* as follows: January, five; February, one; March, eight; April, three; May, 12)

4. Rudall, An,
5. CSL, 7/6/1837, CS to Captain Mitchell
6. J. Blacket, *History of South Australia* (Adelaide: Hussey & Gillingham, 1911) p.153
7. CSMisc (Petition); CS, 1/1838
8. T.H. James, *Six Months in South Australia* (London: J. Cross, 1838) p.53
9. CS, 17/1838; Hawker, 1st Series, p.9
10. *Register*, 1?/1/1838
11. CS, 143/1838 (Sheriff to CS, 2/7/1838)
12. CS, 2?3/1838 (Sheriff to CS, 22/10/1838, and minute by G.M. Stephen)
13. CS, 21?/1838 (Sheriff to CS, 2/11/1838)
14. CS, 162/1838 (Report by Sheriff, 5/8/1838)
15. *Southern Australian*, 1/12/1838
16. CS, 2?/12/1838 (Sheriff to CS)
17. CS, 2??/1838 (Inventory dated 23/11/1838)
18. Archives, A294/B4 (Sheriff to CS, 9/7/1838)
19. CS, 144/1838 (Sheriff to CS, 5/7/1838)
20. *Southern Australian*, ?7/?/1839
21. *Register*, 4/5/1839
22. [indecipherable] (Gawler to Hill, 8/4/1839)
23. [indecipherable]
24. *Southern Australian*, 30/1/1839
25. CSL, 28/8/1839 (to Sheriff)
26. *Southern Australian*, 29/5/1839
27. *Adelaide Chronicle*, 14/4/1840; RSCD 315
28. *Southern Australian*, 7/5/1840
29. *Southern Australian*, 22/5/1840
30. CLCO (Archives 667) p.94, 17/8/1841
31. *Southern Australian*, 10/7/1840; CS, 80/1841 and 107/1841
32. *Southern Australian*, 10/3/1841
33. CS, 80/1841
34. CS, 107/1841
35. Harrison, pp.34-35
36. CS, 151/1841; CS, 9/2/1843, Sheriff to Private Secretary
37. *South Australian Government Gazette*, 22/4/1841
38. Luke XIV.28
39. CS, 15/1/1842
40. Blacket, p.153
41. *South Australian Government Gazette*, 22/4/1841
42. PRSA 116, Grey to Lord John Russell, 10/11/1841
43. CLCO (Archives 667) 28/3/1843
44. *Register*, 23/4/1856 (Supreme Court, *Torrens v. Baker*)

45. *Register*, 8/7/1856 and subsequent days to 12/7/1856
46. *Register*, 17/7/1856 and 2?/7/1856
47. 1857 Hansard 272
48. 1857 Hansard 339
49. 1858 Hansard 335,442
50. *Register*, 14/3/1840
51. Archives, CSP, 404/1840; SA, 19/3/1840, 2/4/1840
52. CSMisc, Blue Book 1840, p.193
53. CSP, 480/1840, 507/1840, 545/1840
54. CSP, 474/1841 and 504/1841
55. PRSA, Grey to Lord John Russell, 4/7/1841
56. Archives 667, p.94, Colonisation Commissioners to CO, 17/8/1841; Rudall, An., CO to Governor, 13/9/1841
57. Blue Books 1840 and 1841, CS, Sheriff to CS, 18/11/1841
58. CS, Sheriff to CS, 14/10/1841
59. *Honorary Magistrate*, October 1905, p.58
60. CSP, Sheriff to CS, 31/5/1842; CSP, 585/1850; PRSA, p.276
61. CS, 353/1841
62. Blue Book 1847, p.219
63. CSP, 1057/1845 and 1510/1845
64. CSP, 1428/1848
65. CSP, 1868/1848; CSL, 29/12/1848 (to Advocate-General); CSP, 167/1850; *Register*, 21/7/1849, 25/7/1849; CSP, 336/1850, 419/1850, 338/1851
66. CSP, 759/1852

Index

n = note p = picture

www.ingramcontent.com/pod-product-compliance
Lightning Source LLC
LaVergne TN
LVHW062128200926
848484LV00007B/1782